Y0-BYZ-119

The GALE
ENCYCLOPEDIA of
MENTAL HEALTH

THIRD EDITION

The GALE ENCYCLOPEDIA of MENTAL HEALTH

THIRD EDITION

VOLUME

2

M–Z
ORGANIZATIONS
GLOSSARY
INDEX

KRISTIN KEY, EDITOR

GALE
CENGAGE Learning

Detroit • New York • San Francisco • New Haven, Conn • Waterville, Maine • London

Gale Encyclopedia of Mental Health, Third Edition

Project Editor: Kristin Key

Editorial: Tara Atterberry, Donna Batten, Jacqueline Longe, Kristin Mallegg, Brigham Narins, Joseph Palmisano, Bob Romaniuk, Alejandro Valtierra

Product Manager: Anne Marie Sumner

Editorial Support Services: Andrea Lopeman

Indexing Services: Laurie Andriot

Rights Acquisition and Management: Margaret Chamberlain-Gaston

Composition: Evi Abou-El-Seoud

Manufacturing: Wendy Blurton

Imaging: John Watkins

Product Design: Kristine Julien

© 2012 Gale, Cengage Learning

ALL RIGHTS RESERVED. No part of this work covered by the copyright herein may be reproduced, transmitted, stored, or used in any form or by any means graphic, electronic, or mechanical, including but not limited to photocopying, recording, scanning, digitizing, taping, Web distribution, information networks, or information storage and retrieval systems, except as permitted under Section 107 or 108 of the 1976 United States Copyright Act, without the prior written permission of the publisher.

For product information and technology assistance, contact us at **Gale Customer Support, 1-800-877-4253.**
For permission to use material from this text or product, submit all requests online at **www.cengage.com/permissions.**
Further permissions questions can be emailed to **permissionrequest@cengage.com**

While every effort has been made to ensure the reliability of the information presented in this publication, Gale, a part of Cengage Learning, does not guarantee the accuracy of the data contained herein. Gale accepts no payment for listing; and inclusion in the publication of any organization, agency, institution, publication, service, or individual does not imply endorsement of the editors or publisher. Errors brought to the attention of the publisher and verified to the satisfaction of the publisher will be corrected in future editions.

LIBRARY OF CONGRESS CATALOGING-IN-PUBLICATION DATA

The Gale encyclopedia of mental health / Kristin Key, editor. -- 3rd ed.
  p. cm.
  Summary: "Alphabetically arranged encyclopedia (500 entries) that covers a wide variety of disorders, treatments, tests, and therapies, focused specifically on topics in mental health"– Provided by publisher.
  Includes bibliographical references and index.
  ISBN 978-1-4144-9012-0 (hardback) -- ISBN 978-1-4144-9013-7 (vol. 1) – ISBN 978-1-4144-9014-4 (vol. 2)
  1. Psychiatry–Encyclopedias. 2. Mental illness–Encyclopedias.
I. Key, Kristin. II. Title: Encyclopedia of mental health.
  RC437.G36 2012
  616.89003–dc23
                                                    2011049279

Gale
27500 Drake Rd.
Farmington Hills, MI, 48331-3535

ISBN-13: 978-1-4144-9012-0 (set)   ISBN-10: 1-4144-9012-7 (set)
ISBN-13: 978-1-4144-9013-7 (vol. 1)   ISBN-10: 1-4144-9013-5 (vol. 1)
ISBN-13: 978-1-4144-9014-4 (vol. 2)   ISBN-10: 1-4144-9014-3 (vol. 2)

This title is also available as an e-book.
ISBN-13: 978-1-4144-9015-1   ISBN-10: 1-4144-9015-1
Contact your Gale, a part of Cengage Learning sales representative for ordering information.

Printed in China
1 2 3 4 5 6 7 16 15 14 13 12

CONTENTS

ALPHABETICAL LIST OF ENTRIES

A

Abnormal Involuntary Movement Scale
Abuse
Acupressure
Acupuncture
Acute stress disorder
Addiction
Adjustment disorders
Adrenaline
Adult ADHD
Advance directives
Affect
Agoraphobia
Alcohol use and related disorders
Alprazolam
Alzheimer's disease
Amantadine
American Academy of Child & Adolescent Psychiatry
American Psychiatric Association
American Psychological Association
Amitriptyline
Amnesia
Amoxapine
Amphetamines
Amphetamines and related disorders
Anorexia nervosa
Anosognosia
Antianxiety drugs and abuse
Antidepressants
Antisocial personality disorder
Anxiety disorders
Anxiety reduction techniques
Apathy
Aprepitant

Aripiprazole
Aromatherapy
Art therapy
Asenapine
Asperger syndrome
Assertive community treatment
Assertiveness training
Atomoxetine
Attention deficit hyperactivity disorder (ADHD)
Autism
Aversion therapy
Avoidant personality disorder

B

Barbiturates
Beck Depression Inventory
Behavior modification
Bender Gestalt Test
Benzodiazepines
Benztropine
Bereavement
Beta blockers
Bibliotherapy
Binge drinking
Binge eating disorder
Biofeedback
Biperiden
Bipolar disorder
Body dysmorphic disorder
Body image
Body integrity identity disorder
Bodywork therapies
Borderline personality disorder
Brain

Breathing-related sleep disorder
Brief psychotic disorder
Bulimia nervosa
Bullying
Bupropion
Buspirone

C

Caffeine-related disorders
Cannabis and related disorders
Capgras syndrome
Carbamazepine
Case management
Catatonia
Catatonic disorders
CATIE
Chamomile
Child abuse
Childhood disintegrative disorder
Children's Apperception Test
Children's Depression Inventory
Chloral hydrate
Chlordiazepoxide
Chlorpromazine
Circadian rhythm sleep disorder
Citalopram
Clinical Assessment Scales for the Elderly
Clinical trials
Clomipramine
Clonazepam
Clonidine
Clorazepate
Clozapine
Cocaine and related disorders

Histrionic personality disorder
Hoarding
Homelessness
Hospitalization
House-tree-person test
Hypersomnia
Hypnotherapy
Hypoactive sexual desire disorder
Hypochondriasis
Hypomania

I

Iloperidone
Imaging studies
Imipramine
Impulse control disorders
Informed consent
Inhalants and related disorders
Insomnia
Intellectual disability
Intelligence tests
Intermittent explosive disorder
Internet addiction disorder
Internet-based therapy
Interpersonal therapy
Intervention
Involuntary hospitalization
Isocarboxazid

J

Journal therapy
Juvenile bipolar disorder
Juvenile depression

K

Kaufman Adolescent and Adult
   Intelligence Test
Kaufman Assessment Battery for
   Children
Kaufman Short Neurological
   Assessment Procedure
Kava kava
Kleine-Levin Syndrome
Kleptomania

L

Lamotrigine
Late-life depression
Lavender
Lead poisoning
Learning disorders
Light therapy
Lisdexamfetamine
Lithium carbonate
Lorazepam
Loxapine
Luria-Nebraska Neuropsychological
   Battery

M

Magnetic resonance imaging
Magnetic seizure therapy
Major depressive disorder
Male orgasmic disorder
Malingering
Managed care
Manic episode
Maprotiline
Marriage counseling
Mathematics disorder
Matrix model
Medication-induced movement
   disorders
Meditation
Memantine
Mental health courts
Mental health law
Mental health and violence
Mental status examination
Mesoridazine
Methadone
Methamphetamine
Methylphenidate
Military mental health
Mind-body medicine
Mini-mental state examination
Minnesota Multiphasic Personality
   Inventory
Mirtazapine
Mixed episode

Mixed receptive-expressive
   language disorder
Modeling
Molindone
Monoamine oxidase inhibitors
   (MAOIs)
Movement disorders
Multisystemic therapy
Music therapy

N

Naltrexone
Narcissistic personality disorder
Narcolepsy
National Institute of Mental Health
Nefazodone
Negative symptoms
Neglect
Neuroleptic malignant syndrome
Neuropsychiatry
Neuropsychological testing
Neurosis
Neurotransmitters
Nicotine and related disorders
Nightmare disorder
Nortriptyline
Nutrition counseling
Nutrition and mental health

O

Obsession
Obsessive-compulsive disorder
Obsessive-compulsive personality
   disorder
Olanzapine
Opioids and related disorders
Oppositional defiant disorder
Origin of mental illnesses
Oxazepam
Oxcarbazepine

P

Pain disorder
Paliperidone

Suicide
Support groups
Systematic desensitization

 T

Tacrine
Talk therapy
Tardive dyskinesia
Temazepam
Thematic Apperception Test
Thioridazine
Thiothixene
Tic disorders
Toilet phobia
Token economy system
Tourette syndrome
Transcranial magnetic stimulation
Transvestic fetishism
Tranylcypromine
Trauma
Traumatic brain injury

Trazodone
Treatment for Adolescents with
    Depression Study
Triazolam
Trichotillomania
Trifluoperazine
Trihexyphenidyl
Trimipramine

 U

Undifferentiated somatoform
    disorder

 V

Vaginismus
Vagus nerve stimulation (VNS)
Valerian
Valproic acid
Vascular dementia
Venlafaxine

Vivitrol
Vocational rehabilitation
Voyeurism

 W

Wechsler intelligence scales
Wernicke-Korsakoff syndrome
Wide range achievement test
Wilson disease

 Y

Yoga

 Z

Zaleplon
Zinc
Ziprasidone
Zolpidem

PLEASE READ—IMPORTANT INFORMATION

The *Gale Encyclopedia of Mental Health, Third Edition* is a health reference product designed to inform and educate readers about mental health, mental disorders, and psychiatry. Gale, Cengage Learning believes the product to be comprehensive, but not necessarily definitive. It is intended to supplement, not replace, consultation with a physician or other healthcare practitioner. While Gale, Cengage Learning has made substantial efforts to provide information that is accurate, comprehensive, and up-to-date, Gale, Cengage Learning makes no representations or warranties of any kind, including without limitation, warranties of merchantability or fitness for a particular purpose, nor does it guarantee the accuracy, comprehensiveness, or timeliness of the information contained in this product. Readers should be aware that the universe of medical knowledge is constantly growing and changing, and that differences of opinion exist among authorities. Readers are also advised to seek professional diagnosis and treatment for any medical condition, and to discuss information obtained from this book with their healthcare provider.

INTRODUCTION

The *Gale Encyclopedia of Mental Health* is a valuable source of information on mental health. The *Encyclopedia* provides in-depth coverage of specific disorders recognized by the American Psychiatric Association in its *Diagnostic and Statistical Manual of Mental Disorders* (*DSM*), as well as other mental health conditions, diagnostic procedures and techniques, therapies, psychiatric medications, alternative treatments, legal concerns, and related topics.

SCOPE

The *Gale Encyclopedia of Mental Health* includes 500 entries on disorders, drugs, tests, and treatments. The *Encyclopedia* minimizes medical jargon and uses language that any reader can understand while still providing thorough coverage, making this text useful to consumers and students alike.

Entries follow a standardized format that provides information at a glance. Categories include:

Disorders and conditions

• Definition
• Demographics
• Description
• Causes and symptoms
• Diagnosis
• Treatment
• Prognosis
• Prevention

Drugs and herbs

• Definition
• Purpose
• Description
• Recommended dosage
• Precautions
• Side effects
• Interactions

Tests and procedures

• Definition
• Purpose
• Description
• Preparation
• Aftercare
• Risks
• Results

Treatments and therapies

• Definition
• Purpose
• Demographics
• Description
• Preparation
• Aftercare
• Risks

Other areas of discussion include Origins, Benefits, Research and general acceptance, and Training and certification, when applicable.

INCLUSION CRITERIA

A preliminary list of mental disorders and related topics was compiled from a wide variety of sources, including professional medical guides and textbooks as well as consumer guides and encyclopedias. An advisory board of professionals from a variety of healthcare fields, including psychology, psychiatry, pharmacy, and social work, evaluated the topics and made suggestions for updates and inclusion. The final selections were determined by Gale editors in conjunction with the advisory board.

ABOUT THE CONTRIBUTORS

The essays in this *Encyclopedia* were written by experienced medical writers, including physicians, pharmacists, and psychologists. All essays were reviewed by advisors to ensure that they are appropriate, up-to-date, and accurate.

HOW TO USE THIS BOOK

The *Gale Encyclopedia of Mental Health* has been designed with ready reference in mind.

- Straight **alphabetical arrangement** of topics allows users to locate information quickly.

- **Bold-faced terms** within entries direct the reader to related articles.

- **Cross-references** placed throughout the *Encyclopedia* direct readers to primary entries from alternate names, drug brand names, and related topics.

- Lists of **key terms** are provided where appropriate to define unfamiliar terms or concepts. A **glossary** of key terms is also included at the back of Volume 2.

- New to this edition, **Questions to Ask Your Doctor** sidebars provide sample questions that patients can ask their physicians.

- **Biographies** of key people recognized for their important work in the field of mental health are profiled in entry sidebars.

- **Resources** at the end of every entry direct readers to additional sources of information on a topic.

- Valuable **contact information** for organizations and support groups is included with each entry and compiled in the back of Volume 2.

- A comprehensive **general index** guides readers to all topics mentioned in the text.

GRAPHICS

The *Gale Encyclopedia of Mental Health* contains 240 color photographs, illustrations, charts, and tables.

ADVISORY BOARD

Several experts in mental health have provided invaluable assistance in the formulation of this encyclopedia, from defining the scope of coverage to reviewing individual entries for accuracy and accessibility. We would like to express our sincere thanks and appreciation for all of their contributions.

Thomas E. Backer
President
Human Interaction Research
    Institute
Associate Clinical Professor of
Medical Psychology
School of Medicine
University of California, Los
    Angeles
Los Angeles, CA

Debra Franko
Professor, Author
Department of Counseling and
    Applied Educational Psychology,
    Bouvé College of Health Sciences
Northeastern University
Boston, MA

Irene S. Levine, PhD
Professor, Author
New York University School of
    Medicine
New York, NY

Susan Mockus, PhD
Medical Writer and Editor
Pawtucket, RI

Chitra Venkatasubramanian, MD
Clinical Assistant Professor,
Neurology and Neurological
Sciences
Stanford University School of
    Medicine
Palo Alto, CA

James E. Waun, MD, MA, RPh
Adjunct Assistant Professor of
Clinical Pharmacy
Ferris State University
Associate Clinical Professor
Michigan State University
Registered Pharmacist
East Lansing, MI

Eric Zehr
Vice President
Addiction & Behavioral Services
Proctor Hospital
Peoria, IL

CONTRIBUTORS

Margaret Alic, PhD
Science Writer
Eastsound, WA

William Atkins
Medical Writer
Pekin, IL

Maria Eve Basile, PhD
Medical Writer
Roselle, NJ

Rosalyn Carson-DeWitt, MD
Medical Writer
Durham, NC

Laura Jean Cataldo, RN, EdD
Medical Writer
Myersville, MD

L. Lee Culvert
Medical Writer
Alna, ME

Tish Davidson, AM
Medical Writer
Fremont, CA

L. Fleming Fallon Jr., MD, DrPH
Professor of Public Health
Bowling Green University
Bowling Green, OH

Paula Ford-Martin
Medical Writer
Warwick, RI

Rebecca J. Frey, PhD
Research and Administrative Associate
East Rock Institute
New Haven, CT

Sandra L. Friedrich, MA
Science Writer
Clinical Psychology
Chicago, IL

Gary Gilles, MA
Medical Writer
Wauconda, IL

Clare Hanrahan
Medical Writer
Asheville, NC

Kelly Karpa, RPh, PhD
Assistant Professor
Department of Pharmacology
Pennsylvania State University
College of Medicine
Hershey, PA

Monique Laberge, PhD
Research Associate
Department of Biochemistry and Biophysics
McGill University
Montreal, Quebec, Canada

Judy Leaver, MA
Behavioral Health Writer and Consultant
Washington, DC

Brenda Wilmoth Lerner, RN
Medical Editor and Writer
Montrose, AL

Mark A. Mitchell, MD
Medical Writer
Seattle, WA

Teresa G. Odle
Medical Writer
Albuquerque, NM

Jack Raber, PharmD
Principal
Clinipharm Services
Seal Beach, CA

Joan Schonbeck, RN
Medical Writer
Massachusetts Department of Mental Health
Marlborough, MA

Genevieve Slomski, PhD
Medical Writer
New Britain, CT

Heidi Splete
Freelance Writer
Washington, DC

Deanna M. Swartout-Corbeil, RN
Medical Writer
Thompsons Station, TN

Samuel Uretsky, PharmD
Medical Writer
Wantagh, NY

Ken R. Wells
Freelance Writer
Laguna Hills, CA

Emily Willingham, PhD
Freelance Writer
Austin, TX

M

Magnetic resonance imaging

Definition

Magnetic resonance imaging (MRI), also referred to as "nuclear magnetic resonance imaging" (NMRI), is one of the most versatile medical imaging technologies currently available for the scanning of the human body. With the use of MRI, doctors can obtain highly refined images (scans) of the body's interior, specifically the nuclei of atoms inside the body, without surgery. By using strong magnets and pulses of radio waves to manipulate the natural magnetic properties in the body, this technique makes higher-quality images of organs and soft tissues than those of other scanning technologies. MRI is particularly useful for imaging the **brain** and spine as well as the soft tissues of joints and the interior structure of bones. The entire body is visible to the technique. Because the technique does not use ionizing radiation, MRI poses no known major health risks.

Purpose

The scientific principle behind MRI, which is also called "nuclear magnetic resonance" (NMR), was discovered independently in 1946 by Swiss physicist Felix Bloch (1905–1983) and American physicist Edward Purcell (1912–1997). In 1952, they were awarded the Nobel Prize in Physics for "their development of new ways and methods for nuclear magnetic precision measurements." Then, in 1971, American-Armenian inventor Raymond Damadian (1936–) developed the first Magnetic Resonance (MR) scanning machine that could be used safety on humans based on the principle of NMR. Damadian showed that magnetic resonance could be applied to the scanning of tissues within the human body. The first MRI image was published in 1973 and the first studies on humans were performed in 1977. In 2003, American chemist Paul Lauterbur (1929–2007) and English physicist Peter Mansfield (1933–) won the Nobel Prize in Physiology or Medicine for "their discoveries concerning magnetic resonance imaging."

The latest additions to MRI technology are magnetic resonance angiography (MRA), magnetic resonance spectroscopy (MRS), functional magnetic resonance imaging (fMRI), interventional magnetic resonance imaging (iMRI), and diffusion tensor imaging (DTI). MRA was developed to study blood flow, while MRS can identify the chemical composition of diseased tissue and produce color images of brain function. The specialized form of MRI called fMRI was developed to measure the change in blood flow as related to neurological activity in the brain and spinal column, while iMRI is used to perform interventional radiology procedures (that is, to produce images during minimally invasive procedures). DTI scans, sometimes also called "diffusion MRI scans," are used to measure water flow within the tissues of the brain.

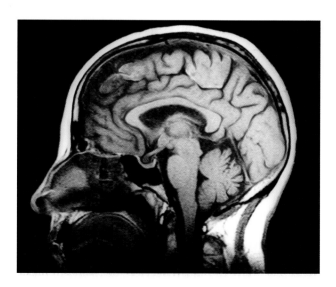

A magnetic resonance imaging (MRI) scan of the human brain; the hypothalamus is highlighted in orange. (© Phototake. All rights reserved.)

The many advantages of MRI include:

• Detail. MRI creates precise images of the body based on the varying proportions of magnetic elements in different tissues. Minor fluctuations in chemical composition can be determined. MRI images have greater natural contrast than standard x rays, computed tomography scan (CT scan), or ultrasound, all of which depend on the differing physical properties of tissues. This sensitivity lets MRI distinguish fine variations in tissues deep within the body. It also is particularly useful for spotting and distinguishing diseased tissues (tumors and other lesions) early in their development. Often, doctors prescribe an MRI scan to more fully investigate earlier findings of the other imaging techniques.

• Scope. The entire body can be scanned, from head to toe and from the skin to the deepest recesses of the brain. Moreover, MRI scans are not obstructed by bone, gas, or body waste, which can hinder other imaging techniques. (Although the scans can be degraded by motion such as breathing, heartbeat, and normal bowel activity.) The MRI process produces cross-sectional images of the body that are as sharp in the middle as on the edges, even of the brain through the skull. A close series of these two-dimensional (2D) images can provide a three-dimensional (3D) view of a targeted area.

• Safety. MRI does not depend on potentially harmful ionizing radiation, as do standard x-ray and CT scans. There are no known risks specific to the procedure, other than for people who might have metal objects in their bodies.

MRI is being used increasingly during surgical operations, particularly those involving very small structures in the head and neck, as well as for preoperative assessment and planning. Intraoperative MRIs (iMRIs) have shown themselves to be safe as well as feasible, and to improve the surgeon's ability to remove the entire tumor or other abnormality. They are valuable because an image can be produced during the procedure so that, for instance, a missed portion of tumor can be removed immediately, during the initial surgery, rather than having to return for a second procedure.

Given all the advantages, doctors would undoubtedly prescribe MRI as frequently as ultrasound scanning, but the MRI process is complex and costly. The process requires large, expensive, and complicated equipment; a highly trained operator; and a doctor specializing in radiology. Generally, MRI is prescribed only when serious symptoms and/or negative results from other tests indicate a need. Many times, another test is appropriate for the type of **diagnosis** needed.

Doctors may prescribe an MRI scan of different areas of the body. Some of these different areas include:

• Brain and head. MRI technology was developed because of the need for brain imaging. It is one of only a few imaging tools that can see through bone (such as the skull). Consequently, it can deliver high-quality pictures of the brain's delicate soft tissue structures. MRI may be needed for patients with symptoms of a brain tumor, stroke, or infection (like meningitis). MRI also may be needed when cognitive and/or psychological symptoms suggest brain disease (like Alzheimer's disease or Huntington's disease, or multiple sclerosis), or when a developmental or intellectual disability suggests a birth defect. MRI can also provide pictures of the sinuses and other areas of the head beneath the face. Recent refinements in MRI technology may make this form of diagnostic imaging even more useful in evaluating patients with brain cancer, stroke, or epilepsy and can be used as an aid in diagnosing schizophrenia. In particular, a new 3D approach to MRI imaging, "known as diffusion tensor imaging" (DTI), or sometimes as "diffusion magnetic resonance imaging" (dMRI, or diffusion MRI), measures the flow of water within brain tissue, allowing the radiologist to tell where the normal flow of fluid is disrupted and to distinguish more clearly between cancerous and normal brain tissue. The introduction of DTI has led to a technique known as "fiber tracking," which allows the neurosurgeon to tell whether a space-occupying brain tumor has damaged or displaced the nerve pathways in the white matter of the brain. This information, in turn, improves the surgeon's accuracy during the actual operation.

• Spine. Spinal problems can create a host of seemingly unrelated symptoms. MRI is particularly useful for identifying and evaluating degenerated or herniated spinal discs. It can also be used to determine the condition of nerve tissue within the spinal cord.

• Joint. MRI scanning is most commonly used to diagnose and assess joint problems. MRI can provide clear images of the bone, cartilage, ligament, and tendon that comprise a joint. MRI can be used to diagnose joint injuries due to sports, advancing age, or arthritis. MRI can also be used to diagnose shoulder problems, like a torn rotator cuff. MRI can also detect the presence of an otherwise hidden tumor or infection in a joint and can be used to diagnose the nature of developmental joint abnormalities in children.

• Skeleton. The properties of MRI that allow it to see through the skull also allow it to view the inside of bones. It can be used to detect bone cancer, inspect the marrow for leukemia and other diseases, assess bone loss (osteoporosis), and examine complex fractures.

• The rest of the body. While CT and ultrasound satisfy most chest, abdominal, and general body imaging needs, MRI may be needed in certain circumstances to provide better pictures or when repeated scanning is required. The progress of some therapies, like liver cancer therapy, needs to be monitored, and the effect of repeated x-ray exposure is a concern.

Description

In essence, MRI produces a map of hydrogen distribution in the body. Hydrogen (chemical symbol H) is the simplest element known, the most abundant in biological tissue, and one that can be magnetized. It will align itself within a strong magnetic field, like the needle of a compass. The Earth's magnetic field is not strong enough to keep a person's hydrogen atoms pointing in the same direction, but the superconducting magnet of an MRI machine can. This comprises the "magnetic" part of MRI.

Once a patient's hydrogen atoms have been aligned in the magnet, pulses of very specific radio wave frequencies are used to knock them back out of alignment. The hydrogen atoms alternately absorb and emit radio wave energy, vibrating back and forth between their resting (magnetized) state and their agitated (radio pulse) state. This comprises the "resonance" part of MRI.

The MRI equipment records the duration, strength, and source location of the signals emitted by the atoms as they relax, and translates the data into an image on a monitor. This relates to the "imaging" part of MRI. The state of hydrogen in diseased tissue differs from healthy tissue of the same type, making MRI particularly good at identifying tumors and other lesions. In some cases, chemical agents such as gadolinium can be injected to improve the contrast between healthy and diseased tissue.

A single MRI exposure produces a two-dimensional (2D) image of a slice through the entire target area. A series of these image slices closely spaced (usually less than half an inch) makes a virtual three-dimensional (3D) view of the area.

Magnetic resonance spectroscopy (MRS) is a specialized type of MRI, slightly different from MRI because MRS uses a continuous band of radio wave frequencies to excite hydrogen atoms in a variety of chemical compounds other than water. These compounds absorb and emit radio energy at characteristic frequencies, or spectra, which can be used to identify them. Generally, a color image is created by assigning a color to each distinctive spectral emission. This comprises the "spectroscopy" part of MRS. Thus, MRS measures biochemical information about the tissues of the body, while MRI only provides structural information about these tissues. MRS is quite new, and it is available in only a few research centers as a way to perform theoretical research and, in some cases, limited studies on humans. However, it is clear to the medical community that MRS has the potential to greatly improve the diagnosis and treatment of diseases.

Doctors primarily use MRS to study the brain and disorders, like epilepsy, **Alzheimer's disease**, brain tumors, and the effects of drugs on brain growth and metabolism. The technique is also useful in evaluating metabolic disorders of the muscles and nervous system.

Magnetic resonance angiography (MRA) is another variation on standard MRI. MRA, like other types of angiography, looks specifically at fluid flow within the blood (vascular) system, but does so without the injection of dyes or radioactive tracers. Standard MRI cannot make a good picture of flowing blood, but MRA uses specific radio pulse sequences to capture usable signals. The technique is generally used in combination with MRI to obtain images that show both vascular structure and flow within the brain and head in cases of **stroke**, or when a blood clot or aneurysm is suspected.

Regardless of the exact type of MRI planned, or area of the body targeted, the procedure involved is basically the same and occurs in a special MRI suite. The patient usually lies on a narrow table and is made as comfortable as possible. Transmitters are positioned on the body, and the cushioned table that the patient is lying on moves into a long tube that houses the magnet. The tube is as long as an average adult lying down, and it is narrow and open at both ends. Once the area to be examined has been properly positioned, a radio pulse is applied. Then a two-dimensional image corresponding to one slice through the area is made. The table then moves a fraction of an inch, and the next image is made. Each image exposure takes several seconds and the entire examination will last anywhere from 30 to 90 minutes. During this time, the patient is not allowed to move. If the patient moves during the scan, the picture will not be clear.

An open MRI scanner is less restrictive and is usually open on two or three sides. Although this type of machine accommodates larger or claustrophobic persons with greater ease, high-field or "closed" MRI machines usually generate more accurate and detailed images. The stand-up type of open MRI generates images of the spine, allowing the physician to evaluate images made in the weight-bearing state.

Depending on the area to be imaged, the radio-wave transmitters will be positioned in different locations. Some of these different locations include:

• For the head and neck, a helmet-like hat is worn.

• For the spine, chest, and abdomen, the patient lies on the transmitters.

KEY TERMS

Angiography—Any of the different methods for investigating the condition of blood vessels, usually via a combination of radiological imaging and injections of chemical tracing and contrasting agents.

Diffusion tensor imaging (DTI)—A refinement of magnetic resonance imaging that allows the doctor to measure the flow of water and track the pathways of white matter in the brain. It can detect abnormalities in the brain that do not show up on standard MRI scans.

Gadolinium—A very rare metallic element useful for its sensitivity to electromagnetic resonance, among other things. Traces of it can be injected into the body to enhance the MRI pictures.

Hydrogen—The simplest, most common element known in the universe. It is composed of a single electron (negatively charged particle) circling a nucleus consisting of a single proton (positively charged particle). It is the nuclear proton of this element that makes MRI possible by reacting resonantly to radio waves while aligned in a magnetic field.

Ionizing radiation—Electromagnetic radiation that can damage living tissue by disrupting and destroying individual cells. All types of nuclear decay radiation (including x rays) are potentially ionizing. Radio waves do not damage organic tissues they pass through.

Magnetic field—The three-dimensional area surrounding a magnet, in which its force is active. During MRI, the patient's body is permeated by the force field of a superconducting magnet.

Radio waves—Electromagnetic energy of the frequency range corresponding to that used in radio communications, usually 10,000 cycles per second to 300 billion cycles per second. Radio waves are the same as visible light, x rays, and all other types of electromagnetic radiation but are of a higher frequency.

• For the knee, shoulder, or other joint, the transmitters are applied directly to the joint.

Additional probes will monitor vital signs (like pulse or respiration).

The process is very noisy and confining. The patient hears a thumping sound for the duration of the procedure.

Since the procedure is noisy, music or videos may be offered as a distraction for the patient. Some patients become anxious or panic because they are in the small, enclosed tube. This is why vital signs are monitored and the patient and medical team can communicate between each other. If the chest or abdomen are to be imaged, the patient will be asked to hold his/her breath as each exposure is made. Other instructions may be given to the patient, as needed. In many cases, an MRI operator, who is not a doctor, will perform the entire examination. However, the supervising radiologist should be available to consult as necessary during the exam and will view and interpret the results later.

Preparation

In some cases (such as for MRI brain scanning or an MRA), a chemical designed to increase image contrast may be given by the radiologist immediately before the exam. If a patient suffers from anxiety or claustrophobia, drugs may be given to help the patient relax.

The patient must remove all metal objects (e.g., watches, jewelry, eye glasses, hair clips). Any magnetized objects (like credit and bank machine cards) should be kept far away from the MRI equipment because they can be erased. Patients may not bring their wallet or keys into the MRI machine. The patient may be asked to wear clothing without metal snaps, buckles, or zippers, unless a medical gown is worn during the procedure. The patient may be asked to remove any hair spray, hair gel, or cosmetics that may interfere with the scan.

Aftercare

No aftercare is necessary unless the patient received medication or had a reaction to a contrast agent. Normally, patients can immediately return to their daily activities. If the examination reveals a serious condition that requires more testing and/or treatment, appropriate information and counseling will be needed.

Risks

MRI poses no known major health risks to the patient and produces no physical side effects. The potential effects of MRI on an unborn baby are not well known. Any woman who is, or may be, pregnant, should carefully discuss this issue with her doctor and radiologist before undergoing a scan. The most common problems are minor bleeding and bruising at the site of contrast injection. Since neither are reportable events, morbidity can only be estimated. Occasionally, an unknown allergy to seafood is discovered after injecting contrast. No deaths have been reported from MRI tests.

QUESTIONS TO ASK YOUR
DOCTOR

- How long will the examination take?
- I have metal in my body from a prior surgery. Can I still have an MRI?
- Is MRI the best option for visualizing my condition?
- Should I expect any side effects?
- How long will it take to receive my results?

MRI scanning should not be used when there is the potential for an interaction between the strong MRI magnet and metal objects that might be imbedded in a patient's body. The force of magnetic attraction on certain types of metal objects (including surgical steel) could move them within the body and cause serious injury. Metal may be imbedded in a person's body for several reasons. Some of these reasons include:

- Medical. People with implanted cardiac pacemakers, metal aneurysm clips, or who have had broken bones repaired with metal pins, screws, rods, or plates must tell their radiologist prior to having an MRI scan. In some cases (like a metal rod in a reconstructed leg) the difficulty may be overcome.

- Injury. Patients must tell their doctors if they have bullet fragments or other metal pieces in their body from old wounds. The suspected presence of metal, whether from an old or recent wound, should be confirmed before scanning.

- Occupational. People with significant work exposure to metal particles (working with a metal grinder, for example) should discuss this with their doctor and radiologist. The patient may need pre-scan testing—usually a single, regular x ray of the eyes to see whether any metal is present.

Chemical agents designed to improve the picture and/or allow for the imaging of blood or other fluid flow during MRA may be injected. In rare cases, patients may be allergic to or intolerant of these agents, and these patients should not receive them. If these chemical agents are to be used, patients should discuss any concerns they have with their doctor and radiologist.

The potential side effects of magnetic and electric fields on human health remain a source of debate. In particular, the possible effects on an unborn baby are not well known. Any woman who is, or may be, pregnant should carefully discuss this issue with her doctor and radiologist before undergoing a scan.

As with all medical imaging techniques, being excessively overweight (obese) greatly interferes with the quality of MRI.

Results

A normal MRI, MRA, or MRS result will show the patient's physical condition to fall within normal ranges for the target area scanned. Generally, MRI is prescribed only when serious symptoms and/or negative results from other tests indicate a need. There often exists strong evidence of a condition that the scan is designed to detect and assess. Thus, the results will often be abnormal, confirming the earlier diagnosis. At that point, further testing and appropriate medical treatment are needed. For example, if the MRI indicates the presence of a brain tumor, an MRS may be prescribed to determine the type of tumor so that aggressive treatment can begin immediately without the need for a surgical biopsy.

Resources

BOOKS
Armstrong, Peter, Martin L. Wastie, and Andrea G. Rockall. *Diagnostic Imaging.* Chichester, U.K.: Wiley-Blackwell, 2009.

Culbreth, L. J., and C. Watson. *Magnetic Resonance Imaging Technology.* New York: Cambridge University Press, 2007.

Kastler, B. *Understanding MRI.* 2nd ed. Berlin: Springer-Verlag, 2008.

McRobbie, D. W., E. A. Moore, M. J. Graves, and M. R. Prince. *MRI from Picture to Proton.* 2nd ed. New York: Cambridge University Press, 2007.

Weishaupt, D., V. D. Koechli, and B. Marincek. *How does MRI work?: An Introduction to the Physics and Function of Magnetic Resonance Imaging.* 2nd ed. Berlin: Springer-Verlag, 2008.

Westbrook, Catherine. *Handbook of MRI Techniques.* Chichester, U.K.: Wiley-Blackwell, 2008.

PERIODICALS
Hara, H., T. Akisue, T. Fujimoto, et al. "Magnetic Resonance Imaging of Medullary Bone Infarction in the Early Stage." *Clinical Imaging* 32, no. 2 (2008): 147–151.

Rumboldt, Z. "Imaging of Topographic Viral CNS Infections." *Neuroimaging Clinics of North America* 18, no. 1 (2002): 85–92.

Wada, R., and W. Kucharczyk. "Prion Infections of the Brain." *Neuroimaging Clinics of North America* 18, no. 1 (2008): 183–191.

Zhao, W., J. H. Choi, G. R. Hon, and M. A. Vannan. "Left Ventricular Relaxation." *Heart Failure Clinics* 4, no. 1 (2008): 37–46.

WEBSITES

"Intraoperative Magnetic Resonance Imaging (iMRI)." Mayo Clinic. http://www.mayoclinic.org/intraoperative-mri (accessed May 24, 2011).

MedlinePlus. "MRI." U.S. National Library of Medicine, National Institutes of Health. http://www.nlm.nih.gov/medlineplus/ency/article/003335.htm (accessed May 25, 2011).

———. "MRI scans." http://www.nlm.nih.gov/medlineplus/mriscans.html (accessed May 25, 2011).

ORGANIZATIONS

American College of Radiology, 1891 Preston White Dr., Reston, VA, 20191, (703) 648-8900, http://www.acr.org.

National Institute of Biomedical Imaging and Bioengineering, 31 Center Dr., 1C14, Bethesda, MD, 20892-8859, (301) 469-8859, http://www.nibib.gov.

Kurt Richard Sternlof
Rosalyn Carson-DeWitt, MD
Brenda W. Lerner
William A. Atkins

Magnetic seizure therapy

Definition

Magnetic seizure therapy (MST) is a newer form of convulsive therapy that was under development between the late 1990s and 2011. Many older forms of convulsive therapy use direct electric shocks; however, MST uses rapidly alternating strong magnetic fields to induce **seizures**. In addition to MST, convulsive therapies include **electroconvulsive therapy** (ECT), **transcranial**

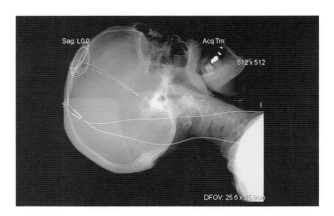

A lateral x ray of a patient's brain, showing the electrodes used in deep brain stimulation. (© Medical Body Scans/ Photo Researchers, Inc.)

magnetic stimulation (TMS), deep **brain** stimulation, and **vagus nerve stimulation**.

Purpose

Convulsive therapies, also called electrotherapies and electrical brain stimulations, generally induce a seizure, or convulsion, in a patient to provide improvement in mental illnesses, the chief among them being major **depression**. MST is one of these convulsive therapies. However, it was developed as a safer and more effective form of convulsive therapies.

Description

Therapeutic magnetic seizure induction, the process of MST, was first performed in Bern, Switzerland, in May 2000. Numerous controlled studies on psychiatric patients were performed after that. Although the results of these studies show promise, researchers continue to investigate the effectiveness and safety of MST. As of 2011, MST was not yet considered an established convulsive therapy in the United States.

During MST, the patient is under a general anesthesia. The process involves a generator that produces multiple short bursts of electricity at a frequency of 50 to 100 hertz (Hz). This creates powerful magnetic fields within a wire coil shaped like a figure eight and attached to a paddle. A technician places the coil/paddle directly onto a patient's forehead, near the forehead, or directly onto the scalp. Because the magnetic fields are not absorbed or scattered by the skull, lower frequency current than in ECT is sufficient; thus, MST is safer than ECT because it uses less electricity.

The magnetic fields reach down about one inch (2.5 cm) into the skull to produce electrical current affecting brain cells directly under the coil. These currents do not reach into areas beneath the cortex. However, researchers are working to increase the distance reached to affect deeper-lying brain regions for greater positive results. The risks associated with MST are smaller than those associated with ECT, but they include the standard risks associated with anesthetics. Additionally, memory loss and disruption of concentration and thinking are shorter and less severe.

The oldest convulsive therapy, ECT, has been the standard treatment for medication-resistant major depression since about 1940. However, ECT sends electricity to the brain and requires general anesthesia and muscle relaxants, subjecting patients to these drugs' associated risks. ECT causes memory loss for events close to the event of therapy and prior to therapy, and this memory does not return to all patients. To avoid the larger risks of anesthesia, muscle relaxants, and memory loss, researchers developed alternative convulsive therapies. A novel alternative, MST shows the most promise and was developed from TMS, which does not induce seizures at its generated electrical frequencies of 0.3 to 20 Hz.

TMS generates lower frequencies than required by ECT, so seizures do not occur. TMS is also focused and more localized to avoid the larger brain areas accessed by ECT. As a result, TMS avoids memory loss. TMS does not require general anesthesia, so those associated risks do not exist. Magnetic seizure therapy comprises TMS administered at higher frequencies to induce seizures, at 50 to 100 Hz, but MST uses magnetic fields instead of electricity, and these fields act directly on the brain. The skull does not absorb or scatter the magnetic fields, making MST more efficient than ECT. MST promises greater safety and diminished cognitive side effects over ECT.

Uses for depression, bipolar disorder, and schizophrenia

MST provides positive outcomes in treatment for a number of mental disorders. While the primary illness treated with MST is the same as for ECT, major depression, MST is also successful in cases of **schizophrenia**, bipolar depression, and bipolar mania. In 2005, Mitchell and Loo studied the safety and effectiveness of repetitive MST. They examined meta-analyses and individual patient reports and found that repetitive MST may be most effective in younger patients with no psychotic features and in depression that is not of the longest duration.

Further, they found that some depression occurring in **bipolar disorder** responds better to repetitive MST than do unipolar depressions (those not part of a bipolar syndrome). The majority of depressed patients receiving repetitive MST do not suffer any side effects or only slight discomfort in the stimulated scalp nerves and muscles or an occasional light headache. Sachdev, Loo, Mitchell, and Mahli found in 2005 that repetitive MST produces significant positive outcomes in patients having the deficit syndrome of schizophrenia, which includes lack of talking, emotion, and motivation. This pilot investigation confirmed the existing research regarding MST as a successful treatment for schizophrenia.

Other applications

Harvard Medical School and Stanford University reported that over 30 ongoing controlled studies examining MST in the United States between October 2005 and late 2011 showed positive outcomes. These studies looked at MST as a treatment for mental illnesses and medical conditions having a mental health

component. As of 2011, these included major depression, schizophrenia, **schizoaffective disorder**, bipolar disorder, **post-traumatic stress disorder** (PTSD), obsessive compulsive disorder (OCD), Tourette syndrome, Parkinson's disease, **stroke**, and cerebral palsy. Additional applications may be found in future research.

Benefits

Sarah H. Lisanby, a professor of clinical psychiatry at Columbia University and the director of the Division of Brain Stimulation and Therapeutic Modulation at the New York State Psychiatric Institute, found that patients were able to remember their own names, current setting, current date, and current location much more quickly after receiving MST than after undergoing ECT. In fact, MST produced only two minutes of memory loss, while ECT caused memory loss for 13 minutes. MST also caused fewer problems with concentration. In task completion, patients finished a simple task in four minutes after receiving ECT, but in only two minutes after MST, and these differences were significant. Lisanby, who is also the leader of the Transcranial Magnetic Stimulation Unit in the fMRI (functional **magnetic resonance imaging**) Research Center at Columbia University, believes that most depressive patients can improve with TMS and without induced seizures but that some depressed patients may need to undergo a seizure to improve and can benefit more from MST, because it offers fewer and smaller side effects than does ECT. Ongoing research may confirm these findings.

Precautions

MST has been a subject of debate since its inception. Its supporters report numerous well-documented successes, while its detractors insist that long-term patient improvement is possible only through seizures induced by ECT. However, researchers have found that MST seizures do not produce the large and intense side effects of ECT. MST produces fewer and shorter disruptions of memory, concentration, and orientation. Overall, MST may be safer and more efficient than ECT, produce fewer side effects, and perhaps reduce treatment costs.

There is debate on whether MST is more effective than TMS. According to the February 23, 2007, issue of the *Harvard Mental Health Letter,* 40% of medication-resistant depression cases improve with TMS, which does not induce any seizures. TMS may also reduce the time needed for psychiatric drugs to work. TMS may provide some improvement for **obsessive-compulsive disorder** (OCD), but as of 2011, the FDA had not yet approved any repetitive transcranial magnetic stimulation device for treatment purposes other than depression.

Preparation

Preparation for magnetic seizure therapy is not necessary.

Aftercare

After MST is used on a patient, the individual is carefully monitored for side effects of the procedure and other possible complications. Although generally perceived as safer than other convulsive therapies, MST is still not without medical risks.

Risks

As with any medical procedure, risks are present. The risks associated with MST are smaller than those associated with ECT. The standard risk is one involving the use of anesthetics. In addition, memory loss and disruption of concentration and thinking can occur but are usually much less than with ECT.

Results

MST has been viewed as useful in nonhuman primates and in humans with depression. Preliminary results with MST show that induced seizures are more focused, result in less overlap into hippocampal and deep brain structures, and produce less side effects than those seizures induced with ECT.

Research & general acceptance

In a 2006 meta-analysis, researchers Loo, Schweitzer, and Pratt found that recent advances and alternative technical approaches have developed in ECT. They examined recent **clinical trials**, case reports, and research updates in ECT's best practices and completed/ongoing research. Loo, Schweitzer, and Pratt found an increasing use of a number of alternative electrode placements useful in ECT, several variations in stimulus configurations, and two altogether new approaches that are successful. These new approaches are MST and focal electrical stimulation. The researchers decided that MST may promise success and safety in treating a variety of mental illnesses but needs further research. Their conclusion confirms the findings of the meta-analysis of Stanford and colleagues in 2005 that includes 69 separate sources and was as of 2011 approved for continuing education credit learning among physicians and researchers.

KEY TERMS

Anesthesia—A drug that induces loss of sensitivity to pain to all or part of a body.

Bipolar depression—The medical condition involving depression with the presence of at least one manic episode.

Bipolar mania—A mental disorder involving manic episodes frequently with depression.

Convulsion—Uncontrollable motions of limbs of the body or the body itself.

Cortex—The outer layer of the cerebrum in the brain.

Depression—A psychiatric disorder involving feelings of hopelessness and symptoms of fatigue, sleeplessness, suicidal tendencies, and poor concentration.

Hertz—A unit of frequency equal to one cycle per second.

Magnetic field—A region or space that is surrounded by a magnetized body or a current-carrying circuit.

Schizophrenia—A mental disorder involving degraded thinking and emotions, often with auditory hallucinations.

In addition to these findings, as of 2011, Lisanby was researching two distinct forms of MST. One of these uses a wire coil to focus seizures in the prefrontal cortex of the brain. The other form uses a coil to stimulate a broader brain area. This research is part of a wider study of MST effects compared with ECT effects in ongoing research at New York State Psychiatric Institute. Lisanby believes that MST can provide fewer side effects and better results than ECT for individuals with depression and a range of other mental illnesses.

In 2010, a clinical study was conducted in the University Hospital at Bonn, Germany. The investigators conducted a single center, clinical pilot efficacy study. Its goal is to show that magnetic seizure therapy can be effective as an add-on therapy for the treatment of refractory major depression as assessed by the Hamilton Depression Rating Scale.

The study's results showed that magnetic seizure therapy produced similar outcomes when compared to electroconvulsive therapy for the treatment of resistant depression. However, the recovery times from the procedures for MST were much faster than for ECT. In addition, fewer cognitive side effects were seen with the

QUESTIONS TO ASK YOUR DOCTOR

- Is MST my best option?
- What are the risks with MST?
- Do the benefits outweigh the risks?

MST. The results of the study were reported at the annual meeting of the European College of Neuropsychopharmacology. The MST device used for the study was the MagPro MST.

The first commercial MST device was developed by MagVenture, a company headquartered in Denmark. As of December 2010, the MagPro MST was considered the most powerful MST device yet to be developed, being about twice as powerful as other such devices. It was shown to be an effective and reliable device for inducing seizures. Earlier devices were not considered reliable for inducing seizures. Sarah Kayser, of the University Hospital and one of the authors of the German study, noted in an interview with *Clinical Psychiatry News* that the MagPro MST was "much smaller and easier to work with" than older devices, which were "large and unwieldy with multiple components."

Resources

BOOKS

Boyer, Bret A., and M. Indira Paharia, eds. *Comprehensive Handbook of Clinical Health Psychology*. Hoboken, NJ: John Wiley and Sons, 2008.

The Duke Encyclopedia of New Medicine: Conventional and Alternative Medicine for All Ages. London: Rodale, 2006.

Fink, Max. *Electroconvulsive Therapy: A Guide for Professionals and Their Patients*. Oxford: Oxford University Press, 2009.

Lisanby, Sarah H., ed. *Brain Stimulation in Psychiatric Treatment*. Washington, DC: American Psychiatric, 2004.

PERIODICALS

Avery, David H., et al. "A Controlled Study of Repetitive Transcranial Magnetic Stimulation in Medication-Resistant Major Depression." *Biological Psychiatry* 59, no. 2 (2006): 187–94.

Harvard Medical School. "Electroconvulsive Therapy." *Harvard Mental Health Letter* 23, no. 8 (2007): 1–3.

Helwick, Caroline. "Magnetic Seizure Therapy Matches ECT for Depression." *Clinical Psychiatry News* 38, no. 10 (October 1, 2010): 1–2.

Lisanby, Sarah H., A. Peterchev, M. A. Marcolin, and F. Padberg, eds. "Transcranial Brain Stimulation for Treatment of Psychiatric Disorders: Magnetic Seizure Therapy for the Treatment of Depression." *Advances in Biological Psychiatry* 23 (2007): 155–71. (DOI: 10.1159/000101036).

Loo, Colleen K, and Philip B. Mitchell. "A Review of the Efficacy of Transcranial Magnetic Stimulation (TMS) Treatment for Depression, and Current and Future Strategies to Optimize Efficacy." *Journal of Affective Disorders* 88, no. 3 (2005): 255–67.

Loo, Colleen K., Isaac Schweitzer, and Chris Pratt. "Recent Advances in Optimizing Electroconvulsive Therapy." *Australian and New Zealand Journal of Psychiatry* 40, no. 8 (2006): 632–38.

Mitchell, Philip B., and Colleen K. Loo. "Transcranial Magnetic Stimulation for Depression." *Australian and New Zealand Journal of Psychiatry* 40, no. 5 (2006): 406–13.

Sachdev, Perminder, Colleen K. Loo, Philip B. Mitchell, and Gin Malhi. "Transcranial Magnetic Stimulation for the Deficit Syndrome of Schizophrenia: A Pilot Investigation." *Psychiatry and Clinical Neurosciences* 5, no. 3 (2005): 354–57.

Stanford, Arielle D., et al. "Magnetic Seizure Therapy and Other Convulsive Therapies." *Primary Psychiatry* 12, no. 10 (2005): 44–50.

ORGANIZATIONS

American Psychiatric Association, 1000 Wilson Blvd., Ste. 1825, Arlington, VA, 22209-3901, (703) 907-7300, apa@psych.org, http://www.psych.org.

Association for Convulsive Therapy, 5454 Wisconsin Ave., Chevy Chase, MD, 20815, (301) 951-7220, http://www.act-ect.org/act/index.php.

New York State Psychiatric Institute, Columbia University Medical Center, 1051 Riverside Dr., New York City, NY, 10032, (212) 543-6000, http://www.nyspi.org.

Patty Inglish, MS

Magnetocephalogram *see* **Electroencephalography**

Major depressive disorder

Definition

Major depressive disorder (MDD) is a condition characterized by a long-lasting depressed mood or marked loss of interest or pleasure (anhedonia) in all or nearly all activities. Children and adolescents with MDD may be irritable instead of sad. These symptoms, along with others described below, must be sufficiently severe to interfere significantly with the patient's daily functioning.

Demographics

According to Mental Health America, depression affects more than 21 million Americans and is the leading cause of disability within this population for persons aged 15–44. Recent research indicates that 4.9% of the population of the United States meets the diagnostic criteria for MDD at any given time, but 17.1% will experience at least one episode of the disorder at some point during their lives. While the disorder may affect people at any age, it is most commonly diagnosed in young adults in their twenties. For reasons that are not well understood, women are twice as likely to develop MDD as are men; prior to puberty, however, MDD is about equally common in girls and boys. Adolescence is a high-risk period for MDD; while suicide may result from impulsive behavior under **stress** rather than from MDD, it is noteworthy that about 14% of all teenage deaths are due to suicide. The figures for gay and lesbian youth indicate that as many as 20%–35% make suicide attempts. Other risk factors include Hispanic ethnicity; younger age at onset; lower levels of education or income; and being separated or divorced.

Depression appears to have become a more common disorder over the past century. Epidemiologists studying the incidence of depression across time compared groups of people born between 1917 and 1936, between 1937 and 1952, and between 1953 and 1966. Their results indicated that the rate of depression increased progressively from one generation to the next. While no single explanation for the rise in depressive disorders emerged, some researchers have suggested that the breakdown of social support networks caused by higher rates of family disruption and greater social mobility may be important contributing factors.

Description

Major depressive disorder is a serious mental disorder that profoundly affects an individual's quality of life. Unlike normal **bereavement** or an occasional episode of "the blues," MDD causes a lengthy period of gloom and hopelessness and may rob the sufferer of the ability to take pleasure in activities or relationships that were previously enjoyable. In some cases, depressive episodes seem to be triggered by an obviously painful event, but MDD may also develop without a specific stressor. Research indicates that an initial episode of **depression** is likely to be a response to a specific stimulus, but later episodes are progressively more likely to start without a triggering event. A person suffering major depression finds job-related and other responsibilities, such as parenting, to be burdensome and carries them out only with great effort. Mental efficiency and memory are affected, causing even simple tasks to be tiring and irritating. Sexual interest dwindles; many people with MDD become withdrawn and avoid any type of social activity. Even the ability to enjoy a good meal

or a sound night's sleep is frequently lost; many depressed people report a chronic sense of malaise (general discomfort or unease). For some, the pain and suffering accompanying MDD become so unendurable that **suicide** is viewed as the only option; MDD has the highest mortality rate of any mental disorder.

Major depressive disorder may be limited to a single episode of depression; more commonly, it may become a chronic condition with many episodes of depressed mood. Other symptoms that may develop include psychotic symptoms (e.g., bizarre thoughts, including delusional beliefs and hallucinations); **catatonia**; postpartum onset (sometimes accompanied by psychotic symptoms); and **seasonal affective disorder**, or SAD.

Such conditions as **postpartum depression** and seasonal affective disorder accompany MDD only under certain circumstances. Postpartum depression begins within four weeks of giving birth. Women with this disorder experience labile mood (frequent drastic mood changes). They may feel helpless and unable to care adequately for their infant, or they may be completely uninterested in the child. The symptoms of postpartum depression are much more severe than those of the relatively common "new baby blues," which affect up to 70% of new mothers. The presence of psychotic symptoms in the mother, too many ruminations (obsessive thoughts), or **delusions** about the infant are associated with a heightened risk of serious harm to the child. The symptoms of postpartum depression are usually attributed to fluctuations in the woman's hormone levels and the emotional impact of bearing a child. The condition is especially likely to occur in women who were highly anxious during pregnancy or had a previous history of mood disorder. SAD is also more common in women than in men; in this case, symptoms of MDD typically begin in fall and winter, especially in northern latitudes in the United States and Canada. Exposure to natural light is limited during the winter in these areas, but the symptoms of SAD typically improve during the spring and summer.

Causes and symptoms

Causes

Because MDD is a relatively common mental disorder, researchers have performed a range of studies to identify possible underlying causes. Three types of causes are commonly identified: intrapsychic, environmental, and biological.

INTRAPSYCHIC. Since Sigmund Freud attributed the development of mental disorders to intrapsychic (occurring inside the mind) conflicts occurring during early childhood, a sizeable number of theorists have suggested that MDD results from a tendency to internalize negative events. Cognitive behavioral treatment models assume that a person's interpretation of situations is responsible for the development of depression rather than the events themselves. Some people blame themselves for negative experiences while attributing positive outcomes to external sources; they may tend to feel guilty, undeserving, and eventually depressed. For example, they may think of their present job as something they obtained by a stroke of good luck; at the same time, they may regard being laid off as something they brought on themselves. When these patterns of thought become habitual, they lead to a style of coping characterized by a view of oneself as worthless, ineffectual, and inferior. In some cases, people pick up these patterns of thinking from their parents or other family members.

Another theory regarding intrapsychic causes attributes depression to so-called "learned helplessness." This theory grew out of research studies on animal learning, comparing dogs that were able to escape from mild electric shocks to dogs that could not escape. The researchers discovered that the dogs who could not escape the mild shocks became passive; later, when they were put in a situation in which they could escape the shocks, they made no attempt to do so but simply lay on their stomachs and whimpered. The animals had, in short, learned to be helpless; they had learned during the first part of the experiment that nothing they had done had any effect on the shocks. Applied to human beings, this theory holds that people tend to become depressed when they have had long-term experiences of helplessness—as would be the case for abused children. Later, when the children have become adults, they do not see themselves as grownups with some control over their lives; they continue to react to setbacks or losses with the same feelings of helplessness that they had as children, and they become depressed.

ENVIRONMENTAL. Environmental theories of the etiology (causation) of MDD emphasize the role of external events in triggering depression. According to this perspective, people become depressed primarily due to unfortunate circumstances that are difficult to change. In some cases, these misfortunes may include environmental disasters or personal losses, but such other factors as low socioeconomic status, oppression associated with one's sex or race, or unpleasant or frustrating relationships are also thought to contribute to depression.

BIOLOGICAL. Ancient medicine alleged that one's state of mind was related to the presence of specific "humors," or fluids, in the body, and various theories have emerged since the eighteenth century regarding possible constitutional factors that affect mood. In recent years, researchers have found numerous abnormalities in the neuroendocrine systems, **neurotransmitters**, and neuroanatomy of the brains of both children and adults with MDD, as well as strong evidence for **genetic factors** in MDD.

Levels of cortisol, a hormone associated with the human "fight-or-flight" response, have long been studied as possible biological markers for depression. In many adults, cortisol levels rise when the person is acutely depressed, and they return to normal when the depression passes. Research findings have been inconsistent regarding cortisol levels in children and adolescents, although there is some evidence that higher levels of cortisol secretion are associated with more severe depressive symptoms and with a higher likelihood of recurrence. However, cortisol levels are not considered reliable enough to be useful in diagnosing MDD.

Another biological factor that has been studied in humans involves changes in the levels of neurotransmitters, which are chemicals that conduct nerve impulses across the tiny gaps between nerve cells. Variations in the levels of certain neurotransmitters have been researched for many years due to their importance in the brain's limbic system, which is the center of emotions and has many important pathways to other parts of the **brain**. In depression, the system that regulates a neurotransmitter called "serotonin" does not function properly. A group of medications known as "serotonin specific reuptake inhibitors," or "SSRIs," are believed to be effective in relieving depression because they prevent **serotonin** from being taken back up too quickly by receptors in the brain.

Differences in the anatomical structure of the brains of children and adults with MDD have suggested several possible explanations for its development. In particular, the prefrontal cortex has been thought to play a role, on the basis of findings in stroke patients with damage to the prefrontal area of the brain, and in children and adults with MDD. Researchers found that stroke patients experienced more severe depression if their stroke occurred closer to the frontal lobe of the brain. Similarly, people with MDD have been found to have decreased frontal lobe volume. Studies of depressed children and adults included subjects who were currently depressed as well as those with a history of depression who were in remission, which suggests that abnormalities in the frontal lobe may be a structural marker of depression. Other neurological studies have reported lower levels of electrical activity in the left frontal cortex among depressed subjects (including the infants of depressed mothers), compared to persons who are not depressed.

Researchers have also been interested in the relationship of genetic factors to depression. It has been known for many years that depression tends to run in families. Convincing evidence of the heritability of depression has been obtained by comparing identical twins (who have identical genetic inheritances) with fraternal twins; these studies have consistently found a higher likelihood of depression between identical than between fraternal twins. Other data indicate that people with a higher genetic risk of depression are more likely to become depressed following a stressful event than are people with fewer genetic risk factors.

Symptoms

The core symptom of major depression is a sad mood that does not go away. While most people have occasional days when they feel out of sorts, persons with MDD experience low feelings that build gradually over a period of days or weeks. They are usually not able to "snap out of it," even when something positive happens. In some cases, the symptoms are preceded by an obvious loss or painful event, such as divorce or a death in the family, but the disorder may also appear to begin "out of the blue." People with MDD often appear sad, irritable, and easily moved to tears. They may sleep poorly and complain of vague physical aches and pains; experience sexual difficulties or loss of interest in sex; drop out of social activities; and come across to others as unhappy or lacking in energy. Some people with MDD may deny that they feel depressed, but they lose their enthusiasm for hobbies or work they once found enjoyable and rewarding. Children and adolescents present with many of these same characteristics, but they may often appear easily frustrated and cranky instead of sad. The symptoms of MDD can be summarized as follows:

- disturbed mood (sad, hopeless, discouraged, "down in the dumps") during most of the day
- loss of interest or pleasure in activities
- change in appetite nearly every day, leading either to weight gain or to loss of 5% of body weight; in children, may appear as a failure to make normal weight gains related to growth
- insomnia (waking in the middle of the night and having difficulty returning to sleep, or waking too early in the morning) or hypersomnia (sleeping much more than normal)
- psychomotor retardation (slowed thinking, speech, body movements) or agitation (inability to sit still, hand-wringing, pulling at clothing, skin, or other objects) that is apparent to others
- sense of worthlessness or unreasonable guilt over minor failings
- problems with clear thinking, concentration, and decision-making
- recurrent thoughts of death or suicide, or making a suicide attempt

KEY TERMS

Anxiety—Can be experienced as a troubled feeling, a sense of dread, fear of the future, or distress over a possible threat to a person's physical or mental well-being.

Cognitive-behavioral therapy—Psychotherapy technique designed to help people change their attitudes, perceptions, and patterns of thinking.

Electroconvulsive therapy (ECT)—Therapy for mood disorders that involves passing electrical current through the brain in order to create a brief convulsion.

Insomnia—Waking in the middle of the night and having difficulty returning to sleep, or waking too early in the morning.

Serotonin—A chemical messenger in the brain, thought to play a role in mood regulation. Low levels of serotonin are associated with depression.

Diagnosis

While many people go through sad or elated moods from time to time, people with major depressive disorder suffer from severe or prolonged mood states that disrupt their daily functioning. Major depressive disorder may be diagnosed when a person visits their family doctor with concerns about their mood, changes in appetite or sleeping patterns, and similar symptoms. Doctors in family practice, in fact, are more likely to be consulted by patients with depression than doctors in any other medical specialty. In addition, a large proportion of people discuss depressed feelings with their clergyperson, who has typically been trained (in the mainstream Christian and Jewish communities) to recognize the signs of depression and to encourage the person to see their doctor. In some cases, a concerned spouse or other family member may take the patient to the doctor.

The **diagnosis** of MDD involves a constellation of symptoms in addition to depressed mood. After taking a careful history, including asking the patient about his or her sleeping patterns, appetite, sex drive, and mood, the doctor will give the patient a physical examination to rule out other possible causes of the symptoms. Certain other disorders may resemble MDD, including cognitive dysfunction caused by the direct effects of a substance (a drug of abuse, medication, or toxic chemical); various medical conditions (e.g., an underactive thyroid gland; strokes; or early stages of **dementia**), or other mental disorders. Such stressful life events as normal bereavement may also produce behaviors similar to those associated with MDD; while a bereaved person may appear to have many of the characteristics of MDD, the disorder would not be diagnosed unless the symptoms continued for more than two months or were extreme in some way. As part of the diagnostic interview, the doctor may give the patient a brief screening questionnaire, such as the **Beck Depression Inventory**, in order to obtain a clearer picture of the symptoms. In addition to interviewing the patient, the doctor may talk to family members or others who can provide information that the patient may forget, deny, or consider unimportant.

The diagnosis of MDD is complicated by the fact that people with MDD frequently suffer from other mental illnesses at the same time, including **anxiety disorders**, **substance abuse** problems, and **personality disorders**. Given that the patient's symptoms may vary according to age, sex, and stage of the illness, some clinicians have suggested that MDD may actually be a collection or group of disorders with a small number of underlying core symptoms rather than a single entity.

The diagnosis of a person with MDD may also include certain specifiers, including the severity and chronicity of the disorder, the presence of psychotic features (delusions or hallucinations); catatonia (remaining motionless for long periods of time, and other peculiarities of posture, movement, or speech); melancholia (depressed mood that is worse in the morning; early-morning wakening; psychomotor retardation or agitation; significant weight loss; or inappropriate guilt); and information regarding postpartum status. If the depression is currently in remission, this fact is also commonly listed as a diagnostic specifier.

DSM

Major depressive disorder is included as a mood disorder in the fourth edition of the *Diagnostic and Statistical Manual of Mental Disorders* (*DSM-IV*), the clinical guideline used by medical professionals in diagnosing mental disorders. The fifth edition of the *DSM* (*DSM-5*) is due for publication in May 2013. Proposed changes for the fifth edition include reclassifying mood disorders as depressive disorders and removing the so-called "grief exclusion," which does not consider bereavement or **grief** as a criteria for major depression. The reasoning behind the removal is that research does not support the separation of loss of a loved one from other stressors; however, the proposal has been met with controversy.

Treatment

Because MDD can have a devastating impact on a person's life, the importance of effective treatment cannot be overestimated. Treatment strategies have evolved over the years, according to researchers' varying opinions of the underlying causes of depression, but the outpouring of interest in MDD allows treatment providers to select from a variety of tested approaches.

Psychotherapy

Cognitive psychotherapies for depression are based on the belief that depressed people perceive themselves and the world in unrealistically negative ways. Considerable research has been done regarding the cognitive dimension of depression; for example, studies find that depressed people pay more attention to negative events than to positive ones, and that dwelling on unpleasant experiences prolongs and worsens depressive episodes. Cognitive therapists help patients identify the automatic thoughts that lead them to anticipate poor outcomes or to interpret neutral events in negative ways. The patient is also encouraged to challenge negative thoughts by comparing his or her expectations of events with actual outcomes.

Evidence that poor interpersonal relationships may heighten vulnerability to depression, along with findings that depressed adults and depressed children tend to provoke negative reactions from other people, has prompted the use of **social skills training** as a form of treatment. In this type of therapy, patients are trained to recognize actions and attitudes that annoy or distance other people, and to replace these behaviors with more appropriate ones. Social skills training may be particularly helpful to depressed persons who tend to isolate themselves and have lost confidence in their ability to develop healthy relationships. This treatment model promotes the idea that depression is likely to lift when the patient becomes adept at making new friends and establishing rewarding social supports.

Psychodynamic psychotherapy is often effective in treating patients with MDD whose depression is related to unresolved issues from the past, particularly abuse or other painful childhood experiences. The growth of insight into one's emotional patterns, as well as the supportive aspects of this form of therapy, offer considerable relief from emotional pain to many patients.

Medications

The use of medications in the treatment of depression began in the late 1950s with the successful introduction of tricyclic **antidepressants** and MAO inhibitors. Treatment of depression with medications has greatly increased since the advent of **selective serotonin reuptake inhibitors (SSRIs)** such as **fluoxetine** (Prozac) or **sertraline** (Zoloft). While these medications are no more effective than their predecessors, they have fewer side effects and are much safer for patients who may be likely to overdose. Selecting the optimal antidepressant medication is not always a straightforward process, however, and the patient may have to try out various drugs for a period of weeks or months before finding one that is effective for him or her. In addition, while the **SSRIs** have comparatively few side effects, such complaints as loss of sexual interest or functioning, nervousness, headaches, gastrointestinal complaints, drowsiness, and **insomnia** can be significant obstacles to the patient's taking the medication as directed.

More recently, **Quetiapine** (Seroquel and Seroquel XR), once used for treatment of **schizophrenia** and **bipolar disorder**, may be used together with other antidepressant medications to treat major depressive disorder in adults who did not have an adequate response to antidepressant therapy.

Other mainstream approaches

The use of **electroconvulsive therapy** (ECT), initially introduced in the 1930s, was virtually abandoned as a treatment for MDD for many years, largely as a result of the effectiveness and convenience of psychotropic (mind-altering) medications. Since the 1980s, however, interest in the procedure has renewed; in 1990, the **American Psychiatric Association** published new guidelines for the use of ECT. Despite media portrayals of ECT as an outdated and cruel form of treatment that causes considerable pain, in actuality the patient is given a sedative, and the electrical stimulation is calibrated precisely to produce the maximum therapeutic effects. ECT may be the first line of treatment when a patient cannot tolerate the customary medications or is at high risk of harming himself or herself; but it is more commonly used with patients who fail to respond to drug treatment. In terms of effectiveness, however, ECT actually outperforms medications even among patients who are helped by antidepressants, as well as those who are resistant to drug treatment.

The use of phototherapy (**light therapy**) has proven to be the treatment of choice for patients diagnosed with seasonal affective disorder. Although the reasons for the effectiveness of phototherapy are not yet clear, treatment involves exposing the eyes to bright (2500 lux) light for several minutes a day. Currently, however, there is little evidence to suggest that phototherapy is useful in the treatment of other types of MDD.

Alternative and complementary treatments

The National Center for Complementary and Alternative Medicine (NCCAM) is conducting an ongoing series of clinical tests of alternative and complementary treatments for depression. Those that have been shown to reduce symptoms of depression and compare favorably with conventional treatments include **acupuncture**; Ayurvedic medicine; **meditation**; and a therapeutic diet designed to be free of caffeine and refined sugar.

Herbal preparations are common alternative treatments for depression; in fact, a NCCAM study found that depression is the single most common reason for people in the United States to purchase herbal remedies. Some, such as St. John's wort, have been used in Europe for decades. The German Commission E, which regulates government approval of herbal preparations in German-speaking Europe, recently approved the use of Ginkgo biloba extract as a treatment for depression. The most important caution is that persons who are using herbal remedies, whether to treat depression or other conditions, should always tell their doctor what they are taking, how much, and how often. This warning is crucial because some herbal preparations that are safe in themselves can interact with prescription medications. In particular, **St. John's wort** has been reported to cause interactions with fluoxetine (Prozac).

Some complementary approaches appear to be helpful to persons with depression because they offer pleasurable experiences for the senses or lift the person's spirit. These include **aromatherapy**; **music therapy**; pet therapy; humor; therapeutic massage; and **yoga**.

Prognosis

Major depression is increasingly viewed as a chronic condition for many people. Left untreated, a depressive episode may last four months or longer, regardless of the age of onset. While most people recover fully from a given depressive episode, eventual recurrence is common. Long-term studies of people with MDD indicate that about 60% of patients who have one episode of depression will have a second episode; with each succeeding episode, the chances of a subsequent episode increase (persons having a third episode stand a 90% chance of having a fourth). Between depressive episodes, the patient's mood may return to a nondepressed state (in about two-thirds of the cases) or continue to show some degree of impairment (one-third of cases). Patients who recover only partially between episodes appear to be at especially high risk of recurrence.

QUESTIONS TO ASK YOUR DOCTOR

- What are the indications that I may have major depressive disorder?

- What physical and psychological diagnostic tests are needed for a thorough assessment?

- What treatment options do you recommend for me?

- What kind of changes can I expect to see with the medications you have prescribed for me?

- What are the side effects associated with the medications you have prescribed for me?

- Will medications for major depressive disorder interact with my current medications?

- What tests or evaluation techniques will you perform to see whether treatment has been beneficial for me?

- Should I see a specialist? If so, what kind of specialist should I contact?

- Does having major depressive disorder put me at risk for other health conditions?

- What tests or evaluation techniques will you perform to see whether treatment has been beneficial for my child?

- What symptoms or adverse effects are important enough that I should seek immediate treatment?

- Can you recommend an organization that will provide me with additional information about major depressive disorder?

- Can you recommend any support groups for me and my family?

Community studies indicate that about 60% of the people diagnosed with MDD are greatly improved or fully recovered by one year after diagnosis. A very severe initial episode of depression, the presence of a coexisting **dysthymic disorder**, or the existence of a serious medical condition are associated with a poorer prognosis.

Prevention

While programs specifically aimed at preventing MDD are not widespread, early interventions with children to address some of the issues related to depression have met with success. In particular, social skills training has been found to reduce symptoms of depression, perhaps by enabling children to develop the kinds of social supports and friendships that promote good mental health. Cognitive behavioral techniques that teach people to challenge dysfunctional thought patterns, such as the tendency to deny responsibility for good outcomes and to feel overly responsible for negative events, has been found to successfully reduce the rates of depressive symptoms in children and college students. In addition, psychoeducational work with parents having mood disorders has been effective in improving the adjustment of their children. Long-term follow-up of such approaches is incomplete, but these studies support the possibility that improved individual and family functioning may help to lower rates of depression in the future.

As the factors that increase an individual's vulnerability to depression become better understood, effective strategies for early **intervention** and possible prevention become possible. Brief therapies that target such symptoms as maladaptive thought patterns or interpersonal problems may lower the risk of serious mood disturbances. Knowledge of the mental health implications of natural or humanly caused disasters has already resulted in much improved mental health services to communities in need. It is realistic to expect that appropriate treatment will become more available and accessible to people experiencing less dramatic setbacks to their ability to function in the future.

Resources

BOOKS

American Psychiatric Association. *Diagnostic and Statistical Manual of Mental Disorders.* 4th ed., Text rev. Washington, DC: American Psychiatric Association, 2000.

American Psychological Association. *Publication Manual of the American Psychological Association,* 6th ed. Washington, DC: American Psychological Association, 2009.

Baldwin, Robert. *Depression in Later Life.* New York: Oxford University Press, 2010.

Gillberg, Christopher, Richard Harrington, and Hans-Christoph Steinhausen, eds. *A Clinician's Handbook of Child and Adolescent Psychiatry.* Cambridge: Cambridge University Press, 2011.

Graham, George. *The Disordered Mind: An Introduction to Philosophy of Mind and Mental Illness.* New York: Routledge, 2010.

Jongsma, Arthur E., Jr., L. Mark Peterson, and William P. McInnis. *The Child Psychotherapy Treatment Planner.* 4th ed. Hoboken, NJ: John Wiley & Sons, 2009.

North, Carol, and Sean Yutzy. *Goodwin and Guze's Psychiatric Diagnosis.* New York, NY: Oxford University Press, 2010.

O'Connor, Richard. *Undoing Depression: What Therapy Doesn't Teach You and Medication Can't Give You,* 2nd ed. New York: Little, Brown and Company, 2010.

Pelletier, Kenneth R., MD. *The Best Alternative Medicine* Kindle Edition, Part II, "CAM Therapies for Specific Conditions: Depression." Lady Lake, FL: Fireside, 2010.

Virani, Adil S., et al., eds. *Clinical Handbook of Psychotropic Drugs,* 19th ed. Cambridge, MA: Hogrefe Publishing, 2011.

PERIODICALS

Brodaty, H., et al. "A 25-year Longitudinal Comparison Study of the Outcome of Depression." *Psychological Medicine* 31 (2001): 1347-1358.

Nolan, Carla L., et al. "Prefrontal Cortical Volume in Childhood-Onset Major Depression." *Archives of General Psychiatry* 59 (2002): 173-175.

Nuland, Sherwin B., M.D. "The Uncertain Art: Lightning on My Mind." *The American Scholar* 71 (Spring 2002): 127-131.

Rush, A.J., et al. "Combining Medications to Enhance Depression Outcomes (CO-MED): Acute and Long-Term Outcomes of a Single-Blind Randomized Study." *American Journal of Psychiatry* 168 (2011): 689–701.

ORGANIZATIONS

American Academy of Child and Adolescent Psychiatry, 3615 Wisconsin Avenue NW, Washington, DC, 20016-3007, (202) 966-7300, Fax: (202) 966-2891, http://www.aacap.org.

American Psychological Association, 750 First Street NE, Washington, DC, 20003, (202) 336-5500, http://www.apa.org/index.aspx.

Depression and Bipolar Support Alliance (DBSA), 730 N. Franklin St., Ste. 501, Chicago, IL, 60654, (800) 826-3632, Fax: (312) 642-7243, http://www.dbsalliance.org.

Families for Depression Awareness, 395 Totten Pond Rd., Suite 404, Waltham, MA, 02451, (781) 890-0220, Fax: (781) 890-2411, http://www.familyaware.org.

Mental Health America, 2000 N. Beauregard Street, 6th Floor, Alexandria, VA, 22311, (703) 684-7722, (800) 969-6642, Fax: (703) 684-5968, http://www1.nmha.org.

National Alliance on Mental Illness (NAMI), Colonial Place Three, 2107 Wilson Blvd., Suite 300, Arlington, VA, 22201, (703) 524-7600, (800) 950-NAMI (6264), Fax: (703) 524-9094, http://www.nami.org/Hometemplate.cfm.

National Institute of Mental Health (NIMH), 6001 Executive Boulevard, Room 8184, MSC 9663, Bethesda, MD, 20892, (301) 443-4513, (866) 615-6464, Fax: (301) 443-4279, nimhinfo@nih.gov, http://www.nimh.nih.gov/index.shtml.

Jane A. Fitzgerald, Ph.D.
Laura Jean Cataldo, RN, Ed.D.

Male erectile disorder *see* **Erectile dysfunction**

Male orgasmic disorder

Definition

Male orgasmic disorder may be defined as a persistent or recurrent inability to achieve orgasm despite lengthy sexual contact or while participating in sexual intercourse.

The mental health professional's handbook, the *Diagnostic and Statistical Manual of Mental Disorders (DSM-IV-TR),* includes this disorder among the **sexual dysfunctions**, along with **premature ejaculation**, **dyspareunia**, and others.

Demographics

Male orgasmic disorder is found in all races and ethnic groups. In the case of the lifelong type of the disorder, manifestations will occur around the age of puberty. In certain genetic hypogonadism disorders, such as Klinefelter's syndrome, certain bodily signs and symptoms may alert the physician. Similarly, in associated thyroid, testicular and pituitary abnormalities, there may be other manifestations of the underlying disorder. In the acquired type of male orgasmic disorder, the patient will have had the previous experience of normal sexual function. In these cases, it is usually a situational factor that precipitates the disorder.

Description

The individual affected by male orgasmic disorder is unable to experience an orgasm following a normal sexual excitement phase. The affected man may regularly experience delays in orgasm or may be unable to experience orgasm altogether.

Normal orgasm

It is important to this discussion to understand the characteristics of a "normal" orgasm. The sensation of orgasm in the male includes emission followed by ejaculation. The term emission refers to a sensation of impending ejaculation produced by contractions of the prostate gland, seminal vesicles, and urethra accompanied by generalized muscular tension, perineal contractions, and involuntary pelvic thrusting. Orgasm is followed by a period of resolution characterized by feelings of well-being and generalized muscular relaxation. During this phase, men may be unable to respond to further sexual stimulation, erection, and orgasm for a variable period of time.

It is also important to distinguish orgasm from ejaculation, although in most instances they occur almost simultaneously. Orgasm is a peak emotional and physical experience, whereas ejaculation is simply a reflex action occurring at the lower portion of the spinal cord and resulting in ejection of semen. Some men have been able to recognize the separation of the two processes, enabling them to experience multiple orgasms without the occurrence of ejaculation. Once ejaculation takes place, a period of recovery time is required prior to a subsequent orgasm.

The sensation of orgasm differs between individuals, and individual orgasms may differ in the same individual. All orgasms share certain characteristics in common including rhythmic body and pelvic contractions, elevation of the heart rate, systemic hypertension, hyperventilation, and muscle tension, followed by the sudden release of tension.

The physiological mechanism of normal orgasm

The cycle of sexual response is under the control of a balanced interplay between the two major nervous systems, the sympathetic and the parasympathetic. In general, the sympathetic nervous system prompts action whereas the parasympathetic system's main action is recovery and calming. In order for a penis to become erect, its smooth muscles are relaxed and it becomes congested with blood vessels. This process is mediated by a complex cascade of humoral, neurological, and circulatory events in which the parasympathetic nervous system plays a key role. Orgasm and ejaculation and subsequent relaxation of the penis are predominantly functions of the sympathetic nervous system.

Thus, whereas emission is a balanced interplay between the parasympathetic and sympathetic nervous systems, orgasm and ejaculation are predominantly under the control of the sympathetic nervous system. The mechanisms of this system may be blocked by impaired function of the **brain** or of the hormonal, circulatory, and neurological systems. Additionally, certain medications may block these actions.

Abnormalities affecting the process of orgasm

Abnormalities in these processes may be "primary" or "secondary." Primary abnormalities are of lifelong duration with effective sexual performance never having been experienced. Secondary abnormalities are acquired after a period of normal function. If an orgasmic problem only occurs under a particular set of circumstances, or only with certain sexual partners, the condition is considered to be "situational" rather than "generalized" (occurring regardless of the circumstances or partner). The defect in sexual function may be total or partial.

The evidence strongly suggests that orgasm has more to do with the brain than with the body. Electrode stimulation of certain parts of the brain will produce

sexual pleasure similar to that produced by physical stimulation. The fact that orgasm occurs during sleep is supportive of this concept.

Causes and symptoms

Causes

The cause of male orgasmic disorders may be organic (related to a condition in the body), but, in most cases, is of psychological origin. It is important for the physician to make every effort to find an underlying cause because the therapy and prognosis depend upon it. A detailed history (including an interview with the sexual partner, if feasible), a general physical examination, the performance of certain laboratory and, in some cases, special tests, are important in the investigation of the underlying cause of the male orgasmic disorder.

Organic causes of male orgasmic disorder include the following:

• hypogonadism, in which the testes do not produce enough testosterone

• thyroid disorders (both hyperthyroidism—too much thyroid hormone—and hypothyroidism, or abnormally low levels of thyroid hormone)

• pituitary conditions (Cushing's syndrome, excessive production of the hormone that induces lactation called prolactin)

• diseases that affect the nervous system, such as strokes, multiple sclerosis, diabetic neuropathy, spinal cord injuries

• surgery affecting the prostate and other pelvic organs

• diseases of the penis

• substance abuse, including alcohol

• certain medications, including: the phenothiazines (antipsychotics such as chlorpromazine [Thorazine] or trifluoperazine [Stelazine]); certain medications used to treat high blood pressure, including the thiazides (such as triamterene [Dyazide] or spironolactone [Aldactone]) and beta blockers (such as propranolol [Inderal]); and tricyclic antidepressants such as doxepin (Sinequan) and protriptyline (Vivactil)

The most common causes of male orgasmic disorder are psychological in nature. The responsible psychological mechanisms may be "intrinsic" (due to basic internal factors), or "extrinsic" (due to external or environmental factors).

Intrinsic psychological factors that may cause male orgasmic disorder include:

• depression

• feelings of guilt, anger, fear, low self-esteem, and anxiety

• fear of getting the partner pregnant or of contracting a sexually-transmitted disease or HIV

Extrinsic psychological factors that may cause male orgasmic disorder include:

• living under conditions that cause undue stress
• unsatisfactory relationship with sexual partner
• past history of traumatic sexual encounters such as sexual abuse, rape, or incest
• having been raised in an atmosphere of strict sexual taboos

Environmental factors may interfere with sexual functioning. There may be no safe, private place in which the patient can exercise sexual activity or he may be too fatigued from other activities to participate sexually. The difficulties in striving for "safe sex" and the psychological effects that may result from homosexuality may also interfere with sexual function.

Symptoms

In order to be diagnosed with male orgasmic disorder, the following symptoms must be present according to the *DSM-IV-TR*:

• Persistent or recurrent delay in, or absence of, orgasm following a normal sexual excitement phase during sexual activity that the clinician judges to be adequate. The affected man's age is considered, as well.
• As with all of the sexual dysfunctions, the manual states that the dysfunction must cause the affected man "distress or interpersonal difficulty." According to the *DSM-IV-TR,* the orgasmic dysfunction cannot be better accounted for by another disorder (except another sexual disorder), and cannot be due exclusively to the direct effects of **substance abuse**, a medication, or a general medical condition. This entry, however, discusses the full scope of male orgasmic difficulties, and so discusses general medical conditions and medications as well as psychological factors.

In addition to specific symptoms involving sexual function (inability or delay in reaching orgasm after sufficient stimulation), most patients complain of anxiety, guilt, shame and frustration, and many develop bodily complaints on a psychological basis. Although sexual dysfunction usually occurs during sexual activity with a partner, the clinician should inquire about sexual function during masturbation. If problems occur during masturbation, the problem probably has nothing to do with the sexual partner.

The physician should differentiate male orgasmic disorder from other sexual disorders such as retarded or delayed ejaculation and retrograde ejaculation. In both of these conditions, orgasm occurs but is delayed or, in the case of retrograde ejaculation, occurs in a retrograde direction (into the bladder).

Diagnosis

The **diagnosis** is usually readily made on the basis of the patient's history and the presence of the *DSM-IV-TR* diagnostic criteria. Male orgasmic disorder may be part of a complex of sexual malfunctioning that may include **erectile dysfunction**, abnormalities in ejaculation (such as premature ejaculation or retrograde ejaculation), and **hypoactive sexual desire disorder**.

In order to differentiate between the various potential disorders, the physician may request laboratory tests and/or may perform further diagnostic evaluations. Blood plasma levels of testosterone are of help in diagnosing hypogonadism. A number of tests of thyroid, pituitary and adrenal function are available to diagnose hormonal abnormalities of those glands. A test for nocturnal penile erections may be performed to diagnose erectile dysfunction.

Treatment

If an extrinsic mechanism is discovered as the cause of the orgasmic disorder, steps should be taken to eliminate or ameliorate the problem. An example would be substance or alcohol abuse or the use of certain provocative medications. In the case of antihypertensives, for example, a number of equally effective agents are available if the one in current use is suspect. Therapy should be directed toward improvement of concurrent conditions such as diabetes that may be having an adverse effect on sexual function. Environmental factors that interfere with sexual activity should be corrected.

In the majority of cases, **psychotherapy** will be suggested even in those cases where psychological factors are secondary rather than the primary mechanism for the disorder. Such treatment should be rendered by therapists with special training in the disorders of sexual function and who can tactfully evaluate the sexual compatibility of the patient and his partner. Treatment usually requires the support of the sexual partner in improving both the psychological as well as the physical aspects of the problem. A step-wise program of partner stimulation of the patient to initially ejaculate outside the vagina, then at the vaginal labia, and finally inside the vagina may be helpful.

Prognosis

The prognosis of the patient with male orgasmic syndrome is dependent on whether the condition is lifelong or acquired and the condition's causes. Prognosis

KEY TERMS

Antihypertensive—An agent used in the treatment of hypertension (high blood pressure).

Diabetes mellitus—A chronic disease affecting the metabolism of carbohydrates that is caused by insufficient production of insulin in the body.

Diabetic neuropathy—Condition existing in people with diabetes in which the nerves at the extremities, especially the feet, are less sensitive to touch and injury.

Humoral—A term describing a hormonal substance secreted by an endocrine gland (such as the thyroid).

Perineal—An anatomical area located between the external genitals and the anus.

Phenothiazine—A class of drugs widely used in the treatment of psychosis.

Prostate gland—The gland at the base of a male's urethra that produces a component of semen.

Retroperitoneal—The anatomical area between the peritoneum (lining of the abdominal cavity) and the muscular and connective tissues of the abdominal wall.

Seminal fluid—Fluid composed of semen from the testes and prostatic secretions.

Seminal vesicles—Sac-like structures bordering the male urethra and serving as storage depots for the seminal fluid.

Urethra—The tubular passage conducting urine from the bladder to the exterior. In the male, the urethra traverses the penis.

is best when it can be demonstrated that the condition is related to some extrinsic or environmental factor that can be corrected or ameliorated. The prognosis is also favorable in those cases that are due to a remedial organic condition such as a thyroid disorder or hypogonadism. The prognosis is guarded when the disorder is found to be secondary to a deep-seated and chronic psychological or actual psychiatric problem that, in itself, carries an unfavorable prognosis.

Prevention

There are no definitive steps that can be taken to prevent the onset of the male orgasmic disorder. Prompt recognition of the syndrome is important so that appropriate therapy can be attempted as early as possible.

As with many chronic conditions, the longer the condition exists, the more difficult therapy becomes.

Resources

BOOKS

American Psychiatric Association. *Diagnostic and Statistical Manual of Mental Disorders.* 4th ed., text rev. Washington, DC: American Psychiatric Publishing, 2000.

Lue, Tom F., et al. *Atlas of Clinical Urology: Impotence and Infertility, Volume I.* New York: Current Medicine Group, 1999.

Masters, William, and Virginia Johnson. *Masters and Johnson on Sex and Human Loving.* New York: Little, Brown, 1988.

Steidle, Christopher P. *The Impotence Source Book.* New York: McGraw-Hill, 1999.

Ralph Myerson, M.D.

Malingering

Definition

In the context of medicine, malingering is the act of intentionally feigning or exaggerating physical or psychological symptoms for motives involving personal or financial gain. Various examples of malingering include fabricating mental or physical disorders in order to avoid school, work, or military service; or to obtain financial compensation, avoid criminal prosecution, or obtain narcotics and other drugs.

Demographics

Malingering can occur within any individual all over the world. Because it is often impossible to determine who is malingering and who is not, it is very difficult to statistically measure how frequently malingering occurs. When not detected and allowed to persist in society, malingering places enormous financial burdens on the health care system. According to the Texas Department of Insurance, fraud that includes malingering costs the U.S. insurance industry approximately $150 billion each year.

Description

People may feign physical or psychological illness for any number of reasons. Faked illness may get them out of work, military duty, or criminal prosecution. It can also help them obtain financial compensation through insurance claims, lawsuits, or workers' compensation.

Feigned symptoms may also be a way of getting a doctor to prescribe certain drugs.

According to the **American Psychiatric Association**, patients who malinger are different from people who invent symptoms for sympathy (**factitious disorder**). Patients who malinger clearly have something tangible to gain. People with factitious disorder appear to have a need to play the "sick" role. They may feign illness for attention or sympathy.

Malingering may take the form of complaints of chronic whiplash pain from automobile accidents. Whiplash claims are controversial. Although some people clearly do suffer from whiplash injury, others may be exaggerating the pain for insurance claims or lawsuits. Some intriguing scientific studies have shown that chronic whiplash pain after automobile accidents is almost nonexistent in countries where the legal systems do not encourage personal injury lawsuits or financial settlements. As specifically related to mental illness, the tendency is to fake more common disorders such as **major depressive disorder**, **post-traumatic stress disorder**, and **panic disorder** with **agoraphobia**. Generalized symptoms, such as headaches, dizziness, low back pain, stomach pain, etc., are easily manufactured, and x rays, **magnetic resonance imaging** (MRIs), or CAT scans (computed axial tomography) are unable to determine a physical cause.

The concept that fakers use less severe symptoms to escape detection was validated in 2001 in a research study. Individuals were asked to fake mental illnesses in such a way as to avoid detection by sophisticated psychological tests. All or portions of the following tests were employed in the research: the Structured Inventory of Malingered Symptomatology, the Psychopathic Personality Inventory, the M-Test, and the **Trauma** Symptom Inventory. Slightly over 11% of the 540 research participants successfully avoided detection and were diagnosed with real disorders instead of with malingering. Questionnaires completed by those who successfully faked symptoms showed that they avoided detection by endorsing fewer actual symptoms, staying away from unduly strange or bizarre symptoms, and responding based upon personal experience.

Although ordinarily an intended fraud, malingering may serve an adaptive purpose under circumstances of duress, such as while being held captive. Faking an illness at such a time may allow a person to avoid cooperating with their captors or to avoid punishment.

Causes and symptoms

People malinger for personal gain. Motivation is always external, and the malingering may be used to:

- evade hard or dangerous situations, punishment, or responsibility
- gain rewards such as free income, a source for drugs, sanctuary from police, or free hospital care
- avenge a monetary loss, legal ruling, or job termination

Mental health practitioners become alert to the possibility of malingering when circumstances exist that might help promote such a facade. The symptoms may vary but generally are similar to symptoms involving chronic **fatigue** syndrome or chronic pain—those for which objective tests such as x rays cannot find any physical cause.

Many dishonest methods are used by individuals feigning symptoms of malingering. Some of these include harming oneself, trying to convince medical professionals one has a disease after learning about its details (such as symptoms) in medical textbooks, taking drugs that provoke certain symptoms common in some diseases, performing excess **exercise** to induce muscle strain or other physical types of ailments, and overdosing on drugs.

Diagnosis

Malingering may be suspected when:

- a patient is referred for examination by an attorney
- the onset of illness coincides with a large financial incentive, such as a new disability policy
- objective medical tests do not confirm the patient's complaints
- the patient does not cooperate with the diagnostic work-up or prescribed treatment
- the patient has antisocial attitudes and behaviors (antisocial personality)

The **diagnosis** of malingering is a challenge for doctors. On the one hand, the doctor does not want to overlook a treatable disease. On the other hand, he or she does not want to continue ordering tests and treatments if the symptoms are faked. Malingering is difficult to distinguish from certain legitimate **personality disorders**, such as factitious disorder or post-traumatic stress disorder. In legal cases, malingering patients may be referred to a **psychiatrist**. Psychiatrists use certain written tests to try to determine whether the patient is faking the symptoms.

Treatment

The ***Diagnostic and Statistical Manual of Mental Disorders*** (*DSM*) does not recognize malingering as a

KEY TERMS

Antisocial personality—A personality characterized by attitudes and behaviors at odds with society's customs and moral standards, including illegal acts.

Factitious diseases—Conditions in which symptoms are deliberately manufactured by patients in order to gain attention and sympathy. Patients with factitious diseases do not fake symptoms for obvious financial gain or to evade the legal system.

Post-traumatic stress disorder (PTSD)—A disorder that occurs among survivors of severe environmental stress such as a tornado, an airplane crash, or military combat. Symptoms include anxiety, insomnia, flashbacks, and nightmares. Patients with PTSD are unnecessarily vigilant; they may experience survivor guilt, and they sometimes cannot concentrate or experience joy.

legitimate disorder, so no structured treatment regimen exists. Patients who are purposefully faking symptoms for gain do not want to be cured. Often, the malingering patient fails to report any improvement with treatment, and the doctor may try many treatments without success. Possible treatments may include **cognitive-behavioral therapy**, **psychotherapy**, **family therapy**, or other such types of psychological treatments.

Prognosis

If the person malingering accepts his or her malady, then treatment can be positively received, and the malingering can be minimized or even eliminated. However, if the person does not wish to admit to malingering, treatment is often difficult and lengthy and ends without resolution. Treatment of malingers by the medical profession has found that most patients do not accept psychiatric help. The person will go to another medical facility where their symptoms and medical history are not known, and they are free to once again pursue their acts of malingering. The recovery of malingers who do not accept and acknowledge their problem is rarely accomplished.

Resources

BOOKS

Dell, Paul F., and John A. O'Neil, eds. *Dissociation and the Dissociative Disorders: DSM-V and Beyond*. New York: Routledge, 2009.

Morgan, Joel E., and Jerry J. Sweet, eds. *Neuropsychology of Malingering Casebook*. New York: Psychology Press, 2008.

Rogers, Richard, ed. *Clinical Assessment of Malingering and Deception*. New York: Guilford Press, 2008.

ORGANIZATIONS

American Psychiatric Association, 1000 Wilson Blvd., Ste 1825, Arlington, VA, 22209-3901, (703) 907-7300, apa@psych.org, http://www.psych.org.

Robert Scott Dinsmoor
Jack H. Booth, Psy.D.

Managed care

Definition

Managed care is a generic term used primarily in the United States for various healthcare payment systems that attempt to contain unnecessary costs by controlling the type and level of services provided. An organization that uses managed care is often called a managed care organization, which is abbreviated MCO. Health maintenance organization (HMO) is a term that is often used synonymously with managed care, but HMOs are actually a particular type of managed care organization. Two other managed-care systems are the preferred provided organization (PPO) and the point-of-service (POS).

Purpose

Healthcare reform has been an increasingly urgent concern in the United States over the past 45 years. Until recently, the primary source of health-care coverage was indemnity insurance, which pays or reimburses the cost of medical services in the event of a person's illness or injury. Indemnity insurance gives health-care providers few reasons to use less expensive forms of treatment—the insurance companies generally pay for any treatment deemed necessary by a physician. Presumably, this type of system encourages providers to overuse expensive, unnecessary treatments and diagnostic procedures. Patient co-pays and deductibles attempt to limit excessive use of medical services. However, costs continue to rise, resulting in insurance companies' frequently raising premium prices.

The primary intent of managed care is to reduce healthcare costs. Emphasis is placed on preventive care and early **intervention**, rather than care provided after an illness or injury has occurred. The responsibility of limiting services is placed on the service provider rather than the consumer. This limitation is achieved by (a) "gatekeeper" policies that require individuals to get referrals for specialized treatment from their primary

Sources of health insurance among persons 18 or older who received mental health treatment* in the past year: 2005–2009

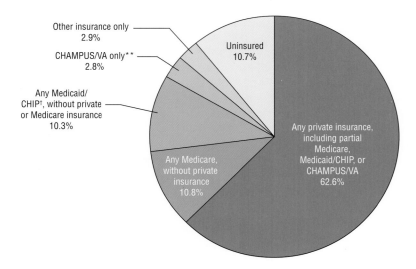

Other insurance only
2.9%

CHAMPUS/VA only**
2.8%

Any Medicaid/
CHIP†, without private
or Medicare insurance
10.3%

Any Medicare,
without private
insurance
10.8%

Uninsured
10.7%

Any private insurance,
including partial
Medicare,
Medicaid/CHIP, or
CHAMPUS/VA
62.6%

Note: Percentages do not add to 100 percent due to rounding.
*Inpatient care or outpatient care for problems with emotions, nerves, or mental health; does not include treatment for drug or alcohol use.
**Civilian Health and Medical Program of the Uniformed Services (CHAMPUS)/Department of Veterans Affairs (VA)
†Children's Health Insurance Program (CHIP)

SOURCE: Center for Behavioral Health Statistics and Quality, Substance Abuse and Mental Health Services Administration (SAMHSA), "Sources of Payment for Mental Health Treatment for Adults," *The NSUDH Report*, July 7, 2011.

Report available online at http://oas.samhsa.gov/2k11/025/WEB_SR_025.htm. *(Chart by PreMediaGlobal. © 2012 Cengage Learning.)*

physicians; (b) financial incentives (either bonuses or withholding money) for providers to restrict services and contain costs; (c) guidelines requiring adherence by providers at the cost of being dropped from the plan for noncompliance; and (d) review of services by the managed care organization and denial of payment if services are considered unnecessary.

Description

Health maintenance organizations have been in existence in the United States since the late 1800s. In the 1950s, however, the federal government began to encourage the development of HMOs. In 1973, the Health Maintenance Organization Act was passed, and in 1978, a Congressional amendment increased federal aid for HMO development. From 1980 to 1989, U.S. enrollment in HMOs increased from 9 million to 36 million. By 1990, 95% of private insurance companies used some form of managed care. In the 1990s, managed care was incorporated into Medicare and Medicaid plans as well. In the early 2010s, managed care is present in many private health benefit programs. However, although managed care is a mainstay in health care in the United States, it continues to generate controversy because it has not been

able to, in most cases, control the costs of medical care in the country. In addition, some critics point out that the quality of medical care has not improved since the introduction of managed care. Such issues were expected to persist in second decade of the twenty-first century.

Managed care organizations frequently contract with a group or panel of healthcare providers. HMOs, preferred provider organizations (PPOs), and point of service (POSs) are examples of these types of contracts. In a health maintenance organization (HMO), the organization enters into a contract with various health-care providers to form a provider network. The providers, such as physicians, hospitals, and other healthcare organizations, under contract to the HMO, provide services to its members at reduced rates in exchange for benefits provided by the HMO, such as the ability to bring in new patients. Members must use the providers in the network in order to receive a reduced rate for services. Each member usually selects a primary care physician (PCP). This PCP, often a family doctor, coordinates all aspects of the patient's care. Because of this role, the patient must see the PCP before being referred to a specialist. These restrictions, along with others, define the HMO plan, but also make it one of the most cost-effective for the patients.

In a preferred provided organization (PPO), the PPO also enters into contracts with healthcare providers to form a provider network. However, in a PPO, a PCP is not used, and members may use any medical professional, within or outside of the network. However, if members use in-network providers, then the costs are less than if an out-of-network provider is used. Although less restrictive than an HMO, the PPO tends to cost more.

The point-of-service (POS) plans are a custom mixture of the HMO and PPO styles. Often members choose which option—HMO or PPO—they wish to use. The POS plan has a provider network that is under contract. A PCP is requested but such coordinators are not required of members. However, if a PCP is not used, then costs are higher. The POS plans usually offer more flexibility than HMOs but may often cost less than PPOs.

Individuals insured under these arrangements may receive care only from providers on the panel. These providers are expected to deliver services according to specific stipulations. Payment is often subject to utilization review, in which delivery of medical services is scrutinized to determine whether the services are necessary. The review may occur with each episode of treatment or may be ongoing by a case manager. If the managed care organization thinks that the services were unnecessary, payment is denied.

Payment arrangements between managed care organizations and care providers are often made in advance. Capitation payment systems are typically used with large healthcare facilities that serve many people. The healthcare provider receives a set amount of money each month based on the number of individuals covered by the plan. The provider may or may not serve that many people in one month. Capitation systems provide a steady, reliable cash flow but involve some economic risk because the services provided may exceed the dollar amount allotted. Another type of payment system uses case rates. The provider receives a predetermined amount of money per individual on a case-by-case basis. The amount of money reflects the estimated service costs to treat the individual patient's condition. Again, the provider takes the risk that unanticipated services will be required.

In the past, mental health services, including **substance abuse** treatment, were routinely excluded from managed care plans. In the 1970s, some mental health care coverage was required in order to meet federal qualifications. Carve-out plans, developed in the 1990s, essentially create a separate managed care plan for mental health services. Mental health services tend to be covered at a lower rate than general health services and, during times of economic troubles, have also been cut back more severely. From 1988 to 1997, mental healthcare spending decreased

---

KEY TERMS

Health maintenance organization—A healthcare organization that provides managed-care group health insurance, in which members pay a stated amount on a regular basis and in response receive medical care from participating physicians, hospitals, and other providers.

Medicaid—A federal program in the United States that pays for the medical expenses of people who are unable to pay for most or all of their own medical expenses due to a disability.

Medicare—A federal health insurance program in the United States that provides medical care and hospital treatment for people over a certain age (usually 65 years).

Point-of-service—A healthcare organization that provides managed-care group health insurance and has characteristics of both health maintenance organizations (HMOs) and preferred provider organizations (PPOs).

Preferred provider organization—A healthcare organization that provides managed-care, group health insurance and is a group of doctors, hospitals, and other providers who have contracted with an insurer or administrator to provide health care at reduced rates for its clients.

---

by 54%, which reflects cutbacks nearly seven times higher than those for general healthcare benefits.

Mental healthcare providers are also subjected to higher levels of utilization review than medical care providers. As mental healthcare services become more popular in managed care packages, issues have developed. For instance, in the first two decades of the twenty-first century, mental health therapists under managed care systems often are overburdened with paperwork required by HMOs and other such plans. In addition, more sensitive information about patients is required by managed care plans in order to be reimbursed, which does not bode well for the highly secure relationships set up by these patients and clients.

Preparation

People interested in getting medical insurance need to discuss all possible managed care plans with a knowledgeable person within each managed care organization being considered. In addition, they ought to discuss with a trusted medical doctor or other medical professional any concerns or questions that they may have before starting such a plan, during the enrollment process, and while they are members. If they intend to switch plans, they may also wish to find out whether their current physicians participate in the plans they are considering.

Risks

Mental health services within managed care can involve some risks. One risk is the reduced amount of confidentiality for the patient. The relationship between doctor and patient was confidential. However, patients and doctors dealing with managed care organizations are often at odds on this point, as these companies require specific information be sent for evaluation and consideration before they decide to pay on claims. The records of clients, once the property of the doctor and the patient, become the property of the managed care organization. The Health Insurance Portability and Accountability Act of 1996 established some safeguards protecting patient information, but if patients are deemed a possible danger to themselves or others, protected confidential health information may be released.

Ethical concerns

Managed care has been in some respects successful in fulfilling its primary purpose of lowering healthcare costs in the United States. Statistics show decreases in the use of inpatient care and accompanying overall reduction in costs. Many observers, however, argue that the quality of care has suffered as a result. Individuals have fewer choices regarding the locations where they can receive treatment. If a managed care organization closes, individuals under that plan must switch to other care providers under a new plan, which can disrupt ongoing treatment. Care providers often feel that their clients are denied essential care in favor of saving money. Many employers are disillusioned because they face increasing disability claims due to employees having received inadequate treatment for illnesses or injuries. In addition to disability claims, inadequate treatment results in hidden costs to employers in terms of lost productivity.

Another factor in decreased quality of care involves conflicting loyalties for healthcare providers. On the one hand, providers want to ensure quality care for their clients. On the other hand, they are encouraged to provide the least amount of care possible in order to receive financial benefits. Just as dishonest practice was suspected in conjunction with indemnity insurance, managed care creates the potential for inappropriately addressing patients' needs based on monetary concerns. Ultimately, the managed care organization has the right to deny or limit

---

QUESTIONS TO ASK YOUR DOCTOR

- What managed care plan is best for me?
- Does my particular health situation mean one plan may be better than another?
- Where can I learn more about my local options for managed care?
- What managed care plans does this office accept?

---

access to a treatment or service, but patients have the right to appeal any care decisions with which they disagree.

Future directions

Due to growing popular discontent with managed care organizations, many critics believe that the system will not continue in its current state. Few people, however, expect managed care to completely disappear and indemnity plans to rise to their former prominence. Changes are expected to occur as managed care programs begin competing among themselves. Cost and efficiency will no longer be the main selling point; quality of services will take precedence. Some suggest that along with new systems of managed care and continuing systems of indemnity plans, healthcare providers may even organize and offer services directly to employers, thus eliminating the middle people. This development would be beneficial to all involved: employers would pay less, providers would be better compensated, and clients would receive better care.

Mental health parity—the equivalent treatment of mental illnesses with physical conditions—has improved in the twenty-first century in the United States. In 1996, the U.S. Congress passed the Mental Health Parity Act (MHPA). The law required that issuers of group health plans—those with over 50 employees—could not set the annual and lifetime dollar limits of mental health benefits any lower than the related limits for other services such as medical and surgical benefits. However, the issuers of such plans bypassed the act's requirements by imposing restrictions on the maximum number of provider visits or on the maximum number of days that could be covered under inpatient psychiatric **hospitalization**.

In 2008, a rider attached to the Troubled Asset Relief Program (TARP), which was sponsored by Senator Paul Wellstone (D-MN), amended the MHPA. The rider closed the loopholes in the 1996 bill by prohibiting all group health plans that offered mental health coverage from instituting any types of maximum limits on co-payments, co-insurance, number of visits, or number of days covered for mental-health related hospital visits. The amended law states any medical insurance that includes mental health coverage must include all mental health conditions listed in the latest edition of the American Psychiatric Association's *Diagnostic and Statistical Manual of Mental Disorders.* According to proponents of the legislation, the improved MHPA will make treatment of mental health benefits equivalent with traditional medical health benefits.

Resources

BOOKS

Codd, R. Trent, III. *Destructive Trends in Mental Health: The Well-Intentioned Path to Harm.* New York: Routledge, 2005.

Foster, Joan, and Antonia Murphy. *Psychological Therapies in Primary Care: Setting Up a Managed Care Service.* London: Karnac, 2005.

Scheid, Teresa L. *Tie a Knot and Hang On: Providing Mental Health Care in a Turbulent Environment.* Hawthorne, NY: Aldine de Gruyter, 2004.

PERIODICALS

Addis, Michael E., et al. "Effectiveness of Cognitive-Behavioral Treatment for Panic Disorder versus Treatment as Usual in a Managed Care Setting: 2-Year Follow-Up." *Journal of Consulting and Clinical Psychology* 74, no. 2 (April 2006): 377–85.

Angelo, Ellen Josephine. "Accountable Care Organizations: Are They the Right Answer?" *Nursing Management* 42, no. 2 (February 2011): 20–24.

Beattie, Martha, Patricia McDaniel, and Jason Bond. "Public Sector Managed Care: A Comparative Evaluation of Substance Abuse Treatment in Three Counties." *Addiction* 101, no. 6 (June 2006): 857–72.

Bobbitt, Bruce L. "The Importance of Professional Psychology: A View from Managed Care." *Professional Psychology: Research and Practice* 37, no. 6 (December 2006): 590–97.

Busch, Alisa B., et al. "Schizophrenia, Co-Occurring Substance Use Disorders and Quality of Care: The Differential Effect of a Managed Behavioral Health Care Carve-Out." *Administration and Policy in Mental Health and Mental Health Services Research* 33, no. 3 (May 2006): 388–97.

Cohen, Julie, Jeanne Marecek, and Jane Gillham. "Is Three a Crowd? Clients, Clinicians, and Managed Care." *American Journal of Orthopsychiatry* 76, no. 2 (April 2006): 251–59.

Kilbourne, Amy M., et al. "Management of Mental Disorders in VA Primary Care Practices." *Adminstration and Policy in Mental Health and Mental Health Services Research* 33, no. 2 (March 2006): 208–14.

Liang, Su-Ying, Kathryn A. Phillips, and Jennifer S. Haas. "Measuring Managed Care and Its Environment Using National Surveys: A Review and Assessment." *Medical Care Research and Review* 63, no. 6 (December 2006): 9S–36S.

McLaughlin, Trent P., et al. "Overlap of Anxiety and Depression in a Managed Care Population: Prevalence and Association with Resource Utilization." *Journal of Clinical Psychiatry* 67, no. 8 (August 2006): 1187–93.

Pear, Robert. "House Approves Bill on Mental Health Parity." *The New York Times*, March 6, 2008. http://www.nytimes.com/2008/03/06/washington/06health.html (accessed September 8, 2011).

Raghavan, Ramesh, et al. "Effects of Medicaid Managed Care Policies on Mental Health Service Use Among a National Probability Sample of Children in the Child Welfare System." *Children and Youth Services Review* 28, no. 12 (December 2006): 1482–96.

WEBSITES

MedlinePlus. "Managed Care." U.S. National Library of Medicine, National Institutes of Health. Last updated December 1, 2010. http://www.nlm.nih.gov/medlineplus/managedcare.html (accessed September 8, 2011).

National Conference of State Legislatures. "State Laws Mandating or Regulating State Mental Health Benefits." http://www.ncsl.org/default.aspx?tabid=14352 (accessed November 14, 2011).

Office of the Assistant Secretary for Planning and Evaluation. "Glossary of Managed Care Terms." U.S. Department of Health and Human Services. http://aspe.hhs.gov/Progsys/forum/mcobib.htm (accessed September 8, 2011).

Office for Civil Rights. "Understanding Health Information Privacy." U.S. Department of Health and Human Services. http://www.hhs.gov/ocr/privacy/hipaa/understanding/index.html (accessed September 8, 2011).

ORGANIZATIONS

America's Health Insurance Plans, 601 Pennsylvania Ave., NW, South Building, Ste. 500, Washington, DC, 20004, (202) 778-3200, Fax: (202) 331-7487, ahip@ahip.org, http://www.ahip.org/default.aspx.

Centers for Medicare & Medicaid Services, 7500 Security Blvd., Baltimore, MD, 21244-1850, (800) 633-4223, http://www.medicare.gov.

Sandra L. Friedrich, MA
Ruth A. Wienclaw, PhD
William A. Atkins

Mania *see* **Manic episode**

Manic depression *see* **Bipolar disorder**

Manic episode

Definition

A manic episode is an abnormally elated mental state characterized by feelings of euphoria, lack of inhibitions, racing thoughts, diminished need for sleep, talkativeness, risk taking, and irritability. In extreme cases, mania can induce hallucinations and other psychotic symptoms.

Description

A person experiencing a manic episode shows persistent and often inappropriate enthusiasm. The affected person may demonstrate unusual behaviors such as taking on new projects for which he or she is ill suited, engaging strangers in detailed conversations, and acting without concern for the consequences of personal actions. Less commonly, a person may be abnormally irritable during a manic episode. On average, manic episodes begin before age 25.

Individuals experiencing a manic episode often have feelings of self-importance, elation, talkativeness, sociability, and a desire to initiate goal-oriented activities, coupled with the less desirable characteristics of irritability, impatience, impulsiveness, hyperactivity, and a decreased need for sleep. (**Hypomania** is a term applied to a condition resembling mania. It is characterized by persistent or elevated expansive mood, hyperactivity, inflated self-esteem, etc., but of less intensity than mania.) Severe mania may have psychotic components.

Causes and symptoms

Manic episodes typically occur as a symptom of **bipolar disorder**, a mood disorder characterized by both manic and depressive episodes. Mania can also be induced by the use or abuse of stimulant drugs, such as **cocaine** and **amphetamines**.

The *Diagnostic and Statistical Manual of Mental Disorders,* fourth edition (*DSM–IV*), the diagnostic standard for mental health professionals in the United States, describes a manic episode as an abnormally elevated mood lasting at least one week (and present for the majority of the time during that week) that is distinguished by at least three of the following symptoms:

- inflated self–esteem
- decreased need for sleep
- increased talkativeness
- racing thoughts
- distractibility
- increase in goal-directed activity
- excessive involvement in activities that have a high potential for negative consequences (e.g., risky sexual behavior or irresponsible spending)

If the mood of the patient is irritable and not elevated, four of these symptoms are required.

Many of these symptoms are also present in a hypomanic episode. A hypomanic episode is similar to a manic episode, but the symptoms may be experienced to

KEY TERMS

Bipolar disorder—Formerly called manic–depressive disorder. A mood disorder characterized alternating periods of overconfidence and activity (manic highs) and depressive lows.

Hypomania—A less severe form of elevated mood state that is a characteristic of bipolar type II disorder.

Mixed mania—A mental state in which symptoms of both depression and mania occur simultaneously.

Psychiatrist—A medical doctor who has completed specialized training in the diagnosis and treatment of mental illness. Psychiatrists can diagnose mental illnesses, provide mental health counseling, and prescribe medications.

Psychologist—A mental health professional who treats mental and behavioral disorders by support and insight to encourage healthy behavior patterns and personality growth. Psychologists also study the brain, behavior, emotions, and learning.

Psychotherapy—The treatment of mental and behavioral disorders by support and insight to encourage healthy behavior patterns and personality growth.

a lesser extent. The main differences between a manic and hypomanic episode are the following:

- A hypomanic episode may only last four days, whereas a manic episode, by definition, lasts one week.
- In a manic episode, psychotic features (hallucinations and delusions) may be present, but in a hypomanic episode, they cannot be.
- A manic episode significantly impairs the affected person's functions, but a hypomanic episode does not.

Both of these kinds of episodes may be seen in patients with bipolar disorder.

Diagnosis

In addition to observable symptoms, to qualify as a manic episode the *DSM* also states that the change in behavior must be either severe enough to disrupt normal functioning at work or at home or to require **hospitalization** to avoid harm to self or others; alternately, the patient may show signs of **psychosis**. Also, the cause of

KAY REDFIELD JAMISON (1946–)

Kay Redfield Jamison is a psychologist and educator who is considered an authority on manic-depressive illness. Her volume *Manic-Depressive Illness*, compiled with Frederick K. Goodwin, is regarded as a key contribution to the study of manic-depressive illness, a biochemical disorder which results in periods of mania alternating with bouts of depression. The book encompasses a range of issues and subjects, including diagnosis, clinical studies, psychological ramifications, and patho-physiological elements. Larry S. Goldman, reviewing the work in the *New England Journal of Medicine*, acknowledged Jamison and Goodwin as "two highly regarded senior clinicians and researchers" and proclaimed their book "thorough and most readable." Goldman concluded, "It is hard to imagine a clinician working with patients with the illness . . . or a researcher in any part of the field of mood disorders who should not have this tour de force available."

Jamison followed *Manic-Depressive Illness* with *Touched with Fire: Manic-Depressive Illness and the Creative Temperament*, a detailed account of the ties between artistic sensibilities and manic-depressive illness. While conceding that not all artists are manic-depressive, Jamison argues that a significant association exists between the artistic and manic-depressive temperaments. There is, for example, a high rate of suicide among both types. In her analysis, Jamison incorporates scientific and medical data, including diagnostic methods and genetic information, and she applies this data to a host of creative individuals, including the composer Robert Schumann, the painter Vincent Van Gogh, and such American writers as Ernest Hemingway, John Berryman, and Hart Crane. Jamison notes that many of the creative individuals considered in *Touched with Fire* had little recourse to any suitable psycho-medical care.

In 1995 Jamison published *An Unquiet Mind*, a memoir of her own experiences with manic depression. In this volume Jamison recounts her extreme moodiness as a child and relates her first exhilarating experience of mania when she was in her mid-teens. She notes that mania and depression sometimes exist simultaneously. It is during these periods, when the depths of despair are coupled with the impulsiveness characteristic of mania, that sufferers, according to Jamison, are more likely to consider suicide. Jamison discloses in *An Unquiet Mind* that she attempted to take her own life, and she credits psychotherapy with helping her realize greater acceptance and stability.

the episode cannot be attributed to side effects from drug abuse, medication, medical treatment, or a medical condition.

Mania is usually diagnosed and treated by a **psychiatrist** and/or a **psychologist** in an outpatient setting. However, most severely manic patients require hospitalization. In addition to an interview, several clinical inventories or scales may be used to assess the patient's mental status and determine the presence and severity of mania. An assessment commonly includes the Young Mania Rating Scale (YMRS). The Mini–Mental State Examination (MMSE) may also be given to screen out other illnesses such as **dementia**.

Treatment

Mania is treated primarily with drugs. The following mood-stabilizing agents are commonly prescribed to regulate manic episodes:

• Lithium (Cibalith-S, Eskalith, Lithane) is one of the oldest and most frequently prescribed drugs available for the treatment of mania. Because the drug takes four to seven days to reach a therapeutic level in the bloodstream, it is sometimes prescribed in conjunction with neuroleptics (antipsychotic drugs) and/or benzodiazepines (tranquilizers) to provide more immediate relief of mania.

• Carbamazepine (Tegretol, Atretol) is an anticonvulsant drug usually prescribed in conjunction with other mood-stabilizing agents. The drug is often used to treat bipolar patients who have not responded well to lithium therapy.

• Valproate (divalproex sodium, or Depakote; valproic acid, or Depakene) is an anticonvulsant drug prescribed alone or in combination with carbamazepine and/or lithium. For patients experiencing "mixed mania," or mania with features of depression, valproate is preferred over lithium.

Clozapine (Clozaril) is an atypical antipsychotic medication used to control manic episodes in patients who have not responded to typical mood-stabilizing agents. The drug has also been a useful preventative treatment in some bipolar patients. Other new anticonvulsants (**lamotrigine**, **gabapentin**) are being investigated for treatment of mania and bipolar disorder.

Prognosis

Patients experiencing mania as a result of bipolar disorder require long-term care to prevent recurrence; bipolar disorder is a chronic condition that requires lifelong observation and treatment after **diagnosis**. Data show that almost 90% of patients who experience one manic episode will go on to have another.

Prevention

Mania as a result of bipolar disorder can only be prevented through ongoing pharmacologic treatment. Patient education in the form of therapy or **self-help groups** is crucial for training patients to recognize signs of mania and to take an active part in their treatment program. **Psychotherapy** is an important adjunctive treatment for patients with bipolar disorder.

Resources

BOOKS

Borch-Jacobsen, Mikkel. *Making Minds and Madness: From Hysteria to Depression.* New York, NY: Cambridge University Press, 2009.

Graham, George. *The Disordered Mind: An Introduction to Philosophy of Mind and Mental Illness.* New York: Routledge, 2010.

North, Carol, and Sean Yutzy. *Goodwin and Guze's Psychiatric Diagnosis.* New York, NY: Oxford University Press, 2010.

Shams, M.D.K. *Human Relation and Personified Relational Disorders.* Raleigh, NC: lulu.com, 2009.

ORGANIZATIONS

American Academy of Child and Adolescent Psychiatry, 3615 Wisconsin Ave. NW, Washington, DC, 20016-3007, (202) 966-7300, Fax: (202) 966-2891, http://aacap.org.

American Psychiatric Association, 1000 Wilson Blvd., Ste. 1825, Arlington, VA, 22209-3901, (703) 907-7300, apa@psych.org, http://www.psych.org.

American Psychological Association, 750 1st St. NE, Washington, DC, 20002-4242, (202) 336-5500; TDD/TTY: (202) 336-6123, (800) 374-2721, http://www.apa.org.

Mental Health America, 2000 North Beauregard St., 6th Floor, Alexandria, VA, 22311, (703) 684-7722, (800) 969-6642, Fax: (703) 684-5968, http://www1.nmha.org.

National Alliance on Mental Illness, 3803 North Fairfax Dr., Ste. 100, Arlington, VA, 22203, (703) 524-7600, Fax: (703) 524-9094, http://www.nami.org.

National Institute of Mental Health, 6001 Executive Blvd., Room 8184, MSC 9663, Bethesda, MD, 20892-9663, (301) 433-4513; TTY: (301) 443-8431, (866) 615-6464; TTY: (866) 415-8051, Fax: (301) 443-4279, nimhinfo@nih.gov, http://www.nimh.nih.gov.

Paula Anne Ford-Martin
Laura Jean Cataldo, RN, Ed.D.

Maprotiline

Definition

Maprotiline is an antidepressant. It is a member of the tetracyclic antidepressant family of compounds and is administered orally. In the United States, it is sold under the trade name Ludiomil.

Purpose

Maprotiline is an antidepressant intended for use by people with depressive **neurosis** and **bipolar disorder**. It is also occasionally used for the relief of anxiety associated with **depression**.

Description

Maprotiline elevates mood. The precise pharmacological mode of action is not fully understood but it is thought to inhibit the absorption of the neurotransmitter norepinephrine at nerve endings in the **brain**. It is prescribed in 25, 50, and 75 mg tablets.

Recommended dosage

The recommended initial dosage of maprotiline is typically 75 mg, given by mouth in three 25 mg administrations, although some patients may start with an initial dose of 25 mg. The initial dosage should be maintained for at least two weeks. Therapeutic results may be observed in three to seven days. Typically, initial administration may have to be continued for two to three weeks before results are observed.

The recommended total dosage is 150 mg per day. Dosage should be increased 25 mg at a time. The maximum daily dosage for people with severe depression is 225 mg.

Precautions

The use of antidepressant drugs, including maprotiline, in children and adults up to age 24 has been linked to an increased risk of suicidal thoughts and behavior. Patients of any age taking maprotiline should be monitored for signs of worsening depression or changes in behavior. The drug may lower the threshold for a **manic episode** among people with bipolar disorders and should be used only with caution and under close supervision in those patients.

Maprotiline may promote seizure activity. Of all the cyclic **antidepressants**, maprotiline probably causes the highest incidence of **seizures** and has thus fallen out of favor with most psychiatrists. Also for this reason, it should not be combined with other neuroleptics (antipsychotics) that can also cause seizures. Maprotiline should be used with caution in persons with heart disease or certain heart conditions. The drug increases the effect of alcohol and should not be taken with products containing alcohol or **barbiturates**. People taking **monoamine oxidase inhibitors (MAOIs)**, such as **tranylcypromine** (Parnate) and **phenelzine** (Nardil), should not take maprotiline.

Side effects

The most commonly reported side effect of maprotiline is dry mouth. Slightly more than one person in five (22%) experiences this effect. Approximately 16% of users experience drowsiness, 8% report dizziness, and 6% report nervousness and constipation. Other less common reported side effects include anxiety, agitation, **insomnia**, blurred vision, tremor, weakness, **fatigue**, nausea, and headache with blurred vision. Other rare side effects are similar to those experienced by people who use tricyclic antidepressants. These include abnormally high or low blood pressure, tachycardia, and syncope. Hallucinations, disorientation, and mania have been reported, as have vomiting, diarrhea, and gastric distress.

Interactions

Maprotiline should be discontinued or reduced in dosage prior to surgery due to the potential for interactions with anesthetic agents. The drugs cimetidine and **fluoxetine** reduce the elimination of maprotiline, resulting in too much of the drug in the body, which can be dangerous. Conversely, barbiturates and phenytoin increase the elimination of maprotiline, leaving too little of the drug in the body and reducing its therapeutic effects. Cardiovascular toxicity has been reported when maprotiline is used simultaneously with thyroid-replacement medications such as levothyroxine, and maprotiline blocks the pharmacological effect of guanethidine. An increased risk of seizures has been reported with the simultaneous use of physostigmine and maprotiline, and a similar effect has been observed when maprotiline is taken simultaneously with phenothiazine compounds; concurrent use should be avoided.

KEY TERMS

Barbiturates—A class of medications (including Seconal and Nembutal) that causes sedation and drowsiness. They may be prescribed legally, but may also be used as drugs of abuse.

Bipolar disorder—An mental condition characterized by periods of intense elation, energy, and activity (mania) followed by periods of inactivity and depression.

Guanethidine—An antihypertensive drug used to treat high blood pressure.

Hallucination—A false sensory perception. A person experiencing a hallucination may "hear" sounds or "see" people or objects that are not really present. Hallucinations can also affect the senses of smell, touch, and taste.

Manic—Referring to mania, a state characterized by excessive activity, excitement, or emotion.

Monoamine oxidase inhibitors—A group of antidepressant drugs that decrease the activity of monoamine oxidase, a neurotransmitter found in the brain that affects mood.

Norepinephrine—A neurotransmitter in the brain that acts to constrict blood vessels and raise blood pressure. It works in combination with serotonin.

Physostigmine—A short-acting drug that enhances levels of a substance (acetylcholine) between neurons in the brain.

Syncope—A brief lapse of consciousness caused by a temporarily insufficient flow of blood to the brain.

Tachycardia—A pulse rate above 100 beats per minute.

Resources
BOOKS
Foreman, John C., and Torben Johansen. *Textbook of Receptor Pharmacology.* 2nd ed. Boca Raton, FL: CRC Press, 2002.

Page, Clive P., et al. *Integrated Pharmacology.* 3rd ed. St. Louis, MO: Elsevier, 2006.

Preston, John D., John H. O'Neal, and Mary C. Talaga. *Handbook of Clinical Psychopharmacology for Therapists.* 5th ed. Oakland, CA: New Harbinger Publications, 2008.

PERIODICALS
Arenas, M. Carmen, et al. "Are the Effects of the Antidepressants Amitriptyline, Maprotiline, and Fluoxetine on

Inhibitory Avoidance State-Dependent?" *Behavioural Brain Research* 166, no. 1 (January 2006): 150–58.

Mayers, Andrew G., and David S. Baldwin. "Antidepressants and Their Effect on Sleep." *Human Psychopharmacology: Clinical and Experimental* 20, no. 8 (December 2005): 533–59.

Rambelomanana, S., et al. "Antidepressants: General Practitioners' Opinions and Clinical Practice." *Acta Psychiatrica Scandinavica* 113, no. 6 (June 2006): 460–67.

WEBSITES

PubMed Health. "Maprotiline." U.S. National Library of Medicine. http://www.ncbi.nlm.nih.gov/pubmedhealth/PMH0000597 (accessed November 12, 2011).

ORGANIZATIONS

American Academy of Clinical Toxicology, 6728 Old McLean Village Dr., McLean, VA, 22101, (703) 556-9222, Fax: (703) 556-8729, admin@clintox.org, http://www.clintox.org.

American Academy of Family Physicians, 11400 Tomahawk Creek Parkway, Leawood, KS, 66211-2672, (913) 906-6000, (800) 274-2237, Fax: (913) 906-6075, contactcenter@aafp.org, http://www.aafp.org.

American Medical Association, 515 N State St., Chicago, IL, 60610, (312) 464-5000, (800) 621-8335, http://www.ama-assn.org.

American Psychiatric Association, 1000 Wilson Blvd., Ste. 1825, Arlington, VA, 22209-3901, (703) 907-7300, apa@psych.org, http://www.psych.org.

American Society for Clinical Pharmacology and Therapeutics, 528 North Washington St., Alexandria, VA, 22314, (703) 836-6981, http://www.ascpt.org.

American Society for Pharmacology and Experimental Therapeutics, 9650 Rockville Pike, Bethesda, MD, 20814-3995, (301) 634-7060, Fax: (301) 634-7061, http://www.aspet.org.

L. Fleming Fallon, Jr., MD, DrPH
Ruth A. Wienclaw, PhD

Marijuana *see* **Cannabis and related disorders**

Marital therapy *see* **Marriage counseling**

Marriage counseling

Definition

Marriage counseling is a type of **psychotherapy** for a married couple or established partners that tries to resolve problems in the relationship. Typically, two people attend counseling sessions together to discuss specific issues; however, in some cases only one partner works within the sessions. It may also be called marital therapy, couple therapy, or relationship counseling.

Before the late twentieth century, close friends, family members, or religious leaders primarily performed marriage counseling. Since then, the guidance most often comes from psychiatrists, psychologists, **social workers**, and marriage/family counselors. With the use of such professionals, certifications and regulations have been established to guide and control these activities. One of the most commonly accepted credentials comes from the American Association for Marriage and **Family Therapy**.

Purpose

Marriage counseling provides help to couples, whether they are married or not, and whether the pair are heterosexual or homosexual. It is based on research showing that individuals and their problems are best handled within the context of their relationships. Marriage counselors are trained in psychotherapy and family systems, and focus on understanding their clients' symptoms and the way their interactions contribute to problems in the relationship.

Various issues are discussed in marriage counseling. Some of the more critical issues addressed include:

• infidelity issues
• sexual problems
• financial difficulties
• physical disabilities
• mental illnesses
• anger management problems
• domestic abuse
• alcohol/substance abuse
• communications difficulties
• interactions with children and other family members

The goal of marital and family therapists is to improve relationships between marital partners or family members, or to help with the dissolution of a difficult relationship with minimum harm to all.

Description

Marriage counseling is usually a short-term therapy that may take only a few sessions to work out problems in the relationship. Longer-term counseling may also occur, with a range of sessions usually from 12 to 24 in number. Typically, marriage counselors ask questions about the couple's roles, patterns, rules, goals, and beliefs. Therapy often begins as the couple analyzes the good and bad aspects of the relationship. The marriage counselor then works with the couple to help them understand that, in most cases, both partners are contributing to problems in the relationship. Various techniques are employed, such as active listening, role-playing, **behavior modification**, and changing expectations concerning the behaviors of others. They are taught techniques to modify their own behaviors, or taught how to more readily accept the behaviors of others. When this is understood, the two can then learn to change how they interact with each other to solve problems. The partners may be encouraged to draw up a contract in which each partner describes the behavior he or she will be trying to maintain. Sometimes counseling is also provided for the entire family, not just for a couple.

Marriage is not a requirement for two people to get help from a marriage counselor. Any one person wishing to improve his or her relationships can acquire help with behavioral problems, relationship issues, or with mental or emotional disorders. Marriage counselors also offer treatment (pre-marital therapy) for couples before they get married to help them understand potential problem areas. A third type of marriage counseling involves post-marital therapy, in which divorcing couples who share children seek help in working out their differences. Couples in the midst of a divorce find that marriage therapy during separation can help them find a common ground as they negotiate interpersonal issues and child custody.

Choosing a therapist

A marriage counselor is trained to use different types of therapy in work with individuals, couples, and groups.

When looking for a marriage counselor, a couple should find out the counselor's training and educational background, professional associations, such as the AAMFT, and state licensure, and whether the person has experience in treating particular kinds of problem. Marital and family therapists receive training in three areas:

• Academic program. A person must earn a master's degree with an emphasis in marital and family therapy from an accredited academic institution. Most programs of study are 48 semester credit hours in length. The curriculum must include theoretical as well as practical training. Specific areas of competency, such as human sexuality, assessing victims of child abuse, and substance abuse, must be embedded in the curriculum. Students must receive 30 hours of directly supervised counseling and an additional 150 hours of directed counseling practice.

• Supervised clinical experience. Prior to becoming eligible to sit for a licensing exam, candidates must complete a total of approximately 3,000 hours of supervised counseling experiences. The 3,000 hours may include activities related to personal psychotherapy, supervision, direct counseling experience, professional enrichment experiences, and maintaining records. Some (approximately one-quarter) of these hours may be included in the graduate degree training curriculum. All of the clinical experiences are closely supervised.

• Licensing examination. The examination has written and oral components. A license to practice is granted with the successful passage of both parts of the exam. A minimum of 36 hours of continuing education training must be completed every two years as a requirement for relicensing.

The American Association for Marriage and Family Therapy (AAMFT) is a professional organization that offers training and nationally recognized accreditation. Patients should also ask questions concerning fees, insurance coverage, and anything else they want to know before committing to therapy sessions.

Results

Marriage counseling helps couples learn to deal more effectively with problems and can help prevent small problems from becoming serious. Research shows that marriage counseling, when effective, tends to improve a person's physical as well as mental health, in addition to improving the relationship.

Resources

BOOKS

Clinton, Tim, and John Trent. *The Quick-Reference Guide to Marriage and Family Counseling.* Grand Rapids, MI: Baker Books, 2009.

Davis, Rebecca L. *More Perfect Unions: The American Search for Marital Bliss.* Cambridge, MA: Harvard University Press, 2010.

Yount, David. *Making a Success of Marriage: Planning for Happily Ever After.* Lanham, MD: Rowman and Littlefield, 2010.

WEBSITES

Mayo Clinic staff. "Marriage Counseling." MayoClinic.com. http://www.mayoclinic.com/health/marriage-counseling/MY00839 (accessed October 22, 2011).

ORGANIZATIONS

American Association for Marriage and Family Therapy, 112 South Alfred St., Alexandria, VA, 22314-3061, (703) 838-9808, Fax: (703) 838-9805, http://www.aamft.org.

American Psychological Association, 750 1st St. NE, Washington, DC, 20002-4242, (202) 336-5500; TDD/TTY: (202) 336-6123, (800) 374-2721, http://www.apa.org.

Carol A. Turkington

Masochism *see* **Sexual masochism**

Massage *see* **Bodywork therapies**

Mathematics disorder

Definition

Mathematics disorder, formerly called developmental arithmetic disorder, developmental acalculia, or dyscalculia, is a learning disorder in which a person's mathematical ability is substantially below the level normally expected based on his or her individual's age, intelligence, life experiences, educational background, and physical impairments. This disability affects the ability to do calculations as well as the ability to understand word problems and mathematical concepts.

Demographics

The number of children with mathematics disorder is not entirely clear. The fourth edition of the **Diagnostic and Statistical Manual of Mental Disorders** (*DSM-IV*), which is the basic manual consulted by mental health professionals in assessing the presence of mental disorders, indicates that about 1% of school age children have mathematics disorder. Other studies, however, have found higher rates of arithmetical dysfunction in children. Likewise, some studies find no gender difference in the prevalence of mathematics disorder, while others find that girls are more likely to be affected. Mathematics disorder, like other learning disabilities, however, does appear to run in families, suggesting the existence of a genetic component to the disorder.

Description

Mathematics disorder was first described as a developmental disorder in 1937. Since then, it has come to encompass a number of distinct types of mathematical deficiencies. These include:

• difficulty reading and writing numbers
• difficulty aligning numbers in order to do calculations
• inability to perform calculations
• inability to comprehend word problems

The range and number of mathematical difficulties that have been documented suggests that there are several different causes for mathematics disorder. In addition, several known physical conditions cause mathematics disorder. Turner syndrome and fragile X syndrome, both genetic disorders that affect girls, are associated with difficulty in mathematics. Injury to certain parts of the **brain** can also cause inability to perform calculations. These conditions appear to be independent of other causes of mathematics disorder. Mathematics disorder is often associated with other **learning disorders** involving reading and language, although it may also exist independently in children whose reading and language skills are average or above average.

Causes and symptoms

The causes of mathematics disorder are not understood. Different manifestations of the disorder may have different causes. Symptoms of the disorder, however, can be grouped into four categories: language symptoms; recognition or perceptual symptoms; mathematical symptoms; and attention symptoms.

People with language symptoms have trouble naming mathematical terms; understanding word problems; or understanding such mathematical concepts as "greater than" or "less than." People with recognition symptoms have difficulty reading numbers and such operational signs as the plus or minus signs, or aligning numbers properly in order to perform accurate calculations. Mathematical symptoms include deficiencies in the ability to count; to memorize such basic arithmetical data as the multiplication tables; or to follow a sequence of steps in problem solving. Attention symptoms are related to failures in copying numbers and ignoring operational signs. Sometimes these failures are the result of a person's carelessness. At other times, however, they appear to result from a lack of understanding of the factors or operations involved in solving the problem.

In practical terms, parents and teachers may see the following signs of mathematics disorder in a child's schoolwork:

• problems counting
• difficulty memorizing multiplication tables
• inability to grasp the difference between such operations as addition and subtraction
• poor computational skills; many errors in simple arithmetic
• slowness in performing calculations
• difficulty arranging numbers in order (from smallest to largest, for example)
• inability to grasp information on graphs
• difficulty copying numbers or problems
• inability to grasp the concept of place value
• inability align two or three digit numbers to do calculations
• difficulty understanding word problems
• inability to understand mathematical symbols

These symptoms must be evaluated in light of the person's age, intelligence, educational experience, exposure to mathematics learning activities, and general cultural and life experience. The person's mathematical ability must fall substantially below the level of others with similar characteristics. In most cases several of these symptoms are present simultaneously.

Diagnosis

Mathematics disorder is not usually diagnosed before a child is in the second or third grade because of the variability with which children acquire mathematical fluency. Many bright children manage to get through to fourth- or fifth-grade level in mathematics by using memorization and calculation tricks (such as counting on fingers or performing repeated addition as a substitute for multiplication) before their disability becomes apparent. Requests for testing usually originate with a teacher or parent who has observed several symptoms of the disorder.

To receive a **diagnosis** of mathematics disorder according to the criteria established by the **American Psychiatric Association**, a child must show substantially lower than expected ability in mathematics based on his or her age, intelligence, and background. In addition, the child's deficiencies must cause significant interference with academic progress or daily living skills.

In addition to an interview with a child **psychiatrist** or other mental health professional, the child's mathematical ability may be evaluated with such individually administered diagnostic tests as the Enright Diagnostic Test of Mathematics, or with curriculum-based assessments. If the results of testing suggest mathematics disorder, such other causes of difficulty as poor vision or hearing, intellectual disability, or lack of fluency in the language of instruction, are ruled out. The child's educational history and exposure to opportunities for learning mathematics are also taken into account. On the basis of this information, a qualified examiner can make the diagnosis of mathematics disorder.

Treatment

Children who receive a diagnosis of mathematics disorder are eligible for an individual education plan (IEP) that details specific accommodations to learning. Because of the wide variety of problems found under the diagnosis of mathematics disorder, plans vary considerably. Generally, instruction emphasizes basic mathematical concepts, while teaching children problem solving skills and ways to eliminate distractions and extraneous information. Concrete, hands-on instruction is more successful than abstract or theoretical instruction. IEPs also address other language or reading disabilities that affect a child's ability to learn mathematics.

KEY TERMS

Individual education plan (IEP)—A plan of instruction drawn up for an individual student who is having specific difficulties with mathematics, reading, or other skills necessary to progress beyond elementary school.

Prognosis

Progress in overcoming mathematics disorder depends on the specific type of difficulties that the child has with mathematics; the learning resources available; and the child's determination to work on overcoming the disorder. Some children work through their disability, while others continue to have trouble with mathematics throughout life. Children who continue to suffer from mathematics disorder may develop low self-esteem and social problems related to their lack of academic achievement. Later in life they may be more likely to drop out of school and find themselves shut out of jobs or occupations that require the ability to perform basic mathematical calculations.

Prevention

There is no known way to prevent mathematics disorder.

Resources

BOOKS

American Psychiatric Association. *Diagnostic and Statistical Manual of Mental Disorders.* 4th ed., text rev. Washington, DC: American Psychiatric Publishing, 2000.

Sadock, Benjamin J., and Virginia A. Sadock, eds. *Comprehensive Textbook of Psychiatry.* Vol. 2. 7th ed. Philadelphia: Lippincott Williams and Wilkins, 2000.

PERIODICALS

Jordan, Nancy, and Laurie B. Hanich. "Mathematical Thinking in Second-Grade Children with Different Forms of LD." *Journal of Learning Disabilities* 33, no. 6 (November 2000): 567–578.

ORGANIZATIONS

Learning Disabilities Association of America, 4156 Library Rd., Pittsburgh, PA, 15234-1349, (412) 341-1515, http://www.ldanatl.org.

National Center for Learning Disabilities, 381 Park Ave. South, Ste. 1401, New York, NY, 10016, (212) 545-7510, Fax: (212) 545-9665, (888) 575-7373, http://www.ncld.org.

Tish Davidson, A.M.

Matrix model

Definition

The Matrix model of **substance abuse** treatment is a multifaceted treatment program designed to help substance abusers stop drug and **alcohol use** and maintain their sobriety through education and monitoring.

Purpose

The Matrix model, while originally designed as a therapeutic approach to treating abuse of such stimulants as **cocaine** and methamphetamines, has subsequently been applied to the treatment of opiate and alcohol abuse.

The Matrix model treatment system was created in the 1980s when cocaine abuse became rampant among members of the middle and upper-middle classes. The Matrix Institute on Addictions is a nonprofit organization based in California. Founded in 1984 to develop the program that became the Matrix model of substance abuse treatment, the Institute itself has several southern California locations. Other private treatment programs are also using the Matrix model, which has the distinct advantage over some treatment programs of having complete and established written treatment protocols as well as a growing body of research supporting its efficacy.

Prior to the early 1980s, cocaine and **methamphetamine** (MA) treatment programs generally followed one of two courses: community-based outpatient drug treatment programs for low-income users, or high-cost, private inpatient institutional treatment programs for those who could afford them. When middle-income drug abuse became epidemic, there was a need for an effective outpatient program that could address the needs of thousands of drug abusers who were neither wealthy nor living on the street.

The 28-day hospital-based treatment programs typically formulated for private health-care treatment of alcoholism were not seen as useful for cocaine users, who rarely needed inpatient programs. Similarly, **psychotherapy** alone has not been universally effective in helping people stop cocaine use or in preventing **relapse**. The Matrix model was designed to treat drug abuse using multiple modalities in as cost-efficient a manner as possible. Its underlying concept was to serve as an outpatient based on a reputable, evaluable protocol. Beginning with cocaine abuse, the Matrix model was extended to cover methamphetamines and other stimulant abuse treatment. Development and subsequent research on the Matrix model has been funded by grants from the National Institute on Drug Abuse, the Center for Substance Abuse Treatment, the **Substance Abuse and Mental Health Services Administration**, and the U.S. Department of Health and Human Services.

Description

The developers of the Matrix model, rather than engaging in the defense of a single theory, used strategies based on several practical approaches that had been shown to work in drug treatment. By using a matrix design rather than a single methodology, the program designers targeted the multiple factors affecting an individual's chances for recovery. Social influences, education for patient and family members, cognitive-behavioral techniques, **support groups**, individual sessions, and urine and breath testing were all included in the treatment model. The goal of this model was to help stimulant abusers 1) stop their drug use, 2) stay in treatment, 3) learn about issues critical to **addiction** and relapse, 4) receive direction and support from a trained therapist, 5) educate family members affected by the patient's addiction, 6) introduce self-help programs to the addicted persons for continued support and 7) continue monitoring with urine testing. The program lasts 16 weeks, and the program administrators conducted several studies to measure the efficacy of the Matrix model for different users, under different conditions and compared to other treatment methods.

The Matrix model recognizes several factors needed for an effective and lasting treatment. The therapeutic relationship, although not as intensive as traditional psychological therapy (only three 45-minute sessions are scheduled over 16 weeks) is used for engaging the patient in a way that will encourage continued participation and engagement in the program. Although the original program consisted of a greater number of individual sessions, they were soon abandoned in favor of additional group sessions, making the program more cost-effective without reducing its efficacy.

Dissemination of information, by way of patient group meetings, helps individuals understand the physiological and psychological effects of drug use. Family-systems theory has shown that, even in cases where change is in the best interest of the family and the patient, family members consciously and unconsciously resist the efforts of any one member who attempts to change. Education of family members in a group setting helps to educate everyone involved, reducing the risk of family dynamics sabotaging the recovery of the patient.

Planning is considered a vital part of **relapse prevention**: patients are taught to schedule their days to stay busy as well as to think about the ways their daily schedule might contribute to sobriety or relapse. Used as a part of the outpatient treatment program, planning promotes positive activity and helps prevent relapse; it is also needed after a patient has completed the program and needs to rebuild a life in which daily activities are not based on drug-addictive behaviors.

Timing is recognized as an important factor in the process of recovery: education sessions are scheduled so as not to interfere with the early stages of treatment, when patients are detoxifying and cannot comprehend much information beyond their own discomfort and shame. As their recovery continues, the program provides more complex information in a set of standardized lectures. Educating patients is part of a cognitive-behavioral approach that teaches them to notice, challenge, and change irrational or unhelpful thought processes, replacing old habits of thought with more productive and positive ones.

Co-occurring dependency is so common in addiction that no comprehensive treatment program should address a single addiction. The Matrix program recognizes that stimulant users often also use alcohol and marijuana. Program research shows significantly greater relapse rates for people who continue using other drugs. Patients are expected to quit all drugs and alcohol. As part of the Matrix model, breath testing and urinalysis address the possibility that some patients may continue drug or alcohol use, and reveal that this contingency needs to be addressed. Urinalysis and breath testing were made part of the Matrix treatment primarily as a way to validate patients in their recovery as well as providing an early warning of difficulty. Testing works with scheduling and other program components to let patients take responsibility for their recovery. There is room in the approach for response to relapse during treatment, and physiological tests will reveal temporary defeat, whereas patients sometimes cannot.

Although one could argue that the Matrix model is focused primarily on relapse prevention, particular coping skills and behaviors are taught to patients to help them identify situations that may test their sobriety. Called "relapse prevention," these established techniques are part of the program and provide social support. In leading relapse-prevention groups, staff members may also be alerted to patients whose behavior in the group may signal a potential relapse.

Aftercare

A vital component of the Matrix model is the recognition that 12-step programs are widely useful for people in aftercare. Substance abuse treatment is notably more effective when patients have resources for maintaining a drug-free lifestyle after leaving treatment.

KEY TERMS

Drug abuse—When an individual's repeated use of controlled substances, prescription or over-the-counter drugs, or alcohol causes damage to their health, thought processes, relationships, or functioning at work or school, they can be said to be practicing drug abuse. Using a substance for purposes other than which it is intended (such as inhaling gasoline fumes recreationally) can also be considered drug abuse.

Matrix—In statistics, variables that may influence a particular outcome are placed into a grid, either in columns or in rows. Statistical calculations can be performed that assign different weights to each variable, and the differential weighting of variables can be seen to affect the outcome. In the Matrix model of drug abuse, the variables that affect a positive outcome (such as behavioral techniques, family education or urinalysis testing) are all considered as important parts of a unified treatment plan.

12-step meetings are held at the Matrix treatment centers, attended by patients who are advancing in their treatment. The Matrix developers realized that some patients would opt out of 12-step meetings because of their format and emphasis on embracing a higher power and spiritual authority: the Matrix program addresses potential resistance by helping patients find ways to reconcile their personal beliefs with the structure of Alcoholics Anonymous, Narcotics Anonymous, or other self-help programs. This serves several purposes. Patients who might otherwise avoid such meetings after leaving the program may choose instead to attend, increasing their chances of maintaining a drug-free lifestyle; patients learn the format and 12-step "rules" while still in a more fully supportive milieu; and patients have a structured system to enter after leaving the program.

Results

The overall expectation of this therapeutic **intervention** is that patients will leave the program drug free and with enough internal and external resources to maintain a life free of drugs and alcohol. Research comparing the Matrix model to other treatment approaches has found that patients who complete the Matrix treatment programs have statistically higher abstinence rates and lower positive results on drug tests than patients who participate in traditional 28-day in-hospital programs.

Resources

BOOKS

Sorensen, James L., et al., eds. *Drug Abuse Treatment Through Collaboration: Practice and Research Partnerships That Work*. Washington, DC: American Psychological Association, 2003.

PERIODICALS

Obert, Jeanne L., et al. "The Matrix Model of Outpatient Stimulant Abuse Treatment." *Journal of Psychoactive Drugs* 32, no. 2 (April–June 2000): 157–64.

"Program Helps Patients Reduce, Discontinue Methamphetamine Use." *The Brown University Digest of Addiction Theory and Application* 21, no. 4 (April 2002): 1–3.

ORGANIZATIONS

National Institute on Drug Abuse, 6001 Executive Blvd., Rm. 5213, Bethesda, MD, 20892, (301) 442-1124; Spanish: (240) 221-4007, information@nida.nih.gov, http://www.nida.nih.gov.

Matrix Institute on Addictions, http://www.matrixinstitute.org.

Lorena S. Covington, MA

MDMA *see* **Ecstasy**

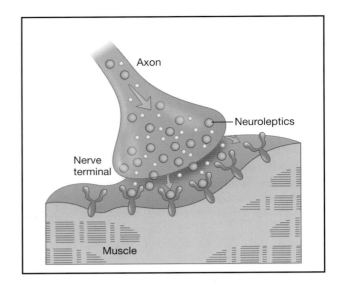

Neuroleptic medications block the action of dopamine, a neurotransmitter that helps coordinate movement. When dopamine cannot reach its receptors (blue channels blocked by neuroleptics), movement-related side effects may occur, including tremor and rigidity. *(Illustration by Electronic Illustrators Group. © 2012 Cengage Learning.)*

Medication-induced movement disorders

Definition

Medication-induced movement disorder occurs due to treatment with antipsychotic medications. Most medication-induced **movement disorders** are caused by medications that block the action of **dopamine**, a neurotransmitter that allows communication between two neurons to take place and that is necessary for coordination of movements of different parts of the body. When the receptor where dopamine is supposed to bind is blocked, certain movement-related side effects occur. All of the medications that block dopamine receptors are called neuroleptics.

Neuroleptics include both conventional or typical antipsychotic agents, such as **chlorpromazine** (Thorazine), **haloperidol** (Haldol), and **fluphenazine** (Prolixin), as well as the newer, or atypical, antipsychotic agents such as **clozapine** (Clozaril), **risperidone** (Risperdal), **olanzapine** (Zyprexa), and **quetiapine** (Seroquel). In general, the newer, atypical antipsychotics appear to have a lower likelihood to cause movement disorders than the older, typical medications. Other neuroleptics include certain drugs used in the treatment of physical symptoms such as nausea, and include prochlorperazine, promethazine, and metoclopramide, as well as **amoxapine** (Asendin), which is marketed as an antidepressant.

There are other medications, however, that do not block dopamine action but still cause movement disorders. They are not referred to as neuroleptics, and they include **lithium carbonate**, **valproic acid** and a class of drugs called **selective serotonin reuptake inhibitors (SSRIs)**. The disorder caused by these medications is called medication-induced postural tremor.

All of the disorders caused by neuroleptics, which include antipsychotics and other medications that block dopamine, as well as disorders caused by non-neuroleptic medications, are collectively referred to as medication-induced movement disorders.

Demographics

Neuroleptic-induced acute dystonia occurs most commonly in young males. It is far less likely to occur with the new medications known as atypical neuroleptic medications, such as clozapine, risperidone, olanzapine, and quetiapine. The possibility of neuroleptic-induced acute dystonia occurring with these atypical medications is less than 5%. The possibility of this side effect occurring with the conventional or typical neuroleptics is about 15%–20%. The incidence is inversely correlated with age, meaning that younger persons are more likely to experience dystonia.

Neuroleptic-induced Parkinsonism is directly correlated with age. This means that older patients are more likely to experience this effect. It occurs in about 30% of patients. Neuroleptic-induced acute akathisia is not related to age and occurs in about 20% of patients being treated with neuroleptics.

The incidence of neuroleptic-induced tardive dyskinesia is related to total lifetime of treatment with antipsychotics. The cumulative incidence is about 5% per year of therapy. This essentially means that there is a 50% chance of developing tardive dyskinesia with 10 years of treatment with neuroleptics.

The incidence of neuroleptic malignant syndrome is about 0.5%. This condition is fatal in about 20% to 30% of cases.

Most available information on medication-induced postural tremor is about lithium-induced tremor. The prevalence of this condition is about 40%.

Description

Neuroleptics

Medication-induced movement disorders caused by neuroleptics are divided into three time periods. The early-onset type, which usually occurs within the first seven days of treatment with neuroleptics, is known as neuroleptic-induced acute dystonia. Neuroleptic-induced acute dystonia is characterized by abnormal contractions of various muscle groups resulting in spasm and/or twisting of the head, neck, jaw, lips, tongue, and eye muscles as well as abnormal movements and postures of the limbs and the trunk.

The intermediate-onset types of movement disorders associated with the use of neuroleptics usually develop within the first three months of treatment. They are known as neuroleptic-induced Parkinsonism and neuroleptic-induced akathisia. Neuroleptic-induced Parkinsonism is associated with difficulty initiating movements. Once movements are initiated, they are very slow. Other characteristics of neuroleptic-induced Parkinsonism are tremor and rigidity in muscles. Neuroleptic-induced akathisia is associated with uncontrollable restlessness that may involve compulsive foot tapping, pacing, and a sense of inner tension.

The late-onset type of neuroleptic-related movement disorder is known as neuroleptic-induced **tardive dyskinesia** and the onset is usually seen many months to years after starting the neuroleptic treatment. Neuroleptic-induced tardive dyskinesia involves grotesque, repetitive, and involuntary movements. They are usually seen in the mouth and face.

A movement disorder that can occur at any time during the course of neuroleptic treatment is known as **neuroleptic malignant syndrome**. It is a serious condition and is characterized by changes in consciousness, ranging from agitation to coma. The patient may experience high fever and increases in blood pressure and heart rate, as well as severe muscular rigidity.

Non-neuroleptics

All of the medication-induced movement disorders are related to the use of neuroleptic medications. However, other drugs, such as lithium, valproic acid, isoproterenol, amphetamine, and theophylline, as well as a class of drugs known as tricyclic **antidepressants**, may also cause a movement disorder that is mainly characterized by postural tremor, a rhythmic alteration in movement. Lithium-induced tremor may take the form of twitching in the arms and legs.

Causes and symptoms

Causes

Neuroleptic-induced movement disorders are caused because the actions of dopamine are blocked. Dopamine is a neurotransmitter necessary for coordination of movements of different parts of the body.

Other medications, which are not classified as neuroleptics, block the action of other **neurotransmitters** as well as dopamine. However, because they essentially block the action of dopamine, they cause similar unwanted effects associated with movements.

Symptoms

Neuroleptic-induced acute dystonia is associated with primarily abnormal postures and muscular spasms. They are usually characterized by abnormal positioning of the head and neck in relation to the body; spasms of the jaw muscles; impaired swallowing, speaking, or breathing; thickened or slurred speech due to a slow movement of the tongue; tongue protrusion or tongue dysfunction; eyes deviated up, down, or sideways; and abnormal positioning of the limbs or trunk. Patients experience pain and cramps in the affected muscles. In addition, many patients experiencing dystonia due to the neuroleptic treatment also experience fear and anxiety. This is especially present in patients who are not aware of the possibility of developing dystonia and who mistakenly associate these side effects as part of their mental illness.

Neuroleptic-induced Parkinsonism includes rigidity, tremor, and bradykinesia (slow movements). The tremor is a rhythmic, three- to six-cycle-per-second motion that is present at rest. The tremor can affect the limbs, head, mouth, or lips. Rigidity signifies the degree of tension present in the muscle. It can be either continuous or intermittent in the affected limbs or joints. Bradykinesia includes decreased arm movements related to walking, as well as difficulty initiating movement. Drooling may occur due to a decrease in pharyngeal motor activity. People experiencing neuroleptic-induced akathisia usually feel anxious, agitated, and unable to relax. They also may pace, rock while sitting and standing, and often rapidly alternate between sitting and standing.

Neuroleptic-induced tardive dyskinesia manifests itself in involuntary movements of the tongue, jaw, trunk, or extremities. It occurs most commonly in patients who have taken older antipsychotic medications for many years, although the condition may appear earlier than that (after one year of treatment with neuroleptics, or even earlier than that, especially in elderly people). The movements can be rapid and jerky, slow and continual, or rhythmic in nature. Over three-fourths of the individuals with neuroleptic-induced tardive dyskinesia have abnormal movements of the face and the mouth. This may include licking, sucking, or smacking of the lips; chewing movements; jaw deviations; grimacing, grunting, and other peculiar sounds; or brow furrowing. About one-half of patients with tardive dyskinesia have abnormal limb movements, while about one-quarter have disposition of the trunk.

The basic features of neuroleptic malignant syndrome is the development of high fever and severe muscle rigidity. These can be accompanied by tremor, changes in level of consciousness ranging from confusion to coma, and increased heart rate and blood pressure. The fever can be mildly elevated (99–100°F) or severe (106°F). Neuroleptic malignant syndrome can be fatal in some cases, while it is relatively benign in others. There are no known predictors of neuroleptic malignant syndrome. However, it usually develops four weeks after starting neuroleptics, and about two-thirds of cases develop within the first week of treatment. A very small number of patients develop neuroleptic malignant syndrome many months after taking the neuroleptic.

Medication-induced postural tremor is characterized by a regular, rhythmic oscillation of hands and fingers, head, mouth, or tongue. The frequency of the tremor ranges from 8 to 12 cycles per second. These are most easily observed when the affected part is in a sustained position (for example if hands are outstretched or the mouth is held open).

Diagnosis

People taking antipsychotic medications and other medications that block dopamine action must be regularly evaluated by a physician to monitor for medication-induced movement disorders. In order for these conditions to be officially diagnosed, certain criteria must be met.

Neuroleptic-induced acute dystonia must have one or more of the following developed in association with the use of neuroleptics: abnormal positioning of the head and neck in relation to the body; spasms of the jaw muscles; impaired swallowing; thickened or slurred speech; tongue protrusion or dysfunction; eyes deviated up, down, or sideways; or abnormal positioning of limbs or trunk. These symptoms need to have developed within seven days of starting the neuroleptic medication. Moreover, the symptoms cannot be associated with an underlying mental disorder, and they cannot be due to a medication other than a neuroleptic. Dystonia due to neuroleptics needs to be distinguished from dystonia due to neuroleptic malignant syndrome.

Neuroleptic-induced Parkinsonism needs to have the triad of symptoms described above which include tremor, rigidity, and bradykinesia (slow movements). These symptoms cannot be related to a non-neuroleptic medication, or a psychiatric condition, such as Parkinson's disease, Wilson's disease, neuroleptic malignant syndrome, or substance withdrawal. Neuroleptic-induced akathisia is due to the use of a neuroleptic and not to anxiety, substance withdrawal, or psychotic agitation. At least one of the symptoms of fidgety movements or swinging the legs, rocking from foot to foot while standing, pacing to relieve restlessness, or inability to sit and stand needs to be present. These symptoms must have developed within four weeks of initiating the therapy with neuroleptics.

Neuroleptic-induced tardive dyskinesia needs to include involuntary movements over a period of at least four weeks that manifest themselves as rapid and jerky, slow and continual, or rhythmic movements. The exposure to neuroleptics needs to be for at least three months, and the symptoms cannot be due to a neurologic condition, such as Huntington's disease, Wilson's disease, Sydenham's (rheumatic) chorea, systemic lupus, or hyperthyroidism.

Neuroleptic malignant syndrome must include severe muscle rigidity and elevated temperature as well as at least two of the following symptoms: sweating, difficulty swallowing, tremor, incontinence, changes in level of consciousness, mutism, increased heart rate, elevated blood pressure, or laboratory evidence of muscle injury. These symptoms cannot be due to another substance or a medical condition, such as viral encephalitis, or mood disorder with catatonic features.

The criteria for diagnosing medication-induced postural tremor includes a development of tremor associated with the use of a medication other than a neuroleptic. The tremor cannot be due to a non-medication condition that was present prior to starting the medication and cannot continue to be present following discontinuation of the medication. These criteria are helpful in distinguishing the tremor due to medication use from the tremor due to anxiety, alcohol withdrawal, **stress**, or **fatigue**. The tremor must have a frequency between 8 and 12 cycles per second, and the tremor must not be caused by neuroleptic-induced Parkinsonism.

Treatment

In an attempt to prevent acute dystonia from developing, physicians may prescribe a preventive medication along with the antipsychotic. Once neuroleptic-induced acute dystonia has appeared, however, there are several treatment options. A medication called **benztropine** in doses ranging from 1 mg to 8 mg is effective in reducing symptoms associated with dystonia. Most patients take 2 mg twice daily for seven days for prevention of dystonia at the time they are starting neuroleptic treatment. When benztropine therapy is initiated, the dose is slowly increased. Moreover, when discontinuing the treatment with benztropine, the dose should be slowly decreased to prevent the nausea and vomiting associated with abrupt withdrawal. Another medication that may be useful in treating neuroleptic-induced acute dystonia is called **trihexyphenidyl**. The doses can vary from 10 mg to 45 mg daily. Younger patients may respond better to the treatment with trihexyphenidyl because they can tolerate higher doses. The third pharmacological option is **diphenhydramine** (Benadryl). This medication can be taken for the period dystonic symptoms last. Another option may include switching the patient to one of the newer antipsychotics, such as clozapine, risperidone, or olanzapine, since each of these has a low incidence of causing dystonia.

There are a couple of ways to treat intermediate-onset movement disorders due to neuroleptics. **Amantadine** is a medication that is approved by the United States Food and Drug Administration for the treatment of Parkinsonian symptoms. Another helpful medication called **propranolol** comes from a class of drugs called **beta blockers**. Propranolol has been reported effective in the treatment of akathisia. The doses that are effective range from 20 mg to 100 mg daily. The response to propranolol is usually seen within the 24 hours of administration. Switching the patient to a newer or atypical antipsychotic, such as clozapine, or decreasing the dose of the current antipsychotic sometimes helps the condition.

There are no effective treatments for tardive dyskinesia once it develops. Tardive dyskinesia is associated and strongly correlated with the cumulative dose of the antipsychotic during years of treatment. Hence, the key to tardive dyskinesia is prevention. If possible, a newer medication, such as clozapine or risperidone, which have only a few case reports of tardive dyskinesia, should be used whenever possible. In many cases, if tardive dyskinesia is noticed early in a regular check-up with the physician, and if the medication causing the condition is stopped, the symptoms of tardive dyskinesia will subside. If the symptoms continue after the antipsychotic has been discontinued, the situation becomes difficult. Treatment will most likely involve movement disorder specialists and may or may not be successful. The medications reserpine and levodopa may be helpful for some patients.

The most common medications used to treat neuroleptic malignant syndrome are dantrolene, (a muscle relaxant that helps with the fever), bromocriptine, and amantadine.

In order to reduce medication-induced postural tremor, the lowest possible dose of the psychiatric drug should be used. Moreover, a medication from the beta blockers, such as propranolol, can be used to help with the symptoms.

Prognosis

The prognoses for the early- and intermediate-onset of movement disorders are very good, especially with the option of switching the patient to a newer antipsychotic such as clozapine.

The prognosis for the late-onset disorder called tardive dyskinesia is very poor. Once the condition occurs, it is essentially irreversible and is very difficult to treat.

Neuroleptic malignant syndrome is a serious condition. It is deadly in about 20%–30% of patients. Those who survive have a good chance of recovering.

Medication-induced postural tremor is very well-controlled with propranolol, and hence the prognosis is good while the patient is being treated with the medication causing the movement disorder.

Prevention

To prevent acute dystonia, some physicians prescribe benztropine diphenhydramine, or other medications that treat dystonia at the outset of treatment with an older antipsychotic.

Dystonia—A neurological disorder characterized by involuntary muscle spasms. The spasms can cause a painful twisting of the body and difficulty walking or moving.

Hyperthyroidism—Condition resulting from the thyroid glands secreting excessive thyroid hormone, causing increased basal metabolic rate, and causing an increased need for food to meet the demand of the metabolic activity; generally, however, weight loss results.

Neuroleptic—Another name for antipsychotic medications, such as haloperidol (Haldol) and chlorpromazine (Thorazine).

Neuroleptic-induced acute dystonia—A severe form of the neurological movement disorder caused by the use of neuroleptic drugs.

Neuroleptic-induced akathisia—Refers to the disorder characterized by a physical restlessness (the inability to sit still, for example), and manifested by excessive voluntary movements, as a result of the use of neuroleptic drugs; research indicates it is likely the most common of neuroleptic-induced movement disorders.

Neuroleptic-induced Parkinsonism—Symptoms similar to Parkinson's disease that may appear in people taking neuroleptic (antipsychotic) medications. These symptoms include tremors in muscles and a shuffling gait.

Neuroleptic-induced tardive dyskinesia—A potentially irreversible neurological disorder caused by the use of antipsychotic/neuroleptic medications, with symptoms involving uncontrollable movement of various body parts.

Neuroleptic malignant syndrome—An unusual but potentially serious complication that develops in some patients who have been treated with antipsychotic medications. NMS is characterized by changes in blood pressure, altered states of consciousness, rigid muscles, and fever. Untreated NMS can result in coma and death.

Postural tremor—A continuous quiver that affects body posture and movement.

SLE (Systemic Lupus Erythematosus)—An autoimmune disease that leads to inflammation and damage to various body tissues and parts, including joints, skin, kidneys, heart, lungs, blood vessels, and brain.

Sydenham's chorea—A serious manifestation of acute rheumatic fever that commonly occurs in children ages 7 through 14, peaking at age 8. This disease of the central nervous system is characterized by emotional instability, purposeless movements, and muscular weakness. At its peak in the 1950s it occurred in nearly 50% of the acute rheumatic fever cases, but by 2002 had subsided to a degree of less than 10% of the acute cases.

The most important component of neuroleptic-induced tardive dyskinesia is prevention. If conventional antipsychotics are used, the drug use, drug dose, and the duration of use therefore should be minimized.

In order to avoid medication-induced postural tremor, patients should limit the amount of caffeine consumption. Also, in order to minimize the amount of daytime tremor they should take the psychiatric drug at bedtime.

Resources

BOOKS

American Psychiatric Association. *Diagnostic and Statistical Manual of Mental Disorders.* 4th ed., text rev. Washington, DC: American Psychiatric Publishing, 2000.

Brunton, Laurence, Bruce Chabner, and Bjorn Knollman. *Goodman & Gilman's The Pharmacological Basis of Therapeutics.* 12th ed. New York: McGraw-Hill, 2010.

Lacy, Charles F. *Drug Information Handbook with International Trade Names Index.* Hudson, OH: Lexi-Comp, Inc. 2011.

Sadock, Benjamin J., and Virginia A. Sadock, eds. *Comprehensive Textbook of Psychiatry.* Vol. 2. 7th ed. Philadelphia: Lippincott Williams and Wilkins, 2000.

PERIODICALS

Heaton, Robert, et al. "Stability and Course of Neuropsychological Deficits in Schizophrenia." *Archives of General Psychiatry.* 58, no. 1 (2001): 24–32.

Littrell, Kimberly. "Marked Reduction of Tardive Dyskinesia With Olanzapine." *Archives of General Psychiatry.* 55, no. 3 (March 1998): 398–403.

ORGANIZATIONS

American Psychiatric Association, 1000 Wilson Blvd., Ste. 1825, Arlington, VA, 22209-3901, (703) 907-7300, apa@psych.org, http://www.psych.org.

American Thyroid Association, 6066 Leesburg Pike, Ste. 550, Falls Church, VA, 22041, (703) 998-8890, Fax: (703) 998-8893, thyroid@thyroid.org, http://www.thyroid.org.

Canadian Movement Disorder Group, affiliate of Canadian Congress of Neurological Sciences, 709 7015 Macleod Trail SW, Calgary, AB, CanadaT2H 2K6, http://www.cmdg.org.

We Move, 5731 Mosholu Ave., Bronx, NY, 10471. wemove@wemove.org, http://www.wemove.org.

Ajna Hamidovic, Pharm.D.

Meditation

Definition

Meditation or contemplation involves focusing the mind upon a sound, phrase, prayer, object, visualized image, breath, ritualized movement, or consciousness in order to increase awareness of the present moment, promote relaxation, reduce **stress**, and enhance personal or spiritual growth. The term refers to a group of widely different types of practices all generally founded within, or related to, ancient religious or spiritual traditions. Since the mid-twentieth century, interest in alternative treatments such as meditation has increased for the treatment and management of mental illnesses. As a part of complementary and alternative medicine, meditation is not considered a part of conventional medicine. However, it is often used with conventional medical treatment.

Purpose

Originally, meditation techniques were intended to develop spiritual understanding, awareness, and direct experience of ultimate reality. Many religious traditions developed meditative practices. These include the contemplative practices of Christian religious orders, the Buddhist practice of sitting meditation, and the whirling movements of the Sufi dervishes. Although distinct from each other, the practices share common aspects, such as using specific postures and practicing focused concentration. Today, meditation is used for both religious and secular purposes. Secular goals include:

- increased physical relaxation
- decreased stress and anxiety and reduced pain
- reduced depression
- reduced insomnia
- increased calmness
- enriched serenity
- enhanced mental consciousness
- improved psychological balance
- improved coping skills in handling physical problems and illness
- reduced physical or emotional symptoms involving chronic illnesses, such as heart disease, cancer, and human immunodeficiency virus/acquired immune deficiency syndrome (HIV/AIDS)
- improved overall health and well-being

Meditation is used in the treatment of both physiological and psychological problems. However, medical researchers do not completely understand what changes when people meditate and whether such changes help to influence positively the user's health. However, as Western medical practitioners began to consider the mind's role in health and disease, interest increased in the use of meditation in medicine. Meditative practices are increasingly offered in medical clinics and hospitals as a tool for improving health and quality of life. Meditation has been used as the primary therapy for treating certain diseases; as an additional therapy in a comprehensive treatment plan; and as a means of improving the quality of life of people with debilitating, chronic, or terminal illnesses. Medical research is ongoing regarding the applicability of meditation within traditional medicine, including how meditation works to counter diseases and conditions.

Demographics

Meditation techniques have been practiced for millennia. Although meditation is an important spiritual practice in many religious and spiritual traditions, it can be practiced by anyone regardless of their religious or cultural background to relieve stress and pain. As reported by the U.S. National Center for Complimentary and Alternative Medicine, a 2007 American study that followed 23,393 adults found that 9.4% of them had used meditation in the past year, compared to a similar study

A young woman practices meditation. (© Angela Hampton Picture Library/Alamy)

performed in 2002 that showed 7.6% of the respondents had used meditation over the past year.

Description

Meditation refers to such specific techniques and approaches as concentration meditation, relaxation response, transcendental meditation, mantra meditation, mindfulness meditation, and Zen Buddhist meditation. Many of these techniques originated in ancient Asian religions and spiritual traditions, such as Buddhism. Although meditation practices continue within religious communities, they also are used in secular settings to promote health and well-being. Meditation can be performed while sitting or lying quietly or while moving.

Sitting meditation is done in an upright seated position, either in a chair or cross-legged on a cushion on the floor. The spine is straight yet relaxed. Sometimes the eyes are closed; sometimes individuals gaze into the distance or at a specific object. Depending on the type of meditation, meditators may concentrate on the breath as it is inhaled and exhaled; they may count their inhalations or repeat a sound or chant. Meditators may visualize a certain image or focus on the center of the body. They may consciously remain open to all sensory experience and note with detachment the flow of thoughts that occur to them. They may also perform stylized ritual movements with their hands.

Movement meditation can be spontaneous or choreographed. Movement meditation is particularly helpful for those people who find it difficult to remain still.

Generally speaking, there are two types of meditation: concentration meditation and mindfulness meditation. Concentration meditation practices involve focusing attention on a single object. Objects of meditation can include the breath; an inner or external image; a movement pattern (as in tai chi or **yoga**); or a sound, word, or phrase that is repeated silently as a mantra. The purpose of concentrative practices is to train one's attention or develop concentration. When thoughts or emotions arise, the meditator gently directs the mind back to the original object of concentration.

Mindfulness meditation practices involve becoming aware of the entire field of attention. The meditator is instructed to be aware of all thoughts, feelings, perceptions, or sensations as they arise in each moment. Mindfulness meditation practices are enhanced by the meditator's ability to focus and quiet the mind. Many meditation practices are a blend of these two forms.

In treating physiological conditions, three types of meditation have been used: (1) transcendental meditation (TM); (2) relaxation response, an approach developed by American cardiologist Herbert Benson (1935–); and (3) mindfulness meditation, specifically the program of mindfulness-based **stress reduction** (MBSR) developed by American molecular biologist Jon Kabat-Zinn (1944–).

Transcendental meditation

Transcendental meditation (TM) has its origins in the Vedic tradition of India and was introduced to the West by Maharishi Mahesh Yogi (1914–2008). TM gained worldwide attention in the 1960s when the rock-and-roll group The Beatles was trained in the technique. It is one of the most widely practiced forms of meditation in the West. In TM, the meditator sits with closed eyes and concentrates on a single syllable or word (mantra) for 20 minutes at a time, twice a day. When thoughts or feelings arise, the attention is brought back to the mantra. According to American **psychologist** Charles N. Alexander, an important TM researcher and professor at Maharishi International University, "During TM, ordinary waking mental activity is said to settle down, until even the subtlest thought is transcended and a completely unified wholeness of awareness . . . is experienced. In this silent, self-referential state of pure wakefulness, consciousness is fully awake to itself alone." TM supporters believe that TM practices are more beneficial than other meditation practices.

Frequently, medical studies of TM have focused on such topics as mental health, **addiction**, rehabilitation, and cognition. A study published in 2006, which was funded by the U.S. National Institutes of Health, found that TM may help to prevent health problems caused by environmental and psychosocial stresses in a variety of people from different ethnic backgrounds. Researchers from the Institute for Natural Medicine and Prevention at Maharishi University of Management in Fairfield, Iowa, looked at how TM and Maharishi consciousness-based health care affects blood pressure, psychosocial stress, surrogate markers for atherosclerotic cardiovascular disease (CVD), and mortality. They concluded that TM could "include enhanced resistance to physiological and psychological stress and improvements in homeostatic and self-repair processes" and "may offer clinical and cost effectiveness advantages for health care, particularly in preventive cardiology."

Relaxation response

The relaxation response involves a similar form of mental focusing. One of the first Western doctors to conduct research on the effects of meditation, Benson developed this approach after observing the health benefits of a state of bodily calm he calls "the relaxation response." In order to elicit this response in the body, Benson teaches patients to focus on the repetition of a word, sound, prayer, phrase, or movement activity (including swimming, jogging, yoga, and even knitting) for 10 to 20 minutes at a time, twice a day. Patients are also taught not to pay attention to distracting thoughts and to return their focus to the original repetition when rising thoughts seem to distract them. The individual chooses the focused repetition. Instead of repeating a prescribed Sanskrit term, the meditator chooses something that is personally meaningful, such as a phrase from a prayer.

Mindfulness meditation

Mindfulness meditation derives from traditional Buddhist meditation practices. Jon Kabat-Zinn (1944–) has been instrumental in bringing this form of meditation into medical settings. In formal mindfulness practice, the meditator sits with eyes closed, focusing the attention on the sensations and movement of the breath for approximately 45 to 60 minutes at a time, at least once a day. Informal mindfulness practice involves bringing awareness to every activity in daily life. Wandering thoughts or distracting feelings are simply noticed without resistance or reaction. The essence of mindfulness meditation is not what one focuses on but rather the quality of awareness the meditator brings to each moment. It is practiced by bringing attention to the experiences of breathing in and out, concentrating on this action while focusing one's mind on the experience itself—all the while not reacting or judging what is being experienced.

According to Kabat-Zinn, in his book *Mind/Body Medicine*, "It is this investigative, discerning observation of whatever comes up in the present moment that is the hallmark of mindfulness and differentiates it most from other forms of meditation. The goal of mindfulness is for you to be more aware, more in touch with life and whatever is happening in your own body and mind at the time it is happening—that is, the present moment." The mindfulness-based stress reduction (MBSR) program, which Kabat-Zinn first established at the University of Massachusetts Medical School, consists of a series of complementary-medicine classes involving meditation, movement, and group process. There are over 200 MBSR programs offered in healthcare settings around the world.

Meditation is not considered a medical procedure or **intervention** by most insurers. Many patients pay directly for meditation training. Frequently, religious groups or meditation centers offer meditation instruction free of charge or for a nominal donation. Hospitals may offer MBSR classes at a reduced rate for their patients and a slightly higher rate for the general public.

Benefits

Meditation benefits people with or without acute medical illness or stress. People who meditate frequently have been shown to feel less anxiety and **depression**. They also report that they experience more enjoyment and appreciation of life and that their relationships with others are improved. Meditation produces a state of deep relaxation and a sense of balance or equanimity. According to physician Michael J. Baime, director of the UPenn Program for Mindfulness at the University of Pennsylvania Health System, "Meditation cultivates an emotional stability that allows the meditator to experience intense emotions fully while simultaneously maintaining perspective on them." Out of this experience of emotional stability, one may gain greater insight and understanding about one's thoughts, feelings, and actions. This insight in turn offers the possibility to feel more confident and in control of life. Meditation facilitates a greater sense of calm, empathy, and acceptance of oneself and others.

Meditation can be used with other forms of medical treatment and is an important complementary therapy for both the treatment and prevention of many stress-related conditions. Regular meditation can reduce the number of symptoms experienced by patients with a wide range of illnesses and disorders. Based upon clinical evidence, as well as theoretical understanding, meditation is considered to be one of the better therapies for **panic disorder**, **generalized anxiety disorder**, substance dependence and abuse, ulcers, colitis, chronic pain, psoriasis, and **dysthymic disorder**. It is considered a valuable adjunctive therapy for moderate hypertension (high blood pressure), prevention of cardiac arrest (heart attack), prevention of atherosclerosis (hardening of arteries), arthritis (including fibromyalgia), cancer, **insomnia**, migraine, and prevention of **stroke**.

Meditation may also be a valuable complementary therapy for allergies and asthma because of the role stress plays in these conditions. Meditative practices have been reported to improve function or reduce symptoms in patients with some neurological disorders as well. These include people with Parkinson's disease, people who experience **fatigue** with multiple sclerosis, and people with epilepsy who are resistant to standard treatment.

Overall, health organizations such as the National Institutes of Health view meditation and similar forms of relaxation as ways to improve health and quality of life and to lower healthcare costs. Many physicians, nurses, and occupational therapists in the United States accept meditation as a beneficial adjunct to conventional medical or surgical treatments.

Meditation

KEY TERMS

Dervish—A member of the Sufi order, in which the practice of meditation involves whirling ecstatic dance.

Mantra—A sacred word or formula repeated over and over to concentrate the mind.

Transcendental meditation—A meditation technique based on Hindu practices that involves the repetition of a mantra.

A March 18, 2011, article in the *New York Times* highlighted the popularity that transcendental meditation in the United States. The article concentrated on the effect that various celebrities, such as Russell Brand, Susan Sarandon, and Martin Scorsese, have had on the TM movement. In addition, the article "Look Who's Meditating Now" noted that many research studies show the positive effects of daily TM for the "mind, body and behavior." The *New York Times* article also mentioned the large number of studies funded by the U.S. National Institutes of Health. Such studies have investigated the effects of meditation on such medical conditions as hypertension (high blood pressure), atherosclerosis, and the risk of cardiac events (such as heart attacks, strokes, and congestive heart failure).

In the early 2000s, numerous studies were funded by the U.S. National Center for Complementary and Alternative Medicine (NCCAM). These studies indicated the benefits of meditation for certain medical conditions, such as "Meditation May Make Information Processing In the Brain More Efficient" (June 2007); "Meditation May Increase Empathy" (March 2008); "Mantram Instruction May Help HIV-Positive Individuals Handle Stress" (January 2009); "Transcendental Meditation Helps Young Adults Cope with Stress" (December 2009); and "Mindfulness Meditation Is Associated with Structural Changes in the Brain" (January 2011).

With respect to stress, which in some cases is seen as a precursor to various mental illnesses, the December 2009 study found that TM helped college students reduce psychological stress and cope more effectively with school-related responsibilities. The group of students with the highest likelihood of developing hypertension (high blood pressure) were found to decrease their blood pressure level when they practiced TM on a regular basis. A NCCAM article stated that "This could be good news for the many students experiencing academic, financial, and social pressures that can lead to psychological distress—especially in light of evidence that college-age people with even

slightly elevated blood pressure are three times more likely to develop hypertension within 30 years."

It is important to note that independent systematic reviews of these studies do not necessarily agree with their findings.

Preparation

People who want to meditate usually make the following preparations:

- Find a quiet location that contains few distractions.
- Assume a comfortable posture, one that may involving sitting, lying down, or standing, as specified by the meditation technique being used.
- Focus attention on a specified object, sense perception, word or phrase (a mantra), or movement of breath.
- Allow distractions to come and go without concern, calmly returning attention to the chosen point of focus after each disruption.

Risks

Meditation appears to be safe for most people. There are, however, case reports and studies noting some adverse effects, such as **depersonalization**, or a sense of being detached from one's experiences. To an extent, this is a goal of meditation, but the effect may progress to the extreme and feel unpleasant or alarming. In one particular study, 33%–50% of the people participating in long silent meditation retreats (two weeks to three months) reported increased tension, anxiety, confusion, and depression. However, most of these same people also reported positive effects from their meditation practice. Kabat-Zinn notes that these studies fail to differentiate between serious psychiatric disturbances and normal emotional mood swings. These studies do suggest, however, that meditation may not be recommended for people with psychotic disorders, severe depression, and other severe **personality disorders** unless they are also receiving psychological or medical treatment.

Research & general acceptance

The scientific study of the physiological effects of meditation began in the early 1960s. Certain studies indicated that meditation affects metabolism, the endocrine system, the central nervous system, and the autonomic nervous system. In one study, three advanced practitioners of Tibetan Buddhist meditation practices demonstrated the ability to increase "inner heat" as much as 61%. During a different meditative practice, they were able to dramatically slow down the rate at which their bodies consumed oxygen. Preliminary research shows

948   GALE ENCYCLOPEDIA OF MENTAL HEALTH, 3ᴿᴰ EDITION

that mindfulness meditation is associated with increased levels of melatonin.

Despite the inherent difficulties in designing research studies, there is significant evidence of the medical benefits of meditation. Meditation is particularly effective as a treatment for chronic pain. Studies have shown meditation reduces symptoms of pain and pain-related drug use. In a 1986 four-year follow-up study conducted by Kabat-Zinn and his colleagues, the majority of patients in an MBSR program reported "moderate to great improvement" in pain as a result of participation in the program. Later studies supported his findings, including a 2011 study published in the *Journal of Neuroscience* that found meditation to be as effective—and in some cases more effective—than pain medications.

Research also suggests that meditation is effective in the treatment of chemical dependency. Numerous studies show that TM is helpful in **smoking cessation** programs and programs for drug and alcohol abuse.

Studies suggest that meditation is helpful in reducing symptoms of anxiety and in treating anxiety-related disorders. Furthermore, a study of patients with psoriasis showed that those practicing mindfulness meditation had more rapid clearing of their skin condition, with standard ultraviolet (UV) light treatment, than the control subjects. Another study found that meditation decreased the symptoms of fibromyalgia; over half of the patients reported significant improvement. Research by a group of ophthalmologists indicated that nearly 60% of a group of patients being treated for glaucoma found meditation helpful in coping with their eye disorder. In addition, meditation was one of several **stress management** techniques used in a small study of men with HIV. The study showed improvements in the T-cell counts (a group of white blood cells that play a key role in immunity) of the men, as well as in several psychological measures of well-being.

Training & certification

There is no program of certification or licensing for instructors who wish to teach meditation as a medical therapy. Meditation teachers within a particular religious tradition usually have extensive experience and expertise with faith questions and religious practices but may not have been trained to work with medical patients. Different programs have varied requirements for someone to teach meditation. In order to be recognized as an instructor of TM, one must receive extensive training. The Center for Mindfulness in Medicine, Health Care and Society at the University of Massachusetts Medical Center offers training and

---

QUESTIONS TO ASK YOUR DOCTOR

- How do you think meditation may benefit me?
- What other treatment options do you recommend for me?
- Will meditation interfere with my current medications?
- Is there an exercise regimen you would recommend to help me cope with my condition?
- What symptoms or behaviors are important enough that I should seek immediate treatment?

---

workshops for health professionals and others interested in teaching mindfulness-based stress reduction. The center does not, however, certify that someone is qualified to teach meditation. The University of Pennsylvania Program for Stress Management suggests that individuals have at least 10 years of personal experience with the practice of mindfulness meditation before receiving additional instruction to teach meditation. Teachers are also expected to spend at least two weeks each year in intensive meditation retreats.

Resources

BOOKS

Bear, Marina. *The Little Book of Meditation: A Guide to Stress-Free Living.* Berkeley, CA: SLG, 2009.

Chopra, Deepak. *Reinventing the Body, Resurrecting the Soul: How to Create a New You.* New York: Harmony, 2009.

Liebler, Nancy, and Sandra Moss. *Healing Depression the Mind-Body Way: Creating Happiness with Meditation, Yoga, and Ayurveda.* Hoboken, NJ: Wiley, 2009.

McNally, Lama Christie. *The Tibetan Book of Meditation.* New York: Doubleday Religion, 2009.

PERIODICALS

Alecksander, Irina. "Look Who's Meditating Now." *New York Times,* March 18, 2011. http://www.nytimes.com/2011/03/20/fashion/20TM.html?_r=1 (accessed August 14, 2011).

Kabat-Zinn, J., L. Lipworth, R. Burney, and W. Sellers, "Four Year Follow-up of a Meditation-based Program for the Self-regulation of Chronic Pain: Treatment Outcomes and Compliance." *Clinical Journal of Pain* 2, no. 3 (1986):159–73.

Zeidan, Fadel. "Brain Mechanisms Supporting the Modulation of Pain by Mindfulness Meditation." *Journal of Neuroscience* 31, no. 14 (2011): 5540–48.

WEBSITES

"Meditation: An Introduction." National Center for Complementary and Alternative Medicine. Last updated June 2010. http://nccam.nih.gov/health/meditation/overview.htm#research (accessed August 14, 2011).

"Research Results for Meditation." National Center for Complementary and Alternative Medicine. Last modified February 24, 2011. http://nccam.nih.gov/research/results/topics/index.php?title=Meditation (accessed August 14, 2011).

Schneider, Robert H., et al. "Cardiovascular Disease Prevention and Health Promotion with the Transcendental Meditation Program and Maharishi Consciousness-based Health Care." National Institutes of Health. http://www.ncbi.nlm.nih.gov/pmc/articles/PMC2267926 (accessed August 14, 2011).

"Transcendental Meditation Helps Young Adults Cope with Stress." National Center for Complementary and Alternative Medicine, December 7, 2009. http://nccam.nih.gov/research/results/spotlight/051410.htm (accessed August 14, 2011).

"What Is Mindfulness-Based Stress Reduction?" Mindful Living Programs. http://www.mindfullivingprograms.com/whatMBSR.php (accessed August 14, 2011).

ORGANIZATIONS

Benson-Henry for Mind Body Medicine, 151 Merrimac St., 4th Fl., Boston, MA, 02114, (617) 643-6090, Fax: (617) 643-6077, mindbody@partners.org, http://www.massgeneral.org/bhi.

Center for Mindfulness in Medicine, Health Care and Society, 55 Lake Ave. N, Worcester, MA, 01655, (508) 856-2656, mindfulness@umassmed.edu, http://www.umassmed.edu/cfm/home/index.aspx.

Insight Meditation Society, 1230 Pleasant St., Barre, MA, 01005, (978) 355-4378, http://www.dharma.org.

Linda Chrisman
Rebecca J. Frey, PhD
Laura Jean Cataldo, RN, EdD
William A. Atkins, BB, BS, MBA

Mellaril *see* **Thioridazine**

Memantine

Purpose

Memantine HCl (trade name Namenda) is an N-methyl-D-aspartate (NMDA) receptor antagonist used to treat moderate to severe **Alzheimer's disease** (AD).

Description

A recent theory concerning the mechanism underlying AD is that abnormal glutamate activity in the **brain**

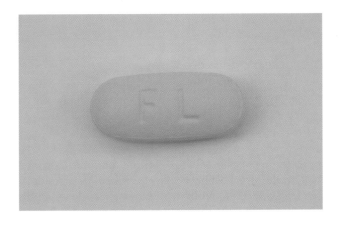

Namenda (memantine), 10 mg. *(© Custom Medical Stock Photo, Inc. Reproduced by permission.)*

causes overexcitation of NMDA receptors, which may play a role in the development and progression of AD. Memantine is a NMDA-receptor antagonist, which hypothetically allows the continued physiological activation of NMDA receptors for continued learning and memory. However, memantine does not appear to prevent or slow the degeneration of brain cells in patients with AD.

Randomized, double-blind, placebo-controlled **clinical trials** of memantine have demonstrated significant improvement of day-to-day functioning in moderate to severe AD.

Recommended dosage

Memantine is available in tablet form, or as an oral solution for patients who have difficulty swallowing tablets. Typically, patients are gradually put on memantine by taking 5 mg once a day for the first week, 5 mg twice a day for the second week (10 mg total per day), and 10 mg in the morning and 5 mg in the evening for the third week (15 mg total per day). After that, the maintenance dosage of memantine is 10 mg twice a day (20 mg total per day). Memantine can be taken with or without food.

Precautions

Clinical trials of memantine found it to be safe and well tolerated. However, anyone with a known hypersensitivity to memantine HCl or any of the inert substances used as a vehicle for the drug should not take memantine. The dosage of memantine should be reduced for patients with severe kidney impairment.

Side effects

No significant difference has been found between patients taking memantine and patients taking a placebo

KEY TERMS

Alzheimer's disease—Alzheimer's disease (AD) is a progressive neurologic disease in which dementia results from the degeneration of brain cells through the formation of senile plaques and neurofibrillary tangles. AD is the most common cause of dementia.

Clinical trial—A controlled scientific experiment designed to investigate the effectiveness of a drug or treatment in curing or lessening the symptoms of a disease or disorder.

Control group—A group in a research study that does not receive the experimental treatment. For example, in an experiment testing the effectiveness of a new drug, the control group might receive the current drug of choice while the experimental group receives the new drug under investigation.

Double-blind study—A research study in which neither the participants nor the professional giving them the drug or treatment know whether they are receiving the experimental treatment or a placebo or control treatment.

Placebo—A preparation without pharmacological effect that is given in place of a drug in clinical trials to determine the effectiveness of the drug under study; a "sugar pill."

Randomization—The process of randomly assigning participants in an experiment to the various conditions (that is, experimental and control groups) so that each individual has an equal chance of being assigned to any of the groups. Randomization helps ensure that each of the groups is roughly the same and that the results are due to the treatment, not to the makeup of the groups.

in vital signs, electrocardiogram values, or laboratory values (serum chemistry, hematology, and urinalysis). The most common adverse reactions to memantine are:

• dizziness

• confusion

• headache

• constipation

• agitation

• falling

• accidental injury

Compared with a placebo, memantine showed a lower level of gastrointestinal side effects (such as constipation, diarrhea, vomiting, or nausea).

Interactions

Studies have revealed that the use of memantine in combination therapy with **donepezil**, a cholinesterase inhibitor, is frequently more effective than the use of donepezil alone in the treatment of moderate to severe AD. Using memantine and donepezil in combination therapy does not affect the actions of either drug. Memantine has been shown to be both safe and effective in such combination therapy.

Studies on memantine have shown low potential for negative interaction with other drugs.

Resources

BOOKS

Burns, Alistair, and Bengt Winblad, eds. *Severe Dementia*. New York: John Wiley & Sons, 2006.

VandenBos, Gary R. ed. *APA Dictionary of Psychology*. Washington, DC: American Psychological Association, 2006.

PERIODICALS

Alexopoulos, G. S., et al. "Treatment of Dementia and Its Behavioral Disturbances." *Postgraduate Medicine* (January 2005): 1–111.

Cummings, Jeffrey L., et al. "Behavioral Effects of Memantine in Alzheimer Disease Patients Receiving Donepezil Treatment." *Neurology* 67, no. 1 (July 2006): 57–63.

Danysz, W., et al. "Neuroprotective and Symptomalogical Action of Memantine Relevant for Alzheimer's Disease." *Neurotoxicity Research* 2 (2000): 85–98.

Doody, R. S. "Refining Treatment Guidelines in Alzheimer's Disease." *Geriatrics* Suppl. (June 2005): 14–20.

Doraiswamy, P. M. "Non-Cholinergic Strategies for Treating and Preventing Alzheimer's Disease." *CNS Drugs* 16, no. 12 (2002): 811–24.

Fox, Chris, et al. "Memantine Combined with an Acetyl Cholinesterase Inhibitor—Hope for the Future?" *Neuropsychiatric Disease and Treatment* 2, no. 2 (2006): 121–25.

Hartmann, S., and H. J. Möbius. "Tolerability of Memantine in Combination with Cholinesterase Inhibitors in Dementia Therapy." *International Clinical Psychopharmacology* 18 (March 2003): 81–85.

Maidment, Ian, et al. "Drug Treatment for Alzheimer's Disease: The Way Forward." *International Journal of Geriatric Psychiatry* 21, no. 1 (2006): 6–8.

Orgogozo, J. M., et al. "Efficacy and Safety of Memantine in Patients with Mild to Moderate Vascular Dementia." *Stroke* 33, no. 7 (July 2002): 1834–39.

Reisberg, B., et al. "Memantine in Moderate-to-Severe Alzheimer's Disease." *New England Journal of Medicine* 348, no. 14 (2003): 1333–41.

Schneider, Lon S., Karen S. Dagerman, Julian P.T. Higgins, and Rupert McShane. "Lack of Evidence for the Efficacy of Memantine in Mild Alzheimer Disease." *Archives of Neurology* 68, no. 8 (2011): 991–998. http://archneur. ama-assn.org/cgi/content/short/archneurol.2011.69 (accessed November 14, 2011).

Tariot, Pierre N., et al. "Memantine Treatment in Patients with Moderate to Severe Alzheimer Disease Already Receiving Donepezil: A Randomized Controlled Trial." *Journal of the American Medical Association* 291, no. 3 (January 21, 2004): 317–24. Available online at http://jama.ama-assn. org/content/291/3/317.full (accessed November 9, 2011).

Xiong, G., and P. M. Doraiswamy. "Combination Drug Therapy for Alzheimer's Disease: What Is Evidence-Based, and What Is Not?" *Geriatrics* 60, no. 6 (2005): 22–26.

WEBSITES

Forest Laboratories, Inc. "Namenda." http://www.namenda. com (accessed October 22, 2011.

Ruth A. Wienclaw, PhD

Men's mental health *see* **Gender issues in mental health**

Mental health courts

Definition

Mental health courts are used to divert criminal offenders with mental health problems from serving sentences in penitentiaries to fulfilling community-based treatment programs combined with court supervision. Because many prisons and jails are overcrowded, the goal of these programs is to help individuals with mental illnesses move forward with their recovery while preserving public safety. Some mental health courts hear felony cases, but most only hear misdemeanor cases. All mental health courts are voluntary. People with mental illnesses that have committed a crime have a choice of prison or program participation.

Qualifying mental illness for the Mental Health Courts Program is defined by law as: "a diagnosable mental, behavioral, or emotional disorder (A) of sufficient duration to meet diagnostic criteria within the most recent edition of the *Diagnostic and Statistical Manual of Mental Disorders*, published by the **American Psychiatric Association**; and (B) that has resulted in functional impairment that substantially interferes with or limits one or more major life activities."

Purpose

The Mental Health Courts Program was established by an act of the U.S. Congress in 2000 to address the particular needs of mentally ill or intellectually disabled defendants. The traditional criminal court system in the United States is designed to process individuals who have been charged with crimes, but it does not account for special considerations, such as mental illness. Mental health courts provide defendants with mental illnesses, who have primarily committed misdemeanor and nonviolent crimes, with supervised treatment in order to reduce the number of incarcerated people with mental illness and to prevent those who have a mental illness from continually cycling through the court system. Those who successfully complete the program avoid prolonged incarceration and may have their charges dismissed.

Demographics

Approximately 1.5 million persons with mental illness are processed by the criminal justice system per year. The National Alliance on Mentally Illness estimates that as many as 40% of mentally ill individuals will encounter the criminal justice system at some point in their lives. Research finds that mentally ill inmates are at greater risk for assault and **suicide** than are other inmates.

Description

Before mental health courts were established, persons with mental illness who broke the law were not differentiated from other criminals. Because of this, the prison population contained about twice as many inmates with mental illness as those in state mental hospitals. In prison, the conditions of mentally ill inmates generally worsened over time, as they often did not receive proper medications or treatment. The criminal justice system had neglected these people, and ignored their mental state. However, their plight was eventually realized, in part due to overcrowding within the prison system, and steps were taken to remedy the situation, resulting in the creation of mental health courts.

After the mental health court system was established, persons with mental illnesses who were being processed through the criminal justice system were eligible to be sent to treatment programs instead of to jail or prison (providing they met the program's eligibility requirements). During their participation in the court program, after being processed through a mental health court, patients are provided treatment and support based on the underlying problems, especially their mental health conditions, that have led to their involvement with the criminal justice system. Time spent within the program is dependent on the terms and conditions of release decided by ongoing mental health assessments.

The mental health court system includes judges, prosecutors, defense attorneys, and other court personnel.

Criminal justice system—The system instituted by federal, state, and local governments to control and deter crime and to punish persons who violate laws.

Felony—A serious crime, such as murder, which is much more serious then a minor crime and much more severely punished than a misdemeanor crime, punishable by at least one year in prison.

Misdemeanor—A minor crime, such as petit larceny (petty theft), which is punishable by not more than one year in prison.

All have an interest or expertise in helping persons with mental illness or **substance abuse** disorders. There are approximately 175 mental health courts operating in the United States, and the program is administered by the Bureau of Justice Assistance and the **Substance Abuse and Mental Health Services Administration**.

The Justice and Mental Health Collaboration Program (JMHCP), a grant program that promotes public safety by facilitating collaboration among the criminal justice, juvenile justice, mental health treatment, and substance abuse systems, increases access to treatment for people with mental illnesses who are inside the criminal justice system by funding grants for mental health courts and similar programs. It was authorized by the Mentally Ill Offender Treatment and Crime Reduction Act of 2004 and is administrated by the Bureau of Justice Assistance (BJA), a division of the Office of Justice Programs.

Origins

In the 1980s, judges, attorneys, and jail officials, realizing that there were a large percentage of persons with mental illness being processed through the criminal justice system, began to call for more specific court-related treatment programs for these individuals. At that time, Judge Evan Dee Goodman, of the Marion Municipal Court in Indianapolis, Indiana, helped to establish a court to deal with mental health cases, which involved psychiatric treatment of criminals arrested on minor charges. The court was terminated in the early 1990s, but is still considered an early version of what came to be called the mental health court system.

In 1997, the first recognized mental health court opened in Broward County, Florida. Three years later, Congress passed the America's Law Enforcement and Mental Health Project Act to relieve the burden on the criminal justice system and on corrective institutions, and to provide individuals with the tools they need to stay out of the criminal justice system. In 2001, the first mental health court for juveniles began operations in Santa Clara, California.

Mental health courts were modeled after drug courts, which since 1989 have been providing drug treatment to addicts who are convicted of crimes. Individuals who complete drug court-mandated programs are eligible to have their criminal charges reduced or dismissed.

Process

Mental health courts generally take between 15 and 375 cases each year, a small percentage of defendants with mental illness. They try individuals with mental illness separately from other cases. Mental health courts vary in the kinds of mental health diagnoses and criminal charges they will accept, how the court monitors a defendant's treatment, and the kinds of pleas an individual can make. In the past, mental health courts would only accept people who were charged with nonviolent offenses, such as trespassing or vandalism. Today, some mental health courts will accept those who have committed more violent crimes, including assault and robbery, but these individuals often require additional supervision.

Although the process can vary from court to court, generally a defendant is referred to a mental health court. Referrals can come from a number of individuals, including family members, law enforcement officials, or judges. Defendants who are too violent or disturbed to appear in court may first be referred to a crisis center for stabilization.

In most mental health courts, defendants are required to plead "guilty" or "no contest" to qualify for treatment (referred to as the post-adjudication model). The defendant then receives a psychiatric evaluation, and, if deemed stable enough and eligible to stand trial in the mental health court, the judge will defer to the treatment decisions of mental health professionals. Mental health professionals under the direction of the court implement the treatment plan, which may include inpatient or outpatient counseling, housing placement, education, vocational training, job placement, health care, and rehabilitation for substance abuse, as needed.

During the treatment period, the patient must return to the court periodically for assessments. When a defendant successfully completes the treatment program, his or her case is considered resolved. Sometimes the charges will be reduced, and sometimes the case will be dismissed. Defendants who do not successfully complete the program are returned to a regular court for another trial, and they may have to face jail time if convicted.

Pros and cons

PROS. For the individuals and communities they serve, as well as for the criminal justice system in general, mental health courts offer several advantages over traditional courts:

• They improve the outcomes for people with mental illness by helping them obtain treatment.

• They lower recidivism rates for people with mental illness who enter the criminal justice system.

• They free jail cells for more serious offenders.

• They are considered a more cost-effective method than correctional institutions to treat defendants with mental illness.

CONS. The program has its critics, however. Some of the arguments against mental health courts, regardless of legitimacy, are as follows:

• They further stigmatize mental illness.

• They provide incentives to mentally ill individuals to commit crimes so that they can receive treatment.

• They could lead police to arrest people with mental illness just to get them into treatment.

• They divert resources used for mental illness treatment from the general community to those with criminal records.

Other arguments question the requirement of a guilty plea, claiming that some individuals with mental illness may not have the ability to make an informed decision. However, only persons deemed competent enough to stand trial are eligible for mental health courts, and participation is completely voluntary.

Results

Although there is little research available to confirm the effectiveness of mental health courts in general, there have been studies conducted on individual mental health courts that suggest positive outcomes. Research overall indicates that participants in mental health courts are less likely to return to jail and generally spend fewer days in jail than those who are processed through the regular court system.

A 1999 study presented at the symposium "Mental Health Courts: Promises and Limitations" followed offenders with mental illness who had spent an average of 18 days in mental hospitals and 85 days in jail in one year. The following year, while on Alaska's mental health court program, they spent only three days in mental hospitals and 16 days in jail. In 2001, in a Pittsburgh, Pennsylvania, mental health court, only 10%

of 223 participants were arrested for a second time after completing their treatment programs.

A study conducted in the Broward County, Florida, mental health court and published in the July 2005 *Psychiatric Services* found that mentally ill defendants had greater access to treatment than they otherwise would have had, and they spent an average of 75% fewer days in jail compared to those who went through the traditional court system.

The August 2006 *Harvard Mental Health Letter* mentions a study conducted in California that found that offenders processed in a mental health court who were rearrested were generally charged with technical violations of parole rather than new crimes. Another California study of a mental health court in San Francisco, conducted in 2007, found that participants who had followed a treatment program for 18 months were 26% less likely to commit new crimes and 55% less likely to commit new violent crimes, compared to individuals with mental illness who had served the same amount of time in a county jail.

A study published in the February 2011 issue of *Archives of General Psychiatry* looked at outcomes of four mental health courts in California, Indiana, and Minnesota. The study found that mental health courts lowered subsequent arrest rates for persons completing treatment programs as part of these courts. In addition, the researchers, headed by Dr. Henry J. Steadman of Policy Research Associates (Delmar, New York), found that the time period during which individuals with serious psychiatric illnesses were incarcerated was also shortened after going through mental health court programs.

However, not all of the research has been positive. A study published in the July 2005 *Psychiatric Services* found a disproportionate balance of gender and ethnic groups represented in the mental health courts. Women and Caucasians in the study were more likely to be referred to mental health courts than were men and other ethnic groups, even though the majority of prison inmates are male (90%–94%) and minorities (63%). That study also found that participants in one mental health court had no significant improvement in clinical symptoms, compared to those who went through the general court system.

Resources

BOOKS

Frank, Richard, and Thomas G. McGuire. *Mental Health Treatment and Criminal Justice Outcomes*. Cambridge, MA: National Bureau of Economic Research, 2010.

Gideon, Lior, and Hung-En Sung, eds. *Rethinking Corrections: Rehabilitation, Reentry, and Reintegration*. Los Angeles: SAGE, 2011.

Johnson, Sandra J. *Assertive Community Treatment: Evidence-Based Practice or Managed Recovery.* New Brunswick, NJ: Transaction, 2011.

Rogers, Richard, and Daniel W. Shuman. *Fundamentals of Forensic Practice: Mental Health and Criminal Law.* New York: Springer, 2005.

Scott, Charles L., ed. *Handbook of Correctional Mental Health.* Washington, DC: American Psychiatric Publishing, 2010.

PERIODICALS

Schwartz, Emma. "Mental Health Courts." *U.S. World News and World Report* (February 7, 2008). http://www.usnews.com/news/national/articles/2008/02/07/mental-health-courts (accessed October 24, 2011).

Steadman, Henry J. "Effect of Mental Health Courts on Arrests and Jail Days: A Multisite Study." *Archives of General Psychiatry* 62, no. 2 (2011): 167–72.

OTHER

Almquist, Lauren, and Elizabeth Dodd. *Mental Health Courts: A Guide To Research-Informed Policy And Practice.* New York: Council of State Governments Justice Center, 2009. http://www.ojp.usdoj.gov/BJA/pdf/CSG_MHC_Research.pdf (accessed October 24, 2011).

Thompson, Michael, Fred Osher, and Denise Tomasini-Joshi. *Improving Responses to People with Mental Illnesses: The Essential Elements of a Mental Health Court.* New York: Council of State Governments Justice Center, 2007. http://www.ojp.usdoj.gov/BJA/pdf/MHC_Essential_Elements.pdf (accessed October 24, 2011).

WEBSITES

Bureau of Justice Assistance. "Mental Health Courts Program." Office of Justice Programs. http://www.ojp.usdoj.gov/BJA/grant/mentalhealth.html (accessed October 24, 2011).

Mental Health America. "Position Statement 53: Mental Health Courts." http://www.nmha.org/go/position-statements/53 (accessed October 24, 2011).

ORGANIZATIONS

Bureau of Justice Assistance, 810 Seventh St. NW, 4th Fl., Washington, DC, 20531, (202) 616-6500, (866) 859-2687, Fax: (202) 305-1367, http://www.ojp.usdoj.gov/BJA/index.html.

Council of State Governments Justice Center, 100 Wall St., 20th Fl., New York, NY, 10005, (212) 482-2320, http://www.justicecenter.csg.org.

National Alliance on Mental Illness, 3803 North Fairfax Drive, Ste. 100, Arlington, VA, 22203, (703) 524-7600, Fax: (703) 524-9094, http://www.nami.org.

National Council for Community Behavioral Healthcare, 1701 K St. NW, Ste. 400, Washington, DC, 20006, (202) 684-7457, Fax: (202) 386-9391, communications@thenationalcouncil.org, http://www.thenationalcouncil.org.

National Institute of Mental Health, 6001 Executive Blvd., Rm. 8184, MSC 9663, Bethesda, MD, 20892-9663, (301) 433-4513; TTY: (301) 443-8431, (866) 615-6464; TTY: (866) 415-8051, Fax: (301) 443-4279, nimhinfo@nih.gov, http://www.nimh.nih.gov.

Stephanie N. Watson
William A. Atkins

Mental health law

Definition

Mental health law is the body of laws and legal standards applied when considering the civil rights of a person with mental illness as defined by law. Key emphases include the areas of involuntary commitment and criminal justice.

Description

Mental health law is involved in the consideration of many issues, including:

- whether a person can be committed against his or her will
- what society's responsibility should be in treating individuals with mental disorders
- whether a mental disorder can serve as evidence that a crime did not involve criminal intent, and if so, at what severity

In legal terms, the concept of mental illness describes a person who is perceived to have impaired thoughts and emotions that may lead to the person being a threat to him/herself or others. The legal concept of mental illness is different from that of a therapist diagnosing a mental disorder. A clinically diagnosed psychological disorder is characterized by identifiable symptoms, clear origins, and recommended treatments. The constantly changing legal concept of mental illness is understandably broader, because it is influenced by societal concerns and the attempt to establish well-accepted criteria of what rights and responsibilities should be afforded someone with a mental illness has proven controversial.

Declaring someone mentally ill can serve as legal grounds for involuntary commitment in a mental hospital or institution. Mental illness also may serve as grounds for avoiding prosecution for a crime if the accused is deemed unable to discern right from wrong or to otherwise conform his or her behavior to societal standards. However, not everyone who demonstrates abnormal behavior has a mental disorder. Even persons with mental disorders have the right to choose their own lifestyle, unless it poses a danger to themselves or others.

Origins

The history of mental health law includes the parallel developments of humane treatment of persons with mental disabilities, respect for people with such disabilities, and recognition of the diminished reasoning ability of some accused criminals. These developments stemmed from an increased awareness of mental illness as a disease, reducing the mystery previously associated with it.

The theory of a biological basis for mental illness dates to ancient times. However, the most common treatments prior to the fifteenth century involved "mystical interventions." While the supernatural approach was gradually rejected over the next few centuries, treatments for mental health disorders were often odd and based upon unproven conjectures.

In the late 1800s, a cure for syphilis unexpectedly brought about the end of hallucinations and **delusions** in those infected. Many took this as a sign that all mental illnesses had a physical basis. A disease model for the cure of mental illness grew in acceptance. John Grey led the movement to make mental hospitals more comfortable and humane. Around the same time, Dorothea Dix worked to raise awareness of "mental hygiene," a humane approach to treating those with mental disabilities by encouraging social interaction.

In England, the M'Naghten rule was developed in response to the controversy that arose when members of a jury acquitted a murderer whom they believed acted out of insanity. To ensure a legal precedent in future cases of this sort, the M'Naghten rule emphasized that such a verdict could only apply if the accused was not aware of reality or the wrongness of his or her actions while committing the crime. This standard was later amended to allow the jury to decide whether the rules applied in each specific trial. The M'Naghten rule was the accepted standard in the United States until 1964, when the case of *Durham v. United States* (214 F.2d 862 (D.C. Cir. 1954)) brought about an analysis that developed new rules.

The Durham rule held that the accused was not guilty if the criminal act was the result of a mental illness or deficiency. This standard at first appeared to be more specific than the M'Naghten rule. However, it proved inadequate, because most mental health professionals could not agree on whether the behavior leading to a crime was the symptom of mental illness. Recognition of the inadequacies of the M'Naghten rule and the Durham rule led the legal profession to reexamine the insanity defense.

The movements for humane treatment of those with mental disabilities developed a focus of treating the person as someone of personal worth. The logical outgrowth of this focus was that, as individuals, persons with mental disabilities were entitled to rights, responsibilities, and privileges. Although it took until the modern era for these attitudes to take root, they originated in the teachings of reformers such as Benjamin Rush, Dorothea Dix, and John Grey. Laws respecting the rights of those with mental disabilities include establishing standards for involuntary commitment, least restrictive environment, and patient privacy.

The insanity defense

The limitation of the M'Naghten rule and the Durham rule led to a professional discussion of how to legally protect people who commit criminal acts while mentally disabled. If a driver is delusional and unaware of pedestrians, his or her actions could hurt or kill one of those pedestrians. However, because there is no criminal intent, the driver should not be punished. The legal question becomes how to distinguish both the effect of mental illness and the lack of criminal intent.

An American Law Institute committee addressed this question in 1962. Taking the position that punishment should deter crime, the American Law Institute suggested that treating the mental disorder would be more likely to deter future crime than would punishing the individual. Their standards focused on mental illness that prevented the person from understanding the wrongness of his or her actions, or from conforming to the requirements of the law. The American Law Institute also noted that mental illness did not apply to any abnormal trait resulting in repeated criminal or antisocial behavior. This seemingly limited the defense; however, another component of the American Law Institute's conclusions, the concept of diminished capacity, broadened the defense in a significant way. Diminished capacity holds that there is no criminal intent if the accused cannot understand the nature of his or her behavior due to mental illness. Diminished capacity made the standards of the M'Naghten rule more liberal and open-ended for the defendants to plea and the juries to decide. As a result, many states accepted diminished capacity as a foundation for the plea, "not guilty by reason of insanity."

This plea or jury finding has been controversial in recent decades due to several high-profile cases that shocked the general public. One case was that of John Hinckley, who attempted to assassinate President Ronald Reagan. Hinckley was found not guilty by reason of insanity. The idea that a would-be presidential assassin could escape punishment enraged many people. As a result, Congress passed the Insanity Defense Law, which moved the standards closer to the M'Naghten rule. The goal of the Insanity Defense Law was to make the insanity plea more difficult to apply.

A few years before Hinckley, another high-profile case was tried in San Francisco. Dan White, a resigned city supervisor, murdered Mayor George Moscone and Supervisor Harvey Milk. At White's trial, he successfully argued that he had suffered diminished capacity at the time of the shootings. The charge of murder was reduced to manslaughter, and he was out of prison in five years. The public outrage led to California eliminating its diminished capacity law, requiring stricter standards for an insanity plea.

The case of Andrea Yates also received much media attention. Yates murdered her five children in the summer of 2001 after years of suffering from clinical **depression** and **psychosis**. In her first trial, the jury could not accept that she did not know the wrongness of her actions, despite her history of mental illness. After a second trial, she was found not guilty by reason of insanity. One important result of Andrea Yates's first trial was the demonstration that a jury could distinguish between delusional thought and moral reasoning.

These cases have led people to protest the insanity plea, because they think it is misused more often than it serves justice. However, the reality is more sobering. A 1994 study by Silver, Cirincione, and Steadman found that random interviewees overestimated by two times the percentage of felonies acquitted by the insanity plea. The public's perception of how many felons attempt an insanity plea was also overestimated by forty times in this study. Further, the estimation of felons being released after a successful insanity plea was consistently higher on the survey than in reality, no matter how the question was qualified.

The "not guilty by reason of insanity" verdict is an awkward decision for many juries, as demonstrated by the Andrea Yates' case. Yates's second verdict was essentially "guilty, but with mental illness." This "guilty, but with mental illness" verdict has been advocated in cases where the jury feels that the accused should receive a prison sentence but urges that they receive treatment for their mental illness as well. Yates's guilty verdict was overturned on the condition that she would be admitted to a mental hospital until she was cured of her mental illness, but she is not expected to leave the mental hospital. Advocates of the "guilty, but with mental illness" verdict feel that if an accused person is cured of the mental disorder, he or she should still serve the remainder of his or her prison sentence.

Involuntary commitment

One key issue in mental health law is the involuntary commitment of people with mental disorders. Most societies feel a responsibility to help those who are unable to take care of themselves. The noble goal of asylums and mental hospitals throughout history has been to ensure that those with mental disabilities are cared for in ways that will reduce their symptoms and enhance their well-being. A lesser historical goal has been to remove these individuals from the daily life of the community. When reformers worked to ensure that the noble goal was met, the asylums tended to become overcrowded and therefore ineffective. Since their institution, many people have abused the asylums as a means of sending away troublesome family members. These considerations perennially raise the question, when is involuntary commitment appropriate for those with mental disabilities?

After the fall of the Soviet Union, many Americans were shocked to learn that political dissidents in the Soviet Union were routinely locked up and declared mentally ill based on their having disagreed with the government. However, similar situations have occurred in the United States. Many people with no diagnosed mental disabilities have been placed in mental hospitals indefinitely. When the Willowbrook hospital, maintained by the state of New York, was investigated in 1972, some of the inmates were found to have no symptoms of mental or developmental disability. Several had cerebral palsy and could not communicate effectively. Others had so little education in their youth that they appeared to have an intellectual disability but could have adapted to adult life had they not been confined. There was no sign of regular professional treatment for any disability. Unfortunately, such problems were found in many mental hospitals across the country.

In the 1970s, the case of Kenneth Donaldson drew the attention of the U.S. Supreme Court. Donaldson was held against his will at the Florida State Hospital for 15 years. During this time, he was diagnosed as paranoid schizophrenic, but the evidence was weak, and there was no follow-up **diagnosis**. During his year of confinement, he received no substantial treatment. In 1972, the Supreme Court ruled that a person's mental disability is not a sufficient reason for involuntary commitment. The decision stated that the government cannot commit someone when he or she is capable of self-care or is able to maintain an independent lifestyle with the willing support of concerned individuals, such as family members or friends. In 1979, the Court clarified the decision and stated that even if the person's quality of life could be improved through involuntary commitment, the state could not lock up a mentally ill person who was not dangerous. The state had to demonstrate that the person was dangerous to himself or others.

Consequently, a person who does need services or treatment for mental illness has a right to refuse them. The perceived effect has been that persons with severe mental disabilities who are not receiving treatment will most likely become involved in the legal system, a trend that has come to be known as the "criminalization of those with mental disabilities."

The Supreme Court rulings did not undermine the legal notion of *parens patriae*, which is the accepted idea that the state can become involved in a person's life to protect him or her from self-harm or **neglect**, even against the person's will. Many people with mental disabilities who might be well served by commitment live on the streets with no identifiable home. Their relatives argue that these homeless people do not understand how they are placing themselves at risk by refusing treatment. The National Alliance on Mental Illness represents such relatives in an effort to allow involuntary commitment out of concern for the individual. Homeless individuals with mental illness fit the description of someone who cannot independently take care of him/herself. Most civil commitment laws justify involuntary commitment in such cases.

Deinstitutionalization

A combination of overcrowding in the mental hospitals and Supreme Court decisions led to a movement of **deinstitutionalization** in the 1970s and early 1980s. The goal of this movement was to reduce the number of persons living in institutions by helping the residents live on their own outside the institution. The goal to close down the institutions was founded on many assumptions, some truer than others. One truth was that many of the institutions were inefficient, callous, and expensive to run. Many mental health advocates felt that the mentally disabled would be better served in a family environment, a group home, or a community-based treatment program.

One misconception behind deinstitutionalization was that new medications could reduce the need for institutions. In some conditions, this may hold true, so long as patients remember to take their medications regularly. However, not all conditions are treatable with medication, and some of the most successful treatments rely on a combination of medication and behavioral therapies. Also, without consistent monitoring, individuals can stop taking their medication and return to a state of disability.

Least restrictive environment

Least restrictive environment is a component of deinstitutionalization and maintains that persons with

---

KEY TERMS

Civil commitment—The involuntary confinement of those who cannot care for themselves.

Criminalization—The de facto societal trend over several decades of sending people with mental disabilities to jails and prisons instead of to institutions.

Deinstitutionalization—The movement to close ineffective, costly institutions with the goal of better serving people with mental disabilities in their homes and communities.

Diminished capacity—The inability of a person to understand the nature of his or her behavior when committing a criminal act.

Insanity defense—The common term for the defense that an accused person makes to argue against his or her actions having criminal intent because of an underlying mental illness.

Parens patriae—The legal concept by which the state has the responsibility to protect those with mental disabilities from self-harm.

---

mental or developmental disabilities should receive services in the setting that most encourages the person's independence. This usually means living in facilities for those with severe disabilities. However, the facilities are expected to teach and encourage self-care, as well as foster dignity and self-respect among the residents. A person who can live independently with some monitoring could, for example, live in a group home with access to 24-hour support. The staff also should recognize the need for the individuals to make as many of their own decisions as they can reasonably handle. States that apply the concept of least restrictive environment tend to better balance the issues of serving those with disabilities without compromising their rights.

Resources

BOOKS

Durand, V. Mark, and David H. Barlow. *Essentials of Abnormal Psychology*. Belmont, CA: Wadsworth, Cengage Learning, 2010.

Erickson, Patricia E., and Stephen K. Erickson. *Crime, Punishment, and Mental Illness: Law and the Behavioral Sciences in Conflict*. New Brunswick, NJ: Rutgers University Press, 2008.

Gostin, Lawrence, et al., eds. *Principles of Mental Health Law and Policy*. New York: Oxford University Press, 2010.

Meyer, Robert G., and Christopher M. Weaver. *Law and Mental Health: A Case-Based Approach.* New York: The Guilford Press, 2005.

PERIODICALS

Atkinson, J. A., and Reilly, J. "The Recent History of Concepts of 'Dangerousness' in Mental Health Law in the UK." *History and Philosophy of Psychology* 13, no. 1 (2011): 45–51.

Bonnie, Richard J., et al. "Mental Health System Transformation after the Virginia Tech Tragedy." *Health Affairs* 28, no. 3 (2009): 793–803.

Taylor, Steven J. "Caught in the Continuum: A Critical Analysis of the Principle of the Least Restrictive Environment." *Research and Practice for Persons with Severe Disabilities* 29, no. 4 (2004).

WEBSITES

Mental Health America. "Position Statement 57: In Support of the Insanity Defense." http://www.nmha.org/go/position-statements/57 (accessed October 24, 2011).

World Health Organization. "Mental Health, Human Rights and Legislation." http://www.who.int/mental_health/policy/legislation/policy/en (accessed October 24, 2011).

ORGANIZATIONS

The Bazelon Center for Mental Health Law, 1101 15th Street NW, Suite 1212, Washington, DC, 20005, (202) 467-5730, info@bazelon.org, http://www.bazelon.org.

National Alliance on Mental Illness, 3803 N Fairfax Dr., Ste. 100, Arlington, VA, 22203, (703) 524-7600, (800) 950-NAMI (6264), http://www.nami.org.

Ray F. Brogan, PhD

Mental health and violence

Definition

As media reports of violent crimes committed by mentally ill persons are prominently featured worldwide, many people have come to associate mental illness with violence and aggression. Research shows that mentally ill persons receiving treatment are no more likely to display violence or aggression against others than people without mental illness, unless **substance abuse** is involved. Substance abuse raises the risk of violent behavior for persons both with and without mental illness. A major study published in 2009 revealed that although persons with mental illness were more likely to be a victim of violence than to commit a violent act, most people still regard people with mental illness as potentially dangerous. This misguided perception contributes to the isolation of persons with serious mental illness and for some helps potentiate a lack of integration into society.

Demographics

Mental illness happens to people in all societies regardless of gender, age, socioeconomic status, or location. According to the World Health Organization (WHO), more than 450 million people, or about 7% of the world's population, have a mental illness at any given time. When including mild **depression** or **anxiety disorders**, this estimate is likely lower than the actual prevalence of mental illness. In the United States and Western Europe, for example, about 25% of the adult population, or one in four adults, is estimated to have a diagnosable mental illness within any given year.

Serious mental illness, defined as any mental disorder that limits participation in the main activities of living including self-care, productive work, or communication with others, occurs much less frequently, or in about 5% of adults in the United States. The U.S. National Institutes of Health reports that females are more likely to be diagnosed with serious mental illness than males, and the peak prevalence of serious mental illness occurs in the 18–25 age group. It is among the seriously mentally ill group that most acts of violence committed by persons with mental illness occur, although this number is small. When a person with severe mental illness is in a period of **psychosis** (out of touch with reality and likely experiencing hallucinations or **delusions**), they are about three times more likely to be violent than when their illness is stabilized with treatment. Nevertheless, persons with serious mental illness are much more likely to harm themselves than to harm others.

Description

Aggression or violence does have a small correlation with **schizophrenia, post-traumatic stress disorder**, and **borderline personality disorder** when the disease remains untreated. Schizophrenia is a chronic **brain** disorder that affects about 1% of the population. People with schizophrenia tend to interpret reality and everyday stimuli in an abnormal fashion. Thinking and communication is sometimes disordered, and hallucinations can be present, as well as delusions and **paranoia**. Schizophrenia tends to be a long-term condition and affected persons rely on medication and supportive therapy to cope with symptoms and maintain daily function in life's activities. In the unlikely event that an untreated person with schizophrenia becomes aggressive toward others, the aggression is usually committed at home and is usually focused toward family members or friends.

Post-traumatic stress disorder (PTSD) is a form of anxiety disorder that stems from the physical and psychological reactions of witnessing a traumatic or dangerous event. When it is in danger, the body releases stress hormones that initiate the "fight-or-flight" response, shunting blood to the major muscle groups, heightening senses, and allowing the body it's best chance to perform in a manner that will survive the threatening situation. In PTSD, the body reacts to everyday stimuli by the same method as if it was still experiencing the danger. A person with PTSD can experience anger and difficulty concentrating or sleeping, can become preoccupied with frightening thoughts, and can experience physical sensations such as a racing heart while they relive the danger during flashbacks. When PTSD is accompanied by depression and left untreated, it can be associated with an increase in aggression or violence toward a domestic partner or rarely toward others. Relationship violence in PTSD has been linked to both men and women with PTSD.

Persons with borderline personality disorder (BPD) experience reoccurring patterns of disordered and unstable mood and self-image. They have difficulty maintaining close relationships; their feelings are intense but also include frequent and marked shifts. People with borderline personality disorder may function highly in an environment such as work or school by manipulating others, but can have difficulty forming attachments. A person with BPD is likely to be impulsive, impatient, and to display anger as in a temper tantrum, or, alternatively, to display brooding and antipathy. Trusting others is difficult. When following impulses, some people with BPD resort to excessive spending, gambling, or substance abuse. Depression and feelings of inadequacy often accompany BPD, as well as fears of abandonment and, occasionally, brief periods of psychosis can occur. Although the vast majority of people with BPD are not violent or criminals, the condition has been linked with criminality and episodes of violent behavior. People with BPD are also more likely to harm themselves than to harm others.

Causes and symptoms

Violent behavior is not a symptom of mental illness. Severe mental illness can include symptoms such as delusions and hallucinations that seem real and are frightening to a person with disordered thoughts. These may be heightened by perceived threats if a person is experiencing paranoia. When a person experiences these symptoms during a period of psychosis, he or she could possibly become aggressive, only because they are afraid and misunderstanding what is happening around them. When a person with PTSD feels the physical symptoms that accompany a sense of danger, he or she could also misinterpret what is happening and react with aggression.

KEY TERMS

Delusion—A fixed and irrational belief.

Hallucination—An unreal perception involving any of the senses that appears real to the person experiencing the hallucination.

Paranoia—An unwarranted sense of suspicion or being persecuted.

Psychosis—A state of impaired, disorganized thought that does not include recognizing reality.

Aggression or violence associated with BPD is usually the result of impulsivity.

Mental illness can happen to anyone and is most likely due to a complex combination of genetic and environmental factors that trigger chemistry changes in the brain. Genetic vulnerabilities likely set the stage for mental illness, which can be potentiated by environmental stressors such as experiencing **neglect**, abuse, violence, or traumatic events. Scientists are also studying the potential roles of vitamin deficiencies, brain injury, complications during birth, drug abuse, and certain infections in the development of mental illness.

Diagnosis

Diagnosis of a serious mental disorder is most often made by a **psychiatrist**, a physician specializing in mental health, mental illness, and brain chemistry. Criteria for each psychiatric diagnosis is set forth in a standard called the *Diagnostic and Statistical Manual of Mental Disorders*, currently in its fourth edition (with the fifth due for publication in 2013). Psychiatrists usually diagnose a psychiatric disorder based upon observation and conversation with their patient, although physical examination, image studies, and lab work can also provide relevant information to support a diagnosis. When a person has a serious mental illness, physicians or therapists routinely assess the potential for self-harm or aggression toward others as part of the overall treatment plan.

Treatment

Treatment for serious mental illness usually involves both psychotropic medicines and **cognitive-behavioral therapy**. Medicines help maintain a balanced mood and reduce the hallucinations and other troubling symptoms of mental illness. This does not cure the mental illness, but it allows the person to better function and to gain the most value from additional therapy. Cognitive-behavioral therapy (**talk therapy**) examines the particular feelings and perceptions that interfere with a person's ability to function in society with a normal sense of self and their environment. Therapists help the person with mental illness to recognize their maladaptive thoughts and to examine their validity, and then to cope with them by adopting alternative thoughts. For most people with severe mental illness, these therapies can be delivered in an outpatient setting. Temporary inpatient care helps during a period of psychosis or acute crisis. Key to reducing or eliminating periods of psychosis is continued medication and therapy and rapid access to a healthcare provider when symptoms increase.

Prognosis

Serious mental illnesses are treatable conditions, and most people experience relief from symptoms and a better quality of life as long as treatment continues. When mental illness is treated and there is no concurrent abuse of drugs or alcohol, then a person with mental illness is no more likely to commit a violent act than the general population. In fact, the majority of violence in the United States is committed by young males aged 18–30, with drugs or alcohol often a contributing factor. Only 1 in 200 persons with schizophrenia is likely to seriously injure someone else over the course of a lifetime, and he or she is many times more likely to commit **suicide** than to seriously harm someone else.

Prevention

Identifying mental illness as early as possible and receiving effective treatment is key to preventing violence among people with serious mental illness. This is particularly important during the first episode of illness, as it sets a pattern for recognizing dealing with the illness in a positive rather than aggressive manner. Treating any substance abuse problems concurrently with the mental illness is also a top priority to help prevent violence. When a rare violent tragedy occurs with a link to mental illness, it is a likely indication that something is wrong with the individual's treatment (or lack of treatment), or even the mental health care system as a whole. Quick access to mental health care and follow up remains a challenge for public health officials. Ideally, a person with serious mental illness would have rapid access to therapy and medications that lasts for as long as they need it.

Since the 2007 shootings at Virginia Tech university in Blacksburg, Virginia, that were carried out by a student diagnosed with a severe mental illness, universities, workplaces, and other and institutions across the United States have taken action to recognize and help members of their communities with mental illness that could be feeling stress or in crisis. Along with rapid communication systems via e-mail or text, counselors are often on call around the clock to enable rapid **intervention**. National and state governments are also re-examining some aspects of privacy laws that currently allow persons diagnosed with severe mental illness to fall between the cracks of the healthcare system regarding follow up. Any change in these laws will be carefully considered in order to balance the privacy rights of the individual with their need for access to continuing treatment.

Removing the **stigma** from mental illness is also important to helping persons with severe mental illness integrate into their communities without fear of persecution. When media outlets sensationalize the rare violent acts made by persons with mental illness, the public tends to distance themselves from people with mental illness and perpetuate inaccurate stereotypes. As the public begins to recognize that people with mental illness are more often the victim of violence, not the perpetrators of violence, mental illness will no longer be considered the first explanation for aggressive or violent behavior.

Resources

BOOKS

Empie, Kristine M. *Workplace Violence and Mental Illness.* New York: LFB Scholarly, 2003.

McFarlane, Alexander C., G. D. Schrader, and C. Bookless. *The Prevalence of Victimization and Violent Behavior in the Seriously Mentally Ill.* Canberra: Australian Institute of Criminology, 2005.

Serper, Mark R., and Andrea J. Bergman. *Psychotic Violence, Methods, Motives, Madness.* Madison, CT: Psychosocial Press, 2003.

Yakeley, Jessica. *Working with Violence: A Contemporary Psychoanalytic Approach.* Basingstoke, UK: Palgrave Macmillan, 2010.

PERIODICALS

American Psychiatric Association. *American Psychiatric Association Fact Sheet: Violence and Mental Illness.* Washington, DC: American Psychiatric Association, 1994.

Corrigan, P. W., A. C. Watson, A. C. Warpinski, and G. Gracia. "Implications of Educating the Public on Mental Illness, Violence, and Stigma." *Psychiatric Services* 55, no. 5 (2004): 577–80.

Douglas, K.S., S. D. Hart, and L. S. Guy. "Psychosis as a Risk Factor for Violence to Others: A Meta-Analysis." *Psychological Bulletin* 135, no. 5 (2009): 679–706.

Friedman, Richard A. "Mental Illness and Violence: How Strong is the Link?" *New England Journal of Medicine* 355, no. 20 (2006): 2064–66.

Langan, J. "Challenging Assumptions About Risk Factors and the Role of Screening for Violence Risk in the Field of

Mental Health." *Health, Risk and Society* 12, no. 2 (2010): 85–100.

Volavka J., and J. Swanson. "Violent Behavior in Mental Illness: the Role of Substance Abuse." *JAMA: the Journal of the American Medical Association* 304, no. 5 (2010): 563–64.

OTHER

Gonzales, Alberto R., Michael O. Leavitt, and Margaret Spellings. "Report to the President on Issues Raised by the Virginia Tech Tragedy." U.S. Department of Health and Human Services. http://www.hhs.gov/vtreport.pdf (accessed February 7, 2011).

"Violence and Mental Illness: Unpacking the Myths." Canadian Mental Health Association. http://www.cmha.bc.ca/files/3-violence_myths.pdf (accessed February 7, 2011).

WEBSITES

National Institute of Mental Health. "New Factors Identified for Predicting Violence in Schizophrenia." Science Update. July 18, 2006. http://www.nimh.nih.gov/science-news/2006/new-factors-identified-for-predicting-violence-in-schizophrenia.shtml (accessed February 7, 2011).

SANE Australia. "Violence and Mental Illness." http://www.sane.org/information/factsheets-podcasts/209-violence-and-mental-illness (accessed February 7, 2011).

Trudeau, Michelle. "Researchers Investigate Aggressive Students' Mental Health." *Morning Edition*, NPR (National Public Radio). http://www.npr.org/templates/story/story.php?storyId=5642298 (accessed February 7, 2011).

Brenda Wilmoth Lerner, RN

Mental retardation *see* **Intellectual disability**

Mental status examination

Definition

A mental status examination (MSE) is an assessment of a patient's level of cognitive (knowledge-related) ability, appearance, emotional mood, and speech and thought patterns at the time of evaluation. It is one part of a full neurologic (nervous system) examination and includes the examiner's observations about the patient's attitude and cooperativeness as well as the patient's answers to specific questions. The most commonly used MSE is the Folstein Mini-Mental Status Examination (MMSE), developed in 1975.

Purpose

The purpose of a mental status examination is to assess the presence and extent of a person's mental impairment. The cognitive functions that are measured during the MSE include the person's sense of time, place, and personal identity; memory; speech; general intellectual level; mathematical ability; insight or judgment; and reasoning or problem-solving ability. Complete MSEs are most commonly given to elderly people and to other patients being evaluated for **dementia** (including AIDS-related dementia). Dementia is an overall decline in a person's intellectual function—including difficulties with language, simple calculations, planning or decision-making, and motor (muscular movement) skills, as well as loss of memory. The MSE is an important part of the differential **diagnosis** of dementia and other psychiatric symptoms or disorders. The MSE results may suggest specific areas for further testing or specific types of required tests. A mental status examination can also be given repeatedly to monitor or document changes in a patient's condition.

Description

The MMSE of Folstein evaluates five areas of mental status, namely, orientation, registration, attention and calculation, recall, and language. A complete MSE is more comprehensive and evaluates the following ten areas of functioning:

- Appearance. The examiner notes the person's age, race, sex, civil status, and overall appearance. These features are significant because poor personal hygiene or grooming may reflect a loss of interest in self-care or physical inability to bathe or dress oneself.

- Movement and behavior. The examiner observes the person's gait (manner of walking), posture, coordination, eye contact, facial expressions, and similar behaviors. Problems with walking or coordination may reflect a disorder of the central nervous system.

- Affect. Affect refers to a person's outwardly observable emotional reactions. It may include either a lack of emotional response to an event or an overreaction.

- Mood. Mood refers to the underlying emotional "atmosphere" or tone of the person's answers.

- Speech. The examiner evaluates the volume of the person's voice, the rate or speed of speech, the length of answers to questions, the appropriateness and clarity of the answers, and similar characteristics.

- Thought content. The examiner assesses what the patient is saying for indications of hallucinations, delusions, obsessions, symptoms of dissociation, or thoughts of suicide. Dissociation refers to the splitting off of certain memories or mental processes from conscious awareness. Dissociative symptoms include feelings of unreality, depersonalization, and confusion about one's identity.

- Thought process. Thought process refers to the logical connections between thoughts and their relevance to the main thread of conversation. Irrelevant detail, repeated words and phrases, interrupted thinking (thought blocking), and loose, illogical connections between thoughts, may be signs of a thought disorder.
- Cognition. Cognition refers to the act or condition of knowing. The evaluation assesses the person's orientation (ability to locate himself or herself) with regard to time, place, and personal identity; long- and short-term memory; ability to perform simple arithmetic (counting backward by threes or sevens); general intellectual level or fund of knowledge (identifying the last five presidents, or similar questions); ability to think abstractly (explaining a proverb); ability to name specified objects and read or write complete sentences; ability to understand and perform a task (showing the examiner how to comb one's hair or throw a ball); ability to draw a simple map or copy a design or geometrical figure; ability to distinguish between right and left.
- Judgment. The examiner asks the person what he or she would do about a common-sense problem, such as running out of a prescription medication.
- Insight. Insight refers to a person's ability to recognize a problem and understand its nature and severity.

The length of time required for an MSE depends on the patient's condition. It may take as little as five minutes to examine a healthy person. Patients with speech problems or intellectual impairments, dementia, or other organic **brain** disorders may require 15 or 20 minutes. The examiner may choose to spend more time on certain portions of the MSE and less time on others, depending on the patient's condition and answers.

Preparation

Preparation for an MSE includes a careful medical and psychiatric history of the patient. The history helps the examiner to interpret the patient's appearance and answers with greater accuracy, because some physical illnesses may produce psychiatric symptoms or require medications that influence the patient's mood or attentiveness. The psychiatric history should include a family history as well as the patient's personal history of development, behavior patterns, and previous treatment for mental disorders (if any). Symptoms of dissociation, for example, often point to a history of childhood **abuse**, rape, or other severe emotional traumas in adult life. The examiner should also include information about the patient's occupation, level of education, marital status, and right- or left-handedness. Information about occupation and education helps in evaluating

the patient's use of language, extent of memory loss, reasoning ability, and similar functions. Handedness is important in determining which half of the patient's brain is involved in writing, picking up a pencil, or other similar tasks that he or she may be asked to perform during the examination.

KEY TERMS

Aphasia—The loss of the ability to speak, or to understand written or spoken language. A person who cannot speak or understand language is said to be aphasic.

Cognition—The mental activities associated with thinking, learning, and memory.

Coma—A state of prolonged unconsciousness in which a person cannot respond to spoken commands or mildly painful physical stimuli.

Delusion—A belief that is resistant to reason or contrary to actual fact. Common delusions include delusions of persecution, delusions about one's importance (sometimes called delusions of grandeur), or delusions of being controlled by others.

Dementia—A decline in a person's level of intellectual functioning. Dementia includes memory loss as well as difficulties with language, simple calculations, planning or decision-making, and motor (muscular movement) skills.

Differential diagnosis—Comparing and contrasting the signs, symptoms, and laboratory findings of two or more diseases to determine which is causing the patient's condition.

Dissociation—The splitting off of certain mental processes from conscious awareness. Specific symptoms of dissociation include feelings of unreality, depersonalization, and confusion about one's identity.

Hallucination—A sensory experience, usually involving either sight or hearing, of something that does not exist outside the mind.

Illusion—A false visual perception of an object that others perceive correctly. A common example is the number of sightings of "UFOs" that turn out to be airplanes or weather balloons.

Obsession—Domination of thoughts or feelings by a persistent idea, desire, or image.

Organic brain disorder—An organic brain disorder refers to impaired brain function due to damage or deterioration of brain tissue.

Aftercare

Depending on the examiner's specific observations, the patient may be given additional tests for follow-up. These tests might include blood or urine samples to test for drug or alcohol abuse, anemia, diabetes, disorders of the liver or kidneys, vitamin or thyroid deficiencies, medication side effects, syphilis, or AIDS. Brain imaging (CT, MRI, or **PET** scans) may be used to look for signs of **seizures**, strokes, head **trauma**, brain tumors, or other evidence of damage to specific parts of the brain. A spinal tap may be performed if the doctor thinks the patient may have an infection of the central nervous system.

Precautions

An MSE cannot be given to a patient who cannot pay attention to the examiner, such as may be the case with a patient who is in a coma or unconscious, completely unable to speak (aphasic), or not fluent in the language of the examiner.

Results

Normal results for a mental status examination depend to some extent on the patient's history, level of education, and recent life events. For example, a depressed mood is appropriate in the context of a recent death or other sad event in the patient's family but inappropriate in the context of a recent pay raise. Speech patterns are often influenced by racial or ethnic background as well as by occupation or schooling. In general, however, the absence of obvious **delusions**, hallucinations, or thought disorders together with the presence of insight, good judgment, and socially appropriate appearance and behavior are considered normal results. A normal numerical score for the MMSE is between 28 and 30.

Abnormal results for a mental status examination include:

• any evidence of organic brain damage

• evidence of thought disorders

• a mood or affect that is clearly inappropriate to its context

• thoughts of suicide

• disturbed speech patterns

• dissociative symptoms

• delusions or hallucinations

A score below 27 on the MMSE usually indicates an organic brain disorder.

Resources

BOOKS

McPhee, Stephen, and Maxine Papadakis. *Current Medical Diagnosis and Treatment, 2010.* 49th ed. New York: McGraw-Hill Medical, 2009.

Porter, Robert S., and Justin L. Kaplan, eds. *The Merck Manual of Diagnosis and Therapy.* 19th ed. Whitehouse Station, NJ: Merck Research Laboratories, 2011.

Rebecca J. Frey, PhD

Mesoridazine

Definition

Mesoridazine is a member of the phenothiazine family of drugs (drugs that reduce the action of the neurotransmitter **dopamine** in the **brain**) and is sold under the brand name Serentil in the United States.

Purpose

Mesoridazine is effective in the treatment of **schizophrenia**, alcoholism, psychoneuroses (disorders of the brain), and organic brain disorders (disorders caused by temporary brain dysfunction or permanent brain damage).

Description

When used for the treatment of schizophrenia, mesoridazine reduces symptoms of emotional withdrawal, anxiety, tension, hallucinations, reduced **affect**, and **paranoia** (suspiciousness). It is often useful in persons for whom other tranquilizers are ineffective. In treating organic brain syndrome, mesoridazine effectively manages hyperactivity and difficult behaviors associated with mental deficiency. Mesoridazine relieves anxiety, nausea, vomiting, tension, and **depression** when used to treat alcoholism. It does not have side effects that affect liver function. It relieves similar symptoms when used to treat persons with psychoneurotic disorders.

Mesoridazine can be taken by mouth or given by intramuscular injection. It is supplied as 25 mg/mL in injection form, and tablets are supplied in 10, 25, 50, and 100 mg strengths.

Recommended dosage

The usual dosage used for treating schizophrenia is 50–400 mg per day and is usually administered three

KEY TERMS

Anxiety—An emotion that can be experienced as a troubled feeling, sense of dread, fear of the future, or distress over a possible threat to a person's physical or mental well-being.

Depression—A mental state characterized by feelings of sadness, despair, discouragement, and low energy, often with overeating and/or over-sleeping.

Dopamine—A chemical in brain tissue that serves as a neurotransmitter (transmitter of nerve impulses) and helps to regulate movement and emotions.

Hallucinations—To hear, see, or otherwise sense things that are not real. Hallucinations can result from nervous system abnormalities, mental disorders, or the use of certain drugs.

Insomnia—The inability to fall asleep or remain asleep.

Schizophrenia—A major mental illness marked by psychotic symptoms, including hallucinations, delusions, and severe disruptions in thinking.

QUESTIONS TO ASK YOUR DOCTOR

- What kind of changes can I expect to see or feel with this medication?
- Does it matter what time of day I take this medication? If so, what is the recommendation?
- Should I take this medication with or without food?
- What are the side effects associated with this medication?
- Will this medication interact or interfere with other medications I am currently taking?
- What symptoms or adverse effects are important enough that I should seek immediate treatment?

times per day. It is begun at a low level and slowly increased until an adequate therapeutic effect is achieved. For persons with organic brain syndrome, an optimum dosage is 75–300 mg per day, administered in three equal amounts. The optimum dosage for persons being treated for alcoholism is 50–300 mg per day, administered in three doses. The usual dosage range for persons with psychoneuroses is 30–150 mg per day, administered in three equal amounts.

Precautions

Before taking mesoridazine, patients should read the accompanying medication guide. Mesoridazine has the potential to produce a serious syndrome called **tardive dyskinesia**. This syndrome consists of involuntary, uncoordinated movements (especially of the tongue, jaw, mouth, or face). It usually develops either late in the course of treatment or after medication has been discontinued and is potentially irreversible. Symptoms similar to those experienced by people with Parkinson's disease have been linked with the administration of mesoridazine. Mesoridazine is inappropriate for use with central nervous system depression, and it should not be administered to persons in a coma.

Side effects

A serious and relatively common side effect of mesoridazine is tardive dyskinesia, a potentially irreversible syndrome for which there is no known effective treatment. The chances of developing tardive dyskinesia increase with both increasing dosage and increasing patient age.

The most common side effects of mesoridazine are drowsiness and low blood pressure and are most frequently reported in persons given relatively high dosages. Side effects also tend to appear relatively early in treatment. Mesoridazine tends to have a remarkably low incidence of side effects compared to other phenothiazine compounds. However, as mentioned, Parkinson-like symptoms have been linked with the administration of mesoridazine. These include restlessness and akathisia (agitation) and dystonia (difficulty walking or moving). These are generally controlled with **benztropine** mesylate or **trihexyphenidyl** hydrochloride.

Other known side effects include:

- anxiety
- restlessness
- agitation
- insomnia
- headache
- euphoria
- drowsiness
- depression
- confusion
- dizziness

Unwanted or unexpected effects associated with the use of mesoridazine have been reported for virtually all organ systems in the body. Although numerous, such side effects are relatively uncommon. An occasionally reported side effect is **neuroleptic malignant syndrome**, a complicated and potentially fatal condition characterized by muscle rigidity, high fever, alterations in mental status, and cardiac symptoms such as irregular pulse or blood pressure, sweating, tachycardia and arrhythmias.

Interactions

Mesoridazine increases the effect of drugs and substances that depress the central nervous system. This class of drugs includes anesthetics, opiates, **barbiturates**, atropine, and alcohol.

Resources

BOOKS

Albers, Lawrence J., Rhoda K. Hahn, and Christopher Reist. *Handbook of Psychiatric Drugs.* Laguna Hills, CA: Current Clinical Strategies, 2010.

American Society of Health-System Pharmacists. *AHFS Drug Information 2011.* Bethesda, MD: ASHP, 2011.

Graham, George. *The Disordered Mind: An Introduction to Philosophy of Mind and Mental Illness.* New York: Routledge, 2010.

Holland, Leland Norman, and Michael Patrick Adams. *Core Concepts in Pharmacology.* 3rd ed. New York: Prentice Hall, 2011.

North, Carol, and Sean Yutzy. *Goodwin and Guze's Psychiatric Diagnosis.* New York: Oxford University Press, 2010.

Preston, John D., John H. O'Neal, and Mary C. Talaga. *Handbook of Clinical Psychopharmacology for Therapists.* 6th ed. Oakland, CA: New Harbinger, 2010.

PERIODICALS

Dallaire, S. "Thioridazine (Mellaril) and Mesoridazine (Serentil): Prolongation of the QTc Interval." *Canadian Medical Association Journal* 164, no. 1 (2001): 91–95.

Nelson, J.C. "Diagnosing and Treating Depression in the Elderly." *Journal of Clinical Psychiatry* 62, Supp. 24 (2001): 18–22.

Ray, W.A., S. Meredith, P.B. Thapa, K.G. Meador, K. Hall, and K.T. Murray. "Antipsychotics and the Risk of Sudden Cardiac Death." *Archives of General Psychiatry* 58, no. 12 (2001): 1161–67.

Varvel A., E. Vann, E. Wise, D. Philibin, and H. Porter. "Effects of Antipsychotic Drugs on Operant Responding After Acute and Repeated Administration." *Psychopharmacology (Berlin)* 160, no. 2 (2002): 182–91.

ORGANIZATIONS

American Academy of Clinical Toxicology, 6728 Old McLean Village Dr., McLean, VA, 22101, (703) 556-9222, Fax: (703) 556-8729, admin@clintox.org, http://www.clintox.org.

American Academy of Family Physicians, 11400 Tomahawk Creek Pkwy., Leawood, KS, 66211-2672, (913) 906-6000, (800) 274-2237, Fax: (913) 906-6075, contactcenter@aafp.org, http://www.aafp.org.

American Psychiatric Association, 1000 Wilson Blvd., Ste. 1825, Arlington, VA, 22209-3901, (703) 907-7300, apa@psych.org, http://www.psych.org.

American Psychological Association, 750 1st St. NE, Washington, DC, 20002-4242, (202) 336-5500; TDD/TTY: (202) 336-6123, (800) 374-2721, http://www.apa.org.

American Society for Clinical Pharmacology and Therapeutics, 528 N Washington St., Alexandria, VA, 22314, (703) 836-6981, info@ascpt.org, http://www.ascpt.org.

National Alliance on Mental Illness, 2107 Wilson Blvd., Ste. 300, Arlington, VA, 22201-3042, Fax: (703) 524-9094, (800) 950-6264, http://www.nami.org.

National Institute of Mental Health, 6001 Executive Blvd., Rm. 8184, MSC 9663, Bethesda, MD, 20892-9663, (301) 433-4513; TTY: (301) 443-8431, Fax: (301) 443-4279, (866) 615-6464; TTY: (866) 415-8051, nimhinfo@nih.gov, http://www.nimh.nih.gov.

U.S. Food and Drug Administration, 10903 New Hampshire Ave., Silver Spring, MD, 20993-0002, (888) INFO-FDA (463-6332), http://www.fda.gov.

L. Fleming Fallon, Jr., MD, DrPH
Laura Jean Cataldo, RN, EdD

Methadone

Definition

Methadone is classified as an opioid (an analgesic that is used for severe pain). In the United States, methadone is also known as dolophine, methenex and methadose.

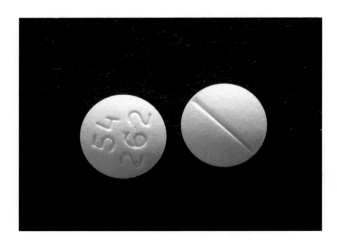

Methadone, 30 mg. (© *Custom Medical Stock Photo, Inc. Reproduced by permission.*)

Purpose

Methadone is used in the long-term maintenance treatment of narcotic **addiction**. Both heroin and methadone are **opioids**; as such, methadone and heroin bind to the same places in the **brain**. Methadone, however, is the opioid of choice for the treatment of narcotic addiction since it is longer lasting and patients do not experience the "high" associated with the drug of abuse. In opioid maintenance therapy, a person addicted to heroin receives methadone instead of heroin. Essentially, the person is switched from an opioid that gives a "high" to an opioid that does not. The dose of methadone may then be decreased over time so that the person can overcome his or her opioid addiction without experiencing withdrawal symptoms, or, after a person has received methadone for a period of time, he or she may choose to go through **detoxification** with **clonidine**. In the United States, methadone treatment is associated with a significant reduction in predatory crime, improvement in socially acceptable behavior and psychological well-being.

Methadone may also be prescribed for pain relief, but in these cases, the physician must note this use on the prescription.

Description

Methadone has been used successfully to treat narcotic addiction for over twenty years in the United States. Methadone is the only FDA-approved agent in its class for the maintenance treatment of narcotic addiction.

Methadone for maintenance treatment is dispensed in methadone clinics. The program needs to be registered with the Drug Enforcement Administration. For admission to methadone treatment in clinical programs, federal standards mandate a minimum of one year of opiate addiction as well as current evidence of addiction. Pregnant, opiate-addicted females can be admitted with less than a one-year history and AIDS patients are routinely accepted. New patients must report daily, take medication under observation, and participate in recommended psychosocial treatments.

Some studies have shown that more than 50% of patients in methadone clinics do not abuse drugs in the first month of treatment. After 10 months, however, the success rate drops to approximately 20%. Moreover, major **depression** is a powerful predictor of **relapse** in methadone treatment. If the patient has dual addictions (alcoholism along with the heroin addiction, for example), management of the other addiction increases the success rate of the methadone therapy. Proper psychiatric and psychological treatment can considerably improve methadone treatment outcome.

In the cases of pregnant women who are addicted to heroin, detoxification (discontinuing the opioid altogether) is associated with a high rate of spontaneous abortions in the first trimester and premature delivery in the third trimester. Therefore, pregnant women can be in methadone maintenance programs if they are at risk of returning to drug dependence. These women should receive the lowest effective dose, receive appropriate prenatal care, and be warned about risks of returning to drug abuse, as well as the dangers associated with withdrawal effects of methadone. Methadone is associated with lower birth weights and smaller head circumference, but it has never been shown that this has any impact on the infants' further development.

Methadone is available in 5, 10, and 40 mg tablets and a solution.

Recommended dosage

The initial dose of methadone is 20 mg daily with additional 10 mg given four to eight hours later. After achieving initial dosing of about 40 mg daily, the dose should be increased since there is evidence that the relapse rate is significantly lower in patients on 80-100 mg daily rather than 40-50 mg daily. The stabilization to maintenance dosing requires one to three months.

The minimum effective dose is 60 mg daily. Patients on lower maintenance doses have recently been studied and have shown shorter treatment retention and have continued heroin use. If patients are stable on methadone for six months or longer, their methadone dose should not be increased by 33% or more, as this sudden increase in dose is associated with an increase in craving for the drugs that were previously abused. Some heroin patients need to be on doses up to 180 mg daily to provide adequate maintenance and to prevent relapse.

Precautions

Methadone should not be used in patients who have had hypersensitivity to methadone. Patients who experience an allergic reaction to other opioids, which may include a generalized rash or shortness of breath, such as morphine, hydromorphone, oxymorphone, or codeine may try methadone. They are less likely to develop the same reaction since methadone has a different chemical structure. Methadone should be administered carefully in patients with pre-existing respiratory problems, history of bowel obstruction, glaucoma, renal problems, and hyperthyroidism.

As stated, pregnant women can be in methadone maintenance programs if they are at risk of returning to drug dependence. Methadone is associated with smaller birth weights and smaller head circumference.

Intentional or accidental overdose of methadone can lead to unconsciousness, coma, or death. The signs of methadone overdose include confusion, difficulty speaking, **seizures**, severe nervousness or restlessness, severe dizziness, severe drowsiness, and/or slow or troubled breathing. These symptoms are increased by alcohol or other central nervous system (CNS) depressants. Anyone who feels that he or she, or someone else, may have overdosed on methadone, or a combination of methadone and other central nervous system depressants, should seek emergency medical attention for that person at once.

Side effects

Most adverse effects of methadone are mild and seen only in the beginning of therapy. Initially patients may develop sedation and analgesia. It takes about four to six weeks for tolerance to these effects to develop. Tolerance to constipation and sweating may take longer to develop.

A few patients who are on larger doses of methadone may experience respiratory problems. These patients also may experience unwanted cardiac effects.

A small number of patients report a decrease in libido, impotence, and premature, delayed, or failed ejaculation. There are a few reports of occasional menstrual irregularities in female patients on methadone.

Interactions

Life-threatening interactions with other drugs have not been identified. One of the initial side effects of methadone could include dizziness and sedation, and these effects are worsened if the patient is also taking other narcotics, **benzodiazepines**, or is consuming alcohol.

Methadone magnifies the effects of alcohol and other central nervous system depressants, such as antihistamines, cold medicines, **sedatives**, tranquilizers, other prescription and over-the-counter (OTC) pain medications, **barbiturates**, seizure medications, muscle relaxants, and certain anesthetics including some dental anesthetics. Alcohol and other central nervous system depressants should not be taken or consumed while methadone is being taken.

Monoamine oxidase inhibitors (MAOIs), such as Parnate (**tranylcypromine**) and Nardil (**phenelzine**), should be avoided by people taking methadone. Medications like **naltrexone** and naloxone should never be used concurrently with methadone. People must stop taking methadone for 7 to 10 days before starting naltrexone or naloxone.

See also Alcohol and related disorders; Disease concept of chemical dependency; Opioids and related disorders

Resources

BOOKS

Albers, Lawrence J., Rhoda K. Hahn, and Christopher Reist. *Handbook of Psychiatric Drugs. 2001–2002.* Laguna Hills, CA: Current Clinical Strategies Publishing, 2008.

Kay, Jerald, Allan Tasman, and Jeffrey A. Lieberman. *Psychiatry: Behavioral Science and Clinical Essentials.* Philadelphia: W.B. Saunders Company, 2000.

PERIODICALS

Curran, Valarie H. "Additional Methadone Increases Craving for Heroin: A Double-Blind, Placebo-Controlled Study of Chronic Opiate Users Receiving Methadone Substitution Treatment." *Addiction* 94, no. 5 (May 1999): 665–74.

Strain, Eric. "Moderate-vs High-Dose Methadone in the Treatment of Opioid Dependence." *Journal of the American Medical Association* 281, no. 11 (1999): 1000–1005.

Ajna Hamidovic, Pharm.D.

Methamphetamine

Definition

Methamphetamine, or meth, is an addictive central nervous system (CNS) stimulant. The U.S. Drug Enforcement Administration (DEA) lists methamphetamine as a Schedule II drug, which means it has high abuse potential but some medical value. Because of this abuse potential, prescriptions for methamphetamine

Methamphetamine in powder form. *(U.S. Drug Enforcement Administration)*

Methamphetamine

Short-term effects:

• Increased alertness
• Rapid and irregular heartbeat
• Rise in blood pressure and body temperature

Long-term effects:

• Anxiety and feelings of confusion
• Dental problems
• Increased risk of contracting diseases such as HIV/AIDS and hepatitis
• Insomnia
• Mood disturbances
• Violent behavior

In 2010, 353,000 Americans aged 12 and older had abused methamphetamine at least once in the past month.

SOURCE: National Institutes of Health, National Institute on Drug Abuse, "Methamphetamine." Available online at: http://www.drugabuse.gov/drugpages/methamphetamine.html; also Substance Abuse and Mental Health Services Administration, *Results from the 2010 National Survey on Drug Use and Health.* Available online at: http://www.oas.samhsa.gov/NSDUH/2k10NSDUH/2k10Results.htm.

(Table by PreMediaGlobal. © 2012 Cengage Learning.)

cannot be refilled. It goes by the street names of ice, crystal, crystal meth, speed, crank, and glass.

Demographics

The national Monitoring the Future survey of 2008 found that in 2007 about 1.3 million Americans had used methamphetamine, a decrease from 1.9 million in 2006. This survey found that 2.3% of eighth graders, 2.4% of 10th graders, and 2.8% of twelfth graders had tried methamphetamine at some time in their lives.

In the United States, methamphetamine use peaks in white men 30–40 years old; however, according to the 2010 *National Survey on Drug Use and Health*, the average age of first use in 2010 was 18.8 years. Methamphetamine use is highest in the western U.S. states. Internationally, methamphetamine use is highest in Eastern Europe and Southeast Asia.

Methamphetamine is produced illegally in many countries, including the United States, and it can be synthesized with readily available materials. The drug's misuse is deemed to be a major social problem.

Purpose

Methamphetamine was first synthesized in Japan in 1919 and was used as a drug therapy in asthma inhalers in the 1930s. **Amphetamines** of all kinds were used during World War II by both sides to increase alertness and prolong wakefulness of military troops. After the war, the government developed stricter regulations for the manufacture and use of amphetamines, but the drugs remained popular among people who wanted to stay awake for long periods (e.g., students, long-haul truckers) and were commonly used by people who wanted to lose weight. In 1970, more restrictions were put on methamphetamine, and it was branded as a Schedule II drug. Despite the dangers, methamphetamine remains a popular drug of abuse.

Description

Methamphetamine is similar to other CNS stimulants, such as amphetamine (its parent drug), **methylphenidate**, and **cocaine**, in that it stimulates **dopamine** reward pathways in the **brain**. Consistent with its stimulant profile, methamphetamine causes increased activity and talkativeness, decreased appetite and **fatigue**, and a general sense of well being. Compared to amphetamine, methamphetamine is more potent and longer lasting, and it has more harmful effects on the brain. In animals, a single high dose of methamphetamine has been shown to damage nerve terminals in the dopamine-containing regions of the brain.

Methamphetamine is a white, odorless, bitter-tasting crystalline powder that easily dissolves in water or alcohol. Misuse occurs in many forms, as methamphetamine can be smoked, snorted, injected, or taken orally. When smoked or injected, methamphetamine enters the brain rapidly and immediately produces an intense but short-lived rush that many abusers find extremely pleasurable. Snorting or oral ingestion produces euphoria—a feeling of being high—within minutes. As with other abused stimulants, methamphetamine is most often used in a binge-and-crash pattern. A "run" of repeated doses may be continued over the course of days (binge) before stopping (crash). Exhaustion occurs with repeated use of methamphetamine, involving intense fatigue and need for sleep after the stimulation phase.

Recommended dosage

Approved medical indications for the drug are the sleep disorder **narcolepsy**, **attention deficit hyperactivity disorder (ADHD)**, and extreme obesity, but in each case methamphetamine is a second-line drug at best and is used only after other, less harmful drugs have failed.

The prescription drug (brand name Desoxyn) comes in the form of a small white tablet, which is orally ingested. Dosing begins at 5 mg once or twice a day and

KEY TERMS

Central nervous system (CNS)—Part of the nervous system consisting of the brain, cranial nerves, and spinal cord. The brain is the center of higher processes, such as thought and emotion, and is responsible for the coordination and control of bodily activities and the interpretation of information from the senses. The cranial nerves and spinal cord link the brain to the peripheral nervous system, that is, the nerves present in the rest of body.

Dopamine—A neurochemical made in the brain that is involved in many brain activities, including movement and emotion.

Hallucination—A false or distorted perception of objects, sounds, or events that seems real. Hallucinations usually result from drugs or mental disorders.

Psychosis—A serious mental disorder characterized by defective or lost contact with reality often with hallucinations or delusions.

Relapse—A recurrence of symptoms after a period of improvement or recovery.

Tolerance—The requirement for higher doses of a substance or more frequent engagement in an activity to achieve the same effect.

QUESTIONS TO ASK YOUR DOCTOR

- How can I tell if someone in my family is using methamphetamine?
- What type of therapy do you recommend for methamphetamine users?
- Can you recommend a treatment center for methamphetamine addiction?
- Will my insurance pay for this treatment?
- What should I tell my friends and family about my family member's methamphetamine problem?
- What should I say to my family member whom I suspect of using methamphetamine?

is increased weekly until the lowest effective dose is attained. Desoxyn should not be taken with other stimulants (including caffeine and decongestants) or antidepressant drugs (especially **monoamine oxidase inhibitors** [MAOIs], but also tricyclic **antidepressants**). Desoxyn should not be taken by patients with glaucoma, cardiovascular disease (including hypertension and arteriosclerosis), or hyperthyroidism.

Precautions

Short-term effects of methamphetamine relate to its stimulation of the brain and the cardiovascular system. Euphoria and rush, alertness, increased physical activity, and decreased sleep and appetite occur from an increase in available dopamine in the brain. Any or all of these effects can lead to compulsive use of the drug. Methamphetamine causes rapid heart beat (tachycardia), increased respiration, and increased blood pressure (hypertension), and with very high doses, increased body temperature (hyperthermia) and convulsions can occur.

Chronic use of methamphetamine can result in two hallmark features of **addiction**: tolerance and dependence. Tolerance to the euphoric effects in particular can prompt abusers to take higher or more frequent doses of the drug. Withdrawal symptoms in chronic users include **depression**, anxiety, fatigue, and an intense craving for the drug. Users who inject methamphetamine risk contracting life-threatening viruses such as HIV and hepatitis through the use of dirty needles.

Addiction is a complex disorder, and prospects for individual addicts vary widely. Chronic methamphetamine use causes changes in brain and mental functions. While some effects are reversible, others are long lasting and possibly permanent. Relapses are common, and cravings may continue for a long time after drug use has stopped.

Side effects

With repeated use, methamphetamine can cause anxiety, **insomnia**, mood disturbances, confusion, hallucinations, **psychosis**, and violent behavior. Psychotic features sometimes emerge, such as **paranoia**, hallucinations, and **delusions**, and can last well after methamphetamine use has stopped. **Stroke** and weight loss are other long-term effects.

Treatment

For acute intoxication accompanied by psychosis, patients may be calmed by reassurance and a quiet setting, but sometimes antipsychotic drugs or **sedatives** are administered. Substances that prevent absorption from the gastrointestinal tract (e.g., activated charcoal) may be used if the drug was taken orally. Additional care is given as needed (e.g., keeping the airways open, treatment of **seizures**). Individual with methamphetamine intoxication may be violent, agitated, and a danger to themselves and others.

The most effective treatment for methamphetamine addiction is cognitive-behavioral **intervention** such as counseling but may also include **family education**, drug testing, and group support in a twelve-step program. The goal of these modalities is to modify the patient's thinking, expectations, and behaviors to increase coping skills in the face of stressors. Contingent management is a promising behavioral intervention, in which incentives are provided in exchange for staying clean and for participating in treatment. Residential programs/therapeutic communities may be helpful, particularly in more severe cases.

Antidepressant drugs such as **bupropion** (Wellbutrin) can be a useful treatment aid, but as of 2011, there were no FDA-approved medications specifically for the treatment of stimulant addiction.

Resources

BOOKS

Lee, Steven J. *Overcoming Crystal Meth Addiction: An Essential Guide to Getting Clean.* New York: Marlowe, 2006.

Weisheit, Ralph A., and William White. *Methamphetamine: Its History, Pharmacology, and Treatment.* Center City, MN: Hazelden, 2009.

WEBSITES

"Methamphetamine." MedlinePlus, September 11, 2010. http://www.nlm.nih.gov/medlineplus/methamphetamine.html (accessed August 14, 2011).

"NIDA InfoFacts: Methamphetamine." National Institute on Drug Abuse, March 2010. http://www.drugabuse.gov/infofacts/methamphetamine.html (accessed August 14, 2011).

Richards, John R. "Toxicity, Methamphetamine." Medscape. http://emedicine.medscape.com/article/820918-overview (accessed August 14, 2011).

Volkow, Nora D. "Methamphetamine Abuse and Addiction." National Institute on Drug Abuse, 2006. http://www.nida.nih.gov/ResearchReports/methamph/methamph.html (accessed August 14, 2011).

ORGANIZATIONS

National Clearinghouse on Alcohol and Drug Information, PO Box 2345, Rockville, MD, 20847, (877) SAMHSA-7; Spanish: (877) 767-8432; TDD: (800) 487-4889, Fax: (240) 221-4292, http://ncadi.samhsa.gov.

National Council on Alcoholism and Drug Dependence Inc., 244 E 58th St., 4th Fl., New York, NY, 10022, (212) 269-7797, (800) NCA-CALL, Fax: (212) 269-7510, national@mcadd.org, http://www.ncadd.org.

The Partnership at Drugfree.org, 352 Park Ave. S., 9th Fl., New York, NY, 10010, (212) 922-1560, Fax: (212) 922-1570, http://www.drugfree.org.

Jill U. Adams
Tish Davidson, AM

Methylphenidate

Definition

Methylphenidate is a mild, central nervous system stimulant. In the United States, the drug is sold under the brand name Ritalin.

Purpose

Methylphenidate is used primarily in the treatment of **attention deficit hyperactivity disorder (ADHD)** in children and adults. It also may be used to treat **narcolepsy**, a sleep disorder. In rare cases, it is used to decrease sedation and lethargy from opioid pain medications and to help improve the mood of a terminally ill person suffering from **depression**.

Description

The mode of action for methylphenidate is not fully understood. It presumably activates the **brain** stem arousal system and cortex to produce a stimulant effect. The brain stem arousal system increases levels of electrical activity in the brain. The effect of methylphenidate is to produce increased alertness and, although

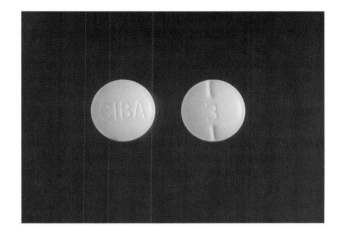

Methylphenidate (Ritalin), 10 mg. *(U.S. Drug Enforcement Administration)*

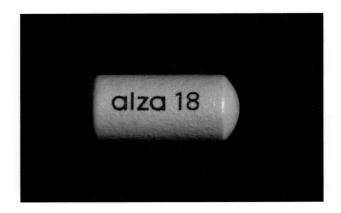

Concerta (methylphenidate). *(© Custom Medical Stock Photo, Inc. Reproduced by permission.)*

children with **ADHD** are overactive and have decreased attention spans, in these children, methylphenidate actually decreases motor restlessness and increases attention span.

Methylphenidate is offered in various forms of administration:

• oral solution and chewable tablets (Methylin, Ritalin)

• extended release (Metadate ER, Metadate CD, Ritalin SR)

• long acting (Concerta, Ritalin LA)

• patch (Daytrana)

Tablets are available in 5, 10, and 20 mg strengths; an extended release form is available as a 20 mg tablet; a long acting form is available in 10, 20, 30, and 40 mg strengths; and the patch is available in 10, 15, 20, and 30 mg strengths.

Recommended dosage

The recommended dosage of methylphenidate is determined by trial and error based on individual responses. Methylphenidate is usually administered in two or three separate doses each day, preferably 45 minutes before a meal. For children with ADHD, the initial recommended dosage is 5 mg twice daily before breakfast and lunch, increased by 5–10 mg per week to a maximum of 60 mg per day. The average total dosage is 20–30 mg per day, although 10–60 mg is not uncommon. For narcolepsy in adults, the recommended dose is 5–20 mg two to three times a day, taken 30–45 minutes before meals.

The drug should be taken exactly as directed. Methylphenidate can become habit forming if taken in greater amounts or for longer periods than necessary. Individuals should take the last dose of the day before 6 P.M. to decrease sleep difficulties. The tablet should

KEY TERMS

Anxiety—An emotion that can be experienced as a troubled feeling, sense of dread, fear of the future, or distress over a possible threat to a person's physical or mental well-being.

Attention deficit hyperactivity disorder (ADHD)—A developmental disorder characterized by distractibility, hyperactivity, impulsive behaviors, and the inability to remain focused on tasks or activities.

Depression—A mental state characterized by feelings of sadness, despair, discouragement, and low energy, often with oversleeping and/or overeating.

Hallucinations—Perceptions without external stimulus. Hallucinations can result from nervous system abnormalities, mental disorders, or the use of certain drugs.

Tourette syndrome—An abnormal condition that causes uncontrollable facial grimaces and tics and arm and shoulder movements. Tourette syndrome is perhaps best known for uncontrollable vocal tics that include grunts, shouts, and use of obscene language (coprolalia).

not be broken or crushed, as doing so changes the time for absorption. If the normal time of administration is missed, persons should take the drug as soon as possible. However, two tablets should not be taken at the same time.

Precautions

Methylphenidate has a great potential to produce physical and mental dependence. Administration should not be stopped abruptly. Such action can cause withdrawal symptoms, including depression, paranoid feelings, thoughts of **suicide**, anxiety, agitation, and sleep disturbances. Methylphenidate should not be given to persons with extreme anxiety, tension, agitation, severe depression, mental or emotional instability, or a history of alcohol or drug abuse. It is not indicated for use by those with **Tourette syndrome**, people with **tic disorders**, glaucoma, or certain mental-health conditions. The drug should be used cautiously in persons with high blood pressure, those with a history of **seizures**, and women who are breastfeeding. Methylphenidate is not typically ordered for women during their childbearing years unless the physician determines that the benefits outweigh the risks.

QUESTIONS TO ASK YOUR DOCTOR

- What kind of changes can I expect to see or feel with this medication?
- Does it matter what time of day I take this medication? If so, what is the recommendation?
- Should I take this medication with or without food?
- What are the side effects associated with this medication?
- Will this medication interact or interfere with other medications I am currently taking?
- What symptoms or adverse effects are important enough that I should seek immediate treatment?

Methylphenidate should not be ordered for children younger than six years of age as its safety has not been determined in this age group. People should not drive or operate machinery or appliances until they understand how this drug affects them. They should not drive if they become lightheaded or dizzy. Methylphenidate may cause irregularities in the composition of the blood and produce changes in liver function. People taking methylphenidate should receive regular blood tests.

Side effects

The most common side effects are nervousness, difficulties with sleep, tachycardia, and increased blood pressure. Reducing the dose or changing the time the drug is taken may reduce some side effects. Affected persons should discuss any adverse reactions with their healthcare professional. Individuals taking methylphenidate should receive regular blood pressure and pulse checks. Methylphenidate also may cause dizziness, irritability, vision changes, drowsiness, and a poor appetite. Less common side effects include chest pain, palpitations, joint pain, skin rash, and uncontrolled movements or speech. Side effects may also include a rapid or irregular heartbeat, stomach upset, nausea, headache, blood in the urine or stool, muscle cramps, red dots on the skin, or bruises. At higher dosages or with long-term use, people may experience weight loss or mental changes such as confusion, false beliefs, mood changes, hallucinations, or feelings that they or their environment are not real.

Interactions

Several drugs may interact adversely with methylphenidate, including anticoagulants and drugs to prevent seizures, combat depression, and treat high blood pressure. The dosages of these drugs may be reduced when taken simultaneously with methylphenidate.

Resources

BOOKS

Albers, Lawrence J., Rhoda K. Hahn, and Christopher Reist. *Handbook of Psychiatric Drugs.* Laguna Hills, CA: Current Clinical Strategies, 2010.

American Society of Health-System Pharmacists. *AHFS Drug Information 2011.* Bethesda, MD: ASHP, 2011.

Barkley, Russell A. *Taking Charge of ADHD: The Complete, Authoritative Guide for Parents.* Rev. ed. New York: Guilford Press, 2000.

Chandler, Chris. *The Science of ADHD: A Guide for Parents and Professionals.* New York: Wiley-Blackwell, 2011.

Graham, George. *The Disordered Mind: An Introduction to Philosophy of Mind and Mental Illness.* New York: Routledge, 2010.

Holland, Leland Norman, and Michael Patrick Adams. *Core Concepts in Pharmacology.* 3rd ed. New York: Prentice Hall, 2011.

North, Carol, and Sean Yutzy. *Goodwin and Guze's Psychiatric Diagnosis.* New York: Oxford University Press, 2010.

Preston, John D., John H. O'Neal, and Mary C. Talaga. *Handbook of Clinical Psychopharmacology for Therapists.* 6th ed. Oakland, CA: New Harbinger, 2010.

PERIODICALS

Miller, A.R., C.E. Lalonde, K.M. McGrail, and R.W. Armstrong. "Prescription of Methylphenidate to Children and Youth, 1990–1996." *Canadian Medical Journal* 165, no. 11 (2001): 1489–94.

Perring C. "Medicating Children: The Case of Ritalin." *Bioethics* 11, no. 3–4 (1997): 228–40.

Sund, A.M., and P. Zeiner. "Does Extended Medication with Amphetamine or Methylphenidate Reduce Growth in Hyperactive Children?" *Norwegian Journal of Psychiatry* 56, no. 1 (2002): 53–57.

ORGANIZATIONS

American Academy of Clinical Toxicology, 6728 Old McLean Village Dr., McLean, VA, 22101, (703) 556-9222, Fax: (703) 556-8729, admin@clintox.org, http://www.clintox.org.

American Academy of Family Physicians, 11400 Tomahawk Creek Pkwy., Leawood, KS, 66211-2672, (913) 906-6000, (800) 274-2237, Fax: (913) 906-6075, contactcenter@aafp.org, http://www.aafp.org.

American Neurological Association, 5841 Cedar Lake Rd., Ste. 204, Minneapolis, MN, 55416, (952) 545-6284, ana@llmsi.com, http://www.aneuroa.org.

American Psychiatric Association, 1000 Wilson Blvd., Ste. 1825, Arlington, VA, 22209-3901, (703) 907-7300, apa@psych.org, http://www.psych.org.

American Psychological Association, 750 1st St., NE, Washington, DC, 20002-4242, (202) 336-5500; TDD/TTY: (202) 336-6123, (800) 374-2721, http://www.apa.org.

American Society for Clinical Pharmacology and Therapeutics, 528 N Washington St., Alexandria, VA, 22314, (703) 836-6981, info@ascpt.org, http://www.ascpt.org.

National Institute of Mental Health, 6001 Executive Blvd., Rm. 8184, MSC 9663, Bethesda, MD, 20892-9663, (301) 433-4513; TTY: (301) 443-8431, (866) 615-6464; TTY: (866) 415-8051, Fax: (301) 443-4279, nimhinfo@nih.gov, http://www.nimh.nih.gov.

L. Fleming Fallon, Jr., MD, DrPH
Laura Jean Cataldo, RN, EdD

Military mental health

Definition

Military health care, or military medicine, is not recognized as a specialty by the American Board of Medical Specialties (ABMS); nonetheless, it is a distinctive category of medical and psychiatric practice. In the twenty-first century, military medicine involves routine health care (including mental health care) for military personnel and their dependents, but it also includes battlefield treatment and evacuation, disease prevention, disaster relief, health care for military personnel in such extreme environments as deserts and the polar regions, and research in these fields—including mental health research. Aerospace medicine and undersea medicine are newer subspecialties that have developed within the larger field of military medicine.

Military physicians are often stationed with the troops they serve, and they must be acquainted with unusual diseases, traumatic injuries, and psychological stressors that are rarely encountered in civilian settings. The Borden Institute of the U.S. Army Medical Department was founded in 1987 to publish textbooks of military medicine on topics ranging from chemical warfare and health care in harsh environments to preventive medicine and medical ethics. As of 2011, the Institute had published 20 separate textbooks; volumes 5 and 6 are titled *Military Psychiatry* and *War Psychiatry*, respectively.

Veterans' health care in the United States dates back to the Revolutionary War, when the first federal military hospital, Hand Hospital, was opened in Pittsburgh in 1778. Contemporary veterans' health care includes a range of different services, from post-deployment counseling and routine medical checkups to inpatient medical and mental health care, including hospice care. The Department of Veterans Affairs (VA) system is currently divided into 21 geographical regions known as Veterans Integrated Service Networks or VISNs. These regions include both VA hospitals and Vet Centers, which are run by the Veterans Health Administration (VHA), and community-based outpatient clinics staffed by civilian physicians who work in partnership with the VA.

Demographics

U.S. military personnel on active duty are under the care of the Military Health System (MHS), which covers approximately 9.5 million beneficiaries, including the families of active duty personnel as well as retirees and their families. The MHS has about 137,000 employees and an annual budget of $42 billion; it operates 65 hospitals, 412 clinics, and 414 dental clinics at facilities across the United States and around the world, as well as facilities in overseas combat theater operations. The health benefits program for active duty personnel, their dependents, and retirees using civilian healthcare providers is known as TRICARE.

The MHS also operates the Uniformed Services University of the Health Sciences (USU), a graduate university established in Bethesda, Maryland, in 1972 that includes a medical school, dental school, school of nursing, and graduate school in the biomedical sciences offering PhD and DPH degrees. USU had about 850 students enrolled in all its graduate programs as of 2011.

Veterans are eligible for benefits from the Veterans Benefits Administration (VBA), depending on their

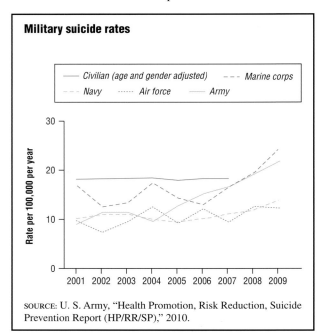

Military suicide rates

SOURCE: U. S. Army, "Health Promotion, Risk Reduction, Suicide Prevention Report (HP/RR/SP)," 2010.

(Graph by PreMediaGlobal. © 2012 Cengage Learning.)

Demographic characteristics of Operation Iraqi Freedom (Iraq) and Operation Enduring Freedom (Afghanistan and surrounding regions) veterans newly utilizing VA healthcare services between October 7, 2001, and March 31, 2007, followed until March 31, 2008, by mental health category

Characteristic	Total veterans	Veterans with no mental health diagnosis		Veterans diagnosed with mental health disorders other than PTSD*		Veterans diagnosed with PTSD*	
Total	**249,440**	**157,844**		**37,868**		**53,728**	
Age group							
15–24	75,715	45,726	(60.4%)	11,859	(15.7%)	18,130	(24.0%)
25–29	65,117	39,734	(61.0%)	10,415	(16.0%)	14,968	(23.0%)
30–39	54,123	33,942	(62.7%)	8,085	(14.9%)	12,096	(22.4%)
40–49	44,059	31,239	(70.9%)	5,869	(13.3%)	6,951	(15.8%)
50–59	9,906	6,815	(68.8%)	1,568	(15.8%)	1,523	(15.4%)
60+	505	374	(74.1%)	71	(14.1%)	60	(11.9%)
Gender							
Male	217,793	137,779	(63.3%)	31,936	(14.7%)	48,078	(22.1%)
Female	31,610	20,032	(63.4%)	5,929	(18.8%)	5,649	(17.9%)
Race/ethnicity							
White	166,509	105,484	(63.4%)	25,113	(15.1%)	35,912	(21.6%)
Black	41,700	26,320	(63.1%)	6,234	(15.0%)	9,146	(21.9%)
Hispanic	27,384	16,837	(61.5%)	4,613	(16.9%)	5,934	(21.7%)
Other	13,847	9,203	(66.5%)	1,908	(13.8%)	2,736	(19.8%)
Marital status							
Married	92,128	52,706	(57.2%)	15,131	(16.4%)	24,291	(26.4%)
Never married	87,565	50,671	(57.9%)	16,137	(18.4%)	20,757	(23.7%)
Divorced, widowed, or separated	22,725	11,119	(48.9%)	4,796	(21.1%)	6,810	(30.0%)
Active duty or reserve							
Active duty	125,836	78,986	(62.8%)	18,949	(15.1%)	27,901	(22.2%)
National Guard/Reserve	123,604	78,858	(63.8%)	18,919	(15.3%)	25,827	(20.9%)
Military rank							
Enlisted (e.g., private, corporal, sergeant)	231,673	143,428	(61.9%)	36,170	(15.6%)	52,075	(22.5%)
Officer (e.g., lieutenant, colonel, general)	17,767	14,416	(81.1%)	1,698	(9.6%)	1,653	(9.3%)
Military branch							
U.S. Army	163,335	97,561	(59.7%)	24,991	(15.3%)	40,783	(25.0%)
U.S. Air Force	28,684	23,093	(80.5%)	3,855	(13.4%)	1,736	(6.0%)
U.S. Marine Corps	30,483	17,631	(57.8%)	4,123	(13.5%)	8,729	(28.6%)
U.S. Navy/Coast Guard	26,938	19,559	(72.6%)	4,899	(18.2%)	2,480	(9.2%)
Multiple deployments							
Yes	78,645	48,832	(62.1%)	11,193	(14.2%)	18,620	(23.7%)
No	170,795	109,012	(63.8%)	26,675	(15.6%)	35,108	(20.6%)
Main VA facility type**							
Medical center	195,133	124,341	(63.7%)	29,597	(15.2%)	41,195	(21.1%)
Outpatient clinic	52,277	31,656	(60.6%)	8,156	(15.6%)	12,465	(23.8%)
Distance to closest VA facility							
Less than 25 miles	130,474	83,934	(64.3%)	20,094	(15.4%)	26,446	(20.3%)
More than 25 miles	117,146	72,779	(62.1%)	17,500	(14.9%)	26,866	(22.9%)

*Post-traumatic stress syndrome
**Veterans Affairs
Notes: Variables may contain missing data; therefore, numbers within each category may not equate to the total number of participants.
PTSD was the most common mental health diagnosis in the study population (21.5%), followed by depression (18.3%), adjustment disorder (11.1%), anxiety disorder (10.6%), substance use disorder (8.4%), and alcohol use disorder (7.3%).

SOURCE: Cohen, Beth E., Kris Gima, Daniel Bertenthal, Sue Kim, Charles R. Marmar and Karen H. Seal. "Mental Health Diagnoses and Utilization of VA Non-Mental Health Medical Services Among Returning Iraq and Afghanistan Veterans." *Journal of General Internal Medicine* 25, no. 1 (January 2010): 18–24.

(Table by PreMediaGlobal. © 2012 Cengage Learning.)

membership in one of eight priority groups. Those retired from long-term military service, those with service-related injuries or conditions, and those awarded the Purple Heart are in the higher-priority groups. Veterans without service-related conditions are eligible for treatment on the basis of financial need. In 2010, there were one million veterans receiving disability benefits, most of them from the period of the Vietnam War (early 1960s–1973).

Description

Historical background

Military medicine and veterans' benefits both originated with Augustus Caesar (63 B.C.–14 A.D.), the first emperor of Rome. Augustus reorganized the Roman army, putting it on a professional footing and creating the first dedicated medical corps in military history. He established a medical school for the training of army physicians (who were responsible for veterinary care for the army's horses and pack animals as well as surgery and medical care for the soldiers), who had to pass detailed course work and examinations to be allowed to join the army. Other innovations were the formation of special groups of soldiers tasked with retrieving the wounded from the battlefield; construction of permanent hospitals (*valetudinaria*) within the army's fortified camps, with special isolation rooms for soldiers with infectious diseases; and the establishment of medical specialties within the army medical corps.

The Civil War was also the first war to bring veterans' mental health issues to the attention of doctors. Jacob Mendez da Costa (1833–1900), a professor at Jefferson Medical College in Philadelphia, identified a disorder that he called the "irritable heart," an anxiety disorder that he observed in Civil War veterans, characterized by breathlessness, panicky feelings, and chest pains on mild exertion. It was sometimes called "soldier's heart" in World War I. Although da Costa's syndrome was not the same as what is now called *post-traumatic stress disorder* (PTSD), recent historical studies of Civil War veterans' health records indicate that many of these men also met contemporary criteria for PTSD. Those at greatest risk were men younger than 18 at the time of service and those who served in units with higher-than-average casualty rates. In addition, doctors and nurses who treated combat casualties developed PTSD even when they were not on the battlefield themselves. Walt Whitman (1819–1892), the famous poet, served as a nurse in a military hospital in Washington, DC between 1862 and 1865; his diary records such symptoms of PTSD as flashbacks, nightmares, **insomnia**, startle reactions, and nausea after his periods on duty.

Mental health issues in the military

Post-traumatic stress disorder

Post-traumatic stress disorder, or PTSD, was not formally introduced as a psychiatric diagnostic category until the third edition of the *Diagnostic and Statistical Manual of Mental Disorders* (*DSM-III*) in 1980, although it has doubtless affected civilians as well as combat veterans for millennia. The earliest recorded case of it concerns an uninjured Athenian hoplite (citizen-soldier) who became blind from emotional shock after witnessing the death of a comrade during the Battle of Marathon in 490 B.C. It is helpful to keep in mind in this context that psychiatry itself is a relatively young medical specialty; Sigmund Freud was a boy of five at the outbreak of the Civil War in 1861.

The notion of evaluating soldiers in combat situations for psychiatric as well as physical symptoms originated in the British army on the Western Front during World War I (1914–1918) when infantrymen in the trenches began to develop what was then called "shell shock"—a combat **stress** reaction marked by indecision, disorientation, inability to set priorities, and a blank and unfocused expression colloquially known as the "thousand-yard stare," a sign of dissociation. During World War II (1939–1945), the condition was generally called "combat fatigue" or "traumatic war neurosis," terms that are now obsolete. It was not until the Vietnam War that studies of combat veterans eventually produced the current definition of PTSD. The **diagnosis** was not applied to civilian survivors of traumatic incidents until the 1980s.

Demographics for PTSD for American veterans of different wars are difficult to estimate because of changing definitions of combat stress reactions as well as differences among branches of the service and the theaters in which they operated. The overall lifetime rate of PTSD for World War II veterans is estimated at 25%, with rates in the Army and Marine Corps higher than in the Navy, Coast Guard, or Air Force (called the "Army Air Corps" before 1947). For World War II veterans who had been prisoners of war, the rate of PTSD was three times higher (36%) for POW veterans of the Pacific Theater than for those taken prisoner in Europe (12%); traumatic memories persisted as long as 65 years after the experience of captivity. The lifetime rate for Vietnam veterans is estimated at 31% for men and 27% for women; for veterans of the Gulf War, from 9% to 24%; for veterans of Operation Iraqi Freedom (OIF) and Operation Enduring Freedom (OEF), 10% to 18%. For purposes of comparison, the lifetime rate of PTSD in the general population is 7% to 8%. Risk factors for PTSD in OIF/OEF veterans include lower service rank, single marital status, female gender, Hispanic ethnicity, longer deployment time, **traumatic brain injury**, family problems at home, prior history of childhood **trauma**, and lower level of education.

The VA established the National Center for PTSD in 1989 to perform research and education on the understanding, treatment, and prevention of PTSD. Although the Center does not provide direct clinical care for veterans with PTSD, it educates both military and civilian physicians about the disorder, maintains a research database called PILOTS (Published International Literature on Traumatic Stress), and has a website with numerous pages about various aspects of PTSD, ranging from self-assessment and self-help to women's issues, post-deployment syndrome, and special programs for Native American, Hispanic, and African American veterans.

Gulf War syndrome

Gulf War syndrome (GWS) is a condition reported by some veterans of the 1991 Gulf War marked by chronic **fatigue**; headaches; memory problems; disturbed sleep; and digestive, skin, muscle, and joint disorders. GWS is a controversial diagnosis because of the wide variety of symptoms claimed as its characteristic features and because of the lack of a standardized definition of the syndrome. A report issued by the Institute of Medicine (IOM) in 2006 concluded, "Although veterans of the first Gulf War report significantly more symptoms of illness than soldiers of the same period who were not deployed, studies have found no cluster of symptoms that constitute a syndrome unique to Gulf War veterans." One reason given for the existence of a distinct syndrome was exposure to a combination of chemicals and contaminants never previously encountered in a war zone. These included bromide pills given to protect troops from the effects of nerve agents, depleted uranium munitions, and anthrax and botulinum vaccines. Another environmental hazard was toxic smoke from hundreds of burning oil wells.

About 700,000 American men and women served in the Gulf War in 1991; about 30% of them have registered with the database set up by the American Legion to track illnesses related to the war. Studies conducted by the Institute of Medicine and the National Academy of Sciences (NAS) in 2005 and 2006 surveyed 19,000 veterans of the Gulf War. Other medical reports by doctors in the field covered an additional 80,000 soldiers. What seems clear is that the medical symptoms of GWS cannot be explained as PTSD. While some veterans of the Gulf War did develop PTSD, a second IOM report in 2010 concluded that "the excess of unexplained medical symptoms reported by deployed Gulf war veterans cannot be reliably ascribed to any known psychiatric disorder." The medical symptoms are now generally described as multisystem illness, or MSI.

Post-deployment syndrome

Post-deployment syndrome (PDS) is sometimes used to describe a combination of PTSD, **depression**, **generalized anxiety disorder** (GAD), chronic pain, and traumatic **brain** injury (TBI) lasting longer than three to six months. It is a condition diagnosed primarily in veterans of the conflicts in Iraq and Afghanistan rather than earlier wars. Research into PDS was ongoing as of 2011, with a focus on finding effective treatments.

Women's issues

Women have served in frontline combat at least occasionally since the nineteenth century. According to diaries from the period and government records, about 750 women successfully disguised themselves as men and served in both Union and Confederate armies during the Civil War. Russian women served in combat in both World War I (the "Women's Battalion of Death" numbered about 2,000 soldiers in 1917) and World War II (about 800,000 women served as snipers, tank crew members, machine gunners, and pilots during the course of the war). Although American women generally served in support roles during earlier conflicts, as of 2011 they were the fastest-growing group of veterans. Women currently account for 11% of all OIF/OEF veterans.

The VA has identified four particular stressors for women in the military: combat missions, military sexual trauma or MST (defined as "any kind of unwanted sexual attention includ[ing] insulting sexual comments, unwanted sexual advances, or even sexual assault"), feeling alone or unsupported in newly formed military units, and concern about children or elderly parents at home. There is evidence that sexual harassment and assault are more common in wartime than in peacetime military duty. A study of MST during the Gulf War reported high rates of sexual assault (7%), physical sexual harassment (33%), and verbal sexual harassment (66%). In another study, 23% of female users of VA healthcare reported experiencing at least one sexual assault while in the military.

One reason that MST is so debilitating is that the military places a very high value on unit cohesion; thus, reporting sexual harassment or assault perpetrated by another member of the unit is considered taboo. Male victims of MST have a higher rate of PTSD (65%) than females (45%), partly because the male gender role causes many men to feel intense shame about their

Combat stress reaction—A general term for mental health symptoms that include depression, fatigue, dissociative symptoms, difficulty focusing, and irritability. It is not identical to PTSD but may be a precursor of it. The condition was sometimes referred to as "combat fatigue" in World War II.

Dissociation—A psychological mechanism in which the mind splits off certain aspects of a traumatic event from conscious awareness. Dissociation can affect the patient's memory, sense of reality, and sense of identity. Dissociative symptoms are commonly experienced by persons with PTSD.

Post-deployment syndrome (PDS)—A term developed recently to describe a constellation of mental disorders found in veterans of the conflicts in Iraq and Afghanistan. PDS includes PTSD, generalized anxiety disorder, major depression, chronic pain, and traumatic brain injury.

Resilience—In psychiatry, the ability of a person to respond positively to, or bounce back from, trauma or hardship. Resilience is considered a process of interaction between the person and his or her environment rather than a one-time action.

Syndrome—A group of signs or symptoms that occur together and characterize or define a particular disease or disorder.

Triage—A process for determining the order and priority of emergency treatment for injured people (civilians or military personnel); the order and priority of emergency transport; and/or the injured person's transport destination.

victimization, making them less likely to seek professional help.

Traumatic brain injury

Traumatic brain injury (TBI) refers to a type of closed-head injury resulting from a blow or jolt to the head; it can result from whiplash injuries as well as a motor vehicle accident, blast, or fall. TBIs can be evaluated as mild, moderate, or severe, depending on whether the person was knocked out and how long they were unconscious. In a mild TBI, the person either does not lose consciousness at all or is unconscious for 30 minutes or less. In a moderate TBI, the person is unconscious for longer than 30 minutes but less than six hours. Unconsciousness lasting longer than six hours indicates a severe TBI.

One of the difficulties of diagnosing a TBI is that some of the emotional and cognitive symptoms overlap with those of PTSD. TBI symptoms may include trouble with concentration, acting without thinking, memory loss, difficulty translating thoughts into words, anger, anxiety, depression, or changes in personality. It is important to make sure that someone who has suffered a TBI together with (or instead of) PTSD receives the proper treatment. People with TBIs should not receive certain types of medications, including several classes of antidepressant drugs, which may aggravate some symptoms of the TBI, such as vertigo. Other drugs that should be avoided include those that may make the patient more susceptible to **seizures** (e.g., **bupropion**) or drugs that may cause confusion (e.g., **benzodiazepines**, lithium).

TBIs are of particular concern to current military and VA doctors because the rate of such injuries is higher (22%) in veterans of Iraq and Afghanistan than in Vietnam veterans (12%). The major causes of TBIs in recent veterans are blasts, motor vehicle accidents, and gunshot wounds. Because many veterans with TBIs have coexisting PTSD or **substance abuse** disorders, they typically take longer than civilians to recover from these head injuries. Veterans with TBIs are also almost twice as likely to attempt **suicide** than veterans who did not suffer such injuries.

Suicide

Statistics kept since World War I indicate that American combat veterans are twice as likely to die from suicide than male adults in the general population. In 2011, the VA reported that there were, on average, 950 suicide attempts each month among veterans receiving some type of VA treatment. Seven percent of these attempts were successful; 11% of attempters were expected to try again within the next nine months. The number of veterans' suicides between 2005 and 2009—1,100—exceeded that of the number of military personnel killed in Afghanistan since 2001.

Access to health care is an important factor in suicide prevention among veterans. Only 8 million of the 23 million veterans in the United States are currently registered with the Department of Veteran Affairs. The data indicate that for veterans between the ages of 18 and 29, the suicide rate is lower for those receiving VA health care than for those who do not seek help. The VA's suicide hotline (800-273-8255, press 1) receives about 10,000 calls per month from current and former service members. One major area of concern is the rising risk of suicide among OIF and OEF veterans. In 2009, there were 1,621 suicide attempts by men and 247 by women veterans of these conflicts, with 94 men and 4 women dying. As in the civilian population, women veterans attempt suicide more often than men, but men are more often successful, mostly because they are more likely to use firearms.

In 2011, the NIMH and the U.S. Army announced the beginning of a suicide-prevention study known as the Army Study to Assess Risk and Resilience in Servicemembers, or the Army STARRS program. The largest study ever conducted to assess mental health issues among military personnel, the Army STARRS program will run through 2014. The study has four separate components: an investigation of historical data, evaluation of new soldiers, an All-Army study, and a health outcomes investigation. Participation is voluntary.

Military mental health services

Statistics indicate that almost half of the 1 million service personnel deployed to Iraq or Afghanistan between 2002 and 2009 sought some form of health care from the VA. Of that fraction, 48% (about 221,000 persons) were diagnosed with mental health issues, including depression and **anxiety disorders** other than PTSD. Treatment is available for veterans at all VA hospitals, Vet Centers, and community clinics working in partnership with the VA.

As of 2011, there were over 200 specialized treatment programs for PTSD within the VA system, covering veterans from World War II and all later conflicts. Several types of therapy are offered, including individualized assessment and **psychotherapy**, medications, **family therapy**, and **group therapy** (including anger management, combat support, and groups for veterans of specific conflicts). Programs range from intensive residential or inpatient treatment programs lasting 28–90 days in day clinics, walk-in community-based clinics, and Vet Center group therapy programs staffed by veterans. A special 60-day residential PTSD program for women veterans, the National Women's Trauma Recovery Program (WTRP), is run by the center in Menlo Park, California.

The National Center for PTSD also has a menu of self-help options on its website, ranging from mindfulness practice and recommendations for a healthy lifestyle to an iPhone app called PTSD Coach that helps users recognize and manage symptoms of PTSD.

According to the VA, there are a number of reasons why veterans are often reluctant to seek help for mental health issues:

• They do not want to be seen as weak.

• They are concerned about privacy.

QUESTIONS TO ASK YOUR DOCTOR

• Have you ever practiced medicine in a military setting?

• Have you ever treated military personnel on active duty?

• What do you consider the distinctive features of military medicine and health care for veterans?

• Have you ever diagnosed or treated a veteran with PTSD?

• Is there a VA health care facility in the area?

• They would rather rely on family and friends.

• They are concerned about possible side effects of medications.

• They do not think treatment will help them.

• They have problems with access to treatment, in terms of cost or geographical location.

• If they are still actively serving, they are concerned about losing future promotions.

As of 2011, there were 322 **clinical trials** under way in the general area of mental health care for veterans. Studies include investigations of various types of psychotherapy and other interventions for PTSD, telephone case monitoring and outreach for World War II veterans as well as younger veterans, Internet- and smartphone-based psychotherapy for rural veterans, suicide-prevention programs, special studies of women veterans, trials of various medications for Gulf War veterans with multisystem illness, and investigations of programs for post-deployment reintegration into civilian life.

Resources

BOOKS

Bradley, Matthew H., ed. *Veterans' Benefits and Care.* Hauppauge, NY: Nova Science Publishers, 2009.

Cifu, David X., and Cory Blake. *Overcoming Post-deployment Syndrome: A Six-Step Mission to Health.* New York: Demos Health, 2011.

Gabriel, Richard A. *Man and Wound in the Ancient World: A History of Military Medicine from Sumer to the Fall of Constantinople.* Washington, DC: Potomac Books, 2012.

McCallum, Jack E. *Military Medicine: From Ancient Times to the 21st Century.* Santa Barbara, CA: ABC-CLIO, 2008.

Rice, Gary H. *A Sketch of Military Medicine in Canada, 1867–2009.* Carleton Place, ON: GEHR Pub. of Mississippi Mills, 2009.

Ritchie, Elspeth Cameron, ed. *Combat and Operational Behavioral Health*. Falls Church, VA: Office of The Surgeon General, United States Army, 2011.

PERIODICALS

Brenner, L.A., et al. "Suicide and Traumatic Brain Injury Among Individuals Seeking Veterans Health Administration Services." *Journal of Head Trauma Rehabilitation* 26 (July–August 2011): 257–64.

Cohen, Beth E., et al. "Mental Health Diagnoses and Utilization of VA Non-Mental Health Medical Services Among Returning Iraq and Afghanistan Veterans." *Journal of General Internal Medicine* 25, no. 1 (2010): 18–24.

Hoge, C.W., et al. "Combat Duty in Iraq and Afghanistan, Mental Health Problems and Barriers to Care." *U.S. Army Medical Department Journal* (July–September 2008): 7–17.

Hsu, David. "Walt Whitman: An American Civil War Nurse Who Witnessed the Advent of Modern American Medicine." *Archives of Environmental and Occupational Health* 65 (October–December 2010): 238–239. http://www.tandfonline.com/doi/pdf/10.1080/19338244.2010.524510 (accessed August 2, 2011).

Jones, E. "Shell Shock at Maghull and the Maudsley: Models of Psychological Medicine in the UK." *Journal of the History of Medicine and Allied Sciences* 65 (July 2010): 368–95.

Kang, H.K., et al. "Health of US Veterans of 1991 Gulf War: A Follow-up Survey in 10 Years." *Journal of Occupational and Environmental Health* 51 (April 2009): 401–10.

Khardis, A., et al. "Posttraumatic Stress, Family Adjustment, and Treatment Preferences among National Guard Soldiers Deployed to OEF/OIF." *Military Medicine* 176 (February 2011): 126–31.

Liberman, Moishe, et al. "The History of Trauma Care Systems from Homer to Telemedicine." *McGill Journal of Medicine* 7, no. 2 (2004). http://www.med.mcgill.ca/mjm/issues/v07n02/feature_rev/feature_rev.htm (accessed August 2, 2011).

Max, Jill. "Medicine and the Military." *Yale Medicine*, Spring 2011. http://www.med.yale.edu/external/pubs/ym_sp11/feature2_military.html (accessed August 1, 2011).

Maze, Rick. "18 Veterans Commit Suicide Each Day." *Army Times*, April 22, 2010. http://www.armytimes.com/news/2010/04/military_veterans_suicide_042210w (accessed August 5, 2011).

Pizarro, Judith, et al. "Physical and Mental Health Costs of Traumatic War Experiences among Civil War Veterans." *Archives of General Psychiatry* 63 (February 2006): 193–200. http://archpsyc.ama-assn.org/cgi/reprint/63/2/193 (accessed August 2, 2011).

Rintamaki, L.S., et al. "Persistence of Traumatic Memories in World War II Prisoners of War." *Journal of the American Geriatrics Society* 57 (December 2009): 2257–62.

Sher, L., and R. Yehuda. "Preventing Suicide among Returning Combat Veterans: A Moral Imperative." *Military Medicine* 176 (June 2011): 601–2.

Street, A.E., et al. "A New Generation of Women Veterans: Stressors Faced by Women Deployed to Iraq and Afghanistan." *Clinical Psychology Review* 29 (December 2009): 685–94.

Wells, T.S., et al. "Mental Health Impact of the Iraq and Afghanistan Conflicts: A Review of US Research, Service Provision, and Programmatic Responses." *International Review of Psychiatry* 23 (April 2011): 144–52.

OTHER

U.S. Army. *Army Health Promotion, Risk Reduction, Suicide Prevention Report 2010*. http://csf.army.mil/downloads/HP-RR-SPReport2010.pdf (accessed November 14, 2011).

WEBSITES

American Psychiatric Association. "Healthy Minds, Healthy Lives: Military." http://www.healthyminds.org/more-info-for/military.aspx (accessed January 5, 2012).

Army STARRS Home Page. http://www.armystarrs.org (accessed August 11, 2011).

Cifu, David, and Cory Blake. "Post-Deployment Syndrome: The Illness of War." BrainLineMilitary.org. http://www.brainlinemilitary.org/content/2011/03/post-deployment-syndrome-the-illness-of-war.html (accessed August 4, 2011).

DoD Live. "Improving the Care of Female Veterans." http://www.dodlive.mil/index.php/2011/07/improving-the-care-of-female-veterans (accessed August 3, 2011).

Military Pathways. "Military Mental Health Screening Program." http://www.militarymentalhealth.org/Welcome.aspx (accessed January 5, 2012).

National Center for PTSD. "Issues Specific to Women." http://www.ptsd.va.gov/public/pages/fslist-specific-women.asp (accessed August 3, 2011).

National Center for PTSD. "PTSD Overview" (includes "Understanding PTSD" Flash player module). http://www.ptsd.va.gov/public/pages/fslist-ptsd-overview.asp (accessed August 3, 2011).

National Center for PTSD. "Return from War." http://www.ptsd.va.gov/public/reintegration/guides-rwz.asp (accessed December 10, 2011).

National Center for PTSD. "Traumatic Brain Injury and PTSD." http://www.ptsd.va.gov/public/pages/traumatic_brain_injury_and_ptsd.asp (accessed August 4, 2011).

U.S. Army Medical Department. "Army Behavioral Health." http://www.behavioralhealth.army.mil (accessed January 5, 2012).

ORGANIZATIONS

Borden Institute, 1546 Porter St., Ste. 207, Fort Detrick, MD, United States 21702, (301) 619-3470, Fax: (301) 619-3471, bordeninfo@amedd.army.mil, http://www.bordeninstitute.army.mil/index.html.

National Center for PTSD, 810 Vermont Avenue NW, Washington, DC, United States 20420, (802) 296-6300, ncptsd@va.gov, http://www.ptsd.va.gov/index.asp.

Uniformed Services University of the Health Sciences (USU), 4301 Jones Bridge Rd., Bethesda, MD, United States 20814, (301) 295-1219, (800) 515-5257, Fax: (301) 295-3757, http://www.usuhs.mil.

U.S. Department of Veterans Affairs (VA), 810 Vermont Avenue NW, Washington, DC, United States 20420, (800) 827-1000; Mental health crisis line: (800) 273-8255 (press 1), http://www.va.gov.

Rebecca J. Frey, Ph.D.

Mind-body medicine

Definition

Mind-body medicine, also known as behavioral medicine, is the field of medicine concerned with the ways that the mind and emotions influence the body and physical health.

Purpose

Mind-body therapies have shown promise in treating cancer, heart disease, hypertension, asthma, and mental illness. They have been used as effective complementary therapies alongside such conventional treatments as surgery and chemotherapy. Mind-body therapies have also been shown to increase quality of life, reduce pain, and improve symptoms for people with chronic diseases and health conditions. They may also help control and reverse certain diseases, particularly those that are stress-related. By reducing **stress**, mind-body therapies may even prevent many diseases. Another benefit of mind-body therapies is that they pose very little risk. Some are inexpensive, and most have few side effects.

Description

Origins

There was a time not long ago when Western medicine believed that health depended solely upon the physical mechanisms of the body—that is, that a person is made up only of physical and chemical reactions that can be measured and manipulated scientifically. The notion that the mind and body live in separate compartments, so to speak, goes back to certain philosophers of classical antiquity. This concept of mind-body separation was also present in such religious groups as the Gnostics and some sects on the fringes of medieval Christianity. The scientific version of this split between mind and body is generally traced back to the seventeenth-century French philosopher Rene Descartes, whose thinking aided the development of science. It has taken a lot of time and research, three centuries after

Descartes, for mainstream medicine to begin to accept that the mind plays a role in health and disease.

The idea that the mind and body interact is not new, however. It can be traced to the Wisdom literature in the Old Testament and to Hippocrates, the father of Western medicine. The ancient Hebrews attributed some physical illnesses to **grief** or anger. Hippocrates believed that health depends upon a balance of the body, mind and environment, and that disease is caused by imbalances in these areas. As modern science progressed, the mind and emotions became neglected, since researchers found it difficult to measure and quantify mental states with the scientific methods and equipment that were so highly valued.

Modern mind-body relationships become apparent

In the early 1900s, Harvard physiologist Walter Cannon coined the term "fight-or-flight response" for the body's reaction to threats, a response that causes increases in heart rate, blood pressure, blood sugar, muscle tension and respiration. During the 1950s, Hans Selye of McGill University pioneered research in what he called stress. Selye determined that the fight-or-flight response could be triggered by psychological factors as well as by physical threats. Stress includes having fight-or-flight reactions in situations where there is no immediate threat except mental perceptions and worries. Stress is not necessarily negative, except when people fail to cope with it effectively. Selye's work laid the groundwork for researchers to determine that stress and reactions to it play an integral role in health and disease.

Other mind-body relationships became apparent to medical researchers. The so-called placebo effect has been studied by doctors and psychologists for years. In clinical experiments, people who are given inert substances made to look like medicines, such as sugar pills, sometimes experience the same improvements as those patients who are given real medications. It is estimated that nearly one out of every three patients improves with medication simply because of the placebo effect and not because of the drug itself. Researchers have also noted that some conditions and illnesses have no physical explanations. Doctors termed these conditions psychosomatic illnesses, as they seem to be caused by the psyche, or mind.

Researchers then theorized that certain personality types are susceptible to particular conditions. For instance, "Type A" personalities tend to be aggressive, ambitious, and always rushed. They tend to cope with stress by getting angry and upset. Researchers have found that these personalities are more prone to heart disease, high blood pressure, and other stress-related conditions. "Type B" personalities are those who cope with stressful situations with communication and balance instead of anger and aggression, and have been found to be less prone to stress-related conditions. Researchers have added a "Type C" personality, who tends to suppress emotions and has trouble with self-expression. Some clinicians have proposed a link between suppressed emotions and the development of cancer.

In the 1970s, Dr. Herbert Benson at Harvard Medical School discovered what he called the "relaxation response." Benson observed that trained **yoga** specialists (yogis) could control bodily functions that had previously been believed to be autonomic, or beyond the control of the mind. During **meditation**, these yogis could reduce their heart rates, blood pressure, metabolism, body temperature, and other physiological processes to surprising levels. Other people who were then taught meditation were able to reach deep states of relaxation and calmness. This relaxation response, as Benson termed it, is essentially the opposite of the fight-or-flight response. The relaxation response reduces blood pressure, respiration, heart rate, oxygen consumption, muscle tension, and other bodily processes that are elevated by stress. Researchers soon began to theorize that if stress could have harmful effects on health, then the relaxation response might have the opposite effect. It was not long before the Harvard Mind-Body Medical Institute was founded, and other major medical clinics followed by integrating mind-body practices and studies into their health programs. A new field opened up in academic medicine called psychoneuroimmunology (PNI), which is the study of how the mind and nervous system affect the immune system. Studies have since shown that the mind and emotions play roles in many diseases, including cancer, diabetes, heart disease, gastrointestinal problems, and asthma.

In the past few decades, researchers have begun to unravel the complex ways in which the mind and body interact. Many findings have demonstrated that the mind and body are intimately interconnected. Medical science has shown that the nervous system works closely with the immune system, systems that were at one time believed to be separate. Nerve endings have been found that connect directly to important components of the immune system called lymph nodes. This connection demonstrates that there is a physical link between the mind and the immune system. Studies have also shown that thoughts and emotions alone can influence the activity of immune system cells.

Methods

There are many alternative techniques that draw upon the interconnections between mind and body. These include **art therapy**, **assertiveness training**, autogenic training, bioenergetics, **biofeedback**, breath therapy, guided imagery, **dance therapy** and movement therapy, dreamwork, **Gestalt therapy**, **group therapy**, hypnosis, meditation, mindfulness training, Jungian **psychoanalysis**, postural integration, prayer and faith healing, progressive relaxation, psychodrama, **psychotherapy**, Reichian therapy, **support groups**, and yoga. Some of the most widely used techniques are meditation, mindfulness training, biofeedback, breath therapy, hypnosis, guided imagery, and movement therapies.

Meditation

There are many forms of meditation, but they all have the same goal, which is to calm and focus the mind. As beginning meditators find out, however, calming and clearing the mind of thoughts and worries is easier said than done. When performed on a regular basis, meditation is an efficient way of promoting the relaxation response. Meditation is used to ease the physical discomfort of many health problems, including stress-related conditions, chronic pain, panic disorders, and tension headaches.

Meditation can be practiced anywhere, but a quiet and peaceful setting is recommended. Persons should sit up straight or lie in a comfortable position. Breathing during meditation should be deep, calm, and slow. The meditator may concentrate on the breath or on a still object such as a flower or candle flame. The meditator often may repeat a soft sound, word, or phrase, known as a mantra. Mantras can be affirmative statements, prayers, or humming sounds. The goal of the meditator is to concentrate deeply in order to reduce the amount of thinking, and to calm the worries and thoughts that typically fill the mind. When thoughts or distractions arise, the meditator should allow them to pass without directing attention toward them.

Meditation is usually practiced twice a day, for 20 minutes at a time, preferably at consistent times to develop discipline. It can be learned from books or tapes, but instruction is widely available and recommended, as beginners can find properly meditating and quieting the mind to be difficult at first.

Mindfulness training

This form of mental discipline was made popular by Dr. Jon Kabat-Zinn, a **psychologist** at the University of Massachusetts Medical Center, who has written some popular books on mind-body medicine. Kabat-Zinn uses mindfulness training to help patients deal with chronic illnesses and pain. Mindfulness training is also good for stress-related conditions and persons undergoing difficult

KEY TERMS

Behavioral medicine—The branch of medicine that studies mind-body relationships.

Fight-or-flight response—The body's reaction to threats.

Mantra—A sacred word or formula repeated over and over to concentrate the mind.

Placebo—A pharmacologically inactive substance disguised as a real medication.

Psychoneuroimmunology—The study of the relationships among mind, nervous system, and immune response.

Psychosomatic—A type of physical illness caused by mental factors.

Relaxation response—The calming of bodily responses through relaxation techniques.

Vipassana—A Buddhist meditative practice that emphasizes deep attentiveness to the present moment.

treatments like surgery or chemotherapy. Practitioners of mindfulness claim it helps them experience more pleasure and less stress in their everyday activities.

Mindfulness training originated from a Buddhist practice called *vipassana*. Its basic idea is that deep awareness of the present moment is the essential discipline. Lack of awareness and attention can lead to stress and bad health habits. To be mindful is to participate fully in whatever one is doing at the present moment, whether reading, walking, working, eating, exercising, relaxing, etc. When a person pays full attention to the present moment without judgment, then worries about the past and future tend to disappear, and stress levels are also significantly reduced.

Mindfulness training teaches that painful situations and emotions should be experienced with full attention as well, which helps people to confront and accept them. Mindfulness training uses techniques like the body scan, in which the patient focuses full attention on each part of the body in succession. This technique helps people become more aware of their bodies and learn to control their reactions to stress, change, and illness.

Biofeedback

Biofeedback uses special instruments that measure and display heart rate, perspiration, muscle tension, **brain** wave activity, body temperature, respiratory patterns, and other indicators of stress and physiological activity. Patients can observe their measurements and learn to consciously control functions that were previously unconsciously controlled. Biofeedback also helps people learn how to initiate the relaxation response quickly and effectively.

Biofeedback is used to treat hypertension, stress-related headaches, migraine headaches, **attention deficit hyperactivity disorder**, and diabetes. Biofeedback is used often in physical therapy to rehabilitate damaged nerves and muscles. It is also an approved treatment for a vascular disorder called Raynaud's syndrome. Patients with this syndrome experience blanching and numbness in their hands and feet in response to cold or emotional stress.

Breath therapy

Breath therapy works on the premise that breathing plays a central role in the body and mind. People who are under stress tend to breathe rapidly and shallowly, whereas slow and deep breathing has been shown to reduce stress and promote the relaxation response. In Ayurvedic medicine and traditional Chinese medicine, the breath is considered the most important metabolic function. In yoga, there is a science of breathing techniques known as pranayama, which is designed to reduce stress and promote health.

Breath therapy is often used in conjunction with meditation and other mind-body techniques. It can be learned from books and tapes or from a yoga or mind-body specialist. It is an inexpensive treatment, and once learned can be practiced easily anywhere.

Hypnosis

Hypnosis is deeply focused attention that brings about a trance state that is somewhere between waking and sleeping. During hypnosis, the mind is very open to suggestion. Mental imagery is often used in conjunction with hypnosis to maximize positive thinking and healing.

Hypnosis, or **hypnotherapy**, is used to reduce stress, anxiety, and pain, and help patients suffering from chronic diseases. It is also used to assist people in overcoming bad health habits and addictions to **nicotine**, alcohol and drugs. Some dentists use hypnosis to help patients relax during dental procedures. Research continues to show the benefits of hypnosis. Hypnosis is best performed by trained hypnotherapists, who can teach techniques of self-hypnosis to the patient.

Guided imagery

This technique uses the imagination to stimulate healing responses in the body, as studies have shown that the imagination can cause the same activity in the brain and immune system as real events. Patients are taught to imagine places or situations in which they have felt happy, healthy, or safe. Patients can also focus on images that increase confidence, reduce stress, and promote healing. Mental imaging techniques are also used in conjunction with many other mind-body techniques like meditation and hypnosis, as it is an efficient means of promoting positive mental attitudes. Mental imaging techniques can be learned from books, audiotapes, videos, and from professional therapists and teachers.

Movement therapy

Movement routines, such as dance therapy, have been shown to have a significant mind-body element. In these therapies, which also include martial arts, yoga, and tai chi, strict routines of physical movements are designed to involve high levels of mental concentration and awareness of the body. Movement therapies are good for people who have trouble sitting still for meditation and are an excellent way of improving physical strength and mental health at the same time.

Precautions

Mind-body practices are safe and have few side effects. They should not, however, be relied upon solely when other medical care is required. Consumers should seek reliable and properly trained practitioners, particularly in those practices and states for which certification is not required by law.

Costs can vary widely for mind-body treatments, depending on the type and the medical training of the practitioner. Consumers should be aware of their insurance provisions, in case their provider does not cover mind-body treatments.

Research & general acceptance

Because of its increasing acceptance by mainstream medicine, mind-body medicine has been the subject of intense research. Studies have shed new light on everything from the minute interactions of the immune and nervous systems to the effective results of individual therapies like meditation and guided imagery. Other studies have indicated relationships between stress and disease. Some eye-opening results have been observed as well, such as studies that have shown that cancer and heart disease patients utilizing mind-body techniques had significantly longer survival rates on average than those patients who did not use mind-body therapies. Despite increasingly proven benefits to

---

QUESTIONS TO ASK YOUR DOCTOR

- How can I benefit from mind-body treatment?
- Is it beneficial to integrate mind-body techniques with my conventional medicines or other therapies?
- What specific practices or treatments would you recommended for me?

---

mind–body medicine, few health plans pay for the treatments.

Resources

BOOKS
Harrington, Anne. *The Cure Within: A History of Mind-Body Medicine*. New York: W.W. Norton & Co, 2009.

Mayo Clinic. *Mayo Clinic Book of Alternative Medicine: The New Approach to Using the Best of Natural Therapies and Conventional Medicine*. New York: Time Inc. Home Entertainment, 2007.

Rotan, Leo W., and Veronika Ospina-Kammerer. *MindBody Medicine: Foundations and Practical Applications*. New York: Taylor & Francis Ltd., 2007.

PERIODICALS
Vaucher, Andrea R., "Doctor's Orders: Cross Your Legs and Say 'Om'." *Los Angeles Times* (October 29, 2007).

Wang, Chenchen, Jean Paul Collett, and Joseph Lau. "The Effect of Tai Chi on Health Outcomes in Patients With Chronic Conditions A Systematic Review." *Archives Internal Medicine* 164 (2004): 493–501.

OTHER
U.S. National Center for Complementary and Alternative Medicine. "Mind-Body Medicine: An Overview." National Institutes of Health. August 2005. http://www.qigonginstitute.org/html/papers/NCCAMmindbody.pdf (accessed November 9, 2011).

ORGANIZATIONS
Academy for Guided Imagery, 10780 Santa Monica Boulevard, Los Angeles, CA, 90025, (800) 726-2070, Fax: (800) 727-2070, info@acadhi.com, http://acadgi.com.

American Society of Clinical Hypnosis, 140 N. Bloomingdale Rd., Bloomingdale, IL, 60108, (630) 980-4740, Fax: (630) 351-8490, http://www.asch.net.

Biofeedback Certification International Alliance, 10200 W 44th Ave., Ste. 304, Wheatridge, CO, 80033, (303) 420-2902, http://www.bcia.org/i4a/pages/index.cfm?pageid=1.

Center for Mind Body Medicine, http://www.cmbm.org.

National Center for Complementary and Alternative Medicine, 9000 Rockville Pike, Bethesda, MD, 20892, info@nccam.nih.gov, http://nccam.nih.gov.

Vipassana Meditation Center, PO Box 24, Shelbourne Falls, MA, 01370, (413) 625-2160, http://www.dhamma.org/en/schedules/schdhara.shtml.

Douglas Dupler
Teresa G. Odle
Brenda W. Lerner

Mini-mental state examination

Definition

The mini-mental state examination, which is also known as the MMSE, standardized MMSE, SMMSE, or the Folstein, is a brief examination consisting of 11 questions, scored with a maximum of 30 points, intended to evaluate an adult patient's level of cognitive functioning, specifically looking for **brain** impairment with respect to **dementia**, such as **Alzheimer's disease**. The test was introduced in 1975 by Marshall Folstein and colleagues and designed for use with elderly patients who are able to cooperate at an optimum level with an examiner for only a brief period, perhaps no more than a few minutes. It tests for cognitive function by assessing attention and calculation, language abilities, orientation, visual-spatial ability, and word recall.

Purpose

The MMSE concentrates on the cognitive aspects of mental functioning, excluding questions about the patient's mood or such abnormal experiences as dissociation. It is used most often to evaluate older adults for **delirium** or dementia. The MMSE can be used to detect the severity of cognitive impairment, to measure decline in cognitive function, to follow the course of the patient's illness, and to monitor responses to treatment. In the early 2000s, it was professionally approved as a measurement of a patient's ability to complete an advance directive, or so-called living will.

The test has been used in research as a screener in epidemiological studies for disorders that affect cognition and to monitor changes in subjects' cognition during **clinical trials**. In 2001, the MMSE was recommended by a special panel of experts for use as a screener in evaluating cognitive function in depressed patients. It has also been used to measure the effects of **acupuncture** in improving mood and some cognitive skills in patients with Alzheimer's disease.

The MMSE evaluates six areas of cognitive function: orientation, attention, immediate recall, short-term recall, language, and the ability to follow simple verbal and written commands. In addition, it provides a total score allowing the examiner to place the patient on a scale of cognitive function. It correlates well with a standard measure of cognition in adults, the Wechsler Adult Intelligence Scale (WAIS). In contrast to the Wechsler, which takes about an hour or more to administer, the MMSE can be completed in ten minutes or less.

Description

The mini-mental state examination identifies serious mental functions, including arithmetic, memory, and orientation. It screens for cognitive impairment in individuals from 18 to 100 years of age. The test is divided into two sections, together taking from 10 to 15 minutes to administer. The first part requires vocal responses to the examiner's questions. The patient is asked to repeat a short phrase after the examiner; to count backward from 100 by 7s; to name the current president of the United States (in Great Britain, the names of the queen and her four children); and similar brief items. It tests the patient's orientation, memory, and attention. The maximum score on this section is 21.

In the second part of the examination, the patient is asked to follow verbal and written instructions, write a sentence spontaneously, and copy a complex geometric figure similar to a Bender-Gestalt figure—a series of nine designs each on separate cards given the test taker who is asked to reproduce them on blank paper. The sentence item usually asks the patient to explain the meaning of a simple proverb such as "People who live in glass houses shouldn't throw stones." The maximum score for the second section is 9. Patients with vision problems can be assisted with large writing. The MMSE is not timed.

The eight categories (and their descriptions and maximum number of points) of the MMSE are:

- orientation to time (questions asked about time, such as "What time is it?"; 5 maximum points)

- orientation to place (questions asked about location, such as "What floor are we on in this building?"; 5 maximum points)

- registration (asked to repeat whatever is stated; 3 maximum points)

- attention and calculation (asked to spell words backwards, count backwards by seven; 5 maximum points)

- recall (asked to recall three words that were previously requested to be remembered; 3 maximum points)

- language (asked to name objects, such as pencil or watch; 2 maximum points)

- repetition (asked to speak back a phrase; 1 maximum point)
- complex commands (asked to draw figures and other various tasks; 6 maximum points)

Little information is available on allowances made in scoring the MMSE for patients whose first language is not English or who have difficulty with standard spoken English. However, in 2010, the Psychological Assessment Resources (PAR), the publisher of the test, released MMSE in a second edition (MMSE-2), with translations in Chinese (simplified), Dutch, French, German, Hindi, Italian, Russian, Spanish (Latin America), Spanish (Europe), and Spanish (United States). This second edition is authored by Marshal F. Folstein and Susan E. Folstein.

The MMSE-2 is similar to the first edition, with the basic structure and scoring retained and problems in the first edition corrected. In addition, some wording for the registration/recall and repetition tasks was changed slightly so that translations could be made. The comprehensive task was also altered to make it easier for persons with physical disabilities.

The second edition MMSE was normalized from a sample of over 1,500 people with either Alzheimer's disease or subcortical dementia. Reliability and validity was established with the use of this normative sample.

Several new features were added to the MMSE-2, including a brief version (BV) of the MMSE-2. The MMSE-2 BV is used when a fast cognitive screening test is required. Administration of the BV takes about five minutes. In addition, an expanded version (EV) of the MMSE-2 is also offered. The 90-item MMSE-2 EV expands on the scoring of the MMSE-2 by increasing the (scoring) sensitivity to individuals with less severe cognitive problems. As such, the expanded version includes two new tasks: story memory (which is an immediate recall of a short story) and processing speed (a symbol-digit coding task). The EV takes about 20 minutes to administer.

The MMSE-2 correlates well with the digit span forward and digit span backward subtests of the Wechsler Memory Scale, third edition; the digit symbol and block design subtests of the Wechsler Adult Intelligence Scale, revised; the Category Naming Test; the Boston Naming Test; the Trail Making Test; the Judgment of Line Orientation; the Stroop Color and Word Test; and the Hopkins Verbal Learning Test, revised.

Preparation

Preparation for the MMSE is neither necessary nor required.

KEY TERMS

Alzheimer's disease—A type of dementia that involves brain disease and progressive degradation of the brain, which involves memory loss and an eventual inability to think and function.

Cognitive—Relating to thoughts and the acquisition of knowledge.

Dementia—The progressive deterioration of intellectual functions, such as memory, within the brain. A type of dementia is Alzheimer's disease.

Schizophrenia—A mental disorder involving degraded thinking and emotions.

Aftercare

There is no aftercare as such for the person who takes this test, but test results are useful to medical professionals and caregivers. The MMSE is used primarily as a valid and reliable way to screen for Alzheimer's disease. Although it is not meant to be used solely as a screening device for such dementia, it can be used as a beginning test to identify persons without the disease. It is also used as a means to chart the course of cognitive declines over time. Consequently, it is a useful way to document a person's response to treatment in the past and to prescribe treatment in the future.

Risks

There is no risk to individuals taking this test. The MMSE should not be used as the sole criterion for assessment during differential **diagnosis** of psychiatric disorders, as there are many disorders and conditions that affect cognitive functioning. The results of the MMSE should be interpreted in the context of the patient's history, a full **mental status examination**, a physical examination, and laboratory findings, if any.

A patient's score on the MMSE must be interpreted according to his or her age and educational level. Scores range from 0 to 30. Whereas the median score is 29 for persons 18–24 years of age, it is 25 for those who are 80 years or older. The median score is 22 for persons with a fourth-grade education or less; 26 for those who completed the eighth grade; and 29 for those who completed high school or college. A complete table within the MMSE Pocket Norms Guide is available for interpreting MMSE scores according to the patient's reference groups for age and education level. Scores of 25 or higher are generally regarded as normal (without cognitive impairment), whereas scores of between 10 and

QUESTIONS TO ASK YOUR DOCTOR

- Do I need to find a qualified health care professional who is knowledgeable at administering the MMSE? If so, who do you recommend?

- Will the MMSE results indicate what treatment is needed?

- Where can I learn more about the MMSE?

- What are the best tests that can be taken to help verify the MMSE's conclusion? Which ones do you recommend?

19 indicate moderate cognitive impairment, and scores of less than 10 indicate severe impairment. It is possible to earn a high score but still have strong cognitive problems.

Precautions

The MMSE should be administered and scored only by a qualified healthcare professional, such as a **psychologist**, physician, or nurse.

Results

The maximum total score on the basic MMSE is 30. As a rule, scores of 20 or lower indicate delirium, dementia, **schizophrenia**, or a mood disorder. Normal subjects and those with a primary diagnosis of personality disorder score close to the median for their age and education level.

The MMSE-2 adds to the original MMSE by allowing for more precise evaluations of individuals with less severe forms of cognitive impairment, such as subcortical dementia. However, the second edition is generally equivalent to the original one, with the addition of the brief version and the expanded version. In fact, administrators can switch between the editions without altering longitudinal data and without changing scoring.

Resources

BOOKS

Barnovitz, Mary Ann, and Pria Joglekar. *Medical Psychiatry: The Quick Reference.* Philadelphia: Wolters Kluwer Health/Lippincott Williams & Wilkins, 2008.

Groth-Marnat, Gary. *Handbook of Psychological Assessment,* 5th ed. Hoboken, NJ: John Wiley and Sons, 2009.

Hersen, Michel, ed. *Industrial and Organizational Assessment.* Vol. 4 of *Comprehensive Handbook of Psychological*

Assessment. Edited by Jay C. Thomas. Hoboken, NJ: John Wiley and Sons, 2004.

Kellerman, Henry, and Anthony Burry. *Handbook of Psychodiagnostic Testing: Analysis of Personality in the Psychological Report,* 4th ed. New York City: Springer, 2010.

Leeming, David A., Kathryn Madden, and Stanton Marlan, eds. *Encyclopedia of Psychology and Religion.* New York City: Springer, 2011.

Lezak, Muriel D., Diane B. Howieson, and David W. Loring. *Neuropsychological Assessment,* 4th ed. New York: Oxford University Press, 2004.

McPhee, Stephen J., and Maxine A. Papadakis, eds. *Current Medical Diagnosis & Treatment 2011.* New York City: McGraw-Hill Medial, 2011.

WEBSITES

"Mini-Mental® State Examination, 2nd Edition." PAR: Creating Connections, Changing Lives. http://www4.parinc.com/Products/Product.aspx?ProductID=MMSE-2 (accessed July 27, 2011).

ORGANIZATIONS

American Psychiatric Association, 1000 Wilson Blvd., Ste. 1825, Arlington, VA, 22209-3901, (703) 907-7300, apa@psych.org, http://www.psych.org.

American Psychological Association, 750 1st St. NE, Washington, DC, 20002, (202) 336-5500, (800) 374-2721, http://www.apa.org.

National Institute of Neurological Disorders and Stroke, PO Box 5801, Bethesda, MD, 20892, (301) 496-5751, (800) 352-9424, http://www.ninds.nih.gov.

Rebecca J. Frey, PhD

Minnesota Multiphasic Personality Inventory

Definition

The Minnesota Multiphasic Personality Inventory, known as the MMPI, and its revised second edition (MMPI-2) are **psychological assessment** instruments used to gather information on the personalities, attitudes, and mental health of persons aged 18 and older to aid in clinical **diagnosis**. The test identifies mental illness and abnormal behavior by evaluating personality traits of the test taker. It is one of the most widely used personality inventory tests used in psychology, especially in the area of mental health.

Purpose

The results of the MMPI-2 allow the test administrator to make inferences about the client's typical behaviors and way of thinking. The clinician evaluates the test taker's personal characteristics by comparing the test taker's answers to those given by various psychiatric and nonpsychiatric comparison groups. By analyzing the test taker's patterns of response to the test items, the examiner is able to draw some tentative conclusions about the client's level of adaptation, behavioral characteristics, and personality traits. The outcomes help the examiner to determine the test taker's severity of impairment, outlook on life, approaches to problem solving, typical mood states, likely diagnoses, and potential problems in treatment. The MMPI-2 is used in a wide range of settings for a variety of procedures. The inventory is often used as part of inpatient psychiatric assessments, differential diagnosis, and outpatient evaluations. In addition, the instrument is often used by expert witnesses in forensic settings as part of an evaluation of a defendant's mental health, particularly in criminal cases. The MMPI has also been used to evaluate candidates for employment in some fields, and in educational counseling.

The MMPI-2 is preferred to the older MMPI because of its larger and more representative community comparison group (also referred to as the "normative" group). The original version of the MMPI is no longer available from the publisher, although some institutions continue to use old copies of it.

Description

The MMPI-2 is composed of 567 true/false items. It can be administered using a printed test booklet and an answer sheet filled in by hand, or by responding to the items on a computer. For the person with limited reading skills or the visually impaired respondent, the MMPI-2 items are available on audiotape. Although the MMPI-2 is frequently referred to as a test, it is not an academic test with "right" and "wrong" answers. Personality inventories like the MMPI-2 are intended to discover what the respondent is like as a person. A number of areas are "tapped into" by the MMPI-2 to answer such questions as: "Who is this person and how would he or she typically feel, think, and behave? What psychological problems and issues are relevant to this person?" Associations between patterns of answers to test items and particular traits or behaviors have been discovered through personality research conducted with the MMPI-2. The inventory items are not arranged into topics or areas on the test. The areas of personality that are measured are interspersed in a somewhat random fashion throughout the MMPI-2 booklet. Some examples of true-or-false statements similar to those on the MMPI-2 are:

- "I wake up with a headache almost every day."
- "I certainly feel worthless sometimes."

- "I have had peculiar and disturbing experiences that most other people have not had."
- "I would like to do the work of a choir director."

The MMPI-2 is intended for use with adults over age 18; a similar test, the MMPI-A, is designed for use with adolescents. The publisher produces the MMPI-2 in English and Spanish versions. The test has also been translated into Dutch-Flemish, two French dialects (France and Canada), German, Hebrew, Hmong, Italian, and three Spanish dialects (for Spain, Mexico, or the United States).

Origins

From the 1940s to the 1980s, the original MMPI was the most widely used and most intensely researched psychological assessment instrument in the United States and worldwide. American **psychologist** Starke R. Hathaway (1903–1984) and American neuropsychiatrist J. Charnley McKinley (1891–1950), both from the University of Minnesota (Minneapolis-St. Paul), developed the MMPI in the late 1930s, and it was first published in 1940. The MMPI utilized a process called empirical keying, which was an innovation. Most assessment tools prior to the MMPI used questions or tasks that were merely assumed by the test designer to realistically assess the behaviors under question. The empirical keying process was radically different. To develop empirical keying, the creators of the original MMPI wrote a wide range of true-or-false statements, many of which did not directly target typical psychiatric topics. Research was then conducted with groups of psychiatric inpatients, hospital visitors, college students and medical inpatients, who took the MMPI in order to determine which test items reliably differentiated the psychiatric patients from the others. The test developers also evaluated the items that reliably distinguished groups of patients with a particular diagnosis from the remaining pool of psychiatric patient respondents; these items were grouped into subsets referred to as clinical scales.

An additional innovation in the original MMPI was the presence of validity scales embedded in the test questions. These sets of items, scattered randomly throughout the MMPI-2, allow the examiner to assess whether the respondent answered questions in an open and honest manner, or tried to exaggerate or conceal information. One means of checking for distortions in responding to the instrument is asking whether the test taker refused to admit to some less-than-ideal actions that most people probably engage in and will admit to doing. An example of this type of question would be (true or false) "If I could sneak into the county fair or an amusement park without paying, I would." Another type of validity check that assesses honesty in responses is whether the client admits to participating in far more unusual behaviors and actions than were admitted to by both the psychiatric comparison group and the general community sample. The validity scales also identify whether the test taker responded inconsistently or randomly.

The MMPI-2, which has demonstrated continuity and comparability with its predecessor, was published in 1989. The revised version was based on a much larger and more racially and culturally diverse normative community comparison group than the original version. Also, more in-depth and stringent research on the qualities and behaviors associated with different patterns of scores allows improved accuracy in predicting test-respondents' traits and behaviors from their test results.

Three years later, in 1992, the MMPI-A was first published, with A standing for Adolescent. The most recent revision, published in 2006, consists of 478 items within 12 test categories; a short form consisting of 350 items is also available. The MMPI-A, administered individually or within a group, targets adolescents 14 to 18 years of age.

In 2003, the MMPI-2-RF (Restructured Form) was introduced. The MMPI-2-RF consists of 338 items and cites itself as being an alternative to, not a replacement for, the MMPI-2. The most recent revision was published in 2008 by Pearson Assessments.

Scoring

The clinical scales within the MMPI-2 are designed to measure common diagnoses. They include:

- Scale 1 (Hypochondriasis [Hs] Scale) measures bodily symptoms as perceived by the person with regards to their health and health issues. It contains 32 items.

- Scale 2 (Depression [D] Scale) measures a person's symptoms with regard to depression. It contains 57 items.

- Scale 3 (Hysteria [Hy] Scale) measures the emotionality of a person, along with their perception of vulnerability and their awareness of such problems. It contains 60 items.

- Scale 4 (Psychopathic Deviate [Pd] Scale) measures the amount of control that a person wants in life, the amount of anger resulting from lack of control in one's life, and the amount of disrespect for the rules of society. It contains 50 items.

- Scale 5 (Masculinity/Femininity [MF] Scale) measures how men and women compare with masculine and feminine (respectively) interests and behaviors of stereotypical characters. It contains 56 items.

- Scale 6 (Paranoia [Pa] Scale) measures a person's level of trust, suspiciousness, and sensitivity to such emotions. It contains 40 items.

- Scale 7 (Psychasthenia [Pt] Scale) measures levels and tendencies of anxiety, worry, doubts, and obsessiveness. It contains 48 items.

- Scale 8 (Schizophrenia [Sc] Scale) measures the unusual cognitive, perceptual, and emotional experiences of a person. It contains 78 items.

- Scale 9 (Mania [Ma] Scale) measures a person's level of energy. It contains 46 items.

- Scale 0 (Social Introversion [Si] Scale) measures the level at which a person enjoys and is comfortable around other people. It contains 69 items.

Specific conditions or syndromes that the test can help identify include **depression**, **hypochondriasis**, hysteria, **paranoia**, and **schizophrenia**. Raw scores based on deviations from standard responses are entered on personality profile forms to obtain the individual results. There is also a validity scale to thwart attempts to "fake" the test. Because the MMPI-2 is a complex test whose results can sometimes be ambiguous (and/or skewed by various factors), professionals tend to be cautious in interpreting it, often preferring broad descriptions to specific psychiatric diagnoses, unless these are supported by further testing and observable behavior. A fifth-grade reading level is required in order to take the test. However, a tape-recorded version is available for those with limited literacy, visual impairments, or other problems.

Risks

Although the MMPI-2 may be administered by trained clerical staff or by computer, for best results the examiner should meet the test taker before giving the test in order to establish the context and reassure the client. Most importantly, the test responses should be interpreted only by a qualified mental health professional with postgraduate education in psychological assessment and specialized training in the use of the MMPI-2. While computer-generated narrative reports are available and can be a useful tool, they should be evaluated (and edited if needed) by the on-site professional to individualize the reported results. Computer scoring and hypothesis generation is complex, and only reputable software programs should be used.

Although the MMPI-2 may yield extensive information about the client, it is not a replacement for a clinical interview. The clinical interview helps the test

KEY TERMS

Battery—A number of separate items (such as tests) used together. In psychology, a group or series of tests given with a common purpose, such as personality assessment or measurement of intelligence.

Biopsychosocial history—A history of significant past and current experiences that influence client behaviors, including medical, educational, employment, and interpersonal experiences. Alcohol or drug use and involvement with the legal system are also assessed in a biopsychosocial history.

Empirical—Verified by actual experience or by scientific experimentation.

Forensic—Pertaining to courtroom procedure or evidence used in courts of law.

Hypothesis—An assumption, proposition, or educated guess that can be tested empirically.

Personality inventory—A type of psychological test that is designed to assess a client's major personality traits, behavioral patterns, coping styles, and similar characteristics. The MMPI-2 is an example of a personality inventory.

Psychological assessment—A process of gathering and synthesizing information about a person's psychological makeup and history for a specific purpose, which may be educational, diagnostic, or forensic.

Scale—A subset of test items from a multi-item test.

administrator to develop conclusions that best apply to the client from the many hypotheses generated from test results. Furthermore, important aspects of the client's behaviors may emerge in an interview that were not reflected in the test results. For similar reasons, the test results should not be interpreted until the clinician has obtained a biopsychosocial history from the client.

The MMPI-2 should be administered as part of a battery, or group, of tests rather than as an isolated assessment measure. A comprehensive assessment of a person will typically include the Rorschach; the **Thematic Apperception Test** (TAT) or the Sentence Completion Test; and the Wechsler Adult Intelligence Scale, Revised (WAIS-R) or similar test of cognitive functioning, as well as the MMPI-2.

The test has been criticized in the past as being too personal when asking many of its questions, with topics pertaining to a person's sex life, religious beliefs, and political viewpoints. Lawsuits attempting to protect the privacy of individuals and the fairness of employment practices have been brought against individuals and organizations that use the test.

Results

The true/false items are organized after scoring into validity, clinical, and content scales. The inventory may be scored manually or by computer. After scoring, the configuration of the test taker's scale scores is marked on a profile form that contrasts each client's responses to results obtained by the representative community comparison group. The clinician is able to compare a respondent's choices to those of a large normative comparison group as well as to the results derived from earlier MMPI and MMPI-2 studies. The clinician forms inferences about the client by analyzing his or her response patterns on the validity, clinical and content scales, using published guidebooks to the MMPI-2. These texts are based on results obtained from over 10,000 MMPI/MMPI-2 research studies.

In addition to the standard validity, clinical, and content scales, numerous additional scales for the MMPI have been created for special purposes over the years by researchers. These special supplementary scale scores are often incorporated into the examiner's interpretation of the test results. Commonly used supplementary scales include the MacAndrews Revised Alcoholism Scale, the Addiction Potential Scale, and the Anxiety Scale. The clinician may also choose to obtain computerized reporting, which yields behavioral hypotheses about the respondent, using scoring and interpretation algorithms applied to a commercial database.

Resources

BOOKS

Andrade, Heidi L., and Gregory J. Cizek, eds. *Handbook of Formative Assessment.* New York: Routledge, 2009.

Butcher, James N., and Carolyn L. Williams. *Essentials of MMPI2 and MMPIA Interpretation.* 2nd ed. Minneapolis: University of Minnesota Press, 2000.

Butcher, J. N., et al. *MMPI-2: Manual for Administration, Scoring and Interpretation.* Revised. Minneapolis: University of Minnesota Press, 2001.

Drummond, Robert J., and Karen Jones. *Assessment Procedures for Counselors and Helping Professionals.* 7th ed. Boston: Pearson, 2010.

Frick, Paul J., Christopher T. Barry, and Randy W. Kamphaus. *Clinical Assessment of Child and Adolescent Personality and Behavior.* 3rd ed. New York: Springer, 2010.

Graham, John R. *MMPI-2: Assessing Personality and Psychopathology.* 5th ed. New York: Oxford University Press, 2011.

Graham, John R., Yossef S. Ben-Porath, and John L. McNulty. *MMPI-2: Correlates for Outpatient Community Mental*

Health Settings. Minneapolis: University of Minnesota Press, 1999.

Green, Susan K., and Robert L. Johnson. *Assessment is Essential.* Boston: McGraw-Hill, 2009.

Kaufman, James C. *Intelligent Testing: Integrating Psychological Theory and Clinical Practice.* Cambridge, UK: Cambridge University Press, 2009.

Spies, Robert A., Janet F. Carlson, and Kurt F. Geisinger. *The Eighteenth Mental Measurements Yearbook.* Buros Center for Testing, 2010.

PERIODICALS

Bennett, Drake. "Against Types." *Boston Globe*, September 12, 2004. http://www.boston.com/news/globe/ideas/articles/2004/09/12/against_types (accessed October 22, 2011).

Butcher, James N. "MMPI-2/MMPI-A Research Project: Research and Clinical Applications," University of Minnesota. http://www1.umn.edu/mmpi (accessed October 22, 2011).

"Dr. Starke R. Hathaway, 80; Invented Psychological Test." *The New York Times,* July 5, 1984. http://www.nytimes.com/1984/07/05/obituaries/dr-starke-r-hathaway-80-invented-psychological-test.html (accessed October 22, 2011).

McNulty, J.L., J.R. Graham, and Y. S. Ben-Porath. "An Empirical Examination of the Correlates of Well-defined and Not Defined MMPI-2 Codetypes." *Journal of Personality Assessment* 71, no. 3 (1998): 393–410.

Paul, Annie Murphy. "Invasion of the Minnesota Normals." *The Believer,* (August 2004), http://www.believermag.com/issues/200408/?read=article_paul (accessed October 22, 2011).

Deborah Rosch Eifert, Ph.D.
William Arthur Atkins

Mirtazapine

Definition

Mirtazapine is most commonly used to treat **depression**. Mirtazapine is available in the United States under the trade names of Remeron and Remeron SolTab.

Mirtazapine, sold under the trade name Remeron, is taken by mouth and swallowed whole. Remeron SolTabs should be allowed to dissolve in the mouth. No water is needed when taking the SolTabs, since these tablets disintegrate in saliva and are not swallowed whole.

Purpose

Mirtazapine is best known for treating depression. However, it may also be used for treating anxiety or to make people drowsy just before surgery.

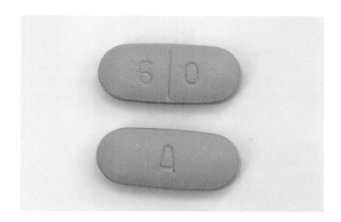

Mirtazapine, 30 mg. (© *Custom Medical Stock Photo, Inc. Reproduced by permission.*)

Description

Mirtazapine is usually thought of as an antidepressant, that is, a drug that alleviates symptoms of depression. Approved by the Federal Drug Administration (FDA) in 1996, it is believed to alter the activities of some chemicals in the **brain** and, in this way, reduce chemical imbalances responsible for causing depression and anxiety. As with all **antidepressants**, it may take several weeks of treatment before full beneficial effects are seen. Mirtazapine is broken down by the liver and eliminated from the body mostly by the kidneys. It is supplied in 15, 30, and 45 mg tablets.

Recommended dosage

The recommended initial dose of mirtazapine in 15 mg taken at bedtime. The dose may be increased in 15 mg increments every one or two weeks as needed until symptoms of depression or anxiety resolve. Typical doses range between 15 and 45 mg. Dosages above 45 mg per day are not recommended. Elderly people or those with liver or kidney disease should use mirtazapine carefully, since they may be more sensitive to some of the drug's side effects.

Precautions

Mirtazapine may cause weight gain and may increase cholesterol levels and should be used carefully in overweight individuals and those with high cholesterol levels. If symptoms of fever, sore throat, or irritation in the mouth occur, a healthcare provider should be notified. Rarely, mirtazapine may lower blood counts, causing people to be at an increased risk of serious complications, including infections. In theory, mirtazapine may increase the tendency for **seizures**. As a result, it should be used carefully in people with epilepsy or

KEY TERMS

Anxiety—An emotion that can be experienced as a troubled feeling, sense of dread, fear of the future, or distress over a possible threat to a person's physical or mental well-being.

Depression—A mental state characterized by feelings of sadness, despair, discouragement, low energy, often with oversleeping and/or overeating.

Monoamine oxidase inhibitors (MAOIs)—A class of antidepressants used to treat certain types of depression. Monoamine oxidase inhibitors are especially useful in treating people whose depression is combined with other problems such as anxiety, panic attacks, phobias, or the desire to sleep too much.

Seizure—A convulsion, or uncontrolled discharge of nerve cells that may spread to other cells throughout the brain.

other seizure disorders. Mirtazapine may alter moods or cause mania. It should be used carefully in people with a history of mania. Mirtazapine may alter liver function and should be used cautiously by those with a history of liver disease. If abdominal pain, yellowing of the skin or eyes, darkening of urine, or itching occurs, a healthcare provider should be notified immediately.

More than 50% of individuals using mirtazapine report feeling sleepier than normal and 7% feel dizzy. As a result, people taking mirtazapine should not participate in activities that require mental alertness, such as driving, until they know how the drug will affect them. Because there is an increased likelihood of **suicide** in depressed individuals, close supervision of those at high risk for suicide attempts using this drug is recommended. Children and young people up to age 24 are particularly affected, especially during the early stages of treatment. Mirtazapine is not recommended in pregnant or breastfeeding women. Use of the medicine should not be abruptly stopped, as withdrawal symptoms may occur.

Side effects

The most common side effects that cause people to stop taking mirtazapine are sleepiness and nausea. Other common side effects are dizziness, increased appetite, and weight gain. Less common adverse effects are weakness and muscle aches, flu-like symptoms, low blood-cell counts, high cholesterol, back pain, chest pain, rapid heartbeats, dry mouth, constipation, water

QUESTIONS TO ASK YOUR DOCTOR

- What kind of changes can I expect to see or feel with this medication?
- Does it matter what time of day I take this medication? If so, what is the recommendation?
- Should I take this medication with or without food?
- What are the side effects associated with this medication?
- Will this medication interact or interfere with other medications I am currently taking?
- What symptoms or adverse effects are important enough that I should seek immediate treatment?

retention, difficulty sleeping, nightmares, abnormal thoughts, vision disturbances, ringing in the ears, abnormal taste in the mouth, tremor, confusion, upset stomach, and increased urination.

Interactions

Use of mirtazapine with **monoamine oxidase inhibitors (MAOIs),** such as Parnate (**tranylcypromine**) and Nardil (**phenelzine**), is prohibited due to the potential for high fever, muscle stiffness, sudden muscle spasms, rapid changes in heart rate and blood pressure, and the possibility of death. In fact, there should be a lapse of at least 14 days between taking an MAOI and taking mirtazapine (and vice versa).

Because mirtazapine may cause drowsiness, it should be used carefully with other medications that also make people prone to sleepiness, such as antidepressants, antipsychotics, antihistamines, antianxiety agents, and alcohol. Increased sleepiness has been reported when mirtazapine was used with both alcohol and the antianxiety drug **diazepam.**

Resources

BOOKS

Albers, Lawrence J., Rhoda K. Hahn, and Christopher Reist. *Handbook of Psychiatric Drugs.* Laguna Hills, CA: Current Clinical Strategies, 2010.

American Society of Health-System Pharmacists. *AHFS Drug Information 2011.* Bethesda, MD: ASHP, 2011.

Graham, George. *The Disordered Mind: An Introduction to Philosophy of Mind and Mental Illness.* New York: Routledge, 2010.

Holland, Leland Norman, and Michael Patrick Adams. *Core Concepts in Pharmacology.* 3rd ed. New York: Prentice Hall, 2011.

North, Carol, and Sean Yutzy. *Goodwin and Guze's Psychiatric Diagnosis.* New York: Oxford University Press, 2010.

Preston, John D., John H. O'Neal, and Mary C. Talaga. *Handbook of Clinical Psychopharmacology for Therapists,* 6th ed. Oakland, CA: New Harbinger, 2010.

ORGANIZATIONS

American Academy of Clinical Toxicology, 6728 Old McLean Village Dr., McLean, VA, 22101, (703) 556-9222, Fax: (703) 556-8729, admin@clintox.org, http://www.clintox.org.

American Psychiatric Association, 1000 Wilson Blvd., Ste. 1825, Arlington, VA, 22209-3901, (703) 907-7300, apa@psych.org, http://www.psych.org.

American Psychological Association, 750 1st St. NE, Washington, DC, 20002-4242, (202) 336-5500; TDD/TTY: (202) 336-6123, (800) 374-2721, http://www.apa.org.

American Society for Clinical Pharmacology and Therapeutics, 528 N Washington St., Alexandria, VA, 22314, (703) 836-6981, info@ascpt.org, http://www.ascpt.org.

Depression and Bipolar Support Alliance, 730 N Franklin St., Ste. 501, Chicago, IL, 60654, (800) 826-3632, Fax: (312) 642-7243, http://www.dbsalliance.org.

National Alliance on Mental Illness, 2107 Wilson Blvd., Ste. 300, Arlington, VA, 22201-3042, Fax: (703) 524-9094, (800) 950-6264, http://www.nami.org.

National Institute of Mental Health, 6001 Executive Blvd., Rm. 8184, MSC 9663, Bethesda, MD, 20892-9663, (301) 433-4513; TTY: (301) 443-8431, Fax: (301) 443-4279, (866) 615-6464; TTY: (866) 415-8051, nimhinfo@nih.gov, http://www.nimh.nih.gov.

U.S. Food and Drug Administration, 10903 New Hampshire Ave., Silver Spring, MD, 20993-0002, (888) INFO-FDA (463-6332), http://www.fda.gov.

Kelly Karpa, RPh, PhD.
Laura Jean Cataldo, RN, EdD

Mixed episode

Definition

A mixed episode is a discrete period during which a person experiences nearly daily fluctuations in mood that qualify for diagnoses of **manic episode** and major depressive episode. Over the course of at least one week, the mood of a person experiencing a mixed episode will rapidly change between abnormal happiness or euphoria and sadness or irritability.

Description

To qualify for a **diagnosis** of mixed episode, symptoms must be severe enough to interfere with an individual's ability to carry out daily routines at work or home, or to require **hospitalization**. Males may be more susceptible to this condition than females. Young people and those more than 60 years of age with **bipolar disorder** may be more prone to mixed episodes than others. A manic episode or a major depressive episode is more likely to turn into a mixed episode than vice versa. Manic episodes can also appear in an individual who does not suffer from these or other disturbances. If the episode can be attributed to side effects related to any medical treatment, medical condition, medication, or drugs of abuse, it is not classified as a mixed episode.

See also Depression

Dean A. Haycock, Ph.D.

Mixed receptive-expressive language disorder

Definition

Mixed receptive-expressive language disorder is diagnosed when a child has problems expressing him- or herself using spoken language and also has problems understanding what people say to him or her.

Demographics

Mixed receptive-expressive language disorder is diagnosed in about 5% of preschool-age children and 3% of children in school. It is less common than expressive language disorder. Children who have mixed receptive-expressive language disorder are more likely to have other disorders as well. Between 40% and 60% of preschoolers who have this disorder may also have phonological disorder (difficulty forming sounds). **Reading disorder** is linked to as many as half the children with mixed receptive-expressive language disorder who are of school age. Children with mixed receptive-expressive language disorder are also more likely to have psychiatric disorders, especially attention deficit disorder (ADD); it is estimated that 30%–60% of children with mixed receptive-expressive language disorder also have ADD. Children from families with a history of language disorders are more likely to have this or other language disorders.

Description

Mixed receptive-expressive language disorder is generally a disorder of childhood. There are two types of mixed receptive-expressive language disorder: developmental and acquired. Developmental mixed receptive-expressive language disorder does not have a known cause and normally appears at the time that a child is learning to talk. Acquired mixed receptive-expressive language disorder is caused by direct damage to the **brain**. It occurs suddenly after such events as a **stroke** or traumatic head injury. The acquired type can occur at any age.

Causes and symptoms

Causes

There is no known cause of developmental mixed receptive-expressive language disorder. Researchers are conducting ongoing studies to determine whether biological or environmental factors may be involved. The acquired form of the disorder results from direct damage to the brain. Damage can be sustained during a stroke, or as the result of traumatic head injury, **seizures**, or other medical conditions. The specific symptoms of the acquired form of the disorder generally depend on the parts of the patient's brain that have been injured and the severity of the damage.

Symptoms

The signs and symptoms of mixed receptive-expressive language disorder are for the most part the same as the symptoms of **expressive language disorder**. The disorder has signs and symptoms that vary considerably from child to child. In general, mixed receptive-expressive language disorder is characterized by a child's difficulty with spoken communication. The child does not have problems with the pronunciation of words, which is found in **phonological disorder**. The child does, however, have problems constructing coherent sentences, using proper grammar, recalling words, or similar communication problems. A child with mixed receptive-expressive language disorder is not able to communicate thoughts, needs, or wants at the same level or with the same complexity as his or her peers. In addition, the child often has a smaller vocabulary than his or her peers.

Children with mixed receptive-expressive language disorder also have significant problems understanding what other people are saying to them. This lack of comprehension may result in inappropriate responses or failure to follow directions. Some people think these children are being deliberately stubborn or obnoxious, but this is not the case. They simply do not understand what is being said. Some children with this disorder have problems understanding such specific types of terms as abstract nouns, complex sentences, or spatial terms.

Diagnosis

The **diagnosis** would be expressive language disorder. If the child is intellectually disabled, hard of hearing, or has other physical problems, the difficulties with speech must be greater than generally occurs with the other disabilities the child may have in order for the child to be diagnosed with this disorder.

The disorder is usually diagnosed in children because a parent or teacher expresses concern about the child's problems with spoken communication. The child's pediatrician may give the child a physical examination to rule out such medical problems as hearing loss. Specific testing for mixed expressive-receptive language disorder requires the examiner to demonstrate that the child not only communicates less well than expected, but also understands speech less well. It can be hard, however, to determine what a child understands. As a result, most examiners will use non-verbal tests in addition to tests that require spoken questions and answers in order to assess the child's condition as accurately as possible. In children who are mildly hearing-impaired, the problem can often be corrected by using hearing aids. Children who speak a language other than English (or the dominant language of their society) at home should be tested in that language if possible. In some cases, the child's ability to understand and communicate in English is the problem, not his or her competence with spoken language in general.

Treatment

Mixed receptive-expressive language disorder should be treated as soon as it is identified. Early **intervention** is the key to a successful outcome. Treatment involves teachers, siblings, parents, and anyone else who interacts regularly with the child. Regularly scheduled one-on-one treatment that focuses on specific language skills can also be effective, especially when combined with a more general approach involving family members and caregivers. Teaching children with this disorder specific communication skills so they can interact with their peers is important, as problems in this area may lead to later social isolation, **depression**, or behavioral problems. Children who are diagnosed early and taught reading skills may benefit especially, because problems with reading are often associated with mixed receptive-expressive language disorder and can cause serious long-term academic problems. There is little information comparing different treatment methods; often several are tried in combination.

KEY TERMS

Phonological disorder—A developmental disorder of childhood in which the child fails to use speech sounds that are appropriate for his or her age level and native language or dialect.

Prognosis

The developmental form of mixed receptive-expressive language disorder is less likely to resolve well than the developmental form of expressive language disorder. Most children with the disorder continue to have problems with language skills. They develop them at a much slower rate than their peers, which puts them at a growing disadvantage throughout their educational career. Some persons diagnosed with the disorder as children have significant problems with expressing themselves and understanding others in adult life.

The prognosis of the acquired type of mixed receptive-expressive language disorder depends on the nature and location of the brain injury. Some people get their language skills back over days or months. For others it takes years, and some people never fully recover expressive language function or the ability to understand speech.

Prevention

Because the causes of developmental mixed receptive-expressive language disorder are unclear, there are no specific ways to prevent it. A healthy diet during pregnancy and regular prenatal care are always recommended. Because the acquired form of the disorder is caused by damage to the brain, anything that helps to prevent brain damage may offer protection against that form of the disorder. Preventive measures include such precautions as lowering blood cholesterol levels, which may help to prevent stroke, or wearing bicycle helmets or automobile seat belts to prevent traumatic head injury.

Resources

BOOKS

American Psychiatric Association. *Diagnostic and Statistical Manual of Mental Disorders*. 4th ed., text rev. Washington, DC: American Psychiatric Publishing, 2000.

Sadock, Benjamin J., and Virginia A. Sadock, eds. *Comprehensive Textbook of Psychiatry*. Vol. 2. 7th ed. Philadelphia: Lippincott Williams and Wilkins, 2000.

PERIODICALS

Stein, Martin T., ed. "Expressive Language Delay in a Toddler." *Journal of Developmental & Behavioral Pediatrics* 22, no. 2 (April 2001): S99–S103.

ORGANIZATIONS

American Academy of Pediatrics, 141 Northwest Point Blvd., Elk Grove Village, IL, 60007-1098, (847) 434-4000, Fax: (847) 434-8000, http://www.aap.org.

American Psychological Association, 750 1st Street NE, Washington, DC, 20002-4242, (202) 336-5500, TDD/TTY: (202) 336-6123, (800) 374-2721, http://www.apa.org.

American Speech-Language-Hearing Association, 2200 Research Blvd., Rockville, MD, 20785, (301) 296-5700, http://www.asha.org.

Tish Davidson, A.M.

MMPI *see* **Minnesota Multiphasic Personality Inventory**

MMSE *see* **Mini-mental state examination**

Moban *see* **Molindone**

Modeling

Definition

Modeling, which is also called observational learning or imitation, is a behaviorally based procedure that involves the use of live or symbolic models to demonstrate a particular behavior, thought, or attitude that a client may want to acquire or change. Modeling is sometimes called vicarious learning, because the client need not actually perform the behavior in order to learn it.

One method of learning is modeling, or imitating another person to learn a skill, as is done in dance classes. (© ImageState/Alamy)

Purpose

Modeling therapy is based on social learning theory. This theory emphasizes the importance of learning that is derived from observing and imitating role models, and learning about rewards and punishments that follow behavior. The technique has been used to eliminate unwanted behaviors, reduce excessive fears, facilitate learning of social behaviors, and many more. Modeling may be used either to strengthen or to weaken previously learned behaviors.

Modeling has been used effectively to treat individuals with **anxiety disorders**; **post-traumatic stress disorder**; **specific phobias**; **obsessive-compulsive disorder**; eating disorders; **attention deficit hyperactivity disorder**; and **conduct disorder**. It has also been used successfully in helping individuals acquire such social skills as public speaking or assertiveness. The effectiveness of modeling has led to its use in behavioral treatment of persons with **substance abuse** disorders, who frequently lack important behavioral skills. These persons may lack assertiveness, including the ability to say "no"; in addition, they may have thought patterns that make them more susceptible to substance abuse.

Modeling when used alone has been shown to be effective for short-term learning. It is, however, insufficient for long-lasting behavior change if the target behavior does not produce rewards that sustain it. Modeling works well when it is combined with role-play and **reinforcement**. These three components are used in a sequence of modeling, role-play, and reinforcement. Role-play is defined as practice or behavioral rehearsal of a skill to be used later in real-life situations. Reinforcement is defined as rewarding the model's performance or the client's performance of the newly acquired skill in practice or in real-life situations.

Several factors increase the effectiveness of modeling therapy in changing behaviors. Modeling effects have been shown to be more powerful when:

• The model is highly skilled in enacting the behavior; is likable or admirable; is friendly; is the same sex and age; and is rewarded immediately for the performance of the particular behavior.

• The target behavior is clearly demonstrated with very few unnecessary details; is presented from the least to the most difficult level of behavior; and several different models are used to perform the same behavior(s).

Description

Types of modeling

Therapy begins with an assessment of the client's presenting problem(s). The assessment usually covers several areas of life, including developmental history (the client's family background, education, employment, social relationships); past traumatic experiences; medical and psychiatric history; and an outline of the client's goals. The client works with the therapist to list specific treatment goals; to determine the target behavior(s) to be learned or changed; and to develop a clear picture of what the behavior(s) will look like. The therapist then explains the rationale and concepts of the treatment. He or she also considers any negative consequences that may arise as the client makes changes in his or her behavior.

The client then observes the model enacting the desired behavior. Some models may demonstrate poor or inadequate behaviors as well as those that are effective. This contrast helps the client to identify ineffective behaviors as well as desired ones. Modeling can be done in several different ways, including live modeling, symbolic modeling, participant modeling, or covert modeling.

Live modeling refers to watching a real person, usually the therapist, perform the desired behavior the client has chosen to learn. For example, the therapist might model good telephone manners for a client who wants a job in a field that requires frequent telephone contact with customers.

Symbolic modeling includes filmed or videotaped models demonstrating the desired behavior. Other examples of symbolic models include photographs, picture books, and plays. A common example of symbolic modeling is a book for children about going to the hospital, intended to reduce a child's anxiety about hospitals and operations. With child clients, cartoon figures or puppets can be used as the models. Self-modeling is another form of symbolic modeling in which clients are videotaped performing the target behavior. The video is than replayed and clients can observe their behaviors and how they appear to others. For example, public speaking is one of the most common feared situations in the general adult population. A law student who is afraid of having to present arguments in a courtroom might be videotaped speaking to classmates who are role-playing the judge and members of the jury. The student can then review the videotape and work on his or her speech problems or other aspects of the performance that he or she would like to change.

In participant modeling, the therapist models anxiety-evoking behaviors for the client, and then prompts the client to engage in the behavior. The client first watches as the therapist approaches the feared object, and then approaches the object in steps or stages with the therapist's encouragement and support. This type of modeling is often used in the treatment of specific phobias. For example, a person who is afraid of dogs might be asked to watch the therapist touch or pet a dog, or perhaps accompany the therapist on a brief walk with a dog. Then, with the therapist's encouragement, the client might begin by touching or holding a stuffed dog, then watching a live dog from a distance, then perhaps walking a small dog on a leash, and eventually by degrees touching and petting a live dog.

In covert modeling, clients are asked to use their imagination, visualizing a particular behavior as the therapist describes the imaginary situation in detail. For example, a child may be asked to imagine one of his or her favorite cartoon characters interacting appropriately with other characters. An adult client is asked to imagine an admired person in his or her life performing a behavior that the client wishes to learn. For example, a person may greatly admire their mother for the way she handled the challenges of coming to the United States from another country. If the client is worried about the challenge of a new situation in their own life (changing careers, having their first child, etc.), the therapist may ask them to imagine how their mother would approach the new situation, and then imagine themselves acting with their mother's courage and wisdom.

Models in any of these forms may be presented as either a coping or a mastery model. The coping model is shown as initially fearful or incompetent and then is shown as gradually becoming comfortable and competent performing the feared behavior. A coping model might show a small child who is afraid of swimming in the ocean, for example. The little boy or girl watches smaller children having fun playing in the waves along the edge of the shore. Gradually the child moves closer and closer to the water and finally follows a child his or her age into the surf. The mastery model shows no fear and is competent from the beginning of the demonstration. Coping models are considered more appropriate for reducing fear because they look more like the client, who will probably make mistakes and have some setbacks when trying the new behavior.

Having the model speak his or her thoughts aloud is more effective than having a model who does not verbalize. As the models speak, they show the client how to think through a particular problem or situation. A common example of this type of modeling is sports or cooking instruction. A golf or tennis pro who is trying to teach a beginner how to hold and swing the club or racquet will often talk as they demonstrate the correct stance and body movements. Similarly, a master chef will often talk to students in a cooking class while he or she is cutting the ingredients for a dish, preparing a sauce, kneading dough, or doing other necessary tasks. The model's talking while performing an action also engages the client's sense of hearing, taste, or smell as well as sight. Multisensory involvement enhances the client's learning.

Role-playing

Role-playing is a technique that allows the client opportunities to imitate the modeled behaviors, which strengthens what has been learned. Role-play can be defined as practice or behavior rehearsal; it allows the client to receive feedback about the practice as well as encouraging the use of the newly learned skill in real-life situations. For example, a group of people who are trying to learn social skills might practice the skills needed for a job interview or for dealing with a minor problem (returning a defective item to a store, asking someone for directions, etc.). Role-play can also be used for modeling, in that the therapist may role-play certain situations with clients. During practice, the therapist frequently coaches, prompts, and shapes the client's enactment of the behavior so the rehearsals come increasingly close to the desired behavior.

Feedback and social reinforcement of the client's performance in the practice phase is an important motivator for behavior change. Feedback may take the form of praise, approval, or encouragement, or it may be corrective, with concrete suggestions for improving the performance. Suggestions are followed by additional practice. Such tangible reinforcements as money, food, candy, or tokens have been used with young children and chronic psychiatric patients. The therapist may teach the client how to use self-reinforcement; that is, using self-praise after performing the desired behavior. The purpose of reinforcement is to shift the client's performance concerns from external evaluation by others to internal evaluation of their own efforts.

Modeling in group settings

Modeling has been shown to be effective in such group programs as **social skills training** and **assertiveness training** as well as in individual therapy. The general approach to both social skills training and assertiveness training is the incorporation of the modeling, role-play, and reinforcement sequence. After assessment of each group member's presenting problem, each member is asked to keep a diary of what happened when the situation occurred during the week. Group members develop goals for dealing with their individual situations, and each person determines how he or she can meet these goals. Modeling is done with either the therapist or other group members role-playing how to deal effectively with a particular problem situation.

Length of treatment

While modeling therapy is a relatively short-term approach to behavioral change, some therapeutic techniques take longer than others. Imagery, for example, requires more sessions than in vivo (real-life) treatments.

In vivo work that takes place outside the therapist's office would require longer time periods for each session. Other considerations include the nature of the client's problem; the client's willingness to do homework; the client's financial resources; and the presence and extent of the client's support network. The therapist's length of experience and personal style also affect the length of therapy.

There are, however, guidelines of treatment length for some disorders. Treatment of obsessive-compulsive disorder may require five weekly sessions for approximately three weeks, with weekly follow-up sessions for several months. Depressive disorders may require 3–6 months, with the client experiencing short-term relief after 3–4 weeks of treatment. General anxiety disorder may also take several months of weekly sessions. The length of treatment depends on the ability to define and assess the target behaviors. Clients may meet with the therapist several times a week at the beginning of treatment; then weekly for several months; then monthly for follow-up sessions that may become fewer in number or spaced more widely until therapy is terminated.

Results

Modeling or observational learning is effective as a method of learning such behaviors as self-assertion, self-disclosure, helping others, empathic behaviors, moral judgment, and many other interpersonal skills. Modeling is also effective in eliminating or reducing such undesirable behaviors as uncontrolled aggression, smoking, weight problems, and single phobias.

The expected outcome is that clients will be able to use their new behaviors outside the treatment setting in real-life situations. This result is called transfer of training, generalization, or maintenance. Homework is the most frequently used technique for transfer of training. Homework may represent a contractual agreement between the therapist and the client in which the client gives a report on his or her progress at each meeting.

To ensure that generalization occurs and that clients will use their new skills, several "transfer enhancers" are used to increase the likelihood of successful transfer of training. Transfer enhancers include:

- Giving clients appropriate rationales and concepts, rules, or strategies for using skills properly.

- Giving clients ample opportunity to practice new skills correctly and successfully.

- Making the treatment setting as much like the real-life situation as possible.

- Giving clients opportunities to practice their new skills in a variety of physical and interpersonal settings.

- Giving clients adequate external social reinforcement and encouraging internal self-reinforcement as they use their skills successfully in real life.

Resources

BOOKS

Braswell, Lauren, and Philip C. Kendall. "Cognitive-Behavioral Therapy with Youth." In *Handbook of Cognitive Behavioral Therapies,* edited by Keith S. Dobson. 2nd ed. New York: The Guilford Press. 2001.

Jinks, Gordon. "Specific Strategies and Techniques." In *Handbook of Counselling and Psychotherapy,* edited by Colin Feltham and Ian Horton. Thousand Oaks, CA: Sage Publications, 2006.

Sharf, Richard S. "Behavior Therapy." Chapter 8 in *Theories of Psychotherapy and Counseling: Concepts and Cases.* 5th ed. Farmington Hills, MI: Cengage Learning, 2012.

ORGANIZATIONS

American Psychological Association, 750 1st Street NE, Washington, DC, 20002-4242, (202) 336-5500, TDD/TTY: (202) 336-6123, (800) 374-2721, http://www.apa.org.

Association for Behavioral and Cognitive Therapies, 305 Seventh Ave., 16th Floor, New York, NY, 10001-6008, (212) 647-1890, Fax: (212) 647-1865, http://www.abct.org.

Mental Health America, 2000 N. Beauregard Street, 6th Floor, Alexandria, VA, 22311, (703) 684-7722, (800) 969-6642, Fax: (703) 684-5968, http://www1.nmha.org.

National Institute of Mental Health, 6001 Executive Blvd., Room 8184, MSC 9663, Bethesda, MD, 20892-9663, (301) 433-4513, TTY: (301) 443-8431, Fax: (301) 443-4279, (866) 615-6464, TTY: (866) 415-8051, nimhinfo@nih.gov, http://www.nimh.nih.gov.

Janice Van Buren, Ph.D.

Molindone

Definition

Molindone is an antipsychotic previously sold under the trade name Moban. In early 2010, the supplier of molindone ceased production on the drug, and by June of the same year, it was no longer available in the United States.

Purpose

Molindone was used to treat psychotic symptoms assosiated with **depression**, mania, or **schizophrenia**.

KEY TERMS

Depression—A mental state characterized by feelings of sadness, despair, discouragement, low energy, and often oversleeping and/or overeating.

Dopamine—A chemical in brain tissue that serves to transmit nerve impulses (is a neurotransmitter) and helps to regulate movement and emotions.

Extrapyramidal symptoms—A group of side effects associated with antipsychotic medications and characterized by involuntary muscle movements, including contraction and tremor.

Hallucinations—A perception without external stimulus. Hallucinations can result from nervous system abnormalities, mental disorders, or the use of certain drugs.

Mania—An abnormal elevation in mood. The individual may appear excessively cheerful and talkative, have grandiose ideas, and may sleep less. Sometimes the elevation in mood is marked by irritability and hostility rather than cheerfulness. Those experiencing mania may seem to be in a frenzy and often will make poor, bizarre, or dangerous choices in their personal and professional lives.

Schizophrenia—A major mental illness marked by psychotic symptoms, including hallucinations, delusions, and severe disruptions in thinking.

Description

Molindone was taken orally and was rapidly absorbed and metabolized. Peak levels were reached within 90 minutes of taking the medication, and its effect lasted 24 to 36 hours. Molindone was available in 5, 10, 25, and 100 mg tablets.

Recommended dosage

The dosage of molindone was adjusted to the lowest level needed to control symptoms. The usual initial dosage was 50 to 75 mg per day. This might have been increased to 100 mg per day three to four days after beginning treatment. A maximal dosage of 225 mg per day was sometimes required.

Precautions

Prolonged or chronic administration of molindone increased the probability of developing **tardive dyskinesia**, a condition characterized by involuntary, uncoordinated movements involving the head, neck, trunk, feet, and hands. Examples of the movements involving the face and head include wormlike movement of the tongue, grimacing, chewing, and lip smacking. Tardive dyskinesia usually disappears once the affected person stops taking the associated medication, but sometimes it is irreversible.

Persons in a coma or experiencing central nervous system depression from alcohol, **barbiturates**, or narcotics were not prescribed molindone.

Drowsiness was often reported by people using molindone. For that reason, persons using molindone were advised not to operate machinery or drive automobiles.

Molindone caused the level of prolactin (a hormone that initiates lactation) in the blood to rise. This was a potential problem for persons with a personal or family history of breast cancer, as the increase could lead to the initiation of breast cancer. For this reason, the benefits of the drug were carefully evaluated before it was administered to persons at risk for breast cancer.

Molindone was associated with an increased risk of death when used in elderly patients with **dementia**. In June 2008, the U.S. Food and Drug Administration (FDA) announced a requirement for manufacturers of molindone (and other antipsychotic drugs) to add a warning label to their packaging stating this risk. The reason for the increase was unclear in studies, but most deaths were found to be related to either cardiovascular complications or complications associated with infection. Molindone was not approved by the FDA for the treatment of behavior problems in older adults with dementia.

In July 2009, the FDA made safety labeling changes to the warnings section for this drug to include information stating that occurrences of leukopenia, neutropenia, and agranulocytosis (issues relating to blood cells) had been reported with the use of molindone. The FDA cautioned that users of this medication should be monitored for signs of infection and also be monitored frequently for changes in blood count values.

Babies born to mothers who took molindone during pregnancy were likely to develop extrapyramidal symptoms (EPS) and withdrawal symptoms, including agitation, trouble breathing, and difficulty feeding. Breastfeeding was not recommended while taking the drug.

Side effects

Molindone had the potential to produce tardive dyskinesia. This syndrome consisting of involuntary, uncoordinated movements is potentially irreversible. The incidence of tardive dyskinesia was higher with increasing age and with increasing dosage of molindone. Tardive dyskinesia is more likely to occur after a long period of taking antipsychotic drugs, such as molindone, but it may also appear after such drug use has been discontinued. Females are at greater risk than males for developing tardive dyskinesia. Involuntary movements of the tongue, jaw, mouth, or face characterize tardive dyskinesia. These may be accompanied by involuntary movements of the arms, legs, and trunk. There is no known effective treatment for tardive dyskinesia.

Parkinson-like symptoms were also linked with the administration of molindone. These included restlessness and agitation (akathisia) and difficulty walking or moving (dystonia). These were generally controlled with **benztropine** mesylate or **trihexyphenidyl** hydrochloride.

An occasionally reported side effect of molindone was **neuroleptic malignant syndrome**, a complicated and potentially fatal condition characterized by muscle rigidity, high fever, alterations in mental status, and cardiac symptoms, including irregular pulse or blood pressure, sweating, tachycardia, or arrhythmias. This condition is considered a medical emergency.

Interactions

Molindone increased the effect of central nervous system depressants (drugs and substances that depress the central nervous system). This class of drugs includes anesthetics, opiates, barbiturates, atropine, and alcohol.

Molindone interfered with the absorption of phenytoin and tetracyclines.

Resources

BOOKS

Albers, Lawrence J., Rhoda K. Hahn, and Christopher Reist. *Handbook of Psychiatric Drugs.* Laguna Hills, CA: Current Clinical Strategies, 2010.

American Society of Health-System Pharmacists. *AHFS Drug Information 2011.* Bethesda, MD: ASHP, 2011.

Graham, George. *The Disordered Mind: An Introduction to Philosophy of Mind and Mental Illness.* New York: Routledge, 2010.

Holland, Leland Norman, and Michael Patrick Adams. *Core Concepts in Pharmacology.* 3rd ed. New York: Prentice Hall, 2011.

North, Carol, and Sean Yutzy. *Goodwin and Guze's Psychiatric Diagnosis.* New York: Oxford University Press, 2010.

Preston, John D., John H. O'Neal, and Mary C. Talaga. *Handbook of Clinical Psychopharmacology for Therapists.* 6th ed. Oakland, CA: New Harbinger, 2010.

PERIODICALS

Bagnall A., et al. "Molindone for Schizophrenia and Severe Mental Illness." *Cochrane Database Systematic Review* no. 2 (2000): CD002083.

Dhaware, B.S., et al. "Effects of Amantadine on Modification of Dopamine-Dependent Behaviours by Molindone." *Indian Journal of Medical Science* 54, no. 8 (2000): 321–24.

Glazer, W.M. "Expected Incidence of Tardive Dyskinesia Associated with Atypical Antipsychotics." *Journal of Clinical Psychiatry* 61, Supp. 4 (2000): 21–26.

ORGANIZATIONS

U.S. Food and Drug Administration, 10903 New Hampshire Ave., Silver Spring, MD, 20993-0002, (888) INFO-FDA (463-6332), http://www.fda.gov.

L. Fleming Fallon, Jr., MD, DrPH
Laura Jean Cataldo, RN, EdD

Monoamine oxidase inhibitors (MAOIs)

Definition

Monoamine oxidase inhibitors (MAOIs) are a class of **antidepressants** most often used to treat atypical **depression**. MAOIs carry the risk of dangerous interactions with certain foods, so they are prescribed only after other antidepressants prove ineffective.

Purpose

The mood-altering effects of MAOIs were initially discovered in the 1940s during efforts to use the first MAOI as a treatment for tuberculosis. The drug was ineffectual against tuberculosis, but the patients taking it reported enhanced mood. Based on these results, MAOIs were used in the 1950s in **clinical trials** for patients with depression. It was discovered that the drugs' common property was inhibition of monoamine oxidase (also called MAO), an enzyme that breaks down mood-regulating **neurotransmitters**, including **dopamine**, **serotonin**, and norepinephrine and epinephrine (also known as noradrenaline and **adrenaline**). By inhibiting the enzyme that breaks down these chemicals, MAOIs allow these neurotransmitters to persist and exert their mood-enhancing effects longer. One class of MAOIs also has recently been developed as a therapy for Parkinson's symptoms.

MAOIs were in widespread use from the 1960s through the 1980s, but fell out of favor as newer drugs with fewer potentially severe side effects and interactions came on the market.

Description

MAOIs can be divided into two main groups. The first group encompasses the nonselective, systemic, irreversible MAOIs and includes **phenelzine** (Nardil), **isocarboxazid** (Marplan), and **tranylcypromine** (Parnate), which are approved by the U.S. Food and Drug Administration for treatment of depression. They are considered nonselective because they target both types of MAOs: MAO-A and MAO-B. Their action is called "irreversible" because they bind the enzyme so strongly that even after a person stops taking them, two or three weeks must pass before the effects of the drugs subside.

The second group consists of the selective inhibitors, which inhibit either MAO-A or MAO-B, as the name implies. Those that inhibit MAO-A, including moclobemide (Aurorix, Manerix) and brofaromine (Consonar), are also known as RIMAS (reversible inhibitors of MAO-A). The use of a selective inhibitor can help prevent some of the food-drug interactions associated with the nonselective inhibitors. RIMAS are not approved for use in the United States.

The other drugs in the second group are inhibitors of MAO-B. These drugs, which include selegiline (Eldepryl) and rasagiline (Azilect), are not used orally for treatment of depression but instead are used in very low doses for treatment of Parkinson's symptoms. Because low dopamine levels are associated with Parkinson's symptoms, and these drugs block the MAO that breaks down dopamine, their effect of increasing dopamine levels has proved beneficial. At higher dosages, however, these MAO-B–inhibiting drugs become nonselective inhibitors, targeting both MAO-A and MAO-B and exerting antidepressant effects. In addition to their potential use in Parkinson's treatment, these MAO-B inhibitors hold promise as therapies for **attention deficit hyperactivity disorder**, stimulant abuse, and **smoking cessation**.

A low-dose, transdermal selegiline patch (Emsam) is also approved by the FDA for treatment of depression.

Recommended dosage

Dosages of MAOIs vary depending on the specific drug. Most are taken orally, but selegiline has been tested in the form of a transdermal patch that lessens exposure in the gastrointestinal tract, preventing some of the food-drug interactions associated with MAOIs.

Nonselective MAOIs

All of the nonselective MAOIs are taken as oral tablets. Isocarboxazid is started at 10 mg taken twice per day. The healthcare provider may gradually increase the dose, but the recommended maximum is no more than 60 mg/day. The adult dose of phenelzine is based on body weight; initially, it is 0.45 mg/lb (1 mg/kg) per day to a maximum dose of no more than 90 mg/day. For older adults, the initial dose is 15 mg in the morning; this dose can be increased, but to no more than 60 mg/day. Tranylcypromine is initially dosed at 30 mg per day and may be increased up to 60 mg/day. In older adults, the regimen is 2.5–5 mg/day to start. This dosage can be increased as needed, but usually to no more than 45 mg/day. For patients younger than 16, the dose should be determined by the practicing physician for all three drugs.

Selective MAOIs

The transdermal selegiline patch is available in three sizes that deliver 6, 9, or 12 mg/day through the skin. It should be applied to dry skin on the upper torso (below the neck and above the waist), upper thigh, or outer surface of the arm every 24 hours. Oral selegiline should not be used at daily doses exceeding 10 mg per day, and this dose should be split into two doses of 5 mg each, taken at breakfast and lunch. Exceeding the 10 mg limit can shift the drug's activity into nonselective inhibition, precipitating food interactions. Oral selegiline is usually taken in conjunction with dopamine-boosting drugs, such as levodopa (also called L-dopa), although it also appears to be effective when used alone. The oral dose for rasagiline is 1 mg once daily if taken alone. If taken in conjunction with levodopa, the recommended starting dose is 0.5 mg once a day, which can be increased to 1 mg a day if necessary.

Precautions

For the nonselective MAOIs (isocarboxazid, phenelzine, tranylcypromine), certain foods should be avoided. These include foods high in tyramine, a chemical found in foods that have been fermented or aged, including cheeses, fava beans, yeast- or meat-based extracts, meat that has been smoked or pickled, some kinds of sausages (e.g., pepperoni or salami), sauerkraut, and overripe fruit. The patient's healthcare provider should supply anyone prescribed these MAOIs with a list of foods to avoid, and patients should also avoid alcohol and large amounts of caffeine.

For people using the selegiline patch with the lowest level of delivery (6 mg/day) or taking oral selegiline at low doses for Parkinson's disease, dietary adjustment is not indicated; however, people using the 9 or 12 mg/day patches should observe dietary restrictions to avoid foods containing tyramine, like those required for the nonselective MAOIs.

In clinical trials, MAOI antidepressants increased the risk of suicidal thinking and behavior in children and adolescents with psychiatric disorders, including major depressive disorder. The average risk in pediatric trials for patients taking these drugs was twice that of patients taking placebo (4% vs. 2%, respectively).

People taking MAOIs must be sure to let their healthcare provider know if they are taking any other medications or drugs, especially the following:

- other antidepressant medications, such as fluoxetine (Prozac) or sertraline (Zoloft)
- some anticonvulsants, such as carbamazepine (Equetro) and oxcarbazepine (Trileptal)
- opioids, such as meperidine (Demerol)
- dextromethorphan, a component of many cough suppressant medications
- decongestants or appetite suppressants containing ephedrine, pseudoephedrine, phenylephrine, or phenylpropanolamine
- antihypertensive medications
- ciprofloxacin (Cipro)
- stimulants, especially amphetamines
- asthma medication
- insulin or antidiabetic medication
- cocaine
- tryptophan as a supplement or as a sleep aid
- St. John's wort

People taking MAOIs must also tell their healthcare provider of any other medical problems, especially alcohol abuse, chest pain, headaches, asthma, diabetes, kidney disease, epilepsy, heart or blood vessel disease, recent heart attack or stroke, high blood pressure, mental illness or a history of mental illness, Parkinson's disease, or hyperthyroidism.

There is an increased risk of birth defects when the nonselective MAOIs are taken during the first three months of pregnancy. Selegiline is classified as a pregnancy category C drug. This category indicates that animal reproduction studies showed an adverse effect on the fetus but there is no sufficient data in humans; however, potential benefits may outweigh potential risks for pregnant women in some cases. Tranylcypromine passes into the breast milk, but the status of the other two nonselective MAOIs is unknown. Selegiline passes into the milk of rodents, but it is unknown whether or not it passes into human breast milk. No studies on rasagiline in human breast milk have been done.

Even after a patient has stopped taking an MAOI, he or she must continue to exercise precautions for at least two weeks due to the time lapse between the end of treatment and the cessation of the drug's effects in the body.

Side effects

A person taking MAOIs must watch for symptoms of very high blood pressure. These include chest pain, enlarged pupils, fast or slow heartbeat, sensitivity to light, increased sweating, nausea or vomiting, and stiff or sore neck. Other potential side effects include dizziness or lightheadedness (can be common), headache, drowsiness, sleep disturbances, **fatigue**, weakness, and tremors. Gastrointestinal side effects can include either constipation or diarrhea and dry mouth. A person taking an MAOI may experience weight gain or, in the case of selegiline, weight loss. A sudden drop in blood pressure with a change in posture is possible, as is swelling in the feet or lower legs. Some people have reported sexual disturbances, including impotence or an inability to experience orgasm. Urinary changes may include decreased fluid volume or more frequent urination.

The only commonly reported side effect for the selegiline patch as of 2011 was an occasional skin reaction at the application site. A less common side effect was lightheadedness related to low blood pressure.

Interactions

One important role of MAO is breaking down tyramine, the compound in foods that have undergone aging or fermentation. Normally, because MAO is active, consuming these foods does not result in much tyramine entering the system. However, when an MAOI interferes with the activity of MAO, tyramine from these foods does enter the system and can elicit what has been called the "cheese reaction" (related to the association of tyramine with aged cheeses). This response can be life-threatening because of tyramine's effects on heart rate and blood pressure; the cheese reaction can produce a severe spike in blood pressure, leading to a hypertensive crisis. For this reason, people taking nonselective MAOIs must avoid foods that contain tyramine and continue this avoidance for at least two weeks after they stop taking the drug. People on the lowest dose (6 mg) of the selegiline patch do not need to exercise any tyramine-related dietary modifications. Users of MAOIs also will be advised about limiting tryptophan consumption, especially in the form of supplements.

Many drugs should not be taken with MAOIs, especially other antidepressants, anticonvulsants, **opioids**, dextromethorphan, decongestants, and **amphetamines**.

Patients using MAOIs should be sure to tell their doctor of any other drugs that they are taking.

Resources

PERIODICALS

Amsterdam, Jay D., and J. Alexander Bodkin. "Selegiline Transdermal System in the Prevention of Relapse of Major Depressive Disorder. A 52-week, Double-blind, Placebo-substitution, Parallel-group Clinical Trial." *Journal of Clinical Psychopharmacology* 26, no. 6 (2006): 579–586.

Howland, Robert H. "MAOI Antidepressant Drugs." *Journal of Psychosocial Nursing* 44, no. 6 (2006): 9–12.

Youdim, Moussa B.H., Dale Edmondson, and Keith F. Tipton. "The Therapeutic Potential of Monoamine Oxidase Inhibitors." *Nature Reviews Neuroscience* 7, no. 4 (2006): 295–309.

WEBSITES

Drugs.com. "Eldepryl Capsules." http://www.drugs.com/pro/eldepryl-capsules.html (accessed October 22, 2011).

Drugs.com. "Nardil" http://www.drugs.com/pro/nardil.html (accessed October 22, 2011.

Mayo Clinic staff. "Depression (major depression): Monoamine Oxidase Inhibitors (MAOIs)." MayoClinic.com. http://www.mayoclinic.com/health/maois/MH00072 (accessed October 22, 2011).

U.S. Food and Drug Administration. "FDA Approves Emsam (selegiline) as First Drug Patch for Depression." FDA News Release. February 28, 2006. http://www.fda.gov/NewsEvents/Newsroom/PressAnnouncements/2006/ucm108607.htm (accessed October 22, 2011).

ORGANIZATIONS

American Parkinson Disease Association, Inc, 135 Parkinson Ave., Staten Island, NY, 10305, (718) 981-8001, Fax: (718) 981-4399, apda@apdaparkinson.org, http://www.apdaparkinson.com.

American Psychiatric Association, 1000 Wilson Blvd., Ste. 1825, Arlington, VA, 22209-3901, (703) 907-7300, apa@psych.org, http://www.psych.org.

Emily Jane Willingham, Ph.D.

Mood disorders *see* **Bipolar disorder;
Depression and depressive disorders**

Mourning *see* **Bereavement; Grief**

Movement disorders

Definition

Movement disorders are a group of diseases and syndromes affecting the ability to produce and control movement.

Description

Although it seems simple and effortless, normal movement in fact requires an astonishingly complex system of control. Disruption of any portion of this system can cause a person to produce movements that are too weak, too forceful, too uncoordinated, or too poorly controlled for the task at hand. Unwanted movements may occur at rest. Intentional movement may become impossible. Such conditions are called movement disorders.

Abnormal movements themselves are symptoms of underlying disorders. In some cases, the abnormal movements are the only symptoms. Disorders causing abnormal movements include:

- Parkinson's disease
- parkinsonism caused by drugs or poisons
- Parkinson-plus syndromes (progressive supranuclear palsy, multiple system atrophy, and cortical-basal ganglionic degeneration)
- Huntington's disease
- Wilson's disease
- inherited ataxias (Friedreich's ataxia, Machado-Joseph disease, and spinocerebellar ataxias)
- Tourette syndrome and other tic disorders
- essential tremor
- restless leg syndrome
- dystonia
- stroke
- cerebral palsy
- encephalopathies
- intoxication
- poisoning by carbon monoxide, cyanide, methanol, or manganese

Causes and symptoms

Causes

Movement is produced and coordinated by several interacting **brain** centers, including the motor cortex, the cerebellum, and a group of structures in the inner portions of the brain called the basal ganglia. Sensory information provides critical input on the current position and velocity of body parts, and spinal nerve cells (neurons) help prevent opposing muscle groups from contracting at the same time.

To understand how movement disorders occur, it is helpful to consider a normal voluntary movement, such as reaching to touch a nearby object with the right index finger. To accomplish the desired movement, the arm

KEY TERMS

Botulinum toxin—Any of a group of potent bacterial toxins or poisons produced by different strains of the bacterium *Clostridium botulinum*. The toxins cause muscle paralysis, and thus force the relaxation of a muscle in spasm.

Cerebral palsy—A movement disorder caused by a permanent brain defect or injury present at birth or shortly after. It is frequently associated with premature birth. Cerebral palsy is not progressive.

Computed tomography (CT)—An imaging technique in which cross-sectional x rays of the body are compiled to create a three-dimensional image of the body's internal structures.

Encephalopathy—An abnormality in the structure or function of tissues of the brain.

Essential tremor—An uncontrollable (involuntary) shaking of the hands, head, and face. Also called familial tremor because it is sometimes inherited, it can begin in the teens or in middle age. The exact cause is not known.

Fetal tissue transplantation—A method of treating Parkinson's and other neurological diseases by grafting brain cells from human fetuses onto the basal ganglia. Human adults cannot grow new brain cells but developing fetuses can. Grafting fetal tissue stimulates the growth of new brain cells in affected adult brains.

Hereditary ataxia—One of a group of hereditary degenerative diseases of the spinal cord or cerebellum. These diseases cause tremor, spasm, and wasting of muscle.

Huntington's disease—A rare hereditary condition that causes progressive chorea and mental deterioration that ends in dementia. Huntington's symptoms usually appear in patients in their 40s. There is no effective treatment.

Levodopa (L-dopa)—A substance used in the treatment of Parkinson's disease. Levodopa can cross the blood-brain barrier that protects the brain. Once in the brain, it is converted to dopamine and thus can replace the dopamine lost in Parkinson's disease.

---

must be lifted and extended. The hand must be held out to align with the forearm, and the forefinger must be extended while the other fingers remain flexed.

THE MOTOR CORTEX. Voluntary motor commands begin in the motor cortex located on the outer, wrinkled surface of the brain. Movement of the right arm is begun by the left motor cortex, which generates a large volley of signals to the involved muscles. These electrical signals pass along upper motor neurons through the midbrain to the spinal cord. Within the spinal cord, they connect to lower motor neurons, which convey the signals out of the spinal cord to the surface of the muscles involved. Electrical stimulation of the muscles causes contraction, and the force of contraction pulling on the skeleton causes movement of the arm, hand, and fingers. Damage to or death of any of the neurons along this path causes weakness or paralysis of the affected muscles.

ANTAGONISTIC MUSCLE PAIRS. Movement is also supported by opposing, or antagonistic, muscle pairs. Contraction of the biceps muscle, located on the top of the upper arm, pulls on the forearm to flex the elbow and bend the arm. Contraction of the triceps, located on the opposite side, extends the elbow and straightens the arm. Within the spine, these muscles are normally wired so that willed (voluntary) contraction of one is automatically accompanied by blocking of the other. The command to

contract the biceps provokes another command within the spine to prevent contraction of the triceps. In this way, these antagonist muscles are kept from resisting one another. Spinal cord or brain injury can damage this control system and cause involuntary simultaneous contraction and spasticity, an increase in resistance to movement during motion.

THE CEREBELLUM. Once the movement of the arm is initiated, sensory information is needed to guide the finger to its precise destination. In addition to sight, the most important source of information comes from the "position sense" provided by the many sensory neurons located within the limbs (proprioception). Proprioception is the response that allows a person to touch the nose with the finger even with the eyes closed. The balance organs in the ears provide important information about posture. Both postural and proprioceptive information are processed by a structure at the rear of the brain called the cerebellum. The cerebellum sends out electrical signals to modify movements as they progress, "sculpting" the barrage of voluntary commands into a tightly controlled, constantly evolving pattern. Cerebellar disorders cause inability to control the force, fine positioning, and speed of movements (ataxia). Disorders of the cerebellum may also impair the ability to judge distance so that a person under- or overreaches the target (dysmetria). Tremor

Magnetic resonance imaging (MRI)—An imaging technique that uses a large circular magnet and radio waves to generate signals from atoms in the body. These signals are used to construct images of internal structures.

Parkinson's disease—A slowly progressive disease that destroys nerve cells in the basal ganglia and thus causes loss of dopamine, a chemical that aids in transmission of nerve signals (neurotransmitter). Parkinson's is characterized by shaking in resting muscles, a stooping posture, slurred speech, muscular stiffness, and weakness.

Positron emission tomography (PET)—A diagnostic technique in which computer-assisted x rays are used to track a radioactive substance inside a patient's body. PET can be used to study the biochemical activity of the brain.

Progressive supranuclear palsy—A rare disease that gradually destroys nerve cells in the parts of the brain that control eye movements, breathing, and muscle coordination. The loss of nerve cells

causes palsy, or paralysis, that slowly gets worse as the disease progresses. The palsy affects ability to move the eyes, relax the muscles, and control balance.

Restless legs syndrome—A condition that causes an annoying feeling of tiredness, uneasiness, and itching deep within the muscle of the leg. It is accompanied by twitching and sometimes pain. The only relief is in walking or moving the legs.

Tourette syndrome—An abnormal condition that causes uncontrollable facial grimaces and tics and arm and shoulder movements. Tourette syndrome is perhaps best known for uncontrollable vocal tics that include grunts, shouts, and use of obscene language (coprolalia).

Wilson's disease—An inborn defect of copper metabolism in which free copper may be deposited in a variety of areas of the body. Deposits in the brain can cause tremor and other symptoms of Parkinson's disease.

during voluntary movements can also result from cerebellar damage.

THE BASAL GANGLIA. Both the cerebellum and the motor cortex send information to a set of structures deep within the brain that help control involuntary components of movement (basal ganglia). The basal ganglia send output messages to the motor cortex, helping to initiate movements, regulate repetitive or patterned movements, and control muscle tone.

Circuits within the basal ganglia are complex. Within this structure, some groups of cells begin the action of other basal ganglia components and some groups of cells block the action. These complicated feedback circuits are not entirely understood. Disruptions of these circuits are known to cause several distinct movement disorders. A portion of the basal ganglia called the substantia nigra sends electrical signals that block output from another structure called the subthalamic nucleus. The subthalamic nucleus sends signals to the globus pallidus, which in turn blocks the thalamic nuclei. Finally, the thalamic nuclei send signals to the motor cortex. The substantia nigra, then, begins movement and the globus pallidus blocks it.

This complicated circuit can be disrupted at several points. For instance, loss of substantia nigra cells, as in

Parkinson's disease, increases blocking of the thalamic nuclei, preventing them from sending signals to the motor cortex. The result is a loss of movement (motor activity), a characteristic of Parkinson's.

In contrast, cell loss in early Huntington's disease decreases blocking of signals from the thalamic nuclei, causing more cortex stimulation and stronger but uncontrolled movements.

Disruptions in other portions of the basal ganglia are thought to cause tics, tremors, dystonia, and a variety of other movement disorders, although the exact mechanisms are not well understood.

Some movement disorders, including Huntington's disease and inherited ataxias, are caused by inherited genetic defects. Some diseases that cause sustained muscle contraction limited to a particular muscle group (focal dystonia) are inherited, but others are caused by **trauma**. The cause of most cases of Parkinson's disease is unknown, although genes have been found for some familial forms.

Symptoms

Movement disorders are usually broken down into two types of movement: hyperkinetic movement and hypokinetic movement. Hyperkinetic movement disorders are characterized by a significant and excessive amount of motor activity. This type also includes cases where there is a significant amount of abnormal involuntary movement. Hypokinetic movement disorders are those in which there is an abnormally reduced amount of intentional motor activity.

Hyperkinetic movement disorders are characterized by two types of behavior: rhythmical and irregular. Tremor is a rhythmic movement that is further divided into three forms: rest, postural, and intention. Rest tremor is most prominent when an individual is at rest and decreases with voluntary activity. Postural tremor occurs when an individual attempts to support a position against gravity (such as holding an arm outstretched). Intention tremor occurs during voluntary movement toward a specific target.

Irregular involuntary movements are classified by their speed and site of occurrence. Tics are rapid irregular movements that are controlled with voluntary effort. The types of rapid irregular movements that cannot be controlled voluntarily are called chorea, hemiballismus, and myoclonus. Chorea is a rapid, jerking movement that most often affects the face or limbs. Hemiballismus is the sudden and extreme swinging of a limb. Myoclonus is a rapid, irregular movement that usually occurs for a short period of time. It usually occurs when the person is at rest, and it often affects more than one area of the body at a time.

One of the most well-known hyperkinetic movement disorders is Huntington's disease, characterized by chorea-type movements. This disease is inherited and usually develops between 30 and 50 years of age. Persons with this condition have progressive **dementia**, and the condition eventually causes death. Children of persons with Huntington's disease have a 50% chance of developing the condition. **Stereotypic movement disorder** is characterized by repetitive behaviors that meet no functional need such as hand waving; rocking; head banging; mouthing of objects; or biting, picking, or hitting oneself. These behaviors interfere with normal activities and are not caused by **substance abuse** or a general medical condition.

The symptoms of hypokinetic movement disorders include a rigid, stone-like face; decreased limb motion during walking; and stiff turning movements. These features are classified as bradykinesia, while akinesia is the absence of purposeful movement. The most common type of hypokinetic movement disorder is Parkinson's disease, caused by the loss of neurons containing **dopamine** in the area of the brain called the substantia nigra pars compacta. The loss of these neurons is a part of the alteration of vital motor circuits in the brain that leads to a slowing of intentional movements.

Diagnosis

Diagnosis of movement disorders requires a careful medical history and a thorough physical and neurological examination. Brain **imaging studies** are usually performed. Imaging techniques include **computed tomography** scan (CT scan), **positron emission tomography** **(PET)**, or **magnetic resonance imaging** (MRI) scans. Routine blood and urine analyses are performed. A lumbar puncture (spinal tap) may be necessary. Video recording of the abnormal movement is often used to analyze movement patterns and to track progress of the disorder and its treatment. Genetic testing is available for some forms of movement disorders.

Treatment

Treatment of a movement disorder begins with determining its cause. Physical and occupational therapy may help make up for lost control and strength. Drug therapy can help compensate for some imbalances of the basal ganglionic circuit. For instance, levodopa (L-dopa) or related compounds can substitute for lost dopamine-producing cells in Parkinson's disease. Conversely, blocking normal dopamine action is a possible treatment in some hyperkinetic disorders, including tics. Oral medications can also help reduce overall muscle tone. Local injections of botulinum toxin can selectively weaken overactive muscles in dystonia and spasticity. Destruction of peripheral nerves through injection of phenol can reduce spasticity. All of these treatments may have some side effects.

Surgical destruction or inactivation of basal ganglionic circuits has proven effective for Parkinson's disease and is being tested for other movement disorders. Transplantation of fetal cells into the basal ganglia has produced mixed results in Parkinson's disease.

Prognosis

The prognosis for a patient with a movement disorder depends on the specific disorder.

Prevention

Prevention depends on the specific disorder.

See also Medication-induced movement disorders

Resources

BOOKS

Chaudhuri, Ray, K., and William Ondo. *Movement Disorders in Clinical Practice.* New York: Springer, 2010.

Newell, Lori A. *The Book of Exercise and Yoga for Those with Parkinson's Disease: Using Movement and Meditation to Manage Symptoms.* Charleston, SC: CreateSpace, 2010.

Truong, Daniel D., Mayank Pathak, and Karen Frei. *Living Well with Dystonia: A Patient Guide.* New York: Demos Health, 2010.

Wyborny, Sheila. *Tourette Syndrome.* Farmington Hills, MI: Gale, Cengage Learning, 2011.

ORGANIZATIONS

American Academy of Neurology, 1080 Montreal Ave., St. Paul, MN, 55116, (651) 695-2717, (800) 879-1960, Fax: (651) 879-2791, memberservices@aan.com, http://www.aan.com.

American Physical Therapy Association, 1111 North Fairfax St., Alexandria, VA, 22314-1488, (703) 684-APTA (2782), TDD: (703) 683-6748, (800) 999-APTA (2782), http://www.apta.org.

The Movement Disorder Society, 555 East Wells St., Ste. 1100, Milwaukee, WI, 53202-3823, (414) 276-2145, http://www.movementdisorders.org.

Worldwide Education and Awareness for Movement Disorders, One Gustave L. Levy Pl., PO Box 1052, New York, NY, 10029, (800) 437-6683, http://www.wemove.org.

Richard Robinson
Laura Jean Cataldo, RN, Ed.D.

Movement therapies *see* **Bodywork therapies**

MRI *see* **Magnetic resonance imaging**

Multi-infarct dementia *see* **Vascular dementia**

Multiple personality disorder *see* **Dissociative identity disorder**

Multisystemic therapy

Definition

Multisystemic therapy (MST) is an intensive family- and community-based treatment program designed to make positive changes in the various social systems (home, school, community, peer) that contribute to the serious antisocial behaviors of children and adolescents who are at risk for out-of-home placement. These out-of-home placements might include foster care, **group homes**, residential care, correctional facilities, or **hospitalization**.

Purpose

MST operates with the fundamental assumption that parents, guardians, or those who have primary caregiving responsibilities to children, have the most important influence in changing problem behaviors in children and adolescents. The primary goals of MST are to:

- develop in parents or caregivers the capacity to manage future difficulties
- reduce juvenile criminal activity
- reduce other types of antisocial behaviors, such as drug abuse
- achieve these outcomes at a cost savings by decreasing rates of incarceration and other out-of-home placements

MST was created approximately 30 years ago as an intensive family- and community-based treatment program to focus on juvenile offenders presenting with serious antisocial behaviors and who were at risk for out-of-home placement. The program has been shown to be effective with targeted populations that include inner-city delinquents, violent and chronic juvenile offenders, juvenile offenders who abuse or are dependent on substances and also have psychiatric disorders, adolescent sex offenders, and abusive and neglectful parents. A more recent focus of MST has been to treat youths who present with psychiatric emergencies, such as suicidal ideation, homicidal ideation, **psychosis**, or threat of harm to self or others due to mental illness. The results are promising and indicate that MST is an effective alternative to psychiatric hospitalization. Some treatment conditions and interventions were modified to take care of this new population, including developing a crisis plan during the initial family assessment and adding child and adolescent psychiatrists, psychiatric residents, and crisis caseworkers to the MST treatment team. Supervision by the treatment team was increased from weekly to daily meetings. Caseloads of MST therapists were reduced from five to three families, increasing the intensity of the **intervention**. When some adolescents were hospitalized for safety, the MST staff maintained clinical responsibility for the adolescent who was insulated from the usual activities due to inpatient care.

MST is licensed by MST Services, Inc., through the Medical University of South Carolina.

Description

MST programs are usually housed in community-based mental health organizations with a focus that is more rehabilitative than punitive. The program staff creates strong working relationships with referral sources, such as persons within the juvenile justice system and the family court. They work closely with deputy juvenile officers, social welfare workers, teachers, and guidance counselors to obtain the perspectives of multiple systems or "stakeholders" who have the common goal of improving children, adolescent, and family treatment. Each youth referred to the program is assigned to an MST therapist who designs individualized interventions in accordance, with the nine MST treatment principles, thereby addressing individual needs of the youth and his or her specific environment.

MST is a time-limited (four to six months) intensive therapeutic program that provides services in the family's home, at other locations (school, neighborhoods), or wherever the family feels most comfortable. After the initial sessions, the family members who attend sessions with the therapist will vary depending on the nature of the particular problem being discussed. For example, children are not included in sessions addressing intimate marital issues between parents or dealing with poor parental discipline, so as not to undermine parental authority.

Characteristics of the MST model—such as availability of the MST staff (24 hours a day, seven days a week), flexible scheduling, and delivery of services in the home—all provide safety for the family, prevent violence, foster a joint working relationship between therapist and family, provide the family with easier access to needed services, increase the likelihood that the family will stay in treatment, and help the family maintain changes in behaviors. The MST staff are full-time practitioners, and they wear pagers, carry cellular telephones, and work in teams of three. They can provide intensive services because of small caseloads and have multiple contacts with the family during the week, sometimes even daily. They stay as long as required and at times most convenient to the family, including weekends, evenings, and holidays. Services provided by staff at unusual times (10 P.M. to 8 A.M.) are discouraged, except in emergencies. The development of an informal support system in which the family can call on a friend or relative at crucial times is part of the treatment goals. Families have less contact with the therapist as they get closer to being discharged from treatment.

MST is designed to be a flexible intervention to provide highly individualized treatment to families. Specific treatment techniques or therapies are used as a part of MST interventions. These include parent-behavior training, structural **family therapy**, and strategic family and **cognitive-behavioral therapy**. In addition, some biological influences, such as **depression** and depressive disorders, may be identified, and psychotropic medications are integrated into treatment. This model does not support one method for obtaining successful changes in behaviors; however, there are nine guiding principles of treatment:

• The primary purpose of assessment is to understand the fit between the identified problems and their broader

systemic context. At the initial visit with the family, the staff begins to assess the family's strengths; capabilities; needs; problems; environmental support systems; and transactions with social systems, such as peers, extended family, friends, teachers, parental workplace, referral resources, and neighbors. The therapist and family work together to identify and prioritize problems to be targeted for change, determine interventions, and develop a treatment plan. The assessment is conducted in a manner that empowers family members by encouraging them to define their problems, needs, strengths, and—except in matters of imminent safety—set their priorities. The assessment is gradually updated until the family has reached its goals and is functioning independently.

• Therapeutic contacts emphasize the positive and should use systemic strengths as levers for change. MST is a strength-based treatment program and adherence to this principle decreases negativity among family members, builds positive expectations and hope, identifies strengths, and decreases therapist and family frustrations by emphasizing problem solving. It also builds the caregiver's confidence. The therapist develops and maintains the focus on the strength of the family and positive thinking through the use of positive language, teaching, and the technique of reframing negative thoughts and beliefs; the liberal use of positive rewards for appropriate behaviors; using a problem-solving stance rather than one of failure and seeing barriers as challenges; and identifying and using what the family does well.

• Interventions are designed to promote responsible behavior and decrease irresponsible behavior among family members. The therapist assists parents and youths in behaving in a responsible manner across a variety of domains. Parental duties include providing support, guidance, and discipline; expressing love and nurturance; protection; advocacy; and meeting basic physical needs. The primary responsibilities of the child and adolescent include complying with family and societal rules, attending school and putting forth reasonable effort, helping around the house, and not harming self or others. Therapists will spend a great deal of time throughout the treatment process enhancing, developing, and maintaining the responsible behaviors of parents through praise and support. Other family members who become engaged in the treatment process are also encouraged by the therapist to reinforce responsible parental behaviors that will help maintain these behaviors when treatment ends. It has been noted that when parents increase their responsibilities, there is almost always improvement in the child's behavior. Parental abdication of responsibilities may be caused by factors such as mental illness or the lack of necessary parenting skills. Interventions are designed to address these influences. For children and adolescents, positive reinforcement and discipline are used to increase responsible behaviors and decrease irresponsible behaviors. Parents are encouraged to clearly outline their expectations for compliance and punishments for noncompliance before putting them into action. For example, the child should know ahead of time that missing curfew will result in being grounded for a week. Parents are also taught to praise often for compliant behaviors.

- Interventions are focused on the present and action oriented, targeting specific and well-defined problems. Due to time limitations of the MST model, family members are required to work intensely to solve often long-standing problems. Once information has been gathered and assessed, therapist and family jointly formalize problem and goals into a treatment plan. The plan specifies which changes in what behavior or skill will be achieved by whom, by what method or action, and in what period of time within the limits of the program. The treatment plan contains the family's ultimate aims that are to be accomplished by the end of the treatment period, and intermediate goals or incremental steps needed to reach the overarching goals. These intermediate goals are measurable and time-limited, and the interventions chosen are those that have been determined to have the most immediate and powerful impact on the problem behavior. The therapist assists families in meeting their specific goals by helping them focus their time, energy, and resources on their assignments. Also, the expected outcome of each intervention is described in observable and measurable terms before the treatment plan is put into action. This aids the MST staff and the family in determining whether the interventions are effective or if alternatives are needed.

- Interventions should target sequences of behavior within and between multiple systems that maintain the identified problem. For example, if an ineffective parenting style (permissive, authoritarian, neglectful) is identified as a factor in influencing the problem behavior, it will be targeted for an intervention. However, if the parents are having marital difficulties that lead to disagreements in child-rearing practices, and these difficulties are sustaining the poor parenting style, the marital issues will be the focus of an additional intervention. The family may also have some practical or concrete needs (housing, heat, transportation) that are affecting parental discipline, and these may require interventions across the family–community support system.

- Interventions are developmentally appropriate and fit the needs of the youth. The nature of the intervention should take into account the age and maturity of the child or adolescent and the caregiver. It is noted that, for children and young adolescents, interventions aimed at increasing parental control are the most appropriate. Such interventions might include introducing systematic monitoring, reward, and discipline systems. For an older adolescent, interventions would most likely focus on preparing the youth for entry into the adult world, such as increasing his or her social maturity. Other interventions may be needed to overcome obstacles to independent living, such as having the teenager participate in GED classes or enter a vocational training school. The developmental stage of the caregiver is also important to consider. For example, grandparents may not have the physical or emotional health to become primary caregivers but may be able to assist parents in other ways, such as helping with homework or sitting with the youth after school for a few hours.

- Interventions are designed to require daily or weekly effort by family members. This leads to a more rapid decrease in the problem behavior and current and continuous evaluation of whether the intervention is working and producing the expected results. For example, if a parent sits near the child while he is doing homework, he or she can gauge the child's progress toward the anticipated goal of better school performance. This design also allows family members to experience immediate success and obtain positive feedback.

- Intervention effectiveness is evaluated continuously from multiple perspectives with providers assuming accountability for overcoming barriers to successful outcomes. Before intervention is implemented the therapist is required to document anticipated outcomes for each intervention by describing the observable and measurable goals of treatment. This information is used to assess the successes achieved or barriers encountered and to assess the impact of the intervention. The MST staff may also be in daily contact with teachers and administrators, deputy juvenile officers, and welfare professionals who provide feedback regarding whether the interventions across systems are successful in changing behaviors.

- Interventions are designed to promote treatment generalization and long-term maintenance of therapeutic change by empowering caregivers to address family members' needs across multiple systemic contexts. The MST therapist, the MST team, and the provider agency are responsible for engaging the family in treatment, making services for the family easier to obtain, and achieving positive outcomes for the child or adolescent and the family in every case. The program's achievement of

KEY TERMS

Psychotropic medication—Medication that has an effect on the mind, brain, behavior, perceptions, or emotions. Psychotropic medications are used to treat mental illnesses because they affect a patient's moods and perceptions.

Punitive—Concerned with, or directed toward, punishment.

Rehabilitative—To restore; to put back into good condition.

successful goals and maintenance of behavior change is due to staff adherence to the treatment model. Research has demonstrated that strong adherence correlates to strong case outcomes. The key to the success of the model is intensive and ongoing staff training. Clinical staff training includes five days of orientation training, weekly supervision with an MST expert, and quarterly booster training. On-site supervisors are also intensively trained to ensure that the MST staff adhere to the MST model.

Results

At the end of MST treatment, parents are provided with the resources needed to parent effectively and maintain better family structure and cohesion. Specifically, parents:

• are able to systematically monitor the behavior of their child or adolescent

• have learned to use appropriate reward and discipline measures to maintain new behavioral changes

• can communicate more effectively with each other and their children

• can advocate for their children and themselves across social systems (e.g., school, social services)

• can problem-solve daily conflicts

• can maintain positive relations with natural social supports such as extended family, friends, and church members

• are able to maintain a positive working relationship with school personnel

• have learned strategies to monitor and promote the child's or adolescent's school performance and/or vocational functioning

Other outcomes to be expected have to do with the youth's relationships with peers and his or her performance in school. Specifically, it is expected that the child or adolescent has decreased his or her association with delinquent and/or drug-using peers; has increased his or her relationships with positive peers and engages in positive activities through after-school activities, organized athletics, or volunteer or paid activities; has better school performance; and has had no days, or fewer days, requiring out-of-home placement.

Resources

BOOKS

Henggeler, Scott W., et al. *Multisystemic Therapy for Antisocial Behavior in Children and Adolescents.* New York: Guilford Press, 2009.

Swenson, Cynthia Cupit, et al. *Multisystemic Therapy and Neighborhood Partnerships: Reducing Adolescent Violence and Substance Abuse.* New York: Guilford Press, 2009.

PERIODICALS

Cox, Kathleen F. "Examining the Role of Social Network Intervention as an Integral Component of Community-Based, Family-Focused Practice." *Journal of Child and Family Studies* 14, no. 3 (September 2005): 443–54.

Ellis, Deborah A., et al. "Multisystemic Therapy for Adolescents With Poorly Controlled Type I Diabetes: Stability of Treatment Effects in a Randomized Controlled Trial." *Journal of Consulting and Clinical Psychology* 75, no. 1 (February 2007): 168–74.

Littell, Julia H. "Lessons from a Systematic Review of Effects of Multisystemic Therapy." *Children and Youth Services Review* 27, no. 4 (April 2005): 445–63.

Schaeffer, Cindy M., and Charles M. Borduin. "Long-Term Follow-Up to a Randomized Clinical Trial of Multisystemic Therapy With Serious and Violent Juvenile Offenders." *Journal of Consulting and Clinical Psychology* 73, no. 3 (June 2005): 445–53.

Schoenwald, Sonja K., Elizabeth J. Letourneau, and Colleen Halliday-Boykins. "Predicting Therapist Adherence to a Transported Family-Based Treatment for Youth." *Journal of Clinical Child and Adolescent Psychology* 34, no. 4 (December 2005): 658–70.

Timmons-Mitchell, Jane, et al. "An Independent Effectiveness Trial of Multisystemic Therapy With Juvenile Justice Youth." *Journal of Clinical Child and Adolescent Psychology* 35, no. 2 (June 2006): 227–36.

ORGANIZATIONS

National Institute of Mental Health, 6001 Executive Blvd., Room 8184, MSC 9663, Bethesda, MD, 20892-9663, (301) 433-4513; TTY: (301) 443-8431, Fax: (301) 443-4279, (866) 615-6464; TTY: (866) 415-8051, nimhinfo@nih.gov, http://www.nimh.nih.gov.

Office of Juvenile Justice and Delinquency Prevention, 810 Seventh St. NW, Washington, DC, 20531, (202) 307-5911, http://www.ojjdp.gov.

Janice VanBuren, PhD
Ruth A. Wienclaw, PhD

Munchausen syndrome *see* **Factitious disorder**

Music therapy

Definition

Music therapy is a technique of complementary medicine that uses music prescribed in a skilled manner by trained therapists. Programs are designed to help patients overcome physical, emotional, intellectual, and social challenges. Applications range from improving the well-being of geriatric patients in nursing homes to lowering the **stress** level and pain of women in labor. Music therapy is used in many settings, including schools, rehabilitation centers, hospitals, hospices, nursing homes, community centers, and sometimes even in the home.

A woman plays the xylophone during a music therapy session for persons with learning disabilities. (© Paula Solloway/Alamy)

Purpose

Music can be beneficial for everyone. Although it can be used therapeutically for people who have physical, emotional, social, or cognitive deficits, even those who are healthy can use music to relax, reduce stress, improve mood, or to accompany **exercise**. There are no potentially harmful or toxic effects. Music therapists help their patients achieve a number of goals through music, including improvement of communication, academic strengths, attention span, and motor skills. They may also assist with behavioral therapy and pain management.

Description

Music has been used throughout human history to express and affect human emotion. In biblical accounts, King Saul was reportedly soothed by David's harp music, and the ancient Greeks expressed views about music having healing effects as well. Many cultures are steeped in musical traditions. It can change mood, have stimulant or sedative effects, and alter physiologic processes such as heart rate and breathing. The apparent health benefits of music to patients in Veterans Administration hospitals following World War II led to it being studied and formalized as a complementary healing practice. Musicians were hired to continue working in the hospitals. Degrees in music therapy became available in the late 1940s, and in 1950, the first professional association of music therapists was formed in the United States. The National Association of Music Therapy merged with the American Association of Music Therapy in 1998 to become the American Music Therapy Association.

Benefits

Brain function physically changes in response to music. The rhythm can guide the body into breathing in slower, deeper patterns that have a calming effect. Heart rate and blood pressure are also responsive to various types of music. The speed of the heartbeat tends to speed or slow depending on the volume and speed of the auditory stimulus. Louder and faster sounds tend to raise both heart rate and blood pressure; slower, softer, and more regular tones produce the opposite result. Music can also relieve muscle tension and improve motor skills. It is often used to help rebuild physical patterning skills in rehabilitation clinics. Levels of endorphins, natural pain relievers, are increased and levels of stress hormones are decreased in individuals while they listen to music. This latter effect may partially explain the ability of music to improve immune function. A study at Michigan State University showed that even 15 minutes of exposure to music can increase interleukin-1 levels, a consequence which also heightens immunity.

Mental effects

Depending on the type and style of sound, music can either sharpen mental acuity or assist in relaxation. Memory and learning can be enhanced, and this effect has been used with good results in children with learning disabilities. This effect may also be partially due to increased concentration that many people have while listening to music. Better productivity is another outcome of an improved ability to concentrate. The term "Mozart effect" was coined after a study showed that college students performed better on math problems when they were listening to classical music.

Emotional effects

The ability of music to influence human emotion is well known and is used extensively by moviemakers. A variety of musical moods may be used to create feelings of calm, tension, excitement, or romance. Lullabies have long been popular for soothing babies as they fall asleep. Music can also be used to express emotion nonverbally, which can be a valuable therapeutic tool in some settings.

Goals

Music is used to form a relationship between the therapist and the patient. The music therapist sets goals on an individual basis, depending on the reasons for treatment, and selects specific activities and exercises to help the patient progress. Objectives may include development of communication, cognitive, motor, emotional, and social skills. Some of the techniques used to achieve this are singing, listening, instrumental music, composition, creative movement, guided imagery, and other methods as appropriate. Other disciplines may be integrated as well, such as dance, art, and psychology. Patients may develop musical abilities as a result of therapy, but this is not a major concern. The primary aim is to improve patients' ability to function.

Techniques

Learning to play an instrument is an excellent activity for developing motor skills in individuals with developmental delays, brain injuries, or other motor impairment. It is also an exercise in impulse control and group cooperation. Creative movement is another activity that can help to improve coordination, as well as strength, balance, and gait. Improvisation facilitates the nonverbal expression of emotion. It encourages socialization and communication about feelings as well. Singing develops articulation, rhythm, and breath control. Remembering lyrics and melody is an exercise in sequencing for **stroke** victims and others who may be intellectually impaired. Composition of words and music is one avenue available to assist patients in working through fears and negative

feelings. Listening is an excellent way to practice attending and remembering. It may also make patients aware of memories and emotions that need to be acknowledged and perhaps talked about. Singing and discussion are related methods, which are used with some patients to encourage dialogue. Guided imagery and music (GIM) is a popular technique developed by music therapist Helen Bonny. Listening to music is used as a path to invoke emotions, pictures, and symbols from patients. This is a bridge to the exploration and expression of feelings.

Music and children

The sensory stimulation and playful nature of music can help to develop children's ability to express emotion, communicate, and develop rhythmic movement. Some evidence shows that speech and language skills can be improved through the stimulation of both hemispheres of the brain. Just as with adults, appropriately selected music can decrease stress, anxiety, and pain among children. Music therapy in a hospital environment with those who are sick, preparing for surgery, or recovering postoperatively is appropriate and beneficial. Children can also experience improved self-esteem through musical activities that allow them to succeed.

Newborns may enjoy even greater benefits from music. Premature infants experience more rapid weight gain and an earlier discharge from the hospital than their peers who are not exposed to music. There is also anecdotal evidence of improved cognitive function in premature infants from listening to music.

Music and rehabilitation

Patients with brain damage from stroke, **traumatic brain injury**, or other neurologic conditions have been shown to exhibit significant improvement as a result of music therapy. This is theorized to be partially the result of entrainment, which is the synchronization of movement with the rhythm of the music. Consistent practice

---

KEY TERMS

Adjunctive—Describes a form of treatment that is not strictly necessary to a therapy regimen but is helpful. Music therapy is an example of an adjunctive form of treatment.

Entrainment—The patterning of body processes and movements to the rhythm of music.

Physiologic—Describes the physiology, particularly normal, healthy, physical functioning.

---

leads to gains in motor skill ability and efficiency. Cognitive processes and language skills often benefit from appropriate musical **intervention**.

Music therapy has also shown effectiveness in rehabilitating the hearing of children and adults who have had cochlear implant surgery to treat impaired hearing. Young children who have never heard sounds face a lengthy rehabilitation in order to learn how to interpret sound and form speech. Music therapy can serve as a bridge between nonverbal communication and the new sounds that toddlers are hearing and processing into language. In older adults with cochlear implants, music therapy can offer relaxation to minimize distortion among new sounds and cues to remembering old sounds. Individualized music therapy is also used to reduce noise levels in people with tinnitus, or ringing in the ears.

Music and the elderly

The geriatric population can be prone to anxiety and **depression**, particularly in nursing home residents. Chronic diseases causing pain are also not uncommon in this setting. Music is an excellent outlet to provide enjoyment, relaxation, relief from pain, and an opportunity to socialize and reminisce about music that has had special importance to individuals. It can have a striking effect on patients with **Alzheimer's disease**, even sometimes allowing them to focus and become more responsive for a time. Music has also been observed to decrease the agitation that is so common with this disease. One study shows that elderly people who play a musical instrument are more physically and emotionally fit as they age than their nonmusical peers are.

Music and psychiatric disorders

Music can be an effective tool for treating the mentally or emotionally ill. **Autism** is one disorder that has been particularly researched. Music therapy has enabled some autistic children to relate to others and have improved learning skills. **Substance abuse, schizophrenia, paranoia**, and disorders of personality, anxiety, and affect have all benefited from music therapy. In these groups, participation and social interaction are promoted through music. Reality orientation is improved. Patients are helped to develop coping skills, reduce stress, and express their feelings.

In the treatment of psychotic disorders, however, the benefits of music therapy appear to be limited. One study of patients diagnosed with schizophrenia or schizoaffective **psychosis** found that while music therapy improved the patients' social relationships, these benefits were relatively short-lived.

Music and hospice care

Pain, anxiety, and depression are major concerns with patients who are terminally ill, whether they are in hospice or not. Music can provide some relief from pain, through the release of endorphins and the promotion of relaxation. It can also provide an opportunity for the patient to reminisce and talk about the fears that are associated with death and dying. Music may help regulate the rapid breathing of a patient who is anxious and soothe the mind. The Chalice of Repose project, headquartered at St. Patrick Hospital in Missoula, Montana, is one organization that attends to and nurtures critical patients through the use of music in a practice called music-thanatology, developed by Therese Schroeder-Sheker. Practitioners in this program work to relieve suffering through music prescribed for the individual patient.

Music and childbirth

Research has proven that women require less pharmaceutical pain relief during labor if they make use of music. Listening to music that is familiar and associated with positive imagery is the most helpful. During early labor, music promotes relaxation. Maternal movement is helpful to get the baby into a proper birthing position and dilate the cervix. Enjoying some "music to move by" can encourage the mother to stay active for as long as possible during labor. The rhythmic auditory stimulation may also prompt the body to release endorphins, which are a natural form of pain relief. Many women select different styles of music for each stage of labor, with a more intense or faster-moving piece as the natural accompaniment to the more difficult parts of labor. Instrumental music is often preferred.

The benefits of music therapy during childbirth have also been shown to apply to other surgical procedures. Women who have listened to music tapes during gynecologic surgery have more restful sleep following the procedure and less postoperative soreness.

Precautions

Patients making use of music therapy should not discontinue medications or therapies prescribed by other health providers without prior consultation.

Research and general acceptance

There is little disagreement among physicians that music can be of some benefit for patients, although the extent of its effects on physical well-being remains a matter of debate among members of the medical community. Acceptance of music therapy as an adjunctive treatment modality is increasing, however, due to the growing diversity of patient populations receiving music therapy. Research has shown that listening to music can decrease anxiety, pain, and recovery time. There is also evidence supporting its use for the specific subpopulations discussed. A therapist referral can be made through the AMTA.

Training and certification

Music therapists are themselves often talented musicians; they also study the ways in which music can be applied to specific groups and circumstances. Coursework includes classes in music history and performance, behavioral science, and education. The American Music Therapy Association dictates what classes must be included in order for a music therapy program to be certified. There are approximately 70 colleges with approved curricula. A six-month internship follows the completion of the formal music therapy program, and graduates are then able to take a national board exam to gain certification.

There are about 5,000 board certified music therapists in the United States. The field is growing rapidly as an increasing number of both inpatient and outpatient healthcare settings incorporate music therapy into their treatment modalities.

Resources

BOOKS

Boxill, Edith Hillman, and Kristen M. Chase. *Music Therapy for Developmental Disabilities*. Austin, Tex: Pro-Ed, Inc. 2007.

Nordoff, Paul, and Clive Robbins. *Creative Music Therapy: A Guide to Fostering Clinical Musicianship*. 2nd ed. Gilsum, N.H.: Barcelona Publishers, 2007.

Oldfield, Amelia, and Claire Flower. *Music Therapy with Children and Their Families*. Gateshead, UK: Athenaeum Press, 2008.

Sacks, Oliver W. *Musicophilia: Tales of Music and the Brain*. New York: Alfred A. Knopf, 2007.

Sekeles, Chava. *Music Therapy: Death and Grief*. Gilsum, NH: Barcelona Publishers, 2007.

Serlin, Ilene A. *Whole Person Healthcare*. Praeger Perspectives. Westport, CT: Praeger, 2007.

PERIODICALS

Avers, Laura, Ambika Mathur, and Deepak Kamat. "Music Therapy in Pediatrics." *Clinical Pediatrics*. 46, no. 7 (October 2007): 575–579.

Lite, Jordan. "Sonic Health Boost: Music Therapy Can Fight Pain and Disease." *Prevention*. (January 2008): 53–57.

Parker, A.B., "Music Therapy Clarifications." *Journal of Psychosocial Nursing and Mental Health Services* 47, no. 4 (April 2009): 15.

Romo, R., and L. Gifford. "A Cost-Benefit Analysis of Music Therapy in a Home Hospice." *Nursing Economics*. (November–December 2007): 34.

Talwar, N., et al. "Music Therapy for In-Patients with Schizophrenia: Exploratory Randomized Controlled Trial." *The British Journal of Psychiatry: the Journal of Mental Science*. 189 (2006): 405–9.

ORGANIZATIONS

American Music Therapy Association, 8455 Colesville Rd., Suite 1000, Silver Spring, MD, 20910, (301) 589-3300, Fax: (301) 589-5175, http://www.musictherapy.org.

Judith Turner
Rebecca J. Frey, PhD
Brenda W. Lerner

Mutual support *see* **Support groups**

Naltrexone

Definition

Naltrexone is classified as a pure opiate antagonist. It is sold in the United States under the brand names ReVia and Depade and is also manufactured and sold under its generic name.

Purpose

Naltrexone is used as part of medically supervised **behavior modification** programs to help patients who have stopped taking narcotics or alcohol to continue to abstain from opiates or alcohol.

Description

Opiates are a group of drugs that are either derived from opium (e.g., morphine, hydromorphone, oxymorphone, heroin, codeine, hydrocodone, oxycodone) or chemically resemble these opium derivatives (such as meperidine). They are commonly referred to as narcotics. Some opiates have medically valid uses, while others are recreational drugs of abuse. All are physically addictive.

The drug naltrexone is an opiate antagonist. This means that it blocks and reverses the physical effects of drugs such as morphine, hydromorphone, oxymorphone, heroin, meperidine, codeine, hydrocodone, oxycodone and other drugs classified as narcotics. When given to patients who have been successfully treated for opiate **addiction**, it not only decreases cravings for these types of drugs, it also helps patients who use opiates while taking naltrexone to avoid experiencing the euphoria associated with their use. In these two ways, naltrexone helps prevent re-addiction to opiates.

Chemically, naltrexone is not an alcohol antagonist. However, when it is used in combination with behavior modification in a person recovering from alcoholism, naltrexone decreases the craving for alcohol. This helps

patients to prevent a return to **alcohol use** or decreases the severity of **relapse** by reducing the amount of alcohol consumed during the relapse or decreasing the length of the relapse.

Naltrexone is available in 50 mg oral tablets.

Recommended dosage

After successful **detoxification** from opiates, people who used them will receive a test dose of 25 mg of naltrexone, then be observed for one hour for symptoms of opiate withdrawal. If no problems occur after this test dose, another 25 mg test dose is administered.

Getting such people to comply with treatment for opiate addiction is the single most important aspect in maintaining an opiate-free state. Different schedules for taking naltrexone have been developed to help meet the needs of individuals complying with taking the drug. Following successful initiation of therapy, naltrexone may be administered in one of the following ways:

- 50 mg daily, Monday through Friday, and 100 mg on Saturday
- 100 mg every other day
- 150 mg every third day
- 100 mg on Monday and Wednesday and 150 mg on Friday
- 150 mg on Monday and 200 mg on Thursday

The duration of treatment with naltrexone for people with opiate dependence varies with patient need, although most patients will require at least six months of treatment.

The usual dose of naltrexone for alcohol dependence is 50 mg daily, although a few patients may require only 25 mg daily. The proper duration of therapy is not known, as studies of the use of naltrexone in people with alcohol dependence did not go beyond 12 weeks.

KEY TERMS

Antagonist—A substance whose actions counteract the effects of or work in the opposite way from another chemical or drug.

Opiates—A class of drugs that is either derived from opium (i.e., morphine, hydromorphone, oxymorphone, heroin, codeine, hydrocodone, oxycodone) or resembles these opium derivatives (such as meperidine) and is commonly referred to as narcotics.

Precautions

In a very small number of patients, naltrexone may be toxic and cause damage to the liver. Before starting naltrexone and throughout treatment, patients should receive monthly liver function tests to assess the drug's effect on the liver.

Patients should be free of all opiates for seven to ten days before starting naltrexone. Naltrexone may cause opiate withdrawal symptoms in people whose bodies are not free from opiates. Patients should be observed for opiate withdrawal immediately following the first dose of the drug.

Patients may have a false sense of security that the presence of naltrexone in their system makes them immune from the effects of opiates. In actuality, patients are more sensitive to the effects of opiates when taking naltrexone, and patients receiving naltrexone who continue to use or receive opiates should be monitored for signs and symptoms of opiate overdose.

Side effects

The following represents the most common side effects associated with naltrexone:

- nausea, vomiting, diarrhea, cramps
- headache, insomnia, anxiety, irritability, depression, dizziness
- joint and muscle pain
- rash

Interactions

Because naltrexone is an opiate antagonist, opiate derivatives that are used medicinally in treating coughs, diarrhea, and pain may no longer be effective.

The combination of naltrexone and **disulfiram**, a drug that is also used for alcohol abuse, may cause increased liver toxicity and liver damage. This combination should be avoided unless, in consultation with a physician, it is decided that the potential benefits of this combination outweigh the risks.

See also Opioids and related disorders

Resources

BOOKS

American Society of Health-System Pharmacists. *AHFS Drug Information 2008*. Bethesda, MD: American Society of Health-System Pharmacists, 2008.

Preston, John D., John H. O'Neal, and Mary C. Talaga. *Handbook of Clinical Psychopharmacology for Therapists*. 5th ed. Oakland, CA: New Harbinger Publications, 2008.

PERIODICALS

Anton, Raymond F., et al. "Combined Pharmacotherapies and Behavioral Interventions for Alcohol Dependence: The COMBINE Study: A Randomized Controlled Trial." *Journal of the American Medical Association* 295, no. 17 (May 2006): 2003–17.

Armeli, Stephen, et al. "The Effects of Naltrexone on Alcohol Consumption and Affect Reactivity to Daily Interpersonal Events Among Heavy Drinkers." *Experimental and Clinical Psychopharmacology* 14, no. 2 (May 2006): 199–208.

Comer, Sandra D., et al. "Injectable, Sustained-Release Naltrexone for the Treatment of Opioid Dependence: A Randomized, Placebo-Controlled Trial." *Archives of General Psychiatry* 63, no. 2 (February 2006): 210–18.

Johansson, Björn Axel, Mats Berglund, and Anna Lindgren. "Efficacy of Maintenance Treatment with Naltrexone for Opioid Dependence: A Meta-Analytical Review." *Addiction* 101, no. 4 (April 2006): 491–503.

Morley, Kirsten C., et al. "Naltrexone Versus Acamprosate in the Treatment of Alcohol Dependence: A Multi-Centre, Randomized, Double-Blind, Placebo-Controlled Trial." *Addiction* 101, no. 10 (October 2006): 1451–62.

Nunes, Edward V., et al. "Behavioral Therapy to Augment Oral Naltrexone for Opioid Dependence: A Ceiling on Effectiveness?" *American Journal of Drug and Alcohol Abuse* 32, no. 4 (2006): 503–17.

O'Brien, Charles, and James W. Cornish. "Naltrexone for Probationers and Parolees." *Journal of Substance Abuse Treatment* 31, no. 2 (September 2006): 107–11.

Petrakis, Ismene L., et al. "Naltrexone and Disulfiram in Patients with Alcohol Dependence and Comorbid Post-Traumatic Stress Disorder." *Biological Psychiatry* 60, no. 7 (October 2006): 777–83.

Pettinati, Helen M., et al. "The Status of Naltrexone in the Treatment of Alcohol Dependence: Specific Effects on Heavy Drinking." *Journal of Clinical Psychopharmacology* 26, no. 6 (December 2006): 610–25.

Rohsenow, Damaris J., et al. "High-Dose Transdermal Nicotine and Naltrexone: Effects on Nicotine Withdrawal, Urges, Smoking, and Effects of Smoking." *Experimental and*

Clinical Psychopharmacology 15, no. 1 (February 2007): 81–92.

Roozen, Hendrik G., et al. "A Systematic Review of the Effectiveness of Naltrexone in the Maintenance Treatment of Opioid and Alcohol Dependence." *European Neuropsychopharmacology* 16, no. 5 (July 2006): 311–23.

Sullivan, Maria A., et al. "Predictors of Retention in Naltrexone Maintenance for Opioid Dependence: Analysis of a Stage I Trial." *The American Journal on Addictions* 15, no. 2 (March–April 2006): 150–59.

Jack Raber, Pharm. D.
Ruth A. Wienclaw, PhD

Narcissistic personality disorder

Definition

Narcissistic personality disorder (NPD) is included in the ***Diagnostic and Statistical Manual of Mental Disorders*** (*DSM*), a handbook that mental health professionals use to diagnose mental disorders, as one of several **personality disorders**. As a group, these disorders are described in the revised fourth edition (*DSM-IV-TR*) as "enduring pattern[s] of inner experience and behavior" that are sufficiently rigid and deep-seated to bring a person into repeated conflicts with his or her social and occupational environment. *DSM-IV-TR* specifies that these dysfunctional patterns must be regarded as nonconforming or deviant by the person's culture, and cause significant emotional pain and/or difficulties in relationships and occupational performance.

To meet the **diagnosis** of a personality disorder, the patient's problematic behaviors must appear in two or more of the following areas:

- perception and interpretation of the self and other people
- intensity and duration of feelings and their appropriateness to situations
- relationships with others
- ability to control impulses

It is important to note that all the personality disorders are considered to have their onset in late adolescence or early adulthood. Doctors rarely give a diagnosis of personality disorder to children on the grounds that children's personalities are still in process of formation and may change considerably by the time they are in their late teens.

NPD is defined more specifically as a pattern of grandiosity (exaggerated claims to talents, importance, or specialness) in the patient's private fantasies or outward behavior; a need for constant admiration from others; and a lack of empathy for others. The term *narcissistic* is derived from an ancient Greek legend, the story of Echo and Narcissus. According to the legend, Echo was a woodland nymph who fell in love with Narcissus, who was an uncommonly handsome but also uncommonly vain young man. He contemptuously rejected her expressions of love. She pined away and died. The god Apollo was angered by Narcissus' pride and self-satisfaction, and condemned him to die without ever knowing human love. One day, Narcissus was feeling thirsty, saw a pool of clear water nearby, and knelt beside it in order to dip his hands in the water and drink. He saw his face reflected on the surface of the water and fell in love with the reflection. Unable to win a response from the image in the water, Narcissus eventually died beside the pool.

Havelock Ellis, a British **psychologist**, first used the story of Echo and Narcissus in 1898 as a capsule summary of pathological self-absorption. The words *narcissist* and *narcissistic* have been part of the vocabulary of psychology and psychiatry ever since. They have, however, been the subjects of several controversies. In order to understand NPD, the reader may find it helpful to have an outline of the different theories about narcissism in human beings, its relation to other psychiatric disorders, and its connections to the wider culture. NPD is unique among the *DSM-IV-TR* personality disorders in that it has been made into a symbol of the problems and discontents of contemporary Western culture as a whole.

Demographics

DSM-IV-TR states that 2% to 16% of the clinical population and slightly less than 1% of the general population of the United States suffers from NPD. Between 50% and 75% of those diagnosed with NPD are males. Little is known about the prevalence of NPD across racial and ethnic groups.

Gender issues

The high preponderance of male patients in studies of narcissism has prompted researchers to explore the effects of gender roles on this particular personality disorder. Some have speculated that the gender imbalance in NPD results from society's disapproval of self-centered and exploitative behavior in women, who are typically socialized to nurture, please, and generally focus their attention on others. Others have remarked that the imbalance is more apparent than real, and that it reflects a basically sexist definition of narcissism. These researchers suggest that definitions of the disorder should be rewritten in future editions of *DSM* to account for ways in which narcissistic personality traits manifest differently in men and in women.

Professional and leadership positions

One important aspect of NPD that should be noted is that it does not prevent people from occupying, as well as aspiring to, positions of power, wealth, and prestige. Many people with NPD, as Kernberg's classification makes clear, are sufficiently talented to secure the credentials of success. In addition, narcissists' preoccupation with a well-packaged exterior means that they often develop an attractive and persuasive social manner. Many high-functioning narcissists are well liked by casual acquaintances and business associates who never get close enough to notice the emptiness or anger underneath the polished surface.

Unfortunately, narcissists in positions of high visibility or power—particularly in the so-called helping professions (medicine, education, and the ministry)—often do great harm to others. In recent years a number of books and articles have been published within the religious, medical, and business communities regarding the problems caused by professionals with NPD. One **psychiatrist** noted in a lecture on substance abuse among physicians that NPD is one of the three most common psychiatric diagnoses among physicians in court-mandated substance abuse programs. A psychologist who serves as a consultant in the evaluation of seminary students and ordained clergy has remarked that the proportion of narcissists in the clergy has risen dramatically since the 1960s. Researchers in the field of business organization and management styles have compiled data on the human and economic costs of executives with undiagnosed NPD.

Description

A good place to begin a discussion of the different theories about narcissism is with the observation that NPD exists as a diagnostic category only in *DSM-IV-TR*, which is an American diagnostic manual. The *International Statistical Classification of Diseases and Related Health Problems, Tenth Revision* (*ICD-10*, the European equivalent of *DSM*) lists only eight personality disorders. What *DSM-IV-TR* defines as narcissistic personality disorder, *ICD-10* lumps together with "eccentric, impulsive-type, immature, passive-aggressive, and psychoneurotic personality disorders."

DSM-IV-TR specifies nine diagnostic criteria for NPD. For the clinician to make the diagnosis, an individual must fit five or more of the following descriptions:

- He or she has a grandiose sense of self-importance (exaggerates accomplishments and demands to be considered superior without real evidence of achievement).

- He or she lives in a dream world of exceptional success, power, beauty, genius, or "perfect" love.

- He or she thinks of him-or herself as "special" or privileged, and that he or she can only be understood by other special or high-status people.

- He or she demands excessive amounts of praise or admiration from others.

- He or she feels entitled to automatic deference, compliance, or favorable treatment from others.

- He or she is exploitative towards others and takes advantage of them.

- He or she lacks empathy and does not recognize or identify with others' feelings.

- He or she is frequently envious of others or thinks that they are envious of him or her.

- He or she "has an attitude" or frequently acts in haughty or arrogant ways.

In addition to these criteria, *DSM-IV-TR* groups NPD together with three other personality disorders in its so-called Cluster B. These four disorders are grouped together on the basis of symptom similarities, insofar as patients with these disorders appear to others as overly emotional, unstable, or self-dramatizing. The other three disorders in Cluster B are antisocial, borderline, and histrionic personality disorders.

The *DSM-IV-TR* clustering system does not mean that all patients can be fitted neatly into one of the three clusters. It is possible for patients to have symptoms of more than one personality disorder or to have symptoms from different clusters. In addition, patients diagnosed with any personality disorder may also meet the criteria for mood, **substance abuse**, or other disorders.

Subtypes of NPD

AGE GROUP SUBTYPES. Ever since the 1950s, when psychiatrists began to notice an increase in the number of their patients that had narcissistic disorders, they have made attempts to define these disorders more precisely. NPD was introduced as a new diagnostic category in *DSM-III*, which was published in 1980. Prior to *DSM-III*, narcissism was a recognized phenomenon but not an official diagnosis. At that time, NPD was considered virtually untreatable because people who suffer from it rarely enter or remain in treatment; typically, they regard themselves as superior to their therapist, and they see their problems as caused by other people's "stupidity" or "lack of appreciation." More recently, however, some psychiatrists have proposed dividing narcissistic patients into two subcategories based roughly on age: those who suffer from the stable form of NPD described by

DSM-IV-TR, and younger adults whose narcissism is often corrected by life experiences.

This age group distinction represents an ongoing controversy about the nature of NPD—whether it is fundamentally a character disorder, or whether it is a matter of learned behavior that can be unlearned. Therapists who incline toward the first viewpoint are usually pessimistic about the results of treatment for patients with NPD.

PERSONALITY SUBTYPES. Other psychiatrists have noted that patients who meet the *DSM-IV-TR* criteria for NPD reflect different clusters of traits within the *DSM-IV-TR* list. One expert in the field of NPD has suggested the following subcategories of narcissistic personalities:

- Craving narcissists. These are people who feel emotionally needy and undernourished, and may well appear clingy or demanding to those around them.

- Paranoid narcissists. This type of narcissist feels intense contempt for him- or herself, but projects it outward onto others. Paranoid narcissists frequently drive other people away from them by hypercritical and jealous comments and behaviors.

- Manipulative narcissists. These people enjoy "putting something over" on others, obtaining their feelings of superiority by lying to and manipulating them.

- Phallic narcissists. Almost all narcissists in this subgroup are male. They tend to be aggressive, athletic, and exhibitionistic; they enjoy showing off their bodies, clothes, and overall "manliness."

Causes and symptoms

Causes

At present there are two major theories about the origin and nature of NPD. One theory regards NPD as a form of arrested psychological development while the other regards it as a young child's defense against psychological pain. The two perspectives have been identified with two major figures in psychoanalytic thought, Heinz Kohut and Otto Kernberg respectively.

Both theories about NPD go back to Sigmund Freud's pioneering work *On Narcissism,* published in 1914. In this essay, Freud introduced a distinction which has been retained by almost all later writers—namely, the distinction between primary and secondary narcissism. Freud thought that all human infants pass through a phase of primary narcissism, in which they assume they are the center of their universe. This phase ends when the baby is forced by the realities of life to recognize that it does not control its parents (or other caregivers) but is in fact entirely dependent on them. In normal circumstances, the baby gives up its fantasy of being all-powerful and becomes emotionally attached to its parents rather than itself. What Freud defined as secondary narcissism is a pathological condition in which the infant does not invest its emotions in its parents but rather redirects them back to itself. He thought that secondary narcissism developed in what he termed the pre-Oedipal phase of childhood; that is, before the age of three. From a Freudian perspective, then, narcissistic disorders originate in very early childhood development, and this early origin is thought to explain why they are so difficult to treat in later life.

CAUSES IN THE FAMILY OF ORIGIN. Kohut and Kernberg agree with Freud in tracing the roots of NPD to disturbances in the patient's family of origin—specifically, to problems in the parent-child relationship before the child turned three. Where they disagree is in their accounts of the nature of these problems. According to Kohut, the child grows out of primary narcissism through opportunities to be mirrored by (i.e., gain approval from) his or her parents and to idealize them, acquiring a more realistic sense of self and a set of personal ideals and values through these two processes. On the other hand, if the parents fail to provide appropriate opportunities for idealization and mirroring, the child remains "stuck" at a developmental stage in which his or her sense of self remains grandiose and unrealistic while at the same time he or she remains dependent on approval from others for self-esteem.

In contrast, Kernberg views NPD as rooted in the child's defense against a cold and unempathetic parent, usually the mother. Emotionally hungry and angry at the depriving parents, the child withdraws into a part of the self that the parents value, whether looks, intellectual ability, or some other skill or talent. This part of the self becomes hyperinflated and grandiose. Any perceived weaknesses are "split off" into a hidden part of the self. Splitting gives rise to a lifelong tendency to swing between extremes of grandiosity and feelings of emptiness and worthlessness.

In both accounts, the child emerges into adult life with a history of unsatisfactory relationships with others. The adult narcissist possesses a grandiose view of the self but has a conflict-ridden psychological dependence on others. At present, however, psychiatrists do not agree in their description of the central defect in NPD; some think that the problem is primarily emotional while others regard it as the result of distorted cognition, or knowing. Some maintain that the person with NPD has an "empty" or hungry sense of self while others argue that the narcissist has a "disorganized" self. Still others regard the core problem as the narcissist's inability to test reality and construct an accurate view of him- or herself.

MACROSOCIAL CAUSES. One dimension of NPD that must be taken into account is its social and historical context. Psychiatrists became interested in narcissism shortly after World War II (1939–45), when the older practitioners in the field noticed that their patient population had changed. Instead of seeing patients who suffered from obsessions and compulsions related to a harsh and punishing super-ego (the part of the psyche that internalizes the standards and moral demands of one's parents and culture), the psychiatrists were treating more patients with character disorders related to a weak sense of self. Instead of having a judgmental and overactive conscience, these patients had a weak or nonexistent code of morals. They were very different from the patients that Freud had treated, described, and analyzed. The younger generation of psychiatrists then began to interpret their patients' character disorders in terms of narcissism.

In the 1960s historians and social critics drew the attention of the general public to narcissism as a metaphorical description of Western culture in general. These writers saw several parallels between trends in the larger society and the personality traits of people diagnosed with narcissistic disorders. In short, they argued that the advanced industrial societies of Europe and the United States were contributing to the development of narcissistic disorders in individuals in a number of respects. Some of the trends they noted include the following:

- The mass media's preoccupation with "lifestyles of the rich and famous" rather than with ordinary or average people.

- Social approval of open displays of money, status, or accomplishments ("if you've got it, flaunt it") rather than modesty and self-restraint.

- Preference for a leadership style that emphasizes the leader's outward appearance and personality rather than his or her inner beliefs and values.

- The growth of large corporations and government bureaucracies that favor a managerial style based on "impression management" rather than objective measurements of performance.

- Social trends that encourage parents to be self-centered and to resent their children's legitimate needs.

- The weakening of churches, synagogues, and other religious or social institutions that traditionally helped children to see themselves as members of a community rather than as isolated individuals.

Although discussion continues about the location and forms of narcissism in the larger society, no one now denies that personality disorders both reflect and influence the culture in which they arise. Family therapists are now reporting on the treatment of families in which the children are replicating the narcissistic disorders of their parents.

Symptoms

Most observers regard grandiosity as the most important single trait of a narcissistic personality. It is important to note that grandiosity implies more than boasting or prideful display as such—it signifies self-aggrandizement that is not borne out by reality. For example, a person who claims that he or she was the most valuable player on a college athletic team may be telling the truth about their undergraduate sports record. Their claim may be bad manners but is not grandiosity. On the other hand, someone who makes the same claim but had an undistinguished record or never even made the team is being grandiose. Grandiosity in NPD is related to some of the diagnostic criteria listed by *DSM-IV-TR*, such as demanding special favors from others or choosing friends and associates on the basis of prestige and high status rather than personal qualities. In addition, grandiosity complicates diagnostic assessment of narcissists because it frequently leads to lying and misrepresentation of one's past history and present accomplishments.

Other symptoms of NPD include:

- a history of intense but short-term relationships with others; inability to make or sustain genuinely intimate relationships

- a tendency to be attracted to leadership or high-profile positions or occupations

- a pattern of alternating between unrealistic idealization of others and equally unrealistic devaluation of them

- assessment of others in terms of usefulness

- a need to be the center of attention or admiration in a working group or social situation

- hypersensitivity to criticism, however mild, or rejection from others

- an unstable view of the self that fluctuates between extremes of self-praise and self-contempt

- preoccupation with outward appearance, "image," or public opinion rather than inner reality

- painful emotions based on shame (dislike of who one is) rather than guilt (regret for what one has done)

People diagnosed with NPD represent a range of levels of functioning. Otto Kernberg has described three levels of narcissistic impairment. At the top are those who are talented or gifted enough to attract all the admiration and attention that they want; these people may never enter therapy because they don't feel the need. On the second level are those who function satisfactorily in their jobs but seek professional help because they cannot form healthy relationships or because they feel generally bored and aimless. Narcissists on the lowest level have frequently been diagnosed with another mental disorder and/or have gotten into trouble with the law. They often have severe difficulties with anxiety and with controlling their impulses.

Diagnosis

The diagnosis of NPD is complicated by a number of factors.

Complications of diagnosis

NPD is difficult to diagnose for several reasons. First, some people with NPD function sufficiently well that they do not come to the attention of therapists. Second, narcissists are prone to lie about themselves; thus it may take a long time for a therapist to notice discrepancies between a patient's version of his or her life and information gained from others or from public records. Third, many traits and behaviors associated with NPD may be attributed to other mental disorders. Low-functioning narcissists are often diagnosed as having **borderline personality disorder** (BPD), particularly if they are female; if they are male, they may be diagnosed as having **antisocial personality disorder** (ASPD). If the person with NPD has a substance abuse disorder, some of their narcissistic behaviors may be written off to the mood-altering substance. More recently, some psychiatrists have pointed to a tendency to confuse narcissistic behaviors in people with NPD who have had a traumatic experience with full-blown **post-traumatic stress disorder** (PTSD). Given the lack of clarity in the differential diagnosis of NPD, some therapists are calling for a fundamental revision of *DSM-IV-TR* definitions of the personality disorders.

An additional complication is posed by economic considerations. The coming of **managed care** has meant that third-party payers (insurance companies) prefer short-term **psychotherapy** that concentrates on a patient's acute problems rather than on underlying chronic issues. Since narcissists are reluctant to trust others or form genuine interpersonal bonds, there is a strong possibility that many therapists do not recognize NPD in patients that they are treating for only a few weeks or months.

Diagnostic interviews

Diagnosis of NPD is usually made on the basis of several sources of information: the patient's history and self-description, information from family members and others, and the results of diagnostic questionnaires. One questionnaire that is often used in the process of differential diagnosis is the Structured Clinical Interview for *DSM-III-R* Disorders, known as the SCID-II.

The most common diagnostic instrument used for narcissistic NPD is the Narcissistic Personality Inventory (NPI). First published by Robert R. Raskin and Calvin S. Hall in 1979, the NPI consists of 223 items consisting of paired statements, one reflecting narcissistic traits and the other nonnarcissistic. Subjects are required to choose one of the two items. The NPI is widely used in research as well as diagnostic assessment.

Treatment

Treatment for NPD focuses primarily on psychotherapy, though medications may be used to alleviate symptoms associated with other disorders.

Medication

There are no medications used specifically for the treatment of NPD. Patients with NPD who are also depressed or anxious may be given drugs for relief of those symptoms. There are anecdotal reports in the medical literature that the **selective serotonin reuptake inhibitors**, or **SSRIs**, which are frequently prescribed for **depression**, may reinforce narcissistic grandiosity and lack of empathy with others.

Psychotherapy

Several different approaches to individual therapy have been tried with NPD patients, ranging from classical **psychoanalysis** and Adlerian therapy to rational-emotive approaches and **Gestalt therapy**. The consensus that has emerged is that therapists should set modest goals for treatment with NPD patients. Most of them cannot form a sufficiently deep bond with a therapist to allow healing of early-childhood injuries. In addition, the tendency of these patients to criticize and devalue their therapists (as well as other authority figures) makes it difficult for therapists to work with them.

An additional factor that complicates psychotherapy with NPD patients is the lack of agreement among psychiatrists about the causes and course of the disorder. Other types of therapy that may be tried include **cognitive-behavioral therapy**, **family therapy**, and **group therapy**.

KEY TERMS

Grandiosity—Exaggerated and unrealistic self-importance; inflated self-assessment. Grandiosity is considered one of the core characteristics of persons diagnosed with NPD.

Macrosocial—Pertaining to the wider society, as distinct from such smaller social groupings as families, neighborhoods, etc.

Narcissistic Personality Inventory (NPI)—The most widely used English-language diagnostic instrument for narcissistic personality disorder. Based on the *DSM-III* criteria for NPD, the NPI is frequently used in research studies as well as patient assessment.

Primary narcissism—Sigmund Freud's term for a normal phase in early childhood development in which the infant has not yet learned to distinguish between itself and its world, and sees other people and things in its environment as extensions of itself.

Projection—A psychological process in which a person unconsciously attributes unacceptable feelings to someone else. Narcissists often project their envy onto other people, claiming that the person in question is envious of them.

Splitting—A psychological process that occurs during the childhood of a person with NPD, in which the child separates aspects of him- or herself that the parents value from those that they disregard.

Superego—According to Freud, the part of the mind that represents traditional parental and societal values. The superego is the source of guilt feelings.

Hospitalization

Low-functioning patients with NPD may require inpatient treatment, particularly those with severe self-harming behaviors or lack of impulse control. Hospital treatment, however, appears to be most helpful when it is focused on the immediate crisis and its symptoms rather than the patient's underlying long-term difficulties.

Prognosis

The prognosis for younger persons with narcissistic disorders is hopeful to the extent that the disturbances reflect a simple lack of life experience. The outlook for long-standing NPD, however, is largely negative. Some narcissists are able, particularly as they approach their midlife years, to accept their own limitations and those of others, to resolve their problems with envy, and to accept their own mortality. Most patients with NPD, on the other hand, become increasingly depressed as they grow older within a youth-oriented culture and lose their looks and overall vitality. The retirement years are especially painful for patients with NPD because they must yield their positions in the working world to the next generation. In addition, they do not have the network of intimate family ties and friendships that sustain most older people.

Prevention

The best hope for prevention of NPD lies with parents and other caregivers who are close to children during the early preschool years. Parents must be able to demonstrate empathy in their interactions with the child and with each other. They must also be able to show that they love their children for who they are, not for their appearance or their achievements. And they must focus their parenting efforts on meeting the child's changing needs as he or she matures, rather than demanding that the child meet their needs for status, comfort, or convenience.

Resources

BOOKS

American Psychiatric Association. *Diagnostic and Statistical Manual of Mental Disorders*. 4th ed., text rev. Washington, DC: American Psychiatric Publishing, 2000.

Capps, Donald. *The Depleted Self: Sin in a Narcissistic Age*. Minneapolis: Augsberg Fortress Press, 1993.

Goodman, Cynthia Lechan, and Barbara Leff. *The Everything Guide to Narcissistic Personality Disorder*. Avon, MA: Adams Media, 2012.

Lowen, Alexander. *Narcissism: Denial of the True Self*. New York: Touchstone, 1985.

World Health Organization (WHO). *The ICD-10 Classification of Mental and Behavioural Disorders*. Geneva: WHO, 1993.

PERIODICALS

Billingham, Robert E., et al. "Narcissistic Injury and Sexual Victimization Among Women College Students." *College Student Journal* 33 (September 1999): 62–70.

Coid, J.W. "Aetiological Risk Factors for Personality Disorders." *British Journal of Psychiatry* 174 (June 1999): 530–538.

Karterud, S., et al. "Validity Aspects of the Diagnostic and Statistical Manual of Mental Disorders, Fourth Edition, Narcissistic Personality Disorder Construct." *Comprehensive Psychiatry* 52, no. 5 (2011): 517–26.

Raskin, R.N., and C.S. Hall. "A Narcissistic Personality Inventory." *Psychological Reports* 45, no. 2 (October 1979): 590.

Ritter, K., et al. "Lack of Empathy in Patients with Narcissistic Personality Disorder." *Psychiatry Research* 187, nos. 1–2 (2011): 241–47.

Ronningstam, E. "Narcissistic Personality Disorder in DSM-V—In Support of Retaining a Significant Diagnosis." *Journal of Personality Disorders* 25, no. 2 (2011): 248–59.

Tschanz, Brian T. "Gender Differences in the Study of Narcissism: A Multi-Sample Analysis of the Narcissistic Personality Inventory." *Sex Roles: A Journal of Research* 38 (May 1998): 209–216.

ORGANIZATIONS

American Psychiatric Association, 1000 Wilson Blvd., Ste. 1825, Arlington, VA, 22209-3901, (703) 907-7300, apa@psych.org, http://www.psych.org.

National Institute of Mental Health, 6001 Executive Blvd., Room 8184, MSC 9663, Bethesda, MD, 20892-9663, (301) 433-4513; TTY: (301) 443-8431, Fax: (301) 443-4279, (866) 615-6464; TTY: (866) 415-8051, nimhinfo@nih.gov, http://www.nimh.nih.gov.

Rebecca J. Frey, Ph.D.

Narcolepsy

Definition

Narcolepsy is a neurological disorder caused by the brain's inability to regulate normal sleep/wake cycles. It is marked by excessive daytime sleepiness, uncontrollable sleep attacks, and cataplexy (a sudden loss of muscle tone, usually lasting up to half an hour). It was first described and named in 1880 by a French physician, Jean-Baptiste-Édouard Gélineau (1828–1906). Gélineau derived the name for the disease from two Greek words that mean "numbness" and "seizure."

Demographics

As of 2011, narcolepsy was the second leading cause of excessive daytime sleepiness diagnosed by sleep centers in North America after obstructive sleep apnea. The rate of narcolepsy in the general population varies widely around the world: in Israel, for example, only about one person per 500,000 is diagnosed with narcolepsy, whereas the rate in Japan is one person in every 600. In the United States, narcolepsy affects about one person in every 2,000–3,000; it is slightly more common among African Americans than among members of other races. According to the National Institute of Neurological Disorders and Stroke (NINDS), there may be cases of the disease that are undiagnosed because they lack the symptom of cataplexy.

Narcolepsy is slightly more common in men than in women; the male/female ratio is 1.64:1. It is not thought to be inherited; however, about 10% of Americans with narcolepsy have a relative with the condition, but this percentage is low compared to other disorders that are known to be purely genetic in origin. Most cases of narcolepsy are sporadic, which means that they occur at random as isolated instances without evidence of contagious transmission or genetic inheritance.

Description

Narcolepsy can affect people in any age group but may not be diagnosed for as long as 10 to 15 years after onset. It can be a disabling condition. Because people with narcolepsy can fall asleep in the daytime in the middle of other activities, including eating, driving, or operating heavy equipment, they can be involved in serious accidents. People with untreated narcolepsy are involved in automobile accidents roughly 10 times more often than the general population. Children or adolescents with narcolepsy can fall behind in school or be judged as lazy even though they are of normal or even superior intelligence.

Having narcolepsy does not mean that people with the disorder sleep more than other people. The disorder is better understood as a disturbance of the normal boundaries between sleeping and waking rather than simply sleeping too much. A normal adult who sleeps for about 8 hours has 4–6 sleep cycles during that time. A sleep cycle is a period of a type of sleep called non-rapid eye movement (NREM) sleep followed by a period of rapid eye movement (REM) sleep. REM sleep is characterized by increased **brain** activity, rapid movement of the eyes below the lids, and sleep paralysis. Individuals who say that they were having a dream when they woke up have been awakened from REM sleep. In normal adults, a sleep cycle is about 100–110 minutes long, 80–100 minutes of NREM sleep followed by 10–20 minutes of REM sleep.

In narcolepsy, however, individuals' sleep cycles do not follow this normal pattern. Instead, individuals falls into REM sleep very shortly after falling asleep. In addition, the short periods of sleep that they have during the daytime are REM sleep. This abnormal entry into REM sleep helps to explain such symptoms of narcolepsy as sleep paralysis and cataplexy.

Risk factors

While there are clusters of cases of narcolepsy in some families, genetics is not a major risk factor. Some researchers believe that **trauma**, immune system dysfunction, hormonal imbalances, and emotional **stress** are possible triggers for the appearance of the disorder, although the associations were not clear enough as of 2011 to identify these conditions as definite risk factors.

Narcolepsy

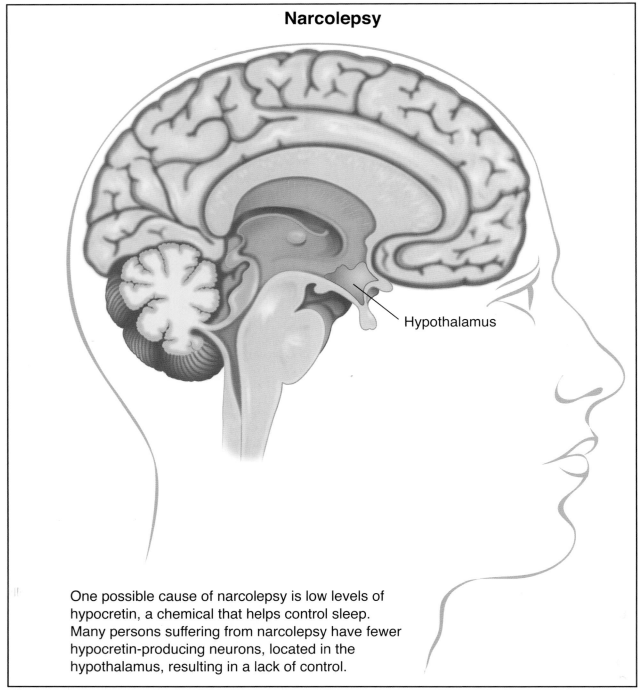

Hypothalamus

One possible cause of narcolepsy is low levels of hypocretin, a chemical that helps control sleep. Many persons suffering from narcolepsy have fewer hypocretin-producing neurons, located in the hypothalamus, resulting in a lack of control.

(Illustration by Electronic Illustrators Group. Reproduced by permission of Gale, a part of Cengage Learning.)

Causes and symptoms

Causes

The cause of narcolepsy was unclear as of 2011, but it is thought to be a combination of genetic, neurotransmitter, and hormonal factors. Some progress has been made since the late 1990s in identifying two pieces of the puzzle. The first is a connection between narcolepsy and changes in a set of genes on chromosome 6 called the HLA complex. The HLA gene family provides instructions for making a group of related proteins known as the human leukocyte antigen (HLA) complex. The HLA complex helps the immune system distinguish the body's own proteins from proteins made by foreign invaders such as viruses and bacteria. From 88% to 98% of patients affected by narcolepsy have been shown to be

HLA DQB1*0602 positive. This allele (form of gene) strongly increases the susceptibility for cataplexy although 41% of patients without cataplexy are carriers. DRB1 and DQB1 genes have been sequenced in narcolepsy patients, but no mutation has been identified. This suggests that these genes strongly confer susceptibility to narcolepsy without their function being defective. Researchers accordingly think that non-HLA genes may also be involved in susceptibility to narcolepsy.

It is thought that changes in the HLA genes may be linked to the loss of cells in the brain that secrete the hypocretins (also called orexins), two closely related hormones secreted by a small group of cells in the hypothalamus that regulate the sleep/wake cycle. In fact, one of the proposed changes in the fifth edition of the *Diagnostic and Statistical Manual of Mental Disorders* (*DSM-5*) is to list the disorder as Narcolepsy/Hypocretin Deficiency. Researchers do not yet know exactly what causes the loss of the brain cells that make the hypocretins. Because the HLA complex has been linked to other autoimmune disorders, however, some doctors think that narcolepsy may be an autoimmune disease. Experiments conducted at Stanford University School of Medicine in 2009 offer some support for this hypothesis. Other researchers think that the hypocretin-producing cells may be damaged by some type of infection, but this theory had not been proven as of 2011.

The third piece of the puzzle is abnormal neurotransmitter function. Some studies of narcolepsy in dogs indicate that abnormally low levels of the neurotransmitter acetylcholine are associated with cataplexy.

Symptoms

Narcolepsy in adults has four primary symptoms known as the narcoleptic tetrad (children, however, rarely have all four):

- Excessive daytime sleepiness (EDS). This symptom may take the form of microsleeps of a few seconds, a long-lasting feeling of drowsiness, or daytime episodes of sleep lasting half an hour or longer.
- Cataplexy. Cataplexy refers to a sudden loss of muscle tone that may result in slurred speech, sagging of the facial muscles, general muscle weakness, inability to hold up the head, buckling of the knees, or loss of strength in the arms. Cataplexy is often triggered by strong emotions, whether positive feelings such as laughter or pleasant surprise or negative emotions such as fear, shock, or anger. Cataplexy can last from a few seconds to as long as 30 minutes. Individuals are awake and alert during an episode of cataplexy even though they may appear unconscious to others.

- Hypnagogic hallucinations. "Hypnagogic" refers to the period of partial alertness that people have when they are waking up or falling asleep. People with narcolepsy experience vivid and sometimes frightening dreams when they are half awake, and they may mistake these dreams for reality.
- Sleep paralysis. Sleep paralysis refers to a temporary inability to move or speak while falling asleep or waking up. These episodes last only one or two minutes and do not affect everyone with narcolepsy, but they can be frightening to patients who do have them.

Other symptoms experienced by some people with narcolepsy are automatic behavior, in which individuals talk to others or perform a routine task such as sorting laundry or making a cup of coffee without conscious awareness or later memory of their action or conversation. People with narcolepsy may also suffer from episodes of **insomnia** or have sleep disturbances in which they thrash about in bed at night or act out their dreams by screaming or waving their arms. Sudden weight gain leading to obesity also occurs in many patients after the symptoms of narcolepsy appear.

Diagnosis

The **diagnosis** of narcolepsy is often delayed because its symptoms resemble those of other disorders such as **depression**, seizure disorders, simple lack of sleep, or even illegal drug use. About 50% of American adults diagnosed with the disorder report that they first noticed its symptoms when they were teenagers. Most cases of narcolepsy first appear in people between the ages of 10 and 25 years, but the disorder has been diagnosed in children as young as three and in adults over 50.

Examination

A routine office physical examination is usually unrevealing, although the patient may be referred to a neurologist to rule out a brain tumor or some other structural abnormality of the brain. The diagnosis of narcolepsy is based on a combination of the patient's history, the results of a screening questionnaire, and overnight testing in a sleep laboratory. The screening questionnaire that is used most commonly is the Epworth Sleepiness Scale, or ESS, which was developed in Australia in the early 1990s. The patient may also be asked to keep a sleep diary for one or two weeks and wear a device called an actigraph, which resembles a wrist watch and measures the person's sleep.

Tests

Imaging tests are not useful in diagnosing narcolepsy. The tests most commonly used to evaluate a

Automatic behavior—Activity that a person with narcolepsy can carry out while partially awake but is not conscious of at the time and cannot recall afterward.

Cataplexy—A sudden episode of muscle weakness triggered by emotions. The muscle weakness may cause the person's knees to buckle or the head to drop. In severe cases, the patient may become paralyzed for a few seconds to minutes.

Eugeroic—A type of medication that promotes wakefulness.

Excessive daytime sleepiness (EDS)—A persistent sense of mental cloudiness, a lack of energy, a depressed mood, or extreme state of exhaustion.

Hypnagogic hallucinations—Auditory or visual hallucinations that occur while falling asleep.

Hypocretins—A pair of closely related neuropeptide hormones that promote wakefulness, secreted by a small group of cells in the hypothalamus. The hypocretins are also called orexins and are identified as hypocretin-1 (orexin-A) and hypocretin-2 (orexin-B).

Hypothalamus—A part of the forebrain that controls heartbeat, body temperature, thirst, hunger, body temperature and pressure, blood sugar levels, and other functions.

Microsleep—A brief episode of sleep lasting from a fraction of a second to 30 seconds. It may result from sleep deprivation, sleep apnea, or oxygen deprivation as well as from narcolepsy.

Non-rapid eye movement (NREM) sleep—The first phase of a sleep cycle, in which there is little or no eye movement.

Off-label—Referring to the use of a prescription medication for an unapproved reason to use it, an unapproved age group, or an unapproved dosage level.

Orexins—Another name for the hypocretins.

Rapid eye movement (REM) sleep—The phase of a sleep cycle in which dreaming occurs; characterized by rapid eye movements.

Sleep cycle—A period of NREM sleep followed by a shorter phase of REM sleep. Most adults have 4–6 sleep cycles per night.

Sleep paralysis—An abnormal episode of sleep in which the patient cannot move for a few minutes, usually occurring on falling asleep or waking up. It is often found in patients with narcolepsy.

person for narcolepsy are sleep tests performed in a specially designed laboratory. The patient will usually be tested overnight in a medical center equipped with a polysomnograph. The polysomnograph is a machine that measures the electrical activity of the heart and brain, breathing, and eye movement while the patient is sleeping. Another sleep test is the multiple sleep latency test or MSLT. The patient is given a chance to sleep every two hours during normal waking time. Observations are made of the time taken to reach various stages of sleep. The MSLT measures the degree of the patient's daytime sleepiness and also detects how soon REM sleep begins.

Another test that may be done in the hospital is a lumbar puncture (spinal tap), which is performed to obtain a sample of the patient's cerebrospinal fluid (CSF). The sample can be tested for its hypocretin level, to determine whether the patient's hypocretin level is abnormally low. DSM-5 specifies a hypocretin level lower than one-third of the normal reference value as one of the diagnostic criteria of narcolepsy. If the diagnosis is uncertain, a genetic blood test can reveal the existence of certain substances in people who have a tendency to develop narcolepsy. Positive test results suggest but do not prove the existence of narcolepsy.

Treatment

There is no cure for narcolepsy. Treatment is multimodal, involving a combination of medications, lifestyle changes, and **psychotherapy**. There were no surgical treatments for narcolepsy as of 2011.

Drugs

Medications given to treat narcolepsy must be tailored to the individual patient because most have side effects, and patients may tolerate some drugs in a given class better than others. Amphetamine-like stimulant drugs are often prescribed to control drowsiness and EDS attacks. Patients who do not like taking high doses of stimulants may choose to take smaller doses and manage their lifestyles, such as by napping every couple of hours, to relieve daytime sleepiness. **Antidepressants**, including **venlafaxine**, **imipramine**, **duloxetine**, and **fluoxetine**, are often effective in treating symptoms of abnormal REM sleep. In 2002, the FDA approved Xyrem (sodium oxybate or gamma hydroxybutyrate, also known as GHB) for treating people with narcolepsy who experience episodes of cataplexy.

Modafinil (brand name Provigil) belongs to a class of stimulants known as eugeroics, which have been used to treat narcolepsy in the United States since the late 1990s. Eugeroic stimulants enhance alertness without many of the physical side effects or potential for dependence or abuse commonly associated with **amphetamines**. Another eugeroic approved by the FDA to treat narcolepsy is armodafinil (Nuvigil), which has fewer side effects than modafinil. It is important, however, for persons taking stimulant medications to notify their employer, because the drugs may show up during pre-employment urine tests. With the discovery of the gene associated with narcolepsy, researchers are hopeful that other treatments can be designed to relieve the symptoms of the disorder.

There were no drugs approved by the FDA as of 2011 to treat narcolepsy in children. In most cases children are treated with lower dosages of drugs approved to treat adults. This type of drug usage (in this case, using a medication for an unapproved age group) is known as off-label prescribing.

Newer drug treatments for narcolepsy include thyrotropin-releasing hormone (TRH), histamine agonists, immunotherapy and hypocretin replacement therapies.

Lifestyle adjustments

Lifestyle changes recommended for patients with narcolepsy include:

- Getting enough sleep at night. Patients are advised to go to bed and get up at the same time every day rather than changing their sleeping schedule frequently.

- Taking scheduled short naps at intervals during waking hours. This practice helps to reduce daytime sleepiness.

- Avoiding the use of alcohol and tobacco. These substances can make it harder to sleep at night.

- Getting regular exercise. Physical exercise 4–5 hours before bedtime helps many people with narcolepsy sleep better. Children in particular benefit from regular sports activities or other forms of exercise.

- Being careful to avoid driving when tired or sleepy.

- Joining a narcolepsy support group. Finding understanding and support from others with the same disorder is particularly helpful to patients who may have waited years to be diagnosed and suffered the

QUESTIONS TO ASK YOUR DOCTOR

- What can be done to control excessive sleepiness during the day?
- What medications can help control symptoms?
- How efficient is sodium oxybate for treatment of cataplexy?
- What are the side effects of the medications you have prescribed for me?
- What lifestyle adjustments can help me cope with the disorder?
- What are some of the newer treatments for narcolepsy?
- Have you ever treated a patient with narcolepsy?

loss of jobs, relationships, or educational opportunities in the meantime.

Prognosis

Narcolepsy is not a degenerative disease, and patients do not develop other neurologic symptoms. People with narcolepsy can expect to live normal life spans (barring accidents). Narcolepsy can, however, interfere with a person's ability to work, play, drive, and perform other daily activities. Early diagnosis is important because the impact of the disorder on a person's education, employment, relationships, and self-esteem can be severe. According to one study, 24% of adults with narcolepsy had to quit working and 18% had been fired from their jobs because of their disease. In severe cases, the disorder prevents people from living a normal life, leading to depression and a loss of independence.

Prevention

There is no known way to prevent narcolepsy, because its causes are not yet understood.

Resources

BOOKS

Baumann, Christian R., ed. *Narcolepsy*. New York: Springer, 2011.

Benca, Ruth M. *Sleep Disorders: The Clinician's Guide to Diagnosis and Management*. Oxford: Oxford University Press, 2011.

Santos, Guillermo, and Lautar Villalba, eds. *Narcolepsy: Symptoms, Causes, and Diagnosis*. New York: Nova Science, 2010.

PERIODICALS

Bogan, R.K. "Armodafinil in the Treatment of Excessive Sleepiness." *Expert Opinion on Pharmacotherapy* 11 (2010): 993–1002.

Cao, M. "Advances in Narcolepsy." *Medical Clinics of North America* 94 (2010): 541–55.

Cao, M., and C. Guilleminault. "Hypocretin and Its Emerging Role as a Target for Treatment of Sleep Disorders." *Current Neurology and Neuroscience Reports* 11 (2011): 227–34.

Golicki, D., et al. "Modafinil for Narcolepsy: Systematic Review and Meta-analysis." *Medical Science Monitor* 16 (2010): RA177–RA186.

Hauw, J.J., et al. "Neuropathology of Sleep Disorders: A Review." *Journal of Neuropathology and Experimental Neurology* 70 (2011): 243–52.

Pack, A.I., and G.W. Pien. "Update on Sleep and Its Disorders." *Annual Review of Medicine* 62 (2011): 447–60.

Raizen, D.M., and M.N. Wu. "Genome-wide Association Studies of Sleep Disorders." *Chest* 139 (2011): 446–52.

Siegel, J.M. "REM Sleep: A Biological and Psychological Paradox." *Sleep Medicine Reviews* 15 (2011): 139–42.

Smolensky, M.H., et al. "Sleep Disorders, Medical Conditions, and Road Accident Risk." *Accident Analysis and Prevention* 43 (2011): 533–48.

Sullivan, S.S. "Narcolepsy in Adolescents." *Adolescent Medicine: State of the Art Reviews* 21 (2010): 542–55.

Zaharna, M., et al. "Expert Opinion on Pharmacotherapy of Narcolepsy." *Expert Opinion on Pharmacotherapy* 11 (J2010): 1633–45.

WEBSITES

American Psychiatric Association. DSM-5 Development. "M 03 Narcolepsy/Hypocretin Deficiency." http://www.dsm5. org/ProposedRevision/Pages/proposedrevision.aspx? rid=196# (accessed October 27, 2011).

Mayo Clinic. " Narcolepsy." http://www.mayoclinic.com/ health/narcolepsy/DS00345 (accessed October 27, 2011).

Medscape. "Narcolepsy." http://emedicine.medscape.com/ article/1188433-overview (accessed October 27, 2011).

Narcolepsy Network. " About Narcolepsy." http://www. narcolepsynetwork.org/about-narcolepsy (accessed October 27, 2011).

National Institute of Neurological Disorders and Stroke (NINDS). " Narcolepsy Fact Sheet." http://www.ninds.nih. gov/disorders/narcolepsy/detail_narcolepsy.htm (accessed October 27, 2011).

National Sleep Foundation. "Narcolepsy and Sleep." http:// www.sleepfoundation.org/article/sleep-related-problems/ narcolepsy-and-sleep (accessed October 27, 2011).

Stanford University School of Medicine Center for Narcolepsy. "About Narcolepsy." http://med.stanford.edu/school/ Psychiatry/narcolepsy/symptoms.html (accessed October 27, 2011).

Stanford University School of Medicine Center for Narcolepsy. "Movies of Narcolepsy/Cataplexy." This is a page with links to seven film clips of narcolepsy or cataplexy in dogs, fish, and mice as well as humans. http://med. stanford.edu/school/Psychiatry/narcolepsy/moviedog.html (accessed October 27, 2011).

ORGANIZATIONS

American Academy of Neurology, 1080 Montreal Ave., St. Paul, MN, 55116, (651) 695-2717, Fax: (651) 695-2791, (800) 879-1960, http://www.aan.com.

American Academy of Sleep Medicine, 2510 North Frontage Rd., Darien, IL, 60561, (630) 737-9700, Fax: (630) 737-9790, inquiries@aasmnet.org, http://www.aasmnet.org.

Narcolepsy Network, 110 Ripple Lane, North Kingstown, RI, 02852, (401) 667-2523, Fax: (401) 633-6567, (888) 292-6522, narnet@narcolepsynetwork.org, http://www. narcolepsynetwork.org.

National Institute of Mental Health, 6001 Executive Blvd., Rm. 8184, MSC 9663, Bethesda, MD, 20892-9663, (301) 443-4513, Fax: (301) 443-4279, (866) 615-6464, nimhinfo@ nih.gov, http://www.nimh.nih.gov/index.shtml.

National Institute of Neurological Disorders and Stroke, PO Box 5801, Bethesda, MD, 20824, (301) 496-5751, (800) 352-9424, http://www.ninds.nih.gov.

National Sleep Foundation, 1010 N. Glebe Rd., Ste. 310, Arlington, VA, 22201, (703) 243-1697, nsf@ sleepfoun dation.org, http://www.sleepfoundation.org.

Stanford University School of Medicine Center for Narcolepsy, 450 Broadway St., Pavilion B, 2nd Fl., Redwood City, CA, 94063, (650) 725-6517 Fax: (650) 725-4913, http://med.stanford.edu/school/ Psychiatry/narcolepsy.

Michelle Lee Brandt
Rebecca J. Frey, PhD
Monique Laberge, PhD

Nardil *see* **Phenelzine**

National Institute of Mental Health

Definition

The National Institute of Mental Health (NIMH) is the U.S. government agency that conducts and supports research on mental illness and mental health. The NIMH is a component of the National Institutes of Health (NIH) and was one of the first four institutes created. Proposed by the National Mental Health Act in 1946, the institute was formally established in 1949. Specific areas of research include the **brain**, behavior, and mental health services.

Purpose

The NIMH is dedicated to improving the mental health of the American people, fostering better understanding, **diagnosis**, treatment, rehabilitation, and prevention of mental and brain disorders. The NIMH's mission is "to transform the understanding and treatment of mental illnesses through basic and clinical research, paving the way for prevention, recovery, and cure."

Description

In order to carry out its mission, the NIMH supports research by awarding more than 2,000 research grants to scientists working in universities or other research facilities. Grants support the study of all aspects of mental illness, from biological to social, and they also help identify specific areas where research is needed. The NIMH also supports a large in-house research program, consisting of more than 500 scientists, that studies the causes of and new treatments for mental illnesses. In addition, the NIMH collects and disseminates statistical information to scientists and researchers, conducts training and career development programs, supports small business research programs, sponsors **clinical trials**, and prepares and distributes a wide variety of educational materials.

Among the key areas of research interest for NIMH are neuroscience and behavioral science, including sciences basic to the understanding of the anatomical and chemical basis of brain disorders, and the most prevalent mental disorders and their causes and prevention, such as **schizophrenia**, mood disorders, **anxiety disorders**, eating disorders, and **Alzheimer's disease**. Specific outside research divisions include the Division of Neuroscience and Basic Behavioral Science (DNBBS), the Division of Adult Translational Research and Treatment Development (DATR), the Division of Developmental Translational Research (DDTR), the Division of AIDS Research (DAR), and the Division of Services and **Intervention** Research (DSIR). Additional research efforts include the NIMH Professional Coalition for Research Progress and the NIMH Alliance for Research Progress.

The NIMH operates under the Office of the NIMH Director. Outside of the five research divisions, additional divisions include the Division of Extramural Activities (DEA) and the Division of Intramural Research Programs (DIRP). Advisory boards and groups include the National Advisory Mental Health Council (NAMHC), peer review committees, a board of scientific counselors (BSC), and the NIMH Outreach Partnership Program, which focuses on improving access to mental health information within communities.

Professional publications

The National Institute of Mental Health communicates current research, diagnosis and treatment information to professionals and the public through conferences, symposia and meetings, and works closely with professional and voluntary organizations and other federal agencies. The institute produces a number of publications, including booklets, brochures, and fact sheets, available in both English and Spanish. The NIMH also produces videos and podcasts on mental health topics, which are available on the NIMH website at: http://www.nimh.nih.gov/news/index.shtml.

ORGANIZATIONS

National Institute of Mental Health, 6001 Executive Blvd., Rm. 8184, MSC 9663, Bethesda, MD, 20892-9663, (301) 433-4513; TTY: (301) 443-8431, (866) 615-6464; TTY: (866) 415-8051, Fax: (301) 443-4279, nimhinfo@nih.gov, http://www.nimh.nih.gov.

Navane *see* **Thiothixene**

Nefazodone

Definition

Nefazodone is a prescription drug commonly used to treat **depression**. Nefazodone was available in the United States under the trade name of Serzone, but its maker is no longer marketing it under that name. It is still available in the United States as generic brands.

Purpose

Nefazodone is considered an antidepressant and is best known for treating depression. It may be used to treat **major depressive disorder**, **dysthymic disorder**, and the depressed phase of **bipolar disorder**. As with all **antidepressants**, it may take several weeks before full beneficial effects are seen.

Description

Nefazodone was approved by the U.S. Food and Drug Administration (FDA) in 1994. It is believed to increase the amounts of some chemicals in the **brain**. By altering the activities of specific brain chemicals, nefazodone may reduce the chemical imbalances responsible for causing depression.

The drug is available as tablets in several different strengths, including 50, 100, 150, 200, and 250 mg tablets.

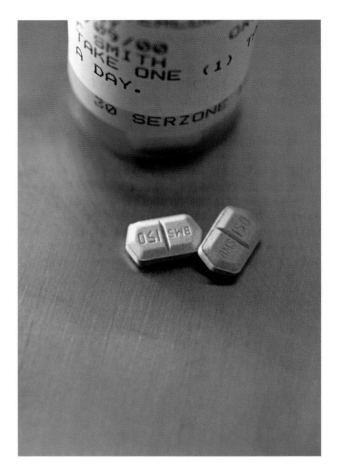

Serzone (nefazodone). *(© Michelle Del Guercio/Photo Researchers, Inc.)*

Nefazodone is broken down by the liver.

Recommended dosage

For most people, the recommended initial dose of nefazodone is 100 mg taken by mouth twice daily. The dose may be increased in 100- or 200 mg increments once a week. Most commonly, final dosages range between 300–600 mg taken by mouth each day.

It is recommended that the initial dose of nefazodone be lowered to 50 mg twice daily for individuals over age 65 or with debilitations, because these individuals may be more sensitive to some of the drug's side effects.

Precautions

Patients should read the medication guide before starting treatment with nefazodone. The drug has been associated with liver failure, which has led the FDA to add a warning to its label, advising of this possibility. People who exhibit symptoms that include yellowing skin or eyes, dark urine, or stomach pain should contact a doctor immediately.

In addition, antidepressants have been associated with an increased risk of patients harming or killing themselves. The FDA has advised that this drug should not be administered to children under the age of 18. If it is prescribed for a child or adolescent, caregivers should watch the patient carefully for signs of intention to commit self-harm or attempt **suicide**. These symptoms can develop suddenly and include new or worsening depression, talk about self-harm or suicide, agitation, panic attacks, aggression, and changes in sleep patterns.

People who have a history of epilepsy or other seizure disorders, heart attack, **stroke**, high blood pressure, or mania may require close physician supervision while taking nefazodone. Nefazodone may increase the tendency to have **seizures**, and it should be used carefully by people with epilepsy or other seizure disorders. Nefazodone may lower blood pressure. This effect may be most noticeable when rising suddenly from a lying or sitting position. People with a history of heart attack or stroke, those taking medications for high blood pressure, or people who are dehydrated may be most sensitive to this effect and may feel dizzy or faint when standing up suddenly. Nefazodone may alter moods or cause mania, so patients with a history of mania should use nefazodone with caution.

In rare situations, men taking nefazodone may experience longlasting, painful erections. If this occurs, a health care provider should be notified immediately.

Because there is an increased likelihood of suicide in individuals with depression, close supervision of those at high risk for suicide attempts is recommended. Nefazodone is not recommended for women who are pregnant or breast-feeding.

Side effects

The most common side effects that cause people to stop taking nefazodone are dizziness, difficulty sleeping, weakness, or agitation. Other common adverse effects include sleepiness, dry mouth, nausea, constipation, blurred vision, and confusion.

Less common adverse effects associated with nefazodone are headache, flu-like symptoms, low blood pressure, itching, rash, upset stomach, fluid retention, muscle aches, thirst, memory impairment, nerve pain, nightmares, difficulty walking, ringing in the ears, urinary difficulties, breast pain, or vaginal irritation.

It has recently been discovered that in rare situations, nefazodone causes liver failure. If nausea, stomach pains, yellowing of the skin or eyes, itching, or darkening of urine occurs while taking nefazodone, a health care professional should be consulted immediately.

Interactions

Use of nefazodone with antidepressants referred to as **monoamine oxidase inhibitors (MAOIs)** is strongly discouraged due to the potential for high fever, muscle stiffness, sudden muscle spasms, rapid changes in heart rate and blood pressure, and the possibility of death. In fact, there should be a lapse of at least 14 days between taking a monoamine oxidase inhibitor and nefazodone, or at least seven days should pass if switching from nefazodone to an MAOI. Some examples of **MAOIs** include **phenelzine** (Nardil) and **tranylcypromine** (Parnate).

Some other drugs such as **trazodone** (Desyrel) and sibutramine may also interact with nefazodone and cause a syndrome characterized by irritability, muscle stiffness, shivering, muscle spasms, and altered consciousness. If nefazodone is used with **buspirone** (BuSpar), the dosage of buspirone should be lowered to prevent adverse effects. Additionally, when nefazodone is used in combination with digoxin (Lanoxin), frequent monitoring of blood levels of digoxin is recommended to prevent toxicity.

Nefazodone should not be used with the drugs **triazolam** (Halcion) and **alprazolam** (Xanax), because the side effects of these drugs are likely to increase. Use of nefazodone should also be avoided with **carbamazepine** (Tegretol), because nefazodone is likely to lose its effectiveness.

It is best to avoid using nefazodone with **pimozide** (Orap) due to an increased tendency for severe and potentially life-threatening irregular heartbeats.

When used with gemfibrozil or other drugs that lower cholesterol levels, the risk of muscle pain and weakness may be increased.

Because nefazodone may cause drowsiness, it should be used carefully with other medications that also make people prone to sleepiness such as antidepressants, antipsychotics, antihistamines, and alcohol.

Resources

BOOKS

Ellsworth, Allan J., et al. *Mosby's Medical Drug Reference.* St. Louis: Mosby, 2007.

Wolters Kluwer Health. *Drug Facts and Comparisons 2012.* 66th ed. St. Louis: Lippincott, Williams & Wilkins, 2011.

PERIODICALS

Ahmad, Syed Rizwanuddin. "Adverse Drug Event Monitoring at the Food and Drug Administration: Your Report Can Make a Difference." *Journal of General Internal Medicine* 18:1 (January 2003): 47–60. http://www.pubmedcentral. nih.gov/articlerender.fcgi?artid=1494803 (accessed October 23, 2011).

WEBSITES

Drugs.com. "Serzone" http://www.drugs.com/pro/serzone.html (accessed October 23, 2011).

MedlinePlus. "Nefazodone." U.S. National Library of Medicine, National Institutes of Health. 2011. http://www.nlm. nih.gov/medlineplus/druginfo/medmaster/a695005.html (accessed October 23, 2011).

U.S. Food and Drug Administration. "Determination That SERZONE (Nefazodone Hydrochloride) Was Not Withdrawn from Sale for Reasons of Safety or Effectiveness." *Federal Register.* October 26, 2004. http://www.federal register.gov/articles/2004/10/26/04-23857/determination-that-serzone-nefazodone-hydrochloride-was-not-withdrawn-from-sale-for-reasons-of (accessed October 23, 2011).

U.S. Food and Drug Administration. "Nefazodone hydrochloride Information. FDA Alert: Suicidal Thoughts or Actions in Children and Adults." 2011. http://www.fda.gov/Drugs/ DrugSafety/PostmarketDrugSafetyInformationforPatients andProviders/ucm108105.htm (accessed October 23, 2011).

Kelly Karpa, RPh, PhD
Emily Jane Willingham, PhD

Negative symptoms

Definition

Negative symptoms are thoughts, feelings, or behaviors normally present which are absent or diminished in a person with a mental disorder.

Description

Examples of negative symptoms are social withdrawal, **apathy** (decreased motivation), poverty of speech (brief replies), inability to experience pleasure (anhedonia), limited emotional expression, or defects in attention control. The term "negative symptoms" is specifically used for describing **schizophrenia**, but sometimes used more generally in reference to disorders such as **depression** or **dementia**. These symptoms may be associated with altered brainwave activity or **brain** damage. They can be more difficult to diagnose than **positive symptoms** (hallucinations, **delusions**, bizarre behavior, or formal thought disorder) because they represent a lesser degree of normal, desirable activity rather than the presence of undesirable or bizarre behavior. Side effects of certain medications, demoralization (loss of positive emotions like hope or confidence usually as the result of situations where one feels powerless), or a lack of stimulation in one's environment can also cause negative symptoms, so these possibilities must be ruled out before attributing the symptoms to a disorder.

Sandra L. Friedrich, M.A.

Neglect

Definition

Neglect occurs when a parent or other primary caretaker chooses not to fulfill their obligations to care for, provide for, or adequately supervise and monitor the activities of their child. Parental and caregiving obligations include the physical, emotional, and educational well-being of the child. Thus, neglect can also occur when the parent or caretaker does not seek adequate medical or dental care for the child. Another definition of neglect is when the parental figure does not provide sufficient food, clothing, or shelter.

Parents are also expected to provide for the emotional needs of the child. Thus, neglect can occur when parents abandon the child, or simply have no time to spend with the child, in essence leaving the child to raise himself. If the child is actually left without supervision, this certainly constitutes neglect as well.

The final feature of neglect includes educational neglect, which often occurs when one child is responsible for other children in the family. Shifting the responsibility of caring for younger children to another child in the family prevents the caregiving child from participating in age-appropriate activities such as attending school. This is a relatively common situation that makes it difficult for the oldest—and perhaps all of the children—to attend school. Parental responsibility includes providing adequate guidance and supervision for the children to regularly attend school. Truancy is not only a problem for children, but may be part of the picture of neglect as well.

Effects of neglect

Consequences of neglect are generally cumulative, and often negatively affect the child's development. For example, poor **nutrition** has negative consequences on the child's physical and psychological development. If proper nutrients are not available at critical growth periods, the child's development will not follow the normal and usual pattern. Common physical and psychological reactions to neglect include stunted growth, chronic medical problems, inadequate bone and muscle growth, and lack of neurological development that negatively affects normal **brain** functioning and information processing. Processing problems may often make it difficult for children to understand directions, may negatively impact the child's ability to understand social relationships, or may make completion of some academic tasks impossible without assistance or **intervention** from others. Lack of adequate medical care may result in long-term health problems or impairments such as hearing loss from untreated ear infections.

Long-term mental health effects of neglect are inconsistent. Effects of neglect can range from chronic **depression** to difficulty with relationships; however, not all adults neglected as children will suffer from these results. Some individuals are more resilient than others and are able to move beyond the emotional neglect they may have experienced. Characteristics of resilient individuals include an optimistic or hopeful outlook on life, and feeling challenged rather than defeated by problems.

Factors associated with neglect

Although each family's situation is unique with regard to stressors and characteristics that might precipitate neglect, there are some general factors that have been associated with neglect of a child. These factors include characteristics of the parental figure and socioeconomic status.

Parental figures who neglect may have been neglected or abused themselves. There is a tendency for parental figures that neglect their children to have low self-esteem, poor impulse control, and to experience anxiety or depression. Other factors associated with neglect often include inadequate information about child development, including age-appropriate expectations of what children may be able to do. The parents may also feel overwhelmed by parenting responsibilities and feel negatively about the child's demands on them. Such parents may never have fully adopted the role of parent or the caregiving the parental role requires. Internal pressures often push the caregivers to take care of their own needs (perhaps inappropriately), while ignoring the needs of the child. **Substance abuse** is often associated with neglect, particularly for those parents who are more self-absorbed and focused on their needs rather than their child's. This characteristic is also consistent with the findings of other studies indicating that some neglectful parents have an inability to be empathic, or to understand the feelings and needs of others.

Although **abuse** may occur across all levels of income and education, neglect is more often associated with severe levels of poverty and lower educational level. The external stressors may feel more extreme in single parent families as well, leading to neglectful behavior. Even in families where the parent is attempting to provide for the children, absence due to multiple work demands may lead to a neglectful situation. Families that are disorganized and socially isolated are more likely to neglect the children in their care.

Unlike victims of abuse, there are few consistent characteristics associated with victims of neglect. Retrospective studies of adults neglected as children indicate that females are slightly less resilient to neglect than men.

Prevalence

The number of children nationwide who are harmed or endangered by neglect is greater than any type of abuse. Neglect is consistently reported in more than half of the substantiated reports of mistreatment handled by the authorities.

Prevention and treatment

Interventions are usually aimed at two levels: community prevention efforts and individual parenting skills. A community-based program that actually combines the two facets of intervention is the "Parents as Teachers" program, which is available through many local school districts throughout the nation and is free of charge. Benefits of the program include its accessibility—parents simply need to call for the free service—and the in-home interventions provided by the program. Although the program is not part of the social service network of agencies, the fact that workers go into the home replicates that aspect of caseworker interventions. The simple act of having a paraprofessional in one's home can reduce the likelihood of neglect. Specific interventions that further reduce the likelihood of neglect include focusing on the parent-child relationship, reviewing appropriate expectations for the child's behavior (based on child development principles), and teaching basic parenting skills.

Other treatment options are generally more formal, and may be initiated by a call from a mandated reporter with concerns about neglect. Mandated reporters include physicians, teachers, and counselors. Any of these professionals may make the initial call if neglect is suspected. Concerned individuals may also call social services to report suspected neglect. In these cases of forced treatment, parents may be less willing participants in treatment efforts aimed at behavioral change for themselves and their families. In other instances, the parent or child may already be in treatment, and the focus on reducing neglectful behaviors may be incorporated into the existing treatment relationship. Factors to focus on in formal treatment aimed at reducing the likelihood of neglect may include specific parenting skills, home visits to allow monitoring of the relationship, as well as other individual needs such as substance abuse treatment, or empathy skill training.

Treatment efforts for the child should include family counseling aimed at communication skills and appropriate expression of affection and emotion within the family. Assertiveness skills training may be helpful for older adolescents in asking for their perceived needs.

Resources

BOOKS

McKenry, P. C., S. J. Price, and C. A. Price eds. *Families & Change*. 4th ed. Thousand Oaks, CA: Sage Publications, 2009.

PERIODICALS

English, D. J. "The Extent and Consequences of Child Maltreatment." *The Future of Children* 8, no. 1 (Spring 1998): 39–53.

Horwitz, A. V., et al. "The Impact of Childhood Abuse and Neglect on Adult Mental Health: A Prospective Study." *Journal of Health & Social Behavior* 42, no. 2 (June 2001): 184–201.

Deanna Pledge, Ph.D.

Neurocognitive disorders *see* **Alzheimer's disease; Delirium; Dementia; Traumatic brain injury; Vascular dementia**

Neuroleptic malignant syndrome

Definition

Neuroleptic malignant syndrome (NMS) is a rare but potentially fatal condition that can occur in people who take neuroleptic medication to treat **schizophrenia**, mania, **delusional disorder**, and other types of mental illnesses. There is evidence that sympathetic nervous system activation or dysfunction may be significantly associated with the underlying pathogenesis of NMS. NMS, which is characterized by motor dysfunction, extremely high fever, and changes in consciousness, is most commonly associated with older generation typical neuroleptics such as **haloperidol** (Haldol) and **chlorpromazine** (Largactil). However, the newer, atypical antipsychotic agents, such as **clozapine** (Clozaril), risperidone (Risperdal), and **olanzapine** (Zyprexa), also have been associated with NMS symptoms. NMS additionally has been reported in patients with Parkinson's disease who have had their medications (such as levodopa) rapidly withdrawn.

Non-neuroleptic agents associated with NMS block central **dopamine** pathways and include metoclopramide (Reglan), lithium, and **amoxapine** (Asendin). The syndrome also shares features with malignant hyperthermia and the **serotonin syndrome**.

Demographics

Neuroleptic malignant syndrome occurs in between 0.02% and 2.44% of people who are treated with neuroleptic medications, although there is no universal agreement on this statistic. The mortality rate with NMS is between 5% and 11.6%, also with no complete consensus on this figure. Mortality from the condition has declined over the years (down from 20% to 30%) but remains significant. Death generally results after respiratory failure, diffuse intravascular coagulation (DIC), cardiovascular collapse, myoglobinuric renal failure, and arrhythmias. There is a predilection toward males but none associated with age. There is a 2:1 male-to-female ratio, which is thought to occur because men are treated with neuroleptic agents more frequently than women.

Description

NMS is believed to be related to the dopaminergic system. Dopamine is a neurotransmitter that transmits messages between nerve cells in the **brain**. It regulates mood, emotion, motivation, and movement. Neuroleptic antipsychotic drugs act as antagonists at dopamine receptors, meaning that they block the receptors, thereby preventing dopamine from attaching to the receptors and causing its response from the decreased availability of dopamine itself. Sometimes, blocking these receptors can result in **movement disorders** and difficulty regulating body heat, both of which are symptoms associated with NMS. NMS typically begins within the first two to four weeks after a patient starts taking antipsychotic medications or is put on a higher dose of the medication, although symptoms may manifest sooner or much later.

Risk factors

A variety of factors may increase an individual's risk of developing this condition, including:

• High environmental temperatures

• Dehydration

• Agitation or catatonia in a patient

• High initial dose or rapid dose increase of neuroleptic, and use of high-potency or intramuscular, long-acting (depot) preparations

• Simultaneous use of more than one causative agent

• Sudden discontinuation of medications for Parkinson disease

• Past history of organic brain syndromes, depression, or bipolar disorder

• Past episode of neuromuscular malignant syndrome (risk of recurrence may be as high as 30%)

Causes and symptoms

Causes

Although researchers have identified several risk factors for NMS, the precise cause is unknown. **Genetic factors** may play a role, however, and NMS has been reported to run in families. Researchers have identified alterations or deletions to the CYP2D6 genes in people with NMS. Changes to these genes may affect the way neuroleptics are metabolized by the liver, resulting in higher blood concentrations.

Symptoms

The **diagnosis** is confirmed, but not excluded, when the following are observed:

• Recent treatment with neuroleptics within the past one to four weeks

• Hypothermia (above 38°C)

• Muscular rigidity

• Exclusion of other drug-induced, system, or neuro-psychiatric illness

• At least five of the following: Change in mental status; Tachycardia (abnormally rapid heartbeat); Hypertension or hypotension; Diaphoresis or sialorrhea; Leukocytosis; Tremor; Incontinence; Increased creatine phosphokinase (CPK) or urinary myoglobin; and Metabolic acidosis

Diagnosis

Early diagnosis of NMS is essential to prevent fatality. Physicians begin by ruling out conditions with similar symptoms. Laboratory studies include a complete blood count; urine myoglobin; CPK; arterial blood gas; liver function tests; blood cultures; serum and urine toxic screening for **cocaine**, **amphetamines**, and other gents; blood urea nitrogen; and calcium and phosphate levels. Blood tests of patients with NMS reveal high levels of creatine kinase, a muscle enzyme, as well as abnormally

KEY TERMS

Atypical antipsychotic—A class of newer generation antipsychotic medications that are used to treat schizophrenia and other psychotic disorders.

Dopamine—A neurotransmitter in the brain that helps regulate emotion and movement.

Dopamine agonist—A drug that binds to dopamine receptors and produces effects that are similar to dopamine.

Dopamine antagonist—A substance that binds to dopamine receptors, preventing dopamine from binding and triggering its response.

Electroencephalogram—A diagnostic technique that measures electrical activity in the brain.

Neuroleptic drugs—The class of drugs used to treat schizophrenia, mania, and other types of mental disorders.

Parkinson's disease—A degenerative condition of the central nervous system that results in reduced dopamine production, leading to symptoms such as tremors, muscle rigidity, and difficulty with balance and coordination.

high levels of leukocytes (white blood cells). An electroencephalogram (EEG), which measures electrical activity in the brain, will show a slowing of brain function. Chest radiography is performed to rule out aspiration pneumonia. A lumbar puncture, sometimes with a preceding CT scan, is performed to diagnose meningitis in patients who have high fever and altered mental status.

Treatment

Because little research has been done on NMS, treatment guidelines are limited. The first line of treatment is to discontinue the medication that is believed to be causing the condition, exclude other medical conditions, begin aggressive supportive care, and administrate pharmacotherapies, such as **benzodiazepines (diazepam)**, muscle relaxants, and dopamine agonists (bromocriptine), which can be used to control symptoms. After the medication is stopped, most patients will improve within two weeks, although symptoms may persist for as long as several months. Doctors typically recommend waiting for at least two weeks after the patient's symptoms have improved before restarting antipsychotic medications, to prevent a **relapse** of NMS. After that period, atypical antipsychotic medications are preferred over the older generation antipsychotic drugs, because they are associated with a lower risk of NMS.

Patients should be carefully monitored while recovering from NMS. Doctors will check the patient's creatine kinase levels, as well as his or her overall health, and will ensure that the patient receives adequate **nutrition** and hydration and does not progress to kidney failure.

Prognosis

With early diagnosis and treatment, mortality from NMS can be prevented. However, because the condition can recur at any time, patients must be monitored over the long term.

Prevention

The only way to entirely prevent NMS is to avoid the use of neuroleptic drugs. But because NMS is rare, and because many patients rely on these drugs for the treatment of mental disorders, avoiding these drugs is neither practical nor feasible in many cases. However, using the newer atypical antipsychotics and/or lowering the dose may reduce the risk of NMS.

Resources

BOOKS

Brunton, Laurence, Bruce Chabner, and Bjorn Knollman. *Goodman & Gilman's The Pharmacological Basis of Therapeutics* 12th ed. New York: McGraw-Hill, 2010.

Caroff, Stanley N., et al. *Neuroleptic Malignant Syndrome and Related Conditions.* 2d ed. Arlington, VA: American Psychiatric Publishing, 2003.

Kring, Ann M., Gerald C. Davison, John M. Neale, and Sheri L. Johnson. *Abnormal Psychology.* 11th ed. Hoboken, NJ: John Wiley & Sons, 2009.

Meyer, Jerrold S., and Linda F. Quenzer. *Psychopharmacology: Drugs, the Brain and Behavior.* Sunderland, MA: Sinauer Associates, Inc., 2005.

ORGANIZATIONS

Mental Health America, 2000 N Beauregard Street, 6th Floor, Alexandria, VA, 22311, (703) 684-7722, (800) 969-6642, Fax: (703) 684-5968, http://www.nmha.org.

National Institute of Mental Health, 6001 Executive Blvd., Room 8184, MSC 9663, Bethesda, MD, 20892-9663, (301) 433-4513; TTY: (301) 443-8431, Fax: (301) 443-4279, (866) 615-6464; TTY: (866) 415-8051, nimhinfo@nih.gov, http://www.nimh.nih.gov.

National Parkinson Foundation, Inc, 1501 NW 9th Ave./Bob Hope Rd., Miami, FL, 33136-1494, (305) 243-6666, Fax: (305) 243-6073, (800) 327-4545, contact@parkinson.org, http://www.parkinson.org.

Neuroleptic Malignant Syndrome Information Service, Box 1069, Sherburne, NY, 13460-1069, (607) 674-7920, Fax: (607) 674-7910, info@nmsis.org, http://www.nmsis.org.

Stephanie N. Watson

Neurolinguistic programming *see* **Hypnotherapy**

Neurontin *see* **Gabapentin**

KEY TERMS

Differential diagnosis—Comparing and contrasting the signs, symptoms, and laboratory findings of two or more diseases to determine which is causing the patient's condition.

Tardive dyskinesia—Involuntary movements of the face and/or body, a side effect of the long-term use of some older antipsychotic drugs.

Neuropsychiatry

Definition

Neuropsychiatry is an integrative, collaborative discipline that deals with the psychiatric aspects of neurological disease. The terms "neuropsychiatry" and "behavioral neurology" are frequently used interchangeably.

Purpose

Patients who may benefit from the services of a neuropsychiatrist are those who have a known neurological disease accompanied by cognitive, emotional, or behavioral deficits, as well as patients who have comorbid psychiatric and neurologic disorders. A neuropsychiatrist may be called upon to consult when a patient exhibits psychiatric symptoms that are unresponsive to the usual treatment approaches, and the differential **diagnosis** extends to a neurological cause, with secondary psychiatric manifestations. Examples of conditions that may be responsive to a neuropsychiatric approach include epilepsy, head injury, **attention deficit hyperactivity disorder**, **dementia**, **tardive dyskinesia**, atypical spells, and irritability.

Description

Neuropsychiatry lies in the interface between the disciplines of neurology and psychiatry. For many centuries, neurology and psychiatry formed a single unified field. Even in the late nineteenth century, many medical practitioners and researchers, such as Sigmund Freud, Jean-Martin Charcot, and Eugen Bleuler, did not distinguish between the study of the mind and the **brain**. In the twentieth century, however, neurology and psychiatry became separate, distinct disciplines. Neurology focused on disorders, such as **stroke**, multiple sclerosis, and Parkinson's disease, that were clearly characterized by disease of, or damage to, the brain and resulted in behavioral and cognitive problems as well as somatic symptoms related to movement and sensation. Psychiatry, on the other hand, concerned itself with behavioral, cognitive, personality, and emotional disorders, such as **depression, schizophrenia**, and **anxiety disorders**. Initially, these conditions were not typically seen as problems related to sensory or motor dysfunction, and consequently revealed few or no pathologic symptoms during standard neurologic examinations.

The impetus for a change in this divide between neurology and psychiatry has come from the advances made in neuroscience during the second half of the twentieth century. With advances in the understanding of the underlying biology of psychiatric disorders, it has become difficult to draw a clear line between the mind and the brain, or the psychological and physical manifestations of a disease. Because of these advances, scientists and clinicians are now able to assess the structure and functioning of the brain in new ways. Many new techniques developed in the latter half of the twentieth century and the beginning of the twenty-first century have shown that behavioral, emotional, and cognitive disorders are often accompanied by physical changes in the brain. For example, **magnetic resonance imaging** studies have revealed structural abnormalities in the brains of patients who suffer from schizophrenia, and functional magnetic resonance imaging and **positron emission tomography** techniques have demonstrated that brain function is abnormal in such patients. Researchers and clinicians are also now more cognizant of the fact that disorders that were traditionally in the domain of neurology, such as Parkinson's disease, are often accompanied by emotional and cognitive symptoms like depression and even dementia.

In addition, treatments that target the brain, such as pharmacotherapy, **transcranial magnetic stimulation**, **vagus nerve stimulation** and deep brain stimulation are being used or are being investigated for their potential to alleviate disorders that have traditionally been considered psychiatric, such as depression and **obsessive-compulsive disorder**. Disorders that are currently recognized as being within the purview of neuropsychiatry include, but are not limited to, neurocognitive disorders, drug-induced **movement disorders**, Tourette syndrome, stroke and head injury, chronic **fatigue** syndrome, Parkinson's disease, attention deficit hyperactivity disorder, and dementia.

Territorial struggles between psychiatry and neurology continue. Modern neuropsychiatry, which has emerged only in the last two decades, is still a discipline with ill-defined boundaries, frequently competitive with both psychiatry and neurology. Training programs in neuropsychiatry are still being developed, but a number of schools have instituted neuropsychiatry programs, including the University of South Carolina, Dartmouh, and the University of Pennsylvania.

Resources

BOOKS

Goldstein, Gerald, Theresa M. Incagnoli, and Antonio E. Puente, eds. *Contemporary Neurobehavioral Syndromes.* New York: Psychology Press, 2011.

Rhawn, Joseph. *Neuropsychology, Neuropsychiatry, and Behavioral Neurology.* Critical Issues in Neuropsychology. New York: Plenum Press, 2010.

Williamson, Peter, and John Allman. *The Human Illnesses: Neuropsychiatric Disorders and the Nature of the Human Brain.* New York: Oxford University Press, 2011.

Yudofsky, Stuart C., and Robert E. Hales. *Essentials of Neuropsychiatry and Behavioral Neurosciences.* Arlington, VA: American Psychiatric Publishing, 2010.

PERIODICALS

Aybek, Selma, Richard Kanaan, and Anthony S. David. "The Neuropsychiatry of Conversion Disorder." *Current Opinion in Psychiatry* 21, no. 3 (2008): 275–80.

Elvevåg, B., and D.R. Weinberger. " Introduction: Genes, Cognition and Neuropsychiatry." *Cognitive Neuropsychiatry* 14, nos. 4–5 (2009): 261–75.

Vaishnavi, Sandeep, et al. "Behavioral Neurology and Neuropsychiatry Fellowship Training: The Johns Hopkins Model." *Journal of Neuropsychiatry and Clinical Neuroscience* 21 (Summer 2009): 335–41. http://dx.doi.org/10.1176/appi.neuropsych.21.3.335 (accessed September 7, 2011).

Yudofsky, Stuart C., ed. *The Journal of Neuropsychiatry and Clinical Neurosciences.* American Neuropsychiatric Association. http://neuro.psychiatryonline.org/index.dtl (accessed September 7, 2011).

ORGANIZATIONS

American Neuropsychiatric Association, 700 Ackerman Road, Suite 625, Columbus, OH, 43202, (614) 447-2077, anpa@osu.edu, http://www.anpaonline.org/home.php.

International Neuropsychiatric Association, INA Secretariat Office Neuropsychiatric Institute Euroa Centre, The Prince of Wales Hospital, Barker St., Randwick, NSW 2031, Australia, 61293823816, Fax: 61293823774, angie.russell@unsw.edu.au, http://www.inawebsite.org.

Ruvanee Pietersz Vilhauer, PhD
Rosalyn Carson-DeWitt

Neuropsychological testing

Definition

Clinical neuropsychology is a field with historical origins in both psychology and neurology. The primary activity of neuropsychologists is assessment of **brain** functioning through structured and systematic behavioral observation. Neuropsychological tests are designed specifically to examine a variety of cognitive abilities, including speed of information processing, attention, memory, language, and executive functions, which are necessary for goal-directed behavior. Such scientifically validated tests are administered generally to individuals to evaluate brain functions. These tests cover a wide range of mental processes from simple motor performance to complex problem solving and reasoning.

By testing a range of cognitive abilities and examining patterns of performance in different cognitive areas, neuropsychologists can make inferences about underlying brain function, including its structure and pathway. Consequently, neuropsychological testing is a primary way that neuropsychologists and other scientists assess neuropsychological function in humans.

Purpose

Neuropsychological testing is an important component of the assessment and treatment of **traumatic brain injury**, attention deficits, developmental milestone failures (in children), **dementia**, neurological conditions, psychiatric disorders, drug or alcohol abuse, and other such problems. Neuropsychological testing is also an important tool for examining the effects of toxic substances and medical conditions on brain functioning.

Testing helps to assess such functions as working memory and attention, short-term and long-term memory, processing speed, reasoning and problem-solving ability, ability to understand and express language, visual-spatial organization, visual-motor coordination, and planning and organizational abilities.

Description

Neuropsychological testing is based on psychometric theory. A sample from a general population (control group) is used as the foundation for scoring, with individual scores compared to the normalized sample.

Origins

As early as the seventeenth century, scientists theorized about associations between regions of the brain and specific functions. French philosopher René

KEY TERMS

Dementia—The progressive deterioration of intellectual functions, such as memory, within the brain. Alzheimer's disease is a type of dementia.

Psychiatric—Relating to psychiatry.

Psychometric—A branch of psychology that deals with measurement of mental capacities, processes, and traits.

Visual-motor—The ability to coordinate vision and bodily movements.

Visual-spatial—The ability to manipulate multi-dimensional figures mentally.

Descartes (1596–1650) believed the human soul could be localized to a specific brain structure, the pineal gland. In the eighteenth century, Austrian physiologist Franz Joseph Gall (1758–1828) advocated the theory that specific mental qualities such as spirituality or aggression were governed by discrete parts of the brain. In contrast, French physiologist Marie Jean Pierre Flourens (1794–1867) contended that the brain was an integrated system that governed cognitive functioning in a holistic manner.

Later discoveries indicated that brain function is both localized and integrated. French physician Pierre Paul Broca (1824–1880) and German physician Karl Wernicke (1848–1905) furthered understanding of localization and integration of function when they reported the loss of language abilities in patients with lesions to two regions in the left hemisphere of the brain.

The modern field of neuropsychology emerged in the twentieth century, combining theories based on anatomical observations of neurology with the techniques of psychology, including objective observation of behavior and the use of statistical analysis to differentiate functional abilities and define impairment. Soviet neuropsychologist Alexander Romanovich Luria (1902–1977) played a major role in defining neuropsychology as it is practiced today. Luria formulated two principal goals of neuropsychology: to localize brain lesions and analyze psychological activities arising from brain function through behavioral observation.

American neuropsychologist Ralph M. Reitan later emphasized the importance of using standardized psychometric tests to guide systematic observations of brain-behavior relationships. Specifically, Dr. Reitan and Dr. Ward Halstead co-developed the Halstead-Reitan Battery—one of many neuropsychological tests used commonly in the twenty-first century—which is used to evaluate brain and nervous system function in individuals 15 years of age and older.

Applications

Before the introduction of neuroimaging techniques such as **computed tomography** (CT), **magnetic resonance imaging** (MRI), **electroencephalography** (EEG), and **positron emission tomography (PET)**, neuropsychological testing was the only way for clinicians to evaluate the condition of the living brain. These neuroimaging techniques allow for the observation of brain lesions or structural abnormalities in living patients. Today, neuropsychological testing and neuroimaging techniques are used together to determine which part of the brain is affected in a given patient.

Neuropsychological tests can identify syndromes associated with problems in a particular area of the brain. For instance, a patient who performs well on tests of attention, memory, and language, but poorly on tests that require visual spatial skills, such as copying a complex geometric figure or making designs with colored blocks, may have dysfunction in the right parietal lobe, the region of the brain involved in complex processing of visual information. When a patient complains of problems with verbal communication after a **stroke**, separate tests that examine production and comprehension of language help neuropsychologists identify the location of the stroke in the left hemisphere. Neuropsychological tests can also be used as screening tests to see whether more extensive diagnostic evaluation is appropriate. Neuropsychological screening of elderly people complaining of memory problems can help identify those at risk for dementia versus those experiencing normal age-related memory loss.

As neuropsychological testing came to play a less vital role in localization of brain dysfunction, clinical neuropsychologists found new uses for their skills and knowledge. By clarifying which cognitive abilities are impaired or preserved in patients with brain injury or illness, neuropsychologists can predict how well individuals will respond to different forms of treatment or rehabilitation. Although patterns of test scores illustrate profiles of cognitive strength and weakness, neuropsychologists can also learn a great deal about patients by observing how they approach a particular test. For example, two patients can complete a test in very different ways yet obtain similar scores. One patient may work slowly and methodically, without making errors, while another rushes through the test, making several errors, but quickly correcting them. Some individuals persevere despite repeated failure on a series of test items, while others refuse to continue after a few failures. These differences might not be apparent in test scores but can help clinicians choose among rehabilitation and treatment approaches.

Performance on neuropsychological tests is usually evaluated through comparison to the average performance of large samples of normal individuals. Most tests include tables of these normal scores, often divided into groups based on demographic variables, like age and education, that appear to affect cognitive functioning. This allows individuals to be compared to appropriate peers.

Evaluation

The typical neuropsychological examination evaluates sensation and perception, gross and fine motor skills, basic and complex attention, visual spatial skills, receptive and productive language abilities, recall and recognition memory, and executive functions such as cognitive flexibility and abstraction. Motivation and personality are often assessed as well, particularly when clients are seeking financial compensation for injuries, or cognitive complaints are not typical of the associated injury or illness.

Test methods

Some neuropsychologists prefer to use fixed test batteries, like the **Halstead-Reitan Battery** or the Luria-Nebraska Battery, for all patients. These batteries include tests of a wide range of cognitive functions, and those who advocate their use believe that all functions must be assessed in each patient in order to avoid diagnostic bias or failure to detect subtle problems. The more common approach today, however, is to use a flexible battery based on hypotheses generated through a clinical interview, observation of the patient, and review of medical records.

While the flexible approach to neuropsychological testing is more prone to bias, it has the advantage of preventing unnecessary testing. Since patients often find neuropsychological testing stressful and fatiguing, and these factors can negatively influence performance, advocates of the flexible battery approach argue that tailoring test batteries to particular patients can provide more accurate information. Moreover, because insurance companies generally have a fixed amount for reimbursement of psychological testing, a more focused approach may assist in payment for testing services.

Numerous neuropsychological tests are available. Some of the more popular ones include (in alphabetical order):

• Ammons Quick Test

• Beck Depression Inventory and Beck Anxiety Inventory

QUESTIONS TO ASK YOUR DOCTOR

• Which test(s) do you recommend in this specific instance?

• Where can I learn more about neuropsychological testing?

• How can I know whether the administrator of any particular test is qualified?

• How can I determine the credentials of the neuropsychologist?

• What happens if the various tests taken come up with different conclusions?

• Clinical Dementia Rating

• Cognitive Assessment Screening Instrument

• Continuous Performance Task

• Finger Tapping Test

• Halstead-Reitan Battery

• Kaufman Assessment Battery for Children

• Luria-Nebraska Battery

• Minnesota Multiphasic Personality Inventory

• Repeatable Battery for the Assessment of Neuropsychological Status

• Rorschach Projective Technique

• Shipley Institute of Living Scale

• Test of Memory and Learning

• Wechsler Adult Intelligence Scale and Wechsler Intelligence Scale for Children

• Wide Range Achievement Test

• Wonderlic Personnel Test

• Word Memory Test

Risks

Neuropsychological testing runs the risk of being biased if a trained and experienced administrator is not used. Therefore, neuropsychological testing should be carried out by a licensed **psychologist** trained in neuropsychology. When qualified personnel are used to collect behavioral, cognitive, language, and executive functioning skills, such data can lead to an accurate **diagnosis** of the individual.

Results

The results of neuropsychological testing are used as a primary way to assess neuropsychological function in humans. Testing includes scores, behavior observations, distinct and consistent patterns, and clinical history, which are all used in combination to provide a final assessment of individuals. Results in neuropsychological testing can be affected due to an individual's age, education, gender, and cultural background.

Different tests may differ based on validity, reliability, sensitivity, and specificity. Validity refers to the degree by which a test measures what it intended to measure. Reliability refers to the consistency and accuracy of the test; that is, how well scores remain consistent when extraneous variables are present (such as illness or injury). Sensitivity refers to the ability of the test to measure abnormalities, while specificity refers to the ability of the test to distinguish individuals with a specific abnormality from other individuals without such abnormality or with other types of abnormalities.

Resources

BOOKS

Feifer, Steven G., and Gurmal Rattan, editors. *Emotional Disorders: A Neuropsychological, Psychopharmacological, and Educational Perspective.* Middletown, MD: School Neuropsych Press, 2009.

Gorske, Tad T. and Steven R. Smith. *Collaborative Therapeutic Neuropsychological Assessment.* New York: Springer, 2009.

Grant, Igor, and Kenneth M. Adams, editors. *Neuropsychological Assessment of Neuropsychiatric and Neuromedical Disorders.* Oxford: Oxford University Press, 2009.

Hebben, Nancy, and William Millberg. *Essentials of Neuropsychological Assessment.* Hoboken, NJ: John Wiley and Sons, 2009.

Lezak, Muriel Deutsh, et al. *Neuropsychological Assessment.* Oxford: Oxford University Press, 2004.

Mitrushina, Maura N., et al. *Handbook of Normative Data for Neuropsychological Assessment.* New York: Oxford University Press, 2005.

Spreen, Otfried, Esther Strauss, and Elisabeth M. S. Sherman. *A Compendium of Neuropsychological Tests: Administration, Norms, and Commentary.* Oxford: Oxford University Press, 2006.

Walsh, Kevin, and David Darby. *Walsh's Neuropsychology: A Clinical Approach.* Edinburgh: Elsevier Churchill Livingstone, 2005.

ORGANIZATIONS

American Psychiatric Association, 1000 Wilson Boulevard, Suite 1825, Arlington, VA, 22209-3901, (703) 907-7300, apa@psych.org, http://www.psych.org.

American Psychological Association, 750 First Street NE, Washington, DC, 20002, (202) 336-5500, (800) 374-2721, http://www.apa.org.

International Neuropsychological Society, 700 Ackerman Road, Suite 625, Columbus, OH, 43202, (614) 263-4200, Fax: (614) 263-4366, http://www.the-ins.org.

National Academy of Neuropsychology, 7555 East Hampden Avenue, Suite 525, Denver, CO, 80231, (303) 691-3694, Fax: (303) 691-5983, office@nanonline.org, http://nanonline.org.

Danielle Barry, M.S.

Neurosis

Definition

Neurosis is a term generally used to describe a nonpsychotic mental illness which triggers feelings of distress and anxiety and impairs functioning.

Description

Origins

The word *neurosis* means "nerve disorder," and was first coined in the late eighteenth century by William Cullen, a Scottish physician. Cullen's concept of neurosis encompassed those nervous disorders and symptoms that do not have a clear organic cause. Sigmund Freud later used the term *anxiety neurosis* to describe mental illness or distress with extreme anxiety as a defining feature.

There is a difference of opinion over the clinical use of the term neurosis today. It is not generally used as a diagnostic category by American psychologists and psychiatrists any longer, and was removed from the American Psychiatric Association's **Diagnostic and Statistical Manual of Mental Disorders** in 1980 with the publication of the third edition (it last appeared as a diagnostic category in *DSM-II*). Some professionals use the term to describe anxious symptoms and associated behavior, or to describe the range of mental illnesses outside of the psychotic disorders (such as **schizophrenia, delusional disorder**). Others, particularly psychoanalysts (psychiatrists and psychologists who follow a psychoanalytical model of treatment, as popularized by Freud and Carl Jung), use the term neurosis to describe the internal process itself (called an unconscious conflict) that triggers the anxiety characteristic.

Categories

The neurotic disorders are distinct from psychotic disorders in that the individual with neurotic symptoms has a firm grip on reality, and the psychotic patient does not. Before their reclassification, there were several major traditional categories of psychological neuroses, including:

KAREN HORNEY (1885–1952)

The German-born American psychoanalyst Karen Danielsen Horney was a pioneer of neo-Freudianism. She believed that every human being has an innate drive toward self-realization and that neurosis is essentially a process obstructing this healthy development.

Horney focused on the central position of conflict and solutions to conflict in neurosis in *Our Inner Conflicts* (1945). She saw the neurotic child feeling helpless and isolated in a potentially hostile world, seeking a feeling of safety in compulsive moves toward, against, and away from others. Each of these moves came to constitute comprehensive philosophies of life and patterns of interpersonal relating. The conflict between these opposed moves she called the basic conflict and recognized that it required the individual to resort to means for restoring a sense of inner unity. These means she called the neurotic solutions.

Neurosis and Human Growth (1950) was Horney's definitive work, in which she placed her concept of healthy development in the foreground. She viewed the real self as the core of the individual, the source of inherent, constructive, evolutionary forces which under favorable circumstances grow and unfold in a dynamic process of self-realization. She presented "a morality of evolution," in which she viewed as moral all that enhances self-realization and as immoral all that hinders it. The most serious obstacle to healthy growth was the neurotic solution, which she called self-idealization, the attempt to see and to mold oneself into a glorified, idealized, illusory image with strivings for superiority, power, perfection, and vindictive triumph over others. This search for glory inevitably leads the individual to move away from himself (alienation) and against himself (self-hate). "At war with himself," his suffering increases, his relationships with others are further impaired, and the self-perpetuating neurotic cycle continues.

---

anxiety neurosis, depressive neurosis, obsessive-compulsive neurosis, somatization, **post-traumatic stress disorder**, and compensation neurosis—not a true neurosis, but a form of **malingering**, or feigning psychological symptoms for monetary or other personal gain.

Resources

BOOKS

American Psychiatric Association. *Diagnostic and Statistical Manual of Mental Disorders*. 4th ed., text rev. Washington, DC: American Psychiatric Publishing, 2000.

Fenichel, Otto M., and Leo Rangell. *The Psychoanalytic Theory of Neurosis: 50th Anniversary Edition*. New York: W.W. Norton and Son. 1995.

Paula Ford-Martin, M.S.

Neurotic excoriation *see* **Dermatillomania**

▌Neurotransmitters

Definition

Neurotransmitters are chemicals located and released in the **brain** to allow an impulse from one nerve cell to pass to another nerve cell.

Description

Approximately 50 neurotransmitters have been identified. There are billions of nerve cells located in the brain, which do not directly touch each other. Nerve cells communicate messages by secreting neurotransmitters. Neurotransmitters can excite or inhibit neurons (nerve cells). Common neurotransmitters include:

- Acetylcholine: Acetylcholine is particularly important in the stimulation of muscle tissue. After stimulation, acetylcholine degrades to acetate and choline, which are absorbed back into the first neuron to form another acetylcholine molecule. The poison curare blocks transmission of acetylcholine. Some nerve gases inhibit the breakdown of acetylcholine, producing a continuous stimulation of the receptor cells and spasms of muscles such as the heart.

- Aspartate: An amino acid that stimulates neurons in the central nervous system, particularly those that transfer information to the area of the brain called the cerebrum.

- Dopamine: Dopamine facilitates critical brain functions and, when unusual quantities are present, abnormal dopamine neurotransmission may play a role in Parkinson's disease, certain addictions, and schizophrenia.

- Epinephrine (adrenaline) and norepinephrine: These compounds are secreted principally from the adrenal gland. Secretion causes an increased heart rate and the enhanced production of glucose as a ready energy source (the fight-or-flight response).

- Gamma aminobutyric acid (GABA): An inhibitory neurotransmitter, GABA is associated with anxiety disorder and mood disorders.

- Insulin: A peptide secreted by the pancreas that stimulates other cells to absorb glucose.

- Oxytocin: A short protein (peptide) that is released within the brain, ovary, and testes. The compound stimulates the release of milk by mammary glands, contractions during birth, and maternal behavior.

- Serotonin: Synthesized from the amino acid tryptophan, serotonin is assumed to play a biochemical role in mood and mood disorders, including anxiety, depression, and bipolar disorder.

- Somatostatin: Another peptide, which is inhibitory to the secretion of growth hormone from the pituitary gland, of insulin, and of a variety of gastrointestinal hormones involved with nutrient absorption.

Mechanism of impulse transmission

Each neurotransmitter can directly or indirectly influence neurons in a specific portion of the brain, thereby affecting behavior. A nerve impulse travels through a nerve in a long, slender cellular structure called an axon, and it eventually reaches a structure called the presynaptic membrane, which contains neurotransmitters to be released in a free space called the synaptic cleft. Freely flowing neurotransmitter molecules are picked up by receptors (structures that appear on cellular surfaces and fit together with molecules like a lock and key) located in a structure called the postsynaptic membrane of another nearby neuron. Once the neurotransmitter is picked up by receptors in the postsynaptic membrane, the molecule is internalized in the neuron and the impulse continues. This process of nerve cell communication is extremely rapid.

Once the neurotransmitter is released from the neurotransmitter vesicles of the presynaptic membrane, the normal movement of molecules should be directed to receptor sites located on the postsynaptic membrane. However, in certain disease states, the flow of the neurotransmitter is defective. For example, in **depression**, the flow of the inhibitory neurotransmitter **serotonin** is defective, and molecules flow back to their originating site (the presynaptic membrane) instead of to receptors on the postsynaptic membrane that will transmit the impulse to a nearby neuron.

The mechanism of action and localization of neurotransmitters in the brain has provided valuable information concerning the cause of many mental disorders, including clinical depression and chemical dependency, and in researching medications that allow normal flow and movement of neurotransmitter molecules.

Neurotransmitters, mental disorders, and medications

SCHIZOPHRENIA. Impairment of dopamine-containing neurons in the brain is implicated in **schizophrenia**, a mental disease marked by disturbances in thinking and emotional reactions. Medications that block **dopamine** receptors in the brain, such as **chlorpromazine** and **clozapine**, have been used to alleviate the symptoms and help patients return to a normal social setting.

DEPRESSION. In depression, there appears to be abnormal excess or inhibition of signals that control mood, thoughts, pain, and other sensations. Depression is treated with **antidepressants** that affect norepinephrine and serotonin in the brain. The antidepressants help correct the abnormal neurotransmitter activity. **Fluoxetine** (Prozac) is a selective serotonin reuptake inhibitor (SSRI) that appears to establish the level of serotonin required to function at a normal level. As the name implies, the drug inhibits the re-uptake of serotonin neurotransmitter from synaptic gaps, thus increasing neurotransmitter action. In the brain, then, the increased serotonin activity alleviates depressive symptoms.

ALZHEIMER'S DISEASE. Alzheimer's disease is characterized by memory loss and the eventual inability for self-care. The disease seems to be caused by a loss of cells that secrete acetylcholine in the basal forebrain (region of brain that is the control center for sensory and associative information processing and motor activities). Some medications to alleviate the symptoms have been developed, but at present there is no known treatment for the disease.

GENERALIZED ANXIETY DISORDER. People with **generalized anxiety disorder** (GAD) experience excessive worry that causes problems at work and in the maintenance of daily responsibilities. Evidence suggests that GAD involves several neurotransmitter systems in the brain, including norepinephrine and serotonin.

ATTENTION DEFICIT HYPERACTIVITY DISORDER. People affected by **attention deficit hyperactivity disorder** (ADHD) experience difficulties in the areas of attention, overactivity, impulse control, and distractibility. Research shows that dopamine and norepinephrine imbalances are strongly implicated in causing **ADHD**.

OTHERS. Substantial research evidence suggests a correlation of neurotransmitter imbalance with other mental disorders, including **borderline personality disorder**, **schizotypal personality disorder**, **avoidant personality disorder**, **social phobia**, **histrionic personality disorder**, and **somatization disorder**.

DRUG ADDICTIONS. **Cocaine** and crack cocaine are psychostimulants that affect neurons containing dopamine in the areas of the brain known as the limbic and frontal cortex. When cocaine is used, it generates a feeling of confidence and power. However, when large amounts are taken, people "crash" and suffer from physical and emotional exhaustion as well as depression.

Opiates, such as heroin and morphine, appear to mimic naturally occurring peptide substances in the brain that act as neurotransmitters with opiate activity called endorphins. Natural endorphins of the brain act to kill pain, cause sensations of pleasure, and cause sleepiness. Endorphins released with extensive aerobic **exercise**, for example, are responsible for the "rush" that long-distance runners experience. It is believed that morphine and heroin combine with the endorphin receptors in the brain, resulting in reduced natural endorphin production. As a result, the drugs are needed to replace the naturally produced endorphins and **addiction** occurs. Attempts to counteract the effects of the drugs involve using medications that mimic them, such as nalorphine, naloxone, and **naltrexone**.

One of the depressant drugs in widest use, alcohol, is believed to cause its effects by interacting with the GABA receptor. Initially anxiety is controlled, but greater amounts reduce muscle control and delay reaction time due to impaired thinking.

Resources

BOOKS

Stern, T.A., et al. *Massachusetts General Hospital Comprehensive Clinical Psychiatry,* 1st ed. Philadelphia: Mosby Elsevier, 2008.

ORGANIZATIONS

American Academy of Neurology, 1080 Montreal Ave., St. Paul, MN, 55116, (651) 695-2717, (800) 879-1960, Fax: (651) 879-2791, memberservices@aan.com, http://www.aan.com.

American Medical Association, 515 N State St., Chicago, IL, 60610, (312) 464-5000, (800) 621-8335, http://www.amaassn.org.

American Neurological Association, 5841 Cedar Lake Rd., Ste. 204, Minneapolis, MN, 55416, (952) 545-6284, ana@llmsi.com, http://www.aneuroa.org.

National Institutes of Health, 9000 Rockville Pike, Bethesda, MD, 20892, (301) 496-4000; TTY: (301) 402-9612, http://www.nih.gov.

National Institute of Neurological Disorders and Stroke (NINDS), PO Box 5801, Bethesda, MD, 20824, (301) 496-5751; TTY: (301) 468-5981, (800) 352-9424, http://www.ninds.nih.gov.

Laith Farid Gulli, MD
Mary Finley

Nicotine and related disorders

Definition

Nicotine is the main psychoactive ingredient in tobacco. It is a physically and psychologically addictive drug. Nicotine is the most influential dependence-producing drug in the United States and worldwide, and its use is associated with many serious health risks.

Demographics

Although the prevalence of smoking has gradually decreased in the United States and many other industrialized countries since the 1970s, the use of tobacco products is rapidly increasing in developing nations, where approximately 80% of current smokers live. Younger populations may be particularly vulnerable. For example, a CDC survey from 2003 found that almost 42% of teenaged boys in one city in Mali were cigarette smokers. The World Health Organization currently attributes more than five million deaths per year globally to tobacco use among the estimated one billion smokers worldwide, a death total expected to increase to eight million by 2030. Another 600,000 deaths occur in nonsmokers as a result of exposure to secondhand smoke. Use of tobacco products in developing countries is of particular concern, because these countries often lack adequate healthcare resources to treat smoking-related diseases, let alone support **smoking cessation** programs.

In the United States, men are more likely to smoke than women (33.7% to 21.5%). In developing countries, male smokers outnumber women smokers, but among adolescent populations, girls and boys are becoming more equal in their rates of smoking. In the United States, people who smoke tend to have less formal education than those who do not, with the lowest smoking rates in persons with college degrees. At least 50% of patients diagnosed with psychiatric problems are smokers, while more than three-quarters of those who abuse other substances also smoke.

According to the National Survey on Drug Use and Health, from 1997 to 2010, smoking among U.S. middle- and high-school students had declined after increasing dramatically in the 1990s. Smoking is most prevalent among adults aged 18 to 25, with an estimated 40.8% of all smokers falling within this age group. Among different ethnic groups, the highest rates of smoking resided in American Indian or Alaskan Native populations (35.8%), followed by persons who were two or more races (32%), Caucasians (29.5%), and African Americans (27.3%).

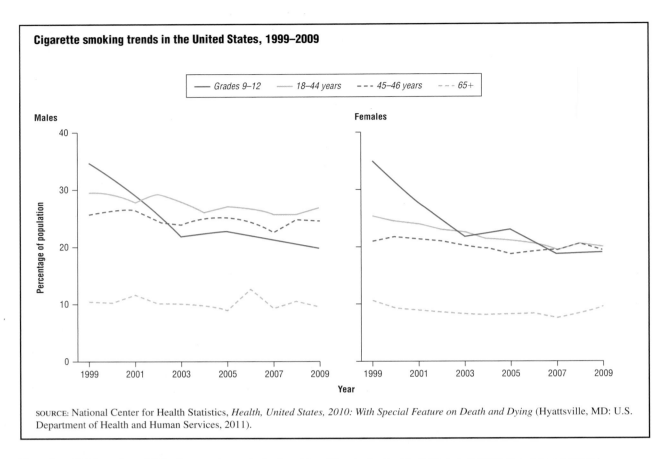

Cigarette smoking trends in the United States, 1999–2009

Grades 9–12 · 18–44 years · 45–46 years · 65+

Males

Females

Percentage of population

Year

SOURCE: National Center for Health Statistics, *Health, United States, 2010: With Special Feature on Death and Dying* (Hyattsville, MD: U.S. Department of Health and Human Services, 2011).

Report available online at http://www.cdc.gov/nchs/hus.htm. *(Graphs by PreMediaGlobal. © 2012 Cengage Learning.)*

Recent research suggests that there may be a genetic component to nicotine dependence, just as there is for alcohol dependence. Studies show that girls (but not boys) whose mothers smoked during pregnancy are four times more likely to smoke than those whose mothers were tobacco-free during pregnancy. Other research suggests that the absence of a certain enzyme in the body protects the body against nicotine dependence.

Description

Nicotine is the most addictive and psychoactive chemical in tobacco, a plant native to North America. Early European explorers learned to smoke its leaves from indigenous peoples who had been using tobacco for hundreds of years. They took tobacco back to Europe, where it became immensely popular. Tobacco became a major source of income for the American colonies and later for the United States. Advances in cigarette-making technology caused a boom in cigarette smoking in the early 1900s. Before the early twentieth century, most people who used tobacco used pipes, cigars, or chewing tobacco.

In the 1950s, researchers began to link cigarette smoking to certain respiratory diseases and cancers.

In 1964, the Surgeon General of the United States issued the first health report on smoking. Cigarette smoking peaked in the United States in the 1960s, then began to decline as health concerns about tobacco increased. In 1971, cigarette advertising was banned from television, although tobacco products are still advertised in other media today. There were about 69.6 million adult smokers in the United States in 2010, and approximately 2.4 million people had smoked their first cigarette in the previous month. Most active smokers are addicted to nicotine.

Pure nicotine is a colorless liquid that turns brown and smells like tobacco when exposed to air. Nicotine can be absorbed through the skin, the lining of the mouth and nose, and the moist tissues lining the lungs. Cigarettes are the most efficient nicotine delivery system. Once tobacco smoke is inhaled, nicotine reaches the **brain** in less than 15 seconds. Because people who smoke pipes and cigars do not inhale, they absorb nicotine more slowly. Nicotine in chewing tobacco and snuff is absorbed through the mucous membranes lining the mouth and nasal passages. There are also several "hard snuff" and other new tobacco products being produced and marketed as alternative to traditional

KEY TERMS

Cold turkey—A slang term for stopping the use of nicotine (or any other addictive drug) suddenly and completely.

Dopamine—A chemical in brain tissue that serves to transmit nerve impulses and helps to regulate movement and emotions.

Epinephrine—Also known as adrenaline, the hormone secreted by the adrenal glands in response to stress.

Neurotransmitter—One of a group of chemicals secreted by a nerve cell (neuron) to carry a chemical message to another nerve cell, often as a way of transmitting a nerve impulse. Examples of neurotransmitters include acetylcholine, dopamine, serotonin, and norepinephrine.

Plaque—A sticky cholesterol-containing substance that builds up on the walls of blood vessels, reducing or blocking blood flow.

Tolerance—A progressive decrease in the effectiveness of a drug with long-term use, requiring higher doses to achieve the desired effect.

Withdrawal—Symptoms experienced by a person who has become physically dependent on a drug, experienced when the drug use is discontinued.

tobacco products. At least one study of the nicotine content of these products has found that some have lower levels of nicotine than regular tobacco products, but others contain comparable levels.

Causes and symptoms

How nicotine works

Nicotine is the main addictive drug among the 4,000 compounds found in tobacco smoke. Other substances in smoke as tar and carbon monoxide present documented health hazards, but they are not addictive and do not cause cravings or withdrawal symptoms to the extent that nicotine does. Neuroimaging technology has shown that levels of monoamine oxidase, the enzyme responsible for boosting mood-enhancing molecule levels in the brain, increase in response to smoking, even though nicotine does not affect levels of this enzyme. Thus, some other compound in cigarette smoke must be acting to exert this effect. In addition, a compound in cigarette smoke called acetaldehyde may contribute to tobacco **addiction** and may have a stronger effect in adolescents.

Nicotine is both a stimulant and a sedative. It is a psychoactive drug, meaning that it works in the brain, alters brain chemistry, and changes mood. Once tobacco smoke is inhaled, nicotine passes rapidly through the linings of the lungs and into the blood. It quickly circulates to the brain where it stimulates release of **dopamine**, a neurotransmitter (nerve signaling molecule) that affects mood. Drugs that elicit an increase in dopamine influence the brain's "reward" pathway, causing the user to turn again to the drug for another pleasurable, rewarding dopamine response. This release accounts for the pleasurable sensation that most smokers feel almost as soon as they light a cigarette. Nicotine also decreases anger and increases the efficiency of a person's performance on long, dull tasks.

As nicotine affects the brain, it also stimulates the adrenal glands. The adrenal glands are small, pea-sized organs located above each kidney that really act as two different endocrine organs. The adrenal gland produces several hormones in the medulla, or inner layer, including epinephrine, also called **adrenaline**. Under normal circumstances, adrenaline is released in response to **stress** or a perceived threat. It is sometimes called the "fight or flight" hormone, because it prepares the body for action. When adrenaline is released, blood pressure, heart rate, blood flow, and oxygen use increase. Glucose, a simple form of sugar used by the body, floods the body to provide extra energy to muscles. The overall effect of the release of the stress hormones is strain on the cardiovascular (heart and blood vessels) system. This response to stress produces inflammation in the blood vessels that ultimately results in buildup of plaque, which can block the vessels and cause **stroke** or heart attack.

Most people begin smoking between the ages of 12 and 20. Few people start smoking as adults over 21. Adolescents who smoke tend to begin as casual smokers, out of rebellion or a perceived need for social acceptance. Dependence on nicotine develops rapidly, however; one study suggests that 85%–90% of adolescents who smoke four or more cigarettes become regular smokers. Nicotine is addictive, so being tobacco-free soon feels uncomfortable for users. In addition, smokers quickly develop tolerance to nicotine. Tolerance is a condition that occurs when the body needs a larger and larger dose of a substance to produce the same effect. For smokers, tolerance to nicotine means more frequent and more rapid smoking. Soon most smokers develop physical withdrawal symptoms when they try to stop smoking. Users of other forms of tobacco experience the same effects; however, the delivery of nicotine is slower and the effects may not be as pronounced.

Nicotine dependence

In addition to the physical dependence caused by the actions of nicotine on the brain, there is a strong psychological component to the dependency of most users of tobacco products, especially cigarette smokers. Most people who start smoking or using smokeless tobacco products do so because of social factors. These include:

• desire to fit in with peers

• acceptance by family members who use tobacco

• rebelliousness

• association of tobacco products with maturity and sophistication

• positive response to tobacco advertising

Such personal factors as mental illness (**depression**, anxiety, **schizophrenia**, or alcoholism), the need to reduce stress and anxiety, or a desire to avoid weight gain also influence people to start smoking. Once smoking has become a habit, whether physical addiction occurs or not, psychological factors play a significant role in a person's continuing to smoke. People who want to stop smoking may be discouraged from doing so because:

• they live or work with people who smoke and who are not supportive of their quitting

• they believe they are incapable of quitting

• they perceive no health benefits to quitting

• they have tried to quit before and failed

• they associate cigarettes with specific pleasurable activities or social situations that they are not willing to give up

• they fear gaining weight

Successful smoking cessation programs must treat both the physical and psychological aspects of nicotine addiction.

Nicotine withdrawal

The **American Psychiatric Association** first recognized nicotine dependence and nicotine withdrawal as serious psychological problems in 1980. Today nicotine is considered an addictive drug, although a common and legalized one.

Quitting nicotine can be difficult. Among people who try, between 75% and 80% **relapse** within six months. Because of this rate, research has found that smoking cessation programs that last longer than six months can greatly enhance quit rates, achieving rates as high as 50% at one year. Combining a nicotine-withdrawal product with a behavioral-modification or support program has produced the greatest success rates.

The combination of physiological and psychological factors make withdrawal from nicotine very difficult. Symptoms of nicotine withdrawal include:

• irritability

• restlessness

• increased anger or frustration

• sleep disturbances

• inability to concentrate

• increased appetite or desire for sweets

• depression

• anxiety

• constant thoughts about smoking

• cravings for cigarettes

• decreased heart rate

• coughing

Withdrawal symptoms are usually more pronounced in smokers than in those who use smokeless tobacco products, and heavy smokers tend to have more symptoms than light smokers when they try to stop smoking. People with depression, schizophrenia, alcoholism, or mood disorders may find it especially difficult to quit, as nicotine offers temporary relief for some of the symptoms of these disorders.

Symptoms of nicotine withdrawal begin rapidly and peak within one to three days. Withdrawal symptoms generally last three to four weeks, but a significant number of smokers have withdrawal symptoms lasting longer than one month. Some people have strong cravings for tobacco that last for months, even though the physical addiction to nicotine is gone. These cravings often occur in settings in which the person formerly smoked, such as at a party, while driving, or after a meal. Researchers believe that much of this extended craving is psychological.

Diagnosis

Smokers usually self-diagnose their nicotine dependence and nicotine withdrawal. Such questionnaires as the Fagerstrom Test for Nicotine Dependence (FTND), a short six-item assessment of cigarette use, help to determine the level of tobacco dependence. Physicians and mental health professionals are less concerned with **diagnosis**, which is usually straightforward, than with determining the physical and psychological factors in each patient that must be addressed for successful smoking cessation.

The ***Diagnostic and Statistical Manual of Mental Disorders***, the handbook used by medical professionals in diagnosing mental health conditions, recognizes two smoking-related disorders: tobacco use disorder and tobacco withdrawal disorder. The criteria for diagnosing a tobacco use disorder is the same for any **substance abuse** disorder. Specific criteria include experiencing symptoms of tolerance or withdrawal, unsuccessful attempts at quitting, and smoking for longer or more often than was originally intended. Criteria for tobacco withdrawal include experiencing withdrawal symptoms within 24 hours after quitting (or reducing intake).

Treatment

Most people do not decide to stop smoking all of the sudden. Instead, they go through several preparatory stages before taking action. First is the precontemplation stage, in which the smoker does not even consider quitting. Precontemplation is followed by the contemplation stage, in which the smoker thinks about quitting, but takes no action. Contemplation eventually turns to preparation, often when counselors or family members encourage or urge the smoker to quit. Now the smoker starts making plans to quit soon. Finally the smoker arrives at the point of taking action.

Having decided to stop smoking, a person has many choices of programs and approaches. When mental health professionals are involved in smoking cessation efforts, one of their first jobs is to identify the physical and psychological factors that keep the person smoking. This identification helps to direct the smoker to the most appropriate type of program. Assessment examines the frequency of the person's smoking, his or her social and emotional attachment to cigarettes, commitment to change, available support system, and barriers to change. These conditions vary from person to person, which is why some smoking cessation programs work for one person and not another.

Medications

Before 1984, there were no medications to help smokers quit. In that year, a nicotine chewing gum (Nicorette) was approved by the U.S. Food and Drug Administration (FDA) as a prescription drug for smoking cessation. In 1996, it became available without prescription. Nicorette was the first of several medications used for nicotine replacement therapy, intended to gradually reduce nicotine dependence to prevent or reduce withdrawal symptoms. This approach, called tapering, is used in withdrawal of other addictive drugs. Studies indicate that people using these replacement therapies do not become addicted to them.

Nicotine gum comes in two strengths, 2 mg and 4 mg. Lozenges (Commit, Nicorette lozenge) are also available in the same doses. As the gum is chewed, nicotine is released and absorbed through the lining of the mouth. Over a 6- to 12-week period, the amount and strength of gum chewed can be decreased until the smoker is weaned away from his or her dependence on nicotine. People trying to quit smoking are instructed to use the gum when they feel a craving. Products with caffeine may limit nicotine absorption and should be avoided in a window of time around the gum "dose." Some people may not like the taste of the gum, and other common side effects include burning mouth and sore jaw. Pregnant or lactating women and persons with heart problems, diabetes, or ulcers should consult with a doctor before beginning any nicotine-replacement product.

Nicotine transdermal patches have been available without prescription since 1996. They are marketed under several brand names, including Habitrol, Nicoderm, NicoDerm CQ, Prostep, and Nicotrol. All but Nicotrol are 24-hour patches; Nicotrol is a 16-hour patch designed to be removed at night. The patches are worn on the skin between the neck and the waist and provide a steady delivery of nicotine through the skin. Patches like Nicoderm come in varying strengths, and after several weeks, users can move down to a patch that delivers a lower dose. With the Nicotrol patch, a user simply ceases use after six weeks. Some people using the 24-hour patches experience sleep disturbances, and a few develop mild skin irritations, but generally side effects are few. Doctors recommend not smoking while using the patch.

Two other nicotine delivery devices are available by prescription only. One is a nicotine nasal spray. It has the advantage of delivering nicotine rapidly, just as a cigarette does, but it delivers a much lower dose than a cigarette. Treatment with nasal spray usually lasts four to six weeks. Side effects include cold-like symptoms (runny nose, sneezing, etc.). A nicotine inhaler is also available that delivers nicotine through the tissues of the mouth. A major advantage of the inhaler is that it provides an alternative to having a cigarette in one's hands while still delivering nicotine. It delivers less nicotine in cold weather (under 50°F). Recommendations for both the spray and the inhaler are that they be used at least hourly at first.

Prescription drugs outside of nicotine replacement therapy have been approved for the treatment of nicotine dependence. The first-approved drug was **bupropion** (Zyban), an antidepressant that acts to cut down withdrawal symptoms. This drug may be used in combination with a nicotine-replacement therapy and behavioral therapy.

A newer drug is varenicline (Chantix), which was developed to help people stop smoking. This drug acts directly on the proteins in the brain that recognize and bind nicotine. Interfering with their action not only stops the brain from sending the pleasurable message of nicotine but also reduces the feelings of nicotine withdrawal. Some studies indicate that this drug can double a person's chances of quitting smoking. Side effects of this drug can include headache, nausea, vomiting, sleep problems, gas, and changes in taste sensation.

Other drugs used in some smoking cessation programs include **nortriptyline** (Pamelor), a tricyclic antidepressant, and **clonidine** (Catapres), a high blood pressure medication. Side effects of these drugs include dry mouth and drowsiness. Both of these drugs are second-line treatments (used only when other treatments have shown no results) and are considered off-label uses (not approved by the FDA for this purpose).

Behavioral treatments

Behavioral treatments are used to help smokers learn to recognize and avoid specific situations that trigger desire for a cigarette. They also help the smoker learn to substitute other activities for smoking. Behavioral treatments are almost always combined with smoker education, and they usually involve forming a support network of other smokers who are trying to quit.

Behavioral treatments often take place in **support groups** either in person or online. They are most effective when combined with nicotine reduction therapy. Other supportive techniques include the use of rewards for achieving certain goals and contracts to clarify and reinforce the goals. Aversive techniques include asking the smoker to inhale the tobacco smoke deeply and repeatedly to the point of nausea, so that smoking is no longer associated with pleasurable sensations. Overall, quit rates are highest when **behavior modification** is combined with nicotine replacement therapy and tapering. Behavior modification once was conducted in person, but with the advent of a telephonic and virtual world on the Internet, behavioral approaches are also available via mail, telephone, and the Web for greater access and flexibility. The U.S. Department of Health and Human Services sponsors a toll-free number for people who want to quit: 800-QUIT-NOW (800-784-8669). This number serves as the point of contact for smokers who want information and help.

Alternative treatments

Many alternative therapies have been tried to help smokers withdraw from nicotine. Hypnosis has proved helpful in some cases, but has not been tested in controlled **clinical trials**. **Acupuncture**, relaxation techniques, restricted environmental stimulation therapy (REST, a combination of relaxation and hypnosis techniques), special **diets**, and herbal supplements have all been used to help people stop smoking. Of these alternative techniques, clinical studies of REST showed substantial promise in helping people stop smoking permanently.

Prognosis

Smoking is a major health risk associated with nicotine dependence, with approximately 50% of long-term smokers dying from smoking-related diseases, according to the FDA. It is the top cause of preventable death in the United States and kills an estimated 443,000 U.S. citizens each year—more than alcohol, illegal drug, homicide, **suicide**, car accidents, and HIV rates combined. Of those 443,000, about 40% will die from cancer, 35% from heart disease and stroke, and 25% from lung disease. Most lung cancers, the leading cause of cancer death in the United States, are linked to smoking, and smoking is linked to about one-third of all cancer deaths. Smoking also causes such other lung problems as chronic bronchitis and emphysema, as well as worsening the symptoms of asthma. Other cancers associated with smoking include cancers of the mouth, esophagus, stomach, kidney, colon, and bladder. Smoking accounts for a large percentage of cardiovascular deaths and significantly increases the risk of heart disease, heart attack, stroke, and aneurysm. Women who smoke during pregnancy have more miscarriages, premature babies, and low–birth weight babies than nonsmokers. In addition, there is an increased risk that a child born to a mother who smokes will die of sudden infant death syndrome (SIDS), making smoking an avoidable factor in this tragic occurrence. Secondhand smoke also endangers the health of nonsmokers in the smoker's family or workplace. Although most of these effects are not caused directly by nicotine, it is the dependence on nicotine that keeps people smoking.

Even though it is difficult for smokers to break their chemical and psychological dependence on nicotine, most of the negative health effects of smoking are reduced or reversed after quitting. Therefore, it is worth trying to quit smoking at any age, regardless of the length of time a person has had the habit.

Mental health problems

Persons with mental health problems, such as depression, anxiety, and schizophrenia, are two to three times more likely to smoke than persons without these conditions. However, smoking has also been associated with the risk of developing mental health problems, which has prompted some researchers to wonder whether smoking is a causal factor in mental illnesses or just prevalent due to effects of nicotine. However, a study published in the *Archives of General Psychiatry* in 2010 suggested that tobacco smoke may have some implications in the development of mental illness. The study focused on the impact of secondhand smoke on individuals and found that nonsmokers were 1.5 times more likely to develop mental health problems if regularly exposed to secondhand smoke. A similar study focused on children, published in the *Archives of Pediatrics & Adolescent Medicine*, found that children exposed to secondhand smoke were more likely to develop behavioral problems such as **attention deficit hyperactivity disorder (ADHD)**. Neither study is definitive of smoking's impact on mental health, and further research is needed, but along with the varied and severe physiological effects of smoking, there is risk of a negative psychological impact, as well.

Prevention

The best way to avoid nicotine dependence and withdrawal is to avoid the use of tobacco products. In September 2012, the FDA will start requiring all cigarette manufacturers to display large, pictographic warning labels on cigarette packaging to deter consumers from purchasing cigarettes. The labels feature images focused on the negative effects of smoking, such as damaged lungs, oral cancer, children affected by secondhand smoke, and even a deceased person. The goal of the new labels is to both help current smokers quit smoking and to prevent others from starting smoking. The images are available on the FDA website: http://www.fda.gov/TobaccoProducts/Labeling/CigaretteWarningLabels/default.htm.

Resources

BOOKS

Bock, Gregory, and Jamie Goode, eds. *Understanding Nicotine and Tobacco Addiction: Novartis Foundation Symposium, 275.* Chichester, UK: John Wiley & Sons, 2006.

Cooper, Grant. *Never Smoke Again: The Top 10 Ways to Stop Smoking Now & Forever.* Garden City Park, NY: Square One Publishers, 2007.

Henningfield, Jack E., Edythe D. London, and Sakire Pogun. *Nicotine Psychopharmacology.* Berlin: Springer, 2009.

Miller, Michael W. *Brain Development: Normal Processes and the Effects of Alcohol and Nicotine.* Oxford: Oxford University Press, 2006.

Naff, Clay Farris. *Nicotine and Tobacco.* San Diego: ReferencePoint Press, Inc, 2007.

PERIODICALS

Berrettini W. "Nicotine Addiction." *The American Journal of Psychiatry* 165 (September 2008): 1089–92.

Caggiula A.R., et al. "The Role of Nicotine in Smoking: a Dual-reinforcement Model." *Nebraska Symposium on Motivation* 55 (2009): 91–109.

DiFranza, J.R. "Hooked From the First Cigarette." *Scientific American.* 298 (April 21, 2008): 82–7.

Glasser, I. "Letters: Nicotine Anonymous May Benefit Nicotine-Dependent Individuals." *American Journal of Public Health.* 100, no. 2 (February 2010): 196.

Oncken C., et al. "Nicotine Gum for Pregnant Smokers: A Randomized Controlled Trial." *Obstetrics and Gynecology.* 112, no. 4 (2008): 859–67.

WEBSITES

Nicotine Anonymous. http://www.nicotine-anonymous.org (accessed October 23, 2011).

Smokefree.gov. "Quit Smoking Today." http://www.smokefree.gov (accessed October 23, 2011).

ORGANIZATIONS

American Cancer Society, 250 Williams Street NW, Atlanta, GA, 30303, http://www.cancer.org.

American Lung Association, 1301 Pennsylvannia Ave. NW, Suite 800, Washington, DC, 20004, (202) 785-3355, Fax: (202) 452-1805, info@lungusa.org, http://www.lungusa.org.

Tish Davidson, AM
Emily Jane Willingham, PhD
Brenda W. Lerner

Nightmare disorder

Definition

Nightmare disorder, which is also called dream anxiety disorder, is characterized by the occurrence of repeated dreams during which the sleeper feels threatened and frightened. The sense of fear causes the person to awake.

Demographics

The actual percentage of people that suffer from nightmare disorder is not known, as many people do not seek treatment for it. There are, however, estimates of the proportion of the population that experience occasional nightmares. Many children suffer from nightmares that concern their parents. Estimates on the number of children who have recurrent nightmares range from 10%–50%. In children, however, nightmares are not usually associated with psychiatric illness.

Nightmares can be caused by psychological traumas or stress and anxiety. (Illustration by Electronic Illustrators Group. © 2012 Cengage Learning.)

The number of children experiencing nightmares decreases as they get older. More than 3% of young adults have frequent nightmares, but only about 1% of mature adults experience nightmares once or twice a week. Half of the adults in the United States who experience regular nightmares have diagnosable psychiatric illnesses. Women are estimated to have nightmares two to four times more frequently than men. There is some uncertainty as to whether this figure reflects an actual difference between the sexes in the frequency of nightmares, or whether women are simply more likely than men to report nightmares. Nightmares typically decrease in frequency as people grow older.

Description

Nightmares are dreams that cause intense fear. These dreams are often complex and fairly long. During the dream the sleeper usually encounters or experiences a threat to their life or safety. Nightmares are also reported that do not involve physical danger but threaten the dreamer's pride or integrity.

As the dream progresses, the threat to the person usually increases, as does their sense of fear. Waking usually occurs just as the threat or danger reaches its climax. It is often difficult for a person to return to sleep after waking from a nightmare. Nightmares usually occur during the second half of the night's sleep.

Causes and symptoms

During the course of a nightmare the sleeper may moan, talk, or move slightly, although these signs do not always appear. The person wakes completely from the nightmare with a profound sense of fear. Waking is usually accompanied by increased heart rate, sweating, and other symptoms of anxiety or fear. Once fully awake, the person usually has a good recall of the dream and what made it so frightening. Because of the physical symptoms of anxiety and because clarity is achieved immediately upon waking, returning to sleep after a nightmare is often difficult. The vividness of the recall and the prominence of the dream images in the person's mind can also make it difficult to calm down and return to sleep.

Sometimes people may avoid going to sleep after a particularly intense nightmare because of the fear of having another bad dream. In addition, people may have problems falling asleep if they are experiencing anxiety caused by the fear of having nightmares. As a result, these people may have the signs and symptoms associated with mild **sleep deprivation**, such as decreased mental clarity, problems paying attention, excessive daytime sleepiness, irritability, or mild **depression**.

The causes of nightmares are not known for certain. Adults who have nightmares on a regular basis constitute a small minority of the American population. About half of these people are thought to suffer from psychiatric disorders that cause nightmares. Nightmares may also be triggered by major psychological traumas, such as those experienced by patients with **post-traumatic stress disorder**. For most patients who do not have an underlying mental disorder, the nightmares are attributed to **stress**. Nightmares that occur on an irregular and occasional basis are usually attributed to life stressors and associated anxiety.

Some researchers think that artistic or creative people are at greater risk for nightmares, as are people who are generally sensitive. These people are considered to have well-developed imaginations and are more sensitive to environmental and social factors.

Nightmares can be a side effect of some medications or drugs of abuse, including drugs given for high blood pressure; levodopa and other drugs given to treat Parkinson's disease; **amphetamines**, **cocaine**, and other stimulants; and some **antidepressants**. Withdrawal from alcohol and other medications can also sometimes cause nightmares.

Diagnosis

A **diagnosis** of nightmare disorder is usually made because the person reports the problem to their family physician or a **psychiatrist**. There are no laboratory tests for nightmare disorder, although the doctor may give the patient a physical examination to rule out any medical conditions that may be causing anxiety or stress.

Nightmares are characterized by awakening with a sense of fear, a clear recollection of the dream, and the physical symptoms of anxiety. Nightmares can occur during nighttime sleep or daytime naps. A patient experiencing nightmares must meet the criteria listed in the *Diagnostic and Statistical Manual of Mental Disorders* (*DSM*) to be diagnosed with nightmare disorder. The manual, which provides guidelines used by the **American Psychiatric Association** for diagnosing psychiatric disturbances, lists four distinct criteria:

• The patient must experience repeated awakenings from frightening or disturbing dreams.

• When the patient awakes, he or she must wake fully and be aware of his or her surroundings.

• The nightmares or the resulting loss of sleep must cause the patient distress in important areas of his or her life.

• The nightmares cannot be directly attributed to another mental disorder or be the direct effects of medications, substance abuse, or a medical condition.

Nightmare disorder can be confused with **sleep terror disorder**. Both disorders are characterized by an arousal during sleep when the patient shows symptoms of anxiety or fear. During a nightmare, the patient may move slightly or moan but does not generally display dramatic or active symptoms. After a nightmare, the patient becomes fully awake and is aware of his or her surroundings. Sleep terror, however, is characterized by a partial arousal from sleep during an episode, in which the patient is generally nonresponsive. Their own cries and screams usually cause them to wake. Patients do not remember either the sleep terror episode or what caused the fear, whereas patients who have nightmares remember them with great clarity and often in considerable detail. Such symptoms of fear or anxiety as increased heart rate, dilated pupils, and sweating are not as dramatic in patients with nightmare disorder as they are in patients experiencing sleep terrors.

Treatment

Nightmares that are associated with a psychiatric disorder are managed by treating the underlying disorder. For patients without psychiatric disorders, psychological counseling to deal with any recurring themes in the nightmares may be helpful. Children may not require treatment for nightmares unless the dreams are causing significant distress, as nightmares generally resolve as children mature.

KEY TERMS

Dream anxiety disorder—Another name for nightmare disorder.

Sleep terror disorder—A sleep disorder that is distinguished from nightmare disorder by the intensity of associated anxiety symptoms, the absence of complete wakefulness, and the person's difficulty recalling the episode.

Because stress is thought to be the most common cause of nightmares, **stress reduction** techniques may prove to be effective complementary treatments. Typical relaxation techniques such as **yoga**, **meditation**, or **exercise** may be helpful. **Psychotherapy** can be an effective way to identify major stressors in the person's life and to explore ways in which they may be reduced or eliminated.

Prognosis

Nightmare disorder can be a lifelong disorder. A general improvement in symptoms often takes place, however, as the patient gets older. Treatment for any underlying psychological disorders can be very successful.

Resources

BOOKS

Aldrich, Michael S. *Sleep Medicine*. New York: Oxford University Press, 1999.

American Psychiatric Association. *Diagnostic and Statistical Manual of Mental Disorders*. 4th ed., text rev. Washington, DC: American Psychiatric Publishing, 2000.

Chokroverty, Sudhansu. *Sleep Disorders Medicine: Basic Science, Technical Considerations, and Clinical Aspects*. 3rd ed. Philadelphia: Saunders Elsevier, 2009.

Sadock, Benjamin J., and Virginia A. Sadock, eds. *Comprehensive Textbook of Psychiatry*. Vol. 2. 7th ed. Philadelphia: Lippincott Williams and Wilkins, 2000.

PERIODICALS

Krakow, Barry, et al. "Imagery Rehearsal Therapy for Chronic Nightmares in Sexual Assault Survivors with Posttraumatic Stress Disorder." *Journal of the American Medical Association* 286, no. 5 (August 2001) 537–45.

ORGANIZATIONS

American Academy of Sleep Medicine, 2510 N Frontage Rd., Darien, IL, 60561, (630) 737-9700, Fax: (630) 737-9790, inquiries@assmnet.org, http://www.aasmnet.org.

National Sleep Foundation, 1010 North Glebe Rd., Suite 310, Arlington, VA, 22201, (703) 243-1697, nsf@sleepfoundation.org, http://www.sleepfoundation.org.

Tish Davidson, A.M.

NIMH *see* **National Institute of Mental Health**

NLP *see* **Hypnotherapy**

Norepinephrine *see* **Adrenaline**

Norpramin *see* **Desipramine**

Nortriptyline

Definition

Nortriptyline is a tricyclic antidepressant. It is sold in the United States under the brand names Aventyl and Pamelor, and is also available under its generic name.

Purpose

Nortriptyline is used to relieve symptoms of **depression**. The drug is more effective for endogenous depression than for other forms of depression. Endogenous depression is depression arising from metabolic changes within a person, such as chemical or hormonal imbalances. Nortriptyline is also used to treat premenstrual depression, **panic disorder**, chronic pain, and some skin conditions. In addition, nortriptyline is being investigated for the treatment of **nicotine** dependence.

Description

Tricyclic **antidepressants** act to change the balance of naturally occurring chemicals in the **brain** that regulate the transmission of nerve impulses between cells. The precise way in which nortriptyline elevates mood is not fully understood. The drug inhibits the activity of **neurotransmitters** such as acetylcholine,

Pamelor (nortriptyline hydrochloride). (© *Custom Medical Stock Photo, Inc. Reproduced by permission.*)

histamine, and 5-hydroxytryptamine. Studies have indicated that nortriptyline interferes with the release, transport, and storage of catecholamines, another group of chemicals involved in nerve impulse transmission.

Recommended dosage

As with any antidepressant, the dose of nortriptyline must be carefully adjusted by the physician to produce the desired therapeutic effect. Nortriptyline is available in 10, 25, 50, and 75 mg capsules, as well as in a 10 mg/5mL solution. The usual dosage for nortriptyline is 25 mg given three or four times each day. The optimum total dose of the drug is 50–150 mg daily. Total dosage in excess of 150 mg is not recommended. The recommended dose for older adults (over age 60) and adolescents is 30–50 mg per day. Nortriptyline is not recommended for use by children.

The therapeutic effects of nortriptyline, like other tricyclic antidepressants, appear slowly. Maximum benefit is often not evident for two to three weeks after starting the drug. People taking nortriptyline should be aware of this and continue taking the drug as directed even if they do not see immediate improvement.

Once symptoms of depression have been controlled, the lowest dosage that maintains the effect should be taken. People who take 100 mg or more of nortriptyline per day should have their blood tested periodically for nortriptyline concentrations. The results of these tests will show whether the dose is appropriate, too high, or too low.

Precautions

Like all tricyclic antidepressants, nortriptyline should be used cautiously and with close physician supervision in people, especially the elderly, who have benign prostatic hypertrophy, urinary retention, and glaucoma, especially angle-closure glaucoma (the most severe form). Before starting treatment, people with these conditions should discuss the relative risks and benefits of treatment with their doctors to help determine if nortriptyline is the right antidepressant for them.

Children and adults up to age 24 taking antidepressant drugs, including nortriptyline, are at increased risk for developing suicidal thoughts and actions. Patients of any age taking nortriptyline should be monitored for signs of worsening depression or changes in behavior.

Nortriptyline may increase the possibility of having **seizures**. Patients should tell their physicians if they have a history of seizures, including seizures brought on by the abuse of drugs or alcohol. These people should use nortriptyline only with caution and be closely monitored by their physicians.

When used by people with **schizophrenia**, nortriptyline may worsen **psychosis**, increase hostility in some patients, or activate other symptoms that had not previously been expressed. When used by people with **bipolar disorder**, symptoms of mania may be magnified. Patients with a history of **suicide** attempts, thoughts of suicide, or drug overdose should be monitored carefully when using nortriptyline. Nortriptyline can either increase or decrease blood sugar levels, depending on the patients and their medical conditions. Nortriptyline should be used with great caution when patients are receiving **electroconvulsive therapy**.

Nortriptyline may increase heart rate and cause irregular heartbeat. It may also raise or lower blood pressure. It may be dangerous for people with cardiovascular disease, especially those who have recently had a heart attack, to take this drug or other antidepressants in the same pharmacological class. In rare cases in which patients with cardiovascular disease must receive nortriptyline, they should be monitored closely for cardiac rhythm disturbances and signs of cardiac **stress** or damage.

A common problem with tricyclic antidepressants such as nortriptyline is sedation (drowsiness and lack of physical or mental alertness). This side effect is especially noticeable early in therapy. In most patients, sedation decreases or disappears entirely with time, but until then patients taking nortriptyline should not perform hazardous activities requiring mental alertness or coordination. The sedative effect is increased when nortriptyline is taken with other central nervous system depressants, such as alcoholic beverages, sleeping medications, other **sedatives**, or antihistamines. It may be dangerous to take nortriptyline in combination with these substances.

Side effects

Nortriptyline shares side effects common to all tricyclic antidepressants. The most frequent of these are dry mouth, constipation, urinary retention, increased heart rate, sedation, irritability, dizziness, and decreased coordination. As with most side effects associated with tricyclic antidepressants, the intensity is highest at the beginning of therapy and tends to decrease with continued use.

Dry mouth, if severe to the point of causing difficulty speaking or swallowing, may be managed by dosage reduction or temporary discontinuation of the drug. Patients may also chew sugarless gum or suck on sugarless candy in order to increase the flow of saliva. Some artificial saliva products may give temporary relief.

Men with prostate enlargement who take nortriptyline may be especially likely to have problems with urinary retention. Symptoms include having difficulty starting a urine flow and more difficulty than usual

---

KEY TERMS

Acetylcholine—A naturally occurring chemical in the body that transmits nerve impulses from cell to cell. Generally, it has opposite effects from dopamine and norepinephrine; it causes blood vessels to dilate, lowers blood pressure, and slows the heartbeat. Central nervous system well-being is dependent on a balance among acetylcholine, dopamine, serotonin, and norepinephrine.

Benign prostate hypertrophy—Enlargement of the prostate gland.

Bipolar syndrome—An abnormal mental condition characterized by periods of intense elation, energy, and activity followed by periods of inactivity and depression.

Catecholamine—A group of neurotransmitters synthesized from the amino acid tyrosine and released by the hypothalamic-pituitary-adrenal system in the brain in response to acute stress. The catecholamines include dopamine, serotonin, norepinephrine, and epinephrine.

Endogenous depression—Depression arising from causes within a person, such as chemical or hormonal imbalances.

Manic—Referring to mania, a state characterized by excessive activity, excitement, or emotion.

Neurotransmitter—A chemical in the brain that transmits messages between neurons, or nerve cells.

---

passing urine. In most cases, urinary retention is managed with dose reduction or by switching to another type of antidepressant.

Problems associated with the skin (loss of sensation, numbness and tingling, rashes, spots, itching, and puffiness), seizures, and ringing in the ears have also been reported. Nausea, vomiting, loss of appetite, diarrhea, and abdominal cramping are associated with nortriptyline usage. Skin rash, sensitivity to sunlight, and itching have been linked to nortriptyline use. People who think they may be experiencing any side effects from this or any other medication should talk to their physicians.

Interactions

Dangerously high blood pressure has resulted from the combination of tricyclic antidepressants, such as nortriptyline, and members of another class of antidepressants known as **monoamine oxidase inhibitors**

(MAOIs). Because of this, nortriptyline should never be taken in combination with **MAOIs**. Patients taking any MAOIs, for example **phenelzine** (Nardil) or **tranylcypromine** (Parnate), should stop taking the MAOI and wait at least 14 days before starting nortriptyline or any other tricyclic antidepressant. The same holds true when discontinuing nortriptyline and starting an MAOI.

Cimetidine (Tagamet) may slow the elimination of nortriptyline, thus increasing the amount of nortriptyline in the body, which can result in toxic levels or increased side effects. Quinidine also raises the circulating levels of the drug, requiring a decrease in the dosage of nortriptyline.

The sedative effects of nortriptyline are increased by other central nervous system depressants such as alcohol, sedatives, sleeping medications, or medications used for other mental disorders such as schizophrenia. The symptoms of increased heart rate, blurred vision, and difficulty urinating are increased when nortriptyline is taken with other drugs such as **benztropine**, **biperiden**, **trihexyphenidyl**, and antihistamines.

Resources

BOOKS

Foreman, John C., and Torben Johansen. *Textbook of Receptor Pharmacology*. 2nd ed. Boca Raton, FL: CRC Press, 2002.

Hall, Sharon M. "Tricyclic Antidepressants in the Treatment of Nicotine Dependence." In *Medication Treatments for Nicotine Dependence*, edited by Tony P. George. Boca Raton, FL: CRC Press, 2007.

Page, Clive P., et al. *Integrated Pharmacology*. 3rd ed. St. Louis: Elsevier, 2006.

Preston, John D., John H. O'Neal, and Mary C. Talaga. *Handbook of Clinical Psychopharmacology for Therapists*. 5th ed. Oakland, CA: New Harbinger Publications, 2008.

PERIODICALS

Foulds, Jonathan, et al. "Developments in Pharmacotherapy for Tobacco Dependence: Past, Present and Future." *Drug and Alcohol Review* 25, no. 1 (January 2006): 59–71.

Hensley, Paula L. "A Review of Bereavement-Related Depression and Complicated Grief." *Psychiatric Annals* 36, no. 9 (September 2006): 619–26.

Hughes, John R., Lindsay F. Stead, and Tim Lancaster. "Nortriptyline for Smoking Cessation: A Review." *Nicotine & Tobacco Research* 7, no. 4 (August 2005): 491–99.

Mulder, Roger T., et al. "Six Months of Treatment for Depression: Outcome and Predictors of the Course of Illness." *American Journal of Psychiatry* 163, no. 1 (January 2006): 95–100.

Shelton, Richard C., et al. "Olanzapine/Fluoxetine Combination for Treatment-Resistant Depression: A Controlled Study of SSRI and Nortriptyline Resistance." *Journal of Clinical Psychiatry* 66, no. 10 (October 2005): 1289–97.

Szanto, Katalin, et al. "Emergence, Persistence, and Resolution of Suicidal Ideation During Treatment of Depression in Old Age." *Journal of Affective Disorders* 98, no. 1–2 (February 2007): 153–61.

Wagena, E. J., P. Knipschild, and M. P. A. Zeegers. "Should Nortriptyline Be Used as a First-Line Aid to Help Smokers Quit? Results from a Systematic Review and Meta-Analysis." *Addiction* 100. no. 3 (March 2005): 317–26.

Wisner, Katherine L., et al. "Postpartum Depression: A Randomized Trial of Sertraline Versus Nortriptyline." *Journal of Clinical Psychopharmacology* 26, no. 4 (August 2006): 353–60.

ORGANIZATIONS

American Medical Association, 515 N State Street, Chicago, IL, 60610, (312) 464-5000, (800) 621-8335, http://www.ama-assn.org.

American Psychiatric Association, 1000 Wilson Blvd., Ste. 1825, Arlington, VA, 22209-3901, (703) 907-7300, apa@psych.org, http://www.psych.org.

American Society for Clinical Pharmacology and Therapeutics, 528 North Washington Street, Alexandria, VA, 22314, (703) 836-6981, http://www.ascpt.org.

American Society for Pharmacology and Experimental Therapeutics, 9650 Rockville Pike, Bethesda, MD, 20814-3995, (301) 634-7060, Fax: (301) 634-7061, http://www.aspet.org.

L. Fleming Fallon, Jr., MD, Dr.P.H.
Ruth A. Wienclaw, PhD

Nutrition counseling

Definition

Nutrition counseling is an ongoing process in which a health professional, usually a registered dietitian, works with an individual to assess his or her usual dietary intake and identify areas where change is needed. The nutrition counselor provides information, educational materials, support, and follow-up to help the individual make and maintain the needed dietary changes.

Purpose

The goal of nutrition counseling is to help a person make and maintain dietary changes. For a person with a mental disorder, dietary change may be needed to promote healthier eating, to adopt a therapeutic diet, or to avoid nutrient-drug interactions. Nutrition counseling is an integral part of treatment for persons with eating disorders or chemical dependencies. Persons taking certain drugs, such as **monoamine oxidase inhibitors**, used to treat

depression and **anxiety disorders**, need to follow a tyramine-controlled diet to avoid dietary interference with their medication. Many drugs used to treat mental disorders can cause weight gain or loss, so persons taking these drugs may also benefit from nutrition counseling.

The nutrition counselor and individual work together to assess current eating patterns and identify areas where change is needed. Registered dietitians have met certain education and experience standards and are well qualified to provide nutrition counseling, but nurses, physicians, and health educators also provide nutrition counseling.

Description

Assessing dietary habits

Nutrition counseling usually begins with an interview in which the counselor asks questions about a person's typical food intake. Nutrition counselors use different methods to assess typical food intake.

The 24-hour recall method is a listing of all the foods and beverages a person consumed within the previous 24-hour period. The nutrition counselor may ask a person to recall the first thing he or she ate or drank the previous morning. The counselor then records the estimated amounts of all the foods and beverages the person consumed the rest of the day. The 24-hour food recall can be used to provide an estimate of energy and nutrient intake. However, people tend to over- or underestimate intake of certain foods, and food intake on one day may not accurately represent typical food intake.

A food frequency questionnaire can sometimes provide a more accurate picture of a person's typical eating patterns. The nutrition counselor may ask the client how often he or she consumes certain food groups. For example, the counselor may ask a person how many servings of dairy products, fruits, vegetables, grains and cereals, meats, or fats he or she consumes in a typical day, week, or month.

Daily food records are also useful in assessing food intake. An individual keeps a written record of the amounts of all foods and beverages consumed over a given period of time. The nutrition counselor can then use the food records to analyze actual energy and nutrient intake. Three-day food records kept over two weekdays and one weekend day are often used.

Assessing body weight

Nutrition counselors may assess an individual's body weight by comparing his or her weight to various weight-for-height tables. A rough rule of thumb for determining a woman's ideal body weight is to allow 100 lb (45 kg) for the first 5 ft (1.5 m) of height plus 5 lb (2.3 kg) for every additional inch. A man is allowed 106 lb (48 kg) for the first 5 ft (1.5 m) of height plus 6 lb (2.7 kg) for every additional inch. However, this guide does not take into account a person's frame size.

Body mass index, or BMI, is another indicator used to assess body weight. BMI is calculated as weight in kilograms divided by height in meters squared. A BMI of 20 to 25 is considered normal weight, a BMI of less than 20 is considered underweight, and a BMI of greater than 25 is considered overweight.

Identifying changes needed

The initial dietary assessment and interview provide the basis for identifying behaviors that need to be changed. Sometimes a person already has a good idea of what dietary changes are needed, but may require help making the changes. Other times the nutrition counselor can help educate a person on the health effects of different dietary choices. The nutrition counselor and client work together to identify areas where change is needed, prioritize changes, and problem-solve as to how to make the changes.

Making dietary change is a gradual process. An individual may start with one or two easier dietary changes the first few weeks and gradually make additional or more difficult changes over several weeks or months. For example, an easy change for a person might be switching from 2% to skim milk, or taking time for a quick yogurt or granola bar in the morning instead of skipping breakfast. More difficult changes might be learning to replace high-fat meat choices with leaner ones, or including more servings of vegetables daily.

In making dietary changes, each individual's situation and background must be carefully considered. Factors that affect food decisions include an individual's ethnic background, religion, group affiliation, socioeconomic status, and world view.

Identifying barriers to change

Once the needed changes have been identified, the client and nutrition counselor think through potential problems that may arise. For example, changing eating behaviors may mean involving others, purchasing different foods, planning ahead for social events, or bringing special foods to work. Some common barriers to changing eating habits include:

- inconvenience
- social gatherings
- food preferences
- lack of knowledge or time
- cost

Setting goals

The nutrition counselor and client set behavior-oriented goals together. Goals should focus on the behaviors needed to achieve the desired dietary change, not on an absolute value, such as achieving a certain body weight. For a person working to prevent weight gain associated with certain medications, for example, his or her goals might be to increase the amount of fruits, vegetables, and whole grains consumed each day. Such changes would help prevent weight gain while placing the emphasis on needed behaviors rather than on actual weight.

Finding support

Family members are encouraged to attend nutrition counseling sessions with the client, especially if they share responsibility for food selection and preparation. Although the individual must make food choices and take responsibility for dietary changes, having the support and understanding of family and friends makes success more likely.

Maintaining changes

The challenge for the nutrition client lies not in making the initial dietary changes, but in maintaining them over the long term. Self-monitoring, realistic expectations, and continued follow-up can help a person maintain dietary changes.

Self-monitoring involves regularly checking eating habits against desired goals and keeping track of eating behaviors. Keeping a food diary on a daily or periodic basis helps the individual be more aware of his or her eating behaviors and provides a ready tool to analyze eating habits. Sometimes a simplified checklist to assure adequate intake of different food groups may be used.

Individuals and nutrition counselors should not expect perfect dietary compliance—slips inevitably occur. The goal is to keep small slips, such as eating a few extra cookies, from becoming big slips, like total abandonment of dietary change. The counselor can help the client identify situations that may lead to **relapse** and plan ways to handle the situations ahead of time.

Nutrition counseling is an ongoing process that can take months or years. In follow-up nutrition counseling sessions, the individual and counselor analyze food records together and problem-solve behaviors that are especially difficult to change. Follow-up counseling also allows the opportunity to reevaluate goals and strategies for achieving those goals.

KEY TERMS

Body mass index, or BMI—A measure of body fat, calculated as weight in kilograms over the square of height in meters.

Food frequency questionnaire—A listing of how often a person consumes foods from certain food groups in a given period of time.

Registered dietitian—A person who has met certain education and experience standards and is well-qualified to provide nutrition counseling.

Twenty-four-hour recall—A listing of the type and amount of all foods and beverages consumed by a person in a 24-hour period.

Resources

BOOKS

American Dietetic Association. *Manual of Clinical Dietetics.* 6th ed. Chicago: American Dietetic Association, 2000.

Hammond, Kathleen A. "Dietary and Clinical Assessment." In *Krause's Food Nutrition, and Diet Therapy,* by L. Kathleen Mahan, Sylvia Escott-Stump, and Janice L. Raymond. Philadelphia: W.B. Saunders Company, 2011.

Hunt, Paula. "Dietary Counseling." In *Essentials of Human Nutrition,* by Jim Mann and A. Stewart Truswell. Oxford: Oxford University Press, 1998.

Mitchell, Mary Kay. *Nutrition Across the Life Span.* Long Grove, IL: Waveland Press, 2008.

PERIODICALS

Harris-Davis, E., and B. Haughton. "Model for Multicultural Nutrition Counseling Competencies." *Journal of the American Dietetic Association* 100, no. 10 (2000): 1178–85.

ORGANIZATIONS

American Dietetic Association, 120 South Riverside Plaza, Ste. 2000, Chicago, IL, 60606, (312) 899-0040, (800) 877-1600, http://www.eatright.org.

Nancy Gustafson, M.S., R.D., F.A.D.A., E.L.S.

Nutrition and mental health

Introduction and overview

A person's food intake affects mood, behavior, and **brain** function. A hungry person may feel irritable and restless, whereas a person who has just eaten a meal may feel calm and satisfied. A sleepy person may feel more productive after a cup of coffee and a light snack. A person who has consistently eaten less food or energy than needed over a long period of time may be apathetic and moody.

Nutrition and the brain

The human brain has high energy and nutrient needs. Changes in energy or nutrient intake can alter both brain chemistry and the functioning of nerves in the brain. Intake of energy and several different nutrients affect levels of chemicals in the brain called **neurotransmitters**. Neurotransmitters transmit nerve impulses from one nerve cell to another, and they influence mood, sleep patterns, and thinking. Deficiencies or excesses of certain vitamins or minerals can damage nerves in the brain, causing changes in memory, limiting problem-solving ability, and impairing brain function.

Nutrition and mental health

Mental health can be influenced by several nutritional factors, including: overall energy intake, intake of the energy-containing nutrients (proteins, carbohydrates, and fats), alcohol intake, and intake of vitamins and minerals. Often deficiencies of multiple nutrients, rather than a single nutrient, are responsible for changes in brain functioning.

In the United States and other developed countries, alcoholism is often responsible for nutritional deficiencies that affect mental functioning. Diseases can also cause nutritional deficiencies by affecting absorption of nutrients into the body or increasing nutritional requirements. Poverty, ignorance, and fad **diets** also contribute to nutritional deficiencies.

Energy intake and mental health

Energy, often referred to as the calorie content of a food, is derived from the carbohydrate, protein, fat, and alcohol found in foods and beverages. Although vitamins and minerals are essential to the body, they provide no energy. The human brain is metabolically very active and uses about 20%–30% of a person's energy intake at rest. Individuals who do not eat adequate calories from food to meet their energy requirements will experience changes in mental functioning. Simply skipping breakfast is associated with lower fluency and problem-solving ability, especially in individuals who are already slightly malnourished. A hungry person may also experience lack of energy or motivation.

Chronic hunger and energy deprivation profoundly affect mood and responsiveness. The body responds to energy deprivation by shutting or slowing down

---

KEY TERMS

Antioxidant—A substance that works to counteract the damage done to human tissue by the breakdown of fatty acids. Dietary antioxidants include beta-carotene and vitamins C and E as well as selenium.

Depression—A mental state characterized by feelings of sadness, despair, and discouragement.

Dopamine—A chemical in brain tissue that serves to transmit nerve impulses (a neurotransmitter) and helps to regulate movement and emotions.

Fat-soluble vitamin—A vitamin that dissolves in, and can be stored in, body fat or the liver.

Hormone—A chemical messenger that is produced by one type of cell and travels through the bloodstream to change the metabolism of a different type of cell.

Mineral—An inorganic substance found in the earth that is necessary in small quantities for the body to maintain health. Examples: zinc, copper, iron.

Neurotransmitter—One of a group of chemicals secreted by a nerve cell (neuron) to carry a chemical message to another nerve cell, often as a way of transmitting a nerve impulse. Examples of neurotransmitters include acetylcholine, dopamine, serotonin, and norepinephrine.

Norepinephrine—A hormone released by nerve cells and the adrenal medulla that causes constriction of blood vessels. Norepinephrine also functions as a neurotransmitter.

Serotonin—A widely distributed neurotransmitter that is found in blood platelets, the lining of the digestive tract, and the brain, and that works in combination with norepinephrine. It causes very powerful contractions of smooth muscle and is associated with mood, attention, emotions, and sleep. Low levels of serotonin are associated with depression.

---

nonessential functions and altering activity levels, hormonal levels, oxygen and nutrient transport, the body's ability to fight infection, and many other bodily functions that directly or indirectly affect brain function. People with a consistently low energy intake often feel apathetic, sad, or hopeless.

Developing fetuses and young infants are particularly susceptible to brain damage from malnutrition. The extent of the damage depends on the timing of the energy deprivation in relation to stage of development. Malnutrition early in life has been associated with below-normal intelligence, and functional and cognitive defects.

Carbohydrates and mental health

Carbohydrates include starches, naturally occurring and refined sugars, and dietary fiber. Foods rich in starches and dietary fiber include grain products like breads, rice, pasta, and cereals, especially whole-grain products; fruits; and vegetables, especially starchy vegetables like potatoes. Foods rich in refined sugars include cakes, cookies, desserts, candy, and soft drinks.

Carbohydrates significantly affect mood and behavior. Eating a meal high in carbohydrates triggers release of a hormone called insulin in the body. Insulin helps let blood sugar into cells, where it can be used for energy, but it also has other effects in the body. As insulin levels rise, more tryptophan enters the brain. Tryptophan is an amino acid, or a building block of protein, that affects levels of neurotransmitters in the brain. As more tryptophan enters the brain, more of the neurotransmitter **serotonin** is produced. Higher serotonin levels in the brain enhance mood and have a sedating effect, promoting sleepiness. This effect is partly responsible for the drowsiness some people experience after a large meal.

Some researchers and many parents claim that a high sugar intake causes hyperactivity in children. Although carefully controlled studies do not support this conclusion, high sugar intake is associated with dental problems. Further, foods high in refined sugars are often low in other nutrients, making it prudent to limit their use.

Proteins and mental health

Proteins are made up of amino acids linked together in various sequences and amounts. The human body can manufacture some of the amino acids, but there are eight essential amino acids that must be supplied in the diet. A complete or high-quality protein contains all eight of the essential amino acids in the amounts needed by the body. Foods rich in high-quality protein include meats, milk and other dairy products, and eggs. Dried beans and peas, grains, and nuts and seeds also contain protein, although the protein in these plant foods may be low in one or more essential amino acid. Generally, combining any two types of plant protein foods together will yield a complete, high-quality protein. For example, a peanut butter and jelly sandwich combines grain protein from the bread with nut protein from the peanut butter to yield

a complete protein. A bean and corn dish, such as refried beans in a corn tortilla, combines bean and grain protein for another complete protein combination.

Protein intake and intake of individual amino acids can affect brain functioning and mental health. Many of the neurotransmitters in the brain are made from amino acids. The neurotransmitter **dopamine** is made from the amino acid tyrosine. The neurotransmitter serotonin is made from the amino acid tryptophan. If the needed amino acid is not available, levels of that particular neurotransmitter in the brain will fall, and brain functioning and mood will be affected. For example, if there is a lack of tryptophan in the body, not enough serotonin will be produced, and low brain levels of serotonin are associated with low mood and even aggression in some individuals. Likewise, some diseases can cause a buildup of certain amino acids in the blood, leading to brain damage and mental defects. For example, a buildup of the amino acid phenylalanine in individuals with a disease called phenylketonuria (PKU) can cause brain damage and **intellectual disability**. States require testing of newborns for the presence of this metabolic disorder.

Fats and mental health

Dietary intake of fats may also play a role in regulating mood and brain function. Dietary fats are found in both animal and plant foods. Meats, regular-fat dairy products, butter, margarine, and plant oils are high in fats. In terms of health, some of these fats are considered "good fats," and some are considered "bad fats." The "good fats" are unsaturated (the fat's carbon chain is not completely filled in every spot with a hydrogen) and polyunsaturated fats. Some "good" fats, such as olive oil, have been shown to offer some protection against heart disease and some cancers. The "bad fats" include saturated fats (all hydrogen spots are full) and trans fats (also called "partially hydrogenated" fats or oils), which have achieved recent notoriety for their apparent role in reducing levels of HDL cholesterol (the "good" cholesterol). The "bad" fats are considered to increase a person's risk of heart disease and other diseases.

Although numerous studies clearly document the benefits of a cholesterol-lowering diet for the reduction of heart disease risk, some studies suggest that reducing fat and cholesterol in the diet may deplete brain serotonin levels, causing mood changes, anger, and aggressive behavior. Some low-carbohydrate diets, such as the "South Beach Diet," have achieved popularity in part because of their link with beneficial changes in cholesterol levels.

Other studies have looked at the effects of a particular kind of fat, the omega-3 fatty acids found in fish oils, and brain functioning. Although a few studies suggest that omega-3 fatty acids are helpful with bipolar affective disorder and **stress**, results are inconclusive.

High levels of saturated fat in the diet contribute to atherosclerosis, or clogging of the arteries. Atherosclerosis can decrease blood flow to the brain, impairing brain functioning. If blood flow to the brain is blocked, a **stroke** occurs.

Alcohol and mental health

A high alcohol intake can interfere with normal sleep patterns and thus can affect mood. Alcoholism is one of the most common causes of nutritional deficiencies in developed countries. Alcoholic beverages provide energy but virtually no vitamins or minerals. A person who consumes large amounts of alcohol will meet their energy needs but not their vitamin and mineral needs. In addition, extra amounts of certain vitamins are needed to break down alcohol in the body, further contributing to nutrient deficiencies.

Vitamins and mental health

Thiamin

Thiamin is a B vitamin found in enriched grain products, pork, legumes, nuts, seeds, and organ meats. It is intricately involved with metabolizing glucose, or blood sugar, in the body. Glucose is the brain's primary energy source. Thiamin is also needed to make several neurotransmitters.

Alcoholism is often associated with thiamine deficiency. Alcohol interferes with thiamin metabolism in the body, and diets high in alcohol are often deficient in vitamins and minerals. Individuals with a thiamin deficiency can develop **Wernicke-Korsakoff syndrome**, which is characterized by confusion, mental changes, abnormal eye movements, and unsteadiness that can progress to severe memory loss.

Vitamin B-12

Vitamin B-12 is found only in foods of animal origin, like milk, meat, or eggs. Strict vegans who consume no animal-based foods need to supplement their diet with vitamin B-12 to meet the body's need for this nutrient.

Vitamin B-12 is needed to maintain the outer coating, called the myelin sheath, on nerve cells. Inadequate myelin results in nerve damage and impaired brain function. Vitamin B-12 deficiency can go undetected in individuals for years, but it eventually causes low blood iron, irreversible nerve damage, **dementia**, and brain atrophy.

Folic acid

Folic acid is another B vitamin found in foods such as liver, yeast, asparagus, fried beans and peas, wheat, broccoli, and some nuts. Many grain products are also fortified with folic acid. In the United States, alcoholism is a common cause of folic acid deficiency.

Folic acid is involved in protein metabolism in the body and in the metabolism of some amino acids, particularly the amino acid methionine. When folic acid levels in the body are low, methionine cannot be metabolized properly, and levels of another chemical, homocysteine, build up in the blood. High blood homocysteine levels increase the risk of heart disease and stroke.

Even modest folic acid deficiency in women causes an increased risk of neural tube defects, such as spina bifida, in developing fetuses. Folic acid deficiency also increases the risk of stroke. Some studies suggest that folic acid deficiency leads to a range of mental disorders, including **depression**, but this concept remains controversial. Folic acid deficiency can lower levels of serotonin in the brain.

Niacin

The B vitamin niacin is found in enriched grains, meat, fish, wheat bran, asparagus, and peanuts. The body can also make niacin from the essential amino acid tryptophan, which is found in high-quality animal protein foods like meat and milk. Niacin deficiency used to be common in the southern United States, but is now common only in countries such as India and China.

Niacin is involved in releasing energy in the body from carbohydrates, proteins, and fats. A deficiency of niacin produces many mental symptoms such as irritability, headaches, loss of memory, inability to sleep, and emotional instability. Severe niacin deficiency progresses to a condition called pellagra, which is characterized by the four D's: dermatitis (a rash resembling a sunburn), diarrhea, dementia, and ultimately, death. The mental symptoms in pellagra can progress to **psychosis**, **delirium**, coma, and death.

Vitamin B-6

Vitamin B-6, also known as pyridoxine, is found in many plant and animal foods, including chicken, fish, pork, whole-wheat products, brown rice, and some fruits and vegetables. In healthy individuals, deficiency of vitamin B-6 is rare, but certain drugs, including some antidepressant drugs, can induce vitamin B-6 deficiency.

Vitamin B-6 is needed by the body to produce most of the brain's neurotransmitters. It is also involved in hormone production. Although rare, vitamin B-6 deficiency is characterized by mental changes such as **fatigue**, nervousness, irritability, depression, **insomnia**, dizziness, and nerve changes. These mental changes are related to the body's decreased ability to manufacture neurotransmitters with vitamin B-6 deficiency.

Just as vitamin B-6 deficiency causes mental changes, so does excess of vitamin B-6. Vitamin B-6 supplements are used by many individuals for a variety of conditions, including carpal tunnel syndrome, **premenstrual syndrome**, and fibrocystic breast disease. Doses of 500 mg per day or more can cause nerve damage, dizziness, sensory loss, and numbness.

Vitamin E

Vitamin E is a fat-soluble vitamin that is found in plant oils, green leafy vegetables, and fortified breakfast cereals. Vitamin E deficiency is very rare, except in disorders that impair absorption of fat-soluble vitamins into the body, such as cystic fibrosis and liver diseases.

Vitamin E deficiency causes changes in red blood cells and nerve tissues. It progresses to dizziness, vision changes, muscle weakness, and sensory changes. If left untreated, the nerve damage from vitamin E deficiency can be irreversible. Because it is an antioxidant, vitamin E has also been studied for treatment of neurological conditions such as Parkinson's and **Alzheimer's disease**. Vitamin E and other antioxidants, such as vitamin C, had shown some promise in treating Alzheimer's, but larger analyses have found no beneficial effect of vitamin E supplements and have in fact identified a greater association between vitamin E supplementation and death from any cause in Alzheimer's patients. This far, vitamin E has shown no effects in slowing the progression of Parkinson's disease, and the only antioxidant that exhibits even minor effectiveness is coenzyme Q10.

Vitamin A

Vitamin A is a fat-soluble vitamin found in meats, fish, and eggs. A form of vitamin A, beta-carotene, is found in orange and green leafy vegetables such as carrots, yellow squash, and spinach. Headache and increased pressure in the head are associated with both deficient and excess vitamin A intake. Among other effects, excess vitamin A intake can cause fatigue, irritability, and loss of appetite. Generally, doses must exceed 25,000 international units of vitamin A over several months to develop such symptoms.

Minerals and mental health

Iron

Iron is a trace mineral that is essential for formation of hemoglobin, the substance that carries oxygen to cells throughout the body. Iron is found in meat, poultry, and fish. Another form of iron that is not as well absorbed as the form in animal foods is found in whole or enriched grains, green leafy vegetables, dried beans and peas, and dried fruits. Consuming a food rich in vitamin C, such as orange juice, at the same time as an iron-containing plant food will enhance iron absorption from the food.

Iron deficiency eventually leads to anemia, with insufficient oxygen reaching the brain. The anemia can cause fatigue and impair mental functioning. Iron deficiency during the first two years of life can lead to permanent brain damage.

Magnesium

The mineral magnesium is found in green leafy vegetables, whole grains, nuts, seeds, and bananas. In areas with hard water, the water may provide a significant amount of magnesium. In addition to its involvement in bone structure, magnesium aids in the transmission of nerve impulses.

Magnesium deficiency can cause restlessness, nervousness, muscular twitching, and unsteadiness. Acute magnesium deficiency can progress to **apathy**, delirium, convulsions, coma, and death.

Manganese

Manganese is a trace mineral found in whole grains and nuts, and to a lesser extent, fruits and vegetables. It is involved in carbohydrate metabolism and brain functioning. Although very rare, manganese deficiency can cause abnormalities in brain function. Miners of manganese in South America have developed manganese toxicity called "manganese madness," with neurological symptoms similar to Parkinson's disease.

Copper

The richest sources of the trace mineral copper in the diet are organ meats, seafood, nuts, seeds, whole-grain breads and cereals, and chocolate. In addition to other functions, copper is involved in iron metabolism in the body and in brain functioning. Deficiency of copper causes anemia, with inadequate oxygen delivery to the brain and other organs. Copper deficiency also impairs

QUESTIONS TO ASK YOUR DOCTOR

- How can I tell if I am getting the right nutrients?
- How do the nutritional choices I make impact my physical and mental health?
- What dietary changes would you recommend for me?
- What tests or evaluation techniques can you perform to see whether my nutritional choices promote a healthy condition?
- Are there foods I should avoid because of the medications I am taking?
- What physical symptoms or behaviors are important enough that I should seek immediate treatment?

brain functioning and immune system response, including changes in certain chemical receptors in the brain and lowered levels of neurotransmitters.

Zinc

The trace mineral **zinc** is found in red meats, liver, eggs, dairy products, vegetables, and some seafood. Among other functions, zinc is involved in maintaining cell membranes and protecting cells from damage. Zinc deficiency can cause neurological impairment, influencing appetite, taste, smell, and vision. It has also been associated with apathy, irritability, jitteriness, and fatigue.

Selenium

Good sources of the trace mineral selenium include seafood, liver, and eggs. Grains and seeds can also be good sources of selenium, depending on the selenium content of the soil they are grown in. Selenium is needed for the synthesis of some hormones and helps protect cell membranes from damage.

Although selenium deficiency is very rare, selenium toxicity has occurred in regions of the world with high selenium soil content. Selenium toxicity causes nervous system changes, fatigue, and irritability.

Increasing interest in the role of nutrition and mental health

Only within the last 100 years have the scientific and medical communities documented the benefits that good nutrition has on physical and mental health. The medical community recognizes that a proper diet is an important factor in maintaining good physical and mental health, and in preventing and managing many diseases.

According to some studies some mental disorders may be triggered by deficiencies of certain nutrients. For instance, the rates of depression are low in countries where people eat a lot of fish, while the rate of depression steadily rises in the United States as Americans eat increasingly more processed food and less fresh fish and vegetables containing omega-3 fats. In one study, 53% of bipolar patients on placebo (olive oil) became ill again within four months, while none of the patients who were given 9.6 g daily of omega-3 fatty acids (as fish oil) did. Furthermore, a 25% decrease in schizophrenic symptoms was observed in patients receiving eicosapentaenoic acid (EPA), one of the omega-3 fatty acids contained in fish oil.

Balanced nutrition plays a role in preventing coronary heart disease, osteoporosis, weakness, diabetes, obesity, and some mental disorders. In addition to good nutrition, a well–balanced **exercise** program can improve general health, build endurance, and slow many of the effects of aging. The benefits of good nutrition have been shown not only to improve physical health but also to enhance emotional well–being.

Resources

BOOKS

Benton, David., ed. *Lifetime Nutritional Influences on Cognition, Behaviour and Psychiatric Illness.* Philadelphia: Woodhead Publishing, 2011.

Katz, David L., M.D., M.P.H. *Nutrition in Clinical Practice.* New York: Lippincott, Williams, and Wilkins, 2008.

North, Carol, and Sean Yutzy. *Goodwin and Guze's Psychiatric Diagnosis.* New York: Oxford University Press, 2010.

Null, Gary, Ph.D. *The Food-Mood Connection: Nutritional and Environmental Approaches to Mental Health and Physical Wellbeing,* Kindle Edition. New York: Seven Stories Press, 2011.

Sharon, Michael, MD. *Nutrient A-Z: A User's Guide to Foods, Herbs, Vitamins, Minerals & Supplements,* 4th ed. New York: Carlton Publishing Group, 2009.

Shils, Maurice E. *Modern Nutrition in Health and Disease,* 11th ed. New York: Williams and Wilkins, 2012.

Smith, Pamela Wartian, M.D. *What You Must Know About Vitamins, Minerals, Herbs, & More: Choosing the Nutrients That Are Right for You.* Garden City Park, NY: Square One Publishers, Inc., 2008.

PERIODICALS

Boothby, Lisa A., and Paul L. Doering. "Vitamin C and vitamin E for Alzheimer's disase." *The Annals of Pharmacotherapy* 39(2005): 2073–2080.

Golomb, Beatric A., Michael H. Criqui, Halbert White, and Joel E. Dimsdale. "Conceptual foundations of the UCSF statin study." *Archives of Internal Medicine* 164 (2004):153–162.

Lakhan, Shaheen E., and Karen F. Vieira. "Nutritional Therapies for Mental Disorders." *Nutrition Journal* 7, no. 2 (2008). http://dx.doi.org/10.1186/1475-2891-7-2 (accessed November 7, 2011).

Lichtenstein, Alice H. "Dietary fat, carbohydrate, and protein: effects on plasma lipoprotein patterns." *Journal of Lipid Research* 47(2006): 1661–1667.

Parker, Gordon, Gibson, Neville A., Brotchie, Heather, Heruc, Gabriella, Rees, Anne-Marie, and Hadzi-Pavlovic, Dusan. "Omega-3 fatty acids and mood disorders." *American Journal of Psychiatry* 163 (2006): 969–978.

Weber, Cynthia A., and Michael E. Ernst. "Antioxidants, supplements, and Parkinson's disease." *The Annals of Pharmacotherapy* 40(2006): 935–938.

Young, Simon N. "Clinical Nutrition: 3. The Fuzzy Boundary Between Nutrition and Psychopharmacology." *Canadian Medical Association Journal* 166 (2002): 205–209.

WEBSITES

American Academy of Family Physicians. "Nutrition and Mental Health." FamilyDoctor.org. http://familydoctor.org/familydoctor/en/prevention-wellness/emotional-well-being/mental-health/nutrition-and-mental-health.html (accessed November 7, 2011).

ORGANIZATIONS

American Academy of Family Physicians, 11400 Tomahawk Creek Pkwy., Leawood, KS, 66211-2672, (913) 906-6000, (800) 274-2237, Fax: (913) 906-6075, contactcenter@aafp.org, http://www.aafp.org.

American Dietetic Association, 120 South Riverside Plaza, Ste. 2000, Chicago, IL, 60606, (312) 899-0040, (800) 877-1600, http://www.eatright.org.

American Psychiatric Association, 1000 Wilson Blvd., Ste. 1825, Arlington, VA, 22209-3901, (703) 907-7300, apa@psych.org, http://www.psych.org.

Mental Health America, 2000 N. Beauregard Street, 6th Floor, Alexandria, VA, 22311, (703) 684-7722, (800) 969-6642, Fax: (703) 684-5968, http://www1.nmha.org.

National Alliance on Mental Illness (NAMI), Colonial Place Three, 2107 Wilson Blvd., Suite 300, Arlington, VA, 22201, (703) 524-7600, (800) 950-NAMI (6264) Fax: (703) 524-9094, http://www.nami.org/Hometemplate.cfm.

National Institute of Mental Health (NIMH), 6001 Executive Boulevard, Room 8184, MSC 9663, Bethesda, MD, 20892, (301) 443-4513, (866) 615-6464, Fax: (301) 443-4279, nimhinfo@nih.gov, http://www.nimh.nih.gov/index.shtml.

U.S. Food and Drug Administration (FDA), 10903 New Hampshire Ave., Silver Spring, MD, 20993, (888) 463-6332, http://www.fda.gov.

Tish Davidson, A.M.
Nancy Gustafson, M.S., R.D., F.A.D.A., E.L.S.
Laura Jean Cataldo, RN, Ed.D.

O

Obsession

Definition

An obsession is an unwelcome, uncontrollable, and persistent idea, thought, image, or emotion that a person can not help thinking even though it creates significant distress or anxiety.

Description

Obsessive ideas seem unnatural or alien to those who have them, but are nevertheless recognized as originating from the person's own thoughts—they are not seen as **delusions** sent or controlled by an outside party.

Typical obsessions include fear of contamination as from doorknobs or handshakes, worry about leaving things in their proper order, persistent doubts about one's responsible behavior, scary images involving violent acts, and images of sexual acts. People with obsessions may find themselves acting in compulsive ways in largely futile attempts to relieve the anxiety associated with their persistent, unpleasant thoughts. Others suffering from obsessions may try very hard to control or ignore them. It is important to note that legitimate worries about daily concerns—paying bills, studying for exams, keeping a job, interpersonal relationships—are not obsessions. Although they can occasionally be carried to obsessive lengths, these concerns can change with circumstances and, in most cases be controlled, with planning, effort, and action. Obsessions relate to problems that most people would consider far removed from normal, daily events and concerns.

Dean A. Haycock, Ph.D.

Obsessive-compulsive disorder

Definition

Obsessive-compulsive disorder (OCD) is classified as an anxiety disorder marked by the recurrence of intrusive or disturbing thoughts, impulses, images, or ideas (obsessions) accompanied by repeated attempts to suppress these thoughts through the performance of certain irrational and ritualistic behaviors or mental acts (compulsions). The obsessions and compulsions take up large amounts of the patient's time (an hour or longer every day) and usually cause significant emotional distress for the patient and difficulties in patient's relationships with others.

OCD should not be confused with **obsessive-compulsive personality disorder** even though the two disorders have similar names. Obsessive-compulsive

A woman undergoes therapy for obsessive-compulsive disorder (OCD). (© Phototake. All rights reserved.)

personality disorder is not characterized by the presence of obsessions and compulsions; rather, it is a lifelong pattern of insistence on control, orderliness, and perfection that begins no later than the early adult years. It is possible, however, for a person to have both disorders.

Demographics

Although descriptions of patients with OCD have been reported since the fifteenth century in religious and medical literature, the condition was widely assumed to be rare until very recently. Epidemiological research since 1980 has now identified OCD as the fourth most common psychiatric illness, after phobias, substance use disorders, and major depressive disorders. OCD is at present classified as a form of anxiety disorder, but current studies indicate that it results from a combination of psychological, neurobiological, genetic, and environmental causes.

According to some estimates, 1 adult in every 50 in North America currently has OCD, and 2 out of 50 have had it at some point in their lives. According to the International OCD foundation, 2–3 million adults in the United States have OCD. It is likely, however, that the disorder is underdiagnosed because many people who suffer from it are embarrassed by their symptoms and often skilled at hiding them from others.

OCD can begin at any age, including childhood; in fact, between one-third and one-half of adults diagnosed with the disorder say that their symptoms began in childhood. The most common age for the emergence of symptoms is between 10 and 24 years, with slightly more women than men being diagnosed with OCD. Childhood OCD is more common in males, and the sex ratio does not favor females until adulthood. People with OCD appear to be less likely to marry than persons diagnosed with other types of mental disorders.

OCD is equally common in all races and ethnic groups in the United States, although patients' specific obsessions are sometimes influenced by their cultural background. For example, fears of violating religious practices or beliefs are reported to be more common among Roman Catholics and Orthodox Jews than among Protestants. Worldwide, cross-cultural studies of OCD indicate that while the incidence of the disorder seems to be about the same in most countries, the symptoms are often shaped by the patient's culture of origin. For example, a patient from a Western country may have a contamination **obsession** that is focused on germs, whereas a patient from India may fear contamination by touching a person from a lower social caste.

Males and females are equally likely to develop OCD; however, males are more likely to begin showing symptoms in childhood and adolescence, and females are more likely to develop symptoms in their early twenties.

Description

OCD is sometimes described as a malfunction of the brain's information processing system. Everyone has upsetting thoughts or impulses from time to time—such as the urge to shout dirty words in public or thinking about hitting someone—but most people are able to let go of these things and not worry about them. A person with OCD, however, gets stuck on the thoughts or impulses and cannot put them aside. These thoughts or impulses are called obsessions. The person who has them may think that he or she is "going crazy" or will not be able to keep from acting on the thoughts. To cope with the anxiety, the person with OCD engages in repetitive behaviors or mental acts to undo, counteract, or control the obsessions. These behaviors are called compulsions.

Common obsessions include fears of contamination by germs or dirt; fear that one has harmed someone; thoughts of violence or of killing a pet or family member; worrying about thoughts that violate one's religious beliefs; and fear of performing sexual acts that the person dislikes. Common compulsions include repeated hand washing or bathing; checking doors or car windows over and over to be sure they are locked; counting objects; insisting that personal possessions like clothes in a closet or items on a desk be arranged "just so"; touching objects in a specific sequence; and **hoarding** items that are not needed.

It is important to recognize that people with OCD are distressed by these behaviors and usually realize that they do not make sense. Compulsions may consume several hours of the patient's day, interfering with work, school, family life, and other activities. They can also be harmful to health; there are instances of people damaging their skin by frequent hand washing or taking long showers. Unlike people with **substance abuse** or eating disorders, people with OCD do not find their rituals pleasurable or satisfying; they are done only to manage their fears.

Studies of families with OCD members indicate that the particular expression of OCD symptoms may be affected by the responses of other people. Families with a high level of tolerance for the symptoms are more likely to have members with more extreme or elaborate symptoms. Problems often occur when the OCD member's obsessions and rituals begin to control the entire family. For example, other family members may find themselves running late for appointments because the OCD member insists on completing their obsessional ritual before they will get in the car.

Risk factors

Known risk factors for OCD include:

- a family history of OCD
- a history of head trauma

- being diagnosed with Tourette syndrome or attention deficit hyperactivity disorder (ADHD)
- a high level of intelligence and education
- higher socioeconomic status
- a pre-existing anxiety disorder, particularly PTSD, phobias, or social anxiety disorder
- high levels of long-term environmental stress

Causes and symptoms

There are various causes and symptoms for obsessive-compulsive disorder.

Causes

At one time it was thought that OCD was caused by childrearing practices that made the person anxious. Such compulsions as repeated washing or checking door locks were explained as rituals intended to please parents who were overly concerned with cleanliness or safety. In the early part of the twentieth century, Sigmund Freud theorized that OCD symptoms were caused by punitive, rigid toilet-training that led to internalized conflicts. This type of psychological explanation is no longer considered useful.

There are several more recent theories about the possible causes of OCD:

- Genetic: It is known that having other family members with OCD increases a person's risk of developing the disorder. Childhood-onset OCD appears to run in families more than adult-onset OCD and is more likely to be associated with tic disorders. Twin studies indicate that monozygotic, or identical twins, are more likely to share the disorder than dizygotic, or fraternal twins. The concordance (match) rate between identical twins is not 100%, however, which suggests that the occurrence of OCD is affected by environmental as well as genetic factors. In addition, it is the general nature of OCD that seems to run in families rather than the specific symptoms; thus, one family member who is affected by the disorder may have a compulsion about washing and cleaning while another is a compulsive counter. Although two genes have been linked to OCD, one discovered in 1994 and the other in 2007, researchers have not yet been able to prove that either or both cause the disorder.
- Abnormally low levels of serotonin in the brain: Serotonin is a chemical produced by the brain that regulates mood, appetite, sleep, and memory. Serotonin affects the efficiency of communication between the front part of the brain (the cortex) and structures that lie deeper in the brain known as the basal ganglia. Dysfunction in the serotonergic system occurs in certain

other mental illnesses, including major depression. OCD appears to have a number of features in common with the so-called obsessive-compulsive spectrum disorders, which include Tourette syndrome, Sydenham's chorea, eating disorders, trichotillomania, and delusional disorders. One piece of evidence that supports the serotonin theory is that patients with OCD who are given a type of antidepressant that makes more serotonin available to brain cells obtain some relief from their symptoms. These antidepressants are called selective serotonin reuptake inhibitors, or SSRIs.

- Differences in brain structure: Researchers who have used magnetic resonance imaging (MRI) to map the regions of the brain have found that patients diagnosed with OCD had significantly less white matter in their brains than did normal control subjects. Other studies using positron emission tomography (PET) scanning indicate that OCD patients have patterns of brain activity that differ from those of people without mental illness or with some other mental illness. These findings suggest that there is a widely distributed brain abnormality in OCD.
- Infections: OCD in children has sometimes been attributed to a complication of strep throat. This theory holds that the affected child's body produces antibodies against the strep throat bacteria. The disorders were sometimes referred to as pediatric autoimmune neuropsychiatric disorders associated with streptococcal infections (PANDAS). It was thought that antibodies in the child's blood cross-react with structures in the basal ganglia, producing or worsening the symptoms of OCD or tic disorders. However, this theory is no longer as widely accepted as it was in the 1990s; it is now controversial and considered unproven.

Symptoms

The symptoms of OCD should not be confused with the ability to focus on detail or to check one's work that is sometimes labeled "compulsive" in everyday life. This type of attentiveness is an important factor in academic achievement and in doing well in such fields that require close attention to detail as accounting, medicine, or engineering. By contrast, the symptoms of OCD are serious enough to interfere with the person's daily functioning. Historical examples of OCD include a medieval Englishman named William of Oseney, who spent twelve hours per day reading religious books in order to be at peace with God, and Freud's Rat Man, a patient who had repeated dreams of cursing Freud and covering him with dung. While the Rat Man was ashamed of these impulses and had no explanation for them, he could not control them.

More recent accounts of OCD symptoms include those of a young man who compulsively touched every electrical outlet as he passed, washed his hands several times an hour, and returned home repeatedly to check that the doors and windows were locked. Another account describes a firefighter who was worried that he had throat cancer. He spent three hours a day examining his throat in the mirror, feeling his lymph nodes, and asking his wife if his throat appeared normal.

More common obsessions and compulsions are described below.

CONTAMINATION. People with contamination obsessions are usually preoccupied with a fear of dirt or germs. They may avoid leaving home or allowing visitors to come inside in order to prevent contact with dirt or germs. Some people with contamination obsessions may wear gloves, coats, or even masks if they are forced to leave their house for some reason. Obsessions with contamination may also include abnormal fears of such environmental toxins as lead, asbestos, or radon.

Washing compulsions are commonly associated with contamination obsessions. For example, a person concerned about contamination from the outside may shower and launder all clothing immediately upon coming home. The **compulsion** may be triggered by direct contact with the feared object, but in many cases, even being in its general vicinity may stir up intense anxiety and a strong need to engage in a washing compulsion. The late Howard Hughes exhibited this kind of washing compulsion; he would even burn his clothing after finding out that he had been in the same room with a sick person. Another man who was afraid of contamination could not take even a short walk down the street without experiencing a compulsion to disinfect the soles of his shoes, launder all his clothing, and wash his hands until they were raw after he returned to his apartment.

Washing compulsions may not always be caused by a fear of germs. That is, a need for perfection or for symmetry may also lead to unnecessary washing. In such cases, the individual may be concerned about being perfectly clean or feel that he cannot leave the shower until his left foot has been washed exactly as many times as his right foot. Other people with washing compulsions may be unable to tolerate feeling sweaty or otherwise not clean.

OBSESSIONAL DOUBTING. Obsessional doubting refers to the fear of having failed to perform some task adequately and that dire consequences will follow as a result. Although individuals with this symptom may try to suppress the worrisome thoughts or images, they usually experiences a rising anxiety which then leads to a compulsion to check the task. For example, they may worry about forgetting to lock the door or turn off the gas burner on the stove and spend hours checking these things before leaving home. In one instance, a man was unable to throw away old grocery bags because he feared he might have left something valuable inside one of them. Immediately after looking into an empty bag, he would again have the thought, "What if I missed something in there?" In many cases, no amount of checking is sufficient to dispel the maddening sense of doubt.

NEED FOR SYMMETRY. Persons suffering from an obsession about symmetry often report feeling acutely uncomfortable unless they perform certain tasks in a symmetrical or balanced manner. Thus, crossing one's legs to the right must be followed by crossing legs to the left; scratching one side of the head must be followed by scratching the other; tapping the wall with a knuckle on the right hand must be followed by tapping with one on the left, and so on. Sometimes the person may have a thought or idea associated with the compulsion, such as a fear that a loved one will be harmed if the action is not balanced, but often there is no clearly defined fear, only a strong sense of unease.

AGGRESSIVE AND SEXUAL OBSESSIONS. Aggressive and sexual obsessions are often particularly horrifying to those who experience them. For some people, obsessive fears of committing a terrible act in the future compete with fears that they may already have done something awful in the past. Compulsions to constantly check and confess cause such individuals to admit to evildoing in which they had no part, a phenomenon familiar to law enforcement following highly publicized crimes. These obsessions often involve violent or graphic imagery that is upsetting and disgusting to the person, such as rape, physical assault, or even murder. One case study concerned a young woman who constantly checked the news to reassure herself that she had not murdered anyone that day; she felt deeply upset by unsolved murder cases. A middle-aged man repeatedly confessed to having molested a woman at work, despite no evidence of such an action ever occurring in his workplace.

SYMPTOMS IN CHILDREN. Obsessions and compulsions in children are often focused on germs and fears of contamination. Other common obsessions include fears of harm coming to self or others, fears of causing harm to another person, obsessions about symmetry, and excessive moralizing or religiosity. Global warming is an increasingly common focus of such obsessive moralizing in the twenty-first century.

Childhood compulsions frequently include washing, repeating, checking, touching, counting, ordering, and

KEY TERMS

Basal ganglia—A group of masses of gray matter located in the cerebral hemispheres of the brain that control movement as well as some aspects of emotion and cognition.

Behavioral therapy—An approach to treatment that focuses on extinguishing undesirable behavior and replacing it with desired behavior.

Cognitive-behavioral therapy (CBT)—An approach to psychotherapy that emphasizes the correction of distorted thinking patterns and changing one's behaviors accordingly.

Compulsion—A repeated behavior or mental act carried out to control or neutralize obsessions.

Neurotransmitter—A chemical in the brain that transmits messages between neurons, or nerve cells.

Obsession—A recurrent, distressing, intrusive thought, image, or impulse.

Selective serotonin reuptake inhibitors (SSRIs)—A group of antidepressants that works by increasing the amount of serotonin available to nerve cells in the brain.

Serotonin—A brain chemical that influences mood, anger, anxiety, body temperature, and appetite.

Sydenham's chorea—A serious manifestation of acute rheumatic fever that commonly occurs in children ages 7 through 14, peaking at age 8. This disease of the central nervous system is characterized by emotional instability, purposeless movements, and muscular weakness.

Tic—A sudden involuntary behavior that is difficult or impossible for the person to suppress. Tics may be either motor (related to movement) or vocal, and may become more pronounced under stress.

Trichotillomania—A disorder marked by repeated pulling and tugging of one's hair, usually resulting in noticeable hair loss on the scalp or elsewhere on the body.

arranging. Younger children are less likely to have full-blown anxiety-producing obsessions, but they often report a sense of relief or strong satisfaction (a "just right" feeling) from completing certain ritualized behaviors. Since children are particularly skillful in disguising their OCD symptoms from adults, they may effectively hide their disorder from parents and teachers for years.

Unusual behaviors in children that may be signs of OCD include:

- Avoidance of scissors or other sharp objects. A child may be obsessed with fears of hurting herself or others.

- Chronic lateness or dawdling. The child may be performing checking rituals (e.g., repeatedly making sure all her school supplies are in her bookbag).

- Daydreaming or preoccupation. The child may be counting or performing balancing rituals mentally.

- Spending long periods of time in the bathroom. The child may have a handwashing compulsion.

- Schoolwork handed in late or papers with holes erased in them. The child may be repeatedly checking and correcting her work.

For both children and adults, the symptoms of OCD wax and wane in severity; the specific content of obsessions and compulsions may change over time. The disorder, however, very seldom goes away by itself without treatment. People with OCD in all age groups typically find that their symptoms worsen during major life changes or following highly stressful events.

Diagnosis

The **diagnosis** of OCD is often delayed because patients are often ashamed of their symptoms and skilled at hiding them. It has been estimated that it takes an average of 17 years from the time that a patient's symptoms begin for that person to be diagnosed correctly and receive treatment for OCD. Another reason for the delay is that a person with OCD often has other disorders, including substance abuse disorders, **bipolar disorder**, **panic disorder**, or **depression**, and the OCD symptoms may be attributed to the other disorders. In children, OCD is sometimes misdiagnosed as **autism** or **Tourette syndrome**.

The diagnosis of OCD may also be complicated because of the number of other conditions that resemble it. For example, major depression may be associated with self-perceptions of being guilty, bad, or worthless, which are excessive and unreasonable. Similarly, eating disorders often include bizarre thoughts about size and weight, ritualized eating habits, or the hoarding of food. Delusional disorders may entail unusual beliefs or behaviors, as do such other mental disorders as **trichotillomania**, **hypochondriasis**, the **paraphilias**, and substance use disorders. Thus, accurate diagnosis of OCD depends on the careful analysis of many variables to determine whether the apparent obsessions and compulsions might be better accounted for by some other disorder or to the direct effects of a substance or a medical condition.

In addition, OCD may coexist with other mental disorders, most commonly depression. It has been estimated that about 34% of patients diagnosed with OCD are depressed at the time of diagnosis and that 65% will develop depression at some point in their lives.

Examination

Persons who are thought to have OCD are given a complete **mental status examination**. They are evaluated for memory, disturbances of mood and emotions, the presence of hallucinations or **delusions**, the risk of **suicide** or homicide, and judgment (whether the persons have insight into their symptoms). They should also be evaluated for the presence of Tourette syndrome or other **tic disorders**, as these comorbid diagnoses may influence treatment decisions.

The presence of hair loss, eczema, or scabs or scratches on the skin caused by compulsive washing, trichotillomania, or picking at the skin may be additional evidence for the diagnosis of OCD. There may not, however, be any physical evidence of the disorder.

Tests

There are no laboratory tests for OCD. The primary care doctor will refer the patient to a **psychiatrist** or **psychologist** for a specialized interview. The diagnosis is based on a combination of the patient's symptom history and their answers to a diagnostic questionnaire. The questionnaire most often used is the Yale-Brown Obsessive Compulsive Scale (Y-BOCS). The Y-BOCS has 10 items, five for obsessions and five for compulsions. The questions evaluate the time consumed by symptoms, the extent to which they interfere with functioning, how much they distress the patient, and what the patient has done to try to control the symptoms.

Treatment

There are various treatments for obsessive-compulsive disorder.

Traditional

Treatment for OCD is usually based on a combination of medications and **psychotherapy**.

PSYCHOTHERAPY. Behavioral treatments using the technique of exposure and response prevention (ERP; sometimes called exposure and ritual prevention) are particularly effective in treating OCD. In this form of therapy, the patient and therapist draw up a list, or hierarchy, of the patient's obsessive and compulsive symptoms. The symptoms are arranged in order from least to most upsetting. The patient is then systematically exposed to the anxiety-producing thoughts or behaviors, beginning with the least upsetting. The patient is asked to endure the feared event or image without engaging in the compulsion normally used to lower anxiety. For example, a person with a contamination obsession might be asked to touch a series of increasingly dirty objects without washing their hands. In this way, the patient learns to tolerate the feared object, reducing both worrisome obsessions and anxiety-reducing compulsions. About 75%–80% of patients respond well to exposure and response prevention, with very significant reductions in symptoms.

Other types of psychotherapy have met with mixed results. **Psychodynamic psychotherapy** is helpful to some patients who are concerned about the relationships between their upbringing and the specific features of their OCD symptoms. Cognitive-behavioral psychotherapy may be valuable in helping the patient to become more comfortable with the prospect of exposure and prevention treatments, as well as helping to identify the role that the patient's particular symptoms may play in his or her own life, and what effects family members may have on the maintenance and continuation of OCD symptoms. Cognitive-behavioral psychotherapy is not intended to replace exposure and response prevention but may be a helpful addition to it. The combination of medication and CBT has been shown to be a particularly helpful form of therapy for OCD.

SURGERY. A very small number of patients with severe OCD that does not respond to medications or ERP are treated surgically. The surgeon makes a small cut in a part of the **brain** called the cingulate bundle. This technique produces significant benefits for about 30% of patients who receive the operation. It is considered a treatment of last resort for OCD.

Researchers are studying the effectiveness of newer drugs in treating OCD as well as deep brain stimulation or DBS. In DBS, thin wires are implanted in the parts of the brain that have been linked to OCD symptoms. A battery-powered stimulator sends electrical pulses to the brain at regular intervals in order to interfere with the activity of the nerve cells in the target areas. DBS has already been used to treat Parkinson's disease and is considered an experimental treatment for Tourette syndrome.

In addition to DBS, current **clinical trials** are also exploring the application of **transcranial magnetic stimulation** (TMS) for OCD as a noninvasive treatment approach. In TMS, weak electric currents are induced in brain tissue by rapidly changing magnetic fields. The

QUESTIONS TO ASK YOUR DOCTOR

- What are the warning signs of OCD?
- I have a close relative with OCD. What are the chances that my child will develop the disorder?
- What treatments do you recommend?

Food and Drug Administration (FDA) approved a TMS device called NeuroStar for use in adults in the United States in October 2008.

Drugs

The medications usually prescribed to treat OCD are the **selective serotonin reuptake inhibitors** or **SSRIs**. These drugs work by increasing the amount of **serotonin** available to some of the nerve endings in the brain. Some patients also benefit from the tricyclic antidepressant **clomipramine**.

It is important, however, to know that the SSRIs must be prescribed with care in treating children and adolescents with OCD. Young patients and adults up to age 24 taking antidepressants for **major depressive disorder** have been found to be at increased risk for developing suicidal thoughts and actions. The risk appears to be reduced in patients taking SSRIs for OCD, but all patients taking SSRIs should be monitored for changes in behavior or worsening depression. According to a 2009 article published in the journal American Family Physician, about 15% of persons with OCD make at least one suicide attempt.

Alternative

Because OCD sometimes responds to selective serotonin reuptake inhibitors (SSRI) **antidepressants**, herbalists believe a botanical medicine called **St. John's wort** (*Hypericum perforatum*) might have some beneficial effect as well. Known popularly as "Nature's Prozac," St. John's wort is prescribed by herbalists for the treatment of anxiety and depression. They believe that this herb affects brain levels of serotonin in the same way that SSRI antidepressants do. Herbalists recommend a dose of 300 mg, three times per day. In about one out of 400 people, St. John's wort (like Prozac) may initially increase the level of anxiety. Homeopathic constitutional therapy can help rebalance the patient's mental, emotional, and physical well-being, allowing the behaviors of OCD to abate over time.

Other alternative treatments for OCD are intended to lower the patient's anxiety level; some are thought to diminish the compulsions themselves. Alternative recommendations include the following:

- Bach flower remedies, such as white chestnut for obsessive thoughts and repetitive thinking.
- Traditional Chinese medicine (TCM), specifically a mixture of bupleurum and dong quai, to strengthen the spleen and regulate the liver. (In TCM, obsessive-compulsive disorder is explained as liver stagnation and a weak spleen.)
- Aromatherapy; a mixture of lavender, rosemary, and valerian is thought to promote for relaxation.
- Yoga; yogis in India developed a special technique of yogic breathing specifically for OCD. The specific yogic technique for treating OCD requires blocking the right nostril with the tip of the thumb; slow deep inspiration through the left nostril; holding the breath; and slow complete expiration through the left nostril. This is followed by a long breath-holding out period.
- Schuessler tissue salts; for OCD, specific doses of *Ferrum phosphorica* and tablets of *Kali phosphorica* are recommended daily.
- Massage therapy, with special emphasis on loosening the muscles in the neck, back, and shoulders.

Prognosis

The prognosis of OCD varies from person to person. The disorder rarely goes away on its own. Few OCD patients become completely symptom-free, but about 70% of patients benefit from treatment; however, symptoms may increase and decrease in a cyclical pattern over time. About 15% of patients get steadily worse over time even with treatment and may eventually become unable to function.

Prevention

There is no known way to prevent OCD; however, early diagnosis and prompt treatment can help to prevent the patient's symptoms from getting worse.

Resources

BOOKS

Cobert, Josiane, and Barton Cobert. *100 Questions and Answers about Your Child's Obsessive Compulsive Disorder.* Sudbury, MA: Jones and Bartlett, 2010.

Deane, Ruth. *Washing My Life Away: Surviving Obsessive-Compulsive Disorder.* Philadelphia: Jessica Kingsley, 2005.

Hyman, Bruce M., and Cherry Pedrick. *Obsessive-Compulsive Disorder*. Minneapolis, MN: Twenty-First Century Books, 2009.

Starcevic, Vladan. *Anxiety Disorders in Adults: A Clinical Guide*, 2nd ed. New York: Oxford University Press, 2009.

PERIODICALS

D'Alessandro, T.M. "Factors Influencing the Onset of Childhood Obsessive-Compulsive Disorder." *Pediatric Nursing* 35 (January-February 2009): 43–46.

Fenske, Jill N., and Thomas L. Schwenk. "Obsessive-Compulsive Disorder: Diagnosis and Management." *American Family Physician* 80, no. 3 (2009): 239–245. http://www.aafp.org/afp/2009/0801/p239.html#afp 20090801p239-b3 (accessed January 11, 2012).

Huyser, C., et al. "Paediatric Obsessive-Compulsive Disorder, a Neurodevelopmental Disorder? Evidence from Neuroimaging." *Neuroscience and Biobehavioral Reviews* 33 (June 2009): 818–30.

Leckman, J.F., et al. "Symptom Dimensions and Subtypes of Obsessive-Compulsive Disorder: A Developmental Perspective." *Dialogues in Clinical Neuroscience* 11 (2009): 21–33.

Schläpfer, T.E., and B.H. Bewernick. "Deep Brain Stimulation for Psychiatric Disorders—State of the Art." *Advances and Technical Standards in Neurosurgery* 34 (2009): 37–57.

Shulman, S.T. "Pediatric Autoimmune Neuropsychiatric Disorders Associated with Streptococci (PANDAS): Update." *Current Opinion in Pediatrics* 21 (February 2009): 127–30.

WEBSITES

"Obsessive-Compulsive Disorder." National Alliance on Mental Illness. Last modified May 2003. http://www.nami.org/Template.cfm?Section=By_Illness&Template=/TaggedPage/TaggedPageDisplay.cfm&TPLID=54&ContentID=23035 (accessed September 16, 2011).

"Obsessive-Compulsive Disorder (OCD)." National Institute of Mental Health. http://www.nimh.nih.gov/health/topics/obsessive-compulsive-disorder-ocd/index.shtml (accessed September 16, 2011).

"Obsessive-Compulsive Disorder: What It Is and How to Treat It." American Academy of Family Physicians. Last modified May 2010. http://familydoctor.org/online/famdocen/home/common/mentalhealth/anxiety/133.html (accessed September 16, 2011).

ORGANIZATIONS

American Psychiatric Association, 1000 Wilson Blvd., Ste. 1825, Arlington, VA, 22209-3901, (703) 907-7300, apa@psych.org, http://www.psych.org.

Anxiety Disorders Association of America, 8730 Georgia Ave., Silver Spring, MD, 20910, (240) 485-1001, Fax: (240) 485-1035, http://www.adaa.org.

National Alliance on Mental Illness, 2107 Wilson Blvd., Ste. 300, Arlington, VA, 22201-3042, Fax: (703) 524-9094, (800) 950-6264, http://www.nami.org.

National Institute of Mental Health, 6001 Executive Blvd., Rm. 8184, MSC 9663, Bethesda, MD, 20892-9663, (301) 433-4513; TTY: (301) 443-8431, Fax: (301) 443-4279, (866) 615-6464; TTY: (866) 415-8051, nimhinfo@nih.gov, http://www.nimh.nih.gov.

Obsessive Compulsive Foundation, PO Box 961029, Boston, MA, 02196, (617) 973-5801, http://www.ocfoundation.org.

Jane A. Fitzgerald
Rebecca J. Frey, PhD

Obsessive-compulsive personality disorder

Definition

Obsessive-compulsive personality disorder (OCPD) is a type of personality disorder marked by rigidity, control, perfectionism, and an overconcern with work at the expense of close interpersonal relationships. Persons with this disorder often have trouble relaxing because they are preoccupied with details, rules, and productivity. They are often perceived by others as stubborn, stingy, self-righteous, and uncooperative.

Obsessive-compulsive personality disorder is included in the *Diagnostic and Statistical Manual of Mental Disorders (DSM)*, a handbook used by medical professionals in diagnosing mental disorders. Personality disorders are defined by the DSM as causing significant impairments in relations with the self (sense of identity) and others. The World Health Organization's *International Classification of Diseases* (ICD), which is the European counterpart of the *DSM*, refers to OCPD as "anankastic personality disorder."

It is important to distinguish between OCPD and **obsessive-compulsive disorder** (OCD), which is an anxiety disorder characterized by the presence of intrusive or disturbing thoughts, impulses, images or ideas (obsessions), accompanied by repeated attempts to suppress these thoughts through the performance of irrational and ritualistic behaviors or mental acts (compulsions). It is unusual but possible, however, for a patient to suffer from both disorders, especially in extreme cases of **hoarding** behavior. In some reported cases of animal hoarding, the people involved appear to have symptoms of both OCD and OCPD.

Demographics

Obsessive-compulsive personality disorder is estimated to occur in about 1% of the population, although rates of 3–10% are reported among psychiatric outpatients. The disorder is usually diagnosed in late adolescence or young adulthood. In the United States, OCPD occurs almost twice as often in men as in women.

Some researchers attribute this disproportion to gender stereotyping, in that men have greater permission from general Western culture to act in stubborn, withholding, and controlling ways.

Description

People suffering from OCPD have careful rules and procedures for conducting many aspects of their everyday lives. While their goal is to accomplish things in a careful, orderly manner, their desire for perfection and insistence on going "by the book" often overrides their ability to complete a task. For example, one patient with OCPD was so preoccupied with finding a mislaid shopping list that he took much more time searching for it than it would have taken him to rewrite the list from memory. This type of inflexibility typically extends to interpersonal relationships. People with OCPD are known for being highly controlling and bossy toward other people, especially subordinates. They will often insist that there is one and only one right way (their way) to fold laundry, cut grass, drive a car, or write a report. In addition, they are so insistent on following rules that they cannot allow for what most people would consider legitimate exceptions. Their attitudes toward their own superiors or supervisors depend on whether they respect these authorities. People with OCPD are often unusually courteous to superiors that they respect, but resistant to or contemptuous of those they do not respect.

While work environments may reward their conscientiousness and attention to detail, people with OCPD do not show much spontaneity or imagination. They may feel paralyzed when immediate action is necessary; they feel overwhelmed by trying to make decisions without concrete guidelines. They expect colleagues to stick to detailed rules and procedures, and often perform poorly in jobs that require flexibility and the ability to compromise. Even when people with OCPD are behind schedule, they are uncomfortable delegating work to others because the others may not do the job "properly." People with OCPD often get so lost in the finer points of a task that they cannot see the larger picture; they are frequently described as "unable to see the forest for the trees." They are often highly anxious in situations without clearly defined rules because such situations arouse their fears of making a mistake and being punished for it. An additional feature of this personality disorder is stinginess or miserliness, frequently combined with an inability to throw out worn-out or useless items. This characteristic has sometimes been described as "pack rat" behavior.

People diagnosed with OCPD come across to others as difficult and demanding. Their rigid expectations of others are also applied to themselves, however; they tend to be intolerant of their own short-comings. Such persons feel bound to present a consistent facade of propriety and control. They feel uncomfortable with expressions of tender feelings and tend to avoid relatives or colleagues who are more emotionally expressive. This strict and ungenerous approach to life limits their ability to relax; they are seldom if ever able to release their needs for control. Even recreational activities frequently become another form of work. A person with OCPD, for example, may turn a tennis game into an opportunity to perfect his or her backhand rather than simply enjoying the **exercise**, the weather, or the companionship of the other players. Many OCPD sufferers bring office work along on vacations in order to avoid "wasting time," and feel a sense of relief upon returning to the structure of their work environment. Not surprisingly, this combination of traits strains their interpersonal relationships and can lead to a lonely existence.

Causes and symptoms

Causes

No single specific cause of OCPD has been identified. Since the early days of Freudian **psychoanalysis**, however, faulty parenting has been viewed as a major factor in the development of personality disorders. Current studies have tended to support the importance of early life experiences, finding that healthy emotional development largely depends on two important variables: parental warmth and appropriate responsiveness to the child's needs. When these qualities are present, the child feels secure and appropriately valued. By contrast, many people with personality disorders did not have parents who were emotionally warm toward them. Patients with OCPD often recall their parents as being emotionally withholding and either overprotective or overcontrolling. One researcher has noted that people with OCPD appear to have been punished by their parents for every transgression of a rule, no matter how minor, and rewarded for almost nothing. As a result, the child is unable to safely develop or express a sense of joy, spontaneity, or independent thought; and begins to develop the symptoms of OCPD as a strategy for avoiding punishment. Children with this type of upbringing are also likely to choke down the anger they feel toward their parents; they may be outwardly obedient and polite to authority figures, but at the same time treat younger children or those they regard as their inferiors harshly.

Genetic contributions to OCPD have not been well documented. Cultural influences may, however, play a part in the development of OCPD. That is, cultures that are highly authoritarian and rule-bound may encourage child-rearing practices that contribute to the development of OCPD. On the other hand, simply because a culture is comparatively strict or has a strong work ethic does not mean it is necessarily unhealthful. In Japanese societies, for example, excessive devotion to work, restricted emotional expression, and moral scrupulosity are highly valued characteristics that are rewarded within that culture. Similarly, certain religions and professions require exactness and careful attention to rules in their members; the military is one example. OCPD is not diagnosed in persons who are simply behaving in accordance with such outside expectations as military regulations or the rule of a religious order. Appropriate evaluation of persons from other cultures requires close examination in order to differentiate people who are merely following culturally prescribed patterns from people whose behaviors are excessive even by the standards of their own culture.

Symptoms

The symptoms of OCPD include a pervasive overconcern with mental, emotional, and behavioral control of the self and others. Excessive conscientiousness means that people with this disorder are generally poor problem-solvers and have trouble making decisions; as a result, they are frequently highly inefficient. Their need for control is easily upset by schedule changes or minor unexpected events. While many people have some of the following characteristics, a person who meets the *DSM-IV-TR* criteria for OCPD must display at least four of them:

- Preoccupation with details, rules, lists, order, organization, or schedules to the point at which the major goal of the activity is lost.

- Excessive concern for perfection in small details that interferes with the completion of projects.

- Dedication to work and productivity that shuts out friendships and leisure-time activities, when the long hours of work cannot be explained by financial necessity.

- Excessive moral rigidity and inflexibility in matters of ethics and values that cannot be accounted for by the standards of the person's religion or culture.

- Hoarding things, or saving worn-out or useless objects even when they have no sentimental or likely monetary value.

- Insistence that tasks be completed according to one's personal preferences.

- Stinginess with the self and others.

- Excessive rigidity and obstinacy.

Diagnosis

It is relatively unusual for OCPD to be diagnosed as the patient's primary reason for making an appointment with their doctor. In many cases the person with OCPD is unaware of the discomfort that his or her stubbornness and rigidity cause other people, precisely because these traits usually enable them to get their way with others. They are more likely to enter therapy because of other issues. **Diagnosis** of OCPD depends on careful observation and appropriate assessment of the individual's behavior; the person must not only give evidence of the attitudes and behaviors associated with OCPD, but these must be severe enough to interfere with their occupational and interpersonal functioning.

The differential diagnosis will include distinguishing between obsessive-compulsive disorder (OCD) and OCPD. A person who has obsessions and compulsions that they experience as alien and irrational is more likely to be suffering from OCD, whereas the person who feels perfectly comfortable with self-imposed systems of extensive rules and procedures for mopping the kitchen floor probably has OCPD. In addition, the thoughts and behaviors that are found in OCD are seldom relevant to real-life problems; by contrast, people with OCPD are preoccupied primarily with managing (however inefficiently) the various tasks they encounter in their daily lives.

Some features of OCPD may occur in other personality disorders. For example, a person with a **narcissistic personality disorder** may be preoccupied with perfection and be critical and stingy toward others; narcissists are usually generous with themselves, however, while people with OCPD are self-critical and reluctant to spend money even on themselves. Likewise, a person with **schizoid personality disorder**, who lacks a fundamental capacity for intimacy, may resemble someone with OCPD in being formal and detached in dealing with others. The difference here is that a person with OCPD, while awkward in emotional situations, is able to experience caring and may long for close relationships. Certain medical conditions may also mimic OCPD, but are distinct in that the onset of the symptoms is directly related to the illness. Certain behaviors related to **substance abuse** may also be mistaken for symptoms of OCPD, especially if the substance problem is unrecognized.

As described earlier, diagnosis may also be complicated by the fact that behaviors similar to OCPD may be normal variants within a given culture, occupation, or religion; however, in order to fulfill criteria for the personality disorder, the behaviors must be sufficiently severe as to impair the patient's functioning.

Treatment

Psychotherapy

Psychotherapeutic approaches to the treatment of OCPD have found insight-oriented psychodynamic techniques and **cognitive-behavioral therapy** to be helpful for many patients. This choice of effective approaches stands in contrast to the limitations of traditional forms of **psychotherapy** with most patients diagnosed with OCD. Learning to find satisfaction in life through close relationships and recreational outlets, instead of only through work-related activities, can greatly enrich the OCPD patient's quality of life. Specific training in relaxation techniques may help patients diagnosed with OCPD who have the so-called "Type A" characteristics of competitiveness and time urgency as well as preoccupation with work.

It is difficult, however, for a psychotherapist to develop a therapeutic alliance with a person with OCPD. The patient comes into therapy with a powerful need to control the situation and the therapist; a reluctance to trust others; and a tendency to doubt or question almost everything about the therapy situation. The therapist must be alert to the patient's defenses against genuine change and work to gain a level of commitment to the therapeutic process. Without this commitment, the therapist may be fooled into thinking that therapy has been successful when, in fact, the patient is simply being superficially compliant.

Medications

For many years, medications for OCPD and other personality disorders were thought to be ineffective since they did not affect the underlying causes of the disorder. More recent studies, however, indicate that treatment with specific drugs may be a useful adjunct (help) to psychotherapy. In particular, the medications known as **selective serotonin reuptake inhibitors (SSRIs)** appear to help the OCPD patient with his or her rigidity and compulsiveness, even when the patient did not show signs of pre-existing **depression**. Medication can also help the patient to think more clearly and make decisions better and faster without being so distracted by minor details. While symptom control may not "cure" the underlying personality disorder, medication does enable some OCPD patients to function with less distress.

Prognosis

Individuals with OCPD often experience a moderate level of professional success, but relationships with a spouse or children may be strained due to their combination of emotional detachment and controlling

KEY TERMS

Anankastic personality disorder—The European term for obsessive-compulsive personality disorder.

Compulsion—A strong impulse to perform an act, particularly one that is irrational or contrary to one's will.

Obsession—A persistent image, idea, or desire that dominates a person's thoughts or feelings.

Therapeutic alliance—The technical term for the cooperative relationship between therapist and patient that is considered essential for successful psychotherapy.

behaviors. In addition, people with OCPD often do not attain the level of professional achievement that might be predicted for their talents and abilities because their rigidity and stubbornness make them poor "team players" or supervisors. Although there are few large-scale outcome studies of treatments for OCPD, existing reports suggest that these patients do benefit from psychotherapy to help them understand the emotional issues underlying their controlling behaviors and to teach them how to relax. Since OCPD sufferers, unlike people with OCD, usually view their compulsive behaviors as voluntary, they are better able to consider change, especially as they come to fully recognize the personal and interpersonal costs of their disorder.

Prevention

Most theories attribute the development of OCPD to early life experiences, including a lack of parental warmth; parental overcontrol and rigidity, and few rewards for spontaneous emotional expression. Little work has been done, however, in identifying preventive strategies.

Resources

BOOKS

Alarcon, Renato D., Edward F. Foulks, and Mark Vakkur. *Personality Disorders and Culture.* New York: John Wiley and Sons, 1998.

Baer, Lee. "Personality Disorders in Obsessive-Compulsive Disorder." In *Obsessive-Compulsive Disorders: Practical Management,* by Michael Jenike, Lee Baer, and William E. Minichiello. 3rd ed. St. Louis: Mosby, 1998.

Jenike, Michael. "Psychotherapy of Obsessive-Compulsive Personality." In *Obsessive-Compulsive Personality Disorders: Practical Management,* edited by Michael Jenike,

Lee Baer, and William E. Minichiello. 3rd ed. St. Louis: Mosby, 1998.

Kay, Jerald, Allen Tasman, and Jeffery Liberman. "Obsessive-Compulsive Disorder." In *Psychiatry: Behavioral Science and Clinical Essentials*, edited by Michael Jenike, Lee Baer, and William Minichiello. Philadelphia: W.B. Saunders, 2000.

Millon, Theodore. *Personality-Guided Therapy*. New York: John Wiley and Sons, 1999.

World Health Organization (WHO). *The ICD-10 Classification of Mental and Behavioural Disorders*. Geneva: WHO, 1993.

PERIODICALS

Barber, Jacques P., et al. "Alliance Predicts Patients' Outcome Beyond In-Treatment change in Symptoms." *Journal of Consulting and Clinical Psychology* 68, no. 6 (December 2000); 1027–1032.

Nordahl, Hans M., and Tore C. Stiles. "Perceptions of Parental Bonding in Patients with Various Personality Disorders, Lifetime Depressive Disorders, and Healthy Controls." *Journal of Personality Disorders* 11, no. 4 (1997): 391–402.

Samuels, Jack, et al. "Personality Disorders and Normal Personality Dimensions in Obsessive-Compulsive Disorder." *British Journal of Psychiatry* 177 (2000) 457–462.

Zaider, Talia, Jeffrey G. Johnson, and Sarah J. Cockell. "Psychiatric Comorbidity Associated with Eating Disorder Symptomatology Among Adolescents in the Community." *International Journal of Eating Disorders* 28, no. 1 (July 2000): 58–67.

ORGANIZATIONS

Anxiety Disorders Association of America, 8730 Georgia Ave., Silver Spring, MD, 20910, (240) 485-1001, Fax: (240) 485-1035, http://www.adaa.org.

Freedom From Fear, 308 Seaview Ave., Staten Island, NY, 10305, (718) 351-1717, help@freedomfromfear.org, http://www.freedomfromfear.org.

Jane A. Fitzgerald, Ph.D.

Olanzapine

Definition

Olanzapine is classified as an atypical antipsychotic drug. It is available in the United States under the brand names Zyprexa and Zyprexa Zydis.

Purpose

Olanzapine is used to treat **schizophrenia** and to control manic episodes of **bipolar disorder**. It may be prescribed off-label to treat symptoms of **dementia** related to **Alzheimer's disease** but is not approved by the U.S. Food and Drug Administration (FDA) for this purpose.

Description

Olanzapine is thought to modify the actions of several chemicals in the **brain**. Olanzapine is chemically related to another atypical antipsychotic agent, **clozapine**, but differs both chemically and pharmacologically from the earlier phenothiazine antipsychotics.

Olanzapine is available as 2.5 mg, 5 mg, 7.5 mg, 10 mg, 15 mg, and 20 mg tablets that can be swallowed (Zyprexa) and 5 mg, 10 mg, 15 mg, and 20 mg tablets that disintegrate when placed under the tongue (Zyprexa Zydis). Olanzapine is broken down by the liver.

A new, long-acting injection form of olanzapine is also available to treat schizophrenia, which obviates some of the issues of medication adherence that often complicate treatment. This form maintains therapeutic levels for 2–4 weeks.

Recommended dosage

Recently, the effectiveness of olanzapine was evaluated in the Clinical Antipsychotic Trials of **Intervention** Effectiveness (**CATIE**) Schizophrenia Study. This study evaluated the effectiveness and side effects of atypical antipsychotics, including olanzapine, in comparison to a conventional antipsychotic drug in the treatment of schizophrenia.

The study found that the conventional antipsychotic generally was equally effective and tolerated as well as the newer, more expensive, atypical antipsychotic medications. Of the atypical antipsychotics, olanzapine performed somewhat better than the other drugs being investigated. Patients taking this drug were less likely to be hospitalized for psychotic **relapse** and tended to stay on their medication longer. However, patients on olanzapine also tended to gain significant weight and experience other metabolic changes associated with diabetes than did patients taking the other drugs in the study.

Olanzapine and another atypical, **risperidone**, tended to be better tolerated than the other atypical antipsychotics investigated, although only 35% of participants on olanzapine were able to continue taking it throughout the entire 18 months of the study. Participants who stopped taking their antipsychotic medication in Phase 1 because it was not adequately controlling their symptoms were more likely to stay on their medication if they were switched to olanzapine or risperidone rather than to **quetiapine** or **ziprasidone**. There was no difference among the four medications

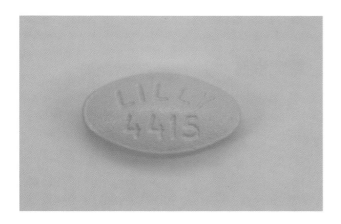

Zyprexa (olanzapine), 15 mg. (© Custom Medical Stock Photo, Inc. Reproduced by permission.)

tested in Phase 2, however, for participants who had stopped taking their Phase 1 medication because they experienced adverse side effects.

In Phase 2 of the study, the drug clozapine was more effective in controlling symptoms than the other atypical antipsychotics under evaluation. For patients whose symptoms were not well controlled on clozapine, olanzapine and risperidone tended to be more effective than the drugs ziprasidone or quetiapine.

The dosage of olanzapine varies depending upon the reason for its use. When used to treat schizophrenia, 5–10 mg is the typical starting dosage. If dosage adjustments are needed, increases are made in 5 mg increments once a week. When treating schizophrenia, a total daily dosage of 10–15 mg is usually effective. When olanzapine is used to treat acute manic episodes, initial doses of olanzapine are often 10–15 mg, and 20 mg per day may be needed for maximum effect. The safety of doses greater than 20 mg per day has not been determined.

Olanzapine is eliminated from the body more quickly in young people than in older (over age 60) individuals, in men more quickly than in women, and in smokers more quickly than in nonsmokers. Dosage adjustments may be needed based upon individual patient characteristics.

Precautions

Caution should be used in patients with heart disease because the drug may cause blood pressure to fall too low, resulting in dizziness, rapid heartbeats, or fainting. Olanzapine should be used carefully in people with known seizure disorders since olanzapine may alter properties of the brain, making **seizures** occur more easily. People with liver disease should have their liver function monitored regularly while taking olanzapine.

Women who are pregnant or breast-feeding should not take olanzapine. Babies born to mothers who took olanzapine during pregnancy may develop extrapyramidal symptoms (EPS) and withdrawal symptoms, including agitation, trouble breathing, and difficulty feeding. People with phenylketonuria, a disorder in which the body is unable to metabolize a protein called phenylalanine, should avoid olanzapine disintegrating tablets, because this form of the drug contains phenylalanine. Olanzapine has also been associated with the risk of developing a blood disorder.

Like other antipsychotic medications, olanzapine carries a warning regarding use in elderly people with dementia, who suffer from an increased risk of death during treatment with these agents. The reason for the increase was unclear in studies, but most deaths were found to be related to either cardiovascular complications or complications associated with infection. Olanzapine is not approved by the FDA for the treatment of behavior problems in older adults with dementia.

Side effects

Side effects that occur in more than 5% of patients taking olanzapine include involuntary movements, weakness, dizziness, extreme drowsiness, nonviolent objectionable behavior, constipation, weight gain, dry mouth, low blood pressure, stomach upset, increased appetite, cold-like symptoms, or fever.

Other side effects that are possible include rash, body aches and pains, elevated liver enzymes, vision abnormalities, chest pain, or rapid heartbeats.

Olanzapine has the potential to produce a serious side effect called **tardive dyskinesia**. This syndrome consists of involuntary, uncoordinated movements that may appear late in therapy and that may not disappear even after the drug is stopped. Tardive dyskinesia involves involuntary movements of the tongue, jaw, mouth, face, or other groups of skeletal muscles. The incidence of tardive dyskinesia increases with increasing age and with increasing dosage of olanzapine. Women are at greater risk than men for developing tardive dyskinesia. There is no known effective treatment for tardive dyskinesia, although gradual (but rarely complete) improvement may occur over a long period.

An occasionally reported side effect of olanzapine is **neuroleptic malignant syndrome**. This is a complicated and potentially fatal condition characterized by muscle rigidity, high fever, alterations in mental status, and cardiac symptoms such as irregular pulse or blood pressure, sweating, tachycardia (fast heartbeat), and arrhythmias (irregular heartbeat).

KEY TERMS

Extrapyramidal symptoms—A group of side effects associated with antipsychotic medications and characterized by involuntary muscle movements, including contraction and tremor.

Off-label use—Drugs in the United States are approved by the Food and Drug Administration (FDA) for specific uses based on the results of clinical trials. However, it is legal for physicians to administer these drugs for other "off-label" uses. It is not legal for pharmaceutical companies to advertise drugs for off-label uses.

Interactions

Any drug that causes drowsiness may lead to decreased mental alertness and impaired motor skills when taken with olanzapine. Some examples include alcohol, **antidepressants** such as **imipramine** (Tofranil) or **paroxetine** (Paxil), antipsychotics such as **thioridazine** (Mellaril), and some antihistamines. Because olanzapine may lower blood pressure, it may reduce blood pressure to dangerously low levels if taken with drugs that are used to treat high blood pressure. **Carbamazepine** (Tegretol), a drug commonly used to treat seizures, may decrease the effectiveness of olanzapine.

Resources

BOOKS

Physicians' Desk Reference 2011. 66th ed. Montvale, NJ: PDR Network, 2011.

Preston, John D., John H. O'Neal, and Mary C. Talaga. *Handbook of Clinical Psychopharmacology for Therapists.* 5th ed. Oakland, CA: New Harbinger Publications, 2008.

Wolters Kluwer Health. *Drug Facts and Comparisons 2012.* 66th ed. St. Louis: Lippincott, Williams & Wilkins, 2011.

PERIODICALS

Casey, Daniel E. "Implications of the CATIE Trial on Treatment: Extrapyramidal Symptoms." *CNS Spectrums* 11, no. 7, Supp. 7 (July 2006): 25–31.

Gentile, Salvatore. "Extrapyramidal Adverse Events Associated with Atypical Antipsychotic Treatment of Bipolar Disorder." *Journal of Clinical Psychopharmacology* 27, no. 1 (February 2007): 35–45.

Glick, Ira D. "Understanding the Results of CATIE in the Context of the Field." *CNS Spectrums* 11, no. 7, Supp. 7 (July 2006): 40–47.

Haro, Josep Maria, et al. "Remission and Relapse in the Outpatient Care of Schizophrenia: Three-Year Results from the Schizophrenia Outpatient Health Outcomes Study." *Journal of Clinical Psychopharmacology* 26, no. 6 (December 2006): 571–78.

Harvey, Philip D., Christopher R. Bowie, and Antony Loebel. "Neuropsychological Normalization with Long-Term Atypical Antipsychotic Treatment: Results of a Six-Month Randomized, Double-Blind Comparison of Ziprasidone vs. Olanzapine." *Journal of Neuropsychiatry & Clinical Neurosciences* 18, no. 1 (February 2006): 54–63.

Jarema, Marek. "Atypical Antipsychotics in the Treatment of Mood Disorders." *Current Opinion in Psychiatry* 20, no. 1 (January 2007): 23–29.

Kinon, Bruce J., et al. "Randomized, Double-Blind 6-Month Comparison of Olanzapine and Quetiapine in Patients with Schizophrenia or Schizoaffective Disorder with Prominent Negative Symptoms and Poor Functioning." *Journal of Clinical Psychopharmacology* 26, no. 5 (October 2006): 453–61.

Lieberman, Jeffrey A., et al. "Effectiveness of Antipsychotic Drugs in Patients with Chronic Schizophrenia." *New England Journal of Medicine* 353, no. 12 (September 2005): 1209–23.

Lipkovich, I., et al. "Predictors of Risk for Relapse in Patients with Schizophrenia or Schizoaffective Disorder During Olanzapine Drug Therapy." *Journal of Psychiatric Research* 41, no. 3–4 (April–June 2007): 305–10.

McCue, Robert E., et al. "Comparative Effectiveness of Second-Generation Antipsychotics and Haloperidol in Acute Schizophrenia." *British Journal of Psychiatry* 189 (November 2006): 433–40.

McEvoy, Joseph P., et al. "Effectiveness of Clozapine Versus Olanzapine, Quetiapine, and Risperidone in Patients with Chronic Schizophrenia Who Did Not Respond to Prior Atypical Antipsychotic Treatment." *American Journal of Psychiatry* 163, no. 4 (April 2006): 600–10.

Meltzer, Herbert Y., and William V. Bobo. "Interpreting the Efficacy Findings in the CATIE Study: What Clinicians Should Know." *CNS Spectrums* 11, Supp. 7 (July 2006): 14–24.

Morrens, Manuel, et al. "Psychomotor and Memory Effects of Haloperidol, Olanzapine, and Paroxetine in Healthy Subjects After Short-Term Administration." *Journal of Clinical Psychopharmacology* 27, no. 1 (February 2007): 15–21.

Nasrallah, Henry A. "Metabolic Findings From the CATIE Trial and Their Relation to Tolerability." *CNS Spectrums* 11, no. 7, Supp. 7 (July 2006): 32–39.

Schneider, Lon S., et al. "Effectiveness of Atypical Antipsychotic Drugs in Patients with Alzheimer's Disease." *New England Journal of Medicine* 355, no. 15 (October 2006): 1525–38.

Stroup, T. Scott, et al. "Effectiveness of Olanzapine, Quetiapine, Risperidone, and Ziprasidone in Patients with Chronic Schizophrenia Following Discontinuation of a Previous Atypical Antipsychotic." *American Journal of Psychiatry* 163, no. 4 (April 2006): 611–22.

Kelly Karpa, R.Ph., PhD
Ruth A. Wienclaw, PhD

Opioids and related disorders

Definition

Opioids are a class of drugs that include both natural and synthetic substances. The natural opioids (referred to as "opiates") include opium and morphine. Heroin, the most abused opioid, is synthesized from opium. Other synthetics (only made in laboratories) and commonly prescribed for pain, such as cough suppressants, or as anti-diarrhea agents, include codeine, oxycodone (Oxy-Contin), meperidine (Demerol), fentanyl (Sublimaze), hydromorphone (Dilaudid), **methadone**, and propoxyphene (Darvon). Heroin is usually injected, either intravenously (into a vein) or subcutaneously (under the skin), but it can be smoked or used intra-nasally (i.e., "snorted"). Other opioids are either injected or taken orally.

The manual that is used by mental health professionals to diagnose mental disorders is the *Diagnostic and Statistical Manual of Mental Disorders*. The latest edition of this manual was published in 2000 and is also known as the *DSM-IV-TR*. It lists opioid dependence and opioid abuse as substance use disorders. In addition, the opioid-induced disorders of opioid intoxication and opioid withdrawal are listed in the substance-related disorders section as well.

The fifth edition of the *Diagnostic and Statistical Manual of Mental Disorders,* also known as the *DSM-5,* is due for publication in May 2013. Proposed changes and revisions to the criteria for psychiatric diagnoses include combining the diagnoses of opioid abuse and opioid dependence into the single diagnosis of opioid use disorder. (The previous diagnoses of opioid intoxication and opioid withdrawal will be retained.)

Opioid dependence

Opioid dependence, or **addiction**, is essentially a syndrome in which a person continues to use opioids in spite of significant problems caused by, or made worse by, the use of opioids. Typically, individuals with opioid dependence are physically dependent on the drug as evidenced by tolerance and/or withdrawal.

Opioid abuse

Opioid abuse is less severe than opioid dependence and typically does not involve physical dependence on the drug. Opioid abuse is essentially repeated significant negative consequences of using opioids recurrently.

Opioid intoxication

When an individual uses a sufficient amount of an opioid, they will get "high" from the drug. Some people, however, have negative experiences when they use an opioid. When too much of an opioid is taken, an individual can overdose.

Opioid withdrawal

Individuals who use opioids on a regular basis, even if only for a few days, may develop a tolerance to the drug and experience physiological and psychological symptoms when they stop using it. The "abstinence syndrome" related to opioids is very similar to a bad case of influenza (or the "flu").

Description

Opioid dependence

Dependence on opioids involves significant physiological and psychological changes, which make it extremely difficult for an individual to stop using them. Recurrent use of opioids causes actual changes in how the **brain** functions. An individual who is addicted to opioids cannot simply just stop using, despite significant negative consequences related to their use. Marital difficulties, including divorce, unemployment, and drug-related legal

---

Classes of narcotics

Narcotics of natural origin
Codeine
Morphine
Opium
Thebaine

Semi-synthetic narcotics
Heroin
Hydrocodone
Hydromorphone
Oxycodone

Synthetic narcotics
Butorphanol
Dextropropoxyphene
Fentanyl
Meperidine
Pentazocine

Narcotics treatment drugs
Buprenorphine
LAAM
Methadone

SOURCE: U.S. Department of Justice, Drug Enforcement Administration, *Drugs of Abuse*, "Chapter 4: Narcotics." Available online at: http://www.justice.gov/dea/pubs/abuse/4-narc .htm (accessed August 19, 2010).

(Table by PreMediaGlobal. © 2012 Cengage Learning.)

problems, are often associated with opioid dependence. People who are dependent on opioids often plan their day around obtaining and using opioids.

Opioid abuse

People who abuse opioids typically use them less frequently than those who are dependent on them. However, despite less frequent use, an individual with opioid abuse can suffer negative consequences. For example, while intoxicated on opioids, an individual may get arrested for their behavior.

Opioid intoxication

An individual who uses opioids typically experiences drowsiness ("nodding off"), mood changes, a feeling of heaviness, dry mouth, itching, and slurred speech. Individuals who use heroin intravenously describe an intense euphoria (or "rush"), a floating feeling, and total indifference to pain. Symptoms of intoxication usually last several hours. Severe intoxication from an overdose of opioids is life-threatening because breathing may stop.

Opioid withdrawal

Tolerance to opioids occurs quickly. Regular users of opioids take doses that would kill someone who has never used before. After regular use, the human body adapts to the regular presence of the drug, and the person feels "normal" only when they have opioids in their system. Therefore, when an opioid-dependent individual stops using opioids abruptly, he or she will experience withdrawal symptoms. Withdrawal symptoms from heroin usually begin six to eight hours after last use and peak after two days. Acute withdrawal typically lasts no more than seven to ten days, but some symptoms of withdrawal (such as craving, **insomnia**, anxiety, or lack of interest) can last six months or longer. Although withdrawal is very uncomfortable, it is not life-threatening unless there is an underlying medical condition, such as heart disease. In addition to physical withdrawal, "psychological withdrawal" often occurs. The individual who is dependent on opioids has difficulty imagining living without the drug, since they were dependent on it to function. This is similar to how someone who is addicted to **nicotine** may feel after giving up cigarettes.

Causes and symptoms

Causes

There are no clear-cut causes of drug use other than the initial choice to use the drug. This decision to use may be highly influenced by peer group. Typically, the age of first use of heroin is about 16, but it has been dropping in recent years.

Certain social and behavioral characteristics, however, are more commonly seen among individuals who become dependent on opioids than those who do not. For instance, many heroin users come from families in which one or more family members use alcohol or drugs excessively or have mental disorders (such as **antisocial personality disorder**). Often heroin users have had health problems early in life, behavioral problems beginning in childhood, low self-confidence, and anti-authoritarian views.

Among opioid-dependent adolescents, a "heroin behavior syndrome" has sometimes been described. This syndrome consists of **depression** (often with anxiety symptoms), impulsiveness, fear of failure, low self-esteem, low frustration tolerance, limited coping skills, and relationships based primarily on mutual drug use.

Symptoms

OPIOID DEPENDENCE. The *DSM-IV-TR* specifies that three or more of the following symptoms must occur at any time during a 12-month period (and cause significant impairment or distress) in order to meet diagnostic criteria for opioid dependence:

- Tolerance: The individual either has to use increasingly higher amounts of the drug over time in order to achieve the same drug effect or finds that the same amount of the drug has much less of an effect over time than before.

- Withdrawal: The individual either experiences the characteristic abstinence syndrome (i.e., opioid-specific withdrawal) or uses opioids or similar-acting drugs in order to avoid or relieve withdrawal symptoms.

- Loss of control: The individual either repeatedly uses more opioids than planned or uses the opioids over longer periods of time than planned.

- Inability to stop using: The individual has either unsuccessfully attempted to cut down or stop using the opioids or has a persistent desire to stop using.

- Time: The individual spends a lot of time obtaining opioids, getting money to buy opioids, using opioids, being under the influence of opioids, and recovering from the effects of opioids.

- Interference with activities: The individual either gives up or reduces the amount of time involved in recreational activities, social activities, and/or occupational activities.

- Harm to self: The individual continues to use opioids despite having either a physical or psychological problem (e.g., depression) that is caused or made worse by the opioid use.

OPIOID ABUSE. The *DSM-IV-TR* specifies that one or more of the following symptoms must occur at any time during a 12-month period (and cause significant impairment or distress) in order to meet diagnostic criteria for opioid abuse:

• Interference with role fulfillment: The individual's use of opioids repeatedly interferes with the ability to fulfill obligations at work, home, or school.

• Danger to self: The individual repeatedly uses opioids in situations in which it may be physically hazardous (e.g., while driving a car).

• Legal problems: The individual has recurrent opioid-related legal problems (e.g., arrests for possession of narcotics).

• Social problems: The individual continues to use opioids despite repeated interpersonal or relationship problems caused by, or made worse by, the use of opioids.

OPIOID INTOXICATION. The *DSM-IV-TR* specifies that the following symptoms must be present in order to meet diagnostic criteria for opioid intoxication:

• Use: The individual recently used an opioid.

• Changes: The individual experiences significant behavioral or psychological changes during, or shortly after, use of an opioid. These changes may include euphoria initially, followed by slowed movements or agitation, impaired judgment, apathy (a "don't care attitude"), dysphoric mood (e.g., depression), or impaired functioning socially or at work.

• Opioid-specific intoxication syndrome: The pupils in the eyes get smaller. In addition, drowsiness or coma, slurred speech, and/or impaired memory or attention during, or shortly after, opioid use occur.

OPIOID WITHDRAWAL. The *DSM-IV-TR* specifies that the following symptoms must be present in order to meet diagnostic criteria for opioid withdrawal:

• Abstinence: Either the individual has stopped using (or has reduced the amount of) opioids, or an opioid antagonist (i.e., a drug, such as naloxone, that blocks the action of opioids) has been administered.

• Opioid-specific withdrawal syndrome: Three or more symptoms develop after abstinence. These symptoms include dysphoric (negative) mood, nausea or vomiting, muscle aches, runny nose or watery eyes, dilated pupils, goosebumps or sweating, diarrhea, yawning, fever, and insomnia.

• Impairment or distress: The withdrawal symptoms must cause significant distress to the individual or

impairment in functioning (socially, at work, or any other important area).

• Not due to other disorder: The withdrawal symptoms cannot be due to a medical condition or other mental disorder.

KEY TERMS

Amphetamines—A group of powerful and highly addictive substances that stimulate the central nervous system. Amphetamines may be prescribed for various medical conditions but are often purchased illicitly and abused.

Anxiety—Can be experienced as a troubled feeling, a sense of dread, fear of the future, or distress over a possible threat to a person's physical or mental well-being.

Depression—A mental state characterized by feelings of sadness, despair, and discouragement.

Demographics

There are at least 600,000 individuals with opioid dependence living in the United States. It has been estimated that almost 1% of the population has met criteria for opioid dependence or abuse at some time in their lives.

In the late 1800s and early 1900s, individuals who were dependent on opioids were primarily white and from middle socioeconomic groups. However, since the 1920s, minorities and those from lower socioeconomic groups have been overrepresented among those with opioid dependence. It appears that availability of opioids and subcultural factors are key in opioid use. Therefore, medical professionals (who have access to opioids) are at higher risk for developing opioid-related disorders.

Males are more commonly affected by opioid disorders than females—they are three to four times more likely than females to be dependent on opioids. Age also is a factor in opioid dependence. There is a tendency for rates of dependence to decrease beginning at 40 years of age. Problems associated with opioid use are usually first seen in the teens and 20s.

Diagnosis

Diagnosis of opioid-related disorders are based on patient interviews and observations of symptoms, including signs of withdrawal, such as dilated pupils, watery eyes, frequent yawning, and anxiety.

Opioid dependence

Other mental disorders are common among individuals with opioid dependence. It has been estimated that 90% of those with opioid dependence have one or more other mental disorders. Depression (usually either major depression or substance-induced mood disorder) is the most common disorder. Opioid-dependent individuals frequently report suicidal ideation (thoughts) and insomnia. Other substance-use disorders (such as alcoholism), **anxiety disorders**, antisocial personality disorder, **posttraumatic stress disorder**, and a history of **conduct disorder** are also fairly common.

Opioid intoxication

Intoxication on other substances, such as alcohol, **sedatives**, hypnotics, and anxiolytics, can resemble intoxication on opioids. Furthermore, dilated pupils can be seen in hallucinogen intoxication, amphetamine intoxication, and **cocaine** intoxication.

Opioid withdrawal

The restlessness and anxiety seen in opioid withdrawal are also seen in withdrawal from sedatives, hypnotics, and anxiolytics.

Treatment

Opioid dependence

Because opioid-related disorders are complex, multiple treatment approaches are often necessary. Generally, the more treatment (e.g., a combination of medication, individual therapy, and **self-help groups**), and the longer the treatment (i.e., at least three months), the better the outcomes. There are a wide variety of treatment options, both inpatient or residential and outpatient:

• Methadone maintenance treatment. Methadone is a long-acting opioid that is generally administered in an outpatient setting (a methadone maintenance clinic). The methadone prevents the individual from experiencing opioid withdrawal, reduces opioid craving, and enables the individual to have access to other services (such as individual counseling, medical services, and HIV-prevention education). A proper dose of methadone also prevents the individual from getting "high" from heroin. Methadone maintenance therapy can decrease criminal activity, decrease HIV-risk behaviors, and increase stability of employment. Low-dose methadone maintenance treatment is preferable for pregnant individuals who would otherwise use illicit opioids. One longer-acting alternative to methadone is LAAM (levo-alphacetylmethadol). Individuals receiving the proper doses of LAAM only need to take it three times per week, instead of every day as with methadone.

• Opioid antagonist treatment. An opioid antagonist is a medication that blocks the effects of opioids. Treatment with an antagonist, usually naltrexone (Trexan), typically takes place on an outpatient basis following an inpatient medical detoxification from opioids. The effects of taking any opioids are blocked by the naltrexone and prevent the individual from getting "high," thereby discouraging individuals from seeking opioids. By itself, this treatment is suitable for individuals who are highly motivated to discontinue opioid use. However, antagonists can be used in addition to other treatment modalities or with individuals who have been abstinent for some time but fear a relapse.

• Opioid agonist-antagonist treatment. An opioid agonist is a drug that has an action similar to morphine. Buprenorphine (Buprenex) is an example of an opioid agonist-antagonist, which means it acts as both an agonist (having some morphine-like action) and antagonist (blocking the effects of additional opioids). Buprenorphine has been shown to reduce opioid use effectively. It is also being studied for opioid detoxification.

• Outpatient drug-free treatment. These are outpatient treatment approaches that do not include medications. There are a number of different types of programs ranging from simple drug education to intensive outpatient programs that offer most of the services of an inpatient setting. Some programs may specialize in treating specific groups of people who are opioid-dependent (e.g., those with co-occurring mental disorders).

• Residential or inpatient treatment. These include inpatient rehabilitation programs (usually seven to 30 days in length) and long-term residential programs (e.g., therapeutic communities). Rehabilitation programs provide an inpatient atmosphere following detoxification and usually offer individual and group counseling as well as medical services. Therapeutic communities are designed to be more than six months long and are highly structured. The primary focus is on resocializing the individual to a drug-free and crime-free lifestyle.

• Individualized drug counseling. Individual counseling is often a part of a methadone maintenance program or inpatient rehabilitation program. The primary focus is on helping the individual learn strategies to reduce or stop their opioid use and learn coping mechanisms to maintain abstinence. Twelve-step participation is encouraged, and referrals for medical, psychiatric, employment, or other services are made as necessary.

• Supportive-expressive psychotherapy. This type of individual psychotherapy may be a part of a methadone maintenance program or offered alone. The focus of this type of therapy is to help individuals feel comfortable talking about themselves, work on relationship issues, and solve problems without resorting to opioids or other drugs.

- Self-help groups. Narcotics Anonymous (NA) is a twelve-step group based on the same model as Alcoholics Anonymous. This self-help group can provide social support to an individual in the process of reducing or stopping opioid use. Participation in NA is often encouraged or is a required component of other types of treatment for opioid dependence. Nar-Anon is a group for family members and friends of opioid-dependent individuals.

- Alternative therapies. Hypnosis, guided imagery, biofeedback, massage, and acupuncture have all been studied as adjunctive treatments for opioid dependence, but none has been proven to be effective.

Opioid abuse

Most of the treatments for opioid dependence would be appropriate for opioid abuse except methadone maintenance and opioid antagonist treatment.

Opioid intoxication

An opioid antagonist, naloxone (Narcan), can be administered to reverse the effects of acute intoxication or overdose on most opioids.

Opioid withdrawal

Opioid withdrawal can be treated on either an inpatient basis (**detoxification**) or an outpatient basis (methadone detoxification):

- Inpatient detoxification program. Typically, this would be from three to seven days. The withdrawal can be medically managed. Clonidine can be administered to help reduce some symptoms of withdrawal.

- Outpatient methadone detoxification. Methadone would be substituted for the illicit opioid, and the dose would be gradually reduced. Detoxification from methadone is easier (i.e., the symptoms are less severe) than from heroin. However, the withdrawal or abstinence syndrome also lasts longer. Clonidine may also be administered during the methadone detoxification to help reduce withdrawal symptoms.

Prognosis

Opioid dependence

Recovering from opioid dependence is a long, difficult process. Typically, multiple treatment attempts

---

QUESTIONS TO ASK YOUR DOCTOR

- What risks are associated with opioid use and opioid abuse?
- What symptoms are associated with opioid dependence?
- Do opioid dependence and abuse put me at risk for other health conditions?
- Can you recommend any treatment and support groups for me?

---

are required. Relapsing, or returning to opioids, is not uncommon even after many years of abstinence. Brief periods of abstinence are common.

Inpatient detoxification from opioids alone, without additional treatment, does not appear to have any effect on opioid use. However, other treatments have been shown to reduce opioid use, decrease illegal activity, decrease rates of HIV-infection, reduce rates of death, and increase rates of employment. Benefits are greatest for those who remain in treatment longer and participate in many different types of treatment (e.g., individual and group counseling in addition to methadone maintenance).

Risk Evaluation and Mitigation Strategy

In February 2009, the U.S. Food and Drug Administration (FDA) announced that it had contacted the manufacturers of opioid pain medications (including fentanyl, morphine, and oxycodone), with plans requiring them to employ a risk evaluation and mitigation strategy (REMS) to ensure that the benefits of these drugs outweigh the risks. The authority for the FDA to require REMS comes from the FDA Amendments Act of 2007 (FDAAA).

The rationale for REMS is that opioid drugs are of benefit when used properly and are a needed component of pain management for specific patient populations; however, these drugs impose serious risks when they are used improperly. Therefore, there is a need for guidelines to be put into place in order to prevent abuse, misuse (intentional or unintentional), and accidental overdose of these drugs. To improve the safe use of these drugs, changes would include new warning labels, risk–management plans, and direct communications to prescribers and patients.

The FDA will require REMS from manufacturers to ensure that the benefits of a drug product outweigh its risks and to establish measures to ensure safe use of these

---

drugs. Establishing REMS will purport to demonstrate a balance between access to the medications and measures to manage and reduce their risks.

Plans and final recommendations to finalize REMS are ongoing. For more information, visit the FDA's website at: http://www.fda.gov/Drugs/DrugSafety/InformationbyDrugClass/ucm163647.htm.

Prevention

The best single thing an individual can do to prevent opioid-related disorders is to never use illicit opioids such as heroin. Opioids are powerfully addicting, especially if used intravenously. The risk of becoming dependent on appropriately prescribed opioids, however, is generally low except for individuals who already have a substance use disorder.

On a larger scale, comprehensive prevention programs that utilize family, schools, communities, and the media can be effective in reducing **substance abuse**. The recurring theme in these programs is not to use drugs in the first place.

Resources

BOOKS

American Psychiatric Association. *Diagnostic and Statistical Manual of Mental Disorders*. 4th ed., text rev. Washington, DC: American Psychiatric Association, 2000.

American Psychological Association. *Publication Manual of the American Psychological Association*. 6th ed. Washington, DC: American Psychological Association, 2009.

Erickson, Carlton K., Ph.D. *Addiction Essentials: The Go-To Guide for Clinicians and Patients*. New York: W. W. Norton & Company, 2011.

Galanter, Marc, and Herbert D. Kleber, eds. *Textbook of Substance Abuse Treatment*. 2nd ed. Washington, DC: American Psychiatric Press, Inc., 2008.

North, Carol, and Sean Yutzy. *Goodwin and Guze's Psychiatric Diagnosis*. New York: Oxford University Press, 2010.

Sadock, Benjamin J., Virginia Alcott Sadock, and Pedro Ruiz, eds. *Kaplan and Sadock's Comprehensive Textbook of Psychiatry,* 2nd ed. New York: Lippincott Williams & Wilkins, 2009.

WEBSITES

National Institute on Drug Abuse. "Prescription Drugs: Abuse and Addiction." U.S. National Institutes of Health. http://drugabuse.gov/ResearchReports/Prescription/prescription2.html

ORGANIZATIONS

American Psychological Association, 750 First Street NE, Washington, DC, 20003, (202) 336-5500, http://www.apa.org/index.aspx.

National Institute on Drug Abuse, 6001 Executive Blvd., Rm. 5213, Bethesda, MD, 20892, (301) 442-1124; Spanish: (240) 221-4007, information@nida.nih.gov, http://www.nida.nih.gov.

The Partnership at Drugfree.org, 352 Park Avenue South, 9th Floor, New York, NY, 10010, (212) 922-1560, (855) DRUGFREE (378-4373; helpline), Fax: (212) 922-1570, webmail@drugfree.org, http://www.drugfree.org.

Substance Abuse and Mental Health Services Administration Referral Resource, 1 Choke Cherry Rd., Rockville, MD, 20857, (877) SAMHSA-7 (726-4727), (800) TTY: 487-4889, Fax: (240) 221-4292, SAMHSAInfo@samhsa.hhs.gov, http://www.samhsa.gov.

Jennifer Hahn, Ph.D.
Laura Jean Cataldo, RN, Ed.D.

Oppositional defiant disorder

Definition

Oppositional defiant disorder (ODD) is a disorder found primarily in children and adolescents. It is characterized by negative, disobedient, or defiant behavior that is worse than the normal "testing" behavior most children display from time to time. Most children go through periods of being difficult, particularly during the period from 18 months to three years, and later during adolescence. These difficult periods are part of the normal developmental process of gaining a stronger sense of individuality and separating from parents. ODD, however, is defiant behavior that lasts longer and is more severe than normal individuation behavior, but is not so extreme that it involves violation of social rules or the rights of others.

The mental health professional's handbook, *Diagnostic and Statistical Manual of Mental Disorders*, fourth edition, text revision (*DSM-IV-TR*), classifies ODD as a disruptive behavior disorder.

Demographics

Oppositional defiant disorder is thought to occur in about 6% of all children and teenagers in the United States, with a range from 2%–16%. It is more common in families of lower socioeconomic status. Boys are more likely to have ODD than are girls. However, in older children, its occurrence is approximately equal with respect to gender. In one study, 8% of children from low-income families were diagnosed with ODD. The disorder is often apparent by the time a child is about six years old. The *Merck Manual* reports that ODD usually develops by the age of eight years. Boys tend to be diagnosed with this disorder more often than girls in the preteen years, but it is equally common in males and females by adolescence.

It is estimated that about one-third of children who have **attention deficit hyperactivity disorder (ADHD)** also have ODD. Children who have ODD are also often diagnosed with anxiety or **depression**.

Description

Children who have ODD are often disobedient. They are easily angered and may seem to be angry much of the time. Very young children with the disorder will throw temper tantrums that last for 30 minutes or longer, over seemingly trivial matters.

In addition, the child with ODD often starts arguments and will not give up. Winning the argument seems to be very important to a child with this disorder. Even if the youth knows that he or she will lose a privilege or otherwise be punished for continuing the tantrum or argument, he or she is unable to stop. Attempting to reason with such a child often backfires, because the child perceives rational discussion as a continuation of the argument.

Most children with ODD, however, do not perceive themselves as being argumentative or difficult. It is usual for such children to blame all of their problems on others. Such children can also be perfectionists and have a strong sense of justice regarding violations of what they consider correct behavior. They are impatient and intolerant of others. They are more likely to argue verbally with other children than to get into physical fights.

Older children or adolescents with ODD may try to provoke others by being deliberately annoying or critical. For example, a teenager may criticize an adult's way of speaking or dressing. This oppositional behavior is usually directed at an authority figure, such as a parent, coach, or teacher. Youths diagnosed with ODD, however, can also be bullies who use their language skills to taunt and abuse other children.

In May 2013, the **American Psychiatric Association** is due to publish the new edition of the *DSM*. Named *DSM-5*, the ADHD and Disruptive Behavior Disorders Work Group, which is co-chaired by Drs. David Shaffer and F. Xavier Castellanos, is working on proposed revisions to ODD, along with other disruptive disorders. According to the group, the definition of ODD is proposed to be: "A persistent pattern of angry and irritable mood along with defiant and vindictive behavior as evidenced by four (or more) of the following

symptoms being displayed with one or more persons other than siblings.":

• Angry/Irritable Mood: (1) Loses temper; (2) Is touchy or easily annoyed by others; (3) Is angry and resentful.

• Defiant/Headstrong Behavior: (4) Argues with adults; (5) Actively defies or refuses to comply with adults' requests or rules; (6) Deliberately annoys people; (7) Blames others for his or her mistakes or misbehavior.

• Vindictiveness: (8) Has been spiteful or vindictive at least twice within the past six months.

The members of the Work Group also make the following statement that is under consideration: "The persistence and frequency of these behaviors should be used to distinguish a behavior that is within normal limits from a behavior that is symptomatic to determine if they should be considered a symptom of the disorder. For children under 5 years of age, the behavior must occur on most days for a period of at least six months unless otherwise noted (see symptom #8). For individuals 5 years or older, the behavior must occur at least once per week for at least six months, unless otherwise noted (see symptom #8). While these frequency criteria provide a minimal level of frequency to define symptoms, other factors should also be considered such as whether the frequency and intensity of the behaviors are non-normative given the person's developmental level, gender, and culture."

The following two statements are also under consideration: "The disturbance in behavior causes clinically significant impairment in social, educational, or vocational activities." and "The behaviors may be confined to only one setting or in more severe cases present in multiple settings."

Causes and symptoms

Causes

The exact cause of ODD is not known for certain within the medical community. However, three causes are thought to contribute to the disorder: biological, genetic, and environmental. Based on previous medical studies, problems found in the **brain**, whether occurring at birth or due to injuries suffered later in life, have been associated with serious psychological problems in children. Abnormalities in the prefrontal cortex of the brain, along with damaged neurotransmitter function in the dopaminergic, noradrenergic, and serotonergic systems, all seem to contribute to ODD. Lower-than-normal cortisol and higher-than-normal testosterone levels are other factors genetically associated with the presence of ODD. In addition, an existing mental illness, such as depression or an anxiety disorder, is thought to add to the risk of developing ODD later in life.

KEY TERMS

Antisocial personality disorder—A psychological condition in which a person appears to be unaware of, or indifferent to, the feelings of others and to normal social rules and standards.

Attention deficit hyperactivity disorder—A disorder that usually begins in childhood and is characterized by an inability to focus on tasks, sit still, and control impulses.

Depression—A disorder that is characterized by such symptoms as feelings of hopelessness, lack of energy, sleeplessness, and, sometimes, thoughts of suicide.

Disruptive behavior disorder—A broader term that includes two similar disorders: oppositional defiant disorder, and conduct disorder.

Genetics are likely to be a factor, meaning that ODD could be an inherited medical disorder. Children and teenagers with close family members who have mental illnesses, such as **anxiety disorders**, mood disorders, and **personality disorders**, are at increased risk of developing ODD. In addition, the environment surrounding a child or teen may increase their risk of ODD. Such environmental factors include **substance abuse**, exposure to toxins, poor **nutrition**, dysfunctional family life, and inconsistent discipline at home or at school.

All three factors—biology, genetics, and environment—could be directly the result of family life. Specifically, ODD has been called a problem of families, not of individuals. It occurs in families in which some or all of the following factors are present:

• Limits set by parents are too harsh or too lax, or an inconsistent mix of both.

• Family life lacks clear structure; rules, limits, and discipline are uncertain or inconsistently applied.

• At least one parent models oppositional behavior in his or her own interactions with others. For example, the mother or father may get into frequent disputes with neighbors, store clerks, other family members, in front of the child.

• At least one parent is emotionally or physically unavailable to the child due to emotional problems of the parent (such as depression); separation or divorce; or work hours.

The defiant behavior may be an attempt by the child to feel safe or to gain control. It may also represent an attempt to get attention from an unresponsive parent.

There may be a genetic factor involved in ODD; the disorder often seems to run in families. However, this pattern may reflect behavior learned from previous generations rather than the effects of a gene or genes for the disorder.

Symptoms

According to *DSM-IV-TR*, a **diagnosis** of ODD may be given to children who meet the following criteria, provided that the behavior occurs more frequently than usual, compared to children of the same age and developmental level.

A pattern of negativistic, hostile, and defiant behavior lasting at least six months, during which four (or more) of the following are present. The child:

• often loses his or her temper

• frequently argues with adults

• often disregards adults' requests or rules

• deliberately tries to provoke people

• frequently blames others for his or her mistakes or misbehavior

• is often easily irritated by others

• is often angry and resentful

• is often spiteful.

In order to make the diagnosis of oppositional defiant disorder, the behavioral disturbances must cause significant impairment in the child's social, academic, or occupational functioning, and the behaviors must not occur exclusively during the course of a psychotic or mood disorder. In addition, the child must not meet criteria for **conduct disorder**, which is a more serious behavioral disorder. If the youth is 18 years or older, he or she must not meet criteria for **antisocial personality disorder**.

Diagnosis

Oppositional defiant disorder is diagnosed when the child's difficult behavior lasts longer than six months. There is no standard test for diagnosing ODD. A full medical checkup may be done to ensure that there is no medical problem causing the child's behavior. The medical examination is followed by a psychological evaluation of the child, which involves an interview with a mental health professional. The mental health professional may also interview the child's parents and teachers. Psychological tests are sometimes given to the child to rule out other disorders.

Evaluation for ODD includes ruling out a more disruptive behavioral disorder known as *conduct disorder* (CD). CD is similar to ODD but also includes physical aggression toward others, such as fighting or deliberately trying to hurt another person. Children with CD also frequently break laws or violate the rights of others (for example, by stealing). They tend to be more covert than children with ODD, lying and keeping some of their unacceptable behavior secret.

The diagnosis of ODD may specify its degree of severity as mild, moderate, or severe.

Treatment

Treatment of ODD focuses on both the child and the parents. The goals of treatment include helping the child to feel protected and safe and to teach him or her appropriate behavior. Parents may need to learn how to set appropriate limits with a child and how to deal with a child who acts out. They may also need to learn how to teach and reinforce desired behavior.

Parents may also need help with problems that may be distancing them from the child. Such problems can include alcoholism or drug dependency, depression, or financial difficulties. In some cases, legal or economic assistance may be necessary. For example, a single mother may need legal help to obtain child support from the child's father so that she will not need to work two jobs and can stay at home in the evenings with the child.

The specific treatment for ODD is determined by the medical professional, based on many factors, including age, severity of symptoms, and the child's ability to participate in, and deal with, the various therapies. Treatment is usually one or more of the following: behavioral therapy, contingency management, cognitive therapy, **parent management training**, **group therapy**, and medication.

Behavioral therapy

Behavioral therapy is usually effective in treating ODD. It focuses on changing specific behaviors, not on analyzing the history of the behaviors or the very early years of the child's life. The theory behind behavioral therapy is that a person can learn a different set of behaviors to replace those that are causing problems. As the person obtains better results from the new behavior, he or she will want to continue that behavior instead of reverting to the old one. To give an example, the child's parents may be asked to identify behaviors that usually start an argument. They are then shown ways to stop or change those behaviors in order to prevent arguments.

Contingency management

Contingency management techniques may be included in behavioral therapy. The child and the parents may be helped to draw up contracts that identify unwanted behaviors and spell out consequences. For example, the child may lose a privilege or part of his or her allowance every time he or she throws a temper tantrum. These contracts can include steps or stages—for example, lowering the punishment if the child begins an argument but manages to stop arguing within a set period of time. The same contract may also specify rewards for desired behavior. For example, if the child has gone for a full week without acting out, he or she may get to choose which movie the family sees that weekend. These contracts may be shared with the child's teachers.

The parents are encouraged to acknowledge good or nonproblematic behavior as much as possible. Attention or praise from the parent when the child is behaving well can reinforce his or her sense that the parent is aware of the child even when he or she is not acting out.

Cognitive therapy

Cognitive therapy may be helpful for older children, adolescents, and parents. In cognitive therapy, the person is guided to greater awareness of problematic thoughts and feelings in certain situations. The therapist can then suggest a way of thinking about the problem that would lead to behaviors that are more likely to bring the person what they want or need. For example, a girl may be helped to see that much of her anger derives from feeling that no one cares about her, but that her angry behavior is the source of her problem because it pushes people away.

Parent management training

Parent management training (PMT) is used as an avenue to train families to better deal with their child with ODD. The PMT has been shown to be effective toward reducing, or even eliminating, negative interactions between parents and children. Training with PMT involves teaching parents to change their behaviors, which indirectly changes the behavior of their children. PMT concentrates on increasing positive attention (such as non-aversive punishment) to the ODD child, while eliminating negative attention. For example, parents are taught not to reinforce disruptive or deviant behaviors with negative attention (such as aversive punishments). In addition, parents are taught to spend more time with their OCD child in order to identify their positive behaviors more easily so they can positively reinforce such actions.

Group therapy

ODD can be treated with group therapy, in which behaviors and reactions are modeled in a classroom setting with other ODD children. Real-life situations are set up in which the children act out situations that promote empathy, listening, and effective problem solving. Often, parents attend with other parents for a combined meeting.

Intervention early in the life of a child is more effective than waiting for the child to grow out of it or intervening later in life. In younger children, combined treatment in which parents attend group therapy sessions while the children go to other meetings has consistently resulted in the best results. Group therapy for adolescents with ODD is most beneficial when it is well organized, structured, and focused on developing the skills of effective problem solving, empathy, and listening.

Medication

Although behavioral therapies are the cornerstone of treatment for ODD, medication may also be helpful in some cases. Children who have concurrent ADHD may need medical treatment to control their impulsivity and extend their attention span. Children who are anxious or depressed may also be helped by appropriate medications.

Prognosis

Treatment for ODD is usually a long-term commitment. Seek help from a qualified medical professional as early as possible in order to provide the best results for a child. It may take a year or more of treatment to notice improvement. It is important for families to continue with treatment even if immediate results are not apparent.

If ODD is not treated, or if treatment is abandoned, the child has a higher likelihood of developing conduct disorder, which is a more serious mental illness. The risk of developing conduct disorder is lower in children who are only mildly defiant. It is higher in children who are more defiant and in children who also have ADHD. In adults, conduct disorder is called antisocial personality disorder (ASD).

Children who have untreated ODD are also at risk for developing passive-aggressive behaviors as adults. Persons with passive-aggressive characteristics tend to see themselves as victims and blame others for their problems.

However, when ODD is identified early and properly, the results of the treatment are usually very effective.

Prevention

Prevention of ODD begins with good parenting. If at all possible, families and the caregivers they encounter should be on the lookout for any problem that may prevent parents from giving children the structure and attention they need.

QUESTIONS TO ASK YOUR DOCTOR

- What treatment options do you recommend for our child?
- In what way do you think medication will benefit my child with ODD?
- What is our first step to treating ODD in my child?
- What can we do as parents to help our child?
- Where can we learn more about ODD?
- How can my child's school help his or her treatment?
- Are there any support groups that could help us understand ODD?

Early identification of ODD and ADHD is necessary to obtain help for the child and family as soon as possible. The earlier ODD is identified and treated, the more likely the child will be able to develop healthy patterns of relating to others.

Resources

BOOKS

American Psychiatric Association. *Diagnostic and Statistical Manual of Mental Disorders.* 4th edition, text revised. Washington, DC: American Psychiatric Association Publishing. 2000.

Beers, Mark H. *Merck Manual of Diagnosis and Therapy.* Rahway: Merck, 2011.

Black, Donald W., and Nancy C. Andreasen. *Introductory Textbook of Psychiatry.* Washington D.C.: American Psychiatric Publishing, 2006.

Corcoran, Jacqueline. *Mental Health Treatment for Children and Adolescents.* Oxford: Oxford University Press, 2011.

Leeming, David A., Kathryn Madden, and Stanton Marlan, editors. *Encyclopedia of Psychology and Religion.* New York: Springer, 2010.

Matthys, Walter, and John E. Lochman. *Oppositional Defiant Disorder and Conduct Disorder in Childhood.* Chichester: Wiley-Blackwell, 2010.

Morrison, James. *DSM-IV Made Easy: The Clinician's Guide to Diagnosis.* New York: Guilford Press, 2006.

Sadock, Benjamin J. *Kaplan & Sadock's Pocket Handbook of Clinical Psychiatry.* Philadelphia: Wolters Kluwer Health/ Lippincott Williams & Wilkins, 2010.

WEBSITES

Helping Children and Youth With Conduct Disorder and Oppositional Defiant Disorder: Systems of Care. U.S. Substance Abuse and Mental Health Services Administration. (January 2006). http://store.samhsa.gov/product/

Helping-Children-and-Youth-With-Conduct-Disorder-and-Oppositional-Defiant-Disorder-Systems-of-Care/SMA06-4200 (accessed July 4, 2011).

Oppositional Defiant Disorder. eMedicine. (February 8, 2008). http://emedicine.medscape.com/article/918095-overview#aw2aab6b2 (accessed July 15, 2011).

Oppositional Defiant Disorder. HealthyPlace.com. (January 2, 2009). httphttp://www.healthyplace.com/other-info/psychiatric-disorder-definitions/oppositional-defiant-disorder/menu-id-71 (accessed July 15, 2011).

Oppositional Defiant Disorder. WebMD. http://www.webmd.com/mental-health/oppositional-defiant-disorder (accessed July 15, 2011).

Q 00 Oppositional Defiant Disorder. American Psychiatric Association. (2010). http://www.dsm5.org/Proposed Revisions/Pages/proposedrevision.aspx?rid=106 (accessed July 15, 2011).

ORGANIZATIONS

American Academy of Child and Adolescent Psychiatry, 3615 Wisconsin Avenue, N.W., Washington, DC, 20016-3007, 1(202) 966-7300, Fax: 1(202) 966-2891, http://aacap.org.

American Psychiatric Association, 1000 Wilson Boulevard, Suite 1825, Arlington, VA, 22209, 1(703) 907-7300, apa@psych.org, http://www.psych.org.

Federation of Families for Children's Mental Health, 9605 Medical Center Drive, Rockville, MD, 20850, 1(240) 403-1901, Fax: 1(240) 403-1909, ffcmh@ffcmh.org, http://ffcmh.org.

Mental Health America, 2000 N. Beauregard Street, 6th Floor, Alexandria, VA, 22311, 1(703) 684-7722, Fax: 1(703) 684-5968, (800) 969-6642, http://www1.nmha.org.

National Alliance on Mental Illness, 3803 North Fairfax Drive, Suite 100, Arlington, VA, 22203, 1(703) 524-7600, Fax: 1(703) 524-9094, http://www.nami.org.

National Institute of Mental Health, 6001 Executive Boulevard, Room 8184, MSC 9663, Bethesda, MD, 20892-9663, 1(301) 443-4513, Fax: 1(301) 443-4279, (866) 615-6464, nimhinfo@nih.gov, http://www.nimh.nih.gov.

Jody Bower, M.S.W.
William Atkins, B.B., B.S., M.B.A.

Orap *see* **Pimozide**

Origin of mental illnesses

Historical background

Mental illness in the ancient world

Over the history of the healing arts, there has been a succession of theories regarding the root causes of mental illness. Early writings from such ancient civilizations as those of Greece, India, and Egypt focused on demonic possession as the cause. This concept eventually disappeared only to resurface again in the Middle Ages in Europe, along with inadequate treatment of the mentally ill. Demons or "foul spirits" were believed to attach themselves to individuals and make them depressed ("poor-spirited") or "mad." The word *mad* became an early synonym for **psychosis**. Unfortunately, the "possessed" included people with seizure disorders as well as others suffering from what are now known to be medical disorders. Few genuinely helpful treatments were available to relieve the suffering of the mentally ill.

The Hippocratic tradition

Hippocrates, a Greek physician who lived around 400 B.C. and is regarded as the source of the Hippocratic Oath taken by modern physicians, first introduced the concept of disturbed physiology (organic processes or functions) as the basis for all illnesses, mental or otherwise. Hippocrates did not describe disturbances of the nervous system as we do today, in terms of a chemical imbalance or a low level of **neurotransmitters** (the chemical messengers sent between **brain** cells). Instead, he used the notion of an imbalance of "humors." Humors were defined as bodily fluids influenced by the environment, the weather, foods, and other external factors, producing various imbalances in a person's state of health. Hippocrates' theory was an early version of the idea that physiological disturbances or body chemistry might play a role in the development of mental illness. Most importantly, perhaps, Hippocrates' concept placed mental illness on the same footing as other medical disorders by highlighting the belief that the mentally ill are genuinely suffering, and therefore need to be treated like other sick persons rather than as moral degenerates. Sadly, modern society has not fully overcome the tendency to stigmatize persons with mental disorders. Hippocrates' perspective, however, meant that someone with **depression** or **schizophrenia** could be viewed as being in a state of disease just like a diabetic or someone with high blood pressure.

The nineteenth century

Toward the end of the nineteenth century, several European neurologists began actively investigating the causes of mental illness. Chief among them, and destined to change forever the understanding of mental illness, was Sigmund Freud. Although psychology and psychiatry have advanced considerably since Freud, his explorations were revolutionary. Freud introduced the concepts of the unconscious and the ego to modern thought, and reintroduced the ancient art of dream

A bust of Hippocrates. (© *The Art Gallery Collection/Alamy*)

interpretation, but from a psychological standpoint. Freud also regarded human psychological states as an energy system in which blockages in the flow of thought (repression or suppression, for example) would result in disease or illness, expressed as mental or emotional loss of balance. He introduced the notion of a "talking cure"; through the use of **talk therapy** alone, many patients would improve. This method of treatment is still used today, although the technique of talk therapy itself has undergone further development. Freud's early advances in understanding the mind, however, awaited further anatomical and biochemical discoveries of the structures and functions of the human brain. As a result, early psychiatry (from two Greek words, *psyche*, meaning "soul" or "mind" and *iatros*, meaning "physician") split into two competing traditions, one that followed Freud in emphasizing thoughts, emotions and dreams as keys to the healing of mental disorders, and another that looked for clues to these disorders in the tissues of the brain.

In the first half of the twentieth century, psychiatry was advanced by the discovery of medications that helped to alleviate depression, mania, and psychosis. As often occurs in the history of medicine, physicians stumbled upon solutions before they understood the mechanisms that made the treatment work. Later studies began to reveal that certain patients responded to medications that increased

certain neurotransmitters. Drugs that increased the levels of the neurotransmitters norepinephrine and **serotonin** seemed to help depressed patients. Similarly, medications that blocked the transmission of **dopamine**, another neurotransmitter, provided relief for patients suffering from hallucinations and **paranoia**. These insights have led to the present emphasis on the biochemistry of the human brain. If, however, the biochemical model becomes the only view of mental health, modern psychiatry risks becoming "mindless." Clearly, a unified theory is needed to understand all the factors that contribute to mental disorders, and to do justice to the complexity of each human being. Understanding all the factors that lead to a disease state has much to do with an adequate treatment response.

Nature and nurture

One attempt to unify the varied theories regarding the origin of mental illness is called simply the "nature versus nurture" theory. It is really the nature *and* nurture theory, however, as it establishes the importance of two forces in the development of mental illness. For example, "nature" refers to biological factors that produce a tendency or predisposition to develop certain diseases. For instance, parents who have high blood pressure have offspring who have a higher probability of developing the same condition. If, on the other hand, these offspring learn to eat properly, **exercise**, and live in a relatively peaceful home, for instance, they may be able to avoid the expression of high blood pressure that runs in their family. This example illustrates the impact that a person's environment may have on the development of physical disease. Researchers believe the same holds true for mental illnesses. For example, researchers know that patients with schizophrenia who return to a family environment in which there is a high level of expressed emotion, such as critical and angry remarks, have more frequent psychotic episodes that require **hospitalization**. Thus, it appears that the interaction between the biological and psychological dimensions of a person and his or her environment determines the likelihood of expressing a mental illness, or perhaps any illness whatsoever. There is, however, no accurate prediction or test that will determine whether a specific person will develop a certain mental illness, even if many members of his or her family are positive for that disease.

Conversely, a child with minimal genetic predisposition to mental illness may develop mental illness if he or she is traumatized in any number of ways, such as being raised in a non-nurturing or a physically, mentally, or emotionally abusive household. As of now, scientists do not know why some people become mentally ill while others do not. Much research remains to be done; although theories abound, the precise etiology or origin of all mental illnesses remains uncertain.

CARL JUNG (1875–1961)

Carl Gustav Jung was born in Kesswil, Switzerland, on July 26, 1875, to a Protestant clergyman who moved his family to Basel when Jung was four. While growing up, Jung exhibited an interest in many diverse areas of study but finally decided to pursue medicine at the University of Basel and the University of Zurich, earning his degree in 1902. He also studied psychology in Paris. In 1903, Jung married Emma Rauschenbach, his companion and collaborator. The couple had five children.

Jung's professional career began in 1900 at the University of Zurich, where he worked as an assistant to Eugene Blueler in the psychiatric clinic. During his internship, he and some co-workers used an experiment that revealed groups of ideas in the unconscious psyche, which he named "complexes." Jung sent his publication *Studies in Word Association* (1904) to Sigmund Freud after finding his own beliefs confirmed by Freud's work. Jung and Freud became friends and collaborators until 1913, when Jung's ideas began to conflict with Freud's. During the time following this split, Jung published *Two Essays on Analytical Psychology* (1916, 1917) and *Psychological Types* (1921). Jung's later work developed from the concepts in his *Two Essays* publication, and he became known as a founder of modern depth psychology.

In 1944, Jung gave up his psychological practice and his explorations after he suffered a severe heart attack. Jung received honorary doctorates from numerous universities, and in 1948 he founded the C. G. Jung Institute in Zurich. He became a controversial figure in his later years because of his association with Nazi sympathizers, his interest in such subjects as alchemy and flying saucers (he wrote a book about the latter in 1959), and revelations of his extramarital affairs with several of his patients. Jung died on June 6, 1961.

Current theories about the origin of mental disorders

Biological theories

GENETIC FACTORS. Genetics is, at this time, an important area of research for psychiatric disorders. For example, a specific gene has been associated with **bipolar disorder** (also known as "manic-depressive disorder"), but unfortunately, the switch that controls the

expression of the disorder is still unknown. It is currently thought that many genes go into the expression or non-expression of any human characteristic, such as a facial feature or a certain aspect of mental health. Research done on identical twins has provided strong support for a genetic component in the development of schizophrenia. For instance, the average person in the United States has a 1% chance of developing schizophrenia, while the identical twin of a person diagnosed with schizophrenia has a 50% chance, even if he or she has been reared by adoptive parents. Other researchers who are studying schizophrenia have found that during embryonic development, there are nerve cells that do not migrate to their proper position in the brain. On the other hand, none of the genetic or embryological findings can account for the rare, but occasional, recoveries from schizophrenia, indicating that biology alone does not determine the occurrence of mental disorders.

Dementias are also noted to run in families, but most of these disorders cannot be predicted with any certainty for the following generation. Only one dementing disorder, Huntington's chorea, which is really a movement disorder with a psychiatric component, appears to be determined by a single gene. **Dementia** of the Alzheimer's type does seem to have a familial pattern, but again, the expression of the disease in any specific individual is not predictable at this time. Scientists believe that similar statements can be made for many mental disorders that run in families, such as **obsessive-compulsive disorder** (OCD), eating disorders, depression, anxiety, and **panic disorder**. The roles of the environment and learning behavior in the ultimate expression of genetically predisposed individuals are, however, undisputed.

EPIGENETICS. **Epigenetics** is a new field of research whose name means "beyond the genome"; it is the study of heritable changes caused by the activation and deactivation of genes without any change in the underlying DNA sequence of the organism. These changes are governed by the epigenome, which is the name given to the group of chemicals in cells that mark or tag the genome (the DNA in the cell) in such a way as to direct its activities.

The epigenome can switch genes on and off in one of two ways. The first way, known as "methylation," involves the attachment of methyl groups (hydrocarbon groups containing one carbon and three hydrogen atoms) to the DNA molecule itself in specific places. Methylation turns genes on and off by affecting the interactions of genes and the proteins they encode. The second process, known as "histone modification," affects DNA indirectly. Histones are proteins that serve as "spools" for winding up the long DNA molecules inside a chromosome. Chemicals in the epigenome can attach themselves to the tails of histones and affect how tightly they "wrap" DNA. Tightly wrapped DNA may result in a gene being silenced, while loosely wrapped DNA may result in the activation of a gene.

While the epigenome can be inherited from parents, it is also flexible over the course of a person's lifetime. Unlike the genome, it can change. The epigenome could be said to represent the intersection between a person's genome and the environment. Diet, emotional **stress**, early life experiences, smoking and drug abuse, prescription medications, environmental pollution, and other factors are known to affect the chemical tags in a person's epigenome. As of 2011, changes in the epigenome had been linked not only to cancer and diabetes, but also to such mental disorders as schizophrenia, substance use disorders, **autism** spectrum disorders, depression, and intellectual disability.

NEUROTRANSMITTER-RELATED CHEMICAL IMBALANCES. This theory of the origin of mental disorders has become the foundation of most psychiatric treatment today. It has legitimated psychiatry by returning it to the world of biological medicine. Diabetes may offer a helpful analogy. In diabetes, a chemical necessary to health (insulin) is missing and can be replaced, essentially restoring the patient's health. In mental illness, the neurotransmitters in the brain may be present in insufficient amounts. These chemicals or transmitters allow communication between nerve cells; as a result, they coordinate information processing throughout the brain. As a person reads, for example, chemical levels rise and fall in response to the letters; the meaning they have; the reader's eye movements, thoughts, reflections and associations; and the feelings the reader may have while reading. Thus, a person's brain chemistry is changed by everything that influences him or her, whether internally or externally. While the discovery of certain neurotransmitters and their roles in mental disorders has led, in turn, to the discovery of effective medications to treat these disorders, it has also resulted in the unfortunate notion that medication is the only method of treatment that is helpful.

Major neurotransmitters identified thus far include acetylcholine, dopamine, epinephrine, norepinephrine, histamine, and serotonin. Serotonin and norepinephrine are most highly implicated in depression, panic disorder and anxiety, as well as OCD. Most of the medications found effective for these disorders are drugs that increase the availability of serotonin and norepinephrine (such as the selective serotonin re-uptake inhibitors, or **SSRIs**). In particular, depression, panic disorder, **anxiety disorders**, and OCD have responded strongly to medications that increase serotonin levels. However, not all people with these disorders respond well to the medications, or they may need a combination of medications and **psychotherapy** to be effectively treated. Medications that block the effects of dopamine in certain parts of the brain are effective in controlling auditory and visual hallucinations as well as paranoia in patients with psychotic disorders.

STRESS-RELATED FACTORS. Stress is something everyone in modern society seems to understand. There are two basic kinds of stress: inner stress from previous traumas or wounds that affect one's present life; and outer stress, or the environmental issues that complicate life on a daily basis, such as work or family problems. The interplay of these two forms of stress affects brain chemistry just as it can affect physical health. Numerous studies have shown that when people are chronically stressed in life, they are vulnerable to depression, anxiety, and other disorders. Seventy percent of the adults in one recent European war situation were found to have depression, which is a normal human response to relentless stress. Researchers currently think that the mechanism that triggers this depression is the depletion of certain neurotransmitters, particularly serotonin and norepinephrine, which may lead to other biochemical imbalances. For instance, most people diagnosed with schizophrenia have their first psychotic episode during such stressful situations as leaving home for college or military service.

Genetic factors may add to a person's susceptibility to mental illness by lowering the body's production of neurotransmitters during difficult life transitions. The same combination of circumstances might affect the development of high blood pressure, diabetes, or ulcers in some families.

GENERAL MEDICAL CONDITIONS. It is important to note that bacterial and viral infections, metabolic illnesses, medications and street drugs can all affect a person's mental status. Insults (injuries) to the brain can cause a person to be disoriented, speak incoherently, have difficulty concentrating, hallucinate, or even act out violently. When clinicians see disorientation and an abrupt change in a person's level of alertness, they refer to the altered mental state as "delirium." **Delirium** is considered a medical emergency because the underlying cause must be identified and treated as quickly as possible. The exact way in which infectious disease and chemical agents change human mental function is unclear and thus might not be visible on **imaging studies**.

The elderly are particularly vulnerable to changes in mental status resulting from apparently minor changes in body chemistry. Fever, dehydration, electrolyte imbalances, and even aspirin or antibiotics can all have an abrupt effect on the mental status of the elderly. Older people are susceptible simply because older brain tissue is more sensitive to the slightest change in metabolism or the presence of toxins.

Certain infectious diseases have severe effects on the brain. One example is HIV/AIDS, in which approximately 70% of patients suffering from full-blown AIDS develop dementia, depression, or delirium. Another sexually transmitted disease (STD) that can end in dementia if untreated is syphilis. Late-stage syphilis, sometimes called "neurosyphilis," might not appear until 4 to 25 years after the initial infection; treatment can halt the progress of the disease at that point but cannot undo damage to the nervous system that has already occurred.

Similarly, at least 50% of patients with multiple sclerosis develop depression from the effects of the disease on brain tissues, not simply as a reaction to knowing that they have MS. Any infectious disease that causes inflammation inside the skull, such as meningitis or encephalitis, will usually result in some change in mental status; fortunately, these changes are usually completely reversible. Other infectious diseases that have been linked to depression and other mental disorders include Lyme disease, toxoplasmosis, and tuberculosis.

Another group of infectious diseases that cause changes in mental status (dementia and eventual death) are the prion diseases, also known as "transmissible spongiform encephalopathies" (TSEs) because of the sponge-like holes they leave in infected brains. Prions are infectious agents that consist of protein in a misfolded form. Prions are distinct from all other infectious materials in that they do not contain any genetic material. Some prion diseases are transmissible among humans or from compatible animal species to humans. These prion diseases, which include kuru and mad cow disease, are classified as zoonoses. Other prion diseases, such as some cases of Creutzfeldt-Jakob disease (CJD), fatal familial **insomnia** (FFI), and Gerstmann-Sträussler-Scheinker disease (GSS), can be inherited; they are caused by a mutation in the *PRNP* gene. Still other cases of prion diseases are sporadic; CJD and FFI sometimes occur in people with no known history of the disease in their family and with no known exposure to infectious materials.

One controversial possible connection between infectious disease and OCD is exemplified by "PANDAS," the acronym for Pediatric Autoimmune Neuropsychiatric Disorder Associated with Group A Streptococcus. Group A streptococcus is an autoimmune disorder thought to cause OCD symptoms (neuropsychiatric symptoms) in children with streptococcal infection of the tonsils and pharynx (more commonly known as strep throat). The neuropsychiatric symptoms are believed to result from an autoimmune reaction, meaning that antibodies made to fight the bacteria mistakenly attack part of the brain, resulting in symptoms of OCD. As of 2011, however, PANDAS had not been validated as a **diagnosis**. The usefulness of the diagnosis has been disputed by some researchers who maintain that this subset of patients does not differ significantly from the remainder of the pediatric population, and that streptococcal infections do not increase the risk of OCD. A study published in early 2011 reported that there was no evidence for a temporal connection between Group A streptococcal infections and **tic disorders** or OCD in children who meet the published PANDAS diagnostic criteria.

Disorders of metabolism can certainly mimic depression, anxiety, and, sometimes, even psychosis. Overproduction of thyroid hormone (thyrotoxicosis) can cause agitation, anxiety, mania and even psychosis; while a lack of thyroid hormone produces symptoms of depression and is routinely checked in patients with depression of recent onset. Imbalances in glucose (sugar) management can result in mood swings and should always be evaluated. Less commonly, malfunctions of the adrenal glands can profoundly affect a person's energy level and mental activity. The role of estrogen in postmenopausal depression has been intensively studied in recent years, but the findings remain inconclusive.

NEUROPATHOLOGY. Neuropathology refers to damage to the brain tissue itself that results in mental illness. The dementias are placed in this category, since the brains of persons diagnosed with dementia exhibit microscopic changes in tissue structure when viewed under a microscope. These changes may ultimately appear on tests such as a CAT scan of the brain. Larger changes are seen with strokes, which result when the blood supply is cut off to a specific area of the brain and causes localized damage. In these instances, a person may have altered speech patterns but retain the ability to think clearly, or vice versa. The losses are somewhat predictable and specific, based on the area of the brain that was affected and the extent of oxygen starvation of the tissue in that region.

Brain tumors and accidental injuries to the head are random in their effects, and the deficits are usually less predictable. Each case must be examined individually. As with strokes, however, the location of the injury or tumor will determine the resulting mental status changes or deficits. Patients suffering **traumatic**

Sigmund Freud (left) with Carl Jung (right). (© *Mary Evans Picture Library/Alamy*)

brain injury (TBI), whether the head wound is closed or penetrating, are at increased risk of mood disorders, personality changes, **substance abuse** disorders, dementia, and psychotic disorders if they survive the accident or criminal attack that caused the wound. The most common causes of TBI in the United States as of 2011 were motor vehicle accidents, falls, and contact sports.

Pancreatic and certain colon cancers are particularly interesting for psychiatrists. These tumors are frequently accompanied by depression even though they are located in organs that are far removed from the brain. Long-term studies of cancer survivors have reported high rates of depression and anxiety as well as cognitive limitations in these persons even though they have been cured of their cancers. More research is needed on the relationship between mood disorders and certain illnesses; it is possible that the tumor releases, into the bloodstream, compounds that have depressive effects or that depression results from the psychological issues of dealing with a serious medical illness.

NUTRITIONAL FACTORS. There is no doubt that poor **nutrition** leads to mental imbalances. While few people in the United States are truly starving or completely depleted nutritionally, instances of mental disorders related to malnutrition still occur in this country. The B vitamins are essential for mental clarity and stability. Insufficient amounts of the B vitamins, which include thiamin, nicotinamide, pyridoxine, and B, can result in confusion, irritability, insomnia, depression, and, in extreme cases, psychosis. The body does not store these vitamins, so persons should monitor their daily intake to ensure a sufficient supply. Tryptophan is an amino acid and supplement that is a building block for serotonin, the neurotransmitter that has been found to be essential in treating depression, anxiety, panic, and OCD, among others. Tryptophan is so important nutritionally that studies have shown that its absence in the diet will result in depression even when the person is taking a prescription antidepressant to increase the availability of serotonin.

Psychological/interpersonal theories

PSYCHODYNAMIC THEORIES. Freud certainly opened the doors for humans to understand themselves in terms of psychology, or the notion that how one thinks and feels affects one's view of the world. He also found that simple conversation could help some very sick people out of depressions and other mental disorders. His work essentially demonstrated that extreme inner conflicts can become a source of mental illness. These extreme internal conflicts can occur, for instance, when one loves another deeply but also feels that that person is hurting them or limiting their development in some way. If the person who is causing pain or hindering growth is a parent or other powerful figure, these intense feelings can be hidden away or repressed. Also, a lack of honesty about reality can lead to any number of illnesses. For instance, feelings of anger and powerlessness, if unrecognized, may place the person at risk for developing aggressive behaviors or depression if insights and appropriate coping skills are not gained. These psychological disharmonies, if ignored, can lead to disease if they are sufficiently intense or associated with central relationships in the person's life.

Freud's view of psychological conflicts as rooted in sexual repression was questioned by Jung, a **psychiatrist** and protégé of Freud, who believed that people's lives are affected by deep spiritual forces that he called "archetypes." Jung's work centered on psychological imbalances stemming from spiritual distress. There were other theorists after Freud, such as Alfred Adler, who regarded power as the central motivating force of human personality, or Melanie Klein, who emphasized the significance of envy.

Following the Second World War, behavioral and cognitive theories have emphasized the role of learning in the development of mental disorders. Children growing up in an abusive home, for example, may be "rewarded" by not being beaten if they learn to be quiet and internalize everything. This internalized state may be a precursor of full-blown depression in later years. Unconscious assumptions based on early experiences may spill over into other situations later in life. As another example, children may learn to be "good" for their parents or society by taking on careers they don't like or belief systems that don't fit them, all for approval by the perceived higher authority.

Cognitive approaches to therapy maintain that people construct their view of the world from beliefs and feelings based on deeper assumptions about their own competencies. Depression, for instance, would be seen as a spiral downward into negative self-talk and feelings of inadequacy. Re-examining these negative assumptions then breaks the cycle based on erroneous thinking (cognition) that is causing the depression, anxiety, or aberrant behavior. Studies have shown that three months of cognitive therapy are as effective as medication in the treatment of depression. This finding clearly shows that talk therapy does change the chemistry of the brain.

TRAUMA-RELATED FACTORS. Psychological traumas are events that are outside the experience of everyday life, although the exact definition of a traumatic experience may vary from person to person, country to country, and century to century. Traumas in early life, such as sexual or physical abuse, can lead to mood disorders and contribute to the development of **personality disorders**. Horrendous early traumas involving torture of a child, other people, or animals, may result in **dissociative identity disorder**, formerly called "multiple personality disorder." Dissociation is a self-protective mechanism for separating conscious awareness from repeated traumas. It has sometimes been described as self-hypnosis, but most clinicians believe that it is not under the patient's control, at least initially.

In later life, such severe traumas as war, rape, natural disasters, or any similar event can lead to psychiatric difficulties. **Post-traumatic stress disorder** (PTSD) is a well-known condition that affects war veterans. Extreme **trauma** causes the brain to record impressions in a way that is different from ordinary formation of memories. These disjointed impressions may re-emerge as flashbacks months or years after the traumatic experience. Chronic and repetitive trauma, exemplified by intermittent abuse or hostage situations, can lead to a chronic form of PTSD as well.

One subcategory of psychiatric disorders that occur in response to traumatic shock is termed "fugue states." Fugue states are poorly understood but can be described as conditions of total memory loss after witnessing an overwhelmingly horrible accident or atrocity. These states of memory loss can last from minutes to years.

SOCIOCULTURAL FACTORS. Some mental disorders are influenced by social values and social interactions shaped by those values. **Anorexia nervosa**, bulimia, and **body dysmorphic disorder** are the most commonly used examples of mental illnesses in this category. With the increased visibility of unnaturally slender women in modern society (as seen everywhere in advertising, television shows, movies, and celebrity fan magazines), doctors have seen a tremendous rise in the occurrence eating disorders. "You can never be too thin or too rich," a saying attributed to the Duchess of Windsor, is a phrase that has many women, and some men, monitoring their every ounce of food intake. The core of the illness is a lack of self-esteem combined with feelings that one's world is out of control. Some clinicians add fear of sexual maturation to this list of psychological causes of eating disorders. The common denominator is that these patients apparently believe they can control their world by controlling their food intake. Although neurotransmitter deficits have been found in patients with bulimia, whose vomiting may actually change their body chemistry, the desire to be thin is the conscious motivating force.

Modern society also values activity over rest, doing over being, thinking over feeling, resulting in many people becoming slaves to work and productivity, and having little respect for their inner life. Many cases of mild stress-related disorders run the risk of developing into full-blown generalized anxiety, panic, and depressive disorders. Mental health requires a reasonable balance between work and activity on the one hand and periods of rest and relaxation on the other.

ALCOHOL AND SUBSTANCE ABUSE. Alcohol is a central nervous system depressant. It plays a prominent role in the development of (at least) depression and is often involved in other mental disorders. In addition, persons who abuse alcohol are at increased risk of mental disorders related to nutritional deficiencies. A lack of thiamin, a B-vitamin, can result in permanent brain damage in the form of severe dementia even at an early age. Persons undergoing withdrawal from alcohol are also at risk for delirium tremens, a serious condition that can result in cardiovascular shock and death.

Street drugs are well known for their effects on young people's mood and behavior. Permanent brain damage may result from the use of some so-called designer drugs. One example is **Ecstasy**, which can cause permanent memory loss and severe depression that responds only slowly to treatment. Street drugs must always be considered as a possible factor in the sudden

KEY TERMS

Biopsychosocial model—An approach to human health that holds that a combination of biological, psychological, and social factors should be taken into account when evaluating a patient rather than physical factors alone.

Dissociation—A condition in which a person's thoughts, emotions, sensations, or memories become compartmentalized, usually as a result of a severe emotional trauma.

Epigenetics—The study of heritable changes in an organism's appearance or gene expression caused by chemical reactions and factors other than changes in the organism's DNA sequences.

Epigenome—The collection of chemical compounds derived from food, medications, and other sources, that mark the genome in ways that affect the DNA in the genome both directly and indirectly.

Genome—The complete set of DNA in a cell.

Histone—A type of protein that serves as a "spool" for wrapping DNA within a chromosome.

Kuru—A prion disease associated with the cannibalism formerly practiced by the Fore people of Papua New Guinea. Its name comes from a word in the Fore language that means "to shake" or "to tremble."

Magnetoencephalography (MEG)—A newer form of brain imaging that captures and records the brain's magnetic fields produced by electrical currents occurring naturally in brain tissue. MEG can identify split-second changes in brain activity.

Methylation—A process in which chemical tags called "methyl groups" (made of one carbon and three hydrogen atoms) attach themselves to a DNA molecule in specific locations, thus affecting the level of a gene's activity.

Neurotransmitter—Any of several chemicals produced in the body that function to convey impulses from nerve cells to target cells.

Prion—An infectious agent consisting of protein in a misfolded form. Its name is a combination of "protein" and "infection."

Sporadic—Occurring at random in persons with no known risk factors or genetic mutations.

Vagus nerve stimulation (VNS)—An experimental treatment for depression that involves implanting a stimulator device which sends electrical impulses at timed intervals to the left vagus nerve.

Zoonosis (plural, zoonoses)—Any disease that can be transmitted from nonhuman animals to humans or from humans to nonhuman animals. Some prion diseases are zoonoses, as are such infectious diseases as toxoplasmosis, Lyme disease, and rabies.

onset of a mental illness in a young person. Moreover, they may precipitate a first psychotic episode in a person with a genetic predisposition to schizophrenia. In this case, the drug is the stressor that reveals the person's dormant susceptibility to the disorder.

Current theory and future directions

The biopsychosocial model of mental illness

All of the above factors are most succinctly summarized in terms of the biopsychosocial model of mental illness. Biological contributions, thoughts and perceptions, social pressures, and environmental stressors, the presence or absence of nurturing and consistency of love, core values, and self-worth, are just a few of the things that contribute to making up the psychological uniqueness of every human being. In addition to the above, researchers are actively examining the role of spirituality in mental health and recovery. No single factor can be said to be the sole cause of mental illness; rather, disorders result from a complex set of forces that act upon each person as an individual. Finding the various elements that contributed to the onset of an illness requires considerable patience from the patient, his or her family, and health professionals. Identifying all factors, if possible, provides the best road map for the healing process.

New directions

In the future, scientists will certainly modify and expand our thought-models about the mind and brain. For example, a new treatment called **transcranial magnetic stimulation** (TMS) is being evaluated as an alternative to electric shock therapy. TMS uses powerful magnets instead of electricity and is delivered to specific areas of the brain. Hence, in the future, scientists must integrate some of the electromagnetic aspects of nature into the mind-brain puzzle. One experimental newer form of TMS is **magnetic seizure therapy** (MST), which resembles TMS in using a magnet to stimulate specific portions of the brain but uses a higher electrical frequency in order to induce a seizure. As of 2011, studies were under way to evaluate the effectiveness of MST as a treatment for depression. Another newer method of direct brain stimulation is **vagus nerve stimulation** (VNS), in which a device implanted under the skin near the shoulder sends electrical impulses to the left vagus nerve, which sends messages to areas in the brain that control sleep and mood. Although the Food and Drug Administration (FDA) approved VNS for the treatment of major depression in 2005, results have been mixed; as of 2011, the treatment was still considered experimental.

New techniques of brain imaging may also lead to a better understanding of the causes of mental illness. **Magnetic resonance imaging** (MRI) has been in use for some years and has led to a range of new specialized forms of MRI that yield new information about the brain's functioning in real time. For example, functional MRI (fMRI) makes use of the different properties of oxygenated and deoxygenated hemoglobin in the blood to produce images of changes in blood flow in the brain associated with neural activity. While fMRI can be used to identify which parts of the brain are activated during performance of certain tasks, it is also extremely sensitive to early signs of **stroke**, thus improving diagnosis of this potentially devastating condition and allowing much earlier treatment. Another new form of brain imaging that is yielding information about the brain's functioning is magnetoencephalography or MEG. MEG maps brain activity by measuring and recording magnetic fields produced by electrical currents occurring naturally in the brain. MEG can capture split-second changes in the brain's functioning. Researchers are currently studying it as a possible tool in the diagnosis of schizophrenia and a way to evaluate the speed of patients' responses to antidepressant medication.

In addition to new forms of neuroimaging, the **National Institute of Mental Health** (NIMH) is researching alternative healing modalities. Prominent among them is **acupuncture**, which has been used to treat depression, anxiety, and panic disorder. Other alternative treatments being studied include the effects of prayer, **meditation**, creative writing, and **yoga**.

Epigenetics offers the potential to evaluate people at risk for certain mental disorders before they occur. For example, the possibility of identifying changes in a person's epigenome resulting from abuse or other forms of trauma in early childhood may lead to strategies to prevent depression in later life, or even to devise treatments that will reverse the chemical changes in the epigenome caused by the abuse. Similarly, changes in the epigenome resulting from drug or alcohol abuse may prove to be reversible, thus opening the way to more effective treatments for **addiction**. Last, the study of the heritability of the chemical tags found on a person's DNA and histones may provide more information about the heritability of mental disorders as well as such diseases as cancer and diabetes.

Deeper exploration of the human condition is both inevitable and desirable. Perhaps researchers will find better answers by asking the question, 'What makes people healthy?' instead of simply looking at what makes us sick. In the end, researchers may find proof of some of the ancient truths taught by spiritual teachers from all traditions, and that the physical changes seen with the naked eye or under a microscope are really just the symptoms, and not the causes, of imbalances.

Resources

BOOKS

American Psychiatric Association. *Diagnostic and Statistical Manual of Mental Disorders.* 4th ed., text rev. Washington, DC: American Psychiatric Association, 2000.

American Psychiatric Association. *Practice Guideline for the Psychiatric Evaluation of Adults,* 2nd ed. Washington, DC: American Psychiatric Association, 2010.

Freeman, Hugh, ed. *A Century of Psychiatry.* St. Louis, MO: Mosby, 1999.

Koch, Jeremias, ed. *Mental Illnesses: Descriptions, Causes, and Treatments.* New York: Nova Science Publishers, 2010.

Susser, Ezra, et al. *Psychiatric Epidemiology: Searching for the Causes of Mental Disorders.* New York: Oxford University Press, 2006.

PERIODICALS

Bale, T.L., et al. "Early Life Programming and Neurodevelopmental Disorders." *Biological Psychiatry* 68 (August 15, 2010): 314–319.

Barak, Y., and D. Aizenberg. "Is Dementia Preventable? Focus on Alzheimer's Disease." *Expert Review of Neurotherapeutics* 10 (November 2010): 1689–1698.

Gannon, P., et al. "Current Understanding of HIV-associated Neurocognitive Disorders Pathogenesis." *Current Opinion in Neurology* 24 (June 2011): 275–283.

Harrington, C.B., et al. "It's Not Over When It's Over: Long-term Symptoms in Cancer Survivors—A Systematic Review." *International Journal of Psychiatry in Medicine* 40 (February 2010): 163–181.

Howland, R.H., et al. "The Emerging Use of Technology for the Treatment of Depression and Other Neuropsychiatric Disorders." *Annals of Clinical Psychiatry* 23 (February 2011): 48–62.

Iwase, S., and Y. Shi. "Histone and DNA Modifications in Mental Retardation." *Progress in Drug Research* 67 (2011): 147–173.

Leckman, J.F., et al. "Streptococcal Upper Respiratory Tract Infections and Exacerbations of Tic and Obsessive-compulsive Symptoms: A Prospective Longitudinal

Study." *Journal of the American Academy of Child and Adolescent Psychiatry* 50 (February 2011): 108–118.

Lee, C.H., et al. "Initially Unrecognized Dementia in a Young Man with Neurosyphilis." *Neurologist* 15 (March 2009): 95–97.

McQuown, S.C., and M.A. Wood. "Epigenetic Regulation in Substance Use Disorders." *Current Psychiatry Reports* 12 (April 2010): 145–153.

Perrin, M., et al. "Critical Periods and the Developmental Origins of Disease: An Epigenetic Perspective of Schizophrenia." *Annals of the New York Academy of Sciences* 1204 (September 2010: Suppl. E8–E13.

Reeves, R.R., and R.L. Panguluri. "Neuropsychiatric Complications of Traumatic Brain Injury." *Journal of Psychosocial Nursing and Mental Health Services* 49 (March 2011): 42–50.

Siekmeier, P.J., and S.M. Stufflebeam. "Patterns of Spontaneous Magnetoencephalographic Activity in Patients with Schizophrenia." *Journal of Clinical Neurophysiology* 27 (June 2010): 179–190.

WEBSITES

Discover Magazine. "The Switches That Can Turn Mental Illness On and Off." http://discovermagazine.com/2010/jun/15-brain-switches-that-can-turn-mental-illness-on-off (accessed June 3, 2011).

National Human Genome Research Institute (NHGRI). "Epigenomics Fact Sheet." http://www.genome.gov/27532724 (accessed June 2, 2011).

National Institute of Mental Health (NIMH). "Brain Basics." http://www.nimh.nih.gov/health/brain-basics/brain-basics.shtml (accessed June 2, 2011).

National Institute of Mental Health (NIMH). "Brain Stimulation Therapies." http://www.nimh.nih.gov/health/topics/brain-stimulation-therapies/brain-stimulation-therapies.shtml (accessed June 2, 2011).

National Institute of Neurological Disorders and Stroke (NINDS). "Traumatic Brain Injury Information Page." http://www.ninds.nih.gov/disorders/tbi/tbi.htm (accessed June 3, 2011).

PBS Nova. "Epigenetics." (13-minute video at link). http://www.pbs.org/wgbh/nova/body/epigenetics.html (accessed May 31, 2011).

University of Utah Genetic Science Learning Center. "Epigenetics and the Human Brain." http://learn.genetics.utah.edu/content/epigenetics/brain (accessed May 31, 2011).

WebMD. "Causes of Mental Illness." http://www.webmd.com/anxiety-panic/mental-health-causes-mental-illness (accessed June 2, 2011).

ORGANIZATIONS

American Psychiatric Association (APA), 1000 Wilson Boulevard, Suite 1825, Arlington, VA, 22209-3901, (703) 907-7300, apa@psych.org, http://www.psych.org

National Human Genome Research Institute (NHGRI), Building 31, Room 4B09, 31 Center Drive, MSC 2152, 9000 Rockville Pike, Bethesda, MD, 20892-2152, (301) 402-0911, Fax: (301) 402-2218, http://www.genome.gov

National Institute of Mental Health (NIMH), 6001 Executive Boulevard, Room 8184, MSC 9663, Bethesda, MD, 20892-9663, (301) 443-4513, Fax: (301) 443-4279, (866) 615-6464, nimhinfo@nih.gov, http://www.nimh.nih.gov/index.shtml

National Institute of Neurological Disorders and Stroke (NINDS), PO Box 5801, Bethesda, MD, 20824, (301) 496-5751, (800) 352-9424, http://www.ninds.nih.gov

Beth A. Bollinger, M.D.
Rebecca J. Frey, Ph.D.

Oxazepam

Definition

Oxazepam is a member of a family of tranquilizers known as **benzodiazepines**. It is sold in the United States under the brand name Serax and in Canada under the brand name Ox-Pam. Generic forms of oxazepam are also available.

Purpose

Oxazepam is prescribed to treat feelings of tension and anxiety. It is also used to calm patients who are suffering from the symptoms of alcohol withdrawal.

Description

Oxazepam slows down certain **brain** functions by blocking specific chemicals that transmit messages among the nerve cells in the brain.

Recommended dosage

The typical starting dose for adults ranges from 5–15 mg per day. The dosage is sometimes increased by

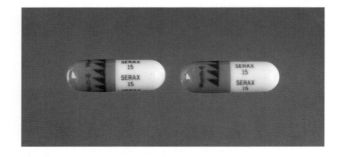

Serax (oxazepam), 15 mg. *(U.S. Drug Enforcement Administration)*

the doctor, but 80 mg is usually the maximum amount prescribed per day. The amount used each day is typically divided into at least two doses. Oxazepam is taken by mouth and is available in tablets and capsules. It can be taken with food if the patient is having side effects in the digestive tract.

Oxazepam is not FDA-approved for use in children under six years. However, in clinical practice, the medication is often used with close physician supervision. The typical starting dose for children aged 2–16 years is 5 mg. The doctor may increase this dose if necessary. Typically, the dose does not exceed 40 mg per day and is given in divided doses. Children under two years of age should receive a dose based on body weight. The doctor must determine whether the child needs the drug, as well as the dosage.

Precautions

The doctor should monitor the patient at regular intervals to ensure that the medicine is not causing troublesome side effects. Monitoring the patient is particularly important if the drug is being taken over a long period of time. Patients should not stop taking oxazepam suddenly, especially if they are taking large doses. The dose should be tapered (gradually decreased), and then stopped. Suddenly discontinuing oxazepam may cause a rebound effect. In a few cases, patients have reported serious withdrawal symptoms when they stopped taking oxazepam, including nausea, vomiting, muscle cramps, and unusual irritability.

Oxazepam should be given with great care to elderly patients; people who are significantly disabled; and people with a history of liver or kidney disease, drug abuse, or breathing problems. Pregnant women should not take oxazepam because of the risk of birth defects in the baby; a woman who becomes pregnant while she is taking the drug should tell her doctor at once. Likewise, nursing mothers should not use oxazepam while they breast feed. Oxazepam and other benzodiazepines should never be combined with alcohol or other drugs that depress (lower the activity of) the central nervous system. Oxazepam and other benzodiazepines may be habit forming and should be used under physician supervision, especially for long-term treatment. Patients who have a history of alcohol abuse, drug abuse, brain disease, mental **depression**, mental illness, sleep apnea, or myasthenia gravis should tell their doctor about their condition. Patients who have been diagnosed with glaucoma or serious psychological disorders should not receive oxazepam. Oxazepam has been associated with the risk of developing anterograde **amnesia**.

KEY TERMS

Anterograde amnesia—The inability to form new memories.

Benzodiazepines—A class of drugs that have a hypnotic and sedative action, used mainly as tranquilizers to control symptoms of anxiety.

Side effects

Rare, but serious, side effects associated with the use of oxazepam include: anxiety, mental depression, reduced memory, and confusion. Even more rare are disorientation, **delusions**, **seizures**, unusually low blood pressure, sleeping difficulties, muscle weakness, and changes in behavior.

Less serious, but more common, side effects include: difficulty talking, dizziness, clumsiness, and drowsiness. Less common, but not particularly serious, side effects include dry mouth, general weakness, headache, mild abdominal pain, constipation, diarrhea, nausea, and vomiting.

When the patient stops taking oxazepam, nervousness, irritability, and sleeping problems are common withdrawal side effects. Less common withdrawal side effects can include confusion, hearing problems, stomach cramps, increased sweating, mental depression, nausea, and vomiting. Rare withdrawal side effects can include seizures, hallucinations, and paranoid ideas.

Interactions

Patients should always inform every health professional that they deal with—doctors, pharmacists, nurses, dentists, and others—about every medication they take. Oxazepam, alcohol, and other medications that cause drowsiness can intensify one another's effects. Some medications that are used to treat viral infections, fungal infections, high blood pressure, and some heart-rhythm problems can increase the effects of oxazepam.

Heavy smoking decreases the effectiveness of oxazepam.

Resources

BOOKS

Brunton, Laurence, Bruce Chabner, and Bjorn Knollman. *Goodman & Gilman's The Pharmacological Basis of Therapeutics* 12th ed. New York: McGraw-Hill, 2010.

Consumer Reports and American Society of Health-System Pharmacists *Consumer Reports Complete Drug Reference.* Yonkers, NY: Consumers Reports, 2009.

Ellsworth, Allan J., et al. *Mosby's Medical Drug Reference.* St. Louis: Mosby, 2007.

Venes, Donald. *Taber's Cyclopedic Medical Dictionary.* 21st ed. Philadelphia: F.A. Davis Company, 2009.

Mark Mitchell, M.D.

Oxcarbazepine

Definition

Oxcarbazepine (Trileptal) belongs to the class of drugs known as anticonvulsants, used to treat seizure disorders. Oxcarbazepine, like other anticonvulsants, works to decrease abnormal neuronal electrical signaling in the **brain**.

Purpose

Oxcarbazepine is used to treat partial **seizures**, which arise from discrete portions of the brain and may cause involuntary movements of a discrete body part such as the fingers. When consciousness is maintained, the seizure is known as a simple partial seizure. When consciousness is lost, the seizure is a complex partial seizure. Oxcarbazepine is used to treat these types of partial seizures in both children and adults. It may be used as monotherapy or in combination with other antiseizure medications.

Description

Oxcarbazepine is an anticonvulsant medication that works by stabilizing abnormal electrical activity in the brain. Brain cells called neurons use electrical signals to

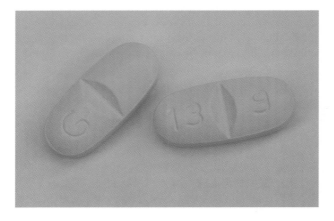

Oxcarbazepine, 60 mg. (© *Custom Medical Stock Photo, Inc. Reproduced by permission.*)

communicate with each other as a part of normal functioning. The electrical signals are created through the use of charged molecules called ions, such as sodium and chloride. The surfaces of neurons contain openings that conduct these ions called ion channels. Neurons propagate electrical signals by opening and closing ion channels on their respective surfaces as the signal travels from one neuron to the next. Seizure disorders are not fully understood, but they are known to involve abnormal electrical signaling between neurons. Anticonvulsants help control seizures by stabilizing both the rate and the amount of signaling that occurs. Oxcarbazepine helps by decreasing the amount of sodium signaling and sodium signal propagation that occurs.

Recommended dosage

Oxcarbazepine is taken as an oral medication. The dosage used varies depending on the medical condition being treated, individual patient response to the medication regarding its effectiveness, and individual patient response to the medication regarding side effects. Some people naturally require a higher dose of oxcarbazepine in order to achieve the desired effect. Other patients require a lower dose either for effect or because they quickly develop side effects that are not tolerable.

Oxcarbazepine used for partial seizures as an adjunct treatment in combination with other anticonvulsants is usually dosed at 600 mg taken twice a day. Patients may start at 300 mg twice daily for the first week of treatment and gradually work their way up to the dose needed for effect. Oxcarbazepine used as monotherapy is started at the same low doses and gradually brought up to 1,200 mg twice a day over a time period of several weeks. Any previous adjunct medications are gradually decreased simultaneously. The maximum dose of oxcarbazepine used is 2,400 mg per day. Children are given lower doses based on their weight, with the same regimen of gradually increasing dosages. Patients are dosed at the lowest possible effective dose to avoid the development of adverse side effects. Slowly increasing the dose helps with minimizing side effects, and some side effects become lessened with continued use. Patients are periodically reassessed to determine whether there is need for continued treatment with oxcarbazepine. All anticonvulsants including oxcarbazepine need to be slowly tapered off if discontinued, to avoid a rebound seizure syndrome.

Precautions

Oxcarbazepine may not be appropriate for use or may require caution in patients with **dementia, depression**, past **suicide** attempts, kidney dysfunction, patients

KEY TERMS

Ion—Charged molecule such as sodium or chloride used in neuronal signaling in the brain.

Ion channel—Physical opening on the surface of neurons that allows the passage of charged ions propagating neuronal signaling in the brain.

Monoamine oxidase inhibitors (MAOIs)—Type of antidepressant medication that affects various kinds of neurotransmitters.

who are dehydrated, have diarrhea or electrolyte abnormalities, and those who are elderly. Kidney and liver function, as well as blood electrolytes and behavioral changes, may be monitored while taking oxcarbazepine. Oxcarbazepine may reduce the amount of sodium in the blood to dangerous levels. When a patient discontinues the use of oxcarbazepine, the dose needs to be tapered down slowly. If oxcarbazepine is abruptly discontinued without tapering, there may be an increase in the incidence of seizures.

Oxcarbazepine may lower the effectiveness of birth control pills; persons taking oral contraceptives should use a second form of protection when taking oxcarbazepine. Oxcarbazepine is classified as category C for pregnancy, which means that either there are no adequate human or animal studies or that adverse fetal effects were found in animal studies but there is no available human data. The decision to use category C drugs in pregnancy is generally based on weighing the critical needs of the mother against the risk to the fetus. Other lower category agents are used whenever possible. Oxcarbazepine is also excreted into breast milk; the safety of use when breast-feeding is unknown and thus is not recommended.

Side effects

Sensitivity to oxcarbazepine varies among patients, and some patients may find lower doses are more than their body system can tolerate. Common side effects of oxcarbazepine include nausea, vomiting, abdominal pain, headache, dizziness, **fatigue**, somnolence, confusion, nervousness, impaired concentration, speech, and coordination, vision and gait changes, tremor, electrolyte abnormalities, changes in liver enzymes, skin rash and acne, hair loss, and sensitivity to sunlight. Rare but serious potential side effects include severe and possibly dangerous electrolyte abnormalities; changes in various types of blood cells, including decrease in immune function and severe anemia; toxic and life-threatening skin

QUESTIONS TO ASK YOUR DOCTOR

- Can I take the full dose right away or do I need to slowly increase the dose up to the full amount?
- Can I stop taking the medication right away or do I need to slowly decrease the dose in order to go off the medication?
- Should I eat before taking this medication?
- Will this medication interact with any of my other prescription medications? Over-the-counter drugs? Herbal supplements?
- What side effects should I watch for that tell me I have taken too much of this medication?
- Can I drink alcoholic beverages when taking this medication?

reactions, severe allergic reactions, inflammation of the pancreas, and suicidality.

Interactions

Patients should make their doctor aware of all medications and supplements they are taking before using oxcarbazepine. Using alcohol while taking oxcarbazepine may create toxic reactions in the body and should be avoided. Drugs that affect the liver may alter the metabolism of oxcarbazepine, resulting in too much or too little of the drug in the body. This could lead to increased side effects or even toxic doses. Likewise, oxcarbazepine may affect the metabolism of other drugs, leading to greater or lower doses of those drugs than therapeutically desired. For example, oxcarbazepine may lower levels of antiviral medications such as rilpivirine; other drugs on which oxcarbazepine has this effect are cholesterol medications such as atorvastatin, oral contraceptives, antibiotics such as clarithromycin, and chemotherapeutics such as temsirolimus.

Oxcarbazepine should not be used at the same time as **monoamine oxidase inhibitors (MAOIs)**, a class of antidepressant drugs Use of these medications during the same period may cause a medical condition called **serotonin syndrome**, which can be severe and life-threatening. Symptoms may include high blood pressure, high fever, nausea, diarrhea, headache, sweating, increased heart rate, tremor, muscle twitching, **delirium**, shock, coma, and death. Switching between drug treatment with an MAOI to oxcarbazepine may require a waiting period of up to several weeks between drugs. Other drugs that cannot be combined with oxcarbazepine due to risk of **serotonin** syndrome include the antibiotic linezolid. Oxcarbazepine should not be used with large doses of the herbal supplements ginkgo biloba or **St. John's wort**, as the combination may decrease the efficacy of oxcarbazepine and induce seizures. The herbal supplements evening primrose, **valerian**, and **kava kava** should also be avoided and may induce seizures.

Resources

BOOKS

Brunton, Laurence, et al. *Goodman and Gilman's the Pharmacological Basis of Therapeutics*. 12th ed. New York: McGraw Hill Medical, 2011.

WEBSITES

PubMed Health. "Oxcarbazepine." U.S. National Library of Medicine. http://www.ncbi.nlm.nih.gov/pubmedhealth/PMH0000176 (accessed November 8, 2011).

ORGANIZATIONS

American Association for Clinical Chemistry, 1850 K St. NW, Ste. 625, Washington, DC, 20006, Fax: (202) 887-5093, (800) 892-1400, http://www.aacc.org.

American Society for Clinical Pharmacology and Therapeutics, 528 N Washington St., Alexandria, VA, 22314, (703) 836-6981, info@ascpt.org, http://www.ascpt.org.

U.S. Food and Drug Administration, 10903 New Hampshire Ave., Silver Spring, MD, 20993-0002, (888) INFO-FDA (463-6332), http://www.fda.gov.

Maria Eve Basile, PhD

P

Pain disorder

Definition

Pain disorder is one of several **somatoform disorders** described in the revised fourth edition of the mental health professional's handbook, the *Diagnostic and Statistical Manual of Mental Disorders* (*DSM-IV-TR*). The term *somatoform* means that symptoms are physical but are not entirely understood as a consequence of a general medical condition or as a direct effect of a substance, such as a drug. Pain in one or more anatomical sites is the predominant complaint and is severe enough to require medical or therapeutic **intervention**. Pain disorder is classified as a mental disorder because psychological factors play an important role in the onset, severity, worsening, or maintenance of pain.

Demographics

There is very little information regarding rates of pain disorder. A major difficulty is that the diagnostic categories for psychogenic pain disorder in *DSM-III*, somatoform pain disorder in *DSM-III-R*, and pain disorder in *DSM-IV* and *DSM-IV-TR* are not equivalent. Further, many criticize the somatoform disorder group (which includes pain disorder) as being an aggregate of disorders that are not truly distinct from one another. This lack of distinctiveness suggests to some researchers that a more appropriate system of classification should be dimensional rather than categorical. If shared dimensions or characteristics of the several somatoform disorders exist, differences among disorders should be a matter of degree along the possible dimensions, similar to spectrum disorders. The critics of the *DSM* categorical approach would prefer a dimensional or multiaxial system, because when classification systems are improved, the reliability and validity of measures assessing disorders also improve, making better prevalence estimates possible.

Description

In 1994, the International Association for the Study of Pain (IASP) defined pain as an unpleasant sensory or emotional experience arising from real or probable tissue damage. The perception of pain is, in part, a psychological response to noxious stimuli. This definition addresses the complex nature of pain and moves away from the earlier dualistic idea that pain is either psychogenic (of mental origin) or somatogenic (of physical origin). The contemporary view characterizes pain as multidimensional, meaning that the central nervous system, emotions, cognitions (thoughts), and beliefs are simultaneously involved.

When a patient's primary complaint is the experience of pain, and when impairment at home, work, or school causes significant distress, a **diagnosis** of pain disorder may be warranted. The diagnosis is further differentiated by a subtype, which is assigned depending on whether or not the pain is primarily accounted for by psychological factors or in combination with a general medical condition, and whether the pain is acute (less than six months) or chronic (six months or more). The classification of pain states is important since the effectiveness of treatment depends on the aptness of the diagnosis of pain disorder and its type.

DSM-5

Earlier names for this disorder include psychogenic pain disorder and somatoform pain disorder. There is some overlap in the meaning of these terms, but views regarding the nature of pain have been changing and they are, therefore, not equivalent diagnostic categories. Sometimes pain disorder is referred to as somatization, but this is an imprecise term and is easily confused with **somatization disorder**. There is a current discussion about recategorizing somatoform or somatization-spectrum disorders, including pain disorder, for the fifth edition of the *DSM* (*DSM-5*, 2013). Proposed changes as of 2011 subsumed pain disorder

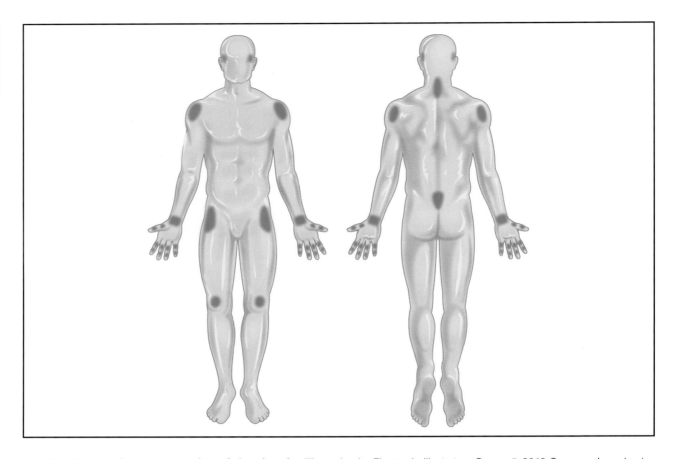

Highlighted areas show common sites of chronic pain. *(Illustration by Electronic Illustrators Group. © 2012 Cengage Learning.)*

into the diagnosis for complex somatic symptom disorder. The reason for the change centers on the complexity of the diagnostic criteria for some of the disorders and the tendency for patients to perceive some of the terms as socially stigmatizing.

Causes and symptoms

Causes

Common sites of pain include the back (especially lower back), head, abdomen, and chest. Causes of pain vary depending on the site; however, in pain disorder, the severity or duration of pain or the degree of associated disability is unexplained by observed medical or psychological problems.

The prevailing biopsychosocial model of mental disorders suggests that multiple causes may be attributed to pain disorder, especially when the pain is chronic. There are four domains of interest when assessing pain:

• The underlying organic problem or medical condition, if there is one. For example, fibromyalgia (a pain syndrome involving fibromuscular tissue), skeletal damage, pathology of an internal organ, migraine

headache, and peptic ulcer all have characteristic patterns of pain and a particular set of causes.

• The experience of the pain. The severity, duration, and pattern of pain are important determinants of distress. Uncontrolled or inadequately managed pain is a significant stressor.

• Functional impairment and disability. Pain is exacerbated by loss of meaningful activities or social relationships. Disruption or loss may lead to isolation and resentment or anger, which further increases pain.

• Emotional distress. Depression and anxiety are the most common correlates of pain, especially when the person suffering feels that the pain is unmanageable, or that the future only holds more severe pain and more losses.

A therapist or team of health professionals will weigh the relative causal contributions, assign priorities for therapeutic intervention, and address the several domains in a multimodal fashion. For example, the design of a treatment plan in a pain clinic may involve a physician, psychotherapist, occupational therapist, physical therapist, anesthesiologist, **psychologist**, and nutritionist.

Symptoms

Symptoms vary depending on the site of pain and are treated medically. However, there are common symptoms associated with pain disorder, regardless of the site:

- negative or distorted cognition, such as feeling helpless or hopeless with respect to pain and its management
- inactivity, passivity, and/or disability
- increased pain requiring clinical intervention
- insomnia and fatigue
- disrupted social relationships at home, work, or school
- depression and/or anxiety

Diagnosis

A **psychiatrist** or mental health professional arrives at the diagnosis of pain disorder after considering several questions. An important preliminary question is whether the pain is entirely accounted for by a general medical condition. If so, the diagnosis of pain disorder is ruled out; if not, the psychiatrist considers whether the pain is feigned. If the psychiatrist believes the patient is pretending to be in pain, the patient is diagnosed as **malingering** for external rewards, such as mood-altering drugs, or as having a **factitious disorder** that reflects the patient's need to adopt a sick role. Neither malingering nor factitious disorder is in the somatoform group.

The psychiatrist may employ a variety of methods to assess the severity of pain and the contribution of psychological factors to the experience of pain. These include structured interviews (where the questions asked are standardized), open or unstructured interviews, numerical rating scales, visual analog scales (where the patient makes a mark along a line to indicate severity of pain or selects a face to represent the degree of pain), and instruments such as the McGill Pain Questionnaire or the West Haven-Yale Multidimensional Pain Inventory.

There are several conditions that rule out a diagnosis of pain disorder:

- dyspareunia, or painful sexual intercourse
- somatization disorder, characterized by a long history of pain that began prior to age 30 and involves the gastrointestinal, reproductive, and nervous systems
- conversion disorder, which includes motor or sensory dysfunction in addition to pain
- a mood, anxiety, or psychotic disorder, if any one of these more fully accounts for the pain

This last exclusion rests upon a very subjective opinion. Subjectivity reduces inter-rater reliability and is one of the points raised by critics of the *DSM* category for pain disorder. A final consideration in diagnosing pain disorder is whether the pain is acute or chronic.

Treatment

Depending on whether the pain is acute or chronic, management may involve one or more of the following: pharmacological treatment (medication), **psychotherapy** (individual or group), and family, behavioral, physical, or occupational therapy. If the pain is acute, the primary goal is to relieve the pain. Customary agents include acetaminophen or nonsteroidal anti-inflammatory drugs (NSAIDs). If opioid analgesics are prescribed, they are often combined with NSAIDs so that a lower dose may be used, as **opioids** have strong addictive potential. Psychotherapy is less important for the treatment of acute pain as compared to chronic pain disorder. In comparison, treatment of chronic pain disorder usually requires some sort of psychotherapy in combination with medication.

Antidepressants

Tricyclic **antidepressants** (TCAs) help reduce pain, improve sleep, and strengthen the effects of opioids (such as codeine and oxycodone), as well as treat moderate **depression**. Relief of pain may occur in a few days while lessening of depression may take several weeks. Usually, TCAs for pain are prescribed at doses 33% to 50% lower than when prescribed for depression. TCAs are particularly effective for neuropathic pain, headache, facial pain, fibromyalgia, and arthritis.

Treatment of sleep dysfunction

Pain and depression diminish the restorative quality of sleep. When the cycle of pain, depression, **insomnia**, and **fatigue** is established, it tends to be self-perpetuating. Treatment may include antidepressants, relaxation training, or education regarding good sleep hygiene.

Cognitive-behavioral therapy

Many people who suffer chronic pain experience isolation, distress, frustration, and a loss of confidence regarding their ability to cope; subsequently, they may adopt a passive, helpless style of problem solving. The goal of **cognitive-behavioral therapy** (CBT) is to restore a sense of self-efficacy by educating patients about the pain-and-tension cycle, by teaching them how to actively manage pain and distress, and by informing them about the therapeutic effects of their medications. CBT is time limited, structured, and goal oriented.

KEY TERMS

Acute—Having a sudden onset and lasting a short time.

Biopsychosocial model—A hypothetical explanation for why something occurs that includes biological, psychological, and social causes or correlates.

Chronic—A disease or condition that progresses slowly but persists or reoccurs over time.

Factitious disorder—A disorder in which the physical or psychological symptoms are produced or controlled by the patient.

Inter-rater reliability—The degree to which judgments about a person are consistent among raters or diagnosticians.

Malingering—Pretending to be sick in order to be relieved of an unwanted duty or obtain some other obvious benefit.

Multiaxial—A type of classification system that involves numeric measurement along more than one dimension and is not based on assignment to mutually exclusive categories.

Multimodal—Several types of therapeutic interventions such as heat or ice packs, electrical stimulation, or ultrasound; sometimes refers to a mix of physical and psychological therapies.

Neuropathic—Relating to neural damage.

Pain states—The four-way classification of pain disorder: (1) acute with psychological factors, (2) acute with psychological factors and a general medical condition, (3) chronic with psychological factors, and (4) chronic with psychological factors and a general medical condition.

Somatization—When mental or emotional distress is expressed physically in a way that disrupts body function.

Some tension-reducing techniques include progressive muscle relaxation, visual imagery, hypnosis, and **biofeedback**. Pain diaries are useful for describing daily patterns of pain and for helping the patient identify any activities, emotions, and thoughts that alleviate or worsen pain. Diaries also are useful in evaluating the effectiveness of medication. Patients may be taught pacing techniques or scheduling strategies to restore and maintain meaningful activities.

The cognitive aspect of CBT is based on cognitive-social learning theory. The focus is on helping the patient to restructure his or her ideas about the nature of pain and the possibility of effective self-management. In particular, the patient is taught to identify and then modify negative or distorted thought patterns of helplessness and hopelessness.

Operant conditioning

The principles of operant conditioning are taught to the patient and family members so that activity and non-pain behaviors are reinforced or encouraged. The goal is to eliminate pain behaviors, such as passivity, inactivity, and over-reliance on medication.

Other treatments

Other treatments used in the management of pain include **acupuncture**, transcutaneous electrical nerve stimulation (TENS), trigger point injections, massage, nerve blocks, surgical ablation (removal of a part or pathway), **meditation**, **exercise**, **yoga**, and music and **art therapy**.

Prognosis

The prognosis for total remission of symptoms is good for acute pain disorder but is not as promising for chronic pain disorder. The typical pattern for chronic pain entails occasional flare-ups alternating with periods of low to moderate pain. The prognosis for remission of symptoms is better when patients are able to continue working; unemployment and the attendant isolation, resentment, and inactivity are correlates of a continuing pain disorder. Additionally, if **reinforcement** of pain behavior is in place (for example, financial compensation for continuing disability, an overly solicitous spouse, or abuse of addictive drugs), remission is less likely.

The results of outcome studies comparing pain disorder treatments point to cognitive-behavioral therapy in conjunction with antidepressants as the most continually effective regimen. However, people in chronic pain may respond better to other treatments, and both the patient and the health professional(s) need to work together to find an individualized mix of effective coping strategies.

Prevention

Pain disorder may be prevented by early intervention at the onset of pain or in the early stages of recurring pain. When pain becomes chronic, it is especially important to find help or learn about and implement strategies to manage the distress before inactivity and hopelessness develop. Most patients in pain first contact their primary care physician, who may make a referral to a mental health professional or pain clinic. Many physicians will reassure the patient that a referral for psychological help is not stigmatizing, does not in any way minimize the experience of pain or the medical condition, and does not imply that the physician believes the pain is imaginary. On the contrary, the accepted IASP definition of pain fully recognizes that all pain is, in part, an emotional response to actual damage or to the threat of damage.

Resources

BOOKS

American Psychiatric Association. *Diagnostic and Statistical Manual of Mental Disorders*. 4th ed., text rev. Washington, DC: American Psychiatric Publishing, 2000.

Martin, Ronald L., and Sean H. Yutzy. "Somatoform Disorders." In *Psychiatry*, edited by Allan Tasman, Jerald Kay, and Jeffrey A. Lieberman. 3rd ed. New York: Wiley and Sons, 2008.

Masheb, Robin M., and Robert D. Kerns. "Pain Disorder." In *Effective Brief Therapies: A Clinician's Guide*, edited by Michael Hersen and Maryka Biaggio. San Diego: Academic Press, 2000.

Simon, Gregory E. "Management of Somatoform and Factitious Disorders." In *A Guide to Treatments that Work*, edited by Peter E. Nathan and Jack M. Gorman. New York: Oxford University Press, 1998.

PERIODICALS

King, Steven. "The Classification and Assessment of Pain." *International Review of Psychiatry* 12, no. 2 (2000): 86–90.

Kroenke, Kurt. "Physical Symptom Disorder: A Simpler Diagnostic Category for Somatization-Spectrum Conditions." *Journal of Psychosomatic Research* 60, no. 4 (April 2006): 335–9.

Merskey, Harold. "Pain, Psychogenesis, and Psychiatric Diagnosis." *International Review of Psychiatry* 12, no. 2 (2000): 99–102.

Sunil, Verma, and Rollin M. Gallagher. "Evaluating and Treating Co-morbid Pain and Depression." *International Review of Psychiatry* 12, no. 2 (2000): 103–14.

WEBSITES

MedlinePlus. "Somatoform Pain Disorder." U.S. National Library of Medicine, National Institutes of Health. http://www.nlm.nih.gov/medlineplus/ency/article/000922.htm (accessed October 23, 2011).

ORGANIZATIONS

American Academy of Pain Medicine, 4700 W. Lake, Glenview, IL, 60025, (847) 375-4731, Fax: (847) 375-6477, info@painmed.org, http://www.painmed.org.

American Chronic Pain Association, PO Box 850, Rocklin, CA, 95677, (800) 533-3231, Fax: (916) 632-3208, ACPA@pacbell.net, http://www.theacpa.org.

American Psychiatric Association, 1000 Wilson Blvd., Ste. 1825, Arlington, VA, 22209-3901, (703) 907-7300, apa@psych.org, http://www.psych.org.

Tanja Bekhuis, Ph.D.
Emily Jane Willingham, Ph.D.

Paliperidone

Definition

Paliperidone (sold under the brand name Invega) is a medication used in the treatment of the psychiatric diseases **schizophrenia** and **schizoaffective disorder**. Paliperidone belongs to a class of drugs known as atypical antipsychotics, which specifically act on two natural body chemicals, **serotonin** and **dopamine**. These chemicals are types of **neurotransmitters** involved in normal **brain** function and can affect the **psychosis** and other symptoms of schizophrenia and schizoaffective disorder. Paliperidone acts as a neurotransmitter blocker, inhibiting the effects of serotonin and dopamine.

Purpose

Paliperidone is a type of drug known as an atypical antipsychotic; atypical antipsychotics are thought to have less adverse side effects than older antipsychotic drugs. The decision to use paliperidone alone or in combination with other drugs depends on the particular medical disorder, the response of the patient to the medication, and individual health parameters.

Description

Paliperidone works by inhibiting the absorption of the neurotransmitters serotonin and norepinephrine. Specifically, paliperidone blocks the signaling of these neurotransmitters in the brain by binding their corresponding neurotransmitter receptors. The pathology of schizophrenia is thought to involve the overactivity of neurotransmitter signaling in some areas of the brain and underactivity in others; antipsychotics such as

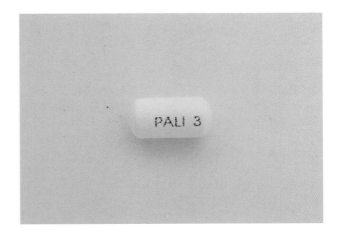

Invega (paliperidone), 3 mg. *(© Custom Medical Stock Photo, Inc. Reproduced by permission.)*

KEY TERMS

Bipolar disorder—Psychiatric mood disorder characterized by periods of manic behavior that may alternate with periods of depression, also known as manic depressive disorder.

Cognitive—Associated with thinking, learning, perception, awareness, and judgment.

Dopamine—A type of neurotransmitter involved in regulation of concentration, impulse control, judgment, mood, attention span, psychostimulation, and disease states such as addiction, and depression.

Insomnia—Disorder involving disturbance of sleep.

Mania—Physiological state of hyperactivity experienced by patients with certain psychiatric illnesses involving inappropriate elevated mood, pressured speech, poor judgment, and sometimes psychotic episodes.

Neuroleptic malignant syndrome—Dangerous reaction to antipsychotic medications that involves temperature instability, muscular rigidity, and altered mental status.

Neuronal signaling—The electrical or chemical pathway by which neurons communicate.

Neurotransmitter—One of a group of chemicals secreted by a nerve cell (neuron) to carry a chemical message to another nerve cell, often as a way of transmitting a nerve impulse. Examples of neurotransmitters include acetylcholine, dopamine, serotonin, and norepinephrine.

Neurotransmitter receptor—A physical recipient for chemicals called neurotransmitters. Receptors sit on the surface of cells that make up body tissues, and once bound to the neurotransmitter, they initiate the chemical signaling pathway associated with neurotransmitters.

Prolactin—Hormone responsible for endocrine function, including lactation.

Psychosis—Loss of contact with reality that may involve false beliefs or hallucinations.

Schizophrenia—Severe psychiatric illness involving the disintegration of thought processes and sometimes including hallucinations.

Serotonin—A type of neurotransmitter involved in regulation of the blood vessels, brain processes, and disease states such as depression.

paliperidone help address the deficits but do not completely treat the disorder. The symptoms of schizophrenia known as **positive symptoms**, such as psychosis, are best treated with paliperidone. The negative and cognitive symptoms such as withdrawal and difficulty reasoning are not as well addressed with paliperidone, but paliperidone has more impact on these types of symptoms than older antipsychotics. Paliperidone is also effective in treating mania, or a mixed state of mood elevation and **depression**.

Recommended dosage

Paliperidone is taken as an oral medication. The available doses are 1.5, 3, 6, and 9 mg pills. The 9 mg dose is an extended release formulation. Patients being treated for schizophrenia are usually started at 6 mg, taken in the morning. The dose is gradually increased to the most effective dose that does not cause intolerable side effects. The daily dose may be increased by 3 mg roughly every 5–7 days. The maximum dose is 12 mg per day. Dosing for schizoaffective disorder is similar. For either disorder, the dose is decreased if the patient has impairment of kidney function or severe liver disease. If side effects develop or if other drugs are to be used in combination with paliperidone, the dose may also be decreased. Side effects impacting the immune system may require a lower dose or complete discontinuation of the drug. Patients are periodically reassessed for the need of treatment.

Precautions

Paliperidone is an atypical antipsychotic medication, a class that was developed for the purpose of avoiding some of the side effects often seen with older, typical antipsychotic medications. As a class, these medications cause fewer **medication-induced movement disorders** than older medications but still have the potential to cause some significant movement-related effects. Patients taking paliperidone must be monitored for the development of **movement disorders** as well as stiffness, mental status changes, and increased temperature associated with a dangerous syndrome known as **neuroleptic malignant syndrome**. However, paliperidone is less likely to cause these disorders than many other types of antipsychotic medications. Patients taking paliperidone must have their immune system function monitored via periodic blood tests, as the drug can cause dangerous decreases in white blood cells. High blood sugar may also develop, especially in patients at risk for diabetes. Blood sugar is measured before initiating paliperidone dosing then monitored periodically. Paliperidone carries a risk of low blood pressure and possible temporary loss of consciousness, especially in older or dehydrated patients rising quickly from a lying down position.

Paliperidone may not be appropriate for use or may require caution in patients with heart abnormalities or disease, liver dysfunction, kidney dysfunction, history of **stroke** or seizure, diabetes, or immune dysfunction; patients who are dehydrated or have diarrhea or electrolyte abnormalities; and the elderly. Paliperidone should not be used in elderly patients to treat symptoms of **dementia**; use of paliperidone for this purpose is not approved by the U.S. Food and Drug Administration, and elderly patients taking paliperidone for dementia-related symptoms are at increased risk of stroke or death.

Paliperidone is classified as category C for pregnancy, which means either there are no adequate human or animal studies or that adverse fetal effects were found in animal studies, but there is no available human data. The decision whether to use category C drugs during pregnancy is generally based on weighing the critical needs of the mother against the risk to the fetus. Other lower category agents are used whenever possible. There are data that suggest paliperidone is considered unsafe for use during breast-feeding, and its use is not recommended.

Side effects

Atypical antipsychotics such as paliperidone are known for having fewer movement-related side effects than other types of older antipsychotic medications that act on neurotransmitter receptors in different parts of the brain. This is one reason why as a general class they tend to be the drug of choice in treatment of schizophrenia or other disorders involving psychosis such as schizoaffective disorder. However, as with all medications, antipsychotics such as paliperidone have side effects. Sensitivity to paliperidone varies between patients, and some patients may find that even lower doses are more than their body system can tolerate. Common side effects of paliperidone include headache, dizziness, dry mouth, cough, nausea, upset stomach, weight gain, **fatigue**, increased heart rate, excess salivation, anxiety, tremor, heart rhythm abnormalities, skin sensitivity to sunlight, and fever. Antipsychotics such as paliperidone that act to antagonize dopamine receptors may cause an increase in prolactin, the hormone that causes lactation in women and impotence in men. Low blood pressure or a drop in

QUESTIONS TO ASK YOUR DOCTOR

- Can I take the full dose right away or do I need to slowly increase the dose up to the full amount?
- Can I stop taking the medication right away or do I need to stop slowly?
- Should I eat before taking this medication?
- Will this medication interact with any of my other prescription medications? Over-the-counter-drugs? Herbal supplements?
- What side effects should I watch for while taking this medication?
- Can I drink alcoholic beverages in the same time frame as taking this medication?

blood pressure upon standing may result in loss of consciousness. Rare but serious potential side effects include severe movement disorders, high blood sugar or overt diabetes, stroke, severe difficulty swallowing, dangerous changes in heart rhythm, **seizures**, and changes in blood cells including anemia and decreased immune function. A rare but dangerous possible side effect is neuroleptic malignant syndrome, a reaction involving very high body temperature, altered mental status, and muscular rigidity.

Interactions

Patients should make their doctor aware of all medications and supplements they are taking before using paliperidone. Using alcohol while taking paliperidone may create toxic reactions in the body and should be avoided. Drugs that affect the liver may alter the metabolism of paliperidone, resulting in too little or too much of the drug in the body. This could lead to increased side effects or even toxic doses. Likewise, paliperidone may affect the metabolism of other drugs, leading to greater or lower doses than therapeutically desired.

Many drugs may cause toxicity and adversely affect heart rhythm when used in combination with paliperidone. These drugs include multiple types of heart medications, including dronedarone and amiodarone; the antimalaria drug mefloquine; the chemotherapeutic toremifene; the antifungal drug voriconazole; the antibiotics azithromycin, clarithromycin, and ciprofloxacin; and antipsychotics such as **pimozide** and **ziprasidone**, among many others. The drug bromocriptine used in various neurological and endocrine disorders may cause dangerously low blood pressure when used with paliperidone. Sedative drugs such as codeine and herbal supplements such as calendula, capsicum, kava, and lemon balm may cause additive effects of severe sedation in patients using paliperidone. The herbal supplement Siberian **ginseng** causes antagonizing effects and decreases the effectiveness of paliperidone, as well as exacerbating many psychiatric conditions.

Resources

BOOKS

Brunton, Laurence L., et al. *Goodman and Gilman's The Pharmacological Basis of Therapeutics.* 12th ed. New York: McGraw Hill Medical, 2011.

Stargrove, Mitchell Bebel, et al. *Herb, Nutrient, and Drug Interactions: Clinical Implications and Therapeutic Strategies.* St. Louis: Mosby, 2007.

WEBSITES

PubMed Health. "Paliperidone." U.S. National Library of Medicine. http://www.ncbi.nlm.nih.gov/pubmedhealth/PMH0000356 (accessed November 8, 2011).

ORGANIZATIONS

American College of Neuropsychopharmacology, 5034-A Thoroughbred Lane, Brentwood, TN, 37027, (615) 324-2360, Fax: (615) 523-1715, acnp@acnp.org, http://www.acnp.org/default.aspx.

American Psychiatric Association, 1000 Wilson Blvd., Ste. 1825, Arlington, VA, 22209-3901, (703) 907-7300, apa@psych.org, http://www.psych.org.

American Society for Clinical Pharmacology and Therapeutics, 528 N Washington St., Alexandria, VA, 22314, (703) 836-6981, info@ascpt.org, http://www.ascpt.org.

Mental Health America, 2000 N Beauregard St., 6th Fl., Alexandria, VA, 22311, (703) 684-7722, (800) 969-6642, Fax: (703) 684-5968, http://www.nmha.org.

U.S. Food and Drug Administration, 10903 New Hampshire Ave., Silver Spring, MD, 20993-0002, (888) INFO-FDA (463-6332), http://www.fda.gov.

Maria Eve Basile, PhD

Pamelor *see* **Nortriptyline**

Panic attack

Definition

Panic attacks, the hallmark of **panic disorder**, are discrete episodes of intense anxiety. Panic attacks can also be experienced by people with **anxiety disorders**, mood disorders, substance-related disorders (e.g.,

cocaine addiction), or general medical conditions (e.g., hyperthyroidism).

Description

Panic attacks are intense anxiety experiences that occur suddenly over discrete periods of time, and are characterized by intense apprehension or fearfulness in situations where there is no actual danger. Physical symptoms of a panic attack may include palpitations, difficulty breathing, chest pain or discomfort, choking or smothering sensations, excessive perspiration, or dizziness. Panic attacks often include the fear of going crazy, losing control, or dying. Panic attacks triggered by a specific experience are called situational panic attacks, since a certain situation (e.g., public speaking, driving, shopping in a crowded store) initiates the intense anxiety.

Persons affected with panic attacks usually exhibit a broad range of clinical signs and symptoms that include:

- heart palpitations (accelerated heart rate)
- shaking or trembling
- sweating
- shortness of breath or sensation of feeling smothered or choked
- feeling of tingling
- chest discomfort or pain
- nausea or abdominal distress
- feeling dizzy, light headed, unsteady or faint
- perceptions of being detached from oneself (depersonalization), or a feeling out of touch with reality (derealization)
- chills or hot flashes
- fear of dying
- fear of going crazy or losing control

A person meets the criteria for a panic attack if the symptoms start abruptly, reach a quick peak (usually within 10 minutes), and if the affected individual has at least four symptoms as listed above. In persons who have less than four symptoms during an attack, the disorder is called a limited symptom attack.

It is typical that affected persons who seek treatment usually have one to two attacks a week and in worse periods may have one daily attacks or several within a week.

As stated, panic attacks can be experienced as a result of stimulant chemical usage, such as cocaine. There is evidence to suggest that persons with panic attacks are sensitive to certain chemicals such as caffeine, carbon dioxide, antihistamines, and, in women, progesterone replacement. Exposure to these substances may precipitate an attack.

Resources

BOOKS

Bope, Edward T., and Rick D. Kellerman. *Conn's Current Therapy.* Philadelphia: Elsevier, 2012.

Schmidt, Leonard J., and Brooke Warner. *Panic: Origins, Insight, and Treatment.* Berkeley, CA: North Atlantic Books, 2002.

Starcevic, Vladan. *Anxiety Disorders in Adults: A Clinical Guide.* 2nd ed. New York: Oxford University Press, 2010.

VandenBos, Gary R., ed. *APA Dictionary of Psychology.* Washington, DC: American Psychological Association, 2006.

ORGANIZATIONS

Anxiety Disorders Association of America, 8730 Georgia Ave., Silver Spring, MD, 20910, (240) 485-1001, Fax: (240) 485-1035, http://www.adaa.org.

Laith Farid Gulli, MD
Jean Suvan, BS, RDH

Panic disorder

Definition

Panic disorder is a condition in which a person suffers recurrent panic attacks. Panic attacks are sudden attacks that are not caused by a substance (such as caffeine), medication, or by a medical condition (such as high blood pressure). During the attack, the sufferer may experience sensations such as accelerated or irregular heartbeats, shortness of breath, dizziness, or a fear of losing control. The sudden attack builds quickly (usually within 10 minutes) and is almost paralyzing in its severity. When a **diagnosis** of panic disorder is given, the disorder can be considered one of two different types—panic disorder with or without **agoraphobia**.

Agoraphobia is a fear of being in a place or situation from which escape might be difficult or embarrassing or in which help may not be available in the case of a **panic attack**. It is not clear why some people develop agoraphobia and other people do not. Many people

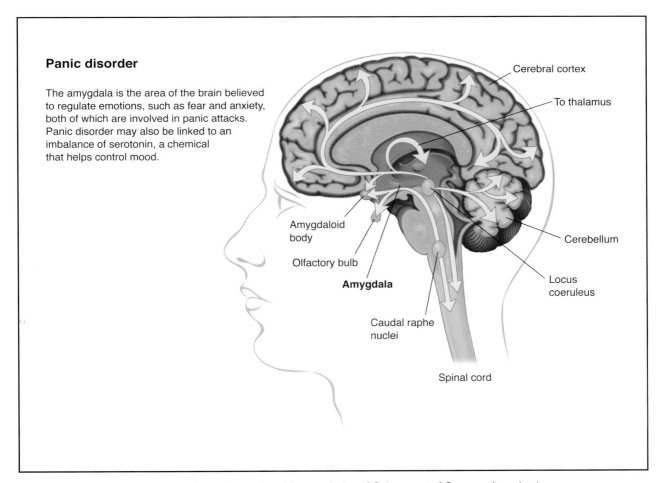

Panic disorder

The amygdala is the area of the brain believed to regulate emotions, such as fear and anxiety, both of which are involved in panic attacks. Panic disorder may also be linked to an imbalance of serotonin, a chemical that helps control mood.

Cerebral cortex

To thalamus

Amygdaloid body

Olfactory bulb

Amygdala

Caudal raphe nuclei

Cerebellum

Locus coeruleus

Spinal cord

(Illustration by Electronic Illustrators Group. Reproduced by permission of Gale, a part of Cengage Learning.)

may develop their agoraphobia symptoms right after their first attack, but others do not develop agoraphobia until years after their attacks began.

The handbook for mental health professionals (called the *Diagnostic and Statistical Manual of Mental Disorders*, or the *DSM*) classifies panic disorder with and without agoraphobia as **anxiety disorders**.

Demographics

Factors such as race, gender, and socioeconomic status are important factors in the development of panic disorder. An individual has a 1%–2% chance of developing panic disorder with or without agoraphobia. The symptoms usually begin when individuals are in their early to mid-twenties. Women are twice as likely as men to develop panic attacks regardless of age. The **National Institute of Mental Health** Epidemiologic Catchment Area Study (ECA) shows no significant differences between the races or ethnic groups, although it appears that African American and Hispanic men between the ages of 40 and 50 have lower rates of panic disorder than white men. Panic disorder patients are at increased risk for major **depression** and the development of agoraphobia. According to ECA studies, an individual with panic disorder has a 33% chance of developing agoraphobia. People without panic disorder only have a 5.5% chance of developing agoraphobia. Again, women were found to be more likely to develop agoraphobia than men. Over the course of their lifetime, African Americans were more likely to develop agoraphobia than whites or Hispanics. Agoraphobia is more prevalent among people with less education and lower economic class.

Description

Panic disorder can be difficult to distinguish from other mental illnesses such as major depression, other anxiety disorders, or medical conditions such as heart attacks. Panic attacks differ from general anxiety in that the episodes last for discrete periods of time, and the symptoms that people suffer are more intense. Panic attacks have three types: unexpected, situationally bound, and situationally predisposed. The unexpected attacks occur without warning and without a trigger. The situationally bound attacks happen repeatedly when the person is performing or preparing to perform some activity or even when the person thinks about doing that activity. For example, a person whose panic attacks are triggered by being in crowds can have an attack just by thinking about going to a shopping mall. Situationally predisposed attacks are similar to the situationally bound attacks, except that they do not always occur when the

trigger stimulus is encountered. For example, someone who experiences panic attacks while in crowds may sometimes be in crowds and not experience attacks or may experience attacks in noncrowded situations as well.

Panic disorder without agoraphobia

Panic disorder without agoraphobia is defined by the fourth edition of the *DSM* (*DSM-IV-TR*) as a disorder in which patients are plagued by panic attacks that occur repeatedly and without warning. After these attacks, affected individuals worry for one month or more about having more embarrassing attacks and may change their behavior with regard to these attacks. For example, patients may fear that they have a cardiac condition and may quit a job or quit exercising because of the fear. Patients may also worry that they are going to lose control or appear insane to other people. Panic disorder without agoraphobia has a less severe set of symptoms than panic disorder with agoraphobia. Patients without agoraphobia do not become housebound; they suffer panic attacks but do not have significant interference in their level of function and are still able to accomplish their daily activities.

Panic disorder with agoraphobia

People who suffer from panic disorder with agoraphobia may experience their agoraphobia in one of two ways. They may experience sudden, unexpected panic attacks that cause them to fear being in a place where help might not be available, or they may experience sudden panic attacks in specific, known situations and fear those situations or places that may trigger attacks. In either case, the fear of further panic attacks restricts affected individuals' ability to complete activities. For example, people whose attacks are triggered by being in crowds may avoid shopping malls for fear that they will be in a crowd and have a panic attack. Individuals may experience sudden, debilitating panic attacks without a particular trigger, and, as a result, they are afraid to go to a supermarket (or similar place) for fear that a panic attack could occur while they are there and no one would be able to help.

Panic disorder in the DSM-5

The fifth edition of the *DSM* (*DSM-5*), due to publish in May 2013, has proposed recategorizing panic disorders and agoraphobia so that each one becomes a separate diagnosis within the category of anxiety disorders. The **American Psychiatric Association** website describing the planned revisions states that panic attack alone will not warrant a separate diagnosis but that both panic disorder and agoraphobia will be treated as separate entities.

Causes and symptoms

Causes

BIOCHEMICAL/PHYSIOLOGICAL CAUSES. It is extremely difficult to study the **brain** and the underlying causes of psychiatric illness; and understanding the chemistry of the brain is the key to unlocking the mystery of panic disorder. The amygdala is the part of the brain that causes fear and the response to **stress**. It has been implicated as a vital part of anxiety disorders. Sodium lactate, a chemical that the body produces when muscles are fatigued, and carbon dioxide are known to induce panic attacks. These substances are thought to inhibit the release of **neurotransmitters** in the brain, which leads to the panic attacks. One hypothesis is that sodium lactate stimulates the amygdala and causes panic attacks. Another hypothesis is that patients with panic disorder have a hypersensitive internal suffocation alarm. This means that the patients's brain sends the body false signals that not enough oxygen is being received, causing the affected persons to increase their breathing rate. Panic disorder patients have attacks when their overly sensitive alarm goes off unpredictably. Yohimbine, a drug used to treat male sexual dysfunction, stimulates a part of the brain called the locus ceruleus and induces panic symptoms thus pointing to this area of the brain's involvement in panic disorder. Brain neurotransmitters **serotonin** and GABA are suspected to be involved in causing the disorder, as well.

GENETICS. Genetics also plays a pivotal role in the development of panic disorder. Twin studies have demonstrated that there is a higher concordance in identical versus fraternal twins thus supporting the idea that panic disorders are inherited. Family studies have also demonstrated that panic attacks run in families. Relatives of patients with panic disorder are four to 10 times more likely to develop panic disorder. People who develop early onset of panic attacks in their mid-20s are more likely to have relatives who have panic disorder. When relatives of patients with panic disorder are exposed to high levels of carbon dioxide, they have panic attacks. Another hypothesis is that patients with panic disorder who develop agoraphobia have a more severe form of the disease. Current efforts to identify a gene for panic disorder have not been successful.

PERSONAL VARIABLES. There are several themes in the psychology of panic disorder. Research has shown that patients who develop panic disorder have difficulty with anger. They also have difficulty when their job responsibilities are increased (as in the case of a promotion) and are sensitive to loss and separation.

People with this disorder often have difficulty getting along with their parents, whom they see as controlling, critical, and demanding, causing the patients to feel inadequate. Early maternal separation is thought to be an underlying cause of panic disorder.

Panic disorder patients also have a pattern of dependency in their interpersonal relationships. As children, people with panic disorder relied on parents to protect them from fear. As a result, they become dependent on their parents and fear detaching from them. They constantly feel as though they are trapped.

There is also an association between **sexual abuse** and patients who have panic attacks. Sixty percent of female patients with panic disorder were sexually abused as children. This explains their difficulty with developing trusting relationships.

Symptoms

PANIC ATTACK. The *DSM-IV-TR* lists thirteen symptoms to meet the criteria for a diagnosis of panic attack. Affected persons must have four or more of these symptoms within ten minutes of the beginning of an attack in order to meet the panic attack criteria:

- bounding or pounding heartbeat or fast heart rate
- sweating
- shaking
- shortness of breath
- feeling of choking
- pains in the chest; many people feel as though they are having a heart attack
- nausea or stomach ache
- feeling dizzy or lightheaded as if they are going to pass out
- feeling of being outside of their body or are detached from reality
- fear that they are out of control or crazy
- fear that they are going to die
- feeling of tingling or numbness
- chills or hot flashes

PANIC DISORDER WITHOUT AGORAPHOBIA. The *DSM-IV-TR* criteria for panic disorder without agoraphobia include:

- recurrent panic attacks (see above) that occur without warning for one month
- persistent worry that panic attacks will recur
- possible change in behavior because of that fear
- no agoraphobia
- not due to a medical condition or substance abuse

• not due other mental illness like specific phobia, social phobia, obsessive-compulsive disorder, separation anxiety disorder, or post-traumatic stress disorder

PANIC DISORDER WITH AGORAPHOBIA. The *DSM-IV-TR* criteria for panic disorder with agoraphobia are the same as panic disorder without agoraphobia, but with the addition of agoraphobia. The symptoms of agoraphobia include fear of being in situations that can trigger panic attacks and avoiding places where attacks have occurred because of the affected persons' fear that they will not be able to leave or will not be able to get help. People with this condition may need to have another person accompany them when going to a place that may trigger anxiety attacks. Sometimes this fear can be so severe that affected individuals become housebound. This fact is important to consider because 15% of the general population can have one spontaneous panic attack without the recurrence of symptoms.

Diagnosis

Differential diagnosis

Differential diagnosis is the process of distinguishing one diagnosis from other, similar diagnoses. Panic disorder can be difficult to distinguish from other anxiety disorders such as specific phobia and **social phobia**. However, in general, specific phobia is cued by a specific trigger or stimulus and social phobia by specific social situations, whereas the panic attacks of panic disorder are completely uncued and unexpected. In certain cases, it may be difficult to distinguish between certain situational phobias and panic disorder with agoraphobia, and mental health professionals must use the *DSM* and professional judgment in these cases. Panic attacks that occur during sleep and wake affected persons up are more characteristic of panic disorder than are the other disorders that include panic attacks. It can be distinguished from **post-traumatic stress disorder** (PTSD), **obsessive-compulsive disorder** (OCD), and **generalized anxiety disorder** (GAD), again by what cues the attacks. In PTSD, thinking about the traumatic event can trigger attacks. In obsessive-compulsive disorder, worries about getting dirty can fuel an attack of anxiety. In generalized anxiety disorder, general worries or concerns can lead to the symptoms of panic. However, in panic disorder, a main component is that the affected individual fears recurrent panic attacks.

Panic attacks can often be difficult to distinguish from other physical problems such as hyperthyroidism, hyperparathyroidism, seizure disorder, and cardiac disease. If patients are middle-aged or older and have other complaints, including dizziness and headaches, their attacks are more likely to be a medical problem and not panic attacks. Panic attacks can also be difficult to distinguish from drug abuse since any drug that stimulates the brain can cause the symptoms. For example, **cocaine**, caffeine, and **amphetamines** can all cause panic attacks. Therefore, individuals must be free of all drugs before a diagnosis of panic disorder can be made. Many patients may attempt to self-medicate with alcohol to try to calm down. Withdrawal from alcohol can lead to worse panic symptoms. Patients may believe that they are reducing symptoms whereas they are actually exacerbating their panic attacks.

Dual diagnosis

Individuals with panic disorders have a high rate of coexisting depression. Patients who have panic disorder have about a 40%–80% chance of developing major depression. In most situations, the panic disorder happens first and the depression comes later. Patients are also at risk for **substance abuse** difficulties as a result of attempts to stop attacks. These attempts may involve the use of alcohol, illicit or unprescribed **sedatives**, or **benzodiazepines** (medications that slow down the central nervous system, having a calming effect). Patients with panic disorder are not at high risk for **suicide** attempts. A recent Harvard-Brown study showed that people with panic disorder with or without agoraphobia are not at risk for suicide unless they have other conditions such as depression or substance abuse.

Psychological measures and diagnostic testing

Currently there is no diagnostic test for panic disorder. Patients who have panic attacks should receive a thorough medical examination to rule out any medical condition. Patients should have baseline blood counts and glucose should be measured. Patients with cardiac symptoms need a cardiac workup and should see their primary medical doctor. Patients who have complaints of dizziness should receive a thorough neurological evaluation. There are several psychological inventories that can help the clinician diagnose panic disorder including the **Beck Depression Inventory** (BDI), Beck Anxiety Inventory (BAI), Specific Fear Inventory, Clinical Anxiety Scale (CAS), and the Clinical Global Inventory (CGI).

Treatment

There are various treatments for panic disorder.

Psychological and social interventions

A psychotherapeutic technique that is critical to the treatment of panic disorder is **cognitive-behavioral** therapy (CBT). Patients are panic-free within six months in about 80–90% of cases. Some people may experience long-term effects after the treatments have been stopped. About half of the patients say that they have rare attacks even two years after treatment has ended.

New studies reveal that the approach to treating panic disorder should have three aspects: the cognitive, the physiological, and the behavioral. The cognitive techniques try to focus on changing the patient's negative thoughts—such as "I will die if I don't get help." Patient education about symptoms is also critical to the treatment of panic attacks. In one physiological approach, patients are taught breathing techniques in an effort to try to help them lower their heart rate and decrease their anxiety. Repeated exposure to physical symptoms associated with the panic disorder is also a part of treatment. For example, patients may cause themselves to hyperventilate in effort to reproduce the panic symptoms. In behavioral approaches, individuals who experience panic attacks need to be exposed to situations that they may have previously feared. Patients can also be taken to places associated with agoraphobia with the therapist.

Some patients may benefit from **psychodynamic psychotherapy** and **group therapy**. Psychodynamic **psychotherapy** explores thoughts and ideas of the person's subconscious. It takes a longer time to achieve efficacy than cognitive-behavioral therapy, but it can be just as effective for patients with panic disorder. Group therapy is also just as helpful to some patients as CBT. **Support groups** can also be helpful to some patients. It can be very therapeutic and healing for individuals to discuss their problems with someone who has actually experienced the same symptoms. Patients can learn from each other's coping styles.

Medical treatments

Panic disorder patients have a 50–80% chance of responding to treatment, which attempts to block the symptoms of panic attacks. Treating the agoraphobia symptoms is more challenging. Developing some anti-panic regimens that address all symptoms is important. The Food and Drug Administration (FDA) approves only five classes of drugs for treating panic disorder. They are:

- benzodiazepines
- Selective serotonin reuptake inhibitors (SSRIs), which cause a buildup of serotonin. This buildup is thought to cause the antidepressant effect.
- Tricyclic antidepressants (TCAs)
- Monoamine oxidase inhibitors (MAOIs) and reversible MAOIs, which inhibit the breakdown of neurotransmitters in the brain, including dopamine and serotonin

- Atypical antidepressants, including bupropion (Wellbutrin), mirtazapine (Remeron), trazodone (Desyrel), and others

Patients should first be started on a low-dose SSRI and then the dose should be increased slowly. Patients with panic disorder are extremely sensitive to the side effects that many patients experience in the first weeks of antidepressant therapy. Patients should also have a benzodiazepine, such as **clonazepam** (Klonopin) or **alprazolam** (Xanax) in the first weeks of treatment until the antidepressant becomes therapeutic. Most people need the same dose of antidepressant as patients with major depression. About 60% of patients will have improvement in their symptoms while taking an antidepressant and a benzodiazepine. Patients with mitral valve prolapse may benefit from a beta blocker. Patients who have tried an SSRI and after six weeks show no improvement can be switched to another SSRI, benzodiazepine, TCA, MAOI, or **venlafaxine** (Effexor). An SSRI should be stopped if patients have intolerable side effects such as loss of sexual libido, weight gain, or mild form of manic depression. When **SSRIs** are stopped, it is important that the dosage is gradually tapered because patients can suffer symptoms when it is abruptly withdrawn. These symptoms may include confusion, anxiety, and poor sleep.

Alternative therapies

Some alternative therapies for panic disorder are hypnosis, **meditation**, **yoga**, proper **nutrition**, **exercise**, and abdominal breathing techniques that foster relaxation, and visualization. Visualization is imagining oneself in the stressful situation while relaxed so that coping strategies can be discovered. The herb kava has been studied in trials to treat anxiety attacks and has been found to be effective in some **clinical trials**, but it has not been studied intensely enough to determine its benefits and side effects and has been associated with liver toxicity.

Prognosis

Patients with panic disorder have a poor prognosis particularly if untreated. Patients often **relapse** when they attempt to discontinue treatment. However, if patients are compliant and willing to stay in treatment, then the long-term prognosis is good. According to one study, eight years after treatment has been completed, 30–40% of patient were doing better. Only 10–20% of patients were doing poorly. Patients with panic attacks have a relapsing and remitting course that can be worsened by significant stressors such as the death of a spouse or divorce. Cognitive-behavioral therapy has an

80–90% chance that the patient will benefit six months after treatment. Medications have a 50–80% efficacy. If patients are committed to staying in treatment, their prognosis is very favorable.

Prevention

Although panic disorder is not totally preventable, individuals with a strong family history of susceptibility to panic attacks are encouraged to be aware of the symptoms and get treatment early. **Compliance** with treatment is important to the recovery from panic disorder.

Resources

BOOKS

American Psychiatric Association. *Diagnostic and Statistical Manual of Mental Disorders.* 4th ed., text rev. Washington DC: American Psychiatric Publishing, 2000.

Burns, David D. *When Panic Attacks: The New, Drug-Free Anxiety Therapy That Can Change Your Life.* New York: Random House, 2007.

Craske, Michelle G., and David H. Barlow. *Mastery of Your Anxiety and Panic: Therapist Guide.* New York: Oxford University Press, 2007.

Wilson, Reid. *Don't Panic: Taking Control of Anxiety Attacks,* 3rd ed. New York: Harper Collins, 2009.

PERIODICALS

Bednar, F., and D.M. Simeone. "Internet-Based Treatment for Panic Disorder: Does Frequency of Therapist Contact Make a Difference?" *Cognitive Behaviour Therapy* (March 18, 2009): 1–14.

Busch, F.N., et al. "A Study Demonstrating Efficacy of a Psychoanalytic Psychotherapy for Panic Disorder: Implications for Psychoanalytic Research, Theory, and Practice." *Journal of the American Psychoanalytic Association* 57, no. 1 (February 2009): 131–48.

Powers, A., and D. Westen. "Personality Subtypes in Patients with Panic Disorder." *Comprehensive Psychiatry* 50, no. 2 (March–April 2009): 164–72.

Starcevic, V. "Treatment of Panic Disorder: Recent Developments and Current Status." *Expert Review of Neurotherapeutics* 8, no. 8 (August 2008): 1219–32.

Teng, E.G., et al. "When Anxiety Symptoms Masquerade as Medical Symptoms: What Medical Specialists Know about Panic Disorder and Available Psychological Treatments." *Journal of Clinical Psychology in Medical Settings* 15, no. 4 (December 2008): 314–21.

WEBSITES

"Answers to Your Questions About Panic Disorder." APA, April 25, 2009. http://www.apa.org/topics/anxietyqanda.html (accessed September 16, 2011).

"Panic Disorder." NIMH, March 31, 2009. http://www.nimh.nih.gov/health/topics/panic-disorder/index.shtml (accessed September 16, 2011).

"Panic Disorder." MedlinePlus, April 13, 2009. http://www.nlm.nih.gov/medlineplus/panicdisorder.html (accessed September 16, 2011).

"Panic Disorder (Panic Attack)." Anxiety Disorders Association of America. Last modified April 25, 2009. http://www.adaa.org/GettingHelp/AnxietyDisorders/Panicattack.asp (accessed September 16, 2011).

"What Is a Panic Attack?" American Psychiatric Association. Last modified April 25, 2009. http://healthyminds.org/factsheets/LTF-Panic.pdf (accessed September 16, 2011).

"When Fear Overwhelms: Panic Disorder." NIMH. Last modified April 25, 2009. http://www.nimh.nih.gov/health/publications/when-fear-overwhelms-panic-disorder/index.shtml (accessed September 16, 2011).

ORGANIZATIONS

American Psychiatric Association, 1000 Wilson Blvd., Ste. 1825, Arlington, VA, 22209-3901, (703) 907-7300, apa@psych.org, http://www.psych.org.

American Psychological Association, 750 1st St., NE, Washington, DC, 20002-4242, (202) 336-5500; TDD/TTY: (202) 336-6123, (800) 374-2721, http://www.apa.org.

Anxiety Disorders Association of America, 8730 Georgia Ave., Silver Spring, MD, 20910, (240) 485-1001, Fax: (240) 485-1035, http://www.adaa.org.

Mental Health America, 2000 N Beauregard St., 6th Fl., Alexandria, VA, 22311, (800) 969-6642, http://www.nmha.org.

National Institute of Mental Health, 6001 Executive Blvd., Rm. 8184, MSC 9663, Bethesda, MD, 20892-9663, (301) 433-4513; TTY: (301) 443-8431, Fax: (301) 443-4279, (866) 615-6464; TTY: (866) 415-8051, nimhinfo@nih.gov, http://www.nimh.nih.gov.

Susan Hobbs, MD

Paranoia

Definition

Paranoia is a symptom in which an individual feels as if the world is "out to get" him or her. When people are paranoid, they feel as if others are always talking about them behind their backs. Paranoia causes intense feelings of distrust, and can sometimes lead to overt or covert hostility.

Demographics

Paranoia is a very human feeling. Nearly everyone has experienced it at some or another time, to varying degrees. Paranoia exists on a continuum, ranging from a feeling of distrust due to an occasional misinterpretation of cues that can be appropriately dealt with and reinterpreted, to an overarching pattern of actual paranoia that affects every interpersonal interaction.

Some research studies have suggested that 6% of all women and 13% of all men have some chronic level of mistrust towards the motivations of others towards them. Only about 0.5% to 0.25% of men and women can actually be diagnosed with **paranoid personality disorder**, however. It remains interesting to researchers that men are more prone to paranoid traits and mental disorders with paranoid features than are women.

Description

An individual suffering from paranoia feels suspicious, and has a sense that other people want to do him or her harm. As a result, the paranoid individual changes his or her actions in response to a world that is perceived as personally threatening. Objective observers may be quite clear on the fact that no one's words or actions are actually threatening the paranoid individual. The hallmark of paranoia is a feeling of intense distrust and suspiciousness that is not in response to input from anybody or anything in the paranoid individual's environment.

Other symptoms of paranoia may include

• Self-referential thinking: The sense that other people in the world (even complete strangers on the street) are always talking about the paranoid individual.

• Thought broadcasting: The sense that other people can read the paranoid individual's mind.

• Magical thinking: The sense that the paranoid individual can use his or her thoughts to influence other people's thoughts and actions.

• Thought withdrawal: The sense that people are stealing the paranoid individual's thoughts.

• Thought insertion: The sense that people are putting thoughts into the paranoid individual's mind.

• Ideas of reference: The sense that the television and/or radio are specifically addressing the paranoid individual.

Causes and symptoms

Researchers do not understand fully what chemical or physical changes in the **brain** cause paranoia. Paranoia is a prominent symptom that occurs in a variety of different mental disorders, as well as a symptom of certain physical diseases. Furthermore, use of certain drugs or chemicals may cause symptoms of paranoia in an otherwise normal individual.

Paranoia is often manifested as part of the symptom complex of **schizophrenia**. In fact, one of the subtypes of schizophrenia is termed "paranoid schizophrenia,"

which actually refers to a type of schizophrenia in which the individual is particularly preoccupied with **delusions** in which the world seems to be pitted against him or her. As with other forms of schizophrenia, sufferers often lack contact with reality, and display hallucinations, flat or emotionless **affect**, and disorganized thinking and behavior.

Paranoid personality disorder is diagnosed when an individual does not have other symptoms of schizophrenia, but a personality that is driven by chronic manifestations of paranoia. These individuals are mistrustful, suspicious, and convinced that the world is out to get them.

In order for an individual to be diagnosed with paranoid personality disorder, he or she must display at least four of the following traits:

• chronically suspicious that people are lying or cheating him or her in some way

• frequently preoccupied with whether people are loyal or trustworthy

• cannot confide in others for fear of being betrayed

• misinterprets benign comments or events as being personally threatening

• harbors long-term grudges against others who are perceived as having been threatening or insulting in some way

• sees others' actions and/or words attacking him or her in some way, and therefore goes on the counterattack

• repeatedly assumes that partner or spouse is unfaithful

Paranoia can also occur as a symptom of other neurological diseases. Individuals suffering from the aftereffects of strokes, brain injuries, various types of **dementia** (including **Alzheimer's disease**), Huntington's disease, and Parkinson's disease may manifest paranoia as part of their symptom complex. The paranoia may decrease in intensity when the underlying disease is effectively treated, although since many of these diseases are progressive, the paranoia may worsen over time along with the progression of the disease's other symptoms.

A number of different medications and drugs can cause paranoia. These include corticosteroid medications, H-2 blockers (cimetidine, ranitidine, famotidine), some muscle relaxants (Baclofen), antiviral/anti-Parkinson drugs (**amantadine**), some **amphetamines** (including Ritalin), anti-HIV medications, **antidepressants** (Nardil). Abused drugs that can prompt paranoia include alcohol, **cocaine**, marijuana, **ecstasy** (MDMA), amphetamines (including Ritalin), LSD, and PCP (angel dust). Withdrawal from addictive drugs may also cause symptoms of paranoia.

Treatment

It can be quite challenging to get an individual who is suffering from paranoia to accept treatment. Their paranoid condition makes them distrustful of people's motivations towards them, so that even a medical doctor appears to be a suspicious party. Medications that may be offered are usually looked at with great distrust, and efforts at **psychotherapy** are considered "mind control" by a profoundly paranoid individual.

The first step to be taken when someone is suffering from paranoia is determining whether an easily reversible situation (such as an adverse reaction to a medication) might be causing the paranoia. If so, discontinuing the drug (either immediately or by gradually weaning the dose) might end the symptoms of paranoia.

Patients who have other diseases, such as Alzheimer's disease or other forms of dementia, Huntington's disease, or Parkinson's disease may notice that their paranoid symptoms improve when their general medical condition is treated. The circumstance that can occur as their underlying disease progresses, is that the paranoia may return or worsen over time.

People who are suffering from diagnosable mental conditions such as schizophrenia or paranoid personality disorder may benefit from the use of typical antipsychotic medications, such as **chlorpromazine** or Haldol, or from the newer, atypical antipsychotic medications, such as **clozapine**, **olanzapine**, or **risperidone**.

Cognitive-behavioral therapy (CBT) or other forms of psychotherapy may be helpful for certain people who have paranoia. CBT attempts to make a person more aware of his or her actions and motivations, and tries to help the individual learn to more accurately interpret cues around him or her, in an effort to help the individual change dysfunctional behaviors. Difficulty can enter into a therapeutic relationship with a paranoid individual, due to the level of mistrust and suspicion that is likely to interfere with their ability to participate in this form of treatment.

Support groups can be helpful for some paranoid individuals and are particularly helpful in assisting family members and friends who must learn to live with or care for individuals experiencing paranoia.

Prognosis

It is difficult to predict the prognosis of an individual who has paranoia. If there is an underlying mental illness, such as schizophrenia or paranoid personality disorder, then the paranoia is likely to be a lifelong condition. It may improve with some treatments (remission), only to become exacerbated under other more stressful conditions, or with changes in medication.

Individuals who have symptoms of paranoia as part of another medical condition may also have a waxing-and-waning-course.

When paranoia is caused by the use of a particular drug or medication, it is possible that discontinuing that substance may completely reverse the symptoms of paranoia.

Resources

BOOKS

Tasman, Allan, et al., eds. *Psychiatry*. 3rd ed. New York: Wiley and Sons, 2008.

ORGANIZATIONS

National Alliance on Mental Illness, 3803 N Fairfax Drive, Ste. 100, Arlington, VA, 22203, (703) 524-7600, http://www.nami.org.

National Institute of Mental Health, 6001 Executive Blvd., Room 8184, MSC 9663, Bethesda, MD, 20892-9663, (301) 433-4513; TTY: (301) 443-8431, Fax: (301) 443-4279, (866) 615-6464; TTY: (866) 415-8051 nimhinfo@nih.gov, http://www.nimh.nih.gov.

Rosalyn Carson-DeWitt, M.D.

Paranoid personality disorder

Definition

People with paranoid personality disorder (PPD) have long-term and unwarranted suspicions that other people are hostile, threatening, or demeaning. These beliefs are steadfastly maintained in the absence of any real supporting evidence. The disorder, named after the Greek word for "madness," is one of ten **personality disorders** described in the fourth edition of the *Diagnostic and Statistical Manual of Mental Disorders* (*DSM-IV-TR*), the guidebook used by mental health professionals to diagnose mental disorders. Proposed changes for the fifth edition (*DSM-5*) include removing PPD as an individual diagnosis.

Despite the pervasive suspicions they have of others, patients with PPD are not delusional (except in rare, brief instances brought on by **stress**). Most of the time, they are in touch with reality, except for their misinterpretation of others' motives and intentions. PPD patients are not psychotic but their conviction that others are trying to "get them" or humiliate them in some way often leads to hostility and social isolation.

Demographics

As of 2011, it was not yet possible to determine the number of people with PPD with any accuracy. This lack of data might be expected for a disorder that is characterized by extreme suspiciousness. Such patients in many cases avoid voluntary contact with such people as mental health workers who have a certain amount of power over them. There are, nonetheless, some estimates of the prevalence of PPD. According to the *DSM-IV-TR*), between 0.5% and 2.5% of the general population of the United States may have PPD, while 2%–10% of outpatients receiving psychiatric care may be affected. A significant percentage of institutionalized psychiatric patients, between 10% and 30%, might have symptoms that qualify for a **diagnosis** of PPD. Finally, the disorder appears to be more common in men than in women.

There are indications in the scientific literature that relatives of patients with chronic schizophrenia may have a greater chance of developing PPD than people in the general population. Also, the incidence of the disorder may be higher among relatives of patients suffering from another psychotic disorder known as delusional disorder of the persecutory type.

Description

People with PPD do not trust other people. In fact, the central characteristic of people with PPD is a high degree of mistrustfulness and suspicion when interacting with others. Even friendly gestures are often interpreted as being manipulative or malevolent. Whether the patterns of distrust and suspicion begin in childhood or in early adulthood, they quickly come to dominate the lives of those suffering from PPD. Such people are unable or afraid to form close relationships with others.

They suspect strangers, and even people they know, of planning to harm or exploit them when there is no good evidence to support this belief. As a result of their constant concern about the lack of trustworthiness of others, patients with this disorder often have few intimate friends or close human contacts. They do not fit in and they do not make good "team players." Interactions with others are characterized by wariness and not infrequently by hostility. If they marry or become otherwise attached to someone, the relationship is often characterized by pathological jealousy and attempts to control their partner. They often assume their sexual partner is "cheating" on them.

People suffering from PPD are very difficult to deal with. They never seem to let down their defenses. They are always looking for and finding evidence that others are against them. Their fear, and the threats they perceive in the innocent statements and actions of others, often contributes to frequent complaining or unfriendly withdrawal or aloofness. They can be confrontational, aggressive and disputatious. It is not unusual for them to sue people they feel have wronged them. In addition, patients with this disorder are known for their tendency to become violent.

Despite all the unpleasant aspects of a paranoid lifestyle, however, it is still not sufficient to drive many people with PPD to seek therapy. They do not usually walk into a therapist's office on their own. They distrust mental health care providers just as they distrust nearly everyone else. If a life crisis, a family member or the judicial system succeeds in getting a patient with PPD to seek help, therapy is often a challenge. Individual counseling seems to work best but it requires a great deal of patience and skill on the part of the therapist. It is not unusual for patients to leave therapy when they perceive some malicious intent on the therapist's part. If the patient can be persuaded to cooperate—something that is not easy to achieve—low-dose medications are recommended for treating such specific problems as anxiety, but only for limited periods of time.

If a mental health care provider is able to gain the trust of a patient with PPD, it may be possible to help the patient deal with the threats that he or she perceives. The disorder, however, usually lasts a lifetime.

Causes and symptoms

Causes

No one knows what causes paranoid personality disorder, although there are hints that familial factors may influence the development of the disorder in some cases. There seem to be more cases of PPD in families that have one or more members who suffer from such psychotic disorders as **schizophrenia** or **delusional disorder**.

Other possible interpersonal causes have been proposed. For example, some therapists believe that the behavior that characterizes PPD might be learned. They suggest that such behavior might be traced back to childhood experiences. According to this view, children who are exposed to adult anger and rage with no way to predict the outbursts and no way to escape or control them develop paranoid ways of thinking in an effort to cope with the stress. PPD would emerge when this type of thinking becomes part of the individual's personality as adulthood approaches.

Studies of identical (or monozygotic) and fraternal (or dizygotic) twins suggest that **genetic factors** may also play an important role in causing the disorder. Twin studies indicate that genes contribute to the development of childhood personality disorders, including PPD. Furthermore, estimates of the degree of genetic contribution to the development of childhood personality disorders are similar to estimates of the genetic contribution to adult versions of the disorders.

Symptoms

A core symptom of PPD is a generalized distrust of other people. Comments and actions that healthy people would not notice come across as full of insults and threats to someone with the disorder. Yet, generally, patients with PPD remain in touch with reality; they don't have any of the hallucinations or **delusions** seen in patients with psychoses. Nevertheless, their suspicions that others are intent on harming or exploiting them are so pervasive and intense that people with PPD often become very isolated. They thus avoid normal social interactions. And because they feel so insecure in what is a very threatening world for them, patients with PPD are capable of becoming violent. Innocuous comments, harmless jokes and other day-to-day communications are often perceived as insults.

Paranoid suspicions carry over into all realms of life. Those burdened with PPD are frequently convinced that their sexual partners are unfaithful. They may misinterpret compliments offered by employers or coworkers as hidden criticisms or attempts to get them to work harder. Complimenting a person with PPD on their clothing or car, for example, could easily be taken as an attack on their materialism or selfishness.

Because they persistently question the motivations and trustworthiness of others, patients with PPD are not inclined to share intimacies. They fear such information might be used against them. As a result, they become hostile and unfriendly, argumentative or aloof. Their unpleasantness often draws negative responses from those around them. These rebuffs become "proof" in the patient's mind that others are, indeed, hostile to them. They have little insight into the effects of their attitude and behavior on their generally unsuccessful interactions with others. Asked if they might be responsible for negative interactions that fill their lives, people with PPD are likely to place all the blame on others.

A brief summary of the typical symptoms of PPD includes:

- suspiciousness and distrust of others
- questioning hidden motives in others
- feelings of certainty, without justification or proof, that others are intent on harming or exploiting them
- social isolation
- aggressiveness and hostility
- little or no sense of humor

Diagnosis

There were no laboratory tests or **imaging studies** as of 2011 that could be used to confirm a diagnosis of PPD. The diagnosis is usually made on the basis of the doctor's interview with the patient, although the doctor may also give the patient a diagnostic questionnaire.

Diagnostic criteria

Mental health care providers look for at least five distinguishing symptoms in patients who they think might suffer from PPD. The first is a pattern of suspiciousness about, and distrust of, other people when there is no good reason for either. This pattern should be present from at least the time of the patient's early adulthood.

In addition to this symptom that is required in order to make the PPD diagnosis, the patient should have at least four of the following seven symptoms as listed in the *DSM-IV-TR*:

- The unfounded suspicion that people want to deceive, exploit or harm the patient.
- The pervasive belief that others are not worthy of trust or that they are not inclined to or capable of offering loyalty.
- A fear that others will use information against the patient with the intention of harming him or her. This fear is demonstrated by a reluctance to share even harmless personal information with others.
- The interpretation of others' innocent remarks as insulting or demeaning; or the interpretation of neutral events as presenting or conveying a threat.
- A strong tendency not to forgive real or imagined slights and insults. People with PPD nurture grudges for a long time.
- An angry and aggressive response in reply to imagined attacks by others. The counterattack for a perceived insult is often rapid.
- Suspicions, in the absence of any real evidence, that a spouse or sexual partner is not sexually faithful, resulting in such repeated questions as "Where have you been?" "Whom did you see?" and other types of jealous behavior.

Differential diagnosis

Psychiatrists and clinical psychologists should be careful not to confuse PPD with other mental disorders or behaviors that have some symptoms in common with the paranoid personality. For example, it is important to make sure that the patient is not a long-term user of amphetamine or **cocaine**. Chronic abuse of these stimulants can produce paranoid behavior. Also, some prescription medications might produce **paranoia** as a side effect; so it is important to find out what drugs, if any, the patient is taking.

There are other conditions that, if present, would mean a patient with paranoid traits does not have PPD. For example, if the patient has symptoms of schizophrenia, hallucinations or a formal thought disorder, a diagnosis of PPD can't be made. The same is true of fixed delusions, which are not a feature of PPD.

Also, the suspiciousness and other characteristic features of PPD must have been present in the patient for a long time, at least since early adulthood. If the symptoms appeared more recently than that, a person can't be given a diagnosis of this disorder.

There are at least a dozen disorders or other mental health conditions listed in the *DSM-IV-TR* that could be confused with PPD after a superficial interview because they share similar or identical symptoms with PPD. It is important to eliminate the following entities before settling on a diagnosis of PPD: paranoid schizophrenia; **schizotypal personality disorder**; **schizoid personality disorder**; persecutory delusional disorder; mood disorder with psychotic features; symptoms and/or personality changes produced by disease, medical conditions, medication or drugs of abuse; paranoia linked to the development of physical disabilities; and borderline, histrionic, avoidant, antisocial or narcissistic personality disorders.

In some individuals, symptoms of PPD may precede the development of schizophrenia. Should a patient who has been correctly diagnosed with PPD later develop schizophrenia, the *DSM-IV-TR* suggests that the diagnosis on the patient's medical record be changed from "Paranoid Personality Disorder" to "Paranoid Personality Disorder (Premorbid)."

If PPD is removed from the *DSM-5* (2013) as a separate diagnosis, it will still be represented and diagnosed by a combination of core impairments in personality functioning and specific pathological personality traits (such as antagonistic, psychotic).

Treatment

Because they are suspicious and untrusting, patients with PPD are not likely to seek therapy on their own. A particularly disturbing development or life crisis may prompt them to get help. More often, however, the legal system or the patient's relatives order or encourage him or her to seek professional treatment. But even after a patient finally agrees or is forced to seek treatment, the nature of the disorder poses very serious challenges to therapists.

Psychotherapy

The primary approach to treatment for such personality disorders as PPD is **psychotherapy**. The problem is that patients with PPD do not readily offer therapists the trust that is needed for successful treatment. As a result, it has been difficult to gather data that would indicate what kind of psychotherapy would work best. Therapists face the challenge of developing rapport with someone who is, by the nature of his or her personality disorder, distrustful and suspicious; someone who often sees malicious intent in the innocuous actions and statements of others. The patient may actively resist or refuse to cooperate with others who are trying to help.

Mental health workers treating patients with PPD must guard against any show of hostility on their part in response to hostility from the patient, which is a common occurrence in people with this disorder. Instead, clinicians are advised to develop trust by persistently demonstrating a nonjudgmental attitude and a professional desire to assist the patient.

It is usually up to the therapist alone to overcome a patient's resistance. **Group therapy** that includes family members or other psychiatric patients, not surprisingly, isn't useful in the treatment of PPD due to the mistrust people with PPD feel towards others. This characteristic also explains why there are no significant **self-help groups** dedicated to recovery from this disorder. It has been suggested, however, that some people with PPD might join cults or extremist groups whose members might share their suspicions.

To gain the trust of PPD patients, therapists must be careful to hide as little as possible from their patients. This transparency should include note taking; details of administrative tasks concerning the patient; correspondence; and medications. Any indication of what the patient would consider "deception" or covert operation can, and often does, lead the patient to drop out of treatment. Patients with paranoid tendencies often don't have a well-developed sense of humor; those who must interact with people with PPD probably should not make jokes in their presence. Attempts at humor may seem like ridicule to people who feel so easily threatened.

With some patients, the most attainable goal may be to help them to learn to analyze their problems in dealing with other people. This approach amounts to supportive therapy and is preferable to psychotherapeutic approaches that attempt to analyze the patient's motivations and possible sources of paranoid traits. Asking about a patient's past can undermine the treatment of PPD patients. Concentrating on the specific issues that are troubling the patient with PPD is usually the wisest course.

With time and a skilled therapist, the patient with PPD who remains in therapy may develop a measure of

KEY TERMS

Delusion—A false belief that is resistant to reason or contrary to actual fact.

Delusional disorder of the persecutory type—A psychotic disorder characterized by a patient's belief that others are conspiring against him or her.

Hallucination—False sensory perceptions. A person experiencing a hallucination may "hear" sounds or "see" people or objects that are not really present. Hallucinations can also affect the senses of smell, touch, and taste.

Neuroleptic—Another name for the older antipsychotic medications, such as haloperidol (Haldol) and chlorpromazine (Thorazine).

Paranoia—A mental disorder characterized by baseless suspicions or distrust of others, often delusional in intensity.

Paranoid personality—A personality disorder characterized by unwarranted suspicion, jealousy, hypersensitivity, social isolation and a tendency to detect malicious intent in the words and actions of others.

Psychosis—Severe state that is characterized by loss of contact with reality and deterioration in normal social functioning; examples are schizophrenia and paranoia. Psychosis is usually one feature of an over-arching disorder, not a disorder in itself. (Plural: psychoses)

Rapport—A relation of empathy and trust between a therapist and patient.

Schizophrenia—A severe mental illness in which a person has difficulty distinguishing what is real from what is not real. It is often characterized by hallucinations, delusions, language and communication disturbances, and withdrawal from people and social activities.

Supportive—An approach to psychotherapy that seeks to encourage the patient or offer emotional support to him or her, as distinct from insight-oriented or exploratory approaches to treatment.

trust. But as the patient reveals more of his or her paranoid thoughts, the clinician will continue to face the difficult task of balancing the need for objectivity about the paranoid ideas and the maintenance of a good rapport with the patient. The therapist thus walks a tightrope with this type of patient. If the therapist is not straightforward enough, the patient may feel deceived. If the therapist

challenges paranoid thoughts too directly, the patient will be threatened and probably drop out of treatment.

Medications

While individual supportive psychotherapy is the treatment of choice for PPD, medications are sometimes used on a limited basis to treat related symptoms. If, for example, the patient is very anxious, **antianxiety drugs** may be prescribed. In addition, during periods of extreme agitation and high stress that produce delusional states, the patient may be given low doses of antipsychotic medications.

Some clinicians have suggested that low doses of neuroleptics should be used in this group of patients; however, medications are not normally part of long-term treatment for PPD. One reason is that no medication has been proven to relieve effectively the long-term symptoms of the disorder, although the **selective serotonin reuptake inhibitors** such as **fluoxetine** (Prozac) have been reported to make patients less angry, irritable and suspicious. **Antidepressants** may even make symptoms worse. A second reason is that people with PPD are suspicious of medications. They fear that others might try to control them through the use of drugs. It can therefore be very difficult to persuade them to take medications unless the potential for relief from another threat, such as extreme anxiety, makes the medications seem relatively appealing. The best use of medication may be for specific complaints, when the patient trusts the therapist enough to ask for relief from particular symptoms.

Prognosis

Paranoid personality disorder is often a chronic, lifelong condition; the long-term prognosis is usually not encouraging. Feelings of paranoia, however, can be controlled to a degree with successful therapy. Unfortunately, many patients suffer the major symptoms of the disorder throughout their lives.

Prevention

With little or no understanding of the cause of PPD, it is not possible to prevent the disorder.

Resources

BOOKS

Allen, Thomas E., et al. *A Primer on Mental Disorders: A Guide for Educators, Families, and Students.* Lantham, MD: Scarecrow Press, 2001.

American Psychiatric Association. *Diagnostic and Statistical Manual of Mental Disorders.* 4th ed., text rev. Washington, DC: American Psychiatric Publishing, 2000.

Frances, Allen, and Michael B. First. *Your Mental Health: A Layman's Guide to the Psychiatrist's Bible*. New York, NY: Scribner, 1998.

"Personality Disorders." In *The Merck Manual of Diagnosis and Therapy*, edited by Robert S. Porter and Justin L. Kaplan. 19th ed. Whitehouse Station, NJ: Merck Research Laboratories, 2011.

Porter, Robert S., and Justin L. Kaplan, eds. *The Merck Manual of Diagnosis and Therapy*. 19th ed. Whitehouse Station, NJ: Merck Research Laboratories, 2011.

Weiner, Alan S. Weiner. *Personality Disorders in Children and Adolescents*. 1st ed. New York, NY: Basic Books, 2000.

PERIODICALS

Coolidge, F.L., L.L. Thede, and K.L. Jang. "Heritability of Personality Disorders in Childhood: A Preliminary Investigation." *Journal of Personality Disorders* 15, no. 1 (February 2001): 33–40.

Webb, C.T., and D.F. Levinson. "Schizotypal and Paranoid Personality Disorder in the Relatives of Patients with Schizophrenia and Affective Disorders: A Review." *Schizophrenia Research* 11, no. 1 (December 1993): 81–92.

WEBSITES

DualDiagnosis.org. "Paranoid Personality Disorder." http://www.dualdiagnosisdrugrehabs.org/116/paranoid-personality-disorder.html (accessed October 24, 2011).

PsychCentral.com. "Paranoid Personality Disorder Treatment." http://psychcentral.com/disorders/sx37t.htm (accessed October 24, 2011).

ORGANIZATIONS

American Psychiatric Association, 1000 Wilson Blvd., Ste. 1825, Arlington, VA, 22209-3901, (703) 907-7300, apa@psych.org, http://www.psych.org.

International Society for the Study of Personality Disorders, University of Michigan Health System, Psychiatry MCHC-6, Box 5295, 1500 East Medical Center Drive, Ann Arbor, MI, 48109-5295, (734) 936-8316, Fax: (734) 936-9761, http://www.isspd.com.

Mental Health America, 2000 N. Beauregard Street, 6th Floor, Alexandria, VA, 22311, (703) 684-7722, (800) 969-6642, Fax: (703) 684-5968, http://www1.nmha.org.

Dean A. Haycock, Ph.D.

Paraphilias

Definition

Paraphilias are sexual feelings or behaviors that may involve sexual partners that are not human, not consenting, or that involve suffering by one or both partners.

Description

According to the *Diagnostic and Statistical Manual of Mental Disorders* (known as the *DSM*) fourth edition text revised (*DSM-IV-TR*), the manual used by mental health professionals to diagnose mental disorders, it is not uncommon for an individual to have more than one paraphilia. The *DSM-IV-TR* lists the following paraphilias: **exhibitionism, fetishism, frotteurism, pedophilia, sexual masochism, sexual sadism, transvestic fetishism,** and **voyeurism**. The *DSM-IV-TR* also includes a category for paraphilia not otherwise specified, which is the category for the less common paraphilias, including necrophilia, zoophilia, and others.

Exhibitionism

Exhibitionism is the exposure of genitals to a nonconsenting stranger. In some cases, the individual may also engage in autoeroticism while exposing himself. Generally, no additional contact with the observer is sought; the individual is stimulated sexually by gaining the attention of and startling the observer.

Fetishism

People with this disorder achieve sexual gratification with the use of objects, most commonly women's undergarments, shoes, stockings, or other clothing item.

Frotteurism

Individuals with this disorder are gratified by touching or rubbing a non-consenting person. This behavior often occurs in busy, crowded places, such as on busy streets or on crowded buses or subways.

Pedophilia

Pedophilia involves sexual activity with a child, generally under age 13. The *DSM-IV-TR* describes a criterion that the individual with pedophilia be over 16 years of age and be at least five years older than the child. Individuals with this disorder may be attracted to either males or females or both, although incidents of pedophilic activity are almost twice as likely to be repeated by those individuals attracted to males. Individuals with this disorder develop procedures and strategies for gaining access to and trust of children.

Sexual masochism

Masochism is a term applied to a specific sexual disorder but which also has a broader usage. The sexual disorder involves pleasure and excitement produced by pain, either inflicted by others or by oneself. It usually begins in childhood or adolescence and is chronic. An individual with this disorder achieves gratification by experiencing pain. Masochism is the only paraphilia in which any noticeable number of women participate—about 5% of masochists are female. The term comes from the name of a nineteenth-century Austrian writer, Leopold von Sacher-Masoch, whose novels often included characters who were obsessed with the combination of sex and pain.

In the broader sense, masochism refers to any experience of receiving pleasure or satisfaction from suffering pain. The psychoanalytic view is that masochism is aggression turned inward, onto the self, when a person feels too guilty or is afraid to express it outwardly.

Sexual sadism

A sadistic individual achieves sexual gratification by inflicting pain on another person.

In psychoanalytic theory, sadism is related to the fear of castration, while the behaviorist explanation of sadomasochism (the deviant sexual practice combining sadism and masochism) is that its constituent feelings are physiologically similar to sexual arousal. Separate but parallel descriptions are given for sexual sadism and sexual masochism in the DSM-IV-TR. The clinical diagnostic criteria for both are recurrence of the behavior over a period of at least six months, and significant distress or impairment of the ability to function as a result of the behavior or associated urges or fantasies. Either type of behavior may be limited to fantasies (sometimes while one is engaged in outwardly nondeviant sex) or acted out with a consenting partner, a non-consenting partner, or in the case of masochism, alone. Sadomasochism occurs in both males and females, and in both heterosexual and homosexual relationships.

Transvestic fetishism

This disorder is characterized by heterosexual males who dress in women's clothing to achieve a sexual response. The activity may begin in adolescence, and in secret; later, as an adult, the man may dress as a woman completely and in public. Not all men who cross-dress are unhappy with their gender, but some are. In a small minority of men with transvestic fetishism, gender dysphoria (unhappiness with original gender) may emerge, and those men may eventually seek hormonal treatments or surgical sex reassignment to enable them to live permanently as women.

Voyeurism

Voyeurism is a paraphilia in which a person finds sexual excitement in watching unsuspecting people who are nude, undressing, or having sex. Voyeurs are almost always male, and the victims are usually strangers. A voyeur may fantasize about having sex with the victim but almost never actually pursues this. The voyeur may return to watch the same stranger repeatedly, but there is rarely any physical contact.

Voyeurs are popularly known as "peeping Toms," based on the eleventh-century legend of Lady Godiva. According to the story, Tom was a tailor who "peeped" at Lady Godiva as she rode naked through the streets of Coventry, England, in a sacrificial act to get her husband to lower taxes. Tom was struck with blindness for not looking away like everyone else.

Uncommon paraphilias

BESTIALITY. Bestiality is a term that describes sexual feelings or behaviors involving animals. Termed zoophilia by DSM-IV this is an uncommon disorder. The disorder does not specify an animal or category of animals; the person with zoophilia may focus sexual feelings on domesticated animals, such as dogs, or farm animals, such as sheep or goats.

NECROPHILIA. Necrophilia is a term that describes sexual feelings or behaviors involving corpses.

Resources

BOOKS

American Psychiatric Association. *Diagnostic and Statistical Manual of Mental Disorders.* 4th ed., text rev. Washington, DC: American Psychiatric Publishing, 2000.

Baumeister, Roy F. *Escaping the Self: Alcoholism, Spirituality, Masochism, and Other Flights from the Burden of Selfhood.* New York: Basic Books, 1993.

Caplan, Paula J. *The Myth of Women's Masochism.* 2nd ed. Toronto: University of Toronto Press, 1993.

Carnes, Patrick. *Out of the Shadows: Understanding Sexual Addiction.* 3rd ed. Center City, MN: Hazelden Publishing, 2001.

PERIODICALS

Guay, D.R. "Drug Treatment of Paraphilic and Nonparaphilic Sexual Disorders." *Clinical Therapeutics* 31, no. 1 (January 2009): 1–31.

WEBSITES

"Paraphilias." The Merck Manual Home Health Handbook. http://www.merckmanuals.com/home/print/mental_health_disorders/sexuality/paraphilias.html (accessed December 12, 2011).

Parental alienation disorder

Definition

Parental alienation disorder (PAD), also called "parental alienation syndrome" (PAS), is a controversial condition that occurs when one parent attempts to negatively affect a

Parental alienation disorder

child's relationship with the other parent (for instance, in child custody disputes). The specific term "parental alienation syndrome" was coined in 1985 by Richard A. Gardner (1931–2003), a child **psychiatrist**. At that time, Gardner defined PAS as a "disorder that arises primarily in the context of child custody disputes. Its primary manifestation is the child's campaign of denigration against a parent with no justification. It is caused by a combination of a programming (brainwashing) parent's indoctrinations and the child's own contributions to the vilification of the targeted parent."

Demographics

There are no reliable statistics for the prevalence of PAD in North America, although discussions of the subject in the mass media as well as professional medical and legal journals suggest that it is largely limited to middle- and upper middle-class families.

There is little agreement about the gender demographic in alienating versus targeted parents. Gardner himself changed his mind about the gender ratio following his initial publications about PAS. In the mid-1980s, Gardner stated that the mother was the alienator in 90% of parental alienation cases, based on the increase in the number of **child abuse** cases that were reported in the 1980s. He theorized that mothers used allegations of physical or **sexual abuse** to win custody, terminate the father's visitation rights, or punish the ex-husband. By 2002, Gardner acknowledged that men and women were equally likely to be alienators.

Description

There is no universally agreed-upon description of PAD, although it is most often described as when one parent's attempts to sway their child's opinion of the other parent, whether consciously or unconsciously, occur concurrently with the child's own words or actions against the other parent. In severe cases, the child will refuse to interact with the alienated parent. Others, however, prefer to avoid defining the condition as a syndrome or disorder, choosing instead to refer simply to parental alienation (PA) and focus on the alienated child and the family situation that has led to the child's estrangement from the rejected parent.

Parental alienation disorder has been proposed by outside sources for addition to the fifth edition of the **Diagnostic and Statistical Manual of Mental Disorders** (*DSM-5*). In 2005, the **American Psychological Association** issued a statement that it would not take a formal stand on the existence of parental alienation syndrome and noted the lack of empirical evidence for

PAD. In November 2010, the *DSM-5* working group on childhood and adolescent disorders stated that there is insufficient scientific evidence to justify the inclusion of parental alienation in the new diagnostic manual. In addition, PAD is not recognized as a disorder in the World Health Organization's *International Statistical Classification of Diseases and Related Health Problems*, tenth edition (ICD-10).

Controversy

The classification of PAD as a mental disorder is highly controversial. One reason is that there has been no agreement among psychiatrists, psychologists, family therapists, and other mental health professionals about its definition: whether PAD is a syndrome (a cluster of symptoms that occur together and are characteristic of a specific disease or disorder), a social dynamic, a mental disorder (in the child), or a relational problem (between parent and child). This fourth definition has been suggested by William Bernet as a justification for including parental alienation disorder under the heading of "Other Conditions That May Be a Focus of Clinical Attention" in *DSM-5*. The changing definitions and descriptions of PAD over the 25 years since Gardner first proposed its existence add to confusion in the courtroom as well as controversy among therapists.

Another major area of controversy is the actual prevalence of the disorder. One 2003 study of 215 California children maintained that PAD is likely to be overreported. The attitudes of the children toward their parents varied, but only a few were considered extreme, either negatively or positively. In addition, a large study of allegations of sexual abuse in child custody cases reported that such allegations are very rare and account for only 2% of child custody lawsuits.

Still another area of disagreement is whether PAD occurs only in separating or divorcing families, or whether it can occur in intact families when one parent (or stepparent or grandparent) seeks power over the other by turning the child or children against the targeted parent. Recent supporters of the existence of the syndrome claim that it can be found in families that are not presently involved in separation or divorce proceedings.

Gardner's own career is a significant source of controversy over PAD. In addition to serving as an expert witness for fathers in child custody cases, he held controversial views on **pedophilia** and other aberrant forms of sexual behavior, maintaining that such behaviors contribute to the survival of the species. Gardner stated in a 1992 article that sexual activities between an adult and a child create a "charged-up child" who will welcome sexual experiences at an early age and be more likely to reproduce. In a 1991 article, Gardner argued that Western society is "excessively moralistic and punitive" toward pedophiles. Gardner was also opposed to mandatory reporting of child abuse and lobbied Congress to abolish legally mandated reporting. He committed **suicide** in 2003 when the symptoms of a chronic neurological pain syndrome became worse.

The remaining reason for ongoing controversy over PAD is its use as a litigation strategy in divorce cases. The fathers' rights movement, a collection of organizations that emerged in the 1980s out of the conviction that the legal system discriminates against men in child custody cases, took up Gardner's early publications. Women's groups generally oppose recognizing PAD as a **diagnosis**, claiming that it has been used in courtroom proceedings to remove children from the custody of a qualified parent and to then stigmatize that parent.

Risk factors

Risk factors for the development of parental alienation disorder can include the following actions or behaviors by the alienating parent:

- severe mental disorder
- alcohol or drug abuse
- inability to control anger in the presence of children
- consistently returning the child or children late (more than 30 minutes) following a visit
- making verbal threats to abduct the children
- withholding visits and/or the child refusing to see the targeted parent

Other risk factors include the presence of an intrusive or controlling stepparent or grandparent in the household or any indications that the child is being mentally, physically, or sexually abused.

Causes and symptoms

Causes

The possible causes of parental alienation disorder (in the alienating parent) are identified as:

- unresolved anger toward the divorcing spouse
- unresolved issues with his or her family of origin
- narcissistic or paranoid personality disorder
- being so wrapped up in the child that he or she has no separate identity and regards the child's relationship with the other parent as a threat
- insecurity about his or her parenting skills, and projecting that insecurity onto the other parent
- the influence of a new spouse or domineering and meddlesome grandparents

---

KEY TERMS

Alienator—The parent attempting to negatively affect the child's opinion of the other (targeted or alienated) parent.

Ambivalence—A state of having conflicting feelings about the same person or situation at the same time.

Fathers' rights movement—A social movement that emerged in the 1980s in response to what members consider gender bias in favor of women in family law.

Syndrome—A group or cluster of symptoms that occur together and are characteristic of a specific disease or disorder.

Symptoms

Gardner listed eight symptoms of parental alienation syndrome in children:

- ongoing denigration of, and hatred toward, the targeted parent
- weak, silly, or frivolous rationalizations of the hateful behavior
- absence of ambivalence (mixed feelings) toward the targeted parent
- maintaining that the decision to reject the targeted parent is his or hers alone (referred to as the "independent thinker phenomenon")
- knee-jerk support of the favored parent
- lack of guilt for treating the rejected parent badly
- using catchphrases or scenarios borrowed from the favored parent
- expanding the rejection of the targeted parent to include his or her extended family and friends

Gardner went on to define three levels of severity of PAS:

- Mild—the child has only six of the eight symptoms; lack of ambivalence and absence of guilt over cruelty to the alienated parent do not appear.
- Moderate—all eight symptoms are present at a moderate intensity.
- Severe—all eight symptoms are present at a high level of severity.

Diagnosis

As of 2011, there were no formally accepted diagnostic criteria for parental alienation disorder, no published and tested assessments or questionnaires to make the diagnosis, and no imaging or laboratory tests to make or confirm the diagnosis. No large-scale controlled studies of the validity and reliability of the concept of parental alienation disorder have yet been conducted. In addition, a survey of 448 mental health and legal professionals reported in 2009 that the respondents were cautious about the applicability of PAD in child custody cases; they were reluctant to support the concept of PAD and did not regard it as meeting admissibility standards for courtroom proceedings.

Bernet proposed the following diagnostic criteria for parental alienation disorder in 2010:

• Criterion A: The child aligns himself or herself with one parent and refuses contact with the alienated parent.

• Criterion B: The child exhibits the first two symptoms listed by Gardner—continuous rejection of the alienated parent, and irrational justifications for the alienation.

• Criterion C: The child manifests two or more of the remaining six symptoms on Gardner's list.

• Criterion D: The "disturbance" lasts for at least two months.

• Criterion E: The "disturbance" causes significant distress or impairment in the child's social, academic, and other areas of functioning.

• Criterion F: The child's refusal to see the rejected parent has no legitimate justification (such as abuse).

Tests

At one point, Gardner published what he called the Sexual Abuse Legitimacy Scale to evaluate children who claimed they had been sexually abused by a parent. The scale was dismissed by child psychologists and psychiatrists and was consequently withdrawn. There was no published and tested diagnostic measure for PAD as of 2011.

Treatment

Gardner's recommendations for treating children with PAD were severe, including complete **denial** of contact between mother and child, and "deprogramming" the child of the belief that he or she has been abused. In some cases, children have become suicidal when forced to live with abusive fathers.

There is no agreement among contemporary therapists who accept the existence of PAD as to what type of therapeutic approach works best with children, nor were there any studies published as of 2011 comparing

different forms of **psychotherapy**. There is, however, a general recognition that Gardner's punitive approach is unacceptable and could possibly lead to violation of the civil rights of parents.

Another aspect of treatment for PAD is the financial benefit to therapists if PAD is included in *DSM-5*. Bernet has been quoted as saying that inclusion of PAS in *DSM-5* "would spur insurance coverage, stimulate more systematic research, lend credence to charge of parental alienation in court, and raise the odds that children would get timely treatment." Opponents of inclusion have charged that proponents of the syndrome are looking for a way to expand their practices. A family lawyer in Florida has maintained that much of the current momentum to add PAS to *DSM-5* is monetary; psychologists and other consultants profit from conducting the evaluations and therapies involved in family court disputes.

Prognosis

Gardner stated in the 1980s that PAD inflicted irreparable harm on the children he diagnosed with the syndrome, in that the relationship between the child and the targeted parent could never be re-established. Other mental health professionals who accept the existence of PAD are less pessimistic but still maintain that it has serious long-term effects on children, including **depression**, **substance abuse**, a history of failed relationships and multiple divorces, and alienation from their own children.

Resources

BOOKS

Bernet, William, ed. *Parental Alienation, DSM-5, and ICD-11*. Springfield, IL: Charles C. Thomas, Publisher, 2010.

Brock, Michael G., and Samuel Saks. *Contemporary Issues in Family Law and Mental Health*. Springfield, IL: Charles C. Thomas, Publisher, 2008.

Darnall, Douglas. *Divorce Casualties: Understanding Parental Alienation*, 2nd ed. Lanham, MD: Taylor Publishing Co., 2008.

Gardner, Richard A. *Therapeutic Interventions for Children with Parental Alienation Syndrome*. Cresskill, NJ: Creative Therapeutics, 2001.

PERIODICALS

Baker, Amy J.L. "Parental Alienation Syndrome: The Parent/Child Disconnect." *Social Work Today* 8 (November–December 2008): 26. http://www.socialworktoday.com/archive/102708p26.shtml (accessed July 12, 2011).

Barton, Adriana. "Diagnosing Divorce: Should Parental Alienation Be a Mental Disorder?" *The Globe and Mail* (May 9, 2011). http://www.theglobeandmail.com/life/the-hot-button/diagnosing-divorce-should-parental-alienation-be-a-mental-disorder/article2015939 (accessed July 12, 2011).

Bernet, W. "Parental Alienation Disorder and DSM-V." *American Journal of Family Therapy* 36 (May 2008): 349–66.

Bow, J.N., et al. "Examining Parental Alienation in Child Custody Cases: A Survey of Mental Health and Legal Professionals." *American Journal of Family Therapy* 37 (February 2009): 127–45.

Bruch, C.S. "Parental Alienation Syndrome and Parental Alienation: Getting It Wrong in Child Custody Cases." *Family Law Quarterly* 35 (2001): 527–52.

Farkas, M.M. "An Introduction to Parental Alienation Syndrome." *Journal of Psychosocial Nursing and Mental Health Services* 49 (April 2011): 20–26.

Gardner, R.A. "Denial of the Parental Alienation Syndrome Also Harms Women." *American Journal of Family Therapy* 30 (March 2002): 191–202.

Hoult, J. "The Evidentiary Admissibility of Parental Alienation Syndrome: Science, Law, and Policy." *Children's Legal Rights Journal* 26 (January 2006): 1–61.

Johnston, J.T. "Parental Alignments and Rejection: An Empirical Study of Alienation in Children of Divorce." *Journal of the American Academy of Psychiatry and the Law* 31 (February 2003): 158–70.

Winter, Mary. "Recognizing Parental Alienation Syndrome." *Denver Post*, December 5, 2010. http://www.denverpost.com/opinion/ci_16763836 (accessed July 11, 2011).

OTHER

Bernet, William, and Joseph N. Kenan. "Proposed Text for Parental Alienation Disorder in DSM-5." Lecture presented to the Forensic Mental Health Association of California, March 24, 2011. http://www.fmhac.net/Assets/Documents/2011/Presentations/BernetParental%20Alienation.pdf (accessed July 12, 2011).

WEBSITES

American Psychiatric Association. "Conditions Proposed by Outside Sources." DSM-5 Development. http://www.dsm5.org/ProposedRevisions/Pages/ConditionsProposedbyOutsideSources.aspx (accessed July 12, 2011).

Crary, David. "Is Parental Alienation a Mental Disorder?" MSNBC.com. October 1, 2010. http://www.msnbc.msn.com/id/39463768/ns/health-mental_health (accessed July 11, 2011).

Dallam, Stephanie J. "Dr. Richard Gardner: A Review of His Theories and Opinions on Atypical Sexuality, Pedophilia, and Treatment Issues." Leadership Council on Child Abuse and Interpersonal Violence. http://www.leadershipcouncil.org/1/res/dallam/2.html (accessed July 11, 2011).

———. "The Parental Alienation Syndrome: Is It Scientific?" Leadership Council on Child Abuse and Interpersonal Violence. http://www.leadershipcouncil.org/1/res/dallam/3.html (accessed July 11, 2011).

Lithwick, Dahlia. "Mommy Hates Daddy and You Should Too." Slate.com. May 17, 2011. http://www.slate.com/id/2294831 (accessed July 12, 2011).

Meier, Joan S. "Parental Alienation Syndrome & Parental Alienation: Research Reviews." VAWnet.org (National Online Resource Center on Violence Against Women).

http://www.vawnet.org/sexual-violence/summary.php?doc_id=1679&find_type=web_desc_AR (accessed August 4, 2011).

ORGANIZATIONS

American Academy of Psychiatry and the Law (AAPL), One Regency Drive, PO Box 30, Bloomfield, CT, 06002, (860) 242-5450, (800) 331-1389, Fax: (860) 286-0787, http://www.aapl.org/contact.htm, http://www.aapl.org.

American Psychiatric Association, 1000 Wilson Boulevard, Suite 1825, Arlington, VA, 22209-3901, (703) 907-7300, apa@psych.org, http://www.psych.org.

Canadian Symposium for Parental Alienation Syndrome (CS-PAS), 150 Hollidge Blvd., Suite 252, Aurora, Canada ONL4G 8A3, (647) 476-3170, info@cspas.ca, http://cspas.ca.

Leadership Council on Child Abuse and Interpersonal Violence, c/o Joyanna Silberg, Ph.D., 6501 North Charles Street, PO Box 6815, Baltimore, MD, 21285-6815. desk1@leadershipcouncil.org, http://www.leadershipcouncil.org/index.html.

National Council of Juvenile and Family Court Judges (NCJFCJ), PO Box 8970, Reno, NV, 89507, (775) 784-6012, Fax: (775) 784-6628, staff@ncjfcj.org, http://www.ncjfcj.org.

Rebecca J. Frey, Ph.D.

Parent management training

Definition

Parent management training (PMT) is an adjunct to treatment that involves educating and coaching parents to change their child's problem behaviors using principles of learning theory and **behavior modification**.

Purpose

The aim of PMT is to decrease or eliminate a child's disruptive or inappropriate behaviors at home or school and to replace problematic ways of acting with positive interactions with peers, parents and authority figures such as teachers. In order to accomplish this goal, PMT focuses on enhancing parenting skills. The PMT therapist coaches parents in applying strategies such as rewarding positive behavior, and responding to negative behavior by removing rewards or enforcing undesirable consequences (punishments). Although PMT focuses on specific targeted behaviors rather than on the child's **diagnosis**, it has come to be associated with the treatment of certain disorders. PMT is used in treating **oppositional defiant disorder**, **conduct disorder**, **intermittent explosive disorder** (age-inappropriate tantrums), and attention deficit disorder with hyperactivity (**attention deficit hyperactivity disorder**). Antisocial behaviors such as firesetting and truancy can also be addressed through PMT.

Description

In PMT, the therapist conducts initial teaching sessions with the parent(s), giving a short summary of foundational concepts in behavior modification; demonstrating interventions for the parents; and coaching parents in carrying out the techniques of PMT. Early meetings with the therapist focus on training in the principles of behavior modification, response-contingent learning, and ways to apply the techniques. Parents are instructed to concretely and specifically define the behavior(s) to be changed. In addition, they learn how to observe and identify relevant behavior and situational factors, and how to chart or otherwise record the child's behavior. Defining, observing and recording behavior are essential to the success of this method, because when behaviors such as fighting or tantrums are highlighted in concrete, specific ways, techniques of **reinforcement** and punishment can be put to use. Progress or its absence is easier to identify when the description of the behavior is defined with enough clarity to be measurable, and when responses to the PMT interventions are tracked on a chart. After the child's parents grasp the basic interventions as well as when and how to apply them, the techniques that the parents practiced with the therapist can be carried out at home.

Learning theory, which is the conceptual foundation of PMT, deals with the ways in which organisms learn to respond to their environment, and the factors that affect the frequency of a specific behavior. The core of learning theory is the notion that actions increase or decrease in frequency depending on the consequences that occur immediately after the actions. Research in parent-child interactions in families with disruptive, difficult, or defiant children shows that parental responses are often unintentionally reinforcing the unwanted behaviors. PMT trains parents to become more aware of their reactions to a child's behavior. The parents learn to provide attention, praise, and increased affection in reaction to the child's desired behaviors, and to withdraw attention, suspend displays of affection, or withdraw privileges in instances of less desirable behavior.

The most critical element of PMT is offering positive reinforcement for socially appropriate (or at least nondeviant) behaviors. An additional component involves responding to any undesired behaviors by removing rewards or applying punishment. These two types of response to the child must be carried out with great consistency. Consistent responding is important because erratic responses to unwanted behavior can actually cause the behavior to increase in frequency. For instance, if a child consistently throws tantrums in stores, hoping to be given something to end the tantrum, inconsistent parent responses can worsen the situation. If a parent is occasionally determined not to give in, but provides a candy bar or a toy to end the tantrum on other occasions, the child learns either to have more tantrums, or to have more dramatic tantrums. The rise in the number or intensity of tantrums occurs because the child is trying to increase the number of opportunities to obtain that infrequent parental reward for the behavior. Planning responses ahead of time to predefined target behaviors by rewarding desired actions and by withdrawing rewards or applying punishment for undesirable behavior is a fundamental principle of PMT. Consistent consequences, which are contingent on (in response to) the child's behavior, result in behavior change. Parents practice therapeutic ways of responding to their child's behavior in the PMT sessions with the therapist.

Through PMT, parents learn that positive rewards for appropriate behaviors can be offered in a variety of ways. Giving praise, providing extra attention, earning points toward obtaining a reward desired by the child, earning stickers or other small indicators of positive behavior, earning additional privileges, hugging (and other affectionate gestures) are all forms of reward. The technical term for the rewarding of desired behavior is *positive reinforcement*. Positive reinforcement refers to consequences that cause the desired target behavior to increase.

PMT instructs parents to cancel rewards or give punishments when the child behaves in undesirable ways. The removal of rewards usually entails time away from the circumstances and situations in which the child can do desired activities or receive attention. The concept of a "time out" is based on this notion of removal of rewards. Time out from rewards customarily means that the child is removed from people and stimulation for a certain period of time; it can also include loss of privileges.

Punishment in PMT is not necessarily what parents typically refer to as punishment; it most emphatically is *not* the use of physical punishment. A punishment in PMT involves a response to the child's negative behavior by exposing the child to something he or she regards as unpleasant. Examples of punishments might include having to redo the correct behavior so many times that it becomes annoying; verbal reproaches; or

Behavior modification—An approach to therapy based on the principles of operant conditioning. Behavior modification seeks to replace undesirable behaviors with preferable behaviors through the use of positive or negative reinforcement.

Positive reinforcement—A procedure or response that rewards a desired behavior.

Response-contingent—An approach to treatment in which rewards or punishments are given in response to a particular behavior to be encouraged or corrected.

Social learning theory—A subset of learning theories based on the concept that human behavior originates in and is affected by the interplay among the person's learned experiences, previous behaviors, and environmental influences.

the military standby—"drop and give me fifty"—having to do pushups or situps or laps around a playing field to the point of discomfort.

The least challenging problems, which have the greatest likelihood of successful change, are tackled first, in hope of giving the family a "success experience." The success experience is a positive reinforcement for the family, increasing the likelihood that they will continue using PMT in efforts to bring about change. In addition, lower-level behavioral problems provide opportunities for parents to become skilled in intervening and to learn consistency in their responses. After the parents have practiced using the skills learned in PMT on the less important problems, more severe issues can be tackled.

In addition to face-to-face sessions with the parents, some PMT therapists make frequent telephone calls to the parents between sessions. The purposes of the calls are to remind parents to continue to be consistent in applying the techniques; to answer questions about the work at home; and to praise the parents' attempts to correct the child's behavior. In addition, ongoing support in sessions and on the telephone helps parents feel less isolated and thus more likely to continue trying to use learning principles in managing their child. Troubleshooting any problems that arise regarding the application of the behavioral techniques is handled over the telephone and in the office sessions.

An additional aspect of learning theory is that rewarding subunits of the ultimately desired behavior can lead to developing more complex new actions. The subunits are finally linked together by changing the ways in which the rewards are given. This process is called "chaining." Sometimes, if the child shows no elements of the desired response, then the desired behavior is demonstrated for the child and subsequent "near hits" or approximations are rewarded. To refine "close but not quite" into the targeted response, rewards are given in a slightly "pickier" manner. Rewarding successive approximations of the desired behavior is also called "shaping."

Risks

The best way to learn to alter parental responses to child behaviors is with the support and assistance of a behavioral health professional (**psychologist, psychiatrist**, clinical social worker). Parents often inadvertently reinforce the problem behaviors, and it is difficult for a parent to see objectively the ways in which he or she is unintentionally supporting the defiant or difficult behavior. Furthermore, inappropriate application of such behavioral techniques as those used in PMT can actually make the problem situation worse. Families should seek therapists with valid credentials, skills, training and experience in PMT.

Results

Typically, the parents should notice a decrease in the unwanted behaviors after they implement the techniques learned in PMT at home. Of the various therapies used to treat childhood disorders, PMT is among those most frequently researched. PMT has shown effectiveness in changing children's behavior in very well-designed and rigorous studies. PMT has a greater effect on behavior than many other treatments, including **family therapy** or **play therapy**. Furthermore, the results—improved child behavior and reduction or elimination of undesirable behavior—are sustained over the long term. When a group of children whose families had used PMT were examined one to fourteen years later, they had maintained higher rates of positive behavior and lower levels of problem behavior.

Resources
BOOKS

Hendren, R. L. *Disruptive Behavior Disorders in Children and Adolescents*. Review of Psychiatry Series, Vol. 18, no. 2. Washington, DC: American Psychiatric Press, 1999.

Webster-Stratton, C., and M. Herbert. *Troubled Families— Problem Children: Working with Parents, a Collaborative Process*. Chichester, England: Wiley, 1995.

PERIODICALS

Feldman, Julie, and Alan E. Kazdin. "Parent Management Training for Oppositional and Conduct Problem Children." *Clinical Psychologist* 48, no. 4 (1995): 3–5. Available online at http://www.apa.org/divisions/div12/Rev_Est/pmt_child.html (accessed November 9, 2011).

Golding, Kim. "Parent Management Training as an Intervention to Promote Adequate Parenting." *Clinical Child Psychology and Psychiatry* 5, no. 3 (2000): 357–372.

Kazdin, A. E. "Parent Management Training: Evidence, Outcome and Issues." *Journal of American Academic Child and Adolescent Psychiatry* 36, no. 10 (October 1997): 1349–1356.

ORGANIZATIONS

American Academy of Child and Adolescent Psychiatry, 3615 Wisconsin Ave. NW, Washington, DC, 20016-3007, (202) 966-7300, Fax: (202) 966-2891, http://aacap.org.

Association for Behavioral and Cognitive Therapies, 305 Seventh Ave., 16th Floor, New York, NY, 10001-6008, (212) 647-1890, Fax: (212) 647-1865, http://www.abct.org.

North American Family Institute, 26 Howley Street, Peabody, MA, 01960, (978) 538-0286, Fax: (978) 531-9313, http://www.nafi.com.

Deborah Rosch Eifert, Ph.D

Parnate *see* Tranylcypromine

Paroxetine

Definition

Paroxetine is an antidepressant of the type known as **selective serotonin reuptake inhibitors (SSRIs)**. It is sold in the United States under the brand name Paxil.

Purpose

Paroxetine is approved by the U.S. Food and Drug Administration (FDA) for treatment of **depression** and for the following **anxiety disorders: obsessive-compulsive disorder**, **panic disorder**, **generalized anxiety disorder**, **post-traumatic stress disorder**, and social anxiety disorder.

Description

Paroxetine increases the amount of **serotonin** (also called "5-HT") available in the **brain**. Serotonin is a neurotransmitter, or chemical in the brain that carries nerve impulses from a sending neuron (nerve cell) to a receiving neuron. The sending neuron releases serotonin into a little gap between neurons, called the synapse. The

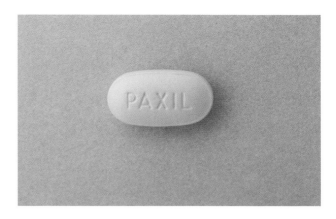

Paxil (paroxetine), 20 mg. (© *Custom Medical Stock Photo, Inc. Reproduced by permission.*)

receiving neuron picks up the serotonin from the synapse, allowing the nerve impulse to continue on its way.

Researchers think that depression and certain other disorders may be caused, in part, because there is not enough available serotonin in the brain. Normally, once a nerve impulse has crossed the synapse, serotonin is reabsorbed by the sending neuron that released it. Once reabsorbed, this serotonin is no longer available and cannot interact with a receiving neuron. Paroxetine blocks the reabsorption, or re-uptake, of serotonin, leaving it available to stimulate receiving neurons. Therefore, paroxetine facilitates the transmission of nerve impulses by increasing available serotonin in the brain and thus increasing its effectiveness.

Paroxetine is an antidepressant that is virtually completely absorbed via oral administration. Food does not reduce its absorption.

The benefits of paroxetine develop slowly over a period of up to four weeks. Patients should be aware of this and continue to take the drug as directed, even if they feel no immediate improvement.

Recommended dosage

The recommended dosage of paroxetine is 20–50 mg per day. The drug should be taken only once per day. An appropriate initial dosage is 20 mg. Dosage changes should not be made more frequently than once per week.

The recommended dosage for older persons or individuals with liver or kidney disease is 10 mg per day. The total dosage for such persons should not exceed 40 mg per day.

Precautions

Paroxetine should never be taken with **monoamine oxidase inhibitors (MAOIs)**.

Paroxetine may lower the threshold for a **manic episode** among people with bipolar (manic-depressive) disorders. For this reason, the drug should be used only with caution and under close supervision in these patients. It may also increase the chance of having a seizure in people with a history of seizure disorders.

The possibility of **suicide** is a component of depression. The minimum number of doses of paroxetine should be dispensed at any one time to minimize the potential for use as a suicide agent.

Hyponatremia (abnormally low concentration of sodium in the blood) has been associated with the use of paroxetine. In all cases, this condition resolved when the drug was discontinued. Most of these instances occurred among older individuals who were also taking diuretics (water pills).

Like other **SSRIs**, paroxetine carries a warning regarding use in children and adults up to the age of 24, who appear to have an increased risk of developing suicidal thoughts or actions while using these agents.

Side effects

Common side effects associated with paroxetine include headache, weakness, chills, malaise, nausea, and sleepiness. Other complaints included dry mouth, dizziness, tremors, constipation, diarrhea, and problems with ejaculation. Adverse reactions to paroxetine have been reported for all organ systems of the body, but all of these side effects are uncommon.

In general, the incidence of side effects increases as the dosage of paroxetine increases.

Interactions

There is the potential for a fatal interaction with another class of antidepressant drugs called monoamine-oxidase inhibitors (**MAOIs**). There have been reports of dangerously elevated body temperature, muscle rigidity, and rapid changes in vital signs, such as heart rate and blood pressure. Mental changes ranging from extreme agitation to **delirium** and coma have also been reported. Because of this, paroxetine should never be taken in combination with MAO inhibitors. Patient taking any MAO inhibitors, for example Nardil (**phenelzine** sulfate) or Parnate (**tranylcypromine** sulfate), should stop the MAO inhibitor then wait at least 14 days before starting paroxetine or any other antidepressant. The same holds true when discontinuing paroxetine and starting an MAO inhibitor.

The combination of paroxetine with the antipsychotic drug **thioridazine** has the potential to cause fatal cardiac arrhythmias (irregular heartbeat). The use of paroxetine in combination with tryptophan may result in unwanted reactions, including agitation, restlessness, and gastrointestinal distress. Paroxetine may also increase the chance of having a seizure in people with a history of seizure disorders. People taking anticonvulsants to control **seizures** should be closely monitored, and a physician may need to adjust the dosage of their seizure medication.

People with **bipolar disorder** are commonly treated with lithium. No interactions between paroxetine and lithium have been reported, nor are there any reported interactions with the common antianxiety drug **diazepam** (Valium).

Phenobarbital at dosages greater than 100 mg per day decreases the bioavailability of paroxetine in some persons. Paroxetine has been reported to increase the systemic bioavailability of procyclidine.

Resources

BOOKS

Adams, Michael, and Norman Holland. *Core Concepts in Pharmacology.* Philadelphia: Lippincott-Raven, 1998.

Foreman, John C., and Torben Johansen. *Textbook of Receptor Pharmacology.* 2nd ed. Boca Raton, FL: CRC Press, 2002.

Von Boxtel, Chris J., Budiono Santoso, and I. Ralph Edwards. *Drug Benefits and Risks: International Textbook of Clinical Pharmacology.* New York: John Wiley and Sons, 2001.

PERIODICALS

Hegeman, J., et al. "Unraveling the Association between SSRI Use and Falls: An Experimental Study of Risk Factors for Accidental Falls in Long-Term Paroxetine Users." *Clinical Neuropharmacology* 34, no. 6 (2011): 210–15.

Tomita, Tetsu, et al. "The Association between Sunshine Duration and Paroxetine Response Time in Patients with Major Depressive Disorder." *Journal of Affective Disorders* (December 6, 2011) [e-pub ahead of print]. http://dx.doi.org/10.1016/j.jad.2011.11.012 (accessed January 6, 2012).

WEBSITES

PubMed Health. "Paroxetine." U.S. National Library of Medicine. http://www.ncbi.nlm.nih.gov/pubmedhealth/PMH0001037 (accessed January 6, 2012).

ORGANIZATIONS

National Institute of Mental Health, 6001 Executive Blvd., Rm. 8184, MSC 9663, Bethesda, MD, 20892-9663, (301) 433-4513; TTY: (301) 443-8431, (866) 615-6464; TTY: (866) 415-8051, Fax: (301) 443-4279, nimhinfo@nih.gov, http://www.nimh.nih.gov.

U.S. Food and Drug Administration, 10903 New Hampshire Ave., Silver Spring, MD, 20993-0002, (888) INFO-FDA (463-6332), http://www.fda.gov.

L. Fleming Fallon, Jr., M.D., Dr.P.H.

Paruresis *see* **Toilet phobia**

Passionflower

Definition

Passionflower (*Passiflora incarnata*) is a vine whose leaves and flowers are widely used in Europe to make a herbal remedy for anxiety and **insomnia**. The plant, which is native to the tropical regions of North America, was first used by the Aztecs of Mexico as a folk remedy for these conditions. Passionflower is also known as maypop, apricot vine, passion vine, and granadilla. It grows as much as 30 ft. (10 m) tall, with a thick, woody stem.

The parts of the plant that grow above the ground are gathered to make passionflower preparations. They may be used either fresh or dried. The most common sources of the passionflower that is used today are India, the West Indies, and the southern United States; the vine can also be grown in Mexico and Latin America.

Purpose

Passionflower is used as a sedative and anxiolytic far more frequently in Great Britain and Europe than in the United States. In Britain, passionflower is the single most common ingredient in herbal **sedatives**, and the German Commission E approved it for use as a tranquilizer. It is also used in homeopathic remedies. In addition to its long-standing uses as a remedy for anxiety and insomnia, passionflower has been shown to be effective in treating narcotic drug withdrawal and adjustment disorder. Passionflower may be recommended for the treatment of gastrointestinal disorders related to anxiety, asthma, tachycardia (an abnormally rapid heartbeat), menstrual cramps, **seizures**, **attention deficit hyperactivity disorder**, and hysteria, but these uses have not yet been proven by **clinical trials**. A topical preparation made from passionflower has been used to treat hemorrhoids.

Description

Passionflower preparations may be made from the flowers, leaves, or shoots of the plant. After the first fruits of the plant have matured, younger shoots growing 12.7–17.8 cm above the ground are harvested and air dried. The plant material is used to prepare infusions, teas, liquid extracts, and tinctures of passionflower. In Europe, passionflower is often combined with lemon balm or **valerian** to make a sedative tea. The standardized formula approved by the German Commission E contains 30% passionflower, 40% valerian root, and 30% lemon balm. Passionflower is also used to make a special sedative tea for children, which typically includes 30% passionflower, 30% lemon balm, 30% **lavender** flower, and 10% **St. John's wort**. Passionflower is sometimes combined with hawthorn to make a remedy for stomach cramps associated with gastritis.

Although passionflower has been shown in animal studies to have sedative and antispasmodic effects, researchers are not yet certain which compounds in the plant have these properties. Passionflower is known to contain flavonoids and a group of alkaloid compounds that include harman, harmine, harmaline, and harmalol. Some researchers have hypothesized that the medicinal

Passionflower plant. (© *iStockPhoto.com/Lidian Neeleman*)

effects of passionflower derive from a combination of these substances rather than from any of them in isolation. A recent Swiss study, however, appears to indicate that a flavonoid called chrysin may be the source of passionflower's anxiolytic properties.

Recommended dosage

As the German recipe indicates, passionflower is considered safe for children. Dosages for children should be calculated on the basis of the child's weight. Since most adult dosages of herbal remedies assume an average adult weight of 150 lb. (70 kg), a child weighing 50 lb. (23 kg) can be given one-third of the adult dose.

Recommended adult doses of passionflower are as follows:

• Infusion: 2–5 g of dried herb, up to three times daily

• Fluid extract (1:1 ratio in a solution of 25% alcohol): 0.5–1.0 mL up to three times daily

• Tincture (1:5 ratio in a solution of 45% alcohol): 0.5–2.0 mL up to three times daily

Precautions

Passionflower should not be used in doses higher than the recommended levels. Because it has a sedative effect, it should not be combined with alcoholic beverages or prescription sedatives. Passionflower should not be used by pregnant or lactating women or for children under six months old, and persons undergoing surgery should stop using passionflower at least two weeks before their procedure.

Side effects

Passionflower is considered generally safe when taken short term. Reported possible side effects include confusion, dizziness or vertigo, vasculitis (blood vessel inflammation), and abnormal muscle contraction or movement.

Interactions

The alkaloids found in passionflower, especially harman and harmaline, may increase the effects of a class of prescription **antidepressants** called **monoamine oxidase inhibitors (MAOIs)**. These drugs are most often prescribed for **depression**, panic attacks, and eating disorders. Passionflower may also increase the effects of sedative medications and should not be used in conjunction with either of these drugs.

KEY TERMS

Antispasmodic—A medication or preparation given to relieve muscle or digestive cramps.

Anxiolytic—A preparation or substance given to relieve anxiety; a tranquilizer.

Flavonoids—Plant pigments that have a variety of effects on human physiology. Some of these pigments have anti-inflammatory, anticarcinogenic, and antioxidant effects.

Gastritis—Inflammation of the lining of the stomach.

Infusion—The most potent form of extraction of a herb into water. Infusions are steeped for a longer period of time than teas.

Tincture—An alcohol-based herbal extract prepared by soaking parts of the plant in a mixture of alcohol and water. Established ratios and dilutions are followed.

Resources

BOOKS

Awang, Dennis, V.C. *Tyler's Herbs of Choice*. New York: CRC Press, 2009.

"Western Herbal Medicine: Nature's Green Pharmacy." In *The Best Alternative Medicine*, by Kenneth R. Pelletier. New York: Touchstone, 2002.

PERIODICALS

Zanoli, P., R. Avallone, and M. Baraldi. "Behavioral Characterisation of the Flavonoids Apigenin and Chrysin." *Fitoterapia* 71, Suppl. 1 (2000): S117–S123.

WEBSITES

MedlinePlus. "Passionflower." U.S. National Library of Medicine, National Institutes of Health. http://www.nlm.nih.gov/medlineplus/druginfo/natural/871.html (accessed November 14, 2011).

ORGANIZATIONS

American Botanical Council, 6200 Manor Rd., Austin, TX, 78723, (512) 926-4900, (800) 373-7105, Fax: (512) 926-2345, abc@herbalgram.org, http://www.herbalgram.org.

National Center for Complementary and Alternative Medicine, 9000 Rockville Pike, Bethesda, MD, 20892, (888) 644-6226, http://nccam.nih.gov.

NIH Office of Dietary Supplements, 6100 Executive Blvd., Room 3B01, MSC 7517, Bethesda, MD, 20892-7517, (301) 435-2920, Fax: (301) 480-1845, ods@nih.gov, http://www.odp.od.nih.gov.

Rebecca J. Frey, Ph.D.

Pathological gambling disorder *see*
Gambling disorder

Paxil *see* **Paroxetine**

Paxipam *see* **Galantamine**

PCP *see* **Phencyclidine and related disorders**

Pedophilia

Definition

Pedophilia is a paraphilia that involves an abnormal interest in children. A paraphilia is a disorder that is characterized by recurrent intense sexual urges and sexually arousing fantasies generally focused on nonhuman objects; the suffering or humiliation of oneself or one's partner (not merely simulated); or animals, children, or other nonconsenting persons. Pedophilia is also a psychosexual disorder in which the fantasy or actual act of engaging in sexual activity with prepubertal children is the preferred or exclusive means of achieving sexual excitement and gratification. It may be directed toward children of the same sex or children of the opposite sex. Some pedophiles are attracted to both boys and girls. Some are attracted only to children, while others are attracted to adults as well as to children.

Pedophilia is defined by mental health professionals as a mental disorder, but the American legal system defines acting on a pedophilic urge as a criminal act.

Demographics

Pedophilia is one of the more common paraphilias; the large worldwide market for child pornography suggests that it is more frequent in the general population than prison statistics would indicate. Together with **voyeurism** and **exhibitionism**, pedophilia is one of the three paraphilias most commonly leading to arrest by the police.

The onset of pedophilia usually occurs during adolescence. Occasional pedophiles begin their activities during middle age but this late onset is uncommon.

The frequency of behavior associated with pedophilia varies with psychosocial **stress**. As the pedophile's stress levels increase, the frequency of his or her acting out generally rises. This manifestation echoes those of a behavioral **addiction**.

Pedophilia is more common among males than among females. In addition, the rate of recidivism for persons with a pedophilic preference for males is approximately twice that of pedophiles who prefer females.

Marital status, socioeconomic level, educational background, and religious observance does not seem to predict pedophilia. Little is known about the incidence of pedophilia in different racial or ethnic groups.

Description

The focus of pedophilia is sexual activity with a child. Many courts interpret this reference to age to mean children under the age of 18. Most mental health professionals, however, confine the definition of pedophilia to sexual activity with prepubescent children, who are generally age 13 or younger. The term *ephebophilia*, derived from the Greek word for "youth," is sometimes used to describe sexual interest in young people in the first stages of puberty.

The sexual behaviors involved in pedophilia cover a range of activities and may or may not involve the use of force. Some pedophiles limit their behaviors to exposing themselves or masturbating in front of the child, or fondling or undressing the child, but without genital contact. Others, however, compel the child to participate in oral sex or full genital intercourse.

The most common overt aspect of pedophilia is an intense interest in children. There is no typical pedophile. Pedophiles may be young or old, male or female, although the great majority are males. Unfortunately, some pedophiles are professionals who are entrusted with educating or maintaining the health and well-being of young persons, while others are entrusted with children to whom they are related by blood or marriage.

Causes and symptoms

Causes

A variety of different theories exist regarding the causes of pedophilia. A few researchers attribute pedophilia, along with the other **paraphilias**, to biology. They hold that testosterone, one of the male sex hormones, predisposes men to develop deviant sexual behaviors. As of 2011, no genes or hereditary factors had been associated with the development of pedophilia.

Pedophilia, as a disorder based in **compulsion** and impulse control, may be related to other disorders associated with obsessive-compulsive and impulsive behaviors. Research, including an imaging study, suggests that abnormalities in an area of the **brain** called the frontal cortex are associated with pedophilia. Other studies have identified similar abnormalities in obsessive-compulsive spectrum disorders. In addition, recent research indicates that pedophilic behavior may be rooted in early disturbances in neurological development, although a clear biological basis for the disorder has not yet been established. Neurotransmitter (nerve signaling molecules) pathways in the brain related to mood regulation have been implicated; these include pathways involving **serotonin** and **dopamine**.

Some experts believe that there is an association between pedophilia and having been sexually abused as a child. Still others think that it derives from the person's interactions with parents during their early years of life. Some researchers attribute pedophilia to arrested emotional development; that is, the pedophile is attracted to children because he or she has never matured psychologically. Some regard pedophilia as the result of a distorted need to dominate a sexual partner. Because children are smaller and usually weaker than adults, they may be regarded as nonthreatening potential partners. This drive for domination is sometimes thought to explain why most pedophiles are males.

Symptoms

A pedophile often seems particularly trustworthy to the children who are potential victims. Potential pedophiles may volunteer their services to athletic teams, Scout troops, or religious or civic organizations that serve youth. In some cases, pedophiles who are attracted to children within their extended family may offer to baby-sit for their relatives. They often have good interpersonal skills with children and can easily gain the children's trust.

Some pedophiles offer rationalizations or excuses that enable them to avoid assuming responsibility for their actions. They may blame the children for being too attractive or sexually provocative. They may also maintain that they are "teaching" the child about "the facts of life" or "love"; this rationalization is frequently offered by pedophiles who have molested children related to them. All these rationalizations may be found in pornography with pedophilic themes.

Diagnosis

According to the *Diagnostic and Statistical Manual of Mental Disorders,* fourth edition text revised, the following criteria must be met to establish a **diagnosis** of pedophilia.

• Over a period of at least six months, the affected person must experience recurrent, intense and sexually arousing fantasies, sexual urges or actual behaviors involving sexual activity with a prepubescent child or children aged 13 or younger.

• The fantasies, sexual urges or behaviors must cause clinically significant distress or impairment in social,

occupational or other important areas of daily functioning.

• The affected person must be at least age sixteen and be at least five years older than the child or children who are the objects or targets of attention or sexual activity.

A diagnosis of pedophilia cannot be assigned to an individual in late adolescence (age 17 to 19) who is involved in an ongoing sexual relationship with a 12- or 13-year-old person.

In establishing a diagnosis of pedophilia, it is important for a mental health professional to determine if the patient is attracted to males, females or both. It is also important to determine whether incest is a factor in the relationship. Finally, the doctor must determine whether the pedophilia is exclusive or nonexclusive; that is, whether the patient is attracted only to children (exclusive pedophilia) or to adults as well as to children (nonexclusive pedophilia).

One difficulty with the diagnosis of the disorder is that persons with pedophilia rarely seek help voluntarily from mental health professionals. Instead, counseling and treatment is often the result of a court order. An interview that establishes the criteria for diagnosis may be enough to diagnose the condition, or surveillance or Internet records obtained through the criminal investigation may also be used.

An additional complication in diagnosis is that the paraphilias as a group have a high rate of comorbidity with one another and an equally high rate of comorbidity with major **depression**, **anxiety disorders**, and **substance abuse** disorders. A person diagnosed with pedophilia may also meet the criteria for exhibitionism or for a substance abuse or mood disorder.

Treatment

In the earliest stages of **behavior modification** therapy, pedophiles may be narrowly viewed as being attracted to inappropriate persons. Such aversive stimuli as electric shocks have been administered to persons undergoing therapy for pedophilia. This approach has not been very successful.

Types of treatment for pedophilia include **psychotherapy** and medication. Therapy is often undergone for many years but still does not have a high rate of success in inducing persons with pedophilia to change their behavior.

The three classes of medications most often used to treat pedophilia (and other paraphilias) are: hormones, particularly the synthetic medroxyprogesterone acetate (MPA); luteinizing hormone-releasing hormone (LHRH) agonists (mimics), which include such drugs as triptorelin (Trelstar), leuprolide acetate, and goserelin acetate; and antiandrogens, which block the uptake and metabolism of testosterone as well as reducing blood levels of this hormone. In particular, these drugs with antiandrogenic effects (interfering with the action of the body's androgenic hormones) have shown some efficacy in reducing the rate of recidivism. Most clinical studies of these drugs have been done in Germany, where the legal system has allowed their use in treating repeat sexual offenders since the 1970s. Researchers have reported some benefit with leuprolide acetate, for example, finding during a two-year study that none of the pedophiles being administered the drug re-offended.

Surgical castration is sometimes offered as a treatment to pedophiles who are repeat offenders or who have pleaded guilty to violent rape.

Increasingly, pedophiles are being prosecuted under criminal statutes and being sentenced to prison terms. Imprisonment removes them from society for a period of time but does not usually remove their pedophilic tendencies. As of 2011, all U.S. states had a registration and tracking system in place for sexual offenders. Legal challenges to this practice are pending in various jurisdictions.

Prognosis

The prognosis of successfully ending pedophilic habits among persons who practice pedophilia is not favorable. Pedophiles have a high rate of recidivism; that is, they tend to repeat their acts often over time.

The rate of prosecution for pedophiles through the criminal justice system has increased in recent years. Pedophiles are at high risk of being beaten or killed by other prison inmates. For this reason, they must often be kept isolated from other members of a prison population. Knowledge of the likelihood of abuse by prison personnel and inmates is not, however, an effective deterrent for most pedophiles.

Prevention

The main method for preventing pedophilia is avoiding situations that may promote pedophilic acts. Children should never be allowed to be in one-on-one situations with any adult other than their parents or trustworthy family members. Having another youth or adult as an observer provides some security for all concerned.

Children should be taught to yell or run if they are faced with an uncomfortable situation and reassured that it is acceptable to scream or call for help.

KEY TERMS

Castration—Desexing a person or animal by surgical removal of the testes (in males) or ovaries (in females). Castration is sometimes offered as a treatment option to pedophiles who are violent rapists and/or repeat offenders.

Comorbidity—Association or presence of two or more mental disorders in the same patient. A disorder that is said to have a high degree of comorbidity is likely to occur in patients diagnosed with other disorders that may share or reinforce some of its symptoms.

Ephebophilia—Sexual desire on the part of an adult for youths in the early stages of puberty, as distinct from prepubertal children.

Incest—Unlawful sexual contact between persons who are biologically related. Many therapists, however, use the term to refer to inappropriate sexual contact between any members of a family, including stepparents and stepsiblings.

Paraphilia—A disorder that is characterized by recurrent intense sexual urges and sexually arousing fantasies generally involving nonhuman objects, the suffering or humiliation of oneself or one's partner (not merely simulated), or children or other non-consenting persons.

Recidivism—A tendency to return to a previously treated activity, or repeated relapse into criminal or deviant behavior.

Voyeurism—A paraphilia that involves watching unsuspecting people, usually strangers, undress or engage in sexual activity.

Another basis of preventing pedophilia is education. Adults who work with youth should be trained on how to avoid situations that may be construed as promoting pedophilia.

All U.S. states conduct some type of background check on childcare providers, but they do not always check for a history of abuse or neglect. A law proposed in 2011 (Child Care Protection Act of 2011) will, if passed, require more extensive background checking.

The Boy Scouts of America has tried to address the problem of pedophilia by creating a training program that is required for all adults in the organization. All applications for volunteers are reviewed and approved by several persons. Adults and youth are required to use separate facilities on all activities.

Secret meetings and one-on-one interactions between adults and youth are prohibited. This program has received several national awards.

Resources

BOOKS

American Psychiatric Association. *Diagnostic and Statistical Manual of Mental Disorders*. 4th ed., text rev. Washington, DC: American Psychiatric Publishing, 2000.

Gelder, Michael, Paul Harrison, and Philip Cowen. *Shorter Oxford Textbook of Psychiatry*. 5th ed. New York: Oxford University Press, 2006.

Wilson, Josephine F. *Biological Foundations of Human Behavior*. Farmington Hills, MI: Cengage Learning, 2002.

PERIODICALS

Berlin, F. S. "Letters to Editor: Treatments to Change Sexual Orientation." *American Journal of Psychiatry* 157, no. 5 (May 2000): 8–9.

Cohen, L.J., et al. "Impulsive Personality Traits in Male Pedophiles Versus Healthy Controls: Is Pedophilia an Impulsive-Aggressive Disorder?" *Comprehensive Psychiatry* 43, no. 2 (March–April 2002): 127–34.

Hill, S.A. "The Man Who Claimed to Be a Paedophile." *Journal of Medical Ethics* 26, no. 2 (2000): 137–8.

O'Donohue, W., L.G. Regev, and A. Hagstrom. "Problems with the DSM-IV Diagnosis of Pedophilia." *Sexual Abuse* 12, no. 2 (2000): 95–105.

Schiffer, Boris, et al. "Structural Brain Abnormalities in the Frontostriatal System and Cerebellum in Pedophilia." *Journal of Psychiatric Research* 41, no. 9 (2007) 753–62.

Schober, Justine M., Peter M. Byrne, and Phyllis J. Kuhn. "Leuprolide Acetate is a Familiar Drug That May Modify Sex-Offender Behavior: The Urologist's Role." *British Journal of Urology International* 97 (2006): 684–6.

ORGANIZATIONS

American Academy of Family Physicians, 11400 Tomahawk Creek Parkway, Leawood, KS, 66211-2672, (913) 906-6000, (800) 274-2237, Fax: (913) 906-6075, contactcenter@aafp.org, http://www.aafp.org.

American Academy of Pediatrics, 141 Northwest Point Blvd., Elk Grove Village, IL, 60007-1098, (847) 434-4000, Fax: (847) 434-8000, http://www.aap.org.

American Medical Association, 515 N State Street, Chicago, IL, 60610, (312) 464-5000, (800) 621-8335, http://www.ama-assn.org.

American Psychiatric Association, 1000 Wilson Blvd., Ste. 1825, Arlington, VA, 22209-3901, (703) 907-7300, apa@psych.org, http://www.psych.org.

American Psychological Association, 750 1st Street NE, Washington, DC, 20002-4242, (202) 336-5500; TDD/TTY: (202) 336-6123, (800) 374-2721, http://www.apa.org.

L. Fleming Fallon, Jr., MD, Dr. P.H.
Emily Jane Willingham, Ph.D.

Peer groups

Description

Peer groups are an important influence throughout one's life, but they are more critical during the developmental years of childhood and adolescence. There is often controversy about the influence of a peer group versus parental influence, particularly during adolescence. Recent studies show that parents continue to have significant influence, even during adolescence, a reassuring finding for many parents. It appears that the power of the peer group becomes more important when the family relationships are not close or supportive. For example, if the parents work extra jobs and are largely unavailable, their children may turn to their peer group for emotional support. This also occurs when the conflict between parents and children during adolescence, or at any time during a child's development, becomes so great that the child feels pushed away and seeks closeness elsewhere. Most children and adolescents in this situation are not discriminating about the kind of group they join. They will often turn to a group simply because that group accepts them, even if the group is involved in illegal or negative activities. Gang involvement, for example, is a common form of organized—often antisocial—peer interaction. Gangs may be based on ethnicity, sex, and/or common activity. Most youths who join gangs come from families where drug and **alcohol use**, financial burdens, and broken relationships are common. The need for affiliation or closeness is often greater than the need to "do the right thing" for some adolescents who feel isolated and abandoned by members of their own family. Being part of a gang provides such individuals with acceptance and security not available at home or in other peer groups.

Membership in peer groups

Despite significant gains in diversity training, current studies continue to show that children are less likely to accept those who are different from themselves. The differences can be as obvious as physical impairments, or as subtle as differences in academic motivation. These rigid standards may create an atmosphere of exclusion for some children and adolescents that pushes them toward peer acceptance of any type.

Peer groups offer children and adults alike the opportunity to develop various social skills, such as leadership, sharing or teamwork, and empathy. Peer groups also offer the opportunity to experiment with new

Peer group interaction has immense influence on adolescents. *(© Frances Roberts/Alamy)*

roles and interactions, similar to treatment groups, although they are less structured. It is for this reason that many children and adolescents drift from one group to another as they "find themselves," or work toward formation of their relatively permanent identity.

Aggression in peer groups

Although **bullying** and teasing have long been part of peer group interactions, these negative behaviors have increased over the last decade, resulting in school violence in many instances. As children and adolescents feel marginalized from their peers, anger builds to a point of rage at times. It is at those times that violence erupts within the school or community setting.

Negative peer interactions also occur more frequently following friendships or romantic relationships that have gone sour. The level of harassment that many of these children—often young women—experience is great enough for parents to become involved. In some cases, it may be necessary to move the child to another school district. A potential remediation for these negative interactions includes more active teacher involvement when negative social interactions are observed.

Influence of peer groups

Peer groups can also have a positive influence—a fact many parents have known for years. Studies support parent's perceptions that the influence of friends can have a positive effect on academic motivation and performance. Conversely, experimentation with drugs, drinking, vandalism, and stealing may also be increased by interaction with the peer group.

Interventions

Since schools are often the site of negative peer interactions, school personnel have a unique opportunity for effective **intervention**. Many schools have peer-mediation programs, in which students are encouraged to resolve conflicts on their own without the use of violence or aggression. School counselors also organize groups within the school to handle various problems, including providing **social skills training** and empathy training.

Risks

Peer groups often provide an example for negative and harmful behaviors. Cluster **suicide** is one such

Schwartz, D. "Subtypes of Victims and Aggressors in Children's Peer Groups." *Journal of Abnormal Child Psychology* 28, no. 2 (April 2000): 181–192.

Deanna Pledge, Ph.D.

KEY TERMS

Cluster suicide—Refers to the phenomenon of additional suicides being attempted or completed after one suicide has occurred within a small community, such as a group of high school students.

example. When a teen realizes that someone he or she knew has attempted or has committed suicide, the teen may see suicide as a viable option for him- or herself as well. For this reason schools and local media should exercise caution when reporting such tragedies. Care must be taken not to portray the suicide glamorously or mythically.

When parents try to protect their children by telling them to stay away from certain friends, they should realize that sometimes this only encourage them to seek out negative role models. Parents should be supportive of their child and redirect their child's activities to more positive and prosocial peers and events. A trusted adult friend, such as a scout leader or a respected coach, may be an important part of the redirection effort.

As noted, children and adolescents without strong family connections, or at least a positive connection with other adults in their life, face a higher risk of negative influence from peer groups. If the child or adolescent has not been able to form bonds with positive peer groups, it is more likely they will be perceived as distant and different from their peers, making them feel more like outsiders. Lower standards of acceptance often exist in less positive peer groups, making it easier for people to join. Unfortunately, many such groups often engage in self-destructive and antisocial activities.

Resources

BOOKS

Juvonen, J., and S. Graham, eds. *Peer Harassment in School: The Plight of the Vulnerable and Victimized*. New York: The Guilford Press, 2001.

PERIODICALS

Pearl, R., et al. "The Social Integration of Students with Mild Disabilities in General Education Classrooms: Peer Group Membership and Peer-assessed Social Behavior." *Elementary School Journal* 99, no. 2 (November 1998): 167–185.

Ryan, A. M. "The Peer Group as a Context for the Development of Young Adolescent Motivation and Achievement." *Child Develoment* 72, no. 4 (July/August 2001): 1135–1150.

Pemoline

Definition

Pemoline is classified as a central nervous system (CNS) stimulant. It is no longer available in the United States but was previously sold under the brand names Cylert and PemADD as well as its generic name.

Purpose

Pemoline was used in combination with psychological, educational, and social support for the treatment of people with **attention deficit hyperactivity disorder (ADHD)**.

Description

Pemoline is a central nervous system stimulant that derives at least some of its effects by increasing levels of **dopamine** in the **brain**. Dopamine is one of several **neurotransmitters** in the brain. Neurotransmitters are naturally occurring chemicals that regulate the transmission of nerve impulses from one cell to another. Mental and physical well-being are partially dependent on

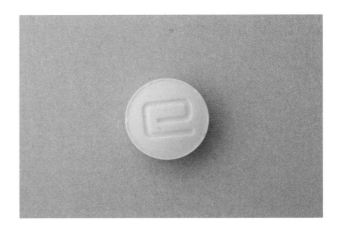

Cylert (pemoline), a drug used to treat attention deficit hyperactivity disorder (ADHD), is no longer available in the United States due to a risk of liver toxicity. (© *Custom Medical Stock Photo, Inc. Reproduced by permission.*)

maintaining the proper balance among the various neurotransmitters in the brain.

Pemoline is similar in its effects to **dextroamphetamine** and **methylphenidate**, two other drugs used to treat **ADHD**, although it is not chemically related to these drugs. The mechanism of action of CNS stimulants in the treatment of ADHD is not totally clear, but likely includes increased mental alertness, decreased mental **fatigue**, and an increased sense of well-being.

Pemoline is no longer manufactured for use, due to its association with potentially life-threatening liver toxicity. Symptoms of liver toxicity range from mild reversible changes in liver function tests to acute liver failure. The risk of liver damage should be weighed against any therapeutic benefit derived from treatment with pemoline.

Resources

BOOKS

American Society of Health-System Pharmacists. *AHFS Drug Information 2002*. Bethesda: American Society of Health-System Pharmacists, 2002.

Preston, John D., John H. O'Neal, and Mary C. Talaga. *Handbook of Clinical Psychopharmacology for Therapists*. 4th ed. Oakland, CA: New Harbinger Publications, 2004.

PERIODICALS

Bonnet, Udo, and Eugen Davids. "A Rare Case of Dependence on Pemoline." *Progress in Neuro-Psychopharmacology & Biological Psychiatry* 30, no. 7 (September 2006): 1340–41.

Krauseneck, Till, and Michael Soyka. "Delusional Parasitosis Associated with Pemoline." *Psychopathology* 38, no. 2 (March–April 2005): 103–4.

Pliszka, Steven R., et al. "The Texas Children's Medication Algorithm Project: Revision of the Algorithm for Pharmacotherapy of Attention-Deficit/Hyperactivity Disorder." *Journal of the American Academy of Child & Adolescent Psychiatry* 45, no. 6 (June 2006): 642–57.

WEBSITES

U.S. Food and Drug Administration. "Information for Healthcare Professionals: Pemoline Tablets and Chewable Tablets (marketed as Cylert)." U.S. Department of Health and Human Services. http://www.fda.gov/Drugs/DrugSafety/PostmarketDrugSafetyInformationforPatientsandProviders/ucm126461.htm (accessed August 18, 2011).

Jack Raber, Pharm.D.
Ruth A. Wienclaw, PhD

Pentobarbital *see* **Barbiturates**

Permitil *see* **Fluphenazine**

Perphenazine

Definition

Perphenazine is a phenothiazine antipsychotic used to treat serious mental disorders. It has also been used to treat severe nausea and vomiting. It is sold in the United States under the brand name Trilafon and is also available under its generic name.

Purpose

Perphenazine is used to treat psychotic disorders and severe nausea and vomiting.

Description

Perphenazine is one of many drugs in the class called phenothiazine derivatives. Phenothiazines work by inhibiting the actions of the **brain** chemicals **dopamine** and norepinephrine, which are overproduced in individuals with **psychosis**. It is a member of the group of "first-generation" antipsychotics, which had fallen out of favor with the advent of the "second-generation" drugs, thought to be more effective and confer fewer side effects. However, a recent study found that perphenazine is as effective as some of the newer drugs and is more cost-effective.

Recommended dosage

For the treatment of psychosis, adults usually receive a total of 4 mg to 16 mg taken as tablets in three or four doses daily, up to a maximum of 64 mg each day. There is also a liquid form available to be taken orally. Injections of perphenazine are also available and are typically given in 5 mg doses every 6 hours, up to 15 mg per day. Hospitalized patients can receive up to 30 mg per day in the injectable form of perphenazine.

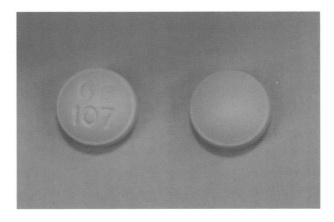

Perphenazine, 4 mg. (© *Custom Medical Stock Photo, Inc. Reproduced by permission.*)

Adult patients with serious nausea and vomiting receive 8 mg to 16 mg per day as tablets, divided into several doses, up to a maximum of 24 mg per day. Injections are typically given in 5 mg to 10 mg doses every 6 hours, up to 15 mg per day in patients who are not confined to bed. Hospitalized patients can receive up to a maximum of 30 mg per day. Intravenous perphenazine can be given to nausea and vomiting patients up to 1 mg every 1 to 2 minutes to a maximum of 5 mg.

The correct dosage of perphenazine must be carefully determined for each patient. Physicians try to find a dose that controls symptoms of the disease without causing intolerable side effects. Dosage guidelines for the treatment of psychosis have not been established for children under the age of 12. In children over age 12, the lowest adult dosage is generally used to treat psychosis. Children with severe nausea and vomiting are usually given 5 mg injections every six hours.

Precautions

Persons who take perphenazine should not stop taking the drug abruptly. Instead, the dose should be decreased gradually, then stopped. People who take perphenazine often develop sunburn easily; sunscreen should be used by persons, especially fair-skinned individuals, taking perphenazine.

Persons who are known to have severe central nervous system **depression** should not take perphenazine or any other drug in its class. In addition, those with a prior history of brain damage, coma, or bone marrow depression should not receive perphenazine without a thorough evaluation by a doctor.

Children under the age of 12, the elderly (over age 65), and those with a history of epilepsy, glaucoma, prostate problems, severe asthma, or other severe breathing problems should receive perphenazine only with great caution and under close supervision of a physician. In addition, persons with a history of heart or blood vessel disease and those with a history of liver or kidney disease should take perphenazine only after a thorough evaluation. Perphenazine should also be used cautiously when taken over a long period. Rarely should perphenazine be taken by pregnant or nursing women; it passes into the breastmilk and can cause drowsiness and adverse side effects in the infant.

Side effects

Serious or life-threatening side effects due to perphenazine are rare. However, if any of these occur, patients should contact their doctors or get immediate medical attention: **seizures**, irregular heartbeat, significant changes in blood pressure, muscle stiffness, weakness, pale skin color, and increased sweating. The treating doctor should be contacted immediately if any of these common side effects develops: rapid movements of the tongue, uncontrolled chewing movement, unusual amounts of lip smacking, and frequent movement of the arms or legs. The treating doctor should be contacted relatively soon if any of the following common side effects develops: reduced balance control, muscle spasms, restlessness, trembling, weakness in the limbs, blurred vision, and decreased night vision.

Less-common side effects that need to be reported to the doctor include severe sunburn, skin rashes, and urination problems. Rare side effects that should be reported to the doctor include abdominal pain, muscle aches, joint aches, fever, chills, muscle weakness, and vomiting. Common, but not serious, side effects include constipation, drowsiness, decreased sweating, mouth dryness, and nasal congestion. Uncommon, and not typically serious, side effects include decreased sexual desire, increased susceptibility to sunburn, menstrual cycle changes, swelling or pain in the breasts, and weight gain.

Perphenazine is not approved for the treatment of psychosis in elderly patients with **dementia**. In 2005, the FDA released a public health advisory warning patients and doctors against using **perphenazine** and other atypical antipsychotics off-label. In studies, these drugs significantly increased the risk of death in older patients with dementia, compared to placebo. Most of the deaths were associated with heart failure or infections such as pneumonia. Atypical antipsychotics also have been associated with an increased risk for **stroke** in elderly patients with dementia-related psychosis.

Interactions

Combining perphenazine with drugs such as the antimalarials amodiaquine, chloroquine, and sulfadoxine-pyrimethamine (Fansidar) can increase the concentrations within the body of these antimalarials.

Perphenazine combined with **barbiturates** tends to lower the concentrations of perphenazine in the body. Combining perphenazine with **clonidine** (Catapress), guanadrel (Hylorel), and guanethidine (Ismelin) can produce dangerously low blood pressure.

Perphenazine should not be combined with alcohol, because alcohol increases the drug's depressive effect on the central nervous system. Perphenazine inhibits the effects of levodopa in Parkinson's patients when the two are combined. Lithium combined with perphenazine lowers the levels of both drugs.

Perphenazine should not be combined with analgesics (pain killers) containing narcotics, because the combination increases depressive effects on the central nervous system. Orphenadrine (Norflex) combined with perphenazine can reduce the beneficial effects of perphenazine.

Resources

BOOKS

Brunton, Laurence, Bruce Chabner, and Bjorn Knollman. *Goodman & Gilman's The Pharmacological Basis of Therapeutics.* 12th ed. New York: McGraw-Hill, 2010.

Consumer Reports and American Society of Health-System Pharmacists. *Consumer Reports Complete Drug Reference.* Yonkers, NY: Consumers Reports, 2009.

Ellsworth, Allan J., et al. *Mosby's Medical Drug Reference.* St. Louis, MO: Mosby, 2007.

Venes, Donald. *Taber's Cyclopedic Medical Dictionary.* 21st ed. Philadelphia: F.A. Davis Company, 2009.

PERIODICALS

Rosenheck, R.A., et al. "Cost-Effectiveness of Second Generation Antipsychotics and Perphenazine in a Randomized Trial of Treatment for Chronic Schizophrenia." *American Journal of Psychiatry* 163 (2006): 2080–89.

WEBSITES

MedlinePlus. "Perphenazine." U.S. National Library of Medicine, National Institutes of Health. http://www.nlm.nih.gov/medlineplus/druginfo/meds/a682165.html (accessed December 19, 2011)

U.S. Food and Drug Administration. "Information on Conventional Antipsychotics." http://www.fda.gov/Drugs/DrugSafety/PostmarketDrugSafetyInformationforPatientsandProviders/ucm107211.htm (accessed December 12, 2011).

Mark Mitchell, MD
Emily Jane Willingham, PhD

Personality disorders

Definition

Personality disorders are a group of mental disturbances defined as ongoing patterns of social behavior that are detrimental to those who display them or to others. The behaviors are generally regarded as being inconsistent with cultural norms and may cause significant emotional pain or difficulties in relationships and occupational performance. In addition, the patient usually sees the disorder as being consistent with his or her self-image (ego-syntonic) and may be resistant to change. The *Diagnostic and Statistical Manual of Mental Disorders* (*DSM*) defines personality disorders as "impairments in personality functioning, [characterized by] pathological personality traits."

Demographics

Personality disorders have their onset in late adolescence or early adulthood. Doctors rarely give a **diagnosis** of personality disorder to children on the grounds that children's personalities are still in the process of formation and may change considerably by the time they are in their late teens. In retrospect, however, many individuals with personality disorders could be judged to have shown evidence of the problems in childhood.

It is difficult to give close estimates of the percentage of the population that has personality disorders. Patients with certain personality disorders, including antisocial and borderline disorders, are more likely to get into trouble with the law or otherwise attract attention than are patients whose disorders chiefly affect their capacity for intimacy. On the other hand, some patients, such as those with narcissistic or obsessive-compulsive personality disorders, may be outwardly successful because their symptoms are useful within their particular occupations. It has been estimated that about 15% of the general population of the United States has a personality disorder, with higher rates in poor or troubled neighborhoods. The rate of personality disorders among patients in psychiatric treatment is between 30% and 50%. It is possible for patients to have a so-called dual diagnosis; for example, they may have more than one personality disorder, or a personality disorder together with a substance abuse problem.

Description

Persons affected by personality disorders, sometimes called "character disorders," have rigid personality traits and coping styles, are unable to adapt to changing situations, and experience impairment in the following areas:

- perception and interpretation of the self and other people
- intensity and duration of feelings and their appropriateness to situations
- relationships with others
- ability to control impulses

The revised fourth edition of the *Diagnostic and Statistical Manual of Mental Disorders* (*DSM-IV-TR*) specifies ten personality disorders: paranoid, schizoid, schizotypal, antisocial, borderline, histrionic, narcissistic, avoidant, dependent, and obsessive-compulsive. Some psychiatrists propose additional categories, including passive-aggressive personality disorder, characterized by a need to control or punish others through frustrating them or sabotaging plans; cyclothymic personality disorder, characterized by intense mood swings alternating between high spirits and moroseness or gloom; and depressive personality disorder, characterized by a negative and pessimistic approach to life. One criticism of the general category of personality disorders is that it is based on Western notions of uniqueness, as different cultures may have different definitions of normalcy.

Paranoid

Patients with **paranoid personality disorder** are characterized by suspiciousness and a belief that others are out to harm or cheat them. They have problems with intimacy and may join cults or groups with paranoid belief systems. Some are litigious, bringing lawsuits against those they believe have wronged them. Although not ordinarily delusional, these patients may develop psychotic symptoms under severe **stress**. According to a 2007 study performed by Dr. Mark F. Lenzenweger (from the Department of Psychology at State University of New York at Binghamton) and colleagues, an estimated 2.3% of the general population meet the *DSM-IV* criteria for paranoid personality disorder. (The statistics provided by the **National Institute of Mental Health** for personality disorders are sourced from Lenzenweger's study.)

Schizoid

Schizoid patients are perceived by others as "loners" without close family relationships or social contacts. Indeed, they are aloof and really do prefer to be alone. They may appear cold to others because they rarely display strong emotions. They may, however, be successful in occupations that do not require personal interaction. About 4.9% of the general population have this disorder (Lenzenweger et al.); it is slightly more common in men than in women.

Schizotypal

Patients diagnosed as schizotypal are often considered odd or eccentric because they pay little attention to their clothing and sometimes have peculiar speech mannerisms. They are socially isolated and uncomfortable at parties or other social gatherings. In addition, people with **schizotypal personality disorder** often have oddities of thought, including "magical" beliefs or peculiar ideas (for example, a belief in telepathy or unidentified flying objects [UFOs]) that are outside of their cultural norms. About 3.3% of the general population have schizotypal personality disorder (Lenzenweger et al.). It is slightly more common in males. Schizotypal disorder should not be confused with **schizophrenia**, although there is some evidence that the disorders are genetically related.

Antisocial

Patients with **antisocial personality disorder** are sometimes referred to as sociopaths or psychopaths. They are characterized by lying, manipulativeness, and a selfish disregard for the rights of others; some may act impulsively. People with antisocial personality disorder are frequently chemically dependent and sexually promiscuous. An estimated 1% of the general population have antisocial personality disorder (Lenzenweger et al.), and the disorder is much more often diagnosed in men than in women.

Borderline

Patients with **borderline personality disorder** (BPD) are highly unstable, with wide mood swings, a history of intense but stormy relationships, impulsive behavior, and confusion about career goals, personal values, or sexual orientation. These often highly conflictual ideas may correspond to an even deeper confusion about their sense of self (identity). People with BPD frequently cut or burn themselves, or threaten or attempt **suicide**. Many of these patients have histories of severe childhood **abuse** or **neglect**. About 1.6% of the general population have BPD (Lenzenweger et al.), with women diagnosed more often than men.

Histrionic

Patients diagnosed with this disorder impress others as overly emotional, overly dramatic, and hungry for attention. They may be flirtatious or seductive as a way of drawing attention to themselves, yet they are emotionally shallow. Histrionic patients often live in a romantic fantasy world and are easily bored with routine. About 2% to 3% of the population is thought to have this disorder. Although historically the disorder has been more associated with women in clinical settings, there may be bias toward diagnosing women with the **histrionic personality disorder**.

Narcissistic

Narcissistic patients are characterized by self-importance, a craving for admiration, and exploitative attitudes toward others. They have unrealistically inflated views of their talents and accomplishments, and may become extremely angry if they are criticized or outshone by others. Narcissists may be professionally successful but rarely have long-lasting intimate relationships. Fewer than 1% of the population has this disorder; about 75% of those diagnosed with it are male.

Avoidant

Patients with **avoidant personality disorder** are fearful of rejection and shy away from situations or occupations that might expose their supposed inadequacy. They may reject opportunities to develop close relationships because of their fears of criticism or humiliation. Patients with this personality disorder are often diagnosed with **dependent personality disorder** as well. Many also fit the criteria for **social phobia**. Approximately 5.2% of the population have avoidant personality disorder (Lenzenweger et al.).

Dependent

Dependent patients are afraid of being on their own and typically develop submissive or compliant behaviors in order to avoid displeasing people. They are afraid to question authority and often ask others for guidance or direction. Dependent personality disorder is diagnosed more often in women, but it has been suggested that this finding reflects social pressures on women to conform to gender stereotyping or bias on the part of clinicians. About 0.6% of the U.S. population have dependent personality disorder (Lenzenweger et al.).

Obsessive-compulsive

Patients diagnosed with this disorder are preoccupied with keeping order, attaining perfection, and maintaining mental and interpersonal control. They may spend a great deal of time adhering to plans, schedules, or rules from which they will not deviate, even at the expense of openness, flexibility, and efficiency. These patients are often unable to relax and may become "workaholics." They may have problems in employment as well as in intimate relationships because they are very stiff and formal, and insist on doing everything their way. About 2.4% of the population have **obsessive-compulsive personality disorder** (Lenzenweger et al.).

Causes and symptoms

Causes

Personality is formed early in life, during childhood. However, disorders in personality can develop during that time of life, based on two factors: heredity and environment.

Heredity is those inherited tendencies that occur because they are passed down from parents to children. There is nothing that can be done to prevent these tendencies (sometimes called a person's temperament) from occurring because they happen naturally—they are within one's genes. However, the experiences that one has in life are due to that person's surrounding environment. They are affected by family, friends, and even complete strangers—along with the situations that are encountered in everyday life.

Personality disorders are thought to result from a bad interface, so to speak, between a child's temperament and character on one hand, and his or her family environment on the other. Temperament can be defined as a person's innate or biologically shaped basic disposition; character is defined as the set of attitudes and behavior patterns that the individual acquires or learns over time. Since children must learn to adapt to their specific families, they may develop personality disorders in the course of struggling to survive psychologically in disturbed or stressful families. For example, nervous or high-strung parents might be unhappy with a baby who is very active and try to restrain him or her at every opportunity. The child might then develop an avoidant personality disorder as the outcome of coping with constant frustration and parental disapproval. As another example, **child abuse** is believed to play a role in shaping borderline personality disorder. One reason that some therapists use the term "developmental damage" instead of "personality disorder" is that it takes the presumed source of the person's problems into account.

Some patients with personality disorders come from families that appear to be stable and healthy. It has been suggested that these patients are biologically hypersensitive to normal family stress. Levels of the **brain** chemical (neurotransmitter) **dopamine** may influence a person's level of novelty-seeking, and **serotonin** levels may influence aggression.

Symptoms

There are many symptoms associated with personality disorder. Generally, they include:

• angry outbursts
• inadequate impulse control
• mistrust and suspicion of others
• need for instant gratification
• problematic relationships
• social isolation
• substance and/or drug abuse
• trouble making friends
• wide and/or frequent mood swings

Diagnosis

A new edition of the *DSM* (*DSM-5*) is due to be published in May 2013. Proposed changes for the *DSM-5* include a reduction of the ten personality disorder types to six:

- antisocial personality disorder (dyssocial personality disorder)
- avoidant personality disorder
- borderline personality disorder
- narcissistic personality disorder
- obsessive-compulsive personality disorder
- schizotypal personality disorder

To account for the disorders that have been removed, a diagnostic category of "Personality Disorder Trait Specified" has been proposed, which accounts for any additional disorders that cause significant impairments in personal and social functioning and that are linked to a specific personality trait:

- negative affectivity, or frequent negative emotions—anxiety, depression, fear, drastic mood swings, paranoia
- detachment, or withdrawal from social interactions—avoidances, depression, lack of joy in social situations
- antagonism, or tendency or desire to hurt others—anger or irritability, manipulation, deceit, aggression
- disinhibition/compulsivity, or impulsive or compulsive behaviors—risk taking, lack of concentration, stubbornness, no sense of responsibility
- psychoticism, or professing "unusual" beliefs—abnormal thoughts, eccentric behavior

The *DSM-5* proposals also include revision of the general diagnosis of *personality disorder,* with the goal of being more specific, being soundly based in clinical observation and experience, and accounting for deviations in cultural norms. The *DSM-IV-TR* criteria defined personality disorder as:

- exhibiting pattern of beliefs and/or behaviors that vary from cultural norms, in the areas (at least two) of cognition, affectivity, interpersonal relations, and impulsivity)
- beliefs/behaviors are inflexible and unaffected by situation or environment
- beliefs/behaviors lead to severe impairment in interpersonal functioning, including social and occupational
- beliefs/behaviors are long-lasting, dating to adolescent/early adulthood
- beliefs/behaviors cannot be attributed to another disorder (physical or mental) or to a substance

By contrast, the proposed *DSM-5* diagnostic criteria require a patient to exhibit all of the following:

- impairments in personal (identity) and interpersonal functioning and relations
- at least one personality trait (negative affectivity, detachment, antagonism, disinhibition/compulsivity, psychoticism)
- consistent behavior, unaffected by situation or environment
- behaviors that are not part of the perceived cultural norm or that are not in line with the individual's level of development
- impairments that are not otherwise explained by substance use or a medical condition

Diagnosis of personality disorders is complicated by the fact that affected persons rarely seek help until they are in serious trouble or until their families (or the law) pressure them to get treatment. The reason for this slowness is that the problematic traits are so deeply entrenched that they seem normal (ego-syntonic) to the patient. Diagnosis of a personality disorder depends, in part, on the patient's age. Although personality disorders originate during the childhood years, they are considered adult disorders. Some patients, in fact, are not diagnosed until late in life because their symptoms had been modified by the demands of their job or by marriage. After retirement or the spouse's death, however, these patients' personality disorders become fully apparent. In general, however, if the onset of the patient's problem is in mid- or late life, the doctor will rule out **substance abuse** or personality change caused by medical or neurological problems before considering the diagnosis of a personality disorder. It is unusual for people to develop personality disorders "out of the blue" in mid-life.

There are no tests that can provide a definitive diagnosis of personality disorder. Most doctors will evaluate a patient on the basis of several sources of information collected over a period of time in order to determine how long the patient has been having difficulties, how many areas of life are affected, and the severity of the dysfunction.

Interviews

The doctor may schedule two or three interviews with the patient, spaced over several weeks or months, in order to rule out an adjustment disorder caused by job loss, **bereavement**, or a similar problem. An office interview allows the doctor to form an impression of the patient's overall personality as well as obtain information about his or her occupation and family.

During the interview, the doctor will note the patient's appearance, tone of voice, body language, eye contact, and other important nonverbal signals, as well as the content of the conversation. In some cases, the doctor may contact other people (family members, employers, close friends) who know the patient well in order to assess the accuracy of the patient's perception of his or her difficulties. It is quite common for people with personality disorders to have distorted views of their situations or to be unaware of the impact of their behavior on others.

Psychological testing

Doctors use psychological testing to help in the diagnosis of a personality disorder. These tests are administered and interpreted by a licensed **psychologist**, and doctors will usually refer patients to specific psychologists for testing.

PERSONALITY INVENTORIES. Personality inventories are tests with true/false or yes/no answers that can be used to compare the patient's scores with those of people with known personality distortions. The single most commonly used test of this type is the **Minnesota Multiphasic Personality Inventory**, or MMPI. Another test that is often used is the Millon Clinical Multiaxial Inventory, or MCMI.

Projective tests are unstructured, meaning that instead of giving one-word answers to questions, the patient is asked to talk at some length about a picture that the psychologist has shown him or her, or to supply an ending for the beginning of a story. Projective tests allow the clinician to assess the patient's patterns of thinking, fantasies, worries or anxieties, moral concerns, values, and habits. Common projective tests include the Rorschach, in which the patient responds to a set of ten inkblots; and the **Thematic Apperception Test** (TAT), in which the patient is shown drawings of people in different situations and then tells a story about the picture.

Treatment

At one time, psychiatrists thought that personality disorders did not respond very well to treatment. This opinion was derived from the notion that human personality is fixed for life once it has been molded in childhood, and from the belief among people with personality disorders that their own views and behaviors are correct, and that others are the ones at fault. More recently, however, doctors have recognized that humans can continue to grow and change throughout life. Most patients with personality disorders are now considered to be treatable, although the degree of improvement may vary depending on the severity and life situation of one's particular personality disorder. The type of treatment recommended depends on the personality characteristics associated with the specific disorder. For the most part, many personality disorders are chronic so treatment is often for an extended period. In addition, a team of medical professionals are often included within the treatment. This professional team may include a primary care provider (such as a family doctor), **psychiatrist**, psychotherapist, pharmacist, and **social workers**. One or more treatments may be needed. These include **hospitalization, psychotherapy**, and medications.

Hospitalization

npatient treatment is rarely required for patients with personality disorders. However, in some cases, a personality disorder may be so severe that psychiatric hospitalization is necessary, as may be the case with patients with borderline personality disorder who are threatening suicide or suffering from drug or alcohol withdrawal, or patients with paranoid personality disorder who are having psychotic symptoms. Psychiatric hospitalization is generally recommended only when persons are not able to care for themselves or are in immediate danger of harming themselves or someone else.

Psychotherapy

Psychoanalytic psychotherapy is suggested for patients who can benefit from insight-oriented treatment. These patients typically include those with dependent, obsessive-compulsive, and avoidant personality disorders. Doctors usually recommend individual psychotherapy for narcissistic and borderline patients, but they often refer these patients to therapists with specialized training in these disorders. Psychotherapeutic treatment for personality disorders may take as long as three to five years. It is considered the primary way to treat personality disorders effectively.

Insight-oriented approaches are not recommended for patients with paranoid or antisocial personality disorders. These patients are likely to resent the therapist and see him or her as trying to control or dominate them.

Supportive therapy is regarded as the most helpful form of psychotherapy for patients with **schizoid personality disorder**.

COGNITIVE-BEHAVIORAL THERAPY. Cognitive-behavioral approaches are often recommended for patients with avoidant or dependent personality disorders. Patients in these groups typically have mistaken beliefs about their competence or likableness.

These assumptions can be successfully challenged by cognitive-behavioral methods. More recently, American psychiatrist Aaron T. Beck (1921–), a professor emeritus in the Department of Psychiatry at the University of Pennsylvania, and his coworkers have successfully extended their approach to cognitive therapy to all ten personality disorders as defined by DSM-IV.

GROUP THERAPY. **Group therapy** is frequently useful for patients with schizoid or avoidant personality disorders because it helps them to break out of their social isolation. It has also been recommended for patients with histrionic and antisocial personality disorders. These patients tend to act out, and pressure from peers in group treatment can motivate them to change. Because patients with antisocial personality disorder can destabilize groups that include people with other disorders, it is usually best if these people meet exclusively with others who have APD in homogeneous groups. However, getting patients with personality disorders to commit and participate to group therapy can be difficult.

FAMILY THERAPY. **Family therapy** may be suggested for patients whose personality disorders cause serious problems for members of their families. It is also sometimes recommended for borderline patients from over-involved or possessive families.

DIALECTICAL BEHAVIOR THERAPY. This type of therapy teaches patients to tolerate and better adapt to stress, along with training that helps with the regulation of emotions and the improvement of relationships with others. Dialectical behavior therapy has the most empirical support of any treatment for personality disorders, particularly with individuals with borderline personality disorder.

PSYCHODYNAMIC PSYCHOTHERAPY. This type of psychotherapy helps those in need to be more aware of unconscious thoughts and behaviors. Along with this new insight, the therapy also helps the patient to understand motivations and conflicts in order to live a more normal life.

PSYCHOEDUCATION. Directed at the patient, along with family and friends, this therapy helps all parties concerned to better understand and deal with the mental illness and develop better coping strategies and problem-solving skills.

Medications

Medications may be prescribed for patients with specific personality disorders. The type of medication depends on the disorder. In general, however, patients with personality disorders are helped only moderately by medications.

ANTIPSYCHOTIC DRUGS. Antipsychotic drugs, such as **haloperidol** (Haldol), may be given to patients with paranoid personality disorder if they are having brief psychotic episodes. Patients with borderline or schizotypal personality disorder are sometimes given antipsychotic drugs in low doses; however, the efficacy of these drugs in treating personality disorder is less clear than in schizophrenia.

MOOD STABILIZERS. **Carbamazepine** (Tegretol) is a drug that is commonly used to treat **seizures**, but is also helpful for borderline patients with rage outbursts and similar behavioral problems. Lithium and valproate may also be used as mood stabilizers, especially among people with borderline personality disorder.

ANTIDEPRESSANTS AND ANTIANXIETY MEDICATIONS. Medications in these categories are sometimes prescribed for patients with schizoid personality disorder to help them manage anxiety symptoms while they are in psychotherapy. **Antidepressants** are also commonly used to treat people with borderline personality disorder.

Treatment with medications is not recommended for patients with avoidant, histrionic, dependent, or narcissistic personality disorders. The use of potentially addictive medications should be avoided in people with borderline or antisocial personality disorders. However, some avoidant patients who also have social phobia may benefit from **monoamine oxidase inhibitors** (MAOIs), a particular class of antidepressant.

Prognosis

The prognosis for recovery depends in part on the specific disorder. Although some patients improve as they grow older and have positive experiences in life, personality disorders are generally lifelong disturbances with periods of worsening (exacerbations) and periods of improvement (remissions). Others, particularly schizoid patients, have better prognoses if they are given appropriate treatment. Beck and his coworkers estimate that effective cognitive therapy with patients with personality disorders takes two to three years on average. Patients with paranoid personality disorder are at some risk for developing delusional disorders or schizophrenia.

The personality disorders with the poorest prognoses are the antisocial and the borderline. Borderline patients are at high risk for developing substance abuse disorders or bulimia. About 80% of hospitalized borderline patients attempt suicide at some point during treatment, and about 5% succeed in committing suicide. Borderline patients

Character—An individual's set of emotional, cognitive, and behavioral patterns learned and accumulated over time.

Cognitive therapy—A form of psychotherapy that focuses on changing people's patterns of emotional reaction by correcting distorted patterns of thinking and perception.

Developmental damage—A term that some therapists prefer to personality disorder, on the grounds that it is more respectful of the patient's capacity for growth and change.

Ego-syntonic—Consistent with one's sense of self, as opposed to ego-alien or dystonic (foreign to one's sense of self). Ego-syntonic traits typify patients with personality disorders.

Personality—The organized pattern of behaviors and attitudes that makes a human being distinctive. Personality is formed by the ongoing interaction of temperament, character, and environment.

Projective tests—Psychological tests that probe into personality by obtaining open-ended responses to such materials as pictures or stories. Projective tests are often used to evaluate patients with personality disorders.

Rorschach test—A well-known projective test that requires the patient to describe what he or she sees in each of ten inkblots. It is named for the Swiss psychiatrist who invented it.

Temperament—A person's natural or genetically determined disposition.

are also the most likely to sue their mental health professional for malpractice.

Prevention

The most effective preventive strategy for personality disorders is early identification and treatment of children at risk. High-risk groups include abused children, children from troubled families, children with close relatives diagnosed with personality disorders, children of substance abusers, and children who grow up in cults or extremist political groups.

Resources

BOOKS

Dobbert, Duane L. *Understanding Personality Disorders: An Introduction*. Westport, CT: Praeger, 2007.

Graham, George. *The Disordered Mind: An Introduction to Philosophy of Mind and Mental Illness*. New York: Routledge, 2010.

North, Carol, and Sean Yutzy. *Goodwin and Guze's Psychiatric Diagnosis*. New York: Oxford University Press, 2010.

O'Donohue, William, Katherine A. Fowler, and Scott O. Lilienfeld. *Personality Disorders: Toward the DSM-V*. Thousand Oaks, CA: Sage Publications, 2007.

PERIODICALS

Hesse, Morten, and Paul Moran. "Screening for Personality Disorder with the Standardised Assessment of Personality: Abbreviated Scale (SAPAS): Further Evidence of Concurrent Validity." *BMC Psychiatry* 10 (January 2010): 10. http://dx.doi.org/10.1186/1471-244X-10-10 (accessed August 31, 2011).

Lenzenweger, Mark F., et al. "DSM-IV Personality Disorders in the National Comorbidity Survey Replication." *Biological Psychiatry* 62, no. 6 (2007): 553–64 http://dx.doi.org/10.1016/j.biopsych.2006.09.019 (accessed August 31, 2011).

Skodol, A.E., et al. "Relationship of Personality Disorders to the Course of Major Depressive Disorder in a Nationally Representative Sample." *American Journal of Psychiatry* 168, no. 3 (2011): 257–64.

OTHER

American Psychiatric Association. "Side By Side Comparison Table of the Criteria for the Personality Disorders." http://www.dsm5.org/Documents/Diagnostic%20Criteria%20for%20Personality%20Disorder%20(Comparison%20of%20DSM-IV%20DSM-5%20old%20DSM-5%20new.pdf (accessed August 31, 2011).

WEBSITES

American Psychiatric Association. "Proposed Revisions: Personality Disorders." DSM-5 Development. http://www.dsm5.org/proposedrevision/Pages/PersonalityDisorders.aspx (accessed August 31, 2011).

Bienenfeld, David. "Personality Disorders." Medscape Reference. (June 14, 2010). http://www.emedicine.com/med/topic3472.htm (accessed August 31, 2011).

Mayo Clinic staff. "Personality Disorders." MayoClinic.com (September 10, 2010). http://www.mayoclinic.com/health/personality-disorders/DS00562 (accessed August 25, 2011).

"Personality Disorders: Statistics." OutOfTheFog.net http://outofthefog.net/Statistics.html#PDPrevalence (accessed August 24, 2011).

ORGANIZATIONS

American Psychiatric Association, 1000 Wilson Boulevard, Suite 1825, Arlington, VA, 22209, (703) 907-7300, apa@psych.org, http://www.psych.org.

Mental Health America, 2000 N. Beauregard Street, 6th Floor, Alexandria, VA, 22311, (703) 684-7722, Fax: (703) 684-5968, (800) 969-6642, http://www1.nmha.org.

National Alliance on Mental Illness, 3803 North Fairfax Drive, Suite 100, Arlington, VA, 22203, (703) 524-7600, Fax: (703) 524-9094, http://www.nami.org.

National Institute of Mental Health, 6001 Executive Boulevard, Room 8184, MSC 9663, Bethesda, MD, 20892-9663, (301) 443-4513, Fax: (301) 443-4279, (866) 615-6464, nimhinfo@nih.gov, http://www.nimh.nih.gov.

Treatment and Research Advancements (National Association for Personality Disorders), 23 Greene Street, New York, NY, 10013, (212) 966-6514, tara4bpd@gmail.com, http://www.tara4bpd.org.

Rebecca J. Frey, Ph.D.
Laura Jean Cataldo, RN, Ed.D.
William A. Atkins, B.B., B.S., M.B.A.

Person-centered therapy

Definition

Person-centered therapy (PCT), also known as "client-centered," "non-directive," or "Rogerian therapy," is an approach to counseling and **psychotherapy** that places much of the responsibility for the treatment process on the "client" (the term preferred over "patient"), with the therapist taking a nondirective role. As such, psychologists and counselors use a non-directive approach to treat their clients.

Purpose

Two primary goals of person-centered therapy are increased self-esteem and greater openness to experience. Some of the related changes that this form of therapy seeks to foster in clients include closer agreement between the client's idealized and actual selves; better self-understanding; lower levels of defensiveness, guilt, and insecurity; more positive and comfortable relationships with others; and an increased capacity to experience and express feelings at the moment they occur.

Description

Developed from the 1930s to the 1950s by American **psychologist** Carl Rogers (1902–1987), client-centered therapy departed from the typically formal, detached role of the therapist emphasized in **psychoanalysis** and other forms of treatment.

Background

Rogers believed that therapy should take place in a supportive environment created by a close personal relationship between client and therapist. Rogers's introduction of the term "client," rather than "patient," expresses his rejection of the traditionally hierarchical relationship between therapist and client and his view of them as equals. In person-centered therapy, the client determines the general direction of therapy, while the therapist seeks to increase the client's insight and self-understanding through informal clarifying questions.

Beginning in the 1960s, person-centered therapy became associated with the human potential movement. This movement, dating back to the beginning of the 1900s, reflected an altered perspective of human nature. Previous psychological theories viewed human beings as inherently selfish and corrupt. For example, Austrian neurologist Sigmund Freud's theory focused on sexual and aggressive tendencies as the primary forces driving human behavior. The human potential movement, by contrast, defined human nature as inherently good. From its perspective, human behavior is motivated by a drive to achieve one's fullest potential.

Self-actualization, a term derived from the human potential movement, is an important concept underlying person-centered therapy. It refers to the tendency of all human beings to move forward, grow, and reach their fullest potential. When humans move toward self-actualization, they are also prosocial; that is, they tend to be concerned for others and behave in honest, dependable, and constructive ways. The concept of self-actualization focuses on human strengths rather than human deficiencies. According to Rogers, self-actualization can be blocked by an unhealthy self-concept (negative or unrealistic attitudes about oneself).

Rogers adopted terms such as "person-centered approach" and "way of being" and began to focus on personal growth and self-actualization. He also pioneered the use of encounter groups, adapting the sensitivity training (T-group) methods developed by German-American psychologist Kurt Lewin (1890–1947) and other researchers at the National Training Laboratories in the 1950s. More recently, two major variations of person-centered therapy have developed: experiential therapy, developed by American psychotherapist Eugene Gendlin in 1979; and process-experiential therapy, developed by Canadian psychologist Leslie Greenberg and colleagues in 1993.

While person-centered therapy is considered one of the major therapeutic approaches, along with psychoanalytic and **cognitive-behavioral therapy**, Rogers's influence is felt in schools of therapy other than his

CARL ROGERS (1902–1987)

Carl Rogers was an American psychotherapist who originated person-centered, nondirective counseling. In 1928, Rogers moved to Rochester, New York, where he began work as a psychologist for the Society for Prevention of Cruelty to Children. In contrast to Teachers College, many colleagues in Rochester emphasized a psychoanalytic approach to behavior. Through the practical and personal experiences in this clinic, however, he began to recognize that the results of both measurement psychologists and psychoanalysts were "never more than superficially effective."

Several incidents in the Rochester clinic helped him "to perceive . . . that it is the client who knows what hurts, what direction to go, what problems are crucial, what experiences have been deeply buried. It began to occur to me that unless I had a need to demonstrate my own cleverness and learning, I would do better to rely upon the client for direction of movement in the therapeutic process." For effective counseling, the psychotherapist, Rogers believed, is "to be genuine and without a facade . . . . and to be empathetic in understanding. As a result the client begins to feel positive and accepting toward himself . . . . his own defenses and facade diminishes . . . . he becomes more open . . . . and he finds that he is free to grow and change in desired directions."

During his lifetime, Rogers published approximately 260 articles and 15 books, which have had a significant influence on the development of psychology in the twentieth century. He was prominent in the human potential movement, and his book on encounter groups had an impressive impact. After the mid-1970s Rogers was especially interested in facilitating groups involving antagonistic factions, whether the hostilities arose out of cultural, racial, religious, or national issues. He facilitated a group from Belfast (Northern Ireland) containing militant Protestants and Catholics from Ireland and the English. He was involved in intercultural groups whose participants came from many nations, including participants from the Eastern European bloc countries. He facilitated black-white groups in South Africa. He was deeply interested in applying the principles of the person-centered approach to international affairs in the interest of world peace. He died in 1987.

own. The concepts and methods he developed are used in an eclectic fashion by many different types of counselors and therapists.

Preparation

Preparing for PCT is as important to the professional therapist as it is to the client.

Process

Rogers believed that the most important factor in successful therapy was not the therapist's skill or training, but rather his or her attitude. Three interrelated attitudes on the part of the therapist are central to the success of person-centered therapy: congruence, unconditional positive regard, and empathy. Congruence refers to the therapist's openness and genuineness—the willingness to relate to clients without hiding behind a professional facade. Therapists who function in this way have all their feelings available to them in therapy sessions and may share significant emotional reactions with their clients. Congruence does *not* mean, however, that therapists disclose their own personal problems to clients in therapy sessions or shift the focus of therapy to themselves in any other way.

Unconditional positive regard means that the therapist accepts the client totally for who he or she is, without evaluating or censoring, and without disapproving of particular feelings, actions, or characteristics. The therapist communicates this attitude to the client by a willingness to listen without interrupting, judging, or giving advice. This attitude of positive regard creates a nonthreatening context in which the client feels free to explore and share painful, hostile, defensive, or abnormal feelings without worrying about personal rejection by the therapist.

The third necessary component of a therapist's attitude is empathy ("accurate empathetic understanding"). The therapist tries to appreciate the client's situation from the client's point of view, showing an emotional understanding of and sensitivity to the client's feelings throughout the therapy session. In other systems of therapy, empathy with the client would be considered a preliminary step to enabling the therapeutic work to proceed; but in person-centered therapy, it actually constitutes a major portion of the therapeutic work itself. One primary way to convey this empathy is by active listening that shows careful and perceptive attention to what the client is saying. In addition to standard techniques, such as eye contact, that are common to any good listener, person-centered therapists employ a special method called "reflection," which consists of paraphrasing and/or summarizing what a client has just said. This technique shows that the therapist is listening carefully and accurately, and gives clients an added opportunity to examine their own thoughts and feelings as they hear them repeated by another person. Generally, clients respond by elaborating further on the thoughts they have just expressed.

According to Rogers, when these three attitudes (congruence, unconditional positive regard, and empathy) are conveyed by a therapist, clients can freely express themselves without having to worry about what the therapist thinks of them. The therapist does not attempt to change the client's thinking in any way. Even negative expressions are validated as legitimate experiences. Because of this nondirective approach, clients can explore the issues that are most important to them—not those considered important by the therapist. Based on the principle of self-actualization, this undirected, uncensored self-exploration allows clients to eventually recognize alternative ways of thinking that will promote personal growth. The therapist merely facilitates self-actualization by providing a climate in which clients can freely engage in focused, in-depth self-exploration.

Applications

Rogers originally developed person-centered therapy in a children's clinic while he was working there; however, person-centered therapy was not intended for a specific age group or subpopulation but has been used to treat a broad range of people. Rogers worked extensively with people with **schizophrenia** later in his career. His therapy has also been applied to persons suffering from **depression**, anxiety, alcohol disorders, cognitive dysfunction, and **personality disorders**. Some therapists argue that person-centered therapy is not effective with nonverbal or poorly educated individuals; others maintain that it can be successfully adapted to any type of person. The person-centered approach can be used in individual, group, or **family therapy**. With young children, it is frequently employed as **play therapy**.

There are no strict guidelines regarding the length or frequency of person-centered therapy. Generally, therapists adhere to a one-hour session once per week. True to the spirit of person-centered therapy, however, scheduling may be adjusted according to the client's expressed needs. The client also decides when to terminate therapy. Termination usually occurs when he or she feels able to better cope with life's difficulties.

KEY TERMS

Depression—A psychiatric disorder involving feelings of hopelessness and symptoms of fatigue, sleeplessness, suicidal tendencies, and poor concentration.

Humanistic therapy—Sometimes also called "humanistic psychology," a perspective that stresses that people are basically good but deviate from that tendency through mental and social problems. It uses a holistic approach that focuses on individual potential and growth, along with self-actualization.

Psychoanalysis—The study of human psychological functioning and behavior.

Schizophrenia—A mental disorder involving degraded thinking and emotions.

Risks

Person-centered therapy has been criticized over the years for its unorthodox style of providing therapy to clients. However, the medical community has proved that it is an effective style of therapy. Clients also view PCT as a widely popular style of treatment.

Results

The expected results of person-centered therapy include:

- improved self-esteem; trust in one's inner feelings and experiences as valuable sources of information for making decisions
- increased ability to learn from (rather than repeat) mistakes
- decreased defensiveness, guilt, and insecurity
- more positive and comfortable relationships with others
- an increased capacity to experience and express feelings at the moment they occur
- openness to new experiences and new ways of thinking about life.

Normal results

Outcome studies of humanistic therapies in general and person-centered therapy in particular indicate that people who have been treated with these approaches maintain stable changes over extended periods of time; that they change substantially compared to untreated

QUESTIONS TO ASK YOUR DOCTOR

- Where can I learn more about person-centered therapy?
- Would person-centered therapy be better for me than traditional therapy?
- Is is helpful to undergo person-centered therapy and traditional therapy at the same time?
- Do you know of any therapists who are trained in person-centered therapy?

persons; and that the changes are roughly comparable to the changes in clients who have been treated by other types of therapy. Humanistic therapies appear to be particularly effective in clients with depression or relationship issues. Person-centered therapy, however, appears to be slightly less effective than other forms of humanistic therapy in which therapists offer more advice to clients and suggest topics to explore.

Abnormal results

If therapy has been unsuccessful, the client will not move in the direction of self-growth and self-acceptance. Instead, he or she may continue to display behaviors that reflect self-defeating attitudes or rigid patterns of thinking.

Several factors may affect the success of person-centered therapy. If an individual is not interested in therapy (for example, he or she was forced to attend therapy), that person might not work well together with the therapist. The skill of the therapist may be another factor. In general, clients tend to overlook occasional therapist failures if a satisfactory relationship has been established. A therapist who continually fails to demonstrate unconditional positive regard, congruence, or empathy cannot effectively use this type of therapy. A third factor is the client's comfort level with nondirective therapy. Some studies have suggested that certain clients may get bored, frustrated, or annoyed with a Rogerian style of therapeutic interaction.

Resources

BOOKS

Cain, David J., ed. *Humanistic Psychotherapies: Handbook of Research and Practice,* Washington, DC: American Psychological Association, 2002.

———. *Person-centered Psychotherapies.* Washington, DC: American Psychological Association, 2010.

———. *Person-centered Therapy Over Time.* Washington, DC: American Psychological Association, 2010.

Purton, Campbell. *Person-centered Therapy: The Focusing-oriented Approach.* Houndmills, Basingstoke, Hampshire: Palgrave Macmillan, 2004.

Rogers, Carl. *Client-Centered Therapy.* Boston: Houghton Mifflin, 1951.

———. *On Becoming a Person.* Boston: Houghton Mifflin, 1961.

———. *A Way of Being.* Boston: Houghton Mifflin, 1980.

Wilkins, Paul. *Person-Centered Therapy: 100 Key Points.* London: Routledge, 2010.

OTHER

Grant, Shelia K. "Person-Centered Therapy." California State University. http://www.csun.edu/~hcpsy002/Psy460_Ch07_Handout_ppt.pdf (accessed December 21, 2010).

ORGANIZATIONS

Association for the Development of the Person-Centered Approach,http://www.adpca.org.

Center for Studies of the Person, 1150 Silverado, Suite 112, La Jolla, CA, 92037, (858) 459-3861, http://www.center-fortheperson.org.

World Association for Person-Centered and Experiential Psychotherapy and Counseling, PO Box 142, Ross-on-Wye, United Kingdom, HR9 9AG, +44 1989 763 901 http://www.pce-world.org.

Sandra L. Friedrich, M.A.

Pervasive developmental disorders

Definition

Pervasive developmental disorders (PDDs) include five different conditions: **Asperger syndrome**, **autism**, **childhood disintegrative disorder** (CDD), pervasive developmental disorder not otherwise specified (PDDNOS), and **Rett syndrome**. The disorders are classified together because of the similarities among them. The three most common shared problems involve communication skills, motor skills, and social skills. Since there are no clear diagnostic boundaries separating these conditions, it is sometimes difficult to distinguish one from the other for diagnostic purposes. Because of this, PDDs (with the exception of Rett syndrome) are sometimes called autism spectrum disorders, meaning that the disorders share symptoms but differ in severity.

Demographics

Asperger syndrome, autism, and childhood disintegrative disorder are four to five times more common in boys, while Rett syndrome has been diagnosed primarily in girls.

All of these disorders are considered rare, though the prevalence of autism has risen in recent years. The U.S. Centers for Disease Control and Prevention estimates that, on average, 1 in 110 children are affected by an autism spectrum disorder, more than those affected by spina bifida, cancer, or **Down syndrome**. The increase in prevalence may be due partly to improved recognition and **diagnosis**.

Description

Asperger syndrome

Children afflicted with Asperger syndrome exhibit difficulties in social relationships and communication. They are reluctant to make eye contact, do not respond to social or emotional contacts, do not initiate play activities with peers, and do not give or receive attention or affection. To receive this diagnosis, an individual must demonstrate normal development of language, thinking, and coping skills. Due to an impaired coordination of muscle movements, children with Asperger syndrome appear to be clumsy. They usually become deeply involved in a select few interests, which tend to occupy most of their time and attention.

Autism

Autism is frequently evident within the first year of life and must be diagnosed before age three. It is associated with moderate intellectual disabilities in three out of four cases. Children with autism generally do not want to be held, rocked, cuddled, or played with. They are unresponsive to affection, show no interest in peers or adults, and have few interests. Other symptoms include avoidance of eye contact, absence of facial expressions, and the use of gestures to express needs. Actions are repetitive, routine, and restricted; rocking, hand and arm flapping, unusual hand and finger movements, and attachment to objects rather than pets and people are common. Speech, play, and other behaviors appear repetitive and without imagination. Children with autism tend to be overactive, aggressive, and self-injurious and do not like changes in routine. They are often highly sensitive to touch, noise, and smells.

Childhood disintegrative disorder

Childhood disintegrative disorder, also called Heller's disease, most often develops between two and ten years of age. Children with CDD develop normally until two to three years of age and then begin to disintegrate rapidly. Signs and symptoms include deterioration of the ability to use and understand language to the point where they are unable to carry on a conversation. This is accompanied by loss of control of the bladder and bowels. Any interest or ability to play and engage in social activities is lost. The behaviors are nearly identical with those of autism. However, childhood disintegrative disorder becomes evident later in life and results in developmental regression, or loss of previously attained skills, whereas autism can be detected as early as the first month of life and results in a failure to progress.

Pervasive developmental disorder not otherwise specified

The term pervasive developmental disorder not otherwise specified (PDDNOS) is also referred to as atypical personality development, atypical PDD, or atypical autism. Individuals with this disorder share some of the same signs and symptoms of autism or related conditions but do not meet all of the criteria for diagnosis for any of the other four syndromes included in PDDs. Because children diagnosed with PDDNOS do not all exhibit the same combination of characteristics, it is difficult to conduct research on this disorder. Limited evidence available suggests that patients are seen by medical professionals later in life than is the case for children with autism, and they are less likely to have intellectual deficits.

Rett syndrome

Rett syndrome was first described in 1966 and is found almost exclusively in girls. In Rett syndrome, the cells in the **brain** experience difficulty in communicating with each other. The growth of the head falls behind the growth of the body, resulting in an **intellectual disability**. These conditions are accompanied by deficits in movement (motor) skills and a loss of interest in social activities. Children with Rett syndrome typically develop normally for 6–18 months (stage one), then development slows down and stops (stage two). Stage three is characterized by a loss of the speech and motor skills already acquired, typically between nine months and three years of age. Stage four begins with a return to learning that will continue across the lifespan but at a very slow rate. Problems with coordination and walking are likely to continue and even worsen. Other conditions that can occur with Rett syndrome are convulsions, constipation, breathing problems, impaired circulation in the feet and legs, and difficulty chewing or swallowing.

Causes and symptoms

Causes

The causes of these disorders are unknown, although brain structure abnormalities, genetic mutation, and alterations in brain function are believed to play a role. Still, no single brain abnormality or location has been connected to a cause. In 2004, scientists reported finding the gene mutation (on gene MECP2) present in 80% of people affected with Rett syndrome. A number of causes have been associated with autism, including genes, environmental factors, and chemical imbalances, but none have been proven. Various neurological conditions, such as convulsions, are commonly found to accompany PDDs.

Symptoms

Because PDDs share similar symptoms, distinctions between conditions must be carefully made to ensure correct diagnosis. Key distinctions are as follows.

PDDNOS:

- impairment of two-way social interaction
- repetitive and predictable behavior patterns and activities

Autism (in addition to the symptoms of PDDNOS):

- severe impairment in communication
- abnormal social interaction and use of language for social communication or imaginative play before age of three
- not better accounted for by another psychiatric disorder

Asperger syndrome (in addition to the symptoms of PDDNOS):

- clinically significant impairment in social, occupational, or other areas of functioning
- no general delay in language
- no delay in cognitive development, self-help skills, or adaptive behavior
- not better accounted for by another pervasive developmental disorder or schizophrenia

Rett syndrome:

- a period of normal development between 6–18 months
- normal head circumference at birth, followed by a slowing of head growth
- intellectual disabilities
- repetitive hand movements

CDD:

- normal development for at least two years
- loss of skills in at least two of the following areas: language, social skills, bowel or bladder control, play, movement skills
- abnormal functioning in at least two of the following areas: social interaction, communication, behavior patterns
- not better accounted for by another PDD or mental illness

KEY TERMS

Hydrotherapy—This term literally means "water treatment" and involves the use of water in physical therapy as well as treatment of physical and emotional illness.

Mutation—A change in a gene. A gene mutation may alter a trait or characteristic of an individual or may manifest as a disease; the mutation can also be transmitted to offspring.

Neurological conditions—A condition that has its origin in some part of the patient's nervous system.

Diagnosis

The diagnosis of a pervasive developmental disorder is made by medical specialists based on a thorough examination of the patient, including observing behavior and gathering information from parents and caregivers.

Treatment

Treatment for children with pervasive developmental disorders is limited. Those who can be enrolled in educational programs will need a highly structured learning environment, a teacher-student ratio of not more than 1:2, and a high level of parental involvement that provides consistent care at home. **Psychotherapy** and **social skills training** may prove helpful to some. There is no specific medication available for treating the core symptoms of any of these disorders, though research is promising. Some psychiatric medications may be helpful in controlling particular behavior difficulties, such as agitation, mood instability, and self-injury. **Music therapy**, massage, and hydrotherapy may exert a calming effect on behavior. Treatment may also include physical and occupational therapy.

Prognosis

In general, the prognosis of all of these conditions is tied to the severity of the illness. The higher the patient's IQ (intelligence quotient) and ability to communicate, the better the prognosis. The prognosis for Asperger syndrome is the most positive, and children with Asperger syndrome are likely to grow up to be functional independent adults, though they will always have problems with social relationships. The prognosis for autism is not as good, though great strides have been made in recent years in its treatment. The prognosis for childhood disintegrative disorder is even less favorable,

QUESTIONS TO ASK YOUR DOCTOR

- What are the indications that my child may have a pervasive developmental disorder?
- What physical and psychiatric diagnostic tests does my child need?
- What treatment options do you recommend for my child?
- What symptoms are important enough that I should seek immediate treatment?
- Can you recommend any support groups for me and my family?

and children with CDD will require intensive and long-term care. Children diagnosed with PDDNOS have a better prognosis, because their initial symptoms are usually milder, their IQ scores are higher, and their language development is stronger.

All persons with PDDs are at greater risk for developing serious mental illness than the general population, and many will always need some level of custodial care. In the past, individuals with PDD were confined to institutions, but many are now able to live in **group homes** or supervised apartments.

Prevention

Until the causes of pervasive developmental disorders are known, it will remain impossible to prevent these conditions.

Resources

BOOKS

American Psychiatric Association. *Diagnostic and Statistical Manual of Mental Disorders.* 4th ed., text rev. Washington, DC: American Psychiatric Association, 2000.

American Psychological Association. *Publication Manual of the American Psychological Association.* 6th ed. Washington, DC: American Psychological Association, 2009.

Coplan, James, MD. *Making Sense of Autistic Spectrum Disorders: Create the Brightest Future for Your Child with the Best Treatment Options.* New York: Bantam, 2010.

Schilling, Shondra, and Curt Schilling. *The Best Kind of Different: Our Family's Journey with Asperger's Syndrome.* New York: HarperCollins, 2010.

Taylor, Paul. *A Beginner's Guide to the Autism Spectrum Disorders: Essential Information for Parents and Professionals.* Philadelphia: Jessica Kingsley Publishers, 2011.

Volkmar, Fred, R., and Lisa A Wiesner. *A Practical Guide to Autism: What Every Parent, Family Member, and Teacher Needs to Know.* Sudbury, MA: Wiley, 2009.

PERIODICALS

Muhle, Rebecca, Stephanie V. Trentacoste, and Isabelle Rapin. "The Genetics of Autism." *Pediatrics* (May 2004): 1389–91.

Tateno, M., et al. "Pervasive Developmental Disorders and Autism Spectrum Disorders: Are These Disorders One and the Same?" *Psychiatric Investigation* 8, no. 1 (2011): 67–70.

Wink, L. K., C. A. Erickson, and C. J. McDougle. "Pharmacologic Treatment of Behavioral Symptoms Associated with Autism and Other Pervasive Developmental Disorders." *Current Treatment Options in Neurology* 12, no. 6 (2010): 529–38.

WEBSITES

National Institute of Mental Health. "Autism Spectrum Disorders (Pervasive Developmental Disorders)." http://mentalhealth.gov/health/publications/autism/complete-index.shtml (accessed November 2, 2011).

Autism Program at Yale. "Information About Pervasive Developmental Disorders (PDD)." Yale School of Medicine. http://medicine.yale.edu/childstudy/autism/information/index.aspx (accessed November 2, 2011).

ORGANIZATIONS

American Academy of Child and Adolescent Psychiatry, 3615 Wisconsin Ave. NW, Washington, DC, 20016-3007, (202) 966-7300, Fax: (202) 966-2891, http://aacap.org.

Autism Society of America, 4340 East-West Hwy, Suite 350, Bethesda, MD, 20814, (301) 657-0881, (800) 3-AUTISM (328-8476), http://www.autism-society.org.

International Rett Syndrome Association, 4600 Devitt Drive, Cincinnati, OH, 45246, (800) 818-7388, Fax: (513) 874-2520, http://www.rettsyndrome.org.

National Organization for Rare Disorders (NORD), PO Box 1968, Danbury, CT, 06813-1968, (203) 744-0100, (800) 999-6673, Fax: (203) 798-2291, orphan@rarediseases.org, http://www.rarediseases.org.

Teresa G. Odle
Donald G. Barstow, RN
Laura Jean Cataldo, RN, EdD

PET *see* **Positron emission tomography**

Phencyclidine and related disorders

Definition

Phencyclidine (PCP) is a street drug known as "angel dust" that causes physiological changes to the nervous and circulatory system, disturbances in thinking and behavior, and can cause hallucinations, psychotic disorder, mood disorder, and anxiety disorder.

Demographics

According to a Drug and Alcohol Services Information System (DASIS) report, in an analysis of PCP admissions, researchers found that 49% of people admitted for a substance-use problem with PCP as the primary substance were African American; another 26% were Hispanic, and 19% were Caucasian. Admissions for PCP as the primary drug were less than 1% of overall admissions for substance-use problems. In addition, admissions for PCP use in the United States were more frequent in the West and Northeast than in the South or Midwest. The average age at admission was 28 years, and most PCP users were male. In terms of education, people admitted for PCP substance-use problems were more likely to have dropped out of high school and less likely to have full-time employment than people admitted for other drugs. However, they were less likely to have an accompanying psychiatric problem than people admitted for other substances.

A study entitled *Monitoring the Future* is conducted every year by the University of Michigan and funded by the National Institute on Drug Abuse (NIDA). The 2007 report revealed that 2.1% of high school seniors had used PCP once, while 0.9% had used PCP at least one time in the previous year. In addition, 21% of high school seniors deemed PCP as *very easy* or *fairly easy* to obtain. The 2009 survey showed that 122,000 Americans age 12 and older had abused PCP at least one time in 2008, and the 2010 report revealed that 1.0% of high school seniors had used PCP at least one time in 2009.

Description

PCP is the best known of several related drugs, including ketamine, cyclohexamine, and dizocilpine. PCP was first synthesized by a pharmaceutical company in the 1950s and sold under the brand names Sernyl and Sernylan until 1967. It was hoped that PCP could be used as a dissociative anesthetic, because it produced a catatonic state in which patients were dissociated from their environment and from pain but not unconscious. Problems with side effects as the drug wore off, including agitated behavior and hallucinations, made PCP unsuitable for medical use. Ketamine (Ketlar, Ketaject) is less potent, has fewer side effects, and is approved for use as a human anesthetic.

PCP became an illicit street drug in the mid-1960s. It was most commonly found in large cities such as New York and San Francisco, and even in the early 2000s, most users lived in urban areas. Into the 1970s, PCP

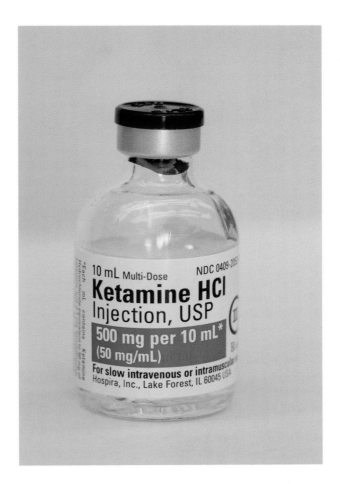

10 mL vial of ketamine; when used illicitly, the liquid is usually evaporated and snorted. *(© Custom Medical Stock Photo, Inc. Reproduced by permission.)*

appeared mainly as a contaminant of other illicit drugs, especially marijuana, and **diagnosis** of PCP use was complicated by the fact that many people did not know they had ingested the drug.

PCP is easy to manufacture and is inexpensive. By the late 1970s, in some urban areas its use equaled that of crack **cocaine**. Use of PCP peaked between 1973 and 1979. After 1980, PCP use declined, although as with many illicit drugs, its popularity increases and decreases in cycles.

People who use PCP exhibit both behavioral and physiological signs. The effects of PCP are erratic, and serious complications can occur at relatively low doses. It is often difficult to distinguish PCP use from the use of other illicit drugs, and many people who use PCP also abuse other substances. According to the *Diagnostic and Statistical Manual of Mental Disorders,* fourth edition, text revision (*DSM-IV-TR*), which presents guidelines used by the **American Psychiatric Association** for diagnosis of mental disorders, phencyclidine can induce mood

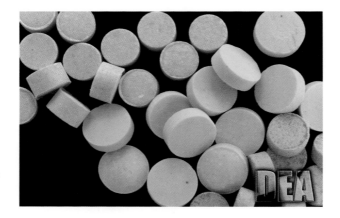

PCP pills. *(U.S. Drug Enforcement Administration)*

disorder, psychotic disorder, and anxiety disorder. These classifications are somewhat controversial and not all are recognized by international psychiatric organizations. Animal studies suggest that both conditions occur, just as they do with many other abused drugs.

PCP is a Schedule II drug under the Controlled Substances Act, which means it has a high potential for abuse and dependence and has severe restrictions for medical use. In its pure form, it is a white powder that dissolves easily in water. Once dissolved, the solution can be sprayed on tobacco or marijuana cigarettes. Less pure forms range from yellowish-tan to brown and can be a sticky mass. On the street PCP has many names, including angel dust, devil dust, tranq, hog, crazy Eddie, rocket fuel, embalming fluid, wack, and ozone. Crack cocaine combined with PCP is sometimes called tragic magic. Marijuana laced with PCP is called love boat, killer weed, or crystal supergrass.

Causes and symptoms

Causes

PCP is easy to manufacture and is inexpensively available on the street in most cities, especially East Coast cities. It can be eaten, smoked, injected, or snorted, and is readily soluble and will cross the skin barrier if in liquid form PCP is spilled on skin or clothing. The most common methods of ingestion are eating and smoking marijuana or tobacco on which liquid PCP has been sprayed. PCP is long-acting. It accumulates in body fat and flashbacks can occur as it is released from fat during **exercise**.

PCP binds to receptors in the **brain** and interferes with the chemical reactions that mediate the transmission of nerve impulses. It is deactivated slowly by the liver and excreted in urine. Although there are no controlled human studies on PCP intoxication, monkeys allowed free use of PCP will dose themselves repeatedly and maintain an almost continuous state of intoxication. They exhibit withdrawal symptoms if their supply of the drug is restricted. PCP is considered to be psychologically and possibly physically addictive in humans.

Symptoms

PCP produces both physiological and psychological symptoms. Effects of the drug are erratic and not always dose-dependent.

Physical symptoms include:

• involuntary rapid movements of the eyes vertically or horizontally
• high blood pressure
• racing heartbeat
• dizziness and shakiness
• drooling
• increased body temperature
• reduced response to pain
• slurred speech
• excessive sensitivity to sound
• lack of muscle coordination
• muscle rigidity or frozen posture
• seizures
• breakdown of muscle and excretion of muscle proteins in urine
• coma
• death

Psychiatric and social symptoms include:

• disordered thinking and confusion
• impaired judgment
• belligerence
• aggressiveness
• agitation
• impulsiveness and unpredictability
• schizophrenic-like psychoses
• hallucinations of sight, sound, or touch
• memory impairment
• difficulty in social-emotional relationships
• chaotic lifestyle, including difficulty functioning at work or school and legal and financial problems

PCP is known for its variability of symptoms, which change both from person to person and from exposure to exposure. In addition, symptoms come and go throughout a period of intoxication that can last 1–2 hours for low-dose exposure to 1–4 days for high-dose exposure. Severity of symptoms is not always related to the size of the dose as measured by blood levels of the drug.

KEY TERMS

Addiction—A strong physical or psychological dependence on a physical substance.

Anxiety—A troubled feeling, a sense of dread, fear of the future, or distress over a possible threat to a person's physical or mental well-being.

Dependence—The adaptation of neurons and other physical processes to the use of a drug, followed by withdrawal symptoms when the drug is removed; physiological and/or psychological addiction.

Hallucinations—Heard, seen, or otherwise sensed perceptions that are not empirically real. Hallucinations can result from nervous system abnormalities, mental disorders, or the use of certain drugs.

Intoxication—The presence of significant problem behaviors or psychological changes following ingestion of a substance.

Schizophrenia—A major mental illness marked by psychotic symptoms, including hallucinations, delusions, and severe disruptions in thinking.

Seizure—A convulsion, or uncontrolled discharge of nerve cells, that may spread to other cells throughout the brain.

Stuporous—A state of sluggishness or impaired consciousness.

Substance abuse—A milder form of addiction than substance dependence. Generally, people who have been diagnosed with substance abuse do not experience the tolerance or withdrawal symptoms—the signs of physiological dependence—that people dependent on a substance experience.

Withdrawal—Symptoms experienced by a person who has become physically dependent on a drug, experienced when the drug use is discontinued.

Three rough phases of intoxication have been established: behavioral toxicity, stuporous stage, and comatose stage. Many users fluctuate between phases, and some have symptoms that do not fit neatly into any phase. In the behavioral toxicity stage, people tend to gaze blankly while their eyes dart horizontally or vertically. Muscle control is poor, and individuals may make repetitive movements, grind their teeth, or grimace. Body temperature, heart rate, and respiration are mildly elevated. Vomiting and drooling may occur.

In the stuporous phase, the eyes are wide open, and individuals appear wide awake but in a stupor. **Seizures**

may occur if individuals are stimulated. The eyes may dart in any direction while the gaze remains fixed. Body temperature is increased substantially. Heart and respiration rate are increased by about 25%. Muscles are rigid with twitching.

In the comatose stage, which may last 1–4 days, individuals are in a deep coma. Their pupils are dilated, and their eyes drift. Body temperature is elevated to the point of being life-threatening. The heart rate is dangerously high, increasing to about twice the normal level, and blood pressure is dangerously low. Breathing may stop for brief periods (apnea). There is no response to pain, and individuals sweat heavily. Death is possible, although most deaths from PCP occur in earlier stages through accidents or **suicide**.

Diagnosis

Diagnosis of PCP abuse or dependence is often complicated by the fact that symptoms are variable. Most people who use PCP also use other drugs (74% of users in one survey used at least one other substance), and PCP can be a contaminant in other street drugs or can itself be contaminated with other chemicals. PCP use is also found among people with psychiatric disorders. In many ways, PCP mimics the symptoms of **schizophrenia**.

The American Psychiatric Association describes two classes of PCP disorders: PCP dependence and PCP abuse. In addition, it recognizes seven other PCP-induced psychiatric disorders.

PCP dependence can be difficult to pinpoint because, unlike many other drugs of abuse, PCP does not invariably cause craving in individuals who use it. In addition, although studies of specific populations have identified signs of tolerance or withdrawal, these symptoms have not been clearly categorized for PCP use. Generally, a person with PCP dependence will engage in PCP use several times a day and persist in using it, even when psychological problems (such as anxiety or rage) and/or medical problems (such as high blood pressure or seizures) occur. Aggression has been identified as a key problem for people dependent on PCP. People with psychiatric disorders are more likely to have bad side effects from PCP than those without psychiatric problems. Because PCP is readily stored in fat and released as fat stores are used, adverse effects of PCP dependence can continue for weeks after the drug is discontinued.

People who exhibit signs of PCP abuse may use the drug less often than those with dependence, but they also may experience interference with their ability to fulfill their responsibilities at school, work, or home. In addition, with the impaired judgment associated with PCP use, individuals may engage in dangerous

QUESTIONS TO ASK YOUR
DOCTOR

- What risks are associated with PCP abuse?
- What symptoms are associated with PCP dependence?
- Does having PCP dependence and abuse put me at risk for other health conditions?
- Can you recommend any treatment and support groups for me?

behaviors, such as driving a car while under the drug's influence. Use of the drug may trigger trouble in personal relationships or with the law.

Phencyclidine-induced disorders include:

• PCP intoxication with or without perceptual disturbances
• PCP intoxication delirium
• PCP-induced psychotic disorder
• PCP-induced mood disorder
• PCP-induced anxiety disorder
• PCP-induced disorders not otherwise specified

PCP intoxication and **delirium** are diagnosed by a history of recent PCP use, behavioral changes, and physical changes that are not accounted for by any other substance use, medical condition, or psychiatric condition. PCP is present in the blood and urine. With PCP intoxication, individuals may have hallucinations but be aware that these are caused by PCP use.

PCP delirium is diagnosed when individuals exhibit muddled thinking, hostility, bouts of hyperactivity and aggressiveness, and schizophrenic-like symptoms, as well as the more severe physical symptoms listed above. PCP delirium can last for hours or days.

It may be difficult initially to separate PCP intoxication or delirium from other mental disorders, as symptoms may mimic **depression**, schizophrenia, mood disorders, **conduct disorder**, and **antisocial personality disorder**. People with PCP intoxication also have physical and psychological symptoms similar to those that occur with the use of other illicit drugs, complicating diagnosis. A complete physical and psychological history helps rule out these other conditions.

Treatment

People experiencing PCP intoxication or delirium often hurt themselves or others. They are generally kept in an environment in which there is as little stimulation as possible. They are restrained only as much as is necessary to keep them from hurting themselves or others until the level of PCP in their bodies can be reduced. Antipsychotic medications may be used to calm patients in cases of PCP delirium.

There are no quick ways to rid the body of PCP. If the PCP has been eaten, stomach pumping or feeding activated charcoal may help keep the drug from being absorbed into the bloodstream. Physical symptoms such as high body temperature are treated as needed.

Most people recover from PCP intoxication or delirium without major medical complications. Many are habitual users who return to use almost immediately. There are no specific behavioral therapies to treat PCP use. **Antidepressants** are sometimes prescribed. Long-term residential treatment or intensive outpatient treatment along with urine monitoring offer some chance of success. Narcotics Anonymous, a self-help group, may be helpful for some patients.

Prognosis

Relapse and return to PCP use is common, even among people who have experienced severe medical and psychiatric complications from the drug. Because many users also abuse other drugs, their success in renouncing PCP is tied to their successful treatment for other addictions. Successful treatment takes persistence, patience, and a functional support system, all of which many users lack.

Prevention

PCP intoxication and related disorders can be prevented by not using the drug.

Resources
BOOKS
American Psychiatric Association. *Diagnostic and Statistical Manual of Mental Disorders,* 4th ed., text rev. Washington, DC: American Psychiatric Publishing, 2000.
American Psychological Association. *Publication Manual of the American Psychological Association,* 6th ed. Washington, DC: American Psychological Association, 2009.
Doweiko, Harold E. *Concepts of Chemical Dependency,* 8th ed. Belmont, CA: Brooks Cole, 2011.
Erickson, Carlton K. *Addiction Essentials: The Go-To Guide for Clinicians and Patients.* New York: Norton, 2011.

WEBSITES
"The DASIS Report: Characteristics of Primary Phencyclidine (PCP) Admissions: 2001." Drug and Alcohol Services Information System (SAMHSA). May 7, 2004. http://

store.samhsa.gov/product/Characteristics-of-Primary-Phencyclidine-PCP-Admissions-2001/SR019 (accessed October 3, 2011).

"NIDA InfoFacts: PCP (Phencylcidine)." National Institute on Drug Abuse. Last modified June 2009. http://www.nida.nih.gov/Infofacts/PCP.html (accessed October 3, 2011).

ORGANIZATIONS

American Council for Drug Education, 50 Jay St., Brooklyn, NY, 11201, (646) 505-2061, acde@phoenixhouse.org, http://www.acde.org.

American Psychiatric Association, 1000 Wilson Blvd., Ste. 1825, Arlington, VA, 22209-3901, (703) 907-7300, apa@psych.org, http://www.psych.org.

American Psychological Association, 750 1st St. NE, Washington, DC, 20002-4242, (202) 336-5500; TDD/TTY: (202) 336-6123, (800) 374-2721, http://www.apa.org.

American Society for Clinical Pharmacology and Therapeutics, 528 N Washington St., Alexandria, VA, 22314, (703) 836-6981, info@ascpt.org, http://www.ascpt.org.

National Institute on Drug Abuse. National Institutes of Health, 6001 Executive Blvd., Rm. 5213, Bethesda, MD, 20892, (301) 442-1124; Spanish: (240) 221-4007, information@nida.nih.gov, http://www.nida.nih.gov.

Tish Davidson, AM
Emily Jane Willingham, PhD
Laura Jean Cataldo, RN, EdD

Phenelzine

Definition

Phenelzine is classified as a monoamine oxidase inhibitor (MAOI). It is used to treat several types of serious **depression**. In the United States, phenelzine is sold under the brand name Nardil.

Purpose

Phenelzine is used to treat certain types forms of serious depression and severe depression complicated by severe anxiety that do not respond to other antidepressant drugs.

Description

Phenelzine is a member of a class of drugs called **monoamine oxidase inhibitors**. Monoamine oxidase, or MAO, is an enzyme found throughout the body. In the **brain**, MAO breaks down norepinephrine and **serotonin**, two naturally occurring chemicals that are important in maintaining mental well-being and preventing

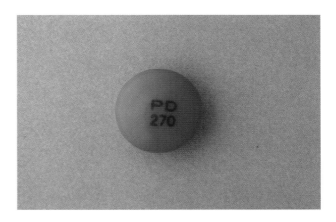

Nardil (phenelzine), 15 mg. (© Custom Medical Stock Photo, Inc. Reproduced by permission.)

depression. Monoamine oxidase inhibitors such as phenelzine reduce the activity of MAO. Less norepinephrine and serotonin are broken down, so their levels rise. This helps to lift depression.

Phenelzine is effective for treating depression, especially complicated types of depression that have not responded to more traditional **antidepressants**. However, phenelzine also affects the MAO enzyme in many other areas of the body. This accounts for the large number of serious side effects and drug interactions caused by the drug.

Recommended dosage

Adults are usually started on 15 mg of phenelzine three times per day. This dosage can be increased to a maximum of 90 mg per day if lower doses are not effective and if the patient can tolerate the higher dose without excessive side effects. After the maximum benefits are achieved, the dosage is usually lowered over several weeks to the lowest level that is effective. This could be as little as 15 mg daily or every other day.

In general, phenelzine is not recommended for people over the age of 60. When it is used by the elderly, the starting dosage is usually 15 mg taken in the morning. This dose may be gradually increased over time to a maximum of 60 mg. Phenelzine is not approved by the U.S. Food and Drug Administration (FDA) for use in patients younger than 18, and recommended dosage in such cases has not been established.

Phenelzine can be taken with food or on an empty stomach. It should not be taken close to bedtime, because it can interfere with sleep. The benefits of this drug may not become apparent for as long as four to eight weeks. Patients should be aware of this and continue taking the drug as directed even if they do not see an immediate improvement.

Precautions

People with a history of congestive heart failure, high blood pressure, cardiovascular disease, headache, kidney disease, or liver disease should not take phenelzine or, if they do take it, they should be under careful medical supervision and monitoring. Children under the age of 18 and people with a history of low blood pressure, **bipolar disorder**, angina, hyperactivity, diabetes mellitus, **seizures**, suicidal thoughts, and overactive thyroid should discuss the risks and benefits of this drug with their physician, and the decision to use phenelzine should be made on an individual case basis. If these patients receive phenelzine, it should be taken only under the careful supervision of a doctor. Evidence suggests that phenelzine should not be used during pregnancy or while nursing.

Children and adults up to age 24 are at an increased risk of developing suicidal thoughts or actions when taking an antidepressant drug, including phenelzine. Patients of any age taking the drug should be monitored for signs of worsening depression or changes in behavior.

People taking phenelzine should get up slowly from a reclining position to prevent dizziness. Caution should be used when operating heavy machinery or performing hazardous activities that require alertness. Patients preparing to undergo surgery should stop taking phenelzine at least ten days before their procedure.

It is very important for the doctor to determine the lowest dosage of phenelzine that produces benefits. When this dosage is exceeded, side effects and interactions increase substantially. Over-the-counter medications that contain decongestants or dextromethorphan (for example, some cough syrups and cold remedies) should not be taken while using phenelzine. In addition, foods and beverages that contain tyramine should not be eaten while using this medication. These foods include yeast or meat extracts, fermented sausage, overripe fruit, sauerkraut, cheese, and fava beans. Phenelzine should not be used within two weeks of undergoing surgery that requires anesthesia.

Side effects

The enzyme monoamine oxidase regulates functions throughout the body. Phenelzine decreases the activity of monoamine oxidase in all the areas of the body where it exists, not just in the brain. This is why phenelzine is capable of causing a wide variety of side effects in many different organ systems.

The most common and unavoidable side effects associated with phenelzine use are swelling of the feet and ankles, low blood pressure upon arising from a reclining position, and **insomnia** if taken near bedtime. Mild side effects and ones that are not frequent include skin rash, headache, dizziness, confusion, memory impairment, drowsiness, weakness, shakiness, muscle twitching, constipation, indigestion, appetite changes, and dry mouth. Although these side effects are considered mild, they should be reported to the patient's physician.

More serious side effects include hepatitis coupled with jaundice, high blood pressure crisis, excessive nervousness, and changes in heart rate. The high blood pressure crisis involves significantly increased blood pressure, severe headache, heart palpitations, nausea, vomiting, and sweating. These symptoms need immediate medical attention. Sexual function can be affected in both men and women.

Interactions

Phenelzine interacts with a long list of drugs. Some of these interactions can cause death. This section is not a complete list of interactions, but it includes the most serious ones. Patients must make sure that every health care professional who takes care of them (for example, doctors, dentists, podiatrists, optometrists, pharmacists, nurses) knows that they take phenelzine, as well as all of the other prescription, nonprescription, and herbal drugs they take.

All foods and beverages containing tyramine need to be avoided while taking this medication. Coffee, tea, and cola beverages should be restricted to one serving per day. Alcohol should not be used while taking phenelzine, because it can significantly increase blood pressure.

Any type of amphetamine and other stimulant should not be used, because this combination can increase blood pressure to dangerously high levels. Phenelzine should not be combined with other antidepressants, because of increased risk of dangerously high blood pressure and manic episodes. Patients taking phenelzine should stop the drug and wait at least 14 days before starting any other antidepressant. The same holds true when discontinuing another antidepressant and starting phenelzine.

Phenelzine combined with **clomipramine** (Anafranil) can cause death. Diet drugs and decongestants containing compounds such as dextromethorphan should not be combined with phenelzine because of an increased

KEY TERMS

Angina—Severe pain and a feeling of constriction around the heart.

Bipolar disorder—A mood disorder marked by alternating episodes of extremely low mood (depression) and exuberant highs (mania).

Hepatitis—An inflammation of the liver that can be caused by a variety of factors.

Jaundice—A yellowing of the skin caused by excess bilirubin in the blood; a liver disorder.

Tyramine—Intermediate product between the chemicals tyrosine and epinephrine in the body and a substance normally found in many foods. Found especially in protein-rich foods that have been aged or fermented, pickled, or bacterially contaminated, such as cheese, beer, yeast, wine, and chicken liver.

risk of seizures and agitation. Phenelzine can decrease the effectiveness of high blood pressure drugs, such as guanadrel (Hylorel) and guanethidine (Ismelin). Phenelzine combined with the Parkinson's disease drug levodopa (Dopar, Larodopa) can produce severely high blood pressure. Lithium should not be used with phenelzine because of the risk of developing an extremely high fever. Phenelzine can prolong the effects of muscle relaxants and **barbiturates** when either of the two are taken with phenelzine.

Resources

BOOKS

Brunton, Laurence, Bruce Chabner, and Bjorn Knollman. *Goodman & Gilman's The Pharmacological Basis of Therapeutics* 12th ed. New York: McGraw-Hill, 2010.

Consumer Reports and American Society of Health-System Pharmacists. *Consumer Reports Complete Drug Reference.* Yonkers, NY: Consumers Reports, 2009.

Ellsworth, Allan J., et al. *Mosby's Medical Drug Reference.* St. Louis, MO: Mosby, 2007.

Venes, Donald. *Taber's Cyclopedic Medical Dictionary.* 21st ed. Philadelphia: F.A. Davis Company, 2009.

WEBSITES

PubMed Health. "Phenelzine." U.S. National Library of Medicine. http://www.ncbi.nlm.nih.gov/pubmedhealth/PMH0000573 (accessed November 13, 2011).

ORGANIZATIONS

National Institute of Mental Health, 6001 Executive Blvd., Rm. 8184, MSC 9663, Bethesda, MD, 20892-9663, (301) 433-4513; TTY: (301) 443-8431, Fax: (301) 443-4279, (866) 615-6464; TTY: (866) 415-8051 nimhinfo@nih.gov, http://www.nimh.nih.gov.

U.S. Food and Drug Administration, 10903 New Hampshire Ave., Silver Spring, MD, 20993-0002, (888) INFO-FDA (463-6332), http://www.fda.gov.

Mark Mitchell, M.D.

Phobias *see* **Agoraphobia; Social phobia; Specific phobias**

Phonological disorder

Definition

Phonological disorder occurs when a child does not develop the ability to produce some or all sounds necessary for speech that are normally used at his or her age.

Demographics

Phonological disorder of unknown cause is considered significantly more common than phonological disorder that is caused by neurological or structural abnormalities. It has been estimated that 7%–8% children who are five years old have phonological disorder with any cause (developmental phonological disorder). About 7.5% of children between the ages of three and eleven are thought to have development phonological disorder. Phonological disorder is more common in boys than it is in girls. Estimates suggest that two to four times as many boys as girls have the disorder. Children who have phonological disorder are more likely to have other language problems and disorders. Children with one or more family members who have this or similar language disorders are also considered to be more likely to have phonological disorders.

Description

Phonological disorder is sometimes referred to as articulation disorder, developmental articulation disorder, or speech sound production disorder. If there is no known cause, it is sometimes called "developmental phonological disorder." If the cause is known to be of neurological origin, the names "dysarthria" or "dyspraxia" are often used. Phonological disorder is characterized by a child's inability to create speech at a level expected of his or her age group because of an inability to form the necessary sounds.

There are many different levels of severity of phonological disorder. These range from speech that is completely incomprehensible, even to a child's immediate family members, to speech that can be understood by everyone but in which some sounds are slightly mispronounced. Treatment for phonological disorder is important not only for the child's development to be able to form speech sounds, but for other reasons, as well. Children who have problems creating speech sounds may have academic problems in subject areas such as spelling or reading. Also, children who sound different than their peers may find themselves frustrated and ridiculed, and may become less willing to participate in play or classroom activities.

Causes

Phonological disorder is often divided into three categories based on the cause of the disorder. One cause is structural problems, or abnormalities in the areas necessary for speech sound production, such as the tongue or the roof of the mouth. These abnormalities make it difficult for children to produce certain sounds, and in some cases make it impossible for a child to produce the sounds at all. The structural problem causing the phonological disorder generally needs to be treated before the child goes into language therapy. This therapy is especially useful, because in many of these cases correction of the structural problem results in correction of the speech sound problem.

The second category of phonological disorder is problems caused by neurological problems or abnormalities. This category includes problems with the muscles of the mouth that do not allow the child sufficient fine motor control over the muscles to produce all speech sounds.

The third category of phonological disorder is phonological disorder of an unknown cause. This is sometimes called " developmental phonological disorder." Although the cause is not known, there is much speculation. Possible causes include slight **brain** abnormalities, causes rooted in the child's environment, and immature development of the neurological system.

Symptoms

The symptoms of phonological disorder differ significantly depending on the age of the child. It is often difficult to detect this disorder, as the child with phonological disorder develops speech sounds more slowly than his or her peers; generally, however, he or she develops them in the same sequence. Therefore, speech that may be normal for a four-year-old child may be a sign of phonological disorder in a six-year-old.

Nearly all children develop speech sounds in the same sequence. The consonant sounds are grouped into three main groups of eight sounds each: the early eight, the middle eight, and the late eight. The early eight include consonant sounds such as "m," "b," and "p." The middle eight include sounds such as "t," "g," and "chi," and the late eight include more complicated sounds such as "sh," "th," "z," and "zh." Many children do not normally finish mastering the late eight until they are seven or eight years old. As children normally develop speech sound skills, there are some very common mistakes that are made. These include the omission of sounds, (e.g., frequently at the end of words), the distortion of sounds, or the substitution of one sound for another. Often the substitution is of a sound that the child can more easily produce for one that he or she cannot.

Diagnosis

The **diagnosis** for phonologic disorder depends greatly on the age of the child in question. Children who are four years old may have speech production difficulties that show normal development for their age, while children who are eight years old and making the same mistakes may have phonological disorder. In children with phonological disorder, the pattern and order of speech sound acquisition is usually similar to that of normally developing children. However, the speech sound skills develop more slowly, so age is an important factor in determining a diagnosis of phonological disorder. Children with phonological disorder may make the same speech sound mistakes as younger, normally developing children. In some cases, however, children with phonological disorder have demonstrated more instances of omissions, substitutions, and distortions in their speech.

When exploring a diagnosis of phonological disorder, it is generally recommended that a physician check for other possible causes of the signs and symptoms. A child's hearing should be checked, because speech sounds that are not heard well by a child cannot be imitated and learned well. In school-age children, reading comprehension should be checked to discover any other language disorders, which are sometimes present in addition to phonological disorder. Any general developmental delays should also be checked by the physician. It is important to remember that for some children whose mother tongue is one other than English, the problems with speech sounds may result from poor crossover of sounds between the child's languages. When diagnosing a child who a different mother tongue, it is recommended that tests involve the child's first language, as well as English. It must be remembered that in some parts of the country, normal pronunciation of some words is different from pronunciation in other parts of the country. Therefore a child's background and history can be very important in making a diagnosis.

The *Diagnostic and Statistical Manual of Mental Disorders* (*DSM-IV-TR*) states that for a diagnosis of phonological disorder to be made, three general criteria must be met. The first criterion is that the child is not developing speech sounds skills considered to be appropriate for his or her age group. Also, this lack of speech sound acquisition must be causing problems for the child at home, at school, or in other important aspects of the child's life. If the child has an intellectual disability, has problems with his or her speech or hearing, or if there is environmental deprivation, a diagnosis of phonological disorder may still be appropriate. The diagnosis can only be made if the lack of speech sounds skill is considered greater than can the child's other problems.

Treatment

Treatment by a speech-language pathologist is generally recommended for children with phonological disorders. The therapy will differ depending on an individual child's needs, but generally takes the form of practicing sounds. Sometimes the child is shown the physical ways that the sound is made, such as where to place the tongue and how to form the lips. Repetition of the difficult sounds with the therapist is an integral part of treatment. There is debate over the way that children with more severe forms of the disorder should be treated. Some therapists believe that the sounds that are learned later in development should be addressed first, even if the child has not developed the more simple sound skills. Other therapists believe that simple sounds should be treated first, as it is easier for children with phonological disorder to master them. One other school of thought is that when the child develops a sense of accomplishment when these sounds are mastered, and he or she will more willingly continue with treatment.

Children who have phonological disorder because of neurological or structural problems that do not allow them to produce some sounds are often helped to find approximate alternatives for the sounds within the range of sounds that they are able to produce.

Prognosis

The prognosis for children with phonological disorder is generally good. For many children, the problem resolves spontaneously. It is reported that in 75% of children with mild or moderate forms of the disorder, and whose problems do not stem from a medical condition, the symptoms resolve before age six. In many other cases, children who receive treatment eventually develop normal or close to normal speech. In some cases, there may be mild effects that

KEY TERMS

Dysarthria—A group of speech disorders caused by disturbances in the strength or coordination of the muscles of the speech mechanism as a result of damage to the brain or nerves. Difficulty talking and speaking.

Dyspraxia—Developmental dyspraxia is an impairment or immaturity of the organization of movement. It is a defect in the way the brain processes information, resulting in messages not being correctly or fully transmitted. The term dyspraxia comes from the word "praxis," meaning "doing" or "acting." Dyspraxia is associated with problems of perception, language, and thought.

last until adulthood, but speech is completely understandable. For children with phonological disorder due to a neurological or structural cause, the outcome generally rests on how well the cause of the problem is treated.

Prevention

There is no known way to prevent phonological disorder. A healthy diet during pregnancy and regular prenatal care may help to prevent some of the neurological or structural problems that can result in the disorder.

Resources

BOOKS

American Psychiatric Association. *Diagnostic and Statistical Manual of Mental Disorders.* 4th ed., text rev. Washington, DC: American Psychiatric Publishing, 2000.

Sadock, Benjamin J., and Virginia A. Sadock, eds. *Comprehensive Textbook of Psychiatry.* Vol. 2. 7th ed. Philadelphia: Lippincott Williams and Wilkins, 2000.

PERIODICALS

Rvachew, Susan, and Michele Nowak. "The Effect of Target-Selection Strategy on Phonological Learning." *Journal of Speech, Language, and Hearing Research* 44, no. 3 (June 2001): 610–623.

Weismer, Susan Ellis, et al. "Nonword Repetition Performance in School-age Children With and Without Language Impairment." *Journal of Speech, Language, and Hearing Research* 43, no. 4 (August 2000) 865–878.

ORGANIZATIONS

American Academy of Child and Adolescent Psychiatry, 3615 Wisconsin Ave. NW, Washington, DC, 20016-3007, (202) 966-7300, Fax: (202) 966-2891, http://aacap.org.

American Speech-Language-Hearing Association, 2200 Research Blvd., Rockville, MD, 20785, (301) 296-5700, http://www.asha.org.

American Academy of Pediatrics, 141 Northwest Point Blvd., Elk Grove Village, IL, 60007-1098, (847) 434-4000, Fax: (847) 434-8000, http://www.aap.org.

Tish Davidson, A.M.

Pica

Definition

Pica is a term that refers to cravings for substances that are not foods. Materials consumed by patients with pica include dirt, ice, clay, glue, sand, chalk, beeswax, chewing gum, laundry starch, and hair.

Demographics

Pica tends to taper off as children grow older. The disorder occasionally continues into adolescence but is rarely observed in adults who are not disabled.

Pica is observed more commonly during the second and third years of life and is considered to be developmentally inappropriate in children older than 18–24 months. Research findings indicate that the disorder occurs in 25%–33% of young children and 20% of children in mental health clinics. Among individuals with intellectual disabilities, pica occurs most often in those between the ages of 10–20 years. Among young pregnant women, the onset of pica is frequently associated with a first pregnancy in late adolescence or early adulthood. Although pica usually stops at the end of the pregnancy, it may continue intermittently for years.

Pica usually occurs with equal frequency among males and females. It is relatively uncommon, however, among adolescent and adult males of average intelligence who live in developed countries.

Description

Pica is the craving or ingestion of nonfood items. The cravings found in patients diagnosed with pica may be associated with a nutritional deficiency state, such as iron-deficiency anemia; with pregnancy; or with an intellectual disability or mental illness. The word *pica* is derived from the Latin word for magpie, a species of bird that feeds on whatever it encounters.

According to the ***Diagnostic and Statistical Manual of Mental Disorders*** (*DSM*) which presents guidelines used by the American Psychiatric Association for diagnosis of mental disorders, a **diagnosis** of pica requires that the patient persists in eating nonfood substances for at least one month. The behavior must be inappropriate for the patient's stage of development. Further, it must not be approved or encouraged by the patient's culture.

Causes and symptoms

Causes

The cause of pica is not known. Many hypotheses have been developed to explain the behavior. These have included a variety of such factors as cultural influences, low socioeconomic status, deficiency diseases, and psychological disorders.

Malnutrition is often diagnosed at the same time as pica. A causal link has not been established. Eating clay has been associated with iron deficiency; however, whether decreased iron absorption is caused by eating clay or whether iron deficiency prompts people to eat clay is not known. Some cultural groups are said to teach youngsters to eat clay. Persons with iron deficiency anemia have also been reported to chew on ice cubes. Again, the mechanism or causal link is not known.

Eating paint is most common among children from families of low socioeconomic status. It is often associated with lack of parental supervision. Hunger also may result in pica.

Among persons with intellectual disabilities, pica has been explained as the result of an inability to tell the difference between food and nonfood items. This explanation, however, is not supported by examples of nonfood items that were deliberately selected and eaten by persons with limited mental faculties.

Pica, iron deficiency, and a number of other physiological disturbances in humans have been associated with decreased activity of the **dopamine** system in the **brain**. Dopamine is a neurotransmitter, or chemical that helps to relay the transmission of nerve impulses from one nerve cell to another. This association has led some researchers to think that there may be a connection between abnormally low levels of dopamine in the brain and the development of pica. No specific underlying biochemical disorders have been identified, however.

Risk factors for pica include the following:

• parental/child psychopathology

• family disorganization

- environmental deprivation
- pregnancy
- epilepsy
- brain damage
- intellectual disabilities
- pervasive developmental disorders

Symptoms

Infants and children diagnosed with pica commonly eat paint, plaster, string, hair, and cloth. Older children may eat animal droppings, sand, insects, leaves, pebbles and cigarette butts. Adolescents and adults most often ingest clay or soil.

The symptoms of pica vary with the item ingested:

- Sand or soil is associated with gastric pain and occasional bleeding.
- Chewing ice may cause abnormal wear on teeth.
- Eating clay may cause constipation.
- Swallowing metal objects may lead to bowel perforation.
- Eating fecal material often leads to such infectious diseases as toxocariasis, toxoplasmosis, and trichuriasis.
- Consuming lead can lead to kidney damage and intellectual disabilities.

Diagnosis

Pica is often diagnosed in a hospital emergency room, when the child or adolescent develops symptoms of **lead poisoning**, bowel perforation, or other medical complications caused by the nonfood items that have been swallowed. Laboratory studies may be used to assess these complications. The choice of imaging or laboratory studies depends on the characteristics of the ingested materials and the resultant medical problems.

The examining doctor may order a variety of **imaging studies** in order to identify the ingested materials and treat the gastrointestinal complications of pica. These imaging studies may include the following:

- abdominal x rays
- barium examinations of the upper and lower gastrointestinal (GI) tracts
- upper GI endoscopy to diagnose the formation of bezoars (solid masses formed in the stomach) or to identify associated injuries to the digestive tract

Films and studies may be repeated at regular intervals to track changes in the location of ingested materials.

KEY TERMS

Behavior modification—An approach to therapy based on the principles of operant conditioning. Behavior modification seeks to replace undesirable behaviors with preferable behaviors through the use of positive or negative reinforcement.

Bezoar—A hard ball of hair or vegetable fiber that may develop in the stomach of humans as the result of ingesting nonfood items.

Chelation—A method of treating lead or mercury poisoning by giving medications that remove heavy metals from the bloodstream. The medications that are used are called chelating agents.

Dopamine—A chemical in brain tissue that serves to transmit nerve impulses (is a neurotransmitter) and helps to regulate movement and emotions.

Neurotransmitter—A chemical in the brain that transmits messages between neurons, or nerve cells.

Toxocariasis—Infection with roundworm larvae, commonly transmitted by the feces of dogs and cats.

Toxoplasmosis—A parasitic infection caused by the intracellular protozoan *Toxoplasmosis gondii*. Humans are most commonly infected by swallowing the oocyte form of the parasite in soil (or kitty litter) contaminated by feces from an infected cat; or by swallowing the cyst form of the parasite in raw or undercooked meat.

Trichuriasis—Infection with the larvae of roundworms. These parasites may live for 10–20 years in humans.

Treatment

The most effective strategies for treatment are based on **behavior modification**, but with limited success. Pica associated with a nutritional deficiency often clears up when the missing nutrient is added to the patient's diet.

Few studies have examined the efficacy of drug treatments for pica. Ongoing research, however, is exploring the relationship between pica and abnormally low levels of the neurotransmitter dopamine. This line of research may help to identify new medications for the treatment of pica. There is some evidence that medications used to manage severe behavioral problems in children may be useful in treating coexisting pica.

Lead poisoning resulting from pica may be treated by chelating medications, which are drugs that remove lead or other heavy metals from the bloodstream. The two medications most often given for lead poisoning are dimercaprol, which is also known as BAL or British Anti-Lewisite; and edetate calcium disodium (EDTA). A medical toxicologist (a doctor who specializes in treating poisoning cases) may be consulted regarding children's dosages of these drugs.

In some cases, surgery may be required to remove metal objects from the patient's digestive tract or to repair tissue injuries. It is particularly important to remove any objects made of lead (fishing weights, lead shot, pieces of printer's type, etc.) as quickly as possible because of the danger of lead poisoning.

Prognosis

Pica frequently ends spontaneously in young children and pregnant women. Untreated pica, however, may persist for years, especially in persons with intellectual and developmental disabilities.

Prevention

There is no known way to prevent pica at the present time. Educating people, particularly young couples with children, about healthy nutritional practices is the best preventive strategy.

Resources

BOOKS

American Psychiatric Association. "Pica." In *Diagnostic and Statistical Manual of Mental Disorders*. 4th ed., text rev. Washington, DC: American Psychiatric Association, 2000.

Herrin, Marcia, and Nancy Matsumoto. *The Parent's Guide to Childhood Eating Disorders*. New York: Henry Holt and Company, 2002.

Palmer, Robert L. *Helping People With Eating Disorders: A Clinical Guide to Assessment and Treatment*. New York: John Wiley and Sons, 2000.

Woolsey, Monika M. *Eating Disorders: A Clinical Guide to Counseling and Treatment*. Chicago: American Dietetic Association, 2002.

PERIODICALS

Grewal P., and B. Fitzgerald. "Pica with Learning Disability." *Journal of the Royal Society of Medicine* 95, no. 1 (January 2002): 39–40.

Hamilton S., et al. "Neonatal Lead Poisoning From Maternal Pica Behavior During Pregnancy." *Journal of the National Medical Association* 93, no. 9 (September 2001): 317–319.

Roberts-Harewood M., and S.C. Davies. "Pica in Sickle Cell Disease: 'She Ate the Headboard.'" *Archives of Diseases of Children* 85, no. 6 (2001): 510.

WEBSITES

Eating-Disorder.org. "Pica Eating Disorders." http://www.eating-disorder.org/pica-eating-disorders.html (accessed October 23, 2011).

PubMed Health. "Pica." U.S. National Library of Medicine, National Institutes of Health. February 28, 2010. http://www.ncbi.nlm.nih.gov/pubmedhealth/PMH0002505 (accessed October 23, 2011).

ORGANIZATIONS

American Academy of Family Physicians, 11400 Tomahawk Creek Parkway, Leawood, KS, 66211-2672, (913) 906-6000, (800) 274-2237, Fax: (913) 906-6075, contactcenter@aafp.org, http://www.aafp.org.

American Academy of Pediatrics, 141 Northwest Point Blvd., Elk Grove Village, IL, 60007-1098, (847) 434-4000, Fax: (847) 434-8000, http://www.aap.org.

American College of Physicians, 190 N Independence Mall W, Philadelphia, PA, 19106-1572, (215) 351-2400, (800) 523-1546, http://www.acponline.org.

American Medical Association, 515 N State Street, Chicago, IL, 60610, (312) 464-5000, (800) 621-8335, http://www.ama-assn.org.

L. Fleming Fallon, Jr., M.D., Dr.P.H.

Pick's disease

Definition

Frontotemporal **dementia** (FTD), originally known as Pick's disease, is a rare form of dementia that is associated with shrinking of the frontal and temporal anterior lobes of the **brain**. The name and classification of FTD has been a topic of discussion for over a century. The current designation of the syndrome groups together Pick's disease, primary progressive aphasia, and semantic dementia as FTD. As it is defined today, the symptoms of FTD fall into two clinical patterns that involve either (1) changes in behavior, or (2) problems with language. The first type features behavior that can be either impulsive (disinhibited) or bored and listless (apathetic) and includes inappropriate social behavior; lack of social tact; lack of empathy; distractibility; loss of insight into the behaviors of oneself and others; an increased interest in sex; changes in food preferences; agitation or, conversely, blunted emotions; neglect of personal hygiene; repetitive or compulsive behavior; and decreased energy and motivation. The second type primarily features symptoms of language disturbance, including difficulty making or understanding speech, often in conjunction with the behavioral type's symptoms. Spatial skills and memory remain intact. Although the exact etiology of Pick's diseases is not known, there is a strong genetic component to the disease; FTD often runs in families.

Demographics

Pick's disease is rare, affecting less than 1% of the U.S. population. It accounts for about 2%–5% of all cases of dementia. Although it sometimes appears in younger or older people, it typically begins in middle age, between the ages of 50 and 60 years. The average age of onset is 54 years and it tends to occur more often in women than in men.

Description

Pick's disease was first described by Arnold Pick, a Czechoslovakian physician who was trained in clinical neurology, psychiatry, and neuropathology. In 1892, Pick reported on a 71-year-old man with progressive loss of language and mental deterioration. After the man died, autopsy revealed asymmetrical atrophy of the frontal cortex of the brain. In 1911, Alois Alzheimer confirmed the pattern of atrophy found in brains of patients with Pick's disease. The term Pick's disease was coined by A. Gans in 1922.

The cortical atrophy seen in Pick's disease is different from **Alzheimer's disease**, although there are major overlaps with Alzheimer's presenile dementia. In Pick's disease, shrinkage is greatest in the frontal and temporal lobes. One of the characteristics of Pick's disease is microtubule-associated tau proteins, which are the main cytoskeletal components modified during the neurodegenerative changes associated with this disease. In Alzheimer's disease, any area of the brain may be affected. Abnormalities called Pick bodies and Pick cells (abnormally swollen nerve cells) are also found in the brains of individuals with Pick's disease. Pick bodies are found inside nerve cells and contain the abnormal form of tau protein that is associated with Pick's disease.

Researchers continue to debate how to classify Pick's disease. Today, few researchers use the term Pick's disease, although it is still used by patients, caregivers, and some health practitioners. Currently, Pick's disease is considered to be part of a syndrome that includes not only Pick's disease but also primary progressive aphasia and semantic dementia, which are two related disorders. The syndrome is known as FTD. Some researchers have suggested that some cases of frontotemporal dementia in which Pick bodies or Pick cells are absent may also represent a form of Pick's disease.

Causes and symptoms

The symptoms of Pick's disease vary among individuals, but changes in behavior, emotions, and language are frequently associated with neurological problems related to movement and memory. Behavioral changes include disinhibition, inappropriate behavior, compulsions such as a tendency to overeat or eat a particular kind of food, repetitive behavior, social withdrawal, inability to keep a job, difficulty initiating tasks and following through, difficulty maintaining personal hygiene, and a short attention span. Emotional changes include mood swings, inappropriate mood, lack of concern for the feelings of others, **apathy**, and indifference to behavioral changes. Language changes include decreased ability to read, write, speak, and understand language. Speech difficulties may range from difficulty finding words and diminished vocabulary to a complete inability to speak. Patients also sometimes display echolalia, or a tendency to repeat the words of others. Patients may also experience difficulty with movement and coordination, muscle weakness or rigidity, and progressively worsening memory loss. Urinary incontinence may also occur.

In the early stages of Pick's disease, patients frequently demonstrate personality changes that are manifested as inappropriate behavior. This is in contrast to Alzheimer's disease, which, in its early stages, is characterized mainly by memory loss. As Pick's disease progresses, patients become aphonic and apathetic. They eventually lapse into a vegetative state and become completely disabled. Death occurs because of malnutrition, infections, or general failure of body systems.

Diagnosis

Diagnosing Pick's disease is difficult, because symptoms overlap with those of other disorders, such as Alzheimer's disease and other dementias that affect the frontal lobes of the brain. According to the National Institutes of Health, at the present time, a definitive **diagnosis** can only be made with a brain biopsy, an invasive procedure in which a small sample of brain tissue is surgically removed for examination. Other diagnostic methods are more commonly used, which allow a diagnosis to be made by ruling out other causes of dementia.

Diagnostic procedures include a detailed clinical evaluation to assess personal and family health history, other medical conditions, overall health status, use of prescription or nonprescription drugs, current symptoms, and changes in daily functioning. Blood tests may be done to detect problems in organ function, hormone levels, and vitamin deficiencies. Neurologic exams may be performed to determine which areas of the brain are affected, and can include **electroencephalography** (EEG), computerized tomography (CT) scans, and **magnetic resonance imaging** (MRI) scans. A psychiatric evaluation may be carried out to determine whether the patient suffers from disorders such as **depression**, which can mimic or worsen the symptoms of Pick's disease.

Treatment

There is no cure for Pick's disease, and currently, there are no known medications that slow the progression of the disease. Medications that are used to treat Alzheimer's disease should not be used to treat Pick's disease, because they may increase aggression in patients.

Treatments for Pick's disease are designed to manage its symptoms. **Behavior modification** strategies, which involve rewarding appropriate behavior, may help to decrease unacceptable or dangerous behaviors. Speech therapy may be helpful for increasing language use. Occupational therapy may be used to help patients improve performance of daily living tasks. Encouraging new hobbies may help to relieve boredom in patients and decrease behavior problems.

Disorders that exacerbate confusion, such as heart failure, hypoxia, thyroid disorders, anemia, nutritional deficiencies, infections, and depression, should be treated. Medications that increase confusion, such as anticholinergics, analgesics, cimetidine, central nervous system depressants, and lidocaine, should be stopped if they are not clearly needed. In some cases, medications may be prescribed to treat aggression, agitation, or dangerous behavior.

In the early stages of Pick's disease, legal advice may help families make ethical decisions about caring for a patient.

As the disease progresses, patients may require constant monitoring and care, either at home or in an institutionalized setting. Help from visiting nurses and aides, volunteer workers, and adult protective services may be needed. Families may benefit from counseling, to help them deal with the difficulties of caring for patients. **Support groups** can also be a helpful resource for families.

Prognosis

The prognosis for Pick's disease is poor. It is a rapidly progressing disease. Death commonly occurs between 2 to 10 years after the onset of the disease.

KEY TERMS

Analgesics—Drugs that reduce pain.

Anticholinergics—Drugs that block the action of acetylcholine, a naturally occurring chemical that is involved in communication between nerve cells.

Atrophy—Shrinkage or deterioration.

Cimetidine—A drug that decreases the amount of acid in the stomach. It is used to treat conditions such as ulcers, gastroesophageal reflux disease, and heartburn.

Computerized tomography (CT) scan—An imaging technique in which x rays are taken of the brain from several different angles and combined through a computer to provide an image of the brain.

Electroencephalography (EEG)—A recording of the electric potentials of the brain from electrodes attached to the scalp.

Frontal lobe—A part of the brain that is involved in processes such as muscle movement, speech production, working memory, planning, reasoning, and judgment.

Hypoxia—Oxygen deficiency.

Lidocaine—A local anesthetic.

Magnetic resonance imaging (MRI) scan—An imaging technique in which magnetic fields, radio waves, and computer enhancement are used to create an image of brain structure.

Primary progressive aphasia—A disorder in which there is progressive loss of language skills.

Semantic dementia—A disorder in which there is progressive loss of knowledge about words and word meanings.

Temporal lobe—A part of the brain that is involved in processing auditory and visual information, emotion and motivation, and understanding language.

Prevention

There are currently no known ways of preventing Pick's disease.

Resources

BOOKS

American Psychiatric Association. *Diagnostic and Statistical Manual of Mental Disorders.* 4th ed., text rev. Washington, DC: American Psychiatric Publishing, 2000.

Brookshire, Robert H. *Introduction to Neurogenic Communication Disorders.* 6th ed. St. Louis, MO: Mosby, 2007.

PERIODICALS

Amano, Nanji. "Editorial: Neuropsychiatric Symptoms and Depression in Neurodegenerative Diseases." *Psychogeriatrics* 4, no. 1 (2004): 1–3.

Hardin, Sonya, and Brenda Schooley. "A Story of Pick's Disease: A Rare Form of Dementia." *Journal of Neuroscience Nursing* 34, no. 3 (June 1, 2002): 117–23.

Odawara, T., et al. "Short Report: Alterations of Muscarinic Acetylcholine Receptors in Atypical Pick's Disease without Pick Bodies." *Journal of Neurology, Neurosurgery and Psychiatry* 74, no. 7 (2003): 965–67.

Pearce, J. M. S. "Historical Note: Pick's Disease." *Journal of Neurology, Neurosurgery and Psychiatry* 74, no. 2 (2003): 169.

WEBSITES

MedlinePlus. "Cimetidine." U.S. National Library of Medicine, National Institutes of Health. September 22, 2011. http://www.nlm.nih.gov/medlineplus/druginfo/meds/a682256.html (accessed October 23, 2011).

MedlinePlus. "Pick's Disease." U.S. National Library of Medicine, National Institutes of Health. October 19, 2011. http://www.nlm.nih.gov/medlineplus/print/ency/article/000744.htm (accessed October 23, 2011).

U.S. National Institute of Neurological Disorders and Stroke. "NINDS Frontotemporal Dementia Information Page." January 21, 2011. http://www.ninds.nih.gov/disorders/picks/picks.htm (accessed October 23, 2011).

ORGANIZATIONS

Association for Frontotemporal Degeneration, Radnor Station Building 2, Ste. 320, 290 King of Prussia Rd., Radnor, PA, 19103, (267) 514-7221, (866) 507-7222, http://www.theaftd.org.

National Aphasia Association, 350 Seventh Ave., Ste. 902, New York, NY, 10001, (800) 922-4622, naa@aphasia.org, http://aphasia.org.

National Institute of Neurological Disorders and Stroke (NINDS), PO Box 5801, Bethesda, MD, 20824, (800) 352-9424; or (301) 496-5751; TTY (301) 468-5981, http://www.ninds.nih.gov.

Pick's Disease Support Group, info@pdsg.org.uk, http://www.pdsg.org.uk.

Ruvanee Pietersz Vilhauer, PhD

Pimozide

Definition

Pimozide is an atypical antipsychotic drug used to treat serious motor and verbal tics associated with **Tourette syndrome**. It is sold under the brand name Orap.

KEY TERMS

Dopamine—A chemical in brain tissue that serves to transmit nerve impulses (neurotransmitter) and helps to regulate movement and emotions. Large amounts of dopamine are released following ingestion of amphetamines.

Extrapyramidal symptoms—A group of side effects associated with antipsychotic medications and characterized by involuntary muscle movements, including contraction and tremor.

Schizophrenia—A major mental illness marked by psychotic symptoms, including hallucinations, delusions, and severe disruptions in thinking.

Seizure—A convulsion or uncontrolled discharge of nerve cells that may spread to other cells throughout the brain.

Tourette syndrome—An abnormal condition that causes uncontrollable facial grimaces and tics and arm and shoulder movements. Tourette syndrome is perhaps best known for uncontrollable vocal tics that include grunts, shouts, and use of obscene language (coprolalia).

Purpose

Pimozide is classified as an atypical antipsychotic drug. It is structurally similar to **haloperidol**, which was the first drug to be used in treating Tourette syndrome. Pimozide is most often used to treat symptoms of Tourette syndrome, although it has also been used for treating **schizophrenia**, mania, and other behavioral disorders.

Description

Excess **dopamine** activity in the **brain** is associated with the verbal and physical tics observed in Tourette syndrome. Like haloperidol, pimozide is believed to inhibit the actions of dopamine, a chemical in the brain.

Pimozide is broken down by the liver and eliminated from the body by the kidneys. Because pimozide is associated with health risks, it should not be used for tics that are simply annoying or cosmetic. Pimozide should be used only in patients with severe symptoms after other drug therapy has been tried and failed.

Pimozide is available in 1 mg and 2 mg tablets.

Recommended dosage

The common starting dose of pimozide in adults is 1–2 mg per day. The dose may be increased every other day until 0.2 mg per 2.2 pounds (1 kg) of body weight per day or 10 mg per day is reached, whichever is less. Doses that exceed 0.2 mg per kg per day or 10 mg daily are not recommended.

In children, the usual initial dose is 0.05 mg per 2.2 pounds (1 kg) daily and increased every 3 days to a maximum dose of 0.2 mg per kg (or 10 mg) per day.

Periodically the dosage of pimozide should be reduced to determine if tics are still present. Patients should be maintained on the lowest dose that is effective in treating this disorder.

Precautions

Pimozide is associated with an increased risk of death when used in elderly patients with **dementia**. In June 2008, the U.S. Food and Drug Administration (FDA) announced a requirement for manufacturers of pimozide (and other antipsychotic drugs) to add a warning label to their packaging stating this risk. The reason for the increase was unclear in studies, but most deaths were found to be related to either cardiovascular complications or complications associated with infection. Pimozide is not approved by the FDA for the treatment of behavior problems in older adults with dementia, and patients in this category (or caregivers of patients in this category) should discuss the risks of taking pimozide with their physician.

Pimozide may alter the rhythm of the heart, resulting in potentially fatal heart arrhythmias. As a result, it should be used with caution in people with heart disease, and these patients should be observed carefully while receiving the drug.

Women should not take pimozide while pregnant or breastfeeding. Babies born to mothers who took pimozide during pregnancy may develop extrapyramidal symptoms (EPS) and withdrawal symptoms, including agitation, trouble breathing, and difficulty feeding.

Pimozide may cause extreme drowsiness and should be used carefully by people who need to be mentally alert.

Pimozide should not be used by people with mild tics, by individuals taking stimulants such as **methylphenidate** (Ritalin), **pemoline** (Cylert), or **dextroamphetamine** (Dexedrine) since these drugs may cause tics. It should be used under close physician supervision by people who have a history of seizure disorders, as it may increase the risk and frequency of **seizures**.

Side effects

The most common side effects associated with pimozide are sleepiness, headache, stomach upset, muscle

QUESTIONS TO ASK YOUR DOCTOR

- What kind of changes can I expect to see or feel with this medication?
- Does it matter what time of day I take this medication? If so, what is the recommendation?
- Should I take this medication with or without food?
- What are the side effects associated with this medication?
- Will this medication interact or interfere with other medications I am currently taking?
- What symptoms or adverse effects are important enough that I should seek immediate treatment?

tightness, muscle weakness, difficulty moving, tremor, abnormal behavior, visual disturbances, and impotence.

Other side effects that might also occur with pimozide are rapid heart rates or irregular heart rhythms, low blood pressure, constipation, dry mouth and eyes, rash, breast pain, breast milk production, loss of bladder control, or low blood cell counts.

Pimozide use cause symptoms that resemble Parkinson's disease. These symptoms may include a tight or mask-like expression on the face, drooling, tremors, pill-rolling motions in the hands, cogwheel rigidity (abnormal rigidity in muscles characterized by jerky movements when the muscle is passively stretched), and a shuffling gait. Taking anti-Parkinson drugs **benztropine** mesylate or **trihexyphenidyl** hydrochloride along with the pimozide usually controls these symptoms.

Pimozide has the potential to produce a serious side effect called **tardive dyskinesia**. This syndrome consists of involuntary, uncoordinated movements that may appear late in therapy and not disappear even after the drug is stopped. Tardive dyskinesia involves involuntary movements of the tongue, jaw, mouth or face or other groups of skeletal muscles. The incidence of tardive dyskinesia increases with increasing age and with increasing dosage of pimozide. Women are at greater risk than men for developing tardive dyskinesia. There is no known effective treatment for tardive dyskinesia, although gradual (but rarely complete) improvement may occur over a long period.

An occasionally reported side effect of pimozide is **neuroleptic malignant syndrome**, a complicated and potentially fatal condition characterized by muscle rigidity, high fever, alterations in mental status, and cardiac symptoms such as irregular pulse or blood pressure, sweating, tachycardia (fast heartbeat), and arrhythmias (irregular heartbeat). People who think they may be experiencing any side effects from pimozide or any other medication should talk to their physician promptly.

Interactions

If pimozide is used with bethanechol (Urecholine), **clonidine** (Catapress), **fluoxetine** (Prozac), indomethacin (Indocin), meperidine (Demerol), **paroxetine** (Paxil), quinidine, or **trazodone** (Desyrel), the side effects associated with pimozide may be increased.

There is an increased risk of irregular heart rhythms if pimozide is used with other antipsychotics, certain **antidepressants**, some heart drugs, and antibiotics such as erythromycin.

The beneficial effects of pimozide may be reduced if used with bromocriptine (Parlodel), **carbamazepine** (Tegretol), levodopa (Larodopa, Sinemet), lithium, or phenobarbital.

Some antibiotics, antifungals, antidepressants, and drugs used for AIDS may prevent the breakdown of pimozide by the liver and thus increase the amount of pimozide in the body. The combination of pimozide and these classes of drugs should be used cautiously if at all.

Pimozide may increase the sedative effects of other central nervous system depressants such as alcohol, sleeping pills, antihistamines, and antidepressants.

Pimozide should not be taken with grapefruit juice, as it inhibits the metabolism of the drug in the body.

Resources

BOOKS

Albers, Lawrence J., Rhoda K. Hahn, and Christopher Reist. *Handbook of Psychiatric Drugs.* Laguna Hills, CA: Current Clinical Strategies, 2010.

American Society of Health-System Pharmacists. *AHFS Drug Information 2011.* Bethesda, MD: ASHP, 2011.

Graham, George. *The Disordered Mind: An Introduction to Philosophy of Mind and Mental Illness.* New York: Routledge, 2010.

Holland, Leland Norman, and Michael Patrick Adams. *Core Concepts in Pharmacology.* 3rd ed. New York: Prentice Hall, 2011.

North, Carol, and Sean Yutzy. *Goodwin and Guze's Psychiatric Diagnosis.* New York: Oxford University Press, 2010.

Preston, John D., John H. O'Neal, and Mary C. Talaga. *Handbook of Clinical Psychopharmacology for Therapists.* 6th ed. Oakland, CA: New Harbinger, 2010.

ORGANIZATIONS

American Academy of Clinical Toxicology, 6728 Old McLean Village Dr., McLean, VA, 22101, (703) 556-9222, Fax: (703) 556-8729, admin@clintox.org, http://www.clintox.org.

American Academy of Family Physicians, 11400 Tomahawk Creek Pkwy., Leawood, KS, 66211-2672, (913) 906-6000, (800) 274-2237, Fax: (913) 906-6075, contactcenter@aafp.org, http://www.aafp.org.

American Academy of Neurology, 1080 Montreal Ave., St. Paul, MN, 55116, (651) 695-2717, (800) 879-1960, Fax: (651) 879-2791, memberservices@aan.com, http://www.aan.com.

American Neurological Association, 5841 Cedar Lake Rd., Ste. 204, Minneapolis, MN, 55416, (952) 545-6284, ana@llmsi.com, http://www.aneuroa.org.

American Psychiatric Association, 1000 Wilson Blvd., Ste. 1825, Arlington, VA, 22209-3901, (703) 907-7300, apa@psych.org, http://www.psych.org.

American Society for Clinical Pharmacology and Therapeutics, 528 N Washington St., Alexandria, VA, 22314, (703) 836-6981, info@ascpt.org, http://www.ascpt.org.

Mental Health America, 2000 N. Beauregard St., 6th Fl., Alexandria, VA, 22311, (703) 684-7722, (800) 969-6642, Fax: (703) 684-5968, http://www1.nmha.org.

National Institute of Neurological Disorders and Stroke (NINDS), PO Box 5801, Bethesda, MD, 20824, (301) 496-5751; TTY: (301) 468-5981, (800) 352-9424, http://www.ninds.nih.gov.

Kelly Karpa, RPh, PhD
Laura Jean Cataldo, RN, EdD

Play therapy

Definition

Play therapy refers to a method of **psychotherapy** with children in which a therapist uses a child's fantasies and the symbolic meanings of his or her play as a medium for understanding and communication with the child.

Purpose

The aim of play therapy is to decrease those behavioral and emotional difficulties that significantly interfere with a child's normal functioning. Inherent in this aim is improved communication and understanding between the child and his or her parents. Less obvious goals include improved verbal expression, ability for self-observation, improved impulse control, more adaptive ways of coping with anxiety and frustration, and

A boy plays in a play area designed to assess children with special needs. (© *James King-Holmes/Photo Researchers, Inc.*)

improved capacity to trust and to relate to others. In this type of treatment, the therapist uses an understanding of cognitive development and the different stages of emotional development as well as the conflicts common to these stages when treating the child.

The use of play therapy relies on the fact that children will process the world in a way that is different from the adult approach. Some researchers describe two stages of function for children at the elementary school level: the "preoperational stage" (ages 2 to 7 years) and the "concrete operations stage" (ages 8 to 11 years). In the preoperational stage, children are still learning how to use language, which employs symbols (words) to mentally represent the things in their world. They tend to have rigid thinking processes, limited only to what is before them, without digging more deeply. Because this results in a lack of true understanding of the world around them, they will provide their own explanations, employing "magical thinking." The child's play, as a result, will increasingly employ imagination and fantasy as he or she ages. Adults who can understand how the play and fantasy translate from a child to an adult world can interpret the child's language.

Play therapy thus relies on the fact that the language of children, especially very young children, is play. Play also serves several other roles for children that can be used in the process of play therapy, including providing a sense of control and a way to develop coping skills. A skilled play therapist will be able to make the most of these factors in using play therapy as a way to translate the child's communications.

Play therapy is used to treat problems that are interfering with the child's normal development. Such difficulties are extreme in degree and have been occurring for many months without resolution. Reasons for treatment include, but are not limited to, temper tantrums, aggressive behavior, nonmedical problems with bowel or bladder control, difficulties with sleeping or having nightmares, and experiencing worries or fears. This type of treatment is also used with children who have experienced sexual or physical **abuse**, **neglect**, the loss of a family member, medical illness, physical injury, or any experience that is traumatic.

At times, children in play therapy will also receive other types of treatment. For instance, youngsters who are unable to control their attention, impulses, tendency to react with violence, or who experience severe anxiety may take medication for these symptoms while participating in play therapy. The play therapy addresses the child's psychological symptoms. Other situations of dual treatment include children with **learning disorders**. These youngsters may receive play therapy to alleviate feelings of low self-esteem, excessive worry, helplessness, and incompetence that are related to their learning problems and academic struggles. In addition, they should receive a special type of tutoring called **cognitive remediation**, which addresses the specific learning issues.

Description

In play therapy, the clinician may meet with the child alone for sessions or with a parent present, and may arrange times to meet with parents separately, depending on the situation. In some forms of play therapy, the therapist may observe the child at play with the parent. The structure of the sessions is maintained in a consistent manner to provide a feeling of safety and stability for the child and parents. Sessions are scheduled for the same day and time each week and occur for the same duration. The frequency of sessions is typically one or two times per week, and meetings with parents occur about two times per month, with some variation. The session length will vary depending on the environment. For example, in private settings, sessions usually last 45 to 50 minutes while in hospitals and mental health clinics the duration is typically 30 minutes. The number of sessions and duration of treatment varies according to the treatment objectives.

MELANIE KLEIN (1882–1960)

The Austrian psychotherapist and child psychologist Melanie Klein developed methods of play technique and play therapy in analyzing and treating child patients. Raised in a Jewish middle-class family, she lacked both the academic background and the medical training usually found in those who choose psychoanalysis for a profession. She was a married woman with children when she began undergoing analysis about 1912. During her analysis she began to observe the behavior of a disturbed child relative and to interpret this behavior in the light of her own psychoanalytic experience. Her analyst, recognizing his patient's aptitude, encouraged her in her efforts at child therapy, a hitherto neglected area.

Originally trained as a Freudian psychoanalyst, Klein made observations and conclusions regarding child behavior that led her to views differing from those held by orthodox Freudian psychoanalysts. She was one of the first to engage in child analysis, beginning in 1920. She evolved a system of play therapy to supplement the usual psychoanalytic procedure, perhaps because the age of her clients indicated more appropriate methods than the exclusively verbal free-association technique then used with adult patients. Gradually she evolved a technique more suitable for probing the deep-layered recesses of the child's mind. By providing the child with small toys representing father, mother, or siblings, she was able to elicit the child's subconscious feelings. Her technique also used the child's free play and spontaneous communications.

Her first paper, "The Development of a Child," was presented to the Budapest Congress of Psychoanalysis in 1919, the year in which she became a member of the Hungarian Psychoanalytic Society. In 1921 she went to the Berlin Psychoanalytic Institute as the first child therapist. In what has been called her second period, beginning in 1934, Klein theorized her previous observations on child behavior, arriving at conceptual conclusions based on them. She then wrote of her earlier findings, on the "depressive position" and the "schizoid-paranoid position," indicating possible ways in which these infancy states relate to psychotic processes in adults.

During the initial meeting with parents, the therapist will want to learn as much as possible about the nature of the child's problems. Parents will be asked for information about the child's developmental, medical, social, and school history, whether or not previous evaluations and interventions were attempted, and the nature of the results. Background information about the parents is also important since it provides the therapist with a larger context from which to understand the child. This process of gathering information may take one to three sessions, depending on the style of the therapist. Some clinicians gather the important aspects of the child's history during the first meeting with parents and will continue to ask relevant questions during subsequent meetings. The clinician also learns important information during the initial sessions with the child.

Sessions with parents are important opportunities to keep the therapist informed about the child's current functioning at home and at school and for the therapist to offer some insight and guidance to parents. At times, the clinician will provide suggestions about parenting techniques and about alternative ways to communicate with their child, and will also serve as a resource for information about child development. Details of child sessions are not routinely discussed with parents. If the child's privacy is maintained, it promotes free expression in the therapist's office and engenders a sense of trust in the therapist. Therapists will, instead, communicate to the parents their understanding of the child's psychological needs or conflicts.

For the purposes of explanation, treatment can be described as occurring in a series of initial, middle, and final stages. The initial phase includes evaluation of the problem and teaching both child and parents about the process of therapy. The middle phase is the period in which the child has become familiar with the treatment process and comfortable with the therapist. The therapist is continuing to evaluate and learn about the child, but has a clearer sense of the youngster's issues and has developed, with the child, a means for the two to communicate. The final phase includes the process of ending treatment and saying goodbye to the therapist.

During the early sessions, the therapist may talk with the child about the reason the youngster was brought in for treatment and explain that the therapist helps make children's problems go away. Youngsters often deny experiencing any problems. It is not necessary for them to acknowledge having any since they may be unable to do so due to normal cognitive and emotional factors or because they are simply not experiencing any problems. The child may be informed about the nature of the sessions, specifically that he or she can say or play or do anything desired while in the office as long as no one gets hurt; what is said and done in the office will be kept private unless the child is in danger of harming himself.

Children communicate their thoughts and feelings through play more naturally than they do through verbal communication. As the child plays, the therapist begins to recognize themes and patterns or ways of using the materials that are important to the child. Over time, the clinician helps the child begin to make meaning out of the play. This is important because the play reflects issues which are important to the child and typically relevant to their difficulties.

When the child's symptoms have subsided for a stable period of time and when functioning is adequate with peers and adults at home, in school, and in extracurricular activities, the focus of treatment will shift away from problems and onto the process of saying goodbye. This last stage is known as the termination phase of treatment and it is reflective of the ongoing change and loss that human beings experience throughout their lives. Since this type of therapy relies heavily on the therapist's relationship with the child and also with parents, ending therapy will signify a change and a loss for all involved, but for the child in particular. In keeping with the therapeutic process of communicating thoughts and feelings, this stage is an opportunity for the child to work through how he or she feels about ending therapy and about leaving the therapist. In addition to allowing for a sense of closure, it also makes it less likely that the youngster will misconstrue the ending of treatment as a rejection by the therapist, which would taint the larger experience of therapy for the child. Parents also need a sense of closure and are usually encouraged to process the treatment experience with the therapist. The therapist also appreciates the opportunity to say goodbye to the parents and child after having become involved in their lives in this important way, and it is often beneficial for parents and children to hear the clinician's thoughts and feelings with regards to ending treatment.

Precautions

Play therapy addresses psychological issues and is not used to alleviate medical or biological problems. Children who are experiencing physical problems should see a physician for a medical evaluation to clarify the nature of the problem and, if necessary, receive the appropriate medical treatment. Likewise, children who experience academic difficulties need to receive a neuropsychological or in-depth psychological evaluation in order to clarify the presence of a biologically based learning disability. In both of these cases, psychological problems may be present in addition to medical ailments and learning disabilities. It is necessary to evaluate and treat both physical and psychological issues. Alternatively, evaluations may show that medical or biological causes are not evident, and this is important information for the parents and therapist.

Preparation

It is recommended that parents explain to the child that they will be going to see a therapist and discuss, if possible, the particular problem and that the therapist is going to teach both parents and child how to make things better. As described earlier, the child may deny even obvious problems, but mainly just needs to agree to meet the therapist and to see what therapy is like.

Aftercare

Children sometimes return to therapy for additional sessions when they experience a setback that cannot be easily resolved.

Results

Normal results include the significant reduction or disappearance of the main problems for which the child was initially seen. The child should also be functioning adequately at home, in school, and with peers, and should be able to participate in and enjoy extracurricular activities.

Sometimes play therapy does not alleviate the child's symptoms. This situation can occur if the child is extremely resistant and refuses to participate in treatment or if the child's ways of coping are so rigidly held that it is not possible for them to learn more adaptive ones.

Resources

BOOKS

Chethik, Morton. *Techniques of Child Therapy*. 2nd ed. New York: The Guilford Press, 2003.

Lovinger, Sophie L. *Child Psychotherapy: From Initial Therapeutic Contact to Termination*. New Jersey: Jason Aronson, 1998.

Webb, Nancy Boyd, ed. *Play Therapy with Children in Crisis*. 3rd ed. New York: The Guilford Press, 2007.

PERIODICALS

Naylor, Angie. "When A Child Plays." *Counselling and Psychotherapy Journal* 16, no. 5 (June 2005): 29–31.

Ray, Dee C., et al. "Play Therapy Practices Among Elementary School Counselors." *Professional School Counseling* 8 (April 2005): 360–65.

ORGANIZATIONS

American Psychological Association, 750 1st Street NE, Washington, DC, 20002-4242, (202) 336-5500; TDD/TTY: (202) 336-6123, (800) 374-2721, http://www.apa.org.

Association for Play Therapy, Inc, 3198 Willow Ave., Ste. 110, Clovis, CA, 93703, (599) 294-2128, Fax: (559) 294-2129, info@a4pt.org, http://www.a4pt.org.

Susan Fine, Psy.D.
Emily Jane Willingham, PhD

PMDD *see* **Premenstrual dysphoric disorder**

PMS *see* **Premenstrual syndrome**

Polysomnography

Definition

Polysomnography is a set of tests performed while a patient sleeps. It is used to diagnose and evaluate **sleep disorders**, and examines at a minimum **brain** wave patterns, the movements of both eyes, and the tone of at least one skeletal muscle.

Purpose

Polysomnography is used to diagnose and evaluate many types of sleep disorders, including disorders of initiating or maintaining sleep (dyssomnias) and disorders

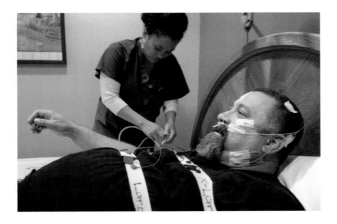

A man prepares to undergo polysomnography at a sleep disorders clinic. (© *Florence Low/MCT/newscom*)

during sleep (parasomnias), including medical, psychiatric, and dental disorders that have symptoms during sleep. A relatively common dyssomnia is sleep apnea, a disorder most prevalent in middle-aged and elderly obese men, in which the muscles of the soft palate in the back of the throat relax and close off the airway during sleep. Sleep apnea may cause the patient to snore loudly and gasp for air at night, and to be excessively sleepy and doze off during the day.

Another dyssomnia often evaluated by polysomnography is **narcolepsy**. Narcoleptics suffer from excessive daytime sleepiness, sudden attacks of muscle weakness (cataplexy), and hallucinations at sleep onset. Some parasomnias that can be detected using polysomnography include disorders of arousal or rapid-eye-movement (REM) sleep problems, such as nightmares. Medical conditions including sleep-related asthma, **depression**, and **panic disorder** can be evaluated. Teeth-grinding (bruxism) or neurological problems such as restless leg syndrome show up during polysomnography. Finally, the tests can also be used to detect or evaluate **seizures** of sleep-related epilepsy that occur in the middle of the night, when the patient and his or her family are unlikely to be aware of them.

Description

Polysomnography is performed during an overnight stay in a sleep laboratory. While the patient sleeps, a wide variety of tests can be performed.

One form of monitoring is **electroencephalography** (EEG), in which electrodes are attached to the patient's scalp in order to record his or her brain wave activity. The electroencephalograph records brain wave activity from different parts of the brain and charts them on a graph. The EEG not only helps doctors establish what stage of sleep the patient is in, but may also detect seizures. Standard tests have at least one central electrode attached to the scalp and one reference electrode attached to the ear. Other electrodes can be added in order to pinpoint the area of the brain where abnormal activity is occurring.

Another form of monitoring is continuous electrooculography (EOG), which records eye movement and is useful in determining when the patient is going through a stage of REM sleep. Both EEG and EOG can be helpful in determining sleep latency (the time that transpires between lights out and the onset of sleep), total sleep time, the time spent in each sleep stage, and the number of arousals from sleep.

The air flow through the patient's nose and mouth is measured by heat-sensitive devices called thermistors. This measurement can help detect episodes of apnea (stopped breathing), or hypopnea (inadequate breathing). Another test, called pulse oximetry, measures the amount of oxygen in the blood and can be used to assess the degree of oxygen starvation during episodes of hypopnea or apnea.

The electrical activity of the patient's heart is also measured using electrocardiography (ECG or EKG). Electrodes are affixed to the patient's chest and pick up electrical activity from various areas of the heart. They help detect cardiac arrhythmias (abnormal heart rhythms), which may occur during periods of sleep apnea. Blood pressure is also measured as episodes of sleep apnea sometimes dangerously elevate blood pressure.

A final standard measurement is the tone of at least one skeletal muscle, often a muscle of the chin (mentalis or submentalis). This is done using electromyography (EMG), which involves placing an electrode on the muscle to record its contractions. If normal, measurements will indicate the general atonia present during REM sleep. Other EMG channels can be placed, particularly on the leg (anterior tibialis), to indicate movement during sleep.

Depending on the suspected disorder, polysomnography can also include sound monitoring to record snoring; video monitoring to document body positions; core body temperature readings; incident light intensities; penile swelling (tumescence); and pressure and pH at various levels of the esophagus.

One test that is often performed in conjunction with polysomnography is a Multiple Sleep Latency Test (MSLT). This test is also performed in a sleep laboratory and involves the recording of the sleep of several naps during the day after the overnight test. The MSLT is particularly important for a complete **diagnosis** of narcolepsy.

Preparation

Patient preparation is necessary to ensure that the night or nights in the sleep laboratory are as close as possible to an unmediated night in the patient's own home. Patients should bring suitable sleepwear and make sure their hair is clean and free from gels or sprays that may interfere with electrode functioning. They should be advised to maintain usual awake-sleep cycles and avoid sleeping pills, alcohol, stimulants, and strenuous **exercise** before the test.

Aftercare

Once the test is over, the monitors are detached from the patient. No special measures need to be taken after polysomnography.

Precautions

The greatest limitation to polysomnography are the differences between the recording conditions and those that are present in the patient's home. The differences between the sleep laboratory and home have the highest effect on the first night of testing. Detection and elimination of this "first night effect" can be accomplished by the rather costly step of recording for multiple nights. Multiple night recordings are also sometimes necessary to obtain information about problems that only appear sporadically.

Results

Standard analysis involves the manual review and scoring of either paper tracings or recordings projected on a computer monitor. Automatic, computer-based systems are becoming more and more common in clinical and research settings.

Overnight parameters such as the times of lights on/ off, total time in bed, and total sleep time are factored into the results. The overnight recording is divided into time periods of approximately 30 seconds. The standard EEG, EMG, and EOG recordings are evaluated, and the predominant stage of sleep, according to the manual of Rechtschaffen and Kales, is assigned to the entire time period.

This data is used to calculate total time and relative proportion of the night spent in each of the six stages of sleep, including REM and non-REM. Latencies to REM and slow-wave sleep (SWS) are also recorded.

Special note is made of such neurophysiologic events as epileptic episodes, intrusion of alpha-type brain waves into sleep, or periodic activity of the tibialis anterior. Respiratory activities, including apneic or hypopneic episodes and oxygen saturation, are correlated with sleep stages. Other parameters measured, such as body position, gastroesophageal reflux, bruxism, and penile tumescence, are recorded.

If a sleep apnea syndrome is diagnosed, primarily through a showing of periodic breathing stoppage and effects on the pulse and heart, a trial of continuous positive airway pressure or a trial of an oral appliance may be undertaken, either in a partial-night or second-night polysomnography recording.

Healthcare team roles

Polysomnography is often performed by a specially trained technician called a polysomnographic technologist. Training programs for this position can involve

KEY TERMS

Apnea—A brief suspension or interruption of breathing.

Arrhythmia—Any disturbance in the normal rhythm of the heartbeat.

Bruxism—Habitual, often unconscious, grinding of the teeth.

Hypopnea—Breathing that is too shallow to maintain adequate levels of oxygen in the blood.

Narcolepsy—A disorder characterized by frequent and uncontrollable attacks of deep sleep.

Oximetry—The measurement of blood oxygen levels.

Parameter—A characteristic or factor that is measured during a test of a complex process or activity like sleep.

Parasomnia—A type of sleep disorder characterized by abnormal changes in behavior or body functions during sleep, specific stages of sleep, or the transition between sleeping and waking.

Thermistor—An electrical device whose resistance decreases with rises in temperature.

one- to two-year programs in training as an electrodiagnostic technologist, with additional time for the polysomnography courses. Some typical courses in this area include:

- fundamentals of polysomnography
- sleep disorders
- infant and pediatric polysomnography
- polysomnography instrumentation
- polysomnography recording and monitoring
- polysomnography record scoring

Registration in polysomnography is available from the Board of Registered Polysomnography Technologists. The certification requires passing a written test.

Resources

BOOKS

Misulis, Karl E. "Polysomnography Basics." In *Essentials of Clinical Neurophysiology,* by Karl E. Misulis and T.C. Head. 3rd ed. London: Butterworth-Heinemann, 2002.

PERIODICALS

Grandjean, Cynthia, and Susanne Gibbons. "Assessing Ambulatory Geriatric Sleep Complaints." *The Nurse Practitioner* 25, no. 9 (September 2000): 25, 29–32, 35.

WEBSITES

Armon, Carmel, K.G. Johnson, and Asim Roy. "Polysomnography." Medscape Reference. November 23, 2009. http://www.emedicine.com/neuro/topic566.htm (accessed October 23, 2011).

ORGANIZATIONS

American Association of Sleep Technologists, 2510 North Frontage Rd., Darien, IL, 60561, (630) 737-9704, Fax: (630) 737-9788, AAST@aastweb.org, http://www.aastweb.org.

National Sleep Foundation, 1010 N Glebe Rd., Ste. 310, Arlington, VA, 22201, (703) 243-1697, nsf@sleep foundation.org, http://www.sleepfoundation.org.

Michelle L. Johnson, M.S., J.D.

Polysubstance dependence

Definition

Polysubstance dependence refers to a type of substance dependence disorder in which an individual uses at least three different classes of substances indiscriminately and does not have a favorite drug that qualifies for dependence on its own.

Demographics

Young adults (between the ages of 18 and 24) have the highest rates of use for all substances. Generally, males tend to be diagnosed with more substance use disorders.

Description

The *Diagnostic and Statistical Manual of Mental Disorders*, fourth edition, text revision (*DSM-IV-TR*), which presents guidelines used by the American Psychiatric Association for diagnosis of mental disorders, defines polysubstance dependence as repeated use of at least three groups of substances (not including caffeine and nicotine) with no single predominate substance. For example, an individual may use **cocaine**, **sedatives**, and **hallucinogens** indiscriminately (i.e., no single drug predominated or no "drug of choice") for a year or more. The individual may not meet criteria for cocaine dependence, sedative dependence, or hallucinogen dependence, but may meet criteria for polysubstance dependence when all three drugs are considered as a group.

Causes and symptoms

Causes

There is very little documented regarding the causes of polysubstance dependence.

Symptoms

The *DSM-IV-TR* specifies that three or more of the following symptoms must occur at any time during a 12-month period (and cause significant impairment or distress) in order to meet diagnostic criteria for substance dependence:

- Tolerance: The individual either has to use increasingly higher amounts of the drugs over time in order to achieve the same drug effect or finds that the same amount of the drug has much less of an effect over time than before. After using several different drugs regularly for a while, an individual may find they need to use at least 50% more of the amount they began using in order to get the same effect.
- Withdrawal: The individual either experiences withdrawal symptoms when he or she stops using the drugs or the individual uses drugs in order to avoid or relieve withdrawal symptoms.
- Loss of control: The individual either repeatedly uses more drugs than planned or uses the drugs over longer periods of time than planned. For instance, an individual may begin using drugs (any combination of three or more types of drugs) on weekdays in addition to weekends.
- Inability to stop using: The individual has either unsuccessfully attempted to cut down or stop using the drugs or has a persistent desire to stop using. An individual may find that, despite efforts to stop using drugs on weekdays, he or she is unable to do so.
- Time: The individual spends a lot of time obtaining drugs, using drugs, being under the influence of drugs, and recovering from the effects of drugs.
- Interference with activities: The individual either gives up or reduces the amount of time involved in recreational activities, social activities, and/or occupational activities because of the use of drugs. An individual may use drugs instead of engaging in hobbies, spending time with friends, or going to work.
- Harm to self: The individual continues to use drugs despite having either a physical or psychological problem that is caused by or made worse by the use of drugs.

Diagnosis

Individuals who abuse alcohol and other drugs usually meet criteria for **substance abuse** and/or dependence for each individual substance used. Multiple diagnoses are given in this situation (cocaine dependence, hallucinogen dependence, and sedative dependence, for example). Polysubstance dependence is reserved only for those situations when an individual uses multiple substances indiscriminately and meets criteria for dependence on these substances, taken as a whole.

Treatment

There is very little documented regarding the treatment of polysubstance dependence. However, several treatments have been tried. Psychological evaluation and tests may be used to assess the affected individual. The person may be admitted into a hospital or treatment center as an inpatient, and/or he or she may receive **cognitive-behavioral therapy**.

Prognosis

The course of substance dependence varies from short-lived episodes to chronic episodes lasting years. The individual with substance dependence may alternate between periods of heavy use with severe problems, periods of no use at all, and periods of use with few problems.

Prevention

The best single thing an individual can do to prevent polysubstance dependence is to avoid using drugs including alcohol altogether. On a larger scale, comprehensive prevention programs that utilize family, schools, communities, and the media (such as television) can be effective in reducing substance abuse.

Resources

BOOKS

American Psychiatric Association. *Diagnostic and Statistical Manual of Mental Disorders*. 4th ed., text rev. Washington, DC: American Psychiatric Publishing, 2000.

Kaplan, Harold, and Benjamin Sadock, eds. *Synopsis of Psychiatry*. 10th ed. Baltimore: Lippincott Williams & Wilkins, 2007.

Jennifer Hahn, Ph.D.

Positive symptoms

Definition

Positive symptoms are thoughts, behaviors, or sensory perceptions present in a person with a mental disorder, but not present in people in the normal population.

Description

Examples of positive symptoms are hallucinations (seeing, hearing, or smelling things not really there), **delusions** (belief in ideas not based on reality), disorganized speech (loose association between ideas, derailment of sentences, incoherence, illogical statements, excessive detail, and rhyming of words), or bizarre behavior. In other disorders, positive symptoms are primarily associated with **schizophrenia** or **psychosis**.

Sandra L. Friedrich, M.A.

Positron emission tomography (PET)

Definition

Positron emission tomography (PET) is a noninvasive scanning/imaging technique that utilizes small amounts of radioactive positrons (positively charged particles; also called "antielectrons") to visualize body function and metabolism. The PET scan uses a special camera and tracer (such as glucose with an added radioactive chemical) to take images of organs and tissues within the body. The camera records the position of the tracer, and the resulting data are then sent to a computer for analysis.

When higher levels of chemical activity occur in the body, the radioactive chemical within the tracer will accumulate in such areas. These areas show up as brighter spots on a PET scan and are useful for evaluating problems within the body. The resulting image is used to evaluate for body disorders such as cancer, neurological

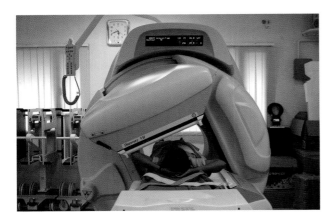

A patient prepares to undergo a positron emission tomography (PET) scan. (© *Dinodia Photos/Alamy*)

problems, and heart disease, along with the flow of blood and the function of organs. PET scans are especially useful to study **brain** activity in mentally ill patients and how mental illness can change activity within the brain.

Purpose

PET is the fastest-growing nuclear medicine tool in terms of increasing acceptance and applications. It is useful in the **diagnosis**, staging, and treatment of cancer because it provides information that cannot be obtained by other techniques, such as **computed tomography** (CT) and **magnetic resonance imaging** (MRI).

PET scans are performed at medical centers equipped with a small cyclotron. Smaller cyclotrons and increasing availability of certain radiopharmaceuticals are making PET a more widely used imaging modality.

Physicians first used PET to obtain information about brain function, and to study brain activity in various neurological diseases and disorders including **stroke**, epilepsy, **Alzheimer's disease**, Parkinson's disease, and Huntington's disease; and in psychiatric disorders such as **schizophrenia**, **depression**, **obsessive-compulsive disorder** (OCD), **attention deficit hyperactivity disorder** (**ADHD**), and **Tourette syndrome**. PET is now used to evaluate patients for types of cancer, including head and neck, brain, lymphoma, melanoma, lung, colorectal, breast, prostate, and esophageal. Cancer is more likely to show up on a PET scan than on a CT or MRI scan.

Because of the clarity of a PET scan, doctors can better see how advanced a cancer is at its place or origin and whether it has spread to other parts of the body. In order to treat cancer, a PET scan is often performed along with a CT or MRI scan. PET also is used to evaluate heart muscle function in patients with coronary artery disease (CAD) or cardiomyopathy. A PET scan is able to determine whether there is poor blood flow to the heart, which is a sign of CAD. If poor blood flow is found, a PET scan also helps to determine the best treatment, for example, coronary artery bypass graft surgery.

PET scans are especially useful for brain-imaging studies. They are often used to illustrate the differences between brains of people without mental disorders and brains of people with mental disorders. For example, because PET scans can detect brain activity (such as blood flow and metabolic activity), PET scans of the brains of depressed and nondepressed persons can show researchers where brain activity is decreased in depressed patients. Similar scans have been taken of brains affected by schizophrenia or Alzheimer's disease. They are also used for people suspected of having amyotrophic lateral sclerosis (ALS), transient ischemic attack (TIA), multiple sclerosis (MS), and other nervous system disorders. Such research can help scientists discover new ways to treat these disorders. Further, once treated, PET scans can tell medical professionals how the activity within specific areas of the brain of mentally ill patients has changed. In psychiatric illness, PET scans are primarily used in research studies rather than as aids to treatment in clinical settings.

Description

While in a nuclear medicine department of a hospital or a specialized PET center, the PET involves injecting a patient with a radiopharmaceutical similar to glucose, a form of sugar. Often fludeoxyglucose (FDG), which contains a radioactive isotope (such as fluorine-18), is used as the trace material. The tracer is a liquid that is placed into the body usually through an intravenous injection into a vein on the arm (or the substance may also be inhaled or swallowed). While the patient lies very still on a table, the tracer moves through the body, collecting at specific organs or tissues. An hour after injection of this tracer, a PET scanner images a specific metabolic function by measuring the concentration and distribution of the tracer throughout the body. The scanner, which is shaped like a doughnut, moves around the patient. The complete test usually takes from one to three hours.

When it enters the body, the tracer courses through the bloodstream to the target organ, where it emits positrons. The positively charged positrons collide with negatively charged electrons, producing gamma rays (a type of electromagnetic radiation). The positrons are absorbed to a different extent by cells varying in their metabolic rate. The gamma rays are detected by photomultiplier-scintillator combinations positioned on opposite sides of the patient. These signals are processed by the computer, and images are generated.

PET scans do not show as much detail as computed tomography (CT) scans or magnetic resonance imaging (MRI) scans. However, PET scans provide an advantage over CT and MRI because they can determine whether a lesion is malignant. The two other modalities provide images of anatomical structures but often cannot provide a determination of malignancy. CT and MRI show structure, while PET shows function. PET has been used in combination with CT and MRI to identify abnormalities with more precision and indicate areas of most active metabolism. This additional information allows for more accurate evaluation of cancer treatment and management.

Precautions

Several precautionary factors may cause the PET scan to be canceled or invalidated. Three of them that might cancel the test are using alcohol, caffeine, or tobacco

KEY TERMS

Computed tomography—An imaging technique that produces images of cross-sections of the body using data acquired through x rays directed in various directions through the body and onto a screen.

Magnetic resonance imaging—An imaging technique that produces images of the body's soft tissues with the use of electromagnetic radiation and a strong magnetic field.

Photomultiplier—A device that is designed to be extremely sensitive to electromagnetic radiation, especially within the ultraviolet, visible, and near-infrared ranges of the electromagnetic spectrum.

Positron—A positively charged particle; also called an "antielectron," the antimatter counterpart of the electron.

Radioactive—Relating to radiation emitted by certain substances.

Radiopharmaceutical—A radioactive drug.

Scintillator—A material that exhibits the property of luminescence (also called "scintillation") when it is excited by ionizing radiation.

within 24 hours of the test; using **sedatives** before the test; or taking medicines such as insulin (which can change a body's metabolism). Two conditions that might invalidate the test include not lying still during the test or being too anxious or nervous during the test. In addition, a PET scan may have to be delayed if a patient recently had a biopsy taken from the body, chemotherapy, radiation therapy, or any type of surgery.

Preparation

Before having or scheduling a PET scan, inform the referring doctor about any of the following: diabetes, pregnancy, or breastfeeding. The dosage of any diabetic medicine on the day of the scan may be reduced or eliminated to accommodate the PET procedure. Do not breastfeed for at least one day before having a PET scan. Discuss this with a medical profession before having the test. In addition, tell the referring doctor about any other medicines or herbal remedies being taken. Such substances may be stopped before the PET test. Do not smoke tobacco products, drink caffeinated beverages or foods, or drink alcoholic beverages for at least 24 hours before the test. Do not eat or drink for at least six hours before the test. Discuss the PET scan with the referring doctor or the attending medical team for other such considerations.

Inform the referring doctor if a fear of enclosed spaces is a problem or of any concerns regarding anxiety or **panic attack** while undergoing the test.

During the test, a small prick or sting may be felt at the injection site. When the tracer liquid is inserted into the body, it may initially make the patient feel warm and slightly flushed. In a small number of instances, patients feel sick to their stomach or may develop a headache. Always inform the medical staff if this occurs.

Aftercare

Resume a normal schedule and level of activity after the scan is complete. Drink plenty of water or other fluids throughout the rest of the day to flush the tracer out of the body.

Risks

A consent form may be required to be signed before the test. Discuss any potential risks with the PET scan with the referring physician or other medical professional. Risk of slight damage to cells or tissue is possible, but minimal, from the low levels of radiation used for the test. Most of the radioactive tracer is flushed out of the body within six to 24 hours. The tracer may cause an allergic reaction, but such incidents are rare. The injection site of the tracer may become sore or swell. If so, the medical staff will apply a warm, moist compress and check the area from time to time for any other medical needs. Benefits usually are considered when talking with a medical professional about this test, and whether they outweigh the risks.

Results

The images produced during these scans are normally sent to the attending physician. Make an appointment with this medical professional to discuss the results of the scan. Results normally are available to the doctor within one to two days. A normal result means that blood flow is normal, and organs and tissues examined are operating as they should. With this result, the tracer has flowed through the body in a normal distribution.

An abnormal result means different things depending on the portion of the body scanned. If the heart has been scanned, then a decreased flow of blood into or out of the heart and increased glucose metabolism may indicate that blood vessels are blocked. One possible diagnosis could be the presence of coronary artery disease; however, a medical professional is best to make that determination. If the brain was scanned, and a decreased flow of blood and oxygen and an increased glucose metabolism were found, then epilepsy is one of several possible diagnoses. If only a decreased flow of

QUESTIONS TO ASK YOUR DOCTOR

- How long will the examination take?
- What may prevent me from having a PET scan?
- Is PET the best option for visualizing my condition?
- When will the results be provided to me?
- Will I need to have someone with me during the imaging study? Will this person need to drive me home?
- What special precautions should be taken with a child?
- Should I expect any side effects?
- How many scans should I have in any one year? How far apart should they be spaced?

blood and oxygen was found, then one probable diagnosis is a stroke. On the other hand, if only a decreased glucose metabolism was discovered, then **dementia** could be a possible diagnosis. In all cases, doctors will thoroughly review the results to make a determination as to why this abnormal result occurred. In many cases, further tests will be performed to validate the results of the PET scan.

Resources

BOOKS

Armstrong, Peter, Martin L. Wastie, and Andrea G. Rockall. *Diagnostic Imaging.* Chichester, U.K.: Wiley-Blackwell, 2009.

Lin, Eugene, and Abass Alavi. *PET and PET/CT: A Clinical Guide.* New York: Thieme, 2009.

Lynch, T. B., J. Clarke, and G. Cook. *PET/CT in Clinical Practice.* London: Springer-Verlag, 2007.

Valk, Peter P., et al., editors. *Positron Emission Tomography: Clinical Practice.* London: Springer, 2006.

Workman, Ronald B., Jr., et al., editors. *PET/CT: Essentials for Clinical Practice.* New York: Springer Science-Business Media, 2006.

WEBSITES

Neuroimaging and Mental Illness: A Window Into the Brain. National Institute of Mental Health. (October 19, 2010). http://www.nimh.nih.gov/health/publications/neuro imaging-and-mental-illness-a-window-into-the-brain/ neuroimaging-and-mental-illness-a-window-into-the-brain.shtml (accessed May 31, 2011).

Positron Emission Tomography (PET) Scan. Mayo Clinic. (May 7, 2011). http://www.mayoclinic.com/health/ pet-scan/MY00238 (accessed May 27, 2011).

ORGANIZATIONS

American College of Physicians, 190 North Independence Mall West, Philadelphia, PA, 19106-1572, (215) 351-2400, (800) 523-1546, http://www.acponline.org.

American College of Radiology, 1891 Preston White Drive, Reston, VA, 20191, (703) 648-8900, http://www.acr.org.

American Heart Association, 7272 Greenville Avenue, Dallas, TX, 75231, (800) 242-8721, http://www.americanheart.org.

American Medical Association, 515 N. State Street, Chicago, IL, 60610, (800) 621-8335, http://www.ama-assn.org.

National Cancer Institute, 6116 Executive Boulevard, Suite 300, Bethesda, MD, 20892-8322, (800) 422-6237, http://www.nci.nih.gov.

National Institute of Biomedical Imaging and Bioengineering, 31 Center Dr., 1C14, Bethesda, MD, 20892-8859, (301) 469-8859, http://www.nibib.gov.

Dan Harvey
Lee A. Shratter, MD
Brenda W. Lerner
William A. Atkins

Postpartum depression

Definition

Postpartum **depression** (PPD) is a mood disorder that begins after childbirth and usually lasts at least six weeks.

Demographics

There is a 20% to 30% risk of postpartum depression for women who have had a previous depressive episode not associated with pregnancy. Additionally, there is an increased risk of recurrence in subsequent pregnancies since more than half of patients have more than one episode.

Description

PPD affects approximately 10% to 20% of all childbearing women. The onset of postpartum depression tends to be gradual and may persist for many months or develop into a second bout following a subsequent pregnancy. Mild to moderate cases are sometimes unrecognized by women themselves. Many women feel ashamed and may conceal their difficulties. This is a serious problem that disrupts women's lives and can affect the baby, other children, partners, and other relationships. Levels of depression for fathers can also increase significantly.

Postpartum depression is often divided into two types: early onset and late onset. Early-onset PPD most often seems like the "blues," a mild brief experience during the first days or weeks after birth. During the first week after the birth, up to 80% of mothers experience the "baby blues." This period is usually a time of extra sensitivity; symptoms include tearfulness, irritability, anxiety, and mood changes, which tend to peak between three to five days after childbirth. The symptoms normally disappear within two weeks without requiring specific treatment apart from understanding, support, skills, and practice. Some depression, **fatigue**, and anxiety may fall within the normal range of reactions to giving birth.

Late-onset PPD appears several weeks after birth. It involves slowly growing feelings of sadness, depression, lack of energy, chronic fatigue, inability to sleep, change in appetite, significant weight loss or gain, and difficulty caring for the baby.

Causes and symptoms

The cause of postpartum depression has been extensively studied. Alterations of hormone levels of prolactin, progesterone, estrogen, and cortisol are not significantly different from those of patients who do not suffer from postpartum depression. However, some research indicates a change in a **brain** chemical that controls the release of cortisol.

Research suggests that postpartum depression is unlikely to occur in a patient with an otherwise psychologically uncomplicated pregnancy and past history. There is no association of postpartum depression with marital status, social class, or the number of live children born to the mother. However, there seems to be an increased chance to develop this disorder after pregnancy loss.

Certain characteristics have been associated with increased risk of developing postpartum depression. These risk factors include:

- medical indigence—that is, being in need of health care and not being able to receive it, possibly due to lack of medical insurance
- being younger than 20 years old at time of delivery
- being unmarried
- having been separated from one or both parents in childhood or adolescence
- receiving poor parental support and attention in childhood
- having had limited parental support in adulthood

Edinburgh Postnatal Depression Scale (EPDS)

As you are pregnant or have recently had a baby, we would like to know how you are feeling. Please check the answer that comes closest to how you have felt **IN THE PAST 7 DAYS**, not just how you feel today.

Here is an example, already completed.

I have felt happy:

☐ Yes, all the time
☒ Yes, most of the time   This would mean: "I have felt happy most of the time" during the past week.
☐ No, not very often   Please complete the other questions in the same way.
☐ No, not at all

In the past 7 days:

1. I have been able to laugh and see the funny side of things
    ☐ As much as I always could
    ☐ Not quite so much now
    ☐ Definitely not so much now
    ☐ Not at all

2. I have looked forward with enjoyment to things
    ☐ As much as I ever did
    ☐ Rather less than I used to
    ☐ Definitely less than I used to
    ☐ Hardly at all

*3. I have blamed myself unnecessarily when things went wrong
    ☐ Yes, most of the time
    ☐ Yes, some of the time
    ☐ Not very often
    ☐ No, never

4. I have been anxious or worried for no good reason
    ☐ No, not at all
    ☐ Hardly ever
    ☐ Yes, sometimes
    ☐ Yes, very often

*5. I have felt scared or panicky for no very good reason
    ☐ Yes, quite a lot
    ☐ Yes, sometimes
    ☐ No, not much
    ☐ No, not at all

*6. Things have been getting on top of me
    ☐ Yes, most of the time I haven't been able to cope at all
    ☐ Yes, sometimes I haven't been coping as well as usual
    ☐ No, most of the time I have coped quite well
    ☐ No, I have been coping as well as ever

*7. I have been so unhappy that I have had difficulty sleeping
    ☐ Yes, most of the time
    ☐ Yes, sometimes
    ☐ Not very often
    ☐ No, not at all

*8. I have felt sad or miserable
    ☐ Yes, most of the time
    ☐ Yes, quite often
    ☐ Not very often
    ☐ No, not at all

*9. I have been so unhappy that I have been crying
    ☐ Yes, most of the time
    ☐ Yes, quite often
    ☐ Only occasionally
    ☐ No, never

*10. The thought of harming myself has occurred to me
    ☐ Yes, quite often
    ☐ Sometimes
    ☐ Hardly ever
    ☐ Never

SOURCE: Cox, J.L., J.M. Holden, and R. Sagovsky, "Detection of Postnatal Depression: Development of the 10-item Edinburgh Postnatal Depression Scale," *British Journal of Psychiatry* 150 (June 1987): 782–86.

Items with an asterisk are reverse scored (3, 2, 1, 0 instead of 0, 1, 2, 3). *(Table by PreMediaGlobal. © 2012 Cengage Learning.)*

- having a poor relationship with the baby's father
- having economic problem with housing or income
- being dissatisfied with amount of education
- having low self-esteem
- having past or current emotional problem(s)
- having a family history of depression

Experts have not determined for certain what causes postpartum depression. Most likely, it is caused by a combination of factors that vary from person to person. Some researchers think that women are vulnerable to depression at all major turning points in their reproductive cycle, childbirth being only one of these markers. Factors before the baby's birth that are associated with a higher risk of PPD include severe vomiting (hyperemesis), premature labor contractions, and psychiatric disorders in the mother. In addition, new mothers commonly experience some degree of depression during the first weeks after birth. Pregnancy and birth are accompanied by sudden hormonal changes that affect emotions. Additionally, the 24-hour responsibility for a newborn infant requires a major psychological and lifestyle adjustment for most mothers, even after the first child. These physical and emotional stresses are usually accompanied by inadequate rest until the baby's routine stabilizes, so fatigue and depression are not unusual.

KEY TERMS

Hyperemesis—Severe vomiting during pregnancy. Hyperemesis appears to increase a woman's risk of postpartum depression.

Postpartum—Following childbirth.

Studies suggest that the hormone oxytocin in particular may play a role in postpartum depression. Oxytocin is associated with feelings of attachment and bonding. In a study conducted in Switzerland and published in 2011, researchers measured oxytocin levels in 74 healthy pregnant women during the third trimester of pregnancy. Overall, women with lower oxytocin levels during the third trimester were at greater risk for postpartum depression two weeks after delivery. However, more research is needed in larger groups to confirm the findings, and some experts argue that two weeks after delivery is too soon to assess postpartum depression.

In addition to hormonal changes and disrupted sleep, certain cultural expectations appear to place women from those cultures at increased risk of postpartum depression. For example, women who bear daughters in societies with a strong preference for sons are at increased risk of postpartum depression. In other cultures, a strained relationship with the husband's family is a risk factor. In Western countries, domestic violence is associated with a higher rate of PPD.

Experiences of PPD vary considerably but usually include several symptoms.

Feelings:

• persistent low mood
• inadequacy, failure, hopelessness, helplessness
• exhaustion, emptiness, sadness, tearfulness
• guilt, shame, worthlessness
• confusion, anxiety, and panic
• fear for the baby and of the baby
• fear of being alone or going out

Behaviors:

• lack of interest or pleasure in usual activities
• insomnia or excessive sleep, nightmares
• not eating or overeating
• decreased energy and motivation
• withdrawal from social contact
• poor self-care
• inability to cope with routine tasks

Thoughts:

• inability to think clearly and make decisions
• lack of concentration and poor memory
• avoidance of decision making
• fear of being rejected by the partner
• worry about harm or death to partner or baby
• ideas about suicide

Some symptoms may not indicate a severe problem. However, persistent low mood or loss of interest or pleasure in activities, along with four other symptoms occurring together for a period of at least two weeks, indicate clinical depression and require treatment.

There are several important risk factors for postpartum depression:

• stress
• lack of sleep
• poor nutrition
• lack of support from one's partner, family, or friends
• family history of depression
• labor/delivery complications for mother or baby
• premature or postmature delivery
• problems with the baby's health
• separation of mother and baby
• a difficult baby (temperament, feeding, sleeping problems)
• preexisting neurosis or psychosis

Physical and emotional **stress** during delivery in conjunction with great demands for infant care may cause the patient to neglect other family members, increasing the woman's feelings of worthlessness, isolation, and being trapped. Patients may also feel as if they are inadequate mothers, causing them guilt and embarrassment.

Diagnosis

Diagnosis of postpartum depression entails a clinical interview with the patient to assess symptoms. A doctor or other professional healthcare provider may ask the mother about thoughts and feelings and take a detailed personal history. Clinical assessment may be conducted by a **psychologist** or **psychiatrist**, who can determine the risk factors and diagnose the condition. A comprehensive **psychological assessment** interview may reveal a previous depressive cycle or a family history of depression—important risk factors. The most widely used standard for diagnosis is the Edinburgh Postnatal Depression Scale (EPDS), a simple and short

10-question scale. A score of 12 or greater on the EPDS is considered high risk for postpartum depression.

Treatment

Several treatment options exist, including medication, **psychotherapy**, counseling, and group treatment and support strategies. Treatment should begin as soon as the diagnosis is established. One effective treatment combines antidepressant medication and psychotherapy. These types of medication are often effective when used for three to four weeks. Any medication use must be carefully considered if the woman is breastfeeding, but with some medications, continuing breastfeeding is safe. There are many classes of antidepressant medications. The two most commonly prescribed for PPD are **selective serotonin reuptake inhibitors (SSRIs)** such as **citalopram** (Celexa), **escitalopram** (Lexapro), **fluoxetine** (Prozac), **paroxetine** (Paxil, Pexeva), and **sertraline** (Zoloft), and tricyclics, such as **amitriptyline** (Elavil), **desipramine** (Norpramin), **imipramine** (Tofranil), and **nortriptyline** (Aventyl, Pamelor). Nevertheless, medication alone is not sufficient and should always be accompanied by counseling or other support services. Also, many women with postpartum depression feel isolated. It is important for these women to know that they are not alone in their feelings. There are various postpartum depression **support groups** available in local communities, often sponsored by nonprofit organizations or hospitals. Support information is available by contacting postpartum depression organizations. Women can find a local support group by calling the Kristin Brooks Hope Center helpline at (800) 442-4673. Women who have thoughts of **suicide** should immediately call the national toll-free 24-hour suicide hotline at (800) 784-2433.

When medications are combined with psychological therapy, the rates for successful treatment are increased. **Interpersonal therapy** and **cognitive-behavioral therapy** have been found to be effective.

Adjunct therapies such as **acupuncture**, traditional Chinese medicine, **yoga**, **meditation**, and herbs may be helpful for mothers suffering from postpartum depression.

An important part of treating postpartum depression is self-care, which should not be underestimated or ignored.

A new mother can apply at-home strategies to help cope with the stress of becoming a parent, such as:

• valuing her role as a mother and trusting her own judgment

• making each day as simple as possible

• avoiding extra pressures or unnecessary tasks

QUESTIONS TO ASK YOUR DOCTOR

• How do I know if I have postpartum depression?

• What type of treatment do you recommend for me?

• What symptoms or behaviors are important enough that I should seek immediate treatment?

• Can you recommend any support groups for me and my family?

• trying to involve her partner more in the care of the baby

• discussing with her partner how both can share the household chores and responsibilities

• scheduling frequent outings, such as walks and short visits with friends

• sharing her feelings with her partner or friends

• talking with other mothers to help keep problems in perspective

• trying to sleep or rest when the baby is sleeping

• taking care of personal health and well-being

Exercise, including yoga, can help enhance a new mother's emotional well-being. New mothers should also try to cultivate good sleeping habits and learn to rest when they feel physically or emotionally tired. It is important for a woman to learn to recognize her own warning signs of fatigue and respond to them by taking a break.

Prognosis

When a woman has supportive friends and family, mild postpartum depression usually disappears quickly. If depression becomes severe and a mother cannot care for herself and the baby, **hospitalization** may be necessary. Medication, counseling, and support from others usually resolve even severe depression in three to six months. The prognosis for postpartum depression is better if it is detected early during its clinical course and a combination of **SSRIs** and psychotherapy is available and initiated.

Prevention

Mothers should be advised prior to hospital discharge that if the "maternity blues" last longer than two weeks or pose tough difficulties with family interactions, they should call the hospital where their baby was delivered and get a referral for a psychological evaluation. Education concerning risk factors and reduction of these is important. Prophylactic (preventive) use of SSRIs is indicated two to three weeks before delivery to prevent the disorder in a patient with a past history of depression, since recurrence rates are high. Use of medication during pregnancy should always take place under careful medical supervision.

Resources

BOOKS

Beck, Cheryl Tatano, and Jeanne Watson Driscoll. *Postpartum Mood and Anxiety Disorders: A Clinician's Guide.* Sudbury, MA: Jones and Bartlett, 2006.

Poulin, Sandra. *The Mother-to-Mother Postpartum Depression Support Book.* New York: Berkley Trade, 2006.

Shields, Brooke. *Down Came the Rain: My Journey Through Postpartum Depression.* New York: Hyperion Books, 2006.

Subcommittee on Health, U.S. House of Representatives. *Improving Women's Health: Understanding Depression after Pregnancy. (Hearing before the Subcommittee on Health of the Committee on Energy and Commerce, House of Representatives, One Hundred Eighth Congress, Second Session, September 29, 2004.)* Washington, DC: U.S. Government Printing Office, 2005.

Venis, Joyce A., and Suzanne McCloskey. *Postpartum Depression Demystified: An Essential Guide for Understanding the Most Common Complication after Childbirth.* New York: Marlowe, 2007.

PERIODICALS

Barnes, Diana Lynn. "Postpartum Depression: Its Impact on Couples and Marital Satisfaction." *Journal of Systemic Therapies* 25, no. 3 (Fall 2006): 25–42.

Gaby, Alan R. "Fish Oil for Postpartum Depression." *Townsend Letter: The Examiner of Alternative Medicine* (October 2006): 40.

Haslam, Divna M., Kenneth I. Pakenham, and Amanda Smith. "Social Support and Postpartum Depressive Symptomatology: The Mediating Role of Maternal Self-Efficacy." *Infant Mental Health Journal* 27, no. 3 (May–June 2006): 276–91.

Hung, Chich-Hsiu. "The Hung Postpartum Stress Scale." *Journal of Nursing Scholarship* (Spring 2007): 71–75.

Klier, Claudia M., et al. "The Role of Estrogen and Progesterone in Depression after Birth." *Journal of Psychiatric Research* 41, no. 3–4 (April–June 2007): 273–79.

Klotter, Jule. "Exercise and Postpartum Depression." *Townsend Letter: The Examiner of Alternative Medicine* (October 2007): 42–44.

McGinnis, Marianne. "Baby Blues? Get Help Early." *Prevention* (January 2006): 107.

Moehler, E., et al. "Maternal Depressive Symptoms in the Postnatal Period Are Associated with Long-Term Impairment of Mother-Child Bonding." *Archives of Women's Mental Health* 9, no. 5 (September 2006): 273–78.

Nylen, Kimberly J., et al. "Maternal Depression: A Review of Relevant Treatment Approaches for Mothers and Infants." *Infant Mental Health Journal* 27, no. 4 (July/August 2006): 327–43.

Ramashwar, S. "In China, Women Who Give Birth to Girls Face an Increased Risk of Postpartum Depression." *International Family Planning Perspectives* (December 2007): 191–93.

Sharma, Verinder. "A Cautionary Note on the Use of Antidepressants in Postpartum Depression." *Bipolar Disorders* 8, no. 4 (August 2006): 411–14.

Skrundtz, M. "Plasma Oxytocin Concentration During Pregnancy is Associated with Development of Postpartum Depression." *Neuropsychopharmacology* 36, no. 9 (August 2011): 1886–93.

ORGANIZATIONS

Kristin Brooks Hope Center, 615 7th St., NE, Washington, DC, 20002, (202) 536-3200, (800) 442-4673, http://www.hopeline.com.

National Institute of Mental Health, 6001 Executive Blvd., Room 8184, MSC 9663, Bethesda, MD, 20892, (866) 615-6464, http://www.nimh.nih.gov.

Postpartum Support International, PO Box 60931, Santa Barbara, CA, 93160, (805) 967-7636, (800) 944-4773, http://www.postpartum.net.

Laith Farid Gulli, MD
Nicole Mallory, MS, PA-C
Laura Jean Cataldo, RN, EdD
Heidi Splete

Post-traumatic stress disorder

Definition

Post-traumatic **stress** disorder (PTSD) is a complex anxiety disorder that may occur when individuals experience or witness an event perceived as a threat and in which they experience fear, terror, or helplessness. PTSD is sometimes summarized as "a normal reaction to abnormal events." It was first defined as a distinctive disorder in 1980. Originally diagnosed in veterans of the Vietnam War, it is now recognized in civilian survivors of rape or other criminal assaults; natural disasters; plane crashes, train collisions, or industrial explosions; acts of terrorism; **child abuse**; or war.

Demographics

PTSD can develop in almost anyone in any age group exposed to a sufficiently terrifying event or chain of events. The **National Institute of Mental Health**

(NIMH) estimated in 2007 that about 7.7 million adults in the United States have PTSD. One study found that 3.7% of a sample of teenage boys and 6.3% of adolescent girls had PTSD. It is estimated that people's risk of developing PTSD over the course of their life is between 8 and 10%. Women are at greater risk of PTSD following sexual assault or domestic violence, whereas men are at greater risk of developing PTSD following military combat. On average, 30% of soldiers who have been in a war zone develop PTSD. Recent statistics on PTSD in U.S. military personnel returning from Iraq demonstrated that, using more inclusive parameters, between 20.7% and 30.5% of troops suffered from PTSD; using stricter parameters, PTSD was present in 5.6–11.3% of troops.

Traumatic experiences are surprisingly common in the general North American population. More than 10% of the men and 6% of the women in one survey reported experiencing four or more types of **trauma** in their lives. The most frequently mentioned traumas are:

• witnessing someone being badly hurt or killed

• being involved in a fire, flood, earthquake, severe hurricane, or other natural disaster

• being involved in a life-threatening accident (work-place explosion or transportation accident)

• being in military combat

PTSD is more likely to develop in response to an intentional human act of violence or cruelty such as a rape or mugging than as a reaction to an impersonal catastrophe like a flood or hurricane. It is not surprising that the traumatic events most frequently mentioned by men diagnosed with PTSD are rape, combat exposure, childhood **neglect**, and childhood physical **abuse**. For women diagnosed with PTSD, the most common traumas are rape, sexual molestation, physical attack, being threatened with a weapon, and childhood physical abuse.

PTSD can also develop in therapists, rescue workers, or witnesses of a frightening event as well as in those who were directly involved. This process is called vicarious traumatization.

Description

The experience of PTSD has sometimes been described as like being in a horror film that keeps replaying and cannot be shut off. It is common for people with PTSD to feel intense fear and helplessness and to relive the frightening event in nightmares or in their waking hours. Sometimes the memory is triggered by a sound, smell, or image that reminds the sufferer of the traumatic event. These re-experiences of the event are called flashbacks. Persons with PTSD are also likely to be jumpy and easily startled or to go numb emotionally

and lose interest in activities they used to enjoy. They may have problems with memory and with getting enough sleep. In some cases they may feel disconnected from the real world or have moments in which their own bodies seem unreal; these symptoms are indications of dissociation, a process in which the mind splits off certain memories or thoughts from conscious awareness. Many people with PTSD turn to alcohol or drugs in order to escape the flashbacks and other symptoms of the disorder, even if only for a few minutes.

Risk factors

Factors that influence the likelihood of a person's developing PTSD include:

• The nature, intensity, and duration of the traumatic experience. For example, someone who just barely escaped from the World Trade Center before the towers collapsed is at greater risk of PTSD than someone who saw the collapse from a distance or on television.

• The person's previous history. People who were abused as children, who were separated from their parents at an early age, or who have a previous history of anxiety or depression are at increased risk of PTSD.

• Genetic factors. Vulnerability to PTSD is known to run in families.

• The availability of social support after the event. People who have no family or friends are more likely to develop PTSD than those who do.

HIGH-RISK POPULATIONS. Some subpopulations in the United States are at greater risk of developing PTSD. The lifetime prevalence of PTSD among persons living in depressed urban areas or on Native American reservations is estimated at 23%. For victims of violent crimes, the estimated rate is 58%.

PTSD also appears to be more common in seniors than in younger people. Thirteen percent of the senior population reports they are affected by PTSD in comparison to 7–10% of the entire population. Reports of **elder abuse** crimes have gone up by 200% since 1986. Also, the incidence of PTSD is known to be higher in Holocaust survivors, war veterans, and cancer or heart surgery survivors, which accounts for a significant portion of older Americans. Of those seniors who are military veterans, there is an increasing number who are isolated and/or in poor health as a result of PTSD.

Children are also susceptible to PTSD and their risk is increased exponentially as their exposure to the event increases. Children experiencing abuse, the death of a parent, or those located in a community suffering a traumatic event can develop PTSD. Two years after the

Oklahoma City bombing of 1995, 16% of children within a 100-mile radius of Oklahoma City with no direct exposure to the bombing had increased symptoms of PTSD. Weak parental response to the event, having a parent suffering from PTSD symptoms, and intensified exposure to the event via the media all increase the possibility of a child's developing PTSD symptoms. In addition, a developmentally inappropriate sexual experience for a child may be considered a traumatic event, even though it may not have actually involved violence or physical injury. Proposed changes to the fifth edition of the *Diagnostic and Statistical Manual of Mental Disorders* (*DSM-5*, 2013) include post-traumatic stress disorder in preschool children among its new diagnoses.

MILITARY VETERANS. Studies conducted between 2004 and 2006 with veteran participants from the wars in Iraq and in Afghanistan found a strong correlation between duration of combat exposure and PTSD. Veterans of combat in Iraq reported a higher rate of PTSD than those deployed to Afghanistan because of longer exposure to warfare.

Information about PTSD in veterans of the Vietnam era is derived from the National Vietnam Veterans Readjustment Survey (NVVRS), conducted between 1986 and 1988. The estimated lifetime prevalence of PTSD among American veterans of this war is 30.9% for men and 26.9% for women. An additional 22.5% of the men and 21.2% of the women have been diagnosed with partial PTSD at some point in their lives. The lifetime prevalence of PTSD among veterans of World War II and the Korean War is estimated at 20%.

CROSS-CULTURAL ISSUES. Further research needs to be done on the effects of ethnicity and culture on post-traumatic symptoms. As of the early 2010s, most PTSD research had been done by Western clinicians working with patients from a similar background. Researchers do not yet know whether persons from non-Western societies have the same psychological reactions to specific traumas or whether they develop the same symptom patterns.

PROTECTIVE OR RESILIENCE FACTORS. As important as the question of *who* gets PTSD is also the question of who does *not* get PTSD. Why do some people who are exposed to traumatic events succumb to the long-lasting aftereffects of PTSD, whereas others seem to endure the trauma and successfully move on. Researchers have identified the following resilience factors, which seem to decrease the likelihood that traumatic exposure will lead to PTSD:

- actively seeking support from friends, family, or others following a traumatic incident
- engaging with a formal support group
- maintaining a positive view of personal actions during the course of or in response to the traumatic incident
- implementing a coping strategy
- feeling as if a lesson has been learned from the traumatic event
- not becoming paralyzed with terror; being able to respond and react effectively despite fear

Causes and symptoms

The causes of PTSD are not completely understood. One major question that has not yet been answered is why some people involved in a major disaster develop PTSD and other survivors of the same event do not. For example, a survey of 988 adults living close to the World Trade Center conducted in November 2001 found that only 7% had been diagnosed with PTSD following the events of September 11; the other 93% were anxious and upset, but they did not develop PTSD. Research into this question is ongoing.

Causes

When PTSD was first suggested as a diagnostic category for *DSM-III* in 1980, it was controversial precisely because of the central role of outside stressors as causes of the disorder. Psychiatry has generally emphasized the internal abnormalities of individuals as the source of mental disorders; prior to the 1970s, war veterans, rape victims, and other trauma survivors were often blamed for their symptoms and regarded as cowards, moral weaklings, or masochists. The high rate of psychiatric casualties among Vietnam veterans, however, led to studies conducted by the Veterans Administration. These studies helped to establish PTSD as a legitimate diagnostic entity with a complex set of causes.

BIOCHEMICAL/PHYSIOLOGICAL CAUSES. Present neurobiological research indicates that traumatic events cause lasting changes in the human nervous system, including abnormal levels of secretion of stress hormones. In addition, in PTSD patients, researchers have found changes in the amygdala and the hippocampus—the parts of the **brain** that form links between fear and memory. Experiments with ketamine, a drug that inactivates one of the **neurotransmitters** in the central nervous system, suggest that trauma works in a similar way to damage associative pathways in the brain. **Positron emission tomography (PET)** scans of PTSD patients suggest that trauma affects the parts of the brain that govern speech and language.

SOCIOCULTURAL CAUSES. Studies of specific populations of PTSD patients (combat veterans, survivors of rape or genocide, former political hostages or prisoners, etc.) have shed light on the social and cultural causes of PTSD. In general, societies that are highly authoritarian, glorify violence, or sexualize violence have high rates of PTSD even among civilians.

OCCUPATIONAL FACTORS. Persons whose work exposes them to traumatic events or who treat trauma survivors may develop secondary PTSD (also known as compassion **fatigue** or burnout). These occupations include specialists in emergency medicine, police officers, firefighters, search-and-rescue personnel, psychotherapists, and disaster investigators. The degree of risk for PTSD is related to three factors: the amount and intensity of exposure to the suffering of trauma victims, the worker's degree of empathy and sensitivity, and unresolved issues from the worker's personal history.

PERSONAL VARIABLES. Although the most important causal factor in PTSD is the traumatic event itself, individuals differ in the intensity of their cognitive and emotional responses to trauma; some persons appear to be more vulnerable than others. In some cases, this greater vulnerability is related to temperament or natural disposition, with shy or introverted people being at greater risk. In other cases, the person's vulnerability results from chronic illness, a physical disability, or previous traumatization— particularly abuse in childhood. Studies done by the U.S. Department of Veterans Affairs have found some evidence that race and ethnicity may also play a factor, with veterans belonging to ethnic minority groups at higher risk of experiencing PTSD after combat.

Symptoms

DSM-IV-TR specifies six diagnostic criteria for PTSD:

- Traumatic stressor: The patient has been exposed to a catastrophic event involving actual or threatened death or injury or a threat to the physical integrity of the self or others. During exposure to the trauma, the person's emotional response was marked by intense fear, feelings of helplessness, or horror. In general, stressors caused intentionally by human beings (genocide, rape, torture, abuse) are experienced as more traumatic than accidents, natural disasters, or "acts of God."

- Intrusive symptoms: Patients experience flashbacks, traumatic daydreams, or nightmares, in which they relive the trauma as if it were recurring in the present. Intrusive symptoms result from an abnormal process of memory formation. Traumatic memories have two distinctive characteristics: they can be triggered by stimuli that remind the patient of the traumatic event, or they may have a "frozen" or wordless quality, consisting of images and sensations rather than verbal descriptions.

KEY TERMS

Benzodiazepines—A class of drugs that have a hypnotic and sedative action, used mainly as tranquilizers to control symptoms of anxiety.

Cognitive-behavioral therapy—A type of psychotherapy used to treat anxiety disorders (including PTSD) that emphasizes behavioral change as well as alteration of negative thought patterns.

Cortisol—A hormone produced by the adrenal glands near the kidneys in response to stress.

Dissociation—The splitting off of certain mental processes from conscious awareness. Many PTSD patients have dissociative symptoms.

Flashback—A temporary reliving of a traumatic event.

Hyperarousal—A state of increased emotional tension and anxiety, often including jitteriness and being easily startled.

Hypervigilance—A condition of abnormally intense watchfulness or wariness. Hypervigilance is one of the most common symptoms of PTSD.

Prevalence—The percentage of a population that is affected by a specific disease at a given time.

Selective serotonin reuptake inhibitors (SSRIs)—A class of antidepressants that works by blocking the reabsorption of serotonin in the brain, raising the levels of serotonin.

Trauma—A severe injury or shock to a person's body or mind.

- Avoidant symptoms: Patients attempt to reduce the possibility of exposure to anything that might trigger memories of the trauma and to minimize their reactions to such memories. This cluster of symptoms includes feeling disconnected from other people, psychic numbing, and avoidance of places, persons, or things associated with the trauma. Patients with PTSD are at increased risk of substance abuse as a form of self-medication to numb painful memories.

- Hyperarousal: Hyperarousal is a condition in which the nervous system is always on "red alert" for the return of danger. This symptom cluster includes hypervigilance, insomnia, difficulty concentrating, general irritability, and an extreme startle response. Some clinicians think that this abnormally intense startle response may be the most characteristic symptom of PTSD.

- Duration of symptoms: The symptoms must persist for at least one month.

- Significance: Patients suffer from significant social, interpersonal, or work-related problems as a result of the PTSD symptoms. A common social symptom of PTSD is a feeling of disconnection from other people (including loved ones), from the larger society, and from spiritual, religious, or other significant sources of meaning.

Diagnosis

The **diagnosis** of PTSD is based on the patient's history, including the timing of the traumatic event and the duration of the patient's symptoms.

Examination

Consultation with a mental health professional for diagnosis and a plan of treatment is always advised. Many of the responses to trauma, such as shock, terror, irritability, blame, guilt, **grief**, sadness, emotional numbing, and feelings of helplessness, are natural reactions. For most people, resilience is an overriding factor, and trauma effects diminish within six to sixteen months. It is when these responses continue or become debilitating that PTSD is often diagnosed.

As outlined in *DSM-IV*, the exposure to a traumatic stressor means that an individual experienced, witnessed, or was confronted by an event or events involving death or threat of death, serious injury or the threat of bodily harm to oneself or others. The individual's response must involve intense fear, helplessness, or horror. A two-pronged approach to evaluation is considered the best way to make a valid diagnosis because it can gauge under-reporting or over-reporting of symptoms. The two primary forms are structured interviews and self-report questionnaires. Spouses, partners, and other family members may also be interviewed. Because the evaluation may involve subtle reminders of the trauma in order to gauge a patient's reactions, individuals should ask for a full description of the evaluation process beforehand. Asking what results can be expected from the evaluation is also advised.

A number of structured interview forms have been devised to facilitate the diagnosis of post-traumatic stress disorder:

- Clinician Administered PTSD Scale (CAPS) developed by the National Center for PTSD
- Structured Clinical Interview for DSM (SCID)
- Anxiety Disorders Interview Schedule-Revised (ADIS)
- PTSD-Interview
- Structured Interview for PTSD (SI-PTSD)
- PTSD Symptom Scale Interview (PSS-I)

Self-reporting checklists provide scores to represent the level of stress experienced. Some of the most commonly used checklists are:

- The PTSD Checklist (PCL), which has one list for civilians and one for military personnel and veterans
- Impact of Event Scale-Revised (IES-R)
- Keane PTSD Scale of the MMPI-2
- Mississippi Scale for Combat Related PTSD and the Mississippi Scale for Civilians
- Post Traumatic Diagnostic Scale (PDS)
- Penn Inventory for Post-Traumatic Stress
- Los Angeles Symptom Checklist (LASC)

Tests

There are no laboratory or imaging tests that can detect PTSD, although the doctor may order **imaging studies** of the brain to rule out head injuries or other physical causes of the patient's symptoms.

Treatment

Various treatments are used for post-traumatic stress disorder.

Traditional

Treatment for PTSD usually involves a combination of medications and **psychotherapy**. If patients have started to abuse alcohol or drugs, they must be treated for the **substance abuse** before being treated for PTSD. If they are diagnosed with coexisting **depression**, treatment should focus on the PTSD because its course, biology, and treatment response are different from those associated with major depression. Patients with the disorder are usually treated as outpatients; they are not hospitalized unless they are threatening to commit **suicide** or harm other people.

Mainstream forms of psychotherapy used to treat patients who have already developed PTSD include:

- Cognitive-behavioral therapy. There are two treatment approaches to PTSD included under this heading: exposure therapy, which seeks to desensitize the patient to reminders of the trauma; and anxiety management training, which teaches the patient strategies for reducing anxiety. These strategies may include relaxation training, biofeedback, social skills training, distraction techniques, or cognitive restructuring.
- Psychodynamic psychotherapy. This approach helps the patient recover a sense of self and learn new coping strategies and ways to deal with intense

emotions related to the trauma. Typically, it consists of three phases: establishing a sense of safety for the patient; exploring the trauma itself in depth; helping the patient re-establish connections with family, friends, the wider society, and other sources of meaning.

- Discussion groups or peer-counseling groups. These groups are usually formed for survivors of specific traumas, such as combat, rape/incest, and natural or transportation disasters. They help patients to recognize that other survivors of the shared experience have had the same emotions and reacted to the trauma in similar ways. They appear to be especially beneficial for patients with guilt issues about their behavior during the trauma (e.g., submitting to rape to save one's life or surviving the event when others did not).
- Family therapy. This form of treatment is recommended for PTSD patients whose family life has been affected by the PTSD symptoms.

Drugs

In general, medications are used most often in patients with severe PTSD to treat the intrusive symptoms of the disorder as well as feelings of anxiety and depression. These drugs are usually given as one part of a treatment plan that includes psychotherapy or **group therapy**. As of 2012, no single medication was considered a primary cure for PTSD. The **selective serotonin reuptake inhibitors (SSRIs)** appear to help the core symptoms when given in higher doses for five to eight weeks, while the tricyclic antidepressants (TCAs) or the **monoamine oxidase inhibitors (MAOIs)** are most useful in treating anxiety and depression.

Sleep problems can be lessened with brief treatment with an antianxiety drug, such as a benzodiazepine like **alprazolam** (Xanax), but long-term usage can lead to disturbing side effects, including increased anger, drug tolerance, dependency, and abuse. **Benzodiazepines** are also not given to PTSD patients diagnosed with coexisting drug or alcohol abuse.

Alternative

Relaxation training, which is sometimes called anxiety management training, includes breathing exercises and similar techniques intended to help the patient prevent hyperventilation and relieve the muscle tension associated with the fight-or-flight reaction of anxiety. **Yoga**, aikido, tai chi, and **dance therapy** help patients work with the physical as well as the emotional tensions that either promote anxiety or are created by the anxiety.

Other alternative or complementary therapies are based on physiological and/or energetic understanding of how the trauma is imprinted in the body. These therapies affect a release of stored emotions and resolution of them by working with the body rather than merely talking through the experience. One example of such a therapy is somatic experiencing (SE), developed by Peter Levine. SE is a short-term, biological, body-oriented approach to PTSD or other trauma. This approach heals by emphasizing physiological and emotional responses, without re-traumatizing the person, without placing the person on medication, and without the long hours of conventional therapy.

When used in conjunction with therapies that address the underlying cause of PTSD, relaxation therapies such as hydrotherapy, massage therapy, and **aromatherapy** are useful to some patients in easing PTSD symptoms. Essential oils of **lavender, chamomile**, neroli, sweet marjoram, and ylang-ylang are commonly recommended by aromatherapists for stress relief and anxiety reduction.

Some patients benefit from spiritual or religious counseling. Because traumatic experiences often affect patients' spiritual views and beliefs, counseling with a trusted religious or spiritual advisor may be part of a treatment plan. A growing number of pastoral counselors in the major Christian and Jewish bodies in North America have advanced credentials in trauma therapy. Native Americans are often helped to recover from PTSD by participating in traditional tribal rituals for cleansing memories of war and other traumatic events. These rituals may include sweat lodges, prayers and chants, or consultation with a shaman or tribal healer.

Several controversial methods of treatment for PTSD have been introduced since the mid-1980s. Some have been developed by mainstream medical researchers while others are derived from various forms of alternative medicine. These methods are controversial because they do not offer any scientifically validated explanations for their effectiveness. They include:

- Eye Movement Desensitization and Reprocessing (EMDR). This is a technique in which the patient re-imagines the trauma while focusing visually on movements of the therapist's finger. It is claimed that the movements of the patient's eyes reprogram the brain and allow emotional healing.
- Tapas Acupressure Technique (TAT). TAT was developed in 1993 by licensed acupuncturist Tapas Fleming. It is derived from traditional Chinese medicine (TCM), and its practitioners maintain that a large number of acupuncture meridians enter the brain at certain points on the face, especially around the eyes. Pressure on these points is thought to release traumatic stress.

QUESTIONS TO ASK YOUR DOCTOR

- What are my chances of recovering completely from PTSD? How long do you think it might take?

- What medications would you recommend and why?

- What should I do when I have a flashback?

- Can you help me explain my symptoms to my family and friends?

- Thought Field Therapy. This therapy combines the acupuncture meridians of TCM with analysis of the patient's voice over the telephone. The therapist then provides an individualized treatment for the patient.

- Traumatic Incident Reduction. This is a technique in which the patient treats the trauma like a videotape and "runs through" it repeatedly with the therapist until all negative emotions have been discharged.

- Emotional Freedom Techniques (EFT). EFT is similar to TAT in that it uses the body's acupuncture meridians, but it emphasizes the body's entire "energy field" rather than just the face.

- Counting Technique. Developed by a physician, this treatment consists of a preparation phase, a counting phase in which the therapist counts from 1 to 100 while the patient re-imagines the trauma and a review phase. Like Traumatic Incident Reduction, it is intended to reduce the patient's hyperarousal.

Healthcare team roles

It is essential for all treatment team members to know their roles and execute them properly throughout the treatment and recovery phases of this disorder. Depending on whether outpatient or inpatient treatment is being provided, the team leaders may include psychiatrists, psychologists, nursing staff, behavior specialists, physical therapists, and other medical/behavioral staff. In some cases it may be appropriate to include the patient's religious or spiritual advisor as a member of the team.

Prognosis

The prognosis of PTSD is difficult to determine because patients' personalities and the experiences they undergo vary widely. A majority of patients get better, including some who do not receive treatment. One study reported that the average length of PTSD symptoms in patients who get treatment is 32 months, compared to 64 months in patients who are not treated.

Factors that improve a patient's chances for full recovery include prompt treatment, early and ongoing support from family and friends, a high level of functioning before the frightening event, and an absence of alcohol or substance abuse.

About 30% of people with PTSD never recover completely, however. A few commit suicide because their symptoms get worse rather than improving.

Prevention

PTSD is impossible to prevent completely because natural disasters and human acts of violence will continue to occur. In addition, it is not possible to tell beforehand how any given individual will react to a specific type of trauma. Prompt treatment after a traumatic event may lower the survivor's risk of developing severe symptoms.

Resources

BOOKS

American Psychiatric Association. *Diagnostic and Statistical Manual of Mental Disorders.* 4th ed., text rev. Washington, DC: American Psychiatric Publishing, 2000.

Antony, Martin M., and Murray B. Stein, eds. *Oxford Handbook of Anxiety and Related Disorders.* New York: Oxford University Press, 2009.

Bradley, W., et al. *Neurology in Clinical Practice,* 5th ed. Philadelphia: Butterworth-Heinemann, 2008.

Brohl, Kathryn. *Working with Traumatized Children: A Handbook for Healing,* rev. ed. Arlington, VA: CWLA Press, 2007.

Grey, Nick, ed. *A Casebook of Cognitive Therapy for Traumatic Stress Reactions.* New York: Routledge, 2009.

Slone, Laurie B., and Matthew J. Friedman. *After the War Zone: A Practical Guide for Returning Troops and Their Families.* Cambridge, MA: Da Capo Lifelong, 2008.

PERIODICALS

Cohen, J.A., and M.S. Scheeringa. "Post-traumatic Stress Disorder Diagnosis in Children: Challenges and Promises." *Dialogues in Clinical Neuroscience* 11 (2009): 91–99.

Evans, S., et al. "Disability and Posttraumatic Stress Disorder in Disaster Relief Workers Responding to September 11, 2001, World Trade Center Disaster." *Journal of Clinical Psychology* 65 (April 22, 2009): 684–94.

Hamblen, J.L., et al. "Cognitive Behavioral Therapy for Postdisaster Distress: A Community-Based Treatment Program for Survivors of Hurricane Katrina." *Administration and Policy in Mental Health* 36 (May 2009): 206–14.

Smith, T.C., et al. "PTSD Prevalence, Associated Exposures, and Functional Health Outcomes in a Large, Population-

Based Military Cohort." *Public Health Reports* 124 (January-February 2009): 90–102.

WEBSITES

"Helping Children Cope with Violence and Disasters: What Parents Can Do." National Institute of Mental Health. http://www.nimh.nih.gov/health/publications/helping-children-and-adolescents-cope-with-violence-and-disasters-what-parents-can-do/index.shtml (accessed September 16, 2011).

Hope for Recovery: Understanding PTSD [video]. National Center for PTSD. http://www.ncptsd.va.gov/ncmain/ncdocs/videos/emv_hoperecovery_gpv.html (accessed September 16, 2011).

"Post-Traumatic Stress Disorder." National Alliance on Mental Illness. http://www.nami.org/Template.cfm?Section=By_Illness&Template=/TaggedPage/TaggedPageDisplay.cfm&TPLID=54&ContentID=23045 (accessed September 16, 2011).

"What Is PTSD?" National Center for PTSD Fact Sheet. http://www.ncptsd.va.gov/ncmain/ncdocs/fact_shts/fs_what_is_ptsd.html (accessed September 16, 2011).

ORGANIZATIONS

American Academy of Experts in Traumatic Stress, 203 Deer Rd., Ronkonkoma, NY, 11779, (631) 543-2217, Fax: (631) 543-6977, info@aaets.org, http://www.aaets.org.

American Psychiatric Association, 1000 Wilson Blvd., Ste. 1825, Arlington, VA, 22209-3901, (703) 907-7300, apa@psych.org, http://www.psych.org.

Anxiety Disorders Association of America, 8730 Georgia Ave., Silver Spring, MD, 20910, (240) 485-1001, Fax: (240) 485-1035, http://www.adaa.org.

National Alliance on Mental Illness, 2107 Wilson Blvd., Ste. 300, Arlington, VA, 22201-3042, Fax: (703) 524-9094, (800) 950-6264, http://www.nami.org.

National Center for PTSD, U.S. Department of Veterans Affairs, 810 Vermont Ave. NW, Washington, DC, 20420, (802) 296-6300, ncptsd@va.gov, http://www.ncptsd.va.gov.

National Institute of Mental Health, 6001 Executive Blvd., Rm. 8184, MSC 9663, Bethesda, MD, 20892-9663, (301) 433-4513; TTY: (301) 443-8431, Fax: (301) 443-4279, (866) 615-6464; TTY: (866) 415-8051, nimhinfo@nih.gov, http://www.nimh.nih.gov.

Rebecca J. Frey, PhD

Premature ejaculation

Definition

Premature ejaculation (PE) refers to the persistent or recurrent discharge of semen with minimal sexual stimulation before, on, or shortly after penetration; before the person wishes it; and earlier than he expects it.

Description

In making the diagnosis of PE, the clinician must take into account factors that affect the length of time that the man feels sexually excited. These factors include the age of the patient and his partner; the newness of the sexual partner; and the location and recent frequency of sexual activity.

Premature ejaculation that takes place before the man's penis enters the woman's vagina will interfere with conception if the couple is planning a pregnancy. Continued lack of ejaculatory control may lead to sexual dissatisfaction for either or both members of the couple. It may become a source of marital tension, disturbed interpersonal relationships, or eventual separation or divorce.

Failure to respond to treatment for PE and the complications that may result from it should encourage the patient to seek further help from a health provider trained and experienced in treating the problem.

Causes and symptoms

Causes

Premature ejaculation (PE) is a common complaint. The available evidence supports the notion that control and modulation of sexual excitement is learned behavior, and if it has been learned incorrectly or inadequately, it can be relearned. PE is only rarely caused by a physical or structural problem; in these cases it is usually associated with other physical symptoms, usually pain. In rare cases, PE may be associated with a neurological condition; infection of the prostate gland; or urethritis (inflammation of the duct that carries urine and semen to the outside of the body). With the rising prevalence of **substance abuse**, an increasing number of cases of PE are being diagnosed in patients withdrawing from drugs, especially **opioids**.

PE may be of lifelong duration or develop in later life, especially if a difficult interpersonal relationship is one of its causes. Although PE is commonly associated with psychological symptoms, especially performance anxiety and guilt, these symptoms are its consequences rather than its causes. Once PE is firmly established, however, the accompanying psychological factors, especially in combination with sexual overstimulation, may form a self-perpetuating cycle that makes the disorder worse.

Premature ejaculation is common in adolescents where it may be made worse by feelings of sinfulness concerning sexual activity, fear of discovery, fear of making the partner pregnant, fear of contracting a sexually transmitted disease (STD), or performance anxiety. Adults may have similar concerns as well as interpersonal factors related to the sexual partner.

Symptoms

In PE, ejaculation occurs earlier than the patient and/or the couple would like, thus preventing full satisfaction from intercourse, especially on the part of the sexual partner, who frequently fails to attain orgasm. PE is almost invariably accompanied by marked emotional upset and interpersonal difficulties that may add frustration to an already tense situation, which makes the loss of sexual fulfillment even worse. It is also important to differentiate male orgasm from ejaculation. Some men are able to distinguish between the two events and enjoy the pleasurable sensations associated with orgasm apart from the emission of semen, which usually ends the moment of orgasm. In these cases, the partner is capable of achieving her own orgasm and sexual satisfaction.

Diagnosis

The physical examination of a patient who is having problems with PE usually results in normal findings. Abnormal findings are unusual. The best source of information for diagnosing the nature of the problem is the patient's sexual history. On taking the patient's history, the clinician should concentrate on the sexual history, making sure that both partners have adequate and accurate sexual information. Ideally, the sexual partner should participate in the history and is often able to contribute valuable information that the patient himself may be unaware of or unwilling to relate. The female partner should also be examined by a gynecologist in order to ascertain her sexual capabilities and to eliminate the possibility that the size or structure of her genitals is part of the reason for the male's premature ejaculation.

Treatment

Preferably, therapy for PE should be conducted under the supervision of a health professional trained in sexual dysfunction. Both partners must participate responsibly in the therapeutic program. Treatment of PE requires patience, dedication and commitment by both partners, and the therapist must convey this message to both. The first part of therapy requires both partners to avoid intercourse for a period of several weeks. This period of abstinence is helpful in relieving any troublesome performance anxiety on the part of the man that may interfere with therapy.

Behavioral techniques, taught either individually, conjointly, or in groups, are effective in the therapy of PE. A preliminary stage of all treatment is termed "sensate focus" and involves the man's concentration on the

---

KEY TERMS

Abstinence—Refraining from sexual intercourse for a period of time.

Ejaculation—The discharge of semen by the male reproductive organs.

Glans—The tip of the penis.

Orgasm—Another word for sexual climax. In the male, orgasm is usually accompanied by ejaculation but may be experienced as distinct from ejaculation.

Prostate—A muscular gland surrounding the urethra in males at the base of the urinary bladder. The prostate gland secretes the fluid that combines with the male sperm cells to form semen.

Semen—A thick whitish fluid containing sperm, produced by the male reproductive organs.

Urethritis—Inflammation of the urethra, which is the duct that carries urine and (in males) semen to the outside of the body.

---

process of sexual arousal and orgasm. He should learn each step in the process, most particularly the moment prior to ejaculation. The sexual partner participates in the process, maintaining an awareness of her partner's sensations and how close he is to ejaculating. At this point, two techniques are commonly used:

- The "stop and start" technique. This approach involves sexual stimulation until the man recognizes that he is about to ejaculate. At this time, the stimulation is discontinued for about thirty seconds and then resumed. This sequence of events is repeated until ejaculation is desired by both partners, with stimulation continuing until ejaculation occurs.

- The "squeeze" technique. This approach involves sexual stimulation, usually by the sexual partner, until the man recognizes that he is about to ejaculate. At this time stimulation ceases. The patient or his partner gently squeezes the end of the penis at the junction of the glans penis (tip of the penis) with the shaft. The squeezing is continued for several seconds. Sexual stimulation is withheld for about 30 seconds and then resumed. This sequence of events is repeated by the patient alone or with the assistance of his partner until ejaculation is desired. At this point stimulation is continued until the man ejaculates.

The patient and his partner should be advised against trying any of the many unproven remedies that are available either over the counter or popularized on the Internet. Certain prescription medications, especially **antidepressants** that produce delayed ejaculation as a side effect, may be useful as therapeutic adjuncts. The use of a class of drugs known as **selective serotonin reuptake inhibitors** (**SSRIs**) has shown promise in the treatment of premature ejaculation. The SSRIs prolong the time it takes the man to ejaculate by as much as 30 minutes. The SSRIs most commonly used to treat PE are **sertraline** (Zoloft) and **fluoxetine** (Prozac), which are currently approved by the Food and Drug Administration (FDA) for use in treating **depression** and panic attacks. It is important to emphasize that the use of these drugs to treat premature ejaculation is still considered experimental, as the FDA had not approved them for this specific use as of 2011.

Prognosis

In most cases (some observers claim a 95% success rate), the patient is able to control ejaculation through education and practice of the techniques recommended by a health professional. In chronic cases that do not respond to treatment, the PE may be related to a serious psychological or psychiatric condition, including depression or anxiety. Patients in this category may benefit from **psychotherapy**.

See also Male orgasmic disorder

Resources

BOOKS

Lue, Tom F., et al. *Atlas of Clinical Urology: Impotence and Infertility, Volume I*. New York: Current Medicine Group, 1999.

Masters, William, and Virginia Johnson. *Masters and Johnson on Sex and Human Loving*. New York: Little, Brown, 1988.

Steidle, Christopher P. *The Impotence Source Book*. New York: McGraw-Hill, 1999.

Ralph Myerson, M.D.

▌ Premenstrual dysphoric disorder

Definition

Premenstrual dysphoric disorder (PMDD) is a collection of physical and emotional symptoms that occurs 5 to 11 days before a woman's period begins and goes away once menstruation starts. PMDD is a severe form of **premenstrual syndrome** (PMS).

> **KEY TERMS**
>
> **Antidepressant**—A medication used to relieve the symptoms of clinical depression.
>
> **Beta blockers**—Class of drug that primarily works by blunting the action of adrenaline, the body's natural fight-or-flight chemical.
>
> **Nonsteroidal anti-inflammatory drugs**—This class of drugs includes aspirin and ibuprofen, and primarily works by interfering with the formation of prostaglandins, enzymes implicated in pain and inflammation.

Demographics

PMS is estimated to affect 30%–80% of childbearing age. The more severe form of the disorder, PMDD, affects 3–8% of women of childbearing age. Up to 40% of women have PMDD symptoms that are so severe they interfere with their daily activities. Individuals are more at risk if they are in their late 20s and early 40s; have a history of **depression**, alcohol abuse, anxiety/tension, affective lability, or irritability/anger; are overweight; are under **stress**; have a maternal history of the disorder; use significant quantities of caffeine; or do not **exercise**. Clinical studies suggest that more than two million women in the United States may be affected by PMDD.

Description

While PMS is mild or moderate in severity, PMDD is considerably more severe. The symptoms of depressed mood, anxiety, lability, and intense irritability or anger result in significant problems with functioning. Like PMS, menstruation results in resolution of PMDD symptomatology.

Causes and symptoms

Although the actual cause of PMDD is not known, it is believed to be related to hormonal changes that occur before menstruation. The most common symptoms include headache; swelling of ankles, feet, and hands; backache; abdominal cramps; heaviness or pain; bloating and/or gas; muscle spasms; breast tenderness; weight gain; recurrent cold sores; acne; nausea; constipation or diarrhea; food cravings; anxiety or panic; confusion; difficulty concentrating or forgetfulness; poor judgment; and depression.

Diagnosis

PMDD is diagnosed when symptoms occur during the second half of the menstrual cycle (14 days or more after the first day of a woman's period), are absent for about seven days after the period ends, increase in severity as the cycle progresses, go away when the menstrual flow begins or shortly thereafter, and occur for at least three consecutive menstrual cycles. There are no tests to diagnose it. The **diagnosis** of PMDD emphasizes and requires psychologically important mood symptoms.

PMDD was listed in the appendix of the fourth edition of the ***Diagnostic and Statistical Manual of Mental Disorders*** (*DSM-IV*), but it is under consideration for its own listing as a depressive disorder in the forthcoming fifth edition (*DSM-5*), due to be published in 2013. The proposed criteria state that a woman may be diagnosed with PMDD if at least five of the following symptoms occur within a week of the onset of menses, and are minimal or absent by the first week after menses. At least one of the five symptoms must be one of the first four listed to meet the criteria for diagnosis and must be severe enough to interfere with normal work and life activities:

• mood swings, including sudden feelings of sadness or increased sensitivity to rejection

• irritability, anger, or an increase in personal conflicts

• depressed mood, including self-deprecating thoughts or a sense of hopelessness

• anxiety and tension

• reduced interest in activities, such as work, school, or social outings

• trouble concentrating

• fatigue, loss of energy

• change in appetite, including binges or cravings

• changes in sleep patterns

• feeling overwhelmed

• physical symptoms, including breast tenderness or swelling, joint pain, bloating, or weight gain

Treatment

Selective serotonin reuptake inhibitors (**SSRIs**) are used to treat the depressive and anxious symptoms of PMDD. These include **fluoxetine**, **sertraline**, **paroxetine**, **fluvoxamine**, **citalopram**, and **escitalopram**. Additionally, nonsteroidal anti-inflammatory drugs, such as ibuprofen and aspirin, may help with bloating and pain; beta blockers may help with migraines. Women with significant fluid retention (manifested by bloating, breast pain, weight gain) may benefit from the use of diuretics.

In October 2006, the FDA approved the use of the birth control pill YAZ for treating PMDD. YAZ contains a synthetic form of progesterone called drospirenone and estrogen in the form of ethinyl estradiol. Reports indicate that YAZ alleviates both physical and emotional symptoms of PMS and PMDD. In 2011, the FDA issued

---

QUESTIONS TO ASK YOUR DOCTOR

• What types of treatments are available?

• What types of side effects from treatments can I expect? What are your recommendations to help me deal with those side effects?

• Are there any lifestyle changes that I should make? Dietary changes? Changes in activity level?

• What type of diet should I follow? Are there foods I should avoid?

---

a safety alert warning that women taking a newer type of birth control containing the progestin hormone drospirenone may be at higher risk for developing potentially deadly blood clots than women taking pills with an older type of progestin hormone.

Alternative treatment

Nonpharmaceutical treatments include a variety of lifestyle changes, such as following a healthy diet, exercise, sufficient rest, decreased caffeine and alcohol intake, stress-relief therapies, and possibly alternative therapies such as **aromatherapy**. Certain vitamins and supplements may also help, such as vitamin B6, calcium, magnesium, and vitamin E. Some experts also suggest increasing consumption of vitamin D and omega-3 fatty acids. Certain herbs may also help with symptom relief, including vitex, black cohosh, **valerian**, **kava kava**, and **St. John's wort**.

Prognosis

The prognosis varies for each woman, and is largely dependent on how much work she is willing to do in terms of lifestyle changes. Additionally, planning for PMDD symptoms, joining a support group, and communicating with her spouse and family can help minimize the negative effects of PMDD and its impact on a woman's home and work environments.

Prevention

Some women may find their PMDD disappears periodically. Exercise, stress relief strategies, diet, and nutritional supplements can have the greatest impact in preventing PMDD.

Resources

Katz, V. L., et al. *Comprehensive Gynecology*. 5th ed. St. Louis: Mosby, 2007.

WEBSITES

PubMed Health. "Premenstrual Dysphoric Disorder." U.S. National Library of Medicine. http://www.ncbi. nlm.nih.gov/pubmedhealth/PMH0004461 (accessed November 14, 2011).

ORGANIZATIONS

Office on Women's Health, U.S. Department of Health and Human Services, 200 Independence Ave. SW, Washington, DC, 20201, (800) 994-9662; TDD: (888) 220-5446, http://www.womenshealth.gov.

Heidi Splete

Premenstrual syndrome

Definition

Premenstrual syndrome (PMS) refers to symptoms that occur between ovulation and the onset of menstruation. The symptoms include both physical symptoms, such as breast tenderness, back pain, abdominal cramps, headache, and changes in appetite, as well as psychological symptoms of anxiety, **depression**, and unrest. Severe forms of this syndrome are referred to as **premenstrual dysphoric disorder** (PMDD). These symptoms may be related to hormones and emotional disorders.

Demographics

As many as 80% of women report that they experience some change in mood, behavior, and physical sensations or functioning in the time period before the onset of menses, although most women do not find these changes troubling. PMDD affects about 5% to 8% of women between puberty and menopause. About 10% to 40% of all menstruating women have PMS, which means that they experience symptoms that are marked enough to impair relationships, work, or family life but do not have symptoms that are severe enough to warrant a **diagnosis** of PMDD. Although many researchers list these and similar estimates of the prevalence of PMS, others point out that such estimates may be inaccurate because PMS is not a well-defined condition, and because prevalence estimates are usually derived from women's retrospective reports. Retrospective reports are often flawed because of memory distortions. For example, it is possible that some women who experience symptoms throughout the menstrual cycle misremember them as occurring only in the period prior to menstruation.

PMS can begin at any age after menarche or at the time of the first menstrual period. PMS occurs most often in women who ovulate, but women who do not ovulate may also experience it. For example, it may occur in women around the time of menopause, when women sometimes have menstrual periods, even when they do not ovulate. According to the National Women's Health Information Center, PMS is most common in women who are between their late 20s and early 40s, have at least one child, have a family history of depression, and have suffered from depression in the past. Some scientists have suggested that PMS is more likely to occur in women who eat large amounts of chocolate, or women who drink heavily. Women with PMS typically seek medical help for the condition in their 30s.

Description

In their reproductive years, women normally have fluctuations of various hormones over the course of the menstrual cycle. An average menstrual cycle lasts about 28 days, although a normal cycle can range from 21 to 35 days. Many hormones are released into the blood during the menstrual cycle, including estrogen and progesterone. Fluctuations in hormone levels cause changes in the ovaries and the uterus. On around day 14 of a 28-day cycle, an egg is released from the ovaries, in a process called ovulation. After ovulation, the luteal phase of the menstrual cycle begins. The luteal phase lasts about 14 days in a normal 28-day menstrual cycle. If the egg is not fertilized by a sperm, the lining of the uterus is shed in the process called menstruation. The onset of menstruation, or menses, marks the end of the luteal phase. The characteristic features of PMS are physical and emotional symptoms that start in the luteal phase and disappear soon after the onset of menses.

The cluster of symptoms associated with premenstrual syndrome was first described in the scientific literature in 1931, by R.T. Frank, the chief of obstetrics and gynecology at New York's Mt. Sinai Hospital. The term "premenstrual syndrome" was coined in 1953, in an article written by the English physician Katharina Dalton, who believed that PMS was due to a deficiency of the hormone progesterone.

PMS occurs in the middle of a symptom continuum that ranges from premenstrual molimina, or the normal signs heralding the onset of menses, to severe distress and dysfunction. The large majority of women between the ages of menarche and menopause experience physical, emotional, and/or behavioral changes during the time period before the start of menses, but many of them do not find these changes troubling. Women who experience severe symptoms are considered to have premenstrual dysphoric disorder, or PMDD, which was formerly called late luteal phase dysphoric disorder. The *Diagnostic and Statistical Manual of Mental Disorders*, fourth edition (*DSM-IV*), describes PMDD as a condition that warrants further study before being granted the status of a specific disorder, but PMDD is used as a diagnostic category. For a woman to be diagnosed as having PMDD, she must have at least 5 of 11 symptoms, which include sadness, tension, mood swings, irritability, reduced interest in usual activities, difficulty concentrating, **fatigue**, appetite and sleep changes, a sense of being overwhelmed, and physical symptoms such as bloating or pain. At least one of the symptoms must be a mood symptom, and symptoms have to be present for most days during the luteal period for most months in the past year. Symptoms must remit shortly after the onset of menses.

Women who experience symptoms that are troubling enough to affect relationships, work, or family life but whose symptoms do not meet the criteria for PMDD are considered to have PMS. PMS is not listed as a psychiatric disorder in the *DSM-IV*. According to the tenth edition of the *International Statistical Classification of Diseases and Related Health Problems*, *ICD-10*, a diagnosis of PMS can be made even if only one distressing symptom is present. The American College of Obstetricians and Gynecologists guidelines for diagnosing PMS require at least one symptom to be present in the five days preceding the menses for three consecutive menstrual cycles.

Some people criticize the characterization of PMS as a disorder. They point out that PMS is not well defined and that many women experience PMS symptoms. They fear that making PMS into a disorder stigmatizes women in general and makes women subject to negative portrayals in popular culture. Women are described as "PMSing," aggressive, hostile, and crazy, and are the frequent targets of jokes about the effects of the menstrual cycle. The idea that women are strongly influenced by their menstrual cycles can have an impact on their professional lives, even though there is little evidence that PMS impairs task performance. Some people even suggest that the promotion of PMS as a disorder is attributable to a profit motive. They claim that the concept of PMS exists partly because it is financially beneficial for hospitals and clinics to provide treatments for PMS, even though many of these treatments are ineffective or unproved.

Others advocate defining PMS as a disorder. They argue that PMS is a significant burden for many women, and that women with PMS are relieved to have the condition recognized as a real problem, rather than have it be dismissed as the product of an overactive imagination.

Symptoms

Symptom type can vary from menstrual cycle to cycle, as can symptom severity. The PMS symptoms most commonly reported by women are bloating, irritability, and difficulty sleeping. Other symptoms include breast discomfort, headaches, swelling of hands or feet, back pain, joint or muscle aches, fatigue, lapses in memory, decreased interest in sex, angry outbursts, restlessness, difficulty concentrating, confusion, depression, anxiety, social withdrawal, and cravings for sweet or salty foods and caffeine.

Causes

The causes of PMS are unclear. Scientists have put forward many theories to explain the etiology of PMS, including low levels of the hormone progesterone, changes in the ratio of the hormone estrogen to progesterone, increases in the activity of the adrenal gland, too much of the hormone prolactin, decreased endorphins, and too little prostaglandin, among others. Research does not provide consistent support for any of these theories.

However, most scientists do agree that abnormal levels of the neurotransmitter **serotonin**, or abnormal bodily responses to serotonin, may be involved in PMS. The fluctuations of hormones during the menstrual cycle may have an effect on serotonin function, but the details of the mechanisms involved are still unclear. Evidence for the involvement of serotonin in PMS comes from the fact that PMS and PMDD have many symptoms in common with disorders such as depression, which involve abnormalities related to serotonin levels. Also, many women with PMDD and PMS find that symptoms are alleviated when they take **selective serotonin reuptake inhibitors (SSRIs)**, which are antidepressant drugs that increase the levels of serotonin available to nerve cells.

Because there are many different kinds of PMS symptoms and many different etiological theories with partial support, some researchers speculate that there may be more than one form and multiple causes of PMS.

Diagnosis

There are no laboratory tests for diagnosing PMS, because the cause of the condition is unknown. A diagnosis of PMS is typically made only after a woman has kept a record of daily symptoms over the course of the menstrual cycle for at least three months. This allows women to determine whether their symptoms occur only during the luteal phase of the cycle or at other times as well.

A diagnosis of PMDD is given only after ruling out the possibility of a premenstrual increase in the symptoms of another disorder. Some women with general medical conditions such as seizure disorders, endocrine dysfunctions, cancer, systemic lupus erythematosus, anemia, endometriosis, and some kinds of infections may experience higher levels of negative mood and fatigue during the premenstrual period. Some women with psychological disorders, such as depression, **anxiety disorders**, **bulimia nervosa**, substance use problems, and **personality disorders**, may also experience exacerbations of their symptoms during the premenstrual period. These women, however, experience symptoms throughout the menstrual cycle, unlike women with PMS, who only experience symptoms during the luteal phase.

Treatment

Treatments for PMS include lifestyle changes, drug therapy, nutritional supplements, and herbal remedies.

Traditional

Changes in lifestyle, rather than drug therapy, are recommended for women who experience mild PMS. For many women, regular **exercise** alleviates PMS symptoms. One theory suggests that a decrease in endorphin levels in the late luteal phase may result in premenstrual symptoms. Exercise causes endorphins to be released, which may help to alleviate the depressive symptoms that some women with PMS experience. Twenty to thirty minutes of aerobic exercise at least three days a week are recommended.

Because **stress** can exacerbate PMS, taking steps to reduce work and family stress, especially in the premenstrual period, can be helpful. Women who experience PMS may find it helpful to avoid scheduling stressful activities on days when they expect to have symptoms. Dealing with issues at work and within relationships that produce conflict may also be helpful, because achieving a sense of control can reduce stress.

Although some researchers point out that there is no evidence that dietary changes can alleviate PMS, others recommend keeping dietary salt levels low to prevent fluid retention and bloating, and reducing caffeine intake to alleviate breast discomfort and reduce jitteriness.

Drugs

The main pharmacological agents used to treat PMS are **SSRIs**, antianxiety medications, drugs that induce chemical menopause, hormones, and oral contraceptives.

The U.S. Food and Drug Administration (FDA) has approved the use of the SSRIs **fluoxetine** and **sertraline** for the treatment of PMDD. Although the FDA has not approved these drugs for PMS, reports indicate that they are helpful for treating PMS. The dose that is prescribed for PMDD and PMS is typically smaller than that used to treat depression. SSRIs typically take two to four weeks before they begin to have an effect on the symptoms of depression, but they alleviate the symptoms of PMS and PMDD in a much shorter time, usually in one or two days. For depression, intermittent dosing with SSRIs is not usually effective, but for PMS and PMDD SSRIs are effective when taken daily only during the luteal phase of the menstrual cycle.

Studies show that SSRIs are not effective for about 40% of women with PMDD. These results may indicate that hormones and **neurotransmitters** other than serotonin are also implicated in PMDD.

Some practitioners report that **alprazolam** is effective for alleviating the anxiety that some women with PMS experience. Alprazolam is a benzodiazepine drug that is sold under the brand name Xanax. Other reports indicate that alprazolam is not an effective treatment for negative premenstrual mood symptoms and that it can also impair task performance. In addition, the use of alprazolam can lead to **addiction**.

Chemically inducing menopause is an effective way of eliminating PMS and PMDD, but because this treatment has many side effects, it is only used as a last resort. Drugs such as leuprolide, which is sold under the brand name Lupron, are used to induce chemical menopause. Leuprolide is similar to a gonadotropin-releasing hormone, a hormone naturally released by the **brain**. Leuprolide reduces estrogen production by the ovaries. Because low estrogen can lead to problems such as thinning of bones, estrogen is sometimes administered to women who take drugs like Lupron, to reduce side effects such as osteoporosis and hot flashes. However, estrogen add-back therapy is very expensive and may result in the return of PMS symptoms.

In the 1950s, the English physician Katharina Dalton treated many women with PMS by giving them supplements of the hormone progesterone. She reported that progesterone was effective in alleviating symptoms in these women. More recent research in the United States has not confirmed Dalton's results. Despite this, gynecologists still sometimes prescribe progesterone for PMS, because some women report benefits. Natural progesterone, or synthetic progesterone in the form of drugs such as Provera, may be used. Progesterone injections can be given in the form of Depo-Provera, which is a contraceptive. A dose of injected Depo-Provera lasts for three months. It prevents women from getting periods. The drug has a sedative effect on some women and so alleviates premenstrual anxiety. The drug can, however, have negative side effects, including bleeding or spotting, depression, and weight gain.

Some women with PMS find that symptoms are alleviated when they take a low-dose birth control pill, although, for unknown reasons, other women actually have worsening of symptoms when they use oral contraceptives. In October 2006, the FDA approved the use of the birth control pill YAZ for treating PMDD. YAZ contains a synthetic form of progesterone called drospirenone and estrogen in the form of ethinyl estradiol. Reports indicate that YAZ alleviates both physical and emotional symptoms of PMS. In 2011 the FDA issued a safety alert warning that women taking a newer type of birth control containing the progestin hormone drospirenone may be at higher risk for developing potentially deadly blood clots than women taking pills with an older type of progestin hormone.

Alternative

Some health practitioners suggest using nutritional and herbal supplements, selected to treat the primary symptoms experienced, although their effectiveness in alleviating PMS is controversial. Some nutritional supplements and herbs can be toxic or may interact with medications. There are varying dosage recommendations for many of these supplements in the scientific literature. For these reasons, women should consult with their physicians before using such substances.

For fluid retention problems, diuretic therapy with 25 mg of spironolactone twice a day is sometimes recommended. Spironolactone is sold under the trade name Aldactone. Other reports indicate that a spironolactone supplement of 100 mg per day improves both the physical and mood symptoms of PMS. Using a calcium supplement of 1,200–1,500 mg daily also appears to reduce PMS symptoms in some women. Some practitioners recommend using vitamin B6 supplements of 50–100 mg daily, but others recommend a higher dose. Vitamin B6 is a natural diuretic and may help to reduce bloating. Furthermore, vitamin B6 appears to suppress the action of prolactin, which is a hormone that may be involved in PMS. Vitamin B6 may also play a role in the metabolism of serotonin, which appears to be involved in PMS. A Vitamin E supplement of about 400–600 units a day is sometimes suggested for helping to alleviate breast discomfort. Daily supplements of magnesium appear to reduce symptoms related to fluid retention such as weight gain, breast tenderness, swelling of hands and feet, and abdominal bloating. Dose recommendations vary from 200–600 mg daily.

Some practitioners report that women who use **evening primrose oil** find that it occasionally alleviates PMS symptoms, although others report that studies have not demonstrated its effectiveness. Evening primrose is a plant that has a fatty acid essential to the body, called gamma-linoleic acid. Some researchers have speculated that gamma-linoleic acid may help PMS symptoms by raising the levels of prostaglandin in the body. Other oils that contain gamma-linoleic acid are borage oil, black currant oil, and rapeseed oil.

The Mexican wild yam (*Dioscorea villosa*) contains a substance that may be converted to progesterone in the body. Because this substance is readily absorbed through

---

KEY TERMS

Adrenal gland—A gland that produces many different hormones, including estrogen, progesterone, and stress hormones.

Anemia—A condition in which red blood cells do not supply enough oxygen to body tissues.

Benzodiazepine—A class of antianxiety drugs.

Bulimia nervosa—An eating disorder in which binge eating is followed by inappropriate and often dangerous efforts to control body weight.

Contraceptive—A method that prevents conception and pregnancy.

Endocrine dysfunction—A problem relating to inadequate or excessive production of hormones.

Endometriosis—A condition in which the tissue that is normally present in the lining of the uterus grows elsewhere in the body.

Endorphin—A neurotransmitter that acts like a natural opiate, relieving pain and producing euphoria.

Gonadotropin-releasing hormone—A hormone produced by the brain that stimulates the pituitary gland to release hormones that trigger ovulation.

Luteal phase—The period of time between ovulation and menstruation.

Menarche—The first menstrual period.

Menopause—The cessation of menstrual periods.

Neurotransmitter—A chemical that sends signals from one nerve cell to another.

Osteoporosis—The thinning of bone and loss of bone density.

Personality disorder—A chronic pattern of behaving and relating to others that causes significant distress and impairs functioning.

Premenstrual molimina—The normal signs that indicate that menses will soon occur.

Prostaglandin—A chemical produced in the body, which is involved in many functions, including blood pressure regulation and inflammation.

Systemic lupus erythematosus—A chronic, inflammatory autoimmune disorder.

---

the skin, it can be found as an ingredient in many skin creams. (Some products also have natural progesterone added to them.) Some herbalists believe that these products can have a progesterone-like effect on the body and decrease some of the symptoms of PMS.

The most important way to alter hormone levels may be by eating more phytoestrogens. These plant-derived compounds have an effect similar to estrogen in the body. One of the richest sources of phytoestrogens is soy products, such as tofu. Additionally, many supplements can be found that contain black cohosh (*Cimicifugaracemosa*) or dong quai (*Angelica sinensis*), which are herbs high in phytoestrogens. Red clover (*Trifolium pratense*), alfalfa (*Medicago sativa*), licorice (*Glycyrrhiza glabra*), hops (*Humulus lupulus*), and legumes are also high in phytoestrogens. Increasing the consumption of phytoestrogens is also associated with decreased risks of osteoporosis, cancer, and heart disease.

Many **antidepressants** act by increasing serotonin levels. An alternative means of achieving this is to eat more carbohydrates. For instance, two cups of cereal or a cup of pasta have enough carbohydrates to effectively increase serotonin levels. An herb known as **St. John's wort** (*Hypericum perforatum*) has stood up to scientific trials as an effective antidepressant. As with the standard antidepressants, however, it must be taken continuously and does not show an effect until used for 46 weeks. There are also herbs, such as skullcap (*Scutellaria lateriflora*) and kava (*Piper methysticum*), that can relieve the anxiety and irritability that often accompany depression. An advantage of these herbs is that they can be taken when symptoms occur rather than continually. Chaste tree (*Vitex agnus-castus*) in addition to helping rebalance estrogen and progesterone in the body, also may relieve the anxiety and depression associated with PMS.

The only alternative therapy that has shown clinical promise in reducing symptoms of PMS is calcium. Regular and increased calcium intake appears to alleviate and even prevent PMS symptoms in women; however, the calcium must be ingested from food sources and not from supplements. Evidence for all other nutritional or herbal therapies is conflicting. Patients should always discuss taking supplements with their physicians before beginning treatment.

Prevention

Maintaining a good diet, one low in sugars and fats and high in phytoestrogens and complex carbohydrates, may prevent some of the symptoms of PMS. Women should try to exercise three times a week, keep in generally good health, and maintain a positive self image. Avoidance of caffeine and/or alcohol may help some women. Because PMS is often associated with stress, avoidance of stress or developing better means to deal with stress can be important.

Prognosis

Women who have PMS typically experience symptoms throughout their reproductive years, except during pregnancy. In some women, PMS can become more severe around the time of menopause, in the perimenopausal time period. PMS generally remits after menopause.

Resources

BOOKS

American Psychiatric Association. *Diagnostic and Statistical Manual of Mental Disorders*. 4th ed., text rev. Washington, DC: American Psychiatric Publishing, 2000.

Minkin, Mary Jane, and Carol V. Wright. *The Yale Guide to Women's Reproductive Health From Menarche to Menopause*. New Haven, CT: Yale University Press, 2003.

Ratcliff, Kathryn Strother. *Women and Health: Power, Technology, Inequality and Conflict in a Gendered World*. Upper Saddle River, NJ: Prentice-Hall, 2008.

Speroff, Leon, and Marc A. Fritz. *Clinical Gynecologic Endocrinology and Infertility*. 7th ed. Philadelphia: Lippincott Williams & Wilkins, 2010.

PERIODICALS

Clayton, A.H., et al. "Exploratory Study of Premenstrual Symptoms and Serotonin Variability." *Archives of Women's Mental Health* 9, no. 1 (January 2006): 51–57.

Hudson, Tori. "Premenstrual Syndrome: A Review of Herbal and Nutritional Supplements." *Townsend Letter for Doctors and Patients* 270 (January 2006): 126–31.

Mishell, Daniel R. "Premenstrual Disorders: Epidemiology and Disease Burden." *American Journal of Managed Care* 11, no. 16 Suppl. (2005): S473–79.

Rapkin, Andrea J. "New Treatment Approaches for Premenstrual Disorders." *American Journal of Managed Care* 11, no. 16 Suppl. (December 2005): S480–91.

Strine, Tara W., Daniel P. Chapman, and Indu B. Ahluwalia. "Menstrual-Related Problems and Psychological Distress among Women in the United States." *Journal of Women's Health* 14, no. 4 (May 2005): 316–23.

Yonkers, Kimberly A. "Management Strategies for PMS/PMDD." *Journal of Family Practice* 53, no. 9 (September 2004): SS15–20.

WEBSITES

Drugs.com. "FDA Approves New Indication for YAZ to Treat Emotional and Physical Symptoms of Premenstrual Dysphoric Disorder (PMDD)." October 5, 2006. http://www.drugs.com/news/fda-approves-yaz-emotional-physical-premenstrual-dysphoric-disorder-1929.html (accessed October 23, 2011).

MEDgle Patient GPS.com. "Premenstrual Syndrome." July 24, 2011. http://www.medgle.com/rw/diagnoses/premenstrual+syndrome (accessed October 23, 2011).

ORGANIZATIONS

American College of Obstetricians and Gynecologists, PO Box 96920, Washington, DC, 20090-6920, (202) 638-5577, http://www.acog.org.

The Hormone Foundation, 8401 Connecticut Ave., Ste. 900, Chevy Chase, MD, 20815-5817, (800) 467-6663, Fax: (301) 941-0259, hormone@endo-society.org, http://www.hormone.org.

National Institute of Mental Health, 6001 Executive Blvd., Room 8184, MSC 9663, Bethesda, MD, 20892-9663, (301) 433-4513; TTY: (301) 443-8431, Fax: (301) 443-4279, (866) 615-6464; TTY: (866) 415-8051 nimhinfo@nih.gov, http://www.nimh.nih.gov.

National Women's Health Information Center, 8270 Willow Oaks Corporate Drive, Ste. 101, Fairfax, VA, 22031, (800) 994-9662, http://www.womenshealth.gov.

Ruvanee Pietersz Vilhauer, PhD

Prescription drug abuse

Definition

Prescription drug abuse is the use of medicine prescribed by a doctor in dosages other than the prescribed dosage; for reasons other than the symptoms for which it was prescribed; by a person other than for whom it was prescribed; or as a recreational drug.

Demographics

According to the National Institute on Drug Abuse (NIDA), the abuse of prescription drugs and over-the-counter medications in the United States more than doubled between 1999 and 2009. More than 7 million Americans were abusing prescription drugs in 2010, according to the National Survey on Drug Use and Health.

Prescription drugs are abused most often by adolescents and young adults in their twenties. In youths aged 12–17, girls are more likely than boys to abuse prescription drugs; the rate is about even in adults. In young people, prescription drug abuse often is recreational. In this group, there is a correlation between **alcohol use**, other types of drug abuse, risky sexual behavior, and prescription drug abuse.

Description

The three categories of prescription drugs that are the most abused are opioid pain relievers, central nervous system depressants prescribed as **sedatives** or tranquilizers, and stimulants used to treat **attention deficit hyperactivity disorder (ADHD)**.

Opioids

Opioids are narcotic pain-relieving drugs that block certain receptors in the **brain** and reduce the individual's perception of pain. Morphine, the first medical opioid, is a natural product derived from the sap of the opium poppy. Today most opioid drugs with medical uses are synthetic compounds that act in ways similar to morphine. Commonly prescribed opioids include codeine, hydrocodone (Vicodin),

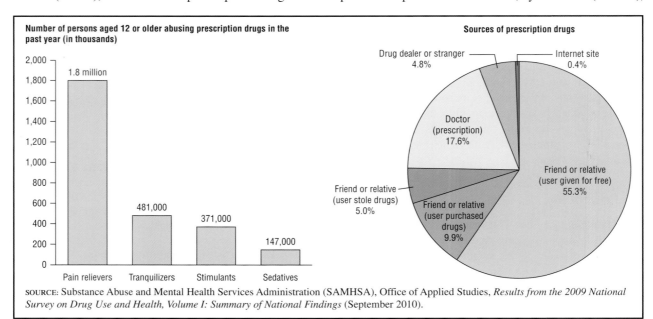

Number of persons aged 12 or older abusing prescription drugs in the past year (in thousands)

- Pain relievers: 1.8 million
- Tranquilizers: 481,000
- Stimulants: 371,000
- Sedatives: 147,000

Sources of prescription drugs

- Friend or relative (user given for free) 55.3%
- Doctor (prescription) 17.6%
- Friend or relative (user purchased drugs) 9.9%
- Friend or relative (user stole drugs) 5.0%
- Drug dealer or stranger 4.8%
- Internet site 0.4%

SOURCE: Substance Abuse and Mental Health Services Administration (SAMHSA), Office of Applied Studies, *Results from the 2009 National Survey on Drug Use and Health, Volume I: Summary of National Findings* (September 2010).

Report available online at http://oas.samhsa.gov/NSDUH/2k9NSDUH/2k9Results.htm. *(Graphs by PreMediaGlobal. © 2012 Cengage Learning.)*

methadone, oxycodone (OxyContin), meperidine (Demerol), propoxyphene (Darvon), hydromorphone (Dilaudid), and fentanyl (Fentora). Of these, hydro-codone, oxycodone, and codeine are the most fre-quently abused. Heroin, another drug in this group, is commonly abused but has no medical use and is never prescribed.

Opioids are very effective in controlling pain. Side effects include drowsiness and constipation. When taken exactly as prescribed, opioids are rarely addictive. When abused, opioids can be physically addictive and tolerance can develop. Large doses can depress breathing and cause death.

In people with a genuine medical need for pain control, abuse can develop by taking a larger or more frequent dose than prescribed. However, most abuse arises from recreational drug use. This is especially true of oxycodone, hydrocodone, and codeine. OxyContin and Vicodin, for example, are tablets that can be crushed into a powder and snorted or dissolved in water and injected. This practice is particularly dangerous as it quickly exposes the abuser to high levels of the drug. Overdoses can be fatal. Codeine usually is taken orally. It is a common component of prescription cough syrups and is found in combination tablets with acetaminophen (e.g., Tylenol with codeine).

Many opioid abusers get their drugs from friends or family members who have had legitimate prescriptions for the drugs but have unused drugs remaining after treatment. Others go prescription shopping, visiting several doctors and claiming severe pain symptoms for which they receive multiple prescriptions for an opioid drug. In some cases, these drugs are bought without a prescription over the Internet from suppliers in countries where a prescription is not required. Opioids also are sold as street drugs.

Central nervous system depressants

Central nervous system (CNS) depressants are prescribed as sedatives and tranquilizers to treat **sleep disorders** and anxiety. Commonly abused drugs in this category include **barbiturates** such as mephobarbital (Mebaral) and sodium phenobarbital (Nebutal); **benzo-diazepines** such as **diazepam** (Valium), **alprazolam** (Xanax), and **estazolam** (Prosom), which are used to treat anxiety; and sleep medications such as **zolpidem** (Ambien), **zaleplon** (Sonata), and eszopiclone (Lunesta). Both barbiturates and benzodiazepine have a fairly high potential for physical **addiction**. The newer sleep medications have less potential to be physically addictive.

CNS depressants increase the amount of a neuro-transmitter in the brain called gamma-aminobutyric acid (GABA). This produces a feeling of calm and drowsiness, which is what makes these drugs effective in treating anxiety and **insomnia**. CNS depressants usually are taken orally (tablets or capsules) and are sometimes taken to counteract the effect of illicit stimulant drugs. Taken with alcohol, these drugs are especially dangerous, as alcohol also is a CNS depressant. Overdose, especially in combination with alcohol, can be fatal. People who take CNS depressants for a long time and then suddenly stop taking them can have withdrawal symptoms and **seizures**. Many people who abuse CNS depressants get them by prescription shopping or from family and friends.

Stimulants

Stimulant prescription drugs are used to treat **ADHD**, **narcolepsy**, and sometimes **depression** that is unrespon-sive to other drug therapies. Stimulant drugs increase alertness, attention, and energy. Common stimulant drugs of abuse include **dextroamphetamine** (Dexedrine), **methylphenidate** (Ritalin, Concerta), and the amphet-amine Adderall. Prescription stimulants are particularly popular among high school and college students who use them to increase concentration and energy when studying. These drugs also are used to get high.

Although stimulants increase focus and concentration by increasing the level of the neurotransmitter **dopamine** in the brain, they also can have serious side effects including increased blood pressure, irregular heartbeat, increased body temperature, insomnia, irritability, and seizures. Heart failure is possible, especially when these drugs are mixed with antidepressant drugs or over-the-counter cold medications containing decongestants.

Many prescription stimulants are acquired through a legitimate prescription and then abused in the way they are taken. Alternately, people who have no medical need for the drugs buy them from friends with legitimate prescriptions. Ritalin and Adderall abuse are especially common on college campuses. **Amphetamines** also can be bought as street drugs, and in some cases prescription stimulant drugs can be ordered through the Internet from countries where prescriptions are not required.

Causes and symptoms

The number of prescriptions written for common drugs of abuse has undergone an eight-fold increase in the past 20 years. Some experts believe that intensive drug advertising on television and in magazines has encouraged patients to ask their doctors for prescriptions for specific drugs, especially pain medicines and sleep aids. In addition, Internet pharmacies have made it easier to acquire these drugs without a proper medical examination and prescription.

KEY TERMS

Attention deficit hyperactivity disorder (ADHD)—A learning and behavioral disorder characterized by difficulty in sustaining attention, impulsive behavior, and excessive activity.

Central nervous system (CNS)—Part of the nervous system consisting of the brain, cranial nerves, and spinal cord. The brain is the center of higher processes, such as thought and emotion and is responsible for the coordination and control of bodily activities and the interpretation of information from the senses. The cranial nerves and spinal cord link the brain to the peripheral nervous system, which consists of the nerves present in the rest of body.

Dopamine—A neurochemical made in the brain that is involved in many brain activities, including movement and emotion.

Narcolepsy—A disorder in which the individual can fall into a deep sleep without warning.

Narcotic—A drug derived from opium or compounds similar to opium. Such drugs are potent pain relievers and can affect mood and behavior. Long-term use of narcotics can lead to dependence and tolerance.

Neurotransmitter—One of a group of chemicals secreted by a nerve cell (neuron) to carry a chemical message to another nerve cell, often as a way of transmitting a nerve impulse. Examples of neurotransmitters include acetylcholine, dopamine, serotonin, and norepinephrine.

Tolerance—A decrease in sensitivity to a drug. When tolerance occurs, a person must take more and more of the drug to get the same effect.

The reasons people abuse prescription drugs are varied but include:

- an attempt to eliminate pain (opioids)
- to increase concentration and focus (stimulants)
- to treat insomnia (CNS depressants)
- to relieve anxiety (CNS depressants)
- to get high
- because they believe prescription drugs, unlike street drugs, to be safe

Behaviors that suggest prescription drug abuse include:

- stealing or forging prescriptions
- stealing drugs from the medicine cabinets of family or friends

- repeatedly claiming to have lost a prescription so that another must be written
- visiting multiple doctors for the same symptoms and getting prescriptions from each one
- an increase in extreme mood swings
- changes in sleep patterns
- changes in energy level
- increased irritability

Diagnosis

Diagnosis can be difficult. Doctors may become alerted to prescription drug abuse through behaviors such as requesting replacement for "lost" prescriptions or early renewal of prescriptions. In other cases, a family member may suggest prescription drug abuse is occurring. Finally there may be physical signs of drug abuse. These will vary depending on the type of drug being abused.

Examination

A complete medical history, especially a medication history, and a physical examination are the starting point of a diagnosis of prescription drug abuse. Blood and urine tests can identify some drugs of abuse, although they are often more helpful in monitoring progress toward recovery than in making an initial diagnosis. Often, however, the patient or a patient's family member will express concern about prescription drug usage that will initiate a conversation leading to a diagnosis of drug abuse.

Treatment

There are two approaches to treatment: drug therapy and **psychotherapy**. For best results, these therapies often are used together. Treatment must take into account the type of drug used, the length of use, the health status of the individual, abuse of other substances such as alcohol or illicit drugs, the mental health status of the individual, and his or her life circumstances.

No single type of treatment is right for all prescription drug abusers. Physically addicted individuals should be in a supervised **detoxification** program. Serious negative health consequences and withdrawal symptoms may occur if the individual simply stops taking the drug of abuse on his or her own initiative.

Drugs

Of the three major categories of abused prescription drugs, only opioids can be treated with drugs. **Naltrexone** is a medication that blocks the effects of opioids drugs. It is used most often to treat overdoses. Serious physical opioid addiction can be treated with methadone or buprenorphine (Buprenex, Subutex) to relieve withdrawal symptoms and help prevent drug cravings. Methadone is a synthetic opioid that eliminates withdrawal symptoms. It is often used to treat heroin addiction but under some circumstances may used to treat addiction to other opioids. Buprenorphine treatment has not been well studied in relation to prescription drug addiction. Both methadone and buprenorphine are tightly controlled and are not be available from all doctors.

No drug therapy exists to treat CNS depressant addiction or prescription stimulant addiction. Nevertheless, some drugs may be used to help stabilize mood swings during withdrawal. It is especially important that people who are addicted to barbiturates or benzodiazepines be treated in a supervised detoxification program. Use of these drugs must be reduced gradually (tapered) to prevent serious health consequences.

Psychotherapy

Group or individual **cognitive-behavioral therapy** and **family therapy** often are used to treat individuals addicted to any type of drug. Cognitive behavioral therapy helps individuals understand the factors that trigger prescription drug abuse and to replace negative behaviors with positive ones. Family therapy helps families deal with underlying tensions in family relationships and to accept and deal with relapses.

Prognosis

Recovery depends on the type and strength of drug the individual is abusing and the length of time the drug has been abused. Relapses are common. Another problem in treating prescription drug addiction involves exchanging one addictive drug for another—for example, eliminating sedative dependence but replacing it with alcohol dependence. The greatest chance of complete recovery comes with early and intensive treatment, with family involvement or other support.

Prevention

The following tips can help prevent prescription drug abuse:

• Take all drugs in the amount and at the time intervals prescribed.

• Properly discard all unused prescription medicines.

• Do not share prescriptions or use drugs prescribed for another person, even if that person shares the same symptoms.

• Monitor children's or teen's prescription drug use.

Resources

BOOKS

Colvin, Rod. *Overcoming Prescription Drug Addiction: A Guide to Coping and Understanding.* 3rd ed. Omaha, NE: Addicus Books, 2008.

WEBSITES

Mayo Clinic. "Prescription Drug Abuse." June 25, 2010. http://www.mayoclinic.com/print/prescription-drug-abuse/DS01079 (accessed October 23, 2011).

MedlinePlus. "Prescription Drug Abuse." U.S. National Library of Medicine, National Institutes of Health. October 19, 2011. http://www.nlm.nih.gov/medlineplus/prescriptiondrugabuse.html (accessed October 23, 2011).

U.S. National Institute on Drug Abuse. "Prescription Drug Abuse." May 2011. http://drugabuse.gov/tib/prescription.html (accessed October 23, 2011).

U.S. National Institute on Drug Abuse. "Prescription Drugs: Abuse and Addiction." http://www.nida.nih.gov/ResearchReports/Prescription/prescription7.html (accessed October 23, 2011).

ORGANIZATIONS

Drug Enforcement Administration, Mailstop AES, 8701 Morrissette Drive, Springfield, VA, 22152, (800) 882-9539, http://www.justice.gov.

National Council on Alcoholism and Drug Dependence, Inc., 244 East 58th Street, 4th Fl., New York, NY, 10022, (212) 269-7797, Fax: (212) 269-7510, http://www.ncadd.org.

National Institute on Drug Abuse, 6001 Executive Blvd., Room 5213, Bethesda, MD, 20892-9561, http://www.nida.nih.gov.

The Partnership at Drugfree.org, 352 Park Ave. South, 9th Floor, New York, NY, 10010, (212) 922-1560, Fax: (212) 922-1570, http://www.drugfree.org.

Tish Davidson, AM

Presenile dementia *see* **Alzheimer's disease**

Primary hypersomnia *see* **Hypersomnia**

Primary insomnia *see* **Insomnia**

Pristiq *see* **Desvenlafaxine**

Problem-solving skills training *see* **Cognitive problem-solving skills training**

Process addiction

Definition

A process **addiction**, also known as behavioral addiction, is the repetitive occurrence of impulsive behaviors regardless of the negative consequences the behaviors may trigger.

Demographics

Adolescence is a period of critical vulnerability in the development of addiction, for both cultural and neurobiological reasons. Age at onset for kleptomania is not known, but it is usually before adulthood, and two-thirds of people with kleptomania are female. Pyromania is both extremely rare and understudied, and no one has established the range of age at onset. The best-studied process addiction is pathological gambling, and its demographics can vary based on environmental factors, including proximity to a gambling location and exposure to gambling. It is more prevalent among males, and rates can be as high as 8% among adolescents and college-age students. The little research done thus far on Internet addiction suggests that it can affect any age or socioeconomic group.

Description

Process or behavioral addiction became a focus of study in the 1980s and 1990s. Researchers hypothesized that changes wrought in the brain's reward system by certain substances (e.g., **cocaine**) and leading to substance use problems or addiction may also underlie the exercise of dysfunctional, directed behaviors that have negative consequences. In other words, the addictions may differ in nature (a process like gambling versus taking a substance like cocaine), but the end result in the brain/body is the same. To paraphrase one researcher, the **brain** does not care whether or not the reward comes from a chemical stimulus or from an experience.

Many of the behaviors listed in the *Diagnostic and Statistical Manual of Mental Disorders,* fourth edition, text revision (also known as the *DSM-IV-TR*) as "Impulsive-Compulsive, Not Elsewhere Classified," may fall under the umbrella of process addiction. An essential feature of an impulse disorder is the inability to resist engaging in an act that can harm the individual or others. For most, if not all, of these disorders, the act or behavior is preceded by a feeling of tension or anticipation. The behavior itself brings on a feeling of pleasure, gratification, or relief, and following the behavior, the person may or not feel regret or self-reproach.

In addition to the impulsive nature of the behaviors, there is also a pattern of behavioral addiction. The features of this group of disorders include the urge to engage in a behavioral sequence that has negative consequences or is counterproductive; a feeling of increasing tension as the execution of the behavior approaches; a resurgence of the urge after a lapse of hours, days, or weeks; and the presence of external cues for the behavior that vary and are specific to a particular behavioral addiction. These patterns are similar to those manifested in substance addiction and can be classified as addictions because they have the same components as substance/chemical addictions, including mood modification, tolerance, withdrawal, and **relapse**.

Among this group of impulsive-compulsive behaviors that may also be classified as behavioral addictions are pathological gambling, **kleptomania**, **pyromania**, **trichotillomania** (recurrent pulling out of one's own hair), compulsive buying, and compulsive sexual behavior. The suite of disorders may also include compulsive Internet/computer use. Of these disorders, pathological gambling has received the most attention and study. These disorders may ultimately be included in a new category in the *DSM-5,* called "Substance and Behavioral Addictions." This category is under review to include pathological gambling, kleptomania, pyromania, and disorders currently listed under "Impulsive-Compulsive Behaviors Not Otherwise Specified," along with compulsive buying and impulsive-compulsive sex behavior.

Causes and symptoms

Causes

Being the child of a person who has an impulsive disorder such as pathological gambling may be a risk factor. Early onset of alcohol or drug use can exacerbate the severity of process addiction, and this pattern also holds true at least for pathological gambling. Adolescence is a critically vulnerable time, primarily because the brain areas affected as addiction develops are immature and susceptible. The immaturity may lead to a greater level of impulsive behaviors.

There have been some genetic links indicated in studies of pathological gambling and compulsive buying.

The mechanism underlying addiction involves disruptions in **serotonin** and **dopamine** signaling and monoamine oxidase (MAO) activity. The MAO gene lies on the X chromosome, which can result in the observed sex differences in some behavioral addiction disorders. Males, who have only one X chromosome, express only the gene their single X chromosome carries; females have two X chromosomes, and having one normal version of MAO on one X chromosome can compensate for having a mutant version on the other chromosome.

Symptoms

Dopamine is a neurotransmitter involved in reward pathways in the brain and in the development or reinforcement of behaviors. This molecule and its associated proteins have been strongly implicated in **substance abuse** and behavioral addiction. People with process addiction may share many symptoms with people who have substance use disorders, including **depression**, loneliness, social impairment, and distraction.

Some symptoms are specific to a given behavior. For example, in impulsive-compulsive sex behavior, the person may have frequent, intrusive thoughts about sex and engage repeatedly in sex behaviors that may spiral out of their control.

Some criteria have been proposed for considering a behavior an addiction. These include the level of significance certain cues have for the person, the manifestation of withdrawal symptoms, tolerance (i.e., the need to engage in the behavior more or longer for the same effect), relapse, and mood modification. According to the World Health Organization and the **American Psychological Association**, another criterion is loss of control.

Diagnosis

These behaviors, although listed as different disorders in the *DSM-IV-TR,* share a suite of similar diagnostic features. These features include failure to resist the associated impulse (e.g., gambling or stealing), feelings of tension before engaging in the behavior, and a feeling of pleasure or relief when the behavior is being performed.

Comorbidities

The specific behavioral or process addiction of pathological gambling has been associated with high rates of psychiatric comorbidity and mortality, one of many similarities between substance and process addictions. There is a frequent co-occurrence of some behavioral addictions with depression, **suicide** attempts, and anxiety.

Association with substance abuse

There are substantial similarities between a disorder like pathological gambling and substance use disorder, from the comorbidities to personality features, behavioral measures, and neurobiological observations; substance use disorder and behavioral or process addiction often occur together. For example, low serotonin levels have been identified in people with pathological **gambling disorder** and in people with alcohol dependency. There is the phenomenon of "cross priming," in which the development of an addiction to a substance primes an individual's neural circuitry for susceptibility to a process

addiction; for example, amphetamine use might prime a person biochemically for developing a gambling problem. Among pathological gamblers, as many as 70% people addicted to gambling are addicted to **nicotine**, 50%–70% have alcohol problems, and up to 40% have problems with abuse of other drugs.

The converse is that people who have substance use disorders can be up to 10 times more likely also to have a pathological gambling problem, and there are similar relationships between substance use disorder and kleptomania or compulsive buying. Compulsive sexual behavior and substance use disorder occur together in 25% and 71% of cases, respectively.

Treatment

As with substance abuse, **denial** can be a key characteristic of the behavior in process addiction, and any treatment begins with recognition and acknowledgment of the problem.

Pharmacologic approaches

The medical establishment is still in the early stages of developing and applying pharmacological treatment for process addiction. **Selective serotonin reuptake inhibitors (SSRIs)** have proven beneficial in some studies, but not in others. More effective, at least for pathological gambling and kleptomania, are opioid antagonists like **naltrexone** and nalmefene. The efficacy of these drugs may result from the interaction of the opioid system with dopamine signaling pathways.

Pharmacological treatments can be based on comorbidities. For example, if **obsessive-compulsive disorder**, depression, or anxiety are present, SSRIs may be effective. Mood stabilizers might be efficacious if **bipolar disorder** is present, and if **attention deficit hyperactivity disorder** (ADHD) is a comorbidity, stimulants or inhibitors of dopamine or noradrenaline reuptake (MAO-B inhibitors) may be beneficial.

Benzodiazepines can actually reduce inhibitions even more but are not recommended except in emergency situations.

Therapeutic approaches

The 12-step programs (e.g., Gamblers Anonymous) are enormously popular and well recognized, but their dropout rates are high and few studies have established their level of effectiveness. Other therapeutic approaches can involve **cognitive-behavioral therapy**, motivational interviewing, or **relapse prevention**, all based on approaches used for substance use disorders. The

KEY TERMS

Dopamine—A neurotransmitter involved in the reward pathways in the brain.

MAO-B inhibitors—Inhibitors of dopamine or noradrenaline reuptake by monoamine oxidase.

SSRI—Selective serotonin reuptake inhibitor.

Trichotillomania—Recurrent pulling out of one's own hair.

therapeutic approach may also need to be disorder specific; for example, for impulsive-compulsive sexual behavior, **couples therapy** may be warranted.

Prognosis

These disorders are considered to be chronic, and relapses in those that have been reasonably well studied, such as pathological gambling, are common. However, at least in the case of pathological gambling, appropriate treatment can help in management of the disorder.

Prevention

Prevention is based on decreased exposure to targets of process addiction; for example, little or no exposure to gambling can be helpful to people at risk. Early **intervention** may also be preventative.

Resources

BOOKS

American Psychiatric Association. *Diagnostic and Statistical Manual of Mental Disorders*. 4th ed., text rev. Washington, DC: American Psychiatric Publishing, 2000.

PERIODICALS

Grant, Jon E., Judson A. Brewer, and Marc N. Potenza. "The Neurobiology of Substance and Behavioral Addictions." *CNS Spectrum* 11, no. 12 (December 2006): 924–930.

Lobo, Daniela S.S., and James L. Kennedy. "The Genetics of Gambling and Behavioral Addictions." *CNS Spectrum* 11, no. 12 (December 2006): 931–939.

Mick, Thomas M., and Eric Hollander. "Impulsive-Compulsive Sexual Behavior." *CNS Spectrum*. 11, no. 12 (December 2006): 944–955.

Pallanti, Stefano. "From Impulse-control Disorders Toward Behavioral Addictions." *CNS Spectrum* 11, no. 12 (December 2006): 921–922.

Pallanti, Stefano, Silvia Bernardi, and Leonardo Quercioli. "The Shorter PROMIS Questionnaire and the Internet Addiction Scale in the Assessment of Multiple Addictions in a High-school Population: Prevalence and Related Disability." *CNS Spectrum* 11, no. 12 (December 2006): 966–974.

WEBSITES

American Psychological Association. "Addictions." http://www.apa.org/topics/addiction/index.aspx (accessed October 24, 2011).

MedlinePlus. "Pathological Gambling." U.S. National Library of Medicine, National Institutes of Health. http://www.nlm.nih.gov/medlineplus/ency/article/001520.htm (accessed October 24, 2011).

ORGANIZATIONS

American Psychiatric Association, 1000 Wilson Blvd., Ste. 1825, Arlington, VA, 22209-3901, (703) 907-7300, apa@psych.org, http://www.psych.org.

Gamblers Anonymous, International Service Office, PO Box 17173, Los Angeles, CA, 90017, (626) 960-3500, Fax: (626) 960-3501, isomain@gamblersanonymous.org, http://www.gamblersanonymous.org.

Sex Addicts Anonymous, ISO of SAA, PO Box 70949, Houston, TX, 77270.info@saa-recovery.org, http://saa-recovery.org.

Emily Jane Willingham, Ph.D.

Program of Assertive Community Treatment (PACT) *see* **Assertive community treatment**

Prolixin *see* **Fluphenazine**

Propranolol

Definition

Propranolol is classified as a beta blocker. It is sold in the United States under the brand name Inderal. When combined with the diuretic, hydrochlorothiazide, it is sold under the brand name Inderide. Propranolol also is

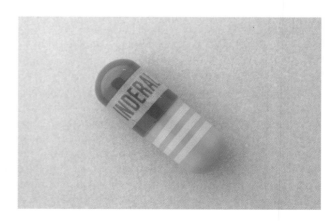

Inderal (propranolol), 120 mg. (© *Custom Medical Stock Photo, Inc. Reproduced by permission.*)

produced as a generic product by a number of generic manufacturers.

Purpose

Propranolol is approved by the U.S. Food and Drug Administration (FDA) for the treatment of hypertension (high blood pressure), angina, certain types of cardiac arrhythmias, certain types of cardiac output diseases, a sympathetic nervous system disorder known as pheo-chromocytoma, hyperthyroid conditions, heart attack, and tremors of a variety of origins. It is also used in the prevention of migraine headaches and on occasion for the treatment of **medication-induced movement disorders** caused by antipsychotic drugs and certain anxiety states in people suffering from a specific form of **social phobia**. **Beta blockers**, such as propranolol, are not useful for people with general social phobia who are anxious in most social situations; instead, propranolol may be more useful for people who are anxious about specific performance situations, such as presenting a speech before an audience.

Description

Propranolol falls into the broad pharmacologic category known as beta blockers. Beta blockers block specific sites in the central nervous system known as beta-adrenergic receptor sites. When these sites are blocked, heart rate and blood pressure are reduced and patients become less anxious. Because of this, propranolol is useful in treating chest pain, high blood pressure, and excessive nervousness. Unfortunately, propranolol often makes breathing disorders, such as asthma, worse because it tends to constrict breathing passages and sometimes causes fluid to build up in the lungs if it excessively depresses the heart.

In the treatment of anxiety, propranolol is usually not administered on a chronic basis but, rather, prior to stressful events such as public speaking or acting. In the treatment of certain types of tremors, especially tremors secondary to a drug, and **movement disorders** second-ary to antipsychotic therapy, propranolol is administered throughout the day in divided doses. Propranolol is available in 10, 20, 40, 60, and 80 mg tablets; in 60, 80, 120, and 160 mg long-acting capsules; and in an injectable form containing 1 mg per mL. It is also combined with the diuretic hydrochlorothiazide in tablets and extended-release capsules.

Recommended dosage

For the treatment of performance anxiety or stage fright, a single dose of 10–40 mg may be administered

---

KEY TERMS

Beta blocker—Drugs that block beta-adrenergic receptors on neurons in the central nervous system. When these sites are blocked, heart rate, blood pressure, and anxiety levels decrease.

Brachycardia—Slow heartbeat, defined as a rate of less than 60 beats per minute.

Diuretic—An agent that increases the amount of urine; often used to decrease fluid retention in bodily tissues.

Epinephrine (adrenaline)—The principal blood pressure–raising hormone and a relaxant of the bronchial and intestinal smooth muscles; pre-scribed to (among other things) stimulate the heart and as a muscle relaxant in bronchial asthma.

Glaucoma—A group of eye diseases characterized by increased pressure within the eye significant enough to damage eye tissue and structures. If untreated, glaucoma results in blindness.

Hypotension—Low blood pressure.

Ischemia—Localized anemia of tissues due to obstructed inflow of blood.

Laryngospasm—Spasms that close the vocal appa-ratus of the larynx (the organ of voice production).

Neurotransmitter—One of a group of chemicals secreted by a nerve cell (neuron) to carry a chemical message to another nerve cell, often as a way of transmitting a nerve impulse.

Norepinephrine (noradrenaline)—A hormone with similar stimulatory effects to epinephrine but, in contrast to epinephrine, has little effect on cardiac (heart) output and in relaxing smooth muscles.

Raynaud's syndrome—A disorder of the circula-tory or vascular system characterized by abnor-mally cold hands and feet because of constricted blood vessels in these areas.

Thrombocytopenia—A condition involving abnor-mally low numbers of platelets (blood-clotting agents) in the blood; usually associated with hemorrhaging (bleeding).

20–30 minutes before the event. For the treatment of tremors, especially tremors secondary to lithium, doses range from 20 to 160 mg per day administered in two or three divided doses. For the treatment of movement disorders secondary to antipsychotic drug therapy, doses range from 10 to 30 mg three times daily.

Precautions

Precautions should be taken when administering propranolol in the following situations:

- liver or renal (kidney) failure
- prior to screening tests for glaucoma
- a history of immediate allergic reaction (known as anaphylaxis) to a beta blocker of any kind

In addition, a person taking propranolol should never suddenly stop taking the drug because of the risk of chest pain or heart attack in some people who do so.

Side effects

The following side effects have been observed with propranolol. Most have been mild and transient and rarely require the withdrawal of therapy:

- cardiovascular: brachycardia, congestive heart failure, hypotension, Raynaud's syndrome
- central nervous system: light-headedness, mental depression, insomnia, vivid dreams, disorientation, memory loss
- gastrointestinal: nausea, vomiting, abdominal pain, cramping, diarrhea, constipation, bowel ischemia
- allergic: fever, rash, laryngospasm, thrombocytopenia
- respiratory: bronchospasm
- hematologic: bone marrow suppression, bleeding under the skin

Interactions

Interactions with drugs that deplete the body of the **neurotransmitters** epinephrine and norepinephrine have been reported with concomitant propranolol. This group includes reserpine and guanethidine. Fainting, hypotension, dizziness, and slow heart rate have occurred under these circumstances. Drugs known as calcium channel blockers may decrease the pumping ability of the heart and lead to the development of cardiac arrhythmias. Nonsteroidal anti-inflammatory agents (e.g., ibuprofen and naproxen) may blunt the blood pressure–lowering effects of propranolol. Aluminum hydroxide antacids greatly reduce the rate of absorption of propranolol, as does alcohol. Interactions have also been reported with the drugs phenytoin, rifampin, phenobarbital, **chlorpromazine**, lidocaine, thyroxin, cimetidine, and theophylline.

Resources

BOOKS

Physicians' Desk Reference 2011. 66th ed. Montvale, NJ: PDR Network, 2011.

Springhouse. *Nursing 2003 Drug Handbook.* Springhouse, PA: Lippincott, Williams and Wilkins, 2002.

Venes, Donald. *Taber's Cyclopedic Medical Dictionary.* 21st ed. Philadelphia: F.A. Davis Company, 2009.

WEBSITES

MedlinePlus. "Propranolol Oral." U.S. National Library of Medicine, National Institutes of Health.http://www.nlm.nih.gov/medlineplus/druginfo/meds/a682607.html (accessed November 13, 2011).

DailyMed. "Inderal La (propranolol hydrochloride) Capsule, Extended Release." U.S. National Library of Medicine, National Institutes of Health. http://dailymed.nlm.nih.gov/dailymed/drugInfo.cfm?id=6143 (accessed October 24, 2011).

ORGANIZATIONS

U.S. Food and Drug Administration, 10903 New Hampshire Ave., Silver Spring, MD, 20993-0002, (888) INFO-FDA (463-6332), http://www.fda.gov.

Ralph Myerson, MD
Emily Jane Willingham, PhD

Prosom *see* **Estazolam**

Protriptyline

Definition

Protriptyline is an oral tricyclic antidepressant. It is sold in the United States under the brand name Vivactil and is also available under its generic name.

Purpose

Protriptyline is used primarily to treat **depression** and to treat the combination of symptoms of anxiety and depression. Like most **antidepressants** of this chemical

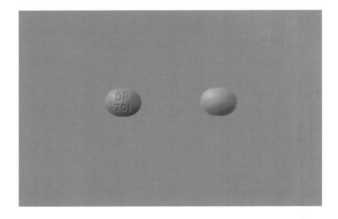

Vivactil (protriptyline). *(Teva Pharmaceuticals USA, Inc.)*

and pharmacological class, protriptyline has also been used in limited numbers of patients to treat **panic disorder**, **obsessive-compulsive disorder**, **attention deficit hyperactivity disorder**, **enuresis** (bed-wetting), eating disorders such as **bulimia nervosa**, **cocaine** dependency, and the depressive phase of **bipolar disorder**; it has also been used to support **smoking cessation** programs. However, not all of these uses are approved by the U.S. Food and Drug Administration (FDA).

Description

Tricyclic antidepressants act to change the balance of naturally occurring chemicals in the **brain** that regulate the transmission of nerve impulses between cells. Protriptyline acts primarily to increase the concentration of norepinephrine and **serotonin** (both chemicals that stimulate nerve cells) and, to a lesser extent, to block the action of another brain chemical, acetylcholine. Protriptyline shares most of the properties of other tricyclic antidepressants, such as **amitriptyline**, **clomipramine**, **desipramine**, **imipramine**, **nortriptyline**, and **trimipramine**. Studies comparing protriptyline with these other drugs have shown that protriptyline is no more or less effective than other antidepressants of its type. Its choice for treatment is as much a function of physician preference as any other factor.

The therapeutic effects of protriptyline, like those of other antidepressants, appear gradually. Maximum benefit is often not evident for at least two weeks after starting the drug. People taking protriptyline should be aware of this and continue taking the drug as directed even if they do not see immediate improvement.

Recommended dosage

As with any antidepressant, protriptyline must be carefully adjusted by the physician to produce the desired therapeutic effect. Protriptyline is available as 5 mg and 10 mg tablets. Doses range from 15 to 40 mg per day and can be taken in one daily dose or divided into up to four doses daily. Some patients with severe depression may require up to 60 mg per day.

In people over age 60, therapy should be initiated at a dose of 5 mg three times a day and increased under supervision of a physician as needed. Patients over age 60 who are taking a daily doses of 20 mg or more should be closely monitored for side effects such as rapid heart rate and urinary retention.

Precautions

Antidepressants have been associated with an increased risk of patients up to age 24 harming themselves or attempting or committing suicide. The FDA has advised that such drugs should not be administered to children under the age of 18. Patients of any age should be monitored carefully for signs of intention to commit self-harm or attempt **suicide** when taking antidepressants. These symptoms can develop suddenly and include new or worsening depression, talk about self-harm or suicide, agitation to panic attacks, aggression, and changes in sleep patterns.

Like all tricyclic antidepressants, protriptyline should be used cautiously and with close physician supervision in people, especially the elderly, who have benign prostatic hypertrophy, urinary retention, and glaucoma, especially angle-closure glaucoma (the most severe form). Before starting treatment, people with these conditions should discuss the relative risks and benefits of treatment with their doctors to help determine if protriptyline is the right antidepressant for them.

A common problem with tricyclic antidepressants is sedation (drowsiness and lack of physical and mental alertness). This side effect is especially noticeable early in therapy. In most patients, sedation decreases or disappears entirely with time, but until then patients taking protriptyline should not perform hazardous activities requiring mental alertness or coordination. The sedative effect is increased when protriptyline is taken with other central nervous system depressants, such as alcoholic beverages, sleeping medications, other **sedatives**, or antihistamines. It may be dangerous to take protriptyline in combination with these substances. Protriptyline may increase the possibility of having **seizures**. Patients should tell their physician if they have a history of seizures, including seizures brought on by the abuse of drugs or alcohol. These people should use protriptyline only with caution and be closely monitored by their physician.

Protriptyline may increase heart rate and stress on the heart. It may be dangerous for people with cardiovascular disease, especially those who have recently had a heart attack, to take this drug or other antidepressants in the same pharmacological class. In rare cases where patients with cardiovascular disease must take protriptyline, they should be monitored closely for cardiac rhythm disturbances and signs of cardiac stress or damage.

Side effects

Protriptyline shares side effects common to all tricyclic antidepressants. The most frequent of these are dry mouth, constipation, urinary retention, increased heart rate, sedation, irritability, dizziness, and decreased coordination. As with most side effects associated with tricyclic antidepressants, the intensity is highest at the

KEY TERMS

Acetylcholine—A naturally occurring chemical in the body that generally produces effects that are the opposite of those produced by dopamine and norepinephrine. Central nervous system well-being is dependent on a balance among acetylcholine, dopamine, serotonin, and norepinephrine.

Anticholinergic—Related to the ability of a drug to block the nervous system chemical acetylcholine. When acetylcholine is blocked, patients often experience dry mouth and skin, increased heart rate, blurred vision, and difficulty urinating. In severe cases, blocking acetylcholine may cloud thinking and cause delirium.

Benign prostate hypertrophy—Enlargement of the prostate gland.

Norepinephrine—A neurotransmitter in the brain that acts to constrict blood vessels and raise blood pressure. It works in combination with serotonin.

Serotonin—A widely distributed neurotransmitter that is found in blood platelets, the lining of the digestive tract, and the brain, and that works in combination with norepinephrine. It causes very powerful contractions of smooth muscle, and is associated with mood, attention, emotions, and sleep. Low levels of serotonin are associated with depression.

beginning of therapy and tends to decrease with continued use.

Dry mouth, if severe to the point of causing difficulty speaking or swallowing, may be managed by dosage reduction or temporary discontinuation of the drug. Patients may also chew sugarless gum or suck on sugarless candy in order to increase the flow of saliva. Some artificial saliva products may give temporary relief.

Men with prostate enlargement who take protriptyline may be especially likely to have problems with urinary retention. Symptoms include having difficulty starting a urine flow and more difficulty than usual passing urine. In most cases, urinary retention is managed with dose reduction or by switching to another type of antidepressant. In extreme cases, patients may require treatment with bethanechol, a drug that reverses this particular side effect. People who think they may be experiencing any side effects from this or any other medication should tell their physicians.

Interactions

Dangerously high blood pressure has resulted from the combination of tricyclic antidepressants, such as protriptyline, and members of another class of antidepressants known as **monoamine oxidase inhibitors** (MAOIs). Because of this, protriptyline should never be taken in combination with MAOIs. Patients taking any MAOIs, for example **phenelzine** (Nardil) or **tranylcypromine** (Parnate), should stop taking the MAOI and wait at least 14 days before starting protriptyline or any other tricyclic antidepressant. The same holds true when discontinuing protriptyline and starting an MAOI.

Protriptyline may decrease the blood pressure–lowering effects of **clonidine**. Patients who take both drugs should be monitored for loss of blood-pressure control, and the dose of clonidine should be increased as needed.

The sedative effects of protriptyline are increased by other central nervous system depressants such as alcohol, sedatives, sleeping medications, or medications used for other mental disorders such as **schizophrenia**. The anticholinergic effects of protriptyline are additive with other anticholinergic drugs such as **benztropine**, **biperiden**, **trihexyphenidyl**, and antihistamines.

Resources

BOOKS

American Society of Health-System Pharmacists. *AHFS Drug Information 2008*. Bethesda, MD: American Society of Health-System Pharmacists, 2008.

DeVane, C. Lindsay, Pharm.D. "Drug Therapy for Mood Disorders." In *Fundamentals of Monitoring Psychoactive Drug Therapy*. Baltimore: Williams and Wilkins, 1990.

WEBSITES

MedlinePlus. "Protriptyline." U.S. National Library of Medicine, National Institutes of Health. http://www.nlm.nih.gov/medlineplus/druginfo/meds/a604025.html (accessed November 13, 2011).

U.S. Food and Drug Administration. "Antidepressant Use in Children, Adolescents, and Adults." http://www.fda.gov/Drugs/DrugSafety/InformationbyDrugClass/ucm096273.htm (accessed October 24, 2011).

U.S. Food and Drug Administration. "Historical Information on Antidepressant Use in Children, Adolescents, and Adults." http://www.fda.gov/Drugs/DrugSafety/InformationbyDrugClass/ucm096293.htm (accessed October 24, 2011).

ORGANIZATIONS

National Institute of Mental Health, 6001 Executive Blvd., Rm. 8184, MSC 9663, Bethesda, MD, 20892-9663, (301) 433-4513; TTY: (301) 443-8431, Fax: (301) 443-4279,

(866) 615-6464; TTY: (866) 415-8051, nimhinfo@nih. gov, http://www.nimh.nih.gov.

U.S. Food and Drug Administration, 10903 New Hampshire Ave., Silver Spring, MD, 20993-0002, (888) INFO-FDA (463-6332), http://www.fda.gov.

Jack Raber, Pharm.D.
Emily Jane Willingham, PhD

Prozac *see* **Fluoxetine**

Pseudocyesis

Definition

Pseudocyesis is the medical term for a false pregnancy. Pseudocyesis can cause many of the signs and symptoms of pregnancy, and often resembles the condition in every way except for the presence of a fetus.

Demographics

The rate of pseudocyesis in the United States has declined significantly in the past century. In the 1940s there was one occurrence for approximately every 250 pregnancies. This rate has since dropped to between one and six occurrences for every 22,000 births. The average age of the affected woman is 33, though cases have been reported for women as young as six-and-a-half and as old as 79. More than two-thirds of women who experience pseudocyesis are married, and about one-third have been pregnant at least once. Women who have been victims of incest may be at greater risk for developing pseudocyesis. Although pseudocyesis is overwhelmingly a disorder of females, there have been at least three reported cases of males with it. Pseudocyesis is found in some mammals other than humans, most often cats, dogs, and rabbits. In these animals, researchers have found that prolactin, the hormone that produces mammalian milk, plays a role in the development of the false pregnancy.

Description

Pseudocyesis has been observed and written about since antiquity. Hippocrates set down the first written account around 300 B.C., and recorded 12 different cases of women with the disorder. One of the most famous historical examples is Mary Tudor (1516–1558), Queen of England, who believed twice that she was pregnant when she was not. Some even attribute the violence that gave her the nickname "Bloody Mary" as a reaction to the disappointment of finding out that she was not carrying a child. Other historians believe that the queen's physicians mistook fibroid tumors in her uterus for a pregnancy, as fibroids can enlarge a nonpregnant uterus. She retired to her chambers for 14 months for the first false pregnancy, only to emerge humiliated, without a child. On the second occasion, the cause of her symptoms may have been advanced ovarian cancer, which some medical historians believe eventually killed her.

Pseudocyesis has become increasingly rare in many parts of the world in which accurate pregnancy tests have become widely available. Cultures that place high value on pregnancy, or that make close associations between fertility and a person's worth, still have high rates of the disorder.

Causes and symptoms

Causes

No single theory about the causes of pseudocyesis is universally accepted by mental health professionals. The first theory attributes the false pregnancy to emotional conflict. It is thought that an intense desire to become pregnant, or an intense fear of becoming pregnant, can create internal conflicts and changes in the endocrine system, which may explain some of the symptoms of pseudocyesis. The second theory concerns wish fulfillment. It holds that if a women desires pregnancy badly enough she may interpret minor changes in her body as signs of pregnancy. The third leading theory is the **depression** theory, which maintains that chemical changes in the nervous system associated with some depressive disorders could trigger the symptoms of pseudocyesis.

Symptoms

The symptoms of pseudocyesis are similar to the symptoms of true pregnancy and are often hard to distinguish from the natural signs of pregnancy such as morning sickness, tender breasts, and weight gain. Many health care professionals can be deceived by the symptoms associated with pseudocyesis. Eighteen percent of women with pseudocyesis were at one time diagnosed as pregnant by a medical professional. In some cases the only difference between pregnancy and pseudocyesis is the presence of a fetus.

The sign of pseudocyesis that is common to all cases is that the affected patient is convinced that she is pregnant. Abdominal distension is the most common physical symptom of pseudocyesis, and 63%–97% of women with pseudocyesis experience it. The abdomen expands in the same manner as it does during pregnancy, so that the affected woman looks pregnant. This phenomenon is thought to be caused by buildup of gas, fat, feces, or urine. These symptoms often resolve under general anesthesia, and the woman's abdomen returns to its normal size.

KEY TERMS

Cervix—The neck or narrow lower end of the uterus. Softening of the cervix is one of the signs of pregnancy.

Distension—The condition of being stretched or expanded, as the abdomen of a pregnant woman.

Quickening—A term that refers to the movements or other signs of life of a fetus in the womb.

The second most common physical sign of pseudocyesis is menstrual irregularity (56–98% of women with the disorder experience this). Between 48% and 75% of women are also reported to experience the sensation of fetal movements known as quickening, even though there is no fetus present. Some of the other common signs and symptoms include gastrointestinal symptoms, breast changes or secretions, labor pains, uterine enlargement, and softening of the cervix. One percent of women eventually experience false labor. In addition, some women actually test positive on pregnancy tests.

Treatment

Because pseudocyesis is not known to have a direct underlying physical cause, there are no general recommendations regarding treatment with medications. In some cases, however, the patient may be given medications for such symptoms as the cessation of menstruation. Because most patients with pseudocyesis have underlying psychological problems, they should be referred to a psychotherapist for the treatment of these problems. At the same time, however, it is important for the treating professional not to minimize the reality of the patient's physical symptoms.

The use of ultrasound or other imaging techniques has had the most success is demonstrating to the patient that she is not really pregnant.

Alternative therapies

There have been reports of patients being cured of pseudocyesis by hypnosis, purgatives, massage, **opioids**, or by experiencing "hysterical childbirth" after nine months of symptoms, but few data are available on the effectiveness of these or similar procedures.

Prognosis

Symptoms of pseudocyesis generally last from a few months to a few years. In most cases, symptoms last for a full nine months. Treatments involving **psychotherapy** have high success rates, as they treat the underlying psychological causes of the disorder.

Resources

BOOKS

Knobil, Ernst, and Jimmy D. Neill, eds. *Encyclopedia of Reproduction.* New York: Elsevier, 1998.

Sadock, Benjamin J., and Virginia A. Sadock, eds. *Comprehensive Textbook of Psychiatry.* Vol. 2. 7th ed. Philadelphia: Lippincott Williams and Wilkins, 2000.

PERIODICALS

Aldrich, Knight. "Sixteenth-Century Psychosomatics." *Psychiatric News.* American Psychiatric Association. April 16, 1999. http://www.psychiatricnews.org/pnews/99-04-16/history.html (accessed October 24, 2011).

Hendricks-Matthews, Marybeth K., and Douglas M. Hoy. "Pseudocyesis in an Adolescent Incest Survivor." *Journal of Family Practice* 36, no. 1, (January 1993): 97–104.

Paulman, Paul M., and Abdul Sadat. "Pseudocyesis." *Journal of Family Practice* 30, no. 5, (May 1990): 575–82.

Tish Davidson, A.M.
Emily Jane Willingham, PhD

Psychiatric assessment *see* **Psychological assessment and diagnosis**

Psychiatrist

Definition

A psychiatrist is a physician who specializes in the **diagnosis** and treatment of mental disorders.

Description

Psychiatrists treat patients privately and in hospital settings through a combination of **psychotherapy** and medication. Their training consists of four years of medical school, followed by three or four years of psychiatric residency. Subspecialities usually involve completion of a fellowship that lasts two or more years following the residency. Psychiatrists may receive certification from the American Board of Psychiatry and Neurology (ABPN), which requires two years of clinical experience beyond residency and the successful completion of a written and an oral test. Unlike a medical license, board certification is not legally required to practice psychiatry.

Psychiatrists may practice general psychiatry or choose a specialty, such as child psychiatry, geriatric psychiatry, treatment of **substance abuse**, forensic (legal) psychiatry, emergency psychiatry, intellectual disabilities, community psychiatry, or public health. Some focus their research and clinical work primarily on psychoactive medication, in which case they are referred to as psychopharmacologists. Psychiatrists may be called upon to address numerous social issues, including juvenile delinquency, family and marital dysfunction, legal competency in criminal and financial matters, and treatment of mental and emotional problems among prison inmates and in the military.

Psychiatrists treat the biological, psychological, and social components of mental illness simultaneously. They can investigate whether symptoms of mental disorders have physical causes, such as a hormone imbalance or an adverse reaction to medication, or whether psychological symptoms are contributing to physical conditions, such as cardiovascular problems and high blood pressure. Because they are licensed physicians, psychiatrists—unlike psychologists and psychiatric social workers—can prescribe medication; they are also able to admit patients to the hospital. Other mental health professionals who cannot prescribe medication themselves often establish a professional relationship with a psychiatrist.

Psychiatrists may work in private offices, private psychiatric hospitals, community hospitals, state and federal hospitals, or community mental centers. Often, they combine work in several settings. In addition to their clinical work, psychiatrists often engage in related professional activities, including teaching, research, and administration. The **American Psychiatric Association**, the oldest medical specialty organization in the United States, supports the profession by offering continuing education and research opportunities, keeping members informed about new research and public policy issues, helping to educate the public about mental health issues, and serving as an advocate for people affected by mental illness.

ORGANIZATIONS

American Psychiatric Association, 1000 Wilson Blvd., Ste. 1825, Arlington, VA, 22209-3901, (703) 907-7300, apa@psych.org, http://www.psych.org.

American Board of Psychiatry and Neurology, 2150 E Lake Cook Rd., Ste. 900, Buffalo Grove, IL, 60089, (847) 229-6500, Fax: (847) 229-6600, http://www.abpn.com.

Emily Jane Willingham, PhD

Psychoanalysis

Definition

Psychoanalysis, as a form of therapy, is based on the understanding that human beings are largely unaware of the mental processes that determine their thoughts, feelings, and behavior, and that psychological suffering can be alleviated by making those processes known to the individual. Psychoanalysis is practiced by a trained psychoanalyst, also referred to as an analyst.

Purpose

Primary goals of psychoanalysis include symptom relief, increased self-awareness, and a more objective capacity for self-observation. Other aims might include improved relationships with others and the capacity to live a more deeply satisfying life. Typically, an individual seeks treatment in order to alleviate some difficulty, such as unhappiness in work or love, disturbances in mood or self-esteem, or troubling personality traits. With the exception of those that are physically based, psychoanalysis views such symptoms as related to unconscious mental processes, and because these mental forces are not within the individual's awareness, symptoms cannot be relieved with perseverance or with the help of friends or family. Through a slowly unfolding process, psychoanalysis demonstrates to the individual how unconscious mental processes affect current modes of thinking, feeling and interacting with others. It also demonstrates that these processes can be traced back to early experiences and relationships with caregivers and family members. This kind of insight enables individuals to identify the sources of their, sometimes, troubling thoughts, feelings and behavior and, as a result, gives new meaning to current modes of functioning. Generally, this type of transformation of character takes several years to accomplish due to the intense nature of the process. It requires a sacrifice of time, money, and mental energy. The resulting transformation offers the means for adaptive, enduring changes in personality. These are changes that enable the individual to live a more productive, satisfying, and pleasurable life.

Description

Austrian neurologist Sigmund Freud (1856–1939) originally developed the theory and technique of psychoanalysis in the 1890s. As such, it is sometimes also called Freudian psychology. Freud's ideas are still used in contemporary practice; however, many have been further developed or refined, and some even abandoned.

ERICH FROMM (1900–1980)

Erich Fromm was born in Frankfurt-am-Main, Germany, the son of Naphtali Fromm, a wine merchant, and Rosa Krause. Throughout his career, Fromm strove toward an understanding of human existence based upon the breaking down of barriers—between individuals as well as between schools of thought. In a *Los Angeles Times* obituary of the famous psychologist, a reviewer summarizes: "Fromm's lifelong concern was how people could come to terms with their isolation, insignificance and doubts about life's meaning." As his theories developed over the decades into what would later be collectively labeled "social humanism," he incorporated knowledge and information culled from such diverse fields as Marxist socialism and Freudian psychology. The psychologist used these schools of thought as building blocks for developing original theories that, like his idiosyncratic life, often ran against popular beliefs. As a psychologist, he diverged from the Freudian school, in which the unconscious was the main factor in understanding human actions, by pointing out the importance of the influence of social and economic factors.

Most of Fromm's work was an application of psychoanalysis, sociology philosophy, and religion to the peculiar problems of man in modern industrialize society. In *Escape from Freedom,* he postulated that "modern man, freed from the bonds of pre-individualistic society, which simultaneously gave him security and limited him, has not gained freedom in the positive sense of the realization of his individual self; that is, the expression of his intellectual, emotional and sensuous potentialities. Freedom, though it has brought him independence and rationality, has made him isolated and, thereby, anxious and powerless." This problem, the individual's tenuous relationship to institutions and society, became the core of such later works as *Man for Himself: An Enquiry into the Psychology of Ethics and The Sane Society.*

Fromm's penultimate book, *To Have or To Be?*, presents "the viewpoint and challenge of radical humanistic psychoanalysis," explains Paul Roazen in *Nation.* The volume has been seen as the culmination of Fromm's work at that time and maintains, according to a publisher's note, "that two modes of existence are struggling for the spirit of humankind; the having mode, which concentrates on material possession, acquisitiveness, power, and aggression and is the basis of such universal evils as greed, envy, and violence; and the being mode, which is based in love, in the pleasure of sharing, and in meaningful and productive rather than wasteful activity. Dr. Fromm sees the having mode bringing the world to the brink of psychological and ecological disaster, and he outlines a program for socio-economic change [to] turn the world away from its catastrophic course."

One such post-Freudian theory is called interpersonal psychoanalysis, which was developed primarily by Erich Fromm, Frieda Fromm-Reichmann, and Clara Thompson. It delves into interpersonal interactions; specifically, the way people handle negative emotions, such as anxiety, and their interactions with others as they deal with such emotions.

The theory and technique of psychoanalysis continues to integrate new insights about human development and behavior based on psychoanalytic research and discoveries from related fields. Different schools of psychoanalytic theory have evolved out of the original Freudian one, reflecting a variety of ideas and perspectives.

In psychoanalysis, an individual in treatment is seen four to five times per week for 45- to 50-minute sessions. The individual lies comfortably on a couch while the analyst sits in a chair behind the person, out of view. The person is then asked to say whatever comes into his or her mind. Although this structure varies depending on the theory and style of the analyst, this is the most typical and traditional manner in which sessions are conducted. These conditions are maintained consistently, making it possible for thoughts and feelings to emerge that had once been outside of the person's awareness. The process of free associating, or saying whatever comes to mind, is challenging because people are taught at a young age to keep many ideas and feelings to themselves. When the analyst is out of view, it removes the possibility for eye contact, making it easier to speak spontaneously. Free association is also made easier by the analyst's nonjudgmental attitude—in listening to the individual, in the attention and interest given to seemingly unimportant details, and in the objective and caring attitude with which the analyst understands the individual.

As the person speaks, unconscious sources of present-day difficulties gradually emerge. Specifically, the analyst begins to notice repetitive aspects of behavior. Some of them may include particular subjects about which the person finds it hard to speak, as well as habitual ways in which the person relates to the psychoanalyst. The analyst begins to reveal these to the person in a gradual and thoughtful manner. Sometimes these revelations are accepted as correct and helpful. At other times they are rejected, corrected, or refined.

During the years of an analysis, the individual will grapple with new insights repeatedly, each time comprehending them in new ways. There will be an enhanced emotional and intellectual understanding, in addition to seeing matters from the perspective of different periods of life. As in all worthwhile learning processes, this one includes times of deep satisfaction and great frustration, periods of growth and regression. Overall, the analyst and individual work together to modify debilitating life patterns, to ameliorate troubling symptoms, and to release emotional and intellectual resources bound up in unconscious psychological processes. A transformation will occur eventually, and be one in which the person's understanding of themselves and of others, along with their productivity in work and capacity to love, changes in profound and enduring ways.

Psychoanalysis is used at times with other forms of treatment. Medication may be warranted in selected situations—if an individual suffers from a severe mood disturbance which interferes with his or her capacity to participate in treatment, for example. In general, medication is used as a tool that allows the individual to benefit from the psychoanalytic process; it is an adjunct therapy, while psychoanalysis is the primary curative one. There are also occasions in which psychoanalysis is provided concurrently with **couples therapy** or **family therapy** or with **group therapy**. Treatment recommendations, whether for psychoanalysis alone or in combination with couples, family, or group therapy, are based both on the individual's particular needs and the practice of the treating psychoanalyst.

Finally, psychoanalysis is not only a type of therapy. It is also a theory of human development from infancy to old age, a method for understanding thought processes. It offers a way of thinking about aspects of society and culture such as religion, prejudice, and war.

Benefits

Anyone interested should seek a consultation with a psychoanalyst in order to determine if this treatment is appropriate. People often begin psychoanalysis after having also participated in psychoanalytic **psychotherapy**, which is a less intense form of treatment.

QUESTIONS TO ASK YOUR DOCTOR

- Can I benefit from psychoanalysis?
- Should I use psychoanalysis with other forms of treatment?
- Does my health insurance pay for psychoanalysis?
- How to I find a qualified and experienced psychoanalyst?
- What happens if psychoanalysis does not help me?
- Will I need medication in addition to psychoanalysis? If so, what kind of medicine, and why?

Individuals who are the most suited for psychoanalysis are those who have experienced satisfactions in work, with friends, in marriage, but who nonetheless experience a general dissatisfaction with their life—suffering from long-standing **depression**, anxiety, sexual difficulties, physical symptoms without physical basis, or typically feel isolated or alone. Some people need analysis because their habitual ways of living interfere with experiencing greater pleasure or productivity in life. Individuals need to be psychologically minded with an interest in becoming more self-aware, and a determination to forgo quick symptom relief in favor of a more gradual therapeutic process.

Psychoanalysis is also practiced with children and adolescents, with some variation in technique. Specifically, fantasy play and drawings are used with children in addition to verbal communication. During the treatment of children and young adolescents, parents are consulted on a regular basis so that the analyst can develop a more holistic understanding of the youngster's world. The goal of child and adolescent psychoanalysis is to alleviate symptoms and to remove any obstacles that interfere with normal development.

Precautions

The term "psychoanalyst" can be used by anyone in the psychological profession, so it is important to know the credentials of an analyst prior to beginning treatment.

Preparation

Potential patients should learn more and gain a basic understanding of psychoanalysis before entering such a

KEY TERMS

Depression—A psychiatric disorder involving feelings of hopelessness and symptoms of fatigue, sleeplessness, suicidal tendencies, and poor concentration.

Holistic—Analysis of the entire system, rather than of individual parts.

Psychotic—Relating to psychosis, or a psychiatric disorder characterized by hallucinations, a distorted view of reality, and other such mental problems.

program. In addition, patients with the following general criteria have been shown to have a better chance for success in their treatment:

• ability to relate to the therapist so that an effective relationship can be established

• average intellect, along with a general understanding of psychological theory

• ability to tolerate sadness, disappointment, and other painful/negative emotions

• capacity to separate real and fantasy situations

Risks

The use of psychoanalysis can be a risk to individuals if professionals are not properly trained. In addition, patients suffering from severe depression or psychotic disorders, such as **schizophrenia**, are considered not to be suitable candidates for psychoanalysis. Persons with addictions or dependencies (such as alcohol **addiction** or prescription drug dependency), aggression or **impulse control disorders** (such as **kleptomania**, or compulsive stealing), or acute mental crises (or personal tragedies, for instance, death of family member) should resolve these serious problems before beginning psychoanalysis.

Results

Normal results include symptom relief and an enduring, adaptive change in personality.

Some individuals do not benefit from this in-depth form of treatment. They instead experience increased distress, or do not progress after a sufficient amount of treatment sessions. In these cases, people are typically transitioned to a less intensive form of treatment such as psychoanalytic psychotherapy.

Training and certification

In addition to having received advanced degrees in mental health (psychiatry, psychology, social work), trained psychoanalysts have also graduated from psychoanalytic training institutes. Institute training consists of three parts: course work on psychoanalytic theory and technique; supervised analyses (meaning that the candidate conducts analyses while being supervised by a seasoned psychoanalyst); and, third, candidates undergo a personal psychoanalysis. A personal analysis is considered a vital part of the training, as it enables candidates to learn about their own psychological processes. In turn, the knowledge enhances their capacity to treat others. This type of training program takes a minimum of four years to complete. Psychoanalysts also practice psychoanalytic psychotherapy, a less intensive form of treatment. It relies on the same theory of human development and a similar technique.

Resources

BOOKS

Britzman, Deborah P. *Freud and Education.* New York: Routledge, 2011.

Corsini, Raymond J., and Danny Wedding, eds. *Current Psychotherapies.* Belmont, CA: Brooks/Cole, 2011.

Kandel, Eric. *Psychiatry, Psychoanalysis, and the New Biology of Mind.* Arlington, VA: American Psychiatric Publishing, 2005.

Lichtenberg, Joseph D., Frank M. Lachmann and James L. Fosshage. *Psychoanalysis and Motivational Systems: A New Look.* New York: Routledge, 2011.

Person, Ethel S., Arnold M. Cooper and Glen O. Gabbard, eds. *The American Psychiatric Publishing Textbook of Psychoanalysis.* Arlington, VA: American Psychiatric Publishing, 2005.

WEBSITES

American Psychoanalytic Association. "About Psychoanalysis."http://www.apsa.org/About_Psychoanalysis.aspx (accessed December 22, 2010).

ORGANIZATIONS

American Psychoanalytic Association, 309 E 49th St., New York City, NY, 10017-1601, (212) 752-0450, Fax: (212) 593-0571, http://www.apsa.org.

International Psychoanalytical Association, Woodside Lane, London, United Kingdom, N12 8UD, 44 20 8446 8324, 44 20 8445 4729, ipa@ipa.org.uk, http://www.ipa.org.uk/Public.

National Psychological Association for Psychoanalysis, 40 W 13th St., New York City, NY, 10011, (212) 924-7440, Fax: (212) 989-7543, info@npap.org, http://www.npap.org.

Susan Fine, Psy.D
Stephanie N. Watson

Psychodynamic psychotherapy

Definition

Psychodynamic **psychotherapy**, sometimes also called psychodynamic therapy, is a method of verbal communication used to help a person find relief from emotional pain. It is based on the theories and techniques of **psychoanalysis**. Psychodynamic psychotherapy is similar to psychoanalysis in that it attributes emotional problems to the patient's unconscious motives and conflicts. It differs from classical psychoanalysis, however, in that psychodynamic psychotherapists do not necessarily accept the view of Austrian neurologist Sigmund Freud (1856–1939) that these unconscious motives and conflicts are ultimately sexual in nature. The method also uses the interaction between client and therapist much more than in other forms of therapy. Psychodynamic psychotherapy is used with individual, group, couples, and **family therapy**.

Oftentimes, when people talk about psychotherapy they really mean psychodynamic psychotherapy. Although psychodynamic psychotherapy is the term used by professionals in the field, it is also commonly called client-centered therapy, existential psychotherapy, Gestalt psychotherapy, Group psychotherapy, and many other such terms.

Purpose

The goals of psychodynamic psychotherapy vary depending on the method of treatment, which can be broadly described as either expressive or supportive. Expressive therapy seeks to relieve symptoms through the development of insight, or the slowly developing awareness of feelings and thoughts that were once outside of the person's awareness. Expressive therapy is based on the rationale that difficulties experienced in adult life originate in childhood; that children do not possess the maturity for making effective choices nor the independence to do so; and that methods of adapting developed in childhood may no longer be effective for adapting to the world as an adult. Through guidance from a therapist, the adult becomes aware of present ways of coping that are ineffective, and how they served a purpose in childhood but are no longer relevant. The person learns that he or she now has a range of new options for solving problems and for living in general that are now based on his or her maturity and independence.

In contrast to expressive therapy which is exploratory, supportive therapy remains closer to the surface of the patient's issues. Supportive therapy is an approach that is used to relieve immediate distress; to return the person to his or her previous level of functioning; and to strengthen adaptive ways of coping that the individual already possesses in order to prevent further discomfort. Expressive and supportive methods of treatment are not completely separate categories because elements of supportive therapy are used in expressive treatment and vice versa, depending on the therapeutic need. For instance, if a person in exploratory treatment is experiencing distress, a supportive approach may be used for a period of time in order to help the person feel more stable.

People seek psychodynamic psychotherapy for a variety of reasons that include but are not limited to the following: prolonged sadness; anxiety and **depression**; sexual difficulties; physical symptoms without physical basis; persistent feelings of isolation and loneliness; and the desire to be more successful in work or love. People seek therapy because they have not been able to develop a stable resolution for their difficulties on their own or with the help of friends and family members.

Description

Sessions of psychodynamic psychotherapy may be scheduled from one to three days per week, with greater frequency allowing for more in-depth treatment. The duration of individual sessions varies, but typically lasts for 45 to 50 minutes. It is not usually possible at the outset of treatment to estimate the number of sessions that will be necessary to achieve the person's goals. It is possible, however, for the person to make arrangements for a specific number of sessions.

Psychodynamic psychotherapy begins with a period of evaluation during which the client discusses with the therapist the reasons for seeking treatment. This process gives the therapist the opportunity to learn about the person, to develop an understanding of his or her troubles, and to formulate ideas about how treatment should proceed. This phase of interviewing and learning may take place in one session or over a series of sessions; or it may be done in a less structured manner, depending on the therapist's style. During the initial sessions, such factors as the frequency and length of sessions and the policy for payment will also be discussed. At some point within the first few sessions, the therapist and the individual will come to a mutual understanding of the goals for treatment. After the initial evaluation, sessions will be devoted to the client discussing what is on his or her mind. It is the therapist's job to listen and to help identify patterns of thinking, feeling and interacting that may be contributing to the patient's current struggles. Consequently, the person: (1) becomes more aware of his or her thoughts and feelings; (2) learns how some present ways of coping are no longer adaptive even though they may have been necessary in childhood; and (3) discovers that he or she as an adult has a greatly expanded repertoire of resources and, consequently, can use far more effective ways to deal with problems. Deeper awareness and new insights stimulate psychological growth and change.

Psychodynamic psychotherapy places great importance on the therapeutic dyad, which is a medical term for the relationship between the therapist and the patient. It is within the context of the therapeutic dyad that positive changes in the patient's outlook and behaviors are able to unfold. This relationship is unique because the therapist maintains a uniform, neutral, and accepting stance. Unlike other well-intentioned people in the person's life, the therapist has been trained to listen objectively and without criticism. This therapeutic attitude makes it easier for the person seeking treatment to speak freely and to therefore provide as much information for the therapist to work with as is possible.

Treatment continues until the troubling symptoms have been reduced or alleviated and the person is consistently making use of more adaptive methods of coping with greater insight. For some people, this positive experience inspires them to proceed with further treatment to bring about additional adaptive changes. For others, meeting the initial goals will be sufficient. If so, the focus of sessions turns to issues related to the end of treatment. This final phase of treatment is as important as the beginning and middle stages because it allows the individual to develop insight about his or her therapeutic experience. People need time to clarify how they feel about leaving the therapeutic relationship, and this termination involves identifying and understanding feelings about separation, maturation, loss, and change. The length of time allotted to the termination phase varies with the type of treatment and the needs of the individual.

While many patients benefit from individual psychotherapy alone, some instances call for such additional therapies as family, couples, or **group therapy** in combination with individual treatment. A second treatment modality might be recommended when the patient's progress in individual treatment is highly dependent on relationships with significant others or with interpersonal relationships in general. Psychotropic (mood- or behavior-altering) medication may also be prescribed as an adjunct (help) to treatment in order to manage disturbances in anxiety and depression level, mood, or

KEY TERMS

Anxiety—A psychological state characterized by strong feelings of worry, nervousness, apprehension, or agitation.

Depression—A psychiatric disorder involving feelings of hopelessness and symptoms of fatigue, sleeplessness, suicidal tendencies, and poor concentration.

Psychoanalysis—A form of therapy based on the understanding that human beings are largely unaware of the mental processes that determine their thoughts, feelings, and behavior, and that psychological suffering can be alleviated by making those processes known to the individual.

thinking. Whether additional treatments are recommended is based on the needs of the individual.

Preparation

Preparation for psychodynamic psychotherapy is not needed nor necessary. However, a period of introduction is often used before treatment begins so the therapist and patient can get to know each other better and the therapist can evaluate the patient as to the reasons for seeking treatment.

Aftercare

After a course of psychodynamic psychotherapy has ended, the person should, overall, continue to handle difficulties in a more adaptive manner; experience improved interpersonal relationships and productivity at work; and continue to develop new insights into his or her thoughts, feelings and behavior. In supportive treatment, insight and personality change are not the primary goals of treatment; therapist and patient work toward a continuation of general stability in the person's life.

Risks

Like all therapies, psychodynamic psychotherapy may or may not work successfully for the individual. Patients may like or dislike the method, depending on their individual conditions, personalities, and other factors. It does have a very good record for effectiveness for certain mental illness conditions, such as depression and **personality disorders**. However, because of its varied nature with which it is carried out psychodynamic psychotherapy is difficult to assess its actual effectiveness on a quantitative basis.

QUESTIONS TO ASK YOUR DOCTOR

- Do you think psychodynamic psychotherapy is suited to my particular problem?
- Where can I learn more about psychodynamic psychotherapy?
- If I get better with the therapy, are there other therapies that can be used as a "next step" in my recovery?
- Will my health insurance pay for it?
- How will I know when I no longer need therapy?
- What happens if I have a relapse after stopping therapy?

Results

Psychodynamic psychotherapy is considered to be an effective way to treat various types of mental health problems. Dr. Jonathan Shedler, from the University of Colorado, published a paper stating that psychodynamic psychotherapy is "highly effective" based on scientific evidence. The paper, entitled "The Efficacy of Psychodynamic Psychotherapy," was published in 2010 in the journal *American Psychologist* (volume 654, number 2). Shedler concluded in the study that psychodynamic psychotherapy is, at the very least, as effective as other forms of therapy. In addition, Shedler found that psychodynamic psychotherapy is a long-lasting type of therapy for patients, allowing them to lead a much healthier life, without all of the major symptoms, before such therapy was performed.

Resources

BOOKS

O'Donohue, William, Nicholas A. Cummings and Janet L. Cummings, eds. *Becoming a Psychotherapist.* Amsterdam; Boston: Elsevier Academic Press, 2006.

Person, Ethel Spector, Arnold M. Cooper and Glen O. Gabbard, eds. *The American Psychiatric Publishing Textbook of Psychoanalysis.* Washington, DC: American Psychiatric Publishing, 2005.

Prochaska, James O., and John C. Norcross. *Systems of Psychotherapy: A Transtheoretical Analysis.* Belmont, CA: Brooks/Cole, 2010.

WEBSITES

American Psychological Association. "Psychodynamic Psychotherapy Brings Lasting Benefits through Self-Knowledge." http://www.apa.org/news/press/releases/2010/01/psychodynamic-therapy.aspx (accessed December 29, 2010).

ORGANIZATIONS

American Psychiatric Association, 1000 Wilson Blvd., Ste. 1825, Arlington, VA, 22209-3901, (703) 907-7300, apa@psych.org, http://www.psych.org.

American Psychoanalytic Association, 309 East 49th Street, New York City, NY, 10017, (212) 752-0450, Fax: (212) 593-0571, info@aspa.org, http://www.apsa.org.

American Psychological Association, 750 1st St. NE, Washington, DC, 20002-4242, (202) 336-5500; TDD/TTY: (202) 336-6123, (800) 374-2721, http://www.apa.org.

Susan Fine, Psy.D.

Psychogenic excoriation *see* **Dermatillomania**

Psychological assessment and diagnosis

Definition

A psychological assessment is the process of gathering and evaluating data about a patient's symptoms, mental state, behaviors, and background. It is also called a biopsychosocial or psychiatric assessment. The assessment is used to diagnose mental disorders and as a first step in determining appropriate treatment.

Purpose

The purpose of a psychological assessment is to organize and evaluate information about a patient in order to arrive at a **diagnosis** and recommend a course of treatment. Nearly half of all Americans experience some type of mental disorder at some point in their lives, and as many as 60% of physical complaints for which patients seek medical advice result from or are affected by psychological problems, often anxiety or **depression**. The process of assessment and diagnosis is typically initiated by a patient or family member seeking help for a primary complaint or problem that is interfering with daily activities or affecting quality of life. Accurate assessment and diagnosis is critical for the selection of appropriate medication or other treatment plan.

Assessment and diagnosis are used for the following psychological and psychiatric conditions and disorders, among others:

- anxiety
- depression
- psychological trauma
- post-traumatic stress disorder (PTSD)

- dissociative conditions
- personality disorders
- bipolar disorder
- psychosis
- schizophrenia
- chronic pain
- substance abuse
- eating disorders
- sleep disorders
- domestic violence
- dementia
- Alzheimer's disease
- neurological disorders
- traumatic brain injury

Childhood and adolescent conditions and disorders that are subject to assessment and diagnosis include:

- behavior/conduct disorders
- social problems
- emotional disorders
- anxiety
- depression
- acute and chronic neurological conditions
- developmental delays
- dyslexia
- learning disorders and disabilities
- autism spectrum disorders
- attention deficit hyperactivity disorder (ADHD)
- eating disorders

Description

Various physiological diseases, disorders, and conditions—such as diabetes and thyroid and seizure disorders—can contribute to or even mask psychological and mental health conditions and interfere with psychological assessment and diagnosis. Therefore, a thorough physical examination and appropriate medical tests and procedures may need to be performed prior to psychological assessment and diagnosis. A neurological assessment and **brain** imaging also may be required.

Assessment and diagnosis usually involve the direct examination of the patient by a **psychologist** or **psychiatrist**, although in some instances this may not be possible. Increasingly, initial assessment occurs in primary-care settings and is followed by in-depth assessment and diagnosis by a mental health professional. Different diagnoses require different types of assessments. However, assessments usually involve

standardized interviews that can assess psychological status or establish a psychiatric diagnosis. Cognitive and/or behavioral assessments may be performed in place of or in addition to a psychological assessment. Psychometric measurements are standardized quantifications of different variables, including personality, emotional status, cognitive functioning, behavior, and academic achievement. The entire process is often referred to as psychological testing.

Structured interview

A biopsychosocial assessment is a standard structured interview that is accepted as an effective diagnostic tool. It includes:

- identifying information
- chief complaint or problem
- history of the current illness or condition
- past medical and psychological history
- personal history
- family history
- substance use and abuse history

The interview opens with general and emotionally neutral questions. These include the patient's name, age, occupation, and marital status. The clinician inquires as to the patient's immediate reasons for seeking help, and the patient is asked to describe the onset of signs and symptoms that comprise the current problem. Information about additional symptoms and any previous mental disorders can assist the clinician in formulating pertinent questions during subsequent sections of the interview.

The patient's medical history may reveal problems—such as thyroid disease, Parkinson's disease, head **trauma**, or brain infections—that could be responsible for current psychological symptoms. The patient is also asked about previous psychological/psychiatric treatments, including hospitalizations, outpatient or **substance abuse** treatments, and medications, and the duration, effectiveness, and outcomes of treatments.

Personal history covers the patient's entire life, beginning with prenatal development. The patient is asked about maternal **nutrition** and drug and **alcohol use** during pregnancy, as well as any maternal abortions or miscarriages, birth trauma, and siblings. The early childhood phase—infancy to three years—may include questions about temperament, developmental milestones (e.g., walking, talking, toilet training), nutrition and feeding, family relationships, behavioral problems, hospitalizations, and separation from caregivers. The middle childhood phase—3 to 11 years—includes pertinent information about education and learning, relationships with peers and family, behavioral problems, and general personality development. Adolescence—12 to 18 years—includes school history, behavioral problems, and sexual development. The adulthood section details the patient's education, sexual history, relationships and/or marriages, peer relationships, occupations, and current circumstances. Family history is also very important, since many mental disorders are inherited or tend to run in families. Family interactions can also affect the manifestation of symptoms.

Substance abuse history delineates the patient's past and current use of alcohol, **nicotine**, caffeine, prescribed medications, and illicit drugs, including **sedatives** and depressants, opiates, **cocaine**, marijuana, and **hallucinogens**. Questions focus on the patient's age at first use, age at last use, period of heaviest use, usage within the past 30 days, and frequency, amounts, and methods of usage. The interviewer takes note of any tolerance, dependence, treatment, medical complications (such as HIV/AIDS), and legal problems (such as driving while impaired) that were associated with substance use or abuse.

Mental status examination

The **mental status examination** (MSE) follows the biopsychosocial history. It includes the clinician's observations of the patient, questions about feelings, and assessments of thought processes, memory, and cognition.

The clinician's observations focus on the patient's appearance, behavior, speech, and affect or emotional state. The patient's general appearance, hygiene, grooming, and attire are noted, as well as behaviors such as abnormal movements, hyperactivity, and eye contact with the interviewer. Fluency, rate, clarity, and tone of speech are all important. They can be indicative of mental state. For example, fast talking may suggest anxiety, as well as speech impairments, oral problems (such as dentures or cleft palate), mania, or intoxication. The patient is questioned about current mood, and affect or emotional state are observed and interpreted by the clinician throughout the interview. Affect is described in standardized terms, such as excitable, flat, inappropriate, or labile (rapidly shifting).

Thought processes—the form and content of thoughts—include basic orientation in time and place, such as the ability to identify oneself and loved ones, the current date, and the route to the medical office. The clinician also observes the connectedness, coherence, and logic of the patient's thoughts and notes any thought disturbances. These include circumstantial thinking (circuitous, persistent storytelling), tangential thinking

(irrelevant responses to questions), black/white (extreme) thinking, or impoverished (minimally responsive) thinking, as well as **delusions**, hallucinations, phobias, obsessions, or suicidal or homicidal thoughts.

The MSE includes assessments of cognition, such as attention; awareness; long-, intermediate-, and short-term memory; general knowledge; abstract thinking ability; insight; and judgment. The patient might be asked to spell a word forward and backward, name the current president, read and/or write a passage, compare two objects, or explain the meaning of common sayings.

Pediatric

Special procedures are used for the assessment and diagnosis of children. If possible, assessment and diagnosis should be performed by a pediatrician, child psychologist or psychiatrist, or pediatric neurologist. The assessment is usually carried out in consultation with the child's family. In addition to observations of the child and standardized assessment instruments or structured interviews, discussions involve both the child and the family. The parents must provide a complete medical and family/social history. The child's social, economic, and cultural environment must be taken into consideration.

Preparation

Choosing a qualified mental health practitioner for assessment and diagnosis is important. Depending on the specific problem, it may be appropriate to seek out a specialist in anxiety/depressive disorders, pain management, chemical dependency, or other disorders, or specific types of treatments, such as **cognitive-behavioral therapy** or **hypnotherapy**. Assessment and diagnosis should take place in a private, quiet, nonthreatening environment. The clinician should attempt to make the patient as comfortable as possible. In the case of a language barrier, a competent translator is essential for accurate assessment and diagnosis.

Aftercare

Aftercare is determined by the assessment and diagnosis. It may include additional assessments and tests, perhaps by a specialist, to confirm a diagnosis and determine appropriate treatment. Treatments may include various interventions, psychoactive medications, and/or **psychotherapy**, cognitive-behavioral therapy, **family therapy**, or some other form of counseling. With pediatric assessment and diagnosis, parents should obtain copies of the clinician's notes, assessments, and diagnosis, and

KEY TERMS

Affect—The expression of emotion through such features as facial expressions, hand gestures, and tone of voice. Types of affect include flat (inanimate, no expression), blunted (minimally responsive), inappropriate relative to the context, and labile (abrupt changes in type and intensity of emotion).

Alzheimer's disease—A progressive, neurodegenerative disease characterized by loss of function and death of nerve cells in several areas of the brain, leading to loss of mental functions, such as memory and learning. Alzheimer's disease is the most common cause of dementia.

Assessment—A psychological assessment, usually via a structured interview, to gather information for diagnosing a mental disorder.

Attention deficit hyperactivity disorder (ADHD)—A persistent pattern of inattention, hyperactivity and/or impulsiveness. The pattern is more frequent and severe than is typically observed in people at a similar level of development.

Autism spectrum disorder (ASD)—A range of variable developmental disorders that includes an impaired ability to communicate and form normal social relationships.

Biopsychosocial history—A history of experiences and other factors that influence behaviors, including medical, educational, occupational, and interpersonal histories, as well as any alcohol or drug use or criminal activity.

Bipolar disorder—A recurrent mood disorder, also known as manic-depressive disorder, in which patients have extreme mood swings from depression to mania or a mixture of both.

Cognition—Conscious intellectual activity, including thinking, imagining, reasoning, remembering, and learning.

Delusion—A strongly held false belief, such that the belief that one is being poisoned or has a fatal illness, despite all evidence to the contrary.

Dementia—A group of symptoms (syndrome) associated with chronic progressive impairment of memory, reasoning ability, and other intellectual functions; personality changes; deterioration in personal grooming; disorientation; and sometimes delusions.

Dependence—Physiological or psychological addiction to alcohol or a drug, possibly followed by withdrawal symptoms when use is terminated.

Dissociation—Disconnection from oneself.

Dyslexia—A variable learning disability that is usually characterized by difficulty reading, writing, and spelling. It often runs in families; also called developmental reading disorder (DRD) or specific reading disability.

Eating disorder—A condition characterized by an abnormal attitude toward food, altered appetite control, and unhealthy eating habits.

Hallucinations—False sensory perceptions, for example, hearing sounds or seeing people or objects that are not there. Hallucinations can also affect the senses of smell, touch, and taste.

Phobia—Irrational fear of places, things, or situations, leading to avoidance.

Post-traumatic stress disorder (PTSD)—A psychological response to a highly stressful event, typically characterized by depression, anxiety, flashbacks, nightmares, and avoidance of reminders of the traumatic experience.

Psychometric—Quantitative methods for mental and psychological measurements.

Schizophrenia—A psychotic disorder characterized by loss of contact with one's environment, deterioration of everyday functioning, and personality disintegration.

Tolerance—Progressive decrease in the effectiveness of a drug with long-term use.

---

ensure that they understand the diagnosis and treatment options.

Risks

The major risk of assessment is a wrong diagnosis. Accurate information gathering and objective note-taking are essential for psychological assessments. However, these can be difficult to obtain if the patient is not forthcoming with information, perhaps out of embarrassment or **denial** of symptoms. For example, although depression is quite common in older people, its assessment and diagnosis can be difficult. Clinical symptoms of depression in the elderly may be very different from those

QUESTIONS TO ASK YOUR DOCTOR

- What type of assessment do you recommend for me?
- Who will perform the assessment?
- What will my assessment involve?
- How long will my assessment take?
- What information will my assessment provide?
- Will I have full access to the assessment report?

in younger individuals. Older people tend to complain of physical rather than psychological symptoms. Symptoms of medical disorders, as well as complications from social isolation and personal loss, can mask signs of depression and other mental disorders. Certain portions of an assessment also are quite subjective. Misperceptions, misunderstandings, or inexperience on the part of the interviewer can lead to misdiagnoses. Improper diagnosis presents the risk of inappropriate treatment.

Results

Complete assessments help establish either a tentative or definitive diagnosis. Based on the assessment and diagnosis, the patient may be declared healthy or referred for psychological therapy or other **intervention** and/or prescribed psychoactive medication.

Resources

BOOKS

Butcher, James Neal, Susan Mineka, and Jill M. Hooley. *Abnormal Psychology,* 14th ed. Boston: Allyn & Bacon, 2010.

Dziegielewski, Sophia F. *DSM-IV-TR in Action,* 2nd ed. Hoboken, NJ: John Wiley & Sons, 2010.

Hersen, Michel, and Alan M. Gross, eds. *Handbook of Clinical Psychology.* Hoboken, NJ: John Wiley & Sons, 2008.

Sue, David, and Diane M. Sue. *Foundations of Counseling and Psychotherapy: Evidence-Based Practices for a Diverse Society.* Hoboken, NJ: John Wiley & Sons, 2008.

PERIODICALS

Jones, Karyn Dayle, Tabitha Young, and Monica Leppma. "Mild Traumatic Brain Injury and Posttraumatic Stress Disorder in Returning Iraq and Afghanistan War Veterans: Implications for Assessment and Diagnosis." *Journal of Counseling and Development* 88, no. 3 (Summer 2010): 372–76.

WEBSITES

"Breaking Ground, Breaking Through: The Strategic Plan for Mood Disorders Research." National Institute of Mental Health. http://www.nimh.nih.gov/about/ strategic-planning-reports/breaking-ground-breaking-through–the-strategic-plan-for-mood-disorders-research.pdf (accessed July 24, 2011).

"Psychology Is a Behavioral and Mental Health Profession." American Psychological Association. http://www.apa.org/about/gr/issues/health-care/profession.aspx (accessed July 24, 2011).

"What Parents Should Know About Treatment of Behavioral and Emotional Disorders in Preschool Children." American Psychological Association. http://www.apa.org/pubs/info/brochures/kids-meds.aspx (accessed July 24, 2011).

ORGANIZATIONS

American Psychiatric Association, 1000 Wilson Blvd., Ste. 1825, Arlington, VA, 22209-3901, (703) 907-7300, apa@psych.org, http://www.psych.org.

American Psychological Association, 750 1st St., NE, Washington, DC, 20002-4242, (202) 336-5500, (800) 374-2721, http://www.apa.org.

Mental Health America, 2000 N Beauregard St., 6th Fl., Alexandria, VA, 22311, (703) 684-7722, (800) 969-6642, Fax: (703) 684-5968, http://www.nmha.org.

National Alliance on Mental Illness, 3803 N Fairfax Dr., Ste. 100, Arlington, VA, 22203, (703) 524-7600, (800) 950-6264, Fax: (703) 524-9094, http://www.nami.org.

National Institute of Mental Health, 6001 Executive Blvd., Rm. 8184, MSC 9663, Bethesda, MD, 20892-9663, (301) 443-4513, (866) 615-6464, Fax: (301) 443-4279, nimhinfo@nih.gov, http://www.nimh.nih.gov.

Sidran Institute, PO Box 436, Brooklandville, MD, 21022-0436, (410) 825-8888, Fax: (410) 560-0134, info@sidran.org, http://www.sidran.org.

Laith Farid Gulli, MD
Bilal Nasser, MD
Robert Ramirez
Margaret Alic, PhD

Psychologist

Definition

A psychologist is a social scientist who studies behavior and mental processes, generally in a research or clinical setting.

Description

As psychology has grown and changed throughout history, it has been defined in numerous ways. As early as 400 B.C., the ancient Greeks philosophized about the relationship of personality characteristics to physiological traits. Since then, philosophers have proposed theories to

SIGMUND FREUD (1856–1939)

The work of Sigmund Freud, the Austrian founder of psychoanalysis, marked the beginning of a modern, dynamic psychology by providing the first systematic explanation of the inner mental forces determining human behavior.

Early in his career Sigmund Freud distinguished himself as a histologist, neuropathologist, and clinical neurologist, and in his later life he was acclaimed as a talented writer and essayist. However, his fame is based on his work in expanding man's knowledge of himself through clinical research and corresponding development of theories to explain the new data. He laid the foundations for modern understanding of unconscious mental processes (processes excluded from awareness), neurosis (a type of mental disorder), the sexual life of infants, and the interpretation of dreams. Under his guidance, psychoanalysis became the dominant modern theory of human psychology and a major tool of research, as well as an important method of psychiatric treatment, which currently has thousands of practitioners all over the world. The application of psychoanalytic thinking to the studies of history, anthropology, religion, art, sociology, and education has greatly changed these fields.

Sigmund Freud was born on May 6, 1856, in Freiberg, Moravia (now Czechoslovakia). Sigmund was the first child of his twice-widowed father's third marriage. His mother, Amalia Nathanson, was 19 years old when she married Jacob Freud, aged 39. Sigmund's two stepbrothers from his father's first marriage were approximately the same age as his mother, and his older stepbrother's son, Sigmund's nephew, was his earliest playmate. Thus the boy grew up in an unusual family structure, his mother halfway in age between himself and his father. Though seven younger children were born, Sigmund always remained his mother's favorite. When he was 4, the family moved to Vienna, the capital of the Austro-Hungarian monarchy and one of the great cultural, scientific, and medical centers of Europe. Freud lived in Vienna until a year before his death.

explain human behavior. In the late nineteenth century the emergence of scientific method gave the study of psychology a new focus. In 1879, the first psychological laboratory was opened in Leipzig, Germany, by Wilhelm Wundt, and soon afterward the first experimental studies of memory were published. Wundt was instrumental in establishing psychology as the study of conscious experience, which he viewed as made up of elemental sensations. In addition to the type of psychology practiced by Wundt—which became known as structuralism—other early schools of psychology were functionalism, which led to the development of behaviorism, and Gestalt psychology. The **American Psychological Association** was founded in 1892 with the goals of encouraging research, enhancing professional competence, and disseminating knowledge about the field.

With the ascendance of the Viennese neurologist Sigmund Freud and his method of **psychoanalysis** early in the twentieth century, emphasis shifted from conscious experience to unconscious processes investigated by means of free association and other techniques. According to Freud, behavior and mental processes were the result of mostly unconscious struggles between the drive to satisfy basic instincts, such as sex or aggression, and the limits imposed by society. At the same time that Freud's views were gaining popularity in Europe, an American psychology professor, John B. Watson, was pioneering the behavioral approach, which focuses on observing and measuring external behaviors rather than the internal workings of the mind. B. F. Skinner, who spent decades studying the effects of reward and punishment on behavior, helped maintain the predominance of behaviorism in the United States through the 1950s and 1960s. Since the 1970s, many psychologists have been influenced by the cognitive approach, which is concerned with the relationship of mental processes to behavior. Cognitive psychology focuses on how people take in, perceive, and store information, and how they process and act on that information.

Additional psychological perspectives include the neurobiological approach, focusing on relating behavior to internal processes within the **brain** and nervous system, and the phenomenological approach, which is most concerned with the individual's subjective experience of the world rather than the application of psychological theory to behavior. Although all these approaches differ in their explanations of individual behavior, each contributes an important perspective to the overall psychological understanding of the total human being. Most psychologists apply the principles of various approaches in studying and understanding human nature.

Along with several approaches to psychology there are also numerous, overlapping subfields in which these approaches may be applied. Most subfields can be categorized under one of two major areas of psychology referred to as basic and applied psychology. Basic psychology encompasses the subfields concerned with the advancement of psychological theory and research. Experimental psychology employs laboratory experiments to study basic behavioral processes, including sensation, perception, learning, memory, communication, and motivation, that different species share. Physiological psychology is concerned with the ways in which biology shapes behavior and mental processes, and developmental psychology is concerned with behavioral development over the entire life span. Other subfields include social psychology, quantitative psychology, and the psychology of personality.

Applied psychology is the area of psychology concerned with applying psychological research and theory to problems posed by everyday life. It includes clinical psychology, the largest single field in psychology. Clinical psychologists—who represent 40% of all psychologists—are involved in **psychotherapy** and psychological testing. Clinical psychologists are trained in research and often work in university or research settings, studying various aspects of psychology. Like clinical psychologists, counseling psychologists apply psychological principles to diagnose and treat individual emotional and behavioral problems. Other subfields of applied psychology include school psychology, which involves the evaluation and placement of students; educational psychology, which investigates the psychological aspects of the learning process; and industrial and organizational psychology, which study the relationship between people and their jobs. Community psychologists investigate environmental factors that contribute to mental and emotional disorders; health psychologists deal with the psychological aspects of physical illness, investigating the connections between the mind and a person's physical condition; and consumer psychologists study the preferences and buying habits of consumers as well as their reactions to certain advertising.

In response to society's changing needs, new fields of psychology are constantly emerging. One type of specialization, called environmental psychology, focuses on the relationship between people and their physical surroundings. Its areas of inquiry include such issues as the effects of overcrowding and noise on urban dwellers and the effects of building design. Another specialty is forensic psychology, involving the application of psychology to law enforcement and the judicial system. Forensic psychologists may help create personality profiles of criminals, formulate principles for jury selection, or study the problems involved in eyewitness testimony. Yet another emerging area is program evaluation, whose practitioners evaluate the effectiveness and cost efficiency of the programs.

Depending on the nature of their work, psychologists may practice in a variety of settings, including colleges and universities, hospitals and **community mental health** centers, schools, and businesses. A growing number of psychologists work in private practice and may also specialize in multiple subfields. Most psychologists earn a PhD degree in the field, which requires completion of a four- to six-year post-bachelors' degree program offered by a university psychology department. The course of study includes a broad overview of the field, as well as specialization in a particular subfield, and completion of a dissertation and an internship (usually needed only for applied psychology, such as clinical, counseling, and school psychology). Students who intend to practice only applied psychology rather than conduct research have the option of obtaining a Psy.D. degree, which differs in the limited emphasis that is put on research and a dissertation that does not have to be based on an empirical research study.

ORGANIZATIONS

American Psychological Association, 750 1st Street NE, Washington, DC, 20002-4242, (202) 336-5500; TDD/TTY: (202) 336-6123, (800) 374-2721, http://www.apa.org.

Emily Jane Willingham, PhD

Psychopharmacology

Definition

Psychopharmacology is the branch of medicine that investigates the properties and legitimate uses of psychoactive substances and their effects on human thinking, emotions, sensations, and behavior. The name comes from three Greek words meaning "mind" or "soul," "drug," and "study of." Although recreational ("street") drugs also have psychoactive properties, psychopharmacology is primarily concerned with the development and testing of drugs for the treatment of mental disorders or their symptoms. Psychoactive drugs are also known as psychopharmaceuticals or psychotropic drugs.

Psychoactive drugs interact with specific molecules found on the surfaces of cells in the central nervous system known as receptors. The action of a psychopharmaceutical on a receptor is called the drug's pharmacodynamics, while the body's use of the drug (the drug's absorption within the body and its eventual excretion) is called its pharmacokinetics.

Purpose

Psychopharmacology has several purposes, including the research and development of new drugs to treat mental disorders, including drugs derived from natural sources as well as those synthesized in the laboratory; improved understanding of the mechanisms of drug activity in the **brain** and central nervous system; and improved understanding of long-term as well as short-term side effects of psychopharmaceuticals and their interactions with other medications.

Demographics

Psychopharmacology has moved over the past half century into a leading subspecialty of biochemistry, largely on account of the increasing use of medications rather than **psychotherapy** to treat mental disorders. The number of Americans diagnosed with mental disorders has risen dramatically since the 1980s—between 1987 and 2007, the number of Americans receiving supplemental Social Security payments for mental disability rose from 1 in every 184 adults to 1 in every 76, an increase of 250%. The increase in diagnoses of mental illness in children is even more remarkable: a 35-fold increase over the same twenty-year period. A survey conducted by the **National Institute of Mental Health** (NIMH) between 2001 and 2003 reported that 46% of the randomly sampled adults met criteria for at least one of four categories of mental illness at some point in their lives: mood disorders, **anxiety disorders**, impulse-control disorders, and **substance abuse** disorders.

The increases are attributed at least in part to the popularity of psychopharmaceuticals; within ten years after the 1987 introduction of Prozac—the first of the **selective serotonin reuptake inhibitors** (SSRIs)—the number of patients diagnosed with **depression** tripled. As of 2011, 10% of Americans over six years of age were taking antidepressant medications. With regard to antipsychotics, the newer so-called atypical antipsychotics are now the top-selling class of drugs in the United States, ahead of cholesterol-lowering medications. This steep climb in the number of patients taking psychotropic medications in less than three decades is a major reason for the reinvestigation of the effectiveness of these drugs.

Description

Origins

PRESCIENTIFIC USE OF PSYCHOACTIVE SUBSTANCES. The use of psychoactive substances goes back to prehistoric times. Before the rise of scientific biochemistry in the nineteenth century, most psychoactive preparations were derived from plants. Tribal cultures made use of psychedelic mushrooms and cacti (such as the peyote cactus) to induce altered states of consciousness; there is evidence that some of these substances were used as early as 10,000 B.C.E. With the development of agriculture and the formation of settled villages during the New Stone Age (around 9,500 B.C.E.), humans began to make use of cultivated plants for both recreational and medicinal purposes.

Most early human societies discovered alcoholic beverages in the form of fermented products such as wine and beer (distilled liquors such as gin and whiskey were not developed until the seventeenth century). With regard to anesthesia, the painkilling properties of the opium poppy were known to the ancient Sumerians, Egyptians, Indians, Greeks, and Romans. In addition to these plant-derived psychoactive substances, ancient societies in both the East and the West collected and studied herbs for their medicinal properties. While medieval European and Native American herbalists generally favored preparations made from a single plant, traditional Chinese medicine developed complex formulas for medicines that required several different herbs to produce the desired result.

In the sixteenth and seventeenth centuries, European settlement of North America and trade with Turkey introduced two new plants containing psychoactive substances to the West: tobacco and coffee beans. In contrast to alcohol and **opioids**, which are depressants, the **nicotine** in tobacco and the caffeine in coffee are stimulants. Caffeine is the most widely used psychoactive substance in the world, with 85% of American adults consuming coffee on a daily basis.

PSYCHOPHARMACOLOGY IN THE MODERN WORLD. It was not until the establishment of organic chemistry as a subdiscipline within chemistry in the late nineteenth century that modern psychopharmaceuticals were made possible. The discovery of the concept of chemical structure, made independently in 1858 by Friedrich August Kekulé (1829–1896) and Archibald Scott Couper (1831–1892), permitted the synthesis of complex molecules in the laboratory through multistep processes. By the end of the nineteenth century, Bayer AG in Germany patented its brand of acetylsalicylic acid under the name of aspirin. Although many of the new pharmaceutical companies that were formed between the 1890s and the outbreak of World War I in 1914 were primarily interested in creating completely new synthetic compounds, others began to investigate the chemical compounds found in herbs and other natural sources. Many of the most important drugs used in psychiatry in the twentieth century resulted from research into herbal lore, including some compounds that were originally developed to treat infections and were found to change a person's mental state only accidentally.

The use of psychopharmaceuticals to treat mental illness was relatively uncommon before the 1950s. From the 1880s onward, **psychoanalysis**, **psychodynamic psychotherapy**, and other forms of the therapy were the primary methods of treatment; although Freud himself experimented with using **cocaine** to relieve depression in his patients between 1883 and 1887 and used it to regulate his own moods until 1896. In the 1950s, however, the discovery of several classes of anxiolytics, particularly the **barbiturates** and the benzodiazepine tranquilizers, made it possible to treat anxiety disorders with medications, and the tricyclic **antidepressants**, first discovered in the mid-1950s, were soon recommended for the treatment of major depression. The oldest antipsychotic drugs, **chlorpromazine** (Thorazine) and the phenothiazines, were used to treat **schizophrenia** as early as 1952.

The rise of the so-called counterculture in the 1960s, with its use of **hallucinogens** and other street drugs to induce altered states of consciousness, led to some psychiatrists' recommending the use of **cannabis** (marijuana), peyote, and psilocybin as adjuncts to traditional psychotherapy. Lysergic acid diethylamide (LSD), first synthesized by the Swiss chemist Albert Hoffman (1906–2008) in 1938, was first used by psychiatrists in 1947, but controversy over its popularity in the drug culture of the 1960s led to restrictions on its use by mainstream therapists.

The success of the first antipsychotics and the tricyclic antidepressants led to the so-called biological psychiatry movement, based on the notion that mental disorders are fundamentally biological in origin. Biological psychiatrists proposed the chemical imbalance theory of mental disorders, namely that mental illnesses are the end result of too little or too much of neurotransmitters— such as **serotonin**, norepinephrine, or dopamine—in the central nervous system. The shift from the older psychoanalytic theories of mental illness to biological psychiatry was reflected in the third edition of the *Diagnostic and Statistical Manual of Mental Disorders* (*DSM-III*), published in 1980.

One major problem with the chemical imbalance theory, however, is that it did not explain the time lag that typically occurs between the biological activity of the first doses of an antidepressant and symptom relief; studies indicated that the neurotransmitter levels in the patient's body began to change within hours, but changes in the patient's mood took weeks. A more recent version of the theory holds that depression and other disorders result from degenerative changes in the neurons (nerve cells) in the central nervous system and/or the loss of functional connections between neurons and that antidepressants work by stimulating the growth of new neurons or repairing their interconnections.

Types of psychoactive drugs

There are seven major classes of psychoactive drugs:

- Antidepressants. These drugs are used to treat major depression and some anxiety disorders. Most of them work by inhibiting the breakdown of serotonin, norepinephrine, or both. The five major types of antidepressants are the monoamine oxidase inhibitors (MAOIs), tricyclic (TCAs) and tetracyclic (TeCAs) antidepressants, selective serotonin reuptake inhibitors (SSRIs), and serotonin-norepinephrine reuptake inhibitors (SNRIs).

- Antipsychotics. These drugs are used to relieve the hallucinations and other psychotic symptoms of schizophrenia. They may also be used to help stabilize moods in patients with bipolar disorder even when no psychotic symptoms are present. The older antipsychotics (also called the typical antipsychotics) were developed in the 1950s and include such drugs as the phenothiazines. Examples of atypical antipsychotics include the drugs risperidone, aripiprazole, and clozapine.

- Anxiolytics and hypnotics. These drugs are prescribed to relieve anxiety. Sometimes called tranquilizers, the anxiolytics include benzodiazepines, some of the SSRIs, barbiturates, and buspirone. Barbiturates are rarely prescribed except as sleeping medications (hypnotics) because of their potential for abuse (including suicide when combined with alcohol). Benzodiazepines are considered safer; they include the drugs diazepam, lorazepam, and chlordiazepoxide. Zolpidem, which is not a benzodiazepine, is frequently prescribed as a hypnotic.

- Depressants. Anxiolytics and antipsychotics are sometimes classified as depressants. Other depressants include ethanol (beverage alcohol), which does not require a prescription, and prescription sedatives, opioid pain relievers (also called narcotics), and anesthetics.

- Hallucinogens. These drugs are generally associated with recreational drug use, but some were being used in clinical trials in 2011 as antianxiety agents. These include LSD, psilocybin, dimethyltryptamine (DMT), and cannabis.

Antidepressant—Any of a group of medications given to relieve mood disorders, including anxiety disorders as well as major depression. Antidepressants include monoamine oxidase inhibitors (MAOIs), tricyclic (TCAs) and tetracyclic (TeCAs) antidepressants, selective serotonin reuptake inhibitors (SSRIs), and serotonin-norepinephrine reuptake inhibitors (SNRIs).

Anxiolytic—Any of a group of medications prescribed to relieve anxiety. Also called tranquilizers, anxiolytics include benzodiazepines, some of the selective serotonin reuptake inhibitors (SSRIs), barbiturates, and buspirone.

Attention deficit hyperactivity disorder (ADHD)—A persistent pattern of inattention, hyperactivity, and/or impulsiveness; the pattern is more frequent and severe than is typically observed in people at a similar level of development.

Biological psychiatry—An approach to psychiatry that attributes mental disorders to biochemical or other biological malfunctions of the central nervous system, as distinct from the patient's childhood issues and life history.

Blood-brain barrier—A specialized, semi-permeable layer of cells around the blood vessels in the brain that controls which substances can leave the circulatory system and enter the brain.

Depressant—Any psychoactive substance that lowers the function or activity level of a specific part of the body or brain. Depressants are sometimes referred to as "downers." These include anxiolytics, sedatives, antipsychotics, opioids, and anesthetics as well as nonprescription substances such as alcohol.

Hallucinogen—A drug that distorts sensory perceptions and disturbs emotion, judgment, and memory.

Hallucinogens are often used to induce trances, meditation, and dream states.

Hypnotic—A medication that causes sleep.

Narcotic—Another term for an opioid drug.

Opioid—Any of a group of potent pain-relieving drugs derived from the opium poppy or synthesized in the laboratory. Opioids bind to opioid receptors in the brain, spinal cord, and digestive tract.

Pharmacodynamics—The study of the effects of drugs on the human body.

Pharmacokinetics—The study of the absorption, distribution, and elimination of drugs from the body.

Placebo—A pill or liquid given during the study of a drug or dietary supplement that contains no medication or active ingredient, used to test the effectiveness of the drug or supplement in question. Usually study participants do not know if they are receiving the drug or the placebo.

Psychoactive—Referring to any substance that crosses the blood-brain barrier and acts primarily upon the central nervous system, leading to changes in mood, perception, thinking, feeling, or behavior.

Receptor—In biochemistry, a substance (usually a protein) found on the surface of a cell that interacts with specific other molecules, drugs, hormones, or antibodies.

Stimulant—A type of psychoactive substance that increases alertness or wakefulness. Stimulants are sometimes referred to as "uppers."

Tardive dyskinesia—A disorder characterized by involuntary and repetitive body movements that sometimes develops after long-term use of antipsychotic medications.

Tranquilizer—Another name for anxiolytic.

• Mood stabilizers. These drugs are used to treat bipolar disorder, particularly manic episodes. Lithium carbonate, the oldest mood stabilizer, was discovered in 1949. Other mood stabilizers belong to the class of drugs used to treat epilepsy known as anticonvulsants. These drugs include such medications as valproic acid, carbamazepine, and gabapentin.

• Stimulants. Stimulants are among the most widely prescribed psychotropic drugs and are used to treat attention deficit hyperactivity disorder (ADHD), narcolepsy, and occasionally depression that does

not respond to other medications. Stimulants can be addictive and are not recommended for patients with substance abuse disorders. Prescription stimulants include such drugs as methylphenidate and various amphetamine compounds.

Benefits

The benefits of psychoactive drugs are a source of considerable controversy. A growing number of psychiatrists prefer to combine prescriptions for psychotropic drugs with cognitive-behavioral or psycho-dynamic psychotherapy rather than relying on drugs by themselves. One reason for preferring a combined approach is the growing recognition that many mood disorders, as well as other mental health problems, are related to dysfunctional behaviors and not just abnormalities in brain structure or function. Correcting the cognitive distortions that reinforce the behavior is more effective over the long run than suppressing or alleviating symptoms via medication. Psychotropic drugs may, however, be prescribed for short-term symptom relief.

Precautions

There are several precautions that patients should observe before taking any psychotropic drug:

- Have a discussion with the doctor about the drug: its benefits, risks, and possible side effects, and whether other forms of treatment are available
- Inform the doctor of any allergic reactions to any medications of any type, and making sure the doctor has a complete list of all other medications (over-the-counter as well as prescription) that the patient is taking
- Read the instructions that come with the drug carefully and ask the doctor or pharmacist to explain anything that is unclear or hard to understand
- Take the medication only as directed; do not increase or decrease the dose or the frequency of the dose without telling the doctor. It is particularly important not to stop taking the drug without consulting the doctor, as some psychotropic medications (particularly benzodiazepines, opioid pain relievers, and SSRIs) can produce withdrawal syndromes if abruptly discontinued.
- Store the drug at the appropriate temperature and away from sunlight. If there are small children in the household, keep the drug in a locked cabinet or other safe place.
- Do not share the medication with other family members. This precaution is particularly important if anyone in the family has a substance abuse disorder.

Risks

There are a number of risks associated with prescription psychoactive drugs:

- Short-term adverse effects. Psychopharmaceuticals have well-known side effects that range from constipation, drowsiness, fluid retention, and nausea to loss of sexual interest, loss of coordination, skin rashes, and liver disorders. Several studies have shown that a majority of patients taking antidepressants stop using them within a year because of the side effects. Many subjects participating in clinical trials of antidepressants were able to figure out that they were receiving the real drug rather than a placebo because they experienced adverse side effects.
- Long-term adverse effects. Researchers are increasingly aware of the potential for long-term adverse effects of psychoactive medications—effects that may not appear for some years. One of the first long-term adverse effects to appear was tardive dyskinesia, a movement disorder that develops in patients taking the older antipsychotics for long periods of time. More recently, there is evidence that antipsychotics lead to shrinkage of tissue in the prefrontal cortex of the brain and that the extent of shrinkage is in direct proportion to the dosage level and duration of treatment.
- Interactions with alcohol and other medications. Depressant medications in general should not be taken with alcohol, which intensifies their effects. MAOIs have been found to have potentially dangerous interactions with amphetamines, SSRIs, SNRIs, and many other drugs.
- Withdrawal effects. Patients should not stop taking any psychoactive drug without consulting their doctor, as many of these medications can produce withdrawal symptoms if they are suddenly discontinued. SSRIs, opioids, and benzodiazepines can produce symptoms ranging from irritability and anxiety to sensory disturbances and seizures if they are suddenly withdrawn. An important aspect of withdrawal effects is that they are often mistaken for a recurrence of the patient's disorder. The result is that the patient is often put back on the medication that caused the withdrawal effects, usually at a higher dosage.
- Dependence and abuse. Many classes of psychoactive drugs are associated with the risk of dependency and abuse, particularly in long-term users. Amphetamines are not recommended for treatment of persons with a history of substance abuse. Opioid dependency is another well-known problem, particularly addiction to such semi-synthetic opioids as oxycodone.

Research and general acceptance

Recent research has led to a reexamination of the widespread use of psychotropic drugs. One reason is increasing questioning of the chemical imbalance theory of mental illness. As researchers have pointed out, the theory does not account for the fact that neurotransmitter levels have been found to be normal in people with mental disorders prior to treatment. It appears increasingly likely that the theory developed when doctors discovered that psychopharmaceuticals changed the levels of certain **neurotransmitters** in the brain; the doctors then assumed that the mental illness was caused by abnormal levels of neurotransmitters. It is entirely possible that any symptom relief by psychoactive drugs is due to some other method entirely.

Another part of the problem is the recent discovery through the Freedom of Information Act that **clinical trials** of psychotropic drugs that yielded negative results were never published, while those with positive findings received considerable publicity. One researcher discovered that of 42 trials of the six most frequently prescribed antidepressants approved by the U.S. Food and Drug Administration (FDA) between 1987 and 1999, most had negative outcomes. Most trials found that placebos were about 82% as effective as the antidepressants when measured by the **Hamilton Depression Scale**, a widely used instrument. Yet because the few positive trials were widely reported, most doctors as well as patients were convinced that the antidepressants were highly effective.

A major study that failed to show the superiority of antidepressants to placebos was the 2006 Sequenced Treatment Alternatives to Relieve Depression (STAR*D) study of depression. One of the largest clinical trials ever undertaken, the study enrolled 4,041 patients across the United States who were diagnosed as moderately to severely depressed. The results showed that after a year's time, all but 108 of the 4,041 patients had either dropped out of treatment or relapsed—only 3% of the original patient group remained. A researcher who investigated the outcome of the **STAR*D study** stated, "The STAR*D analysis found that the effectiveness of antidepressant therapies was probably even lower than the modest one reported by the study authors with an apparent progressively increasing dropout rate across each study phase."

Clinical Antipsychotic Trials in **Intervention** Effectiveness (**CATIE**), a study of antipsychotic medications that was conducted between 2000 and 2004, found that the older antipsychotics were as effective for many patients as the newer and far more expensive atypical antipsychotics. In addition, it is significant that several follow-up CATIE studies were designed specifically to investigate the side effects of antipsychotic medications, in particular weight gain and a rise in blood cholesterol levels.

One question that arises from the recent reevaluation of psychopharmaceuticals is why the effectiveness of the drugs has been potentially overrated for so long. Several reasons have been proposed:

• The use of medications for mental illness removed much of the stigma previously attached to it. By attributing the symptoms of mental disorders to chemical imbalances in the brain, psychopharmacologists helped to reassure patients (and for children, their parents) that they were not "bad" people or the products of "bad parenting," but simply people with malfunctioning nervous systems.

• The discovery of antibiotics, effective vaccines against many diseases, and other "wonder drugs" in the 1940s and 1950s fostered a general cultural belief that many human problems can be solved by the right drug. Whereas previous generations recognized that some forms of grief and loss are normal responses to life events and will heal with time, people who grew up after the 1960s are more likely to have absorbed the belief that they need an antidepressant (or some other drug) to help them over temporary sadness. They then attribute their improvement after a few months to the pill rather than normal resolution of grief.

• The greater willingness of insurance companies to reimburse patients for medications rather than psychotherapy for mental health issues. With the rise of managed care in the 1980s, it became easier for doctors to simply prescribe psychotropic drugs rather than recommending counseling.

• The rapid increase of direct-to-consumer advertising of drugs on American television after 1998 (with the exception of New Zealand, other countries do not permit such advertising on television). Many of these ads exaggerate the effectiveness of antidepressants, hypnotics, and other psychoactive drugs.

• The placebo effect. The placebo effect refers to improvement in a patient's condition brought about by the patient's expectations of and confidence in an inert substance that is believed to be a drug. In other words, the effectiveness of many psychoactive drugs appears to be largely based on the placebo effect.

One sign that criticisms of the overuse of psychopharmaceuticals are having an effect is the appearance of articles in financial journals advising against investment in the companies that manufacture them. Another indication is reports in general scientific journals that pharmaceutical manufacturers are shutting down research into new drugs for psychiatric disorders.

Resources

BOOKS

Kirsch, Irving. *The Emperor's New Drugs: Exploding the Antidepressant Myth.* New York: Basic Books, 2010.

Lichtblau, Leonard. *Psychopharmacology Demystified.* Clifton Park, NY: Delmar Cengage Learning, 2011.

Sinacola, Richard S., and Timothy Peters-Strickland. *Basic Psychopharmacology for Counselors and Psychotherapists,* 2nd ed. Boston: Pearson, 2012.

Stahl, Stephen M. *Stahl's Essential Psychopharmacology: The Prescriber's Guide,* 4th ed. New York: Cambridge University Press, 2011.

Whitaker, Robert. *Anatomy of an Epidemic: Magic Bullets, Psychiatric Drugs, and the Astonishing Rise of Mental Illness in America.* New York: Crown, 2010.

PERIODICALS

Alvarez, P.A., and J. Pahissa. "QT Alterations in Psychopharmacology: Proven Candidates and Suspects." *Current Drug Safety* 5 (January 2010): 97–104.

Angell, Marcia. "The Epidemic of Mental Illness: Why?" [part one of a two-part article]. *New York Review of Books* 58, no. 11 (June 23, 2011). http://www.nybooks.com/articles/archives/2011/jun/23/epidemic-mental-illness-why/?pagination=false (accessed September 16, 2011).

———. "The Illusions of Psychiatry." [part two of a two-part article]. *New York Review of Books* 58, no. 12 (July 14, 2011). http://www.nybooks.com/articles/archives/2011/jul/14/illusions-of-psychiatry/?pagination=false (accessed September 16, 2011).

Cressy, Daniel. "Psychopharmacology in Crisis." *Nature News,* June 14, 2011. http://dx.doi.org/10.1038/news.2011.367 (accessed September 16, 2011).

Claessens, S.E., et al. "Development of Individual Differences in Stress Responsiveness: An Overview of Factors Mediating the Outcome of Early Life Experiences." *Psychopharmacology (Berlin)* 214 (March 2011): 141–54.

Pigott, H.E., et al. "Efficacy and Effectiveness of Antidepressants: Current Status of Research." *Psychotherapy and Psychosomatics* 79 (May 2010): 267–79.

Praharaj, S.K., et al. "Sensory Disturbances Associated with Serotonin Reuptake Inhibitors: Brief Review." *Human Psychopharmacology* 25 (April 2010): 216–21.

Pratt, H.D. "Point-counter-point: Psychotherapy in the Age of Pharmacology." *Pediatric Clinics of North America* 58 (February 2011): 1–9.

WEBSITES

Leventhal, Allan M. "What Underlies Psychopharmacology?" *Dissident Voice,* May 4, 2011. http://dissidentvoice.org/2011/05/what-underlies-psychopharmacology (accessed September 16, 2011).

ORGANIZATIONS

American College of Neuropsychopharmacology, 5034-A Thoroughbred Lane, Brentwood, TN, 37027, (615) 324-2360, Fax: (615) 523-1715, acnp@acnp.org, http://www.acnp.org/default.aspx.

American Society for Clinical Pharmacology and Therapeutics, 528 N Washington St., Alexandria, VA, 22314, (703) 836-6981, info@ascpt.org, http://www.ascpt.org.

European College of Neuropsychopharmacology (ECNP), PO Box 85410, Utrecht, Netherlands3508 AK, +31302538567, Fax: +31302538568, secretariat@ecnp.eu, http://www.ecnp.eu.

Rebecca J. Frey, Ph.D.

Psychosis

Definition

Psychosis is a symptom or feature of mental illness typically characterized by radical changes in personality, impaired functioning, and a distorted or nonexistent sense of objective reality.

Description

Patients suffering from psychosis have impaired reality testing; that is, they are unable to distinguish personal subjective experience from the reality of the external world. They experience hallucinations and/or **delusions** that they believe are real, and may behave and communicate in an inappropriate and incoherent fashion. Psychosis may appear as a symptom of a number of mental disorders, including mood and **personality disorders**. It is also the defining feature of **schizophrenia, schizophreniform disorder, schizoaffective disorder, delusional disorder**, and the psychotic disorders (i.e., **brief psychotic disorder, shared psychotic disorder**, psychotic disorder due to a general medical condition, and **substance-induced psychotic disorder**).

Causes and symptoms

Psychosis may be caused by the interaction of biological and psychosocial factors, depending on the disorder in which it presents; psychosis can also be caused by purely social factors, with no biological component.

Biological factors that are regarded as contributing to the development of psychosis include genetic abnormalities and substance use. With regard to chromosomal abnormalities, studies indicate that 30% of patients diagnosed with a psychotic disorder have a microdeletion at chromosome 22q11. Another group of researchers has identified the gene G72/G30 at chromosome 13q33.2 as a susceptibility gene for childhood-onset schizophrenia and psychosis not otherwise specified.

With regard to **substance abuse**, several different research groups reported in 2004 that **cannabis** (marijuana) use is a risk factor for the onset of psychosis.

Migration is a social factor that influences people's susceptibility to psychotic disorders. Psychiatrists in Europe have noted the increasing rate of schizophrenia and other psychotic disorders among immigrants to almost all Western European countries. Black immigrants from Africa or the Caribbean appear to be especially vulnerable. The stresses involved in migration include family breakup, the need to adjust to living in large urban areas, and social inequalities in the new country.

Schizophrenia, schizophreniform disorder, and schizoaffective disorder

Psychosis in schizophrenia and perhaps schizophreniform disorder appears to be related to abnormalities in the structure and chemistry of the **brain**, and appears to have strong genetic links, but its course and severity can be altered by social factors such as **stress** or a lack of support within the family. The cause of schizoaffective disorder is less clear cut, but biological factors are also suspected.

Delusional disorder

The exact cause of delusional disorder has not been conclusively determined, but potential causes include heredity, neurological abnormalities, and changes in brain chemistry. Some studies have indicated that delusions are generated by abnormalities in the limbic system, the portion of the brain on the inner edge of the cerebral cortex that is believed to regulate emotions. Delusional disorder is also more likely to develop in persons who are isolated from others in their society by language difficulties and/or cultural differences.

Brief psychotic disorder

Trauma and stress can cause a short-term psychosis (less than a month's duration) known as brief psychotic disorder. Major life-changing events such as the death of a family member or a natural disaster have been known to stimulate brief psychotic disorder in patients with no prior history of mental illness.

Psychotic disorder due to a general medical condition

Psychosis may also be triggered by an organic cause, termed a psychotic disorder due to a general medical condition. Organic sources of psychosis include neurological conditions (for example, epilepsy and cerebrovascular disease), metabolic conditions (for example, porphyria), endocrine conditions (for example, hyper- or hypothyroidism), renal failure, electrolyte imbalance, or autoimmune disorders.

Substance-induced psychotic disorder

Psychosis is also a known side effect of the use, abuse, and withdrawal from certain drugs. So-called recreational drugs, such as hallucinogenics, PCP, **amphetamines**, **cocaine**, marijuana, and alcohol, may cause a psychotic reaction during use or withdrawal. Certain prescription medications such as **steroids**, anticonvulsants, chemotherapeutic agents, and antiparkinsonian medications may also induce psychotic symptoms. Toxic substances such as carbon monoxide have also been reported to cause substance-induced psychotic disorder.

Shared psychotic disorder

Shared psychotic disorder, also known as *folie à deux* or psychosis by association, is a relatively rare delusional disorder involving two (or more) people with close emotional ties. In the West, shared psychosis most commonly develops between two sisters or between husband and wife, while in Japan the most common form involves a parent and a son or daughter. Shared psychosis occasionally involves an entire nuclear family.

Psychosis is characterized by the following symptoms:

- Delusions. Those delusions that occur in schizophrenia and its related forms are typically bizarre (i.e., they could not occur in real life). Delusions occurring in delusional disorder are more plausible, but still patently untrue. In some cases, delusions may be accompanied by feelings of paranoia.
- Hallucinations. Psychotic patients see, hear, smell, taste, or feel things that aren't there. Schizophrenic hallucinations are typically auditory or, less commonly, visual; but psychotic hallucinations can involve any of the five senses.
- Disorganized speech. Psychotic patients, especially those with schizophrenia, often ramble on in incoherent, nonsensical speech patterns.
- Disorganized or catatonic behavior. The catatonic patient reacts inappropriately to his/her environment by either remaining rigid and immobile or by engaging in excessive motor activity. Disorganized behavior is behavior or activity that is inappropriate for the situation, or unpredictable.

Diagnosis

Patients with psychotic symptoms should undergo a thorough physical examination and history to rule out such possible organic causes as **seizures**, **delirium**, or alcohol withdrawal, and such other psychiatric conditions as dissociation or panic attacks. If a psychiatric cause such as schizophrenia is suspected, a mental health professional will typically conduct an interview with the patient and administer one of several clinical inventories, or tests, to evaluate mental status. This assessment takes place in either an outpatient or hospital setting.

Psychotic symptoms and behaviors are considered psychiatric emergencies, and persons showing signs of psychosis are frequently taken by family, friends, or the police to a hospital emergency room. A person diagnosed as psychotic can be legally hospitalized

Brief psychotic disorder—An acute, short-term episode of psychosis lasting no longer than one month. This disorder may occur in response to a stressful event.

Delirium—An acute but temporary disturbance of consciousness marked by confusion, difficulty paying attention, delusions, hallucinations, or restlessness. Delirium may be caused by drug intoxication, high fever related to infection, head trauma, brain tumors, kidney or liver failure, or various metabolic disturbances.

Delusional disorder—Individuals with delusional disorder suffer from long-term, complex delusions that fall into one of six categories: persecutory, grandiose, jealous, erotomanic, somatic, or mixed.

Delusions—An unshakable belief in something untrue that cannot be explained by religious or cultural factors. These irrational beliefs defy normal reasoning and remain firm even when overwhelming proof is presented to refute them.

Hallucinations—False or distorted sensory experiences that appear to be real perceptions to the person experiencing them.

Paranoia—An unfounded or exaggerated distrust of others, sometimes reaching delusional proportions.

Porphyria—A disease of the metabolism characterized by skin lesions, urine problems, neurologic disorders, and/or abdominal pain.

Schizoaffective disorder—Schizophrenic symptoms occurring concurrently with a major depressive or manic episode.

Schizophrenia—A debilitating mental illness characterized by delusions, hallucinations, disorganized speech and behavior, and inappropriate or flattened affect (a lack of emotions) that seriously hampers the afflicted individual's social and occupational functioning. Approximately 2 million Americans suffer from schizophrenia.

Schizophreniform disorder—A short-term variation of schizophrenia that has a total duration of one to six months.

Shared psychotic disorder—Also known as *folie à deux,* shared psychotic disorder is an uncommon disorder in which the same delusion is shared by two or more individuals.

Tardive dyskinesia—Involuntary movements of the face and/or body that are a side effect of the long-term use of some older antipsychotic (neuroleptic) drugs. Tardive dyskinesia affects 15%-20% of patients on long-term neuroleptic treatment.

against his or her will, particularly if he or she is violent, threatening to commit **suicide**, or threatening to harm another person. A psychotic person may also be hospitalized if he or she has become malnourished or ill as a result of failure to feed, dress appropriately for the climate, or otherwise take care of him- or herself.

Treatment

Psychosis that is symptomatic of schizophrenia or another psychiatric disorder should be treated by a **psychologist** and/or **psychiatrist**. An appropriate course of medication and/or psychosocial therapy is employed to treat the underlying primary disorder. If the patient is considered to be at risk for harming himself or others, inpatient treatment is usually recommended.

Treatment of shared psychotic disorder involves separating the affected persons from one another as well as using antipsychotic medications and **psychotherapy**.

Antipsychotic medication such as **thioridazine** (Mellaril), **haloperidol** (Haldol), **chlorpromazine**

(Thorazine), **clozapine** (Clozaril), sertindole (Serlect), **olanzapine** (Zyprexa), or **risperidone** (Risperdal) is usually prescribed to bring psychotic symptoms under control and into remission. Possible side effects of antipsychotics include dry mouth, drowsiness, muscle stiffness, and **tardive dyskinesia** (involuntary movements of the body). Agranulocytosis, a potentially serious but reversible health condition in which the white blood cells that fight infection in the body are destroyed, is a possible side effect of clozapine. Patients treated with this drug should undergo weekly blood tests to monitor white blood cell counts for the first six months, then every two weeks thereafter.

After an acute psychotic episode has subsided, antipsychotic drug maintenance treatment is typically employed and psychosocial therapy and living and vocational skills training may be attempted.

Prognosis

Prognosis for brief psychotic disorder is quite good; for schizophrenia, less so. Generally, the longer and more severe a psychotic episode, the poorer the prognosis is for the patient. Early **diagnosis** and treatment are critical to improving outcomes for the patient across all psychotic disorders.

Approximately 10% of America's permanently disabled population is comprised of schizophrenic individuals. The mortality rate of schizophrenic individuals is also high—approximately 10% of schizophrenics commit suicide, and 20% attempt it. However, early diagnosis and long-term follow up care can improve the outlook for these patients considerably. Roughly 60% of patients with schizophrenia will show substantial improvement with appropriate treatment.

Resources

BOOKS

Capps, Donald. *Understanding Psychosis: Issues and Challenges for Sufferers, Families, and Friends*. Lanham, MD: Rowman & Littlefield, 2010.

Porter, Robert S., and Justin L. Kaplan, eds. *The Merck Manual of Diagnosis and Therapy*. 19th ed. Whitehouse Station, NJ: Merck Research Laboratories, 2011.

PERIODICALS

Addington, A. M., et al. "Polymorphisms in the 13q33.2 Gene G72/G30 Are Associated with Childhood-Onset Schizophrenia and Psychosis Not Otherwise Specified." *Biological Psychiatry* 55, no. 10 (May 15, 2004): 976–980.

Hutchinson, G., and C. Haasen. "Migration and Schizophrenia: The Challenges for European Psychiatry and Implications for the Future." *Social Psychiatry and Psychiatric Epidemiology* 39, no. 5 (May 2004): 350–357.

Sim, M.G., E. Khong, and G. Hulse. "Cannabis and Psychosis." *Australian Family Physician* 33, no. 4 (April 2004): 229–232.

Tolmac, J., and M. Hodes. "Ethnic Variation among Adolescent Psychiatric In-Patients with Psychotic Disorders." *British Journal of Psychiatry* 184 (May 2004): 428–431.

Verdoux, H., and M. Tournier. "Cannabis Use and Risk of Psychosis: An Etiological Link?" *Epidemiologia e psichiatria sociale* 13, no. 2 (April–June 2004): 113–119.

Williams, N. M., and M. J. Owen. "Genetic Abnormalities of Chromosome 22 and the Development of Psychosis." *Current Psychiatry Reports* 6, no. 3 (June 2004): 176–182.

ORGANIZATIONS

American Psychiatric Association, 1000 Wilson Blvd., Suite 1825, Arlington, VA, 22209-3901, (703) 907-7300, apa@psych.org, http://www.psych.org.

American Psychological Association, 750 1st Street NE, Washington, DC, 20002-4242, (202) 336-5500; TDD/TTY: (202) 336-6123, (800) 374-2721, http://www.apa.org.

National Alliance on Mental Illness, 3803 North Fairfax Drive, Suite 100, Arlington, VA, 22203, (703) 524-7600, Fax: (703) 524-9094, http://www.nami.org.

National Institute of Mental Health, 6001 Executive Blvd., Room 8184, MSC 9663, Bethesda, MD, 20892-9663, (301) 433-4513; TTY: (301) 443-8431, (866) 615-6464; TTY: (866) 415-8051, Fax: (301) 443-4279, nimhinfo@nih.gov, http://www.nimh.nih.gov.

Paula Anne Ford-Martin
Rebecca Frey, PhD

Psychosurgery

Definition

Psychosurgery is the treatment of a psychiatric disorder using surgical techniques to destroy **brain** tissue and is now rarely used.

Purpose

Psychosurgery is considered a last-resort treatment for extreme and debilitating psychiatric disorders.

Description

Early psychosurgery—historical perspective

Brain surgery, a medical practice requiring extraordinary levels of skill and care, may be one of the oldest of all medical procedures. This surprising observation is supported by physical evidence dating back 40,000 years to Neolithic times. Archaeologists have found numerous human skulls showing signs of a procedure called

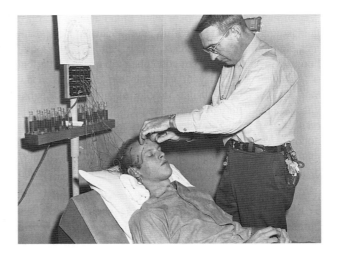

Prisoner at Vacaville Penitentiary in California, 1961, being prepared for a lobotomy. At that time, many psychiatrists believed that criminal behavior was lodged in certain parts of the brain, and lobotomies were frequently practiced on prisoners. (© *Ted Streshinsky/Corbis*)

trepanation or trepanning—an operation in which a hole is cut through the bone that covers the brain (skull) in order to access the brain. A key feature of the wounds found in these ancient skulls is the smoothness and shininess around the edges of the holes. This is a clear sign of new bone growth and evidence that the person whose skull was opened not only survived the operation but lived months or even years afterward while the bone regrew.

Opening a person's skull is a serious procedure, even with today's advanced surgical techniques. The prospect of undergoing the operation in the late Stone Age may appear to us to imply certain death. However, the survival rate of the operation was quite high. Close examination of archeological findings suggests that 75% of those who underwent the procedure lived long enough for new bone to grow around the opening. That number is actually higher than the survival rate for brain surgery during the nineteenth century, when Stone Age trepanned skulls were first identified. Brain surgery during the mid-1860s frequently resulted in infections that killed up to 75% of patients.

Trepanned skulls have been found all over the world, including sites in Peru, China, India, France, and parts of the Middle East and Africa. While trepanning is an effective surgical technique for relieving pressure on the brain caused by bleeding, most archaeologists suspect the operation was carried out in the Stone Age to achieve a different goal. Trepanning, they suspect, was performed to release evil spirits or demons, which the shamans or witch doctors of the time believed produced symptoms of what we know as mental disorders and, perhaps, diseases of the brain. The instruments used in trepanning were likely to have been made of obsidian, a very hard, glass-like, volcanic rock that can hold a very sharp cutting edge. There is also evidence that the end of a wooden stick, hardened by fire and turned back-and-forth rapidly while pressed against the skull may have served as a primitive, but effective, surgical drill.

Neuroscientist and author Elliot Valenstein believes that trepanning did not amount to intentional brain surgery. He quotes from the Latin text by the twelfth-century surgeon Roger of Salerno, who wrote: "For mania and melancholy, the skin of the top of the head should be incised in a cruciate fashion and the skull perforated to allow matter to escape."

A curious example of what might be called pseudo-psychosurgery occurred during the Middle Ages. Some unscrupulous individuals wandered across Europe convincing gullible people that mental disorders were caused by a "stone of madness." To fool others, they faked operating on the brains of mentally ill individuals and, using sleight-of-hand, appeared to produce a real stone from the victim's head, thus "proving" their claim and

effecting a "cure." No doubt, these frauds quickly moved on to other towns before their patients showed signs of continuing psychiatric symptoms.

The impetus for developing a radical treatment

Unfortunately, effective treatments for mental illnesses remained unavailable until the second half of the twentieth century. Before then, psychiatric "care" consisted mostly of imprisonment, neglect, restraint, and/or punishment. During the eighteenth century, more humane conditions of confinement were introduced, but effective treatments remained unavailable. Physicians were desperate for treatments that might make it easier to control violent and deranged patients.

By the end of the nineteenth century, researchers became aware of the role played by the frontal cortex—a part of the brain located behind the forehead—in behavior control. They discovered from the results of animal experiments and by observing humans who suffered damage to this part of the brain that the frontal lobes affect emotions and behavior. This bit of knowledge, combined with the development of effective anesthesia, led to the first modern instances of psychosurgery during the 1890s. A Swiss surgeon named Gottlieb Burkhardt deliberately damaged the frontal lobes of six psychiatric patients in hopes of relieving psychiatric symptoms; at least one of his subjects died and the experimental surgery was discontinued amid criticism from other physicians.

Psychosurgery in the twentieth century

PREFRONTAL LEUCOTOMY. In 1900, an Estonian surgeon, Lodivicus Puusepp, picked up where Burkhardt left off. He cut nerve tracks leading from the frontal lobes to other parts of the brain in psychiatric patients, with unimpressive results. A decade later, he injected tissue-destroying chemicals into the frontal lobes of mentally ill patients through holes drilled over the frontal lobes. Although the procedure accomplished little or nothing in the way of therapy, Puusepp remained optimistic about the ability of this procedure to improve the condition of psychiatric patients. Interest in the frontal lobes as a target for treating mental disorders continued on a small scale until the heyday of psychosurgery began in the 1930s.

In 1935, researchers in the United States reported that damaging the frontal lobes and a nearby region of the brain called the prefrontal cortex could pacify a previously aggressive chimpanzee. A Portuguese **psychiatrist**, Antonio Egas Moniz, learned of these results and recruited neurosurgeon Almeida Lima to operate on some humans suffering from severe psychoses. Moniz's aim was to disconnect nerve pathways running from the frontal lobes to a part of the brain called the thalamus, which is located closer to the center of the brain. By cutting these connections, Moniz hypothesized that he could disconnect a neural circuit that ran from the frontal cortex to the thalamus and then to other parts of the brain's surface. He hoped that interrupting this pathway would disrupt the repetitive thoughts that Moniz believed were responsible for psychotic symptoms.

Despite a lack of supportive evidence behind Moniz's theory, it was both accepted and performed by others in his field, likely because psychiatrists were so desperate for a treatment for severe cases of mental illness that they allowed themselves to support the use of a procedure that was unproven and increasingly subject to abuse.

Moniz and Lima called their procedure leucotomy. It involved trepanning the skull, one hole on each side of the head; inserting a wire knife; and cutting the targeted nerve fibers. Results were mixed enough for Moniz to recommend that the procedure be reserved only for the most seriously mentally ill patients for whom no other course of care or treatment worked. Nevertheless, after 1936, use of the technique spread rapidly, with equally unimpressive results overall. With little evidence of effectiveness and facing opposition from many psychiatrists, particularly psychotherapists, the technique would probably have been abandoned were it not for a pair of American physicians who revived the questionable procedure.

THE PREFRONTAL LOBOTOMY. American neurologist Walter Freeman and neurosurgeon James Watts began operating on patients in 1936 and soon began aggressively promoting its effectiveness. Eventually, they overcame doubts expressed by their colleagues who somewhat reluctantly accepted the procedure now referred to as prefrontal lobotomy. In 1946, Freeman simplified Moniz's leucotomy procedure, reducing it to a less complicated, less messy, and less time-consuming operation known as the "ice-pick lobotomy." This allowed Freeman to literally line up patients and, under local anesthesia, tap an ice pick through the thin bone on the roof of their eye sockets. With the ice pick in the brain, Freeman would sweep it back and forth to cut the frontal lobe's connections to the rest of the brain. This in-and-out procedure required no **hospitalization** but many physicians viewed it with alarm. Watts himself refused to cooperate with Freeman after this technique was developed.

Still, in the 1940s, U.S. physicians performed an estimated 20,000 lobotomies. It was equally popular in other countries, where more than 50,000 operations were conducted during the same period. Moniz's warning was forgotten. The procedure was not reserved for the most hopeless cases but instead applied to "difficult" patients, becoming a way to control behavior rather than to relieve

KEY TERMS

Computed tomography—An imaging technique in which cross-sectional x rays of the body are compiled to create a three-dimensional image of the body's internal structures; also referred to as CT or CAT scan.

Magnetic resonance imaging (MRI)—An imaging technique that uses a large circular magnet and radio waves to generate signals from atoms in the body. These signals are used to construct images of internal structures.

Psychiatrist—A medical doctor who has completed specialized training in the diagnosis and treatment of mental illness. Psychiatrists can diagnose mental illnesses, provide mental health counseling, and prescribe medications.

Trepanation—An operation in which a hole is cut through the bone that covers the brain (skull) in order to access the brain.

symptoms of mental disorder. The abuse often bordered on the criminal. Despite the ethical considerations, Moniz received the 1949 Nobel Prize for Medicine and Physiology for pioneering the procedure.

Critics of the operation began to convince others that there was no scientific proof that lobotomies helped mentally ill patients. It could certainly calm violent patients, but it did so at a terrible cost. As one nurse who recently treated an aged patient who had been lobotomized years before said, "You look in her eyes and you see there is no one there." Victims of the procedure lacked emotions, ambition, social skills, and the ability to plan. The operation was used to control the mentally ill and others, such as uncontrollable children and political dissidents, whose behavior did not conform to society's standards. Arguments against the procedure were powerful: it permanently and severely damaged the brain and often produced unreactive, lifeless individuals whose personalities were forever destroyed. With the introduction of psychotherapeutic drugs—especially **chlorpromazine** (Thorazine)—in the mid-1950s, lobotomies fell out of fashion.

Deep brain stimulation

A surgical procedure called deep brain stimulation (DBS) is currently being used to treat neurological symptoms of Parkinson's disease. DBS is utilized when patients cannot be adequately controlled with medication, and can help treat the neurological symptoms of

Parkinson's such as tremors, slowed movements, rigidity, and unsteady gait.

DBS involves the surgical implantation of an electrode, an extension wire, and a device called a neurostimulator. The electrode is implanted into the brain through a small opening in the skull, and the extension wire is connected between the electrode to the neuro-stimulator (a battery operated device similar to a pacemaker), which is implanted under the skin in the collarbone region. Surgeons use **magnetic resonance imaging** (MRI) or **computed tomography** (CT) scans before the procedure to identify the area of the brain that is causing the neurological symptoms. After the device is in place, electrical impulses are sent from the neuro-stimulator unit and wire system to the brain, where impulses block electrical signals causing the Parkinson's neurological symptoms.

Deep brain stimulation serves to block nerve impulses, but it does not destroy nerve cells or destroy brain tissue, giving it the advantage of being easily programmed or adjusted to the degree of symptoms or being reversed in use altogether. Many patients with Parkinson's disease find they can take fewer medications (reducing the number of medication side effects) when the medications are used in conjunction with DBS. The U.S. Food and Drug Administration (FDA) approved DBS as a treatment for Parkinson's disease in 2002, and it is also being studied for use in treating symptoms of **depression**, obsessive compulsive disorder (OCD), and **Tourette syndrome**. To find out more about medical research studies and these **clinical trials**, visit the U.S. National Institutes of Health website on clinical trials: http://clinicaltrials.gov.

Modern psychosurgery

No one advocates the use of classical lobotomies today as a treatment for mental disorders. Previously, a small minority of neurologists advocated the use of very precise surgical techniques to produce small lesions in defined areas of the brain to treat rare cases of severe mental illness, such as life-threatening depression or incapacitating anxiety or obsessions, but there is little need for such procedures today. Antipsychotic and antidepressant medications are the preferred options for treating mental disorders. Mainstream medicine now classifies psychosurgery as an experimental procedure, and many rules exist to protect patients who might be subjected to it. The majority of mental health profes-sionals believe that psychosurgery is either never justified or should only be considered as a last resort, to be reserved for the most extreme cases of untreatable mental disease when all other therapies have failed and the potential benefits outweigh the risks.

Resources

BOOKS

American Psychiatric Association. *Diagnostic and Statistical Manual of Mental Disorders.* 4th ed., text rev. Washington, DC: American Psychiatric Association, 2000.

American Psychological Association. *Publication Manual of the American Psychological Association.* 6th ed. Washington, DC: American Psychological Association, 2009.

Dowbiggin, Ian. *The Quest for Mental Health: A Tale of Science, Medicine, Scandal, Sorrow, and Mass Society.* New York: Cambridge University Press, 2011.

Kapur, Narinder, ed. *The Paradoxical Brain.* New York: Cambridge University Press, 2011.

Levine, Brian, and Fergus I. M. Craik, eds. *Mind and the Frontal Lobes: Cognition, Behavior, and Brain Imaging.* New York: Oxford University Press, 2011.

Valenstein, Elliot S. *Great and Desperate Cures, The Rise and Decline of Psychosurgery and Other Radical Treatments for Mental Illness.* New York: Basic Books, 1986.

ORGANIZATIONS

American Psychiatric Association, 1000 Wilson Blvd., Ste. 1825, Arlington, VA, 22209-3901, (703) 907-7300, apa@psych.org, http://www.psych.org.

American Psychological Association, 750 1st St. NE, Washington, DC, 20002-4242, (202) 336-5500; TDD/TTY: (202) 336-6123, (800) 374-2721, http://www.apa.org.

Mental Health America, 2000 N. Beauregard St., 6th Fl., Alexandria, VA, 22311, (703) 684-7722, (800) 969-6642, Fax: (703) 684-5968, http://www1.nmha.org.

National Alliance on Mental Illness, 3803 N Fairfax Dr., Ste. 100, Arlington, VA, 22203, (703) 524-7600, http://www.nami.org.

National Institute of Mental Health, 6001 Executive Blvd., Rm. 8184, MSC 9663, Bethesda, MD, 20892-9663, (301) 433-4513; TTY: (301) 443-8431, Fax: (301) 443-4279, (866) 615-6464; TTY: (866) 415-8051, nimhinfo@nih.gov, http://www.nimh.nih.gov.

U.S. National Institutes of Health, 9000 Rockville Pike, Bethesda, MD, 20892, (301) 496-4000; TTY: (301) 402-9612, http://www.nih.gov.

Dean A. Haycock, Ph.D.
Laura Jean Cataldo, RN, Ed.D.

Psychotherapy

Definition

Psychotherapy is the treatment of mental or emotional disorders and adjustment problems through the use of psychological techniques rather than through

A therapist (on the right) in a counselling session with a patient. *(© Photofusion Picture Library/Alamy)*

physical or biological means. Many different approaches to psychotherapy exist. Each approach applies to a specific situation for individuals. Psychotherapy is often commonly called counseling, therapy, or **talk therapy**.

Purpose

Psychotherapy is used to treat mental health issues and problems that occur in daily life. These issues and problems can include mood disorders (including **depression**), **schizophrenia**, addictions (e.g., alcohol, gambling, sex, drug), **anxiety disorders** (e.g., phobias, panic attacks, **stress**), eating disorders (e.g., bulimia, anorexia), and **personality disorders**.

Outside of diagnosed mental health conditions, psychotherapy can help with conflicts at work, in school, at home, and in other situations, such as dealing with grief after the death of a parent or minimizing aggressive behavior. It is also used to deal with serious health problems, such as cancer, and to learn techniques for coping with painful experiences in the past (such as combat in a war or **child abuse**).

Description

Psychoanalysis, the first modern form of psychotherapy, was called the "talking cure," and the many varieties of therapy practiced today are still characterized by their common dependence on a verbal exchange between the counselor or therapist and the person seeking help. The therapeutic interaction is characterized by mutual trust, with the goal of helping individuals change destructive or unhealthy behaviors, thoughts, and emotions. It is common for experienced therapists to combine several different approaches or techniques. Therapy is terminated when the treatment goals have been met or if the client and/or therapist conclude that it is not working. It can be effective to phase out treatment by gradually reducing the frequency of therapy sessions. Even after regular therapy has ended, the client may return for periodic follow-up and reassessment sessions.

Psychodynamic approach

Freudian psychoanalysis places emphasis on uncovering unconscious motivations and breaking down defenses. Therapy sessions may be scheduled once or even twice a week for a year or more. This type of therapy is appropriate when internal conflicts contribute significantly to a person's problems.

Behavioral techniques

In contrast to the psychodynamic approach, behavior-oriented therapy is geared toward helping people see their problems as learned behaviors that can be modified, without looking for unconscious motivations or hidden meanings. According to the theory behind this approach, once behavior is changed, feelings will change as well. Probably the best-known type of behavioral therapy is **behavior modification**, which focuses on eliminating undesirable habits by providing positive **reinforcement** for the more desirable behaviors.

Another behavioral technique is **systematic desensitization**, in which people are deliberately and gradually exposed to a feared object or experience to help them overcome their fears. A person who is afraid of dogs may first be told to visualize a dog, then be given a stuffed toy dog, then be exposed to a real dog seen at a distance, and eventually be forced to interact with a dog at close range. Relaxation training is another popular form of behavior therapy and is used in systematic desensitization. Through techniques such as deep breathing, visualization, and progressive muscle relaxation, clients learn to control fear and anxiety.

Cognitive methods

Some behavior-oriented therapy methods are used to alter not only overt behavior, but also the thought patterns that drive it. This type of treatment is known as **cognitive-behavioral therapy** (or just cognitive therapy). Its goal is to help people break out of distorted, harmful patterns of thinking and replace them with healthier ones. Common examples of negative thought patterns include: magnifying or minimizing the extent of a problem; "all or nothing" thinking (i.e., a person regards himself or herself as either perfect or worthless); overgeneralization (arriving at broad conclusions based

ALFRED ADLER (1870–1937)

Austrian psychiatrist Alfred Adler founded the school of individual psychology, a comprehensive "science of living." His system emphasizes the uniqueness of the individual and his or her relationships with society. In 1902, Austrian neurologist Sigmund Freud (1856–1939) invited Adler to join a small discussion group, which later became the illustrious Vienna Psychoanalytic Society. Adler was an active member but did not consider himself a pupil or disciple of Freud. He could not agree with Freud's basic assumption that sex was the main determinant of personality, and all that this implied: the dominance of biological factors over the psychological; the push of drives, making for identical, predictable patterns; the part commanding the whole; pleasure-seeking as humans' prime motivation. Whereas Freud tried to explain humans in terms of their similarity to machines and animals, Adler sought to understand and influence humans precisely in terms of what makes them different from machines and animals (concepts and values). This humanistic view characterized all the principles of his theory. Adler's views diverged ever more from those of Freud and, in 1911, he resigned from Freud's circle to formulate and found his own school.

Adler's psychology has been judged the first in a social-science direction. "In addition to regarding an individual's life as a unity, we must also take it together with its context of social relations ... [it] is not capable of doing just as it likes but is constantly confronted with tasks ... inseparably tied up with the logic of man's communal life." Adler specified three main tasks of life: occupation, association with others, and love and marriage. He also referred to them as "social ties," for they all require cooperation for their solution. Humankind's very uniqueness is influenced by relations to others: "The style of the child's life cannot be understood without reference to the persons who look after him."

The therapist's function, according to Adler, is not to treat "mental disease" but to divine the error in the patient's way of life and lead him or her to greater maturity. To this end, Adler introduced a number of diagnostic approaches. Among these, his theory of dreams, the meaning of early childhood recollections, and the role of birth order in the family have become widely known and adopted. The understanding of the patient achieved in this way is not one of depth but of context in the larger whole of his or her total transactions. This is the basis for changing the patient's picture of himself or herself and the world. In addition to this reorganization, Adler wished the patient to appreciate his or her own power of self-determination and have the courage to exercise it. To encourage the patient, the therapist must express a disinterested concern that evokes and fosters feelings of trust and fellowship.

on one incident, for example); and personalization (continually seeing oneself as the cause or focus of events).

In cognitive-behavioral therapy, a therapist may talk to the client, pointing out illogical thought patterns, or may use a variety of techniques, such as thought substitution, in which a frightening or otherwise negative thought is driven out by substituting a pleasant thought in its place. Clients may also be taught to use positive self-talk, a repetition of positive affirmations. Cognitive therapy usually takes a longer amount of time than behavior therapy, as it treats more serious problems.

Couples therapy

Couples therapy focuses on the relationship between two people, typically people who have a romantic or sexual connection. The aim of the therapy is to concentrate on the problems of the relationship and make each partner feel that they have an equal role. The therapy can be administered by either a male or female therapist, but many couples feel that having both a male and female therapist in the session is beneficial, though this practice is not typical.

Family and group therapy

Family therapy has proven effective in treating a number of emotional and adjustment problems. While the client's immediate complaint is the initial focus of attention, the ultimate goal of family therapy is to improve the interaction between all family members and enhance communication and coping skills on a long-term basis (although therapy itself need not cover an extended time period). **Group therapy**, which is often combined with individual therapy, offers the support and companionship of other people experiencing the same or similar problems and issues.

KEY TERMS

Anorexia nervosa—An eating disorder highlighted by a person's denial of a healthy body weight, distortion of their outward appearance, and steadfast refusal to eat much food for a fear that they may gain weight.

Attention deficit hyperactivity disorder (ADHD)—A condition found mostly in children, with primary symptoms of an inability to concentrate, inappropriate behaviors, and impulsiveness.

Cognitive behavioral techniques—A type of therapy used to solve problems concerning dysfunctional behaviors (responses), emotions (feelings), and cognitions (abilities to gather knowledge) through a proven systematic set of procedures.

Cognitive therapy—A type of psychiatric treatment involving the treatment of anxiety and/or depression, which encourages patients to confront their problems in order to improve their behavior.

Depression—A psychiatric disorder involving feelings of hopelessness and symptoms of fatigue, sleeplessness, suicidal tendencies, and poor concentration.

Eating disorders—A number of medical conditions characterized by abnormal eating habits that can involve either the lack, or the excessive intake, of food, which results in physical and/or emotional stress. Two types of eating disorders include anorexia nervosa and bulimia nervosa.

Psychodynamic psychotherapy—A method of verbal communication used to help a person find relief from emotional pain.

Schizophrenia—A mental disorder involving degraded thinking and emotions.

Stress—A physical and psychological response that results from being exposed to a demand or pressure.

Preparation

Preparation for psychotherapy should include discussing the problem first with a family doctor or other medical professional. They can help to provide insight into the problem and make recommendations for further treatment. They also can provide information on which type of psychotherapists to use, based on education, background, expertise, and other valid measures.

Aftercare

After psychotherapy sessions are formally ended, the patient may return to the therapist for periodic check-ups and to make sure a **relapse** is not occurring.

Tests

There are several reasons for performing psychological tests after an individual completes psychotherapy, including court requests, rehabilitation, and learning or emotional problems. For instance, a judge may request a person be tested for use within a court case, such as in custody or accident cases. In addition, school officials may request such a test for a child suspected of having a learning or behavioral problem, such as **attention deficit hyperactivity disorder (ADHD)**.

Risks

Psychotherapists use various techniques within psychotherapy to increase self-awareness, improve behavior and cognition, and develop insights within their patients. Individual, couples, group, and family sessions may be given. Various personal and interpersonal problems are treated during these times. Professional psychotherapists—such as clinical psychologists, mental health counselors, **social workers**, family therapists, and many others—are trained, certified, and licensed to perform such therapies, though abilities vary among individual professionals, as they do in any field.

In addition, such professionals may have certifications and licenses in one or more areas of expertise. For instance, licensed professional counselors (LPCs) may have special certifications in mental health, rehabilitation, and school counseling. Specific approaches and methods, along with specific psychotherapists, may or may not be conducive to all individuals. Consequently, the desired results may not be fulfilled in all cases.

It is important to note that any professional can adopt the title of psychotherapist, even if he or she isn't licensed. When seeking therapy, it is best to inquire as to the practitioner's credentials to assure that they are licensed to conduct therapy.

Although such risks are present in psychotherapy, they are usually minor compared with the problem at the central focus of the therapy. During such therapy, these problems will be identified, so serious and/or painful feelings will often cause discomfort, anxiety, or stress. In addition, the therapist may use exposure therapy, which confronts the patient with their problem and may cause additional stress. For instance, if an individual has a fear of confined spaces, part of the therapy might include riding an elevator with the therapist and, eventually,

QUESTIONS TO ASK YOUR DOCTOR

- How can psychotherapy help me?
- What type of specialist do you recommend I use for psychotherapy?
- Will my health insurance pay for psychotherapy?
- How will I know when psychotherapy sessions are no longer needed?
- Will psychotherapy cure my condition?
- Will I need additional sessions in the future once I complete psychotherapy?

alone. In the end, the successful conclusion of therapy often outweighs any risks.

Results

Results may vary in psychotherapy due to wide approach to the treatment of mental or emotional disorders and adjustment. However, it can be successful with the right psychotherapist and a positive attitude from the patient. Before attending the first session, make goals you wish to attain so they can be discussed with the therapist. In addition, therapy works better when the patient attends all appointments made by the therapist. When attending sessions, the more effort and time expended by the patient, the more likely successful results will be attained. In any case, therapy is a good step for identifying and resolving problems in order to live a healthier and happier life.

Resources

BOOKS

Corey, Gerald. *Theory and Practice of Counseling and Psychotherapy,* 7th ed. Belmont, CA: Thomson/Brooks Cole, 2005.

Corsini, Raymond J., and Danny Wedding. *Current Psychotherapies.* Belmont, CA: Wadsworth, 2007.

Seligman, Linda. *Theories of Counseling and Psychotherapy: Systems, Strategies, and Skills,* 2nd ed. Upper Saddle River, NJ: Prentice Hall, 2005.

Sharf, Richard S. *Theories of Psychotherapy & Counseling: Concepts and Cases.* Belmont, CA: Wadsworth, 2007.

PERIODICALS

Anderson, Rebecca A., and Clare S. Rees. "Group Versus Individual Cognitive-Behavioural Treatment for Obsessive-Compulsive Disorder: A Controlled Trial." *Behaviour Research and Therapy* 45, no. 1 (January 2007): 123–37.

Pepper, Robert. "Too Close for Comfort: The Impact of Dual Relationships on Group Therapy and Group Therapy Training." *International Journal of Group Psychotherapy* 57, no. 1 (January 2007): 13–23.

Powles, William E. "Reflections on 'What is a Group?'" *International Journal of Group Psychotherapy* 57, no. 1 (January 2007): 105–113.

Roback, Howard B., and Randall F. Moore. "On the Ethical Group Psychotherapist." *International Journal of Group Psychotherapy* 57, no. 1 (January 2007): 49–59.

WEBSITES

Mayo Clinic staff. "Psychotherapy." MayoClinic.com. http://www.mayoclinic.com/health/psychotherapy/MY00186 (accessed December 31, 2010).

ORGANIZATIONS

American Psychiatric Association, 1000 Wilson Boulevard, Suite 1825, Arlington, VA, 22209-3901, (703) 907-7300, apa@psych.org, http://www.psych.org.

American Psychoanalytic Association, 309 East 49th Street, New York City, NY, 10017, (212) 752-0450, Fax: (212) 593-0571, info@aspa.org, http://www.apsa.org.

American Psychological Association, 750 First Street, N.E., Washington, DC, 20002, (202) 336-5500, (800) 374-2721, http://www.apa.org.

American Psychotherapy Association, 2750 East Sunshine Street, Springfield, MO, 65804, (417) 823-0173, (800) 205-9165, http://www.americanpsychotherapy.com.

Ruth A. Wienclaw, PhD

Psychotherapy integration

Definition

Psychotherapy integration is defined as an approach to **psychotherapy** that includes a variety of attempts to look beyond the confines of single-school approaches to see what can be learned from other perspectives. It is characterized by openness to various ways of integrating diverse theories and techniques. Psychotherapy integration can be differentiated from an eclectic approach in that an eclectic approach is one in which a therapist chooses interventions because they work (the therapist relies solely on supposed efficacy) without looking for a theoretical basis for using the technique. In contrast, psychotherapy integration attends to the relationship between theory and technique.

Purpose

The purpose of psychotherapy integration is to bring together, or integrate, the different schools of psychotherapy so that the personality of an individual is more comprehensively studied. Specifically, it strives to combine the affective, cognitive, behavioral, and physiological systems of a person's personality.

Description

The term "psychotherapy" integration has been used in several different ways. It has been applied to approaches including common factors, assimilative integration, technical eclecticism, and theoretical integration.

Common factors

"Common factors" refers to aspects of psychotherapy that are present in most, if not all, approaches to therapy. These techniques cut across all theoretical lines and appear in all psychotherapeutic activities. Because the techniques are common to all approaches to psychotherapy, the name has been given to this variety of psychotherapy integration. Examples of some common factors include:

- an established therapeutic alliance between the patient and the therapist

- exposure of the patient to prior difficulties, either in imagination or in reality

- a new corrective emotional experience that allows the patient to experience past problems in new and more benign ways

- expectations by both the therapist and the patient that positive change will result from the treatment

- therapist qualities, such as attention, empathy, and positive regard, that are facilitative of change in treatment

- the provision by the therapist, to the patient, of a reason for the problems that are being experienced.

No matter what kind of therapy is practiced, each of these common factors is present. It is difficult to imagine a treatment that does not begin with the establishment of a constructive and positive therapeutic alliance. The therapist and the patient agree to work together, and they both feel committed to a process of change occurring in the patient. Within every approach to treatment, the exposure of the patient to prior difficulties is present. In some instances, the exposure is in vivo (i.e., occurs in real life), and the patient will be asked directly to confront the source of the difficulties. In many cases, the exposure is verbal and in imagination. However, in every case, the patient must express those difficulties in some manner and, by doing so, re-experiences those difficulties through this exposure.

In successful treatment, the exposure usually is followed by a new corrective emotional experience. The "corrective emotional experience" refers to a situation in which an old difficulty is re-experienced in a new and more positive way. As the patient re-experiences the problem in a new way, that problem can be mastered, and the patient can move on to a more successful adjustment.

Having established a therapeutic alliance, and being exposed to the problem in a new and more positive context, both the therapist and the patient always expect positive change to occur. This faith and hope is a common factor that is an integral part of successful therapy. Without this hope and expectation of change, it is unlikely that the therapist can be helpful, and if the patient does not expect to change, it is unlikely that he or she will experience any positive benefit from the treatment. The therapist must possess some essential qualities, such as paying attention to the patient, being empathic with the patient, and making his or her positive regard for the patient clear in the relationship. Finally, the patient must be provided with a credible reason for the problems that he or she is undergoing. This reason is based in the therapist's theory of personality and change. The same patient going to different therapists may be given different reasons for the same problem. As long as the reason is credible, and the patient has a way to understand what had been incomprehensible, that may be sufficient for change to occur.

Assimilative integration

The second major approach to psychotherapy integration is assimilative integration, an approach in which the therapist has a commitment to one theoretical approach but is also willing to use techniques from other therapeutic approaches.

For example, a therapist may try to understand patients in terms of psychodynamic theory, because he or she finds this most helpful in understanding what is happening in the course of the treatment. However, the therapist may also recognize that there are techniques outside psychodynamic theory that work very well, and these may then be used in the treatment plan. The psychodynamic therapist can occasionally use cognitive-behavioral techniques, such as homework, and may occasionally use humanistic approaches, such as a two-chair technique, but always retains a consistent psychodynamic understanding.

The treatment can take place in a way that is beneficial to the patient and is not bound by the restrictions of the therapist's favorite way to intervene. The patient might not be aware that integration is taking place, but he or she does feel that a consistent approach is being maintained. Most patients are not familiar with theory and therefore do not realize that different techniques are generated by different theoretical understandings, and only are concerned with whether the treatment is helpful or not.

Inherent in psychotherapy integration is the conviction that there is no single approach to therapy that is suitable to every patient. Both in single-school approaches and in psychotherapy integration, the treatment must be suitable for the individual patient. In making the treatment suitable for the individual patient, the therapist must understand the patient, and that establishes a place for theory. Assimilative integration is particularly useful in that theory helps in the understanding of the needs of the patient, but then several different approaches to technique can help to design a treatment that fits that particular understanding. The treatment plan then must undergo continuous revision as the understanding of the patient gets fuller and deeper over the course of the treatment.

Technical eclecticism

Technical eclecticism is a variation of assimilative integration and is most common among those practitioners who refer to themselves as eclectic. In technical eclecticism, the same diversity of techniques is displayed as in assimilative integration, but there is no unifying theoretical understanding that underlies the approach. Rather, the therapist relies on previous experience and on knowledge of the theoretical and research literature to choose interventions that are appropriate for the patient.

The obvious similarity between assimilative integration and technical eclecticism is that both rely on a wide variety of therapeutic techniques, focusing on the welfare of the patient rather than on allegiance to any particular school of psychotherapy. The major difference between the two is that assimilative integration is bound by a unifying theoretical understanding, whereas technical eclecticism is free of theory and relies on the experience of the therapist to determine the appropriate interventions.

Theoretical integration

The fourth approach to psychotherapy integration is called "theoretical integration." This is the most difficult level at which to achieve integration because it requires integrating theoretical concepts from different approaches, and these approaches may differ in their fundamental philosophy about human behavior. Whereas assimilative integration begins with a single theory and brings together techniques from different approaches, theoretical integration tries to bring together those theoretical approaches themselves and then to develop what in physics is referred

KEY TERMS

Cognitive behavioral techniques—A type of therapy that is used to solve problems concerning dysfunctional behaviors (responses), emotions (feelings), and cognitions (abilities to gather knowledge) through a proven systematic set of procedures.

Cognitive therapy—A type of psychiatric treatment involving the treatment of anxiety and/or depression, which encourages patients to confront their problems in order to improve their behavior.

Psychoanalysis—A form of therapy based on the understanding that human beings are largely unaware of the mental processes that determine their thoughts, feelings, and behavior, and that psychological suffering can be alleviated by making those processes known to the individual.

Psychodynamic therapy—Sometimes also called "psychodynamic psychotherapy," it is a method of verbal communication that is used to help a person find relief from emotional pain.

to as a "grand unified theory." Neither psychotherapists nor physicists have been successful to date in producing a grand unified theory. It is difficult to imagine a theory that really can combine an approach that has one philosophical understanding, with another that has a different philosophical understanding. For example, a psychodynamic approach believes that an early difficulty leads to a pattern of behavior that is repetitive, destructive, and nearly impossible to resolve. In contrast, behavior therapy sees problems as much more amenable to change. This difference may represent a basic incompatibility between the two theories. Therefore, theoretical integration would be faced with the task of integrating a theory about the stability of behavior with a theory about the ready changeability of behavior, and unless this obstacle can be overcome, theoretical integration will not be achieved.

Conclusions

The general point in three of these approaches—common factors, assimilative integration, and theoretical integration—is that there is a clear value to the role of theory in psychotherapy integration, whether the theory concerns the way integration works (theoretical integration), the framework that governs the choice of interventions (assimilative integration), or the organizing principle for understanding the common factors that are present in all psychotherapy. Technical eclecticism is not

QUESTIONS TO ASK YOUR DOCTOR

- How can psychotherapy integration help me?
- Why will it help?
- What type of specialist do you recommend I use for psychotherapy integration?
- Where can I find more information relating to psychotherapy integration, specifically relating to my condition?
- Will a therapist using psychotherapy integration be better for me rather than a therapist using only one approach to psychotherapy?
- Will my health insurance pay for psychotherapy integration?
- How will I know when psychotherapy integration sessions are no longer needed?
- Will psychotherapy integration cure my condition?
- Will I need additional sessions in the future once completing psychotherapy integration?

concerned with theory, but it does view the benefit of the patient to be of more significance than the adherence to any single theory.

Aftercare

As with any approach to psychotherapy, aftercare is usually necessary even with the most successful of the results.

Risks

About half of therapists mix schools of psychotherapy in their practice, while the other half remain purists. Some controversy exists as to which is better: "purist schools" (those that do not mix the various school of psychotherapy) or "psychotherapy integration schools" (those that do).

Results

For the most part, therapists and patients have benefited from the use of psychotherapy integration, as it allows more flexibility in the therapist to treat patients. In psychotherapy integration, the therapist has the ability to use different approaches based on the specific needs of individual patients. As such, the professional can customize therapy to individual needs. Although usually more complex, psychotherapy integration has more potential to be successful. However, its success is strongly based on

the experience and expertise of the therapist, one in which long-term training is especially important.

Resources

BOOKS

Corey, Gerald. *Theory and Practice of Counseling and Psychotherapy,* 7th ed. Belmont, CA: Thomson/Brooks Cole, 2005.

Corsini, Raymond J., and Danny Wedding. *Current Psychotherapies.* Belmont, CA: Wadsworth, 2007.

Gold, Jerold R. *Key Concepts in Psychotherapy Integration.* New York City: Springer, 2006.

Norcross, John C., and Marvin R. Goldfried, editors. *Handbook of Psychotherapy Integration.* New York City: Oxford University Press, 2005.

Scaturo, Douglas. *Clinical Dilemmas In Psychotherapy: A Transtheoretical Approach To Psychotherapy Integration.* Washington, DC: American Psychological Association, 2005.

Seligman, Linda. *Theories of Counseling and Psychotherapy: Systems, Strategies, and Skills,* 2nd ed. Upper Saddle River, NJ: Prentice Hall, 2005.

Sharf, Richard S. *Theories of Psychotherapy & Counseling: Concepts and Cases.* Belmont, CA: Wadsworth, 2007.

Stricker, George. *Psychotherapy Integration.* Washington, DC: American Psychological Association, 2010.

Stricker, George, and Jerold R. Gold, editors. *Comprehensive Handbook of Psychotherapy Integration.* New York City: Spring, 2004.

PERIODICALS

Allen, David M. "Use of Between-Session Homework in Systems-Oriented Individual Psychotherapy." *Journal of Psychotherapy Integration* 16, no. 2 (June 2006): 238–53.

Beitman, Bernard D., and Angela M. Soth. "Activation of Self-Observation: A Core Process Among the Psychotherapies." *Journal of Psychotherapy Integration* 16, no. 4 (December 2006): 383–97.

Brodley, Barbara T. "Client-Initiated Homework in Client-Centered Therapy." *Journal of Psychotherapy Integration* 16, no. 2 (June 2006): 140–61.

Melito, Richard. "Integrating Individual and Family Therapies: A Structural-Developmental Approach." *Journal of Psychotherapy Integration* 16, no. 3 (September 2006): 346–81.

Watson, Jeanne C. "Reconciling Different Voices—Developing as an Integrative Scientist Practitioner." *Journal of Psychotherapy Integration* 16, no. 1 (March 2006): 20–35.

WEBSITES

Mayo Clinic staff. "Psychotherapy." MayoClinic.com. http://www.mayoclinic.com/health/psychotherapy/MY00186 (accessed December 31, 2011).

ORGANIZATIONS

American Psychiatric Association, 1000 Wilson Boulevard, Suite 1825, Arlington, VA, 22209-3901, (703) 907-7300, apa@psych.org, http://www.psych.org.

American Psychoanalytic Association, 309 East 49th Street, New York City, NY, 10017, (212) 752-0450, Fax: (212) 593-0571, info@aspa.org, http://www.apsa.org.

American Psychological Association, 750 First Street, N.E., Washington, DC, 20002, (202) 336-5500, (800) 374-2721, http://www.apa.org.

American Psychotherapy Association, 2750 East Sunshine Street, Springfield, MO, 65804, (417) 823-0173, (800) 205-9165, http://www.americanpsychotherapy.com.

Society for the Exploration of Psychotherapy Integration, geostricker@gmail.com, http://sepiweb.org.

George Stricker, PhD
Ruth A. Wienclaw, PhD

Pyromania

Definition

Pyromania is defined as a pattern of deliberate setting of fires for pleasure or satisfaction derived from the relief of tension experienced before the firesetting. The name of the disorder comes from two Greek words that mean "fire" and "loss of reason" or "madness." The clinician's handbook *Diagnostic and Statistical Manual of Mental Disorders*, also known as the *DSM*, classifies pyromania as a disorder of impulse control, meaning that a person diagnosed with pyromania fails to resist the impulsive desire to set fires—as opposed to the organized planning of an arsonist or terrorist.

Demographics

The true incidence of pyromania in the general U.S. population remains unknown, but it is considered a rare disorder. Pyromania is diagnosed more frequently in men than in women, and repeated firesetting appears to be more common in children and adolescents than in adult males. In a 2005 review of 600 Finnish male arsonists, led by Finnish **psychiatrist** Nina Lindberg, less than 2% of the arsonists met the *DSM* criteria for pyromania, with the majority attributing alcohol to their firesetting. However, repeated firesetting at the adolescent level is a growing social and economic problem that poses major risks to the health and safety of other people and the protection of their property. In the United States, fires set by children and adolescents are more likely to result in someone's death than any other type of household disaster. The National Fire Protection Association stated that for 2008, fires set by juveniles caused 70 deaths, 910 injuries, and $279 million in property damage.

Some researchers theorize that children and adolescents attracted to firesetting when they are younger "graduate" in adult life to more serious crimes, including serial rape and murder. A number of serial killers, including David Berkowitz, the "Son of Sam" killer, and David Carpenter, the so-called Trailside Killer of the San Francisco Bay area, turned out to have been firesetters in their adolescence. Berkowitz admitted having started more than two thousand fires in Brooklyn-Queens in the early 1970s.

Another hypothesis regarding pyromania in adults is that it is more likely to emerge in the form of workplace violence. The Americans with Disabilities Act (ADA) typically forbids employers to discriminate against workers with mental or physical disabilities as long as they are qualified to perform their job. However, in 1997, the Equal Employment Opportunities Commission (EEOC) excluded pyromania (along with **kleptomania**, compulsive gambling, disorders of sexual behavior, and the use of illegal drugs) from the list of psychiatric conditions for which employers are expected to make "reasonable accommodation." The EEOC's exclusion of pyromania indicates that workers with this disorder are considered a "direct threat" to other people and property that employers are allowed to screen them out during the hiring process.

Description

Pyromania is classified by the *DSM* as an impulse-control disorder, which are disorders characterized by an inability to resist carrying out an action, despite potentially negative or harmful consequences. Some psychiatrists, however, question this classification based on the connection they find between adolescent firesetting and similar behavior in adults. One team of German researchers remarked, "Repeated firesetting, resulting from being fascinated by fire, etc., may be less a disturbance of impulse control but rather the manifestation of a psychoinfantilism, which, supported by alcohol abuse, extends into older age."

Firesetting in children and adolescents

Although most cases of firesetting in the United States involve children or adolescents rather than adults, the *DSM-IV-TR* criteria for pyromania are difficult to apply to this population. Most younger firesetters are diagnosed as having conduct disorders rather than pyromania; significantly, most of the psychiatric literature dealing with this age group speaks of "firesetting" rather than pyromania.

Some observers have attempted to classify children and adolescents who set fires as either pathological or nonpathological. Children in the former group are motivated primarily by curiosity and the desire to experiment with fire. Most are between 5 and 10 years of age and do not understand the dangers of playing with fire, and few have major psychological problems. Those who are considered to be pathological firesetters are further subdivided into five categories, which are not mutually exclusive:

- Firesetting as a cry for help. Children in this category set fires as a way of calling attention to a psychological problem, such as depression, or to an interpersonal problem, including parental separation and divorce or physical and sexual abuse.

- Delinquent firesetters. Firesetters in this category are most likely to be between the ages of 11 and 15. Their firesetting is part of a larger pattern of aggression that may also include vandalism and hate crimes. They are, however, more likely to damage property with their firesetting than to injure people.

- Severely disturbed firesetters. These youths are often diagnosed as either psychotic or paranoid and appear to be reinforced by the sensory aspects of firesetting. Some set fires as part of suicide attempts.

- Cognitively impaired firesetters. This group includes children whose impulse control is damaged by a neurological or medical condition such as fetal alcohol syndrome.

- Sociocultural firesetters. Children in this group are influenced by antisocial adults in their community and set fires in order to win their approval.

Pyromania in adults

Pyromania in adults has a high rate of comorbidity with other disorders, including **substance abuse** disorders, **obsessive-compulsive disorder** (OCD), **anxiety disorders**, and mood disorders. However, few widespread, rigorously controlled studies have been done on adult patients diagnosed with pyromania.

Causes and symptoms

Causes

Most studies of causation regarding pyromania have focused on children and adolescents who set fires. Early studies in the field used the categories of Freudian **psychoanalysis** to explain this behavior. Freud had hypothesized that firesetting represented a regression to a primitive desire to demonstrate power over nature. In addition, some researchers have tried to explain the fact that pyromania is predominantly a male disorder with reference to Freud's notion that fire has a special symbolic relationship to the male sexual urge. A study done in 1940 attributed firesetting to fears of castration in young males, and speculated that adolescents who set fires do so to gain power over adults. The 1940 study is important also because it introduced the notion of an "ego triad" of firesetting, **enuresis** (bed-wetting), and cruelty to animals as a predictor of violent behavior in adult life. Subsequent studies have found that a combination of firesetting and cruelty to animals is a significant predictor of violent behavior in adult life, but that the third member of the triad (bed-wetting) is not.

The causes of firesetting among children and teenagers are complex and not well understood, but theorized causes can be classified as either individual or environmental. Individual factors that may contribute to firesetting include:

- Antisocial behaviors and attitudes. Some adolescent firesetters have also committed other crimes, including forcible rape, nonviolent sexual offenses, and vandalism of property.

- Sensation seeking. Some youths may attracted to firesetting out of boredom or a lack of other forms of recreation.

- Attention seeking. Firesetting may be seen as a way of provoking reactions from parents and other authorities.

- Lack of social skills. Many youths arrested for firesetting are absent significant friendships.

- Lack of fire-safety skills or knowledge of the dangers associated with firesetting.

There are discrepancies between researchers' understanding of individual factors in firesetting and reports from adolescents themselves. One study of 17 teenaged firesetters, 14 males and 3 females, found 6 different self-reported reasons for firesetting: revenge, crime concealment, peer group pressure, accidental firesetting, **denial** of intention, and fascination with fire. The motivations of revenge and crime concealment would exclude these teenagers from being diagnosed with pyromania based on the *DSM* criteria.

Environmental factors that may contribute to adolescent firesetting include:

- Poor supervision on the part of parents or other adults.

- Early learning experiences of watching adults use fire carelessly or inappropriately.

- Parental neglect or lack of emotional involvement.

- Parental psychopathology. Firesetters are significantly more likely to have been physically or sexually abused than children of similar economic or geographic backgrounds. They are also more likely to have witnessed their parents abusing drugs or acting violently.

- Peer pressure. Having peers who smoke or play with fire is a risk factor for a child's setting fires himself.

- Stressful life events. Some children and adolescents resort to firesetting as a way of coping with personal crises or a lack of family support.

Symptoms

Firesetting among children and adolescents and pyromania in adults may be either chronic or episodic; some persons may set fires frequently as a way of relieving

KEY TERMS

Arson—The deliberate setting of fires for criminal purposes, usually to collect insurance money or to cover up evidence of another crime. It is distinguished from pyromania by its connection with planning and forethought rather than failure of impulse control.

Comorbidity—Association or presence of two or more mental disorders in the same patient. A disorder that is said to have a high degree of comorbidity is likely to occur in patients diagnosed with other disorders that may share or reinforce some of its symptoms.

Delusion—A false belief that is resistant to reason or contrary to actual fact. Common delusions include delusions of persecution, delusions of personal importance (sometimes called delusions of grandeur), or delusions of being controlled by others. Pyromania is excluded as a diagnosis if the patient is setting fires on the basis of a delusion.

Kleptomania—A disorder of impulse control characterized by repeated stealing or shoplifting of items that the person does not need.

Spontaneous remission—Recovery from a disease or disorder that cannot be attributed to medical or psychiatric treatments.

tension, while others apparently do so only during periods of unusual **stress** in their lives. Pyromania in adults has also been associated with symptoms of depressed mood, thoughts of **suicide**, repeated conflicts in interpersonal relationships, and poor ability to cope with stress.

Diagnosis

The *DSM* specifies six criteria that must be met for a patient to be diagnosed with pyromania:

- The patient must have set fires deliberately and purposefully on more than one occasion.

- The patient must have experienced feelings of tension or emotional arousal before setting the fires.

- The patient must indicate that he or she is fascinated with, attracted to, or curious about fire and situations surrounding fire (for example, the equipment associated with fire, the uses of fire, or the aftermath of firesetting).

- The patient must experience relief, pleasure, or satisfaction from setting the fire or from witnessing or participating in the aftermath.

- The patient does not have other motives for setting fires, such as financial motives, ideological convictions (such as terrorist or anarchist political beliefs), anger or revenge, the need to cover up another crime, delusions or hallucinations, or impaired judgment resulting from substance abuse, dementia, an intellectual disability, or traumatic brain damage.

- The firesetting cannot be better accounted for by antisocial personality disorder, a conduct disorder, or a manic episode.

Diagnosis of pyromania is complicated by a number of factors; one important factor is the adequacy of the diagnostic category itself. Some psychiatrists are not convinced that the impulse-control disorders should be identified as a separate group, in that problems with self-control are part of the picture in many psychiatric disorders. **Bulimia nervosa**, **borderline personality disorder**, and **antisocial personality disorder** are all defined in part by low levels of self-control but are not considered impulse-control disorders.

Another complication of diagnosis is the lack of experience on the part of mental health professionals in dealing with firesetting. In many cases they are either unaware that the patient is repeatedly setting fires, or they regard the pattern as part of a cluster of antisocial or dysfunctional behaviors.

Treatment

Children and adolescents

Treatment of children and adolescents involved with repeated firesetting appears to be more effective following a case-management approach rather than a medical model, as many young firesetters come from chaotic households. Treatment should begin with a structured interview with the parents as well as the child, in order to evaluate stresses on the family, patterns of supervision and discipline, and similar factors. The next stage in treatment should be tailored to the individual child and his or her home situation. A variety of treatment approaches, including problem-solving skills, anger management, communication skills, aggression replacement training, and cognitive restructuring, may be necessary to address all the emotional and cognitive issues involved in each case.

Adults

Pyromania in adults is considered difficult to treat because of the lack of insight and cooperation on the part of most patients diagnosed with the disorder. Treatment usually consists of a combination of medication—usually one of the **selective serotonin reuptake inhibitors**

(SSRIs), a class of antidepressant drugs—and long-term insight-oriented **psychotherapy**.

Prognosis

The prognosis for recovery from firesetting among children and adolescents depends on the mix of individual and environmental factors involved. Current understanding indicates that children and adolescents who set fires as a cry for help, or who fall into the cognitively impaired or sociocultural categories, benefit the most from therapy and have fairly positive prognoses. The severely disturbed and delinquent types of firesetters have a more guarded outlook.

The prognosis for adults diagnosed with pyromania is generally poor. There are some cases of spontaneous remission among adults, but the rate of spontaneous recovery is not known.

Prevention

Prevention of pyromania requires a broad-based and flexible approach to treatment of children and adolescents who set fires. In addition to better assessments of young people and their families, fire safety education is an important preventive strategy that is often overlooked.

In addition to preventive measures directed specifically at firesetting, recent research into self-control as a general character trait offers hope that it can be taught and practiced like many other human skills. If programs could be developed to improve people's capacity for self-control, they could potentially prevent a wide range of psychiatric disorders.

Resources

BOOKS

American Psychiatric Association. *Diagnostic and Statistical Manual of Mental Disorders.* 4th ed., text rev. Washington, DC: American Psychiatric Publishing, 2000.

Baumeister, Roy F. "Crossing the Line: How Evil Starts." In *Evil: Inside Human Violence and Cruelty,* by Roy F. Baumeister and Aaron Beck. New York: W. H. Freeman and Company, 2001.

Douglas, John, and Mark Olshaker. *Mindhunter: Inside the FBI's Elite Serial Crime Unit.* Audio ed. New York: Simon and Schuster, 2010.

Graham, George. *The Disordered Mind: An Introduction to Philosophy of Mind and Mental Illness.* New York: Routledge, 2010.

McElroy, Susan, and Lesley M. Arnold. "Impulse-Control Disorders." *Treatments of Psychiatric Disorders,* edited by Glen O. Gabbard. 4th ed. Washington, DC: American Psychiatric Publishing, 2007.

North, Carol, and Sean Yutzy. *Goodwin and Guze's Psychiatric Diagnosis.* New York, NY: Oxford University Press, 2010.

PERIODICALS

Evenden, John. "Impulsivity: A Discussion of Clinical and Experimental Findings." *Journal of Psychopharmacology* 13, no. 2 (March 1999): 180–192.

Everall, Ian Paul, and Ann Leconteur. "Firesetting in an Adolescent Boy with Asperger's Syndrome." *British Journal of Psychiatry* 157 (September 1990): 284–287.

Laubichler W., A. Kuhberger, P. Sedlmeier. "'Pyromania' and Arson. A Psychiatric and Criminologic Data Analysis." [in German] *Nervenarzt* 67 (September 1996): 774–780.

Slavkin, Michael L., and Kenneth Fineman. "What Every Professional Who Works with Adolescents Needs to Know About Firesetters." *Adolescence* 35 (Winter 2000): 759–764.

Strayhorn, Joseph M., Jr. "Self-Control: Theory and Research." *Journal of the American Academy of Child and Adolescent Psychiatry* 41, no. 1 (January 2002): 7–16.

Swaffer, Tracey, and Clive R. Hollin. "Adolescent Firesetting: Why Do They Say They Do It?" *Journal of Adolescence* 18, no. 5 (October 1995): 619–624.

Zugelder, Michael T., Steven D. Maurer, and Paul Champagne. "Dangerous Directives? Liability and the Unstable Worker." *Business Horizons* 42, no. 1 (January 1, 1999): 40–48.

WEBSITES

Juvenile Firesetter Intervention Program. "Juvenile Firesetting Statistics." http://www.stopfiresetting.com/florida/Home/JuvenileFiresettingStatistics/tabid/103/Default.aspx (accessed October 24, 2011).

ORGANIZATIONS

American Academy of Child and Adolescent Psychiatry, 3615 Wisconsin Ave. NW, Washington, DC, 20016-3007, (202) 966-7300, Fax: (202) 966-2891, http://aacap.org.

American Psychiatric Association, 1000 Wilson Blvd., Ste. 1825, Arlington, VA, 22209-3901, (703) 907-7300, apa@psych.org, http://www.psych.org.

American Psychological Association, 750 1st Street NE, Washington, DC, 20002-4242, (202) 336-5500; TDD/TTY: (202) 336-6123, (800) 374-2721, http://www.apa.org.

National Alliance for Research on Schizophrenia and Depression, The Brain and Behavior Research Fund, 60 Cutter Mill Rd., Ste. 404, Great Neck, NY, 11021, (516) 829-0091, Fax: (516) 487-6930, info@bbrfoundation.org, http://www.narsad.com.

National Alliance on Mental Illness, 3803 N Fairfax Drive, Ste. 100, Arlington, VA, 22203, (703) 524-7600, http://www.nami.org.

National Institute of Mental Health, 6001 Executive Blvd., Room 8184, MSC 9663, Bethesda, MD, 20892-9663, (301) 433-4513; TTY: (301) 443-8431, Fax: (301) 443-4279, (866) 615-6464; TTY: (866) 415-8051 nimhinfo@nih.gov, http://www.nimh.nih.gov.

Rebecca J. Frey, PhD
Laura Jean Cataldo, RN, EdD

Quazepam

Definition

Quazepam belongs to a class of drugs called **benzodiazepines**. These drugs ease anxiety and slow the central nervous system. In the United States, quazepam is sold under the brand name Doral.

Purpose

Quazepam is approved by the U.S. Food and Drug Administration (FDA) for the treatment of **insomnia**.

Description

Quazepam is unique in its drug properties in two ways. First, some other types of benzodiazepines have an effect called rebound insomnia. This means that the insomnia becomes worse than the original insomnia when the drug is used for extended periods. Quazepam has a minimal tendency to cause rebound insomnia. Second, quazepam is eliminated from the body slowly. This gives quazepam an advantage over certain other medications in the benzodiazepine class, such as **alprazolam** or halazepam, in that patients do not experience early-morning insomnia, since there is still enough medication to induce sleep in the very early morning hours.

Quazepam's sedating effect lasts only for about four weeks of continuous use. The medication is most effective for an intermediate-term treatment of insomnia (two weeks), rather than for a long duration of treatment of more than four weeks. Hence, long-term treatment for insomnia with quazepam should be avoided.

Quazepam comes in 7.5 mg and 15 mg tablets.

Recommended dosage

Effective doses of quazepam for the treatment of insomnia range from 7.5 mg to 30 mg at bedtime. Most patients start by taking 15 mg at bedtime. Adjustments from this dosage can be made as determined by the individual. In some patients, a dosage as low as 7.5 mg is sufficient to reduce insomnia.

Elderly patients (over age 65) should receive a dosage of 7.5 mg, because it takes longer to eliminate the drug from their bodies. Because quazepam is eliminated by the liver, dosage reduction may be necessary in patients with liver problems.

Precautions

Quazepam has an addictive potential when used for too long. Patients can become dependent on quazepam and may experience withdrawal symptoms when they stop taking the drug. Patients preparing to stop treatment with quazepam should gradually decrease the dose over time.

Patients who have a condition known as sleep apnea should not use quazepam. This condition involves episodes of breathing difficulty and oxygen deficiency that occur throughout the night. Patients who are pregnant or who had allergic reactions to quazepam should not take quazepam.

People who need to remain mentally alert, such as those who are driving or operating dangerous machinery, should wait to take quazepam, since it causes drowsiness. Some patients taking sleep aids, including quazepam, have engaged in various behaviors while asleep, such as driving or eating, with no recollection of the events. The sedative effects of quazepam are intensified when the drug is taken with alcohol. It is best not to drink alcoholic beverages while taking quazepam. Patients with compromised respiratory function (breathing problems), as well as patients with a history of drug or alcohol abuse, should be closely monitored during the short-term treatment with quazepam.

Side effects

The effects of quazepam taken at bedtime may last, or hang over, into the next day. This is the most common

Annals of Clinical Psychiatry 18, no. 1 (January–March 2006): 49–56.

KEY TERMS

Benzodiazepines—A group of central nervous system depressants used to relieve anxiety or to induce sleep.

side effect of quazepam. The symptoms of this condition include drowsiness, daytime sleepiness, slurred speech, and mental sluggishness. This effect is dose-related, and seems to occur most frequently in patients taking 30 mg doses. These effects are experienced less commonly with the 15 mg dose, but this dose may not be effective in eliminating insomnia some patients. Some people experience headaches and dizziness when taking quazepam.

A small number of patients experience dry mouth, weight loss, abnormal taste perception, abdominal pain, nausea, vomiting, and either diarrhea or constipation due to quazepam. These effects occur in about 1% to 10% of people taking the drug.

Side effects that occur in less than 1% of patients include skin problems such as rash or skin inflammation, muscle cramps, rigidity, and blurred vision. Patients who experience an allergic reaction (anaphylaxis) or severe facial swelling (angioedema) should contact their physicians immediately.

Interactions

Cimetidine (Tagamet) and ketoconazole increase the levels of quazepam in the body, potentially causing toxicity or increased side effects. Conversely, the drug theophylline decreases the effectiveness of quazepam. **Valerian**, **kava kava**, and alcohol cause increased central nervous system **depression**, which may increase sedation, drowsiness, and slowed reflexes if used while taking quazepam. Patients taking quazepam should not consume any products containing grapefruit, including grapefruit juice, as they may inhibit the absorption of quazepam, resulting in too much of the drug in the body.

Resources

BOOKS

Lacy, Charles F. *Drug Information Handbook with International Trade Names Index.* Hudson, OH: Lexi-Comp, Inc. 2011.

Preston, John D., John H. O'Neal, and Mary C. Talaga. *Handbook of Clinical Psychopharmacology for Therapists.* 5th ed. Oakland, CA: New Harbinger Publications, 2008.

PERIODICALS

Rosenberg, Russell P. "Sleep Maintenance Insomnia: Strengths and Weaknesses of Current Pharmacologic Therapies."

WEBSITES

U.S. Food and Drug Administration. "FDA Requests Label Change for All Sleep Disorder Drug Products." March 14, 2007. http://www.fda.gov/NewsEvents/Newsroom/Press Announcements/2007/ucm108868.htm (accessed November 13, 2011).

ORGANIZATIONS

U.S. Food and Drug Administration, 10903 New Hampshire Ave., Silver Spring, MD, 20993-0002, (888) INFO-FDA (463-6332), http://www.fda.gov.

Ajna Hamidovic, Pharm.D.
Ruth A. Wienclaw, PhD

Quetiapine

Definition

Quetiapine is an atypical antipsychotic drug used to treat symptoms of **schizophrenia**. It works by changing the activity of certain natural substances in the brain. Quetiapine it is available with a prescription under the trade name Seroquel.

Purpose

Quetiapine tablets and extended-release tablets are used to treat the symptoms of schizophrenia, and are used alone or with other medications to treat or prevent episodes of mania or depression in patients with bipolar disorder. The extended-release tablets are also used along with other medication to treat depression. Quetiapine

Seroquel (quetiapine), 25 mg. *(© Custom Medical Stock Photo, Inc. Reproduced by permission.)*

may be used as part of a treatment program to treat biopolar and schizophrenia in children.

Description

Quetiapine is thought to modify the actions of several chemicals in the **brain**. It is chemically related to another atypical antipsychotic agent, **clozapine**, but differs from earlier phenothiazine antipsychotics.

The effectiveness of quetiapine was evaluated in the Clinical Antipsychotic Trials of Intervention Effectiveness (**CATIE**) Schizophrenia Study. The study evaluated the effectiveness and side effects of newer antipsychotic drugs (sometimes referred to as "atypical antipsychotics") in comparison to a conventional antipsychotic drug in the treatment of schizophrenia. Contrary to expectations, the study found that the conventional antipsychotic generally was equally effective and tolerated as well as the newer, more expensive, atypical antipsychotic medications.

Only 16% of participants taking quetiapine in the Phase 1 study were able to continue throughout the entire 18 months. Participants who stopped taking their antipsychotic medication in Phase 1 because it was not adequately controlling their symptoms were more likely to stay on their medication if they were switched to **olanzapine** or **risperidone** rather than quetiapine or **ziprasidone**. There were no differences among the four medications tested in Phase 2, however, for participants who had stopped taking their Phase 1 medication because they experienced adverse side effects.

In Phase 2 of the study, the drug clozapine was more effective in controlling symptoms than the other atypical antipsychotics under evaluation. For patients whose symptoms were not well controlled on clozapine, olanzapine and risperidone tended to be more effective than ziprasidone or quetiapine.

Quetiapine is available in 25 mg, 100 mg, and 200 mg tablets.

Recommended dosage

Initially, a dosage of 25 mg should be taken twice a day. Each dose should be increased by 25–50 mg increments every three to four days until achieving a target dose of 300–400 mg per day, administered in two or three divided doses. It is not known whether doses higher than 800 mg per day are safe.

Precautions

Quetiapine is associated with an increased risk of death when used in elderly patients with **dementia**. In June 2008, the U.S. Food and Drug Administration (FDA) announced

KEY TERMS

Extrapyramidal symptoms—A group of side effects associated with antipsychotic medications and characterized by involuntary muscle movements, including contraction and tremor.

Insomnia—Waking in the middle of the night and having difficulty returning to sleep, or waking too early in the morning.

Seizure—A convulsion, or uncontrolled discharge of nerve cells that may spread to other cells throughout the brain.

a requirement for manufacturers of quetiapine (and other antipsychotic drugs) to add a warning label to their packaging stating this risk. The reason for the increase was unclear in studies, but most deaths were found to be related to either cardiovascular complications or complications associated with infection. Quetiapine is not approved by the FDA for the treatment of behavior problems in older adults with dementia, and patients in this category (or caregivers of patients in this category) should discuss with their physician the risks of taking quetiapine.

Children and adolescents up to age 24 are at increased risk of developing suicidal thoughts and actions while taking quetiapine. It should not be taken by women who are pregnant, trying to become pregnant, or breastfeeding. Babies born to mothers who took quetiapine during pregnancy may develop extrapyramidal symptoms (EPS) and withdrawal symptoms, including agitation, trouble breathing, and difficulty feeding.

Caution should be used in patients with heart disease because the drug may cause blood pressure to fall too low, resulting in dizziness, rapid heartbeat, or fainting. Quetiapine users may also be at risk for potentially fatal heart arrhythmias, especially when taken in combination with other drugs that carry the risk of arrhythmia.

Quetiapine may increase cholesterol levels and contribute to the formation of cataracts. Because of this possibility, cholesterol levels should be checked periodically and yearly eye exams should be performed.

Quetiapine may cause liver damage. As a result, patients should notify their health care providers if they experience flu-like symptoms, notice yellowing of their skin or eyes, or experience abdominal pain. Liver function should be assessed periodically. The drug should be used cautiously in people with a history of liver disease or alcoholic cirrhosis. Quetiapine should be also be used carefully by those with a history of seizure disorders, as it may increase the tendency to have **seizures**.

Quetiapine may alter the function of the thyroid gland. Those taking supplements for low thyroid function may require dosage adjustments in their thyroid medication.

Quetiapine may cause extreme drowsiness and should be used carefully by people who need to be mentally alert.

Side effects

Relatively common side effects that accompany quetiapine usage include drowsiness, dizziness, rash, dry mouth, **insomnia**, **fatigue**, muscular weakness, anorexia, blurred vision, some loss of muscular control, and amenorrhea (lack of menstruation) in women.

Dystonia (difficulty walking or moving) may occur with quetiapine use. This condition may subside in 24 to 48 hours, even when the person continues taking the drug, and it usually disappears when quetiapine is discontinued.

Quetiapine use may lead to the development of symptoms that resemble Parkinson's disease. These symptoms may include a tight or mask-like expression on the face, drooling, tremors, pill-rolling motions in the hands, cogwheel rigidity (abnormal rigidity in muscles characterized by jerky movements when the muscle is passively stretched), and a shuffling gait. Taking the anti-Parkinson's drugs **benztropine** mesylate or **trihexyphenidyl** hydrochloride along with the quetiapine usually controls these symptoms.

Quetiapine has the potential to produce a serious side effect called **tardive dyskinesia**. This syndrome consists of involuntary, uncoordinated movements that may appear late in therapy and not disappear even after the drug is stopped. Tardive dyskinesia involves involuntary movements of the tongue, jaw, mouth, face, or other groups of skeletal muscles. The incidence of tardive dyskinesia increases with age and with dosage of quetiapine. Women are at greater risk than men for developing tardive dyskinesia. There is no known effective treatment for tardive dyskinesia, although gradual (but rarely complete) improvement may occur over a long period.

One occasionally reported side effect of quetiapine use is **neuroleptic malignant syndrome**. This is a complicated and potentially fatal condition characterized by muscle rigidity, high fever, alterations in mental status, and cardiac symptoms such as irregular pulse or blood pressure, sweating, tachycardia (fast heartbeat), and arrhythmias (irregular heartbeat). People who think they may be experiencing any side effects from this or any other medication should talk to their physicians promptly.

QUESTIONS TO ASK YOUR DOCTOR

- What kind of changes can I expect to see or feel with this medication?
- Does it matter what time of day I take this medication? If so, what is the recommendation?
- Should I take this medication with or without food?
- What are the side effects associated with this medication?
- Will this medication interact or interfere with other medications I am currently taking?
- What symptoms or adverse effects are important enough that I should seek immediate treatment?

Interactions

Quetiapine may be less effective when it is taken with drugs like **carbamazepine** (Tegretol), phenytoin (Dilantin), rifampin (Rifadin), **barbiturates**, **thioridazine** (Mellaril), or corticosteroids, such as prednisolone, methylprednisolone, prednisone, and dexamethasone because these drugs increase the breakdown of quetiapine in the liver, causing lower-than-normal levels of the drug.

Antifungal drugs, such as fluconazole (Diflucan) or ketoconazole (Nizoral), and antibiotics, such as erythromycin or clarithromycin (Biaxin), and cimetidine (Tagamet) may decrease the breakdown of quetiapine in the liver, causing higher-than-normal levels of the drug.

Any drug that causes drowsiness may lead to decreased mental alertness and impaired motor skills when taken with quetiapine. Some examples include alcohol, **antidepressants**, such as **imipramine** (Tofranil) or **paroxetine** (Paxil), antipsychotics, such as thioridazine (Mellaril), and some antihistamines.

Resources

BOOKS

Albers, Lawrence J., MD, Rhoda K. Hahn, MD, and Christopher Reist, MD. *Handbook of Psychiatric Drugs.* Laguna Hills, CA: Current Clinical Strategies Publishing, 2010.

American Society of Health-System Pharmacists. *AHFS Drug Information 2011.* Bethesda: American Society of Health-System Pharmacists, 2011.

Graham, George. *The Disordered Mind: An Introduction to Philosophy of Mind and Mental Illness.* New York, NY: Routledge, 2010.

Holland, Leland Norman, and Michael Patrick Adams. *Core Concepts in Pharmacology,*3rd ed. New York, NY: Prentice Hall, 2011.

North, Carol, and Sean Yutzy. *Goodwin and Guze's Psychiatric Diagnosis.*New York, NY: Oxford University Press, 2010.

Preston, John D., John H. O'Neal, and Mary C. Talaga. *Handbook of Clinical Psychopharmacology for Therapists,* 6th ed. Oakland, CA: New Harbinger Publications, 2011.

PERIODICALS

Casey, Daniel E. "Implications of the CATIE Trial on Treatment: Extrapyramidal Symptoms." *CNS Spectrums* 11. no. 7, Supp. 7 (July 2006): 25–31.

El-Mallakh, Rif, et al. "Bipolar II Disorder: Current and Future Treatment Options." *Annals of Clinical Psychiatry* 18, no. 4 (Oct.–Dec. 2006): 259–66.

Gentile, Salvatore. "Extrapyramidal Adverse Events Associated with Atypical Antipsychotic Treatment of Bipolar Disorder." *Journal of Clinical Psychopharmacology* 27, no. 1 (Feb. 2007): 35–45.

Glick, Ira D. "Understanding the Results of CATIE in the Context of the Field." *CNS Spectrums* 11.7, Supp. 7 (July 2006): 40–47.

Haro, Josep Maria, et al. "Remission and Relapse in the Outpatient Care of Schizophrenia: Three-Year Results from the Schizophrenia Outpatient Health Outcomes Study." *Journal of Clinical Psychopharmacology* 26, no. 6 (Dec. 2006): 571–78.

Jarema, Marek. "Atypical Antipsychotics in the Treatment of Mood Disorders." *Current Opinion in Psychiatry* 20, no. 1 (Jan. 2007): 23–29.

Lieberman, Jeffrey A., et al. "Effectiveness of Antipsychotic Drugs in Patients with Chronic Schizophrenia." *New England Journal of Medicine* 353, no. 12 (Sept. 2005): 1209–23.

McEvoy, Joseph P., et al. "Effectiveness of Clozapine Versus Olanzapine, Quetiapine, and Risperidone in Patients with Chronic Schizophrenia Who Did Not Respond to Prior Atypical Antipsychotic Treatment." *American Journal of Psychiatry* 163, no. 4 (Apr. 2006): 600–10.

Meisenzahl, E.M., et al. "Effects of Treatment with the Atypical Neuroleptic Quetiapine on Working Memory Function: A Functional MRI Follow-Up Investigation." *European Archives of Psychiatry and Clinical Neuroscience* 256, no. 8 (Dec. 2006): 522–31.

Meltzer, Herbert Y., and William V. Bobo. "Interpreting the Efficacy Findings in the CATIE Study: What Clinicians Should Know." *CNS Spectrums* 11, no. 7, Supp. 7 (July 2006): 14–24.

Nasrallah, Henry A. "Metabolic Findings from the CATIE Trial and Their Relation to Tolerability." *CNS Spectrums* 11, no. 7, Supp. 7 (July 2006): 32–39.

Nasrallah, Henry A., Martin Brecher, and Björn Paulsson. "Placebo-Level Incidence of Extrapyramidal Symptoms (EPS) with Quetiapine in Controlled Studies of Patients with Bipolar Mania." *Bipolar Disorders* 8.5, part 1 (Oct. 2006): 467–74.

Pae, Chi-Un, et al. "Adjunctive Risperidone, Olanzapine and Quetiapine for the Treatment of Hospitalized Patients with Bipolar I Disorder: A Retrospective Study." *Progress in Neuro-Psychopharmacology & Biological Psychiatry* 30, no. 7 (Sept. 2006): 1322–25.

Savaskan, Egemen, et al. "Treatment of Behavioural, Cognitive and Circadian Rest-Activity Cycle Disturbances in Alzheimer's Disease: Haloperidol vs. Quetiapine." *International Journal of Neuropsychopharmacology* 9, no. 5 (Oct. 2006): 507–16.

Schneider, Lon S., et al. "Effectiveness of Atypical Antipsychotic Drugs in Patients with Alzheimer's Disease." *New England Journal of Medicine* 355, no. 15 (Oct. 2006): 1525–38.

Stroup, T. Scott, et al. "Effectiveness of Olanzapine, Quetiapine, Risperidone, and Ziprasidone in Patients with Chronic Schizophrenia Following Discontinuation of a Previous Atypical Antipsychotic." *American Journal of Psychiatry* 163, no. 4 (Apr. 2006): 611–22.

Tariot, Pierre N., et al. "Quetiapine Treatment of Psychosis Associated With Dementia: A Double-Blind, Randomized, Placebo-Controlled Clinical Trial." *American Journal of Geriatric Psychiatry* 14, no. 9 (Sept. 2006): 767–76.

Thase, Michael E., et al. "Efficacy of Quetiapine Monotherapy in Bipolar I and II Depression: A Double-Blind, Placebo-Controlled Study (The BOLDER II Study)." *Journal of Clinical Psychopharmacology* 26. no. 6 (Dec. 2006): 600–09.

Weiden, Peter J. "EPS Profiles: The Atypical Antipsychotics Are Not All the Same." *Journal of Psychiatric Practice* 13. no. 1 (Jan. 2007): 13–24.

ORGANIZATIONS

American Psychiatric Association, 1000 Wilson Boulevard, Suite 1825, Arlington, VA, 22209, (703) 907-7300, apa@psych.org, http://www.psych.org.

Mental Health America, 2000 N. Beauregard Street, 6th Floor, Alexandria, VA, 22311, (703) 684-7722, (800) 969-6642, Fax: (703) 684-5968, http://www1.nmha.org.

National Alliance on Mental Illness (NAMI), Colonial Place Three, 2107 Wilson Blvd., Suite 300, Arlington, VA, 22201, (703) 524-7600, (800) 950-NAMI (6264), Fax: (703) 524-9094, http://www.nami.org/Hometemplate.cfm.

National Institute of Mental Health (NIMH), 6001 Executive Boulevard, Room 8184, MSC 9663, Bethesda, MD, 20892, (301) 443-4513, (866) 615-6464, Fax: (301) 443-4279, nimhinfo@nih.gov, http://www.nimh.nih.gov/index.shtml.

U.S. Food and Drug Administration, 10903 New Hampshire Ave., Silver Spring, MD, 20993-0002, (888) INFO-FDA (463-6332), http://www.fda.gov.

Kelly Karpa, R.Ph., Ph.D.
Ruth A. Wienclaw, Ph.D.
Laura Jean Cataldo, RN, Ed.D.

R

Rational behavior therapy *see* **Rational emotive therapy**

Rational emotive therapy

Definition

Rational emotive therapy (RET) is a psychotherapeutic approach that proposes that unrealistic and irrational beliefs cause many emotional problems.

Purpose

RET is a form of **cognitive-behavioral therapy** (CBT). The primary focus of this treatment approach is to suggest changes in thinking that will lead to changes in behavior, thereby alleviating or improving symptoms. The therapy emphasizes changing irrational thinking patterns that cause emotional distress into thoughts that are more reasonable and rational. RET can be used to treat persons affected from disorders such as anxiety, **depression**, and **stress**.

Description

Rational emotive therapy was developed by Albert Ellis (1913–2007) in the mid-1950s. Ellis proposed that people become unhappy and develop self-defeating habits because of unrealistic or faulty beliefs. In Ellis's research reports from 1979 and 1987, he introduced the model that most irrational beliefs originate from three core ideas, each one of which is unrealistic. These three core and unrealistic views include:

1. I must perform well to be approved of by others who are perceived significant

2. You must treat me fairly—if not, then it is horrible and I cannot bear it

3. Conditions must be my way and if not I cannot stand to live in such a terrible and awful world

These irrational thoughts can lead to **grief** and needless suffering.

RET is considered an active therapy. The RET therapist will strive to change irrational beliefs, challenge thinking, and promote rational self-talk. Various strategies are used to achieve these goals, including:

• disputing irrational beliefs (the therapist points out how irrational it would be for a client to believe he or she had to be good at everything to be considered a worthwhile person)

• reframing (presenting situations in a more positive angle)

• problem solving

• role playing

• modeling

• use of humor

The client may also be requested to complete certain exercises at home or to read about the disorder (**bibliotherapy**).

Preparation

Before a client begins RET, he or she may undergo an assessment with the therapist. This assessment is called a biopsychosocial assessment, consisting of a structured interview. The questions and information-gathering during this assessment typically cover areas such as past medical and psychological history, family and social history, sex and drug history, employment and education history, and criminal history. The interview provides information for a **diagnosis** or a tentative diagnosis requiring further testing or consultation.

KEY TERMS

Modeling—A behavioral therapy technique in which a patient first observes and then imitates a desired behavior.

Relapse—A recurrence of symptoms after a period of improvement or recovery.

Aftercare

Aftercare may or may not be indicated. This is usually decided on between the patient and mental health practitioner. Aftercare follow-up may be recommended if the affected person is at risk of **relapse** behaviors.

Precautions

There are no major precautions or risks associated with RET. Persons entering treatment must be willing to change their behaviors that promote **negative symptoms**. There is a possibility that treatment may not benefit the affected person; this possibility becomes more likely for patients who have multiple psychological disorders.

Results

If a patient has success with RET, they will begin to understand the repetitive patterns of irrational thoughts and disruption caused by symptoms. The individual in therapy will develop skills to improve his or her specific problems, resulting in improved self-esteem and the development of a sense that life events change and that outcomes may not always be favorable, with the ability to adapt to or accept these changes. Persons who are unwilling to change and adhere to treatment recommendations may not gain any new beneficial behaviors.

Resources

BOOKS

Coon, D. *Essentials of Psychology.* Florence Grove, KY: Wadsworth, 2002.

ORGANIZATIONS

The Albert Ellis Institute, 45 East 65th Street, New York, NY, 10021, (212) 535-0822, Fax: (212) 249-3582, info@ albertellis.org, http://www.rebt.org.

Laith Farid Gulli, MD
Nicole Mallory, MS, PA-C

Reactive attachment disorder of infancy or early childhood

Definition

In reactive attachment disorder (RAD) of infancy or early childhood, the normal healthy bond between infant and parent or caregiver is not established or is broken. Infants normally "bond" or form an emotional attachment, to a parent or other caregiver by the eighth month of life. This includes the child's basic needs for affection, comfort, and nurturing.

From about the second through the eighth month, most infants will respond to attention from a variety of caregivers, if the caregivers are familiar. By the eighth month, however, normal infants have established a strong emotional preference for one or two primary caregivers. They are distressed if separated from these caregivers for even a few hours, even if another familiar person is present. If this bonding process is interfered with, it can have severe emotional and physical consequences for the child. For instance, it can permanently and adversely affect the **brain** of a growing child. Thus, reactive attachment disorder is caused within a child by a history of insufficient care and/or social contact from the child's caregiver, often the parents. This results in the child in never being able to establish caring and loving attachments with others.

Reactive attachment disorder, sometimes called a *post-traumatic disorder,* is considered a severe, but relatively uncommon, disorder that can affect infants and young children well into their adult years by disenabling them from establishing future relationships.

Two internationally based documents are used to classify medical conditions and mental disorders. The *International Statistical Classification of Diseases and Related Health Problems* (ICD), provided for by the World Health Organization, states in its latest version (ICD-10) that the inhibited form of the disorder is called reactive attachment disorder (RAD), while the disinhibited form is called disinhibited attachment disorder (DAD). The **Diagnostic and Statistical Manual of Mental Disorders** (*DSM*), published by the **American Psychiatric Association**, does not differentiate between the two in its latest version (*DSM-IV-TR*); however, that may change with the future version (*DSM-5*).

Demographics

The prevalence of reactive attachment disorder has been estimated at 1% of all children under the age of five years. Children orphaned at a young age have a much higher likelihood of this problem. Otherwise, RAD can appear in any infant or young child without favoring any particular gender, racial, or ethnic group, and without regard to any specific socioeconomic level.

Description

In reactive attachment disorder, an infant or young child has not formed an emotional bond with a parent or other caregiver. Somehow an inability of a child to form normal attachments toward a parent, or parents, has occurred. This affects the child's ability to interact normally with others. Such a problem is likely the result of early experiences of **abuse**, **neglect**, or sudden separation from parents, or caregivers, between the ages of six months to three years. It could also result from a lack of communications or responsiveness between child and caregiver or from a change of caregivers during this span of time. Consequently, the child may develop severe emotional and social problems that extend into adulthood. There may be learning problems and physical problems, such as slow growth and failure to develop as expected.

The mental disorder is characterized by prominent actions that are disturbed and inappropriate within the general social context. In its two basic forms, a person with RAD may have a consistent inability to initiate or respond to social interactions, possess an inhibited behavior, and shun attachments to nearly everyone—what is called the "inhibited" form. This form of RAD occurs most likely when a child does not develop any attachments to any caregiver very early in life. In this other major form, what is called "disinhibited," the person is extremely sociable, to a degree that he or she has an unusual closeness or friendliness with strangers. They aggressively seek out attention, frequently ask for help in performing tasks or activities, have inappropriate age-related behaviors, or appear anxious most of the time. This form of RAD is more likely when a child had multiple caregivers early in life or had various caregivers at different points in childhood.

The forthcoming edition of the *Diagnostic and Statistical Manual of Mental Disorders* (*DSM-5*, 2013) proposes to change some features of how it describes reactive attachment disorder by differentiating RAD into two disorders. This division is likely to include the following two designations: reactive attachment disorder of infancy and early childhood, and disinhibited social engagement disorder.

Proposed criteria (as stated by the American Psychiatric Association's *DSM-5* Development website) for Reactive Attachment Disorder of Infancy or Early Childhood include:

• The child must display a pattern of inappropriate (for developmental level) or disturbing attachment behaviors. Behaviors must be present before five years of age. The attachment behaviors must be consistent, and the child's demeanor must exhibit as inhibited or emotionally withdrawn. The child must rarely demonstrate signs of attachment toward parents or other caregivers, such as not seeking comfort when upset or not responding to comfort when offered.

• The child must exhibit persistent social and emotional disturbances as characterized by at least two of the following:

1. an absence of social or emotional responses in interactions with others

2. limited or lack of positive affect

3. unexplained irritability, sadness, or fearfulness during normal (nonthreating) interactions

• The child's symptoms must not meet the criteria for an autism spectrum disorder

• At least one of the following conditions must be present in the household:

1. child's basic emotional needs are not met by the caregiver

2. child's basic physical needs are not met by the caregiver

3. constant changes in or turnover of primary caregiver are present

4. child is raised in unusual settings

• The child must be at least nine months old.

Proposed criteria (as stated by the American Psychiatric Association's *DSM-5* Development website) for Disinhibited Social Engagement Disorder include:

• The child must regularly interact with strangers and exhibit at least two of the following symptoms:

1. Reduced or no hesitation in approaching strangers

2. Lack of boundaries in interpersonal interactions

3. Failure to check in with caregiver

4. Willingness or lack of hesitation to go off with strangers

• The child's behavior does not meet the criteria for impulsivity in attention deficit hyperactivity disorder.

• At least one of the following conditions must be present in the household:

1. child's basic emotional needs are not met by the caregiver

2. child's basic physical and safety needs are not met by the caregiver

3. constant changes in or turnover of primary caregiver are present

4. child is given frequent and harsh punishments

• The child must be at least nine months old.

Causes and symptoms

Causes

An infant does not know how to form an emotional attachment to another person, any more than it knows how to feed or clean itself. Bonding is a necessary developmental step in a baby's growth. It occurs as the infant is cared for, talked to, played with, and comforted consistently. This helps the infant feel as if it knows what will happen every time it sees a certain person. When this process is interfered with, the infant may never learn how to trust or love.

Many things can interfere with the bonding process. Some of these include:

• Loss of parents. The most common cause of reactive attachment disorder is the child being orphaned or put in foster care at a very early age. The infant may receive care from many people or be moved from place to place often. A bond to a single consistent caregiver, therefore, cannot be formed.

• Neglect or impaired care giving. If the infant is not cared for consistently, he or she will not learn to trust. This includes emotional neglect, where the caregivers may keep the baby clean and fed, but do not allow time for play and bonding. Very often, this occurs when the parent or caregiver has a problem that prevents him or her from giving adequate consistent attention to the infant. Such problems include major depression, psychosis, drug or alcohol abuse, intellectual disability, physical illness, and poverty. The parent may also have been a neglected child or may be very young themselves and simply may not know how to parent adequately. A mother may have postpartum depression after the birth of the child, which may prevent her from adequately taking care of the baby.

• Abuse or pain. Even if an infant is getting love and attention some of the time, he or she may not learn to attach itself to a caregiver if it comes to expect pain on occasion from the caregiver. Illness or pain that the caregiver cannot ease can have the same effect.

• Institutional care. Being in the hospital or other such medical facility for a long period during the early formative years of a child can cause a child not to receive the emotional care it needs.

• Poverty. Being in a situation where extreme poverty is rampant in the family providing care to the child, which may result in the child being ignored due to other pressures within the family.

In disrupted families with more than one child, one child may have reactive attachment disorder while others do not. It is not clear what role personality plays in this problem. It is sometimes suggested that the temperament of the child may play a role. Some young children may be more susceptible to **stress** or unpredictable situations than others, even in the same family, which may cause one child to have RAD in a family while another does not. RAD is a disorder that is not well understood. It is not known what precisely causes it in children but research is ongoing.

Symptoms

Infants with this problem often resist being held or touched and do not reach out when others come near. They are often sad-looking, without any smiling, and may look withdrawn and listless. Such infants may also seem sleepy or "slow." They may not seem aware of what is going on around them, and often they do not follow others with the eyes as they move around the room. These infants often do not have an interest in playing with toys or games involving the actions of others. They may be slow to gain weight. On the other hand, some appear to be overly aware and nervous.

Young children may seem withdrawn and passive. They may ignore others or respond to others in odd ways. For instance, they may dismiss comments or gestures that attempt to provoke comfort or caring. Some may seem overly familiar with strangers and touch or cling to people they have just met. They may also act aggressive toward children around their own age. However, they lack empathy for others. Their behavior comes across to others as needy and strange, unlike the normal friendliness of children. They have a general attitude of being awkward or uncomfortable in situations where such behaviors are not common. Such young children may also try to hide feelings of anger or disgust. They may also not ask for help or assistance when such actions are needed.

Other symptoms of reactive attachment disorder in children can include the following:

• inability to learn from mistakes (poor cause-and-effect thinking)

• learning problems or delays in learning

KEY TERMS

Attention deficit hyperactivity disorder (ADHD)— A disorder primarily in children that is characterized by the inability to concentrate, along with hyperactivity and inappropriate and/or impulsive behaviors.

Autistic spectrum disorder—A mental disorder characterized by abnormal behaviors with regard to social interactions and communications, along with obsessive, repetitive behaviors and only limited perceived interests.

Depression—A disorder characterized by persistent feelings of hopelessness, sadness, and dejection, along with the regular inability to sleep and lack of energy; suicidal tendencies are also sometimes present.

Psychosis—A disorder characterized by hallucinations, distorted ideas of reality, delusions, and other symptoms related to schizophrenia and mania.

- impulsive behavior
- abnormal speech patterns
- destructive or cruel behavior

The ICD-10 describes the following for both RAD and DAD:

- markedly disturbed and developmentally inappropriate social relatedness in most contexts
- disturbance is not accounted for solely by developmental delay and does not meet the criteria for pervasive development disorder
- onset before five years of age
- history of significant neglect
- implicit lack of identifiable, preferred attachment figure

Diagnosis

The standard manual for mental health professionals in the United States is the *Diagnostic and Statistical Manual of Mental Disorders*. This manual lists criteria for diagnosing various mental disorders. The most recent edition, the fourth edition text revised is also known as the *DSM-IV-TR*. According to *DSM-IV-TR*, reactive attachment disorder is diagnosed when the following criteria are met:

- Presence of strange and developmentally inappropriate social interactions, beginning before age five years. The child does not respond to or initiate social interactions in a way that would be developmentally appropriate; instead, the child is either inhibited or is disinhibited in his or her interactions. Inhibited reactions may be excessively vigilant, restrained, or ambivalent. (The child may respond to caregivers with a mixture of approach, avoidance, and resistance to comforting, as an example from the manual.) Disinhibited reactions occur in a variety of social interactions, and the child does not discriminate among people he or she chooses as attachment figures. This child will treat near strangers with inappropriate familiarity.

- The child's inappropriate social skills are not due exclusively to developmental delay (as in intellectual disability) and the child's symptoms do not meet criteria for a pervasive developmental disorder.

- The child has received care in which his or her basic needs—either emotional or physical—are often unmet, or in which stable attachments have not been able to form (such as when primary caregivers change often).

An infant is diagnosed as having reactive attachment disorder when he or she fails to show signs of bonding to a parent or caregiver by the age of eight months. Infants normally start to follow the parent or caregiver with their eyes and smile in response to attention by about two months. By about five months, the child should reach out to be picked up and obviously enjoy simple interactive games like "peekaboo."

Treatment

First, the child's safety and physical health must be attended to. A child who is being abused or has been physically neglected may need to be hospitalized for a while. This is done to separate the child from the harmful situation and to take care of any medical problems resulting from neglect or abuse.

The next step is either to make the child's home environment stable or to place the child in a more stable home. Child protective services may be brought in at this point. The home situation must be evaluated, and the parents or caregivers assessed for emotional fitness to care for the child. The parents or caregivers may be given training in proper childcare and emotional nurturing. **Family therapy** may be needed in some cases to help the parents or caregivers and other children in the family.

With a young infant, the parents or caregivers will be encouraged to have a regular schedule for the infant and to spend time each day simply holding and playing with the infant.

Treatment of children who are past infancy is difficult. It is important to find a therapist experienced in the treatment of children with reactive attachment disorder. Most therapists use a mix of techniques, but primarily psychological counseling and parent or caregiver education. The therapist may seek to help the child relive and work through **grief** and anger from a prior **trauma** or loss. Cognitive therapy may be used to help an older child understand and reframe negative thoughts about himself or herself, or about parents or caregivers. If the child is too young to verbalize or think rationally, techniques such as **play therapy** or **art therapy** may be used to help bring out and work through feelings. Behavioral therapy may be used to help guide development of wanted behaviors.

Although reactive attachment disorder is a permanent condition, treatment can help children to develop better and more stable relationships with parents or caregivers than would be possible without treatment.

Prognosis

There has not been much research to date on the course of this problem. It appears that children who are identified and treated early have a better chance of learning how to form appropriate bonds with other people.

Children who are not treated, or who are treated later in life, have a greater chance of having permanent problems relating to other people. Some of these problems include:

- delayed physical and cognitive development and growth
- poor self-esteem and self-image
- immature behavior
- antisocial or delinquent behavior
- relationship problems with both genders
- anger-management problems along with temper-control problems
- eating disorders, along with resulting malnutrition, which can cause further medical disorders
- depression, anxiety
- learning problems
- addiction to alcohol or drugs
- inability to hold a job, unemployment
- sexual problems or inappropriate sexual behaviors

QUESTIONS TO ASK YOUR DOCTOR

- What treatment options are available?
- Is there a cure for RAD?
- What permanent damage can be caused by RAD?
- What is the best prognosis for my child?
- Are there organizations that specialize in RAD? Is so, where can I learn more?
- Will my insurance cover the treatment?

Prevention

Prevention of reactive attachment disorder begins with good parenting. As far as possible, health care providers and families should be on the lookout for any problem that may prevent parents from giving children the structure and attention they need. If a child loses its primary caregivers, a stable environment with consistent attention from one or two caregivers should be provided as soon as possible.

Early identification of reactive attachment disorder is necessary to get help to the child and family as soon as possible. The earlier this problem is identified and treated, the more likely it is that the child will be able to develop healthy patterns of relating to others.

Resources

BOOKS

American Psychiatric Association. *Diagnostic and Statistical Manual of Mental Disorders,* 4th edition, text revision. Washington, DC: American Psychiatric Press, 2000.

Black, Donald, and Nancy C. Andresen. *Introductory Textbook of Psychiatry.* Washington D.C.: American Psychiatric, 2011.

Dulcan, Mina K., editor. *Dulcan's Textbook of Child and Adolescent Psychiatry.* Washington D.C.: American Psychiatric Press, 2010.

Sadock, Benjamin J., Viginia A. Sadock, Pedro Ruiz, et al., editors. *Kaplan & Sadock's Comprehensive Textbook of Psychology.* Philadelphia: Wolters Kluwer Health/Lippincott Williams & Wilkins; 2009.

World Health Organization. *International Statistical Classification of Diseases and Related Health Problems, Tenth Revision (ICD-10).* Geneva: World Health Organization, 1992.

WEBSITES

"Diagnostic and Statistical Manual." American Psychiatric Association. http://www.psych.org/mainmenu/research/dsmiv.aspx (accessed May 27, 2011).

"G 00 Reactive Attachment Disorder." American Psychiatric Association. http://www.dsm5.org/ProposedRevisions/Pages/proposedrevision.aspx?rid=120 (accessed May 27, 2011).

Mayo Clinic staff. "Reactive Attachment Disorder." Mayo Clinic.com. http://www.mayoclinic.com/health/reactive-attachment-disorder/DS00988 (accessed May 27, 2011).

ORGANIZATIONS

American College of Physicians, 190 North Independence Mall West, Philadelphia, PA, 19106-1572, (215) 351-2400, (800) 523-1546, http://www.acponline.org.

American Medical Association, 515 N. State Street, Chicago, IL, 60610, (800) 621-8335, http://www.ama-assn.org.

American Psychiatric Association, 1000 Wilson Boulevard, Suite 1825, Arlington, VA, 22209, (703) 907-7300, (888) 357-7924, apa@psych.org, http://www.psych.org.

Association for Treatment and Training in the Attachment of Children, PO Box 533, Lake Villao, IL, 60046, (847) 453-8224, Fax: (847) 356-7856, questions@attach.org, http://www.attach.org.

Jody Bower, M.S.W.
William Atkins,

Reading disorder

Definition

Reading disorder is a learning disorder that involves significant impairment of reading accuracy, speed, or comprehension to the extent that the impairment interferes with academic achievement or activities of daily life. Also referred to as reading disability, reading difficulty, and dyslexia, reading disorder is the most commonly diagnosed learning disability in the United States. It is defined by the **American Psychiatric Association** (APA) as "reading achievement . . . that falls substantially below that expected given the individual's chronological age, measured intelligence, and age-appropriate education." Reading disorder is distinct from alexia, which is the term for loss of the ability to read caused by **brain** damage from injury or disease. However, neurological studies of alexia have helped researchers better understand reading disabilities.

Demographics

Estimates of the number of people with **learning disorders** range from 2%–15% of the general population. Most research studies give a figure of 5%. About 80% of people with a learning disorder have reading disorder. Other studies suggest that about 4% of school-age children have reading disorder. People with reading disorder are more likely to have a parent or sibling with the disorder.

Originally it was thought that reading disorder affected more boys than girls (in a ratio of 5:1), but later studies found boys to be only slightly more likely than girls to have reading disorder. Incidence estimates are skewed because boys tend to act out more in class and are consequently referred more frequently for special education. **Diagnosis** is complicated by the fact that anywhere from 20%–55% of dyslexics also suffer from **attention deficit hyperactivity disorder (ADHD)**, a behavioral disorder that may aggravate reading problems. In addition, about one-quarter of children with reading disorder have **conduct disorder**. **Oppositional defiant disorder** and **depression** also occur in higher-than-average rates in children with reading disorder. Almost all people with reading disorder have difficulties spelling, and about 80% of them have other language problems.

Description

Reading disorder is a learning disorder characterized by a significant disparity between an individual's general intelligence and his or her reading skills. Learning disorders, formerly called academic skills disorders, are disorders that account for difficulty learning and poor academic performance when low performance cannot be attributed to **intellectual disability**, low intelligence, lack of learning opportunities, or such specific physical problems as vision or hearing deficits. Common learning disabilities include reading disorder, often called dyslexia; **mathematics disorder**; **disorder of written expression**; and some language processing disorders.

Reading disorder was first recognized in the late nineteenth century. It was initially called pure word blindness and then developmental alexia. Starting in the 1960s, educators commonly referred to reading disorder as dyslexia, from the Greek word *dys*, meaning poor or inadequate, and the word *lexis* meaning words or language.

Reading disorder can cause severe problems in reading, and consequently in academic work, even in people with normal intelligence, educational opportunities, motivation to learn to read, and emotional self-control. Reading disorder is different from slowness in learning or intellectual developmental disorder. In reading disorder, there is a significant gap between the expected level of performance and actual achievement. Difficulties in reading can occur on many levels, and reading disorder may have multiple causes that manifest in different ways.

Types of reading disorders

Reading disabilities have been classified as either dyseidetic, dysphonetic, or mixed. Persons with the dyseidetic type are able to sound out individual letters phonetically but have trouble identifying patterns of letters when they are grouped together. Their spelling tends to be phonetic even when incorrect ("laf" for "laugh"). By comparison, dysphonic readers have difficulty relating letters to sounds, so their spelling is chaotic. They are able to recognize words they have memorized but cannot sound out new ones. They may be able to read near the appropriate grade level but are poor spellers. Persons with mixed reading disabilities have both the dyseidetic and dysphonic types of reading disorder.

Risk factors

Risk factors for reading disorders include a concurrent diagnosis of **attention deficit hyperactivity disorder (ADHD)**, a family history of reading disorder, and delayed early language development. About 40% of boys and 20% of girls with a dyslexic parent develop the disorder. Dyslexia is believed to occur equally in all races.

Causes and symptoms

Causes

The causes of reading disorder are not completely understood but are thought to be related to differences in the structure and functioning of the brain, particularly areas of the brain known as the left perisylvian region, the left temporo-occipital region, and the right fronto-parietal cortex. Persons with reading difficulties appear to process information in different parts of the brain from those without reading disorders. Learning to read is a complex task. It requires coordination of the muscles of the eye to follow a line of print, spatial orientation to interpret letters and words, visual memory to retain the meaning of letters and sight words, sequencing ability, a grasp of sentence structure and grammar, and the ability to categorize and analyze. In addition, the brain must integrate visual cues with memory and associate them with specific sounds. The sounds, or phonemes, must then be associated with specific meanings, and for comprehension, the meanings must be retained while a sentence or passage is read. Reading disorder occurs when any of these processes are disrupted. For that reason, the roots of reading disorder have proved difficult to isolate, and may be different in different individuals.

Reading disorder is known to run in families, and a number of genes linked to dyslexia have been identified. Many participate in gene development, and several genetic studies have found gene linkages on chromosomes 1 and 6 that demonstrate heterogeneous (multiple methods of) transmission. **Positron emission tomography (PET)** studies have shown that dyslexics assigned reading tasks show a lower level of activity than children with normal reading skills in a part of the brain known as the left inferior parietal cortex, a region that is necessary for the rapid perception of word forms. Studies using functional **magnetic resonance imaging** (fMRI) pinpointed the left inferior frontal gyrus, the left inferior parietal lobule, and the left middle temporal gyrus as areas of low activation in children with dyslexia given word tests to complete. Another indication that specific areas of the brain are involved in dyslexia comes from case studies of children who have suffered **stroke**. In one study reported in 2006, a six-year-old boy had suffered a stroke affecting the left hemisphere of his brain. He was able to read words that he had learned prior to the stroke, but attempts to read unfamiliar words were unsuccessful until he received special training.

One surprising finding, reported by a team of researchers at Hong Kong University in 2008, is that the part of the brain affected by dyslexia appears to differ according to the child's primary language. The researchers used magnetic resonance imaging (MRI) to compare a group of children whose first language is English with a second group raised to speak Chinese. The scientists found that the English speakers use a different part of the brain when reading from that used by the Chinese students. The difference is apparently related to the fact that English is an alphabetic language whereas Chinese uses symbols to represent words.

Symptoms

Common characteristics of children with reading disorder include:

- difficulty identifying single words
- problems understanding the sounds in words, sound order, or rhymes
- problems with spelling
- transposing letters in words
- omitting or substituting words
- poor reading comprehension
- slow reading speed (oral or silent)

In addition to these symptoms, children with a reading disorder may also struggle with:

- learning to speak
- organizing thoughts and ideas into clear written and spoken language
- memorizing number facts, such as the multiplication tables
- reading quickly enough to understand what is being read—some children with dyslexia read so slowly that they cannot remember the beginning of a sentence by the time they reach the end of it, particularly if it is a long and complicated sentence
- making their way through longer reading assignments
- spelling words correctly
- making rhymes
- learning foreign languages, which involves a basic understanding of grammar and the parts of speech
- performing mathematical calculations correctly
- opposites and directions

Diagnosis

Evaluation of reading ability must be done on an individual basis in order to make a diagnosis of reading disorder and distinguish it from slow learning or low intelligence. Though reading disorder is rarely diagnosed in children before age five or six, because formal instruction in reading does not begin before kindergarten or first grade in most U.S. schools, preschool-age children may exhibit certain problems, such as trouble sounding out words and difficulty memorizing sequence information such as the days of the week, that may foreshadow a reading disability.

Anyone who is suspected of having reading disorder or any other learning disability should have a comprehensive evaluation, including hearing, vision, and intelligence testing. The test should include all areas of learning and learning processes, not just reading. In school-age children, this evaluation often involves a team of educators, educational psychologists, and child psychiatrists.

Examination

The diagnostic process takes several steps. The first step is an office examination by the child's doctor to rule out any disorders of vision or hearing that could interfere with learning. The child may also be referred to a neurologist (a specialist in disorders of the nervous system) for further evaluation to make sure that the child does not have a brain tumor or other physical disease of the brain.

The next step is usually intelligence testing and an evaluation of the child's reading and speaking skills by a qualified expert. This type of evaluation involves testing the child's short-term memory or asking the child to read nonsense words as a test of their ability to link letters and sounds. In addition, the child may be evaluated psychologically to see whether depression, anxiety, or social problems are causing the learning difficulty. The examiner must take into account the child's age, intelligence, educational opportunities, and such cultural factors as whether the language spoken at home is different from the language used in school instruction.

Reading disorder is diagnosed when reading achievement is substantially below what would be expected after taking into account the above factors. To meet the ***Diagnostic and Statistical Manual of Mental Disorders*** *(DSM)* diagnostic criteria for reading disorder, the reading problems must substantially interfere with his or her schoolwork or daily life. If a physical condition is present (for example, intellectual disability or hearing loss), the reading deficit must be in excess of what one would normally associate with the physical disability.

Treatment

Treatment approaches vary from visual stimulation to special **diets** to enhanced reading instruction. However, it is generally agreed that customized education is the only successful remedy, and the American Academy of Ophthalmology, the American Academy of Pediatrics, and the American Association for Pediatric Ophthalmology and Strabismus have issued a policy statement warning against visual treatments and recommending a cross-disciplinary educational approach. After a child's specific difficulties in reading and understanding language have been analyzed by an expert, a treatment program is drawn up tailored to his or her needs. Under the provisions of the Individuals with Disabilities Education Act (IDEA) of 2004, any child with a diagnosed learning disability, including reading disorder or dyslexia, should be eligible for an Individual Education Program (IEP) that provides customized instruction at school designed to address his or her disability.

The first researcher to identify and study dyslexia, Samuel Torrey Orton, developed the core principles of such an approach in the 1920s. The work of three of his followers—teachers Bessie Stillman, Anna Gillingham, and Beth Slingerland—underlies many of the programs in use today, including Project READ, the Wilson Reading System, and programs based on the Herman method. These and other successful programs have three characteristics in common. They are:

- Sound/symbol (phonics)-based. They break words down into their smallest visual components: letters and the sounds associated with them.

KEY TERMS

Digraph—A pair of letters that represents a single speech sound. In English, the *th* in "thumb" and the *ei* in "vein" are examples of digraphs.

Dyslexia—Another term for reading disorder.

Phonics—A method of teaching reading and spelling based on the phonetic interpretation of ordinary spelling.

• Multisensory. Good programs attempt to form and strengthen mental associations among visual, auditory, and kinesthetic channels of stimulation. The student simultaneously sees, feels, and says the sound-symbol association. For example, a student may trace the letter or letter combination with his or her finger while pronouncing a word out loud.

• Highly structured. Remediation begins at the level of the single letter-sound, then works up to digraphs (a pair of letters representing a single speech sound), syllables, and finally words and sentences in a systematic fashion. Repetitive drills and practice serve to form necessary associations between sounds and written symbols.

When ADHD is co-diagnosed with a reading disorder, special care should be taken to identify specific reading problems and to define cognitive as well as behavioral learning objectives.

Psychotherapy

Persons with reading disorders often need and benefit from **psychotherapy** because of possible struggles with low self-esteem associated with their disability. Many persons with reading disorder feel that they are stupid or less capable than they really are, and are likely to drop out of school if they are not diagnosed and treated early.

Prognosis

Many famous and successful people have suffered from reading disorders, including at least two Presidents of the United States. How well a person compensates for this disorder depends on the severity of the impairment and the type of educational remediation that he or she receives. Generally, people who are identified as having a reading disorder before grade three and who receive intensive reading education can do well. There is, however, a great deal of variation among people in intelligence, educational

opportunities, and the will to overcome a reading disorder, as well as in the type and severity of the problem. All these factors combine to determine the ultimate outcome of this disorder. The prognosis is usually good if the condition is diagnosed early and the person is enrolled in a good remedial program. Learning disabilities can affect a person's self-esteem, and so support from family, friends, and teachers also help improve the chances of overcoming this disorder. Reading disorders can persist into adult life, but many people with reading disorders are able to achieve personal and professional success.

Prevention

There is no known way to prevent reading disorder. Early **intervention** is the key to preventing the associated symptoms of low self-esteem, lack of interest in school, and poor behavior that often accompany low academic achievement.

Resources

BOOKS

American Psychiatric Association. *Diagnostic and Statistical Manual of Mental Disorders.* 4th ed., text rev. Washington, DC: American Psychiatric Publishing, 2000.

Hulme, Charles, and Margaret J. Snowling. *Developmental Disorders of Language Learning and Cognition.* Malden, MA: Wiley-Blackwell, 2009.

PERIODICALS

Bower, Bruce. "Dyslexia Tied to Disrupted Brain Network." *Science News* 153 (March 7, 1998): 150.

Germano, E., A. Gagliano, and P. Curatolo. "Comorbidity of ADHD and Dyslexia." *Developmental Neuropsychology* 35, no. 5 (September 2010): 475–93.

Matvy, Mike. "A Silicon Bullet for Dyslexia: A New Solution for an Old Problem." *The Exceptional Parent* 30 (November 2000) 52–56.

Waldie, K.E., and M. Hausmann. "Right Fronto-parietal Dysfunction in Children with ADHD and Developmental Dyslexia as Determined by Line Bisection Judgements." *Neuropsychologia* 48, no. 12 (October 2010): 3650–3656.

WEBSITES

Crouch, Eric R., Peter M. Dozier, and Angelo P. Giardino. "Reading Learning Disorder." Medscape Reference. http://emedicine.medscape.com/article/1835801-overview (accessed October 24, 2011).

National Center for Learning Disabilities. "What is Dyslexia?" http://www.ncld.org/ld-basics/ld-aamp-language/reading/dyslexia (accessed October 24, 2011).

U.S. National Institute of Neurological Disorders and Stroke. "NINDS Dyslexia Information Page." http://www.ninds.nih.gov/disorders/dyslexia/dyslexia.htm (accessed October 24, 2011).

ORGANIZATIONS

Learning Disabilities Association of America, 4156 Library Rd., Pittsburgh, PA, 15234-1349, (412) 341-1515, http://www.ldanatl.org.

National Center for Learning Disabilities, 381 Park Ave. South, Ste. 1401, New York, NY, 10016, (212) 545-7510, Fax: (212) 545-9665, (888) 575-7373, http://www.ncld.org.

Tish Davidson, A.M.

Reinforcement

Definition

Reinforcement is an act, process, circumstance, or condition that increases the probability of a person repeating a response. A reinforcer is a stimulus that follows some behavior and increases the probability that the behavior will occur. For example, when teaching a child to clean his room, a parent might reinforce him by giving him a reward for doing so without being reminded. The reward reinforces the desired behavior and increases the probability that the child will clean his room again in the future.

Description

In psychology, reinforcement is associated with two types of conditioning: classical (or Pavlovian) conditioning and operant (or Skinnerian) conditioning. Operant conditioning is frequently used to increase the frequency of a desired response by developing positive associations between it and a stimulus or reinforcer. **Behavior modification** uses the principles of operant conditioning or other learning techniques to improve symptoms or to increase desired behavior.

In operant conditioning (as developed by B. F. Skinner), positive reinforcers are rewards that strengthen a conditioned response after it has occurred, such as feeding a hungry pigeon after it has pecked a key. Negative reinforcers are stimuli that are removed when the desired response has been obtained. For example, when a rat is receiving an electric shock and presses a bar that stops the shock, the shock is a negative reinforcer—it is an aversive stimulus that reinforces the bar-pressing behavior. The application of negative reinforcement may be divided into two types: escape and avoidance conditioning. In escape conditioning, the subject learns to escape an unpleasant or aversive stimulus (a dog jumps over a barrier to escape electric shock). In avoidance conditioning, the subject is presented with a warning stimulus, such as a buzzer, just before the aversive stimulus occurs and learns to act on it in order to avoid the stimulus altogether.

Punishment can be used to decrease unwanted behaviors. Punishment is the application of an aversive stimulus in reaction to a particular behavior. For children, a punishment could be the removal of television privileges when they disobey their parents or teachers. The removal of the privileges follows the undesired behavior and decreases its likelihood of occurring again.

Reinforcement may be administered according to various schedules. A particular behavior may be reinforced every time it occurs, which is referred to as continuous reinforcement. In many cases, however, behaviors are reinforced only some of the time, which is termed partial or intermittent reinforcement. Reinforcement may also be based on the number of responses, or scheduled at particular time intervals. In addition, it may be delivered in regularly or irregularly. These variables combine to produce four basic types of partial reinforcement. In fixed-ratio (FR) schedules, reinforcement is provided following a set number of responses (a factory worker is paid for every garment he assembles). With variable-ratio (VR) schedules, reinforcement is provided after a variable number of responses (a slot machine pays off after varying numbers of attempts). Fixed-interval (FI) schedules provide for reinforcement of the first response made within a given interval since the previous one (contest entrants are not eligible for a prize if they have won one within the past 30 days). Finally, with variable-interval (VI) schedules, first responses are rewarded at varying intervals from the previous one.

Resources

BOOKS

Flora, Stephen Ray. *The Power of Reinforcement.* Albany, NY: State University of New York Press, 2004.

VandenBos, Gary R. ed. *APA Dictionary of Psychology.* Washington, DC: American Psychological Association, 2006.

PERIODICALS

Bogdan, Ryan, and Diego A. Pizzagalli. "Acute Stress Reduces Reward Responsiveness: Implications for Depression." *Biological Psychiatry* 60, no. 10 (November 2006): 1147–54.

Dallery, Jesse, Irene M. Glenn, and Bethany R. Raiff. "An Internet-Based Abstinence Reinforcement Treatment for Cigarette Smoking." *Drug and Alcohol Dependence* 86, no. 2–3 (January 12, 2007): 230–38.

Doran, Neal, Dennis McChargue, and Lee Cohen. "Impulsivity and the Reinforcing Value of Cigarette Smoking." *Addictive Behaviors* 32, no. 1 (January 2007): 90–98.

Fernandez, Melanie A., et al. "The Principles of Extinction and Differential Reinforcement of Other Behaviors in the

Intensive Cognitive-Behavioral Treatment of Primarily Obsessional Pediatric OCD." *Clinical Case Studies* 5, no. 6 (December 2006): 511–21.

Hand, Dennis J., Andrew T. Fox, and Mark P. Reilly. "Response Acquisition With Delayed Reinforcement in a Rodent Model of Attention-Deficit/Hyperactivity Disorder (ADHD)." *Behavioural Brain Research* 175, no. 2 (December 2006): 337–42.

Rieskamp, Jörg. "Positive and Negative Recency Effects in Retirement Savings Decisions." *Journal of Experimental Psychology: Applied* 12, no. 4 (December 2006): 233–50.

Ruth A. Wienclaw, PhD

Relapse and relapse prevention

Definition

In the course of illness, relapse is a return of symptoms after a period of time when no symptoms are present. Any strategies or treatments applied in advance to prevent future symptoms are known as relapse prevention.

Purpose

When people seek help for mental disorders, they receive treatment that, hopefully, reduces or eliminates symptoms. However, once they leave treatment, they may gradually revert to old habits and ways of living. This results in a return of symptoms known as relapse. Relapse prevention aims to teach people strategies that will maintain the wellness skills they learned while in treatment.

Prevention of relapse in mental disorders is crucial, not only because symptoms are detrimental to quality of life, but also because the occurrence of relapse increases chances for future relapses. In addition, with each relapse, symptoms tend to be more severe and have more serious consequences.

Description

Relapse is a concern with any disorder, whether physical or psychological. Cancer is a prime example of a physical condition where relapse is common, either after a short period or many years of remission (being symptom free). Psychological disorders can follow a similar pattern, and certain psychological disorders tend to have a higher rate of relapse than others. Addictive disorders, such as alcohol and drug abuse, smoking, overeating, and pathological gambling, are known for having high levels of relapse. Many addictions involve a lifestyle centered around

---

Common early warning signs of relapse

Behavioral changes

- Isolation, avoidance of social situations
- Changes in appetite and/or sleep patterns
- Participation in risky or dangerous behaviors (e.g., alcohol or illicit drug use)
- Increased emotional outbursts, especially when inappropriate for the situation
- Reduced energy levels
- Apathy, loss of motivation
- Disregard for personal hygiene

Cognitive changes

- Lack of concentration
- Loss of memory recall
- Trouble making decisions
- Abnormal thought patterns—racing, slowed, or jumbled
- Constant pessimism and negativity
- Hearing voices
- Thoughts or acts of self-harm
- Excessive dwelling on past events with thoughts of regret

Emotional changes

- Anxiety
- Aggressive behavior
- Depression
- Restlessness
- Increased irritability
- Paranoia

SOURCE: Julie O'Sullivan and Jillian Gilbert, "Early Warning Signs," Inner North Brisbane Mental Health Service, Royal Brisbane Hospital.

Report available online at http://www.health.qld.gov.au/rbwh/docs/early_warning_signs.pdf. *(Table by PreMediaGlobal. © 2012 Cengage Learning.)*

---

the addictive behavior. In such cases, individuals must not only discontinue the addictive habit, they must also restructure their entire lives in order for changes to last. Such vast changes are difficult at best, approaching impossible in the worst scenarios. For example, an individual with a drug addiction may live in a neighborhood where drugs are prevalent but may lack the resources to move. According to recent statistics, relapse rates are approximately 33% for people who gamble pathologically (within three months of treatment), 90% for people who quit smoking, and 50% for people who abuse alcohol. Within one year of treatment, people struggling with obesity typically regain 30% to 50% of the weight they lost.

Affective disorders, such as **depression** and anxiety, also have high rates of relapse. People with affective disorders are thought to engage in self-defeating, negative thought patterns that occur more or less automatically. These thought patterns affect behavior, resulting in unproductive or negative consequences. Negative consequences are regarded by such individuals as proof that their original self-defeating thoughts must be correct. The thought-behavior pattern becomes a repetitive cycle, with negative thoughts resulting in negative behavioral outcomes, and consequences of negative behavior encouraging more self-defeating thoughts. This cycle is extremely difficult to break, because it becomes a habitual way of responding to the world that occurs almost without awareness. Relapse rates for depression are reportedly as high as 80%.

Serious psychiatric disorders such as **bipolar disorder** and **schizophrenia** have high rates of relapse, especially when the conditions are not properly treated. According to the World Federation for Mental Health, rates for bipolar disorder are approximately 40%–50% after one year without a **manic episode** and 70%–75% after five years without episode. In patients with schizophrenia, the risk of relapse is reduced to 20% when treated with antipsychotic drugs, compared to 60% taking a placebo. Without continuing treatment, up to 90% of patients relapse within two years, and 80% of patients who discontinue medication after experiencing an episode will relapse.

Relapse among people who commit sex offenses is a constant safety concern for those in the community. However, some statistics show that this population has a very low rate of relapse. A report by Robin J. Wilson and colleagues indicated rates as low as 3.7% to 6.3%. This same report stated that, among various criminal offenses, those who commit sex offenses relapse at lower rates than those who commit general offenses. Other professionals may not necessarily agree with this study, however. Those who commit sex offenses are considered at a higher risk for relapse if they display little insight into the impact of their crime. Those at high risk of committing a sex offense are not typically released back into the community.

For many types of disorders, initial treatment is often effective at eliminating the unwanted behavior. However, these effects are rarely maintained long-term without some type of preventive planning. Results of medications are similar; symptoms are alleviated, but once the medication is discontinued, symptoms return unless the individual has had some type of training in coping with his or her disorder and that training has been effective. There are various forms of relapse prevention training. Most follow a similar pattern with and employ the following common elements:

• Identifying high-risk situations: Symptoms are often initiated by particular times, places, people, or events. For example, a person with agoraphobia is more likely to experience symptoms of panic in a crowded building. An essential key to preventing relapse is to be aware of the specific situations where one feels vulnerable. These situations are called "triggers," because they trigger the onset of symptoms. While people with the same mental disorder may share similar triggers, triggers can also be highly individual. People tend to react—sometimes unknowingly—to negative experiences in their past. For example, a woman who was sexually abused as a child may have negative emotions when in the presence of men who resemble her abuser. Because some triggers occur without conscious awareness, individuals may not know all their triggers. Many prevention programs encourage individuals to closely monitor their behavior, reflecting on situations where symptoms occurred and determining what was happening immediately before the onset of symptoms. With this kind of analysis, a pattern often emerges that gives clues about the trigger.

• Learning alternate ways to respond to high-risk situations: Once triggers have been identified, one must find new ways of coping with those situations. The easiest coping mechanism for high-risk situations is to avoid them altogether. This may include avoiding certain people who have a negative influence or avoiding locations where the symptom is likely to occur. In some instances, avoidance is a good strategy. For example, individuals who abuse alcohol may successfully reduce their risk by avoiding bars or parties. In other instances, avoidance is not possible or advisable. For example, individuals attempting to lose weight may notice that they are more likely to binge at certain times during the day. One cannot avoid a time of day. Rather, by being aware of this trigger, one can purposely engage in alternate activities during that time. Strategies for coping with unavoidable triggers are generally skills that need to be learned and practiced in order to be effective. Strategies include—but are not limited to—discussion of feelings, whether with a friend, counselor, or via a hotline; distraction, such as music, exercise, or engaging in a hobby; refocusing techniques, such as meditation, deep-breathing exercises, progressive muscle relaxation (focusing on each muscle group separately, and routinely tensing then relaxing that muscle), prayer, or journaling; and cognitive restructuring, such as positive affirmation statements (such as, "I am worthwhile"), active problem solving (defining the problem, generating possible solutions, identifying the consequences of those solutions, choosing the best solution), challenging the validity of negative thoughts, or guided imagery (imagining oneself in a different place or handling a situation appropriately).

• Creating a plan for healthy living: Besides being prepared for high-risk situations, relapse prevention also focuses on general principles of mental health that, if followed, greatly reduce the likelihood of symptoms. These include factors such as balanced nutrition, regular exercise, sufficient sleep, health education, reciprocally caring relationships, productive and recreational interests, and spiritual development.

- Developing a support system: Many research studies have demonstrated the importance of social support in maintaining a healthy lifestyle. Individuals who are socially isolated tend to display more symptoms of mental disorders. Conversely, individuals with mental disorders tend to have more difficultly initiating and maintaining relationships due to inappropriate social behavior. For such people, a support system may be nonexistent. Research suggests that support systems are most effective when they are naturally occurring—in other words, when a circle of family and friends who genuinely care about the individual is already in place. However, artificially created support systems are certainly better than none at all. For this reason, relapse prevention programs strive to involve family members and other significant persons in the treatment program. Everyone in the support system should be knowledgeable about the person's goals, what that person is like when he or she is doing well, and warning signs that the person may be on a path toward relapse. The support system agrees on who will take what role in encouraging, confronting, or otherwise caring for that person. Self-help groups such as Alcoholics Anonymous or Moderation Management are often examples of artificially created support systems.

- Preparing for possible relapse: Although the ultimate goal of relapse prevention is to avoid relapse altogether, statistics demonstrate that relapse potential is very real. Individuals need to be aware that, even when exerting their best efforts, they may occasionally experience lapses (one occurrence of a symptom or behavior) or relapses (return to a previous, undesirable level of symptoms or behavior). Acknowledging the potential for relapse is important, because many people consider a lapse or relapse as evidence of personal failure and give up completely. In their widely acclaimed book for professionals, *Motivational Interviewing*, William R. Miller and Stephen Rollnick cite a study by Prochaska and DiClemente that found that smokers typically relapse between three and seven times before quitting for good. From the perspective of Miller and Rollnick, each relapse can be a step closer to full recovery if relapse is used as a learning experience to improve prevention strategies. Although some argue that such a tolerant attitude invites relapse, general consensus is that individuals need to forgive themselves if relapse occurs and then move on. Some prevention programs include designing a crisis plan to be put into effect if a relapse occurs. The crisis plan involves specific actions to be taken by the individual or members of the support system.

These elements are common to all relapse prevention programs, but programs can be further customized

---

KEY TERMS

Addictive disorder—A disorder involving repetitive participation in a certain activity, in spite of negative consequences and despite attempts to stop the behavior. Alcohol abuse is an example.

Affective disorder—A disorder involving extreme emotional experience that is not congruent with the environmental circumstances (for example, feeling sad when there is no easily identifiable reason, as in depression).

Cognitive restructuring—An approach to psychotherapy that focuses on helping the patient examine distorted patterns of perceiving and thinking in order to change their emotional responses to people and situations.

Guided imagery—Techniques where individuals actively imagine themselves in a scene (usually a different location, such as a relaxing beach, or a trigger situation where one handles the situation successfully), typically guided by another person describing the scene.

Lapse—A single, isolated occurrence of a symptom or negative behavior.

Positive affirmation statements—Statements repeated to oneself, either aloud or mentally, that reflect attitudes of self-worth.

Progressive muscle relaxation—Relaxation exercises where one slowly tenses and then relaxes each muscle group separately in a systematic order.

Refocusing techniques—Techniques that direct one's attention away from overwhelming, negative thoughts and emotions by focusing on inner peace and managing one issue at a time.

Remission—In the course of an illness or disorder, a period of time when symptoms are absent.

Trigger—Any situation (people, places, times, events, etc.) that causes one to experience a negative emotional reaction, which is often accompanied by a display of symptoms or problematic behavior.

---

to meet the particular characteristics of a disorder. For example, prevention of depression or anxiety may focus on becoming aware of thoughts as passing mental events rather than facts about self or reality. Learning to identify bodily sensations that accompany maladaptive thoughts is also important for preventing depression and anxiety. Addictive disorders concentrate on reactions to social pressure, interpersonal conflicts, and negative emotional states as part of a relapse prevention plan.

Preparation

As with any type of therapeutic treatment, success of relapse prevention programs depend heavily on motivation. If an individual is not interested in making life changes, he or she is not likely to follow a prevention plan. Individuals low in motivation may need to participate in group or individual **psychotherapy** before deciding whether to enter a relapse prevention program.

Aftercare

Aftercare typically consists of participation in **support groups**. For addictions, 12-step groups (such as Alcoholics Anonymous) are most commonly recommended. These types of groups can be attended daily. Support groups exist for other types of mental disorders, and may be run by peers or a professional facilitator. Aftercare groups, usually run in treatment facilities by professional staff, may be used to continue practicing skills and to trouble-shoot problems individuals are experiencing with their prevention plans in everyday life. Aftercare groups usually meet less frequently (once a week or month) and may gradually taper off. Some relapse-prevention programs may use telephone contacts or individual therapy sessions to help individuals continue to use prevention skills effectively.

Results

Successful relapse prevention programs will empower individuals to make choices about how they respond in stressful, high-risk situations (triggers) rather than responding in habitual, unhealthy ways. Individuals should be aware of their personal triggers, use positive strategies for coping with **stress**, practice healthy lifestyle choices, involve others in their efforts, and have a realistic attitude regarding relapse. Use of these prevention skills should reduce symptoms and increase the time span between occurrences of lapses or relapses.

If an individual is unmotivated to make life changes, or a relapse prevention program has been ineffective, that individual will demonstrate few (if any) of the prevention skills learned. The individual will show little improvement in symptomatic or problematic behavior. Periods of remission (symptom-free behavior) will be short and relapses will occur frequently.

Resources

BOOKS

Copeland, Mary Ellen. *Winning Against Relapse: A Workbook of Action Plans for Recurring Health and Emotional Problems.* Oakland, CA: New Harbinger Publications, 1999.

Miller, William R. and Stephen Rollnick. *Motivational Interviewing: Preparing People to Change Addictive Behavior.* New York: Guilford Press, 1991.

PERIODICALS

Brandon, Thomas H., et al. "Preventing Relapse Among Former Smokers: A Comparison of Minimal Interventions Through Telephone and Mail." *Journal of Consulting and Clinical Psychology* 68, no. 1 (February 2000): 103–113.

Carich, Mark S., John F. Newbauer, and Mark H. Stone. "Using Relapse Intervention Strategies to Treat Sexual Offenders." *Journal of Individual Psychology* 57, no. 1 (Spring 2001): 26–36.

Echeburua, Enrique, Javier Fernandez-Montalvo, and Concepcion Baez. "Relapse Prevention in the Treatment of Slot-Machine Pathological Gambling: Long-Term Outcome." *Behavior Therapy* 31, no. 2 (2000): 351–364.

Hartzler, Bryan, and Chris Brownson. "The Utility of Change Models in the Design and Delivery of Thematic Group Interventions: Applications to a Self-Defeating Behaviors Group." *Group Dynamics: Theory, Research, and Practice* 5, no. 3 (September 2001): 191–199.

Monti, Peter M., and Damaris J. Rohsenow. "Coping Skills Training and Cue-Exposure Therapy in the Treatment of Alcoholism." *Alcohol Research and Health* 23, no. 2 (Spring 1999): 107–115.

Perri, Michael G., et al. "Relapse Prevention Training and Problem-Solving Therapy in the Long-Term Management of Obesity." *Journal of Consulting and Clinical Psychology* 69, no. 4 (August 2000): 722–726.

Teasdale, John D., et al. "Prevention of Relapse/Recurrence in Major Depression by Mindfulness-Based Cognitive Therapy." *Journal of Consulting and Clinical Psychology* 68, no. 4 (2000): 615–623.

Wilson, Robin J., et al. "Community-Based Sex Offender Management: Combining Parole Supervision and Treatment to Reduce Recidivism." *Canadian Journal of Criminology* 42, no. 2 (2000): 177–188.

OTHER

World Federation for Mental Health. "Serious Mental Illness: Symptoms, Treatment and Causes of Relapse." http://www.wfmh.org/PDF/KEEPINGCARE/Serious%20Mental%20Illness%20fact%20sheet.pdf (accessed October 11, 2011).

ORGANIZATIONS

National Institute of Mental Health, 6001 Executive Blvd., Room 8184, MSC 9663, Bethesda, MD, 20892-9663, (301) 433-4513; TTY: (301) 443-8431, Fax: (301) 443-4279, (866) 615-6464; TTY: (866) 415-8051, nimh info@nih.gov, http://www.nimh.nih.gov.

National Institute on Alcohol Abuse and Alcoholism, 5635 Fishers Lane, MSC 9304, Bethesda, MD, 20892-9304, http://www.niaaa.nih.gov.

National Institute on Drug Abuse, 6001 Executive Blvd., Room 5213, Bethesda, MD, 20892, (301) 442-1124; Spanish: (240) 221-4007, information@nida.nih.gov, http://www.nida.nih.gov.

Sandra L. Friedrich, M.A.

Relaxation therapy

Definition

Relaxation therapy is a broad term used to describe a number of techniques that promote **stress reduction**, the elimination of tension throughout the body, and a calm and peaceful state of mind.

Purpose

Relaxation therapy as a general term includes various forms: transcendental **meditation** (TM), **yoga**, tai chi, qigong, and vipassana (a Buddhist form of meditation meaning insight and also known as mindfulness meditation). Progressive relaxation, a treatment that is designed to rid the body of anxiety and related tension through progressive relaxation of the muscle groups, was first described by Edmund Jacobson in his 1929 book *Progressive Relaxation*. In 1975, Herbert Benson published his groundbreaking work *The Relaxation Response*, which described in detail the stress-reduction mechanism in the body that short-circuits the fight-or-flight response and lowers blood pressure, relieves muscle tension, and controls heart rate. This work gave further credence and legitimacy to the link between mind and body medicine. A number of commonly used relaxation techniques, such as cue-controlled relaxation, are a direct result of Benson's work in this area.

Description

A number of different relaxation methods are available. Some of the most widely taught and most frequently practiced by healthcare providers are progressive relaxation, cue-controlled relaxation, breathing exercises, guided imagery, and **biofeedback**.

Progressive relaxation

Progressive relaxation is performed by first tensing and then relaxing the muscles of the body, one group at a time. Muscle groups can be divided a number of different ways, but a common method is to use the following groupings: (a) hands and arms; (b) head, neck, and shoulders; (c) torso, including chest, stomach and back;

and (d) buttocks, thighs, lower legs, and feet. The patient lies or sits in a comfortable position and then starts with the first muscle group, focusing on the feeling of the muscles and the absence or presence of tension. The patient then tenses the first muscle in the group, holds the tension for approximately five seconds, and releases and relaxes for up to 30 seconds. The contrast allows the individual to notice difference between feelings of tension and those of relaxation. The procedure is repeated with the next muscle in the group and so on, until the first group is completed. The patient then starts on the next muscle group.

Progressive relaxation can be guided with verbal cues and scripts, either memorized by the patient or provided on instructional audiotapes. The procedure remains the same, but the individual is prompted on which muscles to flex and relax and given other cues about noticing the difference between the tense and relaxed state. Some individuals may prefer progressive relaxation that is prompted with a tape because it allows them to completely clear their minds and to just follow instructions.

Deep breathing exercises

Individuals under **stress** often experience fast, shallow breathing. This type of breathing, known as chest breathing, can lead to shortness of breath, increased muscle tension, and inadequate oxygenation of blood. Breathing exercises can both improve respiratory function and relieve stress and tension.

Before starting to learn breathing exercises, individuals should first become aware of their breathing patterns. This can be accomplished by placing one hand on the chest and one hand on the abdomen and observing which hand moves further during breathing. If it is the hand placed on the chest, then chest breathing is occurring, and breathing exercises may be beneficial.

Deep breathing exercises are best performed while lying flat on the back, usually on the floor with a mat. The knees are bent, and the body (particularly the mouth, nose, and face) is relaxed. One hand is placed on the chest and one on the abdomen to monitor breathing technique. The individual takes a series of long, deep breaths through the nose, attempting to raise the abdomen instead of the chest. Air is exhaled through the relaxed mouth. Deep breathing can be continued for up to 20 minutes. After the **exercise** is complete, the individual checks again for body tension and relaxation. Once deep breathing techniques have been mastered, an individual can use deep breathing at any time or place as a quick method of relieving tension.

Release-only relaxation

Like progressive relaxation, release-only relaxation focuses on relieving feelings of tension in the muscles.

However, it eliminates the initial use of muscle tensing as practiced in progressive relaxation, focusing instead solely on muscle relaxation. Release-only relaxation is usually recommended as the next step in relaxation therapy after progressive relaxation has been mastered.

In release-only relaxation, breathing is used as a relaxation tool. The individual sits in a comfortable chair and begins to focus on breathing, envisioning tension leaving the body with each exhale. Once deep abdominal breathing is established, the individual begins to focus on releasing tension in each muscle group, until the entire body is completely relaxed.

Cue-controlled relaxation

Cue-controlled relaxation is an abbreviated tension-relief technique that combines elements of release-only relaxation and deep breathing exercises. It uses a cue, such as a word or mental image, to trigger immediate feelings of muscle relaxation. The cue must first be associated with relaxation in the individual's mind. Individuals choose the cue and then use it in breathing and release-only relaxation exercises repeatedly until the cue starts to automatically trigger feelings of relaxation outside the treatment sessions. Cues can be as simple as a given word such as "one" and are frequently used on relaxation audiotapes. They can also be a visual cue, such as a mental image of a white sand beach, a flower-filled meadow, or clear blue sky. Guided imagery also uses visualization exercises to produce feelings of relaxation.

Guided imagery

Guided imagery is a two-part process. The first component involves reaching a state of deep relaxation through breathing and muscle relaxation techniques. During the relaxation phase, individuals close their eyes and focus on the slow in and out of their breath. Instead, individuals might focus on releasing the feelings of tension from their muscles, starting with the toes and working up to the top of the head. Relaxation tapes often feature soft music or tranquil, natural sounds such as rolling waves and chirping birds in order to promote feelings of relaxation.

Once complete relaxation is achieved, the second component of the exercise is the imagery, or visualization, itself. Relaxation imagery involves conjuring pleasant images that rest the mind and body. These may be past experiences or idealized new situations.

The individual may also use mental rehearsal. Mental rehearsal involves imagining a situation or scenario and its ideal outcome. It can be used to reduce anxiety about an upcoming situation, such as childbirth, surgery, or even a critical event such as an important competition or a job interview. Individuals imagine themselves going through

---

KEY TERMS

Qigong—An exercise practice derived from traditional Chinese medicine and designed to facilitate energy flow throughout the body.

Tai chi—A martial art that uses exercise to balance the body's energy flow to the body center in order to promote physical well-being.

---

each step of the event, visualizing harmony and good will in the whole process and positive outcome.

Biofeedback

Biofeedback, or applied psychophysiological feedback, is a patient-guided treatment that teaches individuals to manipulate muscle tension through relaxation, visualization, and other cognitive techniques. The term biofeedback refers to the biological signals that are fed back, or returned, to the individual in order for that person to develop the relaxation techniques.

During biofeedback, one or more special sensors are placed on the body. These sensors measure muscle tension, **brain** waves, heart rate, and body temperature, and translate the information into a visual and/or audible readout, such as a paper tracing, a light display, or a series of beeps. While viewing the instantaneous feedback from the biofeedback monitors, the individual begins to recognize what thoughts, fears, and mental images influence physical reactions. By monitoring this relationship between mind and body, the individual can then use thoughts and mental images deliberately to manipulate heart beat, brain wave patterns, body temperature, and other bodily functions, and to reduce feelings of stress. This is achieved through relaxation exercises, mental imagery, and other cognitive therapy techniques.

As the biofeedback response takes place, the individual can actually see or hear the results of the relaxation efforts instantly through the sensor readout on the biofeedback equipment. Once these techniques are learned and the individual is able to recognize the state of relaxation or visualization necessary to alleviate symptoms, the biofeedback equipment itself is no longer needed. The person then has a powerful, self-administered treatment technique for dealing with problem symptoms.

Dozens of other effective therapies promote relaxation, including hypnosis, meditation, yoga, **aromatherapy**, hydrotherapy, tai chi, massage, **art therapy**, and others. Individuals should choose a type of relaxation therapy based on their own interests and lifestyle.

HERBERT BENSON (1935–)

Dr. Herbert Benson, the guru of mind/body medicine, was born in 1935. He graduated from Wesleyan University and the Harvard School of Medicine. He nurtured his interest in mind/body relationships and developed expertise in behavioral medicine and spiritual healing. In his research, Benson straddled the thin line between medicine and religion. He conceived of what he called a three-legged approach to health care: self-care, pharmaceuticals, and medical treatment or surgery. His most significant work was his discovery of the relaxation response, which is the connection between lowered blood pressure and transcendental meditation. He was quoted by Daphne Howland of BeWell.com saying that "[B]elief is one of the most powerful healing tools we have in our therapeutic arsenal."

Benson served as the Mind/Body Institute associate professor of medicine at Harvard School

of Medical and worked as the chief of the Division of Behavioral Medicine at the Beth Israel Deaconess Medical Center in Boston, Massachusetts. In 1988 he founded the Mind/Body Medical Institute in Boston, where he served as founding president. He lectured extensively about his work. On November 5, 1997, Benson addressed the Committee on Appropriations of the U.S. House of Representatives and spoke on the topic of "Healing and the Mind." Benson authored scores of scientific papers along with six books pertaining to his years of study, including *The Mind/Body Effect* in 1979, *Relaxation Response* in 1990, and *Timeless Healing: The Power and Biology of Belief* in 1996. Altogether his books sold over four million copies. Among his many honors and awards, Benson received the John Templeton Spirituality and Medicine Curricular Award in 1999.

Benefits

Stress and tension have been linked to numerous ailments, including heart disease, high blood pressure, atherosclerosis, irritable bowel syndrome, ulcers, **anxiety disorders**, **insomnia**, and **substance abuse**. Stress can also trigger a number of distinct physical symptoms, including nausea, headache, hair loss, **fatigue**, and muscle pain. Relaxation therapies have been shown to reduce the incidence and severity of stress-related diseases and disorders in many patients.

Preparations

When considering relaxation therapy to alleviate physical symptoms such as nausea, headache, high blood pressure, fatigue, or gastrointestinal problems, individuals should consult a doctor first to make sure that an underlying disorder or disease is not causing the symptoms. A complete physical examination and comprehensive medical history will be performed, and even if an organic cause for the symptoms is found, relaxation exercises may still be recommended as an adjunct, or complementary, treatment to relieve discomfort.

Relaxation therapy should always take place in a quiet, relaxing atmosphere in which the person has a comfortable place to sit or recline. Some people find that quiet background music improves their relaxation

sessions. If an instructional audiotape or videotape is to be used, the appropriate equipment should be available.

The relaxation session, which can last from a few minutes to an hour, should be uninterrupted. Taking the phone off the hook, turning off cell phones, dimming the lights, and asking family members for privacy and silence can ensure a more successful and relaxing session.

Precautions

Most commonly practiced relaxation techniques are completely safe and free of side effects.

Relaxation techniques that involve special exercises or body manipulation such as massage, tai chi, and yoga should be taught or performed by a qualified healthcare professional or instructor. These treatments may not be suitable for individuals with certain health conditions such as arthritis or fibromyalgia. These individuals should consult with their healthcare professional before engaging in such therapies.

Biofeedback may not be recommended in some individuals who use a pacemaker or other implantable electrical devices. These individuals should inform their biofeedback therapist before starting treatments, as certain types of biofeedback sensors have the potential to interfere with implantable devices.

QUESTIONS TO ASK YOUR DOCTOR

- In what way do you think relaxation therapy will benefit me?
- What tests or evaluation techniques will you perform to see if relaxation therapy has been beneficial for me?
- What other treatment options do you recommend for me?
- Will relaxation therapy interfere with my current medications?
- What symptoms or behaviors are important enough that I should seek immediate treatment?

Relaxation therapy may not be suitable for some patients. Patients must be willing to take an active role in the treatment process and to practice techniques learned in treatment at home.

Some relaxation therapies may also be inappropriate for cognitively impaired individuals (e.g., patients with organic brain disease or a **traumatic brain injury**) depending on their level of functioning. Given the wide range of relaxation therapies available, if one type of relaxation treatment is deemed inappropriate for these patients, a suitable alternative can usually be recommended by a qualified healthcare professional.

Side effects

Relaxation therapy can induce sleepiness, and some individuals may fall asleep during a session. Relaxation therapy should not be performed while a person is operating a motor vehicle or in other situations in which full and alert attention is necessary. Other than this, there are no known adverse side effects to relaxation therapy.

Research and general acceptance

Relaxation therapies are generally well-accepted by the medical community for relief of stress and anxiety.

Some research has also indicated that relaxation therapy may be useful for certain physiological conditions. One study, for example, reported results indicating that relaxation therapy reduced the incidence of preterm labor in women at risk for delivering prematurely. It also found that women who discontinued relaxation exercises for whatever reasons delivered earlier and had lower birth-weight babies than those who continued the treatment. Positive benefits of relaxation therapy have also been reported for persons who have high blood pressure. Another study of 90 individuals who had previously experienced a heart attack reported a more favorable long-term outcome among the patients when they underwent both relaxation therapy and exercise training than exercise training alone. In 2006, researchers conducted a study of the therapy's impact on patients with chronic heart failure. For the study, 121 patients were split into control and experimental groups, with the experimental group receiving training in progressive muscle relaxation. The experimental group reported greater reduction in psychological distress compared to the control group. The researchers concluded that the training might be useful as part of a disease-management program for these patients, although further research would be necessary to discover if any other benefits could be attributed to the relaxation therapy.

Not all research supports relaxation therapy as a treatment option. A report published in 2001 reviewed numerous studies of the effectiveness of relaxation therapies on bronchial asthma. The report concluded that "little evidence in its favor has been presented." It noted, however, that healthcare professionals "continue to include relaxation training as a component in the nonpharmacological treatment of asthma."

Training and certification

Relaxation therapy techniques are used by many licensed therapists, counselors, psychologists, psychiatrists, and other healthcare professionals. Many self-help books, audiotapes, and videos are available that give instruction in relaxation techniques.

Resources

BOOKS

Bear, Marina. *The Little Book of Meditation: A Guide to Stress-Free Living.* Berkeley, CA: SLG Books, 2009.

Davis, Martha, E. R. Eshelman, and Matthew McKay. *The Relaxation & Stress Reduction Workbook,* 6th ed. Oakland, CA: New Harbinger Publications, 2009.

Devereux, Charla. *Aromatherapy: The Essence of Well-being (Book-in-a-Box).* Wilmington, DE: Tower.com, Inc., 2011.

Schenkman, Steven. *Massage Therapy: What It Is and How It Works.* Florence, KY; Cengage Learning, 2009.

PERIODICALS

Yu, Doris. "Abstract 2506: Relaxation Therapy in Patients with Chronic Heart Failure: A Randomized Controlled Trial." *Circulation* 114 (2006): 517.

ORGANIZATIONS

American Psychological Association, 750 1st Street NE, Washington, DC, 20002-4242, (202) 336-5500; TDD/

TTY: (202) 336-6123, (800) 374-2721, http://www.apa. org.

National Association of Holistic Aromatherapy, PO Box 1868, Banner Elk, NC, 28604, (828) 898-6161, Fax: (828) 898-1965, info@naha.org, http://www.naha.org.

Paula Ford-Martin
Laura Jean Cataldo, RN, EdD

Remeron *see* **Mirtazapine**

Respite

Definition

Respite literally means a period of rest or relief. Respite care provides a caregiver temporary relief from the responsibilities of caring for individuals with chronic physical or mental disabilities.

Purpose

Respite was developed in response to the **deinstitutionalization** movement of the 1960s and 1970s. Maintaining individuals in their natural homes rather than placing them in long-term care facilities was viewed as beneficial to the individual, the involved family, and society (in terms of lowered healthcare costs). The primary purpose of respite care is to relieve the **stress** felt by caregivers, enabling them to continue caring for the individual.

Respite care is typically provided for individuals with disorders related to aging (**dementia**, frail health), terminal illnesses, chronic health issues, or developmental disabilities. More recently, children with behavior disorders have also been eligible for respite care. Respite care is usually recreational and does not include therapy or treatment.

Description

Caregivers frequently experience stress in the forms of physical **fatigue**, psychological distress (resentment, frustration, anxiety, guilt, **depression**), and disruption in relations with other family members. The emotional aspects of caring for a family member are often more taxing than the physical demands. Increased caregiver stress may result in health problems such as ulcers, high blood pressure, difficulty sleeping, weight loss or gain, or breathing difficulties. Respite care offers caregivers the opportunity to relax and destress so that they are able to resume their roles.

A respite caregiver carries a boy off of a bus after a camping trip for the disabled. (© *Photofusion Picture Library/ Alamy*)

Length of respite care can be anywhere from a few hours to several weeks. Services may be used frequently or infrequently, such as for emergencies, vacations, one day per week or month, weekends, or everyday. A variety of services are available, and the type of service is often closely related to the characteristics of the facility:

- In-home respite services consist of a worker who comes to the family home while the caregiver is away. These services are usually provided by agencies that recruit, screen, and train workers. This type of respite is usually less disruptive to the individual with the disability, provided there is a good match between the worker and the patient. However, concerns over the reliability and trustworthiness of the worker can be an additional source of stress for the caregiver.

- Respite centers are residential facilities specifically designed for respite care. Adult day care programs and respite camps also fall into this category. This type of respite offers more peace of mind to the caregiver and may provide a stimulating environment for the individual with the disability. However, centers usually restrict length of stay and may exclude individuals based on severity of disability.

- Institutional settings sometimes reserve spaces to be used for respite purposes. These include skilled nursing facilities, intermediate care facilities, group homes, senior housing, regular day care or after-school programs for children, and hospitals. Some of these facilities provide higher levels of care but are less "home-like." The individual with the disability may oppose staying in an institutional setting or may fear abandonment.
- Licensed foster care providers can also provide respite services in their homes.

Funding

Costs of respite care present a financial burden to many families. **Community mental health** centers often fund respite services if the individual meets certain criteria, including eligibility for Medicaid. Wraparound programs (also accessed through community mental health centers) for children with emotional or behavioral disorders also pay for respite services. Veteran's Administration hospitals provide respite care at little or no charge if the individual receiving the care is a veteran (but not if the caregiver is a veteran). Private insurance companies rarely pay for respite, and many respite providers do not accept this form of payment. Some respite facilities have sliding-scale fees. Other facilities operate as a co-op, where caregivers work at the facility in exchange for respite services.

In addition, respite agencies may have difficulty recruiting and retaining qualified employees, because limited funding prevents agencies from offering desirable salaries. The high turnover and unavailability of employees may result in delays in service delivery or family dissatisfaction with services. Advocacy for policy changes regarding funding is needed.

Barriers to using respite services

Recent research suggests that families who use respite tend to have higher levels of perceived stress, lower levels of support from others, and fewer resources. In many of these families, the individuals in need of care have more severe disabilities, problem behaviors such as aggression or self-injury, and communication difficulties; are school-aged; and are more dependent for basic needs such as eating, toileting, and dressing.

It has been well documented that many families eligible for respite care never utilize these services. Many caregivers obtain respite in informal ways not offered by respite services. Some researchers have suggested that respite care should be just one form of service available to caregivers, with other possible services including home-delivered meals, transportation assistance,

KEY TERMS

Behavior disorders—Disorders characterized by disruptive behaviors such as conduct disorder, oppositional defiant disorder, and attention deficit hyperactivity disorder.

Deinstitutionalization—The process of moving people out of mental hospitals and into treatment programs or halfway houses in local communities. With this movement, the responsibility for care shifted from large (often governmental) agencies to families and community organizations.

Developmental disabilities—Disabilities that are present from birth and that delay or prevent normal development, such as intellectual disability or autism.

Intermediate care facility—An inpatient facility that provides periodic nursing care.

Medicaid—A program jointly funded by state and federal governments that reimburses hospitals and physicians for the care of individuals who cannot pay for their own medical expenses. These individuals may be in low-income households or may have chronic disabilities.

Skilled nursing facility—An inpatient facility that provides 24-hour nursing services to individuals in need of extended care.

Veteran's Administration hospitals—Medical facilities operated by the federal government explicitly for veterans of the U.S. military.

Wraparound programs—A relatively new form of mental health service delivery that strives to accommodate all family members based on self-defined needs, flexibly incorporating both formal and informal community services.

recreational resources, or care skills training. Additional reasons for the non-utilization of respite care include:

- Unfamiliarity. Some families are unaware that such services exist, or may be uncertain about how to access services. This implies a need for improved referral services.

- Funding. Limited funding may prevent some families from receiving services.

- Caregiver qualities. Some caregivers experience guilt or anxiety over allowing someone else to care for their loved one. Being able to maintain one's family independently may be tied to gender roles or cultural customs. Relatives and friends may assist in caregiving, making formal respite unnecessary.

• Care recipient qualities. Occasionally the individual with the disability is opposed to respite care; he or she may not trust strangers or may refuse to leave home. In other instances, the individual may have special needs, such as certain behaviors or physical care, that are too challenging for the respite provider to address.

• Program qualities. Many researchers believe that respite programs are not adequately meeting the needs of families. In some cases, times that services are offered are inconvenient. Individuals with severe disabilities who pose the most need for services are sometimes excluded.

In 2006, the U.S. Congress introduced the Lifespan Respite Care Program. The program promotes the funding of respite services, in order to benefit overall care. Objectives of the program include expanding and improving the quality of respite care programs, improving the execution of services among programs, and increasing access to programs. As of 2011, 30 states had been granted funds for respite care programs.

Resources

BOOKS

Ownby, Lisa L., et al. *Partners Plus: Families and Caregivers in Partnerships: A Family-Centered Guide to Respite Care.* Washington, DC: Child Development Resources, U.S. Department of Education, Early Education Program for Children with Disabilities, 1999.

Tepper, Lynn M. and John A. Toner, eds. *Respite Care: Programs, Problems, and Solutions.* Philadelphia: The Charles Press, 1993.

PERIODICALS

Chan, Jeffrey B., and Jeff Sigafoos. "A Review of Child and Family Characteristics Related to the Use of Respite Care in Developmental Disability Services." *Child and Youth Care Forum* 29, no. 1 (2000): 27–37.

Chappell, Neena L., R. Colin Reid, and Elizabeth Dow. "Respite Reconsidered: A Typology of Meanings Based on the Caregiver's Point of View." *Journal of Aging Studies* 15, no. 2 (2001): 201–216.

ORGANIZATIONS

ARCH National Respite Network and Resource Center, Chapel Hill Training-Outreach Project, 800 Eastowne Drive, Ste. 105, Chapel Hill, NC, 27514, (919) 490-5577, Fax: (919) 490-4905, http://www.chtop.com.

National Aging Information Center, One Massachusetts Ave. NW, Washington, DC, 20001, (202) 619-0724 Fax: (202) 357-3555, aoainfo@aoa.hhs.gov, http://www.aoa.gov.

National Dissemination Center for Children with Disabilities, 1825 Connecticut Ave NW, Ste. 700, Washington, DC, 20009, (202) 884-8200, Fax: (202) 884-8441, http://www.nichcy.org.

The Arc National Headquarters, 1660 L Street, NW, Ste. 301, Washington, DC, 20036, (202) 534-3700, Fax: (202) 534-3731, info@thearc.org, http://www.thearc.org.

Sandra L. Friedrich, M.A.

Response prevention *see* **Exposure treatment**

Restless legs syndrome

Definition

Restless legs syndrome (RLS) is a neurological disorder characterized by uncomfortable sensations in the legs and, less commonly, the arms. These sensations are exacerbated (heightened) when the person with RLS is at rest. The sensations are described as crawly, tingly, prickly and occasionally painful. They result in a nearly insuppressible urge to move around. Symptoms are often associated with sleep disturbances.

Demographics

As much as 10% of the population of the United States and Europe may suffer from some degree of restless legs syndrome. Fewer cases are indicated in India, Japan and Singapore, suggesting racial or ethnic factors play a role in the disorder. Although the demographics can vary greatly, the majority of people suffering from RLS are female. The age of onset also varies greatly, but the number of people suffering from RLS increases with age. However, many people with RLS report that they had symptoms of the disorder in their childhood. These symptoms were often disregarded as growing pains or hyperactivity. In addition, some evidence suggests that there is a genetic component to RLS and it may run in families.

Description

Restless legs syndrome is a sensory-motor disorder that causes uncomfortable feelings in the legs, especially during periods of inactivity. Some people also report sensations in the arms, but this occurs much more rarely. The sensations occur deep in the legs and are usually described with terms that imply movement such as prickly, creepy-crawly, boring, itching, achy, pulling, tugging and painful. The symptoms result in an irrepressible urge to move the leg and are relieved when the person suffering from RLS voluntarily moves. Symptoms tend to be worse in the evening or at night.

Restless legs syndrome is associated with another disorder called periodic limb movements in sleep (PLMS). It is estimated that four out of five patients with RLS also suffer from PLMS. PLMS is characterized by jerking leg movements while sleeping that may occur as frequently as every 20 seconds. These jerks disrupt sleep by causing continual arousals throughout the night.

People with both RLS and PLMS are prone to abnormal levels of exhaustion during the day because they are unable to sleep properly at night. They may have trouble concentrating at work, at school or during social activities. They may also have mood swings and difficulty with interpersonal relationships. **Depression** and anxiety may also result from the lack of sleep. RLS affects people who want to travel or attend events that require sitting for long periods of time.

Causes and symptoms

Restless legs syndrome is categorized in two ways. Primary RLS occurs in the absence of other medical symptoms, while secondary RLS is usually associated with some other medical disorder. Although the cause of primary RLS is currently unknown, a large amount of research into the cause of RLS is taking place. Researchers at Johns Hopkins University published a study in July 2003 suggesting that iron deficiencies may be related to the disorder. They dissected brains from cadavers of people who suffered from RLS and found that the cells in the midbrain were not receiving enough iron. Other researchers suggest that RLS may be related to a chemical imbalance of the neurotransmitter **dopamine** in the **brain**. There is also evidence that RLS has a genetic component. RLS occurs three to five times more frequently in an immediate family member of someone who has RLS than in the general population. A site on a chromosome that may contain a gene for RLS has been identified by molecular biologists.

In many people, other medical conditions play a role in RLS and the disorder is therefore termed secondary RLS. People with peripheral neuropathies (injury to nerves in the arms and legs) may experience RLS. Such neuropathies may result from diabetes or alcoholism. Other chronic diseases such as kidney disorders and rheumatoid arthritis may result in RLS. Iron deficiencies and blood anemias are often associated with RLS and symptoms of the disease usually decrease once blood iron levels have been corrected. **Attention deficit hyperactivity disorder** (ADHD) has also been implicated in RLS. Pregnant women often suffer from RLS, especially in the third trimester. Some people find that high levels of caffeine intake may result in RLS.

KEY TERMS

Anemia—A condition that affects the size and number of red blood cells. It often results from lack of iron or certain B vitamins and may be treated with iron or vitamin supplements.

Insomnia—Trouble sleeping. People who suffer from RLS often lose sleep either because they spend time walking to relieve discomfort or because they have PLMS, which causes them to wake often during the night.

Periodic limb movements in sleep (PLMS)—Random movements of the arms or legs that occur at regular intervals of time during sleep.

The symptoms of RLS are all associated with unpleasant feelings in the limbs. The words used to describe these feelings are various, but include such adjectives as deep-seated crawling, jittery, tingling, burning, aching, pulling, painful, itchy or prickly. They are usually not described as a muscle cramp or numbness. Most often the sensations occur during periods of inactivity. They are characterized by an urge to get up and move. Such movements include stretching, walking, jogging or simply jiggling the legs. The feelings worsen in the evening.

A variety of symptoms are associated with RLS, but may not be characteristic of every case. Some people with RLS report involuntary arm and leg movements during the night. Others have difficulty falling asleep and are sleepy or fatigued during the day. Many people with RLS have leg discomfort that is not explained by routine medical exams.

Eighty-five percent of RLS patients either have difficulty falling asleep or wake several times during the night, and almost half experience daytime **fatigue** or sleepiness. It is common for the symptoms to be intermittent. They may disappear for several months and then return for no apparent reason. Two-thirds of patients report that their symptoms become worse with time. Some older patients claim to have had symptoms since they were in their early 20s, but were not diagnosed until their 50s. Suspected under-diagnosis of RLS may be attributed to the difficulty experienced by patients in describing their symptoms.

Diagnosis

A careful history enables the physician to distinguish RLS from similar types of disorders that cause night time discomfort in the limbs, such as muscle cramps, burning feet syndrome, and damage to nerves that detect sensations or cause movement (polyneuropathy).

The most important tool the doctor has in **diagnosis** is the history obtained from the patient. There are several common medical conditions that are known to either cause or to be closely associated with RLS. The doctor may link the patient's symptoms to one of these conditions, which include anemia, diabetes, disease of the spinal nerve roots (lumbosacral radiculopathy), Parkinson's disease, late-stage pregnancy, kidney failure (uremia), and complications of stomach surgery. In order to identify or eliminate such a primary cause, blood tests may be performed to determine the presence of serum iron, ferritin, folate, vitamin B_{12}, creatinine, and thyroid-stimulating hormones. The physician may also ask if symptoms are present in any close family members, since it is common for RLS to run in families and this type is sometimes more difficult to treat.

In some cases, sleep studies such as **polysomnography** are undertaken to identify the presence of PLMS that are reported to affect 70%–80% of people who suffer from RLS. The patient is often unaware of these movements, since they may not cause him to wake. However, the presence of PLMS with RLS can leave the person more tired, because it interferes with deep sleep. A patient who also displays evidence of some neurologic disease may undergo electromyography (EMG). During EMG, a very small, thin needle is inserted into the muscle and electrical activity of the muscle is recorded. A doctor or technician usually performs this test at a hospital outpatient department.

RLS is under consideration for inclusion in the fifth edition of the ***Diagnostic and Statistical Manual of Mental Disorders*** (*DSM-5*, 2013). The proposed diagnostic criteria describes RLS as the urge to move the legs, accompanied by uncomfortable sensations, and requires the following to be present:

- The sensations start or increase during rest or inactivity.
- The sensations are only partly relieved by moving the legs.
- The sensations are worse in the evening or at night, or they only occur in the evening or at night.

In addition, the above symptoms must be accompanied by at least one of the following conditions

- fatigue
- daytime sleepiness
- problems with concentration, memory, or learning
- mood disturbances

- behavioral problems
- problems at work or school due to lack of sleep
- problems with interpersonal relationships

The *DSM-5* notes that these symptoms should occur despite ample opportunities for sleep.

Treatment

The first step in treatment is to treat existing conditions that are known to be associated with RLS and that will be identified by blood tests. If the patient is anemic, iron (iron sulfate) or vitamin supplements (folate or vitamin B_{12}) will be prescribed. If kidney disease is identified as a cause, treatment of the kidney problem will take priority.

After treating underlying disorders, treatment for restless legs syndrome is generally two-pronged, consisting of making lifestyle changes and using medications to relieve some of the symptoms. Lifestyle changes involve altering the diet, exercising and performing other self-directed activities, and practicing good sleep hygiene. Although the United States Food and Drug Administration has not yet approved any drugs for treating RLS, four classes of pharmaceuticals have been found effective for treating RLS: dopaminergic agents, **benzodiazepines**, **opioids** and anticonvulsants.

Drugs

Dopaminergic agents are the first type of drug prescribed in the treatment of RLS. Most commonly doctors prescribe dopamine-receptor agonists that are used to treat Parkinson's disease such as Mirapex (pramipexole), Permax (pergolide) and Requip (ropinirole). Sinemet (carbidopa/levodopa), which is a drug that adds dopamine to the nervous system, is also commonly prescribed. Sinemet has been used the more frequently than other drugs in treating RLS, but recently a problem known as augmentation has been associated with its use. When augmentation develops, symptoms of RLS will return earlier in the day and increasing the dose will not improve the symptoms.

Antiepileptic drugs are those used for people with **seizures**. These are also useful in the treatment of RLS, and include Neurontin (**gabapentin**), Carbatrol (**carbamazepine**), Keppra (levetiracetam), and Topamax (topiramate).

Benzodiazepines are drugs that sedate and are typically taken before bedtime so that a patient with RLS can sleep more soundly. The most commonly prescribed sedative in RLS is Klonopin (**clonazepam**).

Opioids are synthetic narcotics that relieve pain and cause drowsiness. They are usually taken in the evening. The most commonly used opioids prescribed for RLS include Darvon or Darvocet (propoxyphene), Dolophine (**methadone**), Percocet (oxycodone), Ultram (Tramadol) and Vicodin (hydrocodone). One danger associated with opioids is that they can be addicting.

A few drugs have been found to worsen symptoms of RLS and they should be avoided by patients exhibiting RLS symptoms. These include anti-nausea drugs such as Antivert, Atarax, Compazine and Phenergan. Calcium channel blockers that are often used to treat heart conditions should be avoided. In addition, most anti-depressants tend to exacerbate symptoms of RLS. Finally, antihistamines such as Benadryl have been found to aggravate RLS symptoms in some people.

Home remedies

Simple changes to the diet have proven effective for some people suffering from RLS. Vitamin deficiencies are a common problem in RLA patients. In patients with RLS, most physicians will check the levels of blood serum ferritin, which can indicate low iron storage. If these levels are below 50 mcg/L, then supplemental iron should be added to the diet. Other physicians have found that supplements of vitamin E, folic acid and B vitamins, and magnesium provide relief to symptoms or RLS. Reducing or eliminating caffeine and alcohol consumption has been effective in other patients.

Alternative

It is likely that the best alternative therapy will combine both conventional and alternative approaches. Levodopa may be combined with a therapy that relieves pain, relaxes muscles, or focuses in general on the nervous system and the brain. Any such combined therapy that allows a reduction in dosage of levodopa is advantageous, since this will reduce the likelihood of unacceptable levels of drug side effects. Of course, the physician who prescribes the medication should monitor any combined therapy. Alternative methods may include:

- Acupuncture. Patients who also suffer from rheumatoid arthritis may especially benefit from acupuncture to relieve RLS symptoms. Acupuncture is believed to be effective in arthritis treatment and may also stimulate those parts of the brain that are involved in RLS.
- Homeopathy. Homeopaths believe that disorders of the nervous system are especially important because the brain controls so many other bodily functions. The remedy is tailored to the individual patient and is based on individual symptoms as well as the general symptoms of RLS.
- Reflexology. Reflexologists claim that the brain, head, and spine all respond to indirect massage of specific parts of the feet.
- Nutritional supplements. Supplementation of the diet with vitamin E, calcium, magnesium, and folic acid may be helpful for people with RLS.

Some alternative methods may treat the associated condition that is suspected to cause restless legs. These include:

- Anemia or low ferritin levels. Chinese medicine will emphasize stimulation of the spleen as a means of improving blood circulation and vitamin absorption. Other treatments may include acupuncture and herbal therapies, such as ginseng (*Panax ginseng*) for anemia-related fatigue.
- Late-stage pregnancy. There are few conventional therapies available to pregnant women, since most of the drugs prescribed are not recommended for use during pregnancy. Pregnant women may benefit from alternative techniques that focus on body work, including yoga, reflexology, and acupuncture.

Prognosis

RLS usually does not indicate the onset of other neurological disease. However, it is a lifelong condition for most people. It may remain static, although two-thirds of patients get worse with time. The symptoms usually progress gradually. Treatment with Levodopa is effective in moderate to severe cases that may include significant PLMS. However, this drug produces significant side effects, and continued successful treatment may depend on carefully monitored use of combination drug therapy. The prognosis is usually best if RLS symptoms are recent and can be traced to another treatable condition that is associated with RLS. Some associated conditions are not treatable. In these cases, such as for rheumatoid arthritis, alternative therapies such as **acupuncture** may be helpful.

Prevention

Diet is key in preventing RLS. A preventive diet will include an adequate intake of iron and the B vitamins, especially B_{12} and folic acid. Strict vegetarians should take vitamin supplements to obtain sufficient vitamin B_{12}. Ferrous gluconate may be easier on the digestive system than ferrous sulfate, if iron supplements are prescribed. Some medications may cause symptoms of RLS. Patients should check with their doctor about these possible side effects, especially if symptoms first occur after starting a new medication. Caffeine, alcohol, and **nicotine** use should be minimized or eliminated. Even a hot bath before bed has been shown to prevent symptoms for some sufferers.

Resources

BOOKS

Ferri, Fred, ed. *Ferri's Clinical Advisor 2010.* 1st ed. Philadelphia: Mosby Elsevier, 2009.

Goetz, C.G. *Goetz's Textbook of Clinical Neurology.* 3rd ed. Philadelphia: Saunders, 2007.

Goldman, L., and D. Ausiello, eds. *Cecil Textbook of Internal Medicine.* 23rd ed. Philadelphia: Saunders, 2008.

Rakel, R. *Textbook of Family Medicine 2007.* 7th ed. Philadelphia: Saunders Elsevier, 2009.

Rakel, R. E., and E. T. Bope. *Conn's Current Therapy.* 60th ed. Philadelphia: Saunders Elsevier, 2009.

WEBSITES

American Psychiatric Association. "Restless Legs Syndrome." DSM-5 Development. http://www.dsm5.org/proposedrevision/pages/proposedrevision.aspx?rid=403 (accessed September 11, 2011).

National Institute of Neurological Disease and Stroke. "Restless Legs Syndrome Fact Sheet." U.S. National Institutes of Health. http://www.ninds.nih.gov/disorders/restless_legs/detail_restless_legs.htm (accessed September 11, 2011).

ORGANIZATIONS

Restless Legs Syndrome Foundation, 1904 Banbury Road, Raleigh, NC, 27608-4428, (919) 781-4428, http://www.rls.org.

Ann M. Haren
Heidi Splete

Restoril *see* **Temazepam**

Rett syndrome

Definition

Rett syndrome is a progressive neurological disorder seen almost exclusively in females. The disorder is characterized by an early-onset slowing of the infant's head growth and a reduction in **brain** size by as much as 30%; it is the leading cause of genetically based profound **intellectual disability** in girls. The most common symptoms include decreased speech, cognitive disabilities, severe lack of muscle control, small head size, and unusual hand movements.

A mother communicates with her daughter by using flash cards; her daughter has Rett syndrome, a neurological disorder that can affect language abilities. (© *Kimberly P. Mitchell/Detroit Free Press/MCT/newscom*)

Demographics

Rett syndrome affects almost only females. Males who carry the same gene mutation gene typically are miscarried before birth or die as infants. Rett syndrome usually is fatal in males because they have a single X chromosome, and the Y chromosome they carry cannot compensate for this mutation on their X chromosome. Females with a mutation in the gene that causes Rett syndrome are able to survive because the presence of the second normal X chromosome partially compensates for the mutation on the other X chromosome. Rett syndrome is believed to affect all ethnic groups and nationalities with an equal frequency of about one case for every 10,000 to 15,000 live female births.

Description

Rett syndrome was first described by an Austrian physician, Andreas Rett, in 1966; prior to 1983, however, little was known about the syndrome because it was quite rare. Although Rett syndrome was thought at first to result from the destruction or degeneration of brain tissue, genetic research has indicated that it is caused by the failure of the infant's brain to develop normally. This developmental failure is caused by a genetic mutation affecting production of a key protein that regulates brain development.

Rett syndrome has a distinctive onset and course. In classic Rett syndrome, which occurs only in girls, the child develops normally during the first 6 to 18 months of life. In many cases, at around the fifth month, head growth slows or stagnates, and the child loses any purposeful hand movements that she had previously developed. Language and motor skills regress rapidly. Purposeful hand use gives way to repetitive hand-washing or hand-wringing gestures. **Seizures** occur in up to 90% of affected girls,

KEY TERMS

Congenital—Refers to a disorder which is present at birth.

Joint contractures—Stiffness of the joints that prevents full extension.

Mutation—A mutation is a change in a gene. Since genes determine how a body is structured and functions, any change in a gene will produce some change in these areas.

Neurological conditions—A condition that has its origin in some part of the patient's nervous system.

Seizure—A convulsion, or uncontrolled discharge of nerve cells that may spread to other cells throughout the brain.

and 50%–80% of children with the disorder will eventually develop epilepsy. Screaming fits and crying are features that arise by age 18 to 24 months. The disorder can also include characteristics of **autism**, tremors, and panic-like attacks. Rett syndrome is associated with severe or profound intellectual disability.

Some atypical forms of Rett syndrome, including congenital, late-onset, and preserved-speech Rett, are now being diagnosed in people formerly diagnosed with other disorders, such as autism or learning disability, who carry the genetic mutation linked to Rett syndrome. Males who have inherited an extra X chromosome and are carrying the mutation, or in whom the gene is mutated very early in their development, can manifest a form of the disorder. The features of this form of Rett may not be as severe in nature, because only some of the person's cells will carry the mutation. Because males normally inherit only one X chromosome, those with the mutation usually have such severe problems at birth that they do not survive into their second year.

Rett syndrome is included in the fourth edition of the *Diagnostic and Statistical Manual of Mental Disorders* (*DSM-IV-TR*), the handbook used by medical professionals in diagnosing mental disorders, as a pervasive developmental disorder of childhood. However, proposed changes for the fifth edition (*DSM-5*) include removing Rett syndrome as a mental health **diagnosis**.

Causes and symptoms

Causes

A genetic mutation on the X chromosome is the cause of Rett syndrome. Because only a single copy of this mutated gene is required to give rise to the disease, it is considered an X-linked, dominant disorder. About 99.5% of cases of the syndrome arise from a new mutation in the egg or sperm cell line of a parent, rather than existing in the body cells of the parent. It is possible to be a carrier of an X chromosome with this mutation without knowing, because most cells in a woman's body shut down one of her two X chromosomes. If most of the cells shut down the X carrying the disease-causing gene, she will not manifest the severe symptoms and may bear children, who have a 50% chance of inheriting the mutation-carrying X chromosome from her. Because Rett syndrome usually is the result of a new mutation, however, multiple cases in a single family are rare, but if a pregnant woman is found to be an unaffected carrier or if the couple has a child with the condition, prenatal testing is available.

The gene that causes Rett syndrome is MECP2, which lies on the long arm of the X chromosome. The protein that it encodes is required for life and is necessary for appropriate brain development. Its job is to turn off certain genes at specific developmental periods and to ensure that the correct form of a particular protein is made. When MECP2 does not function correctly, the development of the brain does not occur in an appropriately regulated manner. The genes with which it interacts are thought to relate to nerve cell signaling, and the protein that MECP2 encodes exists at high levels in normal nerve cells. In its absence, the parts of the brain responsible for emotion, sensation, and movement do not communicate correctly with one another, leaving the brain in a permanently infantile developmental state.

Symptoms

The symptoms of Rett syndrome have been described in terms of four stages in the child's development:

- Stage 1, early onset (6–18 months of age): The early symptoms of Rett syndrome are not always noticeable in Stage 1. The infant may not make eye contact with family members and may not show much interest in toys. She may be considered a "good baby" because she is so calm and quiet. On the other hand, there may be noticeable hand-wringing and slowing of head growth.

- Stage 2, rapid deterioration (1–4 years old): This stage may be either rapid or gradual in onset. The child loses her ability to speak and to make purposeful hand movements. Hand-to-mouth movements may appear, as well as hand-wringing or hand-clapping gestures. These movements may be nearly constant while the child is awake but disappear during sleep. There may be noticeable episodes of breath holding and hyper-ventilating (rapid shallow breathing). The child may have trouble sleeping and may become irritable. If she is able to walk, she will start to look unsteady on her feet and may have periods of trembling or shaking. Slowed growth of the head is usually most noticeable during this stage.

- Stage 3, plateau (2–10 years): Motor problems and seizures often appear during this stage. The child's behavior, however, often shows some improvement, with less irritability and crying. She may show greater interest in her surroundings, and her attention span and communication skills often improve. Many patients with Rett syndrome remain in stage 3 for most of their lives.

- Stage 4, late deterioration of motor skills (usually after 10 years of age): In stage 4, patients with Rett syndrome gradually lose their mobility; some stop walking while others have never learned to walk. There is, however, no loss of cognitive or communication skills, and repetitive hand movements may decrease. The spine begins to develop an abnormal sideways curvature (scoliosis), and the patient may develop muscle rigidity. Puberty begins at the same age as in most girls.

Diagnosis

Rett syndrome can be diagnosed based on either the diagnostic criteria established in the *DSM-IV-TR* or based on testing of the MECP2 gene for mutations. Molecular analysis of the MECP2 gene for mutations will correctly identify at least four out of five females who have classic Rett syndrome.

Diagnoses based on *DSM-IV-TR* criteria are made after observation of the child—usually over a period of several hours or days—and interviews with the parents. The diagnosis can be made by a pediatrician or primary care physician, but should be confirmed by a pediatric neurologist (specialist in disorders of the nervous system in children) or developmental pediatrician. After the examiner has excluded the possibility of other developmental disorders, there are six criteria that must be met for a diagnosis of the classic form of Rett syndrome, and a secondary group of supportive criteria that are frequently observed in Rett syndrome patients but are not necessary to make the diagnosis.

The diagnostic criteria for Rett syndrome include the following:

- a period of apparently normal development before 6–18 months of age

- a normal-sized head at birth followed by slowing of head growth between 5 months and 4 years

- severe impairment in the use of language and loss of purposeful hand motion

- repetitive hand movements that include one or more of the following: hand-washing, hand-wringing, or hand-clapping gestures

- shaking of the chest or torso, particularly when the child is agitated or upset

- in children able to walk, an unsteady, stiff-legged, wide-based gait

Supportive criteria

Supportive criteria are criteria that are not essential to the diagnosis of a particular disorder, because some people with the disorder do not have them, but they are present in enough cases to be associated with the diagnosis. Supportive criteria provide strong evidence that a person who exhibits these criteria does in fact have the disorder. The supportive criteria for Rett syndrome do not always appear in young children but are often observed as the child grows older. Supportive criteria for Rett syndrome include:

- dysfunctional breathing, which may include hyper-ventilation, breath holding, and air swallowing

- abnormal electroencephalogram (EEG) patterns

- seizures

- difficulties in chewing and swallowing

- constipation

- muscle rigidity and joint contracture that increases with age

- scoliosis (curvature of the spine from side to side)

- teeth grinding (bruxism)

- small feet in relation to overall height

- slow overall growth

- loss of body fat and muscle mass

- abnormal sleeping patterns combined with irritability or agitation

- poor circulation in the feet and legs

Variant Rett syndrome

Because genetic testing has revealed some gradations in the manifestation of Rett syndrome, there also is a list of suggested criteria for the variant form of the condition. These include a set of main criteria, of which three symptoms must be met:

- reduction or lack of hand skills

- reduction or complete loss of speech, including infant babble

- presence of stereotyped hand movements

- lost or diminished communication abilities

- slowed head growth from early childhood
- regression that is followed by recovery of interaction.

There are also 11 suggested supportive criteria for the variant form of Rett syndrome, with the dictate that at least 5 symptoms must be present:

- breathing irregularities
- bruxism
- abnormal locomotion
- spinal deformity that results in a hunched appearance (kyphosis) or scoliosis (curvature of the spine)
- loss of muscle in the lower limbs
- feet that are cold, discolored, and small
- sleep disturbances, including nighttime screaming
- unexpected episodes of screaming or laughing
- the appearance of a reduced awareness of pain
- intense eye contact

Treatment

There is no single treatment regimen that is applicable to all patients with Rett syndrome. A suite of therapies that may be useful include speech, occupational, and physical therapy. While these therapies will not cure Rett syndrome, they may help ameliorate some aspects of the disorder. Some patients benefit from medications for muscular rigidity or for specific mood or behavioral problems, such as anxiety or irritability. Because of the increased risk of a potentially deadly irregular heartbeat, females with Rett syndrome should avoid drugs that can exacerbate the problem, including antipsychotics, anesthetics, and some antibiotics. A child **psychiatrist** should be consulted in regard to medications.

Parents of children with Rett syndrome are often helped by supportive therapy groups for parents of children with **pervasive developmental disorders**. Another type of program that is helpful for parents centers on learning skills for coping with the behaviors of children with Rett syndrome. These programs are usually led by a behavioral **psychologist**.

Prognosis

The prognosis for Rett syndrome patients is poor. In most cases, there is a steady loss of cognition and of movement-related, social, and behavioral skills throughout the patient's lifetime, though some patients do make modest developmental gains in adolescence. The average life expectancy of a person with Rett syndrome is estimated to be around age 40. Females with the classic form of Rett syndrome usually live to adulthood, but

---

QUESTIONS TO ASK YOUR DOCTOR

- What are the indications that my child may have Rett syndrome?
- What diagnostic tests are needed for a thorough assessment?
- What treatment options do you recommend?
- Should I see a specialist? If so, what kind of specialist should I contact?
- How will I know if treatment has been beneficial?
- What physical limitations do you foresee?
- What associated medical problems does my child have that will need treatment along with Rett syndrome?
- What sort of behaviors can I expect from my child?
- Is my child eligible for any early intervention programs available locally?
- What can we do at home to best help our child?
- What should I tell my other children/relatives/friends about this disorder?
- Does having Rett syndrome put my child at risk for other health conditions?
- Can you recommend any support groups for me and my family?

---

there is a high incidence of sudden death among this group, possibly because of irregular heartbeat.

Children who have Rett syndrome can and do attend school. Some attend special schools targeting children with their disabilities, while others attend neighborhood schools and participate in the general classroom environment. In the United States, the Individuals with Disabilities Education Act (IDEA) ensures eligibility for early **intervention** services in a Birth-to-Three program if children are diagnosed before the age of three.

Prevention

Because most cases result from new mutations of the MECP2 gene rather than transmission of a defective gene from the parents, there are no known strategies for preventing Rett syndrome. Though genetic testing is available, it is not usually recommended unless another child in the family has the syndrome.

Resources

BOOKS

American Psychiatric Association. *Diagnostic and Statistical Manual of Mental Disorders.* 4th ed., text rev. Washington, DC: American Psychiatric Association, 2000.

American Psychological Association. *Publication Manual of the American Psychological Association.* 6th ed. Washington, DC: American Psychological Association, 2009.

Bennett, Robin L. *The Practical Guide to the Genetic Family History.* 2nd ed. New York: Wiley-Blackwell, 2010.

Goldstein, Sam, and Cecil R. Reynolds, eds. *Handbook of Neurodevelopmental and Genetic Disorders in Children.* 2nd ed. New York: The Guilford Press, 2010.

Shannon, Joyce Brennfleck, ed. *Autism and Pervasive Developmental Disorders Sourcebook.* 2nd ed. Detroit: Omnigraphics, 2011.

PERIODICALS

Bradbury, Jane. "Advance Made in Understanding Rett's Syndrome." *Neurology, The Lancet* 4 (2005): 83.

Gura, T. "Gene Defect Linked to Rett Syndrome." *Science* 286 (Oct. 1, 1999): 27.

Jan, M., J. M. Dooley, and K. E. Gordon. "A Male Rett Syndrome Variant: Application of Diagnostic Criteria." *Pediatric Neurology* 20 (1999): 238–40.

Lane, J. B., et al. "Clinical Severity and Quality of Life in Children and Adolescents with Rett Syndrome." *Neurology* (Oct. 19, 2011) [e-pub ahead of print]. http://dx.doi.org/10.1212/WNL.0b013e3182377dd2 (accessed November 2, 2011).

Viola, Angèle, et al. "Metabolic Fingerprints of Altered Brain Growth, Osmoregulation and Neurotransmission in a Rett Syndrome Model." *PLOS [Public Library of Science] ONE* 2, no. 1 (2007): e157. http://dx.doi.org/10.1371/journal.pone.0000157 (accessed November 2, 2011).

WEBSITES

ClinicalTrials.gov. "Rett Syndrome Clinical Trials." U.S. National Institutes of Health. http://clinicaltrials.gov/ct2/results?term=Rett+Syndrome+ (accessed September 26, 2011).

Eunice Kennedy Shriver National Institute of Child Health and Human Development. "Rett Syndrome." U.S. National Institutes of Health. http://www.nichd.nih.gov/health/topics/Rett_Syndrome.cfm (accessed November 2, 2011).

MedlinePlus. "Rett Syndrome." U.S. National Library of Medicine. http://www.nlm.nih.gov/medlineplus/rettsyndrome.html (accessed September 26, 2011).

National Institute of Neurological Disorders and Stroke. "Rett Syndrome Fact Sheet." U.S. National Institutes of Health. http://www.ninds.nih.gov/disorders/rett/detail_rett.htm (accessed September 26, 2011).

ORGANIZATIONS

Angelman, Rett & Prader-Willi Syndromes Consortium (ARPWSC), Rare Diseases Clinical Research Network, University of Alabama at Birmingham, Birmingham, AL, (205) 934-1130, Fax: (205) 975-6330, jlane@uab.edu, http://rarediseasesnetwork.epi.usf.edu/arpwsc.

Genetic Alliance, 4301 Connecticut Ave. NW, Suite 404, Washington, DC, 20008-2369, (202) 966-5557, Fax: (202) 966-8553, info@geneticalliance.org, http://www.geneticalliance.org.

International Rett Syndrome Association, 4600 Devitt Drive, Cincinnati, OH, 45246, (800) 818-7388, Fax: (513) 874-2520, http://www.rettsyndrome.org.

National Institute of Neurological Disorders and Stroke, PO Box 5801, Bethesda, MD, 20824, (301) 496-5751; TTY: (301) 468-5981, (800) 352-9424, http://www.ninds.nih.gov.

National Organization for Rare Disorders (NORD), PO Box 1968, Danbury, CT, 06813-1968, (203) 744-0100, (800) 999-6673, Fax: (203) 798-2291, orphan@rarediseases.org, http://www.rarediseases.org.

Rebecca J. Frey, PhD
Emily Jane. Willingham, PhD
Laura Jean Cataldo, RN, EdD

Revia *see* **Naltrexone**

Reward deficiency syndrome (RDS)

Definition

Reward Deficiency Syndrome, or RDS, is related to a number of mental health disorders, rather than standing alone as a separate and distinct mental illness. The mental illnesses to which RDS is related include a wide range of addictions, compulsive behaviors, and impulsive behaviors.

RDS refers to the breakdown of the reward cascade, and resultant aberrant conduct, due to genetic and environmental influences. RDS is a DNA-related gene and chromosome type of syndrome that interferes with the usual achievement of human physiological drives such as food, water, and sexual reproduction. The A1 (minor) allele of the D2 **dopamine** receptor (DRD2) gene has been shown to be associated with alcoholism, particularly its severe form, as well as with smoking, obesity, and other addictive behaviors.

Addiction is a **brain** disorder that causes the compulsive and continued use of and cravings for substances, regardless of negative consequences. These behaviors are related to neurotransmitter dysregulation, notably that of dopamine and **serotonin**. Addiction, along with **compulsion**, affects the nucleus accumbens, the part of the brain that produces pleasure. Because of its biologic basis, these behaviors are chronic with a propensity toward **relapse**. Addiction/compulsion

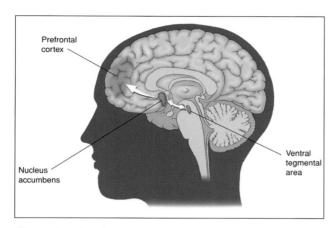

Illustration showing areas of the brain associated with addiction. *(Illustration by Frank Forney. Reproduced by permission of Cengage Learning.)*

causes loss of control over alcohol, **nicotine**, and substance use, so that uncontrollable behaviors occur more quickly as this mental disorder progresses. The name for this particular pattern is Reward Deficiency Syndrome. Defined by pharmacology professor Kenneth Blum in the 1990s, RDS arises in the human genetic units labeled the D2 (dopamine) receptor and the A1 allele. RDS is also linked to such illnesses as **attention deficit hyperactivity disorder** and Tourette syndrome, **conduct disorder**, obesity, gambling, **post-traumatic stress disorder** (PTSD), and **premenstrual syndrome** (PMS).

Demographics

Children of alcohol-addicted or substance-addicted individuals are more highly at risk for developing **alcohol use** and substance use disorders than the general population. Thus, they are more likely to suffer from RDS. There is also evidence of the hereditary nature of some other RDS-related illnesses, especially morbid obesity, attention deficit (ADD/ADHD), and PMS.

Disruptive behavior disorders such as conduct disorder in youth and antisocial personality disorder in adults are related to RDS. The youth-related disorders frequently coexist with substance abuse problems. Other groups that may be affected by RDS are older adults with mood/anxiety disorders who self-medicate in grieving the losses of old age, incarcerated populations, the homeless, and those with eating disorders. Because obesity includes growing proportions of Americans from all demographic classifications in recent decades, and RDS is related to some of these cases, then RDS may affect all demographic designations, but further research is needed to clarify this with certainty.

Description

In the 1950s, researchers experimented placing electrodes into a rat's brain. They discovered that the rat chose pressing a lever attached to the electrodes to provide brain stimulation, even over the basic needs of food and water. This suggested that the implanted brain area is the "pleasure center" of the brain. It contains the nucleus accumbens, a brain structure related to addictions, but also interestingly relevant to processing the rewards of food, sex, and video games (a modern addiction in some individuals). Neurologic reward pathways are very important to human survival, because they provide the drives for pleasure that require eating, love/sex, and reproduction for species survival. These natural rewards facilitate the release of dopamines in both the brain's nucleus accumbens and frontal lobes.

Pharmacologist Kenneth Blum found that individuals with RDS generally possess a specific chromosome sequence in their DNA. This sequence is most often the A1 allele, D2 dopamine receptor. People with this sequence have 20% to 30% fewer D2 reward receptors than in the general population. This makes it more difficult for the pleasure drives to be met, forcing the individuals into high-risk behaviors to gain that fulfillment. In addition, people with the A1 allele are 74% more likely to have one or more of several RDS-related mental illnesses. These illnesses are related to addictions, compulsive behaviors, and impulsive behaviors.

Listed in the 2000 edition of the *Diagnostic and Statistical Manual (DSM-IV)* of the **American Psychiatric Association**, disorders that stem from RDS include alcohol abuse, **substance abuse**, nicotine/tobacco use, compulsive disorder, attention deficit hyperactivity disorder, conduct disorder, **antisocial personality disorder**, obesity, PTSD, and PMS. Such individuals need to stimulate themselves in abundance simply to feel normal. Alcohol and drugs used for stimulation of the pleasure center injures a person's dopamine and endorphin system even more. With each use of drugs or alcohol, the difference between feeling high or even "normal" and being sober becomes larger and larger. Staying sober becomes boring and results in an overarching anxiety and irritability. To alleviate these bad feelings, these individuals often turn back to alcohol and drugs, sometimes overdosing and accidentally or purposefully dying in the process.

Prevalence

It is difficult to estimate the prevalence of RDS among the American population because of its many manifestations. Not only alcohol and substance use disorders but also tobacco/nicotine use, schizoid/avoidant behavior, PTSD, **ADHD**, Tourette syndrome,

KEY TERMS

A1 allele—An allele related to RDS.

A1 D2—A chromosome sequence related to RDS.

Allele—One member of a pair or a series of genes that occupy a specific position on a specific chromosome.

D2—A dopamine receptor.

Dopamine—The neurotransmitter responsible for desire.

Frontal lobes—The large lobes at the front of the brain responsible for reasoning, problem-solving, and logic.

Neurotransmitter—A chemical that relays and amplifies electric signals between brain and central nervous system cells (neurons).

Nucleus accumbens—A structure deep inside and near the center of the brain that makes up a major part of the pathway of pleasure and reward.

Serotonin—The neurotransmitter responsible for satisfaction and inhibition.

aggression, obesity and aberrant weight gain, PMS, and perhaps other mental disorders all fall under the RDS umbrella.

Because the prevalence of **co-occurring disorders** has increased in the last 30 years, the overall prevalence of RDS has also increased, being related to co-occurring disorders (always including substance/alcohol abuse). Further, the co-occurrence of mental illness and substance abuse itself is found in 50% of all individuals suffering from any of the severe mental disorders (SMDs). Therefore, RDS is related to these 50% of cases, possibly a proportion of the other 50% of SMDs, and to the further problems associated with substance and alcohol abuse and impulsive and compulsive behaviors: higher rates of relapse and **hospitalization**, incarceration, violence, **homelessness**, **suicide**, and exposure to infections such as HIV and hepatitis. It is not known how many Americans with obesity and other above-mentioned disorders are RDS-connected, in the absence of genetic testing.

Diagnosis

A thorough multidiscipline assessment is used to establish an individualized treatment plan for alcohol and substance abuse clients and should be used with RDS-related disorders. In addition, it is becoming increasingly important to establish gene involvement via genetic testing. This process begins with a clinical interview of the patient and family, which is vital in recognizing behavior patterns. A number of substance abuse checklists can help determine the presence of a substance abuse disorder. Genetic testing can establish the physical basis for RDS-related disorders. Mental health tests can uncover psychiatric illnesses. These tests include the **Minnesota Multiphasic Personality Inventory** (MMPI), Rorschach inkblot, and other personality and projective tests.

Treatment

Kenneth Blum was awarded U.S. Patent Number 6955873 for *Diagnosis and treatment system for reward deficiency syndrome (RDS) and related behaviors* on October 18, 2005. The diagnostic technique includes four kits for obtaining buccal (inner cheek) swabs for the following primary clusters of disorders: 1) neurotransmitter, tryptophan, and opiate related problems in RDS behaviors, 2) the same problems in relation to weight gain, 3) allele analysis for attention deficit hyperactivity disorder, and 4) substance use disorders (SUDs), obesity, smoking, Tourette syndrome, schizoid/avoidant behavior, aggression, post-traumatic stress disorder (PTSD), and PMS.

In addition to swabs, the **diagnosis** includes the RDS Inventory Scale test, patented under this patent number. Upon analysis of the results of the swab or swabs obtained from a single client, the physician may or may not administer the patented medication formula via injection or oral ingestion for each kit that suggests treatment. Other treatments include a range of psychiatric medications and talking therapies, as well as holistic multidisciplinary techniques traditionally used for RDS-related mental illnesses before genetic testing and Blum's treatment process was established.

Prognosis

Education, prevention, and early diagnosis are all vital to the mental health of individuals who may be at risk for RDS-related disorders. In particular, the earlier that alcohol and substance use disorders can be diagnosed, the better are the chances for successful treatment. Genetic testing for the A1D2 sequence of RDS is available and can be used in early diagnosis in infants and youth.

Resources

PERIODICALS

Baicy, Kate. "Can Food Be Addictive? Insights on Obesity from Neuroimaging and Substance Abuse Treatment and Research." *Nutrition Noteworthy* 7, no. 1 (2005): article 4.

Blum, K., et al. "Genotrimtrade Mark, a DNA-Customized Nutrigenomic Product, Targets Genetic Factors of Obesity: Hypothesizing a Doamine-Glucose Correlation Demonstrating Reward Deficiency Syndrome (RDS)." *Medical Hypotheses* 68, no. 4 (2006): 844–52.

Blum K., et al. "Reward Deficiency Syndrome in Obesity: A Preliminary Cross-Sectional Trial with a Genotrim Variant." *Advances in Therapy* 23, no. 6 (2006):1040–51.

Blum K., et al. "Reward Deficiency Syndrome." *American Scientist* 84, no. 4 (1996): 132–45.

Bowirrat, A., and Oscar-Berman, M. "Relationship between Dopaminergic Neurotransmission, Alcoholism, and Reward Deficiency Syndrome." *American Journal Of Medical Genetics. Part B, Neuropsychiatric Genetics: the Official Publication of the International Society of Psychiatric Genetics* 132, no. 1 (2005): 29–37.

Comings, D. E., et al. "Neurogenetic Interactions and Aberrant Behavioral Co-morbidity of Attention Deficit Hyperactivity Disorder (ADHD): Dispelling Myths." *Theoretical Biology and Medical Modelling* 2, no. 50 (2005): http://www.tbiomed.com/content/pdf/1742-4682-2-50.pdf.

Dick, Danielle M., Richard J. Rose, and Jaakko Kaprio. "The Next Challenge for Psychiatric Genetics: Characterizing the Risk Associated with Identified Genes." *Annals of Clinical Psychiatry* 18, no. 4 (2006): 223–31.

Eisenberg, D. J., et al. "Examining Impulsivity as an Endophenotype Using a Behavioral Approach: A DRD2 TaqI A and DRD4 48-bp VNTR Association Study." *Behavioral and Brain Functions* 3, no. 2 (2007). http://www.behavioralandbrainfunctions.com/content/pdf/1744-9081-3-2.pdf.

Linazaroso, G., N. van Biercom, and A. Lasa. "Hypothesis: Parkinson's Disease, Reward Deficiency Syndrome and Addictive Effects of Levodopa." *Neurlogia* 19, no. 3 (2004):117–27.

Schultz, W. "Behavioral Theories and the Neurophysiology of Reward." *Annual Review of Psychology* 57 (2006): 87–115.

Shaffer, H. J., et al. "Toward a Syndrome Model of Addiction: Multiple Expressions, Common Etiology." *Harvard Review Psychiatry.* 12, no. 6 (2004): 367–74.

Volkow, N. D., et al. "Rain DA D2 Receptors Predict Reinforcing Effects of Stimulants in Humans: Replication Study." *Synapse* 46, no. 2 (2002): 79–82.

Wang, G, N. D. Volkow, P. K. Thanos, and J. S. Fowler. "Similarity Between Obesity and Drug Addiction as Assessed by Neurofunctional Imaging: A Concept Review." *Journal of Addictive Diseases* 23, no. 3 (2004): 39–53.

ORGANIZATIONS

American Psychiatric Association, 1000 Wilson Blvd., Ste. 1825, Arlington, VA, 22209-3901, (703) 907-7300, apa@psych.org, http://www.psych.org.

Patty Inglish, MS

Riluzole

Purpose

Riluzole (brand name Rilutek), a member of the benzothiazole class of drugs, is the only medication that has been proven effective for treating amyotrophic lateral sclerosis (ALS or Lou Gehrig's disease, a degenerative disease that affects neurons in the **brain** and spinal cord). Research indicates that the neuroprotective properties of riluzole might also make it useful for treating **depression**, although it is not approved by the U.S. Food and Drug Administration (FDA) for that purpose.

Description

Riluzole acts on glutamate, an excitatory amino acid neurotransmitter that carries messages to and from nerve cells in the brain. Glutamate is part of the glutamatergic system, which plays a role in memory and information processing. An excess of glutamate is believed to lead to ALS symptoms. Abnormal glutamate levels have also been implicated in depression and other mood disorders. In animal studies, for example, increased glutamate in the brain was associated with feelings of anxiety and fear. Riluzole works by blocking the release of glutamate in the brain. Riluzole also inhibits sodium channels and activates potassium channels leading to alterations in calcium currents. The mechanism responsible for any effect on ALS or depression symptoms may be a combination of an effect on glutamate release and these other effects.

Although **antidepressants** are the mainstay of treatment for mood disorders, studies indicate that about 30% to 40% of patients do not respond to them. Therefore, researchers are investigating new therapeutic agents that are more effective with fewer adverse effects.

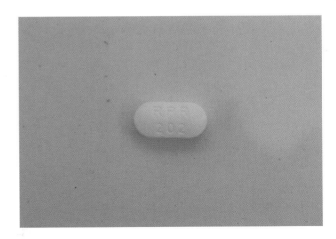

Rilutek (riluzole), 50 mg. (© *Custom Medical Stock Photo, Inc. Reproduced by permission.*)

Preliminary studies have demonstrated the effectiveness of riluzole for treating major depression, **bipolar disorder**, and **generalized anxiety disorder**. A study published in December 2005 in the *American Journal of Psychiatry* found that riluzole was effective in achieving remission in about half of a group of adults who had been diagnosed with generalized anxiety disorder. In a 2004 study that was published in February 2005 in *Biological Psychiatry*, riluzole improved symptoms in patients with treatment-resistant depression (depression that had not responded to antidepressant medications). Riluzole also was well tolerated in these studies.

Researchers say larger, placebo-controlled trials are needed to confirm the results of these preliminary investigations. As of 2011, new research was underway, including controlled studies investigating the potential effects of riluzole on the treatment of bipolar disorder. Research also indicates that riluzole might be effective for the treatment of obsessive-compulsive and panic disorders, but further study is needed.

Recommended dosage

Because riluzole was not yet FDA-approved for treating mood disorders as of 2011, appropriate doses have only been described in research studies. In studies, patients have been given between 50 and 200 mg of riluzole per day.

Precautions

Because riluzole blocks the release of the excitatory neurotransmitter, glutamate, this drug can cause drowsiness. Patients are advised to use caution when driving or operating machinery. Alcohol can increase this side effect, and people who are taking the drug should therefore avoid or use alcohol in moderation. Women who are pregnant, plan to become pregnant, or are breastfeeding should let their doctor know before taking this medication. Smoking cigarettes can decrease the effectiveness of this medication by causing the body to eliminate riluzole more quickly.

People who have liver dysfunction should use caution when taking this drug because it may not metabolize properly. Researchers who have studied the drug recommend that patients who are taking it be monitored for potential liver function problems.

Side effects

The side effects most commonly reported with riluzole include:

- abdominal pain
- constipation
- decreased saliva

> ## KEY TERMS
>
> **Amyotrophic lateral sclerosis (ALS or Lou Gehrig's disease)**—A degenerative disease that affects nerves of the brain and spinal cord, and results in eventual paralysis.
>
> **Bipolar disorder**—A brain disorder that causes rapid mood shifts.
>
> **Generalized anxiety disorder**—A mental disorder characterized by excessive and uncontrollable worry.
>
> **Glutamate**—An excitatory amino acid neurotransmitter that carries messages to and from nerve cells in the brain.
>
> **Glutamatergic system**—The neurotransmitter system in the central nervous system that plays a role in memory formation and information processing, and that is believed to play a role in depression and other mood disorders.
>
> **Obsessive-compulsive disorder**—A disorder marked by persistent thoughts or fears, which lead to the compulsion to repeat a particular task over and over again.

- diarrhea
- dizziness
- drowsiness
- dry mouth
- headache
- insomnia
- muscle weakness
- nausea
- vertigo
- vomiting

These symptoms may be lessened by lowering the dose.

Interactions

The following drugs may decrease the rate at which riluzole is eliminated, which could potentially cause a buildup of the drug in the body:

- amitriptyline
- caffeine
- phenactin
- quinolones
- theophylline

Conversely, the following substances may increase the rate at which riluzole is eliminated from the body, potentially reducing its effectiveness:

- cigarettes

- charcoal-grilled foods

- barbiturates

- rifampicin

Resources

BOOKS

Mondimore, Francis Mark. *Bipolar Disorder: A Guide for Patients and Families*. 2nd ed. Baltimore: The Johns Hopkins University Press, 2006.

Ropper, Allan, MD, and Martin A. Samuels. *Adams and Victor's Principles of Neurology*. 8th ed. New York: The McGraw Hill Companies, 2009.

Swartz, Karen L. *Johns Hopkins White Papers: Depression and Anxiety*. New York: Medletter Associates, 2005.

PERIODICALS

Sanjay, Mathew J., et al. "Open-label Trial of Riluzole in Generalized Anxiety Disorder." *American Journal of Psychiatry*. 162, no. 12 (December 2005): 2379–81.

Zarate, Carlos A. Jr., et al. "An Open-label Trial of the Glutamate-modulating Agent Riluzole in Combination with Lithium for the Treatment of Bipolar Depression." *Biological Psychiatry*. 57, no. 4 (February 15, 2005): 430–32.

Zarate, Carlos Al Jr., et al. "Glutamatergic Modulators: the Future of Treating Mood Disorders?" *Harvard Review of Psychiatry* 18, no. 5 (2010): 293–303.

WEBSITES

Yale School of Medicine. "Depression Treatment Study." Yale Depresion Research Clinic. http://psychiatry.yale.edu/research/programs/clinical_people/trials/sanacora1.aspx (accessed November 13, 2011).

ORGANIZATIONS

American Psychiatric Association, 1000 Wilson Blvd., Ste. 1825, Arlington, VA, 22209-3901, (703) 907-7300, apa@psych.org, http://www.psych.org.

Brain and Behavior Research Foundation, 60 Cutter Mill Rd., Ste. 404, Great Neck, NY, 11021, (516) 829-0091, Fax: (516) 487-6930, http://www.bbrfoundation.org.

National Alliance on Mental Illness, 3803 N Fairfax Drive, Ste. 100, Arlington, VA, 22203, (703) 524-7600, http://www.nami.org.

National Institute of Mental Health, 6001 Executive Blvd., Room 8184, MSC 9663, Bethesda, MD, 20892-9663, (301) 433-4513; TTY: (301) 443-8431, Fax: (301) 443-4279, (866) 615-6464; TTY: (866) 415-8051, nimhinfo@nih.gov, http://www.nimh.nih.gov.

Stephanie N. Watson

Risperdal *see* **Risperidone**

Risperidone

Definition

Risperidone is classified as an atypical antipsychotic drug. It is sold in the United States under the brand name of Risperdal.

Purpose

Risperidone is used for the management of symptoms of psychotic disorders such as **schizophrenia**.

Description

Risperidone is considered an atypical antipsychotic. Atypical antipsychotics are chemically unrelated to the older antipsychotic drugs. Where older antipsychotic drugs primarily inhibit the actions of **dopamine**, a chemical in the **brain**, risperidone may also have some action against another brain chemical, **serotonin**. The proper levels of both dopamine and serotonin are influential in maintaining mental well-being.

One advantage of using risperidone over one of the older antipsychotic drugs is a lower incidence of Parkinsonian-like side effects. These side effects may be sufficiently troublesome, causing patients to discontinue treatment for their schizophrenia. For this reason, patients who have had negative experiences with older antipsychotics may benefit from risperidone. Some patients who showed little improvement with older antipsychotic drugs responded better to risperidone.

Recently, the effectiveness of risperidone was evaluated in the Clinical Antipsychotic Trials of **Intervention** Effectiveness (**CATIE**) Schizophrenia Study. This study evaluated the effectiveness and side

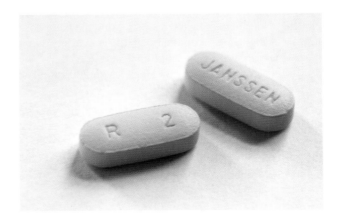

Risperdal (risperidone). (© *Chris Gallagher/Photo Researchers, Inc.*)

effects of atypical antipsychotics, including risperidone, in comparison to a conventional antipsychotic drug in the treatment of schizophrenia.

Contrary to expectations, the study found that the conventional antipsychotic generally was equally effective and tolerated as well as the newer, more expensive, atypical antipsychotic medications. The study showed that risperidone and another atypical, **olanzapine**, tend to be better tolerated than the other atypical antipsychotics investigated, although only 35% of participants on risperidone were able to continue taking it throughout the entire 18 months of the study. Participants who stopped taking an alternate antipsychotic medication in Phase 1 because it was not adequately controlling their symptoms were more likely to stay on their medication if they were switched to risperidone or olanzapine than to the drugs **quetiapine** or **ziprasidone**. There was no difference between the four medications, however, for participants who had stopped because of adverse side effects.

In Phase 2 of the study, the drug **clozapine** was more effective in controlling symptoms than the other atypical antipsychotics. For patients whose symptoms were not well controlled on clozapine, risperidone and olanzapine tended to be more effective than ziprasidone or quetiapine. Of the drugs evaluated, risperidone had the least adverse side effects.

Recommended dosage

Risperidone is available in 0.25 mg, 0.5 mg, 1 mg, 2 mg, 3 mg, and 4 mg tablets and a solution containing 1 mg of drug in each milliliter of solution. For treating psychotic disorders in adults, the usual starting dose of risperidone is 1 mg twice daily. Dosage is increased gradually until a target dose of 3 mg twice daily is reached. Some patients do just as well with a single daily dose (6 mg once a day, for example). There is little clinical evidence to indicate that increasing the daily dose beyond 8 mg offers additional benefit. However, higher doses may contribute to additional side effects. If the dose needs to be adjusted, the changes should be made no more often than once per week.

In older patients (over age 60), starting dosage should not exceed 1 mg daily. Most patients should not take more than 3 mg daily. People with low blood pressure and those who have kidney disease should take a similarly reduced dose.

Precautions

Patients with a history of cardiovascular disease or low blood pressure should take risperidone only after discussing the risks and benefits with their physicians, and then with close physician monitoring. Risperidone may cause abnormal heart rhythm (arrhythmia) that may prove fatal.

Risperidone has occasionally been associated with **seizures**. People with a past history of seizures should discuss with their doctors whether risperidone is the right antipsychotic for them to use.

People taking risperidone should avoid operating a motor vehicle or other dangerous machinery until they see how risperidone affects them.

Some people have trouble regulating their body temperatures while taking risperidone and are at risk of developing malignant hyperthermia. Patients receiving this drug should be aware of this and should avoid extremes in outdoor temperatures.

The use of risperidone and other antipsychotic drugs has been associated with an increased risk of death when used in elderly patients with **dementia**. In studies, these drugs significantly increased death in older patients with dementia, compared to placebo. Most of the deaths were associated with heart failure or infections such as pneumonia. Risperidone has not been approved by the U.S. Food and Drug Administration (FDA) for the treatment of **psychosis** or behavioral problems in elderly patients with dementia.

Women who are pregnant should not take risperidone and should alert their physicians if they become pregnant while on risperidone. Babies born to mothers who took risperidone during pregnancy may develop extrapyramidal symptoms (EPS) and withdrawal symptoms, including agitation, trouble breathing, and difficulty feeding. Breast-feeding is not recommended while taking the drug.

Patients may develop hyperglycemia (high blood sugar) while taking risperidone. People with schizophrenia are more likely to develop diabetes than those without schizophrenia, and taking risperidone increases this risk. Patients should alert their doctors immediately if they experience symptoms of diabetes, including excessive thirst or hunger, frequent urination, blurry vision, or **fatigue**.

Risperidone has been associated with the risk of developing hyperprolactinemia, a blood disorder caused by heightened levels of the hormone prolactin. Symptoms include amenorrhea and lactation in women and breast development and **erectile dysfunction** in men.

Side effects

The most common and bothersome side effect associated with risperidone is decreased blood pressure while standing up (known as "orthostatic hypotension"). This can cause dizziness or fainting. A decrease in blood

KEY TERMS

Amenorrhea—Abnormal cessation of menstruation.

Extrapyramidal symptoms—A group of side effects associated with antipsychotic medications and characterized by involuntary muscle movements, including contraction and tremor.

pressure usually occurs early in therapy, when the proper dose is still being established. It is more common in older patients than in younger ones. Usually this side effect disappears entirely with time. If it continues, the physician may decrease the dose. Meanwhile, people taking risperidone should be aware of this side effect and get up slowly if they have been sitting for an extended time.

The most common nervous system side effects of risperidone include **insomnia**, agitation, anxiety, and headache. Early in therapy, patients may experience an inability to think clearly or perform certain tasks that require mental alertness. High doses of risperidone can cause unwanted sleepiness in about 40% of patients.

Antipsychotic drugs, including risperidone, can cause side effects that are similar to the symptoms of Parkinson's disease, including muscle tremor, difficulty with voluntary movements, and poor muscle tone. They normally disappear if the drug is stopped.

The most common gastrointestinal side effects include nausea, vomiting, constipation, and difficulty digesting food. Risperidone may cause weight gain.

Up to 10% of patients taking risperidone experience rhinitis (runny nose).

Interactions

There is very little information about how risperidone interacts with other drugs. However, because some patients receiving risperidone experience lowered blood pressure while standing, it is expected that other drugs that lower blood pressure may increase the incidence and severity of this side effect when taken with risperidone.

Resources

BOOKS

American Society of Health-System Pharmacists. *AHFS Drug Information 2008*. Bethesda, MD: American Society of Health-System Pharmacists, 2008.

Preston, John D., John H. O'Neal, and Mary C. Talaga. *Handbook of Clinical Psychopharmacology for Therapists*. 5th ed. Oakland, CA: New Harbinger Publications, 2008.

PERIODICALS

Casey, Daniel E. "Implications of the CATIE Trial on Treatment: Extrapyramidal Symptoms." *CNS Spectrums* 11, no. 7, Supp. 7 (July 2006): 25–31.

Gentile, Salvatore. "Extrapyramidal Adverse Events Associated with Atypical Antipsychotic Treatment of Bipolar Disorder." *Journal of Clinical Psychopharmacology* 27, no. 1 (February 2007): 35–45.

Glick, Ira D. "Understanding the Results of CATIE in the Context of the Field." *CNS Spectrums* 11, no. 7, Supp. 7 (July 2006): 40–47.

Haro, Josep Maria et al. "Remission and Relapse in the Outpatient Care of Schizophrenia: Three-Year Results from the Schizophrenia Outpatient Health Outcomes Study." *Journal of Clinical Psychopharmacology* 26, no. 6 (December 2006): 571–78.

Haupt, Martin, Alfonso Cruz-Jentoft, and Dilip Jeste. "Mortality in Elderly Dementia Patients Treated with Risperidone." *Journal of Clinical Psychopharmacology* 26, no. 6 (December 2006): 566–70.

Lieberman, Jeffrey A., et al. "Effectiveness of Antipsychotic Drugs in Patients with Chronic Schizophrenia." *New England Journal of Medicine* 353, no. 12 (September 2005): 1209–23.

Luby, Joan et al. "Risperidone in Preschool Children with Autistic Spectrum Disorders: An Investigation of Safety and Efficacy." *Journal of Child and Adolescent Psychopharmacology* 16, no. 5 (October 2006): 575–87.

McCue, Robert E., et al. "Comparative Effectiveness of Second-Generation Antipsychotics and Haloperidol in Acute Schizophrenia." *British Journal of Psychiatry* 189 (November 2006): 433–40.

Meltzer, Herbert Y., and William V. Bobo. "Interpreting the Efficacy Findings in the CATIE Study: What Clinicians Should Know." *CNS Spectrums* 11, Supp. 7 (July 2006): 14–24.

Nasrallah, Henry A. "Metabolic Findings From the CATIE Trial and Their Relation to Tolerability." *CNS Spectrums* 11, no. 7, Supp. 7 (July 2006): 32–39.

Pandina, Gahan J., Michael G. Aman, and Robert L. Findling. "Risperidone in the Management of Disruptive Behavior Disorders." *Journal of Child and Adolescent Psychopharmacology* 16, no. 4 (August 2006): 379–92.

Savas, Haluk A., et al. "Use of Long-Acting Risperidone in the Treatment of Bipolar Patients." *Journal of Clinical Psychopharmacology* 26, no. 5 (October 2006): 530–31.

Schneider, Lon S., et al. "Effectiveness of Atypical Antipsychotic Drugs in Patients with Alzheimer's Disease." *New England Journal of Medicine* 355, no. 15 (October 2006): 1525–38.

Stroup, T. Scott et al. "Effectiveness of Olanzapine, Quetiapine, Risperidone, and Ziprasidone in Patients with Chronic Schizophrenia Following Discontinuation of a Previous Atypical Antipsychotic." *American Journal of Psychiatry* 163, no. 4 (April 2006): 611–22.

Taylor, David M., Corina Young, and Maxine X. Patel. "Prospective 6-Month Follow-Up of Patients Prescribed Risperidone Long-Acting Injection: Factors Predicting

Favourable Outcome." *International Journal of Neuropsychopharmacology* 9, no. 6 (December 2006): 685–94.

Troost, Pieter W., et al. "Neuropsychological Effects of Risperidone in Children with Pervasive Developmental Disorders: A Blinded Discontinuation Study." *Journal of Child and Adolescent Psychopharmacology* 16, no. 5 (October 2006): 561–73.

Weiden, Peter J. "EPS Profiles: The Atypical Antipsychotics Are Not All the Same." *Journal of Psychiatric Practice* 13, no. 1 (Jan. 2007): 13–24.

Jack Raber, Pharm.D.
Ruth A. Wienclaw, PhD

Ritalin *see* **Methylphenidate**

Rivastigmine

Definition

Rivastigmine is a drug used to treat symptoms of **Alzheimer's disease**. In the United States, rivastigmine is sold as the brand name drug Exelon.

Purpose

Rivastigmine is used to treat symptoms of Alzheimer's disease in individuals with mild to moderate illness. It has also been used to treat **dementia** caused by other conditions such as Lewy body disease or following strokes. The drug may produce mild improvements in symptoms of thinking for a short period of time, but rivastigmine does not cure or stop progression of underlying diseases.

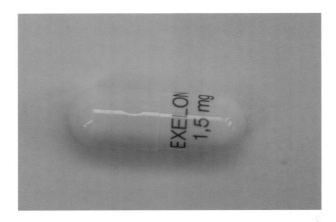

Exelon (rivastigmine), 1.5 mg. (© *Custom Medical Stock Photo, Inc. Reproduced by permission.*)

Description

The U.S. Food and Drug Administration approved rivastigmine in 2000 specifically for treating Alzheimer's disease. In patients with Alzheimer's disease, some cells in specific regions of the **brain** die. Because of this cell death, these brain cells lose their ability to transmit nerve impulses. Brain cells normally transmit nerve impulses to one another by secreting various chemicals known as **neurotransmitters**.

Brain cells that make and secrete a neurotransmitter called acetylcholine are affected early in the course of Alzheimer's disease. Rivastigmine prevents the breakdown of acetylcholine in the brain, thus temporarily increasing its concentration. In doing so, rivastigmine may improve the thinking process by facilitating nerve impulse transmission within the brain.

Rivastigmine is available as capsules in four different strengths and as an oral solution for use by people who have difficulty swallowing. It is also available in a transdermal patch that is applied to the skin. Unlike some other drugs used to treat Alzheimer's disease, rivastigmine is not broken down by the liver. As a result, it may be preferred in the treatment of people with Alzheimer's disease who have liver disease.

Recommended dosage

The initial dosage of rivastigmine is 1.5 mg taken two times per day. If this dose is tolerated without difficulty, the dosage may be increased to 3 mg twice a day after at least two weeks at the lower dosage. Some people are unable to tolerate nausea, vomiting, anorexia, and weight loss that occur with higher dosages. If the drug does not cause significant adverse effects, the dose may be increased to 4.5 mg two times per day, followed by 6 mg two times per day. The dosage should be increased slowly, at two-week intervals. If side effects occur and cannot be tolerated, the drug may be stopped for several doses. When the drug is started again, the same dosage or the next lower dosage may be tried. The maximum daily dosage is 6 mg two times per day.

The patch is applied to dry skin on the back, upper arm, or chest. The patch is left on for 24 hours and then replaced with a new patch. Each new patch should be applied to a new area of skin; the same location should not be used until a two-week period has passed.

Precautions

Rivastigmine may slow heart rates, increase acid in the stomach, make urination difficult, cause breathing difficulties, and may possibly contribute to **seizures**. As a result, it should be used with close physician supervision and monitoring in people with certain heart

KEY TERMS

Acetylcholine—A naturally occurring chemical in the body that transmits nerve impulses from cell to cell. Generally, it has opposite effects from dopamine and norepinephrine; it causes blood vessels to dilate, lowers blood pressure, and slows the heartbeat. Central nervous system well-being is dependent on a balance among acetylcholine, dopamine, serotonin, and norepinephrine.

Dementia—A group of symptoms (syndrome) associated with a progressive loss of memory and other intellectual functions that is serious enough to interfere with a person's ability to perform the tasks of daily life. Dementia impairs memory, alters personality, leads to deterioration in personal grooming, impairs reasoning ability, and causes disorientation.

Lewy body disease—A type of dementia that resembles Alzheimer's disease but progresses more rapidly. Common symptoms include fluctuations in confusion and recurring visual hallucinations. In this disease, abnormal brain cells are distributed throughout the brain.

Neurotransmitter—A chemical in the brain that transmits messages between neurons, or nerve cells.

Placebo—An inactive substance or preparation used as a control in experiments with human subjects to test the effectiveness of a drug or herbal preparation. Some patients may experience a medicinal response or experience side effects to a placebo simply because they have faith in its powers even though it contains no medicine.

conditions, tendencies to stomach ulcers, bladder obstruction, asthma or chronic obstructive pulmonary disease, and a history of seizure disorders.

Individuals taking rivastigmine should be reassessed periodically to determine whether the drug is providing any benefits. If caregivers feel the drug is no longer beneficial, it may be stopped.

Side effects

The most frequent side effects associated with rivastigmine involve stomach upset. Nausea, vomiting, anorexia, heartburn, and weakness occur in more than 5% of people and at twice the rate of people taking placebo pills. Dizziness and headaches also occur in more than 10% of people taking rivastigmine.

Other less common side effects include difficulty sleeping, confusion, **depression**, anxiety, sleepiness, hallucinations, tremors, fainting, aggression, constipation, gas, overwhelming **fatigue**, weight loss, increased sweating, and infections.

Interactions

Drugs such as dicyclomine may inhibit the effects of rivastigmine. Other drugs like bethanechol may possibly increase some of the side effects of rivastigmine. Rivastigmine may interact with some of the drugs used to relax muscles during surgery. The interaction increases the effects of both drugs.

Resources

BOOKS

Tekin, Sibel, and Roger Lane. "Rivastigmine in the Treatment of Dementia Associated with Parkinson's Disease: A Randomized, Double-Blind, Placebo-Controlled Study." In *Progress in Neurotherapeutics and Neuropsychopharmacology,* edited by Jeffrey L. Cummings. New York: Cambridge University Press, 2006.

Wolters Kluwer Health. *Drug Facts and Comparisons 2012.* 66th ed. St. Louis: Lippincott, Williams & Wilkins, 2011.

PERIODICALS

de Tommaso, Marina, et al. "Two Years' Follow-Up of Rivastigmine Treatment in Huntington Disease." *Clinical Neuropharmacology* 30, no. 1 (January–February 2007): 43–46.

Dybicz, Sharon B., et al. "Patterns of Cholinesterase-Inhibitor Use in the Nursing Home Setting: A Retrospective Analysis." *American Journal of Geriatric Pharmacotherapy* 4, no. 2 (June 2006): 154–60.

Eskander, Mariam F., et al. "Rivastigmine Is a Potent Inhibitor of Acetyl- and Butyrylcholinesterase in Alzheimer's Plaques and Tangles." *Brain Research* 1060, no. 1–2 (Oct. 2005): 144–52.

Farlow, Martin R., et al. "Efficacy of Rivastigmine in Alzheimer's Disease Patients with Rapid Disease Progression: Results of a Meta-Analysis." *Dementia and Geriatric Cognitive Disorders* 20, no. 2–3 (August 2005): 192–97.

Guillem, Francois, et al. "Are Cholinergic Enhancers Beneficial for Memory in Schizophrenia? An Event-Related Potentials (ERPs) Study of Rivastigmine Add-On Therapy in a Crossover Trial." *Progress in Neuro-Psychopharmacology & Biological Psychiatry* 30, no. 5 (July 2006): 934–45.

Miyasaki, J.M., et al. "Practice Parameter: Evaluation and Treatment of Depression, Psychosis, and Dementia in Parkinson Disease (an Evidence-Based Review): Report of the Quality Standards Subcommittee of the American Academy of Neurology." *Neurology* 66, no. 7 (April 2006): 996–1002.

Ringman, John M., and Jeffrey L. Cummings. "Current and Emerging Pharmacological Treatment Options for Dementia." *Behavioural Neurology* 17, no. 1 (2006): 5–16.

Rongve, Arvid, and Dag Aarsland. "Management of Parkinson's Disease Dementia: Practical Considerations." *Drugs and Aging* 23, no. 10 (2006): 807–22.

Sharma, Tonmoy, et al. "Cognitive Effects of Adjunctive 24-Weeks Rivastigmine Treatment to Antipsychotics in Schizophrenia: A Randomized, Placebo-Controlled, Double-Blind Investigation." *Schizophrenia Research* 85, no. 1–3 (July 2006): 73–83.

Takeda, A., et al. "A Systematic Review of the Clinical Effectiveness of Donepezil, Rivastigmine and Galantamine on Cognition, Quality of Life and Adverse Events in Alzheimer's Disease." *International Journal of Geriatric Psychiatry* 21, no. 1 (January 2006): 17–28.

WEBSITES

Drugs.com. "Rivastigmine Patch." http://www.drugs.com/cdi/rivastigmine-patch.html (accessed November 13, 2011).

PubMed Health. "Rivastigmine." U.S. National Library of Medicine. http://www.ncbi.nlm.nih.gov/pubmedhealth/PMH0000190 (accessed November 13, 2011).

ORGANIZATIONS

U.S. Food and Drug Administration, 10903 New Hampshire Ave., Silver Spring, MD, 20993-0002, (888) INFO-FDA (463-6332), http://www.fda.gov.

Kelly Karpa, R.Ph.,PhD
Ruth A. Wienclaw, PhD

RLS *see* **Restless legs syndrome**

Road rage

Definition

Road rage is an extreme form of aggressive driving. Road rage is distinguished by its extreme response (often violent or assaultive in nature) and by its intent to harm another individual either physically or psychologically. Road rage is not considered to be a psychiatric disorder.

Demographics

Research indicates that younger drivers tend to be more likely to engage in aggressive and risk-taking driving behaviors, although aggressive driving is observed in all ages. Research does not support the conclusion that males are more aggressive drivers than females.

Description

Although the term "road rage" has been popularized by the media, there is no consensus among researchers over the definition of this term. Aggressive driving—of which road rage is an extreme subset—includes a wide variety of behaviors such as speeding, cutting off another driver in traffic, tailgating, horn honking, and light flashing. Aggressive driving may also include more extreme actions ranging from roadside arguments or rude gestures to even shootings and assaults.

Road rage is differentiated from the more general concept of aggressive driving by both degree and intent. Definitions of road rage often include the concept that the anger is uncontrolled and violent. Road rage is not an isolated phenomenon; similar incidents have been found in the workplace (workplace rage) and airports (airport rage).

Causes and symptoms

There are numerous theories relating to the causes of aggressive driving and road rage. Most of these theories revolve around the concept of driver frustration and anger. It has been hypothesized, for example, that the competitiveness of the driving environment leads to aggressive driving behavior or that aggressive driving is part of a territorial defense reaction.

In some individuals, road rage may be a symptom of **intermittent explosive disorder** (IED). IED is an impulse-control disorder in which the individual acts on his or her impulses in assaultive or destructive ways that are out of proportion to the events or factors that triggered the act. IED is a pattern of aggressive behavior rather than an isolated incident, and is not caused by any other mental disorder, general condition, or chemical substance.

It also has been suggested that road rage can be a result of other underlying causes. These include

---

Aggressive driving and road rage symptoms

- Thoughts of harassment toward other drivers, whether verbal or physical
- Verbally expressing these thoughts to other passengers in the vehicle
- Disregarding traffic safety rules
- Engaging in aggressive and risky driving behaviors, including:
  - Following other cars too closely
  - Speeding
  - Weaving in and out of traffic
  - Speeding up to beat a traffic light
  - Cutting between vehicles to change lanes
  - Using the horn (excessively)
  - Flashing headlights at oncoming traffic (excessively)
  - Braking abruptly or repeatedly to get other drivers to not follow so closely
  - Passing another driver and then purposely slowing down

SOURCE: Washington State Patrol.

(Table by PreMediaGlobal. © 2012 Cengage Learning.)

social maladjustment, personal maladjustment, and psychopathology.

Diagnosis

For those situations where road rage is caused by IED, diagnostic criteria include:

- discrete episodes where the individual acts out aggressive impulses that result in violent assault or destruction of property

- aggressive response to driving stressors that is excessively disproportionate to the provocation

- absence of other disorders that may cause violent outbursts (e.g., antisocial personality disorder, borderline personality disorder, attention deficit hyperactivity disorder)

- absence of a general medical condition that may express itself in aggressiveness (e.g., head injury, Alzheimer's disease)

- individual is not taking medications with the potential side effect of increased aggressive behavior

- no substance abuse

Diagnosis of road rage is made based on a psychiatric interview to assess mental and behavioral symptoms. For road rage stemming from non-psychiatric causes, driving anger scales and driver's **stress** profiles are also available. Individuals may also be referred for treatment by court mandate.

Treatment

For road rage caused by IED, treatment may be achieved through **cognitive-behavioral therapy** (CBT) and/or psychotropic medication. CBT helps individuals recognize and become aware of the impulses that result in aggressive behavior so that they can control the impulses before they are acted upon. This therapy is typically supplemented by teaching the individuals **stress management** skills.

Road rage not related to IED has been successfully treated with desensitization therapy that helps the individual learn to not react to stimuli that provoke an aggressive response, stress management training including relaxation techniques, and other anger management techniques.

Prognosis

With therapy and proper training, the prognosis for controlling road rage is good.

KEY TERMS

Cognitive behavior therapy (CBT)—A form of psychotherapy that aims to identify and modify the individual's inappropriate behavior as well as the underlying maladaptive thought processes.

Psychotropic drug—A drug that acts on or influences the activity of the mind.

Stressor—An internal or external event, force, or condition that results in physical or psychological stress.

Territorial aggression—The response of aggressively defending a defined space perceived as being threatened by a member of the same species.

Prevention

Prevention of road rage is dependent on helping individuals recognize the symptoms of their anger and teaching them techniques to reduce their stress or control their reaction to stressors.

Resources

BOOKS

American Psychiatric Association. *Diagnostic and Statistical Manual of Mental Disorders.* 4th ed., text rev. Washington, DC: American Psychiatric Publishing, 2000.

Galovski, Tara E. *Road Rage: Assessment and Treatment of the Angry, Aggressive Driver.* Washington, DC: American Psychological Association, 2006.

Garase, Maria L. *Road Rage.* New York: LFB Scholarly Publications, 2006.

VandenBos, Gary R. ed. *APA Dictionary of Psychology.* Washington, DC: American Psychological Association, 2006.

Ruth A. Wienclaw, Ph.D.

Rorschach inkblot test

Definition

The Rorschach inkblot test, also known as the Rorschach Technique, the Rorschach psychodiagnostic test, the Rorschach test, and popularly as simply the "Inkblot Test," is a projective personality assessment based on the test taker's reactions to a series of 10 standardized unstructured images or "inkblots." These inkblots are then psychologically interpreted by

An inkblot picture, such as the ones used in the Rorschach inkblot test. *(© Custom Medical Stock Photo, Inc. Reproduced by permission.)*

psychologists and other trained professionals. As a projective psychological test, the Rorschach test was founded on the hypothesis that subjects will interject their own personalities into neutral appearing images, thus revealing their own personality characteristics, hidden emotions, underlying conflicts, reactions to surroundings and the environment, illogical thought processes, and underpinned motivations.

Purpose

The purpose of the Rorschach test is to examine and **diagnosis** the personality characteristics of people, along with the functioning of their emotions. It is also used expressly to better understand thought disorders in people, especially when such persons are unwilling or unable to openly talk about such problems.

Description

The Rorschach test remains one of the most widely used projective psychological test in the world, although its popularity has declined somewhat over the past several decades. It is often included as one of a series of tests used to assess personality, such as for investigations where forensic assessment is needed and in clinical settings where evaluations of mentally disturbed are required. It is generally administered to adolescents and adults but can be used with children as young as three years of age. It must be administered on an individual basis; group evaluations are not possible.

The Rorschach test is used to assess personality structure and identify emotional problems. The test provides information about a child's thought processes, perceptions, motivations, and attitude toward his or her environment, and it can detect internal and external pressures and conflicts as well as illogical or psychotic thought patterns. It can aid in diagnosing and treating a wide range of psychological problems and psychiatric disorders, including **depression, schizophrenia**, and **anxiety disorders**.

The untimed, individually administered test consists of interpreting a series of 10 complicated looking inkblots. The test consists of the test taker being shown inkblots on separate white cards and then being asked a set of standard questions about what he or she sees. The administrator of the test traditionally sits slightly behind the test taker. Five of the ten original inkblots consist entirely of black ink on a white background, while two use black and red ink and three consist of several colors of ink.

The subject observes all of the 10 inkblots, one at a time, in a "free association" phase. Each inkblot is verbally described as to what it resembles. Then the administrator presents all of them again so that the subject has time to make additional responses as to what was originally seen in what is called the "inquiry" phase. The subject is allowed to hold the cards, rotate them, and take other such actions, all of which may add to the final interpretation by the administrator. During this time, the administrator notes all responses and actions by the subject, may ask questions to clarify responses, and maintains a running tabulation of the score.

Responses are tabulated, placed in summary form, and scored according to a set of criteria. Swiss **psychologist** Hermann Rorschach (1884–1922), who pioneered the test in 1921, did not provide a comprehensive scoring system, but many different ones have since been developed. The most thorough and widely used one is the Exner system, which was created by U.S. psychologist John E. Exner Jr. (1928–2006). In 1969 Exner published the book *The Rorschach Systems* and, later, *The Rorschach: A Comprehensive System*. Many consider the Exner system, which was released in 1987, to be the most objective and reliable method of scoring the test, showing especially high reliability among different evaluators. The Exner Comprehensive Rorschach System uses a computer-based scoring system, which includes score summaries and provides possible adjustment and personality descriptions for each subject.

Origins

Dr. Hermann Rorschach was interested in painting and drawing at an early age. By the time he entered graduate school Rorschach was still undecided as to whether to pursue a career in art or science. Although deciding upon science, he incorporated his interest in art within his professional activities; specifically, with his interest in "inkblot pictures" that went back to his childhood experiences.

Rorschach developed his series of inkblots after studying hundreds of introverted and extroverted patients in parallel with a lesser number of normal (control) subjects. Backed with about 10 years of research into using such inkblots to study patients, Rorschach wrote the book *Pscyodiagnostik (Psychodiagnostics)* in 1921, which detailed his studies and research into the use of inkblots to test the personality of people. In the book, he selected 10 specific inkblot cards as the foundation of his test. In 1942, the book was translated into English, and it was published as *Psychodiagnostics: A Diagnostic Test Based on Perception.*

KEY TERMS

Projective psychological test—Any test in psychology that is designed to allow the test subject to respond to ambiguous (those having more than one meaning) stimuli (such as images), which are intended to reveal to the evaluator hidden emotions and personality characteristics of the subject.

Psychodiagnostic—Various methods used to examine and analyze the factors that form human behavior, especially abnormal behavior.

Preparation

Preparation for the test is not necessary nor recommended.

Risks

Though only trained professionals should administer the test and evaluate it afterwards, the subjective nature of the test allows for the possibility of uncertainty in the results. Even though the Exner system is widely used in the scoring of the test, researchers sometimes criticize it for its lack of objectivity, reliability, and validity. Two professionals have the potential for scoring one individual very differently, based on the individual judgments of each person. The test itself is criticized for its inability to accurately assess personality in patients previously exposed to the inkblots.

The test often takes several hours to complete and interpret, which is sometimes seen as a negative for the test.

Results

Overall, the results of the test provide the administrator (evaluator) with information on cognitive and personality characteristics of the subject. Based on the subject's responses and actions, the evaluator should be able to reveal certain underlying characteristics of the individual, such as any conflicts residing within the person and any perceptions that the individual may have of the world or others. Because the evaluator must interpret the responses and actions of the subject, the interpretations of the subject by different evaluators may vary.

The scoring of the Rorschach test is based on several factors, such as the content of the subject's response. The content observed by the subject is usually classified by the evaluator in one of such groupings as humans, animals, nature, clothing, or abstract. A subject seeing a movie star would be grouped under human, while a leaf from a maple tree would be categorized under nature.

However, content alone is not the sole factor used in evaluations. A particular characteristic of the inkblot may determine the response by the subjects. Such a *determinant* includes the shape (or form) of the inkblot, along with subfactors such as color, movement, and shading. For instance, people who see movement (motion) within the inkblots are usually evaluated as introspective or intellectual. Those who see stationary objects in the inkblots are considered more practical by nature.

The Rorschach can be interpreted by the *location* within the inkblot from which the response originated. Location may consist of the entire blot, sections of it, or only specific details within it. Other factors include *popularity* (how common was the response when compared to others) and *originality* (how uncommon was the response).

The final outcome of the test can be affected by the demeanor of the subject, such as if he/she is cooperative or hostile toward the test, and/or the evaluator. These behaviors can influence the evaluator in the final scoring of the test.

The scoring of the Exner system, often considered one of the most reliable ways to score the Rorschach test, uses clusters of Rorschach variables as the centerpiece of its ability to accurately evaluate responses. It also contains a sequential search strategy that forces the evaluator to evaluate in a particular order. The Exner system uses a method that is objective, reliable, and follows a standardized procedure to assure unbiased evaluations.

Resources

BOOKS

Aronow, Edward, Marvin Reznikoff, and Kevin Moreland. *The Rorschach Technique: Perceptual Basics, Content Interpretation, and Applications.* Boston: Allyn and Bacon, 1994.

Drummond, Robert J. *Assessment Procedures for Counselors and Helping Professionals.* Boston: Pearson, 2010.

Frick, Paul J., Christopher T. Barry and Randy W. Kamphaus. *Clinical Assessment of Child and Adolescent Personality and Behavior.* New York: Springer, 2010.

Green, Susan K., and Robert L. Johnson. *Assessment Is Essential.* Boston: McGraw-Hill Higher Education, 2010.

Hart, Diane. *Authentic Assessment: A Handbook for Educators.* Menlo Park, CA: Addison-Wesley, 1994.

Lee, Steven W., ed. *Encyclopedia of School Psychology.* Thousand Oaks, CA: Sage, 2005.

Leichtman, Martin. *The Rorschach: A Developmental Perspective.* Hillsdale, NJ: Analytic Press, 1996.

McAfee, Oralie, and Deborah J. Leong. *Assessing and Guiding Young Children's Development and Learning.* Upper Saddle River, NJ: Pearson, 2011.

McCullough, Virginia E. *Testing and Your Child: What You Should Know about 150 of the Most Common Medical, Educational, and Psychological Tests.* New York: Plume, 1992.

Mindes, Gayle. *Assessing Young Children.* Boston: Pearson, 2011.

Psychodiagnostics: Bibliography. New York: Grune and Stratton, 1954.

Rorschach, Hermann. *Psychodiagnostik.* Bern: Bircher, 1921.

WEBSITES

"Are You Using the Right Assessment Instrument for the Right Child?" State Education Resource Center. http://www.ctserc.org/initiatives/ece/ecetests.shtml (accessed October 4, 2010).

"The Classical Rorschach." Göteborg University. http://www.phil.gu.se/fu/ro.html (accessed October 11, 2010).

Hermann Rorschach Archives and Museum website. http://www.zb.unibe.ch/rorschach/en/index.html (accessed October 11, 2010).

International Society of the Rorschach and Projective Methods website. http://www.rorschach.com (accessed October 11, 2010).

William Arthur Atkins

Rumination disorder

Definition

Rumination disorder may be diagnosed when a person deliberately brings food back up into the mouth and either rechews and reswallows it or spits it out.

Demographics

Rumination disorder occurs primarily in infants. The onset usually occurs before the infant's first birthday. The disorder is also more common in people with intellectual disabilities. The onset of rumination disorder is typically later in persons with intellectual disabilities, and may not appear until puberty or even the early adult years. Rumination disorder is rare and thought to occur more often in males than in females. People who have anorexia or bulimia may begin to ruminate only in adult life. One report found that up to 20% of people with bulimia may ruminate.

Description

Rumination disorder is sometimes called merycism. It is a disorder most commonly found in infants and is associated with intellectual disability. During rumination, previously eaten food is intentionally brought back into the mouth. Sometimes the child spits it out, but in other cases, the food is rechewed and reswallowed. The regurgitation is not caused by a medical condition. In many cases, the child has had an illness associated with vomiting that occurs before the onset of rumination disorder. Rumination has also been observed in severe cases of eating disorders among teenagers as well as adults.

Causes and symptoms

Causes

There is no general agreement on the causes of rumination disorder. In infants, it is thought to be caused by a lack of nurturing or physical contact. The child's rumination may represent an attempt to stimulate or soothe him- or herself. Biological factors are also being explored as possible causes of rumination disorder.

Symptoms

The symptoms of rumination include both the regurgitation of food and, in infants, the effort made to regurgitate that food. In infants, the attempts to bring up food can include putting fingers in the mouth, sucking on the tongue, and arching the back. When food is brought up, the cheeks expand and appear puffed. Sometimes an observer can detect the rechewing; the person often appears to take pleasure in the act. The person's breath may have a foul or sour odor. Some infants, especially those who have just begun ruminating, will expel most or all of the regurgitated food from their mouths. When this expulsion occurs, it is often mistaken for normal infant vomiting. As an infant continues to ruminate, he or she often learns to keep more and more of the regurgitated food in the mouth.

Diagnosis

The *Diagnostic and Statistical Manual of Mental Disorders*, fourth edition, text revision (*DSM-IV-TR*), which is the standard reference work for mental health professionals, gives only three general criteria for diagnosing rumination disorder. The first is that the person's behavior of deliberately bringing up and rechewing food must have lasted for at least a month. The regurgitation and rechewing must happen after a period of time in which the person did not ruminate. In addition, the rumination cannot result from a medical condition such as esophageal reflux. In addition, the manual specifies that the rumination cannot be associated with anorexia or bulimia.

Rumination disorder may be difficult to diagnose. One reason for this difficulty is that infants or adults who do not expel any of their regurgitated food can often be identified only by a puffing of the cheeks when the food is in the mouth or by an unpleasant breath odor. In addition, because many people and infants who ruminate

---

KEY TERMS

Merycism—Another name for rumination disorder.

Regurgitation—The return of partly digested food from the stomach to the mouth. Regurgitation may be either an intentional act or an involuntary physical reaction.

Ruminate—To chew or rechew regurgitated food.

---

find the experience a positive and pleasurable one, there are no physical signs of discomfort to bring the disorder to the attention of caretakers or others.

Some experts disagree with the statement of the *Diagnostic and Statistical Manual* that a **diagnosis** of rumination disorder cannot be made if the rumination is associated with anorexia or bulimia. These experts maintain that diagnosing and treating rumination disorder in patients who have other eating disorders is important for the sake of the patient's health.

Treatment

Treatment for rumination disorder depends on the cause of the behavior. Infants who are thought to ruminate because of a lack of affection may be fed by someone other than their mother or father. This person can be a replacement while their parents receive treatment themselves. Other approaches involve therapy and parenting education to create a stronger bond between the parents and the child.

The treatment of adult patients includes giving them chewing gum to use when rumination might normally occur. Other researchers have found that giving adults with intellectual disabilites filling meals may reduce rumination. Treating such eating disorders as anorexia or bulimia frequently helps to resolve the rumination that may be associated with those disorders. **Behavior modification** techniques that help a patient to unlearn the ruminating behavior have also been used.

Prognosis

In many cases rumination that begins in infancy stops on its own. The disorder should be treated, however, because infants with untreated rumination disorder are at risk of malnutrition and death caused by dehydration. Treatments for rumination disorder are generally very effective. Treatment of associated eating disorders in adults is generally regarded as successful.

Prevention

There is no known way to prevent rumination disorder. It is possible, however, that a strong parent-child bond may reduce the possibility of the disorder occurring in infants.

Resources

BOOKS

American Psychiatric Association. *Diagnostic and Statistical Manual of Mental Disorders*. 4th ed., text rev. Washington, DC: American Psychiatric Publishing, 2000.

Sadock, Benjamin J., and Virginia A. Sadock, eds. *Comprehensive Textbook of Psychiatry*. Vol. 2. 7th ed. Philadelphia: Lippincott Williams and Wilkins, 2000.

PERIODICALS

Weakley, Melinda M., Theodore A. Petti, and George Karwisch. "Case Study: Chewing Gum Treatment of Rumination in an Adolescent with an Eating Disorder." *Journal of the American Academy of Child and Adolescent Psychiatry* 36, no. 8 (August 1997): 1124–1128.

ORGANIZATIONS

American Academy of Pediatrics, 141 Northwest Point Blvd., Elk Grove Village, IL, 60007-1098, (847) 434-4000, Fax: (847) 434-8000, http://www.aap.org.

Tish Davidson, A.M.

S

SAD *see* **Seasonal affective disorder**

Sadism *see* **Sexual sadism**

Saffron

Description

Saffron is an herbal preparation harvested from the stigma of the *Crocus sativus* flower. It is dark orange and threadlike in appearance, with a spicy flavor and pungent odor. The plant is grown in India, Spain, France, Italy, the Middle East, and the eastern Mediterranean region.

Purpose

In addition to its culinary uses, saffron is prescribed as an herbal remedy to stimulate the digestive system, ease colic and stomach discomfort, and minimize gas. It is also used as an emmenagogue, to stimulate and promote menstrual flow in women.

Bowl of saffron. (© *iStockPhoto.com/Dan Bachman*)

Preliminary studies have shown that saffron may also be a useful tool in fighting cancer. According to a 1999 study, use of the herb slowed tumor growth and extended lifespan in female rats. A 2002 study done at Indiana University indicated that saffron may not only be effective in treating certain types of cancer but is significantly less likely to cause birth defects if given to pregnant women than all-trans-retinoic acid (ATRA), the compound most often given to treat these cancers. Saffron may thus be a preferable alternative to treating ATRA-sensitive cancers in women of childbearing age.

A 2004 review of previous research in animal models and with cultured human malignant cell lines concluded that **clinical trials** are warranted to define the possible chemopreventive properties of saffron. A 2006 study at the National Institute of Pediatrics in Mexico concluded that "saffron itself, as well as its carotenoid components, might be used as potential cancer chemopreventive agents."

Additional human studies have indicated that saffron has powerful antioxidant properties; that is, it helps to protect living tissues from free radicals and other harmful effects of oxidation. In Iran and Japan, pharmacology studies in 2000 and 2002 confirmed that saffron extract has an anticonvulsant activity.

Two chemical components of saffron extract, crocetin and crocin, reportedly improved memory and learning skills in learning-impaired rats in a Japanese study published in early 2000. These properties indicate that saffron extract may be a useful treatment for neurodegenerative disorders and related memory impairment.

In 2005 in the *Journal of Ethnopharmacology* researchers reported on the first scientific study to test the effectiveness of saffron as a treatment for symptoms of mild to moderate **depression**. Daily dosages of 30 mg saffron extract (standardized to 0.7 mg of safranal) were compared to 20 mg of **fluoxetine** (Prozac) in 38 people. Participants were aged 18 to 55 years. At the conclusion of the six-week trial, both treatments demonstrated significant improvements in depressive symptoms. There was no significant difference between the herbal treatment and the drug treatment as far as the amount of improvement demonstrated. However, participants who took the saffron extract did not report side effects, such as sexual dysfunction, tremor, or sweating, sometimes attributed to fluoxetine. Symptoms were evaluated with the Hamilton Rating Scale for Depression prior to the study and at intervals of one, two, four, and six weeks.

An Iranian study published in March 2007 revealed that saffron was as effective as fluoxetine (Prozac) in the treatment of depression, noting that both saffron and fluoxetine yielded similar side effects for users of both groups. In fact, scientists at the University of Medical Sciences in Tehran now believe that saffron is as beneficial as fluoxetine in the treatment of mild to moderate depression. In January 2010, the *Journal of Natural Medicines* published findings showing that laboratory mice that were given saffron extracts, exhibited stress-adaptive benefits, supporting beliefs that saffron may be beneficial in treatment for depression.

Saffron has also been found to be beneficial for depression associated with **premenstrual syndrome** (PMS). An Iranian study published in March 2008 determined that women between the age of 20 and 45 reported a significant reduction in their PMS depression. The women (who took 30 mg of saffron a day for two concurrent menstrual cycles) noted relief of these symptoms; however, more research was said to be needed to determine possible negative effects of saffron associated with PMS, before it could be established as a safe and therapeutic treatment regimen for PMS.

As of 2011, saffron was being investigated for the following medicinal uses:

- to help control the effects of mild to moderate Alzheimer's disease

- to help improve mood

- to improve circulation

- to inhibit cancer cell proliferation against breast, liver, pancreatic, and skin cancers

Preparations

Saffron is harvested by drying the orange stigma of the *Crocus sativus* flower over fire. Over 200,000 crocus stigmas must be harvested to produce one pound of saffron. This volume makes the herb extremely expensive, and it is often cut with other substances of a similar color (e.g., marigold) to keep the price down.

Safranal, a terpene aldehyde, is formed during the drying process. It is the component responsible for much of saffron's characteristic fragrance.

KEY TERMS

Antioxidants—Enzymes that bind with free radicals to neutralize their harmful effects.

Crocetin—A reddish-yellow plant pigment found in saffron that has been studied for its anticancer effectiveness.

Decoction—An herbal extract produced by mixing an herb with cold water, bringing the mixture to a boil, and letting it simmer to evaporate the excess water. Decoctions are usually chosen over infusion when the botanical or herb in question is a root, seed, or berry.

Emmenagogue—A medication or substance given to bring on a menstrual period.

Free radicals—Reactive molecules created during cell metabolism that can cause tissue and cell damage like that which occurs in aging and with such disease processes as cancer.

Stigma—The thread-like filament found in the center of a flower where pollen collects.

Tincture—A liquid extract of an herb prepared by steeping the herb in an alcohol and water mixture.

Because saffron is frequently used as a spice to flavor a variety of dishes, particularly in Mediterranean recipes, it can often be purchased by mail order and at gourmet food stores, as well as at health food stores. The herb is usually sold in either powdered form or in its original threadlike stigma form. Saffron is expensive and can cost as much $315 per ounce.

For medicinal purposes, saffron can be taken by mouth in powder, tincture, or liquid form. To make a liquid saffron decoction, mix 6–10 stigmas or strands of saffron in one cup of cold water, bring the mixture to a boil, and then let it simmer. The saffron is then strained out of the decoction, which can be drunk either hot or cold. An average recommended dose of saffron decoction is 0.5–1 cup daily.

Saffron should be stored in an airtight container in a cool location away from bright light to maintain its potency. The herb can be frozen. Properly stored saffron can be used for up to two years. A good measure of the herb's freshness and potency is its odor. If the saffron does not have a noticeable pungent smell, it is probably past its peak.

Precautions

Because saffron can stimulate uterine contractions, pregnant women should never take the herb for medicinal purposes.

QUESTIONS TO ASK YOUR DOCTOR

- In what way do you think saffron will benefit me?
- Will saffron interfere with my current medications?
- What symptoms are important enough that I should seek immediate treatment?

Saffron should always be obtained from a reputable source that observes stringent quality control procedures and industry-accepted good manufacturing practices. Because of its high cost, saffron is sometimes found in adulterated form, so package labeling should be checked carefully for the type and quality of additional ingredients.

Legislation known as the Dietary Supplement Health and Education Act (DSHEA) was passed in 1994 in an effort to standardize the manufacture, labeling, composition, and safety of botanicals and supplements. Botanical supplements are regulated by the FDA; however, they are not required to undergo any approval process before reaching the consumer market and are classified as nutritional supplements rather than drugs.

Side effects

Although there are no known side effects or health hazards associated with recommended dosages of saffron preparations in healthy individuals, people with chronic medical conditions should consult their healthcare professional before taking the herb. In addition, pregnant women should never take saffron, as the herb stimulates uterine contractions and may cause miscarriage.

Despite earlier reports of serious adverse effects from as little as 5 grams of saffron, there is no scientific evidence as to the toxicity of *Crocus sativus*. According to Subhuti Dharmananda, director of the Institute for Traditional Medicine in Portland, Oregon, "all recent research reports indicate that saffron is non-toxic." The so-called meadow saffron *(Colchicum autumnale)* is highly toxic, however, and is sometimes mistaken for the non-toxic medicinal plant *Crocus sativus*.

Interactions

There are no reported negative interactions between saffron and other medications and herbs, but saffron may alter the efficacy of other drugs. Patients should always consult with their physicians before taking any herbs or supplements.

Resources

BOOKS

Awang, Dennis V.C. *Tyler's Herbs of Choice: The Therapeutic Use of Phytomedicinals,* 3rd ed. Boca Raton, FL: CRC Press, 2009.

Barnes, Joanne, et al. *Herbal Medicines (Includes CD-ROM),* 3rd ed. London: Pharmaceutical Press, 2007.

Micozzi, Marc S. *Fundamentals of Complementary and Alternative Medicine.* New York: Saunders, 2010.

Physician's Desk Reference. *PDR for Nonprescription Drugs, Dietary Supplements, and Herbs 2009,* 30th ed. New York: PDR, 2008.

Smith, Pamela Wartian. *What You Must Know About Vitamins, Minerals, Herbs, & More: Choosing the Nutrients That Are Right for You.* Garden City Park, NY: Square One, 2008.

PERIODICALS

Dharmananda, Subhuti. "Saffron: An Anti-Depressant Herb." *Institute for Traditional Medicine* (May 2005). http://www.itmonline.org/articles/saffron/saffron.htm (accessed October 3, 2011).

Noorbala, A.A. "Hydro-alcoholic Extract of Crocus Sativus versus Fluoxetine in the Treatment of Mild to Moderate Depression: A Double-Blind, Randomized Pilot Trial." *Journal of Ethnopharmacology* 97, no. 2 (2005): 281–84.

ORGANIZATIONS

Institute for Traditional Medicine, 2017 SE Hawthorne Blvd., Portland, OR, 97214, (503) 233-4907, http://www.itmonline.org.

National Center for Complementary and Alternative Medicine, 9000 Rockville Pike, Bethesda, MD, 20892, (888) 644-6226, http://nccam.nih.gov.

Office of Dietary Supplements. National Institutes of Health, 6100 Executive Blvd., Rm. 3B01, MSC 7517, Bethesda, MD, 20892-7517, (301) 435-2920, Fax: (301) 480-1845, ods@nih.gov, http://dietary-supplements.info.nih.gov.

Paula Ford-Martin
Laura Jean Cataldo, RN, EdD

Sage

Definition

Common sage is a small, perennial plant or bush with woody stems, aromatic grayish leaves, and white or blue-to-purplish flowers. A member of the Lamiaceae, or mint, family and genus *Salvia*, it is also referred to as garden, meadow, or true sage. More than 750 species of sage exist in Central and South America, Central Asia and the Mediterranean, and Eastern Asia.

Sage plant. (© Elliotte Rusty Harold/Shutterstock.com)

Sage has been used since ancient times for medicinal and culinary purposes; it is commonly used as an herb in poultry stuffing. With regard to mental health, alternative medicine practitioners tout sage as a way to reduce anxiety and other symptoms prevalent in mental disorders.

Purpose

Sage is a celebrated herb long valued for its many uses. The Romans revered the herb as a sacred plant, and the Egyptians used it to treat the plague. Nicholas Culpeper (1616–54), the seventeenth-century herbalist and astrologer, believed sage was under the dominion of the planet Jupiter. Folk belief placed the herb under the influence of Venus, and sage was traditionally used to aid conception. One folk tradition encouraged eating a bit of sage each day during the month of May to assure immortality. Failing to live up to this promise, sage was traditionally planted on graves.

Sage's main constituents are volatile oil, diterpene bitters, thujone, camphor, tannins, triterpenoids, resin, flavonoids, estrogenic substances, saponins, and phenolic acids, including rosmarinic and caffeic acids. The herb purportedly acts as an antiallergen, antibiotic, antiperspirant, antiseptic, antispasmodic, astringent, and carminative.

Sage has been used as a general tonic (a beverage that generally makes one feel better). It is the preferred beverage tea in many cultures, particularly in China, where the root of the species *S. miltiorrhiza*, known as *dan shen*, is used for its soothing and healing qualities.

Description

Sage (*Salvia officinalis*, abbreviated *S. officinalis*) is native to the Mediterranean and naturalized throughout Europe and North America. The genus name is taken from the Latin *salvare,* meaning "to save." The specific name *officinalis* indicates that sage was included on official lists of medicinal herbs.

There are numerous species of sage, but *S. officinalis* is the best known for its medicinal purposes. It often serves as the standard to which other sage species are compared. Other species also noted for medicinal purposes are *S. officinalis purpurascens* ("Purpurea," red or purple common sage), *S. miltiorrhiza* (Chinese sage, red sage), *S. fruticosa* (Greek sage), and *S. lavandulifolia.* (Spanish sage).

Sage thrives in full sun and well-drained soils, growing wild in some areas. It is a hardy, evergreen shrub with a deep taproot and an erect root stalk that produces woody, square, slightly downy, branching stems that may reach a height of 4 feet (1.2 m). The familiar plant has long, light green leaf stalks that bear simple, opposite, lance- or oval-shaped leaves. The strong and pliable leaves are veined, with a velvet-like, somewhat crinkled, texture and may grow to 2 inches (5.1 cm) long in some species. Leaf margins resemble a fine embroidery finish with rounded, minutely toothed edges. They are a gray green on the top and lighter on the underside. The entire plant is strongly aromatic, with a familiar pungency. Fresh leaves are bitter to the taste. Sage blossoms in the middle of summer with small white, blue, or purple flowers.

Among its many virtues, sage has been shown by researchers to help calm the central nervous system and reduce anxiety. Medical research also found that sage helps to enhance mood and improve memory and cognitive skills. Some tout sage as helping to reduce chemical imbalances in the **brain** and thus helping to reduce symptoms commonly associated with Alzheimer's disease (AD), a type of **dementia**. In a 2003 study published in the *Journal of Clinical Pharmacy and Therapeutics*, persons with mild to moderate AD given sage extract for four months experienced improved cognitive functioning. However, further research is needed; the National Center for Complementary and Alternative Medicine (NCCAM) has conducted a trial on the effects of sage on memory and cognitive performance in patients with AD, which was expected to be completed in December 2012.

Recommended dosage

The sage leaf is the medicinal part of the herb. Both the fresh and dried leaves may be used for medicinal purposes. The leaves are harvested when the herb begins to flower in the summer of its second year. The leaves are removed from the woody branches. Then they are spread in a single layer on a tray or screen in a warm, airy, and shady place. Exposure to direct sunlight during the drying process results in a significant loss of the volatile oil. Dried leaves are stored in a dark, airtight container.

KEY TERMS

Central nervous system—The part of the nervous system that includes the brain and spinal cord but excludes the peripheral nerves.

Hypertension—The medical term for high blood pressure.

Thujone—A natural chemical compound found in sage as well as in wormwood and certain other spices. In large quantities it can cause hallucinations and convulsions.

Tonic—A preparation or medicine that invigorates, strengthens, or restores tone to body tissues.

QUESTIONS TO ASK YOUR DOCTOR

- Do you know how effective sage might be for me with regards to my symptoms?
- Are there any underlying medical concerns that need to be addressed or corrected before I take sage?
- Will health insurance cover the use of sage?
- How long may I take sage before noticing any difference?

To make an infusion, 1 pint (0.5 L) of nonchlorinated water that has just reached the boiling point is poured over 2–3 teaspoons (0.3–0.5 fl oz) of dried or fresh sage leaves in a glass container. The mixture is covered and steeped for 10–15 minutes. This liquid can be drunk warm or cold, up to 3 cups (25 fl oz) daily.

For improved cognitive functioning with **Alzheimer's disease**, the suggested dose is 0.04 oz. (1 g) of sage extract per day. Patients should always consult with their physicians before starting any treatment, even alternative or complementary treatments, especially if taking concurrent medications.

Tinctures of sage are available commercially. A standard dose is 16–40 drops, up to three times daily.

Precautions

Sage preparations in medicinal doses should not be used during pregnancy and breastfeeding. Pregnant women should avoid sage because of the possibility that the chemical thujone may be present in various species of sage. Increased amounts of thujone can bring on a menstrual period in women. If a woman is pregnant, such an incident will cause a miscarriage. In addition, some research has shown that thujone may reduce the amount of milk for mothers who are breastfeeding a child.

People with epilepsy should not use sage due to the thujone content in the herb. Thujone may trigger convulsions in these people, with its essential oil containing as much as 25% thujone. These essential oils may accumulate in the body, so long-term or high dose use of sage (for more than two weeks at a time) should be avoided.

In addition, in large enough doses, thujone can be poisonous. Consequently, it can cause **seizures** and damage to the liver and nervous systems in anyone taking the chemical. The amount of thujone in sage varies depending on various factors such as growing conditions and time of harvest.

Diabetics should avoid sage because it can lower their blood sugar levels, which is called hypoglycemia. People with high blood pressure (hypertension) should also avoid sage. Sage can increase blood pressure, which can be dangerous for people already with higher than normal blood pressure. Those allergic to sage or other plants in the mint family should also avoid this herb.

Side effects

There are no adverse side effects when sage is taken in designated therapeutic doses. However, sage may interfere with absorption of iron and other minerals.

Interactions

Various interactions have been reported between sage and prescription medications. Medications used to prevent seizures (anticonvulsants) can interact with sage because both alter the state of certain chemicals in the brain. As such, using both can alter the effectiveness of such medicines. Some antiseizure medicines are **carbamazepine** (Tegretol), **gabapentin** (Neurontin), primidone (Mysoline), and **valproic acid** (Depakene). Sedative medications, which are called central nervous system (CNS) depressants, also interact with sage. When used together they can cause excessive sleepiness and drowsiness. Some sleep aid medicines are **clonazepam** (Klonopin), **lorazepam** (Ativan), and **zolpidem** (Ambien).

Resources

BOOKS

Dasgupta, Amitava, and Catherine A. Hammett-Stabler, eds. *Herbal Supplements: Efficacy, Toxicity, Interactions with Western Drugs and Effects on Clinical Laboratory Tests.* Hoboken, NJ: Wiley, 2011.

PDR for Herbal Medicines. Montvale, NJ: Thomson, 2007.

Tang, Tifan. *Chinese Herbal Medicines: Comparisons and Characteristics.* Edinburgh: Churchill Livingstone/ Elsevier, 2010.

Ulbricht, Catherine E. *Davis's Pocket Guide to Herbs and Supplements.* Philadelphia: F. A. Davis, 2011.

Woods, Michael, and Mary B. Woods. *Ancient Medical Technology: From Herbs to Scalpels.* Minneapolis: Twenty-First Century Books, 2011.

PERIODICALS

Akhondzadeh, S., et al. "*Salvia officinalis* Extract in the Treatment of Patients with Mild to Moderate Alzheimer's Disease: A Double Blind, Randomized and Placebo-controlled Trial." *Journal of Clinical Pharmacy and Therapeutics* 28, no. 1 (2003): 53–59.

WEBSITES

Brett, Jennifer. "Sage: Herbal Remedies." Discovery Health. http://health.howstuffworks.com/wellness/natural-medicine/herbal-remedies/sage-herbal-remedies.htm (accessed September 8, 2011).

National Center for Complementary and Alternative Medicine (NCCAM). "Sage." U.S. National Institutes of Health. http://nccam.nih.gov/health/sage (accessed September 8, 2011).

ORGANIZATIONS

American Botanical Council, 6200 Manor Rd., Austin, TX, 78723, (512) 926-4900, Fax: (512) 926-2345, abc@herbalram.org, http://abc.herbalgram.org.

American Psychiatric Association, 1000 Wilson Blvd., Ste. 1825, Arlington, VA, 22209, (703) 907-7300, apa@psych.org, http://www.psych.org.

National Center for Complementary and Alternative Medicine Clearinghouse, 9000 Rockville Pike, Bethesda, MD, 20892, info@nccam.nih.gov, http://nccam.nih.gov.

Natural Standard, One Davis Sq., Somerville, MA, 02144, (617) 591-3300, Fax: (617) 591-3399, http://naturalstandard.com.

Office of Dietary Supplements, National Institutes of Health, 6100 Executive Blvd., Rm. 3B01, MSC 7517, Rockville, MD, 20892-7517, (301) 435-2920, Fax: (301) 480-1845, ods@nih.gov, http://ods.od.nih.gov.

United States Pharmacopoeia, 12601 Twinbrook Pkwy., Rockville, MD, 20852-1790, (800) 227-8772, http://www.usp.org.

Clare Hanrahan
Rebecca J. Frey, PhD
William A. Atkins, BB, BS, MBA

St. John's wort

Definition

St. John's wort is a perennial, yellow-flowering plant that grows in the wild throughout Europe and is now found also in North America. The plant has been used as a popular

St. John's wort. *(© Jim Dubois/Shutterstock.com)*

herbal folk remedy for centuries, but more recently, practitioners of conventional Western medicine have been exploring its utility for treating **depression** and anxiety.

Purpose

Writings since the Middle Ages have described using St. John's wort as treatment for inflammation, injuries, burns, muscle pain, anxiety, high blood pressure, stomach problems, fluid retention, **insomnia**, hemorrhoids, cancer, and depression. Research conducted over the last decade of the twentieth century in Europe studied the efficacy of St. John's wort for the treatment of depression and anxiety. Research protocols have been developed in the United States to study the same issues, to determine appropriate dosages, to develop standard formulations, and to define whether it can be used for all forms of depression or only for more mild forms of the condition.

Description

Hypericum perforatum is the most medicinally important species of the Hypericum genus, commonly known as St. John's wort or Klamath weed. There are as many as 400 species in the genus, which belongs to the Clusiaceae family. Native to Europe, St. John's wort is found throughout the world. It thrives in sunny fields, open woods, and gravelly roadsides. Early colonists brought this plant to North America, and it has become naturalized in the eastern United States and California, as well as in Australia, New Zealand, eastern Asia, and South America. St. John's wort has long been one of the most commonly used herbs in the United States, especially among women. The popular use of the herb declined in the late 1990s, however, due in part to research reports that the hypericum in the plant may be

KEY TERMS

Immunosuppressant—Medications that suppress or lower the body's immune system, primarily used to help the body accept a transplanted organ.

Monoamine oxidase inhibitors (MAOIs)—A group of antidepressant drugs that decrease the activity of monoamine oxidase, a neurotransmitter found in the brain that affects mood.

Reserpine—Medication to treat high blood pressure. Brand names include Serpalan, Novoreserpine, and Reserfia.

Theophylline—A medication used to treat asthma. Sold under many brand names, including Aerolate Sr, Respbid, and Theolair.

Warfarin—A medication that helps to prevent the formation of clots in the blood vessels. Sold as Coumadin in the U.S.

less effective in treating depression than previously claimed.

Research has yet to completely explain how St. John's wort affects the **brain** in depression. It is, however, thought to change the balance of chemicals in the brain in much the same way as **selective serotonin reuptake inhibitors (SSRIs)** such as **fluoxetine**, and **monoamine oxidase inhibitors (MAOIs)**, such as **isocarboxazid**. The active ingredients are thought to be compounds called hypericin and pseudohypericin, although researchers are attempting to identify other chemicals that may be involved in the herb's effectiveness.

The leaves and flowers of St. John's wort are both used. St. John's wort is available as pills, capsules, extracts, dried herbs for tea, and oil infusions for skin applications.

St. John's wort has been proven clinically effective in treating mild-to-moderate depression. In 2005, the British Journal of Psychiatry reported on 37 previous scientific studies comparing the clinical benefits to adults with depressive disorders of hypericum in St. John's wort and either a placebo or a standard antidepressant. The trials suggested that St. John's wort extract had "minimal beneficial effects" in treating major depression, but showed "similar beneficial effects" in cases of mild depression as when using a standard antidepressant. St. John's wort also shows promise in treating **somatoform disorders**. Research on its treatment of anxiety and other conditions is conflicting and inconclusive.

Recommended dosage

Because dosages of herbal preparations are not always standardized, it is important to discuss with a knowledgeable practitioner the most reliable form of St. John's wort. Recommendations call for 300–500 mg (of a standardized 0.3% hypericin extract) three times daily. It can take four to six weeks to notice the antidepressant effects of this preparation.

Alternatively, one to two teaspoons of dried St. John's wort can be put into a cup of boiling water and steeped for 10 minutes to make tea. The recommended dose of tea is one to two cups daily. Again, four to six weeks may be necessary in order to notice improvement in symptoms of depression.

Precautions

There are a number of important precautions to observe in using St. John's wort. Pregnant or lactating women should not use the herb at all. Animal studies have linked St. John's wort to lower birth weight, and there are studies showing that breastfed infants whose mothers are using St. John's wort may experience drowsiness or colic.

Persons taking prescription **antidepressants** of any kind should not use St. John's wort at the same time, as the herb may precipitate a health crisis known as **serotonin syndrome**. **Serotonin** syndrome is potentially life threatening; it is characterized by changes in level of consciousness, behavior, and neuromotor functioning as a result of increased levels of the neurotransmitter serotonin in the central nervous system. Drug interactions are the most common cause of serotonin syndrome. Several cases of serotonin syndrome have been reported in patients who were taking St. John's wort by itself or in combination with **SSRIs**, fenfluramine (Pondimin), or **nefazodone** (Serzone). Patients taking **MAOIs** must carefully avoid taking St. John's wort due to serious adverse effects of combining the two.

Depression can be a serious, even life-threatening, condition; therefore, it is imperative that depressed patients using St. John's wort are carefully monitored.

Side effects

People taking St. John's wort may develop one or all of the following side effects:

- skin rash due to sun sensitivity (the most common side effect)
- headache, dizziness, dry mouth, constipation
- abdominal pain, confusion, sleep problems, and high blood pressure (less frequently experienced)

Interactions

Again, a knowledgeable professional should be consulted before St. John's wort is taken to determine the appropriateness of its use and avoid serious interactions. Interactions include:

• A possible decrease in effectiveness of reserpine, warfarin, theophylline, immunosuppressant medications such as cyclosporine, and antiviral drugs such as indinavir.

• Dangerous interactions when used with other antidepressant medicines (especially MAOIs), digoxin, and loperamide.

• Interactions with oral birth control pills. St. John's wort may interfere with the effectiveness of birth control pills, increasing the risk of pregnancy; an alternative form of birth control should be considered while taking St. John's wort. In addition, women taking both birth control pills and St. John's wort may notice bleeding between menstrual periods.

Other drugs with reported interactions include **amphetamines**, asthma **inhalants**, decongestants, diet pills, narcotics, and tryptophan and tyrosine (amino acids). Moreover, anesthesiologists have reported that the herb increases bleeding time in patients under general anesthesia. Patients should always consult a mainstream health practitioner before using St. John's wort and should discontinue taking it at least two weeks prior to major surgery.

See also Depression

Resources

BOOKS

Rister, Robert, and Siegrid Klein. *The Complete German Commission E Monographs: Therapeutic Guide to Herbal Medicines*. Austin, TX: American Botanical Council, 1998.

PERIODICALS

Linde, K., M.M. Berner, and L. Kriston. "St. John's Wort for Depression." *Cochrane Database of Systematic Reviews* 8, no. 4 (October 2008): CD000448.

WEBSITES

U.S. National Center for Complementary and Alternative Medicine. "Questions and Answers: A Trial of St. John's Wort (*Hypericum perforatum*) for the Treatment of Major Depression." http://nccam.nih.gov/news/2002/stjohnswort/q-and-a.htm (accessed October 27, 2011).

U.S. National Center for Complementary and Alternative Medicine. "St. John's Wort and Depression." http://nccam.nih.gov/health/stjohnswort/sjw-and-depression.htm (accessed October 27, 2011).

ORGANIZATIONS

National Center for Complementary and Alternative Medicine, 9000 Rockville Pike, Bethesda, MD, 20892, info@nccam.nih.gov, http://nccam.nih.gov.

Rosalyn Carson-DeWitt, M.D.

SAMe

Definition

SAMe (S-adenosyl-L-methionine, sometimes also written as S-adenosylmethionine) is a naturally occurring chemical compound found throughout the entire body. It is involved in many chemical reactions that are necessary for life. For instance, SAMe helps to maintain cell membranes and make **dopamine**, melatonin, and **serotonin** in the body. It is available as a natural dietary supplement and can be purchased without a prescription (over-the-counter). In mental health, it is used to treat conditions such as **attention deficit hyperactivity disorder (ADHD)** and **depression**.

Purpose

People take supplements of SAMe for many reasons, including to relieve symptoms of heart disease, fibromyalgia, osteoarthritis, bursitis, heart disease, tendonitis, chronic lower back pain, chronic fatigue syndrome (CFS), multiple sclerosis, spinal cord injuries, migraine headaches, **lead poisoning**, liver disease, and Parkinson's disease, as well as to improve intellectual performance.

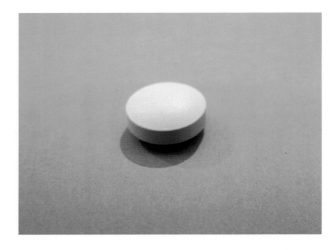

SAMe supplement. (© *Custom Medical Stock Photo, Inc. Reproduced by permission.*)

KEY TERMS

Antioxidant enzyme—An enzyme that can counteract the damaging effects of oxygen in tissues.

Bipolar disorder—Also referred to as manic depression, a mood disorder marked by alternating episodes of extremely low mood (depression) and exuberant highs (mania).

Dopamine—A chemical compound and neurotransmitter, which is a precursor of epinephrine.

Homocysteine—An amino acid with the chemical formula $HSCH_2CH_2CH(NH_2)CO_2H$.

Melatonin—A hormone derived from serotonin that produces changes in the color of the skin.

Serotonin—A chemical that acts as a neurotransmitter, with the formula $C_{10}H_{12}N_2O$.

Within the realm of mental illness, SAMe is used to treat anxiety, depression, **ADHD**, and **dementia**, including Alzheimer's disease. Some evidence suggests that taking SAMe can improve symptoms of depression within two weeks, which is considerably faster than the time it takes for oral antidepressant prescription drugs to work. (Prescription **antidepressants** often take a minimum of two weeks for patients to begin noticing any effect, and many take up to four to six weeks.)

Description

SAMe is a specific form of the amino acid methionine, a substance that, when not metabolized properly, allows homocysteine to build up in the blood. (High levels of homocysteine have been associated with increased risk for cardiovascular disease.) SAMe is also an antioxidant, a substance that protects the body from damaging reactive oxygen molecules. These reactive oxygen molecules can come from inside the body or from environmental pollution and are thought to play a role in the aging process and the development of degenerative disease. In general, SAMe is thought to raise the level of functioning of other amino acids in the body.

Although people use SAMe for many reasons, the best evidence as of 2011 indicated that SAMe may be most effective in relieving symptoms of osteoarthritis. However, it is increasingly used for treating depression. Several studies have indicated that oral SAMe and intravenous SAMe are effective treatments for depression. The studies researching the oral SAMe were mostly small studies of short duration, but they show promise for the use of SAMe in treating depression. Some found that SAMe may almost be as effective as tricyclic antidepressants, traditional medicines used to treat depression. Other research has shown that taking SAMe may be helpful for depression only when prescription antidepressants are not effective. Additional and more extensive studies of SAMe are necessary to validate these results.

Research studies have also been conducted to test the effects of SAMe on ADHD. The conclusions are not definite with respect to SAMe being effective at reducing symptoms of ADHD, as not enough studies have been completed. As of 2011, the medical consensus was that SAMe may possibly reduce symptoms of ADHD; the National Institutes of Health stated that, based on limited research, "SAMe might lessen ADHD symptoms in adults."

Recommended dosage

SAMe can be taken orally or intravenously. Oral administration is more common. When taken by mouth, doses of 400–1,600 mg daily have been suggested based on study results. However, a specific recommended therapeutic dosage had not been established as of 2011.

In treating depression, 200 mg of SAMe has been administered intravenously or intramuscularly for 14 days while simultaneously beginning therapy with prescription antidepressant drugs. If SAMe is used without prescription antidepressants, 200–400 mg per day by intravenous or intramuscular injections has been used. When treating other medical conditions, doses as high as 800 mg daily by injection have been used. Again, intravenous administration is rare in the United States.

Precautions

As a natural supplement, SAMe has not been evaluated by the Food and Drug Administration (FDA). Claims of safety or effectiveness for treating any medical disorder have not been thoroughly studied by any governmental agency, and there is no regulation of natural supplements. This means that potencies and purities may vary between lots or among manufacturers. It is also possible that supplements may not contain the ingredients that are listed on product labels.

SAMe should be used carefully by individuals with a history of **bipolar disorder** since it may aggravate symptoms of mania. When used with prescription antidepressant medications, life-threatening symptoms may occur. It should be used with prescription antidepressant drugs only under close medical supervision. Individuals should not begin taking SAMe until one week or more after stopping an antidepressant medicine, and two weeks or more after taking **phenelzine** (Nardil) or **tranylcypromine** (Parnate).

When users take SAMe by mouth, it may cause stomach upset, including gas, vomiting, diarrhea or soft stool, constipation, and nausea. Although SAMe may cause an upset stomach, it is generally recommended to take on an empty stomach for better absorption. Prospective users ought to ask a doctor to determine what is best in their case. SAMe can also cause dry mouth, headache, mild **insomnia**, anorexia, sweating, increased thirst, blurred vision, restlessness, dizziness, and nervousness. The benefits of the medication may show up within one week; however, it may take as long as four to eight weeks before the full effects are shown. Users should not suddenly discontinue use of SAMe; rather, it is recommended that use be gradually discontinued. In addition, alcohol should not be consumed with SAMe.

Increased anxiety has occurred in people with depression when taking SAMe. Furthermore, a conversion to mania has been reported in those with a history of bipolar disorder. Patients with Parkinson's disease have frequently reported worse symptoms while taking SAMe.

Women who are pregnant or breastfeeding should use extreme caution when using SAMe. Its safety under those situations has not been adequately researched, and the medical community recommends that SAMe not be used by women who are pregnant or breastfeeding.

People scheduled for surgery should stop taking SAMe at least two weeks before surgery because of a heightened risk of complications. Part of this risk involves adverse reactions to the central nervous system when individuals are taking SAMe.

Interactions

Use of SAMe with antidepressant drugs (especially **selective serotonin reuptake inhibitors**, or **SSRIs**) may cause life-threatening symptoms, including agitation, tremors, anxiety, rapid heartbeats, difficulty breathing, diarrhea, shivering, muscle stiffness, and excessive sweating. The combination can also cause insomnia. Use of SAMe with a prescription antidepressant must be approved by a physician, and close medical supervision is required. Medications for depression include **amitriptyline** (Elavil), **clomipramine** (Anafranil), **fluoxetine** (Prozac), **imipramine** (Tofranil), **paroxetine** (Paxil), and **sertraline** (Zoloft).

QUESTIONS TO ASK YOUR DOCTOR

- In what way do you think SAMe will benefit me?
- Will SAMe interfere with my current medications?
- What symptoms or adverse effects are important enough that I should seek immediate treatment?

In addition, **monoamine oxidase inhibitors** (MAOI) drugs also treat depression. Taking SAMe with MAOIs can cause serious symptoms, including anxiety, heart problems, and shivering. Two types of MAOIs are phenelzine (Nardil) and tranylcypromine (Parnate).

People should not take SAMe if they are also taking dextromethorphan (Robitussin DM and others), levodopa (which is used to treat Parkinson's disease), meperidine (Demerol), pentazocine (Talwin), or tramadol (Ultram).

SAMe may offer beneficial drug interactions when used with some medications. More research is needed, but some scientists think that SAMe may protect the liver from damage caused by some drugs, including acetaminophen, alcohol, estrogens, **steroids**, and several other prescription drugs.

SAMe, which increases serotonin in the **brain**, should not be taken with other herbs and supplements that also increase serotonin levels, such as **5-HTP**, Hawaiian baby woodrose, L-tryptophan, and St. John's wort.

Resources

BOOKS

Marian, Mary J., Pamela Williams-Mullen, and Jennifer Muir Bowers. *Integrating Therapeutic and Complementary Nutrition.* Boca Raton, FL: CRC, 2006.

Micozzi, Marc S. *Fundamentals of Complementary and Alternative Medicine.* New York: Saunders, 2010.

Pelletier, Kenneth R. "Western Herbal Medicine: Nature's Green Pharmacy." Chapter 6 in *The Best Alternative Medicine.* New York: Simon and Schuster, 2007.

Physician's Desk Reference. *PDR for Nonprescription Drugs, Dietary Supplements, and Herbs 2009,* 30th ed. New York: PDR, 2008.

Purchon, Nerys. *The Essential Natural Health Bible: The Complete Home Guide to Herbs and Oils, Natural Remedies and Nutrition.* NSW, Australia: Millennium House, 2011.

Therapeutic Research Faculty. *Natural Medicines Comprehensive Database 2007*. Stockton, CA: Natural Medicines Database, 2006.

PERIODICALS

Mischoulon, David, and Maurizio Fava. "Role of S-adenosyl-L-methionine in the Treatment of Depression: A Review of the Evidence." *American Journal of Clinical Nutrition* 76, no. 5 (November 2002): 1158S–61S. http://www.ajcn.org/content/76/5/1158S.full (accessed September 8, 2001).

Nelson, J. Craig. "S-Adenosyl Methionine (SAMe) Augmentation in Major Depressive Disorder." *American Journal of Psychiatry* 167 (August 2010): 889–91.

Rucklidge, J. J., J. Johnstone, and B. J. Kaplan. "Nutrient Supplementation Approaches in the Treatment of ADHD." *Expert Review of Neurotherapeutics* 9, no. 4 (2009): 461–76.

Ryan, Susan, and Karolyn A. Gazella. "Evaluation of S-Adenosyl-L-Methionine (SAMe) as Primary or Adjuvant Treatment of Depression." *Natural Medicine Journal* 3, no. 1 (January 2011): 8–11. http://naturalmedicine journal.com/article_content.asp?article=9 (accessed September 8, 2011).

WEBSITES

MedlinePlus. "SAMe." National Institutes of Health. Last updated March 5, 2011. http://www.nlm.nih.gov/medlineplus/druginfo/natural/786.html (accessed September 8, 2011).

St. John, Don. "S-Adenosyl-L-Methionine (SAMe)." University of Iowa Hospitals and Clinics. Last updated January 31, 2000. http://www.uihealthcare.com/topics/medicalde-partments/psychiatry/medications/same.html (accessed September 8, 2011).

ORGANIZATIONS

American Botanical Council, 6200 Manor Rd., Austin, TX, 78723, (512) 926-4900, Fax: (512) 926-2345, abc@herbalram.org, http://abc.herbalgram.org.

American Psychiatric Association, 1000 Wilson Blvd., Ste. 1825, Arlington, VA, 22209-3901, (703) 907-7300, apa@psych.org, http://www.psych.org.

National Center for Complementary and Alternative Medicine Clearinghouse, 9000 Rockville Pike, Bethesda, MD, 20892, info@nccam.nih.gov, http://nccam.nih.gov.

Natural Standard, One Davis Square, Somerville, MA, 02144, (617) 591-3300, Fax: (617) 591-3399, http://naturalstandard.com.

Office of Dietary Supplements, National Institutes of Health, 6100 Executive Blvd., Rm. 3B01, MSC 7517, Rockville, MD, 20892-7517, (301) 435-2920, Fax: (301) 480-1845, ods@nih.gov, http://ods.od.nih.gov.

United States Pharmacopoeia, 12601 Twinbrook Pkwy., Rockville, MD, 20852-1790, (800) 227-8772, http://www.usp.org.

Kelly Karpa, RPh, PhD
Laura Jean Cataldo, RN, EdD
William A. Atkins, BB, BS, MBA

SAMSHA *see* **Substance Abuse and Mental Health Services Administration**

Saphris *see* **Asenapine**

Savant syndrome

Definition

Below-normal intelligence combined with a special talent or ability in a specific area.

Demographics

It is estimated that there are about 100 persons worldwide with savant syndrome; about 50 of these would be considered prodigious savants, meaning that their special skill is so outstanding that it would be remarkable even in a non-impaired person.

Description

Children who display savant syndrome have traditionally been referred to as "idiot" or autistic savants, because their IQ is usually between 40 and 70, although some have had IQs as high as 114. The negative connotations of the term "idiot" have led to the disuse of "idiot savant"; because the syndrome is often associated with **autism** or **Asperger syndrome**, the latter term is more frequently heard. Persons with savant syndrome have an exceptional talent or skill in a particular area in spite of their low IQ, such as the ability to process mathematical calculations at a phenomenal speed. These special talents are called "splinter skills." Savant syndrome is not recognized as a medical **diagnosis** and is considered more as a phenomenon that occurs with certain developmental disorders.

Persons with savant syndrome

Well-known persons with savant syndrome include Kim Peek (1951–2009), a man who could recite 12,000 complete books from memory but whose IQ was slightly below average and had motor difficulties. The 1988 movie *Rain Man* is based on Peek's early life. Another well-known person is Hikari Oe (1963–), a Japanese composer with epilepsy, visual impairments, and autism. Alonzo Clemons, an American who lives in Colorado, sculpts animal figures in less than 20 minutes from images of animals that he sees briefly on a television or computer screen, yet he could not tie his shoes or feed himself as a child. Since his debut as a sculptor in 1986, Clemons has been able to live independently in his own apartment and compete in the Special Olympics as a weight lifter.

Causes and symptoms

Persons with savant syndrome have been the subject of much scientific study, although the nature and cause of their seemingly contradictory abilities are not well understood. In addition to its association with autism and Asperger syndrome, savant syndrome has also been reported to develop in some persons who have suffered head injuries, usually those that impair functioning in the left side of the **brain**. Another possibility is that savant syndrome is genetic. Studies of families of children with savant syndrome point to a deletion or other abnormality in the region of chromosome 15q11-13.

Savant syndrome is found more often in males than in females; it affects four to six males for every female. This gender disproportion is explained by the theory that savant syndrome in general is caused by damage to the left hemisphere of the brain being compensated for by neurons in the right hemisphere. In the male fetus, the high levels of circulating testosterone can hinder the growth of neurons in the left hemisphere of the brain, which is slower to develop than the right hemisphere and hence more vulnerable to prenatal influences. CT scans and SPECT imaging of several savants has in fact demonstrated damage to or structural abnormalities in the left hemisphere.

Savant skills occur in a number of different areas, including music, the visual arts, and mathematics. Experts believe that the most common skills demonstrated by savants depend on extraordinary memory. Persons with savant syndrome may be able to memorize extensive amounts of data in such areas as sports statistics, population figures, or historical and biographical data. One particular type of memorization common to persons with savant syndrome is the ability to calculate what day of the week a particular date fell on or will fall on. The first account of savant syndrome was published in a German medical journal in 1783, and described a young man who had this ability. Another type of mathematical skill is lightning calculation. In 1789, the eminent American physician Benjamin Rush described the case of Thomas Fuller, who was of distinctly subnormal intelligence but could calculate with astonishing rapidity. When Rush asked Fuller how many seconds a man had lived who was 70 years, 17 days, and 12 hours old, he took only 90 seconds to come up with the correct answer: 2,210,500,800—even making corrections for the 17 leap years included in the man's life span. Other skills include being able to calculate distances and angles with great precision by sight and being able to accurately gauge the passing of time without a clock or watch.

Prognosis

The prognosis of savant syndrome depends on the extent of the underlying disorder.

Resources

BOOKS

Howe, Michael J. *Fragments of Genius: The Strange Feats of Idiots Savants*. London: Routledge, 1989.

Obler, L.K., and D. Fein, eds. *The Exceptional Brain: Neuropsychology of Talent and Special Abilities*. New York: Guilford Press, 1988.

Treffert, Darold A., MD. *Extraordinary People: Understanding Savant Syndrome*. New York: Backinprint.com, 2006.

PERIODICALS

Fitzgerald, M. "Asperger's Disorder and Mathematicians of Genius." *Journal of Autism and Developmental Disorders* 32, no. 1 (February 2002): 59–60.

Newport, G. "How Do They Do It? Insight on Calendar Skills from an Asperger's Savant." *Journal of Autism and Developmental Disorders* 36 (February 2006): 285–286.

Sacks, Oliver. "A Neurologist's Notebook: Prodigies." *The New Yorker* 70 (January 9, 1995): 44.

Treffert, D.A., and D.D. Christensen. "Inside the Mind of a Savant." *Scientific American* 293 (December 2005): 108–113.

WEBSITES

Treffert, Darold A. "Genius Among Us: Alonzo Clemons." Wisconsin Medical Society. http://www.wisconsinmedicalsociety.org/savant_syndrome/savant_profiles/alonzo_clemons (accessed December 11, 2011).

———. "Islands of Genius." Wisconsin Medical Society. http://www.wisconsinmedicalsociety.org/savant_syndrome/savant_articles/islands (accessed October 26, 2011).

Wisconsin Medical Society. "Savant Syndrome: What's New?" http://www.wisconsinmedicalsociety.org/savant_syndrome/whats_new (accessed October 27, 2011).

ORGANIZATIONS

National Institute of Neurological Disorders and Stroke, PO Box 5801, Bethesda, MD, 20824, (301) 496-5751, TTY: (301) 468-5981, (800) 352-9424, http://www.ninds.nih.gov.

▋Schizoaffective disorder

Definition

Schizoaffective disorder is a mental illness that involves both psychotic symptoms and conspicuous, long-enduring, severe symptoms of mood disorder. The cluster of symptoms experienced by people with schizoaffective disorder can resemble—at various times in its course—bipolar disorder, major depressive episode with psychotic features, or **schizophrenia**.

Demographics

Because of the imprecise nature of the **diagnosis**, the actual rate of brief schizoaffective disorder in adults is unknown. The proportion of schizoaffective disorder identified in persons undergoing treatment for psychiatric disorders has ranged from 2% to almost 30%, depending on the study cited. More females than males (overall) suffer from schizoaffective disorder. However, similar to gender ratios in clinical **depression** and **bipolar disorder**, it seems that there is a much higher ratio of women to men in the depressive subtype, whereas the bipolar subtype has a more even gender distribution. Thus, the higher ratio of women overall is primarily caused by the concentration of women within the depressive subtype of schizoaffective disorder.

Description

The schizoaffective disorder classification is applied when a mental health patient meets diagnostic criteria for both schizophrenia and an affective (mood) disorder—either depression or bipolar disorder. In patients with schizoaffective disorder, mood and psychotic symptoms occur predominantly simultaneously and the mood disturbance is long-lasting. However, periods of experiencing serious psychotic symptoms without serious mood disturbance are also a definitive feature. In bipolar disorder and depression with psychotic features, psychotic symptoms only occur during an active episode of mania or severe clinical depression. Schizoaffective disorder is characterized by periods during which psychotic symptoms are experienced without simultaneous severe mood changes. If the patient is encountered for the first time during such a period of psychotic symptoms in the absence of mood changes, it can appear that the individual has schizophrenia. However, in a person who has psychotic symptoms, the presence of long-standing severe mood disturbance suggests possible schizoaffective disorder if they also have periods of psychotic symptoms without concurrent mood fluctuations.

Schizoaffective disorder is typically identified by a process of lengthy observation and elimination of another diagnostic alternative over a long course of care. Because of the need for longitudinal observation and collection of a wealth of information before an accurate diagnosis is possible, most people with schizoaffective disorder have borne other diagnostic labels prior to the schizoaffective diagnosis (usually bipolar disorder).

Symptoms of schizoaffective disorder vary considerably from patient to patient. **Delusions**, hallucinations, and evidence of disturbances in thinking—as observed in full-blown schizophrenia—may be seen. Similarly, mood fluctuations, such as those observed in major depression or bipolar disorder, may also be seen. These symptoms tend to appear in distinct episodes that impair the individual's ability to function well in daily life. Between episodes, some patients with schizoaffective disorder remain chronically impaired, while others may do quite well in day-to-day living.

Causes and symptoms

Causes

Because clear identification of schizoaffective disorder has traditionally been challenging, scientists have conducted far less research relating to the disorder than studies relating to schizophrenia or mood disorders. However, there are indications that there is a genetic component to the disorder. Close relatives of people with schizoaffective disorder have higher rates of both schizophrenia and mood disorder. The disorder most typically strikes in early adulthood; in some cases, there appears to be a major trigger, or some form of life **stress**, initiating the occurrence of the symptoms. In cases where an identifiable stressor is involved, the person tends to have a better outcome than when such is not the case. Some evidence suggests that the bipolar form of schizoaffective disorder is more treatable and yields better outcomes than the depressive form. Similarly, some clinicians believe that "schizomanic" patients are fundamentally different from "schizodepressed" types; the former are similar to bipolar patients, while the latter are a very heterogeneous group.

RELATIONSHIP TO PERSONALITY DISORDER. People with **personality disorders** appear to be more susceptible to developing psychotic reactions in response to stress. One aspect of personality disorder is that when life becomes more demanding and difficult than can be tolerated, the individual with personality disorder may lapse into a brief psychotic episode. For some individuals, personality disorder may be a predecessor to the development of schizoaffective disorder. Those with preexisting schizotypal, paranoid, schizoid, and borderline personality disorders may be more vulnerable to developing a schizoaffective disorder than the general population.

Symptoms

PSYCHOTIC SYMPTOMS. Both psychotic symptoms and mood disorder symptoms are experienced by individuals with schizoaffective disorder. In schizoaffective disorder, at least two of the major symptoms of **psychosis** are evident in the patient. Classic psychotic symptoms can occur during mood disturbances as well as in periods without extreme mood changes.

Hallucinations, delusions, and strange bodily movements or lack of movements (catatonic behavior) are all psychotic symptoms that may be observed. Additionally, minimal or peculiar speech, lack of drive to act on one's behalf, bizarre or primitive (socially inappropriate or immature) behavior, or near-absent emotionality are also typical psychotic symptoms that may occur. Of course, not all of the possible psychotic symptoms will occur concurrently in a single person with schizoaffective disorder. Importantly, to meet the criteria for the schizoaffective disorder diagnosis, delusions or hallucinations (the most "prototypical" of the psychotic symptoms) must be observed within a fairly lengthy period of time during which there is no form of mood disturbance.

MOOD DISTURBANCE. An extremely important and challenging aspect of schizoaffective disorder is that mood problems are prominent. Patients with schizoaffective disorder frequently experience depressed mood or mania within days of the appearance of psychotic symptoms. During mood episodes, psychotic features are simultaneously evident. The disruption of mood may be depressive, manic, or take the form of a **mixed episode** (which includes both depressive and manic features). If only depressed mood occurs, the individual is described as having the depressive subtype of schizoaffective disorder. If mixed episodes or manic episodes are noted, the patient is identified as having the bipolar form of schizoaffective disorder.

Diagnosis

The ***Diagnostic and Statistical Manual of Mental Disorders*** (*DSM-IV-TR*), produced by the **American Psychiatric Association**, is used by most mental health professionals in North America and Europe to diagnose mental disorders. The *DSM-IV-TR* provides these major criteria for diagnosing schizoaffective disorder:

- At least two of the following symptoms of psychosis present for at least one month: delusions, hallucinations, disorganized speech (strange, peculiar, difficult to comprehend), disorganized (bizarre or childlike) behavior, catatonic behavior, minimal speech (approaching mutism), lack of drive to act on one's own behalf, and a perceived absence of emotions.

- Delusions or hallucinations have occurred for at least two weeks in the absence of prominent mood symptoms.

- During a "substantial portion" of the period of active illness, the individual meets criteria for one of the following mood disturbances: major depressive episode, manic episode, mixed episode.

- The symptoms are not caused by a biologically active entity, such as drugs, alcohol, adverse reaction to a medication, physical injury, or medical illness.

Even using the *DSM-IV-TR* criteria, identification of schizoaffective disorder remains difficult and relatively subjective. An unusual condition in this set of diagnostic criteria is the need to weigh the relative prominence of the mood symptoms and to identify a period of psychotic symptoms that occurred without significant mood disturbance. In the various other psychotic disorders, frequently a low level of depression accompanies the symptoms. When depressive symptoms are the sole form of mood disturbance, only subjective clinical judgment determines whether there has been sufficient severity or duration of that disturbance to merit the possibility of schizoaffective disorder. An additional complication is the cultural relativity of "psychotic symptoms." If the psychotic-like behaviors shown are expected and valued in the person's culture or religion, and these behaviors occur in a traditionally affirming context such as religious services or **meditation**, then schizoaffective disorder would not be diagnosed.

As stated, schizoaffective disorder is typically identified by a process of lengthy observation and elimination of other diagnostic alternatives over a long course of care. A very thorough history of the patient's entire past experiences of psychiatric symptoms, mental health treatments, and response to different kinds of medications that have been taken, helps in determining whether that individual is suffering from schizoaffective disorder. Information about current and past experiences is collected in interviews with the patient and possibly in discussion with the patient's immediate family. Data also may be gathered from earlier medical records with the patient's consent. In order to examine the sufferer's ability to concentrate, to remember, to understand his or her situation realistically, and to think logically, the clinician may use a semistructured interview called a **mental status examination**. The mental status examination is designed to uncover psychotic or demented thought processes. **Psychological assessment** instruments, such as the MMPI-2, the **Rorschach Inkblot Test**, various mood disorder questionnaires, or structured diagnostic interviews, are sometimes used aid in diagnosis.

Treatment

Atypical, novel, or newer-generation antipsychotic medications are very effective in schizoaffective disorder treatment. Examples of atypical or novel antipsychotic medications include **aripiprazole** (Abilify), **risperidone** (Risperdal), **quetiapine** (Seroquel), and **olanzapine**

(Zyprexa). If the patient's psychotic symptoms are acute and accompanied by agitation, a number of different antipsychotics can be used to terminate the flare-up of acute agitated psychosis. Agitation is a state of frantic activity that is often accompanied by anger or marked fearfulness; when in an agitated state, the patient is more likely to cause harm to self or others. In agitated psychotic states, the antipsychotic agent **haloperidol** (Haldol) is often given as an injection, accompanied by other medications that decrease anxiety and slow behavior (often **lorazepam**, also known as Ativan). At this time, no atypical antipsychotics are available in an injectable formulation. If the patient is not extremely agitated, usually a novel antipsychotic is used, given orally daily for a lengthier period of time.

In some cases, the antipsychotic medication is not sufficient to overcome the mood disturbance component of the disorder, although some antipsychotics have thymoleptic (mood-affecting) qualities. Some of the atypical antipsychotic medications are thought to have antidepressant properties, and olanzapine has U.S. Food and Drug Administration (FDA) approval for the management of acute manic psychosis.

If there is little response to novel antipsychotic monotherapy (treatment with only one medication), an additional compound may be given to target the mood disorder aspect of the illness. The choice of which drug should be added to the medication regimen to decrease mood disorder problems is determined by the subtype of schizoaffective disorder shown by the patient. If the patient experiences the bipolar form, a mood stabilizer is added, often **valproic acid** (Depakote), **carbamazepine** (Tegretol), or lithium (Eskalith or Lithobid). In schizoaffective disorder of the bipolar type, if little response occurs to the usual antipsychotic/mood stabilizer combinations, the mental health patient may be prescribed **clozapine** (Clozaril or other generic formulations), which appears to be both antipsychotic and mood-stabilizing. However, because clozapine has the potential (in a very minute number of cases) to cause lethal alterations in the composition of blood, and because its use requires regular monitoring with recurrent blood testing, it is reserved as a "last-resort" therapy. In cases of the depressive subtype, psychiatrists may prescribe an antidepressant such as **citalopram** (Celexa), **venlafaxine** (Effexor), **paroxetine** (Paxil), or **fluoxetine** (Prozac) as an adjunct to the antipsychotic. In certain cases of depressive subtypes, where medications have been ineffective in resolving the extreme mood or where psychosis is so severe as to be life-threatening, **electroconvulsive therapy** may be utilized. Electroconvulsive therapy has also been shown to be effective in major depressive episode with psychotic features.

KEY TERMS

Catatonic behavior or catatonia—Catatonic behavior or catatonia is a descriptive term that describes both possible extremes related to movement. Catalepsy is the motionless aspect of catatonia—in which a person with catalepsy may remain fixed in the same position for hours on end. Rapid or persistently repeated movements, frequent grimacing and strange facial expressions, and unusual gestures are the opposite end of the catatonia phenomenon, involving an excess or distorted extreme of movement.

Delusion—A false belief that is resistant to reason or contrary to actual fact.

Hallucinations—False sensory perceptions. A person experiencing a hallucination may "hear" sounds or "see" people or objects that are not really present. Hallucinations can also affect the senses of smell, touch, and taste.

Psychosis or psychotic symptoms—Disruptions in perceiving reality, thinking logically, and speaking or behaving in normal fashion. Hallucinations, delusions, catatonic behavior, and peculiar speech are all symptoms of psychosis. In *DSM-IV-TR*, psychosis is usually one feature of an overarching disorder, not a disorder in itself (with the exception of the diagnosis of psychosis not otherwise specified).

Medication is not the only treatment avenue. Supportive **psychotherapy** and psychoeducation is helpful to decrease the patient's fears and to inform the patient about the psychiatric illness. **Cognitive-behavioral therapy** aims to modify the thoughts and behaviors that provoke mood disturbance or prevent full involvement and collaboration in therapy for the mental illness. Psychoeducation and cognitive-behavioral therapy are not effective in lieu of biological therapy, but are enhancing, meaningful components of a "whole-person" approach used in concert with medications for the best possible outcomes.

Prognosis

The prognosis for patients with schizoaffective disorder is largely dependent on the form of the disorder and the presence or absence of a trigger. If a major life event is a prompting stressor, or an unusual traumatic experience preceded the occurrence of the disorder, chances for improvement are higher. If there is not a particular triggering event, or if the schizoaffective disorder occurred in an individual with a premorbid personality disorder, the outcome is less likely to be positive. The bipolar form of the disorder may respond better to treatment than the depressive form. Generally, the earlier the disorder is identified and treated and the fewer lapses from medications, the more positive the outcome.

Prevention

Given that this disorder appears to have a strong genetic or biologic aspect, society-wide prevention approaches are not likely to be fruitful. However, a promising strategy is to educate physicians, psychologists, and **social workers**, as well as people at higher risk for the disorder, about the characteristics and treatability of schizoaffective disorder. Such education of care providers and high-risk individuals would foster early identification and treatment. In schizoaffective disorder, similar to schizophrenia and bipolar disorder, better response is predicted the earlier treatment begins. Because severe stressors theoretically can trigger this disorder (in some cases), strong social support and immediate postcrisis counseling for severe stress could possibly prevent the development of the disorder in some susceptible people.

Resources

BOOKS

American Psychiatric Association. *Diagnostic and Statistical Manual of Mental Disorders.* 4th ed., text rev. Washington, DC: American Psychiatric Publishing, 2000.

Graham, George. *The Disordered Mind: An Introduction to Philosophy of Mind and Mental Illness.* New York: Routledge, 2010.

Murray, William H., ed. *Schizoaffective Disorders: New Research.* Hauppauge, NY: Nova Science Publishers, 2006.

Nemitz, Susan Beth. *Living with Schizoaffective Disorder.* Frederick, MD: PublishAmerica, 2009.

Texas, Nami, and Deborah Colleen Rose, ed. *Diagnosis— Schizophrenia and Schizoaffective Disorder: Visions for Tomorrow—The Basics.* Charleston, SC: CreateSpace, 2009.

PERIODICALS

Lipkovich, I., et al. "Predictors of Risk for Relapse in Patients with Schizophrenia or Schizoaffective Disorder During Olanzapine Drug Therapy." *Journal of Psychiatric Research* 41, no. 3–4 (April–June 2007): 305–10.

Maier, Wolfgang. "Do Schizoaffective Disorders Exist at All?" *Acta Psychiatrica Scandinavica* 113, no. 5 (May 2006): 369–71.

Pinninti, Narsimha, et al. "Severity of Self-Reported Depression in Patients with a Schizoaffective Disorder." *Journal of Psychopathology and Behavioral Assessment* 28, no. 3 (September 2006): 165–70.

Risch, S. Craig, et al. "Donepezil Effects on Mood in Patients with Schizophrenia and Schizoaffective Disorder."
International Journal of Neuropsychopharmacology 9, no. 5 (October 2006): 603–5.

Simpson, George M., et al. "A 1-Year Double-Blind Study of 2 Doses of Long-Acting Risperidone in Stable Patients with Schizophrenia or Schizoaffective Disorder." *Journal of Clinical Psychiatry* 67, no. 8 (August 2006): 1194–1203.

Strous, Rael D., et al. "Comparison Between Risperidone, Olanzapine, and Clozapine in the Management of Chronic Schizophrenia: A Naturalistic Prospective 12-Week Observational Study." *Human Psychopharmacology: Clinical and Experimental* 21, no. 4 (June 2006): 235–43.

Vollmer-Larsen, A., et al. "Schizoaffective Disorder—The Reliability of Its Clinical Diagnostic Use." *Acta Psychiatrica Scandinavica* 113, no. 5 (May 2006): 402–7.

ORGANIZATIONS

American Psychiatric Association, 1000 Wilson Blvd., Suite 1825, Arlington, VA, 22209-3901, (703) 907-7300, apa@psych.org, http://www.psych.org.

American Psychological Association, 750 1st St. NE, Washington, DC, 20002-4242, (202) 336-5500; TDD/TTY: (202) 336-6123, (800) 374-2721, http://www.apa.org.

Brain and Behavior Research Foundation, 60 Cutter Mill Rd., Suite 404, Great Neck, NY, 11021, (516) 829-0091, Fax: (516) 487-6930, info@bbrfoundation.org, http://www.bbrfoundation.org.

Mental Health America, 2000 North Beauregard St., 6th Fl., Alexandria, VA, 22311, (703) 684-7722, (800) 969-6642, Fax: (703) 684-5968, http://www1.nmha.org.

National Alliance on Mental Illness, 3803 N Fairfax Dr., Suite 100, Arlington, VA, 22203, (703) 524-7600, Fax: (703) 524-9094, http://www.nami.org.

National Institute of Mental Health, 6001 Executive Blvd., Rm. 8184, MSC 9663, Bethesda, MD, 20892-9663, (301) 433-4513; TTY: (301) 443-8431, (866) 615-6464; TTY: (866) 415-8051, Fax: (301) 443-4279, nimhinfo@nih.gov, http://www.nimh.nih.gov.

Deborah Rosch Eifert, PhD
Martha Sajatovic, PhD
Ruth A. Wienclaw, PhD

Schizoid personality disorder

Definition

Schizoid personality disorder is characterized by a persistent withdrawal from social relationships and lack of emotional responsiveness in most situations. Individuals with schizoid personality disorder tend to be consistently emotionally cold, lack tender feelings for others, be indifferent to feelings of others, and are unable to form close relationships with more than two people. Schizoid personality disorder, however, does not include the characteristic patterns of speech, behavior, and thought associated with **schizotypal personality disorder**. Schizoid personality disorder is sometimes referred to as a "pleasure deficiency" because of the seeming inability of the person affected to experience joyful or pleasurable responses to life situations.

Demographics

Of all **personality disorders**, schizoid personality disorder is the least commonly diagnosed personality disorder in the general population. The prevalence is approximately 1%. It is diagnosed slightly more often in males than in females.

Description

People with schizoid personality disorder have little or no interest in developing close interpersonal relationships. They appear aloof, introverted, and prefer being alone. Those who know them often label them as shy or a "loner." They turn inward in an effort to shut out social relationships. It is common for people with schizoid personality disorder to avoid groups of people or appear disinterested in social situations, even when they involve family. They are often perceived by others as socially inept.

A closely related trait is the absence of emotional expression. Others routinely interpret this apparent void of emotion as disinterest, lack of concern, and insensitivity to the needs of others. The person with schizoid personality disorder has particular difficulty expressing anger or hostility. In the absence of any recognizable emotion, the person portrays a dull demeanor and is easily overlooked by others. People with schizoid personality disorder tend to prefer to be viewed as "invisible," which aids their quest to avoid social contact with others.

People with schizoid personality disorder may be able to hold jobs and meet the expectations of employers if the responsibilities do not require more than minimal interpersonal involvement. People with this disorder may be married, but do not develop close intimate relationships with their spouses and typically show no interest in sexual relations. Their speech is typically slow and monotonous with a lethargic demeanor. Because their tendency is to turn inward, they can easily become preoccupied with their own thoughts to the exclusion of what is happening in their environment. Attempts to communicate may drift into tangents or confusing associations. They are also prone to being absentminded.

Causes and symptoms

Causes

The schizoid personality disorder has its roots in the family of the affected person. These families are typically emotionally reserved, have a high degree of formality, and have a communication style that is aloof and impersonal. Parents usually express inadequate amounts of affection to the child and provide insufficient amounts of emotional stimulus. This lack of stimulus during the first year of life is thought to be largely responsible for the person's disinterest in forming close, meaningful relationships later in life.

People with schizoid personality disorder have learned to imitate the style of interpersonal relationships modeled in their families. In this environment, affected people fail to learn basic communication skills that would enable them to develop relationships and interact effectively with others. Their communication is often vague and fragmented, which others find confusing. Many individuals with schizoid personality disorder feel misunderstood by others.

Symptoms

As presented in the *Diagnostic and Statistical Manual of Mental Disorders.* (*DSM-IV-TR*), the following seven diagnostic criteria are assessed in patients who may be diagnosed with schizoid personality disorder:

- Avoids close relationships. People with this disorder show no interest or enjoyment in developing interpersonal relationships; this may also include family members. They perceive themselves as social misfits and believe they can function best when not dependent on anyone except themselves. They rarely date, often do not marry, and have few, if any, friends.

- Prefers solitude. They prefer and choose activities that they can do by themselves without dependence upon or involvement with others. Examples of activities they might choose include mechanical or abstract tasks such as computer or mathematical games.

- Avoids sex. There is typically little or no interest in having a sexual experience with another person. This would include a spouse if the affected person is married.

- Lacks pleasure. There is an absence of pleasure in most activities. A person with schizoid personality disorder seems unable to experience the full range of emotion accessible to most people.

- Lacks close friends. People affected with this disorder typically do not have the social skills necessary to develop meaningful interpersonal relationships. This results in few ongoing social relationships outside of immediate family members.

• Indifferent to praise or criticism. Neither positive nor negative comments made by others elicit an emotionally expressive reaction. Those with schizoid personality disorder do not appear concerned about what others might think of them. Despite their tendency to turn inward to escape social contact, they practice little introspection.

• Emotional detachment. The emotional style of those with schizoid personality disorder is aloof and perceived by others as distant or "cold." They seem unable or uninterested in expressing empathy and concern for others. Emotions are significantly restricted and most social contacts would describe their personality as very bland, dull, or humorless. The person with schizoid personality disorder rarely picks up on or reciprocates normal communicational cues such as facial expressions, head nods, or smiles.

Diagnosis

The symptoms of schizoid personality disorder may begin in childhood or adolescence, showing as poor peer relationships, a tendency toward self-isolation, and underachievement in school. Children with these tendencies appear socially out of step with peers and often become the object of malicious teasing by their peers, which increases the feelings of isolation and social ineptness they feel.

For a **diagnosis** of schizoid personality disorder to be accurately made, the affected person must exhibit an ongoing avoidance of social relationships and a restricted range of emotion in interpersonal relationships that began by early adulthood. There must also be the presence of at least four of the above-mentioned symptoms.

A common difficulty in diagnosing schizoid personality disorder is distinguishing it from autistic disorder and **Asperger syndrome**, which are characterized by more severe deficits in social skills. Other individuals who would display social habits that might be viewed as "isolating" should not be given the diagnosis of schizoid personality disorder unless the personality traits are inflexible and cause significant obstacles to adequate functioning.

The diagnosis is based on a clinical interview to assess symptomatic behavior. Other assessment tools helpful in diagnosing schizoid personality disorder include:

• Minnesota Multiphasic Personality Inventory (MMPI-2)

• Millon Clinical Multiaxial Inventory (MCMI-II)

• Rorschach Psychodiagnostic Test

• Thematic Apperception Test (TAT)

Treatment

A major goal of treating a patient diagnosed with schizoid personality disorder is to combat the tendencies toward social withdrawal. Strategies should focus on enhancing self-awareness and sensitivity to their relational contacts and environment.

Psychodynamically oriented therapies

A psychodynamic approach would typically not be the first choice of treatment due to the patient's poor ability to explore his or her thoughts, emotions, and behavior. When this treatment is used, it usually centers around building a therapeutic relationship with the patient that can act as a model for use in other relationships.

Cognitive-behavioral therapy

Attempting to cognitively restructure the patient's thoughts can enhance self-insight. Constructive ways of accomplishing this would include concrete assignments such as keeping daily records of problematic behaviors or thoughts. Another helpful method can be teaching social skills through role-playing. This might enable individuals to become more conscious of communication cues given by others and sensitize them to others' needs.

Group therapy

Group therapy may provide patients with a socializing experience that exposes them to feedback from others in a safe, controlled environment. It can also provide a means of learning and practicing social skills in which they are deficient. Since patients usually avoid social contact, timing of group therapy is of particular importance. It is best to first develop a therapeutic relationship between therapist and patient before starting a group therapy treatment.

Family and marital therapy

It is unlikely that a person with schizoid personality disorder will seek **family therapy** or marital therapy. If pursued, it is usually on the initiative of the spouse or other family member. Many people with this disorder do not marry and end up living with and are dependent upon immediate family members. In this case, therapy may be recommended for family members to educate them on aspects of change or ways to facilitate communication. Marital therapy (also called **couples therapy**) may focus on helping the couple to become more involved in each other's lives or improve communication patterns.

KEY TERMS

Asperger syndrome—A condition in which young children experience impaired social interactions and develop limited repetitive patterns of behavior.

Autistic disorder—A developmental disability that appears early in life, in which normal brain development is disrupted and social and communication skills are retarded, sometimes severely.

Millon Clinical Multiaxial Inventory (MCMI-II)—A self-report instrument designed to help clinicians assess *DSM-IV*-related personality disorders and clinical syndromes. It provides insight into 14 personality disorders and 10 clinical syndromes.

Minnesota Multiphasic Personality Inventory (MMPI-2)—A comprehensive assessment tool widely used to diagnose personality disorders.

Rorschach Psychodiagnostic Test—This series of 10 "inkblot" images allows patients to project their interpretations that can be used to diagnose particular disorders.

Thematic Apperception Test (TAT)—A projective test using stories and descriptions of pictures to reveal some of the dominant drives, emotions, sentiments, conflicts, and complexes of a personality.

Medications

Some patients with this disorder show signs of anxiety and **depression** that may prompt the use of medication to counteract these symptoms. In general, to date no definitive medication is used to treat schizoid symptoms.

Prognosis

Because people with schizoid personality disorder seek to be isolated from others, which includes those who might provide treatment, there is only a slight chance that most patients will seek help on their own initiative. Those who do may stop treatment prematurely because of their difficulty maintaining a relationship with the professional or their lack of motivation for change.

If the degree of social impairment is mild, treatment might succeed if its focus is on maintenance of relationships related to the patient's employment. The need for patients to support themselves financially can act as a higher incentive for pursuit of treatment outcomes. Once treatment ends, however, it is highly likely the patient will **relapse** into a lifestyle of social isolation similar to that before treatment.

Prevention

Because schizoid personality disorder originates in the patient's family of origin, the only known preventive measure is a nurturing, emotionally stimulating, and expressive caretaking environment.

Resources

BOOKS

American Psychiatric Association. *Diagnostic and Statistical Manual of Mental Disorders*. 4th ed., text rev. Washington, DC: American Psychiatric Publishing, 2000.

Beck, Aaron T., Arthur Freeman, and Denise D. Davis. *Cognitive Therapy of Personality Disorders*. New York: The Guilford Press, 2006.

Livesley, W. John. *Practical Management of Personality Disorder*. New York: The Guilford Press, 2003.

Millon, Theodore, et al. *Personality Disorders in Modern Life*. 2nd ed. New York: John Wiley and Sons, 2004.

VandenBos, Gary R. ed. *APA Dictionary of Psychology*. Washington, DC: American Psychological Association, 2006.

PERIODICALS

Camisa, Kathryn M., et al. "Personality Traits in Schizophrenia and Related Personality Disorders." *Psychiatry Research* 133, no. 1 (January 2005): 23–33.

Kavaler-Adler, Susan. "Anatomy of Regret: A Developmental View of the Depressive Position and a Critical Turn Toward Love and Creativity in the Transforming Schizoid Personality." *American Journal of Psychoanalysis* 64, no. 1 (March 2004): 39–76.

ORGANIZATIONS

American Psychiatric Association, 1000 Wilson Blvd., Ste. 1825, Arlington, VA, 22209-3901, (703) 907-7300, apa@psych.org, http://www.psych.org.

Gary Gilles, MA
Ruth A. Wienclaw, PhD

Schizophrenia

Definition

Schizophrenia is a disorder or group of disorders whose symptoms include disturbances in thinking, emotional responsiveness, and behavior. The word schizophrenia comes from the Greek roots of *skhizein* ("to split") and *phren* ("mind"). At one time, it was thought that the term schizophrenia was synonymous with a multiple personality disorder (split personality), but this is no longer the case. Generally, this disorder is the most chronic and disabling of the severe mental

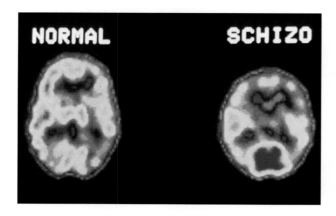

Positron emission tomography (PET) scans comparing a healthy brain (left) with the brain of a person with schizophrenia. (© *Photo Researchers, Inc.*)

disorders and is associated with abnormalities of **brain** structure and function, disorganized speech and behavior, **delusions**, and hallucinations. Schizophrenia is considered a psychotic disorder or a **psychosis**.

Demographics

The World Health Organization (WHO) estimates that schizophrenia affects about 24 million people worldwide. Approximately 2.4–2.7 million Americans are affected by schizophrenia, according to the **National Institute of Mental Health** (NIMH). The incidence of schizophrenia in the United States appears to be uniform across racial and ethnic groups, although there seems to be higher rates within small minority groups in large urban neighborhoods. A study done in the United Kingdom replicated the U.S. findings, with significantly higher rates of schizophrenia among racial minorities living in large cities. The rates of schizophrenia are highest in areas in which these minority groups form the smallest proportion of the local population. The British study included Africans, West Indians of African descent, and Asians.

Schizophrenia is a leading cause of disability around the world; the WHO counts schizophrenia as one of the world's 10 leading causes of disability. Unfortunately, less than half are receiving appropriate and effective care. The situation is worse in developing countries, where about 90% of people with schizophrenia are left untreated. In addition, about 1 in 10 Americans who commit **suicide** have schizophrenia, **depression**, or another mental illness. According to the federal Agency for Healthcare Research and Quality, 70%–80% of people diagnosed with schizophrenia are either unemployed or underemployed (working in jobs well below their actual capabilities). Ten percent of Americans with permanent disabilities have schizophrenia, as well as 20%–30% of the homeless population.

In North America and Western Europe, the gender ratio in schizophrenia is 1.2:1, with males being affected slightly more often than females. There is a significant gender difference in average age at onset; the average for males is between ages 18 and 25 years (late teen years to early 20s), whereas for women there are two peaks: one in the 20s and another in the early 30s. About 15% of all women who develop schizophrenia are diagnosed after age 35. In some women, the first symptoms of the disorder appear postpartum (after giving birth). Many women with schizophrenia are initially misdiagnosed as having depression or **bipolar disorder**, because women with schizophrenia are likely to have more difficulties with emotional regulation than men with the disorder. However, females tend to have higher levels of functioning prior to symptom onset than do males. Although more males acquire schizophrenia in childhood compared to females, this distinction goes away by the time of adolescence with females nearly equal to males in the frequency of the disorder.

In most developed countries, the incidence of schizophrenia appears to be higher among people born in cities than among those born in rural areas. In addition, there appears to be a small generational factor, with the incidence of schizophrenia gradually declining in later-born generations of a family. Paternal age, or the age of the father at conception, may also affect the risk of schizophrenia developing in the offspring, with persons with older fathers being more at risk.

Description

People diagnosed with schizophrenia do not always display the same sets of symptoms; in addition, a given patient's symptoms may change over time. Since the nineteenth century, doctors have recognized different subtypes of the disorder, but no single classification system has gained universal acceptance. Some psychiatrists prefer to speak of schizophrenia as a group or family of disorders ("the schizophrenias") rather than as a single entity.

The symptoms of schizophrenia are usually treatable, but the condition is much more easily treated when diagnosed in its earlier stages and before other functional disabilities arise. Symptoms of schizophrenia can appear at any time after age 6 or 7 years, although onset during adolescence or early adult life is most common. There are a few case studies in the medical literature of schizophrenia in children younger than 5 years, but they are extremely rare. Schizophrenia that appears after age 45 years is considered late-onset schizophrenia, and about 1%–2% of cases are diagnosed in patients over 80 years.

The onset of symptoms in schizophrenia may be either abrupt (sudden) or insidious (gradual). Often, however, the condition goes undetected for two to three years after the onset of diagnosable symptoms, because the symptoms occur in the context of previous cognitive and behavioral problems or diagnoses. In most cases, however, the patient's first psychotic episode is preceded by a prodromal (warning) phase, characterized by a variety of behaviors that may include angry outbursts, withdrawal from social activities, loss of attention to personal hygiene and grooming, anhedonia (loss of enjoyment), and other unusual behaviors. The psychotic episode itself is typically characterized by delusions—false but strongly held beliefs that result from the patient's inability to separate real from unreal events—and hallucinations, which are disturbances of sense perception. Hallucinations can affect any of the senses (sight, smell, taste), but the most common form of **hallucination** in schizophrenia is auditory ("hearing voices"). Autobiographical accounts by people who have recovered from schizophrenia indicate that these hallucinations are frightening and confusing. Patients often find it difficult to concentrate on work, studies, or formerly pleasurable activities because of the constant "static" or "buzz" of hallucinated voices.

There is no "typical" pattern or course of the disorder following the first acute episode. The patient may never have a second psychotic episode; others have occasional episodes over the course of their lives but can lead somewhat normal lives otherwise. About 70% of patients diagnosed with schizophrenia have a second psychotic breakdown within five to seven years after the first one. Some patients remain chronically ill; of these, some remain at a fairly stable level while others grow steadily worse and become severely disabled.

Subtypes of schizophrenia

The revised fourth edition of the *Diagnostic and Statistical Manual of Mental Disorders* (*DSM-IV-TR*), the handbook used by medical professionals in diagnosing mental disorders, specifies five subtypes of schizophrenia:

• Paranoid type. The central feature of this subtype is the presence of auditory hallucinations or delusions alongside relatively unaffected mood and cognitive functions. The patient's delusions usually involve persecution, grandiosity, or both. About a third of schizophrenias diagnosed in the United States belong to this subtype.

• Disorganized type. The core features of this subtype include disorganized speech, disorganized behavior, and flat or inappropriate affect. The person may lose the ability to perform most activities of daily living and may also make faces or display other oddities of behavior. This type of schizophrenia was formerly called "hebephrenic" (derived from the Greek word for

puberty), because some of the patients' actions resemble adolescent behaviors.

• Catatonic type. Catatonia refers to disturbances of movement, whether remaining motionless for long periods of time or excessive and purposeless movement. The absence of movement may take the form of catalepsy, which is a condition in which the patient's body has a kind of waxy flexibility and can be repositioned by others, but where the patient will not initiate the movement, or negativism, a form of postural rigidity in which the patient resists being moved by others. A catatonic patient may assume bizarre postures or imitate the movements of other people.

• Undifferentiated type. Patients in this subtype have some of the characteristic symptoms of schizophrenia but do not meet the full criteria for the paranoid, disorganized, or catatonic subtypes.

• Residual type. Patients in this category have had at least one psychotic episode and continue to have some negative symptoms of schizophrenia but do not have current psychotic symptoms.

Proposed changes for the fifth edition of the *DSM* (*DSM-5*, 2013) include removing the subtypes from the new edition and changing the classification of schizophrenia to schizophrenia spectrum disorders.

Cultural variables

There appear to be some differences across cultures in the symptoms associated with schizophrenia. The catatonic subtype appears to be more common in non-Western countries than in Europe or North America. Other studies indicate that persons diagnosed with schizophrenia in developing countries have a more acute onset of the disorder but better outcomes than patients in industrialized countries.

Association with violence

The connection between schizophrenia and personal assault or violence deserves mention because it is a major factor in the reactions of family members and the general public to a **diagnosis** of schizophrenia and is responsible for some of the **stigma** associated with the disorder. Many patients report that the popular image of a schizophrenic as "a time bomb waiting to explode" is a source of considerable emotional **stress**.

Risk factors for violence in a patient diagnosed with schizophrenia include male gender, age below 30 years, prediagnosis history of violence, paranoid subtype, nonadherence to medication regimen, **homelessness**, and heavy **substance abuse**. On the other hand, it should be noted that most crimes of violence are committed by

E. FULLER TORREY: SCHIZOPHRENIA RESEARCHER

American psychiatrist E. Fuller Torrey (1937–), who has been especially involved in researching and treating schizophrenia, is the author of numerous works of nonfiction dealing with mental illness. In his first major work, *The Mind Game: Witchdoctors and Psychiatrists*, Torrey compares modern psychiatric practices to those of primitive witchdoctors, and in *The Death of Psychiatry* he alleges that modern psychiatry has misdiagnosed maladjustment as mental illness. In the latter work, Torrey advocates support systems for the socially traumatized and recommends neurological help for the truly unbalanced.

Torrey's other writings include *Why Did You Do That? Rainy Day Games for a Post-Industrial Society*, a game-book in which he counsels readers on the importance of recognizing biological, sociological, and psychological factors in assessing human behavior. He also wrote *Surviving Schizophrenia: A Manual for Families, Consumers, and Providers*, in which he supplements a detailed account of the disease's genetic origin and symptoms with testimony from schizophrenics. The fifth edition of *Surviving Schizophrenia* was published in 2006.

In 1998, Torrey founded the Treatment Advocacy Center, a nonprofit organization focused on the proper treatment of severe mental disorders such as schizophrenia. Torrey also serves as a director of the Stanley Medical Research Institute, which conducts research on schizophrenia and bipolar disorder.

people without a diagnosis of schizophrenia, and people with schizophrenia are more likely to be victims of crimes rather than perpetrators.

Causes and symptoms

Causes

Schizophrenia is considered the end result of a combination of genetic, biochemical, developmental, and environmental factors, some of which are still not completely understood. Schizophrenia is often called a "multifactorially inherited" disease, meaning that many factors play roles in its development. There is no known single cause of the disorder.

Researchers have known for many years that first-degree biological relatives (siblings) of patients with schizophrenia have a 10% risk of developing the disorder, as compared with 1% in the general population. If one parent has schizophrenia, his or her child is 10%–15% more likely to also develop the disorder. In larger families, if multiple siblings have schizophrenia, the risk becomes higher for the remaining siblings to develop schizophrenia. The monozygotic (identical) twin of a person with schizophrenia has a 40%–50% risk of developing the disorder; the fact that this risk is not higher, however, indicates that environmental as well as **genetic factors** may be implicated in the development of schizophrenia.

Some specific regions on certain human chromosomes have been linked to schizophrenia, but no one gene can be identified as the direct cause. Scientists believe that the genetic factors underlying schizophrenia vary across different ethnic groups and that the development is likely the result of more than one genetic mutation, making schizophrenia a polygenic disorder. According to the NIMH, persons with schizophrenia have higher rates of rare mutations; hundreds of genes could be involved in the causation of the disorder.

There is some evidence that schizophrenia may be a type of developmental disorder related to the formation of faulty connections between nerve cells during fetal development. In adolescence, the changes in the brain that normally occur during puberty interact with these connections to trigger the symptoms of the disorder. Other researchers have suggested that a difficult childbirth may result in developmental vulnerabilities that eventually lead to schizophrenia; further research is needed on both of these topics.

In 2002, NIMH researchers demonstrated the existence of a connection between two abnormalities of brain functioning in patients with schizophrenia, with the findings published in the January issue of *Nature Neuroscience*. The researchers used radioactive tracers and **positron emission tomography (PET)** to show that reduced activity in a part of the brain called the prefrontal cortex was associated in the patients but not in the control subjects, with abnormally elevated levels of **dopamine** in the striatum. High levels of dopamine are related to the delusions and hallucinations of psychotic episodes in schizophrenia. These findings suggest that treatment directed at the prefrontal cortex might be more effective than present antipsychotic medications, which essentially target dopamine levels without regard to specific areas of the brain.

Certain environmental factors during pregnancy may also be associated with an increased risk of schizophrenia in the offspring. These include the mother's exposure to starvation or famine, influenza during the second trimester of pregnancy, and Rh incompatibility (which involves the Rh antigen, sometimes also called the Rhesus factor) in a second or third pregnancy. Environmental stressors related to home and family life (e.g., parental death or divorce, family dysfunction) or to separation from the family of origin in late adolescence (e.g., going away to college or military training; marriage) may trigger the onset of schizophrenia in individuals with genetic or psychological vulnerabilities.

Some researchers are investigating a possible connection between schizophrenia and viral infections of the hippocampus, a structure in the brain that is associated with memory formation and the human stress response. It is thought that damage to the hippocampus might account for the sensory disturbances found in schizophrenia. Another line of research related to viral causes of schizophrenia concerns a protein deficiency in the brain. The human genome project, a 13-year project that mapped the complete human genome, found that up to 8% of the genome consists of viruses within the deoxyribonucleic acid (DNA), including the borna virus, which supposedly has an association with schizophrenia. The finding remained controversial as of 2011, as further research studies attempted to verify the claim.

The multifactorial and polygenic etiology (origins or causes) of schizophrenia complicates the search for preventive measures against the disorder. It is possible that the human genome mapping will help identify the specific genes that contribute to susceptibility to schizophrenia. The NIMH has compiled the world's largest registry of families affected by schizophrenia in order to attempt to pinpoint specific genes for further study; the institute estimates that at least 60% of the factors that cause schizophrenia may be due to genetic related susceptibility. The NIMH also sponsors a Prevention Research Initiative to identify points in the development of schizophrenia at which patients could benefit from the application of preventive efforts.

Symptoms

The symptoms of schizophrenia are divided into two major categories: **positive symptoms**, which are defined by the *DSM-IV-TR* as excesses or distortions of normal mental functions, and **negative symptoms**, which represent a loss or reduction of normal functioning. Of the two types, the negative symptoms are more difficult to evaluate, because though they account for much of the morbidity (unhealthiness) associated with schizophrenia, they may be influenced by outside factors, such as a concurrent depression or an unstimulating environment.

POSITIVE SYMPTOMS. The positive symptoms of schizophrenia include four so-called "first-rank" or Schneiderian symptoms, named for a German **psychiatrist** who identified them in 1959:

- Delusions. A delusion is a false belief that is resistant to reason or to confrontation with actual facts. The most common form of delusion in patients with schizophrenia is persecutory; the person believes that others—family members, clinical staff, terrorists, etc.—are "out to get" them. Another common delusion is referential, which means that the person interprets objects or occurrences in the environment (a picture on the wall, a song played on the radio, laughter in the corridor, etc.) as being directed at or referring to them.

- Somatic hallucinations. Somatic hallucinations refer to sensations or perceptions about a person's body that have no known medical cause, such as feeling that snakes are crawling around in the intestines or that the eyes are emitting radioactive rays.

- Auditory hallucinations. Auditory hallucinations consist of hearing voices and are the most common form of hallucination in schizophrenia, although visual, tactile, olfactory, and gustatory hallucinations may also occur. Personal accounts of recovery from schizophrenia often mention "the voices" as one of the most frightening aspects of the disorder.

- Thought insertion or withdrawal. These terms refer to the notion that other beings or forces (God, aliens from outer space, the Central Intelligence Agency [CIA], etc.) can put thoughts or ideas into a person's mind or remove them.

Other positive symptoms of schizophrenia include:

- Disorganized speech and thinking. A person with schizophrenia may ramble from one topic to another (derailment or loose associations), give unrelated answers to questions (tangentiality), or say things that cannot be understood because there is no grammatical structure to the language ("word salad" or incoherence).

- Disorganized behavior. This symptom includes such behaviors as agitation, age-inappropriate silliness, inability to maintain personal hygiene, dressing inappropriately for the weather, sexual self-stimulation in public, shouting at people, etc.

- Catatonic behavior. Catatonic behaviors have been described with regard to the catatonic subtype of schizophrenia. This particular symptom is sometimes found in other mental disorders.

NEGATIVE SYMPTOMS. The negative symptoms of schizophrenia include:

• Blunted or flattened affect, or the loss of emotional expressiveness. The person's face may be unresponsive or expressionless, and speech may lack vitality or warmth.

• Alogia, sometimes called poverty of speech. The person has little to say and is not able to expand on their statements. A doctor examining the patient must be able to distinguish between alogia and unwillingness to speak.

• Avolition, or a lack of goal-directed activities. They may sit in one location for long periods of time or show little interest in joining group activities.

• Anhedonia, or the loss of one's capacity for enjoyment or pleasure.

COGNITIVE SYMPTOMS. Persons with schizophrenia also display cognitive deficits, or trouble with tasks involving thought, learning, and memory. Cognitive symptoms of schizophrenia include an inability to apply facts or knowledge when making decisions (**executive function**), lack of concentration, and problems with utilizing new knowledge (working memory).

OTHER SYMPTOMS AND CHARACTERISTICS. Some symptoms and features are not considered diagnostic of schizophrenia, but most patients with the disorder display one or more of the following symptoms or characteristics:

• Dissociative symptoms, particularly depersonalization and derealization.

• Anosognosia. This term originally referred to the inability of stroke patients to recognize their physical disabilities, but it is sometimes used to refer to lack of insight in patients with schizophrenia. Anosognosia is associated with higher rates of noncompliance with treatment, a higher risk of repeated psychotic episodes, and a poorer prognosis for recovery; approximately 50% of individuals with schizophrenia display anosognosia, according to the organization Mental Health America.

• High rates of substance abuse disorders. About 50% of patients diagnosed with schizophrenia meet criteria for substance abuse or dependence. While substance abuse does not cause schizophrenia, it can worsen the symptoms of the disorder. Patients may have particularly bad reactions to amphetamines, cocaine, PCP (phencyclidine, commonly called "angel dust") or marijuana. It is thought that patients with schizophrenia are attracted to drugs of abuse as self-medication

for some of their symptoms. The most common substance abused by patients with schizophrenia is tobacco; 90% of patients are heavy cigarette smokers, compared to 25%–30% in the general adult population. Smoking is a serious problem for people with schizophrenia because it interferes with the effectiveness of their antipsychotic medications as well as increasing their risk of lung cancer and other respiratory diseases.

• High risk of suicide. About 40% of patients with schizophrenia attempt suicide at least once, and 10% eventually complete the act.

• High rates of obsessive-compulsive disorder and panic disorder.

• Downward drift. Downward drift is a sociological term that refers to having lower levels of educational achievement and/or employment than a person's parents.

People with schizophrenia are also more apt to acquire metabolic syndrome, which is a combination of different medical disorders that together increase the risk of developing diabetes, cardiovascular disease, and other related medical maladies. Also known as insulin resistance syndrome, cardiometabolic syndrome, metabolic syndrome X, and Reaven's syndrome, the condition is brought about by a sedentary lifestyle, poor eating habits, and other related factors. Studies have shown that over 30% of people with schizophrenia are also diagnosed with metabolic syndrome. In addition, about 20%–25% of people in the United States are estimated to have metabolic syndrome, with slightly more women having it than men. The risk of developing metabolic syndrome increases with age. Weight gain may also be a side effect of antipsychotic medications.

Diagnosis

There are no symptoms that are unique to schizophrenia and no single symptom that is a diagnostic hallmark of the disorder. In addition, laboratory tests or **imaging studies** are unable to establish or confirm a diagnosis of schizophrenia. The diagnosis is based on a constellation or group of related symptoms and should be completed by a psychiatrist.

As part of the process of diagnosis, the doctor will take a careful medical history and order laboratory tests of the patient's blood or urine in order to rule out general medical conditions or substance abuse disorders that may be accompanied by disturbed behavior. X rays or other imaging studies of the head may also be ordered. Medical conditions to be ruled out include epilepsy, head **trauma**, brain tumor, Cushing's syndrome, Wilson's disease, Huntington's disease, and encephalitis. Drugs of abuse

Antipsychotic medications

Generic name	Trade name	FDA approved age
aripiprazole	Abilify	10+ for bipolar disorder, manic or mixed episodes; 13–17 for schizophrenia and bipolar disorder
chlorpromazine	Thorazine	18+
clozapine	Clozaril	18+
fluoxetine & olanzapine	Symbyax (Prozac & Zyprexa)	18+ (combination antipsychotic and antidepressant)
fluphenazine	(generic only)	18+
haloperidol	Haldol	3+
iloperidone	Fanapt	18+
loxapine	Loxitane	18+
molindone	Moban	18+
olanzapine	Zyprexa	18+; ages 13–17 as second-line treatment for manic or mixed episodes of bipolar disorder and schizophrenia
paliperidone	Invega	18+
perphenazine	(generic only)	18+
pimozide	Orap	12+ for Tourette syndrome
quetiapine	Seroquel	13+ for schizophrenia; 18+ for bipolar disorder; 10–17 for treatment of manic and mixed episodes of bipolar disorder
risperidone	Risperdal	13+ for schizophrenia; 10+ for bipolar mania and mixed episodes; 5–16 for irritability associated with autism
thioridazine	(generic only)	2+
thiothixene	Navane	18+
trifluoperazine	Stelazine	18+
ziprasidone	Geodon	18+

SOURCE: National Institute of Mental Health.

"Alphabetical List of Medications," available online at: http://www.nimh.nih.gov/health/publications/mental-health-medications/alphabetical-list-of-medications.shtml. (Table by PreMediaGlobal. © 2012 Cengage Learning.)

that may cause symptoms resembling schizophrenia include **amphetamines** ("speed"), **cocaine**, and phencyclidine (PCP). In older patients, **dementia** and **delirium** must be ruled out. If the patient has held jobs involving exposure to mercury, polychlorinated biphenyls (PCBs), or other toxic substances, environmental poisoning must also be considered in the differential diagnosis.

The doctor must also rule out other mental disorders that may be accompanied by psychotic symptoms, such as mood disorders; brief psychotic disorders; dissociative disorder not otherwise specified or **dissociative identity disorder**; **delusional disorder**; schizotypal, schizoid, or paranoid **personality disorders**; and **pervasive developmental disorders**. In children, childhood-onset schizophrenia must be distinguished from communication disorders with disorganized speech and from **attention deficit hyperactivity disorder**.

After other organic and mental disorders have been ruled out, it must be determined whether the patient meets the following criteria, as specified by the *DSM*:

• The patient must have two (or more) of the following symptoms during a one-month period: delusions, hallucinations, disorganized speech, disorganized or catatonic behavior, or negative symptoms.

• The patient must exhibit a decline in social, interpersonal, or occupational functioning, including personal hygiene or self-care.

• The symptomatic behavior must last for at least six months.

Treatment

Current treatment of schizophrenia focuses on symptom reduction and **relapse prevention**, since the causes of the disorder have not yet been clearly identified. Unfortunately, not all patients with schizophrenia receive adequate treatment. In addition, many people with schizophrenia do not take their medication, either because they forget, because it does not adequately control their symptoms, because it produces adverse side effects, because they cannot afford it, or because they are not aware of the severity of their condition.

Medications

Antipsychotic medications, namely neuroleptics and atypical antipsychotics, are the primary treatment for schizophrenia. They work to suppress dopamine and **serotonin** activity, respectively, and help to reduce the severity of the positive symptoms. However, they do not help with the negative symptoms or with cognitive problems.

Drug therapy for the disorder is complicated by several factors: the unpredictability of a given patient's response to specific medications, the number of potentially troublesome side effects, the high rate of substance abuse among patients with schizophrenia, and the possibility of drug interactions between antipsychotic medications and **antidepressants** or other medications that may be prescribed for the patient. Therapy is further complicated when patients do not take or do not consistently take their medications. Proper adherence to medication regimens includes always taking the proper dosage within the time frame as determined by the attending medical professional. Medicines may need to be adjusted periodically by the doctor, and the patient should make sure such changes are done without delay.

NEUROLEPTICS. The first antipsychotic medications for schizophrenia were introduced in the 1950s and were known as dopamine antagonists. They are sometimes called neuroleptics and include **haloperidol** (Haldol), **chlorpromazine** (Thorazine), **perphenazine** (Trilafon), and **fluphenazine** (Prolixin). About 40% of patients, however, fail to respond to treatment with these medications. Neuroleptics can control most of the positive symptoms of schizophrenia as well as reduce the frequency and severity of relapses but they have little effect on negative symptoms. In addition, these medications have problematic side effects, ranging from dry mouth, blurry vision, and restlessness (akathisia) to long-term side effects such as **tardive dyskinesia** (TD). TD is a disorder characterized by involuntary movements of the mouth, lips, arms, or legs; it affects about 15%–20% of patients who have been receiving neuroleptic medications over a period of years. Discomfort related to these side effects is one reason why 40% of patients treated with the older antipsychotics do not adhere to their medication regimens.

ATYPICAL ANTIPSYCHOTICS. The atypical antipsychotics, also called second-generation antipsychotics, were introduced in the 1990s. They are sometimes called serotonin dopamine antagonists, or SDAs. These medications include **aripiprazole** (Abilify), **clozapine** (Clozaril), **risperidone** (Risperdal), **quetiapine** (Seroquel), **ziprasidone** (Geodon), and **olanzapine** (Zyprexa). The newer drugs were developed in the hopes that they would be more effective in treating the negative symptoms of schizophrenia and have fewer side effects. Clozapine has been reported to be effective in patients who do not respond to neuroleptics and to reduce the risk of suicide attempts. The atypical antipsychotics, however, do have weight gain as a side effect, and patients taking clozapine must have their blood monitored periodically for signs of agranulocytosis, or a drop in the number of white blood cells.

Prochlorperazine (Buccastem, Compazine, Phenotil, Stemetil, Stemzine), a dopamine receptor antagonist, may be used to treat schizophrenia on a short-term basis when other medicines have not worked effectively. It is not considered to be a first-line treatment for the disorder. The drug works by decreasing abnormal feelings and thoughts within the brain. Prochlorperazine is not approved for the use in treating behavioral problems in older adults with dementia due to an increased risk of death. It should also not be used in anyone younger than two years of age or who weighs less than 20 lb. (9 kg).

The FDA approved lurasidone (Latuda) on October 29, 2010, for the treatment of schizophrenia in adults. **Clinical trials** showed that lurasidone helped to reduce both positive and negative symptoms of schizophrenia. Lurasidone is unique among antipsychotic drugs in that is does not impair learning and memory functions in the patient. The most common side effects in clinical trials included drowsiness or **fatigue**, restlessness, the urge to move (akathisia), nausea, tremors and other abnormal movements, slowed movement, muscle stiffness (Parkinsonism), and agitation. Since lurasidone is a fairly new drug, its general widespread effectiveness and effects of long-term use are not yet known.

The Clinical Antipsychotic Trials of **Intervention** Effectiveness (**CATIE**) Schizophrenia Study was designed to compare the effectiveness of several atypical antipsychotic drugs against the traditional drugs. It was a Phase IV clinical trial funded by the National Institute of Mental Health and coordinated by the University of North Carolina at Chapel Hill. Contrary to expectations, the study found that the new drugs did not perform significantly better than the older drugs. The results of the CATIE study had implications in helping persons with schizophrenia and their physicians make decisions about which other drugs to try, especially when certain medications either did not adequately control symptoms or produced adverse side effects.

OTHER PRESCRIPTION MEDICATIONS. Patients with schizophrenia have a lifetime prevalence of 80% for major depression; others suffer from phobias or other **anxiety disorders**. The doctor may prescribe antidepressants or a short course of **benzodiazepines** along with antipsychotic medications.

Inpatient treatment

Patients with schizophrenia are usually hospitalized during acute psychotic episodes, to prevent harm to themselves or to others and to begin treatment with antipsychotic medications. A patient having a first

KEY TERMS

Attention deficit hyperactivity disorder—A medical condition that primarily occurs within children, which is characterized by the inability to concentrate, along with inappropriate age-related behavior or impulsive behavior.

Brief psychotic disorder—A medical disorder in which the period of psychosis is generally shorter than in other such disorders, is non-reoccurring, and cannot be classified as another related disorder.

Computed tomography—A medical imaging technique in which cross-sectional x rays of the body are compiled to create a three-dimensional image of the body's internal structures.

Delusional disorder—A mental disorder characterized by one or more non-bizarre delusions (such as thinking the police are constantly watching) without the presence of other significant psychopathology.

Dissociative disorder—Medical disorders characterized by disruptions or breakdowns of awareness, identity, memory, and/or perception.

Dissociative identity disorder—Also called multiple personality disorder, a mental condition in which a person displays multiple distinct personalities (alter egos).

DNA (deoxyribonucleic acid)—The hereditary material that makes up genes; influences the development and functioning of the body.

Magnetic resonance imaging—A medical imaging technique that uses electromagnetic radiation, along with a magnetic field, to produce images of the soft tissues within the body, such as the brain and spinal column.

Mood disorder—A medical disorder where a disturbance has occurred in an individual's mood; also called mood affective disorder.

Paranoid personality disorder—A disorder characterized by constant suspicion and mistrust of others.

Pervasive developmental disorder—A disorder involving the lack of development of basic skills of communication and socialization.

Polygenic—A trait or disorder that is determined by several different genes. Most human characteristics, including height, weight, and general body build, are polygenic. Schizophrenia and late-onset AD are considered polygenic disorders.

Positron emission tomography—A medical imaging technique that allows for the scanning of the metabolic activity of the body's organs, which is useful to diagnose cancer, locate brain tumors, and investigate other disorders.

Stigma—A mark or characteristic trait of a disease or disorder generally perceived as negative by society (regardless of fact).

---

psychotic episode is usually given a **computed tomography** (CT) or **magnetic resonance imaging** (MRI) scan to rule out structural brain disease.

Outpatient treatment

In recent years, patients with schizophrenia who have been stabilized on antipsychotic medications have been given psychosocial therapies of various types to assist them with motivation, self-care, and forming relationships with others. In addition, because many patients have had their education or vocational training interrupted by the onset of the disorder, they may be helped by therapies directed toward improving their social functioning and work skills.

Specific outpatient treatments that have been used in patients with schizophrenia include:

• Rehabilitation programs. These programs may offer vocational counseling, job training, problem-solving and money management skills, use of public transportation, and social skills training.

• Cognitive-behavioral therapy and supportive psychotherapy.

• Family psychoeducation. This approach is intended to help family members understand the patient's illness, cope with the problems it creates for other family members, and minimize stresses that may increase the patient's risk of relapse.

• Self-help groups. These groups provide mutual support for family members as well as patients. They can also serve as advocacy groups for better research and treatment, and to protest social stigma and employment discrimination.

• Support groups.

• Group homes or other care facilities. Persons with schizophrenia may be able to live in a residential facility aimed toward helping persons with psychiatric

QUESTIONS TO ASK YOUR DOCTOR

- What medication do you think will be best for me?

- What other treatment options do you recommend for me?

- What symptoms or behaviors are important enough that I should seek immediate treatment?

- Are there any support groups available for my family?

disorders; the patient is able to maintain a sense of independence but is still receiving treatment and has a support system in place.

Prognosis

According to the NIMH, about 20% of patients with schizophrenia recover the full level of functioning that they had before the onset of the disorder, with 10% achieving significant and lasting improvement and 30%–35% showing some improvement with intermittent relapses and some disabilities. The remaining 30% are severely and permanently incapacitated. Even with some improvements, the 80% who do not achieve full recovery of functioning are left with cognitive or intellectual impairments that can lead to problems when reintegrating into mainstream society. Patients may experience difficulty in school, in the workplace, and in forming healthy relationships with others. The majority (60%–70%) of patients with schizophrenia do not marry or have children, and most have very few friends or social contacts. The impact of these social difficulties as well as the stress caused by the symptoms themselves is reflected in the high suicide rate among patients with schizophrenia—about 10% commit suicide within the first ten years after their diagnosis, a rate that is about 20 times higher than that of the general population.

Factors associated with a good prognosis include relatively good functioning prior to the first psychotic episode, a late or sudden onset of illness, female gender, treatment with antipsychotic medications shortly after onset, good **compliance** with treatment, a family history of mood disorders rather than schizophrenia, minimal cognitive impairment, and a diagnosis of paranoid or nondeficit subtype. Factors associated with a poor prognosis include early age of onset, a low level of prior functioning, delayed treatment, heavy substance abuse, noncompliance with treatment, a family history of

schizophrenia, and a diagnosis of disorganized or deficit subtype with many negative symptoms.

Prevention

Schizophrenia cannot be prevented. However, early diagnosis and treatment will help to improve the lives of those afflicted with the disorder. It is especially important to properly diagnose and promptly treat the symptoms of the first episode of schizophrenia. The National Alliance on Mental Illness (NAMI) recently completed the Schizophrenia Patient Outcomes Research (PORT) Team study, which was aimed at determining the most effective treatments for schizophrenia; the results can be found in the *NAMI Consumer and Family Guide to Schizophrenia Treatment.*

Resources

BOOKS

American Psychiatric Association. *Diagnostic and Statistical Manual of Mental Disorders.* 4th ed., text rev. Washington, DC: American Psychiatric Association, 2000.

Beck, Aaron T., et al. *Schizophrenia: Cognitive Therapy, Research, and Therapy.* New York: Guilford Press, 2009.

Beers, Mark H., ed. *Merck Manual of Diagnosis and Therapy.* Rahway, NJ: Merck, 2006.

Lieberman, Jeffrey A., T. Scott Stroup, and Diana O. Perkins, eds. *The American Psychiatric Publishing Textbook of Schizophrenia.* Arlington, VA: American Psychiatric, 2006.

Meyer, Jonathan M., and Henry A. Nasrallah, ed. *Medical Illness and Schizophrenia.* Washington, DC: American Psychiatric, 2009.

Siegel, Steven J., and LaRiena N. Ralph. *Demystifying Schizophrenia for the General Practitioner.* Sudbury, MA: Jones and Bartlett, 2011.

VandenBos, Gary R., ed. *APA Dictionary of Psychology.* Washington, DC: American Psychological Association, 2007.

Williamson, Peter. *Mind, Brain, and Schizophrenia.* Oxford: Oxford University Press, 2006.

PERIODICALS

Meyer-Lindenberg, Andreas. "Reduced Prefrontal Activity Predicts Exaggerated Striatal Dopaminergic Function in Schizophrenia." *Nature Neuroscience* 5, no. 3 (2002): 267–71.

Barrowclough, Christine, et al. "Group Cognitive-Behavioural Therapy for Schizophrenia." *British Journal of Psychiatry* 189, no. 6 (Dec. 2006): 527–32.

Carr, Vaughan J., Terry J. Lewin, and Amanda L. Neil. "What Is the Value of Treating Schizophrenia?" *Australian and New Zealand Journal of Psychiatry* 40, no. 11–12 (Nov. 2006): 963–71.

Gray, Richard, et al. "Adherence Therapy for People with Schizophrenia." *British Journal of Psychiatry* 189, no. 6 (Dec. 2006): 508–14.

Hashimoto, Kenji. "Elevated Glutamine/Glutamate Ratio in Cerebrospinal Fluid of First Episode aAnd Drug Naive Schizophrenic Patients." *BMC Psychiatry* 5, no. 6 (2005).

http://dx.doi.org/10.1186/1471-244X-5-6 (accessed November 5, 2011).

Lawrence, R., T. Bradshaw, and H. Mairs. "Group Cognitive Behavioural Therapy for Schizophrenia: A Systematic Review of the Literature." *Journal of Psychiatric and Mental Health Nursing* 13, no. 6 (Dec. 2006): 673–81.

Lipkovich, I., et al. "Predictors of Risk for Relapse in Patients With Schizophrenia or Schizoaffective Disorder During Olanzapine Drug Therapy." *Journal of Psychiatric Research* 41, no. 3–4 (April–June 2007): 305–10.

Masand, Prakash S., et al. "Polypharmacy in Schizophrenia." *International Journal of Psychiatry in Clinical Practice* 10, no. 4 (Dec. 2006): 258–63.

Yanos, P. T., and R. H. Moos. "Determinants of Functioning and Well-Being Among Individuals With Schizophrenia: An Integrated Model." *Clinical Psychology Review* 27, no. 1 (Jan. 2007): 58–77.

WEBSITES

American Psychiatric Association. "Schizophrenia Spectrum and Other Psychotic Disorders." DSM-5 Development. http://www.dsm5.org/proposedrevision/Pages/Schizophrenia SpectrumandOtherPsychoticDisorders.aspx (accessed July 18, 2011).

"CATIE." University of North Carolina School of Medicine, Department of Psychiatry. http://www.catie.unc.edu (accessed November 5, 2011).

Fox, Stuart. "8 Percent of Human Genome Was Inserted By Virus, and May Cause Schizophrenia." Popular Science (January 7, 2010). http://www.popsci.com/science/article/2010-01/8-percent-human-dna-comes-virus-causes-schizophrenia (accessed July 18, 2011).

MedlinePlus. "Metabolic Syndrome." U.S. National Library of Medicine, National Institutes of Health. http://www.nlm.nih.gov/medlineplus/metabolicsyndrome.html (accessed July 18, 2011).

National Alliance on Mental Illness. "Schizophrenia." http://www.nami.org/Template.cfm?Section=By_Illness&Template=/TaggedPage/TaggedPageDisplay.cfm&TPLID=3&ContentID=10850 (accessed November 5, 2011).

———. "Schizophrenia Patient Outcomes Research Team (PORT)." http://www.nami.org/Template.cfm?Section=eNews_Archive&template=/contentmanagement/contentdisplay.cfm&ContentID=3814 (accessed November 4, 2011).

National Institute of Mental Health. "Clinical Trials: Schizophrenia." http://www.nimh.nih.gov/trials/schizophrenia.shtml (accessed July 18, 2011).

———. "Schizophrenia." http://www.nimh.nih.gov/health/publications/schizophrenia/for-more-information-on-schizophrenia.shtml (accessed July 18, 2011).

Smith, Melinda, and Jeanne Segal. "Schizophrenia Treatment & Recovery." Helpguide.org. http://helpguide.org/mental/schizophrenia_treatment_support.htm (accessed November 5, 2011).

University of Chicago Medical Center. "Schizophrenia." http://www.uchospitals.edu/online-library/content=P00762 (accessed July 18, 2011).

U.S. Food and Drug Administration. "FDA Approves Latuda to Treat Schizophrenia in Adults" (October 28, 2010). http://www.fda.gov/NewsEvents/Newsroom/PressAnnouncements/ucm231512.htm (accessed July 18, 2011).

World Health Organization. "Schizophrenia." http://www.who.int/mental_health/management/schizophrenia/en (accessed July 18, 2011).

ORGANIZATIONS

American Psychiatric Association, 1000 Wilson Blvd., Ste. 1825, Arlington, VA, 22209, (703) 907-7300, apa@psych.org, http://www.psych.org.

Federation of Families for Children's Mental Health, 9605 Medical Center Dr., Rockville, MD, 20850, (240) 403-1901, Fax: (240) 403-1909, ffcmh@ffcmh.org, http://ffcmh.org.

Mental Health America, 2000 N Beauregard St., 6th Fl., Alexandria, VA, 22311, (703) 684-7722, Fax: (703) 684-5968, (800) 969-6642, http://www1.nmha.org.

National Alliance on Mental Illness, 3803 North Fairfax Dr., Ste. 100, Arlington, VA, 22203, (703) 524-7600, Fax: (703) 524-9094, http://www.nami.org.

National Institute of Mental Health, 6001 Executive Blvd., Rm. 8184, MSC 9663, Bethesda, MD, 20892-9663, (301) 443-4513, Fax: (301) 443-4279, (866) 615-6464, nimhinfo@nih.gov, http://www.nimh.nih.gov.

The Stanley Medical Research Institute, Research on Schizophrenia and Bipolar Disorder, info@stanleyresearch.org, http://www.stanleyresearch.org/dnn.

Treatment Advocacy Center, 200 N. Glebe Rd., Ste. 730, Arlington, VA, 22203, (703) 294-6001, Fax: (703) 294-6010, info@treatmentadvocacycenter.org, http://www.treatmentadvocacycenter.org.

Rebecca Frey, PhD
Ruth A. Wienclaw, PhD
William A. Atkins, BB, BS, MBA

Schizophreniform disorder

Definition

Schizophreniform disorder (SFD) is characterized by the same basic features as **diagnosis** is changed to **schizophrenia**.

Demographics

The actual rate of SFD is unknown, mainly because SFD is difficult to measure except in retrospect. In the first few weeks of symptoms, SFD cannot be differentiated from **brief psychotic disorder**. Once the symptoms persist past one month and are identified as SFD, six months or more must pass before one can determine if a mental health consumer had "classic" SFD or was in the early phase of a more chronic mental disorder. Given that a majority of SFD sufferers go on to be diagnosed with schizophrenia, the best inferences about demographics and gender differences in SFD would be drawn from similar information available regarding schizophrenia.

Description

The person experiencing SFD shows at least two psychotic symptoms, which may be either "positive" or "negative." **Positive symptoms** are those that are present but that do not normally occur or which are in excess of what normally occurs. Positive symptoms of **psychosis** include hallucinations, **delusions**, strange bodily movements or frozen movement (catatonic behavior), peculiar speech, and bizarre or primitive (socially inappropriate) behavior. **Negative symptoms** are factors that normally occur but are absent or deficient with the disorder. Various deficiencies in behavior, emotionality, or speech constitute the negative symptoms of psychosis that are observed in some cases of SFD. Negative symptoms of psychosis include avolition, affective flattening, and logia.

Avolition is a lack of effort to act on one's own behalf or to engage in behaviors directed at accomplishing a purpose. Affective flattening or blunted **affect** refers to a decrease or low level of emotion, shown as a wooden quality to one's emotions or a near absence of emotionality. Alogia refers to a disruption in the thought process reflected in the person's speech. One form of alogia is "poverty of speech." Impoverished speech is brief, limited, and terse and generally emerges only in response to questions or prompts rather than flowing spontaneously. An impairment termed "poverty of content" occurs when the information or concepts that the individual is attempting to convey cannot be understood because of limitations in the method of communicating. The meaning behind the phrases is obscured or missing. Typically, in poverty of content, the person's speech, while comprehensible in terms of its orderliness of grammar and vocabulary, does not convey substantial meaning because the phrasing is overly concrete and literal or overly abstract and fanciful.

Among the various positive symptoms of psychosis that can be a part of SFD, delusions are a fairly common. Delusions are strongly held irrational and unrealistic beliefs that are highly resistant to alteration. Even when the person encounters evidence that would invalidate the delusion, the unjustified and improbable belief remains a conviction. Often, delusions are paranoid or persecutory in tone. In these types of delusions, the person is excessively suspicious and continually feels at the mercy of conspirators believed

to be determined to cause harm to the sufferer. However, delusions can also take on other overtones. Some delusions are grandiose, while others may involve elaborate love fantasies (erotomanic delusions). Delusions may involve somatic content, or may revolve around extreme and irrational jealousy.

Peculiar or disorganized speech, catatonic behavior, and bizarre or primitive behavior are all additional positive psychotic symptoms that may occur in SFD. Speech disorganization can involve words blended together into incomprehensible statements, also known as "word salad." In some persons disorganized speech takes the form of echolalia, which is the repetition of another person's exact spoken words, restated either immediately after the initial speaker or after a delay of minutes or hours. Catatonic behavior or **catatonia** involves the presence of one of the possible extremes related to movement. Catalepsy is the motionless end of the catatonic spectrum; in catalepsy, a person may remain unmoving in one fixed position for long periods. The opposite end of the catatonia phenomenon is demonstrated in rapid or persistently repeated movements, recurrent grimacing and odd facial expressions, and contorted or strange gestures. Bizarre or primitive behavior in SFD ranges from childlike behaviors in unsuitable circumstances to unusual practices such as **hoarding** refuse items perceived by the sufferer to be valuable, caching food all over the home, or wandering purposelessly through the streets.

Only rarely would all these various psychotic symptoms be observed simultaneously in one person with SFD. Instead, each individual with SFD has a constellation of symptoms, practices, and thought processes that is unique to that person.

Unlike any other diagnoses offered in the *Diagnostic and Statistical Manual of Mental Disorders* (*DSM-IV-TR*), the SFD diagnosis always includes an indication of the patient's prognosis—the potential outcome for an individual with a particular illness—based on the features observed and the usual course of the illness. If an individual with SFD has several positive prognostic factors, there is a much higher likelihood of complete recovery without **relapse** into psychosis. Such positive prognostic factors include prominent confusion during the illness, rapid (rather than gradual) development of symptoms during a four-week period, good previous interpersonal and goal-oriented functioning, and lack of negative symptoms of psychosis.

Causes and symptoms

Causes

Several views regarding the causes of the disorder have been put forth by researchers and clinicians.

AN EARLY PHASE OF ANOTHER PSYCHIATRIC DISORDER. A number of follow-up studies have examined the relationship between SFD and other disorders such as schizophrenia, **schizoaffective disorder**, and **bipolar disorder**. The majority of these studies have found that between 50% and 75% of persons with SFD eventually develop schizophrenia. Of those persons with a history of SFD who do not subsequently receive a diagnosis of schizophrenia, only a small portion have no further psychiatric disturbance. The other diagnoses that may be observed in persons formerly diagnosed with SFD are schizoaffective disorder or bipolar I disorder.

The most common subsequent diagnosis is schizophrenia, with the next most common being schizoaffective disorder. Because of the high rate of later schizophrenia in SFD sufferers, many clinicians have come to think of SFD as being an initial phase of schizophrenia. It is impossible to identify, during an episode of SFD, whether any one particular case will improve without any relapse into psychotic symptoms, or if the mental health client is actually in the early phase of schizophrenia or schizoaffective disorder. Follow-up studies indicate that being frequently confused during a period of SFD is often associated with gradual complete recovery.

LENGTHY POSTPARTUM PSYCHOSIS. Intense hormonal changes occurring in childbirth and immediately afterward can result in a short-term psychotic disorder often referred to as "postpartum psychosis." When the psychotic symptoms in this condition persist for more than one month but fewer than six months, an SFD diagnosis may be given.

DIATHESIS AND STRESS. "Diathesis" is a medical term meaning that some element of one's physiology makes one particularly prone to develop an illness if exposed to the right conditions. Diathesis is another way of saying there is a personal predisposition to develop a disorder; the predisposition is biologically based and is genetically acquired (inherited in the person's genes). Temporary psychotic reactions may occur in persons who have the diathesis for psychosis, when the individual is placed under marked **stress**. The stress may result from typical life transition experiences such as moving away from home the first time, being widowed, or getting divorced. In some cases, the stressor is more intense or unusual, such as surviving a natural disaster, wartime service, being taken hostage, or surviving a terrorist attack. When the psychotic responses last less than a month, then this reaction is labeled "brief psychotic disorder." Highly susceptible persons may show psychotic symptoms for longer than one month and might be given the SFD diagnosis. If the psychotic symptoms are purely reactive, when the stressor ceases or more support is available, the individual is likely to return to a nonpsychotic mode of functioning. In persons with a strong diathesis or predisposition, the initial psychotic reaction may "tip over" from the category of a brief reaction into a longer-term, persistent psychiatric disorder. The diathesis-stress model is applied not only to SFD, but also to schizophrenia, schizoaffective disorder, and the most severe forms of mood disorders.

CULTURALLY DEFINED DISORDERS. Many cultures have forms of mental disorder, unique to that culture, that would meet criteria for SFD. In culturally defined disorders, a consistent set of features and presumed causes of the syndrome are localized to that community. Such disorders are termed "culture-bound." Examples of culture-bound syndromes that might meet SFD criteria are "amok" (Malaysia), or "locura" (Latino Americans). Amok is a syndrome characterized by brooding, persecutory delusions, and aggressive actions. Locura involves incoherence, agitation, social dysfunction, erratic behavior, and hallucinations.

Symptoms

The *DSM-IV-TR* provides three major criteria for SFD. First, the patient must display at least two persistent positive or negative symptoms of psychosis (delusions; disorganized speech that is strange, peculiar, or difficult to comprehend; disorganized, bizarre, or childlike behavior; catatonic behavior; hallucinations; or negative symptoms). In addition, the symptoms must be manifest for a limited time (i.e., at least one month, but less than six months). Third, the symptoms must not be attributable to biological influences (e.g., drugs, medication, alcohol, physical illness or injury) or another disorder (e.g., schizoaffective disorder or schizophrenia).

Diagnosis

Despite the clarity of the *DSM-IV-TR* criteria, identification of SFD is less than clear-cut. The emphasis on the length of time that symptoms have been evident and the presence or absence of good prognostic factors make SFD one of the most unusually defined of the *DSM-IV-TR* disorders. While duration of symptoms is the major distinction among brief psychotic disorder, SFD, and schizophrenia, it can be difficult to clearly determine the length of time symptoms have existed. An additional complication is that the cultural context in which the "psychotic symptoms" are experienced determines whether the behaviors are viewed as pathological or acceptable. When psychotic-like behaviors are expected to occur normally as part of the person's culture or religion, and when the behaviors occur in a culturally positive context such as a religious service, SFD would not be diagnosed.

Information about current and past experiences is collected in an interview with the client, and possibly in discussion with the client's family. **Psychological assessment** instruments (e.g., Rorschach technique, **Minnesota Multiphasic Personality Inventory**, and mood disorder questionnaires) or structured diagnostic interviews may also be used to aid in the diagnosis.

In addition, part of defining SFD involves examining possible biological influences on the development of the individual's psychotic symptoms. When the psychotic features result from a physical disease, a reaction to medication, or intoxication with drugs or alcohol, then these symptoms are not considered SFD. Also, if hallucinations, delusions, or other psychotic symptoms are experienced solely during episodes of clinical **depression** or mania, the patient is diagnosed with a mood disorder rather than SFD.

Treatment

The main line of treatment for SFD is antipsychotic medication. These medications are often very effective in treating SFD. Mood-stabilizing drugs similar to those used in bipolar disorder may be used if there is little response to other interventions. Postpartum psychosis is also treated with antipsychotics and, possibly, hormones. Supportive therapy and education about mental illness is often valuable. The most useful interventions in culture-bound syndromes are those that are societally prescribed; for example, a sacred ceremony to ease the restless spirits of deceased ancestors might be a usual method of ending the psychotic-like state, in that particular culture.

Prognosis

For the large number of mental health patients with SFD who are later diagnosed with a more chronic form of mental illness, the prognosis is fairly poor. However, when the condition manifests with prominent confusion during the illness, rapid (rather than gradual) development of symptoms during a four-week period, good previous interpersonal and goal-oriented functioning and lack of negative symptoms of psychosis, a full recovery is much more likely.

Prevention

If the SFD is a persistent postpartum psychosis, a prevention option is to avoid having additional children. The physician may anticipate the postpartum problem

---

KEY TERMS

Erotomanic delusions—Erotomanic delusions involve the mistaken conviction that someone is in love with the delusional person. Often, the love object is a public figure of some prominence, such as an actress, rock star, or political figure. David Letterman and Jodie Foster are celebrities who have both been victimized by persons with erotomanic delusions.

Grandiose delusions—Grandiose delusions magnify the person's importance; the delusional person may believe himself or herself to be a famous person, to have magical superpowers, or to be someone in a position of enormous power (such as being the king or president).

Hallucinations—False sensory perceptions. A person experiencing a hallucination may "hear" sounds or "see" people or objects that are not really present. Hallucinations can also affect the senses of smell, touch, and taste.

Psychosis—Severe state that is characterized by loss of contact with reality and deterioration in normal social functioning; examples are schizophrenia and paranoia. Psychosis is usually one feature of an overarching disorder, not a disorder in itself (Plural: psychoses.)

Somatic—Somatic comes from *soma*, the Greek word for body; thus, somatic hallucinations are bodily. Somatic delusions are strongly held but erroneous ideas about the characteristics or functioning of one's body. An example is a mental health client who refuses to eat because of a belief that there is a hole in the stomach that will spill anything consumed into the body cavity, when such is not actually the case.

---

and prescribe an antipsychotic medication regimen to begin immediately after delivery as a preventive measure. Although prevention of psychotic disorders is difficult to accomplish, the earlier treatment begins, the better the outcome. Therefore, efforts are more generally focused on early identification of SFD and other psychotic-spectrum disorders.

Resources

BOOKS

American Psychiatric Association. *Diagnostic and Statistical Manual of Mental Disorders.* 4th ed., text rev. Washington, DC: American Psychiatric Publishing, 2000.

Mueser, Kim T. "Family Intervention for Schizophrenia." In *Innovations in Clinical Practice: Focus on Adults,* edited by Leon VandeCreek. Sarasota, FL: Professional Resource Press/Professional Resource Exchange, 2005.

VandenBos, Gary R., ed. *APA Dictionary of Psychology.* Washington, DC: American Psychological Association, 2006.

PERIODICALS

Norman, Ross M.G., et al. "Early Signs in Schizophrenia Spectrum Disorders." *Journal of Nervous and Mental Disease* 193, no. 1 (January 2005): 17–23.

Deborah Rosch Eifert, PhD
Ruth A. Wienclaw, PhD

Schizotypal personality disorder

Definition

Schizotypal personality disorder is a personality disorder characterized by peculiarities of thought, perception, speech, and behavior. Although schizotypal personality disorder is considered a severe disorder, the symptoms are not severe enough to be classified as schizophrenic.

Demographics

Schizotypal personality disorder appears to occur more frequently in individuals who have an immediate family member with **schizophrenia**. The prevalence of schizotypal personality disorder is approximately 3% of the general population and is believed to occur slightly more often in males.

Symptoms that characterize a typical **diagnosis** of schizotypal personality disorder should be evaluated in the context of the individual's cultural situation, particularly those regarding superstitious or religious beliefs and practices. (Some behaviors that Western cultures may view as psychotic are viewed within the range of normal behavior in other cultures.)

Description

Schizotypal personality disorder is characterized by an ongoing pattern in which the affected person distances him- or herself from social and interpersonal relationships. Affected people typically have acute discomfort when put in circumstances where they must relate to others. These individuals are also prone to cognitive and perceptual distortions and a display a variety of eccentric behaviors that others often find confusing. People with schizotypal personality disorder are more comfortable turning inward, away from others, than learning to have meaningful interpersonal relationships. This preferred isolation contributes to distorted perceptions about how interpersonal relationships are supposed to happen. These individuals remain on the periphery of life and often drift from one aimless activity to another with few, if any, meaningful relationships.

A person with schizotypal personality disorder has odd behaviors, and his or her thoughts are typically viewed by others as eccentric, erratic, and bizarre. They are known on occasion to have brief psychotic episodes. Their speech, while coherent, is marked by a focus on trivial detail. Thought processes of people with schizotypal personality disorder include magical thinking, suspiciousness, and illusions. These thought patterns are believed to be the sufferer's unconscious way of coping with social anxiety. To some extent, these behaviors stem from being socially isolated and having a distorted view of appropriate interpersonal relations.

Causes and symptoms

Causes

Schizotypal personality disorder is believed to stem from the affected person's family of origin. Usually the parents of the affected person were emotionally distant, formal, and displayed confusing parental communication. This **modeling** of remote, unaffectionate relationships is then reenacted in the social relationships encountered in the developing years. The social development of people with schizotypal personality disorder shows that many were also regularly humiliated by their parents, siblings, and peers resulting in significant relational mistrust. Many display low self-esteem, along with self-criticism and self-deprecating behavior. This further contributes to a sense that they are socially incapable of having meaningful interpersonal relationships.

Symptoms

The *Diagnostic and Statistical Manual of Mental Disorders*, the mental health manual, specifies nine diagnostic criteria for schizotypal personality disorder:

• Incorrect interpretations of events. Individuals with schizotypal personality disorder often have difficulty seeing the correct cause and effect of situations and how they affect others. For instance, the schizotypal may misread a simple nonverbal communication cue, such as a frown, as someone being displeased with them, when in reality it may have nothing to do with them. Their perceptions are often distortions of what is really happening externally, but they tend to believe their perceptions more than what others might say or do.

- Odd beliefs or magical thinking. These individuals may be superstitious or preoccupied with the paranormal. They often engage in these behaviors as a desperate means to find some emotional connection with the world they live in. This behavior is seen as a coping mechanism to add meaning in a world devoid of much meaning because of the social isolation these individuals experience.

- Unusual perceptual experiences. These might include having illusions, or attributing a particular event to some mysterious force or person who is not present. Affected people may also feel they have special powers to influence events or predict an event before it happens.

- Odd thinking and speech. People with schizotypal personality disorder may have speech patterns that appear strange in their structure and phrasing. Their ideas are often loosely associated, prone to tangents, or vague in description. Some may verbalize responses by being overly concrete or abstract, and may insert words that serve to confuse rather than clarify a particular situation, yet make sense to the speaker. They are typically unable to have ongoing conversation and tend to talk only about matters that need immediate attention.

- Suspicious or paranoid thoughts. Individuals with schizotypal personality disorder are often suspicious of others and display paranoid tendencies.

- Emotionally inexpressive. Their general social demeanor is to appear aloof and isolated, behaving in a way that communicates they derive little joy from life. Most have an intense fear of being humiliated or rejected, yet repress most of these feelings for protective reasons.

- Eccentric behavior. People with schizotypal personality disorder are often viewed as odd or eccentric due to their unusual mannerisms or unconventional clothing choices. Their personal appearance may look unkempt—they may wear clothes that do not "fit together," clothes that are too small or too large or are noticeably unclean.

- Lack of close friends. Because they lack the skills and confidence to develop meaningful interpersonal relationships, they prefer privacy and isolation. As they withdraw from relationships, they increasingly turn inward to avoid possible social rejection or ridicule. If they do have any ongoing social contact, it is usually restricted to immediate family members.

- Socially anxious. Persons with schizotypal personality disorder are noticeably anxious in social situations, especially with people with whom they are not familiar. They can interact with others when necessary, but prefer to avoid as much interaction as possible because their self-perception is that they do not fit in. Even when exposed to the same group of people over time, their social anxiety does not seem to lessen. In fact, it may progress into distorted perceptions of paranoia involving the people they are in social contact with.

Diagnosis

The symptoms of schizotypal personality disorder may begin showing in childhood or adolescence as a tendency toward solitary pursuit of activities, poor peer relationships, pronounced social anxiety, and under-achievement in school. Other symptoms that may be present during the developmental years are hypersensitivity to criticism or correction, unusual use of language, odd thoughts, or bizarre fantasies. Children with these tendencies appear socially out-of-step with peers and often become the object of malicious teasing by their peers, which increases the feelings of isolation and social ineptness they feel. For a diagnosis of schizotypal personality disorder to be accurately made, there must also be the presence of at least four of the nine diagnostic criteria listed by the *Diagnostic and Statistical Manual of Mental Disorders*.

The symptoms of schizotypal personality disorder can sometimes be confused with the symptoms seen in schizophrenia. The bizarre thinking associated with schizotypal personality disorder can be perceived as a psychotic episode and misdiagnosed. While brief psychotic episodes can occur in the patient with schizotypal personality disorder, the **psychosis** is not as pronounced, frequent, or as intense as in schizophrenia. For an accurate diagnosis of schizotypal personality disorder, the symptoms cannot occur exclusively during the course of schizophrenia or other mood disorder that has psychotic features.

Another common difficulty in diagnosing schizotypal personality disorder is distinguishing it from other the schizoid, avoidant, and paranoid **personality disorders**. Some researchers believe that the schizotypal personality disorder is essentially the same as the schizoid disorder, but many feel there are distinguishing characteristics. Schizoids are deficient in their ability to experience emotion, while people with schizotypal personality disorder are more pronounced in their inability to understand human motivation and communication. While **avoidant**

personality disorder has many of the same symptoms as schizotypal personality disorder, the distinguishing symptom in schizotypal is the presence of behavior that is noticeably eccentric. The schizotypal differs from the paranoid by tangential thinking and eccentric behavior.

The diagnosis of schizotypal personality disorder is based on a clinical interview to assess symptomatic behavior. Other assessment tools helpful in confirming the diagnosis of schizotypal personality disorder include:

• Minnesota Multiphasic Personality Inventory (MMPI-2)
• Millon Clinical Multiaxial Inventory (MCMI-II)
• Rorschach Psychodiagnostic Test
• Thematic Apperception Test (TAT)

Treatment

The patient with schizotypal personality disorder finds it difficult to engage in and remain in treatment. For those higher functioning individuals who seek treatment, the goal will be to help them function more effectively in relationships rather than restructuring their personality.

Psychodynamically oriented therapies

A psychodynamic approach will typically seek to build a therapeutically trusting relationship that attempts to counter the mistrust most people with this disorder intrinsically hold. The hope is that some degree of attachment in a therapeutic relationship could be generalized to other relationships. Offering interpretations about the patient's behavior will not typically be helpful. More highly functioning sufferers who have some capacity for empathy and emotional warmth tend to have better outcomes in psychodynamic approaches to treatment.

Cognitive-behavioral therapy

Cognitive approaches will most likely focus on attempting to identify and alter the content of the thoughts of the person with schizotypal personality disorder. Distortions that occur in both perception and thought processes are addressed. An important foundation for this work is the establishment of a trusting therapeutic relationship. This relaxes some of the social anxiety felt in most interpersonal relationships and allows for some exploration of the thought processes. Constructive ways of accomplishing this might include, among others: communication skills training; the use of videotape feedback to help the affected person perceive his or her behavior and appearance objectively; and practical suggestions about personal hygiene and employment.

Interpersonal therapy

Treatment using an interpersonal approach will allow the individual with schizotypal personality disorder to remain relationally distant while he or she "warms up" to the therapist. Gradually the therapist would hope to engage the patient after becoming "safe" through lack of coercion. The goal is to develop trust in order to help the patient gain insight into the distorted and magical thinking that dominates his/her thought process. New self-talk can be introduced to help orient the individual to reality-based experience. The therapist can mirror this objectivity to the patient.

Group therapy

Group therapy may provide the patient with a socializing experience that exposes them to feedback from others in a safe, controlled environment. It is typically recommended only for patients who do not display severe eccentric or paranoid behavior. Most group members would be uncomfortable with these behavioral displays and it would likely prove destructive to the group dynamic.

Family and marital therapy

It is unlikely that a person with **schizoid personality disorder** will seek family or marital therapy. Many patients do not marry and end up living with and being dependent upon first-degree family members. If they do marry they often have problems centered on insensitivity to their partner's feelings or behavior. Marital therapy (**couples therapy**) may focus on helping the couple to become more involved in each other's lives or improve communication patterns.

Medications

There is considerable research on the use of medications for the treatment of schizotypal personality disorder due to its close symptomatic relationship with schizophrenia. Among the most helpful medications are the antipsychotics that have been shown to control symptoms such as illusions and phobic anxiety, among others. **Amoxapine** (trade name Asendin), is a tricyclic antidepressant with antipsychotic properties, and has been effective in improving schizophrenic-like and depressive symptoms in schizotypal patients. Other **antidepressants** such as **fluoxetine** (Prozac) have also been used successfully to reduce symptoms of anxiety, paranoid thinking, and **depression**.

KEY TERMS

Millon Clinical Multiaxial Inventory (MCMI-II)— A self-report instrument designed to help the clinician assess DSM-IV-related personality disorders and clinical syndromes. It provides insight into 14 personality disorders and 10 clinical syndromes.

Minnesota Multiphasic Personality Inventory (MMPI-2)—A comprehensive assessment tool widely used to diagnosed personality disorders.

Rorschach Psychodiagnostic Test—This series of 10 "inkblot" images allows the patient to project their interpretations which can be used to diagnose particular disorders.

Thematic Apperception Test (TAT)—A projective test using stories and descriptions of pictures to reveal some of the dominant drives, emotions, sentiments, conflicts, and complexes of a personality.

Prognosis

The prognosis for the individual with schizotypal personality disorder is poor due to the ingrained nature of the coping mechanisms already in place. Schizotypal patients who depend heavily on family members or others are likely to regress into a state of **apathy** and further isolation. While some measurable gains can be made with mildly affected individuals, most are not able to alter their ingrained ways of perceiving or interpreting reality. When combined with poor social support structure, most will not enter any type of treatment.

Prevention

Since schizotypal personality disorder originates in the patient's family of origin, the only known preventative measure is a nurturing, emotionally stimulating, and expressive environment.

Resources

BOOKS

American Psychiatric Association. *Diagnostic and Statistical Manual of Mental Disorders*. 4th ed., text rev. Washington, DC: American Psychiatric Publishing, 2000.

Millon, Theodore, et al. *Personality Disorders in Modern Life*. 2nd ed. New York: John Wiley and Sons, 2004.

Silverstein, Marshall L. "Descriptive Psychopathology and Theoretical Viewpoints: Schizoid, Schizotypal,

and Avoidant Personality Disorders." In *Disorders of the Self: A Personality-Guided Approach*. Washington, DC: American Psychological Association, 2007.

VandenBos, Gary R., ed. *APA Dictionary of Psychology*. Washington, DC: American Psychological Association, 2006.

PERIODICALS

Badcock, Johanna C., and Milan Dragovic. "Schizotypal Personality in Mature Adults." *Personality and Individual Differences* 40, no. 1 (January 2006): 77–85.

Harvey, Philip D., et al. "Dual-Task Information Processing in Schizotypal Personality Disorder: Evidence of Impaired Processing Capacity." *Neuropsychology* 20, no. 4 (July 2006): 453–60.

Raine, Adrian. "Schizotypal Personality: Neurodevelopmental and Psychosocial Trajectories." *Annual Review of Clinical Psychology* 2 (2006): 291–326.

Trotman, Hanan, Amanda McMillan, and Elaine Walker. "Cognitive Function and Symptoms in Adolescents with Schizotypal Personality Disorder." *Schizophrenia Bulletin* 32, no. 3 (July 2006): 489–97.

Wuthrich, Viviana M., and Timothy C. Bates. "Confirmatory Factor Analysis of the Three-Factor Structure of the Schizotypal Personality Questionnaire and Chapman Schizotypy Scales." *Journal of Personality Assessment* 87, no. 3 (2006): 292–304.

ORGANIZATIONS

American Psychiatric Association, 1000 Wilson Blvd., Ste. 1825, Arlington, VA, 22209-3901, (703) 907-7300, apa@psych.org, http://www.psych.org.

Gary Gilles, MA
Ruth A. Wienclaw, PhD

Seasonal affective disorder

Definition

Seasonal affective disorder (SAD) is a mood disorder in which major depressive episodes and/or manic episodes occur at predictable times of the year, with depressive episodes typically occurring during the fall and winter months. The term SAD can also be applied to depressive episodes with a seasonal pattern that do not meet the criteria for **major depressive disorder** or a **bipolar disorder** (i.e., subsyndromal). SAD is also sometimes called seasonal mood disorder and seasonal **depression**.

Demographics

SAD is more likely to occur in higher latitudes where there is less sunlight during the fall and winter

KEY TERMS

Bipolar disorder—Formerly called manic-depressive disorder, a mood disorder characterized alternating periods of overconfidence and activity (manic highs) and depressive lows.

Melatonin—A naturally occurring hormone involved in regulating the body's internal clock.

Phototherapy—Also called light therapy, a therapy in which the patient is exposed to a bright light to compensate for reduced exposure to sunlight.

Serotonin—5-Hydroxytryptamine; a substance that occurs throughout the body with numerous effects, including neurotransmission. Inadequate amounts of serotonin are implicated in some forms of depression and obsessive-compulsive disorder.

months. In addition, younger individuals are at higher risk for seasonal depressive episodes than are older persons. In fact, people who are most at risk for developing SAD are those between the ages of 15 to 55 years. Although 60–90% of individuals with a seasonal component to their depressive disorder are women, it is unclear whether this statistic reflects a gender factor specifically for SAD or merely reflects the underlying risks associated with recurrent major depressive disorder. Cases of SAD have been seen in children and adolescents; however, the disorder usually begins when individuals are in their twenties.

Seasonal affective disorder is believed to be relatively common. It is estimated that up to 6% of the population may experience SAD, and up to 20% of Americans may suffer from a mild version of the symptoms (subsyndromal) associated with SAD. One study conducted in the United States and reported in the *New York Times* at the end of 2007 found that in New Hampshire 9.7% of the state's population is affected by SAD, whereas only 1.4% of the population of Florida is affected.

It is not yet known whether a seasonal pattern is more likely in recurrent major depressive disorder or in bipolar disorders. However, the seasonal pattern is more likely to occur in bipolar I disorder (BID) than in bipolar II disorder (BIID).

Description

According to the ***Diagnostic and Statistical Manual of Mental Disorders*** (DSM), published by the **American Psychiatric Association**, a seasonal pattern can exist with major depressive disorder or with major depressive episodes in bipolar I disorder or bipolar II disorder. To be characterized as a seasonal disorder, the onset and remission of the major depressive episodes must occur at characteristic times of year. In most cases of SAD, major depressive episodes occur in the fall and winter months and remit during the spring and summer. Less frequently, some individuals suffer from predictable major depressive episodes during the summer.

Risk factors

Studies have found that women are more likely to be diagnosed with seasonal affective disorder than men; however, men with the disorder are more likely to have severe symptoms. SAD is believed to have a hereditary component, so having a close family member who has been diagnosed with SAD is a significant risk factor for the disorder. SAD is more likely to be diagnosed in young adults than in older adults. Individuals who live in areas far from the equator (at high latitudes) where the duration of sunlight changes substantially during the year are at higher risk for SAD.

SAD can become worse as time goes by, leading to such problems as suicidal thoughts and behaviors; further withdrawal from social activities and society in general; continuing problems at school, home, or at work; and substance and/or alcohol abuse. Such complications from SAD can be corrected with proper **diagnosis** and treatment.

Causes and symptoms

It is not known with certainty what causes SAD. Many theories concerning the origins of SAD link it to irregularities in an individual's biological rhythms. These are triggered by lengthening or shortening of daylight that occurs with the changing seasons. Among these theories, the phase shift hypothesis (PSH) states that SAD patients become depressed in the fall and winter because the later dawn at this time of year causes circadian rhythms to become out of synchronization with respect to clock time and the body's sleep-wake cycle. Specifically, PSH states that SAD is a result of a mismatch between an individual's circadian rhythms related to the sleep-wake cycle and the biological circadian pacemaker in the hypothalamus of the **brain**.

Another theory connects SAD to the body's melatonin levels. The body produces more melatonin at night than during the day, and it helps people feel sleepy at nighttime. There is also more melatonin in the body during winter, when the days are shorter. Some researchers believe that excessive melatonin release during winter causes feelings of drowsiness or depression.

A third theory connects SAD to reduced **serotonin** levels. Serotonin is a neurotransmitter important for the regulation of mood. Reduced levels of sunlight have been shown to be linked to drops in serotonin levels in the brain, which can cause symptoms of depression.

Common symptoms of SAD include:

• anxiety and depression

• moodiness and irritability

• hopelessness

• lack of energy

• difficulty concentrating and coordinating activities

• excessive sleepiness during the day or abnormally prolonged sleep at night (hypersomnia)

• tendency to overeat (hyperphagia), including weight gain and/or craving for carbohydrates

• significant impairment of social and occupational functioning (e.g., lack of interest in social interactions, increased sensitivity to negative reactions from others, or lack of interest in normally enjoyable activities)

Diagnosis

Four criteria must be met for a major depressive disorder, BID, or BIID to be characterized as seasonal. First, there must be a regular relationship between the onset of the depressive episodes and the time of year. For most cases of SAD, depressive episodes occur during the fall and winter seasons. Second, full remission of the depressive episodes (or a change from depression to mania or **hypomania** in the case of bipolar disorders) must also occur at predictable times of the year. Third, the seasonal cycle of onset and remission of major depressive episodes must have occurred within the last two years without any nonseasonal depressive episodes during that time. Fourth, seasonal episodes of depression must occur significantly more frequently than nonseasonal depressive episodes over the course of the person's lifetime.

Other factors used with the four main criteria when diagnosing SAD are sleeping more than usual, being hungry (especially for carbohydrates), and gaining weight—all during periods of SAD. Having a close relative, such as a parent, sister, or brother, with SAD is also a factor used to diagnose the condition.

QUESTIONS TO ASK YOUR DOCTOR

• Is phototherapy an appropriate treatment for me?

• Would the addition of a medication be likely to improve my symptoms?

• What are the side effects?

• Should I seek treatment before I expect my symptoms to appear next year?

• When should I reduce or stop treatment?

During the diagnosis process, it is important to distinguish SAD from depression caused by other factors that may cause depression such as seasonal unemployment or school schedule. In addition, SAD should be distinguished from the so-called holiday blues, a condition not related to circadian rhythms but to such psychosocial factors as increased obligations, expectations that one should be joyous, or early childhood memories or unresolved childhood conflicts.

Treatment

The goal of treatment for SAD is to alleviate the symptoms associated with the disorder. In most cases, the prescribed treatment regimen needs to be followed for the months in which the SAD occurs and can be stopped during the remainder of the year. Many people with SAD can be treated effectively with **light therapy**, although some people may require other therapies or medications as well.

Traditional

The first-line treatment for seasonal affective disorder is phototherapy, also called light therapy, which exposes the patient to bright artificial light to compensate for reduced sunlight in winter. Light therapy uses a device called a light box that contains a set of fluorescent or incandescent lights in front of a reflector. Typically, the patient sits for 30 minutes next to a 10,000-lux box (which is about 50 times brighter than ordinary indoor light) that produces a bright full-spectrum light. (Lux, sometimes abbreviated lx, is a measurement of luminous power per area.) Various wavelengths of light have been tried for the treatment of SAD, and research continued as of 2011 to determine the best possible methods. Light therapy appears to be safe for most people. However, it may be harmful for those with eye diseases. The most common side effects are vision problems such as eyestrain, headaches, irritability, and **insomnia**. In addition, hypomania (elevated or expansive mood, characterized by hyperactivity and inflated self esteem) may occasionally occur.

Counseling, such as **cognitive-behavioral therapy** (CBT), is also helpful in treating the symptoms of SAD. CBT concentrates on an individual's behavioral patterns and thoughts in order to control the symptoms of any medical condition that includes depression and anxiety, such as SAD. It is also useful in controlling such problems as eating disorders, chronic pain, panic disorders, and chronic **fatigue** syndrome.

Drugs

When a major depressive disorder or a bipolar disorder has seasonal characteristics, it may be treated with antidepressant medication. **Fluoxetine** (Prozac) has shown to be as effective as light therapy in controlled **clinical trials**. In 2006, the U.S. Food and Drug Administration (FDA) approved the prescription medication **bupropion** HCl extended release tablets (Wellbutrin XL) for the prevention of SAD. The effectiveness of Wellbutrin XL has been demonstrated in clinical trials with adults having a history of a major depressive disorder occurring in the fall and winter months. Wellbutrin XL, however, is recommended only for individuals whose SAD symptoms meet the criteria for a major depressive disorder. Other **antidepressants** may also be prescribed for SAD.

Alternative

Medical literature also suggests that the over-the-counter compound melatonin may help to alleviate SAD symptoms. Melatonin is a hormone produced by the pineal gland that helps regulate the body's seasonal changes. Research funded by the **National Institute of Mental Health** suggests that a low dose of synthetic or pharmacy-grade melatonin taken in the evening along with exposure to bright light in the morning may be effective in relieving the symptoms of SAD. However, as of 2011, more research was needed to determine the safety and effectiveness of such treatment.

Home remedies

Cases of SAD that do not meet all the criteria for formal diagnosis (subsyndromal cases) may also be improved with phototherapy. Activities such as getting outdoors in the sunshine in the morning or rearranging one's home or office to maximize exposure to sunlight during the day may help mild SAD symptoms. Although a trip to the tropics or other sunny place is also of help in overcoming the effects of SAD, the problem returns once the individual is again exposed to shortened daylight hours.

Prognosis

For cases of subsyndromal SAD, the prognosis for control of symptoms through phototherapy treatment is good. For cases in which SAD is a seasonal characteristic of a major depressive disorder or bipolar disorder, the prognosis is generally the same as for the underlying disorder.

Prevention

There is no known way to prevent SAD. Spending time during waking hours in direct sunlight may help to prevent or reduce symptoms. If an individual has experienced SAD in the past, a doctor or therapist may recommend beginning treatment before the symptoms are expected to occur to help control the symptoms and to minimize the negative effects of the disorder.

Resources

BOOKS

American Psychiatric Association. *Diagnostic and Statistical Manual of Mental Disorders.* 4th ed., text rev. Washington, DC: American Psychiatric Association, 2000.

Dziegielewski, Sophia F. *DSM-IV-TR in Action.* Hoboken, NJ: John Wiley & Sons, 2010.

Partonen, Timo, and Seithikurippu R. Pandi-Perumal, eds. *Seasonal Affective Disorder: Practice and Research,* 2nd ed. New York: Oxford University Press, 2010.

Rohan, Kelly J. *Coping with the Seasons: A Cognitive-Behavioral Approach to Seasonal Affective Disorder.* New York: Oxford University Press, 2009.

Rosenthal, Norman E. *Winter Blues: Everything You Need to Know to Beat Seasonal Affective Disorder.* New York: Guilford Press, 2006.

Smith, Laura L., and Charles H. Elliott. *Seasonal Affective Disorder for Dummies.* Indianapolis, IN: Wiley, 2007.

PERIODICALS

Friedman, Richard A. "Brought on by Darkness, Disorder Needs Light." *New York Times* (December 18, 2007). http://www.nytimes.com/2007/12/18/health/18mind.html (accessed July 27, 2011).

Gill, Jessica M., and Saligan, Leorey N. "Don't Let SAD Get You Down This Season." *Nurse Practitioner* (December 2008): 22–27.

Rankin, Lisa. "Seasonal Affective Order vs. 'Winter Blues.'" *Ohio Nurses Review* 86, no. 1 (January–February 2011):

16. http://www.ohnurses.org/AM/TemplateRedirect.cfm?template=/CM/ContentDisplay.cfm&ContentID=7841 (accessed August 19, 2011).

Rohan, Kelly J., et al. "Winter Depression Recurrence One Year After Cognitive-Behavioral Therapy, Light Therapy, or Combination Treatment." *Behavior Therapy* (September 2009): 225–38.

WEBSITES

Mayo Clinic staff. "Seasonal Affective Disorder (SAD)." MayoClinic.com. http://www.mayoclinic.com/health/seasonal-affective-disorder/DS00195 (accessed July 27, 2011).

MedlinePlus. "Seasonal Affective Disorder." U.S. National Library of Medicine, National Institutes of Health. http://www.nlm.nih.gov/medlineplus/seasonalaffectivedisorder.html (accessed July 27, 2011).

ORGANIZATIONS

Depression and Bipolar Support Alliance, 730 N Franklin St., Ste. 501, Chicago, IL, 60654-7225, (800) 826-3632, Fax: (312) 642-7234, http://www.dbsalliance.org.

Mental Health America, 2000 N Beauregard St., 6th Fl., Alexandria, VA, 22311, (703) 684-7722, (800) 969-6642, Fax: (703) 684-5968, http://www.nmha.org.

National Institute of Mental Health, 6001 Executive Blvd., Rm. 8184, MSC 9663, Bethesda, MD, 20892-9663, (301) 443-4513. TTY (301) 443-8431, (866) 615-6464, TTY (866) 415-8051, Fax: (301) 443-4279, http://www.nimh.nih.gov.

Ruth A. Wienclaw, PhD
Tish Davidson, AM

Sedatives and related disorders

Definition

Sedatives are drugs that depress the central nervous system and produce a calming effect on the body. They are used to relieve anxiety, agitation, or behavioral excitement. When used improperly, sedatives may lead to symptoms of abuse, dependence, and withdrawal. Sedatives are often referred to as "tranquilizers," and the similar classes of sedatives and hypnotics are sometimes referred to as one group: the "sedative-hypnotics."

Demographics

Many people, including about 90% of those who are hospitalized, are given some type of prescription sedative. Of the people who use sedatives, only a few become dependent. People who become dependent usually fall into three categories. Some are drug addicts who use sedatives along with other street drugs. These are usually young people between the ages of 15 and 25. Others are alcoholics who use sedatives to treat chronic anxiety or sleep problems associated with their alcohol dependence. Still others use sedatives under the direction of a doctor to treat long-term pain, anxiety, or sleeplessness. These people may become dependent by increasing the amount of a sedative they take as tolerance develops, without telling their doctor.

Sedative abuse is not a major **addiction** problem with street drug users. Many people who are dependent on sedatives are middle-aged and middle-class people who start taking the drug for a legitimate medical reason. Women may be more at risk than men for developing sedative dependence. Sedative dependence is the most common type of drug addiction among the elderly. Older people do not clear the drug from their bodies as efficiently as younger people and thus may become dependent on lower, therapeutic doses.

Description

Sedatives and similar drugs are available by prescription and have many medical uses. They are used in conjunction with surgery and are prescribed to treat pain, anxiety, panic attacks, **insomnia**, and, in some cases, convulsions. Most people who take prescription sedatives take them responsibly and benefit from their use. Some people misuse these drugs. They may do so unintentionally by increasing their prescribed dose without medical advice. Intentional abusers buy these drugs on the street for recreational use or get them from friends or family members who have prescriptions. Sedatives are not popular street drugs, and when they are used recreationally it is usually in conjunction with other illicit drugs or alcohol. When taken exactly as prescribed, sedatives rarely create major health risks.

A chemically diverse group of drugs are discussed together in this entry because they all appear to work in the body the same way and produce similar problems of abuse, dependence, intoxication, and withdrawal. These drugs work in the **brain** by increasing the amount of the neurotransmitter gamma-aminobutyric acid (GABA). **Neurotransmitters** help to regulate the speed at which nerve impulses travel. When the amount of GABA increases, the speed of nerve transmissions decreases. Thus, these drugs depress the nervous system and cause reduced pain, sleepiness, reduced anxiety, and muscle relaxation.

The most widely prescribed and best-studied sedatives belong to a group called "benzodiazepines." Prescription **benzodiazepines** and their relatives include **alprazolam** (Xanax), **chlordiazepoxide** (Librium), **clonazepam** (Klonopin), **clorazepate** (Tranxene), **diazepam** (Valium), **estazolam** (ProSom), **flurazepam** (Dalmane), halazepam (Paxipam), **lorazepam**, (Ativan), **oxazepam** (Serax), prazepam (Centrax), **quazepam** (Doral), **temazepam** (Restoril), **triazolam** (Halcion). Other drugs that act in a similar manner include the **barbiturates** amobarbital (Amytal), aprobarbital (Alurate), butabarbital (Butisol), phenobarbital, (Nebutal), and secobarbital, (Seconal). In addition, **chloral hydrate** (Notec), ethchlorvynol (Placidyl), glutehimide (Doriden), meprobamate (Miltown, Equanil, Equagesic, Deprol), and **zolpidem** (Ambien) have similar actions. These are meant for short-term use and may cause chemical dependence with prolonged use.

A class of non-benzodiazepine hypnotics for treatment of insomnia are becoming widely popular in the United States. **Zaleplon** (Sonata), zolpidem (Ambien), and eszopiclone (Lunesta) are three such drugs. **Amnesia** and sleepwalking resulting from use of non-benzodiazepine hypnotics to treat **sleep disorders** have been reported. Charges of driving while intoxicated on these drugs, particularly when the patient does not sleep long enough after taking a dose, are a potentially dangerous consequence.

Causes and symptoms

Sedatives and other drugs in this class are physically and sometimes psychologically addicting. People taking sedatives rapidly develop tolerance for the drugs. Tolerance occurs when a larger and larger dose must be taken to produce the same effect. Because sedatives are physically addicting, people with sedative dependence experience physical withdrawal symptoms when these drugs are discontinued.

Sedative abuse occurs when people misuse these drugs but are not addicted to them. Many people who abuse sedatives also use other illicit drugs. They may use sedatives to come down off a **cocaine** high or to enhance the effect of **methadone**, a heroin substitute.

Sedative dependence occurs when there is a physical addiction, when a person actively seeks sedatives (for example, by going to several doctors and getting multiple prescriptions) and continues to use these drugs despite the fact that they cause interpersonal problems and difficulties meeting the responsibilities of daily life.

Sedative intoxication

Sedative intoxication occurs when a person has recently used one of these drugs and shows certain psychosocial symptoms such as hostility or aggression, swings in mood, poor judgment, inability to function in social settings or at work, or inappropriate sexual behavior. Because sedatives depress the central nervous system, physical symptoms include slurred speech, lack of coordination, inattention, impaired memory or "blackouts" and extreme sluggishness, stupor, or coma. Sedative intoxication can appear very similar to alcohol intoxication in its symptoms. Overdoses can be fatal.

Sedative withdrawal

Physical addiction is the main problem with sedative dependence. Sedative withdrawal is similar to alcohol withdrawal. Symptoms of sedative withdrawal are almost the reverse of the symptoms of sedative intoxication. They include:

- increased heart rate
- faster breathing
- elevated blood pressure
- increased body temperature
- sweating
- shaky hands
- inability to sleep
- anxiety
- nausea
- restlessness

About one-quarter of people undergoing sedative withdrawal have **seizures**. If withdrawal is severe, they may also have visual or auditory hallucinations (sedative withdrawal **delirium**). Often, people who experience these more severe symptoms are using additional drugs.

The timeframe for withdrawal symptoms to appear varies depending on the chemical structure of the drug being taken. Withdrawal symptoms can occur hours or days after stopping use. For example, people withdrawing from Valium might not develop withdrawal symptoms for a week and might not have peak symptoms until the second week. Low-level symptoms can linger even longer. Generally, the longer a person takes a drug, and the higher the dose, the more severe the withdrawal symptoms. It is possible to have withdrawal symptoms when a therapeutically prescribed dose is taken for a long time.

Sedative dependence is thought to be able to induce other mental health disorders, although there is some disagreement in the mental health community about how these disorders are defined and classified. Other disorders

KEY TERMS

Anxiety—Can be experienced as a troubled feeling, a sense of dread, fear of the future, or distress over a possible threat to a person's physical or mental well-being.

Anxiolytic—A drug that relieves anxiety.

Hallucinations—Hearing, seeing, or otherwise sensing things that are not real. Hallucinations can result from nervous system abnormalities, mental disorders, or the use of certain drugs.

Insomnia—Waking in the middle of the night and having difficulty returning to sleep, or waking too early in the morning.

Panic attack—A period of intense fear or discomfort with a feeling of doom and a desire to escape. The person may shake, sweat, be short of breath, and experience chest pain.

Seizure—A convulsion, or uncontrolled discharge of nerve cells that may spread to other cells throughout the brain.

that may result from sedative dependence and withdrawal include:

- sedative-induced persisting dementia
- sedative-induced persisting amnestic disorder
- sedative-induced psychotic disorder (with or without hallucinations)
- sedative-induced mood disorder
- sedative-induced anxiety disorder
- sedative-induced sexual dysfunction
- sedative-induced sleep disorder

Diagnosis

Diagnosis of sedative intoxication is made based on recent use of the drug, presence of the symptoms listed above, and presence of the drug in a blood or urine sample. Without a blood or urine test, sedative intoxication can be difficult to distinguish from alcohol intoxication except for the absence of the odor of alcohol. People experiencing sedative intoxication usually remain grounded in reality. However, if they lose touch with reality, they may be diagnosed as having sedative intoxication delirium.

Diagnosis of sedative withdrawal is based on the symptoms listed above. It can be difficult to distinguish from alcohol withdrawal. Withdrawal may occur with or without hallucinations and delirium. Diagnosis depends on whether a person remains grounded in reality during withdrawal.

Diagnosis of other mental disorders induced by sedative dependence requires that the symptoms be in excess of those usually found with sedative intoxication or withdrawal. They cannot be accounted for by other **substance abuse** or another mental or physical disorder.

The fifth edition of the *Diagnostic and Statistical Manual of Mental Disorders*, also known as the *DSM-5*, is due for publication in May 2013. This edition may include proposed changes and revisions to some current diagnostic criteria for psychiatric diagnoses, including combining "Substance Abuse" and "Dependence" into a single disorder, thus modifying "Sedative, Hypnotic, or Anxiolytic Abuse" and "Sedative, Hypnotic, or Anxiolytic Dependence" into one diagnosis of "Sedative, Hypnotic, or Anxiolytic Use Disorder."

Treatment

Treatment depends on how large a dose of sedative the patient is taking, the length of time it has been used, and the patient's individual psychological and physical state.

Physiological treatment

Successful treatment of sedative dependence is based on the idea of gradually decreasing the amount of drug the patient uses in order to keep withdrawal symptoms to a manageable level. This is called a "drug taper." The rate of taper depends on the dependency dose of the drug, the length of time the drug has been taken, a person's individual mental and physical response to drug withdrawal, and any complicating factors such as other substance abuse or other physical or mental illness.

For people dependent on a low dose of sedatives, the current level of use is determined, and then the amount of drug is then reduced by 10 to 25%. If withdrawal symptoms are manageable, reduction is continued on a weekly basis. If withdrawal symptoms are too severe, the patient is stabilized at the lowest dose with manageable symptoms until tapering can be restarted. This gradual reduction of use may take weeks, and the rate must be adjusted to the response of each patient individually.

People dependent on high doses of sedatives are usually hospitalized because of the possibility of life-threatening withdrawal symptoms. A blood or urine test is used to determine the current level of usage. The patient is often switched to an equivalent dose of a different sedative or phenobarbital (a barbiturate) to aid

QUESTIONS TO ASK YOUR DOCTOR

- What risks are associated with abuse of sedative medications?
- What symptoms are associated with sedative dependence?
- Does having sedative dependence and abuse put me at risk for other health conditions?
- Can you recommend any treatment and support groups for me?

in withdrawal while controlling withdrawal symptoms. The tapering process begins, but more gradually than with low-dose dependency. Often, other drugs are given to combat some of the withdrawal symptoms.

Psychological treatment

Cognitive-behavioral therapy (CBT) may be used in conjunction with drug tapering. This type of **talk therapy** aims at two things: to educate patients to recognize and cope with the symptoms of anxiety associated with withdrawal, and to help patients change their behavior in ways that promote coping with **stress**. Patients are taught to mentally talk their way through their anxiety and stress. Some people find **support groups** and journal-keeping to be helpful in their recovery. Recovering from dependency is a slow process, best achieved when a person has a good social support system, patience, and persistence.

Prognosis

The people who have the best chance of becoming sedative-free are those who became dependent through taking long-term therapeutic doses. Although stopping any addiction takes time and work, with a properly managed course of treatment, chances of success are good.

People who abuse multiple street drugs must receive treatment for their multiple drug dependencies. Sedative abuse is low on their list of problems, and the chances of their becoming drug-free are low. Alcoholics also have a difficult time withdrawing from sedatives.

Prevention

The best way to prevent sedative-related disorders is to take these drugs only for the exact length of time, and in the exact amount, prescribed by a doctor.

Resources

BOOKS

American Psychiatric Association. *Diagnostic and Statistical Manual of Mental Disorders.* 4th ed., text rev. Washington, DC: American Psychiatric Association, 2000.

American Psychological Association. *Publication Manual of the American Psychological Association.* 6th ed. Washington, DC: American Psychological Association, 2009.

Erickson, Carlton K, PhD. *Addiction Essentials: The Go-To Guide for Clinicians and Patients.* New York: W. W. Norton & Company, 2011.

PERIODICALS

Compton, Wilson M., et al. "Prevalence, Correlates, and Comorbidity of DSM-IV Antisocial Personality Syndromes and Alcohol and Specific Drug Use Disorders in the United States: Results From the National Epidemiologic Survey on Alcohol and Related Conditions." *Journal of Clinical Psychiatry.* 66, no. 6, Jun. 2005: 677–85.

McCabe, Sean Esteban, and Carol J. Boyd. "Sources of Prescription Drugs for Illicit Use." *Addictive Behaviors.* 30, no. 7, Aug. 2005: 1342–50.

McCabe, Sean Esteban, Christian J. Teter, and Carol J. Boyd. "Medical Use, Illicit Use, and Diversion of Abusable Prescription Drugs." *Journal of American College Health* 54, no. 5, Mar.–Apr. 2006: 269–78.

ORGANIZATIONS

American Psychological Association, 750 First St. NE, Washington, DC, 20003, (202) 336-5500, http://www.apa.org/index.aspx.

National Institute on Drug Abuse, 6001 Executive Blvd., Rm. 5213, Bethesda, MD, 20892, (301) 442-1124; Spanish: (240) 221-4007, information@nida.nih.gov, http://www.nida.nih.gov.

The Partnership at Drugfree.org, 352 Park Ave. S, 9th Fl., New York, NY, 10010, (212) 922-1560, (855) DRUG-FREE (378-4373; helpline), Fax: (212) 922-1570, webmail@drugfree.org, http://www.drugfree.org.

Substance Abuse and Mental Health Services Administration Referral Resource, 1 Choke Cherry Rd., Rockville, MD, 20857, (877) SAMHSA-7 (726-4727), (800) TTY: 487-4889, Fax: (240) 221-4292, SAMHSAInfo@samhsa.hhs.gov, http://www.samhsa.gov.

Tish Davidson, A.M.
Laura Jean Cataldo, RN, Ed.D.

Seizures

Definition

A seizure is a sudden change in behavior characterized by changes in sensory perception (sense of feeling) or motor activity (movement) due to an abnormal firing

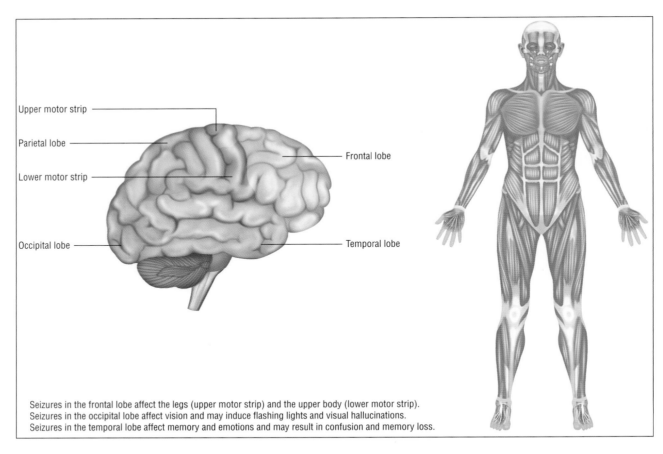

Upper motor strip
Parietal lobe
Lower motor strip
Occipital lobe
Frontal lobe
Temporal lobe

Seizures in the frontal lobe affect the legs (upper motor strip) and the upper body (lower motor strip).
Seizures in the occipital lobe affect vision and may induce flashing lights and visual hallucinations.
Seizures in the temporal lobe affect memory and emotions and may result in confusion and memory loss.

Illustration showing where different types of seizures occur in the brain; the colors of the brain correspond with the body parts affected. *(Illustration by PreMediaGlobal. © 2012 Cengage Learning.)*

of nerve cells in the **brain**. Epilepsy is a condition characterized by recurrent seizures that may include repetitive muscle jerking called convulsions.

Demographics

Epilepsy and seizures affect a reported 3 million—or 1%—of Americans of all ages, although up to 10% of the population may experience at least one seizure during their lives; some of these events are febrile convulsions associated with high fevers in childhood. Every year, about 200,000 new cases are diagnosed and about 300,000 people have their first convulsion. The annual costs of treatment for seizure and epilepsy, in direct and indirect costs, is about $12.5 billion. Men are slightly more likely than women to develop epilepsy, and its prevalence is higher among minority populations in the United States.

Seizures caused by fever have a recurrence rate of 51% if the attack occurred in the first year of life, whereas recurrence rate is decreased to 25% if the seizure took place during the second year. Approximately 88%

of children who experience seizures caused by fever in the first two years experience recurrence.

About 45 million people worldwide are affected by epilepsy. The incidence is highest among young children (under age 2) and the elderly (over age 65). High-risk groups include people with a previous history of brain injury or lesions; children with intellectual disabilities, cerebral palsy, or both; patients with **Alzheimer's disease** or stroke; and children with at least one parent who has epilepsy.

Description

Seizure disorders and their classification date back to the earliest medical literature accounts in history. In 1964, the Commission on Classification and Terminology of the International League Against Epilepsy (ILAE) devised the first official classification of seizures, which was revised in 1981 and again in 1989. They then proposed to use a diagnostic scheme of five diagnostic levels or axes, rather than a classification scheme, for characterizing seizures. These axes are (1) the events that occur during the seizure;

Anticonvulsant and mood-stabilizing medications

Generic name	Trade name	FDA approved age
carbamazepine	Tegretol	Any age (for seizures)
divalproex sodium (valproic acid)	Depakote	2+ (for seizures)
gabapentin	Neurontin	18+
lamotrigine	Lamictal	18+
lithium carbonate	Eskalith, Lithobid	12+
lithium citrate	(generic only)	12+
oxcarbazepine	Trileptal	4+
topiramate	Topamax	18+

SOURCE: National Institute of Mental Health.

"Alphabetical List of Medications," available online at: http://www.nimh.nih.gov/health/publications/mental-health-medications/alphabetical-list-of-medications.shtml. *(Table by PreMediaGlobal. © 2012 Cengage Learning.)*

(2) the type of seizure, chosen from a list that can include where the seizure localizes in the brain and what stimulates it; (3) the type of epileptic syndrome most closely associated with the seizure; (4) the underlying medical or other causes of the syndrome; and (5) the level of impairment the seizure causes. These are proposed recommendations that are still under discussion.

The ILAE classification, meanwhile, is accepted worldwide and is based on electroencephalographic (EEG) studies. Based on this system, seizures can be classified as either focal or generalized. Each of these categories can also be further subdivided.

Focal seizures

A focal (partial) seizure develops when a limited, confined population of nerve cells fire their impulses abnormally on one hemisphere of the brain. (The brain has two portions or cerebral hemispheres—the right and left hemispheres.) Focal seizures are divided into simple or complex based on the level of consciousness (wakefulness) during an attack. Simple partial seizures occur in patients who are conscious, whereas complex partial seizures demonstrate impaired levels of consciousness.

Generalized seizures

A generalized seizure results from initial abnormal firing of brain nerve cells throughout both the left and right hemispheres. Generalized seizures can be classified as follows:

• Tonic-clonic seizures: This is the most common type among all age groups and is categorized into several phases beginning with vague symptoms that appear hours or days before an attack. These seizures are sometimes called grand mal seizures.

• Tonic seizures: These are typically characterized by a sustained nonvibratory contraction of muscles in the legs and arms. Consciousness is also impaired during these episodes.

• Atonic seizures (also called "drop attacks"): These are characterized by sudden, limp posture and a brief period of unconsciousness, and last for one to two seconds.

• Clonic seizures: These are characterized by a rapid loss of consciousness with loss of muscle tone, tonic spasm, and jerks. The muscles become rigid for about 30 seconds during the tonic phase of the seizure and alternately contract and relax during the clonic phase, which lasts 30–60 seconds.

• Absence seizures: These are subdivided into typical and atypical forms based on duration of attack and level of consciousness. Absence (petit mal) seizures generally begin at about the age of four and stop by the time the child becomes an adolescent. They usually begin with a brief loss of consciousness and last 1–10 seconds. People having petit mal seizures become very quiet and may blink, stare blankly, roll their eyes, or move their lips. A petit mal seizure lasts 15–20 seconds. When it ends, individuals resume whatever they were doing before the seizure began, will not remember the seizure, and may not realize that anything unusual happened. Untreated, petit mal seizures can recur as many as 100 times a day and may progress to grand mal seizures.

• Myoclonic seizures: These are characterized by rapid muscular contractions accompanied with jerks in facial and pelvic muscles.

Subcategories are commonly diagnosed based on electroencephalographic (EEG) results. Terminology for classification in infants and newborns is still controversial.

Causes and symptoms

Causes

Simple partial seizures can be caused by congenital abnormalities (abnormalities present at birth), tumor growths, head **trauma**, **stroke**, and infections in the brain or nearby structures. Generalized tonic-clonic seizures are associated with drug and alcohol abuse, and low levels of blood glucose (blood sugar) and sodium. Certain psychiatric medications, antihistamines, and even antibiotics can precipitate tonic-clonic seizures. Absence seizures are implicated with an abnormal imbalance of certain chemicals in the brain that modulate nerve cell activity (one of these **neurotransmitters** is called gamma-aminobutyric acid or GABA, which functions as an inhibitor). Myoclonic seizures are commonly diagnosed in newborns and children.

Symptoms

Symptoms for the different types of seizures are specific.

Partial seizures

SIMPLE PARTIAL SEIZURES. Multiple signs and symptoms may be present during a single simple partial seizure. These symptoms include specific muscles tensing and then alternately contracting and relaxing, speech arrest, vocalizations, and involuntary turning of the eyes or head. There could be changes in vision, hearing, balance, taste, and smell. Additionally, patients with simple partial seizures may have a sensation in the abdomen, sweating, paleness, flushing, hair follicles standing up (piloerection), and dilated pupils (the dark center in the eye enlarges). Seizures with psychological symptoms include thinking disturbances and hallucinations, or illusions of memory, sound, sight, time, and self-image.

COMPLEX PARTIAL SEIZURES. Complex partial seizures often begin with a motionless stare or arrest of activity; this is followed by a series of involuntary movements, speech disturbances, and eye movements.

Generalized seizures

Generalized seizures have a more complex set of signs and symptoms.

TONIC-CLONIC SEIZURES. Tonic-clonic seizures usually have vague prodromal (pre-attack) symptoms that can start hours or days before a seizure. These symptoms include anxiety, mood changes, irritability, weakness, dizziness, lightheadedness, and changes in appetite. The tonic phases may be preceded with brief (lasting only a few seconds in duration) muscle contractions on both sides of affected muscle groups. The tonic phase typically begins with a brief flexing of trunk muscles, upward movement of the eyes, and pupil dilation. Patients usually emit a characteristic vocalization. This sound is caused by contraction of trunk muscles that forces air from the lungs across spasmodic (abnormally tensed) throat muscles. This is followed by a very short period (10–15 seconds) of general muscle relaxation. The clonic phase consists of muscular contractions with alternating periods of no movements (muscle atonia) that gradually increase duration until abnormal muscular contractions stop. Tonic-clonic seizures end in a final generalized spasm. The affected person can lose consciousness during tonic and clonic phases of seizure.

Tonic-clonic seizures can also produce chemical changes in the body. Patients commonly experience lowered carbon dioxide (hypocarbia) due to breathing alterations, increased blood glucose (blood sugar), and an elevated level of a hormone called prolactin. Once affected people regain consciousness, they are usually weak, and have a headache and muscle pain. Tonic-clonic seizures can cause serious medical problems such as trauma to the head and mouth, fractures in the spinal column, pulmonary edema (water in the lungs), aspiration pneumonia (a pneumonia caused by a foreign body being lodged in the lungs), and sudden death. Attacks are generally one minute in duration.

TONIC SEIZURES. Tonic and atonic seizures have distinct differences but are often present in the same patient. Tonic seizures are characterized by nonvibratory muscle contractions, usually involving flexing of arms and relaxing or flexing of legs. The seizure usually lasts less than 10 seconds but may be as long as one minute. Tonic seizures are usually abrupt and patients lose consciousness. Tonic seizures commonly occur during nonrapid eye movement (nonREM) sleep and drowsiness. Tonic seizures that occur during wakeful states commonly produce physical injuries due to abrupt, unexpected falls.

ATONIC SEIZURES. Atonic seizures, also called "drop attacks," are abrupt, with loss of muscle tone lasting one to two seconds, but with rapid recovery. Consciousness is usually impaired. The rapid loss of muscular tone could be limited to head and neck muscles, resulting in head drop, or it may be more extensive involving muscles for balance, causing unexpected falls with physical injury.

CLONIC SEIZURES. Generalized clonic seizures are rare and seen typically in children with elevated fever. These seizures are characterized by a rapid loss of consciousness, decreased muscle tone, and a generalized spasm that is followed by jerky movements.

ABSENCE SEIZURES. Absence seizures are classified as either typical or atypical. The typical absence seizure is characterized by unresponsiveness and behavioral arrest, abnormal muscular movements of the face and eyelids, and lasts less than 10 seconds. In atypical absence seizures, the affected person is generally more conscious, the seizures begin and end more gradually, and do not exceed 10 seconds in duration.

MYOCLONIC SEIZURES. People with myoclonic seizures commonly exhibit rapid muscular contractions. Myoclonic seizures are seen in newborns and children who have either symptomatic or idiopathic (cause is unknown) epilepsy.

Diagnosis

Patients seeking help for seizures should first undergo an EEG that records brain-wave patterns emitted between nerve cells. Electrodes are placed on the head, sometimes for 24 hours, to monitor brain-wave activity and detect both normal and abnormal impulses. **Imaging**

KEY TERMS

Electroencephalograph (EEG)—An instrument that measures the electrical activity of the brain. The EEG traces the electrical activity in the form of wave patterns onto recording paper. Wave patterns that have sudden spikes or sharp waves strongly suggest seizures. An EEG with a seizure-type wave pattern is called an epileptiform EEG.

Hallucination—False sensory perceptions. A person experiencing a hallucination may "hear" sounds or "see" people or objects that are not really present. Hallucinations can also affect the senses of smell, touch, and taste.

Illusion—A misperception or misinterpretation in the presence of a real external stimulus.

studies such as **magnetic resonance imaging** (MRI) and computerized axial tomography (CAT)—that take still "pictures"—are useful in detecting abnormalities in the temporal lobes (parts of the brain associated with hearing) or for helping diagnose tonic-clonic seizures. A complete blood count (CBC) can be helpful in determining whether a seizure is caused by a neurological infection, which is typically accompanied by high fever. If drugs or toxins in the blood are suspected to be the cause of the seizure(s), blood and urine screening tests for these compounds may be necessary.

Antiseizure medication can be altered by many commonly used medications, such as sulfa drugs, erythromycin, warfarin, and cimetidine. Pregnancy may also decrease serum concentration of antiseizure medications; therefore, frequent monitoring and dose adjustments are vital to maintain appropriate blood concentrations of the antiseizure medication—known as the therapeutic blood concentration. Some medications taken during pregnancy could affect the fetus, and women must discuss with their doctors the costs and benefits of any medication taken during pregnancy.

Diagnosis requires a detailed and accurate history, and a physical examination is important because this may help identify neurological or systemic causes. In cases in which a central nervous system (CNS) infection (e.g., meningitis or encephalitis) is suspected, a lumbar puncture (or spinal tap) can help detect an increase in immune cells (white blood cells) that develop to fight the specific infection. (A lumbar puncture involves removing a small amount of cerebrospinal fluid—the fluid that bathes and nourishes the brain and spinal cord—from the spinal chord by syringe.)

Treatment

Treatment is targeted primarily to:

- assist the patient in adjusting psychologically to the diagnosis and in maintaining as normal a lifestyle as possible.
- reduce or eliminate seizure occurrence.
- avoid side effects of long-term drug treatment.

Simple and complex partial seizures respond to drugs such as **carbamazepine**, **valproic acid** (valproate), phenytoin, **gabapentin**, tiagabine, **lamotrigine**, and topiramate. Tonic-clonic seizures tend to respond to valproate, carbamazepine, phenytoin, and lamotrigine. Absence seizures seem to be sensitive to ethosuximide, valproate, and lamotrigine. Myoclonic seizures can be treated with valproate and **clonazepam**. Tonic seizures seem to respond favorably to valproate, felbamate, and clonazepam.

People treated with a class of medications called **barbiturates** (Mysoline, Mebral, phenobarbital) have adverse cognitive (thinking) effects. These cognitive effects can include decreased general intelligence, attention, memory, problem solving, motor speed, and visual motor functions. The drug phenytoin (Dilantin) can adversely affect speed of response, memory, and attention. Other medications used for treatment of seizures do not have substantial cognitive impairment.

Surgical treatment may be considered when medications fail. Advances in medical sciences and techniques have improved methods of identifying the parts of the brain that generate abnormal discharge of nerve impulses. The most common type of surgery is the extratemporal cortical resection. In this procedure, a small part of the brain responsible for causing the seizures is removed. An option of last resort for people with extreme, uncontrollable seizures is functional hemispherectomy, in which communication between the two hemispheres of the brain is severed. Surgical **intervention** may be considered a feasible treatment option if:

- the site of seizures is identifiable and localized.
- surgery can remove the seizure-generating (epileptogenic) area.
- surgical procedure will not cause damage to nearby areas.

Another treatment approach that has been found to reduce seizures in some children is the ketogenic diet. This diet reduces available glucose in the body, forcing the child's body to turn to fat stores for energy. It is a high-fat diet that results in the person getting about 80% of their calories from fat. No one is exactly sure why this diet, which mimics starvation in the body, works to prevent seizures. It also does not work for every child, and the reasons for that also are unclear.

Prognosis

About 30% of patients with severe seizures (starting in early childhood), continue to have attacks and usually never achieve a remission state. In the United States, the prevalence of treatment-resistant seizures is about one to two per 1,000 people. About 60–70% of people achieve a five-year remission within 10 years of initial diagnosis. Approximately half of these patients become seizure-free. Usually the prognosis is better if seizures can be controlled by one medication, the frequency of seizures decreases, and there is a normal EEG and neurological examination prior to medication cessation.

People affected by seizures have increased death rates compared with the general population. Patients who have seizures of unknown cause have an increased chance of dying due to accidents (primarily drowning). Other causes of seizure-associated death include abnormal heart rhythms, water in the lungs, or heart attack.

Prevention

There are no gold-standard recommendations for prevention because seizures can be caused by **genetic factors**, blood abnormalities, many medications, illicit drugs, infection, neurologic conditions, and other systemic diseases. If a person has had a previous attack or has a genetic propensity, care is advised when receiving medical treatment or if diagnosed with an illness correlated with possible seizure development.

Resources

BOOKS

Goetz, Christopher G. *Textbook of Clinical Neurology.* Philadelphia: W. B. Saunders Company, 2003.

Goldman, Lee, and Andrew I. Schafer, eds. *Goldman's Cecil Medicine,* 24th ed. Philadelphia: Elsevier, 2011.

Goroll, Allan H., and Albert G. Mulley. *Primary Care Medicine.* 6th ed. Philadelphia: Lippincott Williams and Wilkins, 2009.

PERIODICALS

Dodrill, C. R., and C. G. Matthew. "The Role of Neuropsychology in the Assessment and Treatment of Persons with Epilepsy." *American Psychologist* 47, no. 9 (September 1992): 1139–42.

ORGANIZATIONS

Epilepsy Foundation, 8301 Professional Pl., Landover, MD, 20785, (800) 332-1000, Fax: (301) 577-2684, http://www.epilepsyfoundation.org.

International League Against Epilepsy, 342 N Main St., West Hartford, CT, 06117-2507, (860) 586-7547, Fax: (860) 586-7550, http://www.ilae-epilepsy.org.

National Institutes of Health, 9000 Rockville Pike, Bethesda, MD, 20892, (301) 496-4000; TTY: (301) 402-9612, http://www.nih.gov.

Laith Farid Gulli, MD
Alfredo Mori, MD, FACEM
Emily Jane Willingham, PhD

Selective mutism

Definition

Selective mutism is a childhood disorder in which a child does not speak in some social situations although he or she is able to talk normally at other times.

Demographics

Selective mutism is generally considered a rare disorder. It is found in about 1% of patients in mental health settings, but it occurs in only about 0.01% of the general United States population. Some researchers maintain, however, that selective mutism occurs more frequently than these data suggest. There may be many unreported cases of selective mutism that resolve with time and require no **intervention**.

In terms of age grouping, selective mutism may appear at the very beginning of a child's social experience or may begin in later childhood. Some cases have been recorded in which selective mutism does not begin until high school. Onset in late adolescence is unusual, however; the most common age of onset for the disorder is the early elementary school years.

Selective mutism is often associated with **social phobia** in adult life. Children with selective mutism disorder may be more likely as adults to have a high level of social anxiety even if they do not meet the diagnostic criteria for social phobia. The disorder appears to run in families Children whose parents are anxious in social settings, were exceptionally timid as children, or suffered from selective mutism themselves in childhood, are at greater risk for developing selective mutism.

Description

Selective mutism was first described in the 1870s, at which time it was called "aphasia voluntaria." This name shows that the absence of speech was considered to lie under the control of the child's will. In 1934 the disorder began to be called selective mutism, a name that still implied purposefulness on the part of the silent child. In the 1994 edition of the *Diagnostic and Statistical Manual of Mental Disorders* (*DSM-IV*) the disorder was renamed selective mutism. This name is considered preferable because it suggests that the child is mute only in certain situations, without the implication that the child remains silent on purpose.

Selective mutism is characterized by a child's inability to speak in one or more types of social situation, although the child is developmentally advanced to the point that speech is possible. The child speaks proficiently in at least one setting, most often at home with one or both parents, and sometimes with siblings or extended family members. Some children also speak to certain friends or to adults that are not related to them; but this variant of selective mutism is somewhat less common.

The most common place for children to exhibit mute behavior is in the classroom, so that the disorder is often first noticed by teachers. Because of this characteristic, selective mutism is most frequently diagnosed in children of preschool age through second grade. As the expectation of speech becomes more evident, selective mutism can have more pronounced negative effects on academic performance. Children who do not talk in classroom settings or other social situations because the language of instruction is not their first tongue are not considered to have the disorder of selective mutism.

Causes and symptoms

The symptoms of selective mutism are fairly obvious. The child does not talk in one or more social situations in which speech is commonly expected and would facilitate understanding. Some children with selective mutism do not communicate in any way in certain settings, and act generally shy and withdrawn. The disorder is also often associated with crying, clinging to the parent, and other signs of social anxiety. Other children with the disorder, however, may smile, gesture, nod, and even giggle, although they do not talk.

Consensus regarding the most common causes of selective mutism has changed significantly over time. When the disorder was first studied, and for many years thereafter, it was thought to be caused by severe **trauma** in early childhood. Some of these causative traumas were thought to include rape, molestation, incest, severe physical or emotional **abuse**, and similar experiences. In addition,

many researchers attributed selective mutism to family dynamics that included an overprotective mother and an abnormally strict or very distant father. While all of these factors may contribute to selective mutism in certain cases, none of them are considered to be common causes of selective mutism.

Selective mutism is instead frequently attributed to high levels of social anxiety in children and not to traumatic events in their early years. Children with selective mutism have been found to be more timid and shy than most children in social situations; and to exhibit signs of **depression, obsessive-compulsive disorder,** and **anxiety disorders**. Some children have been reported to dislike speaking because they are uncomfortable with the sound of their own voice or because they think their voice sounds abnormal.

Many links have also been found between selective mutism and speech development problems. Language reception problems have also been documented in selectively mute children. Although there is no evidence indicating that selective mutism is the direct result of any of these difficulties in language development, possible connections are being explored.

Diagnosis

The criteria for diagnosing selective mutism disorder given by the *Diagnostic and Statistical Manual of Mental Disorders*, fourth edition, text revision (*DSM-IV-TR*) include the failure to speak in some social situations even though the child may talk at other times. This criterion is not met if the child does not speak at all in any situation.

The child's inability to talk must interfere with the achievement of such relevant goals as schoolwork, play with friends, or communication of needs. In addition, the lack of speech must persist for at least one month. The first month of school should not be included in this measurement because many children are shy and unwilling to talk freely until they feel comfortable with their new teacher, classmates, and surroundings.

Furthermore, the child's lack of speech cannot be attributed to unfamiliarity with the language they must use in school or social settings. The **diagnosis** of selective mutism does not apply to children from immigrant families who may not feel comfortable conversing in a second language. Moreover, the child's inability to talk cannot be attributed to **stuttering** or similar speech disorders, which may make the child uncomfortable because they are aware that their speech sounds different from the speech of their peers. The lack of speech also must not be attributable to **schizophrenia**, **autism**, or other mental health disorders.

The disorder of selective mutism is usually noticed first by parents or teachers of affected children. It is often hard for doctors to diagnose selective mutism because it is unlikely that the child in question will talk to them. Therefore it may be difficult for a general practitioner to assess the existence of any underlying language or developmental problems that may be either causing or exacerbating the disorder. Tests that evaluate mental development without verbal responses from the patient may be used successfully to evaluate children with selective mutism.

There are also ways to test the child's speech development in the situations in which he or she does talk. One method involves interviews with the parents or whomever the child does speak to on a regular basis. This method can be fairly subjective, however. It is more useful for the doctor to obtain a tape or video recording of the child talking in a situation in which he or she feels comfortable. The child's hearing should be checked, as speech problems are often related to hearing disorders. Observing the child at play activities or asking him or her to draw pictures offer other effective ways to determine the child's reactions in social situations.

Treatment

A number of different approaches have been used in attempts to treat selective mutism. Recent opinion has moved away from the idea that it is caused by a trauma, and attempts to treat it have followed accordingly. The factors that are most intensively studied at present are underlying anxiety problems. In the few cases in which an underlying trauma is discovered to be the source of the problem, counseling to help treat the underlying problems is recommended. Treatments of any kind are generally found to be more effective when the family of the child is involved in decisions about his or her treatment.

Behavior modification

Selective mutism can be treated by using a **reinforcement** approach. This method gives positive rewards to the child in the form of praise, treats, privileges, or anything else that the child values. In general rewards are given for speech, and withheld for silence. The use of punishments alongside the rewards is not generally recommended because it would place more **stress** on children who are already severely anxious. The positive reinforcement technique is

> ## KEY TERM
>
> **Stimulus fading**—A form of behavior modification used to treat children with selective mutism, in which goals of gradually increasing difficulty are set for the child.

generally found to be at least partially successful in most cases.

Another technique for modifying behavior in children with selective mutism is known as stimulus fading. This technique sets goals of increasing difficulty for the child to meet. For example, the child might be encouraged to start talking by whispering, then work up gradually to talking at full volume. Alternately, the child could start by talking to one person who is not a family member and gradually add names until he or she feels comfortable talking to more than one person at a time. Stimulus fading has been found to be particularly effective when it is used in conjunction with positive reinforcement techniques.

Treatment with medications

In some cases selective mutism is treatable with medication. **Fluoxetine** (Prozac), which is one of the **selective serotonin reuptake inhibitors (SSRIs)** is the drug that has been studied most often as a treatment for selective mutism. Treatment with medication is more successful in younger children. Overall fluoxetine has been found to reduce the symptoms of selective mutism in about three-fourths of children. Other drugs used to treat anxiety and social phobia disorders may also be effective in certain cases.

Prognosis

Selective mutism is considered treatable in that many cases of the disorder are thought to resolve on their own, although treatment can be very effective. There is little information about the long-term outcome of selective mutism. Researchers have noted, however, that while many children with the disorder do show improvement in speech, their anxiety in social situations persists.

Resources

BOOKS

American Psychiatric Association. *Diagnostic and Statistical Manual of Mental Disorders*. 4th ed., text rev. Washington, DC: American Psychiatric Publishing, 2000.

Sadock, Benjamin J., and Virginia A. Sadock, eds. *Comprehensive Textbook of Psychiatry*. Vol. 2. 7th ed. Philadelphia: Lippincott Williams and Wilkins, 2000.

PERIODICALS

Dow, Sara P., et al. "Practical Guidelines for the Assessment and Treatment of Selective Mutism." *Journal of the American Academy of Child and Adolescent Psychiatry* 34, no. 7 (July 1995): 836–847.

Dummit, Steven E. III, et al. "Fluoxetine Treatment of Children with Selective Mutism: An Open Trial." *Journal of the American Academy of Child and Adolescent Psychiatry* 35, no. 5 (May 1996): 615–622.

Joseph, Paul R. "Selective Mutism—The Child Who Doesn't Speak at School." *Pediatrics* 104, no. 2 Part 1 (August 1999): 308–309.

Stein, Martin T., Isabelle Rapin, and Diane Yapko. "Selective Mutism." *Journal of Developmental & Behavioral Pediatrics* 22, no. 2 Suppl. (April 2001): S123.

ORGANIZATIONS

Selective Mutism Group—A Division of Childhood Anxiety Network, Inc, http://www.selectivemutism.org.

Tish Davidson, A.M.

Selective serotonin reuptake inhibitors (SSRIs)

Definition

Selective **serotonin** reuptake inhibitors (SSRIs) are a class of antidepressant medicines that help increase the activity of a chemical in the **brain** called serotonin. They are also called serotonin boosters.

Purpose

Serotonin is a neurotransmitter, which is a substance that helps send messages between nerves in the brain. It is believed that problems with serotonin levels play a role in determining a person's mood and behavior.

SSRIs are used to treat a wide variety of mental disorders, including:

- major depressive disorder
- obsessive-compulsive disorder
- posttraumatic stress disorder (PTSD)
- social and generalized anxiety
- panic disorder
- postmenstrual dysphoric disorder (PMDD)

Sometimes, a health-care provider will prescribe an SSRI for a condition other than the approved ones listed on the drug's label. This is called off-label use. Off-label uses for SSRIs include the treatment of obesity, certain types of irritable bowel syndrome (IBS), and bulimia, an eating disorder. The American Medical Association has reported that SSRI use in persons with **depression** who have had a heart attack reduces the risk of death and repeated heart attacks.

Description

SSRIs act on the central nervous system. They prevent nerve cells in the brain, called receptors, from soaking up serotonin. The action of soaking up, or absorbing, a substance is called reuptake. When serotonin reuptake is blocked, the serotonin has nowhere to go, and the levels of the chemical in the brain increase. SSRIs were released in the U.S. market in 1987. **Fluoxetine** (Prozac) was the first type of SSRI sold in the United States. Ten years later, more than half of Americans receiving outpatient treatment for major depression were prescribed an SSRI.

SSRIs include:

- citalopram (Celexa)
- escitalopram (Lexapro)
- fluoxetine (Prozac)
- fluvoxamine (Luvox)
- paroxetine (Paxil)
- sertraline (Zoloft)

Recommended dosage

SSRIs are taken by mouth. They are available in many different forms. Extended-release (XR) and controlled-release (CR) forms slowly release medicine into the body over several hours. Most SSRIs are taken once a day. The exact dosage needed depends on the specific drug, the person's age, and medical condition being treated. The medicine must be taken regularly for several weeks before an effect is seen. If symptoms continue, a different type of medicine may be prescribed.

Precautions

Pregnant women

Pregnant women should discuss the use and safety of SSRIs with their health care providers. In 2006, the U.S. Food and Drug Administration (FDA) warned that mothers who take SSRIs after the 20th week of pregnancy have an increased risk of giving birth to babies with a serious heart and lung disorder called persistent pulmonary hypertension (PPHN). The FDA classifies a drug according to how it may affect a baby during pregnancy and breastfeeding. Most SSRIs fall into pregnancy category C, which means: 1) no animal and human studies have been done, or 2) animal studies have shown the drugs cause harm to a fetus, but more complete human studies are needed. The SSRI **paroxetine** (Paxil) falls into a higher risk category. The American College of Obstetricians and Gynecologists has recommended that pregnant women avoid taking Paxil. The organization encourages patients and doctors to carefully weigh the possible risk of birth defects against a woman's individual risk of depression during pregnancy.

Children and young adults

Sometimes SSRIs may make depression worse or cause suicidal thoughts or behaviors. A government review of all studies involving antidepressant use among children and adolescents concluded that 4% of those taking SSRIs thought about **suicide** or displayed suicidal behavior. In October 2004, the FDA told the manufacturers of **antidepressants** that they must include a warning on the medicine's label that tells users the drugs have been linked to an increase in suicide in children and young adults. Such an alert is called a "black box warning." According to the FDA, the use of SSRIs among people aged 10 to 19 has risen sharply in recent years. Children and adolescents taking any type of antidepressants should be closely watched for signs of suicidal tendencies, behavior changes, or worsening of depression.

Other medical conditions

SSRIs should be used with caution in people with kidney or liver problems and diabetes, and in women who are producing breast milk (lactating).

Side effects

Side effects depend on the specific type of SSRI, but those most commonly reported are listed below:

Central nervous system

- anxiety
- dizziness
- drowsiness
- headache
- light-headedness
- nervousness
- tremors
- trouble sleeping

KEY TERMS

Metabolism—A series of chemical changes that break down food, medicine, and body tissue.

Monoamine oxidase inhibitor (MAOI)—An older type of antidepressant medicine.

Neurotransmitter—A substance that helps send messages between nerve cells.

Persistent pulmonary hypertension (PPHN)—A life-threatening disorder seen in newborn babies in which blood does not properly enter the lungs.

Tricyclic antidepressant (TCA)—An older group of antidepressants that were introduced in the 1960s. TCAs affect the activity of serotonin and another body chemical called norepinephrine.

Skin

- itching
- rash
- sweating

Gastrointestinal system

- anorexia nervosa (an eating disorder)
- changes in taste
- constipation
- diarrhea
- dry mouth
- indigestion
- nausea and vomiting

Reproductive system

- painful menstruation
- changes in sexual function, such as difficulty becoming aroused or reaching orgasm

Respiratory system

- sore throat
- upper respiratory infections

Other

- increased body temperature
- weakness
- weight loss

Forgetting to take several doses or stopping the drug suddenly can cause symptoms of withdrawal, which may include a flu-like feeling, nausea, headache, dizziness, and tiredness.

Interactions

Taking SSRIs together with other drugs that affect serotonin levels, such as **monoamine oxidase inhibitors (MAOIs)** or tricyclic antidepressants, can lead to a rare but life-threatening drug reaction called "serotonin syndrome." Symptoms of **serotonin syndrome** occur within minutes to hours, and may include high blood pressure, mental status changes, and increased body temperature (hyperthermia).

Taking SSRIs with the herbal remedy **St. John's wort** may also cause this reaction.

SSRIs may slow down the body's metabolism of many other drugs. The following drugs have also been reported to interact with SSRIs and, when taken together, may lead to dangerously high serotonin levels:

- antipsychotics
- benzodiazepines
- beta blockers
- calcium channel blockers
- cocaine
- codeine
- dextromethorphan
- fenfluramine
- levodopa
- pentazocine

Resources

BOOKS

Karch, Amy M. *2012 Lippincott's Nursing Drug Guide.* Baltimore, MD: Lippincott Williams & Wilkins, 2011.

Kasper, Dennis L., et al. *Harrison's Principles of Internal Medicine.* 17th ed. New York, NY: McGraw-Hill, 2008.

Marx, J., R. Hockberger, and R. Walls. *Rosen's Emergency Medicine: Concepts and Clinical Practice.* 7th ed. St. Louis, MO: Mosby, 2010.

ORGANIZATIONS

Mental Health America, 2000 N Beauregard St., 6th Fl., Alexandria, VA, 22311, (703) 684-7722, (800) 969-6642, Fax: (703) 684-5968, http://www.nmha.org.

National Alliance on Mental Illness, 3803 N Fairfax Dr., Ste. 100, Arlington, VA, 22203, (703) 524-7600, http://www.nami.org.

National Institute of Mental Health, 6001 Executive Blvd., Rm. 8184, MSC 9663, Bethesda, MD, 20892-9663, (301) 433-4513, TTY: (301) 443-8431, Fax: (301) 443-4279, (866) 615-6464, TTY: (866) 415-8051, nimhinfo@nih.gov, http://www.nimh.nih.gov.

Kelli Miller Stacy

Self-control strategies

Definition

Self-control strategies are cognitive and behavioral skills used by individuals to maintain self-motivation and achieve personal goals. Initially the skills may be learned from a therapist, text, or self-help book. However, the individual is responsible for using these skills in real-life situations to produce the desired changes.

There are many varieties of self-control strategies. Other terms for self-control strategies are "behavioral self-control training," "cognitive self-regulation," and "self-management techniques." In recent years, the term "self-management" has replaced "self-control," because that term implies changing behavior through sheer willpower. Self-management, on the other hand, involves becoming aware of the natural processes that affect a particular behavior and consciously altering those processes, resulting in the desired behavior change.

Purpose

Most people who decide to use self-control strategies are dissatisfied with a certain aspect of their lives. For example, people may feel they smoke too much, **exercise** too little, or have difficulty controlling anger. Self-control strategies are useful for a wide range of concerns, including medical conditions (such as diabetes, chronic pain, asthma, arthritis, incontinence, or obesity), addictions (such as drug and alcohol abuse, smoking, gambling, or eating disorders), occupational issues (such as study habits, organizational skills, or job productivity), and psychological issues (such as **stress**, anxiety, **depression**, excessive anger, hyperactivity, or **shyness**). If symptoms are severe, self-control strategies may be used in conjunction with other therapies, but they should not be the only form of treatment.

The goal of self-control strategies is to reduce behavioral deficiencies or behavioral excesses. Behavioral deficiencies occur when an individual does not engage in a positive, desirable behavior frequently enough. The result is a missed future benefit. For example, a student who rarely studies might not graduate. Behavioral excesses occur when an individual engages in negative, undesirable behavior too often. This results in a negative consequence. For example, a person who smokes may develop lung cancer.

In the case of behavioral deficiencies, one may fail to engage in a desirable behavior because it does not provide immediate gratification. With behavioral excesses, there is usually some type of immediate gratification and no immediate negative consequence. Self-control strategies help individuals to become aware of their own patterns of behavior and to alter those patterns (usually by creating artificial rewards or punishments) so that the behavior will be more or less likely to occur.

Description

The description of self-control strategies may include the theoretical bases for self-control strategies, the development of a self-control program, and the types of self-control strategies.

Theoretical bases for self-control strategies

Self-control strategies are based primarily on the social cognitive theory of Canadian **psychologist** Albert Bandura (1925–). According to Bandura, one's behavior is influenced by a variety of factors, including one's own thoughts and beliefs, and elements in the environment. Bandura proposed that certain beliefs, self-efficacy, and outcome expectancies are important factors in determining which behaviors an individual will attempt, and how motivated the individual will be when engaging in those behaviors. Self-efficacy is one's belief about how well he or she can perform a given task, regardless of that person's actual ability. Outcome expectancies are what the person believes will happen as a result of engaging in a certain behavior. If self-efficacy and outcome expectancies are inaccurate, the individual may experience behavioral deficits or excesses.

Canadian psychotherapist Donald Meichenbaum developed the idea of self-instructional training, which is a major part of self-control strategies. Meichenbaum believed that learning to control behavior begins in childhood, based on parental instruction. Children eventually control their own behavior by mentally repeating the instructions of their parents. These internal instructions may be positive or negative. Self-instructional training teaches individuals to become aware of their self-statements, evaluate whether these self-statements are helpful or hindering, and replace maladaptive self-statements with adaptive ones.

American psychologist Frederick H. Kanfer (1925–2002) suggested that individuals achieve self-control by using a feedback loop consisting of continuous monitoring, evaluating, and reinforcing of their own behavior. This loop occurs naturally in everyone. However, the loop can be maladaptive if (a) only negative factors are noticed, and positive factors are ignored during the monitoring phase, (b) standards are unrealistic during the evaluation phase, or (c) responsibility is accepted for negative behaviors but not for positive behaviors during the **reinforcement** phase. Self-control strategies help

individuals to be aware of these phases and to make the appropriate changes in monitoring, evaluation, and reinforcement.

Development of a self-control program

Self-control strategies are often taught in treatment centers, group or individual therapies, schools, or vocational settings. However, self-control programs may also be designed without the help of a professional, especially if the problem being addressed is not severe. The use of professionals, at least initially, may increase the likelihood that the program will succeed. Following are the necessary steps for creating a self-control program:

- Making a commitment. A plan cannot succeed unless one is committed to following through. Ways of increasing commitment level include listing the benefits of adhering to the program, telling others about one's intentions, posting written reminders of commitments around one's home, putting a significant amount of time and energy into designing the program, and planning ways to deal with obstacles ahead of time.

- Identifying the problem. The behavior in need of change is referred to as the "target behavior" or the "controlled behavior." A precise definition of the target behavior is a crucial first step. This is usually done by keeping detailed records about when, where, and how the behavior occurs, for one to two weeks. The record-keeping should also focus on other competing behaviors that may be interfering with the target behavior. For example, for a person who is trying to cut down on calorie consumption, a competing behavior would be to eat high-calorie snack foods. It is important to note the antecedents and consequences of the target and competing behaviors; in other words, what typically occurs immediately before (antecedents) and after (consequences) these behaviors? The antecedents and consequences are factors that influence the occurrence of the behavior. Sometimes just the process of record-keeping alters the target behavior by increasing the individual's awareness of what he or she is doing.

- Setting a goal. Once the target behavior has been defined, the individual must decide in what way that behavior should be changed. The goal should be specific so that future progress can be measured. This may entail listing circumstances or behaviors that must be present, as well the degree to which they must be present, in order for a goal to be achieved. For example, a goal to "reduce hyperactivity" in a grade-school student is vague. "Remaining in seat for seven

KEY TERMS

Depression—A psychiatric disorder involving feelings of hopelessness and symptoms of fatigue, sleeplessness, suicidal tendencies, and poor concentration.

Eating disorders—A number of medical conditions characterized by abnormal eating habits that can involve either the lack, or the excessive intake, of food, which results in physical and/or emotional stress. Two types of eating disorders include anorexia nervosa and bulimia nervosa.

Hyperactivity—Activities that are unusually active and restless, and without the person having the ability to concentrate for any extended period.

Stress—A physical and psychological response that results from being exposed to a demand or pressure.

out of fourteen half-hour periods daily" is much more specific. Indicating a period in which the goal can realistically be achieved is also recommended. Goals should be realistic. It is better to set a small goal and to progress to bigger goals than to set a big goal and become quickly discouraged.

- Applying self-control strategies. The self-control strategies are known as "controlling behaviors." Choice of strategies will depend on the target behavior. Types of strategies are discussed later.

- Self-monitoring. While using the self-control strategies, one should continue to keep records regarding the occurrence of the target behavior. Keeping written records is essential for determining whether the strategies are effective. If one is gradually meeting the goal requirements, the strategies can be assumed to be effective. If little progress toward the goal is evident, either the strategies are being used incorrectly or the strategies are ineffective and should be changed. Self-monitoring can be done informally (for example, by making notes on an index card) or formally (for example, by using pre-designed data sheets). In any case, self-monitoring should gather the necessary information but should not become too lengthy or complex. The individual will lose motivation to continue monitoring if the procedures are overly time-consuming or inconvenient.

- Making revisions as necessary. Based on the information gathered during self-monitoring, the individual decides if changes in the plan are necessary. One advantage of self-control programs is that the individual chooses the strategies that will work best for him or her. This freedom of choice increases the likelihood that the individual will adhere to the program. Therefore, self-control programs should always be flexible and adaptable.

Types of self-control strategies

Self-control strategies can be grouped into three broad categories:

ENVIRONMENTAL STRATEGIES. Environmental strategies involve changing times, places, or situations where one experiences problematic behavior. Examples include:

- changing the group of people with whom one socializes
- avoiding situations or settings where an undesirable behavior is more likely to occur
- changing the time of day for participating in a desirable behavior to a time when one will be more productive or successful.

BEHAVIORAL STRATEGIES. Behavioral strategies involve changing the antecedents or consequences of a behavior. Examples include:

- increasing social support by asking others to work towards the same or a similar goal
- placing visual cues or reminders about goal in one's daily environment
- developing reinforcers (rewards) for engaging in desirable behaviors, or punishers for engaging in undesirable behaviors
- eliminating naturally occurring reinforcers for undesirable behavior
- engaging in alternative, positive behaviors when one is inclined to engage in an undesirable behavior
- creating ways to make a desirable behavior more enjoyable or convenient
- scheduling a specific time to engage in a desirable behavior
- writing a behavioral contract to hold oneself accountable for carrying out the self-control program.

COGNITIVE STRATEGIES. Cognitive strategies involve changing one's thoughts or beliefs about a particular behavior. Examples include:

- using self-instructions to cue oneself about what to do and how to do it
- using self-praise to commend oneself for engaging in a desirable behavior

- thinking about the benefits of reaching one's goal

- imagining oneself successfully achieving a goal or using imagery to distract oneself from engaging in an undesirable behavior

- substituting positive self-statements for unproductive, negative self-statements.

In a therapeutic setting, self-control strategies are usually taught in weekly group sessions over a period of several weeks. The sessions typically include an educational lecture regarding a specific strategy, group discussion of how the strategy should be applied and how to cope with potential obstacles (**relapse prevention**), role-playing or rehearsal of the strategy, a review of the session, and a homework assignment for further practice. Sessions usually focus on one strategy at a time. Preferably, an individual should master one strategy before attempting another. After the series of training sessions are complete, the individual is responsible for implementing the strategies in daily life.

Preparation

Individuals must prepare for the use of a self-control strategy because knowledge and skills must be learned in order to produce the desired results.

Aftercare

Relapse is a concern in any therapeutic situation. Current research suggests that individuals are more likely to continue using newly learned self-control strategies if they have periodic follow-up contact with a professional or other designated person. The contact serves at least three purposes: (1) a source of accountability, (2) review of strategy use to ensure proper application, and (3) discussion of problematic situations and development of plans to overcome these situations.

Risks

Self-control strategies are especially prone to short-circuiting of contingencies. This refers to the tendency for individuals to partake of reinforcers at inappropriate occasions, or to avoid punishers designated in their plan. If contingencies are short-circuited, the desired behavior change is unlikely to occur.

Relapse is another risk involved in self-control strategies. Causes of relapse include:

- a poorly defined target behavior (progress cannot be recognized)

- unrealistic or long-term goals without immediate sources of reinforcement

---

QUESTIONS TO ASK YOUR DOCTOR

- Will self-control strategies help me?

- What should I do if self-control strategies do not solve my problem?

- Should I tell my friends and family before starting a self-control strategy?

- Will this type of training help me with other concerns?

- Is it difficult to use a self-control strategy?

- Should medication be used, too?

- Will related support groups help me?

- How long should I use a self-control strategy?

- Is it very expensive?

- failure to anticipate and plan for obstacles to goal-achievement

- overreaction to occasional setbacks

- negative self-talk, especially when one feels that goals are not being satisfactorily met

- failure to use desirable or frequent reinforcers

- ineffective consequences for undesirable behavior

- an inaccurate or unnecessarily complex monitoring system.

Results

Results of self-control strategies vary widely based on individual use.

Normal results

Ideally, individuals will use self-control strategies independently in their everyday surroundings to meet their designated goals. They will decrease behavioral deficiencies and excesses, engaging in desirable behaviors more often, or engaging in undesirable behaviors less frequently or not at all.

Abnormal results

If the self-control strategies are ineffective or used improperly, individuals might not show any changes or may show increases in behavioral deficiencies or excesses.

Resources

BOOKS

Dobson, Keith S., ed. *Handbook of Cognitive-Behavioral Therapies.* 3rd ed. New York City: Guilford Press, 2010.

Martin, Garry, and Joseph Pear. *Behavior Modification: What It Is and How to Do It.* 9th ed. Boston: Prentice Education/ Allyn & Bacon, 2011.

Miltenberger, Raymond G. *Behavior Modification: Principles and Procedures.* 4th ed. Belmont, CA: Thomson Wadsworth, 2008.

PERIODICALS

"Frederick H. Kanfer, 76." *Chicago Tribune* (November 16, 2002). http://articles.chicagotribune.com/2002-11-16/ news/0211160183_1_psychology-behavior-master-s-and-doctorate-degrees (accessed January 3, 2011).

OTHER

Ove R. Myrseth, Kristian, and Ayelet Fishbach. "Self-Control: A Function of Knowing When and How to Exercise Restraint." Booth School of Business, University of Chicago. http://faculty.chicagobooth.edu/ayelet.fishbach/ research/cdir.pdf (accessed January 3, 2011).

WEBSITES

"Donald Meichenbaum, PhD (biography)." Institute for the Advancement of Human Behavior. http://www. iahb.org/html/meichenbaum.html (accessed January 3, 2011).

"Dr. Albert Bandera (biography)." University of Alberta. http:// www.psych.ualberta.ca/~gcpws/Bandura/Biography/ Bandura_bio1.html (accessed January 3, 2011).

ORGANIZATIONS

American Psychotherapy Association, 2750 East Sunshine St., Springfield, MO, 65804, (417) 823-0173, (800) 205-9165, http://www.americanpsychotherapy.com.

Association for Behavioral Analysis International, 550 West Centre Ave., Ste. 1, Portage, MI, 49024, (269) 492-9310, Fax: (269) 492-9316, http://www. abainternational.org.

Beck Institute for Cognitive Therapy and Research, One Belmont Ave., Ste. 700, Bala Cynwyd, PA, 19004-1610, (610) 664-3020, Fax: (610) 664-4437, beckinst@ gim.net, http://www.beckinstitute.org.

Cambridge Center for Behavioral Studies, PO Box 7067, Cummings Center, Ste. 340F, Beverly, MA, 01915, (978) 369-2227, http://www.behavior.org.

Cognitive-Behavioral Therapy Institute, 211 East 43rd St., Ste. 1500, New York City, NY, 10017, (212) 490-3590, http:// www.cbtinstitute.com.

See also Behavior modification; Bibliotherapy; Cognitive-behavioral therapy; Cognitive retraining techniques; Guided imagery therapy; Rational emotive therapy; Social skills training

Sandra L. Friedrich, M.A.

Self-harm *see* **Self-mutilation**

∎ Self-help groups

Definition

Self-help groups—also called mutual help or mutual aid groups—are composed of peers who share a similar mental, emotional, or physical problem, or who are interested in a focal issue, such as education or parenting. Historically, people banded together to improve their chances for survival by pooling their social and economic resources; however, contemporary groups are more likely to organize around a theme or problem.

Purpose

Most self-help groups are voluntary, nonprofit associations open to anyone with a similar need or interest; however, spin-off groups also exist to meet the needs of particular types of people; for example, the elderly, women, or specific ethnic groups. Usually, groups are led by peers, have an informal structure, and are free (except for small donations to cover meeting expenses). However, professionals of various kinds lead some self-help groups.

Description

In the past 30 years or so, the number of self-help organizations and groups operating in communities

---

Substance abuse treatment

In 2010, approximately 4.1 million persons aged 12 or older received treatment for substance abuse.

Locations and methods of treatment included:

Self-help groups	2.3 million treated
Outpatient rehabilitation program	1.7 million
Outpatient mental health center	999,000
Inpatient rehabilitation	986,000
Hospital inpatient	731,000
Private doctor's office	653,000
Hospital emergency room	467,000
Prison or jail	342,000

SOURCE: Substance Abuse and Mental Health Services Administration, Office of Applied Studies, *Results from the 2010 National Survey on Drug Use and Health: Summary of National Findings* (September 2011).

Report available online at http://oas.samhsa.gov/NSDUH/ 2k10NSDUH/2k10Results.htm. *(Table by PreMediaGlobal.* © *2012 Cengage Learning.)*

---

throughout the United States has risen dramatically; some organizations operate in several countries, primarily in the developed world. One of the reasons for the rapid proliferation of groups focusing on health problems may be the advent of managed health care. For individuals with insurance plans offering limited mental health coverage, self-help groups are an economical way to find emotional and social support.

Self-help groups and therapy

Because of the peer-led, informal, and democratic (as opposed to hierarchical and medical) structure, health professionals consider self-help groups for mental or emotional problems to be an adjunct to therapy. While there are therapeutic aspects associated with participation—principally, intimacy as a result of self-disclosure, personal growth in response to others' role **modeling**, and erosion of **denial** as a result of social confrontation—the primary value of contemporary groups is in the mutual aid offered by members to one another. Although the nature of self-help groups is outside the medical realm, doctors and therapists see participation as a way to improve the outcome related to either ongoing or future formal treatment.

Another issue arguing against considering self-help groups as a type of therapy is that the variety of groups is extensive; groups available may include advocacy groups with a focus on legal or social remedies, groups organized around housing or employment needs, and groups focusing on racial or gender issues. Additionally, the self-help movement shares some characteristics with volunteerism and consumerism. In general, members who persevere have experience with other voluntary organizations and believe in the value of donating time and service; also, members may be thought of as consumers who participate in their own care and who have experience and knowledge of relevant goods and services.

Types of self-help groups

TWELVE-STEP GROUPS. The most popular type of self-help group is based on the 12 steps and 12 traditions of Alcoholics Anonymous (AA), founded in 1935. The 12 steps are a guide to recovery from alcoholism or **addiction**, whereas the 12 traditions are a code of ethics. AA and other 12-step programs are based on the spiritual premise that turning one's life and will over to a personally meaningful "higher power," such as God or Spirit, is the key to recovery. Another essential idea is that sobriety or recovery (not cure) depends on the admission of powerlessness with respect to alcohol or

the substance(s) abused. This idea is offensive to critics of 12-step groups, but others believe that this admission accurately reflects the contemporary view of addiction as a disease. Furthermore, people with a familial, genetic vulnerability to addiction are particularly at risk. While some studies suggest that 20% of people suffering from alcoholism will experience remission without benefit of therapy or a 12-step group, most will suffer deteriorating health and dysfunctional, if not ruined, social relationships. In other words, most alcoholics need formal therapy or an informal self-help program to recover. While the dropout rate for AA groups during the first three months is high, alcoholics who persevere have a good chance of attaining and maintaining sobriety or abstinence. This is especially true if the person regularly attends a home group (90 meetings in the first 90 days, slowly diminishing to two or three times per week for years thereafter) and finds an experienced and sympathetic sponsor who also is in recovery.

In addition to AA and its sister organizations, Narcotics Anonymous (NA) and Cocaine Anonymous (CA), a number of 12-step organizations exist for a variety of disorders, including Gamblers Anonymous (GA), Schizophrenics Anonymous (SA), Emotions Anonymous (EA), and Overeaters Anonymous (OA).

HEALTH PROBLEMS AND DISEASES. Self-help organizations also provide support for individuals struggling with the physical and emotional effects of life-threatening or chronic health problems. For example, support exists for people coping with weight management, human immunodeficiency virus/acquired immune deficiency syndrome (HIV/AIDS), multiple sclerosis, muscular dystrophy, cancer, incontinence, and for the families of individuals who suffer from these conditions. Also, support exists for people who share interests or circumstances, such as groups for women who breastfeed (LaLeche League), singles, older adults, and new parents.

Self-help groups for family members of the afflicted person are available, offering support to those whose loved ones may be ill, addicted, or distressed. Family members may unwittingly reinforce illness or addictive behaviors, or may need help coping with the person in distress. Al-Anon, an organization for friends and families of alcoholics, is a companion organization to AA, as is Alateen, a program for teenagers who have been hurt by the alcoholism of significant people in their lives. **Support groups** for caregivers of individuals with life-threatening or terminal illnesses, such as cancer, often meet at treatment centers and hospitals. One popular club for people with cancer, as well as for their friends and family, is Gilda's Club, founded by actor/comedian Gene Wilder

(1933–), Gilda Radner's widower. Gilda Radner (1946–1989), the well-known actress/comedian from *Saturday Night Live*, died at age 42 from ovarian cancer. Gilda's Clubs joined with the Wellness Community to become the Cancer Support Community on June 1, 2011, with clubs all over the world.

ONLINE GROUPS AND CLEARINGHOUSES. A growing trend in the self-help movement is the online support communities, as well as online resource centers and clearinghouses. Chat rooms, bulletin boards, and electronic mailing lists all provide convenient, around-the-clock access to peer support. Many large-scale consumer healthcare websites provide forums for discussions on numerous diseases and disorders, and major online commercial services, such as Google (http://www.google.com/Top/Society/Support_Groups/), provide sites for health care and patient support. In some cases, professionals moderate online groups, although many are exclusively organized and populated by peers. There are self-help groups, such as LaLeche League, that hold some meetings online, often at their own websites.

Features of self-help groups

ACCESSIBILITY. Accessibility and economy are appealing features of self-help groups. Since the groups are free, organizations such as AA and NA are very cost-effective. In addition, meetings are easy to locate through local newspaper announcements, hospitals, health care centers, churches, school counselors, and community agencies. For AA and sister organizations that encourage frequent attendance, hundreds of meetings may be held each week in large metropolitan areas. Furthermore, with the proliferation of online support communities and growth of connectivity to the Internet, self-help groups are becoming as accessible for individuals in rural areas as they are for those in large cities.

ANONYMITY. An important characteristic of 12-step groups is the preservation of anonymity by revealing first names only and by maintaining strict confidentiality of personal details and experiences shared during meetings. Online self-help groups offer even more anonymity since the exchanges are not face-to-face. The virtual anonymity of online experience helps to reduce social discomfort and discrimination, or stereotyping otherwise associated with real-life perceptions of age, disabilities, race, gender, or culture.

SOCIAL SUPPORT AND MUTUAL AID. Self-help groups provide an intact community and a sense of belonging. The social support and mutual aid available in a group may be critical to recovery, rehabilitation, or healthy coping. This is especially true for socially isolated people or people from dysfunctional families, who may have little or no emotional support. Participating in a social network of peers reduces social and emotional isolation and supports healthy behavior. Group members can offer unconditional support and, collectively, are a repository of helpful experiential knowledge.

SELF-ESTEEM AND SELF-EFFICACY. Self-help groups promote self-esteem or self-respect by encouraging reciprocal caring; the concept of self-efficacy, or the belief that one is capable, is promoted by reinforcing appropriate behavior and beliefs and by sharing relevant information regarding the disease or condition. For example, there may be an exchange of information regarding how to cope with failed or disrupted relationships, about what is reasonable to expect from healthcare professionals, about how to manage pain or public embarrassment, about where to go and to whom for a variety of needs. In groups such as AA, self-efficacy also is promoted by sponsors who act as mentors and role models, and by encouraging rotating leadership roles.

INTROSPECTION AND INSIGHT. Introspection, or contemplation, is another fundamental feature of many self-help groups, particularly for groups that follow a 12-step program of recovery. For example, the fourth step of AA states that members make "a searching and fearless moral inventory" of themselves, and the tenth step states that members continue "to take personal inventory" and admit wrongdoing. Introspection is particularly beneficial to individuals who are not entirely aware of the moral repercussions of and motivation for their behavior. In a sense, working through some of the 12 steps resembles the cognitive restructuring learned in **cognitive-behavioral therapy** (CBT), as maladaptive ideas and behaviors are transformed.

SPIRITUAL RECOVERY. The final step in a 12-step program recognizes that recovery entails a spiritual awakening; furthermore, recovering addicts are enjoined to spread the message to others suffering from addiction. Recovery depends on giving up both injurious self-will and denial of maladaptive behavior, and turning to a higher power. Members are urged to seek guidance or inspiration from this higher power. For many addicts, the key to recovery is a spiritually guided movement away from self-centeredness or self-absorption, and a turning towards the "power greater than ourselves" through prayer and **meditation**.

ADVOCACY. Some self-help groups meet to advocate or promote social and legislative remedies with respect to the issue of concern. For example, HIV/AIDS groups have lobbied for improved access to prescription drugs. Groups lobby for reforms by identifying key legislators and policy makers; they submit papers or suggestions for more equitable laws and policies to these key people. They also

KEY TERMS

Anorexia nervosa—An eating disorder highlighted by a person's denial of a healthy body weight, distortion of their outward appearance, and steadfast refusal to eat much food for a fear that they may gain weight.

Cognitive behavioral techniques—A type of therapy that are used to solve problems concerning dysfunctional behaviors (responses), emotions (feelings) and cognitions (abilities to gather knowledge) through a proven systematic set of procedures.

Cognitive therapy—A type of psychiatric treatment involving the treatment of anxiety and/or depression, which encourages patients to confront their problems in order to improve their behavior.

Eating disorders—A number of medical conditions characterized by abnormal eating habits that can involve either the lack, or the excessive intake, of food, which results in physical and/or emotional stress. Two types of eating disorders include anorexia nervosa and bulimia nervosa.

Schizophrenia—A mental disorder involving degraded thinking and emotions.

conduct public education programs (including programs meant to redress the harm of stigmatization). There are groups that advocate for more funds for research and for improved services for people who suffer from one of many diseases or mental disorders. The most important grassroots organization of families and consumers of psychiatric services (former or current patients) is the National Alliance on Mental Illness (NAMI). This organization was founded in 1979, and blends self-help with advocacy efforts for the improvement of research, services, and public awareness of major mental illnesses. Their advocacy efforts target both the federal and state levels.

Preparation

Someone preparing to join a self-help group is advised to learn as much as possible before actually attending a meeting. The more knowledge gained before using a self-help group, the more likely the experience will be positive.

Aftercare

Although individuals may not remain active in self-help groups after recovering from their condition, such groups remain open in aftercare, in case of a **relapse** or other such problems or concerns. For instance, an individual dealing with alcoholism may leave an alcohol rehabilitation program and return to a normal life. However, such sober individuals may return for support activities provided by self-help groups on a periodic basis.

Risks

Risks are always present in self-help groups. However, such help is usually welcomed by individuals needing support from a group so they do not have to deal with their problem alone.

Advocacy versus mutual aid

In some organizations, there is a growing overlap between self-help efforts and community development. Critics maintain that focusing on issues such as crime prevention, affordable housing, and economic development drains time and effort from social support and mutual aid. Nevertheless, some organizations continue to develop both advocacy and support.

Lack of professional involvement

The absence of professional guidance may mean that a member in need of formal **psychotherapy** or treatment may be discouraged from seeking professional help. On the other hand, too much professional involvement in the group may compromise the quality of mutual aid.

The "thirteenth step"

There is a well-known risk associated with attending 12-step groups termed the "thirteenth step." Women new to the groups, especially young women, are at their most vulnerable in the early stages of recovery. Male sexual predators who attend meetings take advantage of the atmosphere of intimacy and mutual trust. To cope with the possibility of sexual exploitation, young females are encouraged to attend meetings with a family member or a trusted adult, and all women are encouraged to find a same-sex sponsor.

Substituting addictions

The early months of a 12-step program are especially difficult. Typically, an addict in early recovery either replaces an addictive substance with a new one, or intensifies his/her concurrent use of another substance.

It is not uncommon for people who are chemically dependent to also have an addictive sexual disorder. (When someone is addicted to sex, there is an intense desire to gratify sexual urges and fantasies or to behave

QUESTIONS TO ASK YOUR DOCTOR

- Will a self-help group help me?
- What should I do if participation in a self-control group does not solve my problem?
- Should I tell my friends and family before starting a self-help group?
- Will this type of training help me with other concerns?
- Is it difficult to be involved with a self-help group?
- Will other related support groups help me in my particular case?
- How long should I be actively involved with a self-help group?
- Is it very expensive?

in ways that cause clinically significant distress; sexual indulgence, often compulsive, is a major disruptive force with respect to social relationships.) In one four-year study of a treatment program, 33% of the chemically addicted patients also were sexually compulsive. Some physicians believe that the predatory "thirteenth step" is evidence of turning from one addiction to another—in this case, addictive sexual disorder.

Members at varying stages of recovery

Another common risk is associated with the varying levels of recovery in a self-help group—that of being actively involved in the abuse of alcohol and/or drugs. Newcomers need to realize that not all members are interested in supporting their recovery, and that people in later stages of recovery may be more reliable. Furthermore, some members are required to attend by disciplinary entities, such as employers or correctional authorities.

Ongoing meetings

One criticism of self-help groups, especially 12-step groups, is that in the eyes of families and friends, members who persevere and attend the meetings seem to become "addicted" to the program. However, physicians who support self-help groups point out that since addiction is a disease, addicts are particularly vulnerable to relapse, and that ongoing involvement with a self-help community surely is better than suffering the recurring misery associated with active addiction.

Alternatives to 12-step groups

For addicts who find the spirituality of 12-step groups offensive and irrational, and who believe that public proclamation of powerlessness at group meetings is demoralizing, alternative groups exist. For example, a well-known organization, Rational Recovery (RR), is based on the cognitive-behavioral principles of American **psychologist** Albert Ellis (1913–2007). RR emphasizes self-reliance, rational thinking as a result of cognitive restructuring, and the development of a new repertoire of behaviors to respond effectively to events that trigger relapse.

Results

Worldwide, self-help groups are becoming increasingly popular. They are effective in providing mutual support and are good resources for finding needed information. However, when searching for an appropriate group prospective members should ask their friends, physicians, and counselors for references, and then visit a few groups before deciding on which one to attend. Also, information clearinghouses on the Internet are a good first step.

See also Co-occurring disorders; Depression; Disease concept of chemical dependency; Gambling disorder; Group therapy; Polysubstance dependence; Substance abuse and related disorders

Resources

BOOKS

Bloch, Douglas. *Healing from Depression: 12 Weeks to a Better Mood (A Body Mind, and Spirit Recovery Program)*. Fort Worth, FL: Nicolas-Hays, 2009.

Brown, Louis, and Scott Wituk, ed. *Mental Health Self-Help: Consumer and Family Driven Initiates*. New York City: Springer, 2010.

Dobson, Keith S., ed. *Handbook of Cognitive-Behavioral Therapies*. 3rd ed. New York City: Guilford Press, 2010.

Gottlieb, Richard, ed. *The Complete Directory for People with Chronic Illness: Condition, Descriptions, Associations, Publications, Research Centers, Support Groups, Websites*. Amenia, NY: Grey House, 2009.

Humphreys, Keith. *Circles of Recovery: Self-help Organizations for Addictions*. Cambridge, UK: Cambridge University Press, 2004.

Martin, Garry, and Joseph Pear. *Behavior Modification: What It Is and How to Do It*. 9th ed. Boston: Prentice Education/ Allyn & Bacon, 2011.

Miltenberger, Raymond G. *Behavior Modification: Principles and Procedures*. 4th ed. Belmont, CA: Thomson Wadsworth, 2008.

Schenker, Mark D. *A Clinician's Guide to 12-step Recovery*. New York City: W. W. Norton, 2009.

WEBSITES

"Self-Help Group Sourcebook Online." American Self-Help Group Clearinghouse. http://www.mentalhelp.net/selfhelp (accessed January 4, 2011).

ORGANIZATIONS

Al-Anon/Alateen, 1600 Corporate Landing Pkwy., Virginia Beach, VA, 23454-5617, (757) 563-1600, Fax: (757) 563-1655, http://www.al-anon.alateen.org.

Alcoholics Anonymous, PO Box 459 (11th Fl., 475 Riverside Dr. at W 120th St., New York City, 10115), New York, NY, 10163, (212) 870-3400, http://www.alcoholics-anonymous.org.

American Psychotherapy Association, 2750 E Sunshine St., Springfield, MO, 65804, (417) 823-0173, (800) 205-9165, http://www.americanpsychotherapy.com.

Association for Behavioral Analysis International, 550 W Centre Ave., Ste. 1, Portage, MI, 49024, (269) 492-9310, Fax: (269) 492-9316, http://www.abainternational.org.

Cancer Support Community (formerly Gilda's Club), 1050 17th St. NW, Washington, DC, 20036, (202) 659–9709, Toll Free: (888) 793-9355, Fax: (202) 974-7999, http://cancersupportcommunity.org.

Cocaine Anonymous, 21720 S Wilmington Ave., Ste. 304 or PO Box 492000, Long Beach or Los Angeles, CA, 90810-1641 or 90049-8000, (310) 559-5833, Fax: (310) 559-2554, cawso@ca.org, http://www.ca.org.

Emotions Anonymous, PO Box 4245, St. Paul, MN, 55104-0245, (651) 647-9712, Fax: (651) 647-1593, http://www.emotionsanonymous.org.

Gamblers Anonymous, PO Box 17173, Los Angeles, CA, 90017, (213) 386-8789, Fax: (213) 386-0030, http://www.alcoholics-anonymous.org.

LaLeche League, 957 North Plum Grove Rd., Schaumburg, IL, 60173, (847) 519-7730, (800) LALECHE (525-3243), Fax: (847) 969-0460, http://www.llli.org.

Narcotics Anonymous, PO Box 9999, Van Nuys, CA, 91409, (818) 773-9999, Fax: (818) 700-0700, http://www.na.org.

National Alliance on Mental Illness, 3803 N Fairfax Dr., Ste. 100, Arlington, VA, 22203, (703) 524-7600, (800) 950-NAMI (6264), Fax: (703) 524-9094, http://www.nami.org.

National Mental Health Consumers' Self-Help Clearinghouse, 1211 Chestnut St., Ste. 1207, Philadelphia, PA, 19107, (215) 751-1810, (800) 553-4539, Fax: (215) 636-6312, info@mhselfhelp.org, http://mhselfhelp.org.

Overeaters Anonymous, PO Box 44020 (6075 Zenith Ct. NE), Rio Rancho, NM, 87174-4020 (87144-6424), (505) 891-2664, Fax: (505) 891-4320, http://www.oa.org.

Rational Recovery, Box 800, Lotus, CA, 95651, (530) 621-2667, Fax: (530) 621-4374, https://rational.org/index.php?id=1.

Schizophrenics Anonymous, http://www.schizophrenia.com.

Tanja Bekhuis, Ph.D.
Paula Ford-Martin, M.A.
Stephanie N. Watson

Self-mutilation

Definition

Self-mutilation, a feature of self-harm or self-injury, is defined as intentional injury to one's own body tissues without an accompanying conscious intention to commit **suicide**. Although this behavior can appear similar to a suicide attempt, the phrase "deliberate self harm" is preferred to "suicide attempt" because the reasons and motivation behind self-harm or mutilation are generally quite different from those that underlie attempted suicide. Self-mutilation is considered a coping mechanism, although not a positive one.

Self-mutilation and self-harm are not explicitly listed as disorders in the 2000 edition of the ***Diagnostic and Statistical Manual of Mental Disorders***, also known as the *DSM*, although some clinicians argue that they should be listed under the category of **impulse control disorders**. The 2000 edition (the fourth edition, text revision, also known as *DSM-IV-TR*) mentions self-injury as a symptom or criterion for **diagnosis** of **borderline personality disorder** (BPD); **stereotypic movement disorder**, which can be a comorbidity of **autism** or intellectual disability; and **factitious disorder** (specifically factitious disorder with predominantly physical signs and symptoms), in which the person fakes a physical illness. For example, the self-mutilation behavior in factitious disorder might involve pulling out one's hair or purposely exacerbating a healing wound

Woman with scars from self-mutilation. (© *Photofusion Picture Library/Alamy*)

to mimic disease symptoms. Self-harm, including self-mutilation, also can be associated with other disorders listed in the *DSM-IV*, including **post-traumatic stress disorder** (PTSD).

Demographics

The incidence of self-harm has received more attention in clinical populations rather than in community or nonclinical groups. Groups at risk of self-harm include depressed adolescents, those experiencing an interpersonal crisis, and those who have done it before. Although reported incidence in the research literature can vary from study to study, there is some overlap. Some studies report a rate of 4% in the general adult population and 21% in the adult clinical population. Adolescents make up the group at greatest risk: In the community, rates have been reported ranging from 14 to 39% of respondents and a range of 14 to 21% among high school students; in adolescent psychiatric inpatient samples, rates are as high as 40 to 61%. Studies have identified self-harm behaviors in 4% of military recruits and 14 to 35% of psychology students at public universities. Research indicates that self-mutilating behavior occurs among nonclinical populations at higher rates than previously thought.

Rates of frequent self-mutilation activity are significantly higher among lesbian and bisexual women, and the behavior was long thought to be more prevalent among females, although recent findings indicate a similar prevalence in both sexes. Although the function of self-mutilation usually differs from the motivations underlying a suicide attempt, one study suggests that 20 to 45% of those who engage in self-harm think about suicide. In addition, someone who experiences one episode of self-harm may be likely to engage in another: As many as 30% of adolescents who report a previous incident of self-harm will do it again.

Description

Self-mutilation can take different forms and have different functions depending on the individual. In some nonpsychiatric subpopulations, self-mutilation is a sanctioned activity; for example, in some adolescents, mutilation of tissues is socially acceptable and done in a group or to gain acceptance from the group. Self-harm or self-mutilation may also accompany cognitive deficits or **psychosis**, and in the most severe expression of the practice can manifest as auto-castration or even self-immolation.

The focus here is self-mutilation that occurs in the absence of cognitive deficits or psychosis. What is known is that this behavior can be a manifestation of anguish that the person cannot otherwise express, or it can be a way for the person to cope with and relieve tension. In some cases, it has been construed as a method of self-punishment. In general, self-mutilation results in so little actual harm to the body that medical professionals and even family members often do not know that the mutilation is taking place. In addition, the person who engages in self-mutilation may go to great lengths to hide the resulting physical signs. The most common forms of self-mutilation are sticking the skin with needles, scratching, or cutting. Other forms of repetitive self-mutilation are punching or slapping the face, burning the skin, and swallowing harmful substances. Matthew Nock has published extensively on studies of self-harm and self-mutilation.

People who engage in self-mutilation often claim that it is accompanied by excitement and that it reduces or relieves such negative feelings as tension, anger, anxiety, **depression**, and loneliness. They also describe it as addictive. Self-mutilating behavior may occur in episodes, with periods of remission, or it may be continuous over a number of years. Characteristics commonly seen in persons with this disorder are perfectionism, dissatisfaction with one's physical appearance, and difficulty controlling and expressing emotions. Repetitive self-mutilation often worsens over time, resulting in increasingly serious forms of injury that may culminate in suicide.

Risk factors

General risk factors for self-mutilation include:

- History of sexual abuse or the death of a parent during childhood
- Parents who are perfectionistic or critical of the child's physical appearance
- Diagnosis of concurrent depression, PTSD, borderline personality disorder, or anxiety disorder
- Female sex
- Age between 12 and 25
- Lesbian or bisexual orientation
- Frequent and excessive use of drugs of abuse or alcohol

There is a correlation between self-harm and suicide attempts, feelings of hopelessness and other symptoms of depression, anxiety, external expectations of perfection, and most often, a history of **abuse**. Risk factors can be classified into two categories: environmental risk factors and individual risk factors. In addition, risk factors from one category can influence those of the other and vice versa.

Environmental risk factors

Some of the most commonly seen environmental risk factors in self-mutilation are associated with abuse experienced in childhood. Most research into the phenomenon of self-harm has focused on **sexual abuse**, but there are some indications that self-harm can also be associated with physical abuse and even emotional abuse, and it is strongly associated with low self-esteem. Almost any discussion about factors directly related to self-harm, however, is theoretical because of the paucity of actual experimental or empirical data.

In what may be a blurring of the distinction between socially sanctioned self-mutilation and the kind of self-mutilation discussed here, another risk factor for engaging in this behavior is awareness that others in one's peer group are doing it. **Substance abuse** also can be a contributing factor, and depression may lead someone to turn to self-mutilation as a coping mechanism. Perfectionism may also be a risk factor. Perfectionism consistently correlates with thoughts and behaviors related to self-injury.

Individual risk factors

The interaction of environmental factors and personal factors arises because of the individual ways in which people respond to environmental risk factors. Researchers have identified alexithymia, which is the inability to express feelings verbally, as an individual risk factor. The importance of this inability to express emotion as a risk factor in self mutilation is underscored by research that suggests that self-harmers who learn to express their feelings verbally decrease their self-harming behavior.

Causes and symptoms

The major cause of self-mutilation is the underlying motivation. Self-injury is closely linked to dysfunctions of emotional expression. For some who self mutilate, the physical pain of cutting or scratching provides a distraction from emotional pain. Others may use self mutilation as a way to punish themselves or relieve a feeling of evil, while for others the practice offers a relief from tension or a way to "feel real" through the physical pain or the visible evidence of physical injury. Causing physical pain to one's body through self mutilation may also provide an outlet for a person who has difficulty communicating emotions like anger or emotional pain. In addition, people who engage in self mutilation may be trying, either consciously or subconsciously, to alter the behavior of someone near them or seek help, although many people who self harm go to great lengths to conceal the signs of the behavior.

KEY TERMS

Borderline personality disorder (BPD)—A pattern of behavior characterized by impulsive acts, intense but chaotic relationships with others, identity problems, and emotional instability.

Comorbidity—The presence of one or more additional diseases or disorders in a patient diagnosed with a primary disorder.

Dissociation—A condition in which a person's thoughts, emotions, sensations, or memories become compartmentalized, usually as a result of a severe emotional trauma.

Impulse control disorders—A group of emotional disorders characterized by the repeated inability to refrain from performing a particular action that is harmful either to oneself or others.

The immediate triggers for self mutilation often center on some kind of interpersonal crisis. A person may have just experienced a separation from a partner, a major confrontation with a parent, or have just run away from home, for example.

The signs that a self-mutilation event has occurred are obvious, but less obvious are the symptoms that one will occur. A recent study found that individuals engaging in self-mutilating behavior usually thought about it for only a few minutes or even less time before completing the act; almost half reported not thinking about it at all before doing it. This association of impulsivity with self-mutilation may be related to the specific characteristics of the population studied, which was a group of adolescents who had previously self-mutilated. High levels of dissociation (a defense mechanism to isolate and protect the psyche from thoughts, emotions, or physical sensations that cause anxiety) may accompany self-mutilating behavior.

There are some signs that may precede an impulsive act of self-mutilation. These signs include trouble with parents, school, partners, or siblings; health problems; trouble with peers, including being bullied; depression; and low self esteem. Again, knowing that others in the peer group are doing it can also be a precipitating factor.

Diagnosis

Many cases of self-mutilation may never come to the attention of a clinician, parent, or caregiver. Often, identified self-mutilation has occurred in the context of a personality disorder, such as BPD. It may also appear as a manifestation of other psychiatric disorders, including substance abuse, **intermittent explosive disorder**, and eating disorders.

Self-mutilation and borderline personality disorder

For a person with BPD, self-mutilating behavior offers relief during a dissociative episode by functioning as an affirmation of the ability to feel or by relieving the person's personal feeling of being bad. Clinical populations with BPD have been the target of most studies focusing on self-harm, and in these populations, emotional vulnerability appears to play an important role in whether an individual will self-harm and in the development of BPD itself. Emotional vulnerability involves two aspects: emotional reactivity (high sensitivity to stimuli) and emotional intensity (extreme reactions to those stimuli). These factors are among the individual characteristics that might interact with environmental factors to elicit self-mutilating behaviors. Persons with BPD may have feel empty or detached to the point of anhedonia, an inability to experience pleasure from things that most people find pleasurable, such as eating good food. In addition, they may exhibit a narrow range of **affect**, the mood that a person displays to others. These signs of emotional inexpressivity may, according to some research, increase the possibility that a person with BPD will engage in self mutilating behavior.

Self-mutilation and suicide

Because self-mutilation can be interpreted as a cry for help, suicide can be a concern for those who become aware that an individual is self mutilating. Research suggests that there is a distinction between the risk of suicide and impulsive self-mutilation compared to self-mutilation that is deliberate and well thought out. Statistically, 20% to 25% of self harmers think about suicide, and the risk of suicide after self-harm ranges from 0.24% to 4.3%. Among the self-harming population, suicide risk factors include being an adolescent male, using a violent method of self-harm, and a history of inpatient treatment at a psychiatric facility. Some other features also are associated with conscious suicidal intent in a person who self-mutilates: self-mutilation performed alone; attempts to hide the behavior; preparations made for death, such as a plan for disposition of effects; or an act of self-harm that was planned considerably in advance (i.e., it was not impulsive).

Proposed diagnostic criteria for DSM-5

The fifth edition of *DSM*, known as *DSM-5*, may contain a new category for self-mutilation, called non-suicidal self injury (NSSI). The proposed criteria for NSSI are as follows:

- The person has on five or more days within the past year engaged in self-injury for purposes of inflicting pain (i.e., not tattooing or body piercing). The person does not intend to commit suicide, and the injury is more severe than minor wound-picking or nail biting.
- The self-injury is associated with at least two of the following four characteristics: negative thoughts preceding the act; a period of preoccupation with self-injury before the act that is difficult to resist; frequent urges to self-injure (which may or may not be acted out); and the self-injury has a purpose (relief from painful feelings or induction of positive feelings).
- The self-injury leads to significant distress or impairment in interpersonal, academic, or other important areas of functioning.
- The behavior is not associated with intoxication, psychosis, or delirium, and cannot be better accounted for by another physical or mental disorder.

The proposed criteria include two subtypes of NSSI, one in which individuals injure themselves fewer than five times per year but think about it often, and one in which the person may have suicidal intent as well as self-injury.

Examination

In some cases, an office examination will disclose physical evidence of self-mutilation, such as needle or burn marks, scars, or bruises. Another clue for the doctor is that the patient is wearing a long-sleeved shirt or long pants in hot weather. The patient may also acknowledge that he or she self-mutilates.

Tests

There are a number of questionnaires and inventories that can be administered in the examiner's office to determine whether the patient meets the criteria for BPD. In addition, a group of therapists in the United Kingdom has evaluated a possible new instrument for self-harming behaviors. There are, however, no laboratory tests (blood or urine samples) that can be used to either diagnose or rule out self-mutilation.

Treatment

Treatment for self-harming behavior tends to be psychological rather than physiological.

Traditional

Psychotherapy treatments for self mutilation include dialectical behavioral therapy, problem-solving therapy, and **cognitive-behavioral therapy**.

DIALECTICAL BEHAVIORAL THERAPY. Dialectical behavioral therapy is a relatively new approach developed by Marsha Linehan at the University of Washington. It focuses on teaching alternative ways to manage emotion and handle distress. The relationship between emotional inexpressivity and self-harm suggests that those who engage in self-mutilating behaviors to express emotions might benefit from a clinical approach involving tutoring in other methods of emotional expression. Dialectical behavioral therapy (DBT), which involves individual therapy and group skills training, was originally developed for individuals with BPD who engage in self-harm, but it is now used for self-harming individuals with a wide variety of other psychological issues, including eating disorders and substance dependence. Research indicates that the approach is helpful in reducing self-harm.

PROBLEM-SOLVING THERAPY. Problem-solving therapy involves developing and rehearsing coping strategies for the situations that may precipitate self harm. The approach can involve the entire family, using structured family interventions over five or six sessions. Focus is on improved cognitive and social skills to facilitate sharing feelings, controlling emotion, and family negotiation. Group treatment can also be a facet of problem-solving therapy. Briefly, this therapeutic approach identifies problems, prioritizes them, defines goals, and establishes and executes a strategy to achieve the goals, addressing any psychological issues that become obstacles along the way.

COGNITIVE-BEHAVIORAL THERAPY. In cases of self-mutilation accompanied by depression, a suggested approach is cognitive-behavioral therapy (CBT), which involves identifying patterns of destructive or negative behaviors or thinking and modifying them to be more realistic and pragmatic.

Other potential treatments for self mutilation in the context of other disorders include treatment for any substance abuse, anger management therapy, or environmental changes.

Drugs

There are no medications specifically indicated for self-injury. The doctor may, however, prescribe **antidepressants** to help the patient cope with strong feelings. The medications most often given to treat self-mutilation are the **selective serotonin reuptake inhibitors (SSRIs)**, which work by increasing the level of **serotonin** in the spaces (synapses) between nerve cells in the central nervous system. The SSRIs include **fluoxetine** (Prozac), **citalopram** (Celexa), **paroxetine** (Paxil), **fluvoxamine** (Luvox), and **sertraline** (Zoloft).

In extreme cases (such as when the patient's self-inflicted injuries are life-threatening), the doctor may

---

QUESTIONS TO ASK YOUR DOCTOR

- I think my teenager is engaging in self-cutting. What steps should I take to get help?
- Have you ever treated an adolescent who engaged in self-mutilation? What was the outcome?
- What is your opinion of psychotherapeutic approaches to treatment for self-mutilation?
- What is your opinion of medications as treatment for impulse control disorders?

---

recommend inpatient psychiatric treatment. Another option is a day hospital program.

Prognosis

Some studies indicate that following self-harm, some adolescents see improvement in their relationship with their parents. In addition, research suggests that self-harm may result in more support from social networks. In terms of decreasing the incidence of self-harm, self-harmers who learn to express their feelings verbally see a decrease in self-mutilating behaviors.

Prevention

Due to the lack of research on the disorder, self mutilation remains a poorly understood phenomenon, and prevention measures have not been thoroughly explored. In addition, the mixed and varied development pathways that lead to self-harm may complicate efforts at prevention. The risk factors for self-harm are often associated with other pathologies, and an awareness of this association might be a potential aid in targeting prevention.

Specific preventive strategies include helping young people with a history of self-injury to expand their social networks; forming peer counseling groups; and educating adolescents about the effects of the mass media in encouraging self-injury.

Resources
BOOKS
Aboujaoude, Elias, and Lorrin M. Koran. *Impulse Control Disorders.* New York: Cambridge University Press, 2010.
American Psychiatric Association. *Diagnostic and Statistical Manual of Mental Disorders.* 4th ed., text rev. Washington, DC: American Psychiatric Association, 2000.

Black, Donald W., and Nancy C. Andreasen. *Introductory Textbook of Psychiatry.* 5th ed. Arlington, VA: American Psychiatric Publishing, 2011.

Favazza, Armando R. *Bodies under Siege: Self-mutilation, Nonsuicidal Self-injury, and Body Modification in Culture and Psychiatry.* 3rd ed. Baltimore: Johns Hopkins University Press, 2011.

Friedman, Lauri S., ed. *Self-mutilation.* Detroit, MI: Greenhaven Press, 2009.

Nock, Matthew, ed. *Understanding Nonsuicidal Self-Injury: Origins, Assessment, and Treatment.* Arlington, VA: American Psychological Association, 2009.

PERIODICALS

Dawood, A. W. "Medicolegal Aspects of 3 Cases of Bizarre Self-mutilation." *American Journal of Forensic Medicine and Pathology* 32 (March 2011): 35–38.

Evren, C., et al. "Self-mutilative Behaviours in Male Alcohol-dependent Inpatients and Relationship with Posttraumatic Stress Disorder." *Psychiatry Research* 186 (March 30, 2011): 91–96.

Hintikka, J., et al. "Mental Disorders in Self-Cutting Adolescents." *Journal of Adolescent Health* 44 (May 2009): 464–67.

Hulbert, C., and R. Thomas. "Predicting Self-injury in BPD: An Investigation of the Experiential Avoidance Model." *Journal of Personality Disorders* 24 (October 2010): 651–53.

Stein, D. J., et al. "Trichotillomania (Hair Pulling Disorder), Skin Picking Disorder, and Stereotypic Movement Disorder: Toward DSM-V." *Depression and Anxiety* 27 (June 2010): 611–26.

Vrouva, I., et al. "The Risk-taking and Self-harm Inventory for Adolescents: Development and Psychometric Evaluation." *Psychological Assessment* 22 (December 2010): 852–65.

WEBSITES

American Psychiatric Association. *DSM-5 Development.* "V 01 Non-Suicidal Self Injury." http://www.dsm5.org/proposedrevision/pages/proposedrevision.aspx?rid=443 (accessed September 8, 2011).

Massachusetts General Hospital for Children. "Self-Mutilation." http://www.massgeneral.org/children/adolescenthealth/articles/aa_self-mutilation.aspx (accessed September 8, 2011).

Mayo Clinic. "Self-injury/Cutting." http://www.mayoclinic.com/health/self-injury/DS00775 (accessed September 8, 2011).

Smith, Melinda, and Jeanne Segal. "Cutting and Self-Harm." Helpguide.org. August 2011. http://www.helpguide.org/mental/self_injury.htm (accessed September 8, 2011).

ORGANIZATIONS

American Psychiatric Association, 1000 Wilson Blvd., Ste. 1825, Arlington, VA, 22209-3901, (703) 907-7300, apa@psych.org, http://www.psych.org.

National Alliance on Mental Illness, 2107 Wilson Blvd., Ste. 300, Arlington, VA, 22201-3042, Fax: (703) 524-9094, (800) 950-6264, http://www.nami.org.

National Institute of Mental Health, 6001 Executive Blvd., Rm. 8184, MSC 9663, Bethesda, MD, 20892-9663, (301) 433-4513; TTY: (301) 443-8431, Fax: (301) 443-4279, (866) 615-6464; TTY: (866) 415-8051, nimhinfo@nih.gov, http://www.nimh.nih.gov.

Emily Jane Willingham, PhD
Rebecca J. Frey, PhD

▌ Senior mental health

Definition

Senior mental health refers to the mental health of persons over the age of 65, including disorders and other mental health issues that are more common later in life. Senior mental health is a rapidly growing field of research and treatment due to the increased proportion of older adults in the general population worldwide.

Senior mental health issues are currently treated by a recognized subspecialty of psychiatry known as *geriatric psychiatry* or *geropsychiatry.* The American Board of Psychiatry and Neurology, which certifies doctors who choose to specialize in this field, established what was then called an "additional qualification" program for geriatric psychiatry in 1989. In 1997, the American Board of Medical Specialties (ABMS) formally renamed the program "Certification in the Subspecialty of Geriatric Psychiatry." As of 2011, psychiatrists in this subspecialty must complete a one-year fellowship in geriatric psychiatry following a four-year residency in general psychiatry and must pass a lengthy written and oral examination.

Demographics

In the United States, longer life expectancy coupled with the size of the post–World War II "baby boomer" generation (76 million people) means that the number of adults over 65 will swell from 13% of the population in 2000 to 20% by 2030. During the same period, the number of older adults with mental illness is expected to double to 15 million. Adults over the age of 85 are currently the fastest-growing segment of the U.S. population.

Women comprise the majority of older adults in Canada and the United States. At age 65, there are 118 women for every 100 men. At age 85, there are 241 women for every 100 men. The proportion of minorities among older adults is also increasing; minorities are expected to account for 25% of seniors in 2030, up from 16% in 1998.

Specialists maintain that mental illness in general is underreported and underdiagnosed in older adults in North America. Nearly 20% of persons 55 years and older experience mental disorders that are not part of normal aging; the most common of these are mood disorders and cognitive impairment. In particular, the rate of **suicide** among seniors is higher than that of any other age group; the rate of suicide among adults 85 and older is twice the national average. In terms of ethnicity, Caucasian seniors have the highest rate of suicide, followed by Asian Americans, Hispanics, and African Americans.

Description

Mental health care for older adults is complicated by several factors that do not affect younger adults as often. The first factor is physical changes, including the effects of aging on sense perception, particularly hearing, sight, and taste. The loss of keenness of sense perception often means that the elderly do not enjoy certain activities as much as they once did, such as dining out; playing, singing, or listening to music; and painting, drawing, or other forms of art. Other changes that affect older adults' outlook on life include problems with sleep, difficulty coping with change, and increased vulnerability to physical injuries from falls or automobile accidents.

Another factor affecting care is the difficulty of prescribing medications for mood disorders or other mental health issues that will not cause problematic interactions with drugs given to treat the physical disorders prevalent in older adults. These conditions include type 2 diabetes, high blood pressure, arthritis, heart disease, cancer, and Parkinson's disease. The practice of taking many different prescription drugs is called *polypharmacy,* and it is more common among the elderly than in any other segment of the population.

A third factor is the social and geographical isolation of many seniors. Older adults must cope with **bereavement** and **grief** more often than younger people. In addition, the loss of a spouse or friends may make getting to regular appointments for mental health care difficult. There are currently 20 million drivers over the age of 65 on American roads, with this number expected to double by 2020. Many older adults, however, often give up driving based on health conditions, loss of eyesight, or recommendations from law enforcement officers, family members, or primary care physicians. Having to stop driving represents a significant loss of independence for many older adults and can worsen **depression** or other mood disorders, as well as complicating access to mental health care.

The mental health issues that are most common among seniors include **anxiety disorders**, **dementia** and Alzheimer's disease, **late-life depression**, suicide, alcoholism, and **substance abuse**.

Anxiety disorders

It is estimated that 11.4% of adults over age 55 meet criteria for an anxiety disorder each year in the United States and Canada. Worries over health, finances, and maintaining independence are common triggers of anxiety disorders in older adults. In contrast to younger people, however, the most common anxiety disorders in seniors are phobias rather than **panic disorder** or **obsessive-compulsive disorder**. Generalized anxiety disorder (GAD) is much more common among younger adults than in seniors, although it may develop in an older adult after he or she is diagnosed with diabetes, heart disease, or another chronic physical disorder.

An increasingly common sign of anxiety among older adults is **hoarding**. While hoarding behavior typically begins in late childhood or adolescence, it usually worsens with age and may reach a critical point in adults over 50.

With regard to treatment, seniors do not respond as well to antianxiety medications as younger people; they usually experience some symptom relief but not the complete elimination of anxiety. Older adults are usually managed on lower doses of these medications than younger patients.

Cognitive impairment

The most common form of dementia among older adults is **Alzheimer's disease** (AD). AD affects about 4.5 million people in the United States alone, and that number is projected to exceed 13 million by the year 2050. It is thought that nearly 10% of all people over age 65, and that up to half of those over age 85 have Alzheimer's disease or another form of dementia. The symptoms of dementia affect about 5% of adults aged 65 to 74 and 40% of those older than 85. About 19 million Americans have a family member with AD or another dementing illness.

Other dementing illnesses that affect older adults include **vascular dementia**, Lewy body dementia, frontotemporal dementia, and dementia associated with HIV infection. Dementia may also accompany Parkinson's disease, Huntington's disease, Creutzfeldt-Jakob disease, and late-stage syphilis. It is possible for a patient to suffer from more than one type of dementia.

KEY TERMS

Dementia—A chronic, global, usually irreversible loss of memory and other aspects of cognition.

Lewy body dementia—A type of dementia characterized by the presence of abnormal sphere-shaped clumps of protein in nerve cells in the brain.

Polypharmacy—The use of a number of different medications by the same patient. Polypharmacy is most common among the elderly and those taking psychiatric medications.

Depression

Depression in older adults is widely misunderstood. On the one hand, there are many aspects of aging, such as bereavement, loss of physical strength, and the appearance or worsening of chronic illness that contribute to "blue" moods or sadness in seniors. However, the assumption that clinical depression is a "normal" or inevitable part of aging is incorrect. The actual rate of major depression in the general population declines with age, although depressive symptoms are more common in older adults. An estimated 6% of Americans aged 65 and older (about two million persons) develop a diagnosable depressive illness each year. Ironically, major depression among seniors is underdiagnosed and undertreated; one study reported that only 11% of depressed seniors in primary care receive adequate antidepressant treatment, with 34% receiving inadequate treatment and 55% receiving no treatment at all.

Major depression in the elderly can be difficult to diagnose because it can mimic the early signs of dementia or Parkinson's disease; it may also coexist with substance abuse disorders or such chronic physical illnesses as thyroid disorders. An older adult with depressive symptoms should be evaluated by a neurologist as well as a geriatric **psychiatrist** to make sure that major depression is adequately diagnosed and treated. One recent development in nonpharmacological treatments of depression in seniors is the growing recognition that cognitive dysfunction needs to be addressed as well as the emotional symptoms of the disorder.

Suicide

As noted above, suicide is a growing problem among older Americans, particularly in men and those over 85 years of age. Research conducted by the **National Institute of**

Mental Health (NIMH) indicates that the following additional factors increase a senior's risk of suicide:

- white race; Asian men, Hispanic men, and African American men are less likely to attempt or commit suicide than Caucasians
- a family history of suicide
- a history of previous suicide attempts
- being a frontline combat veteran
- a history of abuse in childhood
- recent stressful events, such as separation or divorce; job loss or financial difficulty; or death of spouse, partner, friend, or pet
- medical illness, especially terminal illness
- pain, particularly chronic, severe, or intractable pain
- loss of mobility or independence
- alcohol or substance abuse, which can weaken impulse control
- presence of a psychiatric illness

More than 90% of Americans, including seniors, who commit suicide have a significant mental illness. Major depression accounts for 60% of all suicides. Other mental disorders that increase the risk of suicide among seniors include **schizophrenia**, alcoholism, substance abuse, **borderline personality disorder**, Huntington's disease, and epilepsy.

Protective factors that lower a senior's risk of suicide include:

- a significant friendship network
- religious faith and practice; older African American women have a particularly low rate of suicide because of their high rate of church membership
- a stable marriage or close-knit extended family
- a strong interest in, or commitment to, a project or cause that brings people together, such as community service, neighborhood associations, book clubs, hobby groups, other activity groups.

Although seniors are less likely to attempt suicide than younger people, according to the National Strategy for Suicide Prevention (NSSP), they are more likely than younger persons to use highly lethal means of suicide. According to a Canadian study, seniors are most likely to use firearms to commit suicide, followed by hanging, self-poisoning, and leaping from heights.

Alcohol and substance abuse

Alcohol and substance abuse are greater problems among seniors than many people recognize. The National Institute on Alcohol Abuse and Alcoholism (NIAAA) estimates that between 2% and 10% of seniors living in the community meet *DSM-IV* criteria for substance dependence or abuse. Another study reported that 6% of seniors are heavy drinkers, which is defined as having two or more drinks per day. These disorders can trigger a number of health-related problems in seniors and worsen those that already exist. Alcohol abuse is four times more common among men than women ages 65 and older.

One major reason for the negative effects of heavy drinking on health in older adults is that the human body metabolizes (i.e., digests and uses) alcohol much less efficiently as it ages; thus, a senior may get drunk on the same amount of alcohol that he or she could drink without noticeable effects when he or she was younger. Studies have shown that a 65-year-old who consumes the same amount of alcohol as a 20-year-old will have a blood alcohol level 20% higher, and a 90-year-old will have a blood alcohol 50% higher. Some of the specific health risks of substance abuse in the elderly are:

- high blood pressure and increased risk of stroke
- increased risk of cancer of the head, neck, or esophagus
- increased risk of cirrhosis of the liver
- increased risk of falls and fall-related injuries, particularly in women; studies indicate that heavy drinking in older women also increases the risk of osteoporosis
- increased risk of malnutrition
- high risk of interactions with prescription drugs that the senior may be taking for other conditions
- decline in cognitive function; some researchers think that alcohol abuse increases a senior's risk of Alzheimer's disease, but further research is needed

Diagnosis of alcohol or substance abuse in the elderly is complicated by several factors. One is that the signs of alcohol or substance dependence are easy to confuse with age-related changes in muscle coordination, cognition, mood, social functioning, and the like. Older alcoholics are also less likely to be noticed if they no longer drive or work outside the home. In addition, about one-third of seniors who abuse alcohol are so-called late-onset drinkers; they are people who did not abuse alcohol when they were younger but have turned to it out of loneliness or bereavement. Late-onset seniors typically have higher levels of education and income than the two-thirds of older substance abusers with previous histories of alcohol or drug dependence.

In contrast to younger adults, seniors are less likely to use illicit "street" drugs, with rates of less than 0.1% of adults over 65. **Prescription drug abuse**, however, is relatively common among seniors, particularly older women.

QUESTIONS TO ASK YOUR DOCTOR

- Can you give me a referral for a geriatric psychiatrist?
- Have you ever treated a caregiver for emotional stress?
- What can I do to avoid mental health conditions associated with aging?
- Can you recommend any support groups for elderly patients?

Caregiver issues

One significant concern in geriatric psychiatry is the **stress** placed on caregivers for the elderly. Many seniors with Alzheimer's disease and other forms of dementia are cared for by family members or friends, at least in the early stages of the disease. As of 2011, almost 25% of U.S. households were providing care for a family member over the age of 50. The average age of these primary caregivers was over 60 years of age, and more than 75% were women. With regard to mental health issues among caregivers for the elderly, studies indicate that 46% meet the criteria for clinical depression; almost half of those caring for a person with Alzheimer's report significant emotional distress. In many cases, geriatric psychiatrists treat the mental health issues of their patient's caregiver(s) as well as their patient's disorders.

Treatment

Most seniors with mental health issues do not receive care from specialists; only about 3% are seen by geriatric psychiatrists. About half of seniors with mental health issues do not consult any physician for help; those who do, usually ask for help from their primary care physician. Seniors in the United States have the lowest rate of mental health care utilization of any adult age group: older adults account for only 7% of all inpatient mental health services, 6% of community-based mental health services, and 9% of private psychiatric care, even though they represent 13% of the population. The reasons given for seniors' underutilization include the **stigma** attached to mental illness, lack of access to mental health services, poor coordination among mental healthcare providers and services for the elderly, lack of funding, transportation difficulties, and a shortage of health care professionals.

Funding for mental health care among seniors comes from a combination of Medicare, Medicaid, private insurance, state and local governments, and block grants awarded and administered by the Center for Mental Health Services of the **Substance Abuse and Mental Health Services Administration** (SAMHSA). Medicare coverage is not comprehensive; as of 2011, it covered only 50% of the cost of mental health services, and it did not cover the cost of prescription medications.

Specialists in the field of geriatric psychiatry are concerned about the growing shortfall of physicians in the field. About 2,500 psychiatrists have been board-certified in geriatric psychiatry since 1990; there were 56 approved fellowship programs in the field as of 2011. The National Institute on Aging (NIA) estimated in 1997 that 4,000 to 5,000 geriatric psychiatrists will be needed by 2030 to keep up with the growth of the elderly population; however, at the present rate of certification, there will be only about 2,700 physicians in the field at that time (allowing for a 3% loss each year due to death and retirement).

With regard to research, there were 179 **clinical trials** in the general field of geriatric psychiatry under way in 2011. Some of these studies are investigating the effectiveness of telemedicine in meeting the mental health needs of seniors, new screeners to detect depression in older adults, **transcranial magnetic stimulation** as a possible treatment for depression, and various treatments for **sleep disorders** in the elderly. Other researchers are studying various drugs for the treatment of Alzheimer's and other types of dementia, ranging from lithium and the atypical antipsychotics ordinarily used to treat schizophrenia to experimental drugs that have not yet been approved by regulatory agencies.

Resources

BOOKS

Agronin, Marc E., and Gabe J. Maletta, eds. *Principles and Practice of Geriatric Psychiatry.* 2nd ed. Philadelphia: Wolters Kluwer Health/Lippincott Williams and Wilkins, 2011.

American Psychiatric Association. *Diagnostic and Statistical Manual of Mental Disorders.* 4th ed., text rev. Washington, DC: American Psychiatric Association, 2000.

Blazer, Dan G., and David C. Steffens, eds. *The American Psychiatric Publishing Textbook of Geriatric Psychiatry.* 4th ed. Washington, DC: American Psychiatric Pub., 2009.

Craft, Edwin, Saul M. Levin, and Richard K. Ehara, eds. *Substance Abuse among Older Adults: Physicians' Guide.* Rockville, MD: U.S. Dept. of Health and Human Services, Substance Abuse and Mental Health Services Administration, Center for Substance Abuse Treatment, 2010.

Halter, Jeffrey B., et al., eds. *Hazzard's Geriatric Medicine and Gerontology.* 6th ed. New York: McGraw Medical, 2006.

PERIODICALS

Alexopoulos, G.S. "Psychotherapy for Late-Life Depression." *Journal of Clinical Psychiatry* 71 (June 2010): e13.

Baldwin, R.C. "Preventing Late-Life Depression: A Clinical Update." *International Psychogeriatrics* 22 (December 2010): 1216–24.

Kalapatapu, R.K., et al. "Alcohol Use Disorders in Geriatrics." *International Journal of Psychiatry in Medicine* 40 (March 2010): 321–37.

Madhusoodanan, S., et al. "Primary Prevention in Geriatric Psychiatry." *Annals of Clinical Psychiatry* 22 (November 2010): 249–61.

Mahgoub, N., et al. "Self-injurious Behavior in the Nursing Home Setting." *International Journal of Geriatric Psychiatry* 26 (January 2011): 27–30.

Milka, M. "Study Details Lingering Effects of Stroke." *Journal of the American Medical Association* 306 (July 13, 2011): 142–43.

Siemens, I., and L. Hazelton. "Communicating with Families of Dementia Patients: Practical Guide to Relieving Caregiver Stress." *Canadian Family Physician* 57 (July 2011): 801–2.

Tartaglia, M.C., et al. "Neuroimaging in Dementia." *Neurotherapeutics* 8 (January 2011): 82–92.

Voaklander, D.C., et al. "Medical Illness, Medication Use and Suicide in Seniors: A Population-Based Case Control." *Journal of Epidemiology and Community Health* 62 (February 2008): 138–46.

Wilkins, V.M., et al. "Late-life Depression with Comorbid Cognitive Impairment and Disability: Nonpharmacological Interventions." *Clinical Interventions in Aging* 15 (November 2010): 323–31.

WEBSITES

American Association for Geriatric Psychiatry (AAGP). "Geriatrics and Mental Health—The Facts." http://www.aagpgpa.org/prof/facts_mh.asp (accessed August 6, 2011).

National Institute of Mental Health (NIMH). "Older Adults: Depression and Suicide Facts." http://www.nimh.nih.gov/health/publications/older-adults-depression-and-suicide-facts-fact-sheet/index.shtml (accessed August 6, 2011).

National Institute of Mental Health (NIMH). "Older Adults and Mental Health." http://www.nimh.nih.gov/health/topics/older-adults-and-mental-health/index.shtml (accessed August 6, 2011).

ORGANIZATIONS

American Association for Geriatric Psychiatry (AAGP), 7910 Woodmont Ave., Ste. 1050, Bethesda, MD, United States 20814-3004, (301) 654-7850, Fax: (301) 654-4137, main@aagponline.org, http://www.aagpgpa.org.

American Geriatrics Society (AGS), 40 Fulton St., 18th Fl., New York, NY, United States 10038, (212) 308-1414, Fax: (212) 832-8646, info.amger@americangeriatrics.org, http://www.americangeriatrics.org.

International Psychogeriatric Association (IPA), 550 Frontage Rd., Ste. 3759, Northfield, IL, United States 60093, (847) 501-3310, Fax: (847) 501-3317, http://www.ipa-online.org.

National Institute on Aging (NIA), Bldg. 31, Rm. 5C27, 31 Center Dr., MSC 2292, Bethesda, MD, United States 20892, (301) 496-1752, Fax: (301) 496-1072, (800) 222-2225, http://www.nia.nih.gov.

National Institute of Mental Health (NIMH), 6001 Executive Blvd., Rm. 8184, MSC 9663, Bethesda, MD, United States 20892-9663, (301) 443-4513, Fax: (301) 443-4279, (866) 615-6464, nimhinfo@nih.gov, http://www.nimh.nih.gov/index.shtml.

Rebecca J. Frey, Ph.D.

▌ Sensory integration disorder

Definition

Sensory integration disorder or dysfunction (SID) is a neurological disorder that results from the brain's inability to integrate certain information received from the body's five basic sensory systems. These sensory systems are responsible for detecting sights, sounds, smell, tastes, temperatures, pain, and the position and movements of the body. The **brain** then forms a combined picture of this information in order for the body to make sense of its surroundings and react to them appropriately. The ongoing relationship between behavior and brain functioning is called sensory integration (SI), a theory that was first pioneered by A. Jean Ayres, Ph.D., OTR in the 1960s.

Description

Sensory experiences include touch, movement, body awareness, sight, sound, smell, taste, and the pull of gravity. Distinguishing between these is the process of sensory integration (SI). While the process of SI occurs automatically and without effort for most, for some the process is inefficient. Extensive effort and attention are required in these individuals for SI to occur, without a guarantee of it being accomplished. When this happens, goals are not easily completed, resulting in sensory integration disorder (SID).

The normal process of SI begins before birth and continues throughout life, with the majority of SI development occurring before the early teenage years. The ability for SI to become more refined and effective coincides with the aging process as it determines how well motor and speech skills, and emotional stability develop. The beginnings of the SI theory by Ayres instigated ongoing research that looks at the crucial foundation it provides for complex learning and behavior throughout life.

Causes and symptoms

The presence of a sensory integration disorder is typically detected in young children. While most children develop SI during the course of ordinary childhood activities, which helps establish such things as the ability for motor planning and adapting to incoming sensations, others' SI ability does not develop as efficiently. When their process is disordered, a variety of problems in learning, development, or behavior become obvious.

Those who have sensory integration dysfunction may be unable to respond to certain sensory information by planning and organizing what needs to be done in an appropriate and automatic manner. This may cause a primitive survival technique called "fright, flight, and fight," or withdrawal response, which originates from the "primitive" brain. This response often appears extreme and inappropriate for the particular situation.

The neurological disorganization resulting in SID occurs in three different ways: the brain does not receive messages due to a disconnection in the neuron cells; sensory messages are received inconsistently; or sensory messages are received consistently, but do not connect properly with other sensory messages. When the brain poorly processes sensory messages, inefficient motor, language, or emotional output is the result.

According to Sensory Integration International (SII), a nonprofit corporation concerned with the impact of sensory integrative problems on people's lives, the following are some signs of sensory integration disorder (SID):

• oversensitivity to touch, movement, sights, or sounds
• underreactivity to touch, movement, sights, or sounds
• tendency to be easily distracted
• social and/or emotional problems
• activity level that is unusually high or unusually low
• physical clumsiness or apparent carelessness
• impulsive, lacking in self-control
• difficulty in making transitions from one situation to another
• inability to unwind or calm self
• poor self concept
• delays in speech, language, or motor skills
• delays in academic achievement

While research indicates that sensory integrative problems are found in up to 70% of children who are considered learning disabled by schools, the problems of sensory integration are not confined to children with learning disabilities. SID transfers through all age groups, as well as intellectual levels and socioeconomic groups. Factors that contribute to SID include: premature birth;

autism and other developmental disorders; learning disabilities; delinquency and substance abuse due to learning disabilities; stress-related disorders; and brain injury. Two of the biggest contributing conditions are autism and attention deficit hyperactivity disorder (ADHD).

Diagnosis

In order to determine the presence of SID, an evaluation may be conducted by a qualified occupational or physical therapist. An evaluation normally consists of both standardized testing and structured observations of responses to sensory stimulation, posture, balance, coordination, and eye movements. These test results and assessment data, along with information from other professionals and parents, are carefully analyzed by the therapist who then makes recommendations about appropriate treatment.

Treatment

Occupational therapists play a key role in the conventional treatment of SID. By providing sensory integration therapy, occupational therapists are able to supply the vital sensory input and experiences that children with SID need to grow and learn. Also referred to as a "sensory diet," this type of therapy involves a planned and scheduled activity program implemented by an occupational therapist, with each "diet" being designed and developed to meet the needs of the child's nervous system. A sensory diet stimulates the "near" senses (tactile, vestibular, and proprioceptive) with a combination of alerting, organizing, and calming techniques.

Motor skills training methods that normally consist of adaptive physical education, movement education, and gymnastics are often used by occupational and physical therapists. While these are important skills to work on, the sensory integrative approach is vital to treating SID.

The sensory integrative approach is guided by one important aspect—the child's motivation in selection of the activities. By allowing them to be actively involved, and explore activities that provide sensory experiences most beneficial to them, children become more mature and efficient at organizing sensory information.

Alternative treatment

Sensory integration disorder (SID) is treatable with occupational therapy, but some alternative methods are emerging to complement the conventional methods used for SID.

KEY TERMS

Axon—A process of a neuron that conducts impulses away from the cell body. Axons are usually long and straight.

Cortical—Regarding the cortex, or the outer layer of the brain, as distinguished from the inner portion.

Neurotransmission—When a neurotransmitter, or chemical agent released by a particular brain cell, travels across the synapse to act on the target cell to either inhibit or excite it.

Proprioceptive—Pertaining to proprioception, or the awareness of posture, movement, and changes in equilibrium and the knowledge of position, weight, and resistance of objects as they relate to the body.

Tactile—The perception of touch.

Vestibular—Pertaining to the vestibule; regarding the vestibular nerve of the ear which is linked to the ability to hear sounds.

Therapeutic body brushing is often used on children (not infants) who overreact to tactile stimulation. A specific non-scratching surgical brush is used to make firm, brisk movements over most of the body, especially the arms, legs, hands, back and soles of the feet. A technique of deep joint compression follows the brushing. Usually begun by an occupational therapist, the technique is taught to parents who need to complete the process for three to five minutes, six to eight times a day. The time needed for brushing is reduced as the child begins to respond more normally to touch. In order for this therapy to be effective, the correct brush and technique must be used.

A report in 1998 indicated the use of cerebral electrical stimulation (CES) as being helpful to children with conditions such as moderate to severe autistic spectrum disorders, learning disabilities, and sensory integration dysfunction. CES is a modification of Transcutaneous Electrical Nerve Stimulation (TENS) technology that has been used to treat adults with various pain problems, including arthritis and carpal tunnel syndrome. TENS therapy uses a low voltage signal applied to the body through the skin with the goal of replacing painful impressions with a massage-like sensation. A much lower signal is used for CES than that used for traditional TENS, and the electrodes are placed on the scalp or ears. Occupational therapists who have studied the use of CES suggest that CES for children with SID can result in improved brain activity. The device is worn by children at home for 10 minutes at a time, twice per day.

Music therapy helps promote active listening. Hypnosis and **biofeedback** are sometimes used, along with **psychotherapy**, to help those with SID, particularly older patients.

Prognosis

By providing treatment at an early age, sensory integration disorder may be managed successfully. The ultimate goal is for the individual to be better able to interact with his or her environment in a more successful and adaptive way.

Resources

BOOKS

Auer, Christopher, Susan Blumberg, and Lucy Jane Miller. *Parenting a Child with Sensory Processing Disorder: A Family Guide to Understanding and Supporting Your Sensory-Sensitive Child.* Oakland, CA: New Harbinger Publications, 2006.

WEBSITES

Sensory Processing Disorder Foundation. "About SPD." http://www.sinetwork.org/about-sensory-processing-disorder.html (accessed November 14, 2011).

ORGANIZATIONS

Sensory Integration International/The Ayres Clinic, 200 2nd Ave. S, 447, St. Petersburg, FL, 33701-4313, (888) 271-2744.

Sensory Processing Disorder Foundation, 5420 S Quebec St., Ste. 135, Greenwood Village, CO, 80111, (303) 794-1182, Fax: (303) 322-5550, http://www.sinetwork.org.

Beth A. Kapes

Separation anxiety disorder

Definition

Like many childhood concerns, separation anxiety is normal at certain developmental stages. For example, when a child between the ages of 8 and 14 months is separated from her mother or other primary caretaker, she may experience distress. This is normal. However, separation anxiety that occurs at later ages is considered a disorder because it is outside of normal developmental expectations, and because of the intensity of the child's emotional response.

Separation anxiety disorder occurs most frequently from the ages of 5 to 7 and from 11 to 14.

Environmental stimuli and internal cues from the child himself interact in the presentation of separation anxiety disorder. Separation anxiety disorder is defined by the primary expression of excessive anxiety that occurs upon the actual or anticipated separation of the child from adult caregivers—most often the parents. Significant problems in daily functioning for the child and parents can result from the disorder. Common fears observed in the presentation of separation anxiety include concerns about the parents' health or well-being (less frequently the child's own health), general catastrophes, natural disasters, or the child becoming lost/separated from the parents. Disrupted sleep, difficulty falling asleep alone, fear of monsters, or nightmares are also commonly experienced by children with separation anxiety disorder.

Family routines, parents' work schedules, and siblings' activities may all be negatively affected by the excessive anxiety and demands of the child with separation anxiety disorder. Family life is often disrupted by efforts to soothe the child. Parents can become stressed themselves as they try to maintain their daily routines and obligations, while attempting to manage their child's anxiety. The family's adjustment is often made more difficult due to the sudden appearance of symptoms.

Demographics

Prevalence estimates of separation anxiety disorder are 4%–5% of the population. Gender differences have not been observed, although girls do present more often with **anxiety disorders** in general. Of those diagnosed with separation anxiety disorder, approximately 75% experience school refusal. The most frequently observed ages for occurrence of separation anxiety disorder are in children ages 5 to 7 years and again from ages 11 to 14 years. It is at these times the children may feel more challenged by the developmental tasks of entering school or beginning puberty.

Description

Children experiencing separation anxiety disorder display significant distress upon separation from the parent or other primary caregiver. Separation anxiety disorder often becomes problematic for families during elementary school, although it can also occur in older or younger children. The child appears fearful because he or she thinks something horrible will happen to the child or parent while they are apart. The child's responses to separation may include crying or becoming angry with the adult in an attempt to manipulate the situation. When thwarted by the adult's appropriate boundaries, expectations, and structure (the child must attend school, for example), the child's distress may become displaced into other maladaptive or negative behaviors. The child may begin to exhibit behavioral problems at school or at home when there has been no previous history of such problems. The child may seek out a new, negative peer group in order to gain attention or avoid separation.

Many children are unable to describe their specific fear. The feelings may seem more general and engulfing, especially to the younger child, making description more difficult and the feelings more overpowering. Children, and even adolescents, may experience difficulty describing their internal thoughts and feelings, which is normal. The ability to self-monitor, or observe one's own behavior or decision-making process, does not develop until late in adolescence for some individuals. When caregivers press the child experiencing separation anxiety for explanations, the feelings of anxiety can actually become more overwhelming. The intensity of the child's emotional response, accompanied by a lack of explanation, can become very frustrating for parents. Children or adolescents with an angry or frustrated parent may create a reasonable explanation for their fears to appease caregivers, and to keep them from leaving. Lying to take the emphasis off their strong feelings may be one of the early behavioral changes that can accompany separation anxiety.

Although exposure to a specific stressor is not required for the development of separation anxiety disorder, in many cases, a specific incident may precipitate the onset of the disorder (the traumatic events of the terrorist attacks against the United States on September 11, 2001, for example). Another common precipitant is the holiday or summer break from school. Some children experience significant difficulty returning to school after a relatively short break, but certainly after summer and holidays.

Causes and symptoms

Causes

- Environmental change. Separation anxiety disorder is often precipitated by change or stress in the child's life and daily routine, such as a move, death or illness of a close relative or pet, starting a new school, a traumatic event, or even a return to school after summer vacation.
- Genetic influence. Evidence suggests a genetic link between separation anxiety disorders in children and a history of panic disorder, anxiety, or depression in their parents. Infants with anxious temperaments may have a predisposition toward later development of anxiety disorders.

- Parent/child attachment. Quality of attachment between children and their parents has also been identified as a factor in separation anxiety disorder. If the child senses emotional distance, the behaviors may be an attempt to draw the parent in more closely. The problematic behaviors can also draw the attention and care of others as well.
- Developmental considerations. Children develop at different rates when compared to each other (boys mature slower than girls, for example). Furthermore, the rate of development within the same person can vary across different types of functioning (for example, a gifted child is advanced intellectually but may be behind developmental expectations for social and emotional areas of functioning). A slower rate of development in the intellectual, social, emotional, or physical arena can foster anxiety within the child, making the separation more difficult.
- Cognitive factors. Children repeatedly worry about what they are afraid of (getting lost or a parent getting hurt, for example). The thought patterns are repeated within the child's mind until his emotions are beyond his control. The child may feel he is unable to think about anything else other than his fears, which contributes to his anxiety and irrational behaviors.
- Behavioral factors. The child or adolescent's crying and clinging behaviors may be developed by the child to cope with the feelings of anxiety associated with certain people, environment, or situations, such as attending school. The behaviors serve to distract attention away from the child's negative feelings, while nurturing the anxiety and fear into a greater part of the child's daily experience. For children, the behavioral component often becomes the mode of expression for the anxiety. The behavior may appear manipulative at times, due to the quick disappearance of symptoms once the threat of separation passes.
- Stress factors and influence. Symptoms of separation anxiety disorder may be exacerbated by a change in routine, illness, lack of adequate rest, a family move, or change in family structure (such as death, divorce, parent illness, birth of a sibling). The child's symptoms may also be affected by a change in caregivers or changes in parents' response to the child in terms of discipline, availability, or daily routine. Even if changes are positive or exciting, the change may feel uncomfortable and precipitate an anxious response in the child.

Symptoms

The *Diagnostic and Statistical Manual of Mental Disorders (DSM-IV-TR)*, a handbook for mental health professionals that aids in **diagnosis**, lists the following criteria for separation anxiety disorder.

- Recurrent excessive distress upon separation. The child may become focused on the separation long before the actual event, or simply at the time of the anticipated separation. The recurrent behavioral pattern does not respond to intervention. The child experiences extreme distress, a highly charged emotional response that is repeated when the child anticipates separation from the caregiver. The child's fears trigger more anxiety and the emotional response intensifies.

- Persistent and excessive worry. The content of the worry may include some type of harm occurring to the child himself or toward the parents, or it may focus on becoming lost or separated indefinitely from the parent or caregiver.

- Repetitive nightmares. The child may experience repeated nightmares with themes of being chased, harmed, or separated from her family. Some fears are age-appropriate, but in separation anxiety disorder, the intensity of the fears becomes overwhelming to the child, leaving little opportunity for the child to control her emotions or behaviors. Although dreams are often a way of exploring and making sense of daily life, children with separation anxiety disorder report nightmares that represent their irrational fears or preoccupation with disaster.

- Complaints of physical symptoms. The child may feign illness (headaches, stomachaches, etc.) to avoid separation, or the child may actually experience nausea upon separation. If allowed to continue, the child may develop psychosomatic symptoms (physical symptoms with a psychological origin) that prevent the child from attending or fully participating in school activities. In these cases, the separation anxiety may develop into a more serious hypochondriacal state in which the child complains of chronic pain, which results in the child getting what she wants (i.e., not attending school).

- Persistent reluctance or refusal to engage in age-appropriate activities. The child may refuse to attend school because of preoccupation about separation from the parent. The child may also experience reluctance to be alone at home or at school without another adult being immediately available. The child may resist sleep without an adult present. The disorder causes significant disruption in the child's daily routine and may decrease the ability to perform previously mastered tasks. The child may appear to have reverted to behaviors from a younger age. The intensity of her emotions blocks the child's ability to communicate her feelings in ways other than through behaviors. Examples include tantrums, hitting, or clinging. Crying is one of the primary behaviors associated with separation anxiety disorder. The crying can become quite intense, making it difficult for the child to regain composure.

- Enmeshment or unusual interest in parents' schedules. The child wants to know all the details of the daily routine, a behavior which minimizes the anxiety the child is feeling.

- Quick resolution of symptoms (upon meeting child's demands). It may be hard for parents to accept the reality of the disorder because the symptoms often disappear quickly when separation does not occur. It is this component that can feel manipulative to those in the child's life.

Diagnosis

The mental health professional will usually make the diagnosis of separation anxiety disorder based on information gathered during an interview process involving the parent(s) and the child. It is usually preferable for the interviews with the parent and child to occur separately; however that may not be possible because of the child's intense anxiety about separation.

As noted, separation anxiety disorder is generally diagnosed by history, including parental report; however, a few measures of general anxiety exist that can be used to supplement the history. These include Pediatric Anxiety Rating Scale, Children's Global Assessment Scale, Children's Anxiety Scale, Screen for Child Anxiety Related Emotional Disorders (SCARED-R), Multi-Dimensional Anxiety Scale for Children, and Achenbach's Child Behavior Checklist.

Duration of disturbance prior to diagnosis is a minimum of four weeks, occurring prior to the age of 18 years.

The disorder is described as "early onset" prior to the age of 6, and is generally not diagnosed after the age of 18. However, some researchers are describing another type of separation anxiety experienced by parents when their adolescents leave home. Readers may recognize this stage of life as the "empty nest syndrome," however, no such formal diagnosis exists for a parental form of separation anxiety.

Treatment

The most effective treatments for separation anxiety disorder involve parents, as well as school personnel when appropriate. Giving the child a sense of safety and security is key to successful treatment. Current treatment methods combine some form of group or individual cognitive behavioral **intervention**. Treatment options include cognitive-behavioral therapy, imagery, modeling, systematic desensitization, positive role models, behavior modification, reminders, distraction and altruism, and medication management.

Cognitive-behavioral therapy

Cognitive-behavioral therapy is a treatment approach designed to alter a person's thoughts, beliefs, and images as a way of changing behavior. In treating a child with separation anxiety disorder, the goal is to help the child label her fears and identify the irrational beliefs and assumptions underlying her fears. By confronting and correcting her false beliefs, a parent can help his or her child become less anxious about separation.

Imagery

With imagery, a child uses his imagination to see himself being successful in a stressful situation. For example, before heading off to school, a child could imagine how he will handle separation from mom. Instead of crying, he sees himself calmly saying goodbye to his mom. The use of positive mental pictures may help diminish some of the child's anxiety and fear before separation actually occurs.

Modeling

Parents and teachers can be helpful in **modeling** appropriate behaviors and coping mechanisms at home and at school. For example, parents can model being relaxed when saying goodbye to their children and other people.

Systematic desensitization

Systematic desensitization is a **behavior modification** technique in which a person is gradually exposed to an anxiety-provoking or fearful object or situation while learning to be relaxed. A child with separation anxiety disorder may be taught to spend longer and longer periods of time at school without a caregiver present by teaching her relaxation techniques for managing her anxiety.

Positive role models

Using positive role models, whether in real life or in books, can also be helpful for children. Reading books about other children successfully separating from their caregiver can give the anxious child the confidence that he can do it, too. Watching his friends calmly separate from their caregivers can also empower the child to do the same.

Behavior modification

Behavior modification uses a system of rewards and reinforcements to change behavior. This method has been shown to be effective in a majority of cases involving children and separation anxiety disorder, even at one-year follow-up.

Reminders

Small items that remind the child of his bond with his parents can sometimes be helpful in managing the child's anxiety. Typical objects could include a smooth stone in the child's pocket, a picture of the family in the child's notebook, or a friendship bracelet. Allowing phone calls or contact throughout the day is generally not effective, as it provides a more direct reminder of the caregiver's absence.

Distraction and altruism

Distraction and altruism is another strategy that can be useful in treating separation anxiety disorder. Helping the child focus on things outside himself can provide a healthy distraction. For instance, the child may be asked to take care of a pet at school. Such distractions from the child's internal thoughts and feelings coupled with a "fun" responsibility can help the child move away from his internal state of anxiety.

Medication management

Medication is helpful in certain cases where the anxiety is so debilitating that the child is unable to participate in other forms of treatment, or go about his daily routine. Medication management most often involves some type of antianxiety or antidepressant drug. Specific classes include the **selective serotonin re-uptake inhibitors (SSRIs)** that influence **neurotransmitters** in the **brain** to regulate emotional response. Before any medication is given, however, it is essential that a careful medical and psychiatric evaluation be performed by a trained health professional.

Prognosis

More than 60% of children participating with their parents in cognitive-behavioral treatment are successful in managing their symptoms without medication. Symptoms generally do not re-appear in exactly the same way as the initial presentation; however, the child may have a heightened sensitivity to normal life transitions, such as changing schools. Families can help children cope with these transitions by visiting the new school, meeting teachers, and getting to know some students.

Separation anxiety disorder has a poorer prognosis in environments where threat of physical harm or separation actually exist.

Existence of other conditions, such as **autism**, decrease the likelihood of a positive prognosis. Presence of separation anxiety disorder in childhood is sometimes associated with early onset **panic disorder** in adults.

Studies indicate a lower prevalence of **alcohol use** and suicidal ideation in children or adolescents who

KEY TERM

Neurotransmitter—A chemical in the brain that transmits messages between neurons, or nerve cells.

experience separation anxiety disorder. **Depression** is commonly associated with anxiety disorders. Developing social skills can also be negatively affected by separation anxiety disorder.

Prevention

Prevention can be enhanced through parent effectiveness training that emphasizes the child's positive and successful coping strategies when dealing with separation. Overly anxious parents may need to develop their own support mechanisms and systems to manage their feelings and avoid influencing their children negatively.

Resources

BOOKS

American Psychiatric Association. *Diagnostic and Statistical Manual of Mental Disorders*. 4th ed., text rev. Washington, DC: American Psychiatric Publishing, 2000.

Brandt, Amy. *Benjamin Comes Back*. Transl. by Eida de la Vega. St. Paul, MN: Redleaf Press, 2000.

Penn, Audrey. *The Kissing Hand*. Terre Haute, IN: Tanglewood Press, 2007.

Silverman, W.K. and Andy P. Field, eds. *Anxiety Disorders in Children and Adolescents: Research, Assessment and Intervention*. 2nd ed. New York, NY: Cambridge University Press, 2011.

PERIODICALS

Burke, P., and R.C. Baker. "Is Fluvoxamine Safe and Effective for Treating Anxiety Disorders in Children?" *Journal of Family Practice* 50, no. 8 (August 2001).

Goodwin, R., et al. "Obsessive-Compulsive Disorder and Separation Anxiety Co-morbidity in Early Onset Panic Disorder" *Psychological Medicine* 31, no. 7 (October 2001): 1307–1310.

Kaplow, J.B., et al. "The Prospective Relation between Dimensions of Anxiety and the Initiation of Adolescent Alcohol Use." *Journal of Clinical Child Psychology* 30, no. 3 (September 2001): 316–326.

Kendall, P.C., E.V. Brady, and T. Verduin. "Comorbidity in Childhood Anxiety Disorders and Treatment Outcome." *Journal of the American Academy of Child & Adolescent Psychiatry* 40, no. 7 (July 2001): 787–794.

Muris, P., et al. "The Revised Version of the Screen for Child Anxiety Related Emotional Disorders (SCARED:R)." *British Journal of Clinical Psychology* 40, no. 1 (March 2001): 323–336.

Shortt, A.L., P.M. Barrett, and T.L. Fox. "Evaluating the FRIENDS Program: A Cognitive-Behavioral Group Treatment for Anxious Children and Their Parents." *Journal of Clinical Child Psychology* 30, no. 4 (December 2001): 525–535.

Southam-Gerow, M.A., P.C. Kendall, and V.R. Weersing. "Examining Outcome Variability: Correlates of Treatment Response in a Child and Adolescent Anxiety Clinic." *Journal of Clinical Child Psychology* 30, no. 3 (September 2001): 422–436.

Walkup, J.T., et al. "Fluvoxamine for the Treatment of Anxiety Disorders in Children and Adolescents." *The New England Journal of Medicine* 344, no. 17 (April 2001): 1279–85.

ORGANIZATIONS

American Academy of Child and Adolescent Psychiatry, 3615 Wisconsin Ave. NW, Washington, DC, 20016-3007, (202) 966-7300, Fax: (202) 966-2891, http://aacap.org.

Anxiety Disorders Association of America, 8730 Georgia Ave., Silver Spring, MD, 20910, (240) 485-1001, Fax: (240) 485-1035, http://www.adaa.org.

Deanna Pledge, Ph.D.

Serax *see* **Oxazepam**

Serentil *see* **Mesoridazine**

Seroquel *see* **Quetiapine**

Serotonin

Definition

Serotonin (pronounced ser-oh-TOH-nin) is a monoamine neurotransmitter—one of the chemicals naturally produced in the body that serves to convey nerve impulses across the gaps (synapses) between nerve cells. It is also known as 5-hydroxytryptamine or 5-HT. Monoamine means that a molecule of the neurotransmitter contains a single amino group. The chemical formula of serotonin is $C_{10}H_{12}N_2O$.

Purpose

Serotonin conveys nerve impulses across gaps (synapses) between nerve cells. It controls various functions in the body and various psychological characteristics as well.

Description

In its pure form, serotonin is a white powder that is slightly soluble in water. Serotonin was first discovered in blood in 1948 and was found to act as a

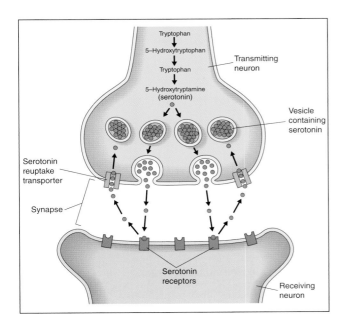

Diagram showing the role of serotonin in neuron (brain cell) communication. *(Illustration by Frank Forney. Reproduced by permission of Cengage Learning.)*

vasoconstrictor, a chemical compound that causes blood vessels to narrow or tighten. Its name comes from a combination of "serum" and "tone." Serotonin is found in a wide variety of plants and animals other than humans; it is an active ingredient in the venom found in stinging nettle plants and wasp, hornet, and scorpion stingers.

As its alternate name suggests, serotonin is derived from tryptophan, an essential amino acid. "Essential" means that the amino acid cannot be synthesized by the organism that needs it and must therefore be part of the organism's diet. Tryptophan is, however, plentiful in many foods, including chocolate, poultry, red meat, oats, dried dates, tofu, papayas, bananas, yogurt, milk, cottage cheese, eggs, sesame, chickpeas, sunflower and pumpkin seeds, peanuts, and fish. Serotonin is synthesized in the body from tryptophan by a short metabolic pathway that involves two enzymes, tryptophan hydroxylase (TPH) and amino acid decarboxylase (DDC). There are two genes in humans that encode TPH, located on chromosomes 11 and 12. The gene in humans that encodes DDC is located on chromosome 7.

Serotonin is synthesized in two different locations in the body, the **brain** and the intestines, and operates along two distinctive pathways depending on its source. About 5–10% of the serotonin in the human body is synthesized by serotonergic neurons (nerve cells) in the brain, where it functions as a neurotransmitter. The serotonin in the central nervous system (CNS) has a variety of functions, including mood regulation, appetite regulation, sexual desire, and sleep. Serotonin in the CNS also has some effect on cognitive functions, including memory, imagination, and learning. The greater part of the body's serotonin (about 90%), however, is secreted by enterochromaffin cells in the lining of the digestive tract. About 80% of the body's serotonin is utilized in the gut or by the smooth muscle tissues of the respiratory and cardiovascular systems, with the remainder stored in the platelets in the bloodstream. The serotonin in the platelets plays a role in the aggregation (clumping) of platelets during the process of blood clotting.

The brain's supply of serotonin is secreted by the raphe nuclei, a collection of nine pairs of neurons located along the length of the brainstem. The lower raphe nuclei have axons (long slender projections that carry nerve impulses away from the cell body) extending into the cerebellum and the spinal cord, while the axons of the upper raphe nuclei extend throughout the remainder of the brain, from the frontal cortex and hypothalamus to the amygdala and the hippocampus. Almost all the 40 million neurons in the human brain are influenced either directly or indirectly by the serotonin secreted by the raphe nuclei.

Serotonin receptors

At least 15 different types of serotonin receptors had been identified as of 2011, grouped into seven families numbered from 5-HT$_1$ through 5-HT$_7$. These receptors are protein molecules found on the surfaces of neurons and other cells that receive and respond to serotonin. The serotonin receptors modulate the release of such other **neurotransmitters** as norepinephrine, GABA, acetylcholine, and **dopamine**. They also regulate the release of a number of different hormones, including oxytocin, prolactin, cortisol, vasopressin, and corticotropin.

The serotonin receptors influence a wide variety of biological processes and neurological functions, including sleep, thermoregulation, nausea, vomiting, mood, aggression, anxiety, memory, cognition, learning, and appetite. Some of the specific 5-HT receptors, the locations of their activity, and their functions are as follows:

- 5-HT$_{1A}$. Active in blood vessels and CNS; affects aggression, anxiety, blood pressure regulation, hunger, memory, imagination, mood, cardiovascular tone, heart rate, respiration, ability to feel pain, sexual behavior, vomiting, temperature regulation, sleep, and addiction

- 5-HT$_{1B}$. Active in blood vessels and CNS; affects movement (locomotion), aggression, anxiety, blood pressure regulation, memory, mood, learning, sexual behavior, and addiction

- 5-HT$_{1D}$. Active in blood vessels and CNS; affects vasoconstriction, movement, and anxiety
- 5-HT$_{1F}$. Active in CNS and involved in migraine headaches.
- 5-HT$_{2A}$. Active in the digestive tract, smooth muscles, blood vessels, CNS, peripheral nervous system, and platelets; affects anxiety, blood pressure regulation, temperature regulation, hunger, learning, memory, mood, cognition, sexual behavior, sleep, and addiction
- 5-HT$_{2B}$. Active in the digestive tract, smooth muscles, blood vessels, CNS, peripheral nervous system, and platelets; affects peristalsis, blood pressure regulation, hunger, anxiety, and sleep.
- 5-HT$_{2C}$. Active in the digestive tract, smooth muscles, blood vessels, CNS, peripheral nervous system, and platelets; affects anxiety, movement, peristalsis, blood pressure regulation, hunger, mood, sexual behavior, temperature regulation, sleep, and addiction
- 5-HT$_3$. Active in the digestive tract, CNS, and peripheral nervous system; affects anxiety, peristalsis, vomiting, learning, memory, and addiction
- 5-HT$_4$. Active in the digestive tract, CNS, and peripheral nervous system; affects breathing, hunger, peristalsis, learning, memory, mood, and anxiety
- 5-HT$_{5A}$. Active in CNS; affects movement and sleep
- 5-HT$_6$. Active in CNS; affects cognition, learning, memory, anxiety, and mood
- 5-HT$_7$. Active in the digestive tract, blood vessels, and CNS; affects blood pressure regulation, breathing, temperature regulation, sleep, memory, mood, and anxiety

The 5-HT receptors are the targets of antipsychotic, antiemetic, antimigraine, and appetite suppressant drugs as well as **antidepressants**, LSD and other **hallucinogens**, and street drugs such as **ecstasy**.

The serotonin transporter

The serotonin transporter, or SERT (also known as 5-HTT), is a monoamine protein that regulates the amount of serotonin in the synapses between neurons. More specifically, it recycles serotonin by conveying (transporting) serotonin from the synaptic space back into the presynaptic neuron, thus ending the activity of the neurotransmitter at the synapse. SERT is the target of many antidepressant drugs, particularly those classified as **selective serotonin reuptake inhibitors**, or **SSRIs**. The SSRIs work by reducing the ability of serotonin to bind to the transporter protein. Changes in the metabolism of the serotonin transporter have been linked to various disorders ranging from **obsessive-compulsive disorder** (OCD), **depression**, and alcoholism to **social phobia** and high blood pressure.

SERT can also be found in platelets in blood serum, where serotonin itself functions as a vasoconstrictor.

SERT is encoded by a gene known as *SLC6A4*, located on chromosome 17 at locus 17q11.1–q12. Variations (polymorphisms) in this gene have been associated with increased susceptibility to depression and **anxiety disorders**. The *SLC6A4* gene has a region known as *5-HTTLPR*, which has two forms: a long form with 16 repeats and a short form with 14 repeats. The short form appears to be associated with a lower rate of gene transcription and a higher risk of anxiety disorders and PTSD in persons with this polymorphism.

Serotonin and mood disorders

Serotonin has been nicknamed the "happiness hormone" because of its association with positive mood. Its role in mood disorders, however, was not completely understood as of 2011. One reason for the ongoing questions is researchers' inability to measure directly the levels of serotonin in the living brain. Although it is thought that low levels of serotonin are associated with depression, the theory has not been proven. While it has been shown that levels of serotonin in the bloodstream are lower in depressed people, no one is certain whether the low levels of serotonin cause depression or whether depression causes blood levels of serotonin to drop.

In addition, it is not yet known how low levels of serotonin activity result in the brain; possible causes include insufficient production of serotonin in the raphe nuclei, too few receptor sites to respond to the serotonin that is produced, a shortage of tryptophan in the body, or inability of the serotonin to reach the HT receptors.

One possible explanation for the association between serotonin and depression focuses on the fact that serotonin boosts the production of new brain cells and that depression—particularly depression caused by stress—suppresses brain cell regeneration. According to this theory, the SSRI antidepressants work by stimulating the growth of new brain cells, which in turn relieves the patient's depressed mood.

Serotonin and antidepressants

A surprising recent finding is the relationship between bone formation or bone loss and serotonin. Serotonin formed in the digestive tract acts like a hormone to inhibit the formation of new bone while serotonin formed in the brain helps to increase bone mass. A related finding is that selective serotonin reuptake inhibitor (SSRI)

KEY TERMS

Agonist—Any chemical that binds to a receptor on a cell surface and stimulates that cell to respond.

Antidepressant—Any of a group of medications given to relieve mood disorders, including anxiety disorders as well as major depression. Antidepressants include monoamine oxidase inhibitors (MAOIs), tricyclic (TCAs) and tetracyclic (TeCAs) antidepressants, selective serotonin reuptake inhibitors (SSRIs), and serotonin-norepinephrine reuptake inhibitors (SNRIs).

Axon—A long, threadlike projection that is part of a nerve cell.

Brainstem—The lowermost portion of the brain, adjoining and continuous with the spinal cord. The brainstem regulates heart and respiratory function, the sleep cycle, and the nerves that convey sensory information to the face and neck.

Enterochromaffin cells—Specialized cells in the thin layer of tissue lining the cavity (lumen) of the digestive tract. Also known as Kulchitsky cells, enterochromaffin cells provide about 90% of the human body's supply of serotonin.

Neurotransmitter—Any of a group of chemicals produced in the body that function to convey impulses from nerve cells (neurons) to target cells. Serotonin is a neurotransmitter.

Peripheral nervous system—The part of the nervous system that lies outside the brain and spinal cord. It connects the central nervous system with sensory organs, muscles, blood vessels, and glands.

Peristalsis—The waves of muscular contraction in the intestines that push the food along during the process of digestion.

Platelet—A small, irregularly shaped cell fragment that plays an important role in blood clotting. Platelets are also called thrombocytes.

Raphe nuclei—A group of nine pairs of compact clusters of nerve cells found in the brainstem that secrete serotonin for use in the brain.

Receptor—In biochemistry, a substance (usually a protein) found on the surface of a cell that interacts with specific other molecules, drugs, hormones, or antibodies.

Serotonin transporter (SERT)—A protein that removes serotonin from the spaces between neurons (synaptic clefts) and thus terminates its action. In effect, SERT recycles serotonin by returning it to the neuron that originally released it (the presynaptic neuron).

Synapse—A connection between a neuron (nerve cell) and another cell (which may be a neuron or another type of cell) that allows the neuron to transmit a chemical or electrical signal to the receiving cell.

Tryptophan—An essential amino acid produced in the body by the action of trypsin (a digestive enzyme) on protein molecules.

Vasoconstrictor—Any substance that causes blood vessels to narrow or tighten. Serotonin is a vasoconstrictor.

antidepressants paradoxically discourage the formation of new bone when given at the dosage levels needed to treat major depression. This finding suggests that the SSRIs should be used with caution in patients with osteoporosis.

Drugs related to serotonin or serotonin receptor regulation

There are several different classes of drugs approved by the Food and Drug Administration (FDA) for use in the United States that work by acting on the serotonin transporter (SERT).

SELECTIVE SEROTONIN REUPTAKE INHIBITORS (SSRIs). There were six drugs in this category approved for the treatment of major depression as of 2011:

• fluoxetine (Prozac)

• sertraline (Zoloft)

• citalopram (Celexa)

• escitalopram (Lexapro)

• paroxetine (Paxil, Pexeva)

• fluoxetine combined with olanzapine, an atypical antipsychotic (Symbyax)

Some SSRIs are available in extended-release (XR) or controlled-release (CR) forms. These formulations allow patients to take the medication only once a day or once a week.

Vilazodone (Viibryd) is a new SSRI approved by the FDA in January 2011 that also acts as a partial receptor agonist. This dual action means that the drug affects the absorption of serotonin by receptors on the postsynaptic neuron as well as limiting the effectiveness of the transporter protein in returning serotonin to the presynaptic neuron. It is thought that vilazodone is less likely than the other SSRIs to produce such side effects as weight gain and sexual problems.

SEROTONIN AND NOREPINEPHRINE REUPTAKE INHIBITORS (SNRIs). There were three SNRIs approved for use in treating major depression as of 2011. These drugs are sometimes referred to as dual reuptake inhibitors:

• venlafaxine (Effexor)

• duloxetine (Cymbalta)

• desvenlafaxine (Pristiq)

Precautions

Serotonin syndrome is an increasingly frequent and potentially life-threatening condition that results from excessive amounts of serotonin in the body. It is most likely to occur when a person takes two drugs that both affect the levels of serotonin that remain in the brain or are released elsewhere in the body. Serotonin syndrome may result from several different drug combinations: a triptan (class of drugs given to relieve migraine headaches) and either an SSRI or an SNRI; a monoamine oxidase inhibitor (MAOI, an older class of antidepressants) and either an SSRI or an SNRI; or a pain reliever (meperidine, fentanyl, or cyclobenzaprine) or dextromethorphan (the active ingredient in many cough medicines) and either an SSRI or an SNRI. Serotonin syndrome has also been reported to occur with street drugs, including **cocaine**, **methamphetamine**, LSD, and ecstasy; herbal supplements, particularly **St. John's wort** and **ginseng**; antinausea drugs, particularly ondansetron and metoclopramide; lithium, a mood stabilizer; linezolid, an antibiotic; and ritonavir, a drug used to treat AIDS.

The symptoms of serotonin syndrome usually appear within minutes or hours (usually about six hours) after taking the drugs. Milder symptoms include diarrhea, shivering, and goose bumps on the skin. The patient may also experience headache, muscle twitching, heavy sweating, restlessness, confusion, rapid heart rate, and high blood pressure. Severe serotonin syndrome can be life-threatening; its symptoms include **seizures**, irregular heartbeat, high fever, and loss of consciousness. The syndrome causes around 125 deaths each year in the United States.

There were no specific tests to diagnose serotonin syndrome as of 2011; the **diagnosis** depends partly on the patient's medication history and partly on the doctor's ruling out other possible diagnoses. A person who notices any of the symptoms of serotonin syndrome shortly after starting a new medication or increasing the dosage of a medication that affects serotonin levels should call the doctor at once or go to the hospital emergency department. If the symptoms are severe or worsening rapidly, it is vital to seek emergency help at once. In the hospital, the patient may be treated with muscle relaxants, **benzodiazepines** to reduce agitation, cyproheptadine to block serotonin production, other drugs to regulate heart rate and blood pressure, and oxygen and intravenous fluids to treat high fever. Patients with very high fever may need to be intubated, given medications that paralyze muscles, and placed on a respirator.

In milder cases, the symptoms of serotonin syndrome usually go away within a day of discontinuing medications that increase serotonin production and/or taking drugs that block serotonin production.

Resources

BOOKS

American Psychiatric Association. *Diagnostic and Statistical Manual of Mental Disorders.* 4th ed., text rev. Washington, DC: American Psychiatric Association, 2000.

Kalueff, Allan V., and Justin L. Laporte, eds. *Experimental Models in Serotonin Transporter Research.* New York: Cambridge University Press, 2010.

Marino, Alessia G., and Ilaria C. Russo, eds. *Serotonin: New Research.* New York: Nova Science, 2009.

Stahl, Stephen M. *Antidepressants.* New York: Cambridge University Press, 2009.

Zorumski, Charles F., and Eugene H. Rubin. *Psychiatry and Clinical Neuroscience: A Primer.* New York: Oxford University Press, 2011.

PERIODICALS

Ables, Adrienne, and Raju Nagubilli. "Prevention, Diagnosis, and Management of Serotonin Syndrome." *American Family Physician* 81 (2010): 1139–42. http://www.aafp.org/afp/2010/0501/p1139.html (accessed October 12, 2011).

Angier, Natalie. "Job Description Grows for Our Utility Hormone." *New York Times*, May 3, 2011. http://www.nytimes.com/2011/05/03/science/03angier.html?_r=1&pagewanted=all (accessed October 12, 2011).

Armbruster, D., et al. "Serotonin Transporter Gene Variation and Stressful Life Events Impact Processing of Fear and Anxiety." *International Journal of Neuropsychopharmacology* 12 (2009): 393–401.

Barton, David A., et al. "Elevated Brain Serotonin Turnover in Patients with Depression: Effect of Genotype and Therapy." *Archives of General Psychiatry* 65, no. 1 (2008): 38–46. http://archpsyc.ama-assn.org/cgi/content/full/65/1/38 (accessed October 12, 2011).

Byrd, L. "Serotonin Syndrome: What Is It? Causes, Recognition, and Management." *Geriatric Nursing* 31 (2010): 387–89.

Ducy, P. "5-HT and Bone Biology." *Current Opinion in Pharmacology* 11 (2011): 34–38.

Khan, A., et al. "A Randomized, Double-blind, Placebo-controlled, 8-week Study of Vilazodone, a Serotonergic

Agent for the Treatment of Major Depressive Disorder." *Journal of Clinical Psychiatry* 72 (2011): 441–47.

Richerson, G.B., and G.F. Buchanan. "The Serotonin Axis: Shared Mechanisms in Seizures, Depression, and SUDEP." *Epilepsia* 52, Suppl. 1 (2011): 28–38.

Wankerl, M., et al. "Current Developments and Controversies: Does the Serotonin Transporter Gene-linked Polymorphic Region (5-HTTLPR) Modulate the Association between Stress and Depression?" *Current Opinion in Psychiatry* 23 (2010): 582–87.

WEBSITES

National Human Genome Research Institute (NHGRI). "Frequently Asked Questions about Pharmacogenomics." National Institutes of Health. http://www.genome.gov/27530645 (accessed October 12, 2011).

"Serotonin Syndrome." MayoClinic.com. http://www.mayoclinic.com/health/serotonin-syndrome/DS00860 (accessed October 12, 2011).

ORGANIZATIONS

American Association for Clinical Chemistry, 1850 K St. NW, Ste. 625, Washington, DC, 20006, Fax: (202) 887-5093, (800) 892-1400, http://www.aacc.org.

American Society for Clinical Pharmacology and Therapeutics, 528 N Washington St., Alexandria, VA, 22314, (703) 836-6981, info@ascpt.org, http://www.ascpt.org.

National Institute of Mental Health, 6001 Executive Blvd., Rm. 8184, MSC 9663, Bethesda, MD, 20892-9663, (301) 433-4513; TTY: (301) 443-8431, Fax: (301) 443-4279, (866) 615-6464; TTY: (866) 415-8051, nimhinfo@nih.gov, http://www.nimh.nih.gov.

Rebecca J. Frey, PhD

Serotonin syndrome

Definition

Serotonin syndrome is a dangerous and potentially life-threatening condition that results from too much of the neurotransmitter serotonin in the body.

Description

Serotonin is a type of neurotransmitter in the nervous system, a chemical that neurons (**brain** cells) use to signal one another in complex pathways for normal brain and body functioning. **Neurotransmitters** such as serotonin bind to chemical receptors on the surface of neurons. Once bound to a receptor, they affect physiological processes. The receptors activate a sequence of cellular events known as a chemical cascade or signaling pathway. Neurotransmitter signaling pathways are responsible for many regulatory processes, including the signaling that affects mood and emotional stability.

It is believed that a decrease in serotonin contributes to illnesses such as **depression** and **anxiety disorders**. Various types of antidepressant medication such as **selective serotonin reuptake inhibitors (SSRIs)** and selective serotonin and norepinephrine reuptake inhibitors (SSNRIs) decrease the absorption of serotonin, resulting in increased levels of serotonin in the body. However, taking some of these **antidepressants** or other medications that increase serotonin at the same time can result in too much serotonin left in the body. Overactivity of serotonin can be dangerous, resulting in serotonin syndrome, also called serotonin toxicity, serotonin poisoning, and serotonin storm.

Causes and symptoms

Causes

Serotonin overdose may be caused by taking multiple drugs that increase the amount of serotonin in the body. Drugs that increase serotonin include **SSRIs**, such as **paroxetine** (Paxil) and **fluoxetine** (Prozac); SSNRIs, such as **duloxetine** (Cymbalta); and antidepressants called **monoamine oxidase inhibitors (MAOIs)**. Other drugs include the antibiotic linezolid and the migraine drug sumatriptan. The combination of any of these drugs increases the amount of serotonin, producing undesirable additive effects or overdose. Other drugs that cannot be combined with these medications due to risk of serotonin syndrome are the antipsychotics **chlorpromazine** and **fluphenazine**, some pain killers such as tramadol, and the herbal supplements yohimbine and **St. John's wort**.

Symptoms

Symptoms of serotonin overdose may range from mild to life-threatening, depending on the individual situation. The intensity of clinical findings seems to correlate with the degree of serotonergic activity, meaning that the more drugs taken, the worse the syndrome. Symptoms may include high blood pressure, high fever, nausea, vomiting, diarrhea, headache, sweating, increased heart rate, tremor, muscle twitching and rigidity, shock, coma, and death. Hyper reflexia are common, especially in the lower extremities. Mental status changes include anxiety, agitated **delirium**, restlessness, and disorientation.

Diagnosis

The **diagnosis** of serotonin syndrome is made based on clinical grounds, as opposed to any diagnostic test. A detailed history and physical exam is necessary for diagnosis. Information regarding the prescription and nonprescription medications, supplements, or illicit drugs the patient is taking is critical. Changes in doses or dose scheduling are also important, including whether extended release preparations are being used. A thorough description of the time of onset and type of symptoms is part of the diagnostic history. Most cases of serotonin syndrome occur within 24 hours of drug overdose, with the first six hours being a common time for onset. Physical exam may demonstrate increased heart rate and blood pressure, increased temperature, and dramatic swings in vital signs. Other physical exam findings include agitation, abnormal eye movements, dilated pupils, tremors, muscle twitching and rigidity, hyper reflexia, flushed skin, dry mucous membranes, and sweating.

The most accurate set of diagnostic criteria for serotonin syndrome is the Hunter Toxicity Criteria Decision Rules. These criteria require the patient to have taken a serotonergic agent and to have one of the following: repeated spontaneous muscular spasms of rhythmic contractions called clonus, inducible clonus plus agitation or sweating, ocular (eye) clonus plus agitation or sweating, tremor with hyper reflexia, severely rigid muscle tone, or high temperature plus inducible or ocular clonus.

Treatment

Serotonin syndrome progresses rapidly and must be treated quickly. The first step in treating the condition is discontinuation of all serotonergic agents. Supportive care is aimed at stabilization and normalization of all vital signs, as well as oxygen and intravenous fluids. Patients may be given **sedatives** such as **diazepam** (Valium) and sometimes short-acting medications for controlling blood pressure and heart rate. These measures are usually sufficient for mild serotonin syndrome.

Patients with more severe illness may require treatment with medications that antagonize or block serotonin signaling. The antidote of choice in these circumstances is cyproheptadine, which blocks serotonin activity and causes sedation. Critically ill patients may even require paralysis and endotracheal intubation with assisted breathing in an intensive care unit. Control of body temperature caused by muscle fasciculation (twitch) is critical for treatment and is accomplished through sedation or paralysis; drugs such as acetaminophen are not used. Once treatment is concluded, the patient is observed for a period to ensure that the illness has subsided and that vital signs are stabilized. Some

KEY TERMS

Clonus—Muscular spasm involving repeated, rhythmic contractions. Clonus may be spontaneous or inducible and may involve major body muscles or eye muscles.

Endotracheal intubation—The insertion of a flexible tube into the trachea for purposes of anesthesia, airway protection, and mechanical lung ventilation.

Monoamine oxidase inhibitors (MAOIs)—Type of antidepressant medication that affects various kinds of neurotransmitters, including serotonin.

Neurotransmitter—One of a group of chemicals secreted by a nerve cell (neuron) to carry a chemical message to another nerve cell, often as a way of transmitting a nerve impulse. Examples of neurotransmitters include acetylcholine, dopamine, serotonin, and norepinephrine.

Neurotransmitter receptor—A physical recipient for chemicals called neurotransmitters. Receptors sit on the surface of cells that make up body tissues, and once bound to the neurotransmitter, they initiate the chemical signaling pathway associated with neurotransmitters.

Selective serotonin norepinephrine reuptake inhibitors (SSNRI)—Drug class that acts to specifically inhibit the reuptake of serotonin and norepinephrine with little effect on other types of neurotransmitters, thereby decreasing side effects associated with broader-acting drugs.

Selective serotonin reuptake inhibitors (SSRI)—Drug class that acts to specifically inhibit the reuptake of serotonin with little effect on other types of neurotransmitters, thereby decreasing side effects associated with broader-acting drugs.

Serotonergic—Related to serotonin.

Serotonin—A type of neurotransmitter involved in regulation of the blood vessels, brain processes, and disease states such as depression.

Serotonin syndrome—A potentially life-threatening drug reaction involving an excess of the neurotransmitter serotonin, usually occurring when too many medications that increase serotonin are taken together.

Synapse—Physical space between neurons that allows the passage of neurotransmitters for chemical signaling pathways.

drugs may cause symptoms for days and require extensive observation. Cardiac activity is monitored continuously. A reassessment of the need for any prescribed serotonergic agents is conducted at the conclusion of treatment.

Prognosis

Prognosis for mild serotonin syndrome is good with proper treatment. For all cases, quick treatment is key to a positive prognosis.

Prevention

Serotonin syndrome is prevented by not taking more than one serotonergic agent at any given time. Patients should follow dosing instructions for all medications exactly as prescribed.

Resources

BOOKS

Brunton, Laurence, et al. *Goodman and Gilman's the Pharmacological Basis of Therapeutics*. 12th ed. New York: McGraw Hill Medical, 2011.

Kalueff, Allan V., and Justin L. Laporte, eds. *Experimental Models in Serotonin Transporter Research*. New York: Cambridge University Press, 2010.

Marino, Alessia G., and Ilaria C. Russo, eds. *Serotonin: New Research*. New York: Nova Science, 2009.

PERIODICALS

Ables, Adrienne, and Raju Nagubilli. "Prevention, Diagnosis, and Management of Serotonin Syndrome." *American Family Physician* 81, no. 9 (2010): 1139–42. http://www.aafp.org/afp/2010/0501/p1139.html (accessed October 12, 2011).

Byrd, L. "Serotonin Syndrome: What Is It? Causes, Recognition, and Management." *Geriatric Nursing* 31, no. 5 (2010): 387–89.

Richerson, G.B., and G.F. Buchanan. "The Serotonin Axis: Shared Mechanisms in Seizures, Depression, and SUDEP." *Epilepsia* 52, Suppl. 1 (2011): 28–38.

WEBSITES

Mayo Clinic staff. "Serotonin Syndrome." MayoClinic.com. http://www.mayoclinic.com/health/serotonin-syndrome/DS00860 (accessed October 12, 2011).

ORGANIZATIONS

American Association for Clinical Chemistry, 1850 K St. NW, Ste. 625, Washington, DC, 20006, Fax: (202) 887-5093, (800) 892-1400, http://www.aacc.org.

American Society for Clinical Pharmacology and Therapeutics, 528 N Washington St., Alexandria, VA, 22314, (703) 836-6981, info@ascpt.org, http://www.ascpt.org.

National Institute of Mental Health, 6001 Executive Blvd., Rm. 8184, MSC 9663, Bethesda, MD, 20892-9663, (301) 433-4513, TTY: (301) 443-8431, Fax: (301) 443-4279, (866) 615-6464, TTY: (866) 415-8051, nimhinfo@nih.gov, http://www.nimh.nih.gov.

Maria Eve Basile, PhD

Sertraline

Definition

Sertraline is an antidepressant that belongs to the class of drugs called **selective serotonin reuptake inhibitors (SSRIs)**. In the United States it is sold under the brand name Zoloft.

Purpose

Sertraline is approved by the U.S. Food and Drug Administration (FDA) for use in adults in treating **major depressive disorder**, **obsessive-compulsive disorder (OCD)**, **panic disorder**, **post-traumatic stress disorder (PTSD)**, **premenstrual dysphoric disorder** (PMDD), and social anxiety disorder. Sertraline is not approved in persons younger than the age of 24 unless used in the treatment of OCD.

Description

Serotonin is a **brain** chemical that carries nerve impulses from one nerve cell to another. Researchers think that **depression** and certain other mental disorders may be caused, in part, because there is not enough serotonin being released and transmitted in the brain. Like the other SSRI **antidepressants**, **fluvoxamine** (Luvox), **fluoxetine** (Prozac), and **paroxetine** (Paxil), sertraline increases the level of brain serotonin (also

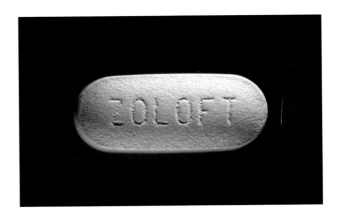

Zoloft (sertraline). (© *Leonard Lessin, FBPA/Photo Researchers, Inc.*)

known as 5-HT). Increased serotonin levels in the brain may be beneficial in patients with obsessive-compulsive disorder, alcoholism, certain types of headaches, post-traumatic **stress** disorder (PTSD), pre-menstrual tension and mood swings, and panic disorder. Sertraline is not more or less effective than the other SSRI drugs although selected characteristics of each drug in this class may offer greater benefits in some patients. Fewer drug interactions have been reported with sertraline, however, than with other medications in the same class.

The benefits of sertraline develop slowly over a period of up to four weeks. Patients should be aware of this and continue to take the drug as directed, even if they feel no immediate improvement.

Controversy still exists regarding the effectiveness of SSRI antidepressants, like sertraline. Some research has shown that other modalities, such as **cognitive-behavioral therapy**, are equally effective.

Sertraline is available in 25 mg, 50 mg and 100 mg tablets, or as a 20 mg per mL solution.

Recommended dosage

The recommended dosage of sertraline depends on the disorder being treated. The initial recommended dosage for depression and obsessive-compulsive disorder is 50 mg daily. This may be increased at intervals of at least one week to the maximum recommended dosage of 200 mg daily. For the treatment of panic disorder and post-traumatic stress disorder, the initial dose is 25 mg once daily. This dosage is increased to 50 mg daily after one week. If there is no therapeutic response, the dosage may be increased to the maximum of 200 mg daily at intervals of at least one week. These dosages may need to be reduced in elderly patients (over age 65) or in people with liver disease.

For the treatment of obsessive-compulsive disorder in the pediatric population, treatment should be initiated at a dose of 25 mg per day in children 6 to 12 years of age and 50 mg per day in children 13 to 17 years of age. Doses may be increased at one-week intervals to a total daily dose of 200 mg.

Precautions

A group of serious side effects, referred to collectively as **serotonin syndrome**, have resulted from the combination of antidepressants such as sertraline and members of another class of antidepressants known as **monoamine oxidase inhibitors (MAOIs)**. Serotonin syndrome usually consists of at least three of the following symptoms: diarrhea, fever, sweatiness, mood or behavior changes, overactive reflexes, fast heart rate,

restlessness, shivering or shaking. Because of this, sertraline should never be taken in combination with **MAOIs**. Patient taking any MAOIs—for example, Nardil (**phenelzine** sulfate) or Parnate (**tranylcypromine** sulfate)—should stop the MAOI and wait at least 14 days before starting sertraline or any other antidepressant. The same holds true when discontinuing sertraline and starting an MAOI. Also, people should not take sertraline oral concentrate while using **disulfiram** (Antabuse). Sertraline should never be taken by people who are taking any other SSRI antidepressants.

Children and adults up to age 24 are at an increased risk of developing suicidal thoughts and behaviors when taking sertraline or any other antidepressant drug. Patients of all ages should be monitored for signs of worsening depression or changes in behavior. Sertraline may precipitate a shift to mania in patients with **bipolar disorder**. The drug should be used with cautiously and with close physician supervision by people with a prior history of **seizures**, people who are at an increased risk of bleeding, and those for whom weight loss is undesirable. The risk of bleeding may increase when taking sertraline with medication that thins the blood, including aspirin.

Side effects

More than 5% of patients experience **insomnia**, dizziness, and headache. About 14% of men report delayed ejaculation while 6% report decreased sex drive while taking this drug. In order to reduce these sexual side effects patients can wait for tolerance to develop (this may take up to 12 weeks), reduce the dose, have drug holidays (where the weekend dose is either decreased or skipped), or discuss with their physician using a different antidepressant.

More than 10% of patients report nausea and diarrhea while taking sertraline. Other possible side effects include agitation, anxiety, rash, constipation, vomiting, tremors, or visual difficulty. Although most side effects eventually subside, it may take up to four weeks for people to adjust to the drug.

Interactions

Sertraline interacts with **St. John's wort**, an herbal remedy for depression. The risk of seizures is increased in patients using tramadol and sertraline. Taking sertra-line with MAO inhibitors may result in the serious side effects discussed above. Erythromycin, an antibiotic, may inhibit the breakdown of sertraline in the liver and cause increased central nervous system effects such as drowsiness and decreasing of mental alertness. Other antidepressants should not be taken by people using sertraline except in rare cases where prescribed by a physician. If a combination of antidepressants is considered beneficial, a low dose of tricyclic antidepressants (10–25 mg daily) should be used.

Sertraline should not be taken with grapefruit juice as the combination may increase sertraline levels in the body.

Resources

BOOKS

Jacobson, J.L., Jacobson, AM. *Psychiatric Secrets.* 2nd ed. Philadelphia: Hanley & Belfus, 2001.

Stern, T.A., et al. *Massachusetts General Hospital Comprehensive Clinical Psychiatry.* 1st ed. Philadelphia: Mosby Elsevier, 2008.

PERIODICALS

Edwards, Guy. "Systemic Review and Guide to Selection of Selective Serotonin Reuptake Inhibitors." *Drugs.* 57 (1999): 507–33.

Hirschfeld, Robert. "Management of Sexual Side Effects of Antidepressant Therapy." *Journal of Clinical Psychiatry.* 60 (1999): 27–30.

WEBSITES

PubMed Health. "Sertraline." U.S. National Library of Medicine. http://www.ncbi.nlm.nih.gov/pubmedhealth/PMH0001017 (accessed January 9, 2012).

Ajna Hamidovic, Pharm.D.

Serzone *see* **Nefazodone**

Sexual abuse

Definition

Sexual **abuse** in general is the forcing of unwanted sexual contact or behavior by one person on another. It may involve two adults, or an adult and an adolescent or a child. In some jurisdictions, it may also be used to describe the abuse of a younger child by an adolescent or older child. Sexual abuse may or may not involve direct physical contact; it also includes such behaviors as **voyeurism** (peeping), exposing one's genitals, showing pornographic materials to the victim, stalking, sexual harassment online or by telephone, and seductive or sexually explicit remarks or comments.

Unwanted sexual contact that is infrequent, brief in duration, or immediate is called sexual assault. Sexual assault includes not only forcible rape but also any other sexual contact that results from coercion, including being touched, grabbed, fondled or kissed against one's will, or

being shown the perpetrator's genitals. Rape is defined as nonconsensual oral, anal, or vaginal penetration of the victim by body parts or objects using force, threats of bodily harm, or by taking advantage of a victim who is incapacitated or otherwise incapable of giving consent. Incapacitation may include mental disability, forced or voluntary intoxication, being a minor, or any other condition defined in law that indicates that the person is unable to give consent.

The seduction of a child through offers of affection or bribes of some kind is also considered sexual assault. Sexual intercourse with a child below the age of consent is defined as statutory rape, while sexual intercourse between two close relatives is called incest. While laws vary somewhat from state to state, sexual assault and rape are generally defined as felonies in most jurisdictions in the United States. Sexual abuse between spouses is considered a form of domestic violence.

Sexual abuse in the workplace, school or college, military facility, or other institutional setting is called sexual harassment or sexual misconduct. It occurs when a person in a position of power or authority compels someone to participate in unwanted sexual activity for fear of job loss, demotion, a failing grade, or a similar penalty.

Demographics

Sexual abuse is increasingly recognized as a cause or trigger of mental health problems in persons of all genders, age groups, and racial and ethnic groups worldwide. The National Crime Victimization Survey reports an average of 280,000 sexual assaults (including rape and attempted rape) each year in the United States. Current estimates indicate that someone is sexually assaulted every two minutes somewhere in North America, and that 1 in 6 women and 1 in 33 men will be the victim of a sexual assault at least once in their lifetimes. According to the Centers for Disease Control and Prevention (CDC), sexual assaults account for 10% of all assault-related visits by women to hospital emergency rooms in North America.

As many as one out of three girls and one out of five boys under age 18 in North America have been sexually abused, according to the U.S. Department of Justice (DOJ). Current estimates of incest and other forms of childhood sexual abuse range from 12% to 40%, depending on settings and population. Most studies have found that among women, approximately 20% report experiencing sexual abuse in childhood. Significant underreporting of abuse occurs because children are too ashamed or afraid to tell anyone or because they think that they will not be believed. Legal procedures for corroborating sexual abuse can also be an impediment.

In recent years, however, increased public awareness of child sexual abuse has resulted in more reporting and more prosecutions.

Rape

More than 100,000 rapes (about 300 episodes every day) are reported in the United States every year. It is thought, however, that many—possibly most—rapes are not reported; according to the American Medical Association, rape is the most underreported violent crime. The Rape, Abuse and Incest National Network (RAINN) estimates that 60% of all rapes are not reported to the police, and that 15 out of every 16 rapists never spend a single day in jail.

Most rapes in North America are committed by males between the ages of 20 and 50. About half of all rapes are committed against females 18 years of age or younger, although rape victims range in age from infants 2 months old to women in their 80s; about 4% of female rape victims are 50 years of age or older. About 50% of rapes involve strangers; the other 50% are committed by men known to their victims. About 5% of rapes involve family members. Forcible rape may involve forcible oral/genital contact or anal rape (sometimes called sodomy) as well as vaginal penetration.

Human trafficking

A growing problem related to the sexual abuse of children is human trafficking, or the commercial sexual exploitation of people. The Trafficking Victims Protection Act, a law passed by Congress in 2000, defines any child under the age of 18 years old who is used for the purpose of exploitation through sexual servitude (prostitution), regardless of the absence of monetary bribes, manipulation, fraud, coercion, threats, force, or violence, as a commercially sexually exploited child and a victim of human trafficking. This means that a child or adolescent does not have to prove that he or she was tricked or forced into prostitution or other forms of sexual exploitation to be considered a victim of human trafficking. According to the DOJ, the average age of entry into prostitution in North America is 12 to 14 years. About 300,000 children in the United States and Canada are thought to be victims of human trafficking each year. The majority are girls, coerced into such activities as stripping, escort services, and posing for pornographic pictures or films as well as prostitution.

Description

Children

Although child sexual abuse can involve violence, it is more likely to involve other forms of coercion. Whereas infants and young children are defenseless, older children may be susceptible to lies, bribes, or threats. Most often they acquiesce to the demands of adults who hold inherent power over them. Abusers may manipulate a child through a process called grooming, which can involve gaining the child's trust, confusing the child about normal forms of "love," preparing the child to accept sexual abuse, and ensuring that the child will not tell others. Grooming can also involve creating a public persona in which the abuser is held in high regard by the child's family and community.

Sexual abuse can overwhelm a child with horror, confusion, disbelief, fear, and shame. Sometimes children become passive in an attempt to dissociate their minds from the physical reality of the abuse. This passivity can be misconstrued as consent. Some children attempt to repress memories of the abuse or rationalize it into insignificance.

Sexual abuse can leave a child emotionally devastated. Even very young children, who may not understand what has happened, are unable to cope with the overstimulation. Children aged five and older may feel caught between loyalty or affection toward their abuser and their knowledge that the sexual activity is wrong. If the abuser is a family member, the child may be afraid of breaking up the family. Some abusers threaten children with withdrawal of love. Children often feel that they are to blame for the abuse and this combination of shame and guilt reinforces the abuser's insistence on secrecy.

Not all forms of child sexual abuse involve adult abusers. Sibling incest is considered the most common form of incest; most cases involve older brothers abusing younger siblings of either sex. Adolescent perpetrators of sibling incest are reported to use violence more frequently and more severely than adult perpetrators; abuse their victims over a longer period of time; are more likely than a father or stepfather to penetrate the victim; and are more likely than a father or stepfather to choose a very young victim.

Adults

Sexual abuse of adults is commonplace worldwide. It includes human trafficking and sexual abuse of incapacitated adults as well as forcible rape, **frotteurism**, and stalking or other nonphysical forms of unwanted sexual advances.

DOMESTIC VIOLENCE. Domestic violence includes sexual violence within families as well as beatings or other forms of physical assault. The term "marital rape" is used to describe nonconsensual intercourse between husband and wife; "intimate partner violence" or IPV is used to refer to sexual violence between former (divorced) spouses, common-law partners, dating partners, or live-in boyfriends or girlfriends. IPV may refer to same-sex as well as opposite-sex violence. Some researchers use the term "family violence" to include sexual violence toward elderly persons living in the household as well as the abuse of children or adolescents.

The CDC estimates that women in the United States experience about 4.8 million intimate-partner related physical assaults and rapes each year, while men are the victims of about 2.9 million intimate-partner related physical assaults per year. About 2,500 people in North America die each year at the hands of intimate partners; 70% are women and 30% are men.

STALKING. Stalking has been recognized in law as a crime only recently. It refers to obsessive and unwanted attention directed by an individual or group to another person. A form of harassment and intimidation, stalking is usually sexual in nature, intended to obtain or force a relationship with someone who is unavailable or unwilling. It can be defined as willful and repeated following, watching and/or harassing of another person. Stalkers may resort to verbal threats or property damage in order to frighten or intimidate the victim. About 3.4 million cases of stalking are reported in the United States each year.

Most cases of stalking involve young adults between the ages of 18 and 24, with 25% of these cases involving cyberstalking, or stalking someone online. Most victims of stalking know the perpetrator(s). According to the DOJ, 43% of male victims report being stalked by a woman, with 41% stalked by another man. Women who are stalked report being stalked by males in 67% of cases, with 24% being stalked by another woman.

Special populations

ELDER ABUSE. Sexual abuse of the elderly is significantly underreported, partly because victims are ashamed and unwilling to speak up, and partly because many people mistakenly believe that older adults are unlikely to be the targets of sexual abuse. In addition, elderly persons suffering from Alzheimer's or another form of **dementia** may be unable to remember the details of the abuse or to report it. A study commissioned by the National Institute of Justice in 2007 reported that:

- Elderly victims of sexual assault are rarely evaluated for psychological aftereffects of the attack.

- The older the victim, the less likely the perpetrator is to be convicted of sexual assault.

- The perpetrator is more likely to be charged with a crime and convicted if the victim shows signs of physical injury.

- Assailants of elderly people living independently are more likely to be charged and convicted than those who attack seniors in assisted living situations.

A study published in the *Journal of the American Geriatrics Society* in 2010 reported that most cases of sexual aggression against elderly people in long-term care facilities are perpetrated by residents rather than staff, and that the most common single cause is hypersexuality associated with dementia. These cases have the potential to cause significant physical injury to the victims as well as emotional distress to perpetrators and victims alike.

ADULTS WITH DEVELOPMENTAL DISABILITIES. People in any age group with developmental disabilities are particularly likely to be abused. One research team estimates that more than 90% of people with developmental disabilities will experience some form of sexual abuse at some time in their lives, while 49% will experience 10 or more abusive incidents. Other studies indicate that 68% of girls and 30% of boys with developmental disabilities are sexually abused before their 18th birthday, yet these crimes go unreported—one attorney in California found that only 4.5% of sexual assaults on the developmentally disabled are reported, compared to 44% for the general population.

According to recent research, 15,000 to 19,000 people with developmental disabilities are raped each year in the United States. A Canadian study reported that 40% of women with disabilities have been assaulted or raped; and that 54% of boys and 50% of girls with hearing disorders have been sexually abused. In most cases, developmentally disabled people are sexually abused by their caregivers, whether paid staff or family members. A study of 162 cases of sexual abuse of disabled people indicated that 28% were perpetrated by direct care staff members, including psychiatrists; 19% were committed by family members; 15.2% by neighbors or family friends; 9.8% by babysitters; and 3% by dates. With regard to gender, 81.7% of the victims were women; 90.8% of the abusers were men.

PRISON RAPE. Prison rape refers to rape of adults committed within prisons. It is used most often to refer to the rape of inmates by other inmates, whether male/male or female/female, but is sometimes used to refer to the rape of inmates by prison staff or the rape of staff members by inmates. Statistics very widely; the most widely accepted estimate is that 1 in 10 male inmates is raped in prison, mostly by fellow prisoners. Another estimate obtained by the FBI is that between 9% and 14% of male inmates are sexually assaulted. For women, the figure is 1 in 40; however, the perpetrators are usually prison staff rather than other inmates.

MILITARY SEXUAL TRAUMA. The U.S. Veterans Administration (VA) defines military sexual **trauma** (MST) as "any kind of unwanted sexual attention includ[ing] insulting sexual comments, unwanted sexual advances, or even sexual assault." Since the 1980s, military sexual trauma (MST) has been increasingly recognized as a mental health issue for servicemen as well as servicewomen on active duty. There is also evidence that sexual harassment and assault are more common in wartime than in peacetime military duty. A study of MST during the Gulf War reported high rates of sexual assault (7%), physical sexual harassment (33%), and verbal sexual harassment (66%). In another study, 23% of female users of VA healthcare reported experiencing at least one sexual assault while in the military.

Male victims of MST have a higher rate of PTSD (65%) than females (45%), partly because the male gender role causes many men to feel intense shame about their victimization, making them less likely to seek professional help. Although male MST is considerably underreported in armies worldwide, the most recent figures for reported cases in the U.S. armed forces are 1.1% of male service members over the course of their military careers, with a range between 0.03% and 12.4%.

Risk factors

Risk factors for sexual abuse include:

- age—both young children and the elderly are at increased risk of sexual abuse because they are perceived as relatively unable to defend themselves
- female sex
- physical or developmental impairments
- homelessness—homeless adolescents of either sex are at high risk of being raped or forced into prostitution within three days of living on the streets
- habitual alcohol or drug abuse—substance abuse increases a person's risk of being assaulted, tricked, or coerced into unprotected voluntary sexual activity, or engaging in prostitution in order to pay for drugs
- African American, Native American, Hispanic, or mixed ethnicity
- imprisonment
- living in overcrowded housing
- war, rioting, the aftermath of a major disaster, or other forms of social breakdown

Causes and symptoms

Causes

Perpetrators of sexual abuse differ in their motivations, degree of psychopathology, past history of trauma, and current mental and physical health status. Some perpetrators of sexual abuse have multiple victims, while others may be obsessed with a single individual—often someone with whom they had or tried to have a relationship. Perpetrators tend to be angry people with a need to control or dominate others, although there are also some offenders who suffer from emotional dependency and neediness, **delusions**, **schizophrenia**, or a narcissistic sense of entitlement to the victim's attention or affection.

Some abusers of adults as well as children suffer from **personality disorders**, **impulse control disorders**, or psychosis. Some abusers of children have a specific psychiatric disorder known as **pedophilia**—sexual attraction to prepubescent children. A related disorder is hebephilia, or sexual attraction to children in the early stages of puberty. This is not to imply, however, that all persons with these conditions engage in sexual abuse, as quite the opposite is true—the majority do not participate in sexual abuse.

Some sexual abuse is situational, such as parents who abuse their children only when they are under the influence of alcohol or drugs or are under severe **stress**, or adults who may not have planned a sexual assault but take advantage of the victim's intoxication, disability, or other form of incapacitation. Prison rape, particularly male/male rape, is often considered a form of situational sexual abuse, as is MST.

Many perpetrators of sexual abuse were themselves abused as children, and may abuse others in adult life as a form of revenge against the parents or other adults who had victimized them. Other perpetrators witnessed family violence and came to regard it as acceptable, or were exposed to cultural beliefs that support or encourage sexual abuse and violence.

Last, there are a few diseases and disorders characterized by hypersexuality (loss of sexual inhibitions and self-control), and people with these conditions may act inappropriately and abusively toward other adults as well as children. These disorders include **Kleine-Levin syndrome**, a rare disorder primarily found in teenage boys; Klüver-Bucy syndrome, another rare behavioral disorder caused by malfunctions in the temporal lobe of the **brain**; **bipolar disorder**; and the side effects of some drugs given to treat Parkinson disease. Researchers disagree, however, as to when hypersexuality should be regarded as a person's primary disorder and when it should be considered a secondary symptom of another disease.

Symptoms

Sexual abuse results in a variety of physical and psychiatric symptoms in survivors that may range from minor injuries to life-threatening conditions.

KEY TERMS

Age of consent—The minimum age at which a person is considered legally competent to consent to sexual acts. It should not be confused with the voting age, driving age, legal drinking age, or marriageable age. In most jurisdictions in the United States, the age of consent is 16 or 18, but it may be set as low as 12 or as high as 21.

Felony—A major crime, such as sexual assault, aggravated assault and battery, grand theft, rape, burglary, arson, and similar acts.

Frotteurism—The practice of rubbing one's pelvis or (for males) erect penis against a nonconsenting person for sexual gratification. It frequently occurs in subway cars or other crowded public places; most perpetrators are strangers to their victims. Frotteurism is considered a form of sexual assault.

Grooming—Deliberately establishing an emotional connection with someone in order to manipulate them psychologically and lower their resistance against sexual activity.

Hebephilia—Sexual attraction on the part of an adult to children in the early stages of puberty.

Human trafficking—Illegal trade in human beings, whether adults or children, for the purposes of reproductive slavery, prostitution, other forms of sexual exploitation, or forced labor.

Hymen—A membrane that partially or completely covers the vaginal opening in females prior to first intercourse.

Hypersexuality—A general term for extremely frequent or suddenly increased sexual urges or activity. It is usually associated with lowered sexual inhibitions.

Incest—Sexual intercourse or inappropriate sexual contact between two people who are too closely related to legally marry.

Pedophilia—A sexual perversion in which children are the preferred sexual object.

Pornography—Sexually explicit pictures, writings, or other material produced for the purpose of sexual arousal.

Sexual assault nurse examiner (SANE)—A nurse with specialized training in the care and forensic examination of victims of sexual assault.

Sodomy—A term that is sometimes used for anal rape.

Stalking—The willful and repeated following, watching and/or harassing of another person, usually with the intent of forcing the victim into a dating or sexual relationship.

Statutory rape—Sexual activity, often coercive, in which one party is below the age of consent.

Syndrome—A group of signs or symptoms that occur together and characterize or define a particular disease or disorder.

Voyeurism—Sexual stimulation by visual means, usually by observing an unsuspecting individual.

PHYSICAL SYMPTOMS. According to the CDC, the physical symptoms of sexual abuse or sexual assault may include one or more of the following:

- unexplained cuts, scratches, and bruises
- unexplained internal injuries, broken bones, or head trauma
- vaginal or rectal bleeding, pain, itching, redness, swelling, or discharge
- painful urination or bowel movements
- difficulty sitting or walking
- rarely, injury to the buttocks, lower abdomen, or extremities
- pregnancy or a sexually transmitted disease (STD), especially in a child under age 14

Many adult survivors of rape experience a variety of physical symptoms ranging from tension headaches and generalized muscle pain to specific symptoms in the parts of the body that were penetrated during the assault. Survivors of oral rape may have a variety of mouth and throat complaints, nausea and vomiting, and bulimia or anorexia, while survivors of vaginal or anal rape may suffer from abdominal cramping, dysmenorrhea, constipation, or diarrhea.

PSYCHIATRIC SYMPTOMS. Almost all survivors of sexual abuse or assault have one or more psychiatric symptoms or full-blown disorders after the abuse, although some symptoms may not appear for months or even years afterward. The symptoms and disorders most commonly experienced by abuse survivors include:

- major depression
- anxiety disorders, including generalized anxiety disorder, panic disorder, and phobias
- sleep disorders

- dissociative disorders, including dissociative identity disorder (formerly known as multiple personality disorder)
- eating and substance abuse disorders
- cutting and other forms of self-injury
- Stockholm syndrome, a group of psychological symptoms that occur in some persons in captive, hostage, or long-term abuse situations, in which the victim develops positive feelings toward the captor or abuser
- suicidal feelings and/or suicide attempts
- borderline personality disorder (BPD)—this disorder is more likely to develop in children who have been sexually abused for long periods of time than in adult survivors
- repeated victimization—some abuse survivors engage in high-risk lifestyles or occasional episodes of risky behavior that increase their chances of being attacked or abused again

RAPE TRAUMA SYNDROME. Rape trauma syndrome (RTS) is a term first coined by Ann Burgess and Lynda Holmstrom in 1974 to describe a complex form of psychological trauma to an adult rape victim (male or female) reflected in disruptions of the survivor's emotional, cognitive, physical, and interpersonal behaviors. RTS is a syndrome with two phases, the first of which is an acute phase that lasts from several days to several weeks after the assault. Survivors react in different ways during the acute phase. Some survivors are expressive, meaning that they show their emotions by crying, yelling, or being openly angry. Others are controlled; they may be completely silent about the rape and go about their daily routines as if nothing has happened. Neither type of response is considered better than the other.

The second phase of RTS is the reorganization phase, in which the survivor tries to recover the sense of safety and ability to trust others that she or he had before the rape. The survivor must cope with intense feelings of guilt and shame as well as fear and anxiety. In some cases the survivor may feel disconnected or dissociated from her or his body. Male survivors are more likely than females to have questions about their sexual identity and orientation; they are also more likely to postpone or avoid treatment. One study of 100 male rape survivors found that the average time interval between the assault and seeking therapy was 16 years.

Diagnosis

The **diagnosis** and examination of victims of sexual abuse or assault is complicated by the involvement of

law enforcement as well as the victim's need for medical care. The time limits for evidence collection depend on the specific jurisdiction but usually range from 72 to 120 hours. With adults, it is important to immediately document as many details of the incident or relationship as possible, including the location of the abuse or assault; duration of the abuse or assault; identity of the perpetrator, if known; the number of perpetrators, if more than one; home address or workplace of the assailant, if known; whether a weapon, drugs, or alcohol were involved; and whether the victim washed, showered, or douched after the abuse or assault. In the case of adult women, the doctor will need to obtain the date of the woman's last menstrual period, birth control method, and time of last consensual intercourse.

Some medical centers have specially trained sexual assault nurse examiners, or SANEs; in others, the emergency room physician will conduct the physical examination of the victim and record the findings, including bruises, cuts, the presence of sperm, and other evidence of resistance to the attack. Most hospitals have prepackaged rape kits with the needed equipment and detailed instructions for evidence collection. Careful documentation is vital to protect the victim if the case goes to trial. Maintaining a chain of custody for legal purposes requires the documentation of each transfer of the evidence kit from the time it is opened until it is sealed and placed in a secure area.

In the case of minors, a child who reports sexual abuse or is suspected of having been abused should have a complete physical examination as soon as possible, preferably within 72 hours. An examination is ordered whenever a case of suspected sexual abuse is reported to the police or child protection agency. Medical professionals, teachers, and childcare professionals are required by law to report suspected cases of sexual abuse.

The physician will look for any signs of physical injury or sexual abuse, particularly in the mouth and throat and around the anus and penis or vagina. The hymen—a thin membrane covering the opening to the vagina—may be affected in abused girls. Most children, however, are not physically harmed during sexual abuse; signs of abuse are usually temporary; and the abuse is often not reported or discovered until some time after the last occurrence. Therefore, diagnostic findings from a physical examination of a child are rare.

Psychological evaluation of sexually abused children by a trained professional is essential to determine whether treatment is required. Children are often afraid to talk openly about their abuse and therefore must be made to feel very safe. The assessment includes the child's:

• abuse history and other life stressors, such as frequent moves or personal losses

• current stressors, such as medical problems or learning disabilities

• present emotional state

• coping strategies, such as withdrawal or behavioral symptoms

• strengths, such as creativity or athletic ability

• communication skills

• friendships

• attachments to adults

Tests

Blood and/or urine tests may be performed to check for STDs, including syphilis and HIV. In some cases, a drug screen may be performed as well. Women of childbearing age may be tested for pregnancy.

Imaging tests will be performed in cases of apparent or suspected head trauma, gunshot wounds, or other injuries involving weapons.

The victim's clothing and any sheets on which he or she may have been placed if transported to the emergency room in an ambulance should be kept and carefully folded. Care is needed to preserve cuts, tears, stains, or other damage to the clothing; fibers, hairs, dried blood and other body fluids found on the victim's body; and other trace evidence that may be useful for microscopic or DNA analysis.

Procedures

In adult victims, endoscopic examination of the vagina (in women) or anus (in victims of either sex) may be done, because it allows the doctor or SANE to photograph injuries to the victim's body. About two-thirds of adult rape victims have trauma to the body outside the genital region, including signs of attempted strangulation; bite marks; blunt traumatic injuries to the head, face, torso, or limbs; and penetrating injuries. Many victims also have defensive injuries, including cuts, abrasions, and bruises.

If sexual abuse of a child included physical harm, injuries may be photographed for use in prosecution of the perpetrator. As with adults, serious injuries to a child may require diagnostic imaging procedures.

Treatment

Almost all survivors of sexual abuse or assault benefit from one or more forms of psychotherapy or counseling. While classical **psychoanalysis** is not helpful, the following approaches are recommended:

• insight-oriented psychodynamic psychotherapy, useful for adults who were abused as children and need to understand how the abuse has affected their later life in order to prevent revictimization

• supportive therapy, intended to reinforce the patient's healthy methods of coping with symptoms rather than exploring deeper psychological issues

• group therapy

• cognitive-behavioral therapy, useful in changing the survivor's beliefs about the abuse that may be contributing to depression or anxiety disorders

• family therapy, recommended for survivors whose intimate relationships have been damaged or otherwise affected by the abuse or assault

• pastoral counseling, beneficial for survivors whose religious or spiritual beliefs and practices have been affected by their traumatic experiences

Drugs

Antibiotics are given to reduce the risk of STD transmission. The usual dose for adults includes intramuscular ceftriaxone in a single dose, metronidazole by mouth in a single dose, and either azithromycin by mouth in a single dose or doxycycline by mouth twice a day for seven days.

Adolescent or adult women of childbearing age may be given the option of taking Ovral (an oral contraceptive) to prevent pregnancy if the results of the hospital pregnancy test are negative. The usual dosage is two tablets by mouth at the time of treatment in the emergency room, followed by a second dose of two tablets 12 hours later.

Alternative

Some survivors of sexual abuse and assault report being helped by **acupuncture**, mindful **meditation**, prayer, relaxation techniques, **biofeedback**, massage therapy, **yoga**, tai chi, and other forms of movement therapy. Other survivors find **art therapy**, **music therapy**, and **journal therapy** helpful as ways of dealing with memories of and feelings about the abuse.

Prognosis

Sexual abuse has a high mortality rate as well as contributing to long-term physical and psychiatric problems for survivors. According to a study done in San Francisco, 25% of children exploited for commercial sex required **hospitalization** for suicide attempts, while 52% had been hospitalized for drug overdoses. Another study reported that the average life expectancy of a child prostitute after entry into prostitution is 7 years, with murder and HIV/AIDS as the leading causes of death.

Prevention

Not all forms of sexual abuse and assault are completely preventable, as children do not choose their families of origin (or adoptive families), and adults can be taken by surprise in a number of apparently safe situations. The CDC and RAINN suggest the following tips for avoiding potentially abusive situations:

• Be aware of your surroundings; avoid the use of headphones, text messaging, ear buds, or other devices that may interfere with situational awareness.

• Keep your car in good working order, cell phone charged, and money for a taxi in your pocket or otherwise readily available.

• Trust your instincts about unsafe neighborhoods or suspicious people and avoid them.

• Choose friends and associates wisely; learn to recognize the signs of possessive or otherwise abusive behavior early, before you become too deeply involved.

• Go with a group of friends to social gatherings rather than alone. Take your drink with you as you move about the party rather than leaving it unattended, and never accept a drink from someone you don't know and trust.

Resources

BOOKS

Barnett, Ola, Cindy L. Miller-Perrin, and Robin D. Perrin. *Family Violence across the Lifespan: An Introduction.* 3rd ed. Thousand Oaks, CA: Sage Publications, 2011.

Giordano, Angelo P., Elizabeth M. Datner, and Janice B. Asher, eds. *Sexual Assault: Victimization across the Life Span: A Clinical Guide.* St. Louis, MO: G.W. Medical Pub., 2003.

Itzin, Catherine, Ann Taket, and Sarah Barter-Godfrey, eds. *Domestic and Sexual Violence and Abuse: Tackling the Health and Mental Health Effects.* New York: Routledge, 2010.

Ledray, Linda, Ann Wolbert Burgess, and Angelo P. Giardino, eds. *Medical Response to Adult Sexual Assault: A Resource for Clinicians and Related Professionals.* St. Louis, MO: STM Learning, 2011.

Smyth, Michael A. *Prison Rape: Law, Media, and Meaning.* El Paso, TX: LFB Scholarly Pub., 2011.

PERIODICALS

Allard, C. B. "Military Sexual Trauma Research: A Proposed Agenda." *Journal of Trauma and Dissociation* 12 (March 2011): 324–345.

Belluardo-Crosby, M. "Mental Illness and Problematic Sexual Behaviors. A Review of the Recent Literature." *Journal of Psychosocial Nursing and Mental Health Services* 49 (February 2011): 24–28.

Carlson, B. E., et al. "Sibling Incest: Reports from Forty-One Survivors." *Journal of Child Sexual Abuse* 15 (April 2006): 19–34.

Cook, S. L., et al. "Emerging Issues in the Measurement of Rape Victimization." *Violence against Women* 17 (February 2011): 201–218.

Garrity, S. E. "Sexual Assault Prevention Programs for College-Aged Men: A Critical Evaluation." *Journal of Forensic Nursing* 7 (March 2011): 40–48.

Greenfield, E. A., et al. "Childhood Abuse as a Risk Factor for Sleep Problems in Adulthood: Evidence from a U.S. National Study." *Annals of Behavioral Medicine* 42 (October 2011): 245–256.

Hoyt, T., et al. "Military Sexual Trauma in Men: a Review of Reported Rates." *Journal of Trauma and Dissociation* 12 (March 2011): 244-260.

Keogh, A. "Rape Trauma Syndrome: Time to Open the Floodgates?" *Journal of Forensic and Legal Medicine* 14 (May 2007): 221–224.

Linden, Judith A. "Care of the Adult Patient after Sexual Assault." *New England Journal of Medicine* 365 (September 1, 2011): 834–841. http://www.nejm.org/doi/full/10.1056/NEJMcp1102869 (accessed October 2, 2011).

Rosen, T., et al. "Sexual Aggression between Residents in Nursing Homes: Literature Synthesis of an Underrecognized Problem." *Journal of the American Geriatrics Society* 58 (October 2010): 1970–1979.

OTHER

Centers for Disease Control and Prevention (CDC). "Fact Sheet: Understanding Sexual Violence." http://www.cdc.gov/violenceprevention/pdf/SV_factsheet_2011-a.pdf (accessed October 3, 2011).

———. "Preventing Intimate Partner and Sexual Violence: Program Activities Guide." http://www.cdc.gov/violenceprevention/pdf/IPV-SV_Program_Activities_Guide-a.pdf (accessed October 3, 2011).

Chicago Alliance Against Sexual Exploitation. "Know the Facts: Commercial Sexual Exploitation of Children." http://www.caase.org/ckfinder/userfiles/files/KtF_CSEC.pdf (accessed October 3, 2011).

WEBSITES

Ernoehazy, William, Jr. "Sexual Assault." Medscape Reference. December 3, 2009. http://emedicine.medscape.com/article/806120-overview (accessed September 4, 2011).

Merck Manual for Health Care Professionals Online. "Child Maltreatment: Sexual Abuse." http://www.merckmanuals.com/professional/pediatrics/child_maltreatment/overview_of_child_maltreatment.html#v1106301 (accessed September 4, 2011).

———. "Medical Examination of the Rape Victim." http://www.merckmanuals.com/professional/sec19/ch267/ch267a.html (accessed August 10, 2011).

National Center for PTSD. "Sexual Assault against Women." U.S. Department of Veterans Affairs. http://www.ptsd.va.gov/public/pages/sexual-assault-females.asp (accessed August 3, 2011).

National Institute of Justice (NIJ). "Rape and Sexual Violence." http://www.nij.gov/topics/crime/rape-sexual-violence/welcome.htm (accessed September 5, 2011).

———. "Sexual Abuse of the Elderly." http://www.nij.gov/topics/crime/elder-abuse/sexual-abuse.htm (accessed September 5, 2011).

———. "Stalking." http://www.nij.gov/topics/crime/stalking/welcome.htm (accessed October 1, 2011).

Rape, Abuse and Incest National Network (RAINN). "Effects of Sexual Assault." http://www.rainn.org/get-information/effects-of-sexual-assault (accessed October 1, 2011).

ORGANIZATIONS

American Academy of Child and Adolescent Psychiatry (AACAP), 3615 Wisconsin Ave. NW, Washington, DC, United States 20016-3007, (202) 966-7300, Fax: (202) 966-2891, http://www.aacap.org

American Psychiatric Association (APA), 1000 Wilson Blvd., Ste. 1825, Arlington, VA, United States 22209-3901, (703) 907-7300, apa@psych.org, http://www.psych.org

Centers for Disease Control and Prevention (CDC), 1600 Clifton Rd., Atlanta, GA, United States 30333, (800) 232-4636, cdcinfo@cdc.gov, http://www.cdc.gov.

Child Welfare Information Gateway, Children's Bureau/ACYF, 1250 Maryland Ave. SW, 8th Fl., Washington, DC, United States 20024, (800) 394-3366; Abuse report line: (800) 422-4453, info@childwelfare.gov, http://www.childwelfare.gov.

National Institute of Justice (NIJ), 810 Seventh Street NW, Washington, DC, United States 20531, http://www.nij.gov.

National Sexual Violence Resource Center (NSVRC), 123 North Enola Dr., Enola, PA, United States 17025, (717) 909-0710, Fax: (717) 909-0714, (877) 739-3895, resources@nsvrc.org, http://www.nsvrc.org.

Rape, Abuse and Incest National Network (RAINN), 2000 L St. NW, Ste. 406, Washington, DC, United States 20036, (202) 544-1034, (800) 656-HOPE, info@rainn.org, http://www.rainn.org.

U.S. Department of Veterans Affairs (VA), 810 Vermont Ave. NW, Washington, DC, United States 20420, (800) 827-1000, Mental health crisis line: (800) 273-8255 (press 1), http://www.va.gov.

Rebecca J. Frey, Ph.D.

Sexual addiction

Definition

Psychiatrists do not agree on the exact definition of sexual **addiction**. The general elements of sexual addiction are a compulsive pattern of sexual behavior that arises from distorted thinking; sexual behavior that interferes with personal relationships, work, or other responsibilities; and often sex with multiple partners who are seen as objects to be used rather than people.

Demographics

Because there is no professional agreement on the definition of sexual addiction, the number of people thought to be addicted to sex is unknown. What is known is that sexual addiction is much more common in men than women. People addicted to sex are not necessarily sex offenders, nor are all sexual molesters and rapists addicted to sex. Many persons with sexual addictions have other mental health and impulse control problems contributing to their addictive behaviors.

Description

Although a healthy interest in sex is normal, sexual addiction goes well beyond normal healthy interest. With sexual addiction, thinking about sexual activity and having sex dominate a person's thoughts to a degree that it interferes with his or her healthy personal relationships and activities. According to the organization Sex Addicts Anonymous, this compulsive interest in sex covers a wide range of activities, including:

- compulsive masturbation
- compulsive viewing of pornography
- compulsive phone sex
- multiple affairs outside of an established relationship
- frequent sex with anonymous partners
- multiple one-night stands
- prostitution or using prostitutes
- exhibitionism
- voyeurism
- sexual stalking
- sexual molestation or rape

Causes and symptoms

The cause of sexual addiction is not known. Some researchers have suggested that abnormal **brain** chemistry is responsible. Others suggest that early experiences and childhood **sexual abuse** contribute to the disorder.

KEY TERMS

Bipolar disorder—A mood disorder characterized by alternating periods of excessive energy and activity (mania) and depression.

Dissociation—A psychological mechanism in which the mind splits off certain aspects of a traumatic event from conscious awareness. Dissociation can affect the patient's memory, sense of reality, and sense of identity.

Obsessive-compulsive disorder (OCD)—An anxiety disorder in which a person cannot prevent himor herself from dwelling on unwanted thoughts, acting on urges, or performing repetitive rituals, such as washing hands repeatedly.

Paraphilia—Recurring strong sexual arousal to fantasies, objects, situations, or individuals that are not considered normal in the individual's culture.

Nevertheless, there is general agreement among psychiatrists that persons with a sexual addiction usually have one or more additional mental health disorders. Where experts disagree is over whether these mental health disorders alone are enough to cause the addictive behavior or whether sexual addiction is a separate disorder present in addition to other psychiatric disorders.

Common psychiatric disorders among individuals exhibiting sexually addictive behavior include:

• obsessive-compulsive disorder (OCD)
• paraphilia
• bipolar disorder
• mania
• impulse control disorders
• substance abuse
• depression
• post traumatic stress disorder (PTSD)

Specific symptoms of sexual addiction vary with the sex act involved—however, a cycle of events appears to be common. In stage one, the individual has some ongoing emotional stressor(s) (e.g., fear, pain, anger, and loneliness). The individual is unable to develop a healthy way to relieve or cope with the stressor(s). As a result, the individual moves on to stage two. In stage two, the individual begins to dissociate and separate thoughts and emotions from contemplated or anticipated actions. It is as if the actions belong to someone else and will have no consequences for the individual. In stage three, the

individual moves from thinking about acting on his or her thoughts to actually acting on them. This may mean making obscene phone calls, viewing pornography, or searching for a sexual partner. The action culminates in sexual release, and then there is a period ranging from hours to weeks before the cycle starts again.

Diagnosis

Diagnosis of sexual addiction is difficult, as many sex addicts deny that they have a problem. It is also complicated by the fact that sexual addiction often is associated with other mental health disorders. Sexual addiction is not recognized as a specific diagnosis in the *Diagnostic and Statistical Manual of Mental Disorders*, fourth edition, text revised (*DSM-IV-TR*), a guidebook produced by the **American Psychiatric Association** (APA) to classify mental disorders. Instead, it is classified as a sexual disorder not otherwise specified (NOS). This designation is intended to be used when other causes for the behavior, such as **impulse control disorders** and **obsessive-compulsive disorder**, have been eliminated.

A fifth edition of the *DSM* (*DSM-5*) is expected to publish in 2013. Within the APA, there has been substantial controversy over whether sexual addiction should be classified as a separate psychiatric disorder. As of 2011, sexual addiction was not a specific diagnosis, but persons with sexual addiction may meet the criteria for hypersexual disorder, a new diagnosis proposed for the *DSM-5*. Hypersexual disorder is characterized by repeated thoughts of and engagement in sexual behaviors, to the extent that the actions significantly interfere with a person's daily life or cause the person distress. The behaviors must not be the result of drug or alcohol use or a psychiatric or medical condition.

Treatment

There are two approaches to treating sexual addiction. Psychiatrists who see the disorder as mainly caused by a compulsive disorder or as a variation on an impulse control disorder may treat the disorder with drugs such as **fluoxetine** (Prozac) or **clomipramine** (Anafranil), along with **psychotherapy**.

Psychiatrists who see sexual addiction as its own disorder are more likely to use psychotherapy to help the individual control addictive behavior. However, unlike addiction to drugs or alcohol, the goal of treating sexual addiction is not complete abstinence from sex, but rather to develop a normal, healthy approach to sex. Psychotherapy for sexual addiction may involve treatment at a residential center or intensive outpatient therapy.

Regardless of where the therapy takes place, the individual should be treated by professionals experienced in dealing with sexual compulsions. Some therapy may involve couples. Often, therapy is supplemented by a 12-step recovery program such as the one designed by Sex Addicts Anonymous. Since many persons addicted to sex have other mental health disorders, such as **substance abuse** or **depression**, these also are treated with drugs and psychotherapy.

Prognosis

Recovery from sexual addiction is difficult. The earlier the addiction is treated (i.e., stage one or two, before thoughts have been translated into actions), the greater the chance for recovery. Most sex addicts, however, do not recognize their disorder in its early stages and thus do not receive early treatment. Often it takes a major life-altering event to propel the sex addicted individual into treatment. Even then, relapses are common. Prognosis is also affected by the success or failure of treatment for other disorders such as substance abuse.

Prevention

Since the causes of sexual addiction are not clear, there is no definitive form of prevention. Recognizing the problem and getting early treatment for stressors can help prevent behaviors from becoming a full-blown sexual addiction.

Resources

BOOKS

Canning, Maureen. *Lust, Anger, and Love: Understanding Sexual Addiction and the Road to Healthy Intimacy.* Naperville, IL: Sourcebooks, 2008.

Steffens, Barbara, and Marsha Means. *Your Sexually Addicted Partner: Ways to Cope and Deal.* Far Hills, NJ: New Horizon Press, 2009.

PERIODICALS

Carnes, P. J., et al. "PATHOS: A Brief Screening Application for Assessing Sexual Addiction." *Journal of Addiction Medicine* (August 3, 2011) [e-pub ahead of print]. http://dx.doi.org/10.1097/ADM.0b013e3182251a28 (accessed November 13, 2011).

Elmore, J. L. "SSRI Reduction of Nonparaphilic Sexual Addiction." *CNS Spectrums* 5, no. 11 (2000): 53–56.

Garcia, F. D., and F. Thibaut. "Sexual Addictions." *American Journal of Drug and Alcohol Abuse* 36, no. 5 (2010): 254–60.

Hook, J. N., et al. "Measuring Sexual Addiction and Compulsivity: A Critical Review of Instruments." 36, no. 3 (2010): 227–60.

Irons, Richard, and Jennifer P. Schneider. "Differential Diagnosis of Addictive Sexual Disorder Using the DSM-IV." In *Sexual Addiction & Compulsivity* 3, (1996): 7–21. http://www.jenniferschneider.com/articles/diagnos.html (accessed October 27, 2011).

WEBSITES

Herkov, Michael. "What Is Sexual Addiction?" PsychCentral.com. 2006. http://psychcentral.com/lib/2006/what-is-sexual-addiction (accessed October 27, 2011).

International Institute for Trauma & Addiction Professionals. "Sexual Addiction Screening Test." SexHelp.com, 2011. http://www.sexhelp.com/sast.cfm (accessed October 27, 2011).

MedicineNet.com. "Sexual Addiction." March 12, 2010. http://www.medicinenet.com/sexual_addiction/article.htm (accessed October 27, 2011).

Morrison, Keith. "Battling Sexual Addiction." MSNBC. February 24, 2004. http://www.msnbc.msn.com/id/4302347/ns/dateline_nbc/t/battling-sexual-addiction (accessed November 13, 2011).

ORGANIZATIONS

American Psychiatric Association, 1000 Wilson Blvd., Ste. 1825, Arlington, VA, 22209-3901, (703) 907-7300, apa@psych.org, http://www.psych.org.

Sex Addicts Anonymous, PO Box 70949, Houston, TX, 77270, (1-800) 477-8191, info@saa-recovery.org, http://www.sexaa.org.

Tish Davidson, AM

Sexual aversion disorder

Definition

Sexual aversion disorder is a disorder characterized by disgust, fear, revulsion, or lack of desire in consensual relationships involving genital contact.

Normal loss of desire

To understand sexual aversion disorder, one should first understand that there are circumstances in which it is normal for people to lose interest in sexual activity. The reader can then compare these situations to the loss of desire associated with serious sexual disorders, including sexual aversion disorder.

There are a number of reasons that people lose interest in sexual intercourse. It is normal to experience a loss of desire during menopause; directly after the birth of a child; before or during menstruation; during recovery from an illness or surgery; and during such major or stressful life changes as death of a loved one, job loss, retirement, or divorce. These are considered normal causes for fluctuations in sexual desire and are generally temporary. Changing roles, such as becoming a parent for the first time or making a career change have also been found to cause loss of desire. Not having enough time for oneself or to be alone with one's partner may also contribute to normal and naturally reversible loss of desire. Loss of privacy resulting from moving a dependent elderly parent into one's home is a common cause of loss of desire in middle-aged couples. **Depression**, **fatigue**, or **stress** also contribute to lessening of sexual interest.

Demographics

Both men and women can experience sexual aversion disorder. It is thought to be more common in women than in men, possibly because women are more likely than men to be victims of rape and other forms of sexual assault. There are relatively few statistics on the number of people with sexual aversion disorder because it is often confused with other disorders, or with the normal fluctuations in desire associated with life stress. Also, many people find sex a difficult subject to discuss even with a physician, so that the number of people who seek help are probably fewer than the number of people with the disorder overall.

Description

Sexual aversion disorder represents a much stronger dislike of and active avoidance of sexual activity than the normal ups and downs in desire described above. Sexual aversion disorder is characterized not only by a lack of desire, but also by fear, revulsion, disgust, or similar emotions when the person with the disorder engages in genital contact with a partner. The aversion may take a number of different forms; it may be related to specific aspects of sexual intercourse, such as the sight of the partner's genitals or the smell of his or her body secretions, but it may include kissing, hugging, and petting, as well as intercourse itself. In some cases the person with sexual aversion disorder avoids any form of sexual contact; others, however, are not upset by kissing and caressing, and are able to proceed normally until genital contact occurs.

There are several subclassifications of sexual aversion disorder. It may be lifelong (always present) or acquired after a traumatic experience; situational (with a specific partner or in a specific set of circumstances) or generalized (occurring with any partner and in all situations). Sexual aversion may be caused by psychological factors or by a combination of physical and psychological factors.

Causes and symptoms

There are a number of causes of sexual aversion disorder. The most common causes are interpersonal problems and traumatic experiences. Interpersonal problems generally cause situation-specific sexual aversion disorder, in which the symptoms occur only with a specific partner or under certain conditions. In such cases underlying tension or discontent with the relationship is often the cause. Reasons for unhappiness with the relationship may include the discovery of marital infidelity; major disagreements over children, money, and family roles; domestic violence; lack of personal hygiene on the partner's side; or similar problems. Interpersonal problems are often the cause if intercourse was once enjoyed but is no longer desired.

Traumatic experiences have also been found to cause sexual aversion disorder, often of the generalized variety. Some possible traumas include rape, incest, molestation, or other forms of **sexual abuse**. The patient then associates intercourse with a painful experience or memory, possibly one that he or she is trying to forget. Sexual aversion disorder may also be caused by religious or cultural teachings that associate sexual activity with excessive feelings of guilt.

The symptoms of sexual aversion disorder can range from mild to severe. Mild symptoms include lack of interest and mild disgust. Severe symptoms can include panic attacks with all the symptoms of such an attack, including dizziness, shortness of breath, intense fear, and rapid heartbeat. People suffering from sexual aversion disorder often go out of their way to avoid situations that could end in sexual contact through any means they can think of, including going to bed at different times from the spouse, spending extra time at work, or trying to make themselves less sexually attractive.

Diagnosis

A **diagnosis** of sexual aversion disorder is usually made when the affected person or his or her partner mentions the problem itself or their dissatisfaction with the relationship to their family physician, gynecologist, or psychotherapist. An important first step in diagnosis is a thorough physical examination, preferably of both partners, to rule out physical causes of the disorder in the affected person, and to rule out a sexually transmitted disease, physical deformity, or lack of personal cleanliness in the partner that may contribute to the affected person's avoidance of sex.

According to the mental health profession's *Diagnostic and Statistical Manual of Mental Disorders* (*DSM-IV-TR*) of the **American Psychiatric Association**, to meet criteria for a diagnosis of sexual aversion disorder the patient must not only avoid nearly all genital contact

KEY TERM

Coitus—Sexual intercourse.

with his or her partner but have strong negative feelings about such contact or its possibility. In addition, the problem must be causing serious difficulties and unhappiness either for the patient or for his or her partner. In addition, there must not be any underlying physical causes, such as certain disorders of the circulatory system, skin diseases, medication side effects, or similar problems that could cause a loss of desire. To be diagnosed with sexual aversion disorder, the affected person does not have to avoid all sexual contact, but must indicate that he or she is actively avoiding genital contact.

Many other sexual disorders have signs and symptoms similar to those of sexual aversion disorder, which complicates the differential diagnosis. Sexual aversion disorder is often found in conjunction with other sexual disorders; in some cases several diagnoses are appropriate for one patient.

One disorder similar in many aspects to sexual aversion disorder is hypoactive sexual disorder. Many of the signs, such as avoiding sexual contact in a variety of ways, are similar. The primary difference between the two disorders is that a patient with hypoactive sexual disorder is not interested in sex at all and does not have sexual fantasies of any variety. A patient with sexual aversion disorder, by comparison, may have normal sexual fantasies, and even function normally with some partners, although not with a specific partner. Also, a patient with hyposexual disorder will not enjoy or desire any anticipation in sexual activities including kissing and caressing. Some, though not all, people with sexual aversion disorder do enjoy sexual foreplay until the point of genital contact.

Sexual aversion disorder and hypoactive sexual disorder are both considered to be caused mainly by psychological factors and to manifest psychological symptoms. Another disorder that can have some similar symptoms is **female sexual arousal disorder** (FSAD). FSAD refers to a woman's recurrent inability to achieve or maintain an adequate lubrication-swelling response during sexual activity. Lack of lubrication is a physical problem that may have either physical or psychological causes. Women with FSAD find intercourse uncomfortable or even painful. As a result of the physical discomfort, the woman often will avoid intercourse and sexual activity with her partner that may lead to intercourse. Although FSAD is a disorder with physical symptoms as well as psychological ones, it is easily confused with sexual aversion disorder because it may manifest as a problem of interest or desire.

Treatment

Sexual aversion disorder is not thought to have any commonplace underlying physiological causes. The usual treatment is a course of **psychotherapy** for the psychological condition(s) that may be causing the problem. **Marriage counseling** is often appropriate if the disorder concerns a spouse. Medications can be used to treat some symptoms that may be associated with sexual aversion disorder, such as panic attacks, if they are severe enough to be causing additional distress.

Prognosis

When sexual aversion disorder is addressed as a psychological disorder treatment can be very successful. Psychotherapy to treat the underlying psychological problems can be successful as long as the patient is willing to attend counseling sessions regularly. For sexual aversion disorder that is situational or acquired, psychotherapy for both the patient and his or her partner (**couples therapy**) may help to resolve interpersonal conflicts that may be contributing to the disorder. Panic attacks caused by or associated with the disorder can be treated successfully by medication if the doctor considers this form of treatment necessary.

If sexual aversion disorder is not diagnosed, discussed, or treated, the result may be infidelity, divorce, or chronic unhappiness in the relationship or marriage.

Resources

BOOKS

American Psychiatric Association. *Diagnostic and Statistical Manual of Mental Disorders*. 4th ed., text rev. Washington, DC: American Psychiatric Publishing, 2000.

Sadock, Benjamin J., and Virginia A. Sadock, eds. *Comprehensive Textbook of Psychiatry*. Vol. 2. 7th ed. Philadelphia: Lippincott Williams and Wilkins, 2000.

PERIODICALS

Brotto, L. A. "The DSM Diagnostic Criteria for Sexual Aversion Disorder." *Archives of Sexual Behavior* 39, no. 2 (2010): 271–77.

Fabre, L. F., and L. C. Smith. "The Effect of Major Depression on Sexual Function in Women." *Journal of Sexual Medicine* 9, no. 1 (2012): 231–39.

Kingsberg, S. A., and G. Knudson. "Female Sexual Disorders: Assessment, Diagnosis, and Treatment." CNS Spectrums 16, no. 2 (2011) [e-pub ahead of print]. http://www.cnsspectrums.com/aspx/articledetail.aspx?articleid=3577 (accessed January 9, 2012).

Tish Davidson, A.M.

Sexual deviance *see* **Paraphilias**

Sexual dysfunctions

Definition

Sexual dysfunction disorders, sometimes also called sexual dysfunctions, are problems (malfunctions) that interfere with any stage of normal sexual activity, such as the desire, arousal, initiation, consummation, orgasm, or satisfaction with sex. Such disorders inhibit, or in some cases stop, the individual or the couple from enjoying sexual activity. They may begin early in life or may develop over time after experiencing many years of fulfilling sexual activity. Such sexual dysfunctions, which may be physical and/or psychological in nature, may cause an individual to have a partial or total inability to participate in one or many stages of the sexual act. **Depression**, guilt, and past sexual experiences may contribute to sexual disorders. A physical malady may also be responsible for not being able to enjoy or participate in sex.

Viagra pills. *(© Garry Gay/Alamy)*

Demographics

Such sexual dysfunction disorders occur in both men and women and are independent of sexual preference or orientation. Such disorders are more common in people who abuse alcohol or drugs, and in those who have chronic medical disorders such as diabetes and degenerative neurological disorders. Psychological problems may cause problems with maintaining relationships, which consequently can cause problems with sex. Couples with an open, honest, and stable relationship are more apt to avoid psychological dysfunction than those without such relationships.

Age is a significant factor in sexual dysfunctions. Most cases appear in people who are in their early adult years, such as beginning around 20 years of age and going throughout their late 30s and early 40s. For women, sexual dysfunction is also more common in women during their perimenopause (transitional period in which a woman's body shifts from regular cycles of ovulation and menstruation to infertility, or menopause) and postmenopause (stage in which menopause is complete).

Description

Probably nowhere in human health do the body and mind interact more than during sex. There are four generally recognized phases of sexual activity, involving both mental and physical responses, which are applicable to both men and women. These phases are in sequence:

- desire or appetite—fantasies or thoughts about sex
- excitement—physical changes to prepare the body for intercourse and accompanying sense of sexual pleasure
- orgasm—physical response that leads to the peak of physical pleasure and release of sexual tension
- resolution—physical relaxation accompanied by a feeling of well-being and satisfaction

Sexual-dysfunction disorders can occur in any of these four phases. Their cause may be physiological or psychological. More than one sexual dysfunction disorder may appear simultaneously. The ***Diagnostic and Statistical Manual of Mental Disorders*** (latest edition *DSM-IV-TR*), produced by the **American Psychiatric Association** and used by most mental health professionals in North America and Europe to diagnose mental disorders, recognizes nine specific sexual dysfunctions:

- Disorders of desire: These interfere with the initiation of sex and include hypoactive sexual desire disorder (low interest in sex, or low libido) and sexual aversion disorder (objections to having the genitals touched). A decreased sexual interest may be caused by a lowered production of estrogen in women or testosterone in both men and women. It also can be caused by the normal aging process, certain medications, stress or depression, fatigue, pregnancy in women and other problems.

• Disorders of excitement or sexual arousal: These are female sexual arousal disorder (when a woman fails to have physiological responses associated with arousal), and male erectile disorder (when a man fails to get an adequate erection, also referred to as erectile dysfunction). Past terms used with such disorders include frigidity in women and impotence in men.

• Disorders of the orgasm phase: These are female orgasmic disorder (when a woman fails to reach orgasm); and male orgasmic disorder (when a man fails to reach orgasm) and premature ejaculation (when a man reaches orgasm too soon).

• Sexual pain disorders (associated with intercourse and orgasm): These disorders are vaginismus (a condition in which the outer part of a woman's vagina causes involuntary spasms that cause pain and interferes with sexual intercourse) and dyspareunia (a condition in which there is pain during intercourse in either men or women, often caused by insufficient lubrication of the vagina in women).

Changes proposed for the fifth edition of the *DSM* (*DSM-5*, 2013) including placing the following disorders within the diagnostic category of Sexual Dysfunctions (previously Sexual and Gender Identity Disorders):

• erectile disorder

• female orgasmic disorder

• delayed ejaculation

• early ejaculation

• sexual interest/arousal disorder in women

• hypoactive sexual desire disorder in men

• genito-pelvis pain/penetration disorder

• substance-induced sexual dysfunction

• sexual dysfunction associated with a known general medical condition

• other specified sexual dysfunction

• unspecified sexual dysfunction

A new category entitled Gender Dysphoria has been proposed to incorporate the remaining disorders previously grouped with the sexual dysfunctions. The members of the American Psychiatric Association working group for the Sexual Dysfunctions chapter are also considering including diagnostic criteria for hypersexual disorder in the appendix.

In addition, medications or illicit drugs may cause substance-induced sexual dysfunction, and sexual dysfunction may be caused by a general medical condition such as diabetes or nerve damage. If the sexual dysfunction falls into none of the above areas, it is classified as sexual dysfunction not otherwise specified.

Causes and symptoms

The causes of sexual dysfunction disorders are varied, as are their symptoms. In general, symptoms prevent the initiation of sex or the completion of the sex act, or they interfere with satisfaction derived from sex. Almost everyone has some problem with sexual functioning or fulfillment at some point in his or her life, but not all problems are considered sexual dysfunction disorders. Sexual satisfaction is very personal and individual, so what may be an annoyance for one couple may be a serious problem for another. However, estimates suggest that roughly one-fourth of the adult population may have a sexual dysfunction disorder. More women than men report having sexual dysfunction disorders, but the difference may be that women are more open and active about seeking help with sexual problems than are men.

Causes

Some physical causes of sexual dysfunctions include:

• enlarged prostate gland

• injuries, such as with the back

• various chronic diseases, such as multiple sclerosis and diabetic neuropathy

• numerous drugs, including alcohol, antihypertensives, anticonvulsants, neuroleptics, antihistamines, narcotics, nicotine, psychotherapeutics, stimulants, and selective serotonin reuptake inhibitors (SSRI) antidepressant drugs

• endocrine disorders (of the adrenal, pituitary, and thyroid)

• organ failure, such as heart and lungs

• hormonal deficiency, such as with estrogen and testosterone

• nerve damage

• decreased blood flow and other such problems

• birth defects, such as abnormalities in the pelvis or the ovaries (in women)

• insufficient vaginal lubrication

Some psychological causes of sexual dysfunctions include such disorders as **bipolar disorder**, depression, epilepsy, and **schizophrenia**. For instance, in bipolar disorder, a person may feel too elated at times, or too depressed at other times, to have or act on sexual desires.

KEY TERMS

Anticonvulsants—Drugs that treat epileptic seizures.

Antihypertensives—Drugs that treat hypertension; that is, high blood pressure.

Kegel exercises—Repetitive contractions to tone the pubococcygeus muscle of the pelvic floor for enhancing sexual response during intercourse or controlling incontinence.

Neuroleptics—Drugs that treat psychosis, such as hallucinations.

Psychotherapeutics—The general term for drugs such as tranquilizers, sedatives, analgesics, and stimulants.

Selective serotonin reuptake inhibitors—Drugs that treat depression, anxiety, and some personality disorders.

Symptoms

Some symptoms of sexual dysfunctions include:

- inability to feel aroused (both men and women)
- lack of interest in sex (both men and women)
- pain with intercourse (both men and women, but more likely in women)
- delay or absence of ejaculation when properly stimulated (men)
- inability to control timing of ejaculation (men)
- inability to get an erection (men)
- inability to keep an erection throughout intercourse (men)
- burning sensation in or around the vulva or in the vagina during sexual contact (women)
- inability to reach orgasm (women)
- inability to relax vaginal muscles (which prevents intercourse) (women)
- inadequate vaginal lubrication before and/or during sexual intercourse (women)
- low libido due to physical or hormonal problems, psychological problems, or relationship problems (women)

Diagnosis

Diagnosis begins when a medical professional conducts a thorough sexual and medical history and often performs a physical examination including laboratory tests. The doctor will conduct tests based on the specific sexual-dysfunction symptoms experienced by the patient.

Treatment

Treatment for sexual dysfunction depends on its cause. It must be individualized based on the cause and the specific dysfunction. Treatment includes physiological treatment, **psychotherapy**, and/or education and communication counseling. Medical causes can be treated, and usually reversed, with medication and/or surgery. Causes from disabilities or physical illnesses can be improved with physical therapy or mechanical aids (such as penile implants). For instance, women can increase blood flow to certain muscles within the pelvic floor, which produce organisms, with the use of Kegel exercises.

Most people can be helped to resolve their problems and improve their sex life. For instance, men can be helped with sildenafil (Viagra), which increases blood flow within the penis, when they have trouble in having an erection. Women can get help, for instance, with lubricating gels, when they are exceptionally dry within the vaginal area. For depression or anxiety associated with sexual dysfunction, **antidepressants** can help to counter the problem in both men and women.

Many behavioral therapies are offered that help with sexual dysfunction. For instance, cognitive behavior therapy offers men with **erectile dysfunction** help to overcome the problem. Therapists teach patients to eliminate distractions during sexual activity and to communicate better with their partner with regard to their special needs. Generally, the sooner the person receives help, the easier the problem is to resolve. Support of a partner is often critical to successful resolution of the problem. The Masters and Johnson treatment strategies have been available since the late 1950s to solve sexual dysfunctions of many types.

Prognosis

People with sexual dysfunction should seek professional medical advice. The probable outcome of such medical advice is generally good for the cases of physical causes. Doctors can successfully diagnose the root of such sexual dysfunction so it can be eliminated or controlled. However, the longer the physical dysfunction is left untreated, the more difficult it is to overcome.

Some types of sexual dysfunction cannot be treated with medical or surgical treatments. These include psychological factors. However, the prognosis for treating these causes is still good for moderate or

---

QUESTIONS TO ASK YOUR DOCTOR

- What is causing my sexual problem?
- What tests can be done to solve my problem?
- Will a lifestyle change help?
- What type of counseling is advised?
- Are impotence and erectile dysfunction the same thing?
- Could menopause cause my sexual dysfunction?

---

temporary dysfunction relating to these factors with the use of psychotherapy. Those with more serious or permanent causes are less likely to have positive outcomes. In any case, people with psychological sexual dysfunctions should seek medical attention immediately, such as victims of sexual **trauma** (such as rape or abuse) whose dysfunction is impairing sexual activities. Counseling to overcome such problems is possible if proper help is found in a timely manner.

Some forms of sexual dysfunction can lead to infertility, including: failure to have sexual intercourse, infrequent sexual intercourse, erectile or ejaculatory dysfunction, and **vaginismus** or dyspareunia.

Prevention

Open and informative communications between parents and children about sex, relationships, and health can help prevent or, at least, minimize physiological problems that may develop in the early years of sexual contact. Such information will also help to maximize the chances of having healthy sexual relationships.

Over-the-counter (nonprescription) and prescription medications, which can have adverse consequences with sexual activities, should be discussed with a medical professional if sexual dysfunctions occur. The medical community recommends drinking alcoholic beverages in moderation or avoiding them altogether.

Resources

BOOKS

American Psychiatric Association. *Diagnostic and Statistical Manual of Mental Disorders.* 4th ed., text revised. Washington, DC: American Psychiatric Association, 2000.

Black, Donald W., and Nancy C. Andreasen. *Introductory Textbook of Psychiatry.* Washington, DC: American Psychiatric Pub., 2011.

Braun-Harvey, Douglas. *Sexual Health in Recovery: A Professional Counselor's Manual.* New York: Springer, 2011.

Leiblum, Sandra R., ed. *Treating Sexual Desire Disorders: A Clinical Casebook.* New York: Guilford 2010.

Levine, Stephen B., et al., eds. *Handbook of Clinical Sexuality for Mental Health Professionals.* New York: Routledge, 2010.

Sadock, Benjamin J., and Virginia A. Sadock, eds. *Kaplan & Sadock's Pocket Handbook of Clinical Psychiatry.* Philadelphia: Wolters Lluwer Health/Lippincott Williams & Wilkins, 2010.

Zaslau, Stanley, ed. *Dx/Rx: Sexual Dysfunction in Men and Women.* Sudbury, MA: Jones & Bartlett Learning, 2011.

WEBSITES

American Psychiatric Association. "Sexual Dysfunctions." DSM-5 Development. http://www.dsm5.org/proposedrevision/Pages/SexualDysfunctions.aspx (accessed May 27, 2011).

MedlinePlus. "Female Sexual Dysfunction." April 24, 2010. http://www.mayoclinic.com/health/female-sexual-dysfunction/DS00701 (accessed May 29, 2011).

———. "Sexual Problems Overview." September 11, 2010. http://www.nlm.nih.gov/medlineplus/ency/article/001951.htm (accessed May 29, 2011).

ORGANIZATIONS

American Association of Sexuality Educators, Counselors, and Therapists, 1444 I St. NW, Ste. 700, Washington, DC, 20005, (202) 449-1099, Fax: (202) 216-9646, http://www.aasect.org.

Sexuality Information and Education Council of the United States, 1706 R St. NW, Washington, DC, 20009, (202) 265-2405, Fax: (202) 462-2340, http://www.aasect.org.

Tish Davidson, A.M.

▌ Sexual masochism

Definition

The essential feature of sexual masochism is the feeling of sexual arousal or excitement resulting from receiving pain, suffering, or humiliation. The pain, suffering, or humiliation is real and not imagined and can be physical or psychological in nature. A person with a **diagnosis** of sexual masochism is sometimes called a masochist.

The *Diagnostic and Statistical Manual of Mental Disorders*, also known as the *DSM*, is used by mental health professionals to diagnose specific mental disorders. In the 2000 edition of this manual (the Fourth Edition Text Revision also known as *DSM-IV-TR*) sexual masochism is one of several **paraphilias**. Paraphilias are intense and recurrent sexually arousing urges, fantasies, or behaviors.

Demographics

Although masochistic sexual fantasies often begin in childhood, the onset of sexual masochism typically occurs during early adulthood. When actual masochistic behavior begins, it will often continue on a chronic course for people with this disorder, especially when no treatment is sought.

Sadomasochism involving consenting partners is not considered rare or unusual in the United States. It often occurs outside of the realm of a mental disorder. More people consider themselves masochistic than sadistic.

Sexual masochism is slightly more prevalent in males than in females.

Death due to hypoxyphilia is a relatively rare phenomenon. Data indicate that less than two people per million in the United States and other countries die from hypoxyphilia.

Description

In addition to the sexual pleasure or excitement derived from receiving pain and humiliation, an individual with sexual masochism often experiences significant impairment or distress in functioning due to masochistic behaviors or fantasies.

With regard to actual masochistic behavior, the person may be receiving the pain, suffering, or humiliation at the hands of another person. This partner may have a diagnosis of **sexual sadism** but this is not necessarily the case. Such behavior involving a partner is sometimes referred to as sadomasochism.

Masochistic acts include being physically restrained through the use of handcuffs, cages, chains, and ropes. Other acts and fantasies related to sexual masochism include receiving punishment or pain by means of paddling, spanking, whipping, burning, beating, electrical shocks, cutting, rape, and mutilation. Psychological humiliation and degradation can also be involved.

Masochistic behavior can also occur in the context of a role-playing fantasy. For example, a sadist can play the role of teacher or master and a masochist can play the role of student or slave.

The person with sexual masochism may also be inflicting the pain or suffering on himself or herself. This can be done through **self-mutilation**, cutting, or burning.

The masochistic acts experienced or fantasized by the person sometimes reflect a sexual or psychological

submission on the part of the masochist. These acts can range from relatively safe behaviors to very physically and psychologically dangerous behavior.

The *DSM* lists one particularly dangerous and deadly form of sexual masochism called hypoxyphilia. People with hypoxyphilia experience sexual arousal by being deprived of oxygen. The deprivation can be caused by chest compression, noose, plastic bag, mask, or other means and can be administered by another person or be self-inflicted.

Causes and symptoms

Causes

There is no universally accepted cause or theory explaining the origin of sexual masochism, or sadomasochism in general. However, there are some theories that attempt to explain the presence of sexual paraphilias in general. One theory is based on learning theory that paraphilias originate because inappropriate sexual fantasies are suppressed. Because they are not acted upon initially, the urge to carry out the fantasies increases and when they are finally acted upon, a person is in a state of considerable distress and/or arousal. In the case of sexual masochism, masochistic behavior becomes associated with and inextricably linked to sexual behavior.

There is also a belief that masochistic individuals truly want to be in the dominating role. This causes them to become conflicted and thus submissive to others.

Another theory suggests that people seek out sadomasochistic behavior as a means of escape. They get to act out fantasies and become new and different persons.

Symptoms

Individuals with sexual masochism experience sexual excitement from physically or psychologically receiving pain, suffering, and/or humiliation. They may be receiving the pain, suffering, or humiliation at the hands of another person, who may or may not be a sadist, or they may be administering the pain, suffering, or humiliation themselves.

They experience distressed or impaired functioning because of the masochistic behaviors, urges, and fantasies. This distress or impairment can impact functioning in social, occupational, or other contexts.

Diagnosis

The *DSM* criteria for sexual masochism include recurrent intense sexual fantasies, urges, or behaviors involving real acts in which the individual with the disorder is receiving psychological or physical suffering, pain, and humiliation. The suffering, pain, and humiliation cause the person with sexual masochism to be sexually aroused. The fantasies, urges, or behaviors must be present for at least six months.

The diagnostic criteria also require that the person has experienced significant distress or impairment because of these behaviors, urges, or fantasies. The distress and impairment can be present in social, occupational, or other functioning.

Sexual masochism must be differentiated from normal sexual arousal, behavior, and experimentation. It should also be differentiated from sadomasochistic behavior involving mild pain and/or the simulation of more dangerous pain. When this is the case, a diagnosis of sexual masochism is not necessarily warranted.

Sexual masochism must also be differentiated from self-defeating or self-mutilating behavior that is performed for reasons other than sexual arousal.

Individuals with sexual masochism often have other sexual disorders or paraphilias. Some individuals, especially males, have diagnoses of both sexual sadism and sexual masochism.

Treatment

Behavior therapy is often used to treat paraphilias. This can include management and conditioning of arousal patterns and masturbation. Therapies involving cognitive restructuring and **social skills training** are also utilized.

Medication is also used to reduce fantasies and behavior relating to paraphilias. This is especially true of people who exhibit severely dangerous masochistic behaviors.

Treatment can also be complicated by health problems relating to sexual behavior. Sexually transmitted diseases and other medical problems, especially when the sadomasochistic behavior involves the release of blood, can be present. Also, people participating in hypoxyphilia and other dangerous behaviors can suffer extreme pain and even death.

Prognosis

Because of the chronic course of sexual masochism and the uncertainty of its causes, treatment is often difficult. The fact that many masochistic fantasies are socially unacceptable or unusual leads some people who may have the disorder to not seek or continue treatment.

Treating a paraphilia is often a sensitive subject for many mental health professionals. Severe or difficult cases of sexual masochism should be referred to professionals who have experience treating such cases.

Prevention

Because it is sometimes unclear whether sadomasochistic behavior is within the realm of normal experimentation or indicative of a diagnosis of sexual masochism, prevention is a tricky issue. Often, prevention refers to managing sadomasochistic behavior so it primarily involves only the simulation of severe pain and it always involves consenting partners familiar with each other's limitations.

Also, because fantasies and urges originating in childhood or adolescence may form the basis for sadomasochistic behavior in adulthood, prevention is made difficult. People may be very unwilling to divulge their urges and discuss their sadistic fantasies as part of treatment.

Resources

BOOKS

American Psychiatric Association. *Diagnostic and Statistical Manual of Mental Disorders*. 4th ed., text rev. Washington, DC: American Psychiatric Publishing, 2000.

Baxter, Lewis R. Jr., and Robert O. Friedel, eds. *Current Psychiatric Diagnosis & Treatment*. Philadelphia: Current Medicine, 1999.

Black, Donald W., and Nancy C. Andreasen. *Introductory Textbook of Psychiatry*. 5th ed. Arlington, VA: American Psychiatric Publishing, 2011.

Ebert, Michael H., et al. *Current Diagnosis & Treatment in Psychiatry*. New York: McGraw-Hill, 2008.

Ali Fahmy, Ph.D.

▌ Sexual sadism

Definition

The essential feature of sexual sadism is a feeling of sexual excitement resulting from administering pain, suffering, or humiliation to another person. The pain, suffering, or humiliation inflicted on the other is real; it is not imagined and may be either physical or psychological in nature. A person with a **diagnosis** of sexual sadism is sometimes called a sadist. The name of the disorder is derived from the proper name of the Marquis Donatien de Sade (1740-1814), a French aristocrat who became notorious for writing novels around the theme of inflicting pain as a source of sexual pleasure.

The ***Diagnostic and Statistical Manual of Mental Disorders***, also known as the *DSM*, is used by mental health professionals to give diagnoses of specific mental disorders. In the 2000 edition of this manual, sexual sadism is listed as one of several **paraphilias**. The paraphilias are a group of mental disorders characterized by **obsession** with unusual sexual practices or with sexual activity involving nonconsenting or inappropriate partners (such as children or animals). The paraphilias may include recurrent sexually arousing urges or fantasies as well as actual behaviors.

Demographics

Although sadistic sexual fantasies often begin in the person's childhood, the onset of active sexual sadism typically occurs during early adult life. When actual sadistic behavior begins, it will often continue on a chronic course for people with this disorder, especially if they do not seek help.

Sexual sadism with consenting partners is much more common than with nonconsensual partners. When consenting partners are involved, the sadist and the masochist may be either male or female. When non-consenting partners are involved, the sadist is almost always a male.

Sadomasochism involving consenting partners is not considered rare or unusual in the United States. It often occurs outside of the realm of a mental disorder. Fewer people consider themselves sadistic than masochistic.

Description

In addition to the sexual pleasure or excitement derived from inflicting pain and humiliation on another, a person diagnosed with sexual sadism often experiences significant impairment or distress in functioning due to actual sadistic behaviors or sadistic fantasies.

With regard to actual sadistic behavior, the person receiving the pain, suffering, or humiliation may or may not be a willing partner. Whether or not the partner is consenting, it is the very real suffering they are experiencing that is arousing to the sadist. When the sexual activity is consensual, the behavior is sometimes referred to as sadomasochism. The consenting partner may be given a diagnosis of **sexual masochism**. Like sadism, masochism is a term derived from a proper name; in this instance, from Leopold von Sacher-Masoch (1836-1895), an Austrian novelist who described the disorder in his books.

The sadistic acts performed or fantasized by a person with sadism often reflect a desire for sexual or psychological domination of another person. These acts range from behavior that is not physically harmful although it may be humiliating to the other person (such as being urinated upon), to criminal and potentially

deadly behavior. Acts of domination may include restraining or imprisoning the partner through the use of handcuffs, cages, chains, or ropes. Other acts and fantasies related to sexual sadism include paddling, spanking, whipping, burning, beating, administering electrical shocks, biting, urinating or defecating on the other person, cutting, rape, murder, and mutilation.

In extreme cases, sexual sadism can lead to serious injury or death for the other person. According to the *DSM* these catastrophic results are more likely when the paraphilia is diagnosed as severe, and when it is associated with **antisocial personality disorder**, a personality disorder that may include psychotic symptoms.

Causes and symptoms

Causes

There is no universally accepted cause or theory explaining the origin of sexual sadism, or of sadomasochism. Some researchers attempt to explain the presence of sexual paraphilias in general as the result of biological factors. Evidence for this viewpoint comes from abnormal findings from neuropsychological and neurological tests of sex offenders.

Some researchers believe that paraphilias are related to such other problems as **brain** injury, **schizophrenia**, or another mental disorder. Often, people with sexual disorders or symptoms of paraphilia are diagnosed with other mental disorders.

Another theory about paraphilias is derived from learning theory. It suggests that paraphilias develop because the person is required to suppress, or squelch, inappropriate sexual fantasies. Because the fantasies are not acted out initially, the urge to carry them out increases. When the person finally acts upon the fantasies, they are in a state of considerable distress and/or arousal. This theory is not accepted by forensic experts at the Federal Bureau of Investigation (FBI) and other researchers who study sexual offenses. Rather than suppressing fantasies, most people who are eventually arrested for crimes involving sexual sadism begin with milder forms of acting on them and progressing to more harmful ways of acting out. For example, the FBI's database indicates that these people— almost always males—start out by collecting pornographic materials that depict sadistic acts, or they may draw ropes and chains on the photographs of models in swimsuit or lingerie advertisements. They then typically progress to following women at a distance, to hiring a prostitute in order to act out the fantasy, and to asking a girlfriend or other willing partner to cooperate with their fantasy. In other words, the severity of sadistic acts tends to increase over time.

Symptoms

Individuals with sexual sadism derive sexual excitement from physically or psychologically administering pain, suffering, and/or humiliation to another person, who may or may not be a consenting partner.

They may experience distressed or impaired functioning because of the sadistic behaviors or fantasies. This distress or impairment may be due to the fact that the partner is not consenting.

Diagnosis

The diagnosis of sexual sadism is complicated by several factors, beginning with the fact that most persons with the disorder do not enter therapy voluntarily. Some are referred to treatment by a court order. Some are motivated by fear of discovery by employers or family members, and a minority enter therapy because their wife or girl friend is distressed by the disorder. The diagnosis of sexual sadism is based on the results of a psychiatrist's interview with the patient. In some cases a person with sexual sadism may be referred to a specialized clinic for the treatment of sexual disorders. In the clinic, he will be given questionnaires intended to measure the presence and extent of cognitive distortions regarding rape and other forms of coercion, aggression, and impulsivity.

DSM-IV-TR criteria for sexual sadism include recurrent intense sexual fantasies, urges, or behaviors involving real acts in which another person is suffering psychological or physical suffering, pain, and humiliation. The victim's suffering, pain, and humiliation cause the person with sexual sadism to become aroused. The fantasies, urges, or behaviors must be present for at least six months.

The diagnostic criteria also require either that the person has acted on these urges or fantasies with a nonconsenting person, or that the person has experienced noticeable distress or interpersonal problems because of these urges or fantasies.

Sexual sadism must be differentiated from normal sexual arousal, behavior, and experimentation. Some forms of mild aggression, such as "love bites" or scratching, are within the range of normal behavior during sexual intercourse. Sadism should also be differentiated from sadomasochistic behavior that involves only mild pain and/or the simulation of more dangerous pain. When these factors are present, a diagnosis of sexual sadism is not necessarily warranted.

Other mental disorders, such as the psychotic disorders, may include elements of sadism or other paraphilias. For example, patients with psychotic symptoms may perform sadistic acts for reasons other than

---

KEY TERMS

Forensic—Pertaining to courtroom procedure or evidence used in courts of law.

Masochism—A mental disorder in which a person obtains sexual satisfaction through pain or humiliation inflicted by the self or by another person. The term is sometimes used more generally to refer to a tendency to find pleasure in submissiveness or self-denial.

Medroxyprogesterone acetate (MPA)—A female hormone that may be prescribed for male patients with sexual sadism or other paraphilias. MPA helps to control sexual urges in men by speeding up the clearance of testosterone from the bloodstream.

Paraphilias—A group of mental disorders that is characterized by recurrent intense sexual urges and sexually arousing fantasies generally involving (1) non-human objects, (2) the suffering or humiliation of oneself or one's partner (not merely simulated), or (3) children or other non-consenting persons.

Sadism—A mental disorder in which sexual arousal and gratification are obtained by inflicting pain or humiliation on another person.

---

sexual excitement. In these cases, an additional diagnosis of sexual sadism is not warranted.

Persons diagnosed with sexual sadism may have other sexual disorders or paraphilias. Some individuals, especially males, have diagnoses of both sexual sadism and sexual masochism.

Treatment

Behavior therapy is often used to treat paraphilias. This approach to treatment may include the management and conditioning of arousal patterns and masturbation. Therapies involving cognitive restructuring and **social skills training** are also often utilized.

Medication may be used to reduce fantasies and behavior relating to paraphilias. This form of treatment is especially recommended for people who exhibit sadistic behaviors that are dangerous to others. The medications that may be used include female hormones (most commonly medroxyprogesterone acetate, or MPA), which speed up the clearance of testosterone from the bloodstream; antiandrogen medications, which block the body's uptake of testosterone; and the **selective serotonin reuptake inhibitors**, or **SSRIs**.

Nonconsensual sadistic behavior often leads to problems with the criminal justice system. Issues related to legal problems may impair or delay the patient's treatment. Persons with sexual sadism may be reluctant to seek or continue treatment because they fear being reported to the police or being named in a lawsuit by an unwilling partner.

Treatment of sexual sadism may also be complicated by health problems related to sexual behavior. Sexually transmitted diseases and other medical problems may be present, especially when the sadistic behavior involves the release of blood or other body fluids.

Prognosis

Because of the chronic course of sexual sadism and the uncertainty of its causes, treatment is often difficult. The fact that many sadistic fantasies are socially unacceptable or unusual leads many people who may have the disorder to avoid or drop out of treatment. Treating a paraphilia is often a sensitive subject for many mental health professionals. Severe or difficult cases of sexual sadism should be referred to a specialized clinic for the treatment of sexual disorders or to professionals with experience in treating such cases.

As was noted previously, acts of sexual sadism tend to grow more violent or bizarre over time. As males with the disorder grow older, however, their ability to commit such acts begins to decrease. Sexual sadism is rarely diagnosed in men over 50.

Prevention

Because it is sometimes unclear whether sadomasochistic behavior is within the realm of normal experimentation or indicative of a diagnosis of sexual sadism, prevention is a tricky issue. Often, prevention refers to managing sadistic behavior so it never involves non-consenting individuals and it primarily involves the simulation of pain and not real pain.

Also, because fantasies and urges originating in childhood or adolescence may form the basis for sadomasochistic behavior in adulthood, prevention is difficult. People may be very unwilling to divulge their urges and discuss their sadistic fantasies.

Resources

BOOKS

American Psychiatric Association. *Diagnostic and Statistical Manual of Mental Disorders*. 4th ed., text rev. Washington, DC: American Psychiatric Publishing, 2000.

Baxter, Lewis R. Jr., and Robert O. Friedel, eds. *Current Psychiatric Diagnosis & Treatment*. Philadelphia: Current Medicine, 1999.

Black, Donald W., and Nancy C. Andreasen. *Introductory Textbook of Psychiatry*. 5th ed. Arlington, VA: American Psychiatric Publishing, 2011.

Douglas, John, and Mark Olshaker. *Mindhunter: Inside the FBI's Elite Serial Crime Unit*. Audio ed. New York: Simon and Schuster, 2010.

Ebert, Michael H., et al. *Current Diagnosis & Treatment in Psychiatry*. New York: McGraw-Hill, 2008.

Ali Fahmy, Ph.D.

Sexual Violence Risk-20

Definition

The Sexual Violence Risk-20, also called the SVR-20, is an assessment instrument used by mental health professionals.

Purpose

The SVR-20 provides a structure for reviewing information important in characterizing an individual's risk of committing sexual violence and for targeting plans to manage that risk. The instrument's authors define sexual violence as, "actual, attempted, or threatened sexual contact with a person who is nonconsenting or unable to give consent."

Precautions

SVR-20 results should be finalized and interpreted by a professional who is familiar with the scientific literature on sexual violence, and who is experienced in conducting individual assessments on sexual and violent offenders. The instrument cannot provide new information about past behavior or profile an examinee as a sexually violent offender. Rather, it helps provide a structure to follow in estimating risk of sexual violence under certain circumstances. The instrument should not be used as a stand-alone measure, and predictions derived from its use should be subject to critical review. It is especially important to place results in the contexts of the examinee's personal style, likely environmental conditions, and base rates of sexual violence in other offenders with similar characteristics.

Description

The SVR-20 is a tool that helps guide a professional in conducting a minimally comprehensive assessment of sexual violence risk. The assessment process is based on six principles:

- It is important to gather a depth of information about the examinee's personal, social, occupational, mental health, illegal, and other relevant behavior.
- Information should be gathered using a variety of sources and methods, including (and not limited to) record reviews, interviews, and psychological, physiological, and medical techniques.
- Information should be gathered from the examinee, his or her relatives and acquaintances, the victim(s), professionals who have interacted with the examinee, and any other sources likely to yield useful information.
- The examinee's history and future exposure to risk factors should be considered.
- The examiner should critically weigh the accuracy, credibility, and applicability of the data that has been gathered.
- The risk assessment process should be ongoing, with regular reassessments for many examinees.

The content of the SVR-20 was developed following a comprehensive review of similar instruments and of the scientific literature on risk for sexual violence and reoffense. The SVR-20 materials consist of a reference manual and protocol sheets that are filled out by the examiner. The instrument includes three major sections: Psychosocial Adjustment, Sexual Offenses, and Future Plans. The SVR-20 items are rated as not present, somewhat or possibly present, or clearly present. The overall pattern is used in forming a professional judgment about the person's risk of sexual recidivism (low, medium, or high). It is intended as a qualitative, not as an absolute, measure. However, the scores of no, maybe/sometimes, and yes can be converted into values (0, 1, and 2, respectively), a method that has been validated in a Swedish study. The SVR-20 has proven again and again to be an excellent tool for evaluating recidivism risk.

The Psychosocial Adjustment section includes 11 risk factors: sexual deviation, victim of **child abuse**, psychopathy, major mental illness, substance use problems, suicidal/homicidal ideation, relationship problems, employment problems, past nonsexual violent offenses, past nonviolent offenses, and past supervision failure.

The Sexual Offenses section includes seven risk factors: high-density sex offenses, multiple sex offense types, physical harm to victim(s) in sex offenses, uses weapons or threats of death in sex offenses, escalation in frequency and severity of sex offenses, extreme minimization or **denial** of sex offenses, and attitudes that support or condone sex offenses.

KEY TERMS

High-density sex offenses—Several offenses within a short period of time.

Risk assessment—The process of gathering and interpreting data useful in estimating the probability that an individual will demonstrate sexual violence.

Risk management—Using the results of a risk assessment to tailor intervention strategies intended to reduce the likelihood that an individual will demonstrate sexual violence.

Sexual violence—Actual, attempted, or threatened sexual contact with a person who is nonconsenting or unable to give consent.

The Future Plans section includes two factors: lacks realistic plans and negative attitude toward **intervention**. Aside from factors related to the examinee's thinking and personality, items found in the first and second sections reference fixed or relatively stable characteristics.

The first and third sections are relevant not only to sexual violence, but also to violence in general. There is also an unstructured supplementary section entitled Other Considerations that can be used to describe unique factors relevant to an examinee's probability of risk.

Results

The SVR-20 does not allow for the definite prediction of sexual violence. Prediction of risk is summarized using a rating of low, moderate, or high. Although the instrument's authors did not provide decision-making guidelines for determining the appropriate rating, they did recommend five questions to consider in communicating a "Risk Message" derived from the results:

- What is the likelihood that the individual will engage in sexual violence, if no efforts are made to manage the risk?
- What is the probable nature, frequency, and severity of any future sexual violence?
- Who are the likely victims of any future sexual violence?
- What steps could be taken to manage the individual's risk for sexual violence?
- What circumstances might exacerbate the individual's risk for sexual violence?

Typically, answers to these and other questions are fashioned in the form of a report for those responsible for making decisions about the examinee. Studies have shown that this evaluative measure works to distinguish recidivists who engage in sexual violence from those who engage in general violence.

Resources

BOOKS

Boer, D., et al. *Manual for the Sexual Violence Risk-20.* Burnaby, British Columbia, Canada: The British Columbia Institute Against Family Violence, copublished with the Mental Health, Law, and Policy Institute at Simon Fraser University, 1997.

Laws, D. Richard, and O'Donohue, William T., eds. *Sexual Deviance: Theory, Assessment, and Treatment.* 2nd ed. New York, Guilford Press, 2008.

Marshall, W., D. Laws, and H. Barbaree, eds. *Handbook of Sexual Assault: Issues, Theories, and Treatment of the Offender.* New York: Springer, 1990.

PERIODICALS

Craig, Leam A., Anthony Beech, and Kevin D. Browne. "Cross-Validation of the Risk Matrix 2000 Sexual and Violent Scales." *Journal of Interpersonal Violence* 21 (May 2006): 612–33.

Menzies, R., and C.D. Webster. "Construction and Validation of Risk Assessments in a Six-Year Follow-Up of Forensic Patients: A Tridimensional Analysis." *Journal of Consulting and Clinical Psychology* 63, no. 5 (October 1995): 766–78.

Monahan, J. "Mental Disorder and Violent Behavior." *American Psychologist* 47, no. 4 (April 1992): 511–21.

ORGANIZATIONS

American Psychological Association, 750 1st St. NE, Washington, DC, 20002-4242, (202) 336-5500; TDD/TTY: (202) 336-6123, (800) 374-2721, http://www.apa.org.

Association for the Treatment of Sexual Abusers, 4900 SW Griffith Dr., Ste. 274, Beaverton, OR, 97005, (503) 643-1023, Fax: (503) 643-5084, atsa@atsa.com, http://www.atsa.com.

British Columbia Institute Against Family Violence, 409 Granville St., Ste. 551, Vancouver, BC, CanadaV6C 1T2, (604) 669-7055, (877) 755-7055, resource@bcifv.org, http://www.bcifv.org.

Geoffrey G. Grimm, PhD, LPC
Emily Jane Willingham, PhD

Shared psychotic disorder

Definition

Shared psychotic disorder, a rare and atypical psychotic disorder, occurs when an otherwise healthy person (secondary partner) begins believing the **delusions** of someone with whom they have a close relationship (primary partner) who is suffering from a psychotic disorder with prominent delusions. This disorder is also referred to as "folie á deux."

Shared psychotic disorder is also referred to by other names, such as **psychosis** of association, contagious insanity, infectious insanity, double insanity, and communicated insanity. There have been cases involving multiple persons, the most significant, being a case involving an entire family of 12 people (folie á douze).

Demographics

Given the fact that the preponderance of cases occur within the same family, the theory about the origins of the disorder come from a psychosocial perspective. Approximately 55% of secondary cases of the disorder have first-degree relatives with psychiatric disorders, not including the primary partner. This is not true of individuals with the primary **diagnosis**, as they showed a roughly 35% incidence.

Little data is available to determine the prevalence of shared psychotic disorder. While it has been argued that some cases go undiagnosed, it is nevertheless a rare finding in clinical settings.

Description

In cases of shared psychotic disorder, the primary partner is most often in a position of strong influence over the other person. This allows the primary partner, over time, to erode the defenses of the secondary partner by forcing their strange belief upon him or her. Most of the time, this disorder occurs within a nuclear family. In fact, more than 95% of the cases reported involved people in the same family. Without regard to the number of persons within the family, shared delusions generally involve two people. There is the primary, most often the dominant person, and the secondary or submissive person. This becomes fertile ground for the primary (dominant) partner to press for understanding and belief by others in the family.

Causes and symptoms

Causes

There are several variables that have great influence on the creation of shared psychotic disorder. For example, family isolation, closeness of the relationship to the person with the primary diagnosis, the length of time the relationship has existed, and the existence of a dominant-submissive factor within the relationship. The submissive partner in the relationship may be predisposed to have a mental disorder. Often the submissive partner meets the criteria for **dependent personality disorder**. Nearly 75% of the delusions are of the persecutory type.

An example of shared psychotic disorder involving the delusion of persecution is a 52-year-old married female and her 48-year-old husband with multiple sclerosis who believed that they were being harassed and watched by the Irish Republican Army (IRA). They were hospitalized and both became stable after two weeks on an antipsychotic medication. However, an interesting point in this case is that they were separated for that two-week period. The general consensus has been that, once separated, the submissive partner will let go of the delusion, that it would resolve itself simply due to separation. That did not happen in this case. Both partners had to be treated with proper medications before the delusion resolved.

In a case involving a middle-aged mother and an adolescent daughter, the delusions were multifaceted. The mother held the persecutory belief that someone in her neighborhood was manufacturing illegal drugs of some sort, and that they were periodically spraying something odorless, tasteless, and invisible into the air. The sprayed substance made her and her teenaged daughter "act crazy." Oddly enough, the effects of the spraying began shortly after the husband left for work in the morning and resolved shortly before he returned in the afternoon. The family raised ducks at their home, and the mother and daughter believed that the men making the illegal drugs were using the family ducks "as a food source" to stay near their hideout and avoid detection by police. Finally, mother and daughter also believed that occasional gunshots in their countryside landscape were meant as warnings to prevent anyone from learning about the misdeeds of the drug makers. This case was revealed when the daughter ran away from home, fearing that men with guns were coming to kill them. She was subsequently placed in the care of a child protective services agency. The bizarre stories began to unfold. Both mother and daughter received psychiatric care.

Symptoms

The principal feature of shared psychotic disorder is the unwavering belief by the secondary partner in the dominant partner's delusion. The delusions experienced by both partners in shared psychotic disorder are far less bizarre than those found in schizophrenic patients; they are, therefore, believable. Since these delusions are often within the realm of possibility, it is easier for the

---

KEY TERMS

Delusions—Irrational beliefs that defy normal reasoning, and remain firm even when overwhelming proof is presented to dispute them. Delusions are distinct from culturally or religiously based beliefs that may be seen as untrue by outsiders.

Schizophrenia—A major mental illness marked by psychotic symptoms, including hallucinations, delusions, and severe disruptions in thinking.

---

dominant partner to impose his/her idea upon the submissive, secondary partner.

Diagnosis

A clinical interview is required to diagnose shared psychotic disorder. There are basically three symptoms required for the determination of the existence of this disorder:

- An otherwise healthy person, in a close relationship with someone who has an established delusion, develops a delusion himself/herself.
- The content of the shared delusion follows exactly or closely resembles that of the established delusion.
- Some other psychotic disorder, such as schizophrenia, is not in place and cannot better account for the delusion manifested by the secondary partner.

Treatment

The treatment approach most recommended is to separate the secondary partner from the source of the delusion. If symptoms have not dissipated within one to two weeks, antipsychotic medications may be required.

Once stabilized, **psychotherapy** should be undertaken with the secondary partner, integrating the dominant partner once he/she has also received medical treatment and is stable.

Prognosis

If the secondary partner is removed from the source of the delusion and proper medical and psychotherapeutic treatment are rendered, the prognosis is good. However, as stated above, the separation alone may not be successful. The secondary partner may require antipsychotic medication. Even after treatment, since

---

QUESTIONS TO ASK YOUR DOCTOR

- What are the indications that I may have shared psychotic disorder?

- What physical and psychiatric diagnostic tests do I need?

- What treatment options do you recommend for me?

- What kind of changes can I expect to see with the medications you have prescribed for me?

- What are the side effects associated with the medications you have prescribed for me?

- What tests or evaluation techniques will you perform to see if treatment has been beneficial for me?

- What symptoms are important enough that I should seek immediate treatment?

- Can you recommend any support groups for me and my family?

this shared psychotic disorder is primarily found in families, the family members tend to reunite following treatment and release. If family dynamics return to pretreatment modes, a **relapse** could occur. Periodic monitoring by a social services agency is advised for as long as a year following treatment.

Prevention

In an effort to prevent relapse, **family therapy** should also be considered to re-establish the nuclear family and to provide social support to modify old family dynamics. This would favor a new behavioral paradigm. The family cannot afford to continue in isolation as it did in the past and will require support from community agencies.

Resources

BOOKS

American Psychiatric Association. *Diagnostic and Statistical Manual of Mental Disorders.* 4th ed. Washington, DC: American Psychiatric Association, 2000.

Cooper, Rachel. *Classifying Madness: A Philosophical Examination of the Diagnostic and Statistical Manual of Mental Disorders.* New York: Springer, 2010.

Graham, George. *The Disordered Mind: An Introduction to Philosophy of Mind and Mental Illness.* New York: Routledge, 2010.

North, Carol, and Sean Yutzy. *Goodwin and Guze's Psychiatric Diagnosis.* New York: Oxford University Press, 2010.

Sadock, Benjamin J., and Virginia A. Sadock. *Kaplan & Sadock's Synopsis of Psychiatry.* 10th ed. New York: Lippincott, Williams and Wilkins, 2007.

PERIODICALS

Lai, Tony T.S., et al. "Folie á Deux in the Aged: A Case Report." *Clinical Gerontologist* 22 (2001): 113–117.

Malik, Mansoor A., and Serena Condon. "Induced Psychosis (Folie á Deux) Associated with Multiple Sclerosis." *Irish Journal of Psychological Medicine* 17 (2000): 73–77.

Mergui, J., et al. "Shared Obsessive-Compulsive Disorder: Broadening the Concept of Shared Psychotic Disorder." *Australian and New Zealand Journal of Psychiatry* 44, no. 9 (2010): 859–62.

ORGANIZATIONS

American Psychological Association, 750 1st St. NE, Washington, DC, 20002-4242, (202) 336-5500, TDD/TTY: (202) 336-6123, (800) 374-2721, http://www.apa.org.

Mental Health America, 2000 N. Beauregard St., 6th Fl., Alexandria, VA, 22311, (703) 684-7722, (800) 969-6642, Fax: (703) 684-5968, http://www1.nmha.org.

National Alliance on Mental Illness, 3803 N Fairfax Dr., Ste. 100, Arlington, VA, 22203, (703) 524-7600, http://www.nami.org.

National Institute of Mental Health, 6001 Executive Blvd., Rm. 8184, MSC 9663, Bethesda, MD, 20892-9663, (301) 433-4513, TTY: (301) 443-8431, Fax: (301) 443-4279, (866) 615-6464, TTY: (866) 415-8051, nimhinfo@nih.gov, http://www.nimh.nih.gov.

Jack H. Booth, Psy.D.
Laura Jean Cataldo, RN, Ed.D.

Shift work sleep disorder *see* **Circadian rhythm sleep disorder**

Shyness

Definition

Shyness is a personality trait that produces behaviors ranging from feeling uncomfortable at a party to an extreme fear of being watched by others while talking on the telephone.

Description

Shyness affects people of all ages. A toddler might run from strangers and cling to his or her parents. While kindergarten is frightening for many children, some students are anxious about the first day of school until they graduate from college. Job interviews are stressful for people uncomfortable talking about themselves. For some people, feelings of self-worth are related to their careers. Retirement may bring feelings of lower self-esteem.

Shyness is linked to **brain** activity, how a person was raised and other experiences, and the person's reaction to those experiences.

Social phobia

Extreme shyness is sometimes referred to as a **social phobia**. Also known as social anxiety disorder, a social phobia is a psychiatric condition defined as a "marked and persistent fear" of some situations. Social phobia may cause a person to remain unemployed, according to the organization Mental Health America. True social phobia affects about 3% of people.

Introversion

Shyness is different from introversion; a person with introversion enjoys being alone and intentionally avoids situations like parties, whereas a shy person wants to be around people. However, shyness is stronger than the desire to be sociable. The shy person is afraid to go to the party and stays home alone.

Causes and symptoms

Causes

A person's temperament is related to the amygdala, the part of the brain related to emotions and new situations. The amygdala evaluates new situations based on memories of past experiences. If the new situation appears threatening, the amygdala sends a warning signal. The amygdala in a shy person is extremely sensitive and much more active than that of an outgoing person. The increased activity causes the person to withdraw either physically or emotionally. This withdrawal is known as inhibition.

Brain activity is one component of shyness, but environment also plays a role. If a child has outgoing, nurturing parents, he or she is more likely to imitate their behavior. If a child has a teacher that is mocking and critical, the child may develop lifelong fear of the first day of school. A person embarrassed in a job interview could become anxious in future interviews.

Symptoms

At the root of shyness is a feeling of self-consciousness. This may cause the person to blush, tense up, or start sweating. Those are some reactions caused when the brain signals its warning. The person may avoid eye contact, look down, become very quiet, or fumble over words.

Symptoms vary because there are degrees of shyness. A person might be very quiet when meeting new people, but then become talkative when he or she feels comfortable with them. A person who is nervous during job interviews may not be afraid of social gatherings.

Social phobia

Social phobia causes an extreme fear of being humiliated or embarrassed in front of people, according to the NMHA. It may be connected to low self-esteem or feelings of inferiority. A person with social phobia is not fearful in all situations and may feel comfortable around people most of the time. However, social phobias have caused people to drop out of school, avoid making friends, and keep away from other fear-provoking situations. Fears range from speaking in pubic and dating to using public restrooms or writing when other people are present.

According to the NMHA, a person with social phobia may feel that everyone is looking at them, A trivial mistake is regarded as much more serious and blushing is painfully embarrassing. Social phobia is frequently accompanied by **depression** or **substance abuse**.

Diagnosis

In many cases, persons will realize on their own that they are shy and may take steps to overcome their shyness. Adults and youths may buy self-help books or take classes on subjects like overcoming shyness and **assertiveness training**. These classes may be taught by counselors, psychologists, or people with experience conquering shyness. Healthcare providers often schedule these classes. They may be taught in settings ranging from adult schools to social service agencies; costs of the classes will vary.

Children may not know that there are treatment solutions for their shyness. Parents and educators should be alert for symptoms of shyness in younger children. Schools and family resource centers can provide referrals if it appears that counseling will help get their child diagnosed.

Medical diagnosis

Based on the child's circumstances, parents may take their children to see a healthcare provider. Some insurance plans require an appointment with a doctor before a referral to a counselor or a **psychologist** is given. The health professional will conduct an assessment and then recommend treatment.

Children and adults may need medical treatment for social phobia. An adult's **diagnosis** will also include a medical exam to determine if there is a physical cause for symptoms. If a medical cause has been ruled out, the patient will undergo a psychiatric evaluation.

Diagnostic fees and the time allocated for evaluation vary for both shyness and social phobia. Diagnosis could span several hour-long sessions that cover an initial evaluation, personality tests, and a meeting to set therapy goals. Insurance may cover part of the costs.

Treatment

Shyness treatment concentrates on changing behavior so that the person feels more at ease in shyness-provoking situations. The person may be guided by a self-help book or participate in individual or **group therapy**.

Traditional

Books and therapy generally focus on behavioral therapy and **cognitive-behavioral therapy**. One method of behavioral therapy is to expose the person to the situation that triggers fear. This could start with rehearsing a job interview with a friend or making eye contact with a store clerk. Over time, the person may go on interviews to gain experience rather than to be hired. Another person might move from eye contact to attending a social event such as a concert to become more at ease around strangers.

Therapy also focuses on developing skills to cope in new situations. These include taking deep breaths to relax and practicing small talk. Cognitive-therapy helps the person learn how thinking patterns contribute to symptoms, according to NMHA. The person is taught techniques to change those thoughts or to stop symptoms. This association maintains this therapy is very effective for people with social phobias.

Therapy sessions may be led by a licensed marriage and family counselor, a psychologist, or a **psychiatrist**. The cost of group therapy is generally an hourly fee with therapy planned for a set time.

Drugs

Treatment may also include medication. Prescription drugs like **paroxetine** (Paxil) are generally only prescribed to people with social **anxiety disorders**. Paxil is traditionally prescribed for depression and other mood disorders. The patient takes one tablet daily.

Insurance may cover part of the costs of therapy and medicine.

Alternative

Alternative treatments for shyness focus on treating accompanying symptoms like tension and **stress**.

Relaxation therapy guides the person through a series of actions to relieve tension. The activity starts with deep breathing, and the person progressively focuses on the head and different parts of the body. The exercise may start with the head, neck, shoulders, moving down to the one foot and then the other. Some techniques involve tightly tensing and then releasing each body part. Another method is to concentrate on relaxing each part or imagining that it becomes warm.

Another self-treatment is **aromatherapy**. **Lavender** is a relaxing scent and is available in liquid form as an essential oil. Stress may be relieved by adding lavender oil to a bath. Some people carry the oil with them; if they become anxious, they can dab the oil on a cotton pad and breathe in the lavender to feel calmer.

Prognosis

Shyness may not be permanent. Children often outgrow shyness, and behavioral changes and therapy can help adults with shyness feel more at ease. Furthermore, some aspects of shyness are positive—persons who are shy are frequently good listeners and are empathetic, or aware of others' feelings.

Prevention

Shyness is a personality trait related to a person's biology and experiences. The part of shyness related to the brain cannot be changed. However, parents can provide a nurturing environment and teach children coping skills, which may help to prevent shyness.

To help combat the avoidance symptom caused by shyness, adults may wish to engage in enjoyable hobbies with social components. Recreational activities like walking groups combine physical exercise with the opportunity to socialize. Enrolling in a class at an adult school or community college provides the opportunity to learn and make new friends. Classes like these can boost confidence as a person learns a hands-on skill or discovers that others value her or his opinion.

Resources

WEBSITES

American Psychological Association. "Shyness." http://www. apa.org/topics/shyness/index.aspx (accessed October 27, 2011).

Cooper, Lisa. "Shy Child, Shy Adult." BabyZone.com. http:// www.babyzone.com/toddler/toddler_development/ social_skills/article/shy-child-shy-adult (accessed October 27, 2011).

KidsHealth.org. "Shyness." http://www.kidshealth.org/teen/ your_mind/emotions/shyness.html (accessed October 27, 2011).

ORGANIZATIONS

American Psychological Association, 750 1st Street NE, Washington, DC, 20002-4242, (202) 336-5500, TDD/TTY: (202) 336-6123, (800) 374-2721, http://www.apa.org.

Mental Health America, 2000 North Beauregard St., 6th Fl., Alexandria, VA, 22311, (703) 684-7722, (800) 969-6642, Fax: (703) 684-5968, http://www.nmha.org.

Shyness Research Institute, 4201 Grant Line Rd., New Albany, IN, 47150, (812) 941-2295, Fax: (812) 941-2591, bcarducc@ius.edu, http://www.ius.edu/shyness.

Liz Swain

Simple phobia *see* **Specific phobias**

Sinequan *see* **Doxepin**

Single photon emission computed tomography

Definition

Single photon emission **computed tomography** (SPECT) is a type of imaging study used in nuclear medicine that uses radioactive materials injected through a vein that pass into the **brain** or other organ generating a high-resolution image. SPECT relies on two technologies: computed tomography (CT) and the use of a radioactive material (radionuclide) to label a compound known as a tracer. Tracking the tracer's movement through body tissues, and the rate of its radioactive decay allows the doctor to obtain 3-D

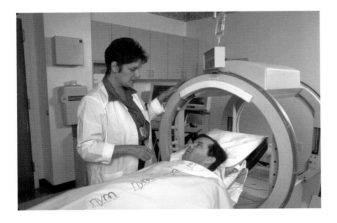

A man prepares to undergo a single photon emission computed tomography (SPECT) scan. (© *David M. Grossman/newscom)*

images of blood flow in the heart, electrical activity in different areas of the brain, or to scan for tumors or bone disease by using a device called a gamma camera contained within the SPECT machine.

Purpose

SPECT is used to diagnose head **trauma**, epilepsy, **dementia**, and cerebrovascular disease. Development of a radiotracer called Tc99m (technetium-99) increased the resolution of brain images generated from SPECT. The images yield accurate spatial and contrast resolutions. Other radioactive isotopes used in SPECT are iodine-123, xenon-133, thallium-201, and fluorine-18. The resulting sharp images enable the clinician to visualize tiny structures within the brain or other parts of the body. The accuracy of SPECT images makes it a useful clinical and research tool.

SPECT is used to diagnose the following disease states:

- Cerebrovascular disease or stroke: SPECT is used to detect ischemia (reduced blood flow), determine stroke causes, evaluate transient ischemia, determine prognosis, and monitor treatment.

- Such forms of dementia as Alzheimer's disease: SPECT studies can be used effectively to rule out other medical causes of dementia.

- Head trauma: SPECT is used to detect increased numbers of lesions following the period after head trauma. The high resolution and accurate brain images of SPECT can detect lesions in the brain that are not possible to visualize using other techniques such as positron emission tomography (PET) scanning. SPECT images give important information concerning prognosis (also sometimes called outcome) and treatment of persons affected with head injury.

- Epilepsy: The radioactive material injected before SPECT imaging concentrates at the seizure locus (the region that contains nerve cells that generate an abnormal impulse). This concentration helps identify the location of seizures and assists clinicians concerning management and outcomes.

- Corpus striatum: SPECT allows clinicians to visualize a specific area of the brain called the corpus striatum, which contains the neurotransmitter dopamine. Circuitry in the corpus striatum and interaction with dopamine can help provide valuable information concerning movement disorders, schizophrenia, mood disorders, and hormone diseases (given that hormones require control and regulation from the brain in the pituitary gland and hypothalamus).

SPECT imaging is a sensitive research tool for measuring blood flow through the brain (cerebral blood flow), in persons who have psychological disorder such as **obsessive-compulsive disorder** (higher blood flow) and alcoholism (lower blood flow).

SPECT has also been used in myocardial perfusion imaging (MPI), which is a test done to evaluate patients for coronary artery disease. It is based on the understanding that diseased heart tissue under stress receives less blood than normal heart tissue (myocardium). A special form of technetium-99 known as Tc-sestamibi is injected. The patient's heart is then stressed by either **exercise** or by the administration of a drug, usually dobutamine, adenosine, or dipyridamole. SPECT imaging performed after the stress reveals the distribution of the Tc-sestamibi within the different regions of the heart muscle. The patient is usually asked to return 1–7 days after the stress test for another set of SPECT images taken while the patient is at rest. Doctors then compare the two sets of images. If the images following the stress test are normal, the patient does not have to return for a second SPECT scan.

Other SPECT diagnostic indications and procedures are similar to other **imaging studies**, such as computed tomography, **magnetic resonance imaging**, and **PET**.

Description

In most cases, the SPECT scan requires injecting the patient with a compound containing the radioactive tracer or administering the tracer through an infusion given intravenously in the arm. In some cases, the patient may inhale the tracer through the nose. The patient is then asked to lie quietly in a room for 15–30 minutes while the radioactive tracer is absorbed by the body.

In the second phase of the scan, the patient is positioned by the healthcare team on a table in the room with the SPECT machine. The exact position depends on the part of the patient's body or the organ system that is being investigated. The SPECT machine itself contains a gamma camera, an imaging device that detects gamma rays given off by the radioactive tracer in the patient's body. The SPECT machine rotates around the patient while the gamma camera records a series of two-dimensional images of the patient's body organs. These images are then sent to a computer that produces 3-D images of the organs in question.

Research studies of the brain utilizing SPECT have been conducted to study changes in and the effects of certain brain receptors. Researchers utilize SPECT scans to map brain metabolism and look at blood flow and activity patterns in the brain, helping assess and evaluate brain function.

KEY TERMS

Gamma camera—A device inside the SPECT machine that forms images of the gamma rays emitted by the radionuclides used in tracers in nuclear medicine.

Gamma rays—Extremely short-wavelength electromagnetic radiation released during the process of radioactive decay.

Myocardium—The specialized involuntary muscle tissue found in the walls of the heart.

Nuclear medicine—A branch of medicine that makes use of radioisotopes (also called radionuclides) to evaluate the rate of radioactive decay in diagnosing and treating various diseases.

Prodromal—The early stage or the start of a disease, before specific or characteristic symptoms occur.

Radionuclide—An atom with an unstable nucleus that emits gamma rays during the process of its radioactive decay. Radionuclides, also known as radioisotopes, are used to make the tracers used in SPECT. The most common radionuclides used in SPECT are iodine-123, technetium-99m, xenon-133, thallium-201, and fluorine-18.

Tracer—A substance containing a radioisotope, injected into the body and followed in order to obtain information about various metabolic processes in the body.

Preparation

Patients wear comfortable clothing for a SPECT scan and expect to stay in the hospital for 1–3 hours. They do not need to fast beforehand or omit the medications they usually take.

Aftercare

Aftercare consists of drinking extra fluids to speed the excretion of the radioactive tracer in the urine. The tracer is usually flushed out in the patient's urine within a few hours after the scan. Any remaining tracer is broken down in the body within the next two days.

Risks

SPECT scans are generally safe and well tolerated by most patients. Some people, however, may experience bruising, bleeding, or pain at the point at which the needle was inserted into their vein. A small number of patients have allergic reactions to the radionuclide.

QUESTIONS TO ASK YOUR DOCTOR

- What are the indications that I should have a SPECT scan performed?
- What kind of diagnostic results can be determined with the use of a SPECT scan?
- Should I have other diagnostics tests in addition to a SPECT scan? If so, what other tests should I have?
- How long will SPECT take?
- Is there anything I can do to help rid my body of the radioactive tracer?
- Is there an alternative to this test?
- Will insurance cover SPECT?

Precautions

Women who are pregnant or breastfeeding should not have SPECT scans because the radioactive tracer can be passed to the fetus or the nursing baby. Women of childbearing age may be asked to have a pregnancy test before a SPECT scan.

Resources

BOOKS

Eisenberg, Ronald, and Alexander Margulis. *A Patient's Guide to Medical Imaging.* New York: Oxford University Press, 2011.

Elgazzar, Abdelhamid E. *A Concise Guide to Nuclear Medicine.* New York: Springer, 2011.

Heller, Gary V., April Mann, and Robert C. Hendel, eds. *Nuclear Cardiology: Technical Applications.* New York: McGraw-Hill Medical, 2009.

Levine, Harry III. *Medical Imaging.* Santa Barbara, CA: ABC-CLIO, 2010.

PERIODICALS

Aggarwal, N.R., et al. "Role of Cardiac MRI and Nuclear Imaging in Cardiac Resynchronization Therapy." *Nature Reviews: Cardiology* 6 (December 2009): 759–70.

Alford, R., et al. "Molecular Probes for the In Vivo Imaging of Cancer." *Molecular Biosystems* 5 (November 2009): 1279–91.

Goffin, K., et al. "Neuronuclear Assessment of Patients with Epilepsy." *Seminars in Nuclear Medicine* 38 (July 2008): 227–39.

Heller, G.V., et al. "Recent Advances in Cardiac PET and PET/CT Myocardial Perfusion Imaging." *Journal of Nuclear Cardiology* 16 (November/December 2009): 962–69.

Placantonakis, D.G., and T.H. Schwartz. "Localization in Epilepsy." *Neurologic Clinics* 27 (November 2009): 1015–30.

Salerno, M., and G.A. Beller. "Noninvasive Assessment of Myocardial Perfusion." *Circulation: Cardiovascular Imaging* 2 (September 2009): 412–24.

Stein, P.D., et al. "SPECT in Acute Pulmonary Embolism." *Journal of Nuclear Medicine* 50 (December 2009): 1999–2007.

ORGANIZATIONS

American College of Physicians, 190 N Independence Mall W, Philadelphia, PA, 19106-1572, (215) 351-2400, (800) 523-1546, http://www.acponline.org.

American Heart Association, 7272 Greenville Ave., Dallas, TX, 75231, (800) 242-8721, http://www.americanheart.org.

American Medical Association, 515 N State St., Chicago, IL, 60610, (312) 464-5000, (800) 621-8335, http://www.ama-assn.org.

National Cancer Institute, 6116 Executive Boulevard, Suite 300, Bethesda, MD, 20892, (800) 422-6237, Fax: (301) 402-0601, http://www.nci.nih.gov.

Laith Farid Gulli, MD
Alfredo Mori, MD
Jean Suvan, BSc, RDH
Laura Jean Cataldo, RN, EdD

Skills training *see* **Social skills training**

Skin picking *see* **Dermatillomania**

Sleep deprivation

Definition

Sleep deprivation is an inadequate amount of sleep for a given individual.

Demographics

Sleep deprivation has become so widespread in industrialized societies that daytime drowsiness may no longer seem abnormal. Between 1998 and 2005, the number of American adults who reported getting eight or more hours of sleep on weekday nights fell from 35% to 26%. Driver **fatigue** causes 100,000 accidents and 1,500 deaths annually in the United States.

Sleep deprivation is considered to be a widespread chronic health problem among American teenagers. A 2006 poll found that only 20% of teens got adequate sleep on school nights: by the end of high school they averaged fewer than seven hours, and most teens reported feeling tired during the day.

Recommended hours of sleep, by age group

Infants	
0–2 months	12–18 hours
2–12 months	14–15 hours
Toddlers/Children	
1–3 years	12–14 hours
3–5 years	11–13 hours
5–10 years	10–11 hours
Adolescents	
10–17 years	8.5–9.25 hours
Adults	
18+	7–9 hours

SOURCE: National Sleep Foundation, "How Much Sleep Do We Really Need?"

Available online at http://www.sleepfoundation.org/article/ how-sleep-works/how-much-sleep-do-we-really-need.
(Table by PreMediaGlobal. © 2012 Cengage Learning.)

Although sleep disturbances and disorders do not necessarily result in sleep deprivation, they can contribute to it:

• About half of all people over age 65 suffer frequent sleep disturbances.

• About 60 million Americans suffer from frequent or extended periods of insomnia resulting in sleep deprivation. The incidence of insomnia increases with age, affecting about 40% of women and 30% of men.

• An estimated 18 million Americans have sleep apnea, although it usually goes undiagnosed.

• Restless legs syndrome (RLS) is one of the most common sleep disorders that causes sleep deprivation, especially among older people. RLS is estimated to affect as many as 12 million Americans.

• Narcolepsy—which affects about 250,000 Americans—can cause nighttime insomnia, resulting in sleep deprivation.

• Most people with mental disorders—including depression and schizophrenia—have sleep disturbances that cause sleep deprivation.

• Many blind people have lifelong sleeping problems, including insomnia and a type of permanent jet lag, which can result in sleep deprivation.

Description

Sleeping and wakefulness are controlled by neurotransmitters—chemical messengers in the brain—that act on different sets of nerve cells or neurons. The **neurotransmitters serotonin** and norepinephrine in the brainstem—the connection between the **brain** and the spinal cord—keep parts of the brain active during wakefulness and are switched off during sleep. Also during wakefulness, an important chemical called adenosine builds up in the blood to the point where it eventually causes drowsiness and is broken down during sleep.

Humans normally cycle through five stages of sleep throughout the night, with one complete sleep cycle averaging 90–120 minutes:

• Stage 1 consists of drowsiness, drifting in and out of sleep, and being easily awakened.

• Stage 2 is light sleep, which accounts for about 50% of total sleeping time.

• Stage 3 is deep sleep.

• Stage 4 is slow-wave deep sleep.

• Stages 1, 3, and 4 together account for about 30% of sleeping time.

• Rapid eye movement (REM) sleep accounts for about 20% of total sleep time.

During the first sleep cycles of the night, deep sleep is relatively long and REM sleep short. REM periods gradually increase in length as deep sleep shortens. Towards waking almost all sleep is stages 1, 2, and REM.

Sleep is essential for survival and sleep deprivation can eventually result in death. However, scientists have only recently begun to understand the many functions of sleep. It is required for proper nervous system functioning. Parts of the brain that are involved in emotions, decision-making, and social interactions are less active during sleep. These neurons may need sleep to repair and replenish themselves, and sleep may also be necessary for growing new neurons and for exercising neuronal functions that are less active during wakefulness.

However, other parts of the brain are very active during sleep. During this period of low sensory input, the brain consolidates recently acquired memories. Nerve-signaling patterns that are generated during the day are repeated during deep sleep. REM sleep is required for learning certain mental skills, and sleep may be necessary for encoding memories and learning.

Many cells in the body produce more protein during deep and REM sleep, so sleep may be necessary for replenishing energy and repairing damage in cells throughout the body. Growth hormones in children and young adults are released during deep sleep, and sleep is required for proper immune system function and cytokines—chemicals that fight infection—are produced during sleep.

Sleep requirements

The amount of sleep required to prevent deprivation depends on a variety of factors, especially age and genetics:

- Infants need about 16 hours of sleep out of every 24 hours, with about 50% spent in REM.
- Toddlers need about 14 hours of sleep, which gradually decreases with age to a requirement of slightly over nine hours in teenagers.
- Most adults need 7–8 hours of sleep each night, although individual requirements may vary from 4 to 12 hours per night.
- Researchers have identified a gene called DEC2 that turns off some genes involved in controlling circadian rhythms—the internal clock that regulates the sleep-wake cycle. People with certain mutations in the DEC2 gene require only about six hours of sleep per night.
- Women often need several extra hours of sleep during the first three months of pregnancy.
- Although older people tend to sleep more lightly and for shorter periods, they need about the same amount of total sleep as when they were younger.

For most people, sleep deprivation accumulates as a "sleep debt," which must be made up. The ability to function relatively well—at least for short periods—under conditions of sleep deprivation appears to be genetically determined. Estimates suggest that 10%–15% of people function adequately on little or no sleep, whereas another 10%–15% cannot function at all without sleep. Most people cannot function at all after 48 hours without sleep, nor do humans appear to adapt to sleep deprivation. One study found that subjects who slept only 4–6 hours per night for 14 consecutive nights showed cognitive impairment equivalent to going without sleep for three consecutive days.

Although people may adjust to a sleep-depriving schedule, daily functioning and physical and mental health suffer, as sleep deprivation interferes with concentration, learning, and problem-solving. At least 6 hours of regular sleep are required for peak memory performance, and sleep deprivation is directly linked to memory loss. In addition, sleep deprivation may:

- interfere with work, school, and social interactions
- cause stress
- slow reaction times; sleep-deprived people perform at least as poorly on driving simulators and hand-eye coordination tasks as people who are intoxicated
- disrupt the decision-making machinery of the brain, impairing judgment, increasing risky behaviors, and reducing sensitivity to loss
- increase the risk of falls and accidents
- increase the risk for many health problems, including hypertension, cardiovascular disease, diabetes, obesity, and infections
- increase appetite and inhibit weight loss, even with proper exercise and diet

- increase the effects of alcohol.
- cause sleep paralysis, a rare but frightening condition in which a person temporarily loses the ability to speak or move while falling asleep or waking up

Teenagers require an average of 9.25 hours of sleep per night for brain development, health, and optimal performance. Sleep-deprived teens are at risk for:

- impaired cognitive function and decision-making
- health problems
- poor grades and athletic performance
- emotional and behavioral problems
- depression
- substance abuse
- violence
- automobile accidents

Risk factors

Risk factors for sleep deprivation include:

- anxiety and stress
- careers with long or irregular working hours
- night or shift work
- work requiring long-distance travel
- multiple jobs
- combining full-time work and school
- being a family caregiver

Causes and symptoms

Causes

Sleep deprivation is most often caused by lifestyle choices or the requirements of work, school, or caregiving. Irregular sleep patterns that differ between weekdays and weekends can harm the quality of sleep. A new baby often results in sleep-deprived parents. Teenagers with hectic schedules of school, homework, athletics, after-school activities, jobs, and family and social obligations find themselves without enough hours for quality sleep. Furthermore, hormonal changes in adolescence set most teens' biological clocks on later schedules than those of children and adults. Teens may be wide awake—albeit exhausted—at bedtime but still have to wake up early for school.

Foods and drugs that change the balance of neurotransmitters in the brain can cause sleep deprivation, including caffeinated drinks, such as coffee, and drugs, such as diet pills and decongestants, which stimulate the brain and can cause **insomnia**. Many **antidepressants** suppress REM sleep, and substances such as alcohol and **nicotine** deprive the brain of REM sleep.

KEY TERMS

Adenosine—A nucleoside that plays multiple physiological roles in energy transfer and molecular signaling, as a component of RNA, and as an inhibitory neurotransmitter that promotes sleep.

Apnea—The transient cessation of breathing.

Circadian rhythm—A 24-hour cycle of physiological or behavioral activities.

Cytokines—A class of proteins, including interferons and interleukins, that are released by cells as part of the immune response and as mediators of intercellular communication.

Insomnia—Prolonged or abnormal inability to obtain adequate sleep.

Melatonin—A hormone involved in regulation of circadian rhythms.

Narcolepsy—A condition characterized by brief attacks of deep sleep.

Neurotransmitters—Chemicals that transmit nerve impulses from one nerve cell to another.

REM—Rapid eye movement; a stage of the normal sleep cycle characterized by rapid eye movements, increased forebrain and midbrain activity, and dreaming.

Restless legs syndrome (RLS)—A neurological disorder characterized by aching, burning, or creeping sensations in the legs and an urge to move the legs, often resulting in insomnia.

Changes in regions of the brain and in neurotransmitters can result in sleep deprivation. Sleeping problems in older people may be a normal part of aging or can be related to underlying medical conditions, medications, medical treatments, or sleep-disrupting hospital routines. Anxiety or chronic pain can cause sleep deprivation, which, in turn, can cause **anxiety disorders** or make it harder to cope with pain. Other conditions that can cause sleep deprivation include menopause, vision loss, **attention deficit hyperactivity disorder (ADHD)**, head injury, **stroke**, cancer, and **Alzheimer's disease**.

Sleep disorders may also result in sleep deprivation. There are more than 70 known sleep disorders; the most common include:

- insomnia, which can have various causes—including stress, jet lag, diet, or an underlying medical condition—and almost always affects next-day functioning

- sleep apnea, or disrupted breathing during sleep, which causes frequent awakenings

- RLS, a condition that causes constant leg movement and insomnia and is either inherited or linked to conditions such as pregnancy, anemia, or diabetes

- periodic limb movement disorder (PLMD), which often accompanies RLS and causes repeated awakenings

- narcolepsy, which is characterized by brief attacks of daytime deep sleep and is usually caused by an inherited malfunction in the regulation of sleep-wake cycles

Symptoms of sleep deprivation include:

- difficulty awakening each morning
- daytime drowsiness
- microsleeps—very brief, often unnoticed—periods of sleep during waking hours
- falling asleep during school or work
- need for frequent naps
- routinely falling asleep within five minutes of lying down
- disrupted sleep
- parasomnias—uncontrollable actions during sleep, such as sleepwalking
- headaches
- poor school or work performance
- inability to concentrate
- inability to perform mathematical calculations
- impaired memory
- problems with decision-making
- clumsiness or impaired physical performance
- irritability or mood swings
- paranoia
- confusion
- hallucinations
- decreased consciousness

Although sleep deprivation can be an effective therapy for people with certain types of **depression**, it can cause depression in otherwise healthy people. Sleep deprivation can also trigger manic episodes of agitation and hyperactivity in people with **bipolar disorder** and **seizures** in patients with some types of epilepsy.

Diagnosis

Examination

Sleep deprivation is usually readily diagnosed from the symptoms accompanying the lack of sleep. Underlying medical problems resulting in sleep deprivation may require further diagnoses.

Procedures

Simple devices are available for detecting sleep apnea. Sleep apnea may be diagnosed at a specialized sleep center using **polysomnography** to record brain waves, heartbeat, and breathing for an entire night.

Treatment

Traditional

The usual treatment for sleep deprivation is sleep. Underlying conditions that result in sleep deprivation require more extensive treatments. For example, severe sleep apnea may require a mask—called a continuous positive airway pressure (CPAP) device—to keep the airways open during sleep. Surgery may be required to correct an airway obstruction.

Drugs

Caffeine and other stimulants cannot overcome the effects of severe sleep deprivation. However, various products are available to treat sleep disturbances that can result in sleep deprivation:

- Over-the-counter sleep aids usually contain antihistamines. Although they are sometimes effective, they have side effects, and tolerance can develop after just a few days of use.
- RLS and PLMD are often relieved with drugs that affect the neurotransmitter dopamine.
- Daily melatonin supplements may improve nighttime sleep in blind patients.

The U.S. Food and Drug Administration (FDA) has approved several sleep aids—called **sedatives** or hypnotics—for indefinite use. However, most sleeping pills are usually prescribed only for short-term insomnia, because they usually become ineffective after several weeks of nightly use and may be habit-forming. If sleeping pills are used for too long, they can actually cause insomnia. Some persons taking sleep aids experience next-day grogginess or engage in behaviors during sleep, such as sleep eating or sleep driving. If medical disorder is causing the sleep deprivation, use of sleep aids may mask the underlying condition, and sleep aids may negatively interact with alcohol or other medications. In persons with sleep apnea, sleep aids may prevent them from waking up to breathe.

Alternative

Alternative treatments for insomnia and other sleep disturbances include **cognitive-behavioral therapy** (CBT); hypnosis; melatonin, a hormone derived from the neurotransmitter serotonin; and tryptophan, an amino acid precursor of serotonin.

Herbal remedies for insomnia include lemon balm, **chamomile**, **valerian** root, **kava kava**, **passionflower**, **lavender**, and **St. John's wort**, although the efficacy of such herbs has not been proven. Patients should discuss the use of herbal supplements with their doctor.

Home remedies

Short-term sleep deprivation may require only a night or two of additional sleep. Longer-term sleep deprivation may require a sleep vacation—a few days devoted to sleeping as much as needed. Mild sleep apnea can be treated effectively by weight loss or by not sleeping on one's back.

Prognosis

Sleep deprivation is usually readily reversible with adequate sleep.

Prevention

Sleep deprivation is preventable by getting as much sleep as an individual requires. Sleep deprivation caused by mild insomnia can often be prevented by:

- sleeping on a schedule—going to bed and rising at the same time every day, including weekends
- structuring daily activities
- exercising 20–30 minutes every day, especially 5–6 hours before sleep
- practicing stress management
- avoiding caffeine, nicotine, and alcohol
- relaxing before bed with activities such as reading or a warm bath that become routinely associated with sleep
- avoiding extreme temperatures that prevent falling or staying asleep
- avoiding lying awake in bed for more than 20 minutes since this can cause anxiety
- reading, watching television, listening to music, or performing an activity until drowsy
- sleeping until sunrise or waking with very bright lights to reset one's internal clock each day
- getting an hour of morning sun exposure

Resources

BOOKS

Bellenir, Karen. *Sleep Information for Teens.* Detroit: Omnigraphics, 2008.

Chokroverty, Sudhansu. *100 Questions & Answers About Sleep and Sleep Disorders.* Sudbury, MA: Jones and Bartlett, 2008.

Epstein, Lawrence J., and Steven Mardon. *The Harvard Medical School Guide to a Good Night's Sleep.* New York: McGraw-Hill, 2007.

Mindell, Jodi A. *Sleep Deprived No More: From Pregnancy to Early Motherhood—Helping You & Your Baby Sleep Through the Night.* New York: DeCapo Press, 2007.

PERIODICALS

Bergin, Christi A., and David A. Bergin. "Sleep: The E-ZZZ Intervention." *Educational Leadership* 67, no. 4 (December 2009/January 2010): 44–47.

He, Ying, et al. "The Transcriptional Repressor DEC2 Regulates Sleep Length in Mammals." *Science* 325, no. 5942 (August 14, 2009): 866–870.

Kowalczyk, Liz. "Turns Out, There's No Magic in that Traditional Number Eight When Figuring Out How Many Hours of Shut-Eye You Need." *The Boston Globe* (December 28, 2009): G6.

Liberatore, Stephanie. "Health Wise: December 2009." *The Science Teacher* 76, no. 9 (December 2009): 62–63.

WEBSITES

Helpguide.org. "How to Stop Snoring." August 2011. http://www.helpguide.org/life/snoring.htm (accessed October 27, 2011).

MedlinePlus. "Sleep Disorders." U.S. National Library of Medicine, National Institutes of Health. http://www.nlm.nih.gov/medline plus/tutorials/sleepdisorders/ htm/index.htm (accessed October 27, 2011).

National Sleep Foundation. "Backgrounder: Later School Start Times." http://www.sleepfoundation.org/article/hot-topics/backgrounder-later-school-start-times (accessed October 27, 2011).

U.S. National Institute of Neurological Disorders and Stroke. "Brain Basics: Understanding Sleep." NIH Publication No.06-3440-c. http://www.ninds. nih.gov/disorders/brain_basics/understanding_sleep.htm (accessed October 27, 2011).

ORGANIZATIONS

American Academy of Sleep Medicine, 2510 N Frontage Rd., Darien, IL, 60561, (630) 737-9700, Fax: (630) 737-9790, inquiries@assmnet.org, http://www.aasmnet.org.

National Institute of Neurological Disorders and Stroke, PO Box 5801, Bethesda, MD, 20824, (301) 496-5751, TTY: (301) 468-5981, (800) 352-9424, http://www.ninds.nih.gov.

National Sleep Foundation, 1010 North Glebe Rd., Suite 310, Arlington, VA, 22201, (703) 243-1697, nsf@sleepfoundation.org, http://www.sleepfoundation.org.

Margaret Alic, PhD

Sleep disorders

Definition

Sleep disorders are various syndromes characterized by disturbance in the amount of sleep, quality or timing of sleep, or in behaviors or physiological conditions associated with sleep, which individuals experience. There are about 81 different sleep disorders, according to the second edition of the *International Classification of Sleep Disorders*. To qualify for the **diagnosis** of sleep disorder, the condition must be a persistent problem, cause individuals significant emotional distress, and interfere with their social or occupational functioning.

Because sleep requirements vary from person to person, there is no specific amount of time spent sleeping that can be used as a cutoff to determine whether individuals have a sleep disorder. Some healthy adults need as much as 10 hours of sleep per night, whereas others need as little as five hours.

Demographics

Sleep disorders are a common problem in the general population of North America. Researchers estimate that 20%–40% of adults report difficulty sleeping at some point each year. About one-third of all Americans have a sleep disorder at some point in their lives. Twenty percent of adults say that they have problems with chronic **insomnia**, and 17% consider their sleeping problem to be serious.

As far as is known, sleep disorders are equally common in all racial and ethnic groups in Canada and the United States.

Description

Normal sleep

Although sleep is a basic behavior in animals as well as humans, researchers still do not completely understand all of its functions in maintaining health. Between 1980 and 2010, however, laboratory studies on human volunteers have yielded information about the different types of sleep. Increasing interest in sleep disorders led to the recognition of sleep medicine as a distinct medical subspecialty with its own board certification procedures in 1978. Researchers have learned about the cyclical patterns of different types of sleep and their relationships to breathing, heart rate, **brain** waves, and other physical functions. These measurements are obtained by a technique called **polysomnography**.

There are five stages of normal human sleep. Four stages consist of non-rapid eye movement (NREM) sleep, with unique brain wave patterns and physical changes occurring. Dreaming occurs in the fifth stage, during rapid eye movement (REM) sleep.

- Stage 1 NREM sleep occurs while a person is falling asleep. It represents about 5% of a normal adult's sleep time.

- Stage 2 NREM sleep is the beginning of "true" sleep, when a person's electroencephalogram (EEG) shows distinctive wave forms called sleep spindles and K complexes. About 50% of sleep time is stage 2 REM sleep.

- Stages 3 and 4 NREM sleep, also called delta or slow wave sleep, are the deepest levels of sleep and represent 10–20% of sleep time. They usually occur during the first 30–50% of the sleeping period.

- REM sleep accounts for 20–25% of total sleep time. It usually begins about 90 minutes after the person falls asleep, an important measure called REM latency. It alternates with NREM sleep about every hour and a half throughout the night. REM periods increase in length over the course of the night.

Sleep cycles vary with a person's age. Children and adolescents have longer periods of stage 3 and stage 4 NREM sleep than do middle-aged or elderly adults. Because of this difference, doctors need to take a patient's age into account when evaluating a sleep disorder. Total REM sleep also declines with age.

The average length of nighttime sleep varies among different age groups. Infants typically need about 16 hours of sleep each day, whereas adolescents need about 9 hours. Most adults sleep 7–9 hours a night, although pregnant women may need as many as 10 or 11 hours of sleep. These population averages appear to be constant throughout the world. In temperate climates, however, people often notice that sleep time varies with the seasons. It is not unusual for people in North America and Europe to sleep about 40 minutes longer per night during the winter.

Primary sleep disorders

Sleep disorders are classified based on what causes them. Primary sleep disorders are distinguished from those that are not caused by other mental disorders, prescription medications, **substance abuse**, or medical conditions. The two major categories of primary sleep disorders are the dyssomnias and the parasomnias.

DYSSOMNIAS. Dyssomnias are primary sleep disorders in which the patient suffers from changes in the amount, restfulness, and timing of sleep. The most important dyssomnia is primary insomnia, which is defined as difficulty in falling asleep or remaining asleep that lasts for at least one month. It is estimated that 35% of adults in the United States experience insomnia during any given year, but the number of these adults who are experiencing true primary insomnia is unknown. Primary insomnia can be caused by a traumatic event related to sleep or bedtime, and it is often associated with increased physical or psychological arousal at night. People who experience primary insomnia are often anxious about not being able to sleep. They may then associate all sleep-related things (their bed, bedtime, etc.) with frustration, making the problem worse. They then become more stressed about not sleeping. Primary insomnia usually begins when individuals are young adults or in middle age.

Hypersomnia is a condition marked by excessive sleepiness during normal waking hours. Individuals have either lengthy episodes of daytime sleep or episodes of daytime sleep on a daily basis even though they are sleeping normally at night. In some cases, patients with primary hypersomnia have difficulty waking in the morning and may appear confused or angry. This condition is sometimes called sleep drunkenness and is more common in males. The number of people with primary hypersomnia is unknown, although 5–10% of patients in sleep disorder clinics have the disorder. Primary hypersomnia usually affects young adults between the ages of 15 and 30.

Nocturnal myoclonus and **restless legs syndrome** (RLS) can cause either insomnia or hypersomnia in adults. Patients with nocturnal myoclonus wake up because of cramps or twitches in their calves. These patients feel sleepy the next day. Nocturnal myoclonus is sometimes called periodic limb movement disorder (PLMD). RLS patients have a crawly or aching feeling in their calves that can be relieved by moving or rubbing the legs. RLS often prevents individuals from falling asleep until the early hours of the morning, when the condition is less intense.

Kleine-Levin syndrome is a recurrent form of hypersomnia that affects a person 3–4 times a year. Doctors do not know the cause of this syndrome. It is marked by 2–3 days of sleeping 18–20 hours per day, hypersexual behavior, compulsive eating, and irritability. Men are three times more likely than women to have the syndrome. There is no cure for this disorder.

Narcolepsy is a dyssomnia characterized by recurrent "sleep attacks" that individuals cannot fight. The sleep attacks are about 10–20 minutes long. Individuals feel refreshed by the sleep, but typically feel sleepy again several hours later. Narcolepsy has three major symptoms in addition to sleep attacks: cataplexy, hallucinations, and sleep paralysis. Cataplexy is the sudden loss of muscle tone and stability ("drop attacks"). Hallucinations may occur just before falling asleep (hypnagogic) or right after waking up (hypnopompic) and are associated with an episode of REM sleep. Sleep paralysis occurs during the transition from being asleep to waking up. About 40% of patients with narcolepsy have or have had another mental disorder. Although narcolepsy is often regarded as an adult disorder, it has been reported in children as young as three years of age. Almost 18% of patients with narcolepsy are 10 years old or younger. It is estimated that 0.02–0.16% of the general population suffer from narcolepsy. Men and women are equally affected.

Breathing-related sleep disorders are syndromes in which patients' sleep is interrupted by problems with their breathing. There are three types of breathing-related sleep disorders:

• Obstructive sleep apnea syndrome is the most common form of breathing-related sleep disorder, marked by episodes of blockage in the upper airway during sleep. It is found primarily in obese people. Patients with this disorder typically alternate between periods of snoring or gasping (when their airway is partly open) and periods of silence (when their airway is blocked). Very loud snoring is a clue to this disorder.

• Central sleep apnea syndrome is primarily found in elderly patients with heart or neurological conditions that affect their ability to breathe properly. It is not associated with airway blockage and may be related to brain disease.

• Central alveolar hypoventilation syndrome is found most often in extremely obese people. These individuals' airway is not blocked, but their blood oxygen level is too low.

• Mixed-type sleep apnea syndrome combines symptoms of both obstructive and central sleep apnea.

Circadian rhythm sleep disorders are dyssomnias resulting from a discrepancy between individuals' daily sleep/wake patterns and demands of social activities, shift work, or travel. The term *circadian* comes from a Latin word meaning "daily." There are three circadian rhythm sleep disorders. Delayed sleep phase type is characterized by going to bed and arising later than most people. Jet lag type is caused by travel to a new time zone. Shift work type is caused by shifts in one's work schedule. People who are ordinarily early risers appear to be more vulnerable to jet lag and shift work-related circadian rhythm disorders than people who are "night owls." Some individuals do not fit the pattern of these three disorders and appear to be the opposite of the delayed sleep phase type. These patients have an advanced sleep phase pattern and cannot stay awake in the evening but wake up on their own in the early morning.

PARASOMNIAS. Parasomnias are primary sleep disorders in which the patient's behavior is affected by specific sleep stages or transitions between sleeping and waking. They are sometimes described as disorders of physiological arousal during sleep.

Nightmare disorder is a parasomnia in which individuals are repeatedly awakened from sleep by frightening dreams and are fully alert on awakening. The actual rate of occurrence of nightmare disorder is unknown. Approximately 10–50% of children between three and five years of age have nightmares. They occur during REM sleep, usually in the second half of the night. These children are usually able to remember the content of the nightmare and may be afraid to go back to sleep. More females than males have this disorder, but it is not known whether the sex difference reflects a difference in occurrence or a difference in reporting. Nightmare disorder is most likely to occur in children or adults under severe or traumatic **stress**.

Sleep terror disorder is a parasomnia in which patients awaken screaming or crying. These individuals also have physical signs of arousal, like sweating or shaking. This disorder is sometimes called pavor nocturnus. Unlike nightmares, sleep terrors typically occur in stage 3 or stage 4 NREM sleep during the first third of the night. Individuals may be confused or disoriented for several minutes and cannot recall the content of the dream. They may fall asleep again and not remember the episode the next morning. Sleep terror disorder is most common in children 4–12 years of age and is outgrown in adolescence. It affects about 3% of children. Less than 1% of adults have the disorder. In adults, it usually begins between the ages of 20 and 30. In children, more males than females have the disorder. In adults, men and women are equally affected.

Sleepwalking disorder, which is sometimes called somnambulism, occurs when individuals are capable of complex movements during sleep, including walking. Like sleep terror disorder, sleepwalking occurs during stage 3 and stage 4 NREM sleep during the first part of the night. If individuals are awakened during a sleepwalking episode, they may be disoriented and have no memory of the behavior. In addition to walking around, patients with sleepwalking disorder have been reported to eat, use the bathroom, unlock doors, or talk to others. It is estimated that 10–30% of children have at least one episode of sleepwalking. However, only 1–5% meet the criteria for sleepwalking disorder. The disorder is most common in children 8–12 years of age. It is unusual for sleepwalking to occur for the first time in adults.

KEY TERMS

Apnea—The temporary absence of breathing. Sleep apnea consists of repeated episodes of temporary suspension of breathing during sleep.

Benzodiazepines—A class of sedative drugs used to treat sleep disorders.

Cataplexy—Sudden loss of muscle tone (often causing a person to fall), usually triggered by intense emotion. It is regarded as a diagnostic sign of narcolepsy.

Circadian rhythm—Any body rhythm that recurs in 24-hour cycles. The sleep-wake cycle is an example of a circadian rhythm.

Cognitive-behavioral therapy (CBT)—A type of psychotherapy that helps patients identify and change problematic thoughts and behaviors.

Dyssomnia—A primary sleep disorder in which the patient suffers from changes in the quantity, quality, or timing of sleep.

Electroencephalogram (EEG)—The record obtained by a device that measures electrical impulses in the brain.

Hypersomnia—An abnormal increase of 25% or more in time spent sleeping. Patients usually have excessive daytime sleepiness.

Hypnotic—A medication that makes a person sleep.

Hypopnea—Shallow or excessively slow breathing usually caused by partial closure of the upper airway during sleep, leading to disruption of sleep.

Insomnia—Difficulty in falling asleep or remaining asleep.

Jet lag—A temporary disruption of the body's sleep-wake rhythm following high-speed air travel across several time zones. Jet lag is most severe in people who have crossed eight or more time zones in 24 hours.

Kleine-Levin syndrome—A disorder that occurs primarily in young males, three or four times a year. The syndrome is marked by episodes of hypersomnia, hypersexual behavior, and excessive eating.

Melatonin—A hormone produced by the pineal gland that is associated with sleep and that may be useful in the treatment of some sleep disorders.

Narcolepsy—A lifelong sleep disorder marked by four symptoms: sudden brief sleep attacks, cataplexy, temporary paralysis, and hallucinations. The hallucinations are associated with falling asleep or the transition from sleeping to waking.

Nocturnal myoclonus—A disorder in which the patient is awakened repeatedly during the night by cramps or twitches in the calf muscles; sometimes called periodic limb movement disorder (PLMD).

Non-rapid eye movement (NREM) sleep—A type of sleep that differs from rapid eye movement (REM) sleep. The four stages of NREM sleep account for 75–80% of total sleeping time.

Parasomnia—A primary sleep disorder in which the person's physiology or behaviors are affected by sleep, the sleep stage, or the transition from sleeping to waking.

Pavor nocturnus—Another term for sleep terror disorder.

Polysomnography—Laboratory measurement of a patient's basic physiological processes during sleep. Polysomnography usually measures eye movement, brain waves, and muscular tension.

Primary sleep disorder—A sleep disorder that cannot be attributed to a medical condition, another mental disorder, or prescription medications or other substances.

Rapid eye movement (REM) sleep—A phase of sleep during which the person's eyes move rapidly beneath the lids. It accounts for 20–25% of sleep time. Dreaming occurs during REM sleep.

REM latency—After a person falls asleep, the amount of time it takes for the first onset of REM sleep.

Restless legs syndrome (RLS)—A disorder in which the patient experiences crawling, aching, or other disagreeable sensations in the calves that can be relieved only by movement. RLS is a frequent cause of difficulty falling asleep at night.

Sedative—A medication given to calm agitated patients; sometimes used as a synonym for hypnotic.

Sleep latency—The amount of time that it takes to fall asleep. Sleep latency is measured in minutes and is important in diagnosing depression.

Somnambulism—Another term for sleepwalking.

Unlike sleepwalking, REM sleep behavior disorder occurs later in the night, and individuals can remember what they were dreaming. The physical activities of these individuals are often violent.

Sleep disorders related to other conditions

In addition to the primary sleep disorders, there are three categories of sleep disorders that are caused by or related to substance use or other physical or mental disorders.

SLEEP DISORDERS RELATED TO MENTAL DISORDERS. Many mental disorders, especially **depression** or one of the **anxiety disorders**, can cause sleep disturbances. Psychiatric disorders are the most common cause of chronic insomnia.

SLEEP DISORDERS DUE TO MEDICAL CONDITIONS. Some patients with chronic neurological conditions such as Parkinson's disease or Huntington's disease may develop sleep disorders. Sleep disorders have also been associated with viral encephalitis, brain disease, and hypo- or hyperthyroidism.

SUBSTANCE-INDUCED SLEEP DISORDERS. The use of drugs, alcohol, and caffeine frequently produces disturbances in sleep patterns. Alcohol abuse is associated with insomnia. Individuals may initially feel sleepy after drinking, but they wake up or sleep fitfully during the second half of the night. Alcohol can also increase the severity of breathing-related sleep disorders. With **amphetamines** or **cocaine** use, individuals typically suffer from insomnia during drug use and hypersomnia during drug withdrawal. **Opioids** usually make short-term users sleepy. However, long-term users develop tolerance and may suffer from insomnia.

In addition to alcohol and drugs that are abused, a variety of prescription medications can affect sleep patterns. These medications include antihistamines, corticosteroids, asthma medicines, and drugs that affect the central nervous system.

Sleep disorders in children and adolescents

Pediatricians estimate that 20–30% of children have difficulties with sleep that are serious enough to disturb their families. Although sleepwalking and night terror disorder occur more frequently in children than in adults, children can also suffer from narcolepsy and sleep apnea syndrome.

Risk factors

Risk factors for sleep disorders include:

- Gender. Primary insomnia is more common in women than in men, while obstructive sleep apnea is twice as common in men as in women.

- Age. Older adults are more likely to develop sleep disorders; the rate rises from 5% of adults between 30 and 50 to 30% in those over 50. One reason for the greater risk of sleep disorders in seniors is that they are more likely to have medical conditions that disturb sleep or to be taking medications that cause sleep disruption.

- Employment that requires frequent travel across time zones or frequent changes in work schedules

- Environmental factors, including noise, high altitude, and abnormally hot or cold temperatures

- Smoking. Heavy smokers often wake up after only a few hours of sleep due to nicotine withdrawal.

- High levels of emotional stress, whether job-related or associated with family or personal problems

- Family history of sleep disorders. Sleepwalking is particularly likely to occur in families.

- Having a disease or disorder that causes physical discomfort

- Genetic factors. There is increasing evidence that obstructive sleep apnea, narcolepsy, and restless legs syndrome are associated with susceptibility genes for these disorders, although no specific genes had been identified as of 2011.

Causes and symptoms

The causes of sleep disorders have already been discussed with respect to the classification of these disorders.

The most important symptoms of sleep disorders are insomnia and sleepiness during waking hours. Insomnia is by far the more common of the two symptoms. It covers a number of different patterns of sleep disturbance. These patterns include inability to fall asleep at bedtime, repeated awakening during the night, and/or inability to go back to sleep once awakened.

Diagnosis

Diagnosis of sleep disorders usually requires a psychological history as well as a medical history. The patient's sex and age are useful starting points in assessing the problem. The doctor may also talk to other family members in order to obtain information about the patient's symptoms. The family's observations are particularly important to evaluate sleepwalking, kicking in bed, snoring loudly, or other behaviors that the patient cannot remember.

Examination

With the exception of sleep apnea syndromes, physical examinations are not usually revealing.

Tests

The doctor may order blood or urine tests to determine whether the patient's sleep disorder is associated with anemia, thyroid dysfunction, alcoholism, or opioid abuse. The patient's blood oxygen level may be tested during sleep in order to determine whether sleep apnea or other types of sleep-disordered breathing are involved. Imaging tests are not routinely done for sleep disorders but may be ordered in some cases to rule out brain tumors or other medical conditions.

Sleep logs

Many doctors ask patients to keep a sleep diary or sleep log for a minimum of one to two weeks in order to evaluate the severity and characteristics of the sleep disturbance. The patient records medications taken as well as the length of time spent in bed, the quality of the sleep, and similar information. Some sleep logs are designed to indicate circadian sleep patterns as well as simple duration or restfulness of sleep.

Psychological testing

The doctor may use psychological tests or inventories to evaluate insomnia because it is frequently associated with mood or affective disorders. The **Minnesota Multiphasic Personality Inventory** (MMPI), the Millon Clinical Multiaxial Inventory (MCMI), the **Beck Depression Inventory**, and the Zung Depression Scale are the tests most commonly used in evaluating this symptom.

Self-report tests

The Epworth Sleepiness Scale, a self-rating form developed in Australia, consists of eight questions used to assess daytime sleepiness. Scores range from 0–24, with scores higher than 16 indicating severe daytime sleepiness.

Laboratory sleep studies

If the doctor is considering breathing-related sleep disorders, myoclonus, or narcolepsy as possible diagnoses, the doctor may ask the patient to be tested in a sleep laboratory or at home with portable instruments.

POLYSOMNOGRAPHY. Polysomnography can be used to help diagnose sleep disorders as well as conduct research into sleep. In some cases the patient is tested in a special sleep laboratory. The advantage of this testing is the availability and expertise of trained technologists, but it is expensive. However, portable equipment is available for home recording of certain specific physiological functions.

MULTIPLE SLEEP LATENCY TEST. The multiple sleep latency test (MSLT) is frequently used to measure the severity of the patient's daytime sleepiness. The test measures sleep latency (the speed with which the patient falls asleep) during a series of planned naps during the day. The test also measures the amount of REM sleep that occurs. Two or more episodes of REM sleep under these conditions indicate narcolepsy. This test can also be used to help diagnose primary hypersomnia.

REPEATED TEST OF SUSTAINED WAKEFULNESS. The repeated test of sustained wakefulness (RTSW) measures sleep latency by challenging the patient's ability to stay awake. In the RTSW, the patient is placed in a quiet room with dim lighting and is asked to stay awake. As with the MSLT, the testing pattern is repeated at intervals during the day.

Treatment

Traditional

Treatment for a sleep disorder depends on what is causing the disorder. For example, if major depression is the cause of insomnia, then treatment of the depression with **antidepressants** should resolve the insomnia. In other cases, a change of environment or work schedule may help.

Drugs

Sedative or hypnotic medications are generally recommended only for insomnia related to a temporary stress (such as surgery or **grief**) because of the potential for **addiction** or overdose. In general, these drugs are given for two weeks or less in order to reduce the risk of dependence. **Trazodone**, a sedating antidepressant, is often used for chronic insomnia that does not respond to other treatments. Sleep medications may also cause problems for elderly patients because of possible interactions with their other prescription medications. Among the safer hypnotic agents are **lorazepam**, **temazepam**, and **zolpidem**. **Chloral hydrate** is often preferred for short-term treatment in elderly patients because of its mildness. Short-term treatment is recommended because this drug may be habit forming.

Narcolepsy is treated with such stimulants as **dextroamphetamine** sulfate or **methylphenidate**. Nocturnal myoclonus has been successfully treated with **clonazepam**.

Children with sleep terror disorder or sleepwalking are usually treated with **benzodiazepines** because this type of medication suppresses stage 3 and stage 4 NREM sleep.

If the cause of insomnia is RLS, treatment includes massage, warm baths, and visualization techniques to distract from the discomfort. The only medication approved by the U.S. Food and Drug Administration (FDA) for the treatment of RLS is ropinirole (Requip), although drugs used for the treatment of Parkinson's disease, benzodiazepines, and anticonvulsant medications also may be effective for this disorder.

Psychotherapy

Psychotherapy is recommended for patients with sleep disorders associated with depression or other mental disorders. In many cases the patient's scores on the Beck or Zung inventories will suggest the appropriate direction of treatment.

Cognitive-behavioral therapy (CBT) is a form of psychotherapy that is often recommended for insomnia as a way of breaking the cycle of anxiety about sleep and sleeplessness associated with insomnia. Patients are typically advised to limit the amount of time they spend in bed and to change certain habits that may contribute to the insomnia. For example, some patients are clock watchers who check their bedside clocks frequently to see how little sleep they are getting. They will be advised to put the clock under the bed or in some other location where they cannot see it during the night.

Sleep education

"Sleep hygiene" or sleep education for sleep disorders often includes instructing the patient in methods to enhance sleep. Patients are advised to do the following:

• wait until they are sleepy before going to bed

• avoid using the bedroom for work, reading, or watching television

• get up at the same time every morning no matter how much or how little they have slept

• avoid smoking and avoid drinking liquids with caffeine

• get some physical exercise early in the day every day

• limit fluid intake after dinner; in particular, avoid alcohol because it frequently causes interrupted sleep

• learn to meditate or practice relaxation techniques

• avoid tossing and turning in bed; instead, get up and listen to relaxing music or read

Lifestyle changes

Patients with sleep apnea or hypopnea are encouraged to stop smoking, avoid alcohol or drugs of abuse, and lose weight in order to improve the stability of the upper airway.

In some cases, patients with sleep disorders related to jet lag or shift work may need to change employment or travel patterns. Patients may need to avoid rapid changes in shifts at work.

Children with nightmare disorder may benefit from limits on television or movies. Violent scenes or frightening science fiction stories appear to influence the frequency and intensity of children's nightmares.

Surgery

Although making a surgical opening into the windpipe (a tracheostomy) for sleep apnea or hypopnea in adults is a treatment of last resort, it is occasionally performed if the patient's disorder is life threatening and cannot be treated by other methods. In children and adolescents, surgical removal of the tonsils and adenoids is a fairly common and successful treatment for sleep apnea. Most sleep apnea patients are treated with continuous positive airway pressure (CPAP). Sometimes an oral prosthesis is used for mild sleep apnea.

Alternative

Some alternative approaches may be effective in treating insomnia caused by anxiety or emotional stress. **Meditation** practice, breathing exercises, and **yoga** can break the vicious cycle of sleeplessness, worry about inability to sleep, and further sleeplessness for some people. Yoga can also help some people to relax muscular tension in a direct fashion. The breathing exercises and meditation can keep some patients from obsessing about sleep.

Homeopathic practitioners recommend that people with chronic insomnia see a professional homeopath. They do, however, prescribe specific remedies for at-home treatment of temporary insomnia: *Nux vomica* for alcohol or substance-related insomnia, *Ignatia* for insomnia caused by grief, *Arsenicum* for insomnia caused by fear or anxiety, and *Passiflora* for insomnia related to mental stress.

Melatonin has also been used as an alternative treatment for sleep disorders. Melatonin is produced in the body by the pineal gland at the base of the brain. This substance is thought to be related to the body's circadian rhythms.

Practitioners of Chinese medicine usually treat insomnia as a symptom of excess yang energy. Cinnabar is recommended for chronic nightmares. Either magnetic magnetite or "dragon bones" is recommended for insomnia associated with hysteria or fear. If the insomnia appears to be associated with excess yang energy arising from the liver, the practitioner will give the patient oyster shells. **Acupuncture** treatments can help bring about balance and facilitate sleep.

Dietary changes, such as eliminating stimulant foods (coffee, cola, chocolate) and late-night meals or snacks, can be effective in treating some sleep disorders. Nutritional supplementation with magnesium, as well as botanical medicines that calm the nervous system, can also be helpful. Among the botanical remedies that may be effective for sleep disorders are **valerian** (*Valeriana officinalis*), **passionflower** (*Passiflora incarnata*), and skullcap (*Scutellaria lateriflora*).

Home remedies

Warm milk before bedtime is a classic home remedy for insomnia. It is thought that this treatment works for many people because milk contains tryptophan, an amino acid that increases the brain's production of melatonin.

Prognosis

The prognosis depends on the specific disorder. Children usually outgrow sleep disorders. Patients with Kleine-Levin syndrome usually get better around age 40. Narcolepsy, however, is a lifelong disorder, although cataplexy can be successfully controlled with medication, and many people find that their symptoms naturally decrease after age 60. The prognosis for sleep disorders related to other conditions depends on successful treatment of the substance abuse, medical condition, or other mental disorder. The prognosis for primary sleep disorders is affected by many things, including the patient's age, sex, occupation, personality characteristics, family circumstances, neighborhood environment, and similar factors.

About 85% of people with insomnia find relief with a combination of sleep hygiene and medication. Although there is no cure for sleep apnea, treatment can reduce the associated risks of high blood pressure and heart disease.

Insomnia and other sleep disorders are not fatal in and of themselves; however, chronic insomnia is associated with an increased risk of depression and **suicide**. In addition, insufficient sleep increases a person's risk of accidents on the road and in the workplace, with the possibility of serious injury or death. Driver **fatigue** is responsible for an estimated 100,000 motor vehicle accidents and 1,500 deaths each year in the

---

QUESTIONS TO ASK YOUR DOCTOR

- How do I know if I am experiencing a sleep disorder?
- What diagnostic tests are needed for a thorough assessment?
- What type of sleep disorder do I have?
- Will I need to go to a sleep laboratory?
- Is the sleep problem related to an underlying physical condition?
- Should I consider psychotherapy?
- What type of treatment do you recommend for me?
- Should I see a specialist? If so, what kind of specialist should I contact?
- What symptoms are important enough that I should seek immediate treatment?

United States, according to the National Highway Traffic Safety Administration.

Prevention

Certain sleep disorders, such as insomnia, can sometimes be prevented by practicing good sleep hygiene. Sleep hygiene involves going to bed at a regular time each night and avoiding stimulating activities, smoking, or heavy meals close to bedtime. Sleep apnea may be prevented in some cases by controlling body weight.

Resources

BOOKS

American Academy of Sleep Medicine. *International Classification of Sleep Disorders: Diagnostic and Coding Manual.* 2nd ed. Westchester, IL: AASM, 2005.

American Psychiatric Association. *Diagnostic and Statistical Manual of Mental Disorders.* 4th ed., text rev. Washington, DC: American Psychiatric Association, 2000.

Berry, Richard B. *Fundamentals of Sleep Medicine.* New York: Saunders, 2011.

Chokroverty, Susan, ed. *Sleep Disorders Medicine: Basic Science, Technical Considerations, and Clinical Aspects.* 3rd ed. New York: Saunders, 2009.

Clete, A. Kushida, ed. *Handbook of Sleep Disorders.* 2nd ed. New York: Informa Healthcare, 2008.

Colligan, L.H. *Sleep Disorders.* New York: Marshall Cavendish Benchmark, 2009.

Foldvary-Schaefer, Nancy. *Cleveland Clinic Guide to Sleep Disorders*. New York: Kaplan, 2009.

Jacobs, Gregg D. *Say Good Night to Insomnia*. New York: Holt Paperbacks, 2009.

Kushida, Clete A., ed. *Handbook of Sleep Disorders*. 2nd ed. New York: Informa Healthcare, 2009.

Lee-Chiong, Teofilo L. *Sleep Medicine Essentials*. Hoboken, NJ: Wiley-Blackwell, 2009.

Mindell, Jodi A., and Judith A. Owens. *A Clinical Guide to Pediatric Sleep: Diagnosis and Management of Sleep Problems*. 2nd ed. New York: Lippincott Williams & Wilkins, 2009.

Pollak, Charles, et al. *Encyclopedia of Sleep and Sleep Disorders*. 3rd ed., rev. New York: Facts On File, 2010.

PERIODICALS

Bae, C.J., et al. "The Use of Sleep Studies in Neurologic Practice." *Seminars in Neurology* 29 (September 2009): 305–19.

Billiard, M. "REM Sleep Behavior Disorder and Narcolepsy." *CNS and Neurological Disorders Drug Targets* 8 (August 2009): 264–70.

Caylak, E. "The Genetics of Sleep Disorders in Humans: Narcolepsy, Restless Legs Syndrome, and Obstructive Sleep Apnea Syndrome." *American Journal of Medical Genetics, Part A* 149A (November 2009): 2612–26.

Fetveit, A. "Late-life Insomnia: A Review." *Geriatrics and Gerontology International* 9 (September 2009): 220–34.

Gallicchio, L., and B. Kalesan. "Sleep Duration and Mortality: A Systematic Review and Meta-analysis." *Journal of Sleep Research* 18 (June 2009): 148–58.

Goodday, R. "Diagnosis, Treatment Planning, and Surgical Correction of Obstructive Sleep Apnea." *Journal of Oral and Maxillofacial Surgery* 67 (October 2009): 2183–96.

Gromov, I., and D. Gromov. "Sleep and Substance Use and Abuse in Adolescents." *Child and Adolescent Psychiatry Clinics of North America* 18 (October 2009): 929–46.

Moyer, D.E., et al. "Restless Legs Syndrome: Diagnostic Time-savers, Tx Tips." *Journal of Family Practice* 58 (August 2009): 415–23.

Uhde, T.W., et al. "Anxiety and Sleep Problems: Emerging Concepts and Theoretical Treatment Implications." *Current Psychiatry Reports* 11 (August 2009): 269–76.

WEBSITES

"Can't Sleep? What to Know about Insomnia." National Sleep Foundation. http://www.sleepfoundation.org/article/sleep-related-problems/insomnia-and-sleep (accessed October 4, 2011).

"Insomnia." Mayo Clinic. Last updated January 7, 2011. http://www.mayoclinic.com/health/insomnia/DS00187 (accessed October 4, 2011).

"Kleine-Levin Syndrome Information Page." National Institute of Neurological Disorders and Stroke. Last updated March 12, 2009. http://www.ninds.nih.gov/disorders/kleine_levin/kleine_levin.htm (accessed October 4, 2011).

Lubit, Roy H., et al. "Sleep Disorders." Medscape Reference, May 21, 2009. http://emedicine.medscape.com/article/287104-overview (accessed October 4, 2011).

"Sleepwalking." Mayo Clinic. Last modified August 12, 2011. http://www.mayoclinic.com/health/sleepwalking/DS01009 (accessed October 4, 2011).

"What Is Sleep?" American Sleep Association, May 2007. http://www.sleepassociation.org/index.php?p=whatissleep (accessed October 4, 2011).

ORGANIZATIONS

American Academy of Sleep Medicine, 2510 N Frontage Rd., Darien, IL, 60561, (630) 737-9700, Fax: (630) 737-9790, inquiries@assmnet.org, http://www.aasmnet.org.

American Psychiatric Association, 1000 Wilson Blvd., Ste. 1825, Arlington, VA, 22209-3901, (703) 907-7300, apa@psych.org, http://www.psych.org.

Anxiety Disorders Association of America, 8730 Georgia Ave., Silver Spring, MD, 20910, (240) 485-1001, Fax: (240) 485-1035, http://www.adaa.org.

National Institute of Neurological Disorders and Stroke, PO Box 5801, Bethesda, MD, 20824, (301) 496-5751; TTY: (301) 468-5981, (800) 352-9424, http://www.ninds.nih.gov.

National Sleep Foundation, 1010 N. Glebe Road, Ste. 310, Arlington, VA, 22201, (703) 243-1697, nsf@sleepfoundation.org, http://www.sleepfoundation.org.

Rebecca J. Frey, PhD
Ruth A. Wienclaw, PhD
Laura Jean Cataldo, RN, EdD

Sleep terror disorder

Definition

Sleep terror disorder is defined as repeated temporary arousal from sleep, during which the affected person appears and acts extremely frightened.

Demographics

Sleep terror disorder is much more common in children than it is in adults. It is estimated that approximately 1%–6% of children in the United States experience sleep terror at some point in their childhood. For most children, sleep terrors begin between the ages of 4 and 12. The problem usually disappears during adolescence. Sleep terror disorder appears to be more common in boys than in girls; some studies have reported that preadolescent boys are the group most commonly affected. No figures are available for the rates of the disorder in different racial or ethnic groups.

Sleep terrors in children are not associated with any psychological disorders.

Fewer than 1% of adults have sleep terror disorder. For most adults, sleep terrors begin in their 20s or 30s, although it is possible for someone to suffer from episodes of sleep terror starting from childhood. In the adult population, sleep terrors affect both sexes equally. They are, however, often associated with psychological disorders, most commonly anxiety, personality, or post-traumatic disorders. People who have a family history of sleep terrors or **sleepwalking disorder** are about 10 times more likely to develop sleep terror disorder than those who do not.

Description

Sleep terror disorder is sometimes referred to as *pavor nocturnus* when it occurs in children, and *incubus* when it occurs in adults. Sleep terrors are also sometimes called night terrors, though sleep terror is the preferred term, as episodes can occur during daytime naps as well as at night.

Sleep terror disorder is frequently confused with **nightmare disorder**. The two are similar in the sense that both are related to bad dreams. Nightmare disorder, however, involves a significantly smaller amount of physical movement than does sleep terror. Normally, people experiencing nightmare disorder do not get out of bed, and people experiencing nightmare disorder often have problems going back to sleep because of the nature of their dream. Most people experiencing sleep terrors, however, go back to deep sleep without ever having fully awakened. People experiencing nightmares can generally remember their dreams and some of the events in the dream leading up to their awakening, and they often awake from nightmares just as they are about to experience the most frightening part of a disturbing dream. People experiencing sleep terrors, however, can sometimes recall a sense of profound fear but often do not remember the episode at all.

Causes and symptoms

Causes

The causes of sleep terror are for the most part unknown. Some researchers suggest that sleep terrors are caused by a delay in the maturation of the child's central nervous system. Such factors as **sleep deprivation**, psychological **stress**, and fever may also trigger episodes of sleep terror.

Symptoms

The symptoms of sleep terror are very similar to the physical symptoms of extreme fear. These include rapid

> ## KEY TERMS
>
> **Nightmare**—A frightening dream that occurs during REM sleep. Nightmares are distinguished from night terrors by the fact that night terrors occur during a different phase of sleep and do not involve dreaming. Children who awaken from nightmares remember them, while children with night terrors often remember nothing about what caused the awakening.
>
> **Non-rapid eye movement (NREM) sleep**—Stages of sleep during which rapid eye movements do not occur. The majority of sleep consists of the four stages of NREM sleep.
>
> **Rapid eye movement (REM) sleep**—A stage of sleep during which the sleeper's eyes move back and forth rapidly. Most dreams occur during REM sleep.

heartbeat, sweating, and rapid breathing (hyperventilation). The heart rate can increase up to two to four times the person's regular rate. Sleep terrors cause people to be jolted into motion, often sitting up suddenly in bed. People sometimes scream or cry. The person's facial expression may be fearful.

People experiencing sleep terror are not fully awake. They are nearly impossible to bring to consciousness or comfort, and sometimes respond violently to attempts to console or restrain them. In many cases, once the episode is over the person returns to sleep without ever waking fully. People often do not have any recollection of the episode after later awaking normally, although they may recall a sense of fear.

People experiencing sleep terror disorder sometimes get out of bed and act as if they are fighting or fleeing something. During this time injuries can occur. Cases have been reported of people falling out of windows or falling down stairs during episodes of sleep terror.

Episodes of sleep terror usually occur during the first third of a person's night sleep, although they can occur even during naps taken in the daytime. Although sleep terror episodes resemble nightmares, they usually occur during NREM (non-rapid eye movement) sleep rather than during the normal dreaming of REM (rapid eye movement) sleep. The average sleep terror episode lasts less than 15 minutes. Usually only one episode occurs per night, but in some cases terror episodes occur in clusters. It is unusual for a person to have many episodes in a single night, although upwards of 40 have been reported. Most persons with the disorder have only one occurrence per week, or just a few per month.

Diagnosis

Sleep terror is diagnosed most often in children when parents express concern to the child's pediatrician. A fact sheet from the American Academy of Child and Adolescent Psychiatry suggests that parents consult a child **psychiatrist** if the child has several episodes of sleep terror each night, if the episodes occur every night for weeks at a time, or if the episodes interfere with the child's daytime activities. The **diagnosis** is usually made on the basis of the child's and parents' description of the symptoms. There are no laboratory tests for sleep terror disorder. In adults, the disorder is usually self-reported to the patient's family doctor. Again, the diagnosis is usually based on the patient's description of the symptoms.

The *Diagnostic and Statistical Manual of Mental Disorders*, the standard reference work used by mental health professionals in diagnosing mental disorders, classifies sleep terror disorder as a disorder of arousal. In order to meet the *DSM* criteria for diagnosis, patients must experience repeated episodes accompanied by fear-related symptoms, such as increased heart rate or sweating; be unable to recall their dreams or the entire episode; and remain asleep during the episode, despite external efforts to awaken them. The episodes must not be attributed to a medical condition or drug use.

Treatment

If sleep terror episodes are infrequent, then treatment may not be necessary as long as the episodes are not interfering significantly with the person's life. Some people may want to rearrange their bedroom furniture to minimize the possibility of hurting themselves or others if they get out of bed during a sleep terror episode. To keep children from becoming overly worried about their sleep terrors, experts suggest that parents avoid placing unnecessary emphasis on the episodes. **Psychotherapy** is often helpful for adults concerned about the specific triggers of sleep terror episodes.

Several different medications have been used to treat sleep terror disorder, with varying degrees of success. One of the most common is **diazepam** (Valium). Diazepam is a hypnotic (sleep-inducing medication) and is thought to be useful in the prevention of sleep terror episodes because it acts as a nervous system depressant. There are many different types of hypnotics, and choosing one for a patient depends on other drugs

---

QUESTIONS TO ASK YOUR DOCTOR

- How do I know if I (or my child) am experiencing sleep terror disorder?
- What diagnostic tests are available for a thorough assessment?
- What symptoms are important enough that I should seek immediate treatment?
- What type of treatment do you recommend?
- Should I see a specialist? If so, what kind of specialist should I contact?

---

that the patient may be taking, any medical or psychological conditions, and other health factors. Most studies of medications as treatments for sleep terror disorder have been done on adult patients; there is little information available on the use of medications to treat the disorder in children.

Prognosis

In most children, sleep terror disorder resolves before or during adolescence without any treatment. Adults often respond well to diazepam or another hypnotic. Psychotherapy and avoidance of any stressors that may precipitate terror episodes may be helpful as well. Episodes of sleep terrors often decrease with age. This decrease is due to the fact that the amount of slow-wave sleep, the sleep phase during which terror episodes usually occur, declines with age.

Resources

BOOKS

American Psychiatric Association. *Diagnostic and Statistical Manual of Mental Disorders.* 4th ed., text rev. Washington, DC: American Psychiatric Publishing, 2000.

Berry, Richard B. *Fundamentals of Sleep Medicine.* New York, NY: Saunders, 2011.

Chokroverty, Sudhansu. *Sleep Disorders Medicine: Basic Science, Technical Considerations, and Clinical Aspects.* 3rd ed. Philadelphia: Saunders Elsevier, 2009.

Cooper, Rachel. *Classifying Madness: A Philosophical Examination of the Diagnostic and Statistical Manual of Mental Disorders.* New York: Springer, 2010.

Kaplan, Harold, and Benjamin Sadock, eds. *Synopsis of Psychiatry.* 10th ed. Baltimore: Lippincott Williams & Wilkins, 2007.

Kushida, Clete, A., ed. *Handbook of Sleep Disorders.* 2nd ed. New York, NY: Informa Healthcare, 2008.

Lee-Chiong, Teofilo L. *Sleep Medicine Essentials*. Hoboken, NJ: Wiley-Blackwell, 2009.

Mindell, Jodi A., and Judith A. Owens. *A Clinical Guide to Pediatric Sleep: Diagnosis and Management of Sleep Problems*. 2nd ed. New York: Lippincott Williams & Wilkins, 2009.

North, Carol, and Sean Yutzy. *Goodwin and Guze's Psychiatric Diagnosis*. New York, NY: Oxford University Press, 2010.

Pollak, Charles P., Michael Thorpy, and Jan Yager. *The Encyclopedia of Sleep and Sleep Disorders*. New York: Facts on File, 2009.

PERIODICALS

Owens, Judith A., Richard P. Millman, and Anthony Spirito. "Sleep Terrors in a 5-Year-Old Girl." *Pediatrics & Adolescent Medicine* 153, no. 3 (March 1999).

WEBSITES

American Academy of Child & Adolescent Psychiatry (AACAP). "Children's Sleep Problems." AACAP Facts For Families Pamphlet #34. Washington, DC: American Academy of Child & Adolescent Psychiatry, 2004.

ORGANIZATIONS

American Academy of Child and Adolescent Psychiatry, 3615 Wisconsin Ave. NW, Washington, DC, 20016-3007, (202) 966-7300, Fax: (202) 966-2891, http://aacap.org.

American Academy of Sleep Medicine, 2510 N Frontage Rd., Darien, IL, 60561, (630) 737-9700, Fax: (630) 737-9790, inquiries@assmnet.org, http://www.aasmnet.org.

National Sleep Foundation, 1010 N Glebe Rd., Ste. 310, Arlington, VA, 22201, (703) 243-1697, nsf@sleepfoundation.org, http://www.sleepfoundation.org.

Tish Davidson, A.M.
Laura Jean Cataldo, RN, Ed.D.

Sleepwalking disorder

Definition

Sleepwalking disorder, also called somnambulism, is characterized by repeated episodes of motor activity during sleep such as sitting up in bed, rising, and walking around, among others. The person appears to be awake because their eyes are usually open and they can maneuver around objects, but is considered asleep.

Sleepwalking disorder is one of several **sleep disorders** listed in the ***Diagnostic and Statistical Manual of Mental Disorders***, produced by the **American Psychiatric Association** and used by most mental health professionals in North America and Europe to diagnose mental disorders.

Demographics

Sleepwalking can occur at any age but is most common in children, with the first episodes usually between the ages of 4 and 8. The peak of sleepwalking behavior occurs at about 12 years of age. Between 10% and 30% of children have had at least one episode of sleepwalking. Sleepwalking disorder is seen in 1%–17% of children and occurs more frequently in boys. It is more frequently found in children if a close relative also has a history of sleepwalking, In fact, identical twins are more likely to sleepwalk than are other siblings. Adults who sleepwalk typically have a history of sleepwalking that stems back to childhood. Sleepwalking events occur in approximately 1%–7% of adults while sleepwalking disorder occurs in about 0.5%.

Description

Sleepwalking episodes usually occur during the first third of the night during the deepest phase of sleep (delta sleep or slow-wave sleep). The episodes can last anywhere from a few minutes up to one hour, with 5 to 15 minutes being average. Sleepwalkers appear to be awake but are typically unresponsive to individuals who attempt to communicate with them. Persons who sleepwalk typically have no memory or awareness of their actions or movement upon waking. However, sleepwalkers sometimes wake up while sleepwalking, remembering a dream they were having, which was being acted out during their sleepwalking episode. After going back to bed, the person will fall back into a light stage of sleep. The next morning, most sleepwalkers do not remember their sleepwalking activities the night before, although some people have vague recollections of what they did or said.

Activities while sleepwalking can be as simple as walking around and talking. However, sometimes activities can be less routine, such as the woman reported in 2008 in the journal *Sleep Medicine* who turned on her computer, logged in with her username and password, and wrote e-mails to friends inviting them to a party. Other such sleepwalking incidents by people include driving a car, taking knives from a kitchen drawer, playing a musical instrument, feeding pets, washing clothes, dressing, talking on the telephone, moving furniture, walking down the street or around the house, painting, cooking, or eating. Physical violence, abusive speech, and even murder has been reported from sleepwalking incidents.

Sometimes night terrors occur with sleepwalking. The person may seem confused or agitated, or extremely fearful or violent. During such terrors, the person may scream or throw their arms up into the air. Frequently, night terrors have a reoccurring theme, possibly from a frightening incident as a child or one that recently occurred as an adult. Although these episodes resemble nightmares, they usually occur during non-rapid eye movement (NREM) sleep rather than during the normal dreaming of rapid eye movement (REM) sleep. The patient often cannot recall the episode the next morning. They are non-REM dream experiences from which the sleeper never fully awakes and which he or she does not recall upon awakening. This condition mostly occurs in children and can be treated with hypnosis or medication in severe cases.

People who frequently sleepwalk often will feel tired and fatigued the next day. They may feel uneasy or restless, have less concentration, and experience some degree of dysfunction, such as delayed response time. Researchers often describe sleepwalking disorder as sleepwalking once or twice a month. Chronic sleepwalking may occur more frequently and may cause serious problems at home, work, or at school due to lack of restful sleep.

During an episode of sleepwalking, a related disorder may occur. For instance, people with nocturnal sleep-related eating disorder (NS-RED) will eat while sleepwalking. Often, the sleepwalker will walk to the kitchen, make a meal, and eat food while still asleep. Another similar sleep disorder is night eating syndrome (NES), which is characterized by a person eating during the night, while fully awake, because they are fearful that they cannot get back to sleep unless they eat food.

Causes and symptoms

Causes

There appears to be a genetic component for individuals who sleepwalk. The condition is 10 times more likely to occur in close relatives of known sleepwalkers than in the general public. These families also tend to be deep sleepers.

Sleepwalking may also be triggered by fever, which directly affects the nervous system, general illness, **alcohol use**, **sleep deprivation**, irregular or chaotic sleep schedule, and emotional **stress**. Certain drugs can also cause sleepwalking disorder such as neuroleptics (drugs that treat **psychosis**), stimulants (drugs that increase physical and/or mental activities), sedative/hypnotics (drugs that increase sleep or relaxation), **antianxiety drugs** (drugs that reduce anxiety), antiseizure drugs (drugs that reduce the chance of **seizures**), antiarrhythmic heart drugs (drugs that reduce or eliminate irregular heartbeat), and antihistamines (drugs that treat allergies). Hormonal changes that occur during adolescence, menstruation, and pregnancy can be also be triggers for sleepwalking. Sleepwalking episodes are more likely during times of physiological or psychological stress.

Certain medical conditions also increase the likelihood of sleepwalking, such as fever, gastroesophageal reflux (when food re-enters the esophagus from the stomach), night asthma, heart arrhythmias, night seizures (convulsions), obstructive sleep apnea (breathing temporarily stops while sleeping), and psychiatric disorders (such as panic attacks).

Symptoms

The *DSM-IV-TR* (fourth edition, text revised) specifies six diagnostic criteria for sleepwalking disorder:

- Repeated episodes of rising from bed during sleep. These episodes may include sitting up in bed, looking around, and walking, and usually occur during the first third of the night.

- Unresponsive to attempts at communication. During sleepwalking, the person typically has his or her eyes open, with dilated pupils, a blank stare, and does not respond to another's attempts at communication. Affected persons typically are only awakened with great difficulty.

- No recollection of the sleepwalking incident. Upon waking, the person typically has no memory of the sleepwalking events. If the individual does awaken from the sleepwalking episode, they may have a vague memory of the incident. Often, sleepwalkers will return to bed, or fall asleep in another place with no recall of how they got there.

- No impairment of mental activity upon waking. If an individual awakens during a sleepwalking episode, there may be a short period of confusion or disorientation, but there is no impairment of mental activity or behavior.

- Causes significant distress to life situations. Sleepwalking causes significant disruption of social and occupational situations or affects other abilities to function.

- Not due to substance use or abuse. Sleepwalking disorder is not diagnosed if the cause is related to drug abuse, medication, or a general medical condition.

Proposed changes for the fifth edition of the *DSM* (*DSM-5*) include subsuming sleepwalking disorder and **sleep terror disorder** into one **diagnosis** called disorder of arousal. The diagnostic criteria is similar but includes subtypes of sleepwalking, sleep terrors, or confusion upon arousal.

Diagnosis

The line that separates periodic sleepwalking from sleepwalking disorder is not clearly defined. Individuals or families most often seek professional help when the episodes of sleepwalking are violent, pose a risk for injury, or impair the person's ability to function. For a diagnosis of sleepwalking disorder to be made, the person must experience a significant amount of social, occupational, or other impairment related to the sleepwalking problem. Episodes that have a long history extending from childhood through adolescence and especially into adulthood are more likely to be diagnosed with sleepwalking disorder.

Since the individual cannot recall the sleepwalking activity, diagnosis by means of interview is of little benefit, unless it involves someone who has witnessed the sleepwalking behavior. The preferred method for accurate diagnosis is through **polysomnography**. This technique involves hooking electrodes to different locations on the affected person's body to monitor **brain** wave activity, heart rate, breathing, and other vital signs while the individual sleeps. Monitoring brain–wave patterns (via an electroencephalogram) and physiologic responses during sleep can usually give sleep specialists an accurate diagnosis of the condition and determine the effective means of treatment, if any.

Sleepwalking disorder can be difficult to distinguish from sleep terror disorder. In both cases, the individual has motor movement, is difficult to awaken, and does not remember the incident. The primary difference is that sleep terror disorder typically has an initial scream and signs of intense fear and panic associated with the other behaviors.

Treatment

Treatment for sleepwalking is often unnecessary, especially if episodes are infrequent and pose no hazard to the sleepwalker or others. If sleepwalking is recurrent, or daytime **fatigue** is suspected to result from disturbed sleep patterns, polysomnography may be recommended to determine whether some form of treatment may be helpful. If stress appears to trigger sleepwalking events in adults, **stress management**, **biofeedback** training, or relaxation techniques can be beneficial. Hypnosis has been used help sleepwalkers awaken once their feet touch the floor. **Psychotherapy** may help individuals who have underlying psychological issues that could be contributing to sleep problems.

Medications are sometimes used in the more severe cases with adults. Benzodiazepines—antianxiety drugs—such as **alprazolam** (Xanax), **clonazepam** (Klonopin),

KEY TERMS

Electroencephalogram (EEG)—A recording of electrical activity in the brain.

Non-rapid eye movement (NREM) sleep—Stages of sleep during which rapid eye movements do not occur. The majority of sleep consists of the four stages of NREM sleep.

Rapid eye movement (REM) sleep—A stage of sleep during which the sleeper's eyes move back and forth rapidly. Most dreams occur during REM sleep.

Sleep terror (or night terror) disorder—A disorder in which the patient wakes up physically aroused and screaming or crying.

or **diazepam** (Valium) can be used to help relax muscles, although these may not result in fewer episodes of sleepwalking. A tricyclic antidepressant (TCA) may also be used, such as **amitriptyline** (Elavil), butriptyline (Evadyne), dibenzepin (Noveril), lofepramine (Lomont), metapramine (Timaxel), **nortriptyline** (Aventyl HCl, Pamelor), or **protriptyline** (Vivactil). When medications are used, they are typically prescribed in the lowest dose necessary and only for a limited period. Such drugs will reduce chemical processes within the brain that affect sleep and, consequently, reduce or eliminate sleepwalking. Hypnosis and biofeedback have also been used effectively in the treatment of sleepwalking disorder.

Sedative drugs used to treat sleep disorders may actually cause sleepwalking and other behaviors during sleep, including sleep eating and sleep driving. In 2007, the U.S. Food and Drug Administration required manufacturers of sedative drugs to add a warning label detailing the risks of engaging in sleep behaviors when taking the medications. Such drugs include **zolpidem** (Ambien), **flurazepam** (Dalmane), **triazolam** (Halcion), eszopiclone (Lunesta), **zaleplon** (Sonata), and **temazepam** (Restoril), among others.

Prognosis

Most cases of sleepwalking subside over time. Sleepwalking in childhood usually disappears without treatment by age 15. If sleepwalking episodes persist into early adulthood, treatment is recommended. With an accurate diagnosis and appropriate treatment, episodes of sleepwalking can be greatly reduced and, in some cases, eliminated. Research into sleepwalking in the 2010s finds that sleepwalking disorder may be based on previous

QUESTIONS TO ASK YOUR DOCTOR

- How do I know if I am experiencing a sleepwalking disorder?
- What role does my family history play in my sleepwalking disorder?
- Could any of the medications I am taking be causing me to sleepwalk?
- What symptoms are important enough that I should seek immediate treatment?
- What diagnostic tests are needed for a thorough assessment?
- What type of treatment do you recommend?
- Should I see a specialist? If so, what kind of specialist should I contact?
- Is there any way I can prevent sleepwalking?
- What safety precautions should I take?

psychiatric issues, and actions performed while sleeping may be dependent on one's past (and not independent, arbitrary activities).

Prevention

Sleepwalking is relatively common and is not cause for concern. The major risk associated with sleepwalking is accidental injury. Persons with sleepwalking disorder should take precautions to block stairways, lock windows, keep floors cleared of harmful objects, etc., before going to sleep at night. Although most sleepwalkers are harmless, their activities can be dangerous to themselves or others. A sleepwalker may become violent if they, for instance, have their path blocked or if they become irritated with their environment. If they are trying to act out a dream or nightmare, they may try to interact with a bystander with aggressive or violent behavior.

If taking certain medications, a medical condition, or exposure to significant stressors are suspected triggers of sleepwalking episodes, a doctor should be consulted for a complete assessment.

Resources

BOOKS

American Psychiatric Association. *Diagnostic and Statistical Manual of Mental Disorders.* 4th ed, text rev. Washington, DC: American Psychiatric Association, 2000.

Berry, Richard B. *Fundamentals of Sleep Medicine.* New York: Saunders, 2011.

Chokroverty, Susan, ed. *Sleep Disorders Medicine: Basic Science, Technical Considerations, and Clinical Aspects.* 3rd ed. New York: Saunders, 2009.

Clete, A. Kushida, ed. *Handbook of Sleep Disorders.* 2nd ed. New York: Informa Healthcare, 2008.

Lee-Chiong, Teofilo L. *Sleep Medicine Essentials.* Hoboken, NJ: Wiley-Blackwell, 2009.

Mindell, Jodi A., and Judith A. Owens. *A Clinical Guide to Pediatric Sleep: Diagnosis and Management of Sleep Problems.* 2nd ed. New York: Lippincott Williams & Wilkins, 2009.

North, Carol, and Sean Yutzy. *Goodwin and Guze's Psychiatric Diagnosis.* New York: Oxford University Press, 2010.

Pollak, Charles P., et al. *A The Encyclopedia of Sleep and Sleep Disorders.* New York: Facts on File, 2009.

PERIODICALS

Dobson, Roger. "Zzz-mail: What Happens When Sleepwalkers Go Online." *The Telegraph* (May 26, 2011). http://www.telegraph.co.uk/news/newstopics/howaboutthat/3743289/Zzz-mail-What-happens-when-sleepwalkers-go-online.html (accessed July 19, 2011).

WEBSITES

American Psychiatry Association. "Sleep-Wake Disorders." DSM-5 Development. http://www.dsm5.org/Proposed-Revision/Pages/Sleep-WakeDisorders.aspx (accessed July 19, 2011).

American Sleep Association. "Sleep Eating." http://www.sleepassociation.org/index.php?p=sleepeating (accessed November 6, 2011).

PubMed Health. "Sleepwalking." U.S. National Library of Medicine. http://www.ncbi.nlm.nih.gov/pubmedhealth/PMH0001811 (accessed November 6, 2011).

U.S. Food and Drug Administration. "FDA Requests Label Change for All Sleep Disorder Drug Products." http://www.fda.gov/NewsEvents/Newsroom/PressAnnouncements/2007/ucm108868.htm (accessed November 6, 2011).

ORGANIZATIONS

American Academy of Child and Adolescent Psychiatry, 3615 Wisconsin Ave. NW, Washington, DC, 20016-3007, (202) 966-7300, Fax: (202) 966-2891, http://www.aacap.org.

American Academy of Sleep Medicine, 2510 N Frontage Rd., Darien, IL, 60561, (630) 737-9700, Fax: (630) 737-9790, http://www.aasmnet.org.

American Medical Association, 515 N State St., Chicago, IL, 60654, (800) 621-8335, http://www.ama-assn.org.

American Psychiatric Association, 1000 Wilson Blvd., Ste. 1825, Arlington, VA, 22209, (703) 907-7300, apa@psych.org, http://www.psych.org.

American Sleep Association, http://www.sleepassociation.org.

Better Sleep Council, 501 Wythe St., Alexandria, VA, 22314-1917, http://www.bettersleep.org.

National Sleep Foundation, 1010 N. Glebe Rd., Ste. 310, Arlington, VA, 22201, (703) 243-1697, nsf@ sleepfoundation.org, http://www.sleepfoundation.org.

Gary Gilles, M.A.
Laura Jean Cataldo, RN, EdD.
William A. Atkins, BS

Smoking *see* **Nicotine and related disorders**

Smoking cessation

Definition

Smoking cessation therapy consists of procedures that educate smokers about the dangers of smoking, motivate them to smoking abstinence, and assist them in their endeavors to quit by way of counseling and pharmaceutical interventions.

Purpose

The goal of smoking cessation is to get smokers to stop smoking or to help them when they **relapse**. Because **nicotine addiction** is strong and the cues to smoke are so prevalent, experts on smoking agree that occasional relapse is normal: One estimate is that smokers who eventually quit for good make at least three or four attempts before freeing themselves of the addiction, and approximately 50% of quitters relapse during the first week or two of trying to quit.

Demographics

Smoking is a key factor in lung cancer, heart attack, cerebrovascular disease, and chronic obstructive pulmonary disease (COPD), which are four of the primary causes of death in the United States. About one-third of deaths due to cancer, heart disease, and **stroke** and around 90% of COPD cases are directly attributable to tobacco use. Individuals who smoke after age 35 have a 50% chance of dying from smoking-related causes, and smokers have an average life span that is shorter by 8 to 10 years than nonsmokers.

Smoking-related illness costs the United States between $96 billion a year in healthcare costs, according to the U.S. Centers for Disease Control and Prevention (CDC). An efficacious treatment approach that significantly cuts the numbers of smokers has a great positive impact on the economy, health care, and insurance costs, and the vast social costs generated by the premature death of approximately 443,000 people per year. The Surgeon General's Office, the U.S. Public Health Service, the National Cancer Institute, and many other governmental and nonprofit organizations, as well as private healthcare agencies, have concerned themselves with the importance of smoking cessation, resulting in established guidelines for clinical practice as well as

Symptom	Cause	Duration	Relief
Craving for cigarette	Nicotine craving	Begins in first week and can linger for months	Distract yourself with other activities (e.g., exercise, hobbies, etc.)
Coughing, dry throat, nasal drip	Body ridding itself of mucus in lungs and airways	Several weeks	Drink plenty of fluids, use cough drops
Irritability, impatience	Nicotine craving	2–4 weeks	Exercise, practice relaxation techniques, avoid caffeine
Lack of concentration	Lack of nicotine stimulation	A few weeks	Reduce workload, avoid stress
Fatigue	Lack of nicotine stimulation	2–4 weeks	Practice relaxation techniques, nap
Insomnia	Nicotine craving temporarily reduces deep sleep	2–4 weeks	Avoid caffeine after 6 p.m.
Hunger	Cigarette cravings confused with hunger pangs	Up to several weeks	Drink water or low-calorie drinks, eat low-calorie snacks
Constipation, gas	Intestinal movement decreases with lack of nicotine	1–2 weeks	Drink plenty of fluids, add fiber to diet, exercise

Side effects of nicotine withdrawal and possible remedies. *(Table by PreMediaGlobal. Reproduced by permission of Gale, a part of Cengage Learning.)*

continuing research on which strategies work and which ones do not.

Description

The U.S. Department of Health and Human Services/Public Health Service Guideline *Treating Tobacco Use and Dependence* (updated in 2008), a comprehensive, evidence-based blueprint for smoking cessation, established the necessity for medical practitioners to take a proactive stance in regard to patients' smoking. This article was based on a review of more than 3,000 articles on tobacco addiction that had been published from 1975 to 1994. The guideline was designed to provide clinicians and others with specific information regarding effective cessation treatments, and it advocated the "frank discussion of personal health risks, the benefits of smoking cessation, and available methods to assist in stopping smoking," an approach designed to raise physician concern about smoking, which had generally not been a topic broached with patients until smoking-related diseases developed. The guidelines provide a strategy by which to approach the problem of patient smoking: The "Five A's" model.

The model of the Five A's specifies:

• Ask to systematically identify all tobacco users at every visit.

• Advise smokers to quit smoking.

• Assess the smoker's willingness to stop; if the smoker is not willing, educate as to the "Five R's."

• Assist smokers who are willing to stop smoking. Tests of nicotine dependence help determine effective treatments.

• Arrange follow-up support. Quick follow-up can prevent or curtail early relapse.

One research estimate is that 5% of smokers will stop smoking if their doctor advises them to, and that educating smokers about the health effects of smoking can motivate them to quit in higher numbers. Motivation to stop smoking can be increased by social support and pharmaceutical interventions, and early relapse can be prevented more easily if the smoker has a follow-up appointment within a week of the stated quitting date.

Smoking cessation methods focus on getting smokers into treatment in the first place by targeting resistance and increasing motivation. If patients are not willing to quit, medical personnel are expected to employ the use of guidelines called the "Five R's":

• Relevance. The medical practitioner discusses the relevance of quitting smoking to the particular individual, perhaps targeting health concerns, family health, or the financial impact of smoking.

• Risks. The medical practitioner engages patients in discussion of the health risks of smoking.

• Rewards. The medical practitioner helps patients identify potential rewards, such as saving money (more than $2,000 a year for a pack-a-day habit), a variety of health improvements, raised self-esteem, improved taste and sense of smell, and setting a good example for children.

• Roadblocks. The practitioner and patient discuss the problems that prevent the patient from quitting, and the practitioner attempts to address the patient's concerns (for example, fear of weight gain). By this time, physicians will also educate patients as to the symptoms of nicotine withdrawal. Irritability, increased food cravings, headaches, lack of concentration, urges to use tobacco, and restlessness are some of the symptoms associated with nicotine withdrawal.

• Repetition. The medical practitioner engages patients unwilling to quit in this discussion at every appointment.

In 2002, a study of **managed care** providers revealed that 71% of the responding plans had written their own guidelines for smoking cessation treatment, and a majority stated that their guidelines were based on the Five A's model. Smoking cessation treatment typically involves primary identification of smokers and their willingness to quit, a behavioral treatment component, and provision of pharmacotherapy.

Once the patient has indicated willingness to take part in a smoking cessation program, the prescribed therapy is generally pharmaceutical. Although telephone counseling has been shown to assist smokers in staying off tobacco, with group or individual counseling also showing some usefulness, it is without doubt that nicotine replacement therapy (NRT) or other drugs greatly contribute to smoking abstinence. Researchers have found that use of any of the drugs currently prescribed for nicotine addiction double or even triple the chances that patients will quit smoking.

Pharmacotherapy

There are currently three primary pharmacologic interventions in smoking cessation: nicotine replacement therapy (NRT), **bupropion** (Wellbutrin, Wellbutrin XL, Zyban), and varenicline (Chantix). The three replacement therapies of choice act differently to affect a similar change: Patients manage to quit smoking with significantly less physiologic distress and less chance of relapse than those who use only behavioral strategies or go "cold turkey."

NRT works by replacing the delivery method of nicotine with chewing gum, lozenges, a nicotine patch, nasal spray, or an "inhaler" that actually works by oral absorption, not by inhalation. Nicotine is delivered to the body in doses that decrease over time, allowing users to eventually end their dependence. Side effects of NRT include nausea, flatulence and other digestive problems, and mouth and jaw soreness from chewing the gum; skin irritation at patch sites; rhinitis, sneezing, and watery eyes for the spray; and throat irritation for the inhaler. Patients' previous health issues determine which, if any, of the NRTs will be prescribed. NRT is not prescribed for patients who have suffered a recent heart attack, who have angina or arrhythmia, or for women who are pregnant or nursing.

Bupropion, an antidepressant drug, inhibits the body's reuptake of the **neurotransmitters dopamine** and norepinephrine. Like **selective serotonin reuptake inhibitors (SSRIs)**, another class of antidepressant drugs, bupropion works because it produces higher levels of neurotransmitters in the **brain**, which in turn create enhanced feelings of well-being. Unlike other **SSRIs**, bupropion has some effect on **serotonin** but has its primary effects on dopamine. Originally used as an antidepressant drug, bupropion has been used in smoking cessation both for those suffering solely from nicotine addiction and for those who have concurrent symptoms of **depression**. Bupropion can be used on its own or together with nicotine replacement products. Several studies have indicated that the combination helps more smokers quit than either method by itself. Bupropion is the only antidepressant currently approved by the FDA for use as a smoking cessation product.

Varenicline, a nicotinic receptor partial agonist, works by targeting nicotine receptors in the brain. The drug attaches itself to the nicotine receptors and blocks nicotine from reaching the receptors. This action blocks the pleasurable sensation smokers derive from smoking. Varenicline is available by prescription only.

Two other drugs, **nortriptyline** (Pamelor) and **clonidine** (Catapres), are sometimes used when the primary treatments are unsuccessful. Nortriptyline is a tricyclic antidepressant that acts by increasing levels of norepinephrine. Clonidine is a drug primarily used for treating high blood pressure. Neither drug is approved by the FDA for treating nicotine dependence, and their uses in smoking cessation are considered off-label.

Behavioral therapy

Smoking cessation programs are more effective when patients learn behavioral coping strategies in addition to using drug therapy; however, given the strength of the physical addiction, if only one therapeutic modality is to be used, pharmacotherapy is generally considered the more effective choice. That said, many smokers find comfort in being able to pick up the phone and talk to someone when cravings become unmanageable. In a best-case scenario (and in most of the managed care programs today), patients have access to behavioral, supportive, and drug therapies.

Alternative treatments

Other approaches that have been used to help smokers quit include hypnosis and **acupuncture**. The evidence for the usefulness of hypnosis is largely anecdotal. It appears to be most helpful when used in combination with nicotine replacement products or bupropion. Although acupuncture has been used in Western countries since the 1970s to help people quit smoking, it does not appear to be particularly effective in this regard.

Precautions

Seeing a physician regularly while using smoking cessation drugs is important. The physician will check to make sure the medicine is working as it should and will watch for unwanted side effects.

Some side effects of smoking cessation drugs include:

- nausea
- vomiting
- severe pain in the stomach or abdomen
- severe diarrhea
- severe dizziness
- fainting
- convulsions (seizures)
- low blood pressure
- fast, weak, or irregular heartbeat
- hearing or vision problems
- severe breathing problems
- severe watering of the mouth or drooling
- cold sweat
- severe headache
- confusion
- severe weakness

Bupropion should not be taken by patients with a history of **seizures**, high blood pressure, anorexia, or **bulimia nervosa**, or patients who are also taking monoamine oxidase inhibitor (MAOI) medications. These include such drugs as furazolidone, **isocarboxazid**, and

KEY TERMS

Nicotine—A poisonous chemical usually derived from the tobacco plant, whose affect on the brain begins within seven seconds after it is inhaled. It causes the adrenal glands to secrete epinephrine, a neurotransmitter that causes the user to experience a nearly immediate feeling of euphoria. The neurotransmitter dopamine is also released, increasing the feeling of well-being. Nicotine also elevates blood pressure, causes the release of glucose into the bloodstream, and increases the heart rate and respiration rate. Nicotine, with its near instant but short duration "high," is extremely addictive, and its presence in tobacco products, such as cigarettes, pipe tobacco, and chewing tobacco, becomes even more dangerous due to other carcinogenic ingredients present in those products.

Neurotransmitter—One of a group of chemicals secreted by a nerve cell (neuron) to carry a chemical message to another nerve cell, often as a way of transmitting a nerve impulse. Neurotransmitters affect various sensations in the body, such as pleasure, pain, hunger, and fear. Examples of neurotransmitters include acetylcholine, dopamine, serotonin, and norepinephrine.

Off-label use—Drugs in the United States are approved by the Food and Drug Administration (FDA) for specific uses based on the results of clinical trials. However, it is legal for physicians to administer these drugs for other off-label uses not approved by the FDA. It is not legal for pharmaceutical companies to advertise drugs for off-label uses.

Selective serotonin reuptake inhibitors (SSRIs)—A class of antidepressants that works by blocking the reabsorption of serotonin in brain cells, raising the level of the chemical in the brain.

phenelzine. Bupropion may also interact with phenytoin, **carbamazepine**, and levodopa.

Bupropion and varenicline are associated with serious mental health side effects including depression, agitation, thoughts of **suicide**, hostility, and attempted suicide. These side effects tend to occur shortly after the patient begins to take the medication and typically stop once the patient stops taking the drug. Patients experiencing these symptoms should be closely monitored by a physician until the side effects stop, and

individuals with known psychiatric or mental health problems are at particularly high risk.

Aftercare

Aftercare consists of maintenance or relapse interventions such as Nicotine Anonymous, a 12-step program that offers support to those who want to quit cigarettes and quit smoking. Maintenance and relapse can be considered lifelong endeavors because a smoker is either not smoking or has suffered a temporary setback that can be addressed by cycling though the stages again. Some researchers say that most smokers will relapse three or four times before quitting; others estimate it to be closer to ten or fifteen times. Aftercare for smoking, like for all addictions, focuses on supportive services and addressing relapse as quickly as possible.

Resources

PERIODICALS

Anczak, John, and Robert Nogler. "Tobacco Cessation in Primary Care: Maximizing Intervention Strategies." *Clinical Medicine & Research* 1, no. 3 (July 2003): 201–16.

Fiore, Michael C., et al. "Clinical Practice Guideline: Treating Tobacco Use and Dependence: 2008 Update." *U.S. Department of Health and Human Services, Public Health Service* May 2008.

Mallin, Robert. "Smoking Cessation: Integration of Behavioral and Drug Therapies." *American Family Physician* 65, no. 6 (March 2002): 1107–15.

McPhillips-Tangum, Carol, et al. "Addressing Tobacco in Managed Care: Results of the 2002 Survey." *Preventing Chronic Disease* 1, no. 4 (October 2004): 1–11.

Rollins, Gina. "With Smoking Cessation Drugs, Dosage is Key." *American College of Physicians-American Society of Internal Medicine Observer*, April 2002. http://www.acpinternist.org/archives/2002/04/smoking.htm (accessed October 27, 2011).

Wu, Ping, et al. "Effectiveness of Smoking Cessation Therapies: a Systematic Review and Meta-Analysis." *BMC Public Health* (December 2006): 1–16.

WEBSITES

Nicotine Anonymous. http://www.nicotine-anonymous.org (accessed October 27, 2011).

U.S. Centers for Disease Control and Prevention. "Smoking & Tobacco Use: How to Quit." http://www.cdc.gov/tobacco/how2quit.htm (accessed October 27, 2011).

U.S. National Cancer Institute. "Free Help to Quit Smoking." http://www.cancer.gov/cancertopics/smoking (accessed October 27, 2011).

Lorena S. Covington, MA

Social anxiety disorder *see* **Social phobia**

Social communication disorder

Definition

Social communication disorder (SCD) is a new concept proposed for addition to the fifth edition of the **Diagnostic and Statistical Manual of Mental Disorders** (*DSM-5*), the guidelines used by medical professionals in diagnosing mental disorders. There is no corresponding disorder in *DSM-IV*. The new criteria are intended to help diagnose children who have unexpected difficulty with pragmatics—the aspect of language skills that concerns the appropriate use of language in social situations—in spite of a relatively normal vocabulary for their age and the ability to form grammatically correct sentences. One additional reason for the new **diagnosis** is to distinguish children with social communication disorder from those diagnosed with **autism** spectrum disorder (ASD). Although children with social communication disorder may share some of the difficulties that children with ASD have in communicating effectively with others, they do not exhibit the repetitive behaviors and limited range of interests found in children with ASD. SCD is proposed to be added as a neurodevelopmental disorder in the category of communication disorders.

Demographics

The demographics of social communication disorder were unknown as of 2011. According to the **National Institute of Mental Health** (NIMH), about one in every 110 eight-year-olds in the United States has an autism spectrum disorder, with boys being four times as likely to be diagnosed with an ASD as girls. The presence of ASD must be completely ruled out before a child can receive the diagnosis of social communication disorder.

Description

To understand the new diagnosis, it is helpful to look at the history of controversy and changes in diagnostic classification that have taken place among child psychiatrists and language specialists since the early 1980s. The controversy concerned whether children with certain types of language impairments belonged to the spectrum of autistic disorders or whether they should be diagnosed as simply having a language disorder that affected their social relationships. The debate began in 1983 with a study by Isabelle Rapin and Doris Allen, professors of neurology and child psychiatry, respectively. Rapin and Allen suggested using the term "semantic pragmatic disorder" (SPD) for children who are excessively talkative, do not seem to fully understand the meaning or words, and lack conversational skills in interacting with others. The word *semantic* refers to the ability to understand the meaning of words and use them correctly, while *pragmatic* refers to practical language skills, namely the ability to understand the rules of conversation, such as knowing what to say and when to say it, taking turns with the conversation partner, and the like. Children with SPD differed from autistic children in that they did not show the full range of symptoms considered characteristic of autism.

The next stage toward the proposed definition of SCD for *DSM-5* was the introduction of the phrase "pragmatic language impairment" (PLI) to describe children whose primary difficulty with social conversation is pragmatic rather than semantic. Whereas a child who has difficulties with the semantics of language may not know the meaning of abstract words (such as "vague" or "freedom"), may have difficulty understanding words referring to emotions (such as "fearful" or "embarrassed"), and often has difficulty with figurative or nonliteral expressions (such as "raining cats and dogs" or "sitting pretty"), the child with PLI has difficulties that typically involve three basic communication skills:

- Using language for different purposes, such as making a request, asking a question, greeting someone, giving information, or promising something.
- Changing the use of language according to the situation or the conversation partner. This aspect of pragmatics includes such skills as talking differently with a baby, another child, or an adult; giving background information to someone unfamiliar with a subject; and talking differently in a classroom compared to home or a playground.
- Following basic rules for polite conversation, such as taking turns, not interrupting the other person, staying on topic, knowing how to change the topic appropriately, knowing how to read such nonverbal signals as body language or facial expression, maintaining appropriate eye contact, and knowing how close to stand to the other person while talking.

The present *DSM-5* proposal for social communication disorder is based on the premise, as stated by the **American Psychiatric Association**, that "pragmatic difficulties (in children) constitute a fundamentally different form of language impairment" and should be distinguished from ASD.

KEY TERMS

Audiologist—A health care professional with special training in testing people for hearing loss or other hearing disorders.

Pragmatic language impairment (PLI)—A term that is used by some researchers as equivalent to social communication disorder. PLI was previously known as *semantic pragmatic disorder* or *SPD*.

Pragmatics—A subfield of linguistics that explores the ways in which context contributes to the meaning of language. In ordinary usage, pragmatics refers to a person's ability to know what is appropriate to say, where and when to say it, and the give-and-take nature of conversation.

Semantics—A subfield of linguistics that focuses on the meaning of words; in ordinary usage, the ability to use words correctly and understand their meanings.

Speech-language pathologist—A professional with special training in the evaluation and treatment of persons with voice, speech, and language disorders.

Risk factors

The risk factors for SCD have not yet been established, because the proposed disorder is considered to be different from ASD.

Causes and symptoms

The causes of SCD were not known as of 2011.

The symptoms of SCD may include the following:

- delayed language development
- difficulty making and maintaining friendships and relationships because of delayed language development
- referring facts to stories and having trouble comprehending jokes, sarcasm, or lies
- communication patterns appearing rude and inconsiderate to others
- talking in long monologues; perhaps telling a story that includes so many details that the listener loses interest
- difficulty extracting the main point of a question or conversation
- frequently missing contextual cues (tone of voice, body language, specific social setting) in a conversation
- difficulty assessing what the other person does or does not already know about the topic of conversation

- little variety in use of language
- difficulty understanding what is socially appropriate (not fitting the criteria for conduct disorder)

Diagnosis

The diagnosis of SCD is complex and difficult. One major problem is that there are no generally accepted assessment tools that are both reliable and practical. Another difficulty is that many children do not fit neatly into any diagnostic category. A child with pragmatic language difficulties may, for example, have 1) only isolated difficulties with pragmatic language skills; 2) both pragmatic and semantic difficulties with language; 3) pragmatic language difficulties together with another disorder on the autism spectrum (such as **Asperger syndrome**); or 4) pragmatic language difficulties together with another disorder that does not belong to the autism spectrum (such as **attention deficit hyperactivity disorder** [ADHD]).

Because of the complexity of diagnosis, a child with symptoms of SCD should be evaluated by a team of specialists, which may include his or her pediatrician, a speech-language pathologist (SLP), an audiologist, a **psychologist**, and possibly the child's teachers, if he or she is of school age.

The proposed *DSM-5* criteria for social communication disorder are as follows:

- Criterion A: The child's language difficulty is one of pragmatics, which affects the child's social relationships and his or her understanding of conversations with others. The child's difficulty cannot be explained on the basis of general cognitive abilities or the child's ability to form sentences and follow the rules of grammar.
- Criterion B: The child's problems with social communication limit his or her ability to function effectively in interpersonal communication, "social participation, academic achievement, or occupational performance, alone or in any combination."
- Criterion C: ASD must be ruled out as a possible diagnosis.
- Criterion D: The symptoms must be present in early childhood, although they may not be fully revealed until the social demands on the child go beyond his or her limited capacities.

No criteria for the severity of social communication disorder had been determined as of 2011.

Examination

In some cases, the child's doctor or a speech-language pathologist may recommend having the child's hearing evaluated to rule out a hearing disorder.

QUESTIONS TO ASK YOUR DOCTOR

- Does my child's problem seem to be one of language only, or are there other areas of concern?
- Would it help my child to see a speech-language pathologist?
- What types of treatment do you suggest?
- How can I help as a parent?
- How can my child's teacher help?

Tests

As of 2011, there were no laboratory or imaging tests being used to diagnose social communication disorder. With regard to psychological tests, there are two instruments that may be used to evaluate a child for ASD. These include the Social Communication Questionnaire (SCQ), which is a 40-item screener for autism spectrum disorder to be filled out by the child's parents. It takes about 10 minutes to complete. Another instrument that was developed in the United Kingdom in 2002 and is more widely used there than in North America is the Diagnostic Interview for Social and Communication Disorders (DISCO). The DISCO is an interview-based instrument for the diagnosis of autism and autism spectrum disorders. It was not clear as of 2011, however, whether either of these tests would be useful in distinguishing between ASD and SCD.

Treatment

Treatment for social communication disorder is highly individualized, as it is for other communication disorders. The therapy is usually conducted by the speech-language pathologist rather than by a pediatrician or other medical doctor. There is no one-size-fits-all approach to treating children with SCD; however, common goals might include helping the child to:

- distinguish between a sincere voice and a sarcastic one, or between a kind voice and a mean or angry one
- recognize and correctly interpret facial expressions and body language
- distinguish between "baby talk" and the kind of language to use with adults
- use verb tenses correctly and distinguish between singular and plural nouns

- take turns in conversations and tell when he or she is going on too long

The SLP may also work with the child's parents or teachers, coaching them on ways to improve the child's communication skills. These may include asking questions or otherwise helping the child to use language for different purposes; taking advantage of everyday situations to practice greetings and farewells, requesting items at the dinner table, and the like; role-playing conversations in which the child pretends to be talking to different people in different situations; and showing the child how important nonverbal signals are in conversation.

Prognosis

The prognosis for SCD depends on the child's overall intelligence and family situation and whether he or she has another medical or mental disorder along with the SCD.

Prevention

There is no known way to prevent social communication disorder, because its causes are not yet understood.

Resources

BOOKS

Bishop, Dorothy V.M., and Laurence B. Leonard. *Speech and Language Impairments in Children: Causes, Characteristics, Intervention and Outcome.* Hove, East Sussex, UK: Psychology Press, 2000.

Damico, Jack S., Nicole Müller, and Martin J. Ball, eds. *Handbook of Language and Speech Disorders.* Malden, MA: Wiley-Blackwell, 2010.

Norbury, Courtney Frazier, J. Bruce Tomblin, and Dorothy V. M. Bishop, eds. *Understanding Developmental Language Disorders in Children.* New York, NY: Psychology Press, 2008.

Rapin I, Allen D. "Developmental Language Disorders: Nosologic Considerations." In *Neuropsychology of Language, Reading, and Spelling,* edited by Ursula Kirk, 155–184. New York: Academic Press, 1982.

PERIODICALS

Freed, J., et al. "Literacy Skills in Primary School-Aged Children with Pragmatic Language Impairment: A Comparison with Children with Specific Language Impairment." *International Journal of Language and Communication Disorders* 46 (May 2011): 334–347.

Van Agt, H., et al. "The Impact on Socio-emotional Development and Quality of Life of Language Impairment in 8-Year-Old Children."*Developmental Medicine and Child Neurology* 53 (January 2011): 81–88.

Wing, L., et al. "The Diagnostic Interview for Social and Communication Disorders: Background, Inter-rater Reliability and Clinical Use." *Journal of Child Psychology and Psychiatry, and Allied Disciplines* 43 (March 2002): 307–325.

WEBSITES

American Psychiatric Association. "A 05 Social Communication Disorder." DSM-5 Development. http://www.dsm5.org/proposedrevision/pages/proposedrevision.aspx?rid=489# (accessed July 19, 2011).

American Speech-Language-Hearing Association (ASHA). "Pragmatic Language Tips." http://www.asha.org/public/speech/development/PragmaticLanguageTips.htm (accessed July 20, 2011).

———. "Social Language Use (Pragmatics)." http://www.asha.org/public/speech/development/pragmatics.htm (accessed July 20, 2011).

Melfi, Renee S. "Communication Disorders." Medscape Reference. http://emedicine.medscape.com/article/317758-overview (accessed July 20, 2011).

National Institute on Deafness and Other Communication Disorders (NIDCD). "Autism and Communication." National Institutes of Health. http://www.nidcd.nih.gov/health/voice/autism.html (accessed July 20, 2011).

National Institute of Mental Health (NIMH). "Autism Spectrum Disorders (Pervasive Developmental Disorders)." National Institutes of Health. http://www.nimh.nih.gov/health/topics/autism-spectrum-disorders-pervasive-developmental-disorders/index.shtml (accessed July 20, 2011).

ORGANIZATIONS

American Psychiatric Association, 1000 Wilson Blvd., Ste. 1825, Arlington, VA, 22209-3901, (703) 907-7300, apa@psych.org, http://www.psych.org.

American Speech-Language-Hearing Association (ASHA), 2200 Research Blvd., Rockville, MD, 20850-3289, (301) 296-5700, (800) 638-8255, Fax: (301) 296-8580, http://www.asha.org.

Callier Center for Communication Disorders, 1966 Inwood Rd., Dallas, TX, 75235, (214) 905-3000, Fax: (214) 905-3022, http://www.utdallas.edu/calliercenter.

I CAN (children's communication charity), 8 Wakley St., London, United Kingdom EC1V 7QE, 011 4420 7(843) 2510, Fax: 011 4420 7(843) 2569, info@ican.org.uk, http://www.ican.org.uk.

National Institute on Deafness and Other Communication Disorders (NIDCD), 31 Center Dr., MSC 2320, Bethesda, MD, 20892-2320, (301) 496-7243, Fax: (301) 402-0018, (800) 241-1044, nidcdinfo@nidcd.nih.gov, http://www.nidcd.nih.gov.

National Institute of Mental Health (NIMH), 6001 Executive Blvd., Rm. 8184, MSC 9663, Bethesda, MD, 20892-9663, (301) 443-4513, Fax: (301) 443-4279, (866) 615-6464, nimhinfo@nih.gov, http://www.nimh.nih.gov/index.shtml.

Rebecca J. Frey, Ph.D.

Social phobia

Definition

According to the handbook used by mental health professionals to diagnose mental disorders, the ***Diagnostic and Statistical Manual of Mental Disorders***, fourth edition, text revision, also known as the *DSM-IV-TR,* social phobia is an anxiety disorder characterized by a strong and persistent fear of social or performance situations in which individuals might feel embarrassment or humiliation. Generalized social phobia refers to a fear of most social interactions combined with fear of most performance situations, such as speaking in public or eating in a restaurant. Persons who are afraid of only one type of performance situation or afraid of only a few rather than most social situations may be described as having nongeneralized, circumscribed, or specific social phobia.

Social phobia, which is also known as social anxiety disorder, is a serious mental health problem in the United States. In any given year, social phobia affects 3.7% of the U.S. population between the ages of 18 and 54, or about 5.3 million people. It is the third most common psychiatric condition after **depression** and alcoholism. Patients diagnosed with social phobia have the highest risk of alcohol abuse of all patients with **anxiety disorders**; in addition, they suffer from worse impairment than patients with major medical illnesses, including congestive heart failure and diabetes.

Demographics

The prevalence of social phobia in the general U.S. population is difficult to evaluate because researchers differ in their estimation of the threshold of "significant interference" with the person's occupational or educational functioning. In addition, different studies have focused on different subtypes of social phobia. One study found that about 20% of the adults surveyed reported high levels of anxiety related to public speaking or other types of public performance, but only 2% indicated sufficient distress to meet the diagnostic criteria of social phobia. Because of these differences in measurement, epidemiological and community-based studies give figures for a lifetime prevalence of social phobia that fall between 3 and 13%.

The types of situations associated with social phobia are different in the general population as contrasted with clinical populations. Surveys of adults in the general population indicate that most people diagnosed with social phobia are afraid of public speaking; only 45% report being afraid of meeting new people or having to talk to strangers. Fears related to eating, drinking, or writing in public, or using a public restroom, are much less common in this group. By contrast, people being treated for social phobia in outpatient clinics are more likely to be afraid of a range of social situations rather than just one. Social phobia accounts for 10–20% of the anxiety disorders diagnosed in patients in outpatient clinics, but it is rarely the reason for hospitalizing a patient.

The same difference between general and clinical populations affects the sex ratios given for social phobia. Community-based studies suggest that social phobia is more common in women, but in most samples of clinical patients, the sex ratio is either 1:1 or males are in the majority. A study of social phobia in prepubertal children found that girls were more likely to verbalize anxiety than boys, but the researchers who observed the children interact with adults and with one another did not observe any behavioral differences between boys and girls. The researchers concluded that the apparently higher rates of social phobia in women may simply reflect women's greater openness about their feelings.

With regard to race, the same study found no statistically significant difference in the incidence of social phobia between Caucasian and African American children. This finding was consistent with a 1995 study that failed to find differences based on race in lists of children's top 10 fears. Further research, however, is necessary in order to determine whether social phobia has different symptom patterns or rates of development in different racial or ethnic groups.

The demographics of social phobia in young children are particularly difficult to determine because of changes in diagnostic categories and criteria in successive editions of *DSM*. Social phobia was introduced as a diagnostic category in *DSM-III*, which was published in 1980. Neither *DSM-III* nor its 1987 revision restricted social phobia to adults, but the disorder was rarely diagnosed in children—most likely because *DSM-III* and *DSM-III-R* listed two diagnoses for children, overanxious disorder and avoidant disorder of childhood, whose symptoms overlapped those of social phobia. Statistics based on *DSM-III-R* criteria for social phobia placed the prevalence of the disorder in children in the general population at about 1%. The revisions of the diagnostic criteria in *DSM-IV*, however, have led to an apparent dramatic increase in the prevalence of social phobia in children. One study done in 1997 reported that 18% of the children in a clinical sample met *DSM-III-R* criteria for social phobia but that 40% of the children in the same sample had social phobia according to *DSM-IV* criteria.

Description

Social phobia varies in its development and initial presentation. In some young people, the disorder grows out of a history of **shyness** or social inhibition. In others, social phobia becomes apparent following a move to a new school or similar developmental challenge. In adults, circumscribed social phobia may be associated with a change of occupation or job promotion, the most common example being the emergence of the disorder with regard to public speaking in a person whose previous jobs did not require them to make presentations or speeches in front of others. The onset of social phobia may be insidious, which means that it gets worse by slow degrees. About one-half of all patients, however, experience a sudden onset of social phobia following a particularly humiliating or frightening experience. For example, in one British case study, the patient's social phobia developed abruptly after her father's sudden death. The patient had had an argument with her father one morning, and he was killed in an accident later in the day. The onset of social phobia almost always occurs in childhood or the midteens; onset after age 25 is unusual. The disorder is often a lifelong problem, although its severity may diminish in adult life.

Adults and adolescents with social phobia, as well as many children with the disorder, have sufficient insight to recognize that their fears are excessive or unwarranted. This factor often adds to their distress and feelings of inferiority.

Social phobia is of major concern to society as a whole for two reasons. One reason is the disorder's very high rate of comorbidity with such other mental health problems as major depression and **substance abuse**. In comparison with patients diagnosed with other anxiety disorders, patients with social phobia have higher averages of concurrent anxiety disorders (1.21 versus 0.45); comorbid depression or other disorders (2.05 versus 1.19); and lifetime disorders (3.11 versus 2.05). The most common comorbid disorders diagnosed in patients with social phobia are major depression (43%); **panic disorder** (33%); **generalized anxiety disorder** (19%); PTSD (36%); alcohol or substance abuse disorder (18%); and attempted **suicide** (23%).

The second reason is the loss to the larger society of the gifts and talents that these patients possess. Social phobia can have a devastating effect on young people's intellectual life and choice of career, causing them to abandon their educations, stay in dead-end jobs, refuse promotions involving travel or relocation, and make similar self-defeating choices because of their fear of classroom participation, job interviews, and other social interactions in educational and workplace settings. One sample of patients diagnosed with social phobia found that almost one-half had failed to finish high school; 70% were in the bottom two quartiles of socioeconomic status (SES); and 22% were on welfare. In addition to their academic and employment-related difficulties, people with social phobia have limited or nonexistent social support networks. They are less likely to marry and start families of their own because of their fear of interpersonal relationships. Many continue to live at home with their parents even as adults or remain in unfulfilling relationships.

Causes and symptoms

Causes

The causes of social phobia appear to be a combination of physical and environmental factors. The symptoms vary among individuals of different ages.

NEUROBIOLOGICAL FACTORS. There is some evidence that social phobia can be inherited. A group of researchers at Yale identified a genetic locus on human chromosome 3 that is linked to **agoraphobia** and two genetic loci on chromosomes 1 and 11q linked to panic disorder. Because social phobia shares some traits with panic disorder, it is likely that there are also genes that govern susceptibility to social phobia. In addition, researchers at the **National Institute of Mental Health** (NIMH) identified a gene in mice that appears to govern fearfulness.

Positron emission tomography (PET) scans of patients diagnosed with social phobia indicate that blood flow is increased in a region of the **brain** (the amygdala) associated with fear responses when the patients are asked to speak in public. In contrast, **PET** scans of control subjects without social phobia show that blood flow during the public speaking exercise is increased in the cerebral cortex, an area of the brain associated with thinking and evaluation rather than emotional arousal. The researchers concluded that patients with social phobia have a different neurochemical response to certain social situations or challenges that activates the limbic system rather than the cerebral cortex.

TEMPERAMENT. A number of researchers have pointed to inborn temperament (natural predisposition) as a broad vulnerability factor in the development of anxiety and mood disorders, including social phobia. More specifically, children who manifest what is known as behavioral inhibition in early infancy are at increased risk for developing more than one anxiety disorder in adult life, particularly if the inhibition remains over time. Behavioral inhibition refers to a group of behaviors that are displayed when the child is confronted with a new situation or unfamiliar people. These behaviors include agitated movement (such as hyperextension), crying, and general irritability, followed by withdrawing, seeking comfort from a familiar person, and stopping what one is doing when one notices the new person or situation. Children of depressed or anxious parents are more likely to develop behavioral inhibition. One study of preadolescent children diagnosed with social phobia reported that many of these children had been identified as behaviorally inhibited in early childhood.

PSYCHOSOCIAL FACTORS. The development of social phobia is also influenced by parent-child interactions in a patient's family of origin. Several studies have found that the children of parents with major depression, whether or not it is comorbid with panic disorder, are at increased risk of developing social phobia. Children of parents with major depression and comorbid panic disorder are at increased risk of developing more than one anxiety disorder. A family pattern of social phobia, however, is stronger for the generalized than for the specific or circumscribed subtype.

It is highly likely that the children of depressed parents may acquire certain attitudes and behaviors from their parents that make them more susceptible to developing social phobia. One study of children with social phobia found that their cognitive assessment of ambiguous situations was strongly negative, not only with regard to the dangerousness of the situation but also in terms of their ability to cope with it. In other words, these children tend to overestimate the threats and dangers in life and to underestimate their strength, intelligence, and other resources for coping. This process of learning from observing the behavior of one's parents or other adults is called social **modeling**.

Still another psychosocial factor related to the development of social phobia in children and adolescents is the general disintegration in the social fabric of the developed countries since World War II. A number of social theorists as well as physicians and therapists have noted that children are exposed more frequently to both real-life and media depictions of aggressive behavior and abrasive language than earlier generations. Children also learn about frightening or unpleasant social realities at earlier and earlier ages. The increased rate of social phobia and school refusal among adolescent girls has been linked to the greater crudity of teasing from boys in junior high and high school. In addition, the fortress mentality reflected in the architecture of high-rise apartment buildings and gated communities for those who can afford them also sends children the message that other people are to be feared. While trends in the larger society may not directly cause social phobia (or other

KEY TERMS

Agoraphobia—Abnormal anxiety regarding public places or situations from which the patient may wish to flee or in which he or she would be helpless in the event of a panic attack.

Panic attack—A time-limited period of intense fear accompanied by physical and cognitive symptoms. Panic attacks may be unexpected or triggered by specific internal or external cues.

mental disorders), they are nonetheless important indirect influences.

Symptoms

The symptoms of social phobia are somewhat different in children and adults, in that the early onset of social phobia typically means that children with the disorder fail to achieve at their predicted level, whereas adults and adolescents show declines from previously achieved levels of functioning.

SYMPTOMS IN CHILDREN. Symptoms of social phobia in children frequently include tantrums, crying, "freezing," clinging to parents or other familiar people, and inhibiting interactions to the point of refusing to talk to others (mutism).

SYMPTOMS IN ADULTS. The symptoms of social phobia in adults include a range of physical signs of anxiety as well as attitudes and behaviors.

- blushing, sweating, nausea, diarrhea, dry mouth, tremors, and other physical indications of anxiety
- difficulties with self-assertion
- extreme sensitivity to criticism, rejection, or negative evaluations
- intense preoccupation with the reactions and responses of others
- heightened fears of being embarrassed or humiliated
- avoidance of the feared situation(s) and anticipatory anxiety

In adults, there is often a "vicious circle" quality to the symptoms, in that the anxiety and symptoms lead to actual or perceived poor performances, which in turn increase the anxiety and avoidance. A common example is performance anxiety related to musical instruments; the person who is afraid of having to play the piano in a recital, for example, may become so anxious that the muscles in the hands become tense, thus producing frequent mistakes in fingering and sound production during the recital performance.

Not all adults with social phobia appear shy or outwardly nervous to other people. Some adults are able to force themselves to attend social events, give public presentations, or interact with others by self-medicating with alcohol or limiting the time period of their interactions. These strategies, however, prevent the underlying fears and disabilities from being addressed.

Diagnosis

The **diagnosis** of social phobia is usually made on the basis of the patient's history and reported symptoms. The doctor may also decide to administer diagnostic questionnaires intended to rule out other phobias, other anxiety disorders, and major depression. In diagnosing a child, the doctor will usually ask the child's parents, teachers, or others who know the child well for their observations.

Children and adolescents

A doctor who is evaluating a child for social phobia must take into account that children do not have the freedom that adults usually have to avoid the situations that frighten them. As a result, they may not be able to explain why they are anxious. It is important to evaluate the child's capacity for social relationships with people that he or she knows; and to assess his or her interactions with peers for indications of social phobia, not only his or her behavior around adults.

A semi-structured interview that a doctor can use to assess social phobia in children is the Anxiety Disorders Interview Schedule for Children (ADIS-C). A newer clinician-administered test is the Liebowitz Social Anxiety Scale for Children and Adolescents (LSAS-CA). Self-report inventories for children include the Child Depression Inventory (CDI), and the Social Phobia and Anxiety Inventory for Children (SPAI-C). Parents can be asked to complete the Child Behavior Checklist (CBL), and teachers may be given the Teacher's Report Form (TRF).

Adults

Diagnostic instruments for assessing social phobia in adults are more problematic. Some general screeners that are used in primary care settings, such as the **Structured Clinical Interview for DSM-IV** Screen (SCID-Screen), do include questions related to social phobia but can take as long as 25 minutes to administer. Others, such as the Primary Care Evaluation of Mental Disorders, or Prime-MD, are not specific for social phobia. Instruments designed to measure social phobia by itself, such as the

Fear of Negative Evaluation Scale and the Social Avoidance and Distress Scale, are lengthy and generally more useful for monitoring the progress of therapy. Another clinician-administered interview for social phobia in adults, the Liebowitz Social Anxiety Scale (LSAS), was not in widespread use as of 2011.

Many physicians, however, have found that the addition of a few selected questions to a general screener for mental disorders is helpful in detecting social phobia. One study found that giving patients three specific statements with yes/no answers detected 89% of cases of social phobia:

- Being embarrassed or looking stupid are among my worst fears.

- Fear of embarrassment causes me to avoid doing things or speaking to people.

- I avoid activities in which I am the center of attention.

Treatment

Social phobia responds well to proper treatment; however, patients with social phobia have a distinctive set of barriers to treatment. Unlike persons with some other types of mental disorders, they are unlikely to deny that they have a problem. What researchers have found is that in comparison to persons suffering from other disorders, persons with social phobia are significantly more likely to say that financial problems, uncertainty over where to go for help, and fear of what others might think prevent them from seeking treatment. The researchers concluded that providing better information about community services as well as easing the psychological and financial burdens of patients with social phobia would significantly improve their chances of recovery. Left untreated, social phobia can become a chronic, disabling disorder that increases the patient's risk of suicide.

Medications

About 53% of patients diagnosed with social phobia are treated with medications. Drug treatment has proven beneficial to patients with this disorder; however, no one type of medication appears to be clearly superior to others. Selection of a medication depends on the subtype of the patient's social phobia; the presence of other mental disorders; and the patient's occupation and personal preferences.

Specific medications that are used to treat social phobia include:

- Benzodiazepine tranquilizers. These are often prescribed for patients who need immediate relief from anxiety. They have two major drawbacks, however;

they are habit-forming, and they are unsuitable for patients with comorbid alcohol or substance abuse disorders. Benzodiazepines are, however, sometimes prescribed for patients who have a low risk for substance abuse and have not responded to other medications.

- Monoamine oxidase inhibitors (MAOIs). About two-thirds of patients with social phobia show significant improvement when treated with these drugs. MAOIs, however, have the disadvantage of requiring patients to stick to a low-tyramine diet that excludes many popular foods, and requiring them to avoid many over-the-counter cold and cough preparations.

- Selective serotonin reuptake inhibitors (SSRIs). About 50–75% of patients with social phobia benefit from treatment with SSRIs. The SSRIs appear to work best in patients with comorbid major depression or panic disorder. Sertraline (Zoloft) has been recommended for patients with generalized social phobia.

- Beta blockers. These medications, which include propranolol (Inderal), are given to patients with mild to moderate circumscribed performance anxiety to suppress the symptoms of panic. The patient takes the medication on an as-needed basis rather than a standing dosage, for instance, when facing a known trigger event (e.g., flying or speaking publicly). Beta-blockers do not appear to be helpful for patients with generalized social phobia.

- Botulism toxin. In conjunction with SSRIs, Botox is helpful for some patients to control sweating, a symptom of panic that may escalate the phobia.

- Alternative drugs. Anti-convulsant drugs such as gabapentin (Neurontin) and levetiracetam (Keppra) show promise as a treatment for social phobia.

Psychotherapy

The type of **psychotherapy** most commonly recommended for treatment of social phobia is **cognitive-behavioral therapy** (CBT). Mild to moderate cases of social phobia often show considerable improvement with CBT alone; patients with more severe social phobia benefit from a combination of CBT and an appropriate medication. Cognitive-behavioral treatment of adults diagnosed with social phobia usually combines exposure therapy with cognitive restructuring techniques. In exposure therapy, the patient is exposed to small "doses" of the feared situation that are gradually lengthened in time. The chief drawback to exposure therapy for social phobia is that some feared situations are easier to replicate for purposes of treatment than others. Patients who are afraid of public speaking or musical performance can practice performing in front of any group of people

QUESTIONS TO ASK YOUR DOCTOR

- What are the indications that I may have social phobia?
- What physical and psychiatric diagnostic tests do I need?
- What treatment options do you recommend for me?
- What kind of changes can I expect to see with the medications you have prescribed for me?
- What are the side effects associated with the medications you have prescribed for me?
- What tests or evaluation techniques will you perform to see if treatment has been beneficial for me?
- What actions or activities would you recommend for dealing with social phobia?
- What symptoms are important enough that I should seek immediate treatment?
- Can you recommend any support groups for me and my family?

that can be collected to help, but it is not so easy to arrange exposure sessions for a patient who is afraid of interactions with a specific teacher, employer, or supervisor. The other aspect of CBT that is used in treating social phobia in adults is cognitive restructuring. This approach challenges patients to reconsider and then replace the biased cognitions that have led them to overestimate the dangers in social situations and to underestimate his or her own resources for coping with them.

Several trial programs of CBT **group therapy** have been used with adolescents with social phobia. One pilot program situated the group meetings in the school rather than in a clinic, on the grounds that most of the fears of adolescents with social phobia revolve around school activities. Another CBT group for adolescents was conducted in a clinical setting. Both programs included **social skills training** alongside exposure therapy and cognitive restructuring, and both were reported to be moderately successful at one-year follow-up.

Other approaches

Other approaches that have been used to treat social phobia include **family therapy** and relaxation techniques.

Prognosis

The prognosis for recovery from social phobia is good, given early diagnosis and appropriate treatment. The prognosis for persons with untreated social phobia, however, is poor. In most cases, these individuals become long-term underachievers, at high risk for alcoholism, major depression, and suicide.

Prevention

Given that some of the factors implicated in social phobia are neurobiological or genetic, the best preventive strategy is early identification of children with behavioral inhibition and developing techniques for assisting their social development.

Resources

BOOKS

American Psychiatric Association. *Diagnostic and Statistical Manual of Mental Disorders.* 4th ed., text rev. Washington, DC: American Psychiatric Association, 2000.

Cooper, Rachel. *Classifying Madness: A Philosophical Examination of the Diagnostic and Statistical Manual of Mental Disorders.* New York: Springer, 2010.

Graham, George. *The Disordered Mind: An Introduction to Philosophy of Mind and Mental Illness.* New York: Routledge, 2010.

Heimberg, Richard G., et al., eds. *Social Phobia: Diagnosis, Assessment, and Treatment.* New York: Guilford Press, 2006.

Hofmann, Stefan. *Cognitive-Behavior Therapy of Social Phobia: Evidence-Based and Disorder-Specific Treatment Techniques.* Oxford: Routledge, 2007.

North, Carol, and Sean Yutzy. *Goodwin and Guze's Psychiatric Diagnosis.* New York: Oxford University Press, 2010.

Otto, Michal, and Stefan Hofmann, eds. *Avoiding Treatment Failures in the Anxiety Disorders (Series in Anxiety and Related Disorders).* New York: Springer, 2009.

Sadock, Benjamin J., and Virginia A. Sadock. *Kaplan & Sadock's Synopsis of Psychiatry.* 10th ed. New York: Lippincott, Williams and Wilkins, 2007.

Stravynski, Ariel. *Fearing Others: The Nature and Treatment of Social Phobia.* New York: Cambridge University Press, 2007.

PERIODICALS

Andersson, Gerhard, et al. "Internet-Based Self-Help with Therapist Feedback and in Vivo Group Exposure for Social Phobia: A Randomized Controlled Trial." *Journal of Consulting and Clinical Psychology* 74, no. 4 (2006): 677–86.

Black, Donald W. "Efficacy of Combined Pharmacotherapy and Psychotherapy versus Monotherapy in the Treatment of Anxiety Disorders." *CNS Spectrums* 11, no. 10 Suppl. 12 (2006): 29–33.

Smits, Jasper A., et al. "The Efficacy of Videotape Feedback for Enhancing the Effects of Exposure-Based Treatment for

Social Anxiety Disorder: A Controlled Investigation." *Behaviour Research and Therapy* 44, no. 12 (2006): 1773–85.

Voncken, Marisol J., et al. "Hiding Anxiety versus Acknowledgment of Anxiety in Social Interaction: Relationship with Social Anxiety." *Behaviour Research and Therapy* 44, no. 11 (2006): 1673–79.

ORGANIZATIONS

American Psychiatric Association, 1000 Wilson Blvd., Ste. 1825, Arlington, VA, 22209-3901, (703) 907-7300, apa@psych.org, http://www.psych.org.

American Psychological Association, 750 1st St. NE, Washington, DC, 20002-4242, (202) 336-5500, TDD/TTY: (202) 336-6123, (800) 374-2721, http://www.apa.org.

Anxiety Disorders Association of America, 8730 Georgia Ave., Silver Spring, MD, 20910, (240) 485-1001, Fax: (240) 485-1035, http://www.adaa.org.

Association for Behavioral and Cognitive Therapies, 305 7th Ave., 16th Fl., New York, NY, 10001, (212) 647-1890, Fax: (212) 647-1865, (866) 615-6464, http://www.abct.org.

Rebecca J. Frey, PhD
Laura Jean Cataldo, RN, EdD

Social skills training

Definition

Social skills training (SST) is a form of individual or **group therapy** used by teachers, therapists, and trainers to help those who need to learn to overcome inhibition or social ineffectiveness in their interactions with others. SST may use any of a number of techniques, including behavior rehearsal, cognitive rehearsal, and **assertiveness training**.

Purpose

Goals

One major goal of social skills training is to teach persons who may or may not have emotional problems about the verbal as well as nonverbal behaviors involved in social interactions. There are many people who have never been taught such interpersonal skills as making "small talk" in social settings, or the importance of good eye contact during a conversation. In addition, many people have not learned to "read" the many subtle cues contained in social interactions, such as how to tell when someone wants to change the topic of conversation or shift to another activity. Social skills training helps patients learn to interpret these and other social signals so they can determine how to act appropriately in the company of other people in a variety of different situations. SST proceeds on the assumption that when people improve their social skills or change selected behaviors, they will raise their self-esteem and increase the likelihood that others will respond favorably to them. Trainees learn to change their social behavior patterns by practicing selected behaviors in individual or group therapy sessions. Another goal of social skills training is to improve a patient's ability to function in everyday social situations. Social skills training can help patients to work on specific issues—for example, improving one's telephone manners—that interfere with their jobs or daily lives.

Treatment of specific disorders

A person who lacks certain social skills may have great difficulty building a network of supportive friends and acquaintances as he or she grows older, and may become socially isolated. Moreover, one of the consequences of loneliness is an increased risk of developing emotional problems or mental disorders. Social skills training has been shown to be effective in treating patients with a broad range of emotional problems and diagnoses. Some of the disorders treated by social skills trainers include **shyness**; **adjustment disorders**; marital and family conflicts, **anxiety disorders**, **attention deficit hyperactivity disorder**, **social phobia**, alcohol dependence; **depression**; **bipolar disorder**; **schizophrenia**; developmental disabilities; **avoidant personality disorder**; **paranoid personality disorder**; **obsessive-compulsive disorder**; and **schizotypal personality disorder**.

One specific example of the ways in which social skills training can be helpful is its application to alcohol dependence. In treating patients with alcohol dependence, a therapist who is using social skills training focuses on teaching the patients ways to avoid drinking when they go to parties where alcohol is served or when they find themselves in other situations in which others may pressure them to drink.

Another example is the application of social skills training to social phobia or shyness. People who suffer from social phobia or shyness are not ignorant of social cues, but they tend to avoid specific situations in which their limitations might cause them embarrassment. Social skills training can help these patients to improve their communication and social skills so that they will be able to mingle with others or go to job interviews with greater ease and self-confidence. Some studies indicate that the social skills training given to patients with shyness and social phobia can be applied to those with avoidant personality disorder, but more research is needed to differentiate among the particular types of social skills that benefit specific groups of patients, rather than treating social skills as a single entity. When trainers apply social skills training to the treatment of other **personality disorders**, they focus on the specific skills required to handle the issues that emerge with each disorder. For example, in the treatment of **obsessive-compulsive personality disorder** (OCD), social skills trainers focus on helping patients with OCD to deal with heavy responsibilities and **stress**.

People with disabilities in any age group can benefit from social skills training. Several studies demonstrate that children with developmental disabilities can acquire positive social skills with training. Extensive research on the effects of social skills training on children with attention deficit hyperactivity disorder shows that SST programs are effective in reducing these children's experiences of school failure or rejection as well as the aggressiveness and isolation that often develop in them because they have problems relating to others.

SST can be adapted to the treatment of depression with a focus on assertiveness training. Depressed patients often benefit from learning to set limits to others, to obtain satisfaction for their own needs, and to feel more self-confident in social interactions. Research suggests that patients who are depressed because they tend to withdraw from others can benefit from social skills training by learning to increase positive social interactions with others instead of pulling back.

There has been extensive research on the effective use of social skills training for the treatment of schizophrenia, in outpatient clinics as well as inpatient units. SST can be used to help patients with schizophrenia make better eye contact with other people, increase assertiveness, and improve their general conversational skills.

Social skills training with other therapies

Social skills training is often used in combination with other therapies in the treatment of mental disorders. For example, in the treatment of individuals with alcohol dependence, social skills training has been used together with cognitive restructuring and coping skills training. Social skills training has also been integrated with exposure therapy, cognitive restructuring, and medication in the treatment of social phobia. Social skills training has been used within **family therapy** itself in the treatment of marital and family conflicts. Moreover, SST works well together with medication for the treatment of depression. For the treatment of schizophrenia, social skills training has often been combined with pharmacotherapy, family therapy, and assertive **case management**.

Description

Techniques in social skills training

Therapists who use social skills training begin by breaking down complex social behaviors into smaller portions. Next, they arrange these smaller parts in order of difficulty, and gradually introduce them to the patients. For example, a therapist who is helping a patient learn to feel more comfortable at parties might make a list of specific behaviors that belong to the complex behavior called "acting appropriately at a party," such as introducing oneself to others; making conversation with several people at the party rather than just one other guest; keeping one's conversation pleasant and interesting; thanking the host or hostess before leaving; and so on. The patient would then work on one specific behavior at a time rather than trying to learn them all at once.

Such specific techniques as instruction, **modeling**, role-playing, shaping, feedback, and **reinforcement** of positive interactions may be used in SST. For example, instruction may be used to convey the differences among assertive, passive, and aggressive styles of communication. The technique of monitoring may be used to ask patients to increase their eye contact during a conversation. In role-playing exercises, group members have the opportunity to offer feedback to one another about their performances in simulated situations. For example, two members of the group may role-play a situation in which a customer is trying to return a defective purchase to a store. The others can then give feedback about the "customer's" assertiveness or the "clerk's" responses.

Content of social skills training

SST may be used to teach people specific sets of social competencies. A common focus of SST programs is communication skills. A program designed to improve people's skills in this area might include helping them with nonverbal and assertive communication and with making conversation. It might also include conversational skills that are needed in different specific situations; for example, job interviews, informal parties, and dating. The skills might be divided further into such subjects as beginning, holding, and ending conversations, or expressing feelings in appropriate ways.

Another common focus of SST programs involves improving a patient's ability to perceive and act on social cues. Many people have problems communicating with others because they fail to notice or do not understand other people's cues, whether verbal or nonverbal. For example, some children become unpopular with their peers because they force their way into small play groups, when a child who has learned to read social signals would know that the children in the small group do not want someone else to join them, at least not at that moment. Learning to understand another person's spoken or unspoken messages is as important as learning conversational skills. A social skills program may include skills related to the perceptual processing of the conversation of other individuals.

Scheduling

Social skills training may be given as an individual or as a group treatment once or twice a week, or more often depending upon the severity of a patient's disorder and the level of his or her social skills. Generally speaking, children appear to gain more from SST in a peer group setting than in individual therapy. Social skill training groups usually consist of approximately 10 patients, a therapist, and a cotherapist.

Cultural and gender issues

Social skills training programs may be modified somewhat to allow for cultural and gender differences. For example, eye contact is a frequently targeted behavior to be taught during social skills training. In some cultures, however, downcast eyes are a sign of respect rather than an indication of social anxiety or shyness. In addition, girls or women in some cultures may be considered immodest if they look at others, particularly adult males, too directly. These modifications can usually be made without changing the basic format of the SST program.

Generalization or transfer of skills

Current trends in social skills training are aimed at developing training programs that meet the demands of specific roles or situations. This need developed from studies that found that social skills acquired in one setting or situation are not easily generalized or transferred to another setting or situation. To assist patients in using their new skills in real-life situations, trainers use role-playing, teaching, modeling, and practice.

Precautions

Social skills training should rest on an objective assessment of the patient's actual problems in relating to other people.

It is important for therapists who are using SST to move slowly so that the patient is not overwhelmed by trying to change too many behaviors at one time.

KEY TERMS

Antisocial—Behaving in ways that purposefully disregard the rights of others and break society's rules or laws.

Antisocial behavior—Behavior that differs significantly from the norms of society and is considered harmful to society.

Anxiety disorder—A group of conditions that cause people to feel extreme fear or worry that sometimes is accompanied by symptoms such as dizziness, chest pain, or difficulty sleeping or concentrating.

Attention deficit hyperactivity disorder (ADHD)—A condition that makes it hard for a person to pay attention, sit still, or think before acting.

Obsessive-compulsive disorder (OCD)—A condition that causes people to become trapped in a pattern of repeated, unwanted thoughts, called "obsessions," and a pattern of repetitive behaviors, called "compulsions."

Schizophrenia—A serious mental disorder that causes people to experience hallucinations, delusions, and other confusing thoughts and behaviors, which distort their view of reality.

Social phobia—An anxiety disorder characterized by a strong and persistent fear of social or performance situations in which the patient might feel embarrassment or humiliation.

In addition, social skill trainers should be careful not to intensify the patient's feelings of social incompetence. This caution is particularly important in treating patients with social phobia, who are already worried about others' opinions of them.

One additional precaution is related to the transfer of social skills from the therapy setting to real-life situations. This transfer is called "generalization" or "maintenance." Generalization takes place more readily when the social skills training has a clear focus and the patient is highly motivated to reach a realistic goal. In addition, social skills trainers should be sure that the new skills being taught are suitable for the specific patients involved.

Preparation

Preparation for social skills training requires tact on the therapist's part, as patients with such disorders as social phobia or paranoid personality disorder may be discouraged or upset by being told that they need help with their social skills. One possible approach is through reading. The social skills therapist may recommend some self-help books on social skills in preparation for the treatment. Second, the therapist can ease the patient's self-consciousness or embarrassment by explaining that no one has perfect social skills. One additional consideration before starting treatment is the possibility of interference from medication side effects. The therapist will usually ask the patient for a list of all medications that he or she takes regularly.

One of the most critical tasks in preparation for social skills training is the selection of suitable target behaviors. It is often more helpful for the therapist to ask the patient to identify behaviors that he or she would like to change, rather than pointing to problem areas that the therapist has identified. The treatment should consider the patient's particular needs and interests. Whereas social skills training for some patients may include learning assertiveness on the job, training for others may include learning strategies for dating. Therapists can prepare patients for homework by explaining that the homework is the practice of new skills in other settings; and that it is as relevant as the therapy session itself.

Aftercare

Some studies strongly suggest the need for follow-up support after an initial course of social skills training. One study showed that follow-up support doubled the rate of employment for a group of patients with schizophrenia, compared to a group that had no follow-up.

Results

Outcome studies indicate that social skills training has moderate short-term effects but limited long-term effects. SST programs that include social perspective-taking may have greater long-term effects than traditional SST programs based on cognitive-behavioral models. In general, social skills training tends to generalize or transfer to similar contexts rather than to contexts that are not similar to the training. SST programs for patients with developmental disabilities should include programming for generalization so that the patients can transfer their newly acquired skills more effectively to real-life settings. One approach to improving generalization is to situate the training exercises within the patient's work, living, or social environment.

One of the benefits of social skills training programs is flexibility. The treatment can take place either as individual or group therapy, and new trainers can learn the techniques of SST fairly quickly. One additional advantage of SST is that it focuses on teaching skills that can be learned rather than emphasizing the internal or biological determinants of social adequacy. Future research should explore the integration of social skills training with the needs of families from different cultural backgrounds; the relationship between social skills training and different categories of mental disorders; the transfer of skills from therapeutic contexts to daily life; and improving patients' long-term gains from SST.

Resources

BOOKS

Center, Frostig. *The Six Success Factors for Children with Learning Disabilities: Ready-to-Use Activities to Help Kids with LD Succeed in School and in Life.* New York: Jossey-Bass, 2009.

Taffe, Richard. *Social Skills Training with Aggressive-Rejected Children.* Saarbrücken, Germany: Lambert Academic Publishing, 2010.

VandenBos, Gary R., ed. *APA Concise Dictionary of Psychology.* Washington D.C.: American Psychological Association, 2009.

White, Susan Williams, PhD. *Social Skills Training for Children with Asperger Syndrome and High-Functioning Autism.* New York: The Guilford Press, 2011.

PERIODICALS

Chronis, Andrea M., Heather A. Jones, and Veronica L. Raggi. "Evidence-Based Psychosocial Treatments for Children and Adolescents with Attention-Deficit/Hyperactivity Disorder." *Clinical Psychology Review* 26, no. 4 (June 2006): 486–502.

de Boo, Gerly M., and Pier J. M. Prins. "Social Incompetence in Children with ADHD: Possible Moderators and Mediators in Social-Skills Training." *Clinical Psychology Review* 27, no. 1 (January 2007): 78–97.

Fenstermacher, Kevin, Daniel Olympia, and Susan M. Sheridan. "Effectiveness of a Computer-Facilitated Interactive Social Skills Training Program for Boys with Attention Deficit Hyperactivity Disorder." *School Psychology Quarterly* 21, no. 2 (Summer 2006): 197–224.

Gresham, Frank M., Mai Bao Van, and Clayton R. Cook. "Social Skills Training for Teaching Replacement Behaviors: Remediating Acquisition Deficits in At-Risk Students." *Behavioral Disorders* 31, no. 4 (August 2006): 363–77.

Konstantareas, M. Mary. "Social Skills Training in High Functioning Autism and Asperger's Disorder." *Hellenic Journal of Psychology* 3, no. 1 (April 2006) 39–56.

Kopelowicz, Alex, Robert Paul Liberman, and Roberto Zarate. "Recent Advances in Social Skills Training for Schizophrenia." *Schizophrenia Bulletin* 32, Supplement 1, (October 2006): S12–23.

Pfammatter, Mario; Junghan, Ulrich Martin, and Hans Dieter Brenner. "Efficacy of Psychological Therapy in

Schizophrenia: Conclusions From Meta-Analyses." *Schizophrenia Bulletin* 32, Supplement 1, (October 2006): S64–80.

Sim, Leslie, et al. "Effectiveness of a Social Skills Training Program with School Age Children: Transition to the Clinical Setting." *Journal of Child and Family Studies* 15, no. 4 (August 2006): 409–18.

ORGANIZATIONS

American Psychiatric Association, 1000 Wilson Blvd., Ste. 1825, Arlington, VA, 22209-3901, (703) 907-7300, apa@psych.org, http://www.psych.org.

American Psychological Association, 750 1st St. NE, Washington, DC, 20002-4242, (202) 336-5500; TDD/TTY: (202) 336-6123, (800) 374-2721, http://www.apa.org.

Judy Koenigsberg, Ph.D.
Ruth A. Wienclaw, Ph.D.
Laura Jean Cataldo, RN, Ed.D.

Social workers

Definition

A social worker is a helping professional who is distinguished from other human service professionals by a focus on both the individual and his or her environment. Generally, social workers have at least a bachelor's degree from an accredited education program and in most states they must be licensed, certified, or registered. A Master's in Social Work is required for those who provide **psychotherapy** or work in specific settings such as hospitals or nursing homes.

Description

Social workers comprise a profession that had its beginnings in 1889 when Jane Addams founded Hull House and the American settlement house movement in Chicago's West Side. The ethics and values that informed her work became the basis for the social work profession. They include respect for the dignity of human beings, especially those who are vulnerable, an understanding that people are influenced by their environment, and a desire to work for social change that rectifies gross or unjust differences.

The social work profession is broader than most disciplines with regard to the range and types of problems addressed, the settings in which the work takes place, the levels of practice, interventions used, and populations served. It has been observed that social work is defined in its own place in the larger social environment, continuously evolving to respond to and address a changing world. Although several definitions of social work have been provided throughout its history, common to all definitions is the focus on both the individual and the environment, distinguishing it from other helping professions.

Social workers may be engaged in a variety of occupations ranging from hospitals, schools, clinics, police departments, public agencies, court systems to private practices or businesses. They provide the majority of mental health care to persons of all ages in this country, and in rural areas they are often the sole providers of services. In general, they assist people to obtain tangible services; help communities or groups provide or improve social and health services; provide counseling and psychotherapy with individuals, families, and groups; and participate in policy change through legislative processes. The practice of social work requires knowledge of human development and behavior; of social, economic and cultural institutions; and of the interaction of all these factors.

Resources

PERIODICALS

Gibelman, Margaret. "The Search for Identity: Defining Social Work—Past, Present, Future." *Social Work* 44, no. 4 (July 1999).

WEBSITES

National Association of Social Workers. "Choices: Careers in Social Work" (2011). http://www.naswdc.org/pubs/choices/choices.htm (accessed October 27, 2011).

ORGANIZATIONS

National Association of Social Workers, 750 First St. NE, Ste. 700, Washington, DC, 20002-4241, (202) 408-8600, http://www.naswdc.org.

Judy Leaver, M.A.

Sodium amobarbital *see* **Barbiturates**
Sodium pentobarbital *see* **Barbiturates**

Somatization disorder

Definition

Somatization disorder is a psychiatric condition marked by multiple medically unexplained physical, or somatic, symptoms. In order to qualify for the **diagnosis** of somatization disorder, somatic complaints must be serious enough to interfere significantly with a person's ability to perform important activities, such as work, school, or family and social responsibilities, or lead the person experiencing the symptoms to seek medical treatment.

Somatization disorder has long been recognized by psychiatrists and psychologists and was originally called Briquet's syndrome in honor of Paul Briquet, a French physician who first described the disorder in the nineteenth century. It is included in the category of somatic symptom disorders in the **Diagnostic and Statistical Manual of Mental Disorders**, the professional handbook that aids clinicians in diagnosing mental disorders. Somatic symptom disorders are characterized as disorders with psychological origins that manifest in physical symptoms.

Demographics

According to the *DSM-IV-TR* (fourth edition, text revised), somatization disorder is rare in males in the United States, although higher rates are seen among males from some cultural and ethnic groups. The *DSM-IV-TR* estimates that between 0.2% and 2% of women and less than 0.2% of men suffer from somatization disorder in the United States. Sex ratios may arise from different rates of seeking treatment. However, studies of unexplained somatic symptoms in the general population find less striking differences in rates between men and women. Specific symptoms may vary across cultures. For example, the *DSM-IV-TR* notes that the sensation of worms in the head or ants crawling under the skin are sometimes reported in African and South Asian countries, but rarely seen in North American patients.

Description

Individuals with somatization disorder suffer from a number of vague physical symptoms, involving at least four different physical functions or parts of the body. The physical symptoms that characterize somatization disorder cannot be attributed to medical conditions or to the use of drugs, and individuals with somatization disorder often undergo numerous medical tests (with negative results) before the psychological cause of their distress is identified. Symptoms are often described as burning sensations, pains that move from place to place, strange tastes on the tongue, tingling, or tremors. While many symptoms resemble those associated with genuine diseases, some of the symptoms reported by people with somatization disorder are not. The individual usually visits many different physicians in hopes of finding a treatment but may be met with several different results or diagnoses. This can be dangerous if the patient ends up taking several different medications, which risks harmful drug interactions.

While the physical symptoms of somatization disorder frequently lack medical explanations, they are not fabricated by the patient. A person with somatization disorder has suffered from physical pain, discomfort, and dysfunction for an extended period of time and wishes to identify the cause of their illness and find relief.

Causes and symptoms

Causes

DEFENSE AGAINST PSYCHOLOGICAL DISTRESS. One of the oldest theories about the cause of somatization disorder suggests that it is a way of avoiding psychological distress. Rather than experiencing **depression** or anxiety, some individuals will develop physical symptoms. According to this model, somatization disorder is a defense against psychological pain that allows some people to avoid the **stigma** of a psychiatric diagnosis. While getting the care and nurturing they need from doctors and others who are responsive to their apparent medical illnesses, many patients are encouraged to continue their manipulative behavior.

Many patients described by Sigmund Freud would be diagnosed today with somatization disorder. His patients were usually young women who complained of numerous physical symptoms. In the process of speaking with Freud, they would often recall a number of distressing memories; discussing these memories frequently led to the relief of physical symptoms. These cases formed the foundation of Freud's psychoanalytic treatment. Although this theory offers a plausible explanation for somatization disorder, research indicates that people with multiple physical symptoms are actually more likely to report psychiatric symptoms than those with few physical problems. These findings appear to support a connection between psychological and physical distress, but are inconsistent with the idea that physical symptoms offer a defense against overt psychiatric symptoms.

HEIGHTENED SENSITIVITY. An alternative theory suggests that somatization disorder arises from a heightened sensitivity to internal sensations. People with somatization disorder may be keenly aware of the minor pains and discomforts that most people simply ignore. A similar theory has been offered to account for **panic disorder**. Studies have shown that people with panic disorder are particularly sensitive to internal sensations like breathing rate and heartbeats, which may lead them to react with intense fear to minor internal changes. The physiological or psychological origins of this hypersensitivity to internal sensations and their relevance to somatization disorder are still not well understood.

CATASTROPHIC THINKING. According to this theory, somatization disorder results from negative beliefs and exaggerated fears about the significance of physical sensations. Individuals with somatization disorder are more likely to believe that vague physical symptoms are indicators of serious disease and to seek treatment for them. For instance, someone with somatization disorder may fear that a headache signals a **brain** tumor, or that shortness of breath indicates the onset of asthma. When their doctors can find no medical explanation for the symptoms, the patients may fear that they have a rare disease; they frantically look for specialists who can provide a diagnosis. Anxiety causes them to focus even more intensely on their symptoms, which in turn become more salient and disabling. Many people with somatization disorder reduce or eliminate many activities out of fear that exertion will worsen their symptoms. With fewer activities to distract them from their symptoms, they spend more time worrying about physical problems, resulting in greater distress and disability.

Symptoms

Gastrointestinal (GI) complaints, such as nausea, bloating, diarrhea, and sensitivities to certain foods are common, and at least two different GI symptoms are required for the diagnosis. Sexual or reproductive symptoms, including pain during intercourse, menstrual problems, and **erectile dysfunction** are also necessary features for a diagnosis of somatization disorder. Other frequent symptoms are headaches, pain in the back or joints, difficulty swallowing or speaking, and urinary retention. To qualify for the diagnosis, at least one symptom must resemble a neurological disorder, such as **seizures**, problems with coordination or balance, or paralysis.

Diagnosis

To meet the *DSM-IV-TR* diagnostic criteria for somatization disorder, the patient must have a history of multiple physical complaints that began before age 30 and continued for several years. These symptoms must cause significant impairment to social, occupational, or other areas of functioning or lead the patient to seek medical treatment.

The *DSM-IV-TR* also specifies the following:

- The individual must report a history of pain affecting at least four different parts or functions of the body. Examples include headaches, back, joint, chest or abdominal pain, or pain during menstruation or sexual intercourse.

- A history of at least two gastrointestinal symptoms, such as nausea, bloating, vomiting, diarrhea, or food intolerance must be reported.

- There must be a history of at least one sexual or reproductive symptom, such as lack of interest in sex, problems achieving erection or ejaculation, irregular menstrual periods, excessive menstrual bleeding, or vomiting throughout pregnancy.

- One symptom must mimic a neurological condition. Examples include weakness; paralysis; problems with balance or coordination; seizures; hallucinations; loss of sensations such as touch, seeing, hearing, tasting, or smelling; difficulty swallowing or speaking; or amnesia and loss of consciousness. Pseudo-neurologic symptoms like these are the primary characteristics of another somatoform disorder known as conversion disorder.

If a thorough medical evaluation reveals no evidence of an underlying medical or drug- or medication-induced condition, the diagnosis of somatization disorder is likely. People with genuine medical conditions can qualify for the diagnosis if the level of functional impairment reported is more than would be expected based on medical findings. The symptoms must not be intentionally produced. If the patient is feigning symptoms, a diagnosis of **factitious disorder** or **malingering** would most likely be considered.

DSM-5

Revisions for the fifth edition of the *DSM* (*DSM-5*, 2013) propose subsuming the symptoms of somatization disorder into the diagnosis of complex somatic symptom disorder, which will also include the diagnoses of **hypochondriasis** and **pain disorder**. Proposed criteria include experiencing at least one somatic symptom that significantly interferes with the patient's daily life; excessive occupation with the symptom(s), such as obsessive anxiety or worry over the cause; and occurrence of the symptom(s) for at least six months.

Treatment

Cognitive behavior therapy

Cognitive-behavioral therapy (CBT) for somatization disorder focuses on changing negative patterns of thoughts, feelings, or behaviors that contribute to somatic symptoms. The cognitive component of the treatment focuses on helping patients identify dysfunctional thinking about physical sensations. With practice, patients learn to recognize catastrophic thinking and develop more rational explanations for their feelings. The behavioral component aims to increase activity. Patients with somatization

KEY TERMS

Factitious disorder—A feigned disorder in which the physical or psychological symptoms are controlled or produced by the patient.

Malingering—Pretending to be sick in order to be relieved of an unwanted duty or obtain some other obvious benefit.

disorder have usually reduced their activity levels as a result of discomfort or out of fear that activity will worsen symptoms. CBT patients are instructed to increase activity gradually while avoiding overexertion that could reinforce fears. Other important types of treatment include relaxation training, sleep hygiene, and communication skills training. Preliminary findings suggest that CBT may help reduce distress and discomfort associated with somatic symptoms; however, it has not yet been systematically compared with other forms of therapy.

Medications

Antidepressant medications may help to alleviate symptoms of somatization disorder. According to one study, patients with somatization disorder who took the antidepressant **nefazodone** (Serzone) showed reductions in physical symptoms, increased activity levels, and lower levels of anxiety and depression at the end of treatment.

Prognosis

Untreated somatization disorder is usually a chronic condition, though specific symptoms can come and go and severity may fluctuate over time. Somatization disorder poses a serious problem for society, since many who suffer from it become functionally disabled and unable to work. In addition, patients with unexplained physical symptoms strain already overburdened healthcare resources. Unexplained physical symptoms are extremely common among patients visiting general practitioners, with some estimates suggesting that more than two-thirds of general medical patients have symptoms that cannot be explained by medical tests. Fortunately, there is preliminary evidence that **psychotherapy** and medication can effectively reduce symptoms and disability.

Prevention

Greater awareness of somatization disorder, particularly among physicians, can help identify individuals with somatization disorder and deliver appropriate psychological or psychiatric treatments.

Resources

BOOKS

American Psychiatric Association. *Diagnostic and Statistical Manual of Mental Disorders*. 4th ed., text rev. Washington, DC: American Psychiatric Publishing, 2000.

Breuer, Josef, and Sigmund Freud. *Studies on Hysteria*. New York: Basic Books, 2000.

Butcher, James N., and Carolyn L. Williams. *Essentials of MMPI2 and MMPIA Interpretation*. 2nd ed. Minneapolis: University of Minnesota Press, 2000.

PERIODICALS

Allen, Lesley A., et al. "Cognitive Behavior Therapy for Somatization Disorder: A Preliminary Investigation." *Journal of Behaviour Therapy and Experimental Psychiatry* 32, no. 2 (June 2001): 53–62.

Cameron, Oliver G. "Interoception: The Inside Story—A Model for Psychosomatic Process." *Psychosomatic Medicine* 63 (2001): 697–710.

Hotopf, Matthew, Michael Wadsworth, and Simon Wessely. "Is 'Somatisation' a Defense Against the Acknowledgement of Psychiatric Disorder?" *Journal of Psychosomatic Research* 50 (2001): 119–124.

Menza, Matthew, et al. "Treatment of Somatization Disorder with Nefazodone: A Prospective, Open-label Study." *Annals of Clinical Psychiatry* 13, no. 3 (September 2001): 153–158.

Nimnuan, Chaichana, Matthew Hotopf, and Simon Wessely. "Medically Unexplained Symptoms: An Epidemiological Study in Seven Specialties." *Journal of Psychosomatic Research* 51 (2001): 361–367.

Rief, Winfred, Aike Hessel, and Elmar Braehler. "Somatization Symptoms and Hypochondriacal Features in the General Population." *Psychosomatic Medicine* 63 (2001): 595–602.

Danielle Barry, M.S.

Somatoform disorders

Definition

Somatoform disorders are a group of disorders characterized by the occurrence of somatization, a term that describes the expression of psychological or mental difficulties through physical symptoms. Somatization takes a number of forms, ranging from preoccupation with potential or genuine but mild physical problems to the development of actual physical pain, discomfort, or dysfunction. Somatization appears to be fairly common, but a somatoform disorder **diagnosis** is not warranted unless symptoms cause significant distress or disability.

Description

Somatization disorder is characterized by a history of multiple unexplained medical problems or physical complaints beginning prior to age 30. In the nineteenth and early twentieth centuries, somatization disorder was known as Briquet's syndrome or hysteria—a more generic term for such a condition. People with somatization disorder report symptoms affecting multiple organ systems or physical functions, including pain, gastrointestinal distress, sexual problems, and symptoms that mimic neurological disorders. Although medical explanations for their symptoms cannot be identified, individuals with somatization disorder experience genuine physical discomfort and distress. Review of their medical histories will usually reveal visits to a number of medical specialists, and many patients take numerous medications prescribed by different doctors, running the risk of dangerous drug interactions.

DSM-IV-TR

The revised fourth edition of the *Diagnostic and Statistical Manual of Mental Disorders* (*DSM-IV-TR*), the professional handbook clinicians use to diagnose mental disorders, describes seven disorders under the category of somatoform disorders. These disorders are somatization disorder, **undifferentiated somatoform disorder**, **conversion disorder**, **pain disorder**, **hypochondriasis**, **body dysmorphic disorder**, and somatoform disorder not otherwise specified.

- Undifferentiated somatoform disorder is similar to somatization disorder but may involve fewer symptoms, have a shorter duration, or begin after the age of 30. Common symptoms include chronic fatigue, loss of appetite, gastrointestinal distress, or problems involving the genitals or urinary tract. This diagnosis is appropriate for patients with symptoms of somatization disorder who do not meet all diagnostic criteria.

- Conversion disorder is marked by unexplained sensory or motor symptoms that resemble those of a neurological or medical illness or injury. Common symptoms include paralysis, loss of sensation, double vision, seizures, inability to speak or swallow, and problems with coordination and balance. Symptoms often reflect a naive understanding of the nervous system, and physicians often detect conversion disorder when symptoms do not make sense anatomically. For instance, a patient may report loss of both touch and pain sensation on one side of the body, when a genuine lesion would result in loss of touch and pain

sense on opposite sides of the body. The name conversion disorder reflects a theoretical understanding of the disorder as a symbolic conversion of a psychological conflict into a concrete physical representation. Patients with conversion disorder may not express the level of distress one would expect from someone with a disabling neurological condition. This phenomenon is traditionally called *la belle indifference*.

- The primary feature of pain disorder is physical pain that causes significant distress or disability or leads an individual to seek medical attention. Pain may be medically unexplained, or it may be associated with an identifiable medical condition but manifest more severely than the condition would warrant. Common symptoms include headache, backache, and generalized pain in muscles and joints. Pain disorder can be severely disabling, causing immobility that prevents patients from working, fulfilling family responsibilities, or engaging in social activities. Like patients with somatization disorder, people with pain disorder often have a history of consultations with numerous physicians.

- Hypochondriasis is diagnosed when a person is excessively concerned by fears of having a physical disease or injury. Individuals with hypochondriasis usually do not complain of disabling or painful symptoms. Instead, they tend to overreact to minor physical symptoms or sensations, like rapid heartbeat, sweating, small sores or fatigue. Many people with hypochondriasis develop fears in response to the illness or death of a friend or family member, or after reading about a condition or seeing a feature on television. Hypochondriacal fears can be confined to a single disease or involve a number of different physical concerns. Individuals with hypochondriasis seek frequent reassurance by consulting with physicians or talking about their fears, yet these efforts provide only temporary relief from their fears. Although hypochondriasis is usually not as disabling as somatoform disorders involving the development of actual physical symptoms, it can put stress on relationships or reduce work productivity through time lost to frequent medical appointments and tests.

- Body dysmorphic disorder is characterized by preoccupation with a defect in physical appearance. Often the defect of concern is not apparent to other observers, or if there is a genuine defect, it is far less disfiguring than the patient imagines. Common preoccupations include concerns about the size or shape of the nose, skin blemishes, body or facial hair, hair loss, or "ugly" hands or feet. Individuals with body dysmorphic disorder may be extremely self-conscious, avoiding social situations because they fear others will notice their physical defects or even make fun of them. They may spend hours examining the imagined defect or avoid mirrors altogether. Time-consuming efforts to hide the defect, such as application of cosmetics or adjustments of clothing or hair, are common. Many people with body dysmorphic disorder undergo procedures like plastic surgery or cosmetic dentistry, but are seldom satisfied with the results.

- Somatoform disorder not otherwise specified is diagnosed when somatoform symptoms are present but criteria for another somatoform disorder are not met. *DSM-IV-TR* includes several examples of symptoms that could merit this diagnosis, including false pregnancy and hypochondriacal fears or unexplained physical symptoms of recent onset or short duration.

DSM-5

There is some disagreement among researchers about the *DSM-IV-TR* somatoform disorders category. Some have argued that hypochondriasis and body dysmorphic disorder are more similar to obsessive compulsive disorder than to other somatoform disorders, while others think hypochondriasis may be more appropriately classified with the **anxiety disorders**. Proposed changes for the fifth edition of the *DSM* (*DSM-5*, 2013) have addressed some of these concerns by reorganizing the category of somatoform disorders under the new name of somatic symptom disorders. If approved, the new category will include seven disorders, with body dysmorphic disorder moved to the category of obsessive-compulsive and related disorders:

- complex somatic symptom disorder (subsumes diagnoses of pain disorder, somatization disorder, undifferentiated somatoform disorder, and some aspects of hypochondriasis)
- simple somatic symptom disorder (includes previous diagnosis of somatoform disorder not otherwise specified)
- illness anxiety disorder (hypochondriasis)
- functional neurological disorder (conversion disorder)
- psychological factors affecting medical condition
- other specified somatic symptom disorder
- unspecified somatic symptom disorder

Resources

BOOKS

American Psychiatric Association. *Diagnostic and Statistical Manual of Mental Disorders.* 4th ed., text rev. Washington, DC: American Psychiatric Publishing, 2000.

Phillips, Katherine A. *The Broken Mirror: Understanding and Treating Body Dysmorphic Disorder.* New York: Oxford University Press, 2005.

Pilowsky, Issy. *Abnormal Illness Behaviour.* Chichester, UK: John Wiley and Sons, 1997.

PERIODICALS

Neziroglu, Fugen, Dean McKay, and Jose A. Yaryura-Tobias. "Overlapping and Distinctive Features of Hypochondriasis and Obsessive-Compulsive Disorder." *Journal of Anxiety Disorders* 14, no. 6 (November–December 2000): 603–614.

Danielle Barry, M.S.

Somnambulism *see* **Sleepwalking disorder**

Somnote *see* **Chloral hydrate**

Sonata *see* **Zaleplon**

Specific phobias

Definition

Specific phobia is a disorder in which the affected individual displays a marked and enduring fear of specific situations or objects. The *Diagnostic and Statistical Manual of Mental Disorders, Fourth Edition Text Revision* (*DSM-IV-TR*), used by mental health professionals to diagnose mental disorders, classifies specific phobia as a type of anxiety disorder. Formerly, specific phobia was known as simple phobia.

Demographics

Specific phobias are common. The prevalence rates of specific phobia in community samples range from 4–8%. Over the course of a lifetime, the prevalence estimates in community samples range from 7.2–11.3%. Individuals whose family members have specific phobia are at a higher risk for developing this disorder.

There are approximately twice as many women with specific phobia as there are men with this disorder. The specific gender ratio variable varies depending upon the type of specific phobia. Approximately 75–90% of people with the animal, situational, and natural environment triggers are female. Approximately 55–70% of people with the blood-injection-injury subtype are female. For height phobias, there is a reduced ration of women to men, although the phobias are still more common in women. Illness phobias are more common in men.

Description

Specific phobia has a unique position among the **anxiety disorders** in that individuals with this disorder do not experience pervasive anxiety, nor do they seek treatment as readily as individuals with other anxiety disorders. Unlike individuals with other anxiety disorders, individuals with specific phobias experience extreme fear as soon as they encounter a defined situation or object, a phobic stimulus. For example, an individual with a specific phobia of dogs will become extremely anxious when confronting a dog. Individuals with specific phobias experience impairment or a significant amount of anguish. They may lead restricted lifestyles depending upon the phobia trigger. Adults and adolescents with specific phobias recognize that their fear is unreasonable. Children, by contrast, may not recognize that their fear of the phobic stimulus is unreasonable or extreme.

Types of specific phobias include situational, object, and other. Situational specific phobia is diagnosed if an individual's fear is triggered by a defined situation, such as flying, enclosed places, tunnels, driving, bridges, elevators, or using public transportation. Object specific phobias include animal, natural environment, and blood-injection-injury type triggers. Animal type is diagnosed if an individual's fear is triggered by animals or insects. Natural environment type is diagnosed if an individual's fear is cued by storms, water, or heights. Blood-injection-injury type is diagnosed if an individual's fear is cued by seeing an injury or blood or by an injection or other invasive medical treatment. Other type specific phobia is diagnosed if an individual's fear is triggered by other stimuli such as fear of vomiting, choking, becoming ill, falling down if far from a means of physical support, and a child's fears of loud noises or characters in costume.

Researchers have found that the frequency of type for adults in clinical settings, from least to most frequent, is: animal, blood-injection-injury, natural environment, and situational. The most common phobias for community samples, however, are phobias of heights, mice, spiders, and insects.

Causes and symptoms

There are numerous causes for specific phobias, and the symptoms are also numerous.

Causes

The development of a specific phobia may be determined by a variety of factors. Behavioral, cognitive, and social theories of learning and conditioning, psychodynamic models such as the psychoanalytic theory of Freud, physiological studies of the **brain**, family background, and genetic predisposition, variations in sociocultural themes, and **trauma** can influence the development of specific phobia disorder. In some cases, a specific traumatic event triggers the development of a

specific phobia; however, in most cases no single underlying cause can be pinpointed.

LEARNING AND CONDITIONING CAUSES. As of 2011, research on phobias focused primarily on information processing, learning, and conditioning themes. Learning to experience fear is the core of a conditioning perspective. Informational and instructional factors can result in the formation of fears. For example, an individual who frequently hears of plane crashes in the news may develop a specific phobia of flying. Research shows that individuals with specific phobias pay more attention to information about danger than do individuals who do not have specific phobias. Vicarious acquisition occurs when an individual witnesses a traumatic event or sees another individual behave with fear when confronting a phobic stimulus. Direct conditioning occurs when an individual is frightened by a phobic stimulus.

A major determinant of specific phobias is conditioning. Association and avoidance are types of conditioning. In association conditioning, a stimulus that was initially neutral begins to trigger an anxiety response. For example, if an individual is driving one day and experiences a strong anxiety response, an association may form between driving and anxiety. Individuals do not become phobic until they begin to avoid. In avoidance conditioning, individuals learn to avoid a stimulus that triggers anxiety. Every time individuals avoid the phobic stimulus, driving, for example, they are rewarded by the relief from anxiety.

TRAUMATIC CAUSES. Another determinant of specific phobias is trauma. For example, individuals who have been attacked by a dog may develop a specific phobia disorder and become conditioned to fear dogs. Individuals who observe others experiencing a trauma also may be more likely to develop specific phobia disorder. For example, individuals who witness people falling from a building may develop a specific phobia disorder of falling from heights. Phobias with a traumatic origin may have a sudden onset and develop rapidly.

PHYSIOLOGICAL CAUSES. Some research has suggested that the high activation of brain pathways that correspond to the cognitive and emotional constituents of anxiety biologically predispose individuals to specific phobias.

GENETIC AND FAMILY CAUSES. Although specific phobia is frequently attributed to environmental causes such as **modeling**, learning by association, and negative **reinforcement**, genetic predisposition can influence this disorder. An individual who has a family member with a specific phobia is at an increased risk for developing this disorder. Some research indicates that the pattern of types is similar within families. For example, a first-degree

KEY TERMS

Agoraphobia—Abnormal anxiety regarding public places or situations from which the individual may feel compelled to flee or in which he or she would be helpless in the event of a panic attack.

Beta blocker—An anti-hypertensive (blood pressure-lowering) drug that limits the activity of epinephrine, a hormone that increases blood pressure.

Cognitive-behavioral therapy—A type of psychotherapy in which people learn to recognize and change negative and self-defeating patterns of thinking and behavior.

Hypochondriasis—An anxiety disorder in which the individual believes real or imagined symptoms are indicative of a serious or life-threatening illness or condition.

Schizophrenia—A severe mental disorder in which a person loses touch with reality and may have illogical thoughts, delusions, hallucinations, behavioral problems and other disturbances.

biological relative of individuals with a situational type phobia is more likely to have a situational phobia. Studies indicate that the blood and injury phobias have strong familial patterns.

SOCIOCULTURAL CAUSES. There is not much information about cultural differences in specific phobias. Phobia content may vary by culture. Fear of a phobic stimulus such as magic or spirits, present in several cultures, is diagnosed as a specific phobia only if the fear is excessive for a particular culture and if the fear triggers major distress or interferes with functioning. Some research indicates that African Americans are more likely than whites to report specific phobias. Some studies show that specific phobias are less common among whites born in the United States and immigrant Mexican Americans than among Mexican Americans born in the United States. Research suggests mixed data with regard to the role of socioeconomic status, with some data associating specific phobia disorder with a lower socioeconomic level.

PERSONAL VARIABLES. Studies suggest a relationship between age and specific phobia. Research indicates some connections between the age of individuals with specific phobias and insight into the extreme quality of their fears. Insight increases with age. Children, unlike adults and adolescents, often do not report feelings of distress about having phobias. Insight into the

unreasonable nature of the fear is not required for a **diagnosis** of specific phobia in children. The animal and natural environment types of specific phobia are common and generally transitory in children. Some studies indicate a connection between gender and specific phobia. Research shows that specific phobias from the animal type are more common among women. Some studies suggest, however, that women are more likely to report specific phobias and to seek treatment than men.

Symptoms

DSM-IV-TR delineates seven diagnostic criteria for specific phobia:

- Significant and enduring fear of phobic stimulus: Patients with specific phobia display marked and enduring fear when they encounter a defined situation or object, the phobic stimulus.

- Anxiety response to phobic stimulus: Patients with specific phobia display anxiety as soon as they confront the phobic stimulus. When they confront the phobic stimulus, a defined situation or object, patients with specific phobia may experience a panic attack related to the specific situation. Children may cry, cling, freeze, or have tantrums when they express their anxiety in the face of the phobic stimulus.

- Recognition: Although adolescents and adults realize that their fear is unreasonable and disproportionate to the situation, children may not recognize that their fear is excessive.

- Avoidance: Individuals with specific phobia avoid the phobic stimulus or endure it with deep distress and anxiety.

- Impairment and distress: Individuals with specific phobia display avoidance, distress, and anxious anticipation when they encounter the phobic stimulus. Their avoidance reactions interfere with their daily functioning, or they express significant distress about having a phobia.

- Duration: To diagnose specific phobia in a patient who is under 18 years of age, the duration of the disorder needs to be at least six months.

- Not accounted for by another disorder: A diagnosis of specific phobia is assigned if the phobic avoidance, panic attacks, or anxiety related to the defined situation or object are not better accounted for by other disorders.

Diagnosis

The diagnosis of specific phobia is complicated by factors such as degree of impairment and differential diagnosis, that is, fear caused by another mental disorder.

Although fears of specified situations or objects are common, a diagnosis of specific phobia relies on the degree of impairment.

With regard to differentiating specific phobia types, factors such as the focus of fear and the predictability and timing of the reaction to the phobic stimulus across the specific phobia types can assist clinicians to differentiate. With regard to differentiating specific phobia from other disorders, there are several disorders with similar symptoms. They include **panic disorder** with **agoraphobia**, **social phobia**, **post-traumatic stress disorder**, **obsessive-compulsive disorder**, **hypochondriasis**, **schizophrenia**, and delusional and other psychotic disorders.

Generally, a diagnosis of specific phobia rather than panic disorder is made when there are no spontaneous panic attacks and no fear of panic attacks. It is often difficult to differentiate specific phobia, situational type, from panic disorder with agoraphobia. Specific phobia, situational type, is commonly diagnosed when an individual displays situational avoidance without unexpected and recurrent panic attacks. By contrast, panic disorder with agoraphobia is diagnosed if an individual experiences an initial onset of panic attacks that are not anticipated and subsequently experiences avoidance of several situations considered triggers of panic attacks. Although individuals with specific phobia, unlike individuals with panic disorder with agoraphobia, do not display enduring anxiety, anxious anticipation may occur when confrontation with a phobic stimulus is likely to occur. The *DSM-IV-TR* outlines differentiating factors as to the type and number of panic attacks, the number of avoided contexts, and the focus of the fear. At times, both diagnoses, specific phobia and panic disorder with agoraphobia, need to be assigned.

Psychological measures

Measures used to diagnose specific phobia include behavioral observation, clinical interviews, physiological evaluation, and self-report measures. The behavioral avoidance task (BAT) is a common behavioral observation method used to assess specific phobia. Often the diagnosis of specific phobia is made on the basis of an individual's responses to semistructured interviews, such as the Anxiety Disorders Interview Schedule for *DSM-IV* (ADIS-IV) and the **Structured Clinical Interview for *DSM-IV*** Axis I disorders (SCID-IV). To assist in differential diagnosis between specific phobias and other disorders with similar characteristics, clinicians use the anxiety disorders interview schedule for *DSM-IV* (ADIS-IV). Physiological evaluations usually include heart-rate monitors. Self-report questionnaires include measures such as the subjective units of discomfort/distress scale (SUDS), the most frequently used self-report measure,

the fear survey schedule (FSS-III), and the mutilation questionnaire, specifically for measuring fear of the blood type of specific phobia.

Time of onset and symptom duration

Generally, the initial symptoms of specific phobia occur when an individual is a child or a young adolescent. The type of phobia determines the typical age of onset. The blood, animal, and natural environment types typically begin when an individual is a child; however, many new cases of the natural environment type occur when an individual is a young adult. The onset for the height type usually begins in adolescence. The onset age for the situational type often occurs in childhood and peaks in the mid-twenties. There is no specific onset age for phobias with a traumatic origin.

Individual variations in specific phobia

Classification systems distinguish between individuals with different types of specific phobias. The types of specific phobia, situation, object, and other, relate to particular features such as the age, gender, and culture of an individual. Some researchers propose that to distinguish individual differences in treatment planning, it is more helpful to simply name the specific phobia rather than to use the type classification system.

Dual diagnoses

Specific phobia often occurs with other disorders of mood and anxiety and with substance-related disorders. When specific phobias occur with other disorders in clinical contexts, the primary diagnosis is associated with greater distress. The blood-injury-injection type of specific phobia may occur with physical symptoms such as vasovagal fainting, which is characterized by a short heart rate acceleration and blood pressure elevation. Then the heart rate decelerates and the blood pressure drops. Research shows that individuals who have one specific phobia type are more likely to have other phobias of the same type.

Treatment

Specific phobias are highly treatable. They are most effectively treated by psychological rather than pharmaceutical treatments. The primary goal of most treatments of specific phobias is to reduce fear, phobic avoidance, impairment, and distress.

Cognitive-behavioral therapy

Cognitive-behavioral therapy has been effective in treating specific phobias. There has not been much research on the effects of cognitive therapy alone on specific phobias. Cognitive therapists challenge fearful thoughts and replace them with more positive thoughts. Although some studies show that cognitive therapy may assist patients in decreasing anxiety related to their exposure exercises, research indicates that cognitive therapy alone is probably not an effective treatment for specific phobia. Researchers suggest adding panic management strategies, such as cognitive restructuring, to assist with behavioral treatments.

Several studies indicate that real-life desensitization or exposure is the most effective and long-lasting treatment for a broad range of specific phobias. Desensitization includes a process by which individuals unlearn the association between the phobic stimulus and anxiety. Incremental exposure involves the patient's gradual facing of the phobic stimulus through a series of graded steps. Wolpe's imagery desensitization is suggested so that patients with specific phobias can face the fear in imagery before attempting real-life exposure. Unlike many of the other treatments, the treatment gains of real-life exposure are maintained upon follow-up. Some desensitization treatments employ flooding as a useful strategy. When flooding is used, patients maintain a high anxiety level without retreating. Similar to desensitization, flooding can be used both in imagination and in real life encounters. Flooding may not be appropriate for many individuals because it can trigger a higher level of sensitization and fear reinforcement. For real-life exposure, a patient needs to be highly motivated because the treatment may lead to temporary discomfort. Primary reasons for poor **compliance** with cognitive-behavioral treatment include lack of time, anxiety, and low motivation.

Psychodynamic therapy

Psychodynamic therapy, or insight-oriented therapy, assists patients in becoming aware of the symbolic nature of their anxiety and in exploring traumatic past events. Insight-oriented therapy aims to expose and reduce patients' unconscious conflicts, increase patients' understanding of their underlying thoughts, and assist patients in gaining conscious control over their psychological conflicts. In psychodynamic therapy, for example, patients may discover that their anxiety may be connected to aggressive or sexual feelings and thoughts.

Group therapy

There is little research on **group therapy** for specific phobia disorder. Some studies suggest that group treatment has been effective for dental and spider phobias.

Drugs

Little research has been devoted to the relationship between medication and specific phobia. Generally, pharmacotherapy has not been considered a treatment of choice for individuals with specific phobias. **Benzodiazepines** (sedative drugs that slow the central nervous system to ease nervousness and tension) may decrease anxiety the occurs before an individual enters a phobic situation. A low dose of a benzodiazepine, such as **clonazepam** (Klonopin) or **alprazolam** (Xanax), may be indicated to decrease some fear arousal before real-life exposure to a phobic trigger. The reduction of symptoms, however, may interfere with the treatment. Before beginning real-life exposure, an antidepressant, such as **sertraline** (Zoloft) or **paroxetine** (Paxil), may be suggested to increase motivation for undertaking an uncomfortable treatment. **Beta blockers** also can assist individuals to confront the specific phobia.

Alternative therapies

Research shows some benefits for specific phobias with applied relaxation. Relaxation training includes abdominal breathing and muscle relaxation on a regular basis. Studies have indicated that applied muscle tension helps individuals with blood type phobias to avoid fainting. When patients tense their muscles several times they temporarily increase their blood pressure and keep from fainting when they see blood. Similar to real-life exposure, the gains from applied tension are maintained upon follow-up. Other alternative therapies include immersive virtual reality, **hypnotherapy**, eye-movement desensitization and reprocessing (EMDR), and energy balance approaches such as massage and **acupuncture**.

Prognosis

If specific phobias exist in adolescence, they have a greater chance of persisting in early adulthood. Specific phobias that continue into adulthood generally become chronic if they are not treated. Furthermore, there is a greater chance for an individual diagnosed with specific phobia to develop new phobias as a young adult. Phobias contracted during childhood or adolescence that continue into young adulthood remit approximately 20% of the time. Individuals with specific phobias often fail to seek treatment. For those who seek treatment, research suggests that compared to individuals with specific phobias whose fear diminishes slowly during exposure, individuals with specific phobias whose fear diminishes more rapidly have a better prognosis for recovery.

One factor in prognosis is the distinction between fear onset and phobia onset. Individuals with specific phobias of animal, blood, heights, and driving have a fear

QUESTIONS TO ASK YOUR DOCTOR

- Can you recommend a psychotherapist or other mental health professional for me?
- Is there a mental health professional in your practice with experience in treating phobias?
- Are there any support groups for my phobia in this area?
- How can I tell if my phobia is severe enough to require treatment?
- Will my insurance cover treatment for my phobia?

onset nine years earlier than their phobia onset. Some studies have shown that generalized anxiety level, severity of symptoms, and prior experience with the phobic stimulus are factors that have been associated with treatment outcome.

Although most mental health professionals consider specific phobia that begins in childhood to be a benign disorder, it can last for years if left untreated. Some studies indicate, however, that specific phobia does not become worse and usually diminishes as an individual ages. Without treatment, the prognosis is poor for an individual who has multiple phobias.

Prevention

Early detection is a key to assisting individuals with mild cases of specific phobia to seek treatment to prevent the development of full-blown cases of the disorder. Individuals who are at risk for developing specific phobia as well as individuals who already have been diagnosed with specific phobia need to avoid caffeine because caffeine can increase arousal, causing increased anxiety. Further research is needed to discover variables that predict the reason that only certain individuals will develop specific phobias after conditioning or acquiring information that leads to fear.

Resources

BOOKS

Daitch, Carolyn. *Anxiety Disorders: The Go-To Guide for Clients and Therapists.* New York: Norton, 2011.

Doctor, Ronald M., Ada P. Kahn, and Christine Adamec. *The Encyclopedia of Phobias, Fears, and Anxieties,* 3rd ed. New York: Facts on File, 2008.

Korgeski, Gregory P. *The Compete Idiot's Guide to Phobias.* New York: Alpha, 2009.

PERIODICALS

Baker, Aaron, et al. "Does Habituation Matter? Emotional Processing Theory and Exposure Therapy for Acrophobia." *Behaviour Research and Therapy,* 48, no. 11 (November 2010): 1139–43.

Coelho, Carlos M., and Guy Wallis. "Deconstructing Acrophobia: Physiological and Psychological Precursors to Developing a Fear of Heights." *Depression and Anxiety* 27, no. 9 (September 2010): 864–70.

Trumpf, Julia, et al. "Specific Phobia Predicts Psychopathology in Young Women." *Social Psychiatry and Psychiatric Epidemiology,* 45, no. 12 (December 2010): 1161–66.

ORGANIZATIONS

American Psychiatric Association, 1000 Wilson Blvd., Ste. 1825, Arlington, VA, 22209-3901, (703)907-7300, (888) 357-7924, apa@psych.org, http://www.psych.org.

American Psychological Association, 750 1st St. NE, Washington, DC, 20002-4242, (202) 336-5500, (800) 374-2721, apa@psych.org, http://www.apa.org.

Anxiety Disorders Association of America, 8730 Georgia Ave., Ste. 600, Silver Spring, MD, 20910, (240) 485-1001, Fax: (240) 485-1035, information@adaa.org, http://www.adaa.org.

Judy Koenigsberg, PhD
Tish Davidson, AM

SPECT *see* **Single photon emission computed tomography**

Speech-language pathology

Definition

Treatment for the improvement or cure of communication disorders, including speech, language, and swallowing disorders. The term used to describe professionals in this discipline is speech and language pathologist (SLP).

Description

The discipline of speech-language pathology includes professionals that are trained in the techniques, strategies, and interventions designed to improve or correct communication disorders. Communication disorders include disorders of speech, language, and swallowing.

In 2012, there were more than 126,000 speech-language pathologists in the United States certified by the American Speech-Language-Hearing Association (ASHA), and nearly 20,000 audiologists, who often work with speech pathologists to diagnose disorders. Speech disorders

A speech therapist works with a young boy. (© Hattie Young/ Photo Researchers, Inc.)

treated by speech-language pathologists include voice disorders (abnormalities in pitch, volume, vocal quality, or resonance or duration of sounds), articulation disorders (problems producing speech sounds), and fluency disorders (impairment in speech fluency, such as **stuttering**). Language disorders include developmental or acquired conditions that lead to difficulties in understanding or producing language. Speech-language pathologists participate in the screening, assessment, and treatment of patients who experience one or a combination of these disorders.

Persons with isolated speech sound disorders are often helped by articulation therapy, in which they practice repeating specific sounds, words, phrases, and sentences. For individuals experiencing voice disorders, a combination of medical and behavioral treatments are often helpful. For stuttering and other fluency disorders, treatment approaches usually help individuals develop techniques to both reduce the severity of stuttering and allow the individual to produce more fluent speech. For all of these therapies, individuals are taught to cope more effectively with their speech in progressively difficult situations, starting with speaking alone to the pathologist and ending with speaking to a group of people. In treating children with developmental language disorders, treatment often focusses on **modeling** and stimulation of correct productions of language. This type of approach may also be useful for adults with language disorders, secondary to a **stroke** or degenerative neurological disorder. For people with severe communication disorders, those due to either a speech or language problem, speech pathologists can assist with alternate means of communication, such as manual signing and computer-synthesized speech. Finally, speech-language pathologists have become increasingly involved with the assessment and treatment of individuals with swallowing disorders, or dysphagia.

The majority of speech-language pathologists work in public schools. They are also found at both residential health care facilities and outpatient clinics that specialize in communication disorders. Finally, speech-language pathologists are often employed at hospitals and universities. Professional training programs in speech-language pathology are offered at both the undergraduate and graduate levels. Undergraduate training may include classes in biology, anatomy, psychology, linguistics, education, and special education. Graduate training, at both the masters and doctoral level, provides much deeper opportunities to study communication disorders and their treatment. To receive the Certificate of Clinical Competence(CCC) in speech-language pathology individuals must hold a master's degree in communications sciences and disorders from a program accredited by the ASHA and complete their Clinical Fellowship Year (CFY).

Resources

ORGANIZATIONS

American Academy of Private Practice in Speech-Language Pathology and Audiology, 7349 Topanga Canyon Blvd., Canoga Park, CA, 91303,

American Speech-Language-Hearing Association, 2200 Research Blvd., Rockville, MD, 20785, (301) 296-5700, http://www.asha.org.

National Black Association for Speech-Language and Hearing, 700 McKnight Park Dr., Ste. 708, Pittsburgh, PA, 15237, (412) 366-1177, Fax: (412) 366-8804, NBASLH@nbaslh. org, http://www.nbaslh.org.

Rodney Gabel, Ph.D.

Speech sound disorder *see* **Phonological disorder**

Speech therapy *see* **Speech-language pathology**

Split personality disorder *see* **Dissociative identity disorder**

∎ Stanford-Binet intelligence scales

Definition

The Stanford-Binet Intelligence Scales is a widely used intelligence test. It is a comprehensive, norm-referenced individually administered examination.

Purpose

The purpose of the Stanford-Binet Intelligence Scales, sometimes also called the Stanford-Binet test or simply the "Stanford-Binet," is to assess general intelligence and cognitive abilities in children and adults from the ages of 2 to over 85. Specifically, it tests intelligence in four areas: abstract and visual reasoning, quantitative reasoning, short-term memory skills, and verbal reasoning.

Description

Origins

Considered the oldest and most influential intelligence test, the Stanford-Binet Intelligence Scales was devised in 1916 by Stanford University **psychologist** Lewis Terman (1877–1956), using the Binet-Simon model. French psychologist Alfred Binet (1857–1911) created what is considered the first usable intelligence test. Dr. Binet was given this task by the French government for the purpose of developing a method to assess and identify intellectually deficient children so they could be eventually placed in special needs classes.

Later, in 1908 and 1911, Binet and French psychologist Theodore Simon (1872–1961) revised what is today called the Binet-Simon Scale. The test consisted of various activities (such as touching one's ear and drawing objects or figures from memory) that were commonly performed by children at various ages. Binet and Simon selected these activities based on numerous years of observing children as they played and lived their lives. The two psychologists used 50 children—10 children in five age groupings who were considered of average intelligence by their teachers—to validate 30 activities of increasing difficulties.

Although many psychologists and other professionals question some of the test's concepts, such as mental age and intelligence quotient (IQ), the test is still widely used to assess cognitive development, and often to determine placement in special education classes. The Stanford-Binet Intelligence Scales is considered to have introduced the modern era of intelligence testing (or IQ testing) that continues now into the twenty-first century. The scoring of this test is based on the performance of age-related tasks. For example, a five-year-old child, who successfully completed all of the assigned tasks that a normal five-year-old could pass, would be scored as having a mental age that was equivalent to his/her chronological age.

Specifics

Most recently revised in 2003, the Stanford-Binet Intelligence Scales, Revision Five (Stanford-Binet 5, or SB5), can be used with children, from ages two years and older, and adults. Consisting of questions and short tasks arranged from easy to difficult, the Stanford-Binet measures a wide variety of verbal and nonverbal skills. Its structure is divided into four areas (1) hybrid structure, (2) verbal routing test, (3) nonverbal routing test, and (4) verbal and nonverbal age scales.

The abilities measured by the Stanford-Binet 5 include scales involving (1) Full Scale IQ (a comprehensive measure of cognitive ability, is based on the taking of the subtests), (2) two domain scores (nonverbal IQ and verbal IQ), and (3) five factor indexes (both nonverbal and verbal). The five factor indexes include:

- nonverbal fluid reasoning
- verbal fluid reasoning
- nonverbal knowledge
- verbal knowledge
- nonverbal quantitative reasoning
- verbal quantitative reasoning
- nonverbal visual-spatial processing
- verbal visual-spatial processing
- nonverbal working memory
- verbal working memory

Besides the five factor indexes, two special routing subtests—Nonverbal-Fluid Reasoning: Object Series/ Matrices; and Verbal-Knowledge: Vocabulary—are also provided—together called the Abbreviated Battery. These two subtests are taken before the Stanford-Binet 5 test. Depending on the scores of these two routing subtests, the administrator may begin the SB5 test at Level 1, 2, 3, 4, or 5.

The SB5 Nonverbal subtests, which require minimal receptive language skills and fine-motor coordination, include:

- Nonverbal Knowledge (Picture Absurdities [Levels 4–6] and Procedural Knowledge [Levels 2–3])
- Nonverbal Quantitative Reasoning [Levels 2–6]
- Nonverbal Visual-Spatial Processing (Form Board [Levels 1–2] and Form Patterns [Levels 3–6])
- Nonverbal Working Memory (Block Span [Levels 2–6] and Delayed Response [Level 1])

The Verbal subtests, which require the reading, speaking and comprehending of age-appropriate English, include:

- Verbal Fluid Reasoning (Early Reasoning [Levels 2–3], Verbal Absurdities [Level 4], and Verbal Analogies [Levels 5–6])
- Verbal Quantitative Reasoning [Levels 2–6]
- Verbal Visual-Spatial Processing (Position and Direction [Levels 2–6])

KEY TERMS

Abstract reasoning—The ability to analyze information and to solve problems.

IQ—The acronym for intelligence quotient.

Quantitative reasoning—The ability to complete mathematical problems and to apply mathematics on a practical level.

Verbal reasoning—The ability to understand and reason using concepts involving words (within a particular language).

• Verbal Working Memory (Memory for Sentences [Levels 2–3] and Last Word [Levels 4–6])

Total testing time of the SB5 is 45 to 75 minutes for the Full Scale IQ Battery, with the time variance depending on the test taker's age and the number of subtests given. About 30 minutes is required to administer the Verbal and Nonverbal IQ scales. The Abbreviated Battery test takes from 15 to 20 minutes to complete.

While the test taker's attitude and behavior during the test are noted, they are not used to determine the result, which is arrived at by converting a single raw score for the entire test to a figure indicating "mental age" (the average age of a child achieving that score). A formula is then used to arrive at the intelligence quotient, or IQ. An IQ of 100 means that the child's chronological and mental ages match. Traditionally, IQ scores of from 90 to 109 are considered average, scores below 70 indicate mental disability, and scores of 140 or above place a child into the "gifted" category.

The Stanford-Binet 5 was standardized using a sample of 4,800 individuals (selected at random from all part of the country) from the U.S. Census taken in 2000. A Stanford-Binet Intelligence Scales for Early Childhood is also available for children two years to seven years, three months. In its fifth edition, the test is also called the Early SBS. Both the Stanford-Net 5 and the Early SBS are published by Riverside Publishing, which is headquartered in Rolling Meadows, Illinois.

Preparation

Preparation for the test is neither needed nor recommended.

Results

The SB5 requires that all administrators be skilled at administering the test. Such skill comes from administering a sufficient number of practice tests to establish a reliable knowledge of the testing procedure. Workshops are often used for the training of personnel used to administer the SB5, as are graduate-level testing courses.

The technical manual provided with the SB5 provides sufficient evidence that the scoring process is reliable. The review of the SB5 by the Mental Measurements Yearbook (MMY), Buros Institute, stated that internal consistency reliability coefficients for the IQ scores were from 0.95 to 0.98, while the coefficients for the five Factor Index scores ranged from 0.90 to 0.92. The MMY review added, "...all reliability coefficients were quite high and appropriate for an instrument of this magnitude."

The MMY review concluded with the following summary: "The publication of the newest revision of this well-established test of intelligence continues an almost 100-year-old tradition of evolution and refinement. Despite some technical and statistical limitations (e.g., lower stability for young children and individuals with low cognitive abilities, problematically high correlations with achievement, uncertain factor structure) the SB5 offers important improvements over the previous version of the scale and remains one of the premier instruments for the assessment of cognitive abilities of children, adolescents, and adults."

Resources

BOOKS

Becker, K.A. *History of the Stanford-Binet intelligence scales: Content and psychometrics.* Itasca, IL: Riverside Publishing, 2003.

Binet, Alfred, and Théodore Simon (translated by Elizabeth S. Kite). *The Development of Intelligence in Children (the Binet-Simon Scale).* Baltimore: Williams and Wilkins, 1916.

Drummond, Robert J. *Assessment Procedures for Counselors and Helping Professionals.* Boston: Pearson, 2010.

Green, Susan K., and Robert L. Johnson. *Assessment is Essential.* Boston: McGraw-Hill Higher Education, 2010.

Hart, Diane. *Authentic Assessment: A Handbook for Educators.* Menlo Park, CA: Addison-Wesley, 1994.

McAfee, Oralie, and Deborah J. Leong. *Assessing and Guiding Young Children's Development and Learning.* Upper Saddle River, NJ: Pearson, 2011.

McCullough, Virginia E. *Testing and Your Child: What You Should Know about 150 of the Most Common Medical, Educational, and Psychological Tests.* New York: Plume, 1992.

Mindes, Gayle. *Assessing Young Children.* Boston: Pearson, 2011.

Santrock, John W. *Concept of Intelligence.* New York: McGraw-Hill, 2008.

OTHER

"Stanford-Binet Intelligence Scales, Fifth Edition Assessment Service Bulletin Number 1." Nelson Education, http://www.assess.nelson.com/pdf/sb5-asb1.pdf (accessed October 19, 2010).

WEBSITES

"Alfred Binet." Indiana University. (July 25, 2007), http://www.indiana.edu/~intell/binet.shtml (accessed October 19, 2010).

"Mental Measurements Yearbook, Buros Center for Testing." Buros Institute for Mental Measurements, http://www.unl.edu/buros (accessed October 5, 2010).

"Stanford-Binet Intelligence Scales, Fifth Edition (SB5)." Nelson Education, http://www.assess.nelson.com/test-ind/stan-b5.html (accessed October 19, 2010).

"Stanford-Binet Intelligence Scales for Early Childhood (Early SB5)." Nelson Education, http://www.riversidepublishing.com/products/earlySB5/index.html (accessed October 19, 2010).

William Arthur Atkins

STAR*D study

Definition

The Sequenced Treatment Alternatives to Relieve **Depression** (STAR*D) Study was the largest and longest national trial ever designed to determine which treatments work best in people with **major depressive disorder** (MDD) who have not responded to an antidepressant. MDD is characterized by feelings of persistent sadness, worthlessness, guilt, and lack of interest in daily activities severe enough to interfere with such daily activities.

Purpose

The goal of the study was to help doctors better understand how to treat depression. Previously, the medical literature had provided doctors with little guidance on which treatments to use on their patients who do not respond to initial treatments. The STAR*D study was designed to help doctors learn which treatment plans (including medication dose and duration) are most effective for improving symptoms in patients with chronic depression and have the fewest side effects. The study also may enable doctors to determine how long they should attempt one therapy before moving on to another type of treatment. In addition, STAR*D provided information about the risk of **relapse**, which is defined as the return of depressive symptoms.

Description

The STAR*D study was a seven-year, $35 million-effort funded by the **National Institute of Mental Health** (NIMH) that began in 1999. It involved more than 4,000 participants, ages 18 to 75, with chronic or recurrent major depression. The patients were being or were about to be treated for depressive symptoms at primary care or psychiatric facilities. Major depression is of significant concern to doctors, because it can lead to significant functional impairment and mortality.

To reflect real-life treatment situations, STAR*D was conducted at private practices and public clinics, rather than in universities or other research facilities. In addition, participants were able to choose their own range of treatments. Researchers selected drugs that were the safest, easiest to take, and most commonly used, so the results could immediately be applied to clinical practice.

Researchers

The study was led by Dr. John Rush of the University of Texas Southwestern Medical Center. The following 13 other research centers also participated in the trial:

• Clinical Research Institute—Kansas
• Laureate Psychiatric Hospital & Clinic (Oklahoma)
• Massachusetts General Hospital
• New York State Psychiatric Institute
• Northwestern University (Illinois)
• Oklahoma Tuscaloosa VA Medical Center
• University of California at Los Angeles
• University of California at San Diego
• University of Michigan
• University of North Carolina at Chapel Hill
• University of Pittsburgh
• Vanderbilt University (Tennessee)
• Virginia Commonwealth University

Participants

More than 4,000 participants were initially involved in the study. The average age was 41 years. About 64% of participants were female and 36% were male. About 76% were Caucasian, 18% were African American, 13% were Hispanic, and 6% were of other races.

Participants were either being treated for depression or were entering into treatment at 41 primary care and psychiatric clinics throughout the United States. All of those involved in the study had moderate to severe depression. Seventy-five percent had had two or more depressive episodes in their lifetime. The other 25% were

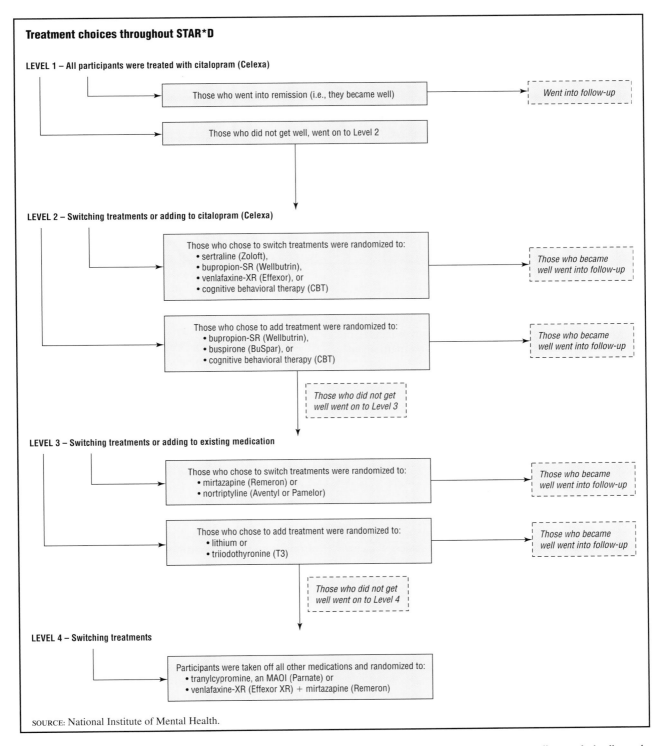

Treatment choices throughout STAR*D

LEVEL 1 – All participants were treated with citalopram (Celexa)

Those who went into remission (i.e., they became well) → *Went into follow-up*

Those who did not get well, went on to Level 2

LEVEL 2 – Switching treatments or adding to citalopram (Celexa)

Those who chose to switch treatments were randomized to:
• sertraline (Zoloft),
• bupropion-SR (Wellbutrin),
• venlafaxine-XR (Effexor), or
• cognitive behavioral therapy (CBT)
→ *Those who became well went into follow-up*

Those who chose to add treatment were randomized to:
• bupropion-SR (Wellbutrin),
• buspirone (BuSpar), or
• cognitive behavioral therapy (CBT)
→ *Those who became well went into follow-up*

Those who did not get well went on to Level 3

LEVEL 3 – Switching treatments or adding to existing medication

Those who chose to switch treatments were randomized to:
• mirtazapine (Remeron) or
• nortriptyline (Aventyl or Pamelor)
→ *Those who became well went into follow-up*

Those who chose to add treatment were randomized to:
• lithium or
• triiodothyronine (T3)
→ *Those who became well went into follow-up*

Those who did not get well went on to Level 4

LEVEL 4 – Switching treatments

Participants were taken off all other medications and randomized to:
• tranylcypromine, an MAOI (Parnate) or
• venlafaxine-XR (Effexor XR) + mirtazapine (Remeron)

SOURCE: National Institute of Mental Health.

Additional information on the STAR*D study available from the National Institute of Mental Health at http://www.nimh.nih.gov/ trials/practical/stard/allmedicationlevels.shtml. *(Diagram by PreMediaGlobal. © 2012 Cengage Learning.)*

currently experiencing an episode of depression that had lasted for at least two years.

The STAR*D study had broader participation than most studies of its kind. However, people with **schizophrenia**, **schizoaffective disorder**, **bipolar disorder**, an eating disorder, **obsessive-compulsive disorder**, or a **substance abuse** problem were not eligible for the study. Also, those who were already participating in **cognitive-behavioral therapy** or who were taking psychotropic medications could not participate.

Out of the 4,041 initial participants who entered Level 1 of STAR*D, 1,438 progressed to Level 2, 376 entered Level 3, and 108 moved on to Level 4 (see level descriptions below). Participants left the program because they entered remission, or they desired to leave the program because of side effects, or they opted to leave for personal reasons.

Preparation

Participants prepared for the study by first meeting with a trained professional who assessed their condition and, later, with a medical doctor.

Examination: Assessments

At the first visit, participants met with a trained clinical research coordinator (CRC), who did not have knowledge of the treatment they were about to receive or were already receiving. The CRC asked the participants about the following:

- history of depression symptoms
- family history of MDD, bipolar disorder, or alcohol and substance abuse
- duration of current depressive episode
- treatment history for the current depressive episode
- past and current substance abuse
- history of suicide attempts
- current mental illnesses.

The CRC also rated the participants' symptom severity using established psychological scales. Patients completed self-questionnaires to determine their psychiatric disorders and depression score. Participants were later given phone interviews by a computer-based voice response system to ascertain their functioning and quality of life.

At doctor visits, the participants were evaluated for medication effectiveness and side effects. The STAR*D researchers also evaluated the patients to determine whether a change in dosage was necessary.

Medications

The following medications were used in the STAR*D study:

- bupropion SR (Wellbutrin SR)
- buspirone (BuSpar;)
- citalopram (Celexa)
- lithium (Eskalith, Lithobid)

- mirtazapine (Remeron)
- nortriptyline (Pamelor, Aventyl)
- sertraline (Zoloft)
- tranylcypromine (Parnate)
- triiodothyronine (T3, Cytomel)
- venlafaxine XR (Effexor XR).

Treatments

The treatments used in STAR*D were the same as those typically used by doctors to treat clinical depression. Participants received only active medications; therefore, placebos were not used.

The study included four treatment levels, each of which could continue for up to 14 weeks. Participants progressed to the next level when their symptoms did not respond to the their current treatment.

The four levels were as follows:

- Level 1: All participants received the antidepressant citalopram (brand name, Celexa). Citalopram is a selective serotonin reuptake inhibitor (SSRI). It works by interfering with the ability of nerve cells in the brain to take up the neurotransmitter, serotonin. This neurotransmitter has been associated with symptoms of depression.
- Level 2: Participants who did not become symptom-free, or who experienced side effects on citalopram, had a choice of seven different treatment options. Four options involved taking either a new medication or engaging in cognitive-behavioral therapy. The other three options added a new medication or cognitive-behavioral therapy to the citalopram participants were already taking. All treatments were randomly chosen from those that the participant had deemed acceptable.
- Level 3: Participants who did not become symptom-free at the previous level were allowed to try one of four other treatment options. They could switch to therapy with either nortriptyline or mirtazapine, or continue taking their current antidepressant along with either lithium or triiodothyronine.
- Level 4: Participants who did not become symptom-free at the previous level were randomly assigned to take either tranylcypromine or a combination of venlafaxine and mirtazapine.

Once participants went into full remission, in which they no longer experienced symptoms of depression, they began a 12-month follow-up process.

Results

The results of the STAR*D study were published in medical and scientific journals in 2006, including the

KEY TERMS

Bipolar disorder—A mood disorder characterized by abnormally high energy levels and moodiness, usually without depression.

Cognitive-behavioral therapy—A type of therapy used to solve problems concerning dysfunctional behaviors (responses), emotions (feelings) and cognitions (abilities to gather knowledge) through a proven systematic set of procedures.

Cognitive therapy—A type of psychiatric treatment involving the treatment of anxiety and/or depression, which encourages patients to confront their problems in order to improve their behavior.

Depression—A psychiatric disorder involving feelings of hopelessness and symptoms of fatigue, sleeplessness, suicidal tendencies, and poor concentration.

Eating disorders—A number of medical conditions characterized by abnormal eating habits that can involve either the lack, or the excessive intake, of food, which results in physical and/or emotional stress. Two types of eating disorders include anorexia nervosa and bulimia nervosa.

Psychotropic medication—A drug that is used to treat mental disorders.

Schizophrenia—A mental disorder involving degraded thinking and emotions.

Substance abuse—Overuse of a drug or alcohol, which leads to addiction.

American Journal of Psychiatry on November 1, 2006. Outcomes included measures of depressive symptoms, social function, and patient satisfaction.

Researchers found that remission rates were about 37% for participants in Level 1, 31% in Level 2, and 13% in Levels 3 and 4. However, some patients dropped out of the study early.

Overall, the findings suggested that more than half of patients who stayed in treatment for one or two steps will achieve remission. But those patients who do not respond after two different treatment courses have a much lower chance of remission, and a higher risk of relapse.

The results of STAR*D emphasized the need for improved and individualized treatment plans when treating major depression. Research topics prompted by the STAR*D results include learning to predict how

patients will respond to treatments and treatment sequences, so as to treat them more effectively, and assessing the use of combination medication therapies earlier in treatment. In 2007, a study based on STAR*D discovered that a slight gene variation predisposed patients to respond to **citalopram**. Using the genetic material of patients who had participated in STAR*D, researchers found that those with the variation (in genes *GRIK4* or *HTR2A*) were 23% more likely to be treated successfully with citalopram.

Resources

BOOKS

Appleton, William S. *The New Antidepressants and Antianxieties.* New York: Plume, 2004.

Beers, Mark H. *The Merck Manual of Medical Information,* 2nd Home Ed. New York: Pocket, 2004.

McCullough, James P. Jr. *Treating Chronic Depression with Disciplined Personal Involvement: Cognitive Behavioral Analysis System of Psychotherapy (CBASP),* first ed. New York: Springer, 2006.

Pettit, Jeremy W., and Thomas E. Joiner.*Chronic Depression: Interpersonal Sources, Therapeutic Solutions.* Washington, DC: American Psychological Association, 2005.

PERIODICALS

Asparouhov, Tihomir, et al. "Growth Modeling with Non-ignorable Dropout: Alternative Analyses of the STAR*D Antidepressant Trial." *Psychological Methods* 16, no. 1 (2011): 17.

Fava, Maurizio, et al. "The Impact of Nonclinical Factors on Care Use for Patients with Depression: A STAR*D Report." *CNS Neuroscience & Therapeutics* 15, no. 4 (2009): 320.

Gaynes, B.N., et al. "A Direct Comparison of Presenting Characteristics of Depressed Outpatients from Primary vs. Specialty Care Settings: Preliminary Findings from the STAR*D Clinical Trial." *General Hospital Psychiatry* 27, no. 2 (March–April 2005): 87–96.

Pigott, H. Edmund, et al. "Efficacy and Effectiveness of Antidepressants: Current Status of Research." *Psychotherapy and Psychosomatics* 79, no. 5 (2010): 267–79.

Rush, A.J. "STAR*D: What We Have Learned." *American Journal of Psychiatry* 164 (2007): 201–4.

Rush, A.J., et al. (STAR*D Investigators Group). "Sequenced Treatment Alternatives to Relieve Depression (STAR*D): Rationale and Design." *Controlled Clinical Trials* 25, no. 1 (February 2004): 119–42.

Wisniewski, S.R., et al. "Can Phase III Trial Results and Antidepressant Medications Be Generalized to Clinical Practice? A STAR*D Report." *American Journal of Psychiatry* 166, no. 5 (2009): 599–607.

Young, E.A., et al. "Sex Differences in Response to Citalopram: A STAR*D Report." *Journal of Psychiatric Research* 43 (2009): 503–11.

WEBSITES

"Sequenced Treatment Alternatives to Relieve Depression (STAR∗D) Study." National Institute of Mental Health. http://www.nimh.nih.gov/trials/practical/stard/index.shtml (accessed July 21, 2011).

"STAR∗D (Sequenced Treatment Alternatives to Relieve Depression)." University of Pittsburgh. http://www.edc.pitt.edu/stard (accessed July 21, 2011).

ORGANIZATIONS

American Psychological Association, 750 1st St. NE, Washington, DC, 20002-4242, (202) 336-5500, TDD/TTY: (202) 336-6123, (800) 374-2721, http://www.apa.org.

National Alliance on Mental Illness, 3803 N Fairfax Dr., Ste. 100, Arlington, VA, 22203, (703) 524-7600, http://www.nami.org.

National Institute of Mental Health, 6001 Executive Blvd., Rm. 8184, MSC 9663, Bethesda, MD, 20892-9663, (301) 433-4513, TTY: (301) 443-8431, Fax: (301) 443-4279, (866) 615-6464, TTY: (866) 415-8051, nimhinfo@nih.gov, http://www.nimh.nih.gov.

Stephanie N. Watson
William Atkins

Stelazine *see* **Trifluoperazine**

STEP-BD study

Definition

The Systematic Treatment Enhancement Program for **Bipolar Disorder** (STEP-BD) was a long-term, outpatient research study conducted within the United States that aimed to find out which treatments, or treatment combinations, are most effective for countering **depression** and mania and for preventing recurrent episodes in people with bipolar disorder.

Purpose

The STEP-BD is one of the largest studies to have evaluated treatments for bipolar disorder. This chronic condition, which is characterized by repeated swings in mood between mania (a state of elation and high energy) and depression, can significantly affect quality of life if not properly treated.

Researchers with the STEP-BD investigated the most effective treatment methods for bipolar episodes (mania and depression), including medication, psychological therapies, and other modalities. The researchers evaluated treatments based on cost-effectiveness,

improvements in patients' social functioning and quality of life, and prevention of recurrence. As part of the study, the investigators also looked at the characteristics of patients with bipolar disorder.

Demographics

The study began in September 1998 and ended in September 2005. It included approximately 4,350 participants with bipolar disorder, who were being treated at 20 clinical treatment centers throughout the United States.

Description

The STEP-BD study was a $28-million, seven-year effort funded by the National Institutes of Mental Health (NIMH). Researchers followed 4,360 participants with bipolar disorder to determine which treatments were most effective for mania and depressive episodes, and for preventing recurrence.

The study offered two treatment arms, called pathways—a real-world, non-controlled Best Practice Pathway, and a randomized and controlled Randomized Care Pathway. Participants had the opportunity to join in both pathways. Researchers were able to compare the two pathways to see how the evaluated treatments worked both in clinical and real-world settings.

Best Practice Pathway

In the "Best Practice Pathway," participants were followed by a STEP-BD certified doctor, and all treatment choices were individualized. Everyone enrolled in STEP-BD was able to participate in this pathway. Participants and their doctors worked together to decide on the best treatment plans and to change these plans if needed. In addition, anyone who wished to stay on his or her current treatment upon entering STEP-BD was permitted do so in this pathway. Adolescents and adults aged 15 years or older were eligible to participate in the Best Practice Pathway.

Randomized Care Pathway

Patients ages 18 years or older had the option of entering the "Randomized Care Pathway" portion of the trial. Patients in this pathway remained on their mood-stabilizing medication, but some were also started on another medication or **talk therapy**. The patients were randomly assigned to treatments, and the study was double-blinded, meaning that neither the doctors nor their patients were aware of which treatment was given. (Double-blinding is done to prevent bias among both researchers and patients.) Approximately 1,500 patients were involved in at least one Randomized Care Pathway. Patients remained with the same physician throughout the course of the study.

Researchers

All researchers involved in STEP-BD were specially trained for the project in the treatment of bipolar disorder. The study was coordinated by Massachusetts General Hospital and the University of Pittsburgh School of Medicine.

The following research centers served as clinical sites for the study:

- Baylor College of Medicine (Texas)
- Case Western Reserve University (Ohio)
- Cornell University (New York)
- Howard University (Washington, DC)
- Massachusetts General Hospital
- New York Presbyterian Hospital
- New York University
- Rush-Presbyterian-St. Luke's Medical Center (Illinois; now named the Rush University Medical Center)
- Stanford University (California)
- State University of New York, Buffalo
- University of Arizona
- University of California, San Diego
- University of Colorado
- University of Louisville (Kentucky)
- University of Massachusetts
- University of Missouri
- University of Oklahoma
- University of Pennsylvania
- University of Pittsburgh (Pennsylvania)
- University of Texas, San Antonio

Participants

STEP-BD enrolled 4,360 patients with bipolar disorder in the United States. To enter the study, participants had to be at least 15 years of age and meet the *Diagnostic and Statistical Manual of Mental Disorders*, fourth edition (*DSM-IV*) criteria for bipolar I disorder, bipolar II disorder, cyclothymia, bipolar disorder not otherwise specified (BD-NOS), or **schizoaffective disorder**, bipolar subtype. The goal of STEP-BD was to evaluate all of the best-practice treatment options used for bipolar disorder: mood-stabilizing medications, **antidepressants**, atypical antipsychotics, and psychosocial interventions—or "talk" therapies—including **cognitive-behavioral therapy**, family-focused therapy,

interpersonal and social rhythm therapy, and collaborative care (psychoeducation).

Some of the patients had already been treated for bipolar disorder before entering the study, whereas others had not received prior treatment. Many of the patients had other mental illnesses, such as anxiety or **substance abuse** problems. Doctors evaluated the participants upon entry (baseline) and monitored their progress throughout the study. Patients were considered to be recovering if they had no more than two moderate symptoms for at least one week. They were considered recovered if they had no more than two moderate symptoms for at least eight weeks.

Treatments

Drugs and behavioral therapies were used in the STEP-BD study.

Drugs included:

- lithium (a mood-stabilizing medication)
- valproate (an anticonvulsant medication that has mood-stabilizing effects)
- lamotrigine (a newer anticonvulsant medication)
- risperidone (an atypical antipsychotic medication)
- bupropion (an antidepressant)
- paroxetine (a type of antidepressant called a selective serotonin reuptake inhibitor [SSRI])
- tranylcypromine (a type of antidepressant known as a monoamine oxidase inhibitor [MAOI])
- inositol (a natural substance that acts as a chemical messenger)

Behavioral therapies included:

- cognitive-behavioral therapy
- family-focused therapy
- interpersonal and social rhythms therapy

Preparation

Participants prepared for the study by first meeting with their family doctor and/or STEP-BD certified doctor, who then assessed their condition and later assisted them throughout their treatment within the STEP-BD study.

Results

In addition to evaluating treatment outcomes, the STEP-BD study looked at the coexistence of other mental disorders, types of medications commonly prescribed for bipolar disorder, and recurrence rates, among other areas of study.

The following were some of the research findings to come out of the STEP-BD study:

- Coexistence of other mental disorders: Among a subgroup of the first 500 patients in the STEP-BD study, more than 50% had a lifetime history of anxiety disorder, 38% had a history of alcohol abuse or dependence, and 26% had a history of substance of abuse or dependence.

- Most common existing treatments for bipolar disorder: Researchers looked at the first 500 patients entering the study and found that the majority (72%)were taking mood-stabilizer medications, such as lithium or carbamazepine, when they began STEP-BD. The next most common class of medications taken was antidepressants (40%), followed by anticonvulsants (32%) and antipsychotic agents (31%).

- Treatment-resistant bipolar depression: Researchers tested three different medications, lamotrigine, inositol, and risperidone, on a subgroup of 66 participants with bipolar depression who had not previously responded to treatment. The recovery rate was 24% with lamotrigine, 17% with inositol, and 4.6% with risperidone. The researchers said their results suggested that lamotrigine may be superior to inositol and risperidone for improving symptoms of treatment-resistant bipolar depression.

- The effectiveness of psychotherapy on bipolar disorder: Researchers looked at a subgroup of the first 1,000 people enrolled in the STEP-BD study. About 60% of these patients had at least one psychotherapy session during the first year of the study. Among participants with more severe depressive symptoms at the outset of the study, more frequent psychotherapy sessions were associated with less severe mood symptoms and better functioning. The researchers said that these results suggest that patients with more severe bipolar disorder might benefit from more frequent psychotherapy sessions.

- Bipolar disorder recurrence: In a prospective study of 1,469 STEP-BD participants, more than half of the patients (58%) achieved recovery. However, almost half of those who recovered experienced a recurrence during the two-year follow-up period. Researchers said that these findings indicate that bipolar disorder has a strong likelihood of recurrence.

STEP-BD Acute Depression Medication Trial

The Acute Depression Medication Trial was a part of the STEP-BD. The trial's results were reported online on March 28, 2007, in the *New England Journal of Medicine*. Participants who had originally enrolled in

---

> ## KEY TERMS
>
> **Bipolar disorder**—A mood disorder characterized by abnormally high energy levels and moodiness, usually without depression.
>
> **Cognitive behavioral techniques**—A type of therapy used to solve problems concerning dysfunctional behaviors (responses), emotions (feelings), and cognitions (abilities to gather knowledge) through a proven systematic set of procedures.
>
> **Cognitive therapy**—A type of psychiatric treatment involving the treatment of anxiety and/or depression, which encourages patients to confront their problems in order to improve their behavior.
>
> **Depression**—A psychiatric disorder involving feelings of hopelessness and symptoms of fatigue, sleeplessness, suicidal tendencies, and poor concentration.
>
> **Mania**—An intense and/or excessive interest for something that leads to a psychiatric disorder characterized by impulsive behavior, excessive physical activities, and other such impulsive actions.
>
> **Substance abuse**—Overuse of a drug or alcohol, which leads to addiction.

---

the STEP-BD Best Practice Pathway (BPP), but whose depression had not improved or who had experienced additional depressive episodes while in the study, could opt out of the study with the option of entering the Acute Depression Medication Trial (ADMT).

In all, 366 people (18 years of age or older) participated in the ADMT, a randomized controlled trial that looked at antidepressant medication treatment options for acute depressive episodes. Specifically, researchers wanted to determine whether an antidepressant added to a mood-stabilizing treatment program was more effective at treating bipolar depressive episodes than using a mood-stabilizer drug by itself, and whether a standard antidepressant medication could lead a person from depression to mania.

Within the ADMT, 179 of the participants received up to 26 weeks of one of two antidepressant medications (**paroxetine** or **bupropion**), along with a mood stabilizer, to treat their depression. The other 187 people (the control group) received a placebo (sugar pill), along with a mood stabilizer, for their depression treatment.

QUESTIONS TO ASK YOUR DOCTOR

- How can the STEP-BD study help me in my problems?
- Where can I learn more about STEP-BD?
- Has more research been performed relating to the STEP-BD?

The group that received the antidepressant medication and a mood stabilizer achieved a 24% "durable recovery," which was defined to be at least eight weeks with no more than two depressive or two manic symptoms. The placebo/mood stabilizer group had a 27% durable recovery rate. The researchers concluded that the antidepressant medication added to a mood stabilizer did not improve the recovery from bipolar depression when compared to using only a mood stabilizer. They also noted that adding an antidepressant to the mood stabilizer did not increase the risk of a person switching from depression to mania or **hypomania**.

The **National Institute of Mental Health** added, " . . . because study participants tolerated both treatments well—less than 1 percent of participants suffered severe adverse effects—the results indicate that properly administered mood-stabilizing medication is an acceptable first-line treatment for outpatients with bipolar depression."

Resources

BOOKS

Basco, Monica Ramirez, and A. John Rush. *Cognitive Behavioral Therapy for Bipolar Disorder.* 2nd ed. New York: Guilford Press, 2005.

Borch-Jacobsen, Mikkel. *Making Minds and Madness: From Hysteria to Depression.* Cambridge: Cambridge University Press, 2009.

Dziegielewski, Sophia F. *DSM-IV-TR in Action.* Hoboken, NJ: John Wiley & Sons, 2010.

Evans, Dwight L., Dennis S. Charney, and Lydia Lewis. *The Physician's Guide to Depression & Bipolar Disorders.* New York: McGraw-Hill, 2005.

Freeman, Hugh, ed. *A Century of Psychiatry.* St. Louis: Mosby, 1999.

Peterson, David B. *Psychological Aspects of Functioning, Disability, and Health.* New York: Springer, 2011.

Schulte-Markwort, Michael, Kathrin Marutt, and Peter Riedesser, eds. *Cross-walks ICD-10-DSM IV-TR: A Synopsis of Classifications of Mental Disorders.* Cambridge, MA: Hogrefe & Huber, 2003.

Suppes, Trisha, and Ellen B. Dennehy. *Bipolar Disorder: The Latest Assessment and Treatment Strategies.* Kansas City: Compact Clinicals, 2005.

Suppes, Trisha, and Paul E. Keck Jr. *Bipolar Disorder: Treatment and Management.* Kansas City: Compact Clinicals, 2005.

VandenBos, Gary R., ed. *APA Dictionary of Psychology.* Washington, DC: American Psychological Association, 2007.

PERIODICALS

American Psychiatric Association. *Diagnostic and Statistical Manual of Mental Disorders.* 4th ed, text rev. Washington, DC: American Psychiatric Association, 2000.

Simon, Naomi, et al. "Anxiety Disorder Comorbidity in Bipolar Disorder Patients: Data From the First 500 Participants in the Systematic Treatment Enhancement Program for Bipolar Disorder (STEP-BD)." *American Journal of Psychiatry* December 2004: 2222–29.

Ghaemi, S. Nassir, et al. "Pharmacological Treatment Patterns at Study Entry for the First 500 STEP-BD Participants." *Psychiatric Services* May 2006: 660–65.

Miklowitz, David J., et al. "Psychotherapy, Symptom Outcomes, and Role Functioning Over One Year Among Patients With Bipolar Disorder." *Psychiatric Services* July 2006: 959–65.

Nierenberg, Andrew, et al. "Treatment-Resistant Bipolar Depression: A STEP-BD Equipoise Randomized Effectiveness Trial of Antidepressant Augmentation With Lamotrigine, Inositol, or Risperidone." *The American Journal of Psychiatry* February 2006: 210–16.

Perlis, Roy, et al. "Predictors of Recurrence in Bipolar Disorder: Primary Outcomes From the Systematic Treatment Enhancement Program for Bipolar Disorder (STEP-BD)." *The American Journal of Psychiatry* February 2006: 217–24.

Tamminga, Carol A., et al., eds. *Deconstructing Psychosis: Refining the Research Agenda for DSM-V.* Arlington, VA: American Psychiatric Association, 2010.

WEBSITES

"Questions and Answers About the STEP-BD Acute Depression Medication Trial." National Institute of Mental Health. (March 18, 2010). http://www.nimh.nih.gov/trials/practical/step-bd/questions-and-answers-about-the-step-bd-acute-depression-medication-trial.shtml (accessed August 30, 2011).

"Systematic Treatment Enhancement Program for Bipolar Disorder (STEP-BD)." National Institute of Mental Health. (March 31, 2011). http://www.nimh.nih.gov/trials/practical/step-bd/index.shtml (accessed August 30, 2011).

ORGANIZATIONS

American Psychiatric Association, 1000 Wilson Boulevard, Suite 1825, Arlington, VA, 22209-3901, (703) 907-7300, apa@psych.org, http://www.psych.org.

American Psychological Association, 750 First St. NE, Washington, DC, 20002-4242, (202) 336-5500, (800) 374-2721, http://www.apa.org.

American Sociological Association, 1430 K St. NW, Ste. 600, Washington, DC, 20005, (202) 383-9005, Fax: 1(202) 638-0882, http://www.asanet.org.

Depression and Bipolar Support Alliance, 730 N Franklin St., Ste. 501, Chicago, IL, 60654-7225, Fax: (312) 642-7243, (800) 826-3632, http://www.dbsalliance.org.

National Alliance on Mental Illness, 3803 N Fairfax Dr., Ste. 100, Arlington, VA, 22203, (703) 524-7600, Fax: (703) 524-9094, (800) 950-6264, http://www.nami.org.

National Institute of Mental Health, 6001 Executive Blvd., Rm. 8184, MSC 9663, Bethesda, MD, 20892-9663, (301) 443-4513, Fax: (301) 443-4279, (866) 615-6464, nimhinfo@nih.gov, http://www.nimh.nih.gov.

Substance Abuse and Mental Health Services Administration, PO Box 2345, Bethesda, MD, 20847-2345, Fax: (240) 221-4292, (877) 726-4727, SAMHSAInfo@samhsa.hhs.gov, http://www.samhsa.gov.

Stephanie N. Watson
William A. Atkins

Stereotypic movement disorder

Definition

Stereotypic movement disorder is characterized by repeated, rhythmic, purposeless movements or activities such as head banging, nail biting, or body rocking. These movements either cause self-injury or severely interfere with normal activities. Until 1994, the **American Psychiatric Association** referred to stereotypic movement disorder as stereotypy/habit disorder.

Demographics

Stereotypic movement disorder is most strongly associated with severe or profound intellectual disabilities, especially among people who are institutionalized and perhaps deprived of adequate sensory stimulation. It is estimated that 1%–3% of people with moderate **intellectual disability** living in the community have stereotypic movement disorder. About 25% of all people with intellectual disabilities who are institutionalized have the disorder. Among those with severe or profound intellectual disability, the rate is between 40% and 60%, with 15% showing behavior that causes self-injury.

Stereotypic movements are common among children with **pervasive developmental disorders,** such as autism, childhood degenerative disorder, and **Asperger syndrome**. These movements also can be seen in people with **Tourette syndrome** or with tics. Head banging is estimated to affect about 5% of children, with boys outnumbering girls three to one, although other stereotypic behaviors appear to be distributed equally between males and females. Despite its association with psychiatric disorders, there are some people with normal intelligence and who develop stereotypic movement disorder.

Description

Stereotypic movements were first described as a psychiatric symptom in the early 1900s. Since then, they have been recognized as a symptom of both psychotic and neurological disorders. They may also arise from unexplained causes. These movements may include:

- head banging
- nail biting
- playing with hair (but not hair pulling, which is considered the separate disorder of trichotillomania)
- thumb sucking
- hand flapping
- nose picking
- whirling
- body rocking
- picking at the body
- self-biting
- object biting
- self-hitting
- compulsive scratching
- eye gouging
- teeth grinding (bruxism)
- breath holding
- stereotyped sound production

The precise definition of stereotypic movement disorder changed between 1990 and 2010. The new definition limits the disorder to repetitive movements that cause physical harm or severely interfere with normal activities. These movements cannot be better described by another psychiatric condition such as anxiety disorder, a general medical condition such as Huntington's disease, or as the side effect of a medication or illicit drug (for example, **cocaine** use).

Stereotypic movements occur in people of any age, including the very young, but they are most prevalent among adolescents. People may exhibit only one particular stereotyped movement or several. The movements may be slow and gentle, fast and frenetic, or varied in intensity. They typically increase with boredom, tension, or frustration, and it appears that the movements are self-stimulatory and sometimes pleasurable. The root causes are unknown.

Stereotypic movements are common in infants and toddlers. Some estimates suggest that 15–20% of children under age three exhibit some kind of rhythmic, repetitive movements. Thumb sucking and body rocking are common self-comforting mechanisms in the very young. This type of repeated movement is temporary and usually ends by age three or four. It is not the same as stereotypic movement disorder.

Causes and symptoms

Although the root causes are unknown, inadequate caregiving and institutionalization are implicated as contributing factors in many cases. The symptoms are noted for their excessive and obsessive nature and for the tendency of individuals to hurt themselves.

Causes

Causes of stereotypic movements include the following:

- sensory deprivation (blindness or deafness)
- drug use (cocaine, amphetamines)
- brain disease (seizures, infection)
- major psychiatric disorders (anxiety disorder, obsessive-compulsive disorder, autism)
- intellectual disability

It has also been suggested that inadequate caregiving may cause the disorder. Although many situations can give rise to stereotypic movements, the root causes of stereotypic movement disorder are unknown. Different theories propose that the causes are behavioral, neurological, and/or genetic. Although there are many theories to account for this disorder, as of 2011 no evidence clearly supported one line of reasoning or specific cause.

Symptoms

Symptoms of stereotypic movement disorder include all the activities listed above. It should be noted that many of these activities are normal in infants. They usually begin between 5 and 11 months and disappear on their own by age 3. About 55% of very young children grind their teeth. These passing phases of repetitive movement are not the same as stereotypic movement disorder. They do not cause harm and often serve the

KEY TERMS

Autism—A syndrome characterized by a lack of responsiveness to other people or outside stimulus, often in conjunction with a severe impairment of verbal and nonverbal communication skills.

Huntington's disease—A hereditary disease that typically appears in midlife, marked by gradual loss of brain function and voluntary movement. Some of its symptoms resemble those of schizophrenia.

Obsessive-compulsive disorder (OCD)—An anxiety disorder in which a person cannot prevent himself from dwelling on unwanted thoughts, acting on urges, or performing repetitious rituals, such as washing his hands or checking to make sure he turned off the lights.

Trichotillomania—A disorder characterized by compulsive hair pulling.

purpose of self-comforting or helping the child learn a new motor skill.

People with stereotypic movement disorder often hurt themselves. They may pick their nail cuticles or skin until they bleed. They may repeatedly gouge their eyes or bite or hit themselves causing bleeding, bruising, and sometimes, as in the case of eye gouging or head banging, even more severe damage. Some people develop behaviors such as keeping their hands in their pockets, to prevent these movements. In other cases, those who hurt themselves appear to welcome, rather than fight, physical restraints that keep them safe. However, when these restraints are removed, they return to their harmful behaviors.

Diagnosis

Stereotypic movements are diagnosed by the presence of the activities mentioned above. Young children rarely try to hide these movements, although older children may, and the first sign of them may be the physical harm they cause (bleeding skin, chewed nails). Often parents mention these repetitive movements when the physician takes a history of the child.

The difficulty in diagnosing stereotypic movement disorder comes from distinguishing it from other disorders where rhythmic, repetitive movements occur. The disorder may be classified as either with self-injurious behavior or without self-harm. To be diagnosed

QUESTIONS TO ASK YOUR DOCTOR

- Are the repetitive movements normal for a child this age?
- Can you recommend a specialist who has experience dealing with repetitive movement disorders?
- Is there an underlying medical disorder that may explain the repetitive movements?
- Will my insurance pay for the assistance of a behavioral or other therapist?
- Could the repetitive movements be the side effect of a medication?

with stereotypic movement disorder, the following conditions must be met.

- The patient must show repeated, purposeless motor behavior.
- The patient must experience physical harm from this behavior, or it must seriously interfere with activities.
- If the patient is intellectually disabled, the behavior must be serious enough to require treatment.
- The behavior must not be a symptom of another psychiatric disorder.
- The behavior must not be a side effect of medicinal or illicit substance use.
- The behavior must not be caused by a diagnosed medical condition.
- The behavior must last at least four weeks.

This definition of stereotypic movement disorder rules out many people who show repetitive movement because of autism or other pervasive developmental disorders. It also rules out those with **obsessive-compulsive disorder**, among whom movements are apt to be ritualistic and follow rigid rules or patterns. In addition, specific disorders such as **trichotillomania** (hair pulling) do not receive the **diagnosis** of stereotypic movement disorder nor do developmentally appropriate self-stimulatory behaviors among young children, such as thumb-sucking, rocking, or transient head banging.

Treatment

There are few successful treatments for stereotypic movement disorder. When the behaviors are harmful to the patient, physical restraints may be required. In less severe situations, behavioral modification techniques may help decrease the intensity of the behavior. Drugs that have been used with some success to treat stereotypic movement disorder are **clomipramine** (Anafranil), **desipramine** (Norpramin), **haloperidol** (Haldol), and **chlorpromazine** (Thorazine).

Prognosis

Stereotypic movements peak in adolescence, then decline, and sometimes disappear. Although **behavior modification** may reduce the intensity of the stereotypic movements, rarely does it eliminate them. **Stress** and physical pain may bring on these movements, which may come and go for years, especially among those patients with severe intellectual disability.

Prevention

Stereotypic movement disorder cannot be prevented. Interventions should be made to prevent self-injury.

Resources

BOOKS

Larsen, Barbara J., ed. *Movement Disorders: Causes, Diagnoses, and Treatments.* Hauppauge, NY: Nova Science Publishers, 2010.

Schapira, Anthony H. V., Anthony E. T. Lang, and Stanley Fahn. *Movement Disorders.* 4th ed. Philadelphia: Saunders/Elsevier, 2010.

Watts, Ray L., David G. Standarett, and Jose A. Obeso, eds. *Movement Disorders.* 3rd ed. New York: McGraw-Hill, 2011.

PERIODICALS

Freeman, Roger D., Atefeh Soltanifar, and Susan Baer. "Stereotypic Movement Disorder: Easily Missed." *Developmental Medicine and Child Neurology* 52, no. 8 (August 2010):733–38.

Singer, Harvey S. "Movement Stereotypies." *Seminars in Pediatric Neurology* 16, no. 2 (June 2009): 77–81.

Zinner, Samuel H., and Jonathan W. Mink. "Movement Disorders I: Tics and Stereotypies." *Pediatrics in Review* 31, no. 6 (June 2010): 223–33.

ORGANIZATIONS

American Association on Intellectual and Developmental Disabilities, 501 3rd St. NW, Ste. 200, Washington, DC, 20001, (202) 387-1968, (800) 424-3688, Fax: (202) 387-2193, http://www.aaidd.org.

The Arc, 1660 L St. NW, Ste. 301, Washington, DC, 20036, (202) 534-3700, (800) 433-5255, Fax: (202) 534-3731, info@thearc.org, http://www.thearc.org.

Movement Disorder Society, 555 E Wells St., Ste. 1100, Milwaukee, WI, 53202, (414) 276-2145, Fax: (414) 276-3349, info@movementdisorders.org, http://www.movementdisorders.org.

Tish Davidson, AM

Steroids

Definition

Steroids constitute a large class of naturally occurring and synthetic chemicals, including sterols, such as cholesterol, and various corticosteroid and sex hormones that have wide-ranging effects. There are five classes of steroid hormones: mineralocorticoids, glucocorticoids, estrogens, progestins, and androgens. However, the term "steroid" commonly refers to anabolic-androgenic steroids (AASs), which are synthetic derivatives of the male sex hormone testosterone.

Purpose

Anabolic-androgenic steroids are growth inducers. They were first developed in Europe in the 1930s to treat malnourishment and to promote healing following surgery. They are most commonly prescribed for hormone-replacement therapy, but may also prescribed for several other conditions, including muscle wasting (cachexia), anemia, and malnutrition, among others.

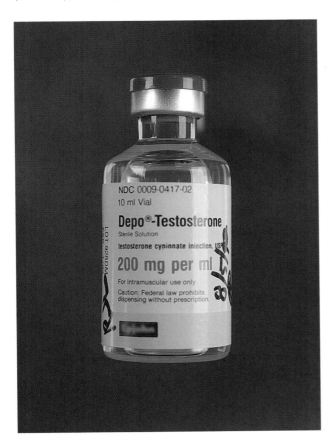

Depo-Testosterone, 10 mL. (*U.S. Drug Enforcement Administration*)

In addition to their legitimate medical uses, AASs are widely abused for building muscle, increasing strength, losing fat, enhancing athletic performance, and otherwise engaging in high-risk behavior. Their anabolic effects build muscle and their androgenic effects develop male sexual characteristics in both males and females. At medically prescribed dosages, the growth effects of anabolic steroids are slow or unnoticeable. However, at high abusive doses, muscles increase rapidly in size and strength, and AAS may increase energy and libido.

Competitive weightlifters began using AASs in the 1950s, and their use gradually spread to other sports. Most major athletic competitions, including the Olympic Games, the Wimbledon tennis tournament, the Tour de France bicycle race, and major-league professional sports teams, now routinely screen athletes for steroid use. Some steroids are easily detectable with a urine screen; the products of steroid metabolism can be identified in the urine for six months or longer after the drugs are discontinued. However, the technology for detecting steroids in blood or urine—and distinguishing the use of AASs from the products of normal metabolism or legitimate medications—is often one step behind the design of new steroid drugs.

Description

Steroids are chemicals containing a steroid nucleus that consists of four rings of 17 carbon atoms. They are fat-soluble compounds found in both plants and animals that function as hormones, or chemical messengers. In humans, steroids are produced from cholesterol in the endocrine glands, such as the adrenal cortex and the gonads (ovary and testis). Glands secrete the hormones directly into the bloodstream, where they are transported to distant parts of the body and control various vital physiologic functions ranging from suppressing inflammation to regulating physiological changes during pregnancy.

Anabolic-androgenic steroids have three mechanisms of action:

- protein metabolism
- increased synthesis of skeletal muscle tissue
- athletic endurance (allowing athletes to train harder and longer)

Common AASs preparations include:

- testosterone esters—testosterone propionate, cypionate, and enanthate
- testosterone derivatives—methyltestosterone (which is rarely used), methandrostenolone, and fluoxymesterone (which is rarely used clinically but is abused)
- nandrolone derivatives—nandrolone decanoate, ethylestrenol, and trenbolone

• dihydrotestosterone (DHT) derivatives—oxandrolone, stanozolol, and oxymetholone

AASs are taken orally as tablets or capsules, injected into muscles, or applied through the skin via ointments or transdermal patches. They are sometimes combined with creatine, protein powders, and/or various antioxidant formulations. These are considered to be ergogenic aids—substances that enhance the body's production, use, or recovery of energy and provide athletes with a competitive advantage.

U.S. brand names

AASs that are prescribed for medical purposes in the United States include:

• Depo-Testosterone (testosterone cypionate) for low testosterone levels

• Android (methyltestosterone) for treating hot flashes in postmenopausal women

• nandrolone decanoate, an injectable preparation available only as a generic and relatively safe at clinical doses for treating osteoporosis, but one of the most widely abused AASs

• Oxandrin (oxandrolone), oral tablets prescribed for HIV/AIDS-related conditions, bone pain from osteoporosis, to prevent certain side effects of corticosteroids, and sometimes abused by female athletes

• Anadrol-50 (oxymetholone), oral tablets that are abused worldwide and are considered to be carcinogenic

In the past, steroidal supplements such as androstenedione ("Andro") were commercially available in the United States. They were declared illegal in 2004 in an amendment to the Controlled Substances Act. The only remaining legal steroidal supplement in the United States is dehydroepiandrosterone (**DHEA**), which may or may not be converted to testosterone in the body.

Many athletes and other people obtain and use AASs illegally. Estimates of steroid abuse in the general adult population of the United States range from 0.5–5%. Although most anabolic steroid users are adult males, misuse is increasing among women and adolescents.

Street names for veterinary steroids that are abused include:

• Abolic
• Dianabol
• Equipoise
• Finajet/Finaject
• Parabolin
• Trenbolone
• Winstrol V

Street names for oral steroids that are abused include:

• Anadrol
• Anavar
• Maxibolin
• Methyltestosterone
• Parabolin
• Primbolin
• Primobolin
• Proviron
• Winstrol

Street names for abused injectable steroids include:

• Anatrofin
• Bolasterone
• Deca-Duabolin
• Delatestryl
• Depo-testosterone
• Dihydrolone
• Durabolin
• Dymethzine
• Enoltestovis
• Methatriol
• Primbolin
• Primobolin
• Quinolone
• Sustanon 250
• Therobolin
• Trophobolene

So-called designer steroids include:

• THG (tetrahydrogestrinone)
• Madol (desoxymethyltestosterone)
• Genabol (norbolethone)
• Equipoise and others (boldenone undecylenate)

Canadian brand names

Canadian AASs include Deca-Durabolin (nandrolone decanoate) and Anapolon 50 (oxymetholone).

International brand names

There are thousands of international brand names for AASs, and in some countries they are available over the counter. Methandrostenolone (Dianabol, Danabol, DBOL, Reforvit-b) and ethylestrenol (Maxibolin) have been discontinued in the United States but are still manufactured internationally. Trenbolone, a veterinary drug in the United States, is a widely abused

KEY TERMS

Anabolic—Causing muscle and bone growth and a shift from fat to muscle in the body.

Androgenic—Causing testosterone-like, masculinizing effects.

Angioedema—Patches of swelling of the skin, subcutaneous layers, mucus membranes, and sometimes internal organs.

Cachexia—Physical wasting and malnutrition, usually from chronic disease.

Cholesterol—A steroid alcohol in cells and body fluids that serves as a precursor for hormones and other steroids.

Corticosteroid—A steroid, such as cortisone, produced by the adrenal cortex.

Creatine—A nitrogen-containing substance found in muscle.

Estrogen—The primary female sex hormone.

Hormones—Chemical messengers that are carried by the bloodstream to various organs where they affect functioning, often by stimulatory action.

Sex hormones—Hormones that are responsible for sexual characteristics and reproductive functioning.

Steroids—A class of hormones and drugs that includes sex and stress hormones and anti-inflammatory medications, contraceptives, and growth-promoting substances.

Sterols—Steroid alcohols, such as cholesterol, that are widely distributed in the body.

Testosterone—The primary male sex hormone.

European prescription drug. Winstrol (stanozolol) is marketed internationally as well as in the United States, comes in both oral and injectable forms, and is widely abused.

Recommended dosage

Dosages used by AAS abusers are often 50–100 times higher than those for treating medical conditions. In one survey of 500 AAS users, more than half reported taking 1,000 mg or more every week. In addition 13% acknowledged using unsafe injection practices such as sharing needles, reusing needles, or sharing multi-dose vials of steroids.

In addition to higher doses, AAS abusers may practice:

• stacking—taking two or more AASs together, using more than one route of administration, or mixing AASs with other drugs such as stimulants or painkillers

• cycling—alternating periods of steroid use with periods of abstinence

• pyramiding—cycling of increasing doses over several weeks followed by decreasing doses

Some users believe that cycling and pyramiding maximize the desirable effects of steroids while reducing the undesirable effects, although there is no scientific evidence to support this claim, and cycling may build tolerance, requiring higher dosages.

Precautions

Although AASs are considered to be relatively safe at the usual prescribed dosages, at abusive dosages they can result in a wide range of serious health problems:

• abnormal lipid profiles

• early heart attacks

• strokes

• kidney failure

• severe liver problems including jaundice, tumors, and cancer

• depression

• severe psychiatric disturbances

Unsafe injection of AASs can result in HIV and hepatitis B and C infections. It has also been suggested that steroids may be gateway drugs for narcotics abuse, and it is possible to become psychologically addicted to them.

Withdrawal from high doses of AASs may require:

• medication to relieve withdrawal symptoms

• antidepressants

• hormones to restore normal hormonal function

Pediatric

AASs should be used with extreme caution in children. They can cause early puberty and lead to premature cessation of bone growth, resulting in permanent short stature.

QUESTIONS TO ASK YOUR DOCTOR

- When should I take this medication?
- Should I take it with food?
- What if I miss a dose?
- What side effects might I experience?
- Can I become addicted to this drug?

A 2008 survey by the National Institute on Drug Abuse found that 1.4% of eighth graders, 1.4% of tenth graders, and 2.2% of twelfth graders had used AASs. Some were athletes attempting to increase their strength and size; others were simply attempting to speed up their growth to keep pace with their peers. Many teenagers are also attracted by the psychological rush that comes with steroid abuse. Prevention programs often target school- or community-sponsored athletic teams, team leaders, and coaches. It has been recommended that educational prevention programs start with middle-school athletes.

Side effects

AASs usually have few side effects at medical dosages. However, at the much higher doses used to improve **body image** or athletic performance, side effects can be serious and sometimes irreversible. Excessive use can cause harmful imbalances in hormones and body chemistry. Side effects of AAS abuse can include:

- shrinking testicles, falling sperm counts, gynecomastia (swelling and enlargement of the breasts), increased urination, and enlarged prostate glands in males

- virilization in females, including hirsutism (growth of body and facial hair), male-pattern baldness, cessation of menstruation, decreased breast size, deepening of the voice, and abnormal enlargement of the clitoris

- an increase in "bad" cholesterol (LDL) and a decrease in "good" cholesterol (HDL)

- water retention leading to high blood pressure and stroke

- heart attacks

- liver and kidney tumors

- insomnia

- drastic mood swings ranging from mania to depression

- aggression, paranoia, irritability, delusions, hostility, psychosis

Treatment

Treatment of steroid abuse may include counseling to address the reasons for steroid use and medications to alleviate any symptoms associated with withdrawal. Hormones may be used to restore normal hormonal functioning in the body, and **antidepressants** may be used to alleviate **depression** that can occur when steroid use is terminated.

Resources

BOOKS

Fourcroy, Jean L., ed. *Pharmacology, Doping, and Sports: A Scientific Guide for Athletes, Coaches, Physicians, Scientists, and Administrators.* New York: Routledge, 2009.

Freedman, Jeri. *Steroids: High-Risk Performance Drugs.* New York: Rosen, 2009.

Kiesbye, Stefan. *Steroids.* Detroit: Greenhaven Press, 2007.

Thompson, Teri, et al. *American Icon: The Fall of Roger Clemens and the Rise of Steroids in America's Pastime.* New York: Alfred A. Knopf, 2009.

Walker, Ida. *Steroids: Pumped Up and Dangerous.* Philadelphia: Mason Crest, 2008.

PERIODICALS

Dines, Josh, and Rock Positano. "Steroid Talk Rages On." *New York Daily News* (June 21, 2009): 55.

Kokkevi, A., et al. "Daily Exercise and Anabolic Steroids Use in Adolescents: A Cross-National European Study." *Substance Use and Misuse* 43, no. 14 (2008): 2053–65.

Talih, F., et al. "Anabolic Steroid Abuse: Psychiatric and Physical Costs." *Cleveland Clinic Journal of Medicine* 74, no. 5 (2007): 341–52.

WEBSITES

Kishner, Stephen. "Anabolic Steroid Use and Abuse." Medscape Reference. Last updated July 6, 2011. http:// emedicine.medscape.com/article/128655-overview (accessed August 15, 2011).

Mayo Clinic staff. "Performance-Enhancing Drugs: Are They a Risk to Your Health?" MayoClinic.com. December 23, 2010. http://www.mayoclinic.com/print/performance-enhancing-drugs/HQ01105/METHOD=print (accessed August 15, 2011).

National Institute on Drug Abuse. "Anabolic Steroid Abuse." http://www.steroidabuse.org (accessed August 15, 2011).

———. "Steroids (Anabolic-Androgenic)." *NIDA InfoFacts,* July 2009. http://www.drugabuse.gov/infofacts/steroids. html (accessed August 15, 2011).

ORGANIZATIONS

American College of Sports Medicine, PO Box 1440, Indianapolis, IN, 46202-1440, (317) 637-9200, Fax: (317) 634-7817, http://www.acsm.org.

National Institute on Drug Abuse, 6001 Executive Blvd., Rm. 5213, Bethesda, MD, 20892-9561, (301) 443-1124, information@nida.nih.gov, http://www.drugabuse.gov/NIDAHome.html.

Jill U. Adams
Margaret Alic, PhD

Stigma

Definitions

Stigma (plural, stigmas) is a Greek word that in its origins referred to a kind of tattoo mark that was cut or burned into the skin of criminals, slaves, or traitors in order to visibly identify them as blemished or morally polluted persons. These individuals were to be avoided or shunned, particularly in public places. The word was later applied to other personal attributes that are considered shameful or discrediting.

Social psychologists have distinguished three large classes, or categories, of stigma:

- Physical deformities. These include extremes of height and weight and such conditions as albinism and facial disfigurements or missing limbs. In the developed countries, this category also includes such signs of aging as gray hair, wrinkles, and stooped posture.

- Weaknesses or defects of individual character. This category includes biographical data that are held to indicate personal moral defect, such as a criminal record, addiction, divorce, unemployment, suicide attempts, or psychiatric disorders.

- Tribal stigma. This type of stigma refers to a person's membership in a race, ethnic group, religion, or (for women) gender that is thought to devalue all members of the group.

The second category, weaknesses or defects of an individual's character, is particularly relevant to treatment for mental illness. The 1999 report on mental health by the Surgeon General of the United States was regarded as a landmark document in the United Kingdom as well as the United States because of its straightforward identification of the stigma associated with mental illness as the chief obstacle to effective treatment of persons with mental disorders. Chapter 1 of the report noted that "Stigma leads others to avoid living, socializing or working with, renting to, or employing people with mental disorders... It reduces patients' access to resources and opportunities (e.g., housing, jobs) and leads to low self-esteem, isolation, and hopelessness. It deters the public from seeking, and wanting to pay for, care. In its most overt and egregious form, stigma results in outright discrimination and **abuse**. More tragically, it deprives people of their dignity and interferes with their full participation in society."

The report attributed the stigma attached to mental illness in the United States to three major factors:

- A misguided philosophical separation of mind and body going back to René Descartes (1596–1650) in the seventeenth century that led to a tendency to regard mental health issues as completely separate from physical disorders.

- Separation of treatment systems in which the mentally ill were isolated from the rest of society in "asylums" or mental hospitals.

- Fear of violent behavior on the part of the mentally ill. The report stated that public perception of those diagnosed with psychotic disorders in particular as dangerous was much stronger in the late 1990s than in the 1950s, even though the general public appeared to have a better understanding of the various causes of mental disorders than had been the case in the 1950s.

Psychiatrists who have studied the social stigma associated with mental illness maintain that it is important to distinguish two types of stigma: public stigma, which they define as prejudice and discrimination on the part of the general population against those diagnosed with mental disorders, and self-stigma, which is a person's internalization of public discrimination and disapproval.

The nature of stigma

Origins

One explanation for the origin of stigmas is that it is rooted in humans' concern for group survival at earlier times in their evolutionary journey. According to this theory, stigmatizing people who were perceived as unable to contribute to the group's survival, or who were seen as threats to its well-being, were stigmatized in order to justify isolating or forcing them out of the group.

The group survival theory is also thought to explain why certain human attributes seem to be universally regarded as stigmas, while others are specific to certain cultures or periods of history. Mental illness appears to be a characteristic that has nearly always led to the stigmatization and exclusion of its victims. The primary influences on Western culture, the classical philosophical tradition of Greece and Rome, and the religious traditions of Judaism and Christianity, indicate that mental illness was a feared affliction that carried a heavy stigma.

Contemporary contexts

The core feature of stigma in the modern world is defined by social psychologists as the possession of an attribute "that conveys a devalued social identity within a particular context." Context is important in assessing the nature and severity of **stress** that a person suffers with regard to stigma. Certain attributes, such as race, sex, level of education, or occupation, affect an individual's interactions with other people in so many different situations that they have been termed "master status attributes." These have become the classic identifying characteristics of the person who possesses them.

Other forms of devalued social identity are relative to specific cultures or subcultures. In one social context, a person who is stigmatized for an attribute devalued by a particular group may find acceptance in another group that values that particular attribute. One common example is that of an artistically or athletically talented child who grows up in a family that values only intellectual accomplishment. When the youngster is old enough to leave the family of origin, he or she can find a school or program for other students who share the same interest. A less marked contrast, but one that is relevant to the treatment of mental illness, is the cultural differences with regard to the degree of response to certain symptoms of mental illness. A study of **dementia** patients from minority ethnic groups reported in 2011 that members of these groups were much slower to seek **diagnosis** and treatment than members of the general public, in large measure because of the greater stigma attached to dementia in the ethnic minority communities.

One additional complicating feature of stigma is the issue of overlapping stigmas. Many people belong to several stigmatized groups or categories, and it is not always easy to determine which category triggers the unkind or discriminatory treatment encountered. For example, one study of the inadequate medical treatment that is offered to most HIV-positive Native Americans noted that the stigma of Acquired Immune Deficiency Syndrome (AIDS) provides a strong motivation for not seeking treatment. The study protocol, however, did not seek to investigate whether young Native American men are afraid of being stigmatized for their sexual orientation, their race, their low socioeconomic status, or all three. A later Canadian study, however, did attempt to account for the overlapping layers of stigma in this population.

Stigma and mental illness

Stigma and specific disorders

The stigma that is still attached to mental illness in the developed countries does not represent a simple or straightforward problem. Public health experts who have studied the stigmatization of mental illness in recent years have noted that the general public's perception of mental illness varies according to the nature of the disorder. While in general the stigma of mental illness in contemporary society is primarily associated with the second of the three categories of stigma, supposed character failings, it also spills over into the first category, physical deformities. Mental disorders that

affect a person's physical appearance, particularly weight gain, are more heavily stigmatized than those that do not. Obese persons are also a stigmatized group even without the context of a mental disorder.

The stigma related to certain types of mental disorders has declined since the 1950s, most notably in regard to **depression** and **anxiety disorders**. It is thought that the reason for this change is that people are now more likely to attribute these disorders to stress, with which most people can identify. Moreover, there has been greater awareness and education about mental disorders and their treatments in the past decade. On the other hand, the stigma associated with psychotic disorders appears to be worse than it was in the 1950s. Changes in public attitude are also reflected in age-group patterns in seeking or dropping out of treatment for mental disorders. One study demonstrated that older adults being treated for depression were more likely than younger adults to drop out of treatment because they felt stigmatized. The difference in behavior is related to public attitudes toward mental illness that were widespread when the older adults were adolescents.

The types of mental disorders that carry the heaviest stigma fall into the following categories:

- Disorders associated in the popular mind with violence and/or illegal activity. These include schizophrenia, mental problems associated with HIV infection or other sexually transmitted diseases, and substance abuse disorders. Veterans of military service are particularly likely to be stigmatized by treatment for PTSD as well as substance abuse.

- Disorders in which the patient's behavior in public may embarrass family members. These include dementia in the elderly, borderline personality disorder or schizophrenia in adults, and the autistic spectrum disorders in children.

- Disorders treated with medications that cause weight gain, facial puffiness, tardive dyskinesia, or other visible side effects. Pharmacy students in particular are reported to hold strongly negative opinions of persons diagnosed with these disorders.

- Disorders treated with medications that can be abused for mood alteration. One survey of U.S. college students reported in 2011 that 13% of the students surveyed admitted to misusing psychiatric medications to improve studying (usually stimulants) or to get "high" (usually benzodiazepine tranquilizers).

Role of the media

The role of the media in perpetuating the stigmatization of mental illness has received increasing attention from public health researchers, particularly in Great

Britain. In 1998, the Royal College of Psychiatrists launched a five-year campaign intended to educate the general public about the nature and treatment of mental illness. Surveys conducted among present and former mental patients found that they considered media coverage of their disorders to be strongly biased toward the sensational and the negative. One-third of patients said that they felt more depressed or anxious as a result of news stories about the mentally ill, and 22% felt more withdrawn. The main complaint from mental health professionals, as well as patients, is that the media presented mentally ill people as "dangerous time bombs waiting to explode" when in fact 95% of murders in the United Kingdom are committed by people with no mental illness. The proportion of homicides committed by the mentally ill has decreased by 3% per year since 1957, but this statistic goes unreported. Much of the same unfair stigmatization in the media occurs in the United States according to a 1999 report of the Surgeon General.

Physicians' attitudes toward mental illness

Physicians' attitudes toward the mentally ill are also increasingly recognized as part of the problem of stigmatization. The patronizing attitude of moral superiority toward the mentally ill in the early 1960s, specifically in mental hospitals, has not disappeared. This was reported by Erving Goffman in his classic study. An American physician who specializes in the treatment of substance addicts cites three reasons for the persistence of stigmatizing attitudes among his colleagues: their tendency to see **substance abuse** as a social issue, rather than a health issue; their lack of training in detecting substance abuse; and their mistaken belief that no effective treatments exist. A similar lack of information about effective treatments characterizes many psychiatrists' attitudes toward **borderline personality disorder**.

Negative attitudes on the part of physicians toward the mentally ill can be found in Europe and Asia as well as North America. For example, a survey of Turkish medical students reported in 2011 that 90% would not want a person with a history of **suicide** attempts to care for their children, and 73% would not rent a room to such a person.

Stigma as cause of mental illness

It is significant that researchers in the field of social psychology have moved in recent years to analyzing stigma in terms of stress. Newer studies in this field now refer to membership in a stigmatized group as a stressor that increases a person's risk of developing a mental illness. The physiological and psychological effects of stress caused by racist behavior, for example, have been

documented in African Americans. Similar studies of obese people have found that the stigmatization of obesity is the single most important factor in the psychological problems of these patients. To give still another example, the high rates of depression among postmenopausal women have been attributed to the fact that aging is a much heavier stigma for women than for men in contemporary society.

Stigma has a secondary effect on rates of mental illness in that members of stigmatized groups have less access to educational opportunities, well-paying jobs, and adequate health care. They are therefore exposed to more environmental stressors in addition to the stigma itself.

Stigma as effect

Stigma resulting from mental illness has been shown to increase the likelihood of a patient's **relapse**. Since a mental disorder is not as immediately apparent as race, sex, or physical disabilities, many people with mental disorders undergo considerable strain trying to conceal their condition from strangers or casual acquaintances. More seriously, the stigma causes problems in the job market, leading to stress caused by lying to a potential employer and fears of being found out. Erving Goffman, a sociologist who wrote a landmark study of mental institutions, reported in the 1960s that one common way around the dilemma involved taking a job for about six months after discharge from a mental institution, then quitting that job and applying for another with a recommendation from the first employer that did not mention the history of mental illness.

The stigmatization of the patient with mental illness extends to family members, partly because they are often seen, or see themselves, as the source of the patient's disorder. A study done in Israel reported in 2011 that the parents of individuals with severe mental illness carry a heavy burden of self-stigma. An editorial published in the *Journal of the American Medical Association* in 2001 tells the story of two sets of parents coping with the stress caused by other people's reactions to their children's mental illness, and the different responses they received when the children's disorders were thought to be a physical problem. The writer also recounts the problems encountered by the parents of an autistic child. The writer stated that family excursions were difficult, and continued, "My friend's wife was reprimanded by strangers for not being able to control her son. The boy was stared at and ridiculed. The inventive parent, fed up with the situation, bought a wheelchair to take the child out. The family was now asked about their child's disability. They were praised for their tolerance of his physical hardship and for their courage; the son was commended for his bravery. Same parents, same child, different view."

Results of stigma

The stigmatization of mental disorders has a number of consequences for the larger society. Patients' refusal to seek treatment, noncompliance with treatment, and inability to find work carry a high price tag. Disability related to mental illness accounts for fully 15% of the economic burden caused by *all* diseases in developed countries.

Seeking treatment

Stigmatization of mental illness is an important factor in preventing persons with mental disorders from asking for help. This factor affects even mental health services on university campuses; interviews with Harvard students following a 1995 murder in which a depressed student killed a classmate found that students hesitated to consult mental health professionals because many of their concerns were treated as disciplinary infractions rather than illnesses. The tendency to stigmatize mental disorders as character faults is as prevalent among educators as among medical professionals. Another institution in which persons are reluctant to seek help is the military, including veterans as well as service personnel on active duty; many soldiers, sailors, and airmen mention the possible effect of mental health treatment records on promotion or career advancement as a major reason for not seeking help.

In addition, studies of large corporations indicate that employees frequently hesitate to seek treatment for depression and other stress-related disorders for fear of receiving negative evaluations of job performance and possible termination. These fears are especially acute during economic downturns and periods of corporate downsizing.

Compliance with treatment

Another link between mental disorders and stigma is the low rates of treatment **compliance** among patients. To a large extent, patient compliance is a direct reflection of the quality of the doctor-patient relationship. Other reasons for low compliance with treatment regimens are related to stigmatized side effects. Many patients, particularly women, discontinue medications that cause weight gain because of the social stigma attached to obesity in females.

Social and economic consequences

Persons with a history of treatment for mental disorders frequently encounter prejudice in the job market and the likelihood of long periods of unemployment; this can result in lower socioeconomic status as

---

KEY TERMS

Asylum—An older term for psychiatric hospitals; it is rarely used except in historical studies of psychiatric treatment.

Master status attribute—A term used in sociology for a characteristic that is the most important definer of an individual's social status or identity; one that overshadows other traits and affects the person's behavior in most situations. Common master status attributes are race, sex, sexual orientation, level of education, age, and mental illness or disability.

Medical model of mental illness—An approach to psychiatric diagnosis and treatment patterned on the process of diagnosis and treatment of physical disease.

Self-stigma—Loss of self-esteem and personal effectiveness that develops when a person being treated for a mental health issue internalizes public prejudice against people diagnosed with mental disorders.

Tardive dyskinesia—A disorder characterized by involuntary and repetitive body movements that sometimes develops after long-term use of antipsychotic medications.

---

well as loss of self-esteem. These problems are not limited to North America. In 1990, the U.S. Congress included mental disorders (with a few exceptions for disorders related to substance abuse and compulsive sexual behaviors) in the anti-discriminatory provisions of the Americans with Disabilities Act (ADA). As of 2011, mental disorders constituted the third-largest category of discrimination claims against employers.

Stigmatization of mental disorders also affects funding for research into the causes and treatment of mental disorders. Records of recent debates at the federal and state levels indicate that money for mental health research was still apportioned as of 2011. Increasing such funding is one of the goals of the National Consortium on Stigma and Empowerment (NCSE), an organization of mental health researchers founded in the late 1990s.

Future prospects

The stigma of mental illness will not disappear overnight. Slow changes in attitudes toward other social issues have occurred in the past three decades, giving

---

QUESTIONS TO ASK YOUR DOCTOR

- Do you think people still fear being stigmatized if they seek help for mental health problems?
- Have you ever had difficulty referring a patient to a psychiatrist because they were afraid of stigma?
- Do you think that the situation is gradually improving and that the general public is more understanding of mental health issues?
- What is your opinion of media treatment of people with mental disorders?

hope to the lessening of stigma borne by people with mental illness. In addition, the stigmatizing of mental conditions has become a major topic of sociological as well as psychiatric research and publication since the early 2000s. However, economic limitations are an ongoing reason for concern. As the economic "pie" has to be divided among a larger number of advocacy groups, causing stiffer competition for public funding, persons with mental disorders will need skilled and committed advocates if their many serious needs are to receive adequate attention and help. Such groups as the National Alliance on Mental Illness (NAMI), which has launched a "StigmaBusters" campaign, have stepped up their efforts to educate the public as well as press for increases in funding to reduce the stigma of mental illness.

Another approach to reducing the stigma of mental illness is setting up education groups for caregivers of patients diagnosed with such severe disorders as **schizophrenia** and **Alzheimer's disease**; the groups include helping caregivers cope with the stigma of their loved one's illness as well as providing direct care for him or her. Online courses for caregivers as well as some for patients themselves are also available; these resources appear to be particularly useful to high school and college students with mental health problems. Readers interested in educating themselves about stigma or in advocacy at the local community level can find resources on the NAMI website as well as on the website of the National Consortium on Stigma and Empowerment (NCSE), listed under Organizations below.

The proposed change in the definition of a mental disorder for DSM-5 may also help to reduce the stigma associated with mental health problems. The new definition represents a move away from the traditional medical model of mental disorders by referring to them as "behavioral or psychological syndrome[s] or pattern[s] that occur in an individual" and that reflect "an underlying psychological dysfunction." One of the rationales given for the new definition is the growing recognition that human behavior and psychology cannot be separated from the biological dimension of human beings. This recognition is a clear rejection of the Cartesian separation of mind and body noted earlier.

Resources

BOOKS

Arboleda-Flórez, Julio, and Norman Sartorius, eds. *Understanding the Stigma of Mental Illness: Theory and Interventions*. Hoboken, NJ: John Wiley and Sons, 2008.

Corrigan, Patrick William, David Roe, and Hector W.H. Stang. *Challenging the Stigma of Mental Illness: Lessons for Therapists and Advocates*. Hoboken, NJ: John Wiley and Sons, 2011.

Goffman, Erving. *Asylums: Essays on the Social Situation of Mental Patients and Other Inmates*. New York: Anchor Books, 1961.

Goffman, Erving. *Stigma: Notes on the Management of Spoiled Identity*. New York: Simon and Schuster, Inc., 1963.

PERIODICALS

Barnes, E., et al. "Developing an Online Education Package for Bipolar Disorder." *Journal of Mental Health* 20 (February 2011): 21–31.

Emul, M., et al. "The Attitudes of Preclinical and Clinical Turkish Medical Students toward Suicide Attempters." *Crisis* 32 (January 1, 2011): 128–133.

Galletly, C., and C. Burton. "Improving Medical Student Attitudes towards People with Schizophrenia." *Australian and New Zealand Journal of Psychiatry* 45 (June 2011): 473–476.

Gorman, L.A., et al. "National Guard Families after Combat: Mental Health, Use of Mental Health Services, and Perceived Treatment Barriers." *Psychiatric Services* 62 (January 2011): 28–34.

Hasson-Ohayon, I., et al. "Insight into Mental Illness, Self-stigma, and the Family Burden of Parents of Persons with a Severe Mental Illness." *Comprehensive Psychiatry* 52 (January-February 2011): 75–80.

Horgan, A., and J. Sweeney. "Young Students' Use of the Internet for Mental Health Information and Support." *Journal of Psychiatric and Mental Health Nursing* 17 (March 2010): 117–123.

Mill, J., et al. "Accessing Health Services While Living with HIV: Intersections of Stigma." *Canadian Journal of Nursing Research* 41 (September 2009): 168–185.

Mukadam, N., et al. "A Systematic Review of Ethnicity and Pathways to Care in Dementia." *International Journal of Geriatric Psychiatry* 26 (January 2011): 12–20.

O'Reilly, C.L., et al. "Consumer-led Mental Health Education for Pharmacy Students." *American Journal of Pharmaceutical Education* 74 (November 10, 2010): 167.

Riley, G., et al. "Carer's Education Groups for Relatives with a First Episode of Psychosis: An Evaluation of an Eight-week Education Group." *Early Intervention in Psychiatry* 5 (February 2011): 57–63.

Schomerus, G., et al. "The Stigma of Alcohol Dependence Compared with Other Mental Disorders: A Review of Population Studies." *Alcohol and Alcoholism* 46 (March-April 2011): 105–112.

Skidmore, W.C., and M. Roy. "Practical Considerations for Addressing Substance Use Disorders in Veterans and Service Members." *Social Work in Health Care* 50 (January 2011): 85–107.

Stone, A.M., and L.J. Merlo. "Attitudes of College Students toward Mental Illness Stigma and the Misuse of Psychiatric Medications." *Journal of Clinical Psychiatry* 72 (February 2011): 134–139.

Vogt, D. "Mental Health-related Beliefs as a Barrier to Service Use for Military Personnel and Veterans: A Review." *Psychiatric Services* 62 (February 2011): 135–142.

Weissman, Myrna M. "Stigma." *Journal of the American Medical Association* 285 (January 17, 2001): 261.

WEBSITES

American Psychiatric Association. DSM-5 Development. "Definition of a Mental Disorder." http://www.dsm5.org/ProposedRevisions/Pages/proposedrevision.aspx?rid=465 (accessed May 23, 2011).

Mental Health: A Report of the Surgeon General, Chapter 1, "Introduction and Themes," section 5, "The Roots of Stigma." http://www.surgeongeneral.gov/library/mentalhealth/chapter1/sec1.html#roots_stigma (accessed May 29, 2011).

National Alliance on Mental Illness (NAMI). "The ADAA-mericans with Disabilities Act." http://www.nami.org/Template.cfm?Section=Helpline1&template=/ContentManagement/ContentDisplay.cfm&ContentID=47065 (accessed May 29, 2011).

ORGANIZATIONS

American Psychiatric Association (APA), 1000 Wilson Blvd., Ste. 1825, Arlington, VA, 22209-3901, (703) 907-7300, apa@psych.org, http://www.psych.org

National Alliance on Mental Illness (NAMI), 3803 N Fairfax Dr., Ste. 100, Arlington, VA, 22203, (703) 524-7600, Fax: (703) 524-9094, (800) 950-NAMI, http://www.nami.org

National Consortium on Stigma and Empowerment (NCSE), Illinois Institute of Technology, Institute of Psychology, 3424 S State St., First Fl., Chicago, IL, 60616, (312) 567-6751, Fax: (312) 567-6753, corrigan@iit.edu, http://www.stigmaandempowerment.org

National Institute of Mental Health (NIMH), 6001 Executive Blvd., Rm. 8184, MSC 9663, Bethesda, MD, 20892-9663, (301) 443-4513, Fax: (301) 443-4279, (866) 615-6464, nimhinfo@nih.gov, http://www.nimh.nih.gov/index.shtml

Rebecca J. Frey, Ph.D.

Stockholm syndrome

Definition

Stockholm syndrome refers to a group of psychological symptoms that occur in some persons in a captive or hostage situation. It has been used to explain the behavior of such well-known kidnapping victims as Patty Hearst (1974) and Elizabeth Smart (2002). The term takes its name from a bank robbery in Stockholm, Sweden, in August 1973. The robber took four employees of the bank (three women and one man) into the vault with him and kept them hostage for 131 hours. After the employees were finally released, they appeared to have formed a paradoxical emotional bond with their captor; they told reporters that they saw the police as their enemy rather than the bank robber and that they had positive feelings toward the criminal. The syndrome was first named by Nils Bejerot (1921–1988), a medical professor who specialized in **addiction** research and served as a psychiatric consultant to the Swedish police during the standoff at the bank. Stockholm syndrome is also known as Survival Identification Syndrome.

Description

Stockholm syndrome is considered a complex reaction to a frightening situation and experts do not agree completely on all of its characteristic features or on the factors that make some people more susceptible than others to developing it. One reason for the disagreement is that it would be unethical to test theories about the syndrome by experimenting on human beings. The data for understanding the syndrome derive from actual hostage situations since 1973 that differ considerably from one another in terms of location, number of people involved, and time frame. Another source of disagreement concerns the extent to which the syndrome can be used to explain other historical phenomena or more commonplace types of abusive relationships. Many researchers believe that Stockholm syndrome helps to explain certain behaviors of survivors of World War II concentration camps, members of religious cults, battered wives, incest survivors, and physically or emotionally abused children, as well as persons taken hostage by criminals or terrorists.

Most experts, however, agree that Stockholm syndrome has three central characteristics:

• The hostages have negative feelings about the police or other authorities.

• The hostages have positive feelings toward their captor(s).

• The captors develop positive feelings toward the hostages.

Causes & symptoms

Stockholm syndrome does not affect all hostages (or persons in comparable situations); in fact, a Federal Bureau of Investigation (FBI) study of more than 1,200 hostage-taking incidents found that 92% of the hostages did *not* develop Stockholm syndrome. FBI researchers then interviewed flight attendants who had been taken hostage during airplane hijackings, and concluded that three factors are necessary for the syndrome to develop:

- The crisis situation lasts for several days or longer.

- The hostage takers remain in contact with the hostages; that is, the hostages are not placed in a separate room.

- The hostage takers show some kindness toward the hostages or at least refrain from harming them. Hostages abused by captors typically feel anger toward them and do not usually develop the syndrome.

In addition, people who often feel helpless in other stressful life situations or are willing to do anything in order to survive seem to be more susceptible to developing Stockholm syndrome if they are taken hostage.

People with Stockholm syndrome report the same symptoms as those diagnosed with **post-traumatic stress disorder** (PTSD): **insomnia**, nightmares, general irritability, difficulty concentrating, being easily startled, feelings of unreality or confusion, inability to enjoy previously pleasurable experiences, increased distrust of others, and flashbacks.

Diagnosis

Stockholm syndrome is a descriptive term for a pattern of coping with a traumatic situation rather than a diagnostic category. Most psychiatrists would use the diagnostic criteria for **acute stress disorder** or post-traumatic **stress** disorder when evaluating a person with Stockholm syndrome.

Treatment

Treatment of Stockholm syndrome is the same as for PTSD, most commonly a combination of medications for short-term sleep disturbances and **psychotherapy** for the longer-term symptoms.

Prognosis

The prognosis for recovery from Stockholm syndrome is generally good, but the length of treatment needed depends on several variables. These include the nature of the hostage situation; the length of time the

KEY TERMS

Coping—In psychology, a term that refers to a person's patterns of response to stress. Some patterns of coping may lower a person's risk of developing Stockholm syndrome in a hostage situation.

Flashback—The re-emergence of a traumatic memory as a vivid recollection of sounds, images, and sensations associated with the trauma. The person having the flashback typically feels as if they are reliving the event. Flashbacks were first described by doctors treating combat veterans of World War I (1914–1918).

Identification with an aggressor—In psychology, an unconscious process in which a person adopts the perspective or behavior patterns of a captor or abuser. Some researchers consider it a partial explanation of Stockholm syndrome.

Regression—In psychology, a return to earlier, usually childish or infantile, patterns of thought or behavior.

Syndrome—A set of symptoms that occur together.

crisis lasted; and the individual patient's general coping style and previous experience(s) of **trauma**.

Prevention

Prevention of Stockholm syndrome at the level of the larger society includes further development of **crisis intervention** skills on the part of law enforcement, as well as strategies to prevent kidnapping or hostage-taking incidents in the first place. Prevention at the individual level is difficult, because researchers have not been able to identify all of the factors that may place some persons at greater risk than others; in addition, they disagree on the specific psychological mechanisms involved in Stockholm syndrome. Some regard the syndrome as a form of regression, while others explain it in terms of emotional paralysis ("frozen fright") or identification with the aggressor.

Resources

BOOKS

Ledwig, Marion. *Emotions: Their Rationality & Consistency.* New York: Peter Lang, 2006.

McMains, Michael J. *Crisis Negotiations: Managing Critical Incidents and Hostage Situations in Law Enforcement and Corrections.* Newark, NJ: LexisNexis, 2006.

PERIODICALS

Bejerot, Nils. "The Six-Day War in Stockholm." *New Scientist* 61, no. 886 (1974): 486–487. http://www.nilsbejerot.se/sexdagar_eng.htm (accessed October 27, 2011).

Grady, Denise. "Experts Look to Stockholm Syndrome on Why Girl Stayed." *The New York Times* March 17, 2003. http://www.dannyhaszard.com/smartbackup.htm (accessed October 27, 2011).

ORGANIZATIONS

American Psychiatric Association, 1000 Wilson Blvd., Ste. 1825, Arlington, VA, 22209-3901, (703) 907-7300, apa@psych.org, http://www.psych.org.

Federal Bureau of Investigation, 935 Pennsylvania Ave. NW, Washington, DC, 20535-0001, http://www.fbi.gov.

Rebecca Frey, PhD

Strattera *see* **Atomoxetine**

Stress

Definition

Stress is defined as an organism's total response to physical, mental, emotional, or environmental demands or pressures. A stressor is defined as the stimulus or event that provokes a stress response. Stressors can be categorized as acute or chronic and as external or internal to the organism.

Demographics

Nearly everyone experiences stress in their lives at some time. One study found that about 75% of those surveyed reported experiencing at least some stress in the previous two weeks. Occasional stress is an expected part of life for most people, and while often unpleasant, it does not lead to long-term negative outcomes. In some cases, however, severe or prolonged stress can lead to illness.

Work plays a highly visible role in the stress burden among Americans; in a 2010 survey conducted by the **American Psychological Association**, 70% of those surveyed included work as a top source of stress, with the other top two being money (76%) and the economy (65%). Forty-nine percent of workers cited job insecurity as a major source of stress, and only 32% felt their employers helped them attain a satisfactory work-life balance. Only one-third of respondents felt they were successful in managing their stress levels.

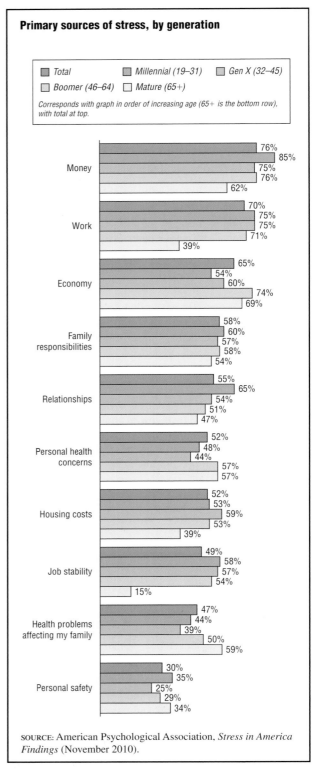

Primary sources of stress, by generation

- ▇ Total
- ▇ Millennial (19–31)
- ▇ Gen X (32–45)
- ▢ Boomer (46–64)
- ▢ Mature (65+)

Corresponds with graph in order of increasing age (65+ is the bottom row), with total at top.

Money: 76%, 85%, 75%, 76%, 62%
Work: 70%, 75%, 75%, 71%, 39%
Economy: 65%, 54%, 60%, 74%, 69%
Family responsibilities: 58%, 60%, 57%, 58%, 54%
Relationships: 55%, 65%, 54%, 51%, 47%
Personal health concerns: 52%, 48%, 44%, 57%, 57%
Housing costs: 52%, 53%, 59%, 53%, 39%
Job stability: 49%, 58%, 57%, 54%, 15%
Health problems affecting my family: 47%, 44%, 39%, 50%, 59%
Personal safety: 30%, 35%, 25%, 29%, 34%

SOURCE: American Psychological Association, *Stress in America Findings* (November 2010).

Report available online at http://www.apa.org/news/press/releases/stress/index.aspx. *(Graph by PreMediaGlobal. © 2012 Cengage Learning.)*

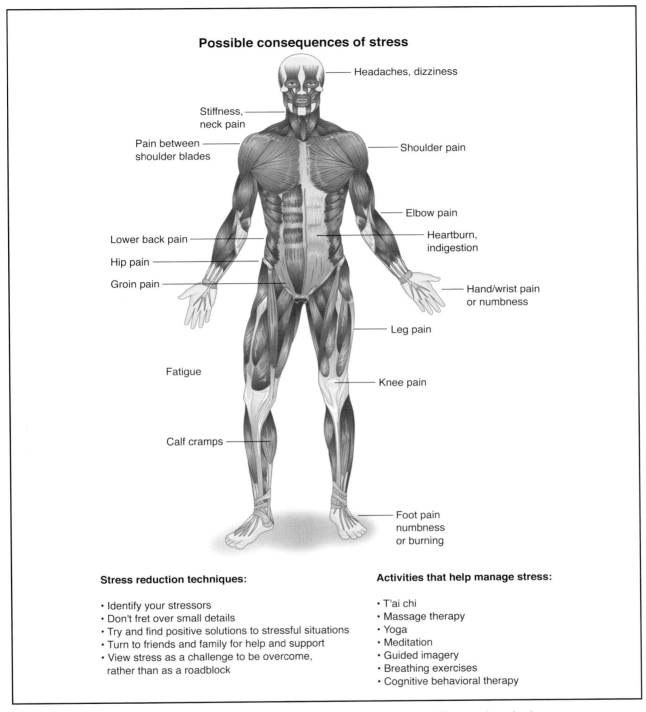

Possible consequences of stress

- Headaches, dizziness
- Stiffness, neck pain
- Pain between shoulder blades
- Shoulder pain
- Elbow pain
- Lower back pain
- Heartburn, indigestion
- Hip pain
- Groin pain
- Hand/wrist pain or numbness
- Leg pain
- Fatigue
- Knee pain
- Calf cramps
- Foot pain numbness or burning

Stress reduction techniques:

- Identify your stressors
- Don't fret over small details
- Try and find positive solutions to stressful situations
- Turn to friends and family for help and support
- View stress as a challenge to be overcome, rather than as a roadblock

Activities that help manage stress:

- T'ai chi
- Massage therapy
- Yoga
- Meditation
- Guided imagery
- Breathing exercises
- Cognitive behavioral therapy

(Illustration by Electronic Illustrators Group. Reproduced by permission of Gale, a part of Cengage Learning.)

Description

Stress results from interactions between persons and their environment that are perceived as straining or exceeding the individuals' adaptive capacities or threatening their well-being. A certain degree of stress is a normal part of life; it comprises individuals' responses to inevitable changes in their physical or social environment. Moreover, positive as well as negative events can generate stress. Graduating from college, for example, is accompanied by stress related to the challenge of finding employment or saying good-bye to friends and family, as well as feelings of positive accomplishment. Some researchers refer to stress associated with positive events as eustress.

Stress may be acute or chronic. Acute stress is defined as a reaction to something believed to be an immediate threat. Acute stress reactions can occur to a falsely perceived danger as well as to a genuine threat; they can also occur in response to memories. For example, a war veteran who hears a car backfire may drop to the ground because the noise triggers vivid memories, called flashbacks, of combat experience. Common acute stressors are loud, sudden noises; being in a crowded space, such as an elevator; being cut off in heavy traffic; and being exposed to dangerous weather. Chronic stress is a reaction to a stressful situation that is ongoing, such as financial insecurity or caring for a dependent elderly parent.

Stress-related disease results from chronic stress resulting from excessive and prolonged demands on an individual's ability to cope with the stressor(s). Canadian researcher Hans Selye (1907–1982), a pioneer in studying stress, observed that an increasing number of people, particularly in developed countries, died of so-called diseases of civilization, or degenerative diseases, which are primarily caused by stress.

The role of perception in identifying stressors indicates that human stress responses reflect differences in personality, as well as differences in physical strength or general health. Selye affirmed that stress in humans depends partly on people's evaluation of a situation and their emotional reaction to it; thus, an experience that one person finds stimulating and exciting, for example, bungee jumping, may produce harmful stress in another.

One recurrent disagreement among researchers concerns the definition of stress in humans. The debate centers on whether stress is primarily an external response that can be measured by changes in glandular secretions, skin reactions, and other physical functions or a solely an internal interpretation of, or reaction to, a stressor. Perhaps, in some cases, it is both.

Risk factors

Risk factors for stress-related illnesses are a mix of personal, interpersonal, and social variables. These factors include lack or loss of control over one's physical environment and lack or loss of social support networks. People who are dependent on others, such as children, the elderly, or those who are socially disadvantaged, are at greater risk of developing stress-related illnesses. Other risk factors are feelings of helplessness, hopelessness, extreme fear or anger, and cynicism or distrust of others.

Research indicates that some vulnerability to stress is genetic. Scientists at the University of Wisconsin and King's College London discovered that people who inherited a short, or stress-sensitive, version of the **serotonin** transporter gene were almost three times as likely to experience **depression** following a stressful event as people with the long version of the gene. Further research is likely to identify other genes that affect susceptibility to stress.

Stress and mental disorders

The **Diagnostic and Statistical Manual of Mental Disorders**, fourth edition, text revised (*DSM-IV-TR*) specifies two major categories of mental disorders directly related to stress: the post-traumatic syndromes and **adjustment disorders**. Proposed changes for the *Diagnostic and Statistical Manual of Mental Disorders*, fifth edition (*DSM-5*), scheduled for publication in 2013, combine these categories into one: trauma- and stressor-related disorders. Stress is closely associated with depression and can worsen the symptoms of most other disorders.

POST-TRAUMATIC DISORDERS. Post-traumatic stress disorder (PTSD) and **acute stress disorder** (ASD) are defined by their connection to a traumatic event in an individual's life, whether experienced or witnessed. The post-traumatic disorders are characterized by a cluster of anxiety and dissociative symptoms and by their interference with the patient's normal level of functioning. **Magnetic resonance imaging** (MRI) studies have shown that the high levels of sustained stress in some PTSD patients cause demonstrable damage to the hippocampus. Excessive amounts of stress hormones in **brain** tissue cause the nerve cells, or neurons, in parts of the hippocampus to wither and eventually die. One group of Vietnam veterans with PTSD lost as much as 8% of the tissue in the hippocampus.

SUBSTANCE ABUSE DISORDERS. Stress is related to **substance abuse** disorders in that chronic stress frequently leads people to self-medicate with drugs of abuse or alcohol. Substance abuse disorders are associated with a specific type of strategy for dealing with stress called emotion-focused coping. Emotion-focused coping strategies concentrate on regulating painful emotions related to stress, as distinct from problem-focused coping strategies, which involve efforts to change or eliminate the impact of a stressful event. Persons who handle stress from a problem-oriented perspective are less likely to turn to mood-altering substances when they are under stress.

ADJUSTMENT DISORDERS. The *DSM-IV-TR* defines adjustment disorders as psychological responses to stressors that are excessive given the nature of the stressor or that result in impairment of a person's academic, occupational, or social functioning. The most important difference between the post-traumatic disorders and adjustment disorders is that most people would not regard stressors involved in the latter disorder as traumatic. Adjustment disorders appear to be more common following divorce, the birth of a child, or retirement from work.

Causes and symptoms

The human stress response began as a biologically conditioned set of reactions that was necessary during earlier points in human evolution but is now less adaptive under the circumstances of modern life. In humans, the biochemical response to acute stress is known as the fight-or-flight reaction. It begins with the activation of a section of the brain called the hypothalamic-pituitary-adrenal system, or HPA. This system first activates the release of steroid hormones, which are also known as glucocorticoids. These hormones include cortisol, the primary stress hormone in humans.

Following the stress hormones, the HPA system releases a set of **neurotransmitters** known as catecholamines, which include **dopamine**, norepinephrine, and epinephrine (also known as **adrenaline**). Catecholamines have three important effects:

• They activate the amygdala, an almond-shaped structure in the limbic system that triggers an emotional response of fear.

• They signal the hippocampus, another part of the limbic system, to store the emotional experience in long-term memory.

• They suppress activity in parts of the brain associated with short-term memory, concentration, and rational thinking. This suppression allows a human to react quickly to a stressful situation, but it also lowers ability to deal with complex social or intellectual tasks that may be part of the situation.

In reaction to stress, heart rate, blood pressure, and breathing intake rise, allowing the lungs to take in more oxygen. Blood flow to the muscles, lungs, and brain may triple or quadruple. The spleen releases more blood cells into circulation, which increases the blood's ability to transport oxygen. The immune system redirects white blood cells to the skin, bone marrow, and lymph nodes, where injury or infection are most likely to occur.

At the same time, nonessential body systems shut down. The skin becomes cool and sweaty as blood is drawn away toward the heart and muscles. The mouth becomes dry, and the digestive system slows.

After the crisis passes, the levels of stress hormones drop, and the body's various organ systems return to normal, a process known as the relaxation response. Some people are more vulnerable to stress than others because their hormone levels do not return to normal after a stressful event. An absent or incomplete relaxation response is most likely to occur in professional athletes and in people with a history of depression.

Causes

Any event or occurrence that puts pressure on a person's coping mechanisms or resources can produce stress. Events such as a job interview, work-related presentation, or final exam can cause significant stress. Persons who dread a future event may experience an increased level of agitation and fretfulness. They may visualize the event negatively, worrying about what may go wrong. It is often hard to stop thinking about the event. This type of stress can take a significant toll if it persists for a long time.

Stress also may be caused by negative world news. Events such as the terrorist attacks on the United States, on September 11, 2001, are believed to increase stress both among Americans and people living elsewhere in the world. Events like terrorist attacks can prompt people to worry about the safety of family members and to fret about potential future attacks. These kinds of worries, when they occur over a long period of time, can produce chronic stress and related negative symptoms.

One study conducted telephone interviews following the September 11 terrorist attacks to assess stress reactions among the general U.S. population. The team found that the single most important factor was not geographical location relative to the attacks but the amount of time spent watching televised reports of the attacks. The interviewers discovered that 49% of the adults had watched at least eight hours of television on September 11, and the researchers considered extensive television viewing a reaction to stress.

Experiencing directly or witnessing a traumatic event such as a car accident, earthquake, or an attack of physical violence can cause severe stress. In these cases, an individual may mentally relive the event repeatedly. This is a normal response to a traumatic event, but if it persists for more than a short time or does not seem to get better, the individual may have PTSD or ASD.

Stress can also be caused by the presence of issues and problems that are upsetting or frustrating in day-to-day life. These can include worries about money, pressure at work, and problems in a relationship. Events such as divorce or the death of a loved one can also cause stress for many months or years but are not generally suggestive of PTSD or ASD.

Other causes of stress can include:

- social changes, such as living far away from family members or growing apart from childhood friends
- economic issues, such as a recession or lowered socioeconomic status
- technology, including constant access to news and events or feeling tied to work via e-mail or mobile devices
- environmental changes, such as pollution or nuclear disasters apparently due to chronic emotional stress rather than physiological exposure to harmful chemicals or radioactivity
- changes in mainstream beliefs and attitudes

Symptoms

The symptoms of stress can be physical, psychological, or both. Physical symptoms may include problems sleeping, indigestion, stomach pain or chest pain, **fatigue**, headache, back or neck pain, and many others. Psychological signs of stress include anxiety, frustration, irritability, and even depression. These symptoms may not be problematic if they occur for a brief time, but in cases of chronic stress, the body's organ systems do not have the opportunity to return fully to normal functioning. Different organs become under- or overactivated on a long-term basis. In time, these abnormal levels of activity can damage an organ or organ system.

In the workplace, stress-related illness often takes the form of burnout, a loss of interest in or ability to perform one's job due to long-term high stress levels. For example, palliative care nurses are at high risk of burnout due to their inability to prevent their patients from dying or even to relieve their physical suffering in some circumstances.

Effects of chronic stress on body systems

CARDIOVASCULAR SYSTEM. Stress has a number of negative effects on the heart and circulatory system. Acute, sudden stress increases the heart rate but also causes the arteries to narrow, which may block the flow of blood to the heart. The emotional effects of stress can alter the rhythm of the heart. In addition, stress triggers an inflammatory response in the blood vessels that can ultimately result in injury to the lining of the arteries. Markers of inflammation, linked to the development of cardiovascular disease, are also markers of the acute-phase response to stress. Stress also can cause a change in cholesterol levels, increasing fats in the blood that can eventually lead to clogged arteries and heart attack or **stroke**.

GASTROINTESTINAL SYSTEM. The effects of chronic stress on the gastrointestinal system include diarrhea, constipation, bloating, and irritable bowel syndrome. Although stress does not cause ulcers, which arise from an infection with *Helicobacter pylori* bacteria, it can exacerbate them. Stress can also influence inflammatory bowel disease, stimulating colon spasms and possibly interacting with the immune system in producing flare ups.

Stress is the cause of abnormal weight loss in some people and of weight gain in others, largely related to stress-related inability to eat or to control eating. It is thought that stress related to the physical and emotional changes of puberty is a major factor in the development of eating disorders.

REPRODUCTIVE SYSTEM. Stress affects sexual desire in both men and women and can cause impotence in men. It appears to worsen the symptoms of **premenstrual syndrome** (PMS) in women. Stress affects fertility because the high levels of cortisol in the blood can affect the hypothalamus, which produces hormones related to reproduction. Very high levels of cortisol can cause amenorrhea or cessation of menstrual periods.

In pregnancy, stress has been strongly associated with miscarriage during the earliest weeks of gestation; in one study, 90% of women with high cortisol levels experienced a miscarriage in the first three weeks of pregnancy, compared to 33% of women with normal cortisol levels. High stress levels of the mother during pregnancy are also related to higher rates of premature births and babies of lower-than-average birth weight; both are risk factors for infant mortality. In addition, stress during pregnancy is also associated with negative effects that persist after the baby is born.

MUSCULOSKELETAL SYSTEM. Stress intensifies the chronic pain of arthritis and other joint disorders. It also produces tension headaches, caused by the tightening of the muscles in the neck and scalp. Research indicates that people who have frequent tension headaches have a biological predisposition for converting emotional stress into muscle contraction.

BRAIN. The physical effects of stress hormones on the brain include interference with memory and learning. Acute stress interferes with short-term memory, although this effect goes away after the stress is resolved. People who are under severe stress are unable to concentrate and may become physically inefficient and accident prone. In children, the brain's biochemical responses to stress hampers the ability to learn.

KEY TERMS

Adjustment disorder—A psychiatric disorder marked by inappropriate or inadequate responses to a change in life circumstances. Depression following retirement from work is an example of adjustment disorder.

Biofeedback—A technique in which patients learn to modify certain body functions, such as temperature or pulse rate, with the help of a monitoring machine.

Burnout—An emotional condition, marked by fatigue, loss of interest, or frustration, that interferes with job performance. Burnout is usually regarded as the result of prolonged work-related stress.

Stress hardiness—A personality characteristic that enables persons to stay healthy in stressful circumstances. It includes belief in one's ability to influence the situation; commitment to or full engagement with one's activities; and a positive view of change.

Stress management—A category of popularized programs and techniques intended to help people deal more effectively with stress.

Stressor—A stimulus, or event, that provokes a stress response in an organism. Stressors can be categorized as acute or chronic and as external or internal to the organism.

Chronic stress appears to be a more important factor than aging in the loss of memory in older adults. Older people with low levels of stress hormones perform as well as younger people in tests of cognitive (knowledge-related) skills, but those with high levels of stress hormones test between 20% and 50% lower than the younger test subjects.

IMMUNE SYSTEM. Chronic stress affects the human immune system and increases a person's risk of getting an infectious disease. Several research studies have shown that people under chronic stress have lower-than-normal white blood cell counts and are more vulnerable to colds and influenza. Men with HIV infection and high stress levels progress more rapidly to AIDS than infected men with lower stress levels.

Diagnosis

To identify a stress-related illness, doctors take a careful medical history that includes stressors in the patient's life (e.g., family or employment problems, other illnesses, recent major life changes). Many physicians evaluate patients' personality as well, in order to assess their coping resources and emotional response patterns. Many clinicians think that differences in attitudes toward stressful events are the single most important factor in assessing individuals' vulnerability to stress-related illnesses. The ability to cope with stress depends in part on a person's perception of the stressor. The person's resources, previous physical and psychological health, and previous life experiences all affect this interpretation. Someone who has had good experiences of overcoming hardships is more likely to develop a positive interpretation of stressful events than someone who has repeatedly faced traumas and discouragement in solving problems.

There are several personality inventories and psychological tests that doctors can use to help diagnose the amount of stress that the patient experiences and the coping strategies that the patient uses to deal with them. Doctors also try to identify what the patient perceives as threatening and stressful.

The ways in which people cope with stress can be categorized according to two different sets of distinctions. One is the distinction between emotion-focused and problem-focused styles of coping. Problem-focused coping is believed to lower the impact of stress on health; people who use problem-focused coping have fewer illnesses, are less likely to become emotionally exhausted, and report higher levels of satisfaction in their work and feelings of personal accomplishment. Emotion-focused coping, in contrast, is associated with higher levels of interpersonal problems, depression, and social isolation. Although some studies reported that men are more likely to use problem-focused coping and women to use emotion-focused coping, other research done in the early 2000s found no significant gender differences in coping styles.

The second set of categories distinguishes between control-related and escape-related coping styles. Control-related coping styles include direct-action behaviors that can be done alone, help-seeking behaviors that involve social support, and positive thinking. Escape-related coping styles include avoidance of or resignation from the stressful event and substance abuse.

Stress-related illness can be diagnosed by primary care doctors, as well as by those who specialize in psychiatry. The doctor will need to distinguish between adjustment disorders and anxiety or mood disorders, and between psychiatric disorders and physical illnesses that have psychological side effects (e.g., abnormal thyroid activity).

Treatment

Advances in the understanding of the many complex connections between the human mind and body have

QUESTIONS TO ASK YOUR DOCTOR

- Are there any lifestyle changes that I can make to reduce stress?
- How can I tell the difference between a symptom of stress and being sick with an illness?
- What type of support is there to help me handle the stressors in my life?
- Can you recommend any support groups for me and my family?

produced a variety of mainstream approaches to treating stress and stress-related illness. Present treatment regimens may include one or more of the following:

- Medications may include drugs to control blood pressure or other physical symptoms of stress, as well as drugs that affect the patient's mood (antianxiety drugs or tranquilizers, antidepressants).
- Stress management programs may be either individual or group treatments and usually involve analysis of the stressors in the patient's life. They often focus on job or workplace-related stress.
- Behavioral approaches include relaxation techniques, breathing exercises, and physical exercise programs, including walking.
- Cognitive therapies teach patients to reframe or mentally reinterpret the stressors in their lives in order to modify the body's physical reactions. Anger management techniques are recommended for people who have stress-related symptoms due to chronic anger.

Alternative treatment

Treatment of stress is one area in which the boundaries between traditional and alternative therapies have changed in recent years, in part because some forms of physical **exercise** (**yoga**, tai chi, aikido) that were once associated with the counterculture have become widely accepted as useful parts of mainstream **stress reduction** programs. **Meditation**, **music therapy**, and relaxation techniques have been clinically proven to alleviate symptoms of stress. Other alternative therapies for stress that are occasionally recommended are **aromatherapy**, **dance therapy**, **biofeedback**, nutrition-based treatments (including dietary guidelines and nutritional supplements), **acupuncture**, homeopathy, pranayama (controlled breathing), massage and other **bodywork therapies**, and herbal medicine. Eating a well-balanced diet, exercising regularly, and receiving adequate sleep each night promote good health in general but may also provide stress relief.

Prognosis

The prognosis for recovery from a stress-related illness is dependent on a wide variety of factors in a person's life, many of which are genetically determined (e.g., race, sex, illnesses that run in families) or beyond the individual's control (e.g., economic trends, cultural stereotypes and prejudices, death of a loved one). It is possible, however, for individuals to learn new responses to stress and, thus, change their perceptions and experiences. A person's ability to remain healthy in stressful situations is sometimes referred to as stress hardiness. Stress-hardy people have a cluster of personality traits that strengthen their ability to cope. These traits include believing in the importance of what they are doing, believing that they have some power to influence their situation, and viewing life's changes as positive opportunities rather than as threats.

Prevention

Complete prevention of stress is neither possible nor desirable because stress is an important stimulus of human growth and creativity, as well as an inevitable part of life. Specific strategies for stress prevention vary widely from person to person, depending on the nature and number of the stressors in an individual's life and the amount of control he or she has over these factors. In general, a combination of attitudinal and behavioral changes works well for most patients. An important form of prevention may be parental **modeling** of healthy attitudes and behaviors within the family.

Resources

BOOKS

Al' Absi, Mustafa. *Stress and Addiction: Biological and Psychological Mechanisms.* Boston: Academic Press, 2007.

Greenberg, Jerrold S. *Comprehensive Stress Management.* Boston: McGraw-Hill, 2010.

Miller, Allen R. *Living with Stress.* New York: Facts on File, 2010.

Romas, John A., and Sharma, Manoj. *Practical Stress Management: A Comprehensive Workbook for Managing Change and Promoting Health.* 5th ed. San Francisco: Pearson Benjamin Cummings, 2010.

Seaward, Brian Luke. *Essentials of Managing Stress.* 2nd ed. Sudbury, MA: Jones and Bartlett, 2010.

ORGANIZATIONS

American Institute of Stress, 124 Park Ave., Yonkers, NY, 10703, (914) 963-1200, Fax: (914) 965-6267, Stress125@optonline.net, http://www.stress.org.

Centers for Disease Control and Prevention, 1600 Clifton Rd., Atlanta, GA, 30333, (404) 639-3534, 800-232-4636, inquiry@cdc.gov, http://www.cdc.gov.

National Institute of Mental Health, 6001 Executive Blvd., Rm. 8184, MSC 9663, Bethesda, MD, 20892-9663, (301) 443-4513, (866) 615-6464 TTY (866) 415-8051, Fax: (301) 443-4279, nimhinfo@nih.gov, http://www.nimh.nih.gov/index.shtml.

Rebecca J. Frey, PhD
Tish Davidson, AM
Laura Jean Cataldo, RN, EdD

Stress management/reduction

Definition

Stress management and stress reduction comprise a set of techniques and programs intended to help people deal more effectively with stress by identifying and analyzing the specific stressors that affect them and taking positive actions to minimize the effects of these stressors. Most organized stress management programs deal with job stress and workplace issues.

Purpose

The purpose of stress management and reduction is to protect the physical and mental health of people; within businesses and large organizations, it has the additional purpose of reducing employee burnout and turnover.

Demographics

Stress affects the lives of most adults in developed countries in many ways. It is a major factor in rising healthcare costs; one public health expert maintains that 90% of all diseases and disorders in the United States are stress-related. Stress plays a part in many social problems, such as child and **elder abuse**, workplace violence, juvenile crime, **suicide**, substance **addiction**, "road rage," and the like.

Stress also affects the productivity of businesses and industries. One nationwide survey conducted in the early 2000s reported that 80% of workers experience stress on the job; 53% of American workers name their job as the greatest single source of stress in their lives; nearly half report that they need help in learning how to manage

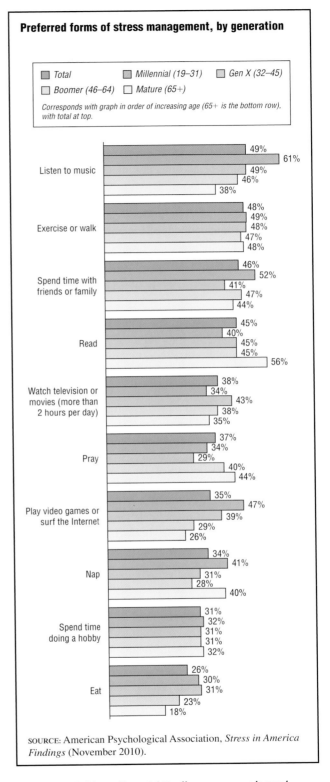

Preferred forms of stress management, by generation

- Total
- Millennial (19–31)
- Gen X (32–45)
- Boomer (46–64)
- Mature (65+)

Corresponds with graph in order of increasing age (65+ is the bottom row), with total at top.

Listen to music: 49%, 61%, 49%, 46%, 38%

Exercise or walk: 48%, 49%, 48%, 47%, 48%

Spend time with friends or family: 46%, 52%, 41%, 47%, 44%

Read: 45%, 40%, 45%, 45%, 56%

Watch television or movies (more than 2 hours per day): 38%, 34%, 43%, 38%, 35%

Pray: 37%, 34%, 29%, 40%, 44%

Play video games or surf the Internet: 35%, 47%, 39%, 29%, 26%

Nap: 34%, 41%, 31%, 28%, 40%

Spend time doing a hobby: 31%, 32%, 31%, 31%, 32%

Eat: 26%, 30%, 31%, 23%, 18%

SOURCE: American Psychological Association, *Stress in America Findings* (November 2010).

Report available online at http://www.apa.org/news/press/releases/stress/index.aspx. *(Graph by PreMediaGlobal. © 2012 Cengage Learning.)*

stress; 42% say their coworkers need such help; 25% have felt like screaming or shouting because of job stress; 10% are concerned about an individual at work they fear could become violent; and 9% know of an assault or violent act in their workplace within the past year.

Precautions

People considering a stress management program or technique on their own should inform themselves about its basic approach and underlying assumptions, and consult their physician if it is a movement-oriented therapy. Those participating in a workplace stress management program may wish to question the organizers or trainers conducting the program about the types of stress reduction techniques the program will involve and whether there is a choice of activities.

Description

In order to understand stress management and stress reduction programs and techniques, it is important to understand the nature of stress, its effects on the human organism, and the ways people try to cope with it prior to learning about stress reduction.

What stress is

Most researchers consider the human stress response a biologically conditioned set of reactions that was a necessary adaptation at earlier points in human evolution but is less adaptive under the circumstances of modern life. In humans, the biochemical response to acute stress is known as the "fight-or-flight" reaction. It begins with the activation of a section of the **brain** called the hypothalamic-pituitary-adrenal system, or HPA. This system first activates the release of steroid hormones, which include cortisol, the primary stress hormone in humans.

The HPA system then releases a set of **neurotransmitters** known as catecholamines. The catecholamines include **dopamine**, norepinephrine, and epinephrine (also known as **adrenaline**). Catecholamines have three important effects:

• They activate the amygdala, an almond-shaped structure in the limbic system that triggers an emotional response of fear.

• They signal the hippocampus, another part of the limbic system, to store the emotional experience in long-term memory.

• They suppress activity in parts of the brain associated with short-term memory, concentration, and rational thinking. This suppression allows a human to react quickly to a stressful situation, but it also lowers the

person's ability to deal with complex social or intellectual tasks that may be part of the situation.

Heart rate and blood pressure rise; the person breathes more rapidly, which allows the lungs to take in more oxygen. Blood flow to the muscles, lungs, and brain may increase 3–4 times the at rest pace. The spleen releases more blood cells into the circulation, which increases the blood's ability to transport oxygen. The immune system redirects white blood cells to the skin, bone marrow, and lymph nodes. At the same time, nonessential body systems shut down. The skin becomes cool and sweaty as blood is drawn away from it toward the heart and muscles. The mouth becomes dry, and the digestive system slows down.

After the crisis passes, the levels of stress hormones drop and the body's various organ systems return to normal. This return is called the relaxation response. In chronic stress, the organ systems of the body do not have the opportunity to return fully to normal levels. Different organs become under- or overactivated on a long-term basis. In time, these abnormal levels of activity can damage an organ or organ system.

Ways of coping

Psychologists define coping is as a person's habitual patterns of response to stress. Many clinicians think that differences in attitudes toward and approaches to stressful events are the single most important factor in assessing a person's vulnerability to stress-related illnesses. A person's ability to cope with stress depends in part on that person's interpretation of the event. One person may regard a stressful event as a challenge that can be surmounted, whereas another views it as a problem with no solution. Interpretation of the event in turn is affected by the person's resources, previous physical and psychological health, and previous experience. Someone who has benefited from overcoming setbacks and hardships is more likely to develop a positive interpretation of stressful events than someone who has been repeatedly beaten down by **abuse** and traumas.

People cope with stress in basically two ways. One is a distinction between emotion-focused and problem-focused styles of coping. Emotion-focused coping strategies focus on changing painful emotions related to stress, whereas problem-focused coping strategies involve efforts to change or eliminate the impact of a stressful event. Persons who handle stress from a problem-oriented perspective are less likely to turn to mood-altering substances when they are under stress.

The second way distinguishes between control-related and escape-related coping styles. Control-related coping styles include such behaviors as direct action (behavior that the person can carry out alone), help-seeking (behavior that involves social support), and positive thinking. Escape-related coping styles include avoidance or resignation (distancing oneself from the stressful event) and alcohol or drug use.

Some specific approaches to stress management

Most contemporary approaches to stress management involve various mind/body interventions associated with complementary and alternative medicine as well as mainstream cognitive behavioral techniques. Some people look into stress management techniques on their own, as there are a number of books and workbooks designed for the general public; others participate in **clinical trials** of various stress reduction techniques; and still others may enroll in workplace stress management programs. These programs have become increasingly widespread in large corporations since the 1980s; most combine education about the nature of stress and its effects on the body with training in some specific stress reduction techniques, including tai chi, massage, and relaxation techniques.

No single approach to stress management, prevention, or reduction works for everyone. Just as people vary in their reactions to stressful events and situations, they vary in what they find calming or relaxing.

COGNITIVE-BEHAVIORAL THERAPY. Cognitive-behavioral therapy (CBT) is the most common form of **psychotherapy** used in stress management. Sometimes called cognitive restructuring, CBT begins with the premise that a person's perceptions of a stressor are a major factor in that person's ability to cope and that perceptions are often distorted by dysfunctional thoughts and emotions. Typical thought distortions include overgeneralization (one mistake on the job means that the person cannot do anything right); catastrophizing (assuming that minor errors will always lead to major disasters); and selective abstraction (a minor detail becomes the focus of attention while the larger context is ignored).

By learning to identify and correct their distorted thinking, individuals can then move on to challenge their dysfunctional thinking and substitute positive thoughts and beliefs. Behavioral changes then follow as individuals feel less overwhelmed by the stressors in their life and adopts a problem-solving style of coping rather than an emotion-driven one. A CBT therapist typically gives homework assignments so that participants can practice their new behaviors and coping strategies. CBT therapy is one of the most commonly recommended approaches to stress management and

appears to be particularly helpful in treating children and adolescents.

STRESS INOCULATION TRAINING. Stress inoculation training (SIT) is a technique of stress management developed by Donald Meichenbaum, a Canadian researcher and teacher. Like CBT, SIT is based on the assumption that individuals' thoughts about and perceptions of a stressor are a critical element in the way they cope. The SIT approach is intended to help people expand their present repertoire of coping skills, acquire greater flexibility in their application of these skills, gain confidence in their overall ability to cope with stressors, and practice applying their new skills. SIT has been used with families and groups as well as individuals. A recent development in SIT methods is the use of virtual reality for practice exercises in coping with stress.

RELAXATION TECHNIQUES. Many relaxation techniques are based on the work of Herbert Benson (1935–), a professor of medicine at Harvard who published *The Relaxation Response* in 1975, a book now considered a classic in mind/body medicine. *The Relaxation Response* outlines six simple steps that people can take to relax when under stress:

- sit quietly in a comfortable position
- close the eyes
- deeply relax all muscles and keep them relaxed
- breathe through the nose and focus on the breathing. While breathing out, silently say the word "one" (or any other one-syllable word). Breathe easily and naturally.
- continue for 10–20 minutes. One may open the eyes to check the time but an alarm should not be used. When the time is up, sit quietly for a few minutes, at first with eyes closed and later with eyes open. Do not stand up right away.
- avoid worrying about the depth of the relaxation. Relaxation comes at its own pace. When distracting thoughts occur, one should not dwell on them but simply return to repeating "one" on each exhalation.

Other relaxation techniques include autogenic training; deep breathing exercises; self-hypnosis; **biofeedback**; progressive muscle relaxation; and visualization.

MOVEMENT-RELATED MIND/BODY INTERVENTIONS. Many stress management programs incorporate movement-related CAM therapies into their activities even when the primary focus of the program may be cognitive-behavioral or mindfulness practice. Research indicates that active mind/body techniques such as **yoga**, tai chi, qigong, or gentle stretching are more effective in reducing stress than passive bodywork techniques such as massage therapy, shiatsu, or chiropractic.

KEY TERMS

Amygdala—An almond-shaped brain structure in the limbic system that is activated in acute stress situations to trigger the emotion of fear.

Autogenic training—A relaxation technique with parallels to hypnosis and meditation. It consists of six exercises in which the person uses visualization and verbal cues to relax the body.

Biofeedback—A technique for helping a user gain control over such body processes as heart rate, blood pressure, skin temperature, and muscle tension by obtaining real-time information about these processes and using thoughts and will to influence them.

Burnout—An emotional condition that interferes with job performance, marked by tiredness, loss of interest, or frustration. Burnout is usually regarded as the result of prolonged stress.

Catecholamines—A set of neurotransmitters released by the hypothalamic-pituitary-adrenal system in the brain in response to acute stress. The catecholamines include dopamine, norepinephrine, and epinephrine.

Coping—In psychology, a term that refers to a person's patterns of response to stress.

Hippocampus—A curved ridge in the mammalian brain that is part of the limbic system. The hippocampus stores long-term memories of stressful experiences.

Homeostasis—The tendency of the physiological system in humans and other mammals to maintain its internal stability by means of a coordinated response to any stimulus that disturbs its normal condition. The term was invented by Walter Cannon.

Johrei—A form of energy therapy that originated in Japan in the 1920s. It emphasizes the channeling of spiritual energy to heal people of the toxins that accumulate in their physical bodies through raising their spiritual vibrations.

Limbic system—A group of structures in the brain that includes the amygdala, hippocampus, olfactory bulbs, and hypothalamus. The limbic system is associated with homeostasis and the regulation of emotions.

Progressive muscle relaxation—A technique for lowering stress-related anxiety by alternately tensing and relaxing the muscles.

Relaxation response—The body's inactivation of stress responses and return of stress hormone levels to normal after a threat has passed.

Stressor—A stimulus or event that provokes a stress response in an organism. Stressors can be categorized as acute or chronic and as external or internal to the organism.

Visualization—A technique that employs the imagination to visualize specific events or behaviors occurring in one's life. An example of visualization in stress management is picturing oneself handling a stressful situation in the present with confidence and competence.

SPIRITUAL APPROACHES. Spiritual approaches to stress management include traditional Western prayer and worship rituals, both corporate and private, and Eastern forms of mindfulness **meditation**. Some Christian churches have special healing services that appeal to members suffering from stress-related illnesses as well as other injuries and disorders.

Mindfulness meditation originated in Buddhism centuries ago. The application of mindfulness practice to stress management is usually credited to Jon Kabat-Zinn (1944–), the founding director of the Stress Reduction Clinic and the Center for Mindfulness in Medicine, Health Care, and Society at the University of Massachusetts Medical School. The center conducts programs in mindfulness-based stress reduction, or MBSR. Since 1976, over 18,000 people have completed the program.

The central notion of the program is that people can reduce the impact of stress on their lives by paying attention to what is going on inside and outside them in the moment, rather than reacting mindlessly to the outside world and living on automatic pilot, so to speak.

Origins

Modern interest in stress and its effects on the body began with Walter Cannon (1871–1945), a Harvard physiologist who used animal studies to measure the effects of stress related to thirst, heat and cold, and prolonged restraint. Hans Selye (1907–1982), a Canadian researcher, continued Cannon's work by extending it to humans. Selye defined stress as essentially the rate of wear and tear on the body. He observed that an increasing number of people, particularly in developed countries, die of so-called diseases of civilization, or degenerative diseases, which are primarily caused by stress. Selye also observed that stress in humans depends partly on a person's evaluation of a situation and that person's emotional reaction to it; thus an experience that one person finds stimulating and exciting—for example, bungee jumping—may produce harmful stress in another.

In 1967 psychiatrists Thomas Holmes and Richard Rahe devised a scale to measure the impact of life events as stressors on humans. The Holmes and Rahe Stress Scale is still used to evaluate the likelihood of a person's becoming physically ill as the result of accumulating too many stressors in the course of a calendar year. Holmes and Rahe graded the death of a spouse as 100 life change units or LCUs, imprisonment as 73, job loss as 47, down to Christmas, which rated 12 LCUs. A person who scores 300 or higher on this scale has "a high or very high risk of becoming ill in the near future"; a score between 150 and 299 carries a moderate risk; and a score below 150 carries a low risk. Holmes and Rahe's work has since been modified by researchers who argue that the specific stressors are less important than the individual's perceptions of and responses to them. For example, some people may be more relieved than upset by the loss of a spouse if the marriage itself had been stressful or if the spouse was suffering slowly in a terminal affliction.

Preparation

Preparation for a mainstream stress management or reduction program usually includes an evaluation of individuals using the Holmes and Rahe scale or a similar instrument, the nature of the stressors in their life or workplace, and their typical ways of coping with stress.

Risks

There are few risks to participation in a well-designed stress management program led or conducted by a competent professional. Movement-oriented mind/body interventions that are used in stress management programs are usually gentle, slow-paced, and unlikely to lead to physical injury.

Results

Most stress management techniques are helpful to at least some of those who try them. The degree of success, however, depends in part on whether individuals are using an approach that appeal to them and is well suited to their circumstances.

QUESTIONS TO ASK YOUR DOCTOR

- How are the stresses in my life affecting my physical and mental health?
- Would you recommend a formal stress management program for me? If so, what type?
- What is your opinion of CAM approaches to stress management and stress reduction?
- Are there any forms of stress management that you consider unproven or risky?

Healthcare team roles

Healthcare team roles in stress management and reduction may include a baseline physical examination by the participant's primary care physician to evaluate his or her general health status and possibly identify specific stress-related symptoms or disorders. The participant may also be evaluated by a clinical **psychologist** or **psychiatrist** to analyze his or her habitual responses to stress, preferred coping styles, and the types of situations or experiences that the person finds particularly stressful.

Research & general acceptance

There is a high level of interest among researchers in stress management and stress reduction programs and techniques, reflected in the fact that there were at least 429 clinical trials under way in early 2010. A number of different modalities of stress reduction are represented in these studies, ranging from cognitive-behavioral and relaxation training approaches to biofeedback, yoga, mindfulness meditation, Johrei, anger management, mantra repetition, self-hypnosis, and Healing Rhythms meditation.

Caregiver concerns

Caregivers of seniors or others in their care who are interested in stress management should consult with the person's doctor to make sure that the technique(s) chosen are taught or guided by certified or licensed instructors and are appropriate to the person's overall health status.

Resources

BOOKS

Greenberg, Jerrold S. *Comprehensive Stress Management*. 12th ed. New York: McGraw-Hill, 2010.

Meichenbaum, Donald. "Stress Inoculation Training: A Preventative and Treatment Approach." In *Principals and*

Practices of Stress Management. 3rd ed. New York: Guilford Press, 2007.

Olpin, Michael, and Margie Hesson. *Stress Management for Life: a Research-based Experiential Approach*. 2nd ed. Belmont, CA: Wadsworth/Cengage Learning, 2009.

Oxington, Kimberly V., ed. *Psychology of Stress*. New York: Nova Science Publishers, 2008.

Romas, John A., and Manoj Sharma. *Practical Stress Management: A Comprehensive Workbook for Managing Change and Promoting Health*. 5th ed. San Francisco, CA: Pearson Benjamin Cummings, 2009.

Selye, Hans. *The Stress of Life*. 2nd ed. New York: McGraw-Hill, 1978.

PERIODICALS

Agee, D., et al. "Comparing Brief Stress Management Courses in a Community Sample: Mindfulness Skills and Progressive Muscle Relaxation." *Explore* (NY) 5, no. 2 (March–April 2009): 104–09.

Esch, T., et al. "Mind/body Techniques for Physiological and Psychological Stress Reduction: Stress Management via Tai Chi Training—A Pilot Study." *Medical Science Monitor* 13, no. 11 (November 2007): CR488–CR497.

Lucini, D., et al. "Complementary Medicine for the Management of Chronic Stress: Superiority of Active versus Passive Techniques." *Journal of Hypertension* 27, no. 12 (December 2009): 2421–2428.

McKee, M.G. "Biofeedback: An Overview in the Context of Heart-brain Medicine." *Cleveland Clinic Journal of Medicine* 75 Suppl. 2 (March 2008): Suppl. 2, S31–S34.

Oman, D., et al. "Meditation Lowers Stress and Supports Forgiveness among College Students: A Randomized Controlled Trial." *Journal of American College Health* 56, no. 5 (March–April 2008): 569–78.

Ruzek, J., et al. "Cognitive-Behavioral Psychology: Implications for Disaster and Terrorism Response." *Prehospital and Disaster Medicine* 23, no. 5 (September–October 2008): 397–410.

Sierpina, Victor, John Astin, and James Giordano. "Mind-Body Therapies for Headache." *American Family Physician* 76, no. 10 (November 15, 2007): 1518–22. http://www.aafp.org/afp/2007/1115/p1518.html (accessed October 27, 2011).

Stetz, M.C., et al. "Stress, Mental Health, and Cognition: A Brief Review of Relationships and Countermeasures." *Aviation, Space, and Environmental Medicine* 78, Suppl. 1 (May 2007): B252–B260.

Wethington, H.R., et al. "The Effectiveness of Interventions to Reduce Psychological Harm from Traumatic Events among Children and Adolescents: A Systematic Review." *American Journal of Preventive Medicine* 35, no. 3 (September 2008): 287–313.

WEBSITES

American Institute of Stress. *Stress Reduction, Stress Relievers*. http://www.stress.org/topic-reduction.htm (accessed October 27, 2011).

Center for Mindfulness in Medicine, Health Care, and Society. *Stress Reduction Program*. http://www.umassmed.edu/uploadedFiles/cfm2/SRP_for_desktop_printing.pdf (accessed October 27, 2011).

Consortium for Research on Emotional Intelligence in Organizations. "Stress Management Training." http://www.eiconsortium.org/model_programs/stress_management_training.html (accessed October 27, 2011).

Health.com. "Autogenic Training." June 30, 2009. http://www.health.com/health/library/topic/0,ta7045spec_tp21225,00.html (accessed October 27, 2011).

Holmes, Thomas, and Richard Rahe. "The Holmes and Rahe Stress Scale: Understanding the Impact of Long-Term Stress." Mind Tools, Ltd. 1967. http://www.mindtools.com/pages/article/newTCS_82.htm (accessed October 27, 2011).

Mayo Clinic. "In-Depth: Stress Management." http://www.mayoclinic.com/health/stress-management/MY00435/TAB=indepth (accessed October 27, 2011).

ORGANIZATIONS

American Institute of Stress, 124 Park Ave., Yonkers, NY, 10703, (914) 963-1200, Fax: (914) 965-6267, stress125@optonline.net, http://www.stress.org.

Benson-Henry Institute for Mind/Body Medicine, 151 Merrimac St., 4th Fl., Boston, MA, 02114, (617) 643-6090, Fax: (617) 643-6077, mindbody@partners.org, http://www.massgeneral.org.

Center for Mindfulness in Medicine, Health Care, and Society, University of Massachusetts Medical School, 55 Lake Ave. N., Worcester, MA, 01655, (508) 856-2656, Fax: (508) 856-1977, mindfulness@umassmed.edu, http://www.umassmed.edu.

Rebecca J. Frey, PhD

| Stroke

Definition

A stroke, also called a cerebral vascular accident (CVA), is the sudden death of cells in a specific area of the **brain** due to inadequate blood flow.

Demographics

According to the U.S. Centers for Disease Control and Prevention (CDC), stroke is one of the leading causes of death in the United States and is responsible for about 130,000 deaths each year. About 795,000 Americans have strokes each year, with 610,000 having a stroke for the first time and 185,000 having a second or third stroke. Of these cases, approximately 87% are ischemic strokes. The total cost of stroke to the American economy in 2010 was approximately $53.9 billion. By the year 2025, the annual number of strokes is expected to reach 1 million. According ages of 45 and 55 die from stroke 4–5 times more often that Caucasians in the same age group.

Description

A stroke occurs when blood flow is interrupted to a part of the brain, either when an artery bursts or becomes closed when a blood clot lodges in it. Blood circulation to the area of the brain served by that artery stops at the point of disturbance, and the brain tissue beyond that is damaged or dies. (Brain cells need blood to supply oxygen and nutrients and to remove waste products.) Depending on the region of the brain affected, a stroke can cause paralysis, loss of vision, speech impairment, memory loss and reasoning ability, coma, or death. The effects of a stroke are determined by how much damage occurs, and which portion of the brain is affected.

About a third of all strokes are preceded by transient ischemic attacks (TIAs), or mini-strokes, that temporarily interrupt blood flow to the brain. While TIAs cause similar symptoms (such as sudden vision loss or temporary weakness in a limb), they abate much more quickly than full-fledged strokes, usually within a few hours and sometimes as quickly as a few minutes.

Stroke is a medical emergency requiring immediate treatment. Prompt treatment improves the chances of survival and increases the degree of recovery that may be expected. A person who may have suffered a stroke should be seen in a hospital emergency room without delay. Treatment to break up a blood clot, the major cause of stroke, must begin within three hours of the stroke to be most effective. Improved medical treatment of all types of stroke has resulted in a dramatic decline in death rates in recent decades. In 1950, 9 in 10 stroke victims died, compared to slightly less than 1 in 3 today. However, about two-thirds of stroke survivors will have disabilities ranging from moderate to severe.

Risk factors

Risk factors for stroke involve:

- Age and sex—the risk of stroke increases with age, doubling for each decade after age 55. Men are more likely to have a stroke than women.

- Heredity—people with a family history of stroke have an increased risk of stroke themselves. In addition, African Americans, Asians, and Hispanics all have higher rates of stroke than whites, related partly to higher blood pressure.

- Diseases—people with diabetes, heart disease (especially atrial fibrillation), high blood pressure, or prior

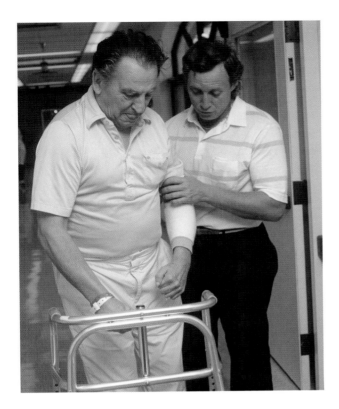

A male therapist works with a stroke victim. (© Custom Medical Stock Photo, Inc. Reproduced by permission.)

to the National Stroke Association, more than 7 million people in the United States are stroke survivors. Worldwide, the World Health Organization estimates that 15 million people suffer a stroke each year, resulting in 5 million deaths and 5 million permanently disabled survivors.

About 50,000 Americans have a transient ischemic attack (TIA) in an average year; of this group, 35% will have a severe stroke at some point in the future.

Strokes can affect people in any age group; however, the risk increases sharply in people over 55 years of age. Seventy-five percent of all strokes in Canada and the United States occur in people over 64. Men are 1.25 times more likely to have strokes than women; however, women are more likely to die of stroke because they are usually older when they have their first stroke.

Strokes in children are rare—about 6 cases per 100,000 children per year in North America. About a third of these cases are in newborns.

African Americans have an increased risk of stroke compared to other racial and ethnic groups in the United States, and they are also more likely to suffer a stroke at younger ages. Hispanics are at lesser risk of stroke than African Americans, but they also tend to have strokes at relatively young ages. African Americans between the

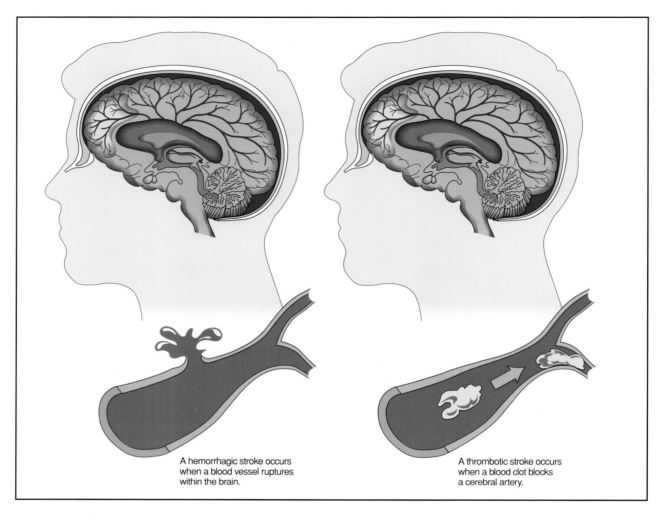

A hemorrhagic stroke occurs when a blood vessel ruptures within the brain.

A thrombotic stroke occurs when a blood clot blocks a cerebral artery.

Illustration of a hemorrhagic and a thrombotic stroke. *(Illustration by Hans & Cassady.)*

stroke are at greater risk for stroke. Patients with one or more TIAs have ten times the risk.

• Other medical conditions—stroke risk increases with obesity, high blood cholesterol, or high red blood cell count.

• Lifestyle choices—stroke risk increases with cigarette smoking (especially if combined with the use of oral contraceptives), a sedentary lifestyle, alcohol consumption above two drinks per day, and/or the use of cocaine or intravenous drugs.

Causes and symptoms

Causes

There are four main types of stroke: cerebral thrombosis, cerebral embolism, subarachnoid hemorrhage, and intracerebral hemorrhage. Cerebral thrombosis and cerebral embolism, known as ischemic strokes, are caused by blood clots that block an artery supplying the brain, either in the brain itself or in the neck. They account for 70%–80% of all strokes. Subarachnoid hemorrhage and intracerebral hemorrhage are hemorrhagic strokes, which occur when a blood vessel bursts around or in the brain, either from **trauma** or excess internal pressure. Hypertension (high blood pressure) and atherosclerosis are usually contributing factors in these types of strokes.

CEREBRAL THROMBOSIS. Cerebral thrombosis, the most common type of stroke, occurs when a blood clot, or thrombus, forms within the brain itself, blocking blood flow through the affected vessel. This is usually due to atherosclerosis (hardening) of brain arteries, caused by a buildup of fatty deposits inside the blood vessels. Cerebral thrombosis occurs most often at night or early in the morning, and is often preceded by a TIA. Recognizing the occurrence of a TIA and seeking immediate treatment is an important step in stroke prevention.

CEREBRAL EMBOLISM. Cerebral embolism occurs when a blood clot from elsewhere in the circulatory system breaks free. If it becomes lodged in an artery supplying the brain, either in the brain or in the neck, it can cause a stroke. The most common cause of cerebral embolism is atrial fibrillation, which occurs when the upper chambers (atria) of the heart beat weakly and rapidly, instead of slowly and steadily. Blood within the atria does not empty completely, and may form clots that can then break off and enter the circulation. Atrial fibrillation is a factor in about 15% of all strokes, but this risk can be dramatically reduced with daily use of anticoagulant medication (such as Heparin or Coumadin).

SUBARACHNOID HEMORRHAGE. In this type of stroke, blood spills into the subarachnoid space between the brain and cranium. As fluid builds up, pressure on the brain increases, impairing its function. Hypertension is a frequent cause of these types of stroke, but vessels with preexisting defects, such as an aneurysm, are also at risk for rupture. Aneurysms are most likely to burst when blood pressure is highest, and controlling blood pressure is an important preventive strategy. Subarachnoid hemorrhages account for about 7% of all strokes.

INTRACEREBRAL HEMORRHAGE. Representing about 10% of all strokes, intracerebral hemorrhage affects vessels and tissue within the brain itself. As with subarachnoid hemorrhage, bleeding deprives affected tissues of blood supply, and the accumulation of fluid within the inflexible skull creates pressure on the brain that can quickly become fatal. Despite this, recovery may be more complete for a person who survives hemorrhage than for one who survives a clot, because the effects of blood deprivation are usually not as severe.

Symptoms

Knowing the symptoms of stroke is as important as knowing those of a heart attack. Patients with stroke symptoms should seek emergency treatment without delay, which may mean dialing 911 rather than their family physician. Specific symptoms of a stroke depend on the type, but all types share some characteristics in common.

An embolic stroke usually comes on quite suddenly and is intense right from the start, while symptoms of a thrombotic stroke come on more gradually. Symptoms for these ischemic strokes may include:

• blurring or decreased vision in one or both eyes
• severe headache, often described as "the worst headache of my life"
• weakness, numbness, or paralysis of the face, arm, or leg, usually confined to one side of the body
• dizziness, loss of balance or coordination, especially when combined with other symptoms

Hemorrhagic strokes are somewhat different. An intracranial hemorrhage exhibits any or all of the following symptoms:

• loss of consciousness
• altered mental state
• seizure
• vomiting or severe nausea
• extreme hypertension
• weakness, numbness, or paralysis, especially on one side of the body
• sudden, severe headache

Symptoms of a subarachnoid hemorrhage include:

• severe headache that begins suddenly
• nausea or vomiting
• stiff neck
• light intolerance
• loss of consciousness

In addition, the American Stroke Association has a quick symptom checklist called "Give Me 5" that can be used by a friend, relative, coworker, or caregiver, as well as by a person who thinks they may be having a stroke:

• Walk: Is the person having trouble with balance or coordination?
• Talk: Is speech difficult or slurred? Is the person's face drooping?
• Reach: Is one side of the body weak or numb?
• See: Is vision partly or entirely lost?
• Feel: Does the person have a sudden severe headache with no obvious cause?

If any of these symptoms are observed and stroke is suspected, call 911 immediately.

Diagnosis

Diagnosing a stroke begins with a careful medical history, especially concerning the onset and distribution of symptoms and presence of risk factors; in this way, other possible causes are excluded. The next step is a complete physical and neurological examination to rule out the possibility that the patient's symptoms are being caused by a brain tumor. The examination has several purposes: checking the patient's airway, breathing, and circulation; identifying any neurological deficits; identifying the potential cause(s) of the stroke; and identifying any comorbid conditions the patient may have. The neurologist may use the National Institutes of Health Stroke Scale (NIHSS), which is a checklist that allows the doctor to record the patient's level of consciousness; visual function; ability to move; ability to feel sensations; ability to move the facial muscles; and ability to talk.

Once stroke is suspected, imaging technology is used to determine what type the patient has suffered—a critical distinction that guides therapy. A noncontrast **computed tomography** scan (CT scan) can reliably identify hemorrhagic strokes, caused by uncontrolled bleeding in the brain. **Magnetic resonance imaging** (MRI), on the other hand, particularly diffusion-weighted imaging, can detect ischemic strokes, caused by blood clots, earlier and more reliably than CT scanning.

Blood and urine tests are also run to look for possible abnormalities. Other investigations that may be performed to guide treatment include electrocardiogram, angiography, ultrasound, and electroencephalogram.

Treatment

When brain cells die during a stroke, they release toxic chemicals that can trigger a chain reaction that can injure or kill other nearby cells. Damage from stroke may be significantly reduced by emergency treatment, a significant factor in how fully a patient will recover.

Emergency treatment

Emergency treatment of an ischemic stroke attempts to dissolve the clot. This "thrombolytic therapy" is performed most often with tissue plasminogen activator (t-PA), which must be administered within three hours of the stroke event. (Patients who awaken with stroke symptoms are ineligible for this type of therapy, since the time of onset cannot be reliably determined.) t-PA therapy has been shown to improve recovery and decrease long-term disability in patients. It carries a 6.4% risk of inducing a cerebral hemorrhage, however, and is not appropriate for patients with bleeding disorders, very high blood pressure, known aneurysms, any evidence of intracranial hemorrhage, or incidence of stroke, head trauma, or intracranial surgery within the past three months. Patients with clot-related stroke who are ineligible for t-PA treatment may be treated with heparin or other blood thinners, or with aspirin or other anticlotting agents in some cases.

Emergency treatment of hemorrhagic stroke is aimed at controlling intracranial pressure that accompanies these types of strokes. New surgical techniques can effectively relieve the pressure, especially when begun soon after the stroke event occurs. Surgery for hemorrhage due to aneurysm may be performed if the aneurysm is close enough to the cranial surface to allow access. Ruptured vessels are closed off to prevent rebleeding. For aneurysms

that are difficult to reach surgically, endovascular treatment, in which a catheter is guided from a larger artery up into the brain to reach the aneurysm, may be effective. Small coils of wire are discharged into the aneurysm, which plug it up and block off blood flow from the main artery.

Rehabilitation

Rehabilitation refers to a comprehensive program designed to regain as much function as possible and compensate for permanent losses. Approximately 10% of stroke survivors recover without any significant disability and are able to function independently. Another 10% are so severely affected that they must remain institutionalized for severe disability. The remaining 80% can return home with appropriate therapy, training, support, and care.

Rehabilitation is coordinated by a team of medical professionals and may include the services of a neurologist, a physician who specializes in rehabilitation medicine, a physical therapist, an occupational therapist, a speech-language pathologist, a nutritionist, a mental health professional, and a social worker. Rehabilitation services may be provided in an acute care hospital, rehabilitation hospital, long-term care facility, outpatient clinic, or at home.

The rehabilitation program is based on the patient's individual deficits and strengths. Strokes on the left side of the brain primarily affect the right half of the body, and vice versa. In addition, in left brain–dominant people, who constitute a significant majority of the population, left-brain strokes usually lead to speech and language deficits, while right-brain strokes may affect spatial perception. Patients with right-brain strokes may also deny their illness, neglect the affected side of their body, and behave impulsively.

Rehabilitation may be complicated by cognitive losses, including diminished ability to understand and follow directions. Poor results are more likely in patients whose strokes left them with significant or prolonged cognitive changes, sensory losses, language deficits, or incontinence.

PREVENTING COMPLICATIONS. Rehabilitation begins with prevention of medical complications, including stroke recurrence, using many of the same measures used to prevent stroke, such as **smoking cessation** and getting hypertension under control.

One of the most common medical complications following stroke is deep venous thrombosis, in which a clot forms within a limb immobilized by paralysis. Clots can also become lodged in an artery feeding the lungs, a condition called pulmonary embolism, that is a common cause of death in the weeks following a stroke. Resuming activity within a day or two after the stroke is an important preventive measure, along with use of elastic

KEY TERMS

Aneurysm—A symptomless bulging of a weak arterial wall that can rupture, leading to stroke.

Angiography—A procedure in which a contrast medium is injected into the bloodstream (through an artery in the neck) and its progress through the brain is tracked. This illustrates where a blockage or hemorrhage has occurred.

Anticoagulant—A medication (such as warfarin [Coumadin], or Heparin) that decreases the blood's clotting ability preventing the formation of new clots. Although anticoagulants will not dissolve existing clots, they can stop them from getting larger. These drugs are commonly called blood thinners.

Atrial fibrillation—A disorder in which the upper chambers (atria) of the heart do not completely empty with each contraction (heartbeat). This can allow blood clots to form and is associated with a higher risk of stroke.

Electrocardiogram—(EKG) A test that measures the electrical activity of the heart as it beats. An abnormal EKG can indicate possible cardiac disease.

Electroencephalogram—(EEG) A test that measures the electrical activity of the brain by means of electrodes placed on the scalp or on or in the brain itself. It may be used to determine whether or not a stroke victim has had a seizure.

Hypertension—High blood pressure, often brought on by smoking, obesity, or other causes; one of the major causes of strokes.

Pressure ulcers—Also known as pressure sores or bed sores, these can develop in stroke patients who are unable to move. If not treated properly, they can become infected.

Tissue plasminogen activator (tPA)—A drug that is sometimes given to patients within three hours of a stroke to dissolve blood clots within the brain; also used to treat heart attack victims.

Ultrasound—A noninvasive test in which high-frequency sound waves are reflected off a patient's internal organs allowing them to be viewed. In stroke victims, a cardiac ultrasound, or echocardiogram, allows the beating heart to be examined.

stockings on the lower limbs. Drugs that prevent clotting may also be given, including intravenous heparin and oral warfarin.

Weakness and loss of coordination of the swallowing muscles may impair swallowing (dysphagia), and allow food to enter the lower airway. This may lead to aspiration pneumonia, another common cause of death shortly after a stroke. Dysphagia may be treated with retraining exercises and temporary use of pureed foods.

Other medical complications include urinary tract infections, pressure ulcers, falls, and **seizures**. **Depression** occurs in 30–60% of stroke patients; its severity is usually related to the level of permanent functional impairment. Depression may be treated with **antidepressants** and **psychotherapy**.

TYPES OF REHABILITATIVE THERAPY. Brain tissue that dies in a stroke cannot regenerate. In some cases, however, rehabilitation training can help other brain regions perform the same functions of that tissue. In other cases, compensatory actions may be developed to replace lost abilities.

Physical therapy is used to maintain and restore range of motion and strength in affected limbs, and to maximize mobility in walking, wheelchair use, and transferring (from wheelchair to toilet or from standing to sitting, for instance). The physical therapist advises patients on mobility aids such as wheelchairs, braces, and canes. In the recovery period, a stroke patient may develop muscle spasticity and contractures (abnormal muscle contractions) that can be treated with a combination of stretching and splinting.

Occupational therapy improves self-care skills, such as feeding, bathing, and dressing, and helps develop effective compensatory strategies and devices for activities of daily living. A speech-language pathologist focuses on communication and swallowing skills. When dysphagia is a problem, a nutritionist can advise alternative meals that provide adequate **nutrition**.

Psychological therapy can help treat depression or loss of thinking (cognitive) skills. A social worker may help coordinate services and ease the transition out of the hospital back into the home. Both **social workers** and mental health professionals help counsel the patient and family during the difficult rehabilitation period. Caring for a person affected with stroke requires a new set of skills and adaptation to new demands and limitations. Home caregivers may develop **stress**, anxiety, and depression—caring for the caregiver is an important part of the overall stroke treatment program. **Support groups** can provide an important source of information, advice, and comfort for stroke patients and caregivers; joining one can be an important step in the rehabilitation process.

Prognosis

The prognosis of stroke depends on the person's age, the type and location of the stroke, and the amount of time elapsed between **diagnosis** and treatment. In general, patients with ischemic stroke have a better prognosis than those with hemorrhagic stroke. In one study in the Boston area, 19% of patients with ischemic stroke died within the first 30 days of the attack compared to 35% with hemorrhagic stroke.

Stroke is fatal for about 26% of white males, 51% of African American males, 39% of white females, and 39% of African American females. However, recent research suggests that African Americans may have a better chance of survival following acute ischemic stroke. Those who do survive a stroke may be left with significant deficits. Emergency treatment and comprehensive rehabilitation can significantly improve both survival and recovery. One recent study found that treating stroke survivors with certain antidepressant medications, even if they were not depressed, could increase their chances of living longer. People who received the treatment were less likely to die from cardiovascular events than those who did not receive antidepressant drugs.

About 10% of stroke patients recover enough function to live independently without help; another 50% can remain at home with outside assistance. The remaining 40% require long-term care in a nursing home.

Stroke in children can be devastating. Between 20% and 35% of newborns who survive a stroke will go on to have a second stroke. More than 66% of older children who suffer strokes will have cognitive deficits, seizures, behavioral problems, changes in personality, or physical disabilities. Unlike adult survivors, children who survive strokes may develop intellectual disabilities, epilepsy, or cerebral palsy.

Prevention

The risk of stroke can be reduced by quitting smoking, controlling blood pressure, exercising regularly, maintaining a healthy weight, avoiding excessive alcohol consumption, getting regular checkups, and following physician advice regarding diet and medications.

Use of high-estrogen dose oral contraceptives increase the chances for developing stroke, particularly in women who smoke and/or who are over 35. Currently, there are low-estrogen dose oral contraceptives, for which a clear relationship with stroke development is unclear.

Treatment of atrial fibrillation may also significantly reduce the risk of stroke. Preventive anticoagulant therapy may benefit those with untreated atrial fibrillation. Warfarin (Coumadin) has proven to be more effective than aspirin for those with higher risk. Warfarin is, however, complicated to use because it interacts with a large number of other drugs and requires frequent monitoring by the patient's physician.

Screening for aneurysms may be an effective preventive measure in those with a family history of aneurysms or autosomal polycystic kidney disease, which tends to be associated with aneurysms.

People with no previous history of stroke may be given certain drugs as preventive measures. These drugs include statins (drugs that lower blood cholesterol levels) and platelet antiaggregants (medications intended to prevent platelets in the blood from forming clumps that may lead to clots).

A recent innovation is the use of computer technology to allow stroke experts in one hospital to evaluate and diagnose a patient in another hospital that might not have a specialist available. Called TeleStroke, the network allows a patient to be evaluated for ischemic stroke within the three-hour time limit for the effective use of tPA. More recently, stroke specialists have proposed an updated version of TeleStroke called TeleStroke 2.0, which would be a Web-based system that could be accessed from any desktop or laptop computer, not just those connected to videoconferencing equipment.

Resources

BOOKS

American Heart Association. *American Heart Association Family Guide to Stroke Treatment, Recovery, and Prevention.* New York: Clarkson Potter, 1996.

Duthie, Edmund H., Jr., and Paul Katz. *Practice of Geriatrics.* 3rd ed. Philadelphia: W. B. Saunders, 2007.

Goetz, Christopher G. *Textbook of Clinical Neurology.* Philadelphia: W. B. Saunders Company, 2003.

McEwen, Mark. *Change in the Weather: Life after Stroke.* New York: Gotham Books, 2008.

Warlow, C. P., et al. *Stroke: A Practical Guide to Management.* Boston: Wiley-Blackwell, 2008.

Williams, Olajide. *Stroke Diaries: A Guide for Survivors and Their Families.* New York: Oxford University Press, 2010.

PERIODICALS

Alvarez-Sabin, J., et al. "Therapeutic Interventions and Success in Risk Factor Control for Secondary Prevention of Stroke." *Journal of Stroke and Cerebrovascular Diseases* 18, no. 6 (November–December 2009): 460–65.

Krishnan, K. Ranga Rama. "Depression as a Contributing Factor in Cerebrovascular Disease." *American Heart Journal* 140, no. 4 Suppl. (October 2000): 70–76.

Mathews, M.S., et al. "Safety, Effectiveness, and Practicality of Endovascular Therapy within the First 3 Hours of Acute Ischemic Stroke Onset." *Neurosurgery* 65, no. 5 (November 2009): 860–65.

Xian, Ying, et al. "Racial Differences in Mortality Among Patients with Acute Ischemic Stroke: An Observational Study." *Annals of Internal Medicine* 154, no. 3 (January 2011): 152–159.

WEBSITES

Jausch, Edward C. "Acute Management of Stroke." Medscape Reference. http://emedicine.medscape.com/article/1159752-overview (accessed October 27, 2011).

Mayo Clinic. "Stroke." July 2010. http://www.mayoclinic.com/health/stroke/DS00150 (accessed October 27, 2011).

U.S. Centers for Disease Control and Prevention. "Stroke." http://www.cdc.gov/stroke/index.htm (accessed October 27, 2011).

U.S. National Institute of Neurological Disorders and Stroke. "Stroke: Hope through Research." http://www.ninds.nih.gov/disorders/stroke/detail_stroke.htm (accessed October 27, 2011).

ORGANIZATIONS

American Academy of Neurology, 1080 Montreal Ave., St. Paul, MN, 55116, (651) 695-2717, (800) 879-1960, Fax: (651) 879-2791, memberservices@aan.com, http://www.aan.com.

American Stroke Association, 7272 Greenville Ave., Dallas, TX, 75231, (800) 242-8721, http://www.heart.org.

Brain Aneurysm Foundation, 269 Hanover St., Bldg. 3, Hanover, MA, 02339, (781) 826-5556, Fax: (781) 826-5566, office@bafound.org, http://www.bafound.org.

National Heart, Lung, and Blood Institute, Health Information Center, PO Box 30105, Bethesda, MD, 20824-0105, (301) 592-8573; TTY: (240) 629-3255, Fax: (240) 629-3246, nhlbiinfo@nhlbi.nih.gov, http://www.nhlbi.nih.gov.

National Institute of Neurological Disorders and Stroke, PO Box 5801, Bethesda, MD, 20824, (301) 496-5751; TTY: (301) 468-5981, (800) 352-9424, http://www.ninds.nih.gov.

National Stroke Association, 9707 E Easter Ln., Ste. B, Centennial, CO, 80112, (800) 787-6537, Fax: (303) 649-1328, Info@stroke.org, http://www.stroke.org.

Laith Farid Gulli, M.D.
Bilal Nasser, M.D.

Structured Clinical Interview for DSM-IV

Definition

The Structured Clinical Interview for *DSM-IV* (SCID) is the generic term for a series of **psychological assessment** instruments used by clinicians and researchers to make diagnoses of mental disorders listed in the *Diagnostic and Statistical Manual of Mental Disorders*, fourth edition (*DSM-IV*), produced by the **American Psychiatric Association**. Its primary authors are Michael First and Robert L. Spitzer. Dr. Spitzer was the primary author of an earlier version of the SCID created in 1990 for the third edition of the *DSM* (*DSM-III*).

Purpose

The primary purpose of the SCID is the differential **diagnosis** of mental disorders according to *DSM-IV* categories. There are two parts to the SCID. The choice of which part is administered depends on what general type of disorder is suspected in the patient. The SCID-I is designed for use by clinicians to accurately and consistently diagnose 37 of the most frequently seen *DSM-IV* Axis I clinical disorders. The disorders fall into the following categories:

• disorders usually first diagnosed in infancy, childhood, or adolescence (excluding intellectual disability)

• delirium, dementia, and amnestic and other cognitive disorders

• mental disorders due to a general medical condition

• substance-related disorders

• schizophrenia and other psychotic disorders

• mood disorders

• anxiety disorders

• somatoform disorders

• factitious disorders

• dissociative disorders

• sexual and gender identity disorders

• eating disorders

• sleep disorders

• impulse-control disorders not elsewhere classified

• adjustment disorders

• other conditions that may be a focus of clinical attention

The SCID-II is designed to measure disorders that are part of Axis II (**personality disorders**) of the *DSM-IV*. These are:

• paranoid personality disorder

• schizoid personality disorder

• schizotypal personality disorder

• antisocial personality disorder

• borderline personality disorder

• histrionic personality disorder

• narcissistic personality disorder

KEY TERMS

Reliability—The ability of a psychological test or diagnostic instrument to consistently measure the concept or entity that it has been designed to measure.

Structured interview—A type of interview often used by researchers to gather data, in which subjects are asked a series of standardized questions in the same order with the same wording. The questions are usually closed-ended (the choice of answers is fixed in advance), although some structured interviews include a few open-ended questions.

Validity—The ability of a test or instrument to measure accurately what it is supposed to measure.

- avoidant personality disorder dependent personality disorder
- obsessive-compulsive personality disorder
- personality disorder not otherwise specified

In addition, the SCID-II is designed to diagnose depressive personality disorder, passive-aggressive personality disorder, and **dependent personality disorder**. Neither the SCID-I nor the SCID-II diagnoses disorders included on Axis III (general medical conditions) or Axis IV (psychosocial and environmental problems) as defined in *DSM-IV*.

Description

The SCID is designed to help clinicians and researchers consistently and accurately diagnose mental disorders and to avoid making a premature diagnosis based on insufficient data or preconceived notions. The SCID uses a standard set of questions that are asked in patient interviews. The diagnosis is made on the basis of the answers to these questions.

The SCID has been translated into numerous other languages, including Chinese (Mandarin), Danish, Dutch, French, German, Greek, Hebrew, Italian, Persian, Portuguese, Romanian, Russian, Spanish, Swedish, and Turkish. Depending on the complexity of the patient's psychiatric history and his or her ability to clearly describe episodes and symptoms, it takes approximately one to two hours to complete the SCID-I and 30 minutes to an hour to complete the SCID-II. These times tend to be shorter than for other comprehensive assessment instruments of this type.

A version of the SCID for use with children-the KID-SCID-was developed by Dr. Fred Matzner in 1993 and is available to researchers on request from Dr. Matzner at 718-920-9362. This version includes most of the disorders included on the SCID-I and SCID-II (with questions rewritten for applicability to children) as well as many childhood disorders, including disruptive behavior disorders and separation **anxiety disorders**. The author expects to add eating disorders and **Tourette syndrome** to the KID-SCID at some point in the future. The KID-SCID has not been formally published as of mid-2011.

Reliability and validity

When determining whether a psychological assessment instrument such as the SCID is useful for the purpose for which it is designed, two factors should be considered: the instrument's reliability and its validity. Reliability is the ability of the assessment instrument to consistently measure the idea or concept it has been designed to measure. Validity is the ability of the instrument to accurately measure what it is intended to measure. Unless a test is reliable, it cannot be valid.

Research studies investigating the reliability of the SCID-I and the SCID-II have shown wide variation in the reliability of the SCID, ranging from poor to good. These findings may be due to such factors as the varying designs of research studies, level of training of the individuals administering the SCID, and the types of disorders represented in those interviewed.

To determine the validity of such assessment instruments as the SCID, researchers typically look at the agreement between diagnoses made using the instrument and diagnoses using an objective standard. Unfortunately, such an objective standard for mental disorders has yet to be developed. However, given the fact that the reliability of the SCID is not consistent, the validity of the instrument must also be called into question.

Versions of the SCID

There are several different versions of the SCID:

- Clinician version (SCID-CV). The clinician version of the SCID is a streamlined form of the research version of the SCID that omits some disorders and covers the remainder in less detail than the research version.

- Research version (SCID-I-RV). This is the standard version of the SCID and comes in three forms: a patient edition (SCID-I-RV/P), for use with subjects who are psychiatric patients; an abridged patient version that includes screening for psychotic disorders; and a nonpatient edition (SCID-I-RV/NP) for use with subjects who are not psychiatric patients (community samples, family studies, etc.)

- Clinical trials version (SCID-CT). The SCID-CT is a streamlined form of the research version designed for use in clinical trials, particularly trials of medications for mental disorders. There are forms of the SCID-CT available to test drugs for major depressive disorder, bipolar disorder, schizophrenia, and generalized anxiety disorder.

- Electronic versions. There are computer-assisted versions of the SCID-CV that require a clinician to be present while the subject answers the questions on a computer. A computer-assisted version of the SCID-I-RV was in development as of 2011.

A series of revisions and fixes of the various versions of the SCID has been posted on the instrument's website. The latest entry, made in January 2010, covers all changes made since October 2008. The details are available at http://cpmcnet.columbia.edu/dept/scid/revisions/jan10.html.

There was no information available as of 2011 about whether the SCID will be updated or altered for the forthcoming fifth edition of *DSM* (*DSM-5*), scheduled for publication in 2013.

Preparation

There is no specific preparation required on the patient or research subject's part for receiving the SCID.

Aftercare

There is no aftercare necessary for the SCID.

Risks

The only significant risk regarding the SCID is receiving the interview from an untrained or unqualified interviewer. While most interviewers who administer the SCID are physicians, psychologists, or other mental health professionals with advanced degrees who have been trained to use the instrument, in some cases, research assistants without clinical experience have been trained to administer the SCID. The less clinical experience the potential interviewer has had, the longer the training period required. According to the authors of the SCID, at least 20 hours of training are required to learn how to administer the instrument.

Results

While the SCID is used in many diagnostic situations, it is not the only assessment instrument

QUESTIONS TO ASK YOUR DOCTOR

- What is your opinion of the SCID? Is it a reliable diagnostic test?
- Have you ever administered the SCID?

available. Other instruments include the Personality Disorder Examination, Structured Clinical Interview for DSM-IV Personality, Diagnostic Interview for Personality Disorders, Brief Psychiatric Rating Scale, Composite International Diagnostic Interview, and Present State Examination. Researchers and clinicians should choose which assessment instrument to use, based on what they are trying to measure and the comparative strengths and weaknesses of the instruments. Note, however, that the lack of objective standards against which to measure validity affects the veracity of the results from all of these instruments, and the problems attendant with using human interviewers affect all interview techniques.

Some clinicians have found that the **depression** module of the SCID has drawbacks for use with depressed patients in that they are likely to leave some questions unanswered, leading to a missed diagnosis.

Resources

BOOKS

American Psychiatric Association. *Diagnostic and Statistical Manual of Mental Disorders.* 4th ed., Text rev. Washington, DC: American Psychiatric Association, 2000.

Benjamin, Lorna Smith, and Michael B. First. *Structured Clinical Interview for DSM-IV Axis II Personality Disorders (SCID-II), User's Guide.* Arlington, VA: American Psychiatric Publishing, 1997.

First, Michael B., ed. *Standardized Evaluation in Clinical Practice.* Washington, DC: American Psychiatric Publishing, 2003.

First, Michael B., et al. *Structured Clinical Interview for DSM-IV Axis I Disorders (SCID-I), Clinician Version, User's Guide.* Arlington, VA: American Psychiatric Publishing, 1997.

First, Michael B., and Alan Tasman. *Clinical Guide to the Diagnosis and Treatment of Mental Disorders.* Hoboken, NJ: Wiley, 2006.

Kupfer, David J., Michael B. First, and Darrel A. Regier, eds. *A Research Agenda for DSM-V.* Washington, DC: American Psychiatric Association, 2002.

Phillips, Katharine A., Michael B. First, and Harold Alan Pincus, eds. *Advancing DSM: Dilemmas in Psychiatric Diagnosis.* Washington, DC: American Psychiatric Association, 2003.

VandenBos, Gary R., ed. *APA Dictionary of Psychology.* Washington, DC: American Psychological Association, 2006.

PERIODICALS

Galione, J., and M. Zimmerman. "A Comparison of Depressed Patients with and without Borderline Personality Disorder: Implications for Interpreting Studies of the Validity of the Bipolar Spectrum." *Journal of Personality Disorders* 24 (December 2010): 763–772.

Gjerdingen, D., et al. "Problems with a Diagnostic Depression Interview in a Postpartum Depression Trial." *Journal of the American Board of Family Medicine* 24 (March-April 2011): 187–193.

Lobbestael, J., et al. "Inter-rater Reliability of the Structured Clinical Interview for DSM-IV Axis I Disorders (SCID I) and Axis II Disorders (SCID II)." *Clinical Psychology and Psychotherapy* 18 (January 2011): 75–79.

Sharifi, V., et al. "A Persian Translation of the Structured Clinical Interview for Diagnostic and Statistical Manual of Mental Disorders, Fourth Edition: Psychometric Properties." *Comprehensive Psychiatry* 50 (January 2009): 86–91.

Torres, L.R., et al. "Diagnosing Co-occurring Substance-related Disorders: Agreement between SCID, Hispanic Clinicians, and Non-Hispanic Clinicians." *Journal of Clinical Psychiatry* 68 (November 2007): 1655–1662.

WEBSITES

American Psychiatric Association. DSM-5 Development Home Page. http://www.dsm5.org/Pages/Default.aspx (accessed May 12, 2011).

SCID. "SCID-Frequently Asked Questions." http://www.scid4.org/faq/scidfaq.html (accessed May 17, 2011).

ORGANIZATIONS

American Psychiatric Association (APA), 1000 Wilson Blvd., Ste. 1825, Arlington, VA, 22209-3901, (703) 907-7300, apa@psych.org, http://www.psych.org.

SCID, c/o Biometrics Research Department, Columbia University at NYSPI, 1051 Riverside Dr., Unit 60, New York, NY, 10032, (212) 543-5524, Fax: (212) 543-5525, scid4@columbia.edu, http://www.scid4.org.

Ruth A. Wienclaw, Ph.D.
Rebecca J. Frey, Ph.D.

Stuttering

Definition

There is no standard definition of stuttering (sometimes called "stammering"), but most attempt to define stuttering as blockages, discoordination, or fragmentations of the forward flow of speech (fluency). These stoppages, referred to as "disfluencies," are often excessive and characterized by specific types, such as repetitions of sounds and syllables, prolongation of sounds, and blockages of airflow. Individuals who stutter are often aware of their stuttering and feel a loss of control when they are disfluent. Both children and adults who stutter expend an excessive amount of physical and mental energy when speaking. Older children and adults who stutter show myriad negative reactive behaviors, feelings, and attitudes. These behaviors, referred to as "secondary behaviors," make the disorder more severe and difficult.

Demographics

Stuttering is a relatively low-prevalence disorder. According to the National Institute on Deafness and Other Communication Disorders (NIDCD), about three million people in the United States stuttered as of 2011, or about 1% of the population. Worldwide estimates total approximately 60 million. This figure differs from incidence, or the number of individuals who have been diagnosed with stuttering at some point in their lives. Research suggests that roughly 5% of the U.S. population has been diagnosed with a stuttering disorder at some point during their lifespan. This difference suggests that a significant number of individuals who stutter develop through or outgrow the problem.

Stuttering is most common in children between the ages of two and five, the period when they are learning to speak. The majority of these children will eventually stop stuttering. In adults, approximately three times as many men stutter as women. The sex ratio seems to be lower in early childhood, with a similar number of girls and boys stuttering. The ratio of boys to girls appears to increase as children become older. This phenomenon suggests that males are more likely to continue to stutter than females.

Description

Stuttering is a confusing and often misunderstood developmental speech and language disorder. Before discussing stuttering, it is important to understand the concepts of speech fluency and disfluency. Fluency is generally described as the forward flow of speech. For most speakers, fluent speech is easy and effortless. It is free of any interruptions, blockages, or fragmentations. Disfluency is defined as a breakdown or blockage in fluency. For all speakers, some occurrence of disfluency is normal. For example, people may insert short sounds or words, referred to as "interjections" or "fillers" when speaking; examples include "um," "like," or "uh." Also, speakers might repeat phrases, revise words or phrases, or sometimes repeat whole words for the purpose of clarification. For young children, disfluency is a part of the normal development of speech and language, especially during the preschool years (between the ages of two and five years).

The occurrence of disfluency is not the same as stuttering, though stuttered speech is characterized by an excessive amount of disfluency. The disfluencies produced by people who stutter will often be similar to those in the speech of individuals who do not stutter; however, certain types of disfluent behavior are likely to appear only in the speech of people who stutter. These disfluencies are sound and syllable repetitions (e.g., ca- ca-ca-cat), sound prolongations (e.g., "sssss–salad," "fffff-fish"), and complete blockages of airflow. These behaviors, often referred to as "stuttering-type disfluencies," distinguish stuttered speech from nonstuttered speech.

Stuttering behaviors can develop and vary throughout the lifespan. Sometimes, children will experience periods when stuttering appears to go away for a time, only to return in a more severe pattern. Many children (estimates range between 50% and 80%) will develop normal fluency after periods of stuttering. For those who continue to stutter during late childhood, adolescence, and into adulthood, stuttering can become a chronic problem. Lifelong efforts are needed to cope successfully with the behavior.

Unlike speakers who do not stutter, most people who stutter react negatively to their disfluencies. A person may develop a number of physical reactions, including tension of the muscles involved in speech (in the tongue, jaw, lips, or chest, for example) and tension in muscles not related to speech (such as shoulders, limbs, and forehead). In addition to these physiological reactions, people who stutter often have negative emotional reactions to the disorder. Among the emotions reported by people who stutter are embarrassment, guilt, and frustration. Many who stutter develop a number of negative attitudes and beliefs regarding themselves and speaking, because of their stuttering. These may be negative attitudes and beliefs in certain speaking situations, with people with whom they interact, and in their own abilities. These physiological, emotional, and attitudinal (cognitive) reactions to stuttering, described as secondary stuttering behaviors, are often very disruptive to the communication process and the person's life.

Due to the effect that stuttering has on communication, the person who stutters may experience difficulty in other parts of his or her life. These problems might result from internal or external factors, such as self-doubt or society's attitudes toward stuttering and other barriers. The 2010 Oscar-winning film *The King's Speech* drew widespread attention to the social stigma that accompanies stuttering, which places undue pressure on the speaker. The film profiles King George VI and his stammer. Persons who stutter may feel increased **stress** or anxiety when faced with speaking situations. Many report difficulties in social settings and as a result may withdraw from social environments to avoid having to speak. Children who stutter often experience teasing and other social penalties that carry through to adolescence and adulthood. Academic settings may be difficult for children who stutter because of the emphasis most schools place on verbal performance in the classroom.

There is some evidence that people who stutter confront barriers in employment, at least for jobs that require interacting with the public. These barriers may take the form of inability to do certain tasks easily (talking on the phone, for example), limitations in job choices, and discrimination in the hiring and promotion processes.

Risk factors

According to the Stuttering Foundation of America (SFA), the following are known risk factors for stuttering:

- Family history of stuttering.
- Gender. Boys are at greater risk of stuttering than girls.
- Age when stuttering begins. Children who begin to stutter before age three are more likely to outgrow it than those who begin to stutter later.
- Time elapsed since onset of stuttering. Children who have been stuttering longer than six months are less likely to outgrow the condition.

As far as was known as of 2011, race, ethnicity, and native language are not risk factors for stuttering. The rate of stuttering and sex ratio are thought to be similar throughout the world, although some researchers believe that rates of stuttering are higher in Africa than elsewhere. What does seem to vary most widely from country to country is cultural attitude toward stuttering.

DSM-5

Stuttering is classified as a mental disorder in the ***Diagnostic and Statistical Manual of Mental Disorders*** (*DSM*), the clinical reference manual used by mental health professionals. Previously listed as a disorder usually diagnosed in infancy, childhood, and adolescence, proposed changes for the fifth edition (*DSM-5*, 2013) refer to stuttering as childhood onset fluency disorder, a neurodevelopmental communication disorder. Other communication disorders include language impairment, late language emergence, **social communication disorder**, speech sound disorder (**phonological disorder**), and voice disorder.

Causes and symptoms

Although research has not identified a single cause of stuttering, there appear to be several factors that are viewed as being important to the onset and development of stuttering. Therefore, stuttering is often described as multifactorial and having possibly multiple causes. First, there is a genetic predisposition to stutter, as evidenced by studies of families and twins. Approximately 60% of children who stutter have family members with the same condition. In 2010, researchers at NIDCD identified three specific genes—one on chromosome 12 and two on chromosome 16—that are linked to stuttering. The genes are known as GNPTAB, GNPTG, and NAGPA.

A second important factor in stuttering the onset of stuttering is the physiological makeup of people who stutter. Research suggests that the brains of people who stutter may function abnormally during speech production. These differences in functioning may lead to breakdowns in speech production and to the development of disfluent speech.

Third, there is some evidence that speech and language development is an important issue in understanding the development of stuttering. Studies have found some evidence that children who show stuttering-type behaviors may also have other difficulties with speech-language. Additionally, children with speech-language delays often show stuttering-type behaviors. Finally, environmental issues have a significant impact on the development of stuttering behaviors. An environment that is overly stressful or demanding may cause children to have difficulties developing fluent speech. Although the environment, in particular parental behaviors, does not cause stuttering, it is an important factor that might adversely affect a child who is operating at a reduced capacity for developing fluent speech.

There is no evidence that stuttering is secondary to a psychological disturbance. It is reasonable to assume that stuttering might have some effect on psychological adjustment and a person's ability to cope with speaking situations. People who stutter might experience a lower self-esteem, and some might report feeling depressed. These feelings and difficulties with coping are most likely the result and not the cause of stuttering. In addition, several research studies have reported that many people who stutter report high levels of anxiety and stress when they are talking and stuttering. These feelings, psychological states, and difficulties with coping are most likely the result and not the cause of stuttering.

Generally, children begin to stutter between the ages of two and five years. This type of stuttering is categorized as developmental stuttering. Another major

KEY TERMS

Developmental—Referring to a speech problem or other disorder that arises during a specific stage in human development.

Disfluency—Any difficulty in fluent speech, including stuttering.

Neurogenic—Referring to a disorder associated with damage to the central nervous system.

Psychogenic—Referring to a disorder associated with mental or emotional conflict. At one time, most stuttering was considered psychogenic, but recent research indicates that psychogenic stuttering is the least common form.

category of stuttering is called "neurogenic stuttering." Neurogenic stuttering results from **brain** damage, such as a **stroke**, a traumatic injury to the brain, or a degenerative neurological disease. In other cases, stuttering may be secondary to a psychological **conversion disorder** due to a psychologically traumatic event. When stuttering has abrupt onset secondary to a psychological **trauma**, it is described as "psychogenic stuttering." This is considered the least common type.

The primary symptoms of stuttering include excessive disfluency, both stuttering and normal types (core behaviors), as well as physical, emotional, and cognitive reactions to the problem. These behaviors vary in severity across people who stutter, from very mild to very severe. Additionally, behaviors will vary considerably across different speaking situations. There are specific situations when people tend to experience more stuttering (such as talking on the phone or with an authority figure) or less stuttering (speaking with a pet or to themselves, for example). It is likely that this variability might even extend to people having periods (days and even weeks) when they can maintain normally fluent or nonstuttered speech.

Other symptoms that may be associated with stuttering in children include eye blinking, tremor in the lips or jaw, and tension or movement of the face or upper body.

Diagnosis

The *DSM* diagnostic criteria for stuttering requires that disfluencies persist over time; be incongruous with the patient's age and language ability; impede communication and/or social, academic, or occupational performance; and not be brought on by trauma, injury, or

malingering. One or more of the following characteristics must also be present:

• repetitions of sounds and syllables

• prolongation of letter pronunciation

• pauses within spoken words

• general pauses in speech, with or without sound

• avoidance of problematic words

• physical tension when speaking

• repetitions of monosyllabic words (e.g., "I," "a")

• anxiety over, and avoidance of, speaking

Examination

Speech-language pathologists (SLPs) are responsible for making the **diagnosis** and managing the treatment of adults and children who stutter. Preferably, a board-certified speech-language pathologist should be sought for direct **intervention** or consulting. Diagnosis of stuttering, or identifying children at risk for stuttering, is difficult because most children show excessive disfluencies in their speech. With children, diagnostic procedures include the collection and analysis of speech and disfluent behaviors in a variety of situations. In addition, the child's general speech-language abilities will be evaluated.

Finally, the speech-language pathologist will interview parents and teachers regarding the child's general development and speech-language development, and their perceptions of the child's stuttering behaviors. For adults and older children, diagnostic procedures will also include gathering and analyzing speech samples from a variety of settings. In addition, the speech-language pathologist will conduct a lengthy interview with the person about their stuttering and history of their stuttering problem. Finally, the person who stutters might be asked to report his or her attitudes and feelings related to stuttering, either while being interviewed or by completing a series of questionnaires.

Tests

In some cases, the child may be referred to an otolaryngologist (specialist in ear, nose, and throat disorders) or a neurologist to rule out the possibility that abnormalities in the structure of the child's tongue or mouth, or a brain disorder, are related to the stuttering.

Treatment

Traditional

GENERAL CONSIDERATIONS. Experts generally accept the view that conducting interventions with children and families early in childhood (preschool) is the most effective means of total recovery from stuttering. Up to 80% of children recover from stuttering if treated between the ages of two and five. The chances for a person to recover fully from stuttering by obtaining near-normal fluency are reduced as the person ages. This is why early intervention is critical. For older children and adults for whom stuttering has become a chronic disorder, the focus of therapy is on developing positive coping mechanisms for dealing with the problem. This therapy varies in success based on the individual.

YOUNG CHILDREN. Treatment of young children generally follows one of two basic approaches. These approaches may also be combined into a single treatment program. The first type of approach, often referred to as "indirect therapy," focuses on altering the environment to allow the child opportunities to develop fluent speech. With this approach, counseling parents regarding the alteration of behaviors that affect fluency is the focus. For example, parents may be taught to reduce the amount of household stress or the level of speech-language demands being placed on the child. In addition, parents may be advised to change characteristics of their speech, such as their speech rate and turn-taking style; this is done to help their children develop more fluent speech.

The other basic approach in treatment with young children targets the development of fluent speech. This type of approach, often referred to as "direct therapy," teaches children to use skills that will help them improve fluency, and they are sometimes given verbal rewards for producing fluent speech.

OLDER CHILDREN AND ADULTS. Treatment approaches for older children and adults usually take one of two forms. These approaches target either helping the person to modify his or her stuttering or fluency. Approaches that focus on modifying stuttering usually teach individuals to reduce the severity of their stuttering behaviors by identifying and eliminating all of the secondary or reactive behaviors. Individuals also work to reduce the amount of emotional reaction toward stuttering.

Finally, the speech-language pathologist will help the individual to learn techniques that allow them to stutter in an easier manner. Therapy does not focus on helping the individual to speak fluently, although most individuals will attain higher levels of fluency if this approach is successful. The other groups of approaches focus on helping adults and children who stutter to speak more fluently. This type of therapy, which focuses less on changing secondary and emotional reactions, helps the person to modify their speech movements in a specific manner that allows for fluent-sounding speech. These procedures require the individual to focus on developing new speech patterns. This often requires a significant amount of practice and skill. The successful outcome of these approaches is nonstuttered, fluent-sounding speech. Many therapists integrate stuttering modification and fluency shaping approaches into more complete treatment programs. In addition, psychological counseling may be used to supplement traditional speech therapy.

Drugs

There is no drug that has been approved by the U.S. Food and Drug Administration (FDA) for the treatment of stuttering as 2011. Although various medications used to treat epilepsy, **depression**, and **anxiety disorders** have been tried as therapy for stuttering, all of these agents have problematic side effects, and none has been particularly successful in treating stuttering. There are, however, isolated case studies of successful treatment of neurogenic stuttering using antipsychotic drugs, such as **asenapine**. In 2011, the FDA was conducting a clinical trial on the anxiolytic (antianxiety) drug pagoclone, after a pilot trial produced positive results, though its sample size was too small to consider as substantial evidence. The trial was expected to finish at the end of 2011. With no FDA-approved medications, the NIDCD advises utilizing therapy or similar methods.

Another method of therapy for stuttering is the use of electronic devices to improve fluency. One type of device fits into the ear like a hearing aid and digitally replays the child's voice so that it sounds as if the child is speaking in unison with someone else. Another type of device, called "delayed auditory feedback," forces the child to speak more slowly so that his or her voice will not sound distorted through the machine. NIDCD researchers maintain that the evidence about the success of these devices is mixed, as it is not clear how long the effects will last or whether the devices are practical.

Prognosis

The prognosis for developmental stuttering is generally good. About 65% of preschool children who stutter outgrow the condition, and 74% recover by their early teens. In general, girls have a better prognosis than boys.

According to the American Speech-Language-Hearing Association (ASHA), no single factor can be used to estimate a given child's prognosis for full recovery from stuttering. Complete recovery from severe stuttering is most likely when children and their families receive treatment close to the time of onset. Thus, early

identification and treatment of stuttering is critical. For older children and adults, stuttering becomes a chronic problem that requires a lifetime of formal and self–directed therapy. For individuals who show this more chronic form of the disorder, internal motivation for change and support from significant others will be an important part of recovery.

Friends, an association for young people who stutter, was founded in 1997 by John Ahlbach, an adult who stutters, and Lee Caggiano, a speech-language therapist who specializes in stuttering and is the mother of a son who stutters. Friends offers online support to young people who stutter, their parents, and speech-language professionals who work with them. The group also publishes books and a bi-monthly newsletter as well as holding an annual convention.

Prevention

With the exception of the small number of cases in which stuttering is caused by a **traumatic brain injury**, the condition is not preventable.

Resources

BOOKS

Guitar, Barry, and Rebecca McCauley, eds. *Treatment of Stuttering: Established and Emerging Approaches.* Baltimore, MD: Lippincott Williams and Wilkins, 2010.

Harrison, Alan E., ed. *Speech Disorders: Causes, Treatment and Social Effects.* Hauppauge, NY: Nova Science Publishers, 2009.

Ramig, Peter R., and Darrell Dodge. *The Child and Adolescent Stuttering Treatment and Activity Resource Guide*, 2nd ed. Clifton Park, NY: Delmar Cengage Learning, 2010.

PERIODICALS

Catalano, G., et al. "Olanzapine for the Treatment of Acquired Neurogenic Stuttering." *Journal of Psychiatric Practice* 15 (November 2009): 484–88.

Changsoo, Kang, et al. "Mutations in the Lysosomal Enzyme-Targeting Pathway and Persistent Stuttering." *New England Journal of Medicine* 362, no. 8 (February 25, 2010): 677–685.

Iverach, L., et al. "The Relationship between Mental Health Disorders and Treatment Outcomes among Adults Who Stutter." *Journal of Fluency Disorders* 34 (March 2009): 29–43.

Jenkins, H. "Attitudes of Teachers towards Dysfluency Training and Resources." *International Journal of Speech–Language Pathology* 12 (June 2010): 253–58.

Kang, C., et al. "Mutations in the Lysosomal Enzyme–targeting Pathway and Persistent Stuttering." *New England Journal of Medicine* 362 (February 25, 2010): 677–85.

Maguire, G., et al. "Exploratory Randomized Clinical Study of Pagoclone in Persistent Developmental Stuttering: the Examining Pagoclone for peRsistent dEvelopmental

Stuttering Study [EXPRESS]." *Journal of Clinical Psychopharmacology* 30, no. 1 (February 2010): 48–56.

Menzies, R.G., et al. "Cognitive Behavior Therapy for Adults Who Stutter: A Tutorial for Speech-Language Pathologists." *Journal of Fluency Disorders* 34 (September 2009): 187–200.

Prasse, J.E., and G.E. Kikano. "Stuttering: An Overview." *American Family Physician* 77 (May 1, 2008): 1271–76.

Prins, D., and R.J. Ingham. "Evidence-based Treatment and Stuttering—Historical Perspective." *Journal of Speech, Language, and Hearing Research* 52 (February 2009): 254–63.

WEBSITES

American Speech–Language–Hearing Association (ASHA). "Stuttering." http://www.asha.org/public/speech/disorders/stuttering (accessed September 23, 2010).

Friends: The National Association of Young People Who Stutter. "Friends Stuttering Presentation Guide." http://www.friendswhostutter.org/pdfs/FRIENDS_Stuttering_Presentation_Guide.pdf (accessed September 23, 2010).

Guitar, Barry, and Edward G. Conture. "If You Think Your Child Is Stuttering . . . " http://www.stutteringhelp.org/Default.aspx?tabid=6 (accessed September 23, 2010).

Mayo Clinic. "Stuttering." http://www.mayoclinic.com/health/stuttering/DS01027 (accessed September 23, 2010).

National Institute on Deafness and Other Communication Disorders (NIDCD). "Stuttering." http://www.nidcd.nih.gov/health/voice/stutter.html (accessed September 23, 2010).

ORGANIZATIONS

American Academy of Otolaryngology—Head and Neck Surgery, 1650 Diagonal Rd., Alexandria, VA, 22314-2857, (703) 836-4444, http://www.entnet.org.

American Speech–Language–Hearing Association (ASHA), 2200 Research Blvd., Rockville, MD, 20850-3289, (301) 296-5700, http://www.asha.org/default.htm.

Friends: The National Association of Young People Who Stutter, [c/o Lee Caggiano] 38 South Oyster Bay Rd., Syosset, NY, 11791, (866) 866-8335, LCAGGIANO@aol.com, http://www.friendswhostutter.org.

International Stuttering Association (ISA), [c/o Joseph Lukong Tardzenyuy, Secretary] PO Box 9598, Douala, Cameroonadmin@stutterisa.org, http://www.stutterisa.org/index.html.

National Institute on Deafness and Other Communication Disorders (NIDCD), 31 Center Dr., MSC 2320, Bethesda, MD, 20892-2320, (800) 241-1044, Fax: (301) 770–8977, nidcdinfo@nidcd.nih.gov, http://www.nidcd.nih.gov/index.asp.

Stuttering Foundation of America (SFA), 3100 Walnut Grove Rd., Suite 603, Memphis, TN, 38111-0749, (901) 452-7343, (800) 992-9392, Fax: (901) 452-3931, info@stutteringhelp.org, http://www.stutteringhelp.org/Default.aspx?tabid=4.

Rodney Gabel, PhD
Rebecca J. Frey, PhD

Substance Abuse and Mental Health Services Administration

Definition

The **Substance Abuse** and Mental Health Services Administration (SAMHSA) is an agency of the U.S. Department of Health and Human Services. It was established by an act of Congress in 1992 to focus attention, programs and funding on improving the lives of people with or at risk for mental and substance abuse disorders.

Description

SAMHSA began as part of a realignment of federal antidrug services centered on the Alcohol, Drug, and Mental Health Administration (ADAMHA). ADAMHA, was originally founded in the early 1970s as a direct response to the awareness of the growing problem of illegal drug abuse. The ADAMHA Reorganization Act in 1992 created SAMHSA to take over the prevention and treatment functions related to mental health and substance abuse. ADAMHA's three research institutes—the National Institute on Alcohol Abuse and Alcoholism, the National Institute on Drug Abuse, and the National Institute of Mental Health— were placed under the National Institutes of Health (NIH) to carry out research. The newly formed SAMHSA had a clear focus for providing resources and leadership in coordination with the states' efforts to prevent and treat mental disorders and substance abuse.

Program centers

The three original centers of SAMHSA are the Center for Mental Health Services, the Center for Substance Abuse Prevention, and the Center for Substance Abuse Treatment. In the early 2000s, a fourth center was added, the Center for Behavioral Health Statistics and Quality to replace the managerial division the Office of Applied Studies.

CENTER FOR MENTAL HEALTH SERVICES. The Center for Mental Health Services (CMHS) has the stated mission of preventing and treating mental illness. The goal of the Center is to work with local service providers through the state to identify the causes of mental illness and to undermine the effect of negative influences. When prevention is not possible, the appropriate treatment is recommended to ease the effect of the mental illness. The CMHS provides funding for services and program development mainly by offering block grants.

Even in states not receiving funding, CMHS influences mental health services by setting goals for mental health prevention and advising on improving treatment. The CMHS has advisors available to the states for training staff and improving services. The CMHS also serves as an advocate for the mentally ill and their families. In fulfilling its mandate to provide timely information on mental health promotion, the center maintains a clearinghouse of publications and documents related to its mission. While the CMHS sponsors its own research conferences, the center also sends experts to other relevant conferences.

CENTER FOR SUBSTANCE ABUSE PREVENTION. The Center for Substance Abuse Prevention (CSAP) was instituted to be the federal leader in providing services and information regarding substance problems. The goal of the Center is to be the primary driver of actions promoting the reduction in the problem use of alcohol, tobacco, and drugs. To this end, CSAP advises legislators and federal agencies on the issues of substance use, while providing services and programs to states in the form of models and block grants.

A main program of CSAP is the Strategic Prevention Framework, which is a community-based model encouraging the implementation of research on effective prevention. The framework takes into consideration the challenges of youth among all lifespan development stages. The problems specific to youth include challenges to self esteem and self autonomy when facing peer pressure. Other problems include the adolescent tendency for risk taking.

CENTER FOR SUBSTANCE ABUSE TREATMENT. The Center for Substance Abuse Treatment (CSAT) is charged with identifying and providing effective treatment for those with substance-based disorders by providing grants for the development of treatments to the states and communities. The center also manages a referral service to help those seeking treatment to find appropriate help. The referral service provides detailed information to address individual situations such as lack of insurance or court-ordered treatment.

In funding and promoting community-based treatment, CSAT emphasizes flexibility of delivery. As the needs of the community and individuals vary, the processes of the funded programs must be matched to the identified needs. The treatment models recommended by CSAT are those that have been found by research to be effective for most people. However, to encourage innovation, CSAT also promotes and funds evaluation of new programs.

CENTER FOR BEHAVIORAL HEALTH STATISTICS AND QUALITY. The Center for Behavioral Health Statistics and Quality (CBHSQ) disseminates information and

---

KEY TERMS

Behavioral health—A broad term for any condition related in any way to mental health.

Community-based—Used to describe any organization or initiative stemming from non-government, local, and independent sources.

Mental disorder—Any illness interfering with perceptions, consciousness, and adjustment.

Mental health—Appropriate adaptation to everyday psychosocial challenges.

Prevention—Successful encouragement of individuals and communities to avoid the use of substances that lead to abuse or dependence.

Recovery—State of being in which someone has changed lifestyle and dependency to the point of not using the previous addictive substance.

Substance abuse—The illicit use of drugs or other psychotropic chemicals to change cognitive or emotional perceptions.

Treatment—The process of helping those with a mental disorder to adapt to life challenges by changing lifestyle and dependency.

---

statistics regarding substance abuse, including the number and types of medical situations involving drug abuse. The CBHSQ collects data from various sources. While the center analyzes its own data, it also has access to substance abuse data analysis from outside sources. Abuse data include not only legal substances, such as alcohol, tobacco, and prescription drugs, but also illegal drugs. The center's information includes the availability, growth, and use of substance abuse treatment.

Typical reports updated regularly include topics such as the level of substance abuse among various ethnic groups. The data systems producing reports include Drug and Alcohol Service Information System, Drug Abuse Warning network, National Survey on Drug Use and Health. The CBHSQ also provides independent analysts appropriate data related to substance abuse and mental health.

Strategic initiatives

In an effort to improve behavioral health services in a community setting, SAMHSA has identified eight strategic initiatives. These strategic initiatives provide a means to focus agency resources in areas that have the greatest need or the greatest chance for impact. Each strategic initiative provides funding and expertise in the assigned area.

PREVENTION OF SUBSTANCE ABUSE AND MENTAL ILLNESS. The Prevention of Substance Abuse and Mental Illness initiative is predominantly covered through the efforts of CSAP. The goal of this initiative is to encourage community based organizations to promote the education and **intervention** necessary to avoid and reduce substance abuse. These organizations include schools, workplaces and faith-based organizations. All qualified groups are invited to apply for grants to support their efforts and to accept SAMHSA's programs in this effort. The main thrust of this effort is toward prevention among children and adolescents.

TRAUMA AND JUSTICE. The **trauma** and justice initiative, which is covered by all the centers, is focused on efforts to reduce the effects of violence and the resulting trauma. The main effort is directed toward sharing important research on dealing with trauma with all health and mental services. Related to sharing information to offset unexpected crisis is the effort to negotiate in the justice system to protect the rights of the mentally ill, promoting treatment rather than harsh punishments for these persons, particularly when crimes stem from a person's disorder.

MILITARY FAMILIES. The military families initiative, which is predominantly covered by CMHS, aims to promote mental health and adjustment in military families facing crises. The CMHS primarily ensure that military families have community services available when needed and that these families are aware of what is available. When mental illness results from the constant challenges of the military families, CMHS informs through community services that treatment is available and follows up to be sure that the treatment is effective.

HEALTH REFORM IMPLEMENTATION. The health reform implementation initiative is a cross-center effort to assure that any healthcare reform legislation includes coverage for mental conditions and substance abuse treatment. Beyond influencing legislation, the effort is on informing mental health consumers of their rights and opportunities when facing funding problems for mental health treatment. In negotiating with insurance and healthcare providers, SAMHSA centers address the disparity between coverage for mental health care and other conditions.

RECOVERY SUPPORT. The recovery support initiative, which is predominantly covered by CMHS, aims to encourage follow-up treatment for those with a mental or substance use disorder. The follow-up treatment is especially important to help those who are in recovery avoid conditions leading to a **relapse**. The importance of avoiding relapse is stressed through this initiative to all levels of the behavioral health system. Other support covers access to housing education and employment coordinated with a decrease of social barriers.

HEALTH INFORMATION TECHNOLOGY. The health information technology initiative is predominantly handled by CSAT. The goal of this initiative is to promote the use of electronic systems for maintaining and updating health records. The concept behind this initiative is that with an accessible electronic file system of behavioral health records, service to individuals will be less complex and less redundant. The two systems promoted by this initiative are Health Information Technology and Electronic Health Records.

DATA, OUTCOMES, AND QUALITY. The data, outcomes, and quality initiative is predominantly covered by CBHSQ. The goal of this initiative is to disseminate timely, accurate information to the public and to policy makers. The data are collected from many sources; they are analyzed within SAMHSA but made available for analysis by independent researchers. Information regarding program evaluation and effectiveness is also collected and circulated. With greater availability of information, it is hoped that better policy will lead to greater improvement in the behavioral healthcare system.

PUBLIC AWARENESS AND SUPPORT. The public awareness and support initiative is a cross-center effort to communicate and market the information and approaches to better improve behavioral health services. One of the tools used in this effort is the strategic communications framework that is designed to coordinate the many information services within SAMHSA. The Office of Communication within SAMHSA operates a blog on SAMHSA's website. The blog is updated as necessary, usually once a week. This initiative is in support of the others, particularly in advertising innovations and successes.

Resources

BOOKS

Hanson, Glen R., et al. *Drugs and Society.* Burlington, MA: Jones & Bartlett Learning, 2011

Levin, Bruce Lebotsky, et al. *Mental Health Services: A Public Health Perspective.* New York: Oxford University Press, 2010.

PERIODICALS

Knopf, Alison. "Senate Appropriations Committee Rejects SAMHSA's 'New Vision'." *Alcoholism & Drug Abuse Weekly* (October 3, 2011). http://www.alcoholismdruga-buseweekly.com/sample-articles/senate-committee-rejects-samhsa-vision.aspx (accessed October 27, 2011).

Torrey, E. Fuller. "Bureaucratic Insanity." *National Review Online* (June 29, 2011). http://www.freerepublic.com/focus/f-news/2742321/posts (accessed October 27, 2011).

ORGANIZATIONS

Substance Abuse and Mental Health Services Administration Referral Resource, 1 Choke Cherry Rd., Rockville, MD, 20857, (877) SAMHSA-7 (726-4727), (800) TTY: 487-4889, Fax: (240) 221-4292, SAMHSAInfo@samhsa.hhs.gov, http://www.samhsa.gov.

U.S. Department of Health & Human Services, 200 Independence Ave. SW, Washington, DC, 20201, (202) 619-7800, (877) 696-6775, http://www.hhs.gov.

Ray F. Brogan, PhD

Substance abuse and related disorders

Definition

Substance abuse, also referred to as alcoholism, **addiction**, drug abuse, or drug misuse, is the continued, compulsive use of mind-altering substances despite personal, social, and/or physical problems caused by the use. Such use, which may involve illegal or legal substances, is for nontherapeutic or nonmedical purposes. Chronic abuse may lead to substance dependence, meaning that the user is physically dependent on the substance and often requires increased amounts of the abused substance to achieve the desired effect or level of intoxication. If use of the substance is suddenly ceased, the user will undergo a period of withdrawal.

Demographics

In 2010, in the United States, approximately 22.6 million people (8.9% of the U.S. population) were using illegal drugs, according to the *National Survey on Drug Use and Health* performed by the **Substance Abuse and Mental Health Services Administration** (SAMHSA), an agency of the U.S. Department of Health and Human Services (HHS). The number of persons receiving treatment for abuse is much lower, estimated at 2.6 million.

Marijuana is the most commonly used drug, with 17.4 million Americans using it in 2010, compared to 14.4 million in 2007. Use of other substances has dropped, however, with an estimated 353,000 people using **methamphetamine** (down from 731,000 in 2006) and 1.5 million using **cocaine** (down from 2.4 million in 2006). Still, there is a substantial problem in the United States, with drug use among 18- to 25-year-olds rising from 19.6% in 2008 to 21.5% in 2010.

Substance abuse and dependence cut across all lines of race, culture, education, and socioeconomic status. In addition to the toll that substance abuse can take on a person's physical health, substance abuse is considered an important factor in a wide variety of social problems, affecting rates of crime, domestic violence, sexually transmitted diseases (including human immunodeficiency virus/acquired immune deficiency syndrome [HIV/AIDS]), unemployment, **homelessness**, teen pregnancy, and failure in school. One study estimated that 20% of the total yearly cost of health care in the United States is spent on the effects of drug and alcohol abuse.

Description

According to the mental health clinician's handbook, the *Diagnostic and Statistical Manual of Mental Disorders* (*DSM*), substance-related disorders include disorders of use and abuse, intoxication, and withdrawal, as well as the various mental states (e.g., **dementia**, **psychosis**, anxiety, mood disorder) that the substance may induce when it is used. Intoxication is the direct effect of the substance; different substances produce different reactions, but some common effects include impaired judgment, emotional instability, increase or decrease in appetite, and altered sleep habits.

Substance abuse and dependence

Approximately 22.1 million people* were classified as having a substance dependence or abuse disorder in 2010.

Dependence on specific drugs included:

Alcohol	17.0 million**
Marijuana	4.5 million
Pain relievers	1.9 million
Cocaine	1.0 million
Tranquilizers	521,000
Hallucinogens	397,000
Heroin	359,000
Stimulants	357,000
Sedatives	162,000
Inhalants	161,000

*Aged 12 and older
**Users may have abused more than one substance, so the number of users of each substance may be higher than the total estimated number of people with a substance abuse disorder.

SOURCE: Substance Abuse and Mental Health Services Administration, Office of Applied Studies, *Results from the 2010 National Survey on Drug Use and Health: Summary of National Findings* (September 2011).

Report available online at http://oas.samhsa.gov/NSDUH/ 2k10NSDUH/2k10Results.htm. (*Table by PreMediaGlobal.* © 2012 Cengage Learning.)

Substance abuse is commonly defined as the use of illegal drugs or misuse of prescribed drugs. If a person consistently abuses a drug for a period of time, they will become physically dependent on it. A substance-dependent person must have a particular dose or concentration of the substance in his or her bloodstream at any given moment in order to avoid the unpleasant symptoms associated with withdrawal from that substance. This amount of the dosage increases as the person becomes tolerant of the substance; as his or her body adapts to the presence of the substance, higher amounts are needed to produce the same effects. If the substance-dependent person abruptly stops using the substance, his or her body will respond by over-compensating for the substance's absence. Functions slowed by the abused substance will be suddenly sped up, while previously stimulated functions will be suddenly slowed. This results in a number of unpleasant effects, known as "withdrawal symptoms." Withdrawal symptoms vary with the substance, but common symptoms include increased heart rate, tremor, **insomnia**, **fatigue**, and irritability.

"Substance addiction" refers to the mind-state of a person who reaches a point where he or she must have a specific substance, despite any negative social, physical, and legal consequences (e.g., deteriorating health or loss of relationships, employment, or housing). "Craving" refers to an intense hunger for a specific substance, to the point where this need essentially directs the individual's behavior. Craving is usually seen in both dependence and addiction and can be so strong that it overwhelms a person's ability to make decisions that will deprive him or her of the substance. Drug possession and use become the most important goals, and other forces (including the law) have little effect on the individual's substance-seeking behavior.

Common classes of substances of abuse include:

- alcohol, such as beer, liquor, and wine

- amphetamines, such as 3,4-Methylenedioxymethamphetamine (MDMA, commonly called "Ecstasy"), ephedrine, and methamphetamine

- barbiturates, such as amobarbital (Amytal), pentobarbital (Nembutal), and secobarbital (Seconal)

- benzodiazepines, including prescription drugs used for treating anxiety, such as diazepam (Valium), and baclofen (Kemstro, Lioesal, and Gablofen)

- caffeine, contained in coffee, tea, and energy drinks

- cannabinoid drugs obtained from the hemp plant, including marijuana and hashish

- cocaine-based drugs (also called "crack" or "coke")

- hallucinogenic or "psychedelic" drugs, including lysergic acid diethylamide (LSD), phencyclidine (PCP, or angel dust), and other PCP-type drugs

- inhalants, including gaseous drugs used in the medical practice of anesthesia, as well as such common substances as paint thinner, gasoline, and glue

- methamphetamines, also called "meth," "ice," "speed," or "crystal"

- methaqualone, such as Quaaludes

- nicotine, such as contained in cigarettes

- opioids, including such prescription pain killers as morphine and Demerol, as well as illegal substances such as heroin

- prescription medications, including other types of sedatives ("downers," such as tranquilizers) and stimulant drugs ("uppers," such as methylphenidate [Ritalin])

The *DSM* does not recognize caffeine abuse or dependence, but it does recognize the effects of caffeine intoxication (e.g., restlessness, nervousness, or excitement after caffeine consumption), caffeine-induced anxiety disorder (feelings of anxiety or panic attacks after caffeine consumption), and caffeine-induced sleep disorder (usually insomnia, but some may experience excessive sleepiness when caffeine is not consumed), and caffeine withdrawal.

In May 2013, the next edition of *DSM* will be available (*DSM-5*). Proposed changes include combining the former categories of substance abuse and substance dependence into one category, *substance use;* adding caffeine and **cannabis** withdrawal disorders; adding non-substance addictions, such as **gambling disorder** (formerly considered an impulse-control disorder); and adding to the list of substance-induced disorders, including substance-induced **obsessive-compulsive disorder** and mild or major neurocognitive disorder associated with substance use.

Causes and symptoms

Causes

It is generally believed that there is not one single cause of substance abuse, though scientists are increasingly convinced that certain people possess a genetic predisposition that can affect the development of addictive behaviors, along with a number of other biological, psychological, and social factors. One theory holds that a particular nerve pathway in the **brain** (dubbed the "mesolimbic reward pathway") holds certain chemical characteristics, which can increase the likelihood that substance use will ultimately lead to substance addiction. Certainly, however, other social factors are involved, including family problems and peer pressure. Primary mood disorders (**bipolar disorder**), **personality disorders**, and the role of learned behavior can be influential on the likelihood that a person will become substance dependent.

Research from the late 2000s and early 2010s continues to investigate the causes of substance abuse. Although concrete facts have yet to determine an exact cause, or causes, of substance abuse, researchers contend that certain risk factors predispose some children early in their developmental years to be more likely to abuse substances later in life, compared to the general population. Medical research has found that the presence of substance abuse disorder is higher for children who come from families where it is already present, making genetics a potential contributing factor for causing such disorders. Common risk factors, within the home and outside, found to increase the presence of substance abuse include:

- disorganized or chaotic home environment
- ineffective parenting skills
- insufficient nurturing and parental attachment
- aggressive or shy behavior
- poor coping skills in society
- general perception that drug and alcohol use is acceptable
- poor school achievement and performance
- association with children showing deviant or socially inappropriate behaviors

Symptoms

The symptoms of substance abuse may be related to its social effects as well as its physical effects. The social effects of substance abuse may include dropping out of school or losing a series of jobs, engaging in fighting or violence in relationships, and legal problems (ranging from driving under the influence to the commission of crimes designed to obtain the money needed to support a drug habit).

Physical effects of substance abuse are related to the specific drug being abused:

- Opioid drug users may appear slowed in their physical movements and speech, lose weight, exhibit mood swings, and have constricted (small) pupils.
- Benzodiazepine and barbiturate users may appear sleepy and slowed, with slurred speech, small pupils, and occasional confusion.
- Amphetamine users may have excessively high energy, inability to sleep, weight loss, rapid pulse,

elevated blood pressure, occasional psychotic behavior, and dilated (enlarged) pupils.

- Marijuana users may be sluggish and slow to react, exhibiting mood swings, changes in weight, and red eyes with dilated pupils.
- Cocaine users may have wide variations in their energy level, severe mood disturbances, psychosis, paranoia, and a constantly runny nose. "Crack" cocaine use may cause aggressive or violent behavior.
- Hallucinogenic drug users may display bizarre behavior due to hallucinations (imagined sights, voices, sounds, or smells that seem completely real to the individual experiencing them) and dilated pupils. LSD use can cause flashbacks.

Other symptoms of substance abuse may be related to the form in which the substance is used. For example, heroin, certain other opioid drugs, and certain forms of cocaine may be injected using a needle and a hypodermic syringe. A person abusing an injectable substance may have "track marks," outwardly visible signs of the site of an injection, with possible redness and swelling of the vein in which the substance was injected. Furthermore, poor judgment brought on by substance use can result in the injections being made under dirty conditions. These unsanitary conditions and the use of shared needles can cause infections of the injection sites, major infections of the heart, infection with HIV (the virus that causes AIDS), certain forms of hepatitis (a liver infection), and tuberculosis.

Cocaine is often taken as a powdery substance that is "snorted" through the nose. This can result in frequent nosebleeds, sores in the nose, and even erosion (an eating away) of the nasal septum (the structure that separates the two nostrils). Other forms of cocaine include smokable or injectable forms, such as freebase and crack cocaine.

Overdosing on a substance is a frequent complication of substance abuse. Drug overdose can be purposeful (with **suicide** as a goal) or the result of carelessness, such as when purchasing from street dealers, where the strength or composition of the drugs are unpredictable; when mixing more than one type of substance or mixing a substance with alcohol; or because of the ever-increasing doses the person must take once he or she has become tolerant. A substance overdose can be a life-threatening emergency, with the specific symptoms dependent on the type of substance used. Substances with depressive effects may dangerously slow the breathing and heart rate, drop the body temperature, and result in general unresponsiveness. Substances with stimulatory effects may dangerously increase the heart rate and blood pressure, increase body temperature, and cause bizarre behavior. With cocaine, there are risks of **stroke** and heart attack.

Diagnosis

The most difficult aspect of **diagnosis** involves overcoming the patient's **denial**. Denial is a psychological trait whereby a person is unable to allow himself or herself to acknowledge the reality of a situation. This may lead a person to completely deny his or her substance use, or it may cause the person to greatly underestimate the degree of the problem and its effects on his or her life.

The *DSM-5* diagnostic criteria for a substance use disorder requires a person to display two or more of the following symptoms within a 12-month period:

• an inability to fulfill obligations, including work, school, and home or family responsibilities
• repeated use of the substance in dangerous situations (e.g., driving under the influence)
• recurrent use despite a negative effect on personal and social life or physical health
• tolerance—either a need for increased amounts of the substance to achieve the intended effect, or loss of effect when continuing to take the same amount
• withdrawal syndrome or continuing use to avoid withdrawal
• substance is taken in higher doses or continued for longer than originally intended
• unsuccessful attempts or intention to cut down on use
• significant time is spent around the substance or activity (obtaining, participating/using, recovering)
• substance use is favored over other activities, including work, hobbies, or social outings
• persistent craving to use substance

Fulfillment of criteria may be revealed during a physical examination or psychiatric test, or suspected abuse may be brought up by the patient's family member or friend. Meeting two or three criteria is considered moderate abuse, while four or more signifies severe substance abuse.

Examination

A physical examination may reveal signs of substance abuse in the form of needle marks, **trauma** to the inside of the nostrils from snorting drugs, or unusually large or small pupils. With the person's permission, substance use can also be detected by examining blood, urine, or hair in a laboratory. Drug testing is affected by drug sensitivity, specificity, and the time elapsed since the person last used the drug.

Tests

One of the simplest and most common screening tools that practitioners use to begin the process of diagnosing substance abuse is the CAGE questionnaire. CAGE (Cut, Annoyed, Guilty, Eye) refers to the first letters of each word that forms the basis of the four questions in the screening examination:

• Have you ever tried to cut down on your substance use?
• Have you ever been annoyed by people trying to talk to you about your substance use?
• Do you ever feel guilty about your substance use?
• Do you ever need an eye opener (use of the substance first thing in the morning) in order to start your day?

Longer questionnaires exist to assess the severity and effects of a person's substance abuse. It is also relevant to determine whether anyone else in the user's family has ever suffered from substance or alcohol addiction.

Treatment

Treatment is difficult if the abuser does not believe they have a problem. Most substance abusers think they can stop using drugs without outside help. However, only a small minority are successful on their own. Medical research shows that the brains of long-time substance abusers are altered due to their habit, resulting in cravings, withdrawal symptoms, and difficulty quitting without help. Therefore, treatment has several goals, which include helping a person deal with the uncomfortable and possibly life-threatening symptoms associated with withdrawal from an addictive substance (called "detoxification"), helping an abuser deal with the social effects that substance abuse has had on his or her life, and working to prevent **relapse** (resumed use of the substance).

Traditional

Detoxification is the halting of substance use, a process that may take from several days to many weeks. It can be accomplished "cold turkey," by complete and immediate cessation of all substance use, or by slowly decreasing (tapering) the dose that a person is taking, to minimize the side effects of withdrawal. Individual or group **psychotherapy** is often recommended and is likely to be important after detoxification.

The most important part of treatment is preventing the abuser from relapsing back to his or her former habits. Behavioral therapies help people cope with their drug cravings and develop strategies so as to not return to using substances. Sometimes the person with the substance abuse disorder also has mental disorders that are exaggerating the problem. Treatment then involves treating the mental disorder(s) with psychiatric medications and/or psychotherapy, along with the substance abuse problem.

Because substance abuse has severe effects on the functioning of the user's family, and because research has shown that family members can accidentally develop behaviors that inadvertently support a person's substance habit, most successful treatment programs will involve family members or close friends to help ensure the patient's recovery.

Drugs

Some abused substances absolutely must be tapered back, because "cold turkey" methods of detoxification are potentially life threatening. Alternatively, a variety of medications may be utilized to combat the unpleasant and threatening physical symptoms of withdrawal. A substance (such as **methadone** in the case of heroin addiction, or **nicotine** patches with cigarette smokers) may be substituted for the original substance of abuse, with gradual tapering of this substituted drug. In practice, many patients may be maintained on methadone and lead a reasonably normal lifestyle. Because of the rebound effects of wildly fluctuating blood pressure, body temperature, and heart and breathing rates, as well as the potential for bizarre behavior and hallucinations, a person undergoing withdrawal must be carefully monitored.

Pharmacological remediation is being investigated for the treatment of stimulant abuse disorders. In the same way that medications are prescribed to treat the cognitive deficits present in psychiatric disorders, research is ongoing as to whether this same theory can be applied to substance abuse disorders. As of 2011, a vaccine was in development (TA-CD, or Therapy for Addiction—Cocaine Addiction) with the goal of helping cocaine addicts reduce consumption by at least half. A similar vaccine is also being developed for nicotine use (TA-NIC).

Prognosis

After a person has successfully withdrawn from substance use, the even-more-difficult task of recovery begins. "Recovery" refers to the lifelong efforts of a person to avoid returning to substance use. Cravings can continue for years after the initial withdrawal and might never completely cease. Triggers for relapse include any number of life stresses (problems on the job or in the

---

KEY TERMS

Addiction—The state of being both physically and psychologically dependent on a substance.

AIDS—Acquired immunodeficiency syndrome.

Dependence—A state in which a person requires a steady concentration of a particular substance in order to avoid experiencing withdrawal symptoms.

Detoxification—A process whereby an addict is withdrawn from a substance.

HIV—Human immunodeficiency virus.

Street drug—A substance purchased from a drug dealer. It may be a legal substance, sold illicitly (without a prescription and not for medical use), or it may be a substance that is illegal to possess.

Tolerance—A phenomenon whereby a drug user becomes physically accustomed to a particular dose of a substance and requires ever-increasing dosages in order to obtain the same effects.

Withdrawal—Those side effects experienced by a person who has become physically dependent on a substance, upon decreasing the substance's dosage or discontinuing its use.

---

marriage, loss of a relationship, death of a loved one, financial stresses) in addition to exposure to a place or an acquaintance associated with previous substance use. While some people remain in counseling indefinitely as a way of maintaining contact with a professional to help monitor behavior, others find that various **support groups** or 12-step programs, such as Alcoholics Anonymous (AA) and Narcotics Anonymous (NA), are the most helpful in monitoring the recovery process and avoiding relapse.

Prevention

Prevention is best aimed at childhood or adolescence. Teenagers are at very high risk for substance experimentation. Education regarding the risks and consequences of substance use, as well as teaching methods of resisting peer pressure, are both important components of a prevention program. Such education includes teaching the penalties associated with substance abuse, along with the social, physical, and psychological harm that it can cause an individual. Substance abuse efforts should occur in schools and communities, and parents should be actively involved in such programs to better communicate the risks to their children. Misperceptions about readily available

QUESTIONS TO ASK YOUR DOCTOR

- What treatment options are available?
- Where can I find support groups in my area?
- Will my insurance handle the expenses of treatment?
- Would you recommend seeing a therapist?

substances such as cigarettes and alcohol can be quickly corrected with proper communication. Furthermore, it is important to identify children at higher risk for substance abuse (including victims of physical or **sexual abuse**; children of parents who have a history of substance abuse, especially alcohol; and children with school failure and/or attention deficit disorder). These children may require a more intensive prevention program.

See also Alcohol use and related disorders; Amnestic disorders; Amphetamines and related disorders; Anti-anxiety drugs and abuse-related disorders; Caffeine and related disorders; Cannabis and related disorders; Cocaine and related disorders; Disease concept of chemical dependency; Hallucinogens and related disorders; Inhalants and related disorders; Nicotine and related disorders; Opioids and related disorders; Phencyclidine and related disorders; Polysubstance dependence; Sedatives and related disorders; Substance Abuse Subtle Screening Inventory; Substance-induced anxiety disorder; Substance-induced psychotic disorder; Wernicke-Korsakoff syndrome

Resources

BOOKS

Ferri, Fred, ed. *Ferri's Clinical Advisor 2010,* 1st ed. Philadelphia: Mosby Elsevier, 2009.

Goldman L, and D. Ausiello, eds. *Cecil Textbook of Internal Medicine,* 23rd ed. Philadelphia: Saunders, 2008.

Kaminer, Yifrah, and Ken C. Winters, eds. *Clinical Manual of Adolescent Substance Abuse Treatment.* Washington, DC: American Psychiatric, 2011.

Rakel, R. *Textbook of Family Medicine,* 7th ed. Philadelphia: Saunders Elsevier, 2007.

Rakel, R.E., and E.T. Bope. *Conn's Current Therapy,* 60th ed. Philadelphia: Saunders Elsevier, 2009.

Stern, T.A., et al. *Massachusetts General Hospital Comprehensive Clinical Psychiatry,* 1st ed. Philadelphia: Mosby Elsevier, 2008.

Wilson, Richard, and Cheryl A. Kolander. *Drug Abuse Prevention: A School and Community Partnership.* Sudbury, MA: Jones and Bartlett, 2011.

PERIODICALS

Hylton, Hilary. "A Drug to End Drug Addiction." *New York Times,* January 9, 2008. http://www.time.com/time/health/article/0,8599,1701864,00.html (accessed September 16, 2011).

Vocci, Frank J. "Cognitive Remediation in the Treatment of Stimulant Abuse Disorders: A Research Agenda." *Experimental and Clinical Psychopharmacology* 16, no. 6 (2008): 484–97.

OTHER

Substance Abuse and Mental Health Services Administration. *Results from the 2010 National Survey on Drug Use and Health: Summary of National Findings.* NSDUH Series H-41, HHS Publication no. (SMA) 11-4658. Rockville, MD: Substance Abuse and Mental Health Services Administration, 2011. http://oas.samhsa.gov/NSDUH/2k10NSDUH/2k10Results.htm (accessed September 16, 2011).

WEBSITES

Mayo Clinic staff. "Drug Addiction." MayoClinic.com (October 2, 2009). http://www.mayoclinic.com/health/drug-addiction/DS00183 (accessed July 19, 2011).

MedlinePlus. "Drug Abuse." U.S. National Library of Medicine, National Institutes of Health. http://www.nlm.nih.gov/medlineplus/drugabuse.html (accessed September 16, 2011).

National Institute on Drug Abuse. "Drugs, Brains, and Behavior: The Science of Addiction." August 2010. http://www.nida.nih.gov/scienceofaddiction (accessed September 16, 2011).

Office of Applied Studies. "Substance Abuse and Mental Health Statistics." Substance Abuse and Mental Health Services Administration (SAMHSA). http://oas.samhsa.gov (accessed September 16, 2011).

"Substance Abuse Treatment Facility Locator." SAMHSA. http://dasis3.samhsa.gov (accessed September 16, 2011).

American Psychiatric Association. "Substance Use and Addictive Disorders." DSM-5 Development. http://www.dsm5.org/ProposedRevision/Pages/SubstanceUseandAddictiveDisorders.aspx (accessed September 16, 2011).

Times Health Guide. "Drug Abuse." *New York Times.* http://health.nytimes.com/health/guides/specialtopic/drug-abuse/overview.html (accessed September 16, 2011).

ORGANIZATIONS

National Council on Alcoholism and Drug Dependence, Inc. (NCADD), 244 E 58th St., 4th Fl., New York, NY, 10022, (800) 622-2255, (212) 269-7797, Fax: (212) 269-7510, national@ncadd.org, http://www.ncadd.org.

National Institute on Drug Abuse, 6001 Executive Blvd., Rm. 5213, Bethesda, MD, 20892, (301) 443-1124; Spanish: (240) 221-4007, information@nida.nih.gov, http://drugabuse.gov.

Substance Abuse and Mental Health Services Administration (SAMHSA), 1 Choke Cherry Rd., Rockville, MD, 20857, (877) SAMHSA-7 (786-4727), TTY: (800) 487-4889, Fax: (240) 221-4292, SAMHSAInfo@samhsa.hhs.gov, http://www.samhsa.gov.

Substance Abuse Subtle Screening Inventory

Definition

The **Substance Abuse** Subtle Screening Inventory is also referred to as the SASSI. Dr. Glenn A. Miller developed the SASSI as a screening questionnaire for identifying people with a high probability of having a substance dependence disorder.

Purpose

The SASSI is intended for gathering information, organizing it, and using it to help make decisions about the likelihood of an individual having a substance dependence disorder, even if the individual does not acknowledge symptoms of the disorder or misuse of substances. Guidelines are available for professionals to flag individuals with a potential substance abuse disorder for further evaluation. Interpreting the results of the SASSI helps professionals understand their clients better and plan their treatment.

Precautions

When used by trained professionals, the SASSI can be an important tool in the assessment of substance use disorders. The SASSI is not intended to prove or diagnose an individual as an alcoholic or addict; it is intended to screen for a person who has a "high probability of having a substance dependence disorder." It should be kept in mind that a thorough assessment integrates other available information, such as self-report and family history, and is done by a skilled professional. This comprehensive assessment is required to determine if an individual meets the accepted standards in the mental health professional's handbook, **diagnosis** of a substance-related disorder.

The accuracy rate of the SASSI is 94%. Although that is very high, this means that there is a 6% probability that an individual will be misclassified based on SASSI scores. While the SASSI is a popular and widely used screening questionnaire, independent research on it has been limited. Some researchers have questions about the SASSI regarding the extent to which subscales measure what they are intended to measure and the accuracy of classification based on direct versus indirect scales. In addition, the SASSI is not to be used to discriminate against individuals, including disqualifying job applicants. It would be a violation of the Americans With Disabilities Act to eliminate a job applicant based on SASSI scores.

Description

The SASSI is a simple, brief one-page paper-and-pencil questionnaire that can be answered in 10 to 15 minutes. The SASSI is easy to administer, to individuals or groups, and can be objectively scored by hand and interpreted, based on objective decision rules, in a minute or two. Optical scanning equipment is available for mass scoring and interpretation. The SASSI does not require a high level of reading ability. The SASSI may be used by a variety of programs and professionals, including school counselors, student assistance programs, employee assistance programs, vocational counselors, psychotherapists, medical personnel, criminal justice programs, and other human service providers.

The SASSI went through rigorous scientific development over a 16-year period before it was first published in 1988. Two new scales were added, and the SASSI-2 was published in 1994. In 1997 the SASSI-3 was published with a new scale and increased accuracy. Items on the SASSI were selected based on established research methods and statistical analysis. Items were included that identified individuals with substance dependence disorders. The selected items were consistently answered differently by individuals with a substance dependence disorder compared to individuals without a substance dependence disorder.

In 1996, a Spanish version was made available. In addition to the paper and pencil format, computer versions of the SASSI, in several formats, are available.

Some questions on the SASSI ask how frequently clients have had certain experiences directly related to alcohol and other drugs. These are answered on a four-point scale, ranging from never to repeatedly. Some items that may appear to be unrelated to substance use (indirect or subtle items) are in a true/false format. Overall, the items make up 10 subscales. The results are reported on a profile form that is discussed with the client. There are separate profile forms for males and females. The objective scoring system results in a yes or no answer about whether the client has a high probability of having a substance dependence disorder. The SASSI-3 has been empirically tested and can identify substance dependence disorder with an overall accuracy of 94%. More specifically, the SASSI identifies individuals with a substance dependence disorder with 94% accuracy, and it identifies those without a substance dependence disorder with 94% accuracy. The accuracy of the SASSI is not significantly affected by gender, age, socioeconomic status, ethnicity, occupational status, marital status, educational level, drug of choice, and general level of functioning. Research is ongoing to improve the accuracy and usefulness of the SASSI.

Since 1990 an adolescent version of the SASSI has been available. The second version of the Adolescent SASSI (SASSI-A2) has a 94% overall accuracy of identifying an adolescent with a substance dependence disorder, including both substance abuse and substance dependence. The SASSI-A2 is designed to screen individuals who are 12 to 18 years old. The accuracy of the SASSI-A2 is not affected by the respondent's gender, age, ethnicity, education, employment status, living situation, prior legal history, or general level of functioning.

Results

A profile of the SASSI results will be reviewed with the client. The actual scores are plotted on a profile graph in comparison to a sample of people who were not being evaluated or treated for addictions or other clinical problems (also called a normative sample). Feedback is then given in terms of whether the individual has a high or low probability of having a substance dependence disorder. Individual scale scores may be used to come up with ideas or hypotheses for further evaluation and treatment. This information is based on clinical experience with the SASSI. The results may indicate issues that are important for treatment (such as difficulty acknowledging personal shortcomings, or primarily focusing on others' needs while unaware of one's own needs). The results may suggest an approach to take with the client (such as increasing awareness, or acknowledging and validating their feelings). The results may suggest a treatment plan that the client may respond to (such as addiction self-help groups or an education-focused program). Finally, the results may indicate appropriate treatment goals for the client (anger management and/ or social skills, for example). The goal of providing feedback about SASSI results is to have a two-way sharing and understanding of information that is descriptive and not judgmental.

Resources

BOOKS

Laux, John M., and Kathleen M. Salyers. "The SASSI-3 Face Valid Other Drugs Scale: A Psychometric investigation." *Psychology* 26 (October 2005) 15–22.

PERIODICALS

Gray, B. Thomas. "A Factor Analytic Study of the Substance Abuse Subtle Screening Inventory (SASSI)." *Educational and Psychological Measurement* 61 (2001): 102–118.

OTHER

U.S. National Institute of Alcohol Abuse and Alcoholism. "Substance Abuse Subtle Screening Inventory (SASSI)." http://pubs.niaaa.nih.gov/publications/Assesing%20 Alcohol/InstrumentPDFs/66_SASSI.pdf (accessed October 30, 2011).

WEBSITES

One Click Pharmacy.com "Substance Abuse Subtle Screening Inventory—Mental Health." http://www.oneclick pharmacy.co.uk/product_article_detail.php?id=6098 (accessed October 27, 2011).

Joneis Thomas, Ph.D.

Substance-induced anxiety disorder

Definition

A substance-induced anxiety disorder occurs when prominent anxiety symptoms (e.g., generalized anxiety, panic attacks, obsessive-compulsive symptoms, or phobia symptoms) are caused by the effects of a psychoactive substance. A substance may induce anxiety symptoms during intoxication (while the individual is under the influence of the drug) or during withdrawal (after an individual stops using the drug).

Demographics

Little is known regarding the demographics of substance-induced **anxiety disorders**. About 40 million American adults have an anxiety disorder, but there are not any reliable statistics indicating what percentage of these individuals have an anxiety disorder induced by substance use. However, it is clear that anxiety disorders occur more commonly in individuals who abuse alcohol or illicit drugs.

Description

A substance-induced anxiety disorder is subtyped or categorized based on whether the prominent feature is generalized anxiety, panic attacks, obsessive-compulsive symptoms, or phobia symptoms. In addition, the disorder is subtyped based on whether it began during intoxication on a substance or during withdrawal from a substance. A substance-induced anxiety disorder that begins during substance use can last as long as the drug is used. A substance-induced anxiety disorder that begins during withdrawal may first manifest up to four weeks after an individual stops using the substance.

Causes and symptoms

Substance-induced anxiety disorder is caused by the effects of certain drugs and alcohol, and the symptoms may look like other anxiety disorders except that in these cases, the conditions are linked to drug use or withdrawal.

Causes

A substance-induced anxiety disorder, by definition, is directly caused by the effects of drugs, including alcohol, prescription medications, illicit drugs, and toxins. Anxiety symptoms can result from intoxication on alcohol, **amphetamines** (and related substances), caffeine, **cannabis** (marijuana), **cocaine**, **hallucinogens**, **inhalants**, phencyclidine (PCP) and related substances, and other or unknown substances. Anxiety symptoms also can result from withdrawal from alcohol, **sedatives**, hypnotics, and anxiolytics (**antianxiety drugs**), cocaine, and other known or unknown substances.

Prescription drugs that may induce anxiety symptoms include anesthetics, analgesics, sympathomimetics (e.g., epinephrine or norepinephrine), bronchodilators, anticholinergic agents, anticonvulsants, antihistamines, insulin, thyroid preparations, oral contraceptives, antihypertensive and cardiovascular medications, antiparkinsonian medications, corticosteroids, **antidepressants**, **lithium carbonate**, and antipsychotic medications. Heavy metals and toxins, such as fuel, paint, organophosphate insecticides, nerve gases, carbon monoxide, and carbon dioxide may also induce anxiety.

Symptoms

The **diagnosis** is made only when the anxiety symptoms are above and beyond what would be expected during intoxication or withdrawal and when the symptoms are severe. The following list comprises the criteria necessary for the diagnosis of a substance-induced anxiety disorder as listed in the *Diagnostic and Statistical Manual of Mental Disorders*, fourth edition, text revision (*DSM-IV-TR*):

- prominent anxiety, panic attacks, or obsessions or compulsions

- symptoms developing during or within one month of intoxication or withdrawal from a substance or medication known to cause anxiety symptoms

- symptoms not part of another anxiety disorder (such as generalized anxiety disorder, phobias, panic disorder, or obsessive-compulsive personality disorder) and not substance induced (For instance, if the anxiety symptoms began prior to substance or medication use, then another anxiety disorder is likely.)

- symptoms not occurring only during delirium

- symptoms causing significant distress or impairment in functioning.

KEY TERMS

Analgesic—Medicine used to relieve pain.

Anticonvulsants—A class of drugs given to control seizures.

Corticosteroid—A steroid hormone produced by the adrenal gland and involved in metabolism and immune response.

Corticosteroid drug—A medication that acts like a type of hormone (cortisol) produced by the adrenal gland of the body. Corticosteroids produced by the body stimulate specific types of functional activity. As a drug, a corticosteroid (sometimes just called steroid) helps treat inflammation, infection, or trauma to the body.

Insulin—A hormone made by the pancreas that controls blood glucose (sugar) levels by moving excess glucose into muscle, liver, and other cells for storage.

Diagnosis

Diagnosis of a substance-induced anxiety disorder requires the case being differentiated from an anxiety disorder due to a general medical condition. Some medical conditions (e.g., hyperthyroidism, hypothyroidism, and hypoglycemia) also can produce anxiety symptoms. Since individuals are likely to be taking medications for these conditions, it can be difficult to determine the cause of the anxiety symptoms. If the symptoms are determined to be due to the medical condition, then a diagnosis of an anxiety disorder due to a general medical condition is warranted. Substance-induced anxiety disorders also need to be distinguished from **delirium**, **dementia**, primary psychotic disorders, and substance intoxication and withdrawal.

Clinical history and physical examination are the best methods to help diagnose anxiety disorders in general; however, appropriate laboratory testing will most likely be necessary to specifically identify substance-induced anxiety disorder. Lab tests may include:

- complete blood count (CBC)
- chemistry panels
- serum and/or urine screens for drugs

Treatment

The underlying cause of the anxiety symptoms, as well as the specific type of symptoms, determine course of treatment. Treatment often is similar to that

QUESTIONS TO ASK YOUR DOCTOR

- Could any of my medications be causing my anxiety symptoms?
- What programs can you recommend to help me stop using the substance causing my anxiety?
- Can you refer me to a mental health professional?
- Will my insurance cover an alternative medication if this one is causing anxiety symptoms?
- What other steps can I take to help reduce my anxiety?
- Are there any support groups in this area that might be right for me?

used to treat a primary anxiety disorder such as **generalized anxiety disorder**, phobias, **panic disorder**, or **obsessive-compulsive disorder**. Appropriate treatment usually includes medication (e.g., antianxiety or antidepressant medication). Additional treatment may be needed to address symptoms of withdrawal when substance use is stopped, a process that should be conducted under the care of a physician.

Prognosis

Anxiety symptoms induced by substance intoxication usually subside once the substance responsible is eliminated. The length of time symptoms persist depends on how long it takes before the substance is no longer present in an individual's body (intoxication-induced anxiety) or how long it takes the body to adjust to no longer having the substance (withdrawal-induced anxiety). Symptoms, therefore, can persist for hours, days, or weeks after a substance is last used. Obsessive-compulsive symptoms induced by substances sometimes do not disappear, even though the substance inducing them has been eliminated. More intensive treatment for the obsessive-compulsive symptoms is then necessary and typically includes a combination of medication and behavioral therapy.

Prevention

Little is documented regarding the prevention of substance-induced anxiety disorder. However, abstaining from illicit drugs and alcohol sharply reduces the risk of developing this disorder. In addition, taking medication under the supervision of an appropriately trained physician should reduce the likelihood of a medication-induced anxiety disorder. Finally, reducing one's exposure to toxins and heavy metals reduces the risk of toxin-induced anxiety disorder.

Resources

BOOKS

Daitch, Carolyn. *Anxiety Disorders: The Go-To Guide for Clients and Therapists.* New York: Norton, 2011.

Doctor, Ronald M., Ada P. Kahn, and Christine Adamec. *The Encyclopedia of Phobias, Fears, and Anxieties,* 3rd ed. New York: Facts on File, 2008.

Fisher, Gary L., and Nancy A. Roget, eds. *Encyclopedia of Substance Abuse Prevention, Treatment, and Recovery.* Los Angeles: SAGE, 2009.

PERIODICALS

Leeies, Murdoch, et al. "The Use of Alcohol and Drugs to Self-Medicate Symptoms of Post-traumatic Stress Disorder." *Depression and Anxiety* 27, no. 8 (August 2010):731–36.

Torrens, Marti, et al. "Psychiatric Comorbidity in Illicit Drug Users: Substance-Induced versus Independent Disorders." *Drug and Alcohol Dependence* (2011).

ORGANIZATIONS

American Psychiatric Association, 1000 Wilson Blvd., Ste. 1825, Arlington, VA, 22209-3901, (703) 907-7300, apa@psych.org, http://www.psych.org.

American Psychological Association, 750 1st St. NE, Washington, DC, 20002-4242, (202) 336-5500; TDD/TTY: (202) 336-6123, (800) 374-2721, http://www.apa.org.

National Council on Alcoholism and Drug Dependence, Inc., 244 E 58th St., 4th Fl., New York, NY, 10022, (212) 269-7797, (800) NCA-CALL, Fax: (212) 269-7510, national@ mcadd.org, http://www.ncadd.org.

Substance Abuse and Mental Health Services Administration Referral Resource, 1 Choke Cherry Rd., Rockville, MD, 20857, (877) SAMHSA-7 (726-4727), (800) TTY: 487-4889, Fax: (240) 221-4292, SAMHSAInfo@samhsa.hhs.gov, http://www.samhsa.gov.

Jennifer Hahn, PhD
Tish Davidson, AM

Substance-induced persisting amnestic disorder *see* **Amnesia and amnestic disorders; Wernicke-Korsakoff syndrome**

Substance-induced psychotic disorder

Definition

The primary feature of a substance-induced psychotic disorder is prominent psychotic symptoms (i.e., hallucinations and/or **delusions**) determined to be caused by the effects of a psychoactive substance. A substance may induce psychotic symptoms during intoxication (while the individual is under the influence of the drug) or during withdrawal (after an individual stops using the drug.

Demographics

Little is known regarding how common substance-induced **psychosis** is across all substances. Approximately 3% of individuals who are dependent on alcohol experience psychosis at some time, either while severely intoxicated or during withdrawal. Substance-induced first episodes of psychosis are more common in men than women. Approximately 51% of individuals experiencing a first episode of psychosis caused by non-medication substance use report having used marijuana. The next most common substance to induce psychosis is alcohol, at 43%, with other substances accounting for the remaining 6% of instances.

Description

A substance-induced psychotic disorder is subtyped or categorized based on whether the prominent feature is delusions or hallucinations. Delusions are fixed, false beliefs. Hallucinations are seeing, hearing, feeling, tasting, or smelling things that are not there. In addition, the disorder is subtyped based on whether it began during intoxication on a substance or during withdrawal from a substance. A substance-induced psychotic disorder that begins during substance use can last as long as the drug is used. A substance-induced psychotic disorder that begins during withdrawal may first manifest up to four weeks after an individual stops using the substance.

Causes and symptoms

Substance-induced psychotic disorder is caused by using certain substances or withdrawing from that use. Symptoms are of two basic sorts: delusions or hallucinations.

Causes

A substance-induced psychotic disorder, by definition, is directly caused by the effects of drugs, including alcohol, illicit drugs, prescription medications, or toxins. Psychotic symptoms can result from intoxication on alcohol, **amphetamines** (and related substances), **cannabis** (marijuana), **cocaine**, **hallucinogens**, **inhalants**, **opioids**, phencyclidine (PCP) and related substances, **sedatives**, hypnotics, anxiolytics, and other or unknown substances. Psychotic symptoms can also result from withdrawal from alcohol, sedatives, hypnotics, anxiolytics, and other or unknown substances.

Medications that may induce psychotic symptoms include anesthetics and analgesics, anticholinergic agents, anticonvulsants, antihistamines, antihypertensive and cardiovascular medications, antimicrobial medications, antiparkinsonian medications, chemotherapeutic agents, corticosteroids, gastrointestinal medications, muscle relaxants, nonsteroidal anti-inflammatory medications, other over-the-counter medications, antidepressant medications, and **disulfiram**. Toxins that may induce psychotic symptoms include anticholinesterase, organophosphate insecticides, nerve gases, carbon monoxide, carbon dioxide, and volatile substances (such as fuel or paint).

The speed of onset of psychotic symptoms varies depending on the type of substance. For example, a large quantity of cocaine can produce psychotic symptoms within minutes. In contrast, psychotic symptoms may result from **alcohol use** only after days or weeks of intensive use.

The type of psychotic symptoms also tends to vary according to the type of substance. For instance, auditory hallucinations (specifically, hearing voices), visual hallucinations, and tactile hallucinations are most common in an alcohol-induced psychotic disorder, whereas persecutory delusions and tactile hallucinations (especially formication, which is the sensation that bugs are crawling on the skin) are commonly seen in a cocaine- or amphetamine-induced psychotic disorder.

Symptoms

The **diagnosis** is made only when the psychotic symptoms are above and beyond what would be expected during intoxication or withdrawal and when the psychotic symptoms are severe. The following are criteria necessary for diagnosis of a substance-induced psychotic disorder as listed in the *Diagnostic and Statistical Manual of Mental Disorders*, fourth edition, text revision (*DSM-IV-TR*):

• Presence of prominent hallucinations or delusions.

• Hallucinations and/or delusions developing during, or within one month of, intoxication or withdrawal from a substance or medication known to cause psychotic symptoms.

• Psychotic symptoms not part of another psychotic disorder (such as schizophrenia, schizophreniform disorder, schizoaffective disorder) that is not substance induced. For instance, if the psychotic symptoms began before substance or medication use, then another psychotic disorder is likely.

KEY TERMS

Dementia—A chronic condition in which thinking and memory are progressively impaired. Other symptoms may also occur, including personality changes and depression.

Hallucination—A false or distorted perception of objects, sounds, or events that seems real. Hallucinations usually result from drugs or mental disorders.

Huntington's chorea—An hereditary disease that typically appears in midlife, marked by gradual loss of brain function and voluntary movement. Some of its symptoms resemble those of schizophrenia.

Schizophrenia—A severe mental disorder in which a person loses touch with reality and may have illogical thoughts, delusions, hallucinations, behavioral problems, and other disturbances.

- Psychotic symptoms not only occurring during delirium.

Diagnosis

Diagnosis of a substance-induced psychotic disorder must be differentiated from a psychotic disorder due to a general medical condition. Some medical conditions (such as temporal lobe epilepsy or Huntington's chorea) can produce psychotic symptoms, and, since individuals are likely to be taking medications for these conditions, it can be difficult to determine the cause of the psychotic symptoms. If the symptoms are determined to be due to the medical condition, then a diagnosis of a psychotic disorder due to a general medical condition is warranted.

Substance-induced psychotic disorder also needs to be distinguished from **delirium**, **dementia**, primary psychotic disorders, and substance intoxication and withdrawal. While there are no absolute means of determining substance use as a cause, a thorough patient history, including a careful assessment of onset and course of symptoms, along with that of substance use, is imperative. Often, the patient's testimony is unreliable, necessitating the gathering of information from family, friends, coworkers, employment records, medical records, and the like. Differentiating between substance-induced disorder and a psychiatric disorder may be aided by the following:

- Time of onset: If symptoms began before substance use, it is most likely a psychiatric disorder.

- Substance use patterns: If symptoms persist for three months or longer after substance is discontinued, a psychiatric disorder is probable.

- Consistency of symptoms: If symptoms are more exaggerated than one would expect with a particular substance type and dose, then the condition most likely is a psychiatric disorder.

- Family history: A family history of mental illness may indicate a psychiatric disorder.

- Response to substance abuse treatment: Clients with both psychiatric and substance use disorders often have serious difficulty with traditional substance abuse treatment programs and relapse during or shortly after treatment cessation.

- Client's stated reason for substance use: Those with a primary psychiatric diagnosis and secondary substance use disorder will often indicate they "medicate symptoms," for example, drink to dispel auditory hallucinations, use stimulants to combat depression, or use depressants to reduce anxiety or soothe a manic phase. While such substance use most often exacerbates the psychotic condition, it does not necessarily mean the client has a substance-induced psychotic disorder.

Unfortunately, psychological tests are not always helpful in determining if a psychotic disorder is caused by substance use or is being exacerbated by it. However, evaluations, such as the MMPI-2 MAC-R scale or the Wechsler Memory Scale—Revised, can be useful in making a differential diagnosis.

Treatment

Treatment is determined by the underlying cause and severity of psychotic symptoms. However, treatment of a substance-induced psychotic disorder often is similar to treatment for a primary psychotic disorder such as **schizophrenia**. Appropriate treatments may include psychiatric **hospitalization** and antipsychotic medication. Concurrent treatment will also be conducted for the **substance abuse** problem.

Prognosis

Psychotic symptoms induced by substance intoxication usually subside once the substance is eliminated. Symptoms persist depending on how long it takes before the substance is no longer present in an individual's system. Symptoms, therefore, can persist for hours, days, or weeks after a substance is last used.

QUESTIONS TO ASK YOUR DOCTOR

- Is the psychosis likely to be the result of substance use?
- Could changing a medication reduce the psychosis symptoms?
- Will my insurance pay for a rehabilitation center?
- Can you recommend a psychiatrist or other specialist experienced in treating this disorder?
- Are there any support groups that might be appropriate for me in this area?
- If I stop using the substance, how long can I expect the symptoms to last?
- Where can I find help for my substance use?

Prevention

There is very little documented regarding prevention of substance-induced psychotic disorder. However, abstaining from drugs and alcohol or using these substances only in moderation clearly reduces the risk of developing this disorder. In addition, taking medication under the supervision of an appropriately trained physician should reduce the likelihood of a medication-induced psychotic disorder. Finally, reducing one's exposure to toxins reduces the risk of toxin-induced psychotic disorder.

Resources

BOOKS

Fisher, Gary L., and Nancy A. Roget, eds. *Encyclopedia of Substance Abuse Prevention, Treatment, and Recovery.* Los Angeles: SAGE, 2009.

Meaden, Alan, and David Hacker. *Problematic and Risk Behaviours in Psychosis: A Shared Formulation Approach.* Hove, East Sussex: Routledge, 2010.

Stern, Theodore A., et al., eds. *Massachusetts General Hospital Handbook of General Hospital Psychiatry,* 6th ed. Philadelphia: Saunders/Elsevier, 2010.

PERIODICALS

Jordaan, Gerhard P., et al. "Alcohol-Induced Psychotic Disorder: A Comparative Study on the Clinical Characteristics of Patients with Alcohol Dependence and Schizophrenia." *Journal of Studies on Alcohol and Drugs* 70, no. 6 (November 2009):870–76.

Pierre, Joseph M. "Psychosis Associated with Medical Marijuana: Risk vs. Benefits of Medical Cannabis Use." *American Journal of Psychiatry* 167, no. 5 (May 2010): 598–99.

Torrens, Marti, et al. "Psychiatric Comorbidity in Illicit Drug Users: Substance-Induced versus Independent Disorders." *Drug and Alcohol Dependence* (2011).

ORGANIZATIONS

American Psychiatric Association, 1000 Wilson Blvd., Ste. 1825, Arlington, VA, 22209-3901, (703) 907-7300, apa@psych.org, http://www.psych.org.

American Psychological Association, 750 1st St. NE, Washington, DC, 20002-4242, (202) 336-5500; TDD/TTY: (202) 336-6123, (800) 374-2721, http://www.apa.org.

National Council on Alcoholism and Drug Dependence Inc., 244 E 58th St., 4th Fl., New York, NY, 10022, (212) 269-7797, (800) NCA-CALL, Fax: (212) 269-7510, national@mcadd.org, http://www.ncadd.org.

Substance Abuse and Mental Health Services Administration Referral Resource, 1 Choke Cherry Rd., Rockville, MD, 20857, (877) SAMHSA-7 (726-4727), (800) TTY: 487-4889, Fax: (240) 221-4292, SAMHSAInfo@samhsa.hhs.gov, http://www.samhsa.gov.

Jennifer Hahn, PhD
Tish Davidson, AM

Suicide

Definition

Suicide is defined as the intentional taking of one's own life. In some European languages, including German, the word for suicide translates into English as "self-murder." In Latin, suicide is derived from *suicidium,* or "to kill oneself." Until approximately the end of the twentieth century, suicide was considered a criminal act; legal terminology used the Latin phrase *felo-de-se,* which means "a crime against the self." Much of the social **stigma** that is still associated with suicide derives from its former connection with legal judgment as well as with religious condemnation.

Demographics

In the United States, the rate of suicide has continued to rise since the 1950s. More people in the general population die from suicide than homicide in North America. There are 11.3 suicide deaths each year for every 100,000 people living in the United States, according to the **National Institute of Mental Health** (NIMH), and for every suicide, there are approximately 11.5 attempts. In any given year, there are approximately 40,000 suicide-based deaths, along with up to 500,000 suicide attempts. The U.S. Centers for Disease Control

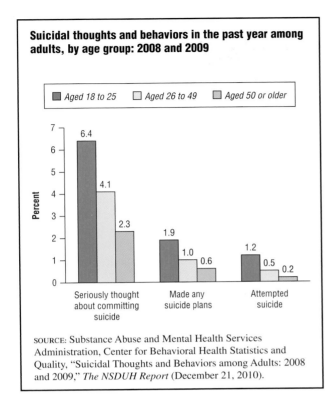

Suicidal thoughts and behaviors in the past year among adults, by age group: 2008 and 2009

■ Aged 18 to 25 ☐ Aged 26 to 49 ☐ Aged 50 or older

Percent

Seriously thought about committing suicide: 6.4, 4.1, 2.3

Made any suicide plans: 1.9, 1.0, 0.6

Attempted suicide: 1.2, 0.5, 0.2

SOURCE: Substance Abuse and Mental Health Services Administration, Center for Behavioral Health Statistics and Quality, "Suicidal Thoughts and Behaviors among Adults: 2008 and 2009," *The NSDUH Report* (December 21, 2010).

Report available online at http://www.oas.samhsa.gov/2k10/212/SuicidalThoughts.htm. *(Graph by PreMediaGlobal. © 2012 Cengage Learning.)*

and Prevention (CDC) states that in 2009, suicide was the tenth-leading cause of death in the United States. According to the U.S. Department of Defense/Veterans Affairs website, more years of life are lost due to suicide than to any other single cause except for heart disease and cancer. Substance abuse is a major factor associated with suicide. Statistics show that substance abuse is thought to be involved in as many as one-half of all suicide cases. In fact, the abuse of alcohol is involved with about 20% of all suicide attempts. Completed suicides are most likely to involve a man over the age of 45 years who is suffering from depression or alcoholism.

By state, region

The demographics of suicide in the United States vary considerably from state to state, with rates higher than the national average in the West and lower in the Midwest and Northeast. Some states, like Alaska, have suicide rates that are almost twice the national average; others, such as Massachusetts, have notably lower rates.

Age and gender

These variations from state to state, and region to region, result in part from differences in age and ethnic distributions and gender ratios among the states. In 2008, suicide was the eighth-leading cause of death among males and sixteenth-leading cause of death among females. Males are four times more likely than females to succeed in their suicide attempts, but females report attempting suicide at some point in their lives three times as often as men do. An increase in the overall suicide rate in the United States between 1999 and 2009 was due primarily to an increase in suicides among Caucasians aged 40–64 years, with white middle-aged women experiencing the largest annual increases.

In terms of age, the highest number of suicides are committed by people under age 40 years, but suicide rates (percentages in a given group) increase with age. People over age 65 years have high suicide rates, with men outnumbering women who commit suicide nearly four to one.

SENIORS. The incidence of suicide and attempted suicide among seniors is widely perceived as a growing public health problem in the United States; in 2009, older adults represented about 13% of the U.S. population but accounted for 20% of suicides. According to the NIMH, the highest suicide rate in the nation is for Caucasian men aged 85 years and older, at 65.3 deaths per 100,000 persons—about six times the national U.S. rate of 10.8 per 100,000.

The ratio of attempted suicides to completed suicides among people over 65 is thought to be around 4:1. According to the National Strategy for Suicide Prevention (NSSP), seniors are more likely than are younger persons to use highly lethal means of suicide. According to a Canadian study published in 2008, seniors are most likely to use firearms to commit suicide, followed by hanging, self-poisoning, and leaping from heights.

YOUNG PEOPLE. The overall rate of suicide among young people has declined slowly since 1992, but it still remains the third-leading cause of death in age groups spanning children 10 years old to young adults up to age 24. Suicidal behavior is rare in prepubertal children, probably because of their relative inability to plan and execute a suicide attempt. Children as young as 5 years, however, have succeeded in killing themselves by leaping out of windows or shooting themselves—as happened with one five-year-old who witnessed his mother kill herself with a gun and imitated her behavior several months later. According to the NIMH, the rates of suicide for American youth in 2007 (the most recent data available) were as follows:

• children between the ages of 10 and 14: 0.9 suicides per 100,000

- teenagers between the ages of 15 and 19: 6.9 per 100,000
- young adults between the ages of 20 and 24: 12.7 per 100,000

Race or ethnicity

In 2007, the NIMH reported the highest suicide rates among American Indians and Alaska Natives, at 14.3 per 100,000, and Non-Hispanic whites, at 13.5 per 100,000. The lowest suicide rates were found among Hispanics, at 6.0 per 100,000; Non-Hispanic blacks, at 5.1 per 100,000; and Asian and Pacific Islanders, at 6.2 per 100,000. Suicide rates among American Indian and Alaskan natives between 15 and 34 years are almost twice the national average for this age range. Young Hispanic females make significantly more suicide attempts than their male or non-Hispanic counterparts.

In the military

In 2008, the rate of suicides in the U.S. Army surpassed the civilian (non-military) rate (19.2 per 100,000), hitting an all-time high of 20.2 suicides per 100,000 people. In that year, at least 128 soldiers committed suicide (with other deaths being investigated as possible suicide cases); suicide deaths numbered 115 and 102 in the two years prior, respectively.

According to 2009 data, five members of the military were unsuccessful in their suicide attempt for every one that was successful. The U.S. Veterans Affairs Department (VA) reported in 2010 that the suicide rate for 17–29 year old male veterans increased by 26% from 2005 to 2007. Statistics show that one of the major causes of suicide within these military personnel was substance abuse (drug or alcohol). Between 2005 and 2009, the use of drugs or alcohol contributed to over 45% of unsuccessful suicide attempts and 30% of suicide deaths. The Defense Survey of Health-Related Behaviors found that 12% of military personnel had the presence of "dangerous levels" of alcohol or illicit drugs within their bodies. Relationship problems were also a major cause of suicide, with 58% of suicide deaths in 2009 believed caused by such stressful situations.

International

Suicide has become a major social and medical problem around the world, not just in North America. Worldwide suicide rates have increased by 60% since 1960. The World Health Organization (WHO) reports that nearly one million people worldwide die annually from suicide, more than the number of people murdered or killed in war. That number of suicides breaks down to 16 deaths per 100,000 people, or one death every 40 seconds. According to WHO, more suicides occur in Asia than in any other region of the world, with China, Japan, and India accounting for 40% of the world's suicides. China is also the only country in the world where more women than men take their own lives, with female suicides representing 58% of the total.

Rates among young people have risen even faster, to the point where they are now the age group at highest risk in 35% of the world's countries. Among people 10 to 24 years of age, suicide is the third-leading cause of death in the world, and it is the second-leading cause in persons aged 15 to 44 years. For every 20 attempted tries at suicide, there is one death. In Europe and North America, mental disorders are particularly high in the cause of suicides. All over the world, suicide involves a complex play of biological (genetic), cultural, environmental, psychological, and social factors.

Description

Suicidal behavior is most commonly regarded—and responded to—as a psychiatric or medical emergency, one often committed due to a mental disorder such as **bipolar disorder**, **depression**, **schizophrenia**, or **substance abuse**. At other times, suicide may be contemplated due to pressures in life, such as financial or legal difficulties or a troubling interpersonal relationship such as a crumbling marriage. Law enforcement personnel may be involved in preventing an attempted suicide or taking suicidal individuals to a hospital emergency department but not in arresting these persons for breaking the law.

Historical background

Attitudes toward suicide have varied throughout history. The ancient Greeks considered it an offense against the state, which was deprived of contributions by potentially useful citizens. The Romans, by comparison, thought that suicide could be a noble form of death, although they legislated against persons taking their own lives before an impending criminal conviction in order to insure their families' financial inheritance. Early Christianity, which downplayed the importance of life on Earth, was not critical of suicide until the fourth century, when Algerian philosopher St. Augustine (354–430) condemned it as a sin because it violated the sixth commandment ("Thou shalt not kill."). Eventually, the Roman Catholic Church excommunicated and even denied funeral rites to people who killed themselves. The view of suicide as a sin prevailed in Western societies for hundreds of years, and many people are still influenced by it, either consciously or unconsciously. For instance, suicide was a felony and attempted suicide a misdemeanor in England until 1961.

Austrian neurologist Sigmund Freud (1856–1939) provided the first theory that addressed suicide in terms of a person's inner mental and emotional state. In *Mourning and Melancholia* (1917), he proposed that suicide was the result of turning hostility toward a loved one back on oneself. In *Man against Himself* (1936), American **psychiatrist** Karl Menninger (1893–1990) extended Freud's contribution to the psychodynamic study of suicide, relating it to such other forms of self-destructive behavior as alcoholism or drug abuse. Some people still refer to such behavior as "slow-motion suicide."

Types of suicidal behavior

Some mental health professionals distinguish five levels of suicidal behavior: completed suicide; suicide attempts, which are potentially fatal; suicide gestures, which involve acting-out behavior that is not necessarily lethal; suicide gambles; and suicidal ideation, or thinking about suicide. An example of a suicide gesture would be cutting one's wrist just deeply enough to draw blood from the skin but not deeply enough to sever veins and arteries. The suicide gamble is a type of suicidal behavior in which the person takes the risk that he or she will be discovered in time and that the discoverer will save them. The suicide of American poet Sylvia Plath (1932–1963) is considered an example of a suicide gamble. Plath gassed herself in the kitchen by turning on her oven without lighting it, but left a note on the door for her children's new nanny, had opened the windows in the children's bedroom to protect them, and had sealed the door to the kitchen with dish towels.

Suicidal ideation, or thinking about suicide, is even more common than suicide gestures or attempted suicide. Suicidal ideation spans a continuum from nonspecific thoughts such as "life is not worth living" to specific ideation. Community surveys indicate that 12%–25% of primary and high school children have some form of suicidal ideation, whereas 5%–10% combine suicidal ideation with a plan or intent to make a suicide attempt. Specific ideation is more closely associated with risk for attempted suicide and frequently occurs in combination with other risk factors.

Risk factors

Some factors increase a person's risk of suicide:

- male gender
- age over 75 years
- family history of suicide or mental illness
- history of suicide attempts
- Caucasian race
- history of abuse
- traumatic experiences after childhood
- recent stressful events, such as separation or divorce, job loss, or death of spouse
- dealing with homosexuality in an unsupportive environment
- lack of a support network, poor relationships with parents or peers, and feelings of social isolation
- chronic medical illness—patients with acquired immune deficiency syndrome (AIDS) have a rate of suicide 20 times that of the general population
- chronic, severe, or intractable pain
- loss of mobility or independence
- access to a firearm—death by firearms accounts for the majority of suicides in the United States
- alcohol or substance abuse—while mood-altering substances do not cause a person to kill himself or herself, they do weaken impulse control
- high blood cholesterol levels
- presence of a psychiatric illness

More than 90% of Americans who commit suicide have a mental illness. Major depression accounts for 60% of suicides, followed by schizophrenia, alcoholism, substance abuse, **borderline personality disorder**, Huntington's disease, and epilepsy. The lifetime mortality due to suicide in psychiatric patients is 15% for major depression, 20% for bipolar disorder, 18% for alcoholism, 10% for schizophrenia, and 5–10% for borderline and certain other **personality disorders**. In children and adolescents, the most common triggers of suicidal behavior involve interpersonal conflict or loss, most frequently with parents or romantic attachment figures. Family discord, physical or **sexual abuse**, and an upcoming legal or disciplinary crisis are also commonly associated with completed and attempted suicides. The most serious suicide attempts involve suicide notes, evidence of planning, and an irreversible method. Most adolescent suicide attempts are of relatively low intent and lethality, and only a minority actually want to die. Usually, children and adolescents who attempt suicide want to escape psychological pain or unbearable circumstances, gain attention, influence others, or communicate such strong feelings as rage or love.

Factors that lower the risk of suicide include:

- significant friendship network outside the workplace
- religious faith and practice, especially those that discourage suicide and value life
- stable marriage
- close-knit extended family
- strong interest in or commitment to a project or cause that brings people together—community service,

environmental concerns, neighborhood associations, animal rescue groups, etc.

Ethical issues related to suicide

Several ethical issues related to suicide have emerged as public policy matters in the early twenty-first century. The most controversial of these are the notion of a "right to suicide" and the question of assisted suicide.

RIGHT TO SUICIDE. The idea that suicide is a right among the elderly or those with terminal illnesses surfaced with the 1991 publication of English-born American journalist Derek Humphry's (1930–) *Final Exit*, a controversial book described by its author as a how-to manual for suicide and assisted suicide. Humphry is the founder of the Euthanasia Research and Guidance Organization (ERGO), known until 2003 as the Hemlock Society. Humphry maintains that people have a right to choose the time, place, and method of their death and that rational suicide is a legitimate and even reasonable choice.

People who are often overlooked in discussions of the right to commit suicide, however, are the relatives and friends who are bereaved by the suicide. It is estimated that each person who commits suicide leaves six survivors to deal with the aftermath. On the basis of this figure, there are at least 4.5 million survivors of suicide in the United States. In addition to the **grief** that ordinarily accompanies death, survivors of suicide often struggle with feelings of guilt and shame as well. Some people have blamed Humphry and his book for their loved one's decision to commit suicide.

ASSISTED SUICIDE. Questions pertaining to the legalization of assisted suicide for persons suffering from a terminal illness are connected in part to increases in the average lifespan. Physician-assisted suicide (also known as physician-assisted death or PAD) was legalized in the Netherlands in April 2001, and in the states of Oregon, Washington, and Montana. As of 2011, it was also legal in Belgium and Luxembourg and was practiced openly in Switzerland. It is important to distinguish between physician-assisted suicide and euthanasia, or "mercy killing." Assisted suicide, which is called "self-deliverance" in Britain, refers to individuals bringing about their own death with the help of another person. Because the other person is often a physician, the act is often called doctor-assisted suicide.

Euthanasia strictly speaking means that the physician or other person is the one who performs the last act that causes death. For example, if a physician injects a patient with a lethal dose of a pain-killing medication, the physician is performing euthanasia. If the physician leaves the patient with a loaded syringe and the patient injects himself or herself with it, the act is an assisted suicide. Euthanasia is illegal in all 50 states.

Causes and symptoms

Causes

One model that has been used by clinicians to explain why people suffering under the same life stresses respond differently is known as the stress/diathesis model. Diathesis is a medical term for a predisposition that makes some people more vulnerable to thoughts of suicide. In addition to factors at the individual level, factors in the wider society have been identified as contributing to the rising rate of suicide in the United States, including:

- Stresses on the nuclear family, including more frequent divorce and economic hardship.
- Loss of a set of moral values held in common by the entire society.
- Weakening of churches, synagogues, neighborhood associations, and other mid-range social groups outside the family. In the past, these institutions often provided a sense of belonging for people from troubled or emotionally distant families.
- Frequent geographical moves, which makes it difficult for people to make and keep long-term friendships outside their immediate family.
- Sensationalized treatment of suicide in the mass media. A number of research studies have shown that there is a definite risk of "contagion" or copycat suicides from irresponsible reporting, particularly among impressionable adolescents. One group of researchers has estimated that as many as 6% of all suicides in the developed countries are copycat suicides.
- Development of medications that allow relatively painless suicide. For most of human history, the available means of suicide were uncertain, painful, or both.
- Easy availability of lethal methods of suicide, most notably firearms, and so-called suicide magnets such as bridges or tall buildings that do not have suicide barriers and are easy to reach. The Golden Gate Bridge in San Francisco, California, is the most notorious public suicide location in the United States; others include the Aurora Bridge in Seattle, Washington, the Sunshine Skyway Bridge in Florida, and the Duke Ellington Bridge in Washington, DC. Other popular suicide locations elsewhere

in the world include the Aokigahara Forest at the base of Mount Fuji in Japan, and Beachy Head in the United Kingdom.

The role of the Internet in the rate of adolescent suicide has been debated. On the one hand, there are websites and chat rooms that foster preoccupation with suicide and offer detailed descriptions of suicide methods. There are even instances of adolescents recruiting other adolescents over the Internet to join them in a suicide pact. For instance, seven young people who had met via the Internet committed group suicide by inhaling carbon monoxide from a charcoal burner inside a locked van. Other websites attack psychiatry and mental health professionals, which may steer some vulnerable young people away from seeking help. On the other hand, there are many supportive websites for teens that offer resources (including peer counseling) and contact information for getting help if they are considering suicide.

Media treatment of suicide

In 1989, the CDC sponsored a national workshop to address the connection between sensationalized media treatments of suicide and the rising rate of suicide among American youth. The CDC and the American Association of Suicidology subsequently adopted a set of guidelines for media coverage of suicide intended to reduce the risk of copycat suicides.

The CDC guidelines point out that the following types of reporting may increase the risk of copycat suicides:

- Presenting oversimplified explanations of suicide, when in fact many factors usually contribute to it. One example concerns the suicide of the widow of a man who was killed in the collapse of the World Trade Center on September 11, 2001. Most newspapers that covered the story described her death as due solely to the act of terrorism, even though she had a history of depressive illness.
- Giving excessive, ongoing, or repetitive coverage of the suicide.
- Sensationalizing the suicide by including morbid details or dramatic photographs.
- Giving "how-to" descriptions of the method of suicide.
- Referring to suicide as an effective coping strategy or as a way to achieve temporary fame or other goals.
- Glorifying the act of suicide or the person who commits suicide.
- Focusing on the person's positive traits without mentioning his or her problems.

Symptoms

Potential warning signs of suicidal thinking may include:

- reading a lot of books or articles on death and suicide
- talking a lot about death or suicide or expressing feelings of hopelessness
- stockpiling medications
- refusing to take care of oneself
- sudden interest in guns
- giving away cherished possessions, writing long letters, or making other elaborate farewells
- disrupted sleep patterns
- hurriedly revising a will
- increased intake of alcohol or prescription drugs

Diagnosis

The **diagnosis** of a suicide attempt is often made when the patient either goes to the emergency room of a hospital to seek help or is taken there by family members or first responders. In many cases, the patient will have written a suicide note, talked about his or her intention, or begun to carry out a plan to kill him- or herself. If the patient is not conscious, the doctor will obtain as much information as possible from family members or first responders.

Treatment

Suicide attempts are treated as a psychiatric emergency by police or other rescue personnel. Treatment in a hospital emergency room includes a complete psychiatric evaluation, a **mental status examination**, and a detailed assessment of the circumstances surrounding the attempt. The physician will interview the person's relatives or anyone else who accompanied the patient in order to obtain as much information as possible. Some questions that the physician will ask include whether the patient had a detailed plan for suicide; whether he or she had the means of suicide at hand; what the patient hoped to gain by killing themselves (freedom from pain, reunion with a dead loved one, solution to financial problems, etc.); and whether the patient had any tendencies toward homicide. As a rule, suicide attempts requiring advance planning and the use of violent or highly lethal methods are regarded as the most serious. The patient will be kept under observation while decisions are made about the need for **hospitalization**.

People who have attempted suicide and who are considered a serious danger to themselves or to others can be legally hospitalized against their will. The doctor bases the decision on the severity of the patient's depression or agitation; the presence of other suicide risk factors, including a history of previous suicide attempts, substance abuse, recent stressful events, and symptoms of **psychosis**; and the availability of friends, relatives, or other social support. If the attempt is judged to be a nonlethal suicide gesture, and the patient has adequate support outside the hospital, he or she may be released after the psychiatric assessment is completed.

Traditional

People who survive a suicide attempt are usually treated with a combination of antidepressant medications and **psychotherapy**.

Drugs

In 2003, the Food and Drug Administration (FDA) approved the use of **clozapine** (Clozaril), an antipsychotic medication, for the treatment of patients with schizophrenia who have attempted suicide.

Treatment of suicide survivors

In addition to the grief that ordinarily accompanies death, survivors of a friend or relative's suicide often struggle with feelings of guilt and shame as well. In spite of a general liberalization of social attitudes since World War II (1939–1945), suicide is still stigmatized in many parts of Europe and the United States. Survivors often benefit from group or individual psychotherapy in order to work through such issues as wondering whether they could have prevented the suicide or whether they are at increased risk of committing suicide themselves. Increasing numbers of clergy as well as mental health professionals are trained in counseling survivors of suicide.

Prognosis

The prognosis for a person who has attempted suicide is generally favorable, although further research needs to be done. Many different studies have followed individuals who attempted suicide to determine how likely they are to die by suicide. These studies have generally found that the likelihood is less than 10%. A doctor who studied 515 people who attempted suicide between 1937 and 1971 found that 94% were still alive at the time of his study or had died of natural causes. In general, individuals who attempt suicide and rate highly on intent to commit suicide and hopelessness may be more likely to commit suicide later. These findings may indicate that suicidal behavior is more likely to be a

passing response to an acute crisis than a reflection of a permanent state of mind.

Prevention

One reason that suicide is such a tragedy is that most self-inflicted deaths are potentially preventable. Many suicidal people change their minds if they can be

---

KEY TERMS

Assisted suicide—A form of self-inflicted death in which individuals voluntarily bring about their own death with the help of another, usually a physician, relative, or friend. Assisted suicide is sometimes called physician-assisted death (PAD).

Cortisol—A hormone released by the cortex (outer portion) of the adrenal gland when a person is under stress. Such levels are now considered a biological marker of suicide risk.

Diathesis—The medical term for predisposition. The stress/diathesis model is a diagram that is used to explain why some people are at greater risk of suicidal behavior than others.

Euthanasia—The act of putting individuals or animals to death painlessly or allowing them to die by withholding medical services, usually because of an incurable disease.

Frontal cortex—The part of the human brain associated with aggressiveness and impulse control. Abnormalities in this part of the brain are associated with an increased risk of suicide.

Self-deliverance—Another term for assisted suicide, more commonly used in Great Britain than in the United States.

Serotonin—A chemical that occurs in the blood and nervous tissue and functions to transmit signals across the gaps between neurons in the central nervous system. Abnormally low levels of this chemical are associated with depression and an increased risk of suicide.

Suicide gesture—Attempted suicide characterized by a low-lethality method, low level of intent or planning, and little physical damage; sometimes called pseudocide.

Suicide magnet—A bridge, tall building, or geographic location that acquires a reputation for attracting people who want to commit suicide and attempt it.

QUESTIONS TO ASK YOUR DOCTOR

- There have been a number of suicides in my family. Does that mean that I am at increased risk of suicide?
- How can I help a depressed friend who says that he or she has nothing to live for?
- How can I tell the difference between an occasional blue spell and the kind of depression that can lead to suicide?
- What would you recommend as good ways to deal with occasional thoughts of suicide?

helped through their immediate crisis; Dr. Richard Seiden, from the University of California at Berkeley, a specialist in treating survivors of suicide attempts, puts the high-risk period at 90 days after the crisis. Some potential suicides change their minds during the actual attempt; for example, a number of people who survived jumping off the Golden Gate Bridge told interviewers afterward that they regretted their action even as they were falling and that they were grateful they survived.

Brain research is an important means of suicide prevention. Known biological markers for an increased risk of suicide may be correlated with personality profiles linked to suicidal behavior under **stress** to help identify individuals at risk. Brain **imaging studies** using **positron emission tomography (PET)** are being used to detect abnormal patterns of **serotonin** uptake in specific regions of the brain. Genetic studies are also yielding new information about inherited predispositions to suicide.

Research is ongoing to discover better methods of treating depression and other disorders that may influence a person's decision to commit suicide. Primary care physicians are continually learning how to better identify and intervene when treating suicidal patients. An estimated 67% of all adults and 80% of seniors who complete suicide have seen a physician within a month of their death, placing primary care physicians in a good position to evaluate patients for signs of depression. The good news is that depression in adults in any age group is highly treatable, particularly when antidepressant medications are combined with psychotherapy.

People who are concerned about a friend or relative at risk of self-harm should take the following steps:

- Become educated about warning signs and risk factors.
- Identify physicians and other healthcare professionals who know the person and can provide help.
- Talk openly with the person about his or her feelings—although many people are afraid to ask whether someone is thinking about suicide for fear of angering them or giving them an idea, in many cases honest concern is welcomed by the individual.
- Call the local hospital emergency department or 911 if the person seems to be at immediate risk of suicide.

Resources

BOOKS

American Psychiatric Association. *Diagnostic and Statistical Manual of Mental Disorders*. 4th ed., text rev. Washington, DC: American Psychiatric Association, 2000.

Beers, Mark H., and Robert Berkow, eds. *Merck Manual of Geriatrics*. 3rd ed. Whitehouse Station, NJ: Merck, 2005.

Giddens, Sandra. *Suicide*. New York: Rosen Publishing, 2007.

Goldney, Robert D. *Suicide Prevention*. New York: Oxford University Press, 2008.

Kutcher, Stanley P., and Sonia Chehil. *Suicide Risk Management: A Manual for Health Professionals*. Malden, MA: Blackwell Publishing, 2007.

Paris, Joel. *Half in Love with Death: Managing the Chronically Suicidal Patient*. Mahwah, NJ: Lawrence Erlbaum Associates, 2007.

PERIODICALS

Ajdacic-Gross, V., et al. "Methods of Suicide: International Suicide Patterns Derived from the WHO Mortality Database." *Bulletin of the World Health Organization* 86 (September 2008): 726–32.

Alao, A. O., M. Soderberg, E. L. Pohl, and A. L. Alao. "Cybersuicide: Review of the Role of the Internet on Suicide." *Cyberpsychology and Behavior* 9 (August 2006): 489–93.

American Academy of Hospice and Palliative Medicine. "Position Statement on Physician-Assisted Death." *Journal of Pain and Palliative Care Pharmacotherapy* 21 (April 2007): 55–57.

Apter, A., and R. A. King. "Management of the Depressed, Suicidal Child or Adolescent." *Child and Adolescent Psychiatric Clinics of North America* 15 (October 2006): 999–1013.

Beyer, J. L. "Managing Depression in Geriatric Populations." *Annals of Clinical Psychiatry* 19 (October/December 2007): 221–38.

Centers for Disease Control and Prevention (CDC). "Alcohol and Suicide among Racial/Ethnic Populations—17 States, 2005–2006." *Morbidity and Mortality Weekly Report* 58 (June 19, 2009): 637–41.

———. "Increases in Age-Group-Specific Injury Mortality—United States, 1999–2004." *Morbidity and Mortality Weekly Report* 56 (December 14, 2007): 1281–84.

Coryell, William H. "Clinical Assessment of Suicide Risk in Depressive Disorder." *CNS Spectrums* 11, no. 6 (2006): 255–461. http://www.cnsspectrums.com/aspx/articledetail. aspx?articleid=474 (accessed November 13, 2011).

Friend, Tad. "Jumpers: The Fatal Grandeur of the Golden Gate Bridge." *New Yorker* (October 13, 2003). http://www. newyorker.com/archive/2003/10/13/031013fa_fact?currentPage=all (accessed July 20, 2011).

Fu, K. W., et al. "Estimating the Risk for Suicide Following the Suicide Deaths of 3 Asian Entertainment Celebrities: A Meta-Analytic Approach." *Journal of Clinical Psychiatry* 70 (June 2009): 869–78.

Guthmann, Edward, et al. "Lethal Beauty." *San Francisco Chronicle* (October 30, 2005). http://www.sfgate.com/ cgi-bin/article.cgi?f=/c/a/2005/10/30/MNG2NFF7KI1. DTL (accessed July 20, 2011).

Jelinek, Pauline, and Kimberly Hefling. "Army Suicide Rates Hit Record High." *Huffington Post* (January 29, 2009). http://www.huffingtonpost.com/2009/01/30/army-suicide-rates-hit-re_n_162484.html (accessed July 20, 2011).

Jokinen, A., et al. "HPA Axis Hyperactivity and Attempted Suicide in Young Adult Mood Disorder Inpatients." *Journal of Affective Disorders* 116 (July 2009): 117–20.

Liu, X., A. L. Gentzler, P. Tepper, et al. "Clinical Features of Depressed Children and Adolescents with Various Forms of Suicidality." *Journal of Clinical Psychiatry* 67 (September 2006): 1442–50.

Voaklander, D. C., et al. "Medical Illness, Medication Use, and Suicide in Seniors: A Population-Based Case Control Study." *Journal of Epidemiology and Community Health* 62 (February 2008): 138–46.

Yip, P.S., et al. "Years of Life Lost from Suicide in China, 1990–2000." *Crisis* 29 (March 2008): 131–36.

OTHER

Centers for Disease Control and Prevention. "Deaths: Preliminary Data for 2009." *National Vital Statistics Report* 59, no. 4 (March 16, 2011). http://www.cdc.gov/ nchs/data/nvsr/nvsr59/nvsr59_04.pdf (accessed July 20, 2011).

WEBSITES

American Academy of Child and Adolescent Psychiatry. "Teen Suicide." *Facts for Families* 10 (May 2008). http://www. aacap.org/cs/root/facts_for_families/teen_suicide (accessed July 20, 2011).

American Association of Suicidology. "Fact Sheets." http:// www.suicidology.org/web/guest/stats-and-tools/ fact-sheets (accessed July 20, 2011).

———. "If You Are Considering Suicide." http://www. suicidology.org/web/guest/thinking-about-suicide (accessed July 20, 2011).

American Foundation for Suicide Prevention. "About Suicide: Frequently Asked Questions." http://www.afsp.org/index. cfm?fuseaction=home.viewPage&page_id= 052618D2-02D2-04B4-00EDA31CFC336B63 (accessed July 20, 2011).

Andrew, Louise B. "Depression and Suicide." Medscape Reference. May 9, 2011. http://emedicine.medscape.com/ article/805459-overview (accessed July 20, 2011).

Centers for Disease Control and Prevention. "National Suicide Statistics: At a Glance." September 30, 2009. http://www. cdc.gov/violenceprevention/suicide/statistics/index.html (accessed July 20, 2011).

National Institute of Mental Health. "Suicide Prevention." July 20, 2011. http://www.nimh.nih.gov/health/ topics/suicide-prevention/index.shtml (accessed July 20, 2011).

———. "Suicide in the U.S.: Statistics and Prevention." September 30, 2009. http://www.nimh.nih.gov/health/ publications/suicide-in-the-us-statistics-and-prevention/ index.shtml (accessed July 20, 2011).

Soreff, Stephen. "Suicide." Medscape Reference. January 11, 2011. http://emedicine.medscape.com/article/288598-overview (accessed July 20, 2011).

U.S. Department of Defense and Veterans Administration. "About Suicide." DoD/VA Suicide Outreach. http://www. suicideoutreach.org/about_suicide (accessed July 20, 2011).

ORGANIZATIONS

American Academy of Child and Adolescent Psychiatry, 3615 Wisconsin Ave. NW, Washington, DC, 20016-3007, (202) 966-7300, Fax: (202) 966-2891, http://www. aacap.org.

American Association of Suicidology, 5221 Wisconsin Ave. NW, Washington, DC, 20015, (202) 237-2280, Fax: (202) 237-2282, http://www.suicidology.org/web/guest/ home.

American Foundation for Suicide Prevention, 120 Wall St., 29th Fl., New York, NY, 20016-3007, (212) 363-3500, (888) 333-2377, Fax: (212) 363-6237, inquiry@afsp.org, http://www.afsp.org.

American Psychiatric Association, 1000 Wilson Blvd., Ste. 1825, Arlington, VA, 22209, (703) 907-7300, apa@psych. org, http://www.psych.org.

Mental Health America, 2000 N Beauregard St., 6th Fl., Alexandria, VA, 22311, (703) 684-7722, Fax: (703) 684-5968, (800) 969-6642, http://www1.nmha. org.

National Alliance on Mental Illness, 3803 N Fairfax Dr., Ste. 100, Arlington, VA, 22203, (703) 524-7600, Fax: (703) 524-9094, http://www.nami.org.

National Institute of Mental Health, 6001 Executive Blvd., Rm. 8184, MSC 9663, Bethesda, MD, 20892-9663, (301) 443-4513, (866) 615-6464, Fax: (301) 443-4279, nimhinfo@-nih.gov, http://www.nimh.nih.gov.

National Suicide Prevention Lifeline, (800) 274-TALK (8255), http://www.suicidepreventionlifeline.org.

U.S. Department of Veterans Affairs (VA), 810 Vermont Ave. NW, Washington, DC, United States 20420, (800) 827-1000; Mental health crisis line: (800) 273-8255 (press 1), http://www.va.gov.

Rebecca J. Frey, PhD
David A. Brent, MD
William A. Atkins, BB, BS, MBA

Support groups

Definition

Support groups are an informal resource that attempts to provide healing components to a variety of problems and challenges. An informal support outside of family, friends, or professionals often provides greater understanding, more similarity (from individuals experiencing similar life events), an opportunity for empathy and altruism, and a sense of identity for participants. Learning new ways to handle challenges, cope with changes, and maintain new behaviors are all important aspects of the support group experience.

A characteristic unique to support groups is the mutual support members are able to provide one another. This support and validation from other group members help facilitate personal growth and change in a way that individual therapy cannot. Although experts and professionals can provide support and positive direction, the mutual exchange of information between group members is a powerful experience that often induces lasting change.

Description

Most support groups are facilitated or led by lay persons, often in conjunction with existing organizations (such as the National Alliance on Mental Illness [NAMI] or Alcoholics Anonymous [AA]). Support groups usually have a set meeting time (generally weekly or monthly), and an open format. Open format means that the groups are ongoing, and members have the option of attending when it is convenient for them. This is in contrast to other types of structured treatment or psycho-educational groups that may meet for a certain number of sessions, with the expectation that participants attend every meeting. The open format allows members to feel some degree of anonymity, and to participate as they are comfortable. For some people, simply attending meetings and listening to the experiences of others can be helpful.

The healing power of groups is well documented, and support groups offer many of the same therapeutic characteristics as more structured groups. These factors include: altruism (chance to help others), belongingness, universality (there are others who struggle with similar challenges), interpersonal learning, guidance, catharsis,

A group of women listen to another woman speak at a support group for victims of domestic violence. (© Lynn Johnson/ National Geographic Image Collection/Alamy)

identification, self-understanding, instillation of hope, and existential factors (such as the search for larger meaning in life). Each of these factors is directly related to the mutual support that members provide one another.

Support groups are generally less structured than psycho-educational groups or therapy groups, however, as each group usually sets its own norms, rules, and schedules. Some groups, such as AA, traditionally reserve time for individual members to discuss their own challenges and progress in front of the group. Others bring in speakers periodically to provide information about disorders or specific coping skills. However, the strength of support groups lies in its members, and their willingness to share their own experiences, challenges, and solutions in the context of the group.

In addition to these traditional, face-to-face support groups, technology has had an impact on the functioning and availability of support groups. There are many listserves, e-mail groups, and chat groups that provide information about specific life problems (adoption of children outside the United States, for example), certain types of mental illness, and specific health problems. While there is always the risk of communicating with others who are not honest, many people benefit from these Internet interactions. Some individuals are actually more comfortable participating in Internet support groups due to the greater anonymity they offer.

There are a variety of problems and challenges that are addressed in support groups. Generally speaking, the severity of the symptom, as well as the phase of the illness or disorder, will determine whether participation in a support group is appropriate. For more severe types of mental illness, such as **schizophrenia**, or **depression** with psychotic episodes, a support group is probably not the optimal **intervention**, particularly at initial onset. After stabilization through therapy and medication (as appropriate), a support group may offer an important addition to more formal treatment. In these cases, the socialization, interpersonal relationships, and social support that can be gained through the group may not be available elsewhere, and as such, it can be a very positive experience for the participant. In a group situation, a participant can learn how to express feelings in a healthy and positive way, practice assertive communication, receive feedback about appropriate and inappropriate content for conversation, receive feedback about nonverbal communication, learn new ways to ask for help from others, be able to help others, learn how to form friendships, and learn new coping skills and behaviors.

Types of support groups

Various types of support groups exist. Some groups provide support for very specific types of loss, illness, or life adjustment. A representative sample is listed below.

BEREAVEMENT/GRIEF COUNSELING GROUPS. Bereavement and **grief counseling** groups provide support to people who have experienced a loss. There are groups for people who have lost a spouse or partner, parents, children, or pets. There are specific groups for people who have lost a loved one due to homicide, **suicide**, SIDS, cancer, or miscarriage. These groups help individuals adjust to the death of a family member or friend, learn how to accept the loss, honor the memory of their loved one, and adjust to life after the loss.

MEDICAL SUPPORT GROUPS. Medical support groups may be more short-term than other types of support groups, depending on the specific disorder. Some groups are formed to help patients adjust to specific treatments, such as chemotherapy or radiation, while others focus on longer-term adjustment and recovery issues, such as a breast cancer support group. These groups may have a stronger educational component to help members understand physical changes they may be experiencing as a result of their medical procedures.

WEIGHT LOSS GROUPS. Although these groups are very specific in their focus, their individual structures can vary greatly. Some weight loss support groups are actively involved in the process of losing weight, and may include monitoring of diet and **exercise**, while others focus on maintaining weight loss, and, therefore, may focus more on social support.

MENTAL HEALTH/ILLNESS SUPPORT GROUPS. These groups usually focus on specific disorders, such as bipolar or eating disorders. Members of these support groups are often at different phases in dealing with their illnesses, and, therefore, the needs and contributions of individual members may vary greatly from meeting to meeting.

FAMILY SUPPORT GROUPS. Family support groups, such as CHADD for parents of children with ADD or NAMI for families with members who struggle with any type of mental illness, provide support from other parents and children who may be feeling the same level of frustration and exasperation. Meeting others who truly understand one's experience has a very powerful effect. For many parents, participation in a support group is the first opportunity to learn that there are other parents who are experiencing the same challenges and frustrations.

LIFE TRANSITIONS GROUPS. Life transitions groups include divorce and aging support groups. Support groups for children of divorce also exist in many communities and schools.

ADDICTIONS SUPPORT GROUPS. Traditional **addiction** support groups include Alcoholics Anonymous (AA), Narcotics Anonymous (NA), and Gambler's Anonymous (GA). Many of these groups follow the traditional "12-step" program of working through various aspects of the addiction, and, as such, are more structured than many other types of support groups.

Support group locations

Support groups meet in many different locations within a community. Hospitals and medical centers may provide meeting locations for medical support groups. **Community mental health** centers, inpatient psychiatric programs, and residential treatment centers are common locations for mental health and mental illness-related support groups. Life transition groups are often provided through schools, senior centers, and daycare centers. **Bereavement** groups and addiction support groups often meet in churches, community meeting rooms of local businesses, and mental health agencies.

Structure of support groups

Support groups are most successful when composed of persons close in age who are experiencing similar life challenges. Support groups are usually led by members of the group, such as the chapter president or another member of the organizing group. Some support groups may be led by paraprofessionals if they are offered as part of an aftercare program associated with a treatment facility.

Support groups usually have explicit norms and expectations for member participation, such as respecting members' feelings and opinions, and coming to meetings free from drugs or alcohol. Due to the open nature of most support groups, members typically feel free to miss a session here or there, which is usually not acceptable in a treatment or therapy group.

Conclusion

Group experiences can be very powerful in changing behavior and maintaining that change. The support group becomes part of the individual's daily life, and promotes healthy functioning by providing reminders about change and support when he or she is feeling down or is drawn toward old patterns. It also provides opportunities to own one's change by helping others. These factors contribute to the positive prognosis for most who participate in a group experience. However, a person could be harmed by a group experience as well. Much of this risk is dependent on the characteristics of individual members, particularly in support groups that operate without professional guidance. For example, if certain individuals dominate the group with their own agenda, perhaps at the expense of other group members, then the experience may have a negative impact on more vulnerable individuals.

See also Grief counseling

Resources

BOOKS

Giuseppe, R., and G. Riva, eds. *Towards Cyberpsychology: Mind, Cognition and Society in the Internet Age* Amsterdam, Netherlands: IOS Press, 2001.

Kaduson, H.G., and Schaefer, C.E., eds. *Short-term Play Therapy for Children*. 2nd ed. New York: The Guilford Press, 2009.

Yalom, I.D. *The Theory and Practice of Group Psychotherapy*. 5th ed. New York: Basic Books, Inc., 2005.

PERIODICALS

Evans, J., J. Jones, and I. Mansell. "Supporting Siblings: Evaluation of Support Groups for Brothers and Sisters of Children with Learning Disabilities and Challenging Behavior." *Journal of Learning Disabilities* 5, no. 1 (March 2001): 69–78.

Gottlieb, B.H. "Self-help, Mutual Aid, and Support Groups Among Older Adults." *Canadian Journal on Aging* 19, Suppl 1 (Summer 2000): 58–74

Martin, D.J., et al. "Support Group Participation, HIV Viral Lead and Sexual Risk Behavior." *American Journal of Health Behavior* 25, no. 6 (November–December 2001): 513–527.

Montazeri, A., et al. "Anxiety and Depression in Breast Cancer Patients Before and After Participation in a Cancer Support Group." *Patient Education & Counseling* 45, no. 3 (December 2001): 195–198.

Sansone, R. A. "Patient-to-Patient E-mail: Support for Clinical Practices." *Eating Disorders* 9, no. 4 (Winter 2001): 373–375.

ORGANIZATIONS

Children and Adults with Attention Deficit/Hyperactivity Disorder, 8181 Professional Pl., Ste. 150, Landover, MD, 20785, (301) 306-7070, Fax: (301) 306-7090, http://www.chadd.org.

National Alliance on Mental Illness, 3803 N Fairfax Dr., Ste. 100, Arlington, VA, 22203, (703) 524-7600, http://www.nami.org.

Deanna Pledge, Ph.D.

Surmontil *see* **Trimipramine**

SVR-20 *see* **Sexual Violence Risk-20**

Sycrest *see* **Asenapine**

Symmetrel *see* **Amantadine**

Systematic desensitization

Definition

Systematic desensitization is a technique used to treat phobias and other extreme or erroneous fears based on principles of **behavior modification**.

Purpose

Systematic desensitization is used to help the client cope with phobias and other fears, and to induce relaxation. In progressive relaxation, one first tightens and then relaxes various muscle groups in the body. During the alternating clenching and relaxing, the client should be focusing on the contrast between the initial tension and the subsequent feelings of relaxation and softening that develop once the tightened muscles are released. After discovering how muscles feel when they are deeply relaxed, repeated practice enables a person to recreate the relaxed sensation intentionally in a variety of situations.

After learning relaxation skills, the client and therapist create an "anxiety hierarchy." The hierarchy is a catalogue of anxiety-provoking situations or stimuli arranged in order from least to most distressing. For a person who is frightened by snakes, the anxiety hierarchy might start with seeing a picture of a snake, eventually move to viewing a caged snake from a distance, and culminate in actually handling a snake. With the therapist's support and assistance, the client proceeds through the anxiety hierarchy, responding to the presentation of each fearful image or act by producing the state of relaxation. The person undergoing treatment stays with each step until a relaxed state is reliably produced when faced with each item. As tolerance develops for each identified item in the series, the client moves on to the next. In facing more menacing situations progressively, and developing a consistent pairing of relaxation with the feared object, relaxation rather than anxiety becomes associated with the source of their anxiety. Thus, a gradual desensitization occurs, with relaxation replacing alarm. Several means of confronting the feared situations can be used. In the pre-computer era, the exposure occurred either through imagination and visualization (imagining a plane flight) or through actual real-life—or so-called *in vivo*—encounters with the feared situation (going on an actual plane flight). More recently, during the 1990s, virtual reality or computer simulated exposure has come to be utilized in lieu of *in vivo* exposure. Research findings indicate that mental imagery is the least effective means of exposure; *in vivo* and virtual reality exposure appear to be indistinguishable in terms of effectiveness.

Description

Systematic desensitization is a therapeutic **intervention** which reduces the learned link between anxiety and objects or situations that are typically fear-producing. The aim of systematic desensitization is to reduce or eliminate fears or phobias that sufferers

KEY TERMS

Behavior modification—An approach to therapy based on the principles of operant conditioning. Behavior modification seeks to replace undesirable behaviors with preferable behaviors through the use of positive or negative reinforcement.

Classical conditioning—In psychology, a process in which a previously neutral stimulus eventually produces a specific response by being paired repeatedly with another stimulus that produces that response. The best-known example of classical conditioning is Pavlov's dogs, who were conditioned to salivate when they heard a bell ring (the previously neutral stimulus) because the sound had been paired repeatedly with their feeding time.

find are distressing or that impair their ability to manage daily life. By substituting a new response to a feared situation—a trained contradictory response of relaxation which is irreconcilable with an anxious response—phobic reactions are diminished or eradicated.

This behavior modification technique, which is founded on the principles of classical conditioning, was developed by Joseph Wolpe in the 1950s. Some of the most common fears treated with desensitization include fear of public speaking, fear of flying, stage fright, elevator phobias, driving phobias and animal phobias. Relaxation responses are trained to occur through *progressive relaxation training*, a technique initially perfected by Edmund Jacobson during the 1930s.

Precautions

Because of the potential for extreme panic reactions to occur, which can increase the phobia, this technique should only be conducted by a well-qualified, trained professional. Also, the relaxation response should be thoroughly learned before confronting the anxiety-provoking hierarchy.

Results

Desensitization is an effective form of therapy. Individuals who have a positive response are enabled to resume daily activities that were previously avoided. The majority of persons undergoing this treatment show symptom reduction.

Resources

BOOKS

Craighead, W. Edward, and Michael J. Mahoney. *Behavior Modification: Principles, Issues, and Applications.* New York: Houghton Mifflin, 1981.

Wolpe, Joseph. *The Practice of Behavior Therapy.* Tarrytown, NY: Pergamon Press, 1990.

PERIODICALS

North, M.M., S.M. North, and J.R. Coble. "Virtual Reality Therapy: An Effective Treatment for Psychological Disorders." *Student Health Technology and Information* 44 (1997), 59–70.

Rothbaum, B., et al. "A Controlled Study of Virtual Reality Exposure Therapy for the Fear of Flying." *Journal of Consulting and Clinical Psychology* 68, no. 6 (December 2000), 1020–1026.

Deborah Rosch Eifert, Ph.D.

T

Tacrine

Definition

Tacrine is a drug used to treat **dementia** associated with **Alzheimer's disease**. It was sold in the United States under the brand name Cognex but is no longer widely prescribed due to the risk of liver toxicity; however, it remains on the market.

Purpose

Tacrine is used to treat symptoms of Alzheimer's disease in people with mild to moderate illness. The drug may result in mild improvements in thinking for a short period. Tacrine does not cure or stop the progression of Alzheimer's disease.

Description

The U.S. Food and Drug Administration (FDA) approved tacrine in 1993 for treating Alzheimer's disease. In Alzheimer's disease, some cells in specific

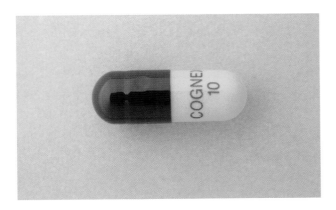

Cognex (tacrine), 10 mg. (© Custom Medical Stock Photo, Inc. Reproduced by permission.)

regions of the **brain** die. Because of this cell death, some brain cells lose their ability to transmit nerve impulses. Brain cells normally transmit nerve impulses by secreting various chemicals known as **neurotransmitters**.

Brain cells that make and secrete a neurotransmitter called acetylcholine are affected early in the course of Alzheimer's disease. Tacrine helps prevent the breakdown of acetylcholine in the brain, thus temporarily increasing its concentration. In doing so, tacrine may improve the thinking process by facilitating nerve impulse transmission within the brain.

Recommended dosage

Tacrine is available as capsules in several different strengths. Tacrine is broken down (metabolized) in the liver.

The proper dose of tacrine will be different for different people. An initial dosage of tacrine is usually 10 mg taken four times per day. This dose should be continued for four weeks while liver function is monitored. If no adverse liver effects are detected, the dosage should be increased to 20 mg taken four times per day. Higher dosages such as 30–40 mg given four times per day may also be used. Liver function must be monitored every other week during the first 16 weeks of treatment. After 16 weeks of tacrine therapy, liver function can be assessed every three months. Dosage increases should not occur more often than every four weeks. Tacrine should be taken on an empty stomach between meals, but if stomach upset occurs, it may be taken with food.

If problems in liver function arise, tacrine may be stopped, or the dosage reduced, until liver function returns to normal. Very specific guidelines should be followed by physicians with regard to dosage adjustments based upon the severity of liver effects. Newer drugs that work in the same manner as tacrine are not as toxic to the liver and may be preferred for patients just beginning therapy for Alzheimer's-type dementia.

Precautions

Tacrine may cause liver damage. It may not be the best drug to treat symptoms of Alzheimer's disease in people with known liver damage. If these individuals take tacrine, their liver function should be closely monitored. Tacrine may also slow heart rates, increase acid secretion in the stomach, make urination difficult, cause breathing difficulties, or contribute to **seizures**. As a result, it should be used carefully in people with certain heart conditions, those who are prone to stomach ulcers, people with bladder obstruction, individuals with asthma, and those with a history of seizure disorders.

People should not stop taking tacrine suddenly, as this could cause behavioral disturbances. The drug may be stopped slowly if improvements are not noted by caregivers or physicians.

Side effects

The most common side effect of tacrine is impaired liver function. This causes 8% of people to stop taking the drug. Other common side effects occurring in at least 5% of people and at twice the rate of placebo are stomach upset (nausea, vomiting, diarrhea, indigestion, or anorexia), muscle aches, and difficulty walking. Side effects affecting the stomach appear to be more severe at higher dosages.

Side effects that occur less often are behavioral disturbances, abnormal thinking, hostility, tremor, inability to sleep, slow heart rates, changes in blood pressure, urinary difficulties, rash, flushing, aggravation of asthma, or cold-like symptoms.

Healthcare providers should be informed immediately if nausea, vomiting, loose stools, or diarrhea occur soon after the dose of tacrine is increased or if rash, jaundice (yellow tinge to eyes or skin), or changes in stool color occur at any time.

Interactions

Many drugs can alter the effects of tacrine. Some drugs such as dicyclomine may lessen the effects of tacrine. Other drugs such as **propranolol**, cimetidine, ciprofloxacin, **fluoxetine**, **fluvoxamine**, neostigmine, or bethanechol may increase some of tacrine's side effects. **Rivastigmine** may interact with some of the drugs used to relax muscles during surgery. The interaction increases the effects of both drugs.

Tacrine may also diminish the effects of levodopa and increase the side effects of theophylline. Smoking cigarettes may reduce the effectiveness of tacrine.

KEY TERMS

Acetylcholine—A naturally occurring chemical in the body that transmits nerve impulses from cell to cell. Generally, it has opposite effects from dopamine and norepinephrine; it causes blood vessels to dilate, lowers blood pressure, and slows the heartbeat. Central nervous system well-being is dependent on a balance among acetylcholine, dopamine, serotonin, and norepinephrine.

Dementia—A group of symptoms (syndrome) associated with a progressive loss of memory and other intellectual functions that is serious enough to interfere with a person's ability to perform the tasks of daily life. Dementia impairs memory, alters personality, leads to deterioration in personal grooming, impairs reasoning ability, and causes disorientation.

Neurotransmitter—A chemical in the brain that transmits messages between neurons, or nerve cells.

Placebo—An inactive substance or preparation used as a control in experiments with human subjects to test the effectiveness of a drug or herbal preparation. Some patients may experience a medicinal response or experience side effects to a placebo simply because they have faith in its powers even though it contains no medicine.

Resources

BOOKS

Ellsworth, Allan J., et al. *Mosby's Medical Drug Reference.* St. Louis, MO: Mosby, 2007.

Physicians' Desk Reference 2011. 66th ed. Montvale, NJ: PDR Network, 2011.

Wolters Kluwer Health. *Drug Facts and Comparisons 2012.* 66th ed. St. Louis: Lippincott, Williams & Wilkins, 2011.

OTHER

Alzheimer's Association. "FDA-Approved Treatments for Alzheimer's." July 2007. http://www.alz.org/national/documents/topicsheet_treatments.pdf (accessed November 13, 2011).

ORGANIZATIONS

U.S. Food and Drug Administration, 10903 New Hampshire Ave., Silver Spring, MD, 20993-0002, (888) INFO-FDA (463-6332), http://www.fda.gov.

Kelly Karpa, RPh, Ph.D.

Tai chi *see* **Bodywork therapies**

Talk therapy

Definition

Talk therapy is an alternate name for the various forms of **psychotherapy** that emphasize the importance of the client or patient speaking to the therapist as the main means of expressing and resolving issues.

Purpose

The purpose of talk therapy is to foster verbal exchange and expression between a client and a therapist. Talk therapy may be conducive in helping individuals work through a variety of feelings, thoughts, and memories.

Description

Psychoanalysis, the first modern form of psychotherapy, was called the "talking cure," and the many varieties of therapy practiced today are still characterized by their common dependence on a verbal exchange between the counselor or therapist and the person seeking help. Some of these therapies that are characterized by the verbal exchange include: **cognitive-behavioral therapy**, behavior therapy, **couples therapy**, **family therapy**, **grief counseling** and therapy, **group therapy**, **interpersonal therapy**, **person-centered therapy**, **psychodynamic psychotherapy**, and **rational emotive therapy**. Both **self-help groups** and **support groups** also rely on the discussion of an issue as a main part of the cure.

Benefits

Talk therapy may allow an individual to candidly describe thoughts, feelings, and concerns relating to fears, memories, upcoming events, or anxiety-provoking situations. In addition, the exchange of verbal communication allows the individual to listen to feedback from the therapist, who may offer insightful advice and further direction to the individual.

Precautions

Most commonly practiced talk therapy is safe and free of side effects.

Preparation

Talk therapy should take place in a quiet, relaxing atmosphere in which the person has a comfortable place to sit or recline. Some people find that quiet background music improves their talk therapy sessions. If an instructional audiotape or videotape is to be used, the appropriate equipment should be available.

The talk therapy session, which can last anywhere from a few minutes to an hour, should be uninterrupted. Taking the phone off the hook, turning off cell phones, and asking family members for privacy and silence can ensure a more successful talk therapy session.

Aftercare

Aftercare may be provided through informal support systems, which may include family and friends, as well as support groups.

Risks

On occasion, individuals may find some discussion during talk therapy to be emotionally forthright and intense; however, there are no risks associated with talk therapy.

Resources

BOOKS

Burns, Donna M. *When Kids Are Grieving: Addressing Grief and Loss in School.* Thousand Oaks, CA: Corwin Press, 2010.

James, John W., and Russell Friedman. *The Grief Recovery Handbook,* 20th Anniversary ed. New York: Harper Paperbacks, 2009.

Jeffreys, J. Shep. *Helping Grieving People—When Tears Are Not Enough: A Handbook for Care Providers,* 2nd ed. New York, NY: Routledge, 2011.

Meier, Scott T., and Susan R. Davis. *The Elements of Counseling,* 7th ed. Belmont, CA: Brooks Cole, 2010.

Noel, Brook., and Pamela D. Blair. *I Wasn't Ready to Say Goodbye: Surviving, Coping and Healing After the Sudden Death of a Loved One.* Naperville, IL: Sourcebooks, 2008.

ORGANIZATIONS

American Psychiatric Association, 1000 Wilson Blvd., Ste. 1825, Arlington, VA, 22209-3901, (703) 907-7300, apa@psych.org, http://www.psych.org.

American Psychoanalytic Association, 309 East 49th Street, New York City, NY, 10017, (212) 752-0450, Fax: (212) 593-0571, info@aspa.org, http://www.apsa.org.

American Psychological Association, 750 1st St. NE, Washington, DC, 20002-4242, (202) 336-5500; TDD/TTY: (202) 336-6123, (800) 374-2721, http://www.apa.org.

Paula Ford-Martin
Laura Jean Cataldo, RN, Ed.D.

Tardive dyskinesia

Definition

Tardive dyskinesia is a neurological disorder consisting of abnormal, involuntary body movements. It usually is associated with taking antipsychotic medications, although it can occur in the absence of drug administration.

Demographics

Tardive dyskinesia is much more common in clinical populations than in the general population. It has been identified as a rare disorder by the National Organization for Rare Disorders. Diseases and disorders are classified as "rare" if they affect fewer than 200,000 individuals in the United States. Prevalence rates are believed to be approximately the same for populations outside the United States.

The majority of individuals with tardive dyskinesia are receiving antipsychotic medications. Estimates of the percentage of individuals in clinical populations with tardive dyskinesia vary widely, from as low as 5.9% to as high as 65%. Risk is greater in older patients, who exhibit a prevalence rate that is five or six times higher than that of people under 50 years of age. Post-menopausal women taking antipsychotics are believed to be at the greatest risk for developing the disorder. The risk of tardive dyskinesia is greater for individuals taking antipsychotic medications for more than three months than for individuals taking the medications for shorter durations.

Description

Tardive means "late" and *dyskinesia* means "abnormal movements." The term refers to abnormal body movements that occur usually after a person has been taking an antipsychotic medication for a long time. The symptoms can sometimes arise even after the medication has been discontinued. In the early stages, the movements may be so subtle that neither the person nor others notice them. For instance, the person may blink rapidly or lick his or her lips often. In later stages, the movements become noticeable and may affect the person's physical abilities.

Other subtypes of tardive dyskinesia can occur. In tardive dystonia, there are abnormal contractions of the neck and shoulder muscles. In tardive akathisia, the person feels restless all the time.

Causes and symptoms

The cause of tardive dyskinesia is uncertain. Because antipsychotics block the proteins that recognize and transmit the signals from **dopamine**, a neurotransmitter, hypotheses about the causes of tardive dyskinesia center on these dopamine pathways in the **brain**. The leading hypothesis is that after an extended period of blocked dopamine signaling, nerves become hypersensitive to dopamine, and stimulation by even a small amount of dopamine results in abnormal movements. The parts of the brain that send signals to the muscles and use dopamine signaling may be affected.

Causes

The types of drugs most commonly associated with the development of tardive dyskinesia are:

- Antipsychotic drugs used to treat schizophrenia and other psychoses. These are also known as neuroleptic medicines. "First-generation" or older versions of these drugs were strongly linked to tardive dyskinesia and other movement disorders. With "second-generation" or so-called atypical antipsychotics, which generally block dopamine receptors more weakly and briefly, clinicians expected to see a reduction in the incidence of tardive dyskinesia. Although a reduction in other motor symptoms related to antipsychotics was observed, it has not yet been clearly established whether tardive dyskinesia rates have fallen. It does appear, however, that the atypical neuroleptics carry a lower risk.
- L-dopa, which is used to treat Parkinson's disease (although paradoxically, high doses of L-dopa may actually help control tardive dyskinesia).
- Antiemetic drugs used to control nausea and vomiting.
- Tricyclic antidepressants used to treat depression and other mood disorders.
- Other drugs that block dopamine signaling.

Symptoms

Symptoms of tardive dyskinesia include:

- involuntary movements of the face (orofacial dyskinesia), including frowning, blinking, smiling, lip licking, mouth puckering, biting or chewing, clenching the jaw, and tongue thrusting or rolling the tongue around in the mouth
- involuntary movements of the hands, arms, feet, or legs, such as twitching the hands or tapping the feet
- trunk movements, such as rocking, twisting, or squirming
- grunting or trouble speaking because of involuntary movements of the diaphragm

Movements may be rapid or slow and complicated. They usually are irregular and do not follow a pattern.

KEY TERMS

Antiemetic—A preparation or medication given to stop vomiting.

Antipsychotic—A drug used to treat symptoms of schizophrenia or other psychotic disorders.

Dopamine—A neurochemical made in the brain that is involved in many brain activities, including movement and emotion.

Neurotransmitter—One of a group of chemicals secreted by a nerve cell (neuron) to carry a chemical message to another nerve cell, often as a way of transmitting a nerve impulse. Examples of neurotransmitters are acetylcholine, dopamine, serotonin, and norepinephrine.

Orofacial dyskinesia—Involuntary movements of the face.

Tardive akathisia—A disorder in which the individual continuously feels restless.

Tardive dystonia—Involuntary, abnormal movements of the neck and shoulder muscles.

QUESTIONS TO ASK YOUR DOCTOR

- Is it likely that my symptoms are being caused by a medication I am taking?
- Is there an alternative medication I could try that has a lower risk of tardive dyskinesia?
- Could my involuntary movements be caused by another underlying medical condition?
- Could we try reducing the dosage of my medication?
- Are there any vitamins or supplements that might help reduce my symptoms?

Diagnosis

The **diagnosis** of TD is suspected upon observation of involuntary movements of the head, neck, face, and tongue in individuals who have a history of antipsychotic drug prescription.

Treatment

Each case is treated differently. In some cases, the drug causing the problem can be stopped, reduced, or changed. However, most people taking antipsychotic drugs cannot stop taking them because of the high risk that their **psychosis** will return. The atypical antipsychotic drug associated with the lowest incidence of tardive dyskinesia is **clozapine** (Clozaril, Fazaclo). The atypical antipsychotics that have been more frequently associated with tardive dyskinesia are **risperidone** (Risperdal) and **olanzapine** (Zyprexa); in the case of risperidone, its longer history of clinical use may be an explanation. It may be possible to lower the dose to a level that does not cause the movements. One study has found that low-potency first-generation antipsychotics taken at moderate doses may carry no increased risk of eliciting tardive dyskinesia compared to second-generation drugs. There is controversy about whether so-called "drug holidays" reduce the likelihood of developing tardive dyskinesia. Drug holidays are planned periods in which the person goes off the medicine, then later resumes it.

Vitamin E has been shown to be helpful in patients, especially those who have had the problem for less than five years. L-dopa and some other medicines are sometimes helpful.

Prognosis

The earlier the problem is noticed and treatment is begun, the better chance of eliminating abnormal movements. Reports indicate that in most cases, tardive dyskinesia is not progressive and can be reversed. Most patients have a noticeable improvement in their symptoms within 18 months; however, some abnormal movements may remain. People who are over age 60 have a greater chance of having the problem go away on its own.

Resources

BOOKS

Mignon, Laurence, ed. *Antipsychotics.* New York: Cambridge University Press, 2009.

Rothschild, Anthony J. *The Evidence-Based Guide to Antipsychotic Mediations.* Washington, DC: American Psychiatric Publishing, 2010.

Watts, Ray L., David G. Standarett, and Jose A. Obeso, eds. *Movement Disorders,* 3rd ed. New York: McGraw-Hill, 2011.

PERIODICALS

Chan, Hung-Yu, et al. "A Randomized Controlled Trial of Risperidone and Olanzapine for Schizophrenic Patients with Neuroleptic-Induced Tardive Dyskinesia." *Journal of Clinical Psychiatry* 71, no. 9 (September 2010): 1226–33.

Peritogiannis, V., and S. Tsouli. "Can Atypical Antipsychotics Improve Tardive Dyskinesia Associated with Other

Atypical Antipsychotics?" *Journal of Psychopharmacology* 24, no. 7 (July 2010): 1121–25.

Tenback, D.E., et al. "Incidence and Persistence of Tardive Dyskinesia and Extrapyramidal Symptoms in Schizophrenia." *Journal of Psychopharmacology* 24, no. 7 (July 2010):1031–35.

ORGANIZATIONS

American Psychiatric Association, 1000 Wilson Blvd., Ste. 1825, Arlington, VA, 22209-3901, (703) 907-7300, (888) 35-PSYCH (357-7924), apa@psych.org, http://www.psych.org.

American Psychological Association, 750 1st St. NE, Washington, DC, 20002-4242, (202) 336-5500; TDD/TTY: (202) 336-6123, (800) 374-2721, apa@psych.org, http://www.apa.org.

Movement Disorder Society, 555 East Wells St., Ste. 1100, Milwaukee, WI, 53202, (414) 276-2145, Fax: (414) 276-3349, info@movementdisorders.org, http://www.movementdisorders.org.

National Organization for Rare Diseases, PO Box 1968, Danbury, CT, 06813-1968, (203) 744-0100, (800) 999-NORD (6673), orphan@rarediseases.org, http://www.rarediseases.org.

Jody Bower, MSW
Tish Davidson, AM

TAT *see* **Thematic Apperception Test**

Tegretol *see* **Carbamazepine**

Temazepam

Definition

Temazepam is a drug that belongs to a family of drugs known as **benzodiazepines**. Temazepam is sold under the brand name Restoril in the United States and is also available under its generic name.

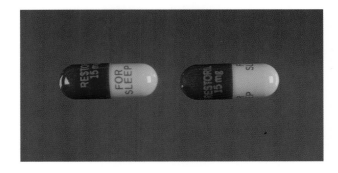

Temazepam (Restoril), 15 mg. *(U.S. Drug Enforcement Administration)*

Purpose

Temazepam is given to patients with sleeping problems. It is often prescribed for **insomnia** characterized by frequent awakening during the night or by awakening early in the morning.

Description

Temazepam is one of several drugs in the class known as benzodiazepines. These drugs produce a variety of effects, but most cause some degree of drowsiness (sedation). Temazepam is used almost exclusively as a hypnotic, or drug given to help people fall asleep. It is nearly always taken just before bedtime. The drug works by slowing down certain impulses in the **brain**, allowing the patient to fall asleep.

Recommended dosage

The typical starting dose for adults is 7.5–15 mg taken just before bedtime. The maximum recommended dose is 30 mg. Elderly patients and those in a weakened condition may need only 7.5 mg. The doctor should determine the dose in children 18 years of age and younger on an individual basis.

Precautions

Patients taking this drug should be monitored by their physicians to ensure that significant side effects do not develop. Insomnia that lasts longer than 7–10 days may point to a significant medical problem that should be thoroughly evaluated. Temazepam should not be combined with alcohol or other drugs that lower the level of activity in the central nervous system. Examples of such drugs include prescription pain medications, antihistamines, **barbiturates**, and muscle relaxants. Some persons may develop dizziness, lightheadedness, and clumsiness after taking temazepam. These side effects are especially common in the elderly.

Persons with a history of anemia, liver disease, kidney disease, drug abuse, serious psychological disorders, and **suicide** attempts should be given temazepam only after being thoroughly evaluated by their physician. This caution also applies to persons with a history of lung disease, seizure disorders, and narrow-angle glaucoma.

People who are taking temazepam should not stop taking it abruptly. Instead, the dose should be reduced gradually. Withdrawal symptoms, including depressed mood, sweating, abdominal cramps, muscle cramps, vomiting, **seizures**, and shakiness can develop if the medication is stopped suddenly.

Although patients are instructed to take temazepam in the evening before bedtime, they often experience side effects the next day, particularly drowsiness and loss of coordination or clumsiness. Pregnant women should not use this drug because it increases the risk of birth defects in the baby. Nursing mothers should not be given temazepam because it can make their babies drowsy and unable to nurse properly. Patients should not operate heavy machinery or drive a car while they are taking temazepam or any other benzodiazepine.

Side effects

Temazepam is a relatively safe drug, safer than most of the benzodiazepines. Its less serious but more common side effects include clumsiness or unsteady behavior, dizziness, drowsiness, and slurred speech. Some patients taking temazepam experience abdominal cramps, dry mouth, constipation, diarrhea, headache, nausea, vomiting, a giddy sense of well-being, and changes in sexual drive.

A small number of patients taking temazepam have experienced anger outbursts, confusion, mental **depression**, unusually low blood pressure, memory difficulties, nervousness, irritability, and muscle weakness. Symptoms of a temazepam overdose include extreme drowsiness, significant confusion, breathing difficulties, a very slow heartbeat, and staggering.

Rebound insomnia is one of the more common side effects of tapering a patient's dose of temazepam. Rebound insomnia is a reaction characterized by the recurrence of the symptom that the drug was originally given to suppress, namely problems with falling or staying asleep. When a person takes a medication for sleep on a regular basis, the body adjusts to the presence of the drug. As a result, when the person stops taking the sleeping medication, the body will take a few nights to return to its normal condition. During this period of readjustment, the person may experience a few sleepless hours each night. People often mistake the rebound insomnia for regular insomnia and consider it a good reason to continue taking temazepam, even though the drug is no longer needed.

People can also develop withdrawal symptoms even when they are gradually decreasing their dose of temazepam, particularly if the original dose was high. The more common withdrawal symptoms include sleeping difficulties, irritability, and nervousness. Less common withdrawal side effects include abdominal cramps, confusion, sweating, nausea, trembling, increased heart rate, and mental depression.

Interactions

Patients should always inform any healthcare provider that they see—doctors, dentists, nurses, and

KEY TERMS

Antihistamine—A medication used to alleviate allergy or cold symptoms such as runny nose, itching, hives, watering eyes, or sneezing.

Barbiturates—A class of medications that causes sedation and drowsiness. They may be prescribed legally but are also used as drugs of abuse.

Generic—A term that refers to a medication that is not protected by a registered trademark.

Hypnotic—A type of medication that induces sleep.

Insomnia—A chronic inability to sleep or to remain asleep throughout the night.

Narrow-angle glaucoma—An eye disorder caused by a buildup of fluid pressure inside the eyeball due to an abnormally small angle between the iris (the colored portion of the eye) and the cornea (the transparent front part of the eye).

Rebound—A physical reaction to stopping a medication characterized by the reappearance of the symptom(s) that the medication was given to suppress. For example, people who stop taking temazepam may experience rebound excitability and sleeping problems.

Sedation—A state of emotional or physical relaxation. The term is usually used to refer to this condition when it is produced by a medication.

Withdrawal—Symptoms experienced by a person who has become physically dependent on a drug, experienced when the drug use is discontinued.

others—about all the medications they are taking, including temazepam. Temazepam interacts with certain other drugs, including cimetidine (an antihistamine), **disulfiram** (a drug given to help patients control cravings for alcohol), and **clozapine** (an antipsychotic medication). Rifampin, which is an antibiotic, may decrease the effectiveness of the temazepam if the two are taken together. Persons taking temazepam should not eat grapefruit or drink grapefruit juice, as the fruit may inhibit the metabolism of the drug, resulting in potentially toxic levels. Also, patients should avoid drinking alcohol or taking other medications that cause drowsiness (such as antihistamines) while taking temazepam, because these substances will intensify the drug's sedative effects. Heavy smoking interferes with the effectiveness of temazepam.

Resources

BOOKS

Brunton, Laurence, Bruce Chabner, and Bjorn Knollman. *Goodman & Gilman's The Pharmacological Basis of Therapeutics* 12th ed. New York: McGraw-Hill, 2010.

Consumer Reports and American Society of Health-System Pharmacists. *Consumer Reports Complete Drug Reference.* Yonkers, NY: Consumers Reports, 2009.

Ellsworth, Allan J., et al. *Mosby's Medical Drug Reference.* St. Louis, MO: Mosby, 2007.

Venes, Donald. *Taber's Cyclopedic Medical Dictionary.* 21st ed. Philadelphia: F.A. Davis Company, 2009.

WEBSITES

PubMed Health. "Temazepam." U.S. National Library of Medicine. http://www.ncbi.nlm.nih.gov/pubmedhealth/PMH0000808 (accessed November 13, 2011).

ORGANIZATIONS

U.S. Food and Drug Administration, 10903 New Hampshire Ave., Silver Spring, MD, 20993-0002, (888) INFO-FDA (463-6332), http://www.fda.gov.

Mark Mitchell, M.D.

Tenex *see* **Guanfacine**

Thematic Apperception Test

Definition

The Thematic Apperception Test, or TAT, is a projective measure intended to evaluate a person's patterns of thought, attitudes, observational capacity, and emotional responses to ambiguous test materials. In the case of the TAT, the ambiguous materials consist of a set of cards that portray human figures in a variety of settings and situations. The subject is asked to tell the examiner a story about each card that includes the following elements: the event shown in the picture; what has led up to it; what the characters in the picture are feeling and thinking; and the outcome of the event.

Because the TAT is an example of a *projective* instrument—that is, it asks the subject to project his or her habitual patterns of thought and emotional responses onto the pictures on the cards—many psychologists prefer not to call it a "test," because it implies that there are "right" and "wrong" answers to the questions. They consider the term "technique" to be a more accurate description of the TAT and other projective assessments.

Purpose

Individual assessments

The TAT is often administered to individuals as part of a battery, or group, of tests intended to evaluate personality. It is considered to be effective in eliciting information about a person's view of the world and his or her attitudes toward the self and other persons. As persons taking the TAT proceed through the various cards and tell stories about the pictures, they reveal their expectations of relationships with peers, parents or other authority figures, subordinates, and possible romantic partners. In addition to assessing the content of the stories that the subject is telling, the examiner evaluates the subject's manner, vocal tone, posture, hesitations, and other signs of an emotional response to a particular story picture. For example, a person who is made anxious by a certain picture may make comments about the artistic style of the picture, or remark that he or she does not like the picture; this is a way of avoiding telling a story about it.

The TAT is often used in individual assessments of candidates for employment in fields requiring a high degree of skill in dealing with other people and/or ability to cope with high levels of psychological stress—such as law enforcement, military leadership positions, religious ministry, education, diplomatic service, etc. Although the TAT should not be used in the differential **diagnosis** of mental disorders, it is often administered to individuals who have already received a diagnosis in order to match them with the type of **psychotherapy** best suited to their personality. Lastly, the TAT is sometimes used for forensic purposes in evaluating the motivations and general attitudes of persons accused of violent crimes. For example, the TAT was recently administered to a 24-year-old man in prison for a series of sexual murders. The results indicated that his attitudes toward other people are not only outside normal limits but are similar to those of other persons found guilty of the same type of crime.

The TAT can be given repeatedly to an individual as a way of measuring progress in psychotherapy or, in some cases, to help the therapist understand why the treatment seems to be stalled or blocked.

Research

In addition to its application in individual assessments, the TAT is frequently used for research into specific aspects of human personality, usually including needs for achievement, fears of failure, hostility and aggression, and interpersonal object relations. "Object relations" is a phrase used in psychiatry and psychology to refer to the ways people internalize their relationships with others and the emotional tone of their relationships. Research into object relations using the TAT investigates a variety of different topics, including the extent to which people are emotionally involved in relationships with others; their ability to understand the complexities of human relationships; their ability to distinguish between their viewpoint on a situation and the perspectives of others involved; their ability to control aggressive impulses; self-esteem issues; and issues of personal identity. For example, one recent study compared responses to the TAT from a group of psychiatric inpatients diagnosed with **dissociative disorders** with responses from a group of non-dissociative inpatients, in order to investigate some of the controversies about **dissociative identity disorder** (formerly called multiple personality disorder).

Precautions

Students in medicine, psychology, or other fields who are learning to administer and interpret the TAT receive detailed instructions about the number of factors that can influence a person's responses to the story cards. In general, they are advised to be conservative in their interpretations, and to err "on the side of health" rather than of psychopathology when evaluating a subject's responses. In addition, the 1992 Code of Ethics of the **American Psychological Association** requires examiners to be knowledgeable about cultural and social differences, and to be responsible in interpreting test results with regard to these differences.

Experts in the use of the TAT recommend obtaining a personal and medical history from the subject before giving the TAT, in order to have some context for evaluating what might otherwise appear to be abnormal or unusual responses. For example, frequent references to death or **grief** in the stories would not be particularly surprising from a subject who had recently been bereaved. In addition, the TAT should not be used as the sole examination in evaluating an individual; it should be combined with other interviews and tests.

Cultural, gender, and class issues

The large number of research studies that have used the TAT have indicated that cultural, gender, and class issues must be taken into account when determining whether a specific response to a story card is "abnormal" strictly speaking, or whether it may be a normal response from a person in a particular group. For example, the card labeled 6GF shows a younger woman who is seated turning toward a somewhat older man who is standing behind her and smoking a pipe. Most male subjects do not react to this picture as implying aggressiveness, but most female subjects regard it as a very aggressive picture, with unpleasant overtones of intrusiveness and danger. Many researchers consider the gender difference in responses to this card as a reflection of the general imbalance in power between men and women in the larger society.

Race is another issue related to the TAT story cards. The original story cards, which were created in 1935, all involved Caucasian figures. As early as 1949, researchers who were administering the TAT to African Americans asked whether the race of the figures in the cards would influence the subjects' responses. Newer sets of TAT story cards have introduced figures representing a wider variety of races and ethnic groups. It is not known, however, whether a subject's ability to identify with the race of the figures in the story cards improves the results of a TAT assessment.

Multiplicity of scoring systems

One problem in assessing the TAT is the absence of a normative scoring system for responses. The original scoring system devised in 1943 by Henry Murray, one of the authors of the TAT, attempted to account for every variable that it measures. Murray's scoring system is time-consuming and unwieldy, and as a result has been little used by later interpreters. Other scoring systems have since been introduced that focus on one or two specific variables, for example hostility or **depression**. While these systems are more practical for clinical use, they lack comprehensiveness. No single system presently used for scoring the TAT has achieved widespread acceptance. The basic drawback of any scoring system in evaluating responses to the TAT story cards is that information that is not relevant to that particular system is simply lost.

Computer scoring

A recent subject of controversy in TAT interpretation concerns the use of computers to evaluate responses. While computers were used initially only to score tests with simple yes/no answers, they were soon applied to interpretation of projective measures. A computerized system for interpreting the **Rorschach**, for example, was devised as early as 1964. There are no computerized systems for evaluating responses to the TAT; however, users of the TAT should be aware of the controversies in this field. Computers have two basic limitations for use with the TAT: the first is that they cannot observe and record the subject's vocal tone, eye contact, and other aspects of behavior that a human examiner can note. Second, computers are not adequate for the interpretation of unusual subject profiles.

Description

The TAT is one of the oldest projective measures in continuous use. It has become the most popular projective technique among English-speaking psychiatrists and psychologists, and is better accepted among clinicians than the Rorschach.

History of the TAT

The TAT was first developed in 1935 by Henry Murray, Christiana Morgan, and their colleagues at the Harvard Psychological Clinic. The early versions of the TAT listed Morgan as the first author, but later versions dropped her name. One of the controversies surrounding the history of the TAT concerns the long and conflict-ridden extramarital relationship between Morgan and Murray, and its reinforcement of the prejudices that existed in the 1930s against women in academic psychology and psychiatry.

It is generally agreed, however, that the basic idea behind the TAT came from one of Murray's undergraduate students. The student mentioned that her son had spent his time recuperating from an illness by cutting pictures out of magazines and making up stories about them. The student wondered whether similar pictures could be used in therapy to tap into the nature of a patient's fantasies.

Administration

The TAT is usually administered to individuals in a quiet room free from interruptions or distractions. The subject sits at the edge of a table or desk next to the examiner. The examiner shows the subject a series of story cards taken from the full set of 31 TAT cards. The usual number of cards shown to the subject is between 10 and 14, although Murray recommended the use of 20 cards, administered in two separate one-hour sessions with the subject. The original 31 cards were divided into three categories, for use with men only, with women only, or for use with subjects of either sex. Recent practice has moved away from the use of separate sets of cards for men and women.

The subject is then instructed to tell a story about the picture on each card, with specific instructions to include a description of the event in the picture, the developments that led up to the event, the thoughts and feelings of the people in the picture, and the outcome of the story. The examiner keeps the cards in a pile face down in front of him or her, gives them to the subject one at a time, and asks the subject to place each card face down as its story is completed. Administration of the TAT usually takes about an hour.

Recording

Murray's original practice was to take notes by hand on the subject's responses, including his or her nonverbal behaviors. Research has indicated, however, that a great deal

KEY TERMS

Apperception—The process of understanding through linkage with previous experience. The term was coined by one of the authors of the TAT to underscore the fact that people don't "perceive" the story cards in a vacuum; rather, they construct their stories on the basis of past experiences as well as present personality traits.

Battery—A number of separate items (such as tests) used together. In psychology, a group or series of tests given with a common purpose, such as personality assessment or measurement of intelligence.

Forensic—Pertaining to courtroom procedure or evidence used in courts of law.

Idiographic—An approach to interpreting the results of a projective test within the context of the individual subject's record.

Nomothetic—An approach to interpreting the results of a projective test in which the subject's answers are measured against a normative comparison sample.

Object relations—In psychology, a phrase that refers to the way in which a subject describes relationships with other people in their environment, and the ways in which he or she has internalized interpersonal relationships.

Projective test or projective measure—A type of psychological evaluation that assesses a person's thinking patterns, observational ability, feelings, and attitudes on the basis of responses to ambiguous test materials. Projective measures are not intended to diagnose psychiatric disorders, although they are often used in outcome studies to compare the effectiveness of different forms of psychotherapy.

Rorschach test—A commonly administered projective measure in which subjects are asked to describe a series of black or colored inkblots.

of significant material is lost when notes are recorded in this way. As a result, some examiners now use a tape recorder to record subjects' answers. Another option involves asking the subject to write down his or her answers.

Interpretation

There are two basic approaches to interpreting responses to the TAT, called *nomothetic* and *idiographic* respectively. Nomothetic interpretation refers to the practice of establishing norms for answers from subjects in specific age, gender, racial, or educational level groups and then measuring a given subject's responses against those norms. Idiographic interpretation refers to evaluating the unique features of the subject's view of the world and relationships. Most psychologists would classify the TAT as better suited to idiographic than nomothetic interpretation.

In interpreting responses to the TAT, examiners typically focus their attention on one of three areas: the content of the stories that the subject tells; the feeling tone of the stories; or the subject's behaviors apart from responses. These behaviors may include verbal remarks (for example, comments about feeling stressed by the situation or not being a good storyteller) as well as nonverbal actions or signs (blushing, stammering, fidgeting in the chair, difficulties making eye contact with the examiner, etc.) The story content usually reveals the subject's attitudes, fantasies, wishes, inner conflicts, and view of the outside world. The story structure typically reflects the subject's feelings, assumptions about the world, and an underlying attitude of optimism or pessimism.

Results

The results of the TAT must be interpreted in the context of the subject's personal history, age, sex, level of education, occupation, racial or ethnic identification, first language, and other characteristics that may be important. "Normal" results are difficult to define in a complex multicultural society like the contemporary United States.

Resources

BOOKS

Aronow, Edward, Kim Altman Weiss, and Marvin Reznikoff. *A Practical Guide to the Thematic Apperception Test: The TAT in Clinical Practice.* Philadelphia, PA: Taylor and Francis, 2001.

Dana, Richard H. "Thematic Apperception Test." In *International Encyclopedia of Psychiatry, Psychology, Psychoanalysis, & Neurology,* edited by Benjamin B. Wolman. New York: Aesculapius Publishers, Inc., 1983.

Douglas, Claire. *Translate This Darkness: The Life of Christiana Morgan.* Princeton,NJ: Princeton University Press, 1997.

Geiser, Lon, and Morris I. Stein. *Evocative Images: The Thematic Apperception Test and the Art of Projection.* Washington, DC: American Psychological Association, 1999.

Maddox, Taddy. *Tests: A Comprehensive Reference for Assessments in Psychology, Education, and Business.* 4th ed. Austin, TX: Pro Ed, 1997.

PERIODICALS

Hatayama, Toshiteru, et al. "Guilt and Shame in Japan: Data Provided by the Thematic Apperception Test in Experimental Settings." *North American Journal of Psychology* 8, no. 1 (2006): 85.

Pica, M., et al. "The Responses of Dissociative Patients on the Thematic Apperception Test." *Journal of Clinical Psychology* 57, no. 7 (July 2001): 847–864.

Porcerelli, J.H., et al. "Object Relations and Defense Mechanisms of a Psychopathic Serial Sexual Homicide Perpetrator: A TAT Analysis." *Journal of Personality Assessment* 77, no. 1 (August 2001): 87–104.

Schultheiss, O.C., and J.C. Brunstein. "Assessment of Implicit Motives with a Research Version of the TAT: Picture Profiles, Gender Differences, and Relations to Other Personality Measures." *Journal of Personality Assessment* 77, no. 1 (August 2001): 71–86.

ORGANIZATIONS

American Psychological Association, 750 1st Street NE, Washington, DC, 20002-4242, (202) 336-5500; TDD/TTY: (202) 336-6123, (800) 374-2721, http://www.apa.org.

Rebecca J. Frey, Ph.D.

Thioridazine

Definition

Thioridazine is a potent antianxiety and antipsychotic agent. It is a member of the phenothiazine family of compounds. In the United States, thioridazine is sold under the brand name of Mellaril and is also available under its generic name.

Purpose

Thioridazine is used to manage psychotic disorders, such as **schizophrenia**. It reduces excitement, abnormal levels of energy, excessive movements (hypermotility),

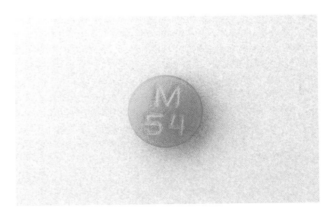

Mellaril (thioridazine), 10 mg. (© *Custom Medical Stock Photo, Inc. Reproduced by permission.*)

and agitation. It is also used in the short-term treatment of **depression** when accompanied by anxiety, sleep disturbances, agitation, and tension, and in children who display seriously inappropriate responses to exciting stimuli. Because of a number of serious side effects associated with thioridazine use, it is only prescribed when other medications have been unsuccessful or when the benefits significantly outweigh the risks.

Description

Thioridazine is used in treating anxiety and **psychosis**. When used for the treatment of schizophrenia, thioridazine reduces the symptoms of emotional withdrawal, anxiety, tension, hallucinations, and suspiciousness. Compared to other phenothiazine drugs, it is less likely to cause vomiting and Parkinson-like symptoms.

Recommended dosage

The dosage of thioridazine is determined based on the individual. The usual initial dosage for adults is 50 to 100 mg three times a day. This may be gradually increased to a maximum of 800 mg per day. Once the desired therapeutic effect has been achieved, the dosage should be stabilized. A typical maintenance dosage is 200 to 800 mg per day, given in three to four doses.

The usual initial dosage for adults being treated for symptoms of anxiety is 25 mg three times per day. After reaching equilibrium and controlling undesired symptoms, the typical maintenance dosage is 20 to 200 mg per day divided into three or four doses.

For children between the ages of 2 and 12, the usual daily dosage of thioridazine is 0.5 to 3.0 mg per 2 lb (1 kg) of body weight. Severely psychotic children who are hospitalized may receive 25 mg twice each day.

Precautions

Thioridazine may cause dangerous heart arrhythmias (irregular heartbeat) that can be fatal. Patients with a history of heart disease or a heart condition, low or high blood pressure, or low levels of potassium in the blood are particularly at risk. If a person taking thioridazine experiences irregular heartbeat, dizziness, light-headedness, or fainting, the patient should call his or her doctor immediately.

It is dangerous to give thioridazine to persons in a comatose state. **Seizures** due to thioridazine therapy have been reported but are unusual. A sudden decrease in blood pressure due to a change in body position (orthostatic hypotension) with accompanying lightheadedness, may

occur in people who have taken the drug. This is more common among women than among men.

Thioridazine is not approved for use in treating the behavioral symptoms of dementia in elderly adults. Patients taking thioridazine for this purpose are at an increased risk of death during treatment.

Thioridazine increases the level of prolactin in the blood; prolactin is a hormone that stimulates the mammary glands in the breast. This is a potential problem for persons with a personal or family history of breast cancer and may increase the risk of breast cancer. Thioridazine is also associated with malignant hyperthermia, vision and urinary problems, and blood dyscrasias (abnormal levels of blood cells).

Some babies born to mothers who took thioridazine during pregnancy exhibited withdrawal symptoms, including increased agitation and trouble breathing; women who are pregnant or planning to become pregnant should not take thioridazine.

Long-term use of thioridazine increases the probability of developing **tardive dyskinesia** (TD). Because of the many serious side effects associated with thioridazine, the risks and benefits of thioridazine must be carefully explained and understood before the drug is started.

Side effects

A common side effect of thioridazine is drowsiness and lack of physical and mental alertness. This side effect is especially noticeable early in therapy. Patients taking thioridazine should refrain from performing hazardous activities requiring mental alertness or coordination. Other common side effects include greater sensitivity to the sun and increased risk of serious sunburn, dry mouth, constipation, and urinary retention. Urinary retention (difficulty starting a urine flow or passing urine,) is a particular problem in men with enlarged prostates.

Thioridazine use may lead to the development of symptoms that resemble Parkinson's disease, but which are not caused by Parkinson's. These symptoms may include a taut or mask-like expression on the face, drooling, tremors, pill-rolling motions in the hands, cogwheel rigidity (abnormal rigidity in muscles, characterized by jerky movements when the muscle is passively stretched), and a shuffling gait. Taking the anti-Parkinson drugs **benztropine** mesylate or **trihexyphenidyl** hydrochloride along with thioridazine usually readily controls these symptoms.

Thioridazine has the potential to produce a serious side effect called tardive dyskinesia. This syndrome consists of involuntary, uncoordinated movements that may not disappear or may only partially improve after the drug is stopped. Tardive dyskinesia involves involuntary

KEY TERMS

Orthostatic hypotension—A sudden decrease in blood pressure due to a change in body position, as when moving from a sitting to standing position.

Prolactin—A hormone that stimulates milk production and breast development.

Schizophrenia—A severe mental illness in which a person has difficulty distinguishing what is real from what is not real. It is often characterized by hallucinations, delusions, language and communication disturbances, and withdrawal from people and social activities.

Tardive dyskinesia—A condition that involves involuntary movements of the tongue, jaw, mouth or face or other groups of skeletal muscles that usually occurs either late in antipsychotic therapy or even after the therapy is discontinued. It may be irreversible.

movements of the tongue, jaw, mouth or face or other groups of skeletal muscles. The incidence of TD increases with patient age and higher doses. It may also appear after thioridazine use has been discontinues. Women are at greater risk than men for developing TD. There is no known effective treatment for tardive dyskinesia, although gradual (but rarely complete) improvement may occur over a long period.

An occasionally reported side effect of thioridazine is **neuroleptic malignant syndrome**. This is a complicated and potentially fatal condition characterized by muscle rigidity, high fever, alterations in mental status, and cardiac symptoms such as irregular pulse or blood pressure, sweating, tachycardia (fast heartbeat), and arrhythmias (irregular heartbeat). People who think they may be experiencing any side effects from this or any other medication should talk to their physician promptly.

Interactions

Thioridazine increases the effect of drugs and substances that depress the central nervous system. This class of drugs includes anesthetics, opiates, **barbiturates**, atropine, and alcohol. These substances should be avoided or used sparingly by people taking thioridazine.

Propranolol increases the concentration of thioridazine. Concurrent administration of pindolol also increases the concentration of thioridazine, and thioridazine increases the concentration of pindolol in the body. Thioridazine may interact with other drugs used to treat

mental disorders. People planning to take this drug should let their physicians know of all other drugs they are taking, including amiodarone (Cordarone), cisapride (Propulsid), disopyramide (Norpace), dofetilide (Tikosyn), erythromycin (E.E.S., E-Mycin, Erythrocin), fluoxetine (Prozac, Sarafem), **fluvoxamine** (Luvox), moxifloxacin (Avelox), **paroxetine** (Paxil, Pexeva), **pimozide** (Orap), pindolol (Visken), procainamide, propranolol (Inderal), quinidine, and sotalol (Betapace, Betapace AF), any of which may be dangerous if used in combination with thioridazine.

Resources

BOOKS

Jacobson, J. L., and A. M. Jacobson. *Psychiatric Secrets*. 2nd ed. Philadelphia: Hanley & Belfus, 2001.

Stern, T. A., et al. *Massachusetts General Hospital Comprehensive Clinical Psychiatry*. 1st ed. Philadelphia: Mosby Elsevier, 2008.

PERIODICALS

Dallaire, S. "Thioridazine (Mellaril) and Mesoridazine (Serentil): Prolongation of the QTc Interval." *Canadian Medical Association Journal* 164, no 1 (2001): 91–95.

Pisani, F., et al. "Effects of Psychotropic Drugs on Seizure Threshold." *Drug Safety* 25, no. 2 (2002): 91–110.

Ray, W. A., et al. "Antipsychotics and the Risk of Sudden Cardiac Death." *Archives of General Psychiatry* 58, no. 12 (2001): 1161–67.

WEBSITES

PubMed Health. "Thioridazine." U.S. National Library of Medicine. http://www.ncbi.nlm.nih.gov/pubmedhealth/PMH0000584 (accessed November 13, 2011).

ORGANIZATIONS

U.S. Food and Drug Administration, 10903 New Hampshire Ave., Silver Spring, MD, 20993-0002, (888) INFO-FDA (463-6332), http://www.fda.gov.

L. Fleming Fallon, Jr., M.D., Dr.P.H.

Thiothixene

Definition

Thiothixene is in a class of drugs called antipsychotics. It is available with a prescription under the generic name of thiothixene or the brand name Navane.

Purpose

Thiothixene is a drug used to treat symptoms of **schizophrenia**. It is also sometimes used to calm severely agitated people.

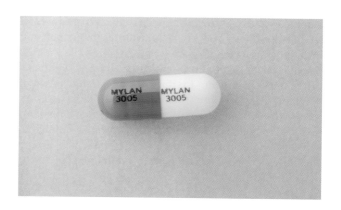

Thiothixene, 5 mg. (© *Custom Medical Stock Photo, Inc. Reproduced by permission.*)

Description

Thiothixene has been used in the United States for many years as a treatment for schizophrenia. It is believed to modify the balance of naturally occurring chemicals in the **brain** called **neurotransmitters** that regulate the transmission of nerve impulses from cell to cell. The proper balance between neurotransmitters is responsible, in part, for maintaining mental well-being. Thiothixene is thought to alter the balance among neurotransmitters in a way that improves symptoms of schizophrenia.

Thiothixene is available in several different strengths as capsules, as an injection, and as a concentrated liquid form taken by mouth. It is broken down by the liver and eliminated from the body by the kidneys.

Recommended dosage

The dosage of thiothixene varies widely from one individual to another. Initially, 2 mg of thiothixene taken by mouth three times daily is used in milder cases. This dosage may be increased slowly. Fifteen to 30 mg per day is often an effective range.

For more severe cases, 5 mg taken by mouth twice per day is a common starting dosage, with slow increases to 20–30 mg per day. Up to 60 mg of thiothixene may be taken daily. Doses greater than 60 mg per day usually do not provide any additional benefit and may increase side effects.

Precautions

Thiothixene may alter the rhythm of the heart. As a result, it should not be used by people with a history of irregular or prolonged heart rhythms (long QT syndrome), those with heart failure, or people who have recently had a heart attack. People with other heart conditions should discuss with their physician whether thiothixene is the right antipsychotic drug for them.

Thiothixene may increase the tendency to have **seizures**. People who have had seizures in the past, including alcohol or drug-induced seizures, should take thiothixene only after discussing the risks and benefits with their physician. People taking thiothixene should call their doctor immediately if they experience any abnormal, involuntary muscle movements, because this adverse effect may be permanent. The risk of abnormal, involuntary muscle movements is believed to increase with long-term use of thiothixene and high dosages.

Thiothixene may increase body temperatures to dangerously high levels. People who **exercise** strenuously, those exposed to extreme heat, individuals taking drugs with anticholinergic effects (this includes many common **antidepressants**), and persons prone to dehydration should be alert to increased body temperatures and dehydration-related side effects. Fevers, difficulty moving muscles, irregular heartbeats, rapid heartbeats, or excessive sweating are warning signs of possible overheating that should be addressed by a physician immediately.

Thiothixene is not approved by the U.S. Food and Drug Administration (FDA) for use in treating the behavioral symptoms of elderly patients with dementia; patients taking thiothixene for this purpose are at an increased risk of death during treatment.

People taking thiothixene should have regular eye examinations, since use of thiothixene has been associated with abnormalities of the retina, the light-sensitive layer of the eye. Thiothixene may also alter reproductive hormone levels causing irregular menstrual periods, difficulty getting pregnant, enlarged breasts, and breast milk production. Thiothixene can cause enlarged breasts and breast milk secretion in men as well as women. People who have had breast cancer should not take thiothixene unless the benefits of this drug substantially outweigh the risks.

Thiothixene may cause drowsiness. People should not perform hazardous tasks that require mental alertness and until they see how the drug affects them. This side effect usually diminishes with continued use of the drug. Thiothixene may make it more difficult to make a patient vomit after a drug overdose or accidental poisoning. Because there is a high incidence of **suicide** in all patients with psychotic illnesses, people using thiothixene should be observed carefully for signs of suicidal behavior. Women who are pregnant or breast-feeding should not take thiothixene; some babies born to mothers who took thiothixene during pregnancy exhibited withdrawal symptoms, including increased agitation and respiratory problems.

KEY TERMS

Anticholinergic—Related to the ability of a drug to block the nervous system chemical acetylcholine. When acetylcholine is blocked, patients often experience dry mouth and skin, increased heart rate, blurred vision, and difficulty in urinating. In severe cases, blocking acetylcholine may cloud thinking and cause delirium.

Antihistamine—A medication used to alleviate allergy or cold symptoms such as runny nose, itching, hives, watering eyes, or sneezing.

Antipsychotic—A medication used to treat psychotic symptoms of schizophrenia such as hallucinations, delusions and delirium. May be used to treat symptoms in other disorders, as well.

Neurotransmitter—A chemical in the brain that transmits messages between neurons, or nerve cells.

Schizophrenia—A severe mental illness in which a person has difficulty distinguishing what is real from what is not real. It is often characterized by hallucinations, delusions, language and communication disturbances, and withdrawal from people and social activities.

Side effects

Common side effects associated with the use of thiothixene include abnormal muscle movements and muscle stiffness, muscle tremors, weight gain, sleepiness, dry mouth, dry eyes, difficulty urinating, constipation, and sudden decreases in blood pressure that cause dizziness when standing up suddenly. Other side effects that may occur when using thiothixene are headaches, seizures, high blood pressure, rapid heartbeats, blurred vision, liver changes, irregular menstrual periods, abnormal blood cell counts, difficulty breathing, and rash.

Uncommon and serious side effects include **neuroleptic malignant syndrome** and **tardive dyskinesia**. Neuroleptic malignant syndrome is an unusual but potentially life-threatening condition. The person with this syndrome becomes extremely rigid, has a high fever, rapid heart rate, and abnormalities on blood tests. The affected person also may have a difficult time breathing and may sweat, and will need to be admitted to the hospital. Tardive dyskinesia (TD) is a condition that may occur after a long period of using antipsychotic medications. TD is characterized by involuntary movements of the facial muscles and tongue, and may also involve muscles in the trunk or hands or feet. TD may disappear as soon as the medication is stopped, but if it does not, it is difficult to treat. All potential side effects should be discussed with the patient's doctor before starting treatment with thiothixene.

Interactions

When thiothixene is used with drugs such as bethanechol, **propranolol**, levodopa, and some antidepressants, some of the side effects associated with thiothixene may increase. Use of narcotic drugs with thiothixene may cause blood pressure to fall to dangerously low levels. If thiothixene is used with levodopa, the actions of levodopa with be diminished.

When thiothixene is used with **barbiturates** or lithium, thiothixene may be less effective. Because thiothixene may cause sleepiness, it should rarely be used with other drugs that also cause drowsiness, such as antidepressants, antihistamines, some pain relievers, and alcohol.

Resources

BOOKS

Stern, T. A., et al. *Massachusetts General Hospital Comprehensive Clinical Psychiatry*. Philadelphia: Mosby Elsevier, 2008.

WEBSITES

PubMed Health. "Thiothixene." http://www.ncbi.nlm.nih.gov/pubmedhealth/PMH0000797 (accessed November 13, 2011).

ORGANIZATIONS

U.S. Food and Drug Administration, 10903 New Hampshire Ave., Silver Spring, MD, 20993-0002, (888) INFO-FDA (463-6332), http://www.fda.gov.

Kelly Karpa, RPh, Ph.D.

Thorazine *see* **Chlorpromazine**

Tic disorders

Definition

Tic disorders are characterized by the persistent presence of abrupt, repetitive involuntary movements and sounds (tics) that have been described as caricatures of normal physical acts. The revised fourth edition of the *Diagnostic and Statistical Manual of Mental Disorders* (*DSM-IV-TR*) lists three main types of tic disorders: **Tourette syndrome**, chronic motor or vocal tic disorder, and transient tic disorder. The best known of these disorders is Tourette syndrome, named after Georges Gilles de la Tourette (1857–1904), who first described its symptoms in 1885.

Demographics

An estimated 200,000 Americans have the most severe form of Tourette syndrome, but as many as one in 100 people exhibit minor tics. Tourette syndrome is three-to-five times more common in males than females. Tic disorders have been reported in people of all races, ethnic groups, and socioeconomic classes, but they appear to occur more frequently in Caucasians than African Americans.

Description

Tics are sudden, painless, nonrhythmic behaviors that are either motor (related to movement) or vocal and that appear out of context—for example, knee bends in science class. They are fairly common in childhood; in the vast majority of cases, they are temporary conditions that resolve on their own. In some children, however, the tics persist over time, becoming more complex and severe.

Tics may be simple (using only a few muscles or simple sounds) or complex (using many muscle groups or full words and sentences). Simple motor tics are brief, meaningless movements like eye blinking, facial grimacing, head jerks, or shoulder shrugs. They usually last less than one second. Complex motor tics involve slower, longer, and more purposeful movements like sustained looks, facial gestures, biting, banging, whirling or twisting around, or copropraxia (obscene gestures).

Simple phonic tics are meaningless sounds or noises like throat clearing, coughing, sniffling, barking, or hissing. Complex phonic tics include syllables, words, phrases, and such statements as "Shut up!" or "Now you've done it!" The child's speech may be abnormal, with unusual rhythms, tones, accents, or intensities. The echo phenomenon is a tic characterized by the immediate repetition of one's own or another's words. Coprolalia is a tic made up of obscene, inappropriate, or aggressive words and statements. It occurs in fewer than 10% of people with tic disorders.

Children under the age of 10 with simple tics find them to be difficult to suppress, or control. Many older patients and children with complex tics describe feeling strong sensory urges in their joints, muscles, and bones that are relieved by the performance of a motor tic in that particular body part. These patients also report inner conflict over whether and when to yield to these urges. A sensation of relief and reduction of anxiety frequently follows the performance of a tic. Unless the tic disorder is very severe, most people with tics can suppress them for varying periods of time.

Motor and vocal tics may be worsened by anxiety, **stress**, boredom, **fatigue**, or excitement. Some people have reported that tics are intensified by **premenstrual syndrome**, additives in food, and stimulants. The symptoms of tic disorders may be lessened while the patient is asleep. **Cannabis** (marijuana), alcohol, relaxation, playing a sport, or concentrating on an enjoyable task are also reported to reduce the severity and frequency of symptoms.

Tics are the core symptom shared by transient tic disorder, chronic motor or vocal tic disorder, and Tourette syndrome. The age of onset for these disorders is between two and 15 years. It is the severity and course that distinguishes these disorders from one another. Tourette symptoms typically appear before the age of 18. In most patients, Tourette symptoms subside after adolescence.

Causes and symptoms

Causes

Emotional factors were once viewed as the cause of tics, but this explanation has been largely discounted. The search for causes now focuses on biological, chemical, and environmental factors. No definitive cause of tics has yet been identified.

There appear to be both functional and structural abnormalities in the brains of people with tic disorders. While the exact neurochemical cause is unknown, it is believed that abnormal **neurotransmitters** (chemical messengers within the **brain**) contribute to the disorders. The affected neurotransmitters are **dopamine**, **serotonin**, and cyclic AMP. Researchers have also found changes within the brain itself, for example in the basal ganglia (an area of the brain concerned with movement) and the anterior cingulate cortex. Functional imaging using **positron emission tomography (PET)** and single photon emission computerized tomography (SPECT) has highlighted abnormal patterns of blood flow and metabolism in the basal ganglia, thalamus, and frontal and temporal cortical areas of the brain. **Magnetic resonance imaging** (MRI) has identified a reduction in frontal lobe tissue in patients with Tourette. Researchers have also shown a correlation between reduced corpus callosum size and the severity of tics in children with Tourette.

Evidence from twin and family studies suggests that vulnerability to tic disorders is genetic, or transmitted within families. Several genes have been suspected as contributing to the development of Tourette, including variations to the SLITRK1 gene. Gender-related inheritance patterns play a role in determining symptoms. Males are more likely to develop tics, while females are more likely to develop the related **obsessive-compulsive disorder**. Researchers have not found a pattern suggesting that certain types of parenting or childhood experiences lead to the development of tic disorders, although some think that there is an interaction between genetic and environmental factors. Researchers are paying close attention to prenatal factors, which are thought to influence the development of the disorders. Some research has indicated that maternal smoking increases the severity of symptoms in Tourette syndrome.

In some cases, tic disorders appear to be caused or worsened by recreational drugs or prescription medications. The drugs most commonly involved are such psychomotor stimulants as **methylphenidate** (Ritalin), **pemoline** (Cylert), **amphetamines**, and **cocaine**. It is not clear whether tics would have developed in these cases if stimulants had not been used. In a smaller percentage of cases, antihistamines, tricyclic **antidepressants**, antiseizure medications, and **opioids** have been shown to worsen tics.

Some forms of tics may be triggered by the environment. A cough that began during an upper respiratory infection may continue as an involuntary vocal tic. New tics may also begin as imitations of normally occurring events, such as mimicking a dog barking. How these particular triggers come to form enduring symptoms is a matter for further study.

Tourette syndrome often occurs together with obsessive-compulsive disorder (OCD) and **attention deficit hyperactivity disorder** (ADHD). People with Tourette syndrome are about 20 times more likely than those in the general population to develop OCD. Tic disorders are also associated with behaviors such as **depression**, rage, sexual aggressiveness, and anxiety.

In some cases, neuropsychiatric disorders, such as tic disorders and obsessive-compulsive disorder, have been shown to develop after streptococcal infection. No precise mechanism for this connection has been determined, although it appears to be related to the autoimmune system. There are other illness-related causes of tics, though they appear to be rare. These include the development of tics after head **trauma**, viral encephalitis, or **stroke**.

Symptoms

The diagnostic criteria of all tic disorders specify that the symptoms must appear before the age of 18 and that they cannot result from ingestion of such substances as stimulants or from such general medical conditions as Huntington's disease. Tic disorders can be seen as occurring along a continuum of severity in terms of disruption and impairment, with transient tic disorder being the least severe and Tourette disorder being the most severe.

Tics increase in frequency when a person is under any form of mental or physical stress, even if it is of a positive nature (e.g., excitement about a party). Some people's tics are most obvious when the person is in a relaxed situation, such as quietly watching television. Tics tend to diminish when the person is placed in a new or highly structured situation, such as a doctor's office— a factor that can complicate **diagnosis**. When the symptoms of a tic are present over long time periods, they do not remain constant but will wax and wane in their severity.

Transient tic disorder occurs in approximately 4–24% of schoolchildren. It is the mildest form of tic disorder, and may be underreported because of its temporary nature. In transient tic disorder, there may be single or multiple motor and/or vocal tics that occur many times a day nearly every day for at least four weeks, but not for longer than one year. If the criteria have been met at one time for Tourette disorder or for chronic motor or vocal tic disorder, transient tic disorder may not be diagnosed.

Chronic motor or vocal tic disorder is characterized by either motor tics or vocal tics, but not both. The tics occur many times a day nearly every day, or intermittently for a period of more than one year. During that time, the patient is never without symptoms for more than three consecutive months. The severity of the symptoms and functional impairment is usually much less than for patients with Tourette disorder.

Tourette is defined by the *DSM-IV-TR* as the presence of both vocal and motor tics for a period of more than one year. The tics occur many times a day, usually in bouts, nearly every day or intermittently. The patient is never symptom-free for more than three months at a time.

Children and adolescents with Tourette disorder frequently experience additional problems including aggressiveness, self-harming behaviors, emotional immaturity, social withdrawal, physical complaints, conduct disorders, affective disorders, anxiety, panic attacks, **stuttering**, **sleep disorders**, migraine headaches, and inappropriate sexual behaviors.

Tics seem to worsen during the patient's adolescence, although some clinicians think that the symptoms become more problematic rather than more severe, because the patient experiences more embarrassment than he or she did before. The symptoms do become more unpredictable from day to day during adolescence. Many teenagers may refuse to go to school when their tics are severe. Coprolalia (uttering obscene, hostile, or inappropriate words) often appears first in adolescence; this symptom causes considerable distress for individuals and their families.

Behavioral problems also become more prominent in adolescence. There is some evidence that temper tantrums, aggressiveness, and explosive behavior appear in preadolescence, intensify in adolescence, and gradually diminish by early adulthood. Aggression appears to increase at approximately the same time that the tics decrease in severity.

Diagnosis

There are no diagnostic laboratory tests to screen for tic disorders. Except for the tics, the results of the patient's physical and neurological examinations are normal. The doctor takes a complete medical history including a detailed account of prenatal events, birth history, head injuries, episodes of encephalitis or meningitis, poisonings, and medication or drug use. The patient's developmental, behavioral, and academic histories are also important. Measurement of thyroid-stimulating hormone levels can be helpful, because tics are often associated with hyperthyroidism (overactive thyroid gland). Also, a strep-A test is useful if the patient suddenly developed tic symptoms after a throat or ear infection.

There is an average delay of 5 to 12 years between the initial symptoms of a tic disorder and the correct diagnosis. This delay is largely related to the misperception that tics are caused by anxiety and should be treated by **psychotherapy**. This misperception in turn is fueled by the fact that tics tend to increase in severity when the affected person is angry, anxious, excited, or fatigued. It is also common for the patient to manifest fewer tics in a doctor's office than at home, leaving parents feeling frustrated and undermined and physicians confused. In addition, children quickly learn to mask their symptoms by converting them to more socially acceptable movements and sounds. The diagnosis of a tic disorder can be aided in some cases by directly observing, videotaping, or audiotaping the patient in a more natural setting.

Clinicians can also become confused by such additional symptoms of tic disorders as touching, hitting, jumping, smelling hands or objects, stomping, twirling, and doing deep-knee bends. They disagree, however, as to whether such symptoms should be classified as tics or compulsions. There appears to be a significant overlap between the symptoms of tic disorders and those of obsessive-compulsive disorder (OCD).

Abnormal obsessive-compulsive behavior has been found in 40% of patients with Tourette disorder between the ages of 6 and 10 years. Obsessions are persistent ideas, thoughts, impulses, or images that are experienced as intrusive, inappropriate, senseless, and repetitive. Compulsions are defined as repetitive behaviors performed to reduce the anxiety or distress caused by the obsessions. For those diagnosed with OCD, common obsessions have to do with dirt, germs, and contamination. Patients with Tourette disorder often have obsessions that involve violent scenes, sexual thoughts, and counting; their compulsions are often related to symmetry (e.g., lining things up and getting them "just right"). OCD symptoms occur considerably later than tics and appear to worsen with age. Some theorists have suggested that obsessive thoughts are cognitive tics.

Tic disorders can be differentiated from **movement disorders** by the following characteristics: they are suppressible; they tend to persist during sleep; they are preceded by sensory symptoms; they have both phonic and motor components; and they wax and wane.

Dual diagnoses

Children and adults with tic disorders are at increased risk for depression and other mood disorders, as well as **anxiety disorders**. This comorbidity may be due to the burden of dealing with a chronic, disruptive, and often stigmatizing disorder. The energy and watchfulness required to suppress tic symptoms may contribute to social anxiety, social withdrawal, self-preoccupation, and fatigue. Low self-esteem and feelings of hopelessness are common in patients diagnosed with tic disorders.

While OCD behaviors have been noted in as many as 80% of individuals with tic disorders, only 30% meet the full criteria for OCD. Distinguishing complex tics from simple compulsions can be difficult. Touching compulsions appear to be characteristic of the tic-related type of OCD. Compared to obsessive-compulsive disorder in persons without a history of tics, there will likely be an earlier age of onset, a greater proportion of male sufferers, a more frequent family history of chronic tics, and a poorer therapeutic response to **selective serotonin reuptake inhibitors** (SSRIs)—although the addition of a neuroleptic to the treatment regimen sometimes brings about improvement.

More than 25% of children with Tourette syndrome also have ADHD, including a short attention span, restlessness, poor concentration, and diminished impulse control. On average, ADHD will manifest two-and-a-half years before the tics appear. A dual diagnosis of ADHD and tic disorder is associated with more severe tics and greater social impairment than for tic disorder by itself. Over time, the problems caused by the inattention, impulsivity, motor overactivity, and the resultant under-achievement in school associated with ADHD are often more disabling than the tics themselves.

Children with tic disorders are five times as likely as other children to require special education programs. The tics may be disruptive and mistakenly interpreted by teachers as intended to disturb the class. Often, children with tic disorders have underlying learning disabilities as well. While there does not appear to be any impairment in general intellectual functioning, researchers have identified patterns of specific learning problems in children with tic disorders. These problems include abnormal visual-perceptual performance, reduced visual-motor skills, and discrepancies between verbal and performance IQ. Many of these learning difficulties are also commonly found in children with ADHD.

Increasing numbers of children with tic disorders are also diagnosed with a **conduct disorder**. Children with conduct disorder show inappropriate and sometimes severe aggression toward people and animals. They may also act out other destructive impulses. Unfortunately, some of these children grow up to develop a personality disorder.

Treatment

A holistic approach is recommended for the treatment of tic disorders. A multidisciplinary team should work together with the affected child's parents and teachers to put together a comprehensive treatment plan. Treatment should include:

- Educating the patient and family about the course of the disorder in a reassuring manner.
- Completion of necessary diagnostic tests, including self-reports (by child and parents); clinician-administered ratings; and direct observational methods.
- Comprehensive assessment, including the child's cognitive abilities, perception, motor skills, behavior and adaptive functioning.
- Collaboration with school personnel to create a learning environment conducive to academic success.
- Therapy, most often behavioral or cognitive-behavioral, though other modalities may be appropriate.
- If necessary, evaluation for medication.

Behavioral and cognitive-behavioral therapy

Habit reversal is the most commonly used technique, combining relaxation exercises, awareness training, and contingency management for positive **reinforcement**. This method shows a 64–100% success rate. Adding a cognitive component to habit reversal involves the introduction of flexibility into rigid thinking, and confronting the child's irrational expectations and unrealistic anticipations. The specific cognitive technique of distraction has been shown to help patients resist sensory urges and to restore the patient's sense of control over the tic.

Massed negative practice is a behavioral therapy technique used in the treatment of children with tic disorder. The patient is asked to deliberately perform the tic movement for specified periods of time interspersed with brief periods of rest. Patients have shown some decrease in tic frequency, but the long-term benefits of massed negative practice are unclear.

Contingency management is another behavioral treatment. It is based on positive reinforcement, usually administered by parents. Children are praised and rewarded for not performing tics and for replacing them with alternative behaviors. Contingency management, however, appears to be of limited use outside of such controlled settings as schools or institutions.

Self-monitoring consists of having the patient record tics by using a wrist counter or small notebook. It is fairly effective in reducing some tics by increasing the child's awareness.

Medications

Medication is the main treatment for motor and vocal tics. Because medications can cause side effects, patients and their families should be evaluated fully and use other treatment methods in conjunction with medication. Because the symptoms of tic disorders overlap those of OCD and ADHD, it is essential to determine which symptoms are causing the greatest concern and impairment, and treat the patient according to the single diagnostic category that best fits him or her, whether it is a tic disorder, OCD, or ADHD.

These medications may be prescribed for patients with tic disorders:

- Typical neuroleptics (antipsychotic medications), including haloperidol (Haldol), risperidone (Risperdal), and pimozide (Orap). Neuroleptics can have significant side effects, which include concentration problems, cognitive blunting, sedation, and, more rarely, tardive dyskinesia (a movement disorder that consists of lip, mouth, and tongue movements).
- Alpha-adrenergic receptor agonists, including clonidine (Catapres) and guanfacine (Tenex). Clonidine has fewer and milder side effects than the neuroleptics in

general, with the most common being sedation. Sedation occurs in 10–20% of cases and can often be controlled by adjusting the dosage.

- The phenothiazines may be used when haloperidol or pimozide has proven ineffective.

- Atypical antipsychotics such as aripiprazole (Abilify) and other agents that block dopamine receptors including risperidone (Risperdal) and clozapine (Clozaril).

- Tetrabenazine is a promising new medication with fewer side effects than other typical neuroleptics. It can be used in combination with the older antipsychotic medications, allowing for lower doses of both medications with substantial relief. However, it may cause depression and Parkinson's-like symptoms.

- Selective serotonin reuptake inhibitors (SSRIs), which include medications such as fluoxetine (Prozac) and sertraline (Zoloft), can be used to treat the obsessive-compulsive behaviors associated with Tourette disorder. They can also be helpful with depression and difficulties with impulse control, though they must be given at higher dosages for OCD than for depression. The SSRIs, however, can cause gastric upset and nausea.

- Benzodiazepines are used in some cases to decrease tic severity and lower the patient's anxiety level, but are often avoided because they can cause dependence and tolerance.

- Nicotine chewing gum appears to reduce tics when added to ongoing treatment with haloperidol, but is in need of further study.

- Calcium channel blockers, such as verapamil (Calan) and nifedipine (Adalat) may ease symptoms by reducing the release of neurotransmitters in the brain.

Surgical treatments

Surgery to the frontal lobe (prefrontal lobotomy) and limbic system (limbic lencotomy) have not been shown effective in treating tic disorders. However, deep brain stimulation—the high-frequency stimulation of the brain with electrodes—has been shown in studies to reduce tic severity by 70%.

Alternative therapies

There is growing interest in dietary changes and nutritional supplements to prevent and manage the symptoms of tic disorders, although formal studies have not yet been conducted in this area. Some theorists have suggested that hidden food and chemical allergies or nutritional deficiencies may influence the development and maintenance of tic disorders. Recommendations include eating organic food and avoiding pesticides, taking antioxidants, increasing intake of folic acid and the B vitamins, eating foods high in **zinc** and magnesium, eliminating caffeine from the diet, and avoiding artificial sweeteners, colors and dyes.

Prognosis

There is presently no cure for tic disorders, and there is no evidence that early treatment alters prognosis. When a child is first evaluated, it is not possible to determine whether the tics will be chronic or transient, mild or severe.

As recently as twenty years ago, tic disorders were considered to be lifelong conditions, with remissions believed to be rare. There is now a general consensus that if a tic disorder is the only diagnosis, the prognosis is favorable. Up to 73% of patients report that their tics decreased markedly or disappeared as they entered the later years of adolescence or early adulthood.

In a small number of patients, the most severe and debilitating forms of a tic disorder occur in adult life. In addition, stress in later life can cause tics to re-emerge. The tics may be new developments in adulthood, a phenomenon that may be more common than previously thought. Remission rates for tic disorders are difficult to pinpoint among this seldom-studied population, but appear to be extremely low.

Although the tics themselves may decline, the associated problems often continue into adult life. Obsessive-compulsive symptoms and other behavioral problems, as well as learning disabilities, may grow worse. Obsessive-compulsive behaviors become most pronounced at age 15 and remain at that level. Panic attacks, depression, **agoraphobia**, and alcoholism are most significant in the early adult years, while a tendency toward obesity increases steadily with age, particularly in women.

In adulthood, a patient's repertoire of tics is reduced and becomes predictable during periods of fatigue and heightened emotionality. Some studies suggest remission rates, with the complete cessation of symptoms, to be as high as 50%. Cases of total remission appear to be related to the family's treatment of the patient when he or she was a child. Persons who were punished, misunderstood and stigmatized because of their tics experience greater functional impairment as adults than those who were supported and understood as children.

Prevention

There are few preventive strategies for tic disorders. There is some evidence that maternal emotional stress

KEY TERMS

Atypical antipsychotics—A group of medications for the treatment of psychotic symptoms that were introduced in the 1990s. The atypical antipsychotics include clozapine, risperidone, quetiapine, ziprasidone, and olanzapine. They are sometimes called serotonin dopamine antagonists, or SDAs.

Basal ganglia—A group of masses of gray matter located in the cerebral hemispheres of the brain that control movement as well as some aspects of emotion and cognition.

Behavioral therapy—An approach to treatment that focuses on extinguishing undesirable behavior and replacing it with desired behavior.

Benzodiazepines—A group of central nervous system depressants used to relieve anxiety or to induce sleep.

Cognitive-behavioral therapy—An approach to psychotherapy that emphasizes the correction of distorted thinking patterns and changing one's behaviors accordingly.

Comorbidity—Association or presence of two or more mental disorders in the same patient. A disorder that is said to have a high degree of comorbidity is likely to occur in patients diagnosed with other disorders that may share or reinforce some of its symptoms.

Compulsion—A strong impulse to perform an act, particularly one that is irrational or contrary to one's will.

Coprolalia—A vocal tic characterized by uttering obscene, hostile, or inappropriate words. A motor tic characterized by obscene gestures is called copropraxia.

Cyclic AMP—A small molecule of adenosine monophosphate (AMP) that activates enzymes and increases the effects of hormones and other neurotransmitters.

Dopamine—A chemical in brain tissue that serves to transmit nerve impulses (is a neurotransmitter) and helps to regulate movement and emotions.

Holistic—A treatment approach that is comprehensive and respectful of a person's emotional, social, cognitive, and interpersonal needs.

Neuroleptic—Another name for the older antipsychotic medications, such as haloperidol (Haldol) and chlorpromazine (Thorazine).

Neurotransmitter—A chemical in the brain that transmits messages between neurons, or nerve cells.

Obsession—A persistent image, idea, or desire that dominates a person's thoughts or feelings.

Onset—The point in time at which the symptoms of a disorder first became apparent.

Phenothiazines—A class of drugs widely used in the treatment of psychosis.

Remission—In the course of an illness or disorder, a period of time when symptoms are absent.

Serotonin—A widely distributed neurotransmitter that is found in blood platelets, the lining of the digestive tract, and the brain, and that works in combination with norepinephrine. It causes very powerful contractions of smooth muscle, and is associated with mood, attention, emotions, and sleep. Low levels of serotonin are associated with depression.

Stigma—A mark or characteristic trait of a disease or defect; by extension, a cause for reproach or a stain on one's reputation. Tic disorders are sometimes regarded as a stigma by the patient's family.

Tardive dyskinesia—A condition that involves involuntary movements of the tongue, jaw, mouth, or face or other groups of skeletal muscles that usually occurs either late in antipsychotic therapy or even after the therapy is discontinued. It may be irreversible.

Thalamus—The middle part of the diencephalon (a part of the human forebrain), responsible for transmitting and integrating information from the senses.

Tic—A sudden involuntary behavior that is difficult or impossible for the person to suppress. Tics may be either motor (related to movement) or vocal, and may become more pronounced under stress.

during pregnancy and severe nausea and vomiting during the first trimester may affect tic severity. Attempting to minimize prenatal stress may possibly serve a limited preventive function.

Similarly, because people with tic disorders are sensitive to stress, efforts to maintain a low-stress environment can help minimize the number or severity of tics (e.g., reducing the number of social gatherings, which can provoke anxiety). This approach cannot prevent tics altogether, and must be undertaken with an awareness that it is neither healthful nor advisable to attempt to eliminate all stressful events in life.

Resources

BOOKS

American Psychiatric Association. *Diagnostic and Statistical Manual of Mental Disorders.* 4th ed., text rev. Washington, DC: American Psychiatric Publishing, 2000.

Chowdhury, Uttom, and Isobel Heyman. *Tics and Tourette Syndrome: A Handbook for Parents and Professionals.* London: Jessica Kingsley Publishers, 2004.

Kurlan, Roger, ed. *Handbook of Tourette's Syndrome and Related Tic and Behavioral Disorder.* New York: Marcel Dekker, 2005.

Woods, Douglas W., and Raymond G. Miltenberger, eds. *Tic Disorders, Trichotillomania, and Other Repetitive Behavior Disorders: Behavioral Approaches to Analysis and Treatment.* New York: Springer, 2006.

PERIODICALS

Balen, George M., et al. "An overview of the treatment of Tourette's disorder and tics." *Journal of Child and Adolescent Psychopharmacology* 20, no. 4 (2010): 249.

Fan, Wenqing, et al. "Association between antipsychotics and body mass index when treating patients with tics." *Journal of Child and Adolescent Psychopharmacology* 20, no. 4 (2010): 277.

Gilbert, Donald L., Elana Harris, and Steve W. Wu. "Tic suppression: the medical model." *Journal of Child and Adolescent Psychopharmacology* 20, no. 4 (2010): 263.

Otto, M. Alexander. "Habit reversal training can bring end to tics: treatment sometimes works as a 'useful adjunct' to drug therapy and can be 'good place to start.'" *Clinical Psychiatry News.* (March 2011): 20.

Piacentini, John C., John T. Walkup, and Douglas W. Woods. "Comprehensive behavioral intervention for tics in children with Tourette syndrome." *Communique* (Oct. 2010): 1.

ORGANIZATIONS

Association for Comprehensive Neurotherapy, PO Box 2198, Broken Arrow, OK, 34688-1967, (561) 798-0472, Fax: (561) 798-9820, acn@latitudes.org, http://www.latitudes.org.

National Institute of Neurological Disorders and Stroke, PO Box 5801, Bethesda, MD, 20824, (301) 496-5751; TTY: (301) 468-5981, (800) 352-9424, http://www.ninds.nih.gov.

Tourette Syndrome Association, Inc, 42-40 Bell Blvd., Bayside, NY, 11361-2861, (718) 224-2999, http://www.tsa-usa.org.

Holly Scherstuhl, M.Ed.
Stephanie N. Watson

Tofranil *see* **Imipramine**

Toilet phobia

Definition

Toilet phobia is an often debilitating psychological condition that affects an individual's ability to urinate or defecate in public facilities. It is an inclusive term that encompasses two different phobias—paruresis, the fear of urinating in public places (also referred to as "bashful bladder syndrome," "shy bladder syndrome," or "pee-phobia") and parcopresis, the fear of having a bowel movement in a public place or when other people are nearby. Many psychologists consider toilet phobias to be a form of social anxiety disorder.

Demographics

An estimated 7%, or 17 million Americans, experience paruresis. Although paruresis can occur in both men and women, approximately 90% of those who seek treatment for the condition are male. This may be because public men's restrooms are much more open (urinals, rather than closed stalls) than women's restrooms. The severity of paruresis can vary widely. It is estimated that between 1 and 2 million Americans have such severe paruresis that it has a significant negative effect on their daily personal and professional lives.

Description

Many people occasionally experience difficulty urinating or having a bowel movement. Often, these difficulties stem from an underlying medical condition, such as a blockage in the urinary system, constipation, illness, or a side effect of medication. However, when an individual is able to urinate or defecate normally at home but not in a public facility, the cause is likely psychological (paruresis or parcopresis). Individuals with these conditions feel embarrassed at the thought that they might be heard or criticized while using the toilet, and their anxiety can gradually worsen as the inability to use public bathrooms persists.

Different degrees of toilet phobias exist. People who have the most severe form are totally unable to use a public restroom and may even be unable to use the bathroom at the home of a friend or family member. Other people with toilet phobias can only use a public restroom if no one else is using it at the same time. Still others can go in a public facility if they are enclosed in a private stall rather than standing at a urinal.

To prevent the urge to urinate when away from home, individuals with toilet phobia may restrict fluids or take medications that prevent them from going to the bathroom. They may refuse to attend social functions and avoid traveling, for fear that they will be unable to find an empty restroom.

Young children may experience phobias during toilet training. The primary causes of toilet phobias in children are the fears of passing a painful bowel movement or being punished for making a mess. In

KEY TERMS

Biofeedback—A technique in which patients learn to modify certain body functions, such as temperature or pulse rate, with the help of a monitoring machine.

Obsessive-compulsive disorder (OCD)—An anxiety disorder in which a person cannot prevent himself from dwelling on unwanted thoughts, acting on urges, or performing repetitious rituals, such as washing his hands or checking to make sure he turned off the lights.

Parcopresis—Fear of having a bowel movement in a public place.

Paruresis—Fear of urinating in a public place.

Prostate—A gland found in men that surrounds the neck of the bladder and secretes fluid that when mixed with sperm becomes semen.

Sympathetic nervous system—The part of the autonomic nervous system that is concerned especially with preparing the body to react to situations of stress or emergency; it contains chiefly adrenergic fibers and tends to depress secretion, decrease the tone and contractility of smooth muscle, and increase heart rate.

most people with paruresis, the condition develops during the adolescent or teenage years, although it can arise at any time.

Causes and symptoms

Toilet phobias are believed to have genetic, physical, and psychological components. The symptoms include various levels of inability in using public toilets.

Causes

Paruresis and parcopresis tend to occur in families, as do social anxiety disorder and **depression**, which also commonly coexist in those individuals with toilet phobias.

The physical component of the disorder occurs when an individual experiences anxiety using a public restroom. That anxiety awakens the sympathetic nervous system, which causes smooth muscles in the urinary tract to contract, shutting off the flow of urine. The level of anxiety the person feels may grow with each subsequent attempt to use a public restroom.

Theories regarding the psychological triggers for toilet phobias include:

- memories of harassment, bullying, or teasing during a childhood or adolescent bathroom experience
- sexual abuse
- a subconscious association between using the bathroom and sexuality
- obsessive-compulsive disorder connected to a fear of contamination
- critical parents or an upbringing that associated shame with the toileting process

Because of the embarrassment involved with toilet phobias, most people who experience them do not seek professional help for their condition.

Symptoms

The following are symptoms of toilet phobias:

- limiting or avoiding fluids
- taking medication to prevent urination or a bowel movement
- avoiding travel, social situations, and jobs that require the use of a public restroom
- having a distended bladder from holding in urine for long periods of time or having other bladder or kidney problems
- feeling sweaty, dizzy, faint, or shaky when attempting to use a public restroom
- being embarrassed or ashamed of using the toilet and of the phobia itself

Diagnosis

Individuals with toilet phobias are often referred to a urologist for an initial evaluation. The urologist will do a series of tests to identify whether the problem stems from a condition such as diabetes or an enlarged prostate gland or is the side effect of a medication. The doctor may do a urodynamic evaluation, which measures urine flow rate, bladder pressure, and residual urine volume to see how well the bladder is filling and emptying. If the urological assessment is negative, the patient may be referred to a **psychiatrist**. For a **diagnosis** of toilet phobia to be made, the phobia must be significant enough to affect the individual's daily life. For example, the person must be going out of his or her way to avoid public restrooms.

Treatment

Several treatments have been proposed for toilet phobias, including **cognitive-behavioral therapy**, **hypnotherapy**, **biofeedback**, medication, and self-

QUESTIONS TO ASK YOUR DOCTOR

- Can you refer me to a therapist or other mental health professional?
- What tests are necessary to rule out an underlying physical condition?
- Is medication to treat anxiety appropriate for me?
- Is there a support group available for this problem?
- Do you have anyone on staff experienced in treating this condition?
- Is cognitive-behavior therapy right for me?

catheterization. The most commonly used treatment for paruresis is graduated behavior therapy, in which patients learn to overcome their phobia by progressing through increasingly public bathroom scenarios. For example, someone may first urinate in a private bathroom while someone is standing in another room in the house and gradually work their way up to voiding while in a public bathroom with someone right outside the stall.

Toilet phobias also may be treated with medication, although no clinical evidence exists to prove its effectiveness. Sometimes the drug **diazepam** (Valium) can relax the pelvic floor muscles to relieve urinary retention. **Selective serotonin reuptake inhibitors (SSRIs)** may be used to treat the underlying anxiety that is causing the toilet phobia.

For children who experience toilet phobias, several possible interventions can be used. If the child fears having a painful bowel movement, stool softeners can help ensure that the bowel movement is not uncomfortable. Parents can reassure their child about using the toilet or use small rewards and incentives. If the phobia stems from anxiety or depression, the child may require counseling from a psychiatrist or **psychologist**.

Prognosis

Although cognitive-behavioral therapy, **psychotherapy**, and other treatments are not effective in every case, these techniques help some people overcome toilet phobias. No randomized, controlled studies have been done to evaluate toilet phobia treatments; however, surveys and case studies suggest that behavioral therapies can at least improve symptoms in more than half of patients and can have complete success in many cases.

Prevention

There is no sure way to prevent toilet phobias. However, treatments such as graduated behavior therapy may be effective in reducing the anxiety associated with using public restrooms.

Resources

BOOKS

Axelby, Clayton P., ed. *Social Phobia: Etiology, Diagnosis, and Treatment.* New York: Nova Biomedical Books, 2009.

Olmert, Carol. *Bathrooms Make Me Nervous: A Guidebook for Women with Urination Anxiety (Shy Bladder).* Walnut Creek, CA: CJOB, 2008.

Robinson, Theresa M., ed. *Social Anxiety: Symptoms, Causes, and Techniques.* Hauppauge, NY: Nova Science, 2010.

PERIODICALS

Soifer, S., J. Himle, and K. Walsh. "Paruresis (Shy Bladder Syndrome): A Cognitive-Behavioral Treatment Approach." *Social Work in Health Care* 49, no. 5 (May 2010): 494–507.

Soifer, Steven, et al. "Paruresis or Shy Bladder Syndrome: An Unknown Urologic Malady?" *Urologic Nursing* 29, no. 2 (March/April 2009): 87–94.

ORGANIZATIONS

Anxiety Disorders Association of America, 8730 Georgia Ave., Ste. 600, Silver Spring, MD, 20910, (240) 485-1001, http://www.adaa.org.

International Paruresis Association, PO Box 65111, Baltimore, MD, 21209, (800) 247-3864, http://www.paruresis.org.

National Institute of Mental Health, 6001 Executive Blvd., Rm. 8184, MSC 9663 , Bethesda, MD, 20892-9663, (301) 443-4513, Fax: (301) 443-4279, (866) 615-6464; TTY: (301) 443-8431; TTY tollfree: (866) 415-8051, http://www.nimh.nih.gov.

Stephanie N. Watson
Tish Davidson, AM

Token economy system

Definition

A token economy is a form of **behavior modification** designed to increase desirable behavior and decrease undesirable behavior with the use of tokens. Individuals receive tokens immediately after displaying desirable behavior. The tokens are collected and later exchanged for a meaningful object or privilege.

Purpose

The primary goal of a token economy is to increase desirable behavior and decrease undesirable behavior. Often token economies are used in institutional settings (such as psychiatric hospitals or correctional facilities) to manage the behavior of individuals who may be aggressive or unpredictable. However, the larger goal of token economies is to teach appropriate behavior and social skills that can be used in one's natural environment. Token economies are often used in special education (for children with developmental or learning disabilities, hyperactivity, attention deficit, or behavioral disorders), regular education, colleges, various types of **group homes**, military divisions, nursing homes, **addiction** treatment programs, occupational settings, family homes (for marital or parenting difficulties), and hospitals. Token economies can be used individually or in groups.

Description

Several elements are necessary in every token economy:

- Tokens: Anything that is visible and countable can be used as a token. Tokens should preferably be attractive, easy to carry and dispense, and difficult to counterfeit. Commonly used items include poker chips, stickers, point tallies, or play money. When an individual displays desirable behavior, he or she is immediately given a designated number of tokens. Tokens have no value of their own. They are collected and later exchanged for meaningful objects, privileges or activities. Individuals can also lose tokens (response cost) for displaying undesirable behavior.

- A clearly defined target behavior: Individuals participating in a token economy need to know exactly what they must do in order to receive tokens. Desirable and undesirable behavior is explained ahead of time in simple, specific terms. The number of tokens awarded or lost for each particular behavior is also specified.

- Back-up reinforcers: Back-up reinforcers are the meaningful objects, privileges, or activities that individuals receive in exchange for their tokens. Examples include food items, toys, extra free time, or outings. The success of a token economy depends on the appeal of the back-up reinforcers. Individuals will only be motivated to earn tokens if they anticipate the future reward represented by the tokens. A well-designed token economy will use back-up reinforcers chosen by individuals in treatment rather than by staff.

- A system for exchanging tokens: A time and place for purchasing back-up reinforcers is necessary. The token value of each back-up reinforcer is pre-determined based on monetary value, demand, or therapeutic value. For example, if the reinforcer is expensive or highly attractive, the token value should be higher. If possession of or participation in the reinforcer would aid in the individual's acquisition of skills, the token value should be lower. If the token value is set too low, individuals will be less motivated to earn tokens. Conversely, if the value is set too high, individuals may become easily discouraged. It is important that each individual can earn at least some tokens.

- A system for recording data: Before treatment begins, information (baseline data) is gathered about each individual's current behavior. Changes in behavior are then recorded on daily data sheets. This information is used to measure individual progress, as well as the effectiveness of the token economy. Information regarding the exchange of tokens also needs to be recorded.

- Consistent implementation of the token economy by staff: In order for a token economy to succeed, all involved staff members must reward the same behaviors, use the appropriate amount of tokens, avoid dispensing back-up reinforcers for free, and prevent tokens from being counterfeited, stolen, or otherwise unjustly obtained. Staff responsibilities and the rules of the token economy should be described in a written manual. Staff members should also be evaluated periodically and given the opportunity to raise questions or concerns.

Initially tokens are awarded frequently and in higher amounts, but as individuals learn the desirable behavior, opportunities to earn tokens decrease. (The amount and frequency of token dispensing is called a **reinforcement** schedule.) For example, in a classroom, each student may earn 25 to 75 tokens the first day, so that they quickly learn the value of the tokens. Later, students may earn 15 to 30 tokens per day. By gradually decreasing the availability of tokens (fading), students should learn to display the desirable behavior independently, without the unnatural use of tokens. Reinforcers that individuals would normally encounter in society, such as verbal praise, should accompany the awarding of tokens to aid in the fading process.

Advantages of token economies are that behaviors can be rewarded immediately, rewards are the same for all members of a group, use of punishment (response cost) is less restrictive than other forms of punishment, and individuals can learn skills related to planning for the future. Disadvantages include considerable cost, effort, and extensive staff training and management. Some professionals find token economies to be time-consuming and impractical.

Risks

Risks involved in token economies are similar to those in other forms of behavior modification. Staff members implementing the therapy may intentionally or

KEY TERMS

Back-up reinforcer—A desirable item, privilege, or activity that is purchased with tokens and serves as a delayed reward and subsequent motivation for target (desired) behavior.

Baseline data—Information regarding the frequency and severity of behavior, gathered before treatment begins.

Behavior modification—An approach to therapy based on the principles of operant conditioning. Behavior modification seeks to replace undesirable behaviors with preferable behaviors through the use of positive or negative reinforcement.

Fading—Gradually decreasing the amount or frequency of a reinforcer so that the target behavior will begin to occur independent of any rewards.

Reinforcement schedule—The frequency and amount of reinforcers administered.

Reinforcer—Anything that causes an increase of a particular behavior.

Response cost—A behavioral technique that involves removing a stimulus from an individual's environment so that the response that directly precedes the removal is weakened. In a token economy system, response cost is a form of punishment involving loss of tokens due to inappropriate behavior, which consequently results in decreased ability to purchase back-up reinforcers.

Target behavior—The specific behavior to be increased or decreased during treatment.

Therapeutic value—The potential benefit of an object or situation, in terms of its ability to enhance functioning (social, emotional, intellectual, occupational, etc.) in an individual.

Token—Any item that can be seen and collected (such as stickers or points in a point tally) that has no value of its own, but is used as an immediate reward for desirable behavior that is later exchanged for back-up reinforcers.

unintentionally neglect the rights of individuals receiving treatment. Token economies should never deprive individuals of their basic needs, such as sufficient food, comfortable bedding, or reasonable opportunities for leisure. If staff members are inadequately trained or there is a shortage of staff, desirable behaviors may not be rewarded or undesirable behaviors may be inadvertently rewarded, resulting in an increase of negative behavior. Controversy exists regarding placing individuals in treatment against their will (such as in a psychiatric hospital), and deciding which behaviors should be considered desirable and which should be considered undesirable.

Results

Ideally, individuals will use the skills learned in a token economy in their everyday surroundings. They will display the undesirable behavior less frequently or not at all. They will also engage in positive, adaptive behaviors more often.

If the token economy was ineffective, or time spent in the token economy was limited, individuals may show either no changes or even increases in the undesirable behavior.

Resources

BOOKS

Martin, Garry. *Behavior Modification: What It Is and How to Do It*. 9th ed. Upper Saddle River, New Jersey: Prentice-Hall, 2010.

Miltenberger, Raymond G. *Behavior Modification: Principles and Procedures*. 5thed. Belmont, California: Wadsworth/Thomson Learning, 2011.

Reinke, Wendy M., Keith C. Herman, and Randy Sprick. *Motivational Interviewing for Effective Classroom Management: The Classroom Check-Up*. New York: The Guilford Press: 2011.

Young, Ellie L., Paul Caldarella, Michael J. Richardson, and K. Richard Young. *Positive Behavior Support in Secondary Schools: A Practical Guide*. New York: The Guilford Press: 2011.

PERIODICALS

Fortson, Beverly L., et al. "Managing Classroom Behavior of Head Start Children Using Response Cost and Token Economy Procedures." *The Journal of Early and Intensive Behavioral Intervention* 2, no. 1 (2005): 28.

Moore, James W., et al. "Restructuring an Existing Token Economy in a Psychiatric Facility for Children." *Child & Family Behavior Therapy* 23, no. 3 (2001): 53–59.

Nelson, Karl G. "Exploration of Classroom Participation in the Presence of a Token Economy." *Journal of Instructional Psychology* 37, no. 1 (2010): 49.

ORGANIZATIONS

Association for Behavioral Analysis International, 550 West Centre Ave., Ste. 1, Portage, MI, 49024, (269) 492-9310, Fax: (269) 492-9316, http://www.abainternational.org.

Cambridge Center for Behavioral Studies, PO Box 7067, Cummings Center, Ste. 340F, Beverly, MA, 01915, (978) 369-2227, Fax: (978) 369-8584, http://www.behavior.org.

Sandra L. Friedrich, M.A.

Tourette syndrome

Definition

Tourette syndrome (TS) is an inherited disorder of the nervous system that typically appears in childhood. The main features of TS are repeated movements and vocalizations called tics. TS can also be associated with behavioral and developmental problems.

Demographics

Tourette syndrome is a relatively common disorder found in all populations and all ethnic groups. TS is three to four times more common in males than females. The exact incidence of Tourette syndrome is unknown, but it is estimated to affect 1–10 per 1,000 children. According to the National Institute for Neurological Disorders and Stroke (NINDS), an estimated 200,000 Americans have the most severe form of TS, and as many as one in 100 have milder symptoms such as chronic motor or vocal tics. Early TS symptoms are almost always noticed first in childhood, with the average onset between 7–10 years.

Description

Tourette syndrome is a variable disorder with onset in childhood. Though symptoms can appear anywhere between 2–18 years of age, typical onset is around age 6 or 7. Tics, which may be motor or vocal, tend to wax and wane (increase and decrease) in severity over time. The first references in the literature to what might today be classified as TS largely describe individuals who were wrongly believed to be possessed by the devil. In 1885 Gilles de la Tourette, a French neurologist, provided the first formal description of this syndrome, which he described as an inherited neurological condition characterized by motor and vocal tics.

Although vocal and motor tics are the hallmark of Tourette syndrome, other symptoms such as the expression of socially inappropriate comments or behaviors, obsessive compulsive disorder, attention deficit disorder, self injuring behavior, **depression**, and anxiety also appear to be associated with Tourette syndrome. Symptoms usually intensify during teenage years and diminish in late adolescence or early adulthood. Patients may also develop co-occurring behavioral disorders, namely **obsessive-compulsive disorder** (OCD), **attention deficit hyperactivity disorder (ADHD)** or attention deficit disorder (ADD), poor impulse control, or **sleep disorders**. Though some children have learning disabilities, intelligence is not impaired. TS is not degenerative and life span is normal.

Risk factors

TS risk factors are unknown, and researchers are studying risk factors before and after birth that may contribute to this complex disorder. Some of the suggested factors are severe psychological **trauma**, recurrent daily stresses, extreme emotional excitement, PANDAS (pediatric autoimmune neuropsychiatric disorder with streptococcal infection), and drug abuse.

Causes and symptoms

A variety of genetic and environmental factors likely play a role in causing TS. Studies suggest that the tics in Tourette syndrome are caused by an increased amount of a neurotransmitter called **dopamine**. A neurotransmitter is a chemical found in the **brain** that helps to transmit information from one brain cell to another. Other studies suggest that the defect in Tourette syndrome involves the neurotransmitter **serotonin** or involves other chemicals required for normal functioning of the brain.

Genetic factors are believed to play a major role in the development of TS. Several chromosomal regions have been identified as possible locations of genes that confer susceptibility to TS. Some family studies have indicated that TS may be inherited in an autosomal dominant manner, but other studies have shown that this is not the case. Mutations involving the SLITRK1 gene have been identified in a small number of TS patients. This gene provides instructions for making a brain protein called SLITRK1. This protein probably plays a role in the development of nerve cells, including the growth of axons and dendrites that allow each nerve cell to communicate with nearby cells. It is unclear how mutations in the SLITRK1 gene can lead to this disorder. The inheritance pattern of Tourette syndrome remains unknown. Although the features of TS can cluster in families, many genetic and environmental factors are likely to be involved. Some researchers believe that Tourette syndrome has different causes in different individuals or is caused by changes in more than one gene. Further research is needed to establish the cause of Tourette syndrome.

Motor and vocal tics

The principal symptoms of Tourette syndrome are simple and complex motor and vocal tics. Simple motor tics are characterized by brief muscle contractions of one or more limited muscle groups. An eye twitch is an example of a simple motor tic. Complex motor tics tend to appear more complicated and purposeful than simple tics and involve coordinated contractions of several muscle groups. Some examples of complex motor tics are the act of hitting oneself and jumping. Copropraxia, the involuntary display of unacceptable or obscene gestures, and echopraxia, the imitation of the movement of another individual, are other examples of complex motor tics.

Vocal tics are actually manifestations of motor tics that involve the muscles required for vocalization. Simple vocal tics include **stuttering**, stammering, abnormal emphasis of part of a word or phrase, and inarticulate noises such as throat clearing, grunts, and high-pitched sounds. Complex vocal tics typically involve the involuntary expression of words. Perhaps the most striking example of this is coprolalia, the involuntary expression of obscene words or phrases, which occurs in fewer than one-third of people with Tourette syndrome. The involuntary echoing of the last word, phrase, sentence or sound vocalized by oneself (palilalia) or of another person or sound in the environment (echolalia) are also classified as complex tics.

The type, frequency, and severity of tics exhibited varies tremendously among individuals with Tourette syndrome. Tourette syndrome has a variable age of onset, and tics can start anytime between infancy and age 18. Initial symptoms usually occur before the early teens, and the mean age of onset for both males and females is approximately seven years of age. Most individuals with symptoms initially experience simple muscle tics involving the eyes and the head. These symptoms can progress to tics involving the upper torso, neck, arms, hands, and occasionally the legs and feet. Complex motor tics are usually the latest onset muscle tics. Vocal tics usually have a later onset then motor tics. In some rare cases, people with Tourette syndrome suddenly present with multiple, severe, or bizarre symptoms.

Not only is there extreme variability in clinical symptoms among individuals with Tourette syndrome, but individuals commonly experience a variability in type, frequency, and severity of symptoms within the course of their lifetime. Adolescents with Tourette syndrome often experience unpredictable and variable symptoms, which may be related to fluctuating hormone levels and decreased **compliance** in taking medications. Adults often experience a decrease in symptoms or a complete end to symptoms.

A number of factors appear to affect the severity and frequency of tics. **Stress** appears to increase the frequency and severity of tics while concentration on another part of the body that is not taking part in a tic can result in the temporary alleviation of symptoms. Relaxation, following attempts to suppress the occurrence of tics, may result in an increased frequency of tics. An increased frequency and severity of tics can also result from exposure to drugs such as **steroids**, **cocaine**, **amphetamines**, and caffeine. Hormonal changes such as those that occur prior to the menstrual cycle can also increase the severity of symptoms.

KEY TERMS

Attention deficit disorder (ADD)—Disorder characterized by a short attention span, impulsivity, and in some cases hyperactivity.

Autosomal dominant—A pattern of genetic inheritance where only one abnormal gene is needed to display the trait or disease.

Axon—The long extension of a nerve fiber that generally conducts impulses away from the body of the nerve cell.

Coprolalia—The involuntary expression of obscene words or phrases.

Copropraxia—The involuntary display of unacceptable/obscene gestures.

Decreased penetrance—Individuals who inherit a changed disease gene but do not develop symptoms.

Dendrites—Fibers of a brain cell that receive signals from other brain cells.

Dysphoria—Feelings of anxiety, restlessness, and dissatisfaction.

Echolalia—Involuntary echoing of the last word, phrase, or sentence spoken by someone else or sound in the environment.

Echopraxia—The imitation of the movement of another individual.

Neurotransmitter—Chemical in the brain that transmits information from one nerve cell to another.

Obsessive compulsive disorder (OCD)—Disorder characterized by persistent, intrusive, and senseless thoughts (obsessions) or compulsions to perform repetitive behaviors that interfere with normal functioning.

Palilalia—Involuntary echoing of the last word, phrase, sentence, or sound vocalized by oneself.

Tic—Brief and intermittent involuntary movement or sound.

Other associated symptoms

People with Tourette syndrome are more likely to exhibit socially inappropriate behaviors such as expressing insulting or socially unacceptable comments or socially unacceptable actions. It is not known whether these symptoms stem from a more general dysfunction of impulse control that might be part of Tourette syndrome.

Tourette syndrome appears to also be associated with attention deficit disorder (ADD). ADD is characterized by a short attention span and impulsivity and in some cases hyperactivity. Researchers have found that 21%–90% of individuals with Tourette syndrome also exhibit symptoms of ADD, whereas 2%–15% of the general population exhibit symptoms of ADD.

People with Tourette syndrome are also at higher risk for having symptoms of obsessive-compulsive disorder (OCD). OCD is characterized by persistent, intrusive, and senseless thoughts (obsessions) or compulsions to perform repetitive behaviors that interfere with normal functioning. A person with OCD, for example, may be obsessed with germs and may counteract this **obsession** with continual hand washing. Symptoms of OCD are present in 1.9%–3% of the general population, whereas 28%–50% of people with Tourette syndrome have symptoms of OCD.

Self-injurious behavior (SIB) is also seen more frequently in those with Tourette syndrome. Approximately 34%–53% of individuals with Tourette syndrome exhibit some form of self-injuring behavior. The SIB is often related to OCD but can also occur in those with Tourette syndrome who do not have OCD.

Symptoms of anxiety and depression are also found more commonly in people with Tourette syndrome. It is not clear, however, whether these symptoms are symptoms of Tourette syndrome or occur as a result of having to deal with the symptoms of moderate to severe Tourette syndrome.

People with Tourette syndrome may also be at increased risk for having learning disabilities and **personality disorders** and may be more predisposed to behaviors such as aggression, antisocial behaviors, severe temper outbursts, and inappropriate sexual behavior. Further controlled studies need to be performed, however, to ascertain whether these behaviors are symptoms of Tourette syndrome.

Diagnosis

The TS **diagnosis** is made through observation and interview of the patient and discussions with other family members. The diagnosis of Tourette syndrome is complicated by a variety of factors. The extreme range of symptoms of this disorder makes it difficult to differentiate Tourette syndrome from other disorders with similar symptoms. Diagnosis is further complicated by the fact that some tics appear to be within the range of normal behavior. For example, an individual who only exhibits tics such as throat clearing and sniffing may be misdiagnosed with a medical problem such as allergies. In addition, bizarre and complex tics such as coprolalia may be mistaken for psychotic or "bad" behavior. Diagnosis is also confounded by individuals who attempt to control tics in public and in front of healthcare professionals and deny the existence of symptoms. Although there is disagreement over what criteria should be used to diagnose Tourette syndrome, one aide is the ***Diagnostic and Statistical Manual of Mental Disorders*** (*DSM-IV*). The *DSM-IV* outlines suggest diagnostic criteria for a variety of conditions including Tourette syndrome:

- presence of both motor and vocal tics at some time during the course of the illness
- occurrence of multiple tics nearly every day through a period of more than one year, without a remission of tics for a period of greater than three consecutive months
- symptoms cause distress or impairment in functioning
- age of onset is prior to 18 years of age
- symptoms not due to medications or drugs and are not related to another medical condition

Some physicians criticize the *DSM-IV* criteria, citing that they do not include the full range of behaviors and symptoms seen in Tourette syndrome. Others criticize the criteria because it limits the diagnosis to those who experience a significant impairment, which may not be true for individuals with milder symptoms. For this reason many physicians use their clinical judgment as well as the *DSM-IV* criteria as a guide to diagnosing Tourette syndrome.

Tests

Patients may undergo blood tests, **imaging studies** such as **magnetic resonance imaging** (MRI), or an electroencephalogram (EEG) scan in order to rule out other possible explanations for the symptoms.

Treatment

There is no cure for Tourette syndrome, and treatment involves the control of symptoms through educational and psychological interventions and/or medications. The treatment and management of Tourette syndrome varies from patient to patient and is typically focused on the alleviation of the symptoms that are most bothersome to the patient or that cause the most interference with daily functioning.

Traditional

Psychological treatments such as counseling are not generally useful for the treatment of tics but can be beneficial in the treatment of associated symptoms such as obsessive-compulsive behavior and attention deficit disorder. Counseling may also help individuals to cope better with the symptoms of this disorder and to have more positive social interactions. Psychological interventions may also help people cope better with stressors that can normally be triggers for tics and negative behaviors. Relaxation therapies may, however, increase the occurrence of tics. Treatment is crucial in helping the affected person avoid depression, social isolation, and strained family relationships. The education of family members, teachers, and peers about Tourette syndrome can be helpful and may help to foster acceptance and prevent social isolation.

Drugs

Many people with mild symptoms of Tourette syndrome never require medications. Those with severe symptoms may require medications for all or part of their lifetime. No single or combination drug therapy offers complete cessation of symptoms without adverse effects. The most effective treatment of tics associated with Tourette syndrome involves the use of drugs such as **Haloperidol**, **Pimozide**, Sulpiride, and Tiapride, which decrease the amount of dopamine in the body. Unfortunately, the incidence of side effects, even at low dosages, is quite high. The short-term side effects can include sedation, dysphoria, weight gain, movement abnormalities, depression, and poor school performance. Long-term side effects can include phobias, memory difficulties, and personality changes. These drugs are therefore better candidates for short-term rather than long-term therapy.

Tourette syndrome can also be treated with other drugs such as **clonidine**, **clonazepam**, and **risperidone**, but the efficacy of these treatments is unknown. In many cases, treatment of associated conditions such as ADD and OCD is often more of a concern than the tics themselves. Clonidine used in conjunction with stimulants such as Ritalin may be useful for treating people with Tourette syndrome who also have symptoms of ADD. Stimulants should be used with caution in individuals with Tourette syndrome since they can sometimes increase the frequency and severity of tics. OCD symptoms in those with Tourette syndrome are often treated with drugs such as Prozac, Luvox, Paxil, and Zoloft.

In many cases the treatment of Tourette syndrome with medications can be discontinued after adolescence. Trials should be performed through the gradual tapering off of medications and should always be done under a doctor's supervision.

Alternative

Clinical trials for the treatment of Tourette syndrome are often sponsored by the National Institutes of Health (NIH) and other agencies. Clinical trial information is constantly updated by NIH, and the most recent information on Tourette syndrome trials can be found at http://clinicaltrials.gov.

Prognosis

The prognosis for Tourette syndrome in individuals without associated psychological conditions is often quite good, and only approximately 10% of Tourette syndrome individuals experience severe tic symptoms. Approximately 30% of people with Tourette syndrome experience a decrease in the frequency and severity of tics, and another 30–40% experience a complete end of symptoms by late adolescence. The other 30–40% continue to exhibit moderate to severe symptoms in adulthood. There does not appear to be a definite correlation between the type, frequency, and severity of symptoms and the eventual prognosis. Patients with severe tics may experience social difficulties and may isolate themselves from others for fear of shocking and embarrassing them. People with Tourette syndrome who have other symptoms such as obsessive compulsive disorder, attention deficit disorder, and self-injurious behavior usually have a poorer prognosis.

Prevention

There is no known way to prevent Tourette syndrome.

Resources

BOOKS

Buffolano, Sandra. *Coping with Tourette Syndrome: A Workbook to Help Kids With Tic Disorders.*Oakland, CA: Instant Help Books (New Harbinger), 2008.

Buzbuzian, Denise. *Victory Over Tourette's Syndrome and Tic Disorders.* Truro, NS: Woodland Publishing, 2007.

Chowdhury, Uttom, and Isobel Heyman. *Tics and Tourette Syndrome: A Handbook for Parents and Professionals.* London: Jessica Kingsley Publishers, 2004.

Marsh, Tracy L., ed. *Children with Tourette Syndrome: A Parent's Guide,* 2nd ed. Bethesda, MD: Woodbine House, 2006.

Peters, Dylan. *Tic Talk: Living with Tourette Syndrome: A 9–Year–Old Boy's Story in His Own Words.* Chandler, AZ: Little Five Star, 2009.

Woods, Douglas W., et al. *Managing Tourette Syndrome: A Behavioral Intervention Adult Workbook.* New York: Oxford University Press, 2008.

PERIODICALS

Altman, G., J.D. Staley, and P. Wener. "Children with Tourette Disorder: A Follow-up Study in Adulthood." *Journal of Nervous and Mental Disease* 197, no. 5 (May 2009): 305–310.

Bernard, B. A., et al. "Determinants of Quality of Life in Children with Gilles de la Tourette Syndrome." *Movement Disorders* 24, no. 7 (May 2009): 1070–1073.

Cavanna, A. E., et al. "The Behavioral Spectrum of Gilles de la Tourette Syndrome." *Journal of Neuropsychiatry and Clinical Neurosciences* 21, no. 1 (Winter 2009): 13–23.

Hedderick, E. F., C. M. Morris, and H. S. Singer. "Double-blind, Crossover Study of Clonidine and Levetiracetam in Tourette Syndrome." *Pediatric Neurology* 40, no. 6 (June 2009): 420–425.

Jimenez-Shahed, J. "Tourette Syndrome." *Neurologic Clinics* 27, no. 3 (August 2009): 737–755.

Verdellen, C. W., et al. "Habituation of Premonitory Sensations during Exposure and Response Prevention Treatment in Tourette's Syndrome." *Behavior Modification* 32, no. 2 (March 2008): 215–227.

OTHER

National Tourette Syndrome Association. "Facts About Tourette Syndrome." http://www.tsa-usa.org/aPeople/LivingWithTS/Images/Fact_Sheet.pdf (accessed October 27, 2011).

WEBSITES

Genetics Home Reference, Lister Hill National Center for Biomedical Communications. "Tourette Syndrome." U.S. National Library of Medicine, National Institutes of Health. http://ghr.nlm.nih.gov/condition=tourettesyndrome (accessed October 27, 2011.)

MedlinePlus. "Tourette Syndrome." U.S. National Library of Medicine, National Institutes of Health. http://www.nlm.nih.gov/medlineplus/tourettesyndrome.html (accessed October 27, 2011)

U.S. Centers for Disease Control. "Tourette Syndrome (TS)." http://www.cdc.gov/ncbddd/tourette/default.htm (accessed October 27, 2011).

ORGANIZATIONS

National Institute of Neurological Disorders and Stroke, PO Box 5801, Bethesda, MD, 20824, (301) 496-5751; TTY: (301) 468-5981, (800) 352-9424, http://www.ninds.nih.gov.

Tourette Syndrome Association, 42-40 Bell Blvd., Bayside, NY, 11361, (718) 224-2999, http://www.tsa-usa.org.

Tourette Syndrome Foundation of Canada, 5945 Airport Rd., Suite 195, Mississauga, ON, L4V 1R9, (905) 673-2255, (1-800) 361-3120, Fax: (905) 673-2638, http://www.tourette.ca.

Lisa Maria Andres, MS, CGC
Dawn J. Cardeiro, MS, CGC
Monique Laberge, PhD

Tranquilizers *see* **Antianxiety drugs and abuse; Sedatives and related disorders**

Transcranial magnetic stimulation

Definition

Transcranial magnetic stimulation (TMS) is a noninvasive experimental procedure that gently stimulates the **brain** using short bursts of electromagnetic energy.

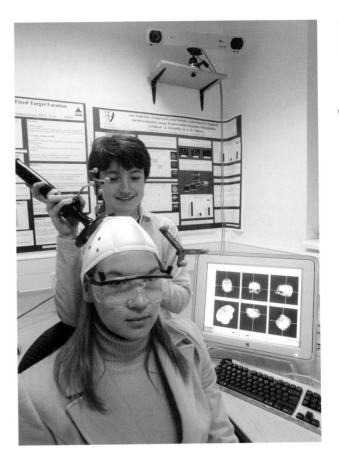

A woman undergoes transcranial magnetic stimulation (TMS). *(© Simon Fraser/University of Durham/Photo Researchers, Inc.)*

Purpose

Originally, TMS was a research tool used to map the brain and to study the differences between a normal brain and a brain with pathology. TMS has been used to study how various functions, such as perception, memory, or attention, are organized in the brain.

More recently, TMS research has also begun to focus on practical applications for the technology in the treatment of various disorders. In October 2008, the Food and Drug Administration (FDA) cleared the first transcranial magnetic stimulation device for treating **depression** in adults who failed to respond favorably to **antidepressants**. Called the NeuroStar device (from a company called Neuronetics), patients receiving TMS would not require sedation (the method is noninvasive) and would have treatment administered on an outpatient basis.

Description

TMS uses specialized electromagnets that are placed on the patient's scalp. The magnets generate short bursts of magnetic energy of approximately the same strength as a **magnetic resonance imaging** (MRI) scanner, but over a more focused area. These pulses produce electrical currents in the brain that change the brain's activity in the area of focus. Repetitive transcranial magnetic stimulation (rTMS) is treatment using a series of TMS pulses.

Use of TMS in the treatment of depression

Much of the application research in TMS has focused on its effectiveness in the treatment of severe and treatment-resistant depression. Although antidepressants, **psychotherapy**, and **electroconvulsive therapy** (ECT) are usually effective in the treatment of depression, not all cases can be successfully treated using these methods. In **clinical trials**, TMS has been found to be effective in many, but not all, of the more difficult cases.

Since the use of antidepressants in children and adolescents is not recommended due to safety issues, TMS offers a promising alternative treatment. However, most research studies to date have focused only on depression in adults. The effectiveness of TMS for children and adolescents cannot be assumed to be the same.

Use of TMS in the treatment of other illnesses

Although most research in the clinical application of TMS and rTMS is focused on the treatment of depression, experimental research and clinical case studies also point to the possibility of TMS being an effective treatment in a number of other disorders. Among these are:

• chronic pain

• epilepsy

• migraine

• obsessive-compulsive disorder

• panic disorder

• Parkinson's disease

• post-traumatic stress disorder

• rehabilitation following a stroke

• tinnitus

• Tourette syndrome

• various psychiatric symptoms, particularly auditory hallucinations associated with schizophrenia

Further research is needed in neuroimaging technology, as well as advances in our understanding of neurocircuitry in mental disorders and how TMS shifts or alters circuitry in the brain.

KEY TERMS

Depression—A mental state characterized by feelings of sadness, despair, and discouragement.

Electroconvulsive therapy (ECT)—Therapy for mood disorders that involves passing electrical current through the brain in order to create a brief convulsion.

Hallucination—To hear, see, or otherwise sense things that are not real. Hallucinations can result from nervous system abnormalities, mental disorders, or the use of certain drugs.

Magnetic resonance imaging (MRI)—An imaging technique that uses a large circular magnet and radio waves to generate signals from atoms in the body. These signals are used to construct images of internal structures.

Psychotherapy—The treatment of mental and behavioral disorders by support and insight to encourage healthy behavior patterns and personality growth.

Seizure—A convulsion, or uncontrolled discharge of nerve cells that may spread to other cells throughout the brain.

Tinnitus—Perceived ringing, buzzing, whistling, or other noise heard in one or both ears that has no external source. A number of conditions may cause this.

Tourette syndrome—An abnormal condition that causes uncontrollable facial grimaces and tics and arm and shoulder movements. Tourette syndrome is perhaps best known for uncontrollable vocal tics that include grunts, shouts, and use of obscene language (coprolalia).

Risks

At this time, it is generally thought that there are no harmful side effects to TMS or rTMS. The main risk of treatment with TMS is of inducing a seizure. Even in cases where **seizures** resulted from TMS, the seizures occurred either during the treatment or immediately thereafter and did not lead to the development of epilepsy. In general, the research shows this risk to be low, and safety guidelines have been put in place to minimize seizure risk.

Although there is the potential risk of TMS to affect the normal functioning of the brain, the literature to date reports few side effects. Unlike the potential memory loss, inability to concentrate, and similar side effects

QUESTIONS TO ASK YOUR DOCTOR

- What are the indications that I should have transcranial magnetic stimulation performed?
- What kind of results can occur with the use of transcranial magnetic stimulation?
- Should I have other procedures in addition to transcranial magnetic stimulation? If so, what other procedures should I have done?

often associated with ECT, the side effects of TMS tend to be very rare, mild, and transient.

Potential side effects of TMS include neckaches or headaches. These tend to be mild reactions that respond well to common over-the-counter analgesics. rTMS has been shown to cause tinnitus or temporary hearing loss. However, the use of earplugs during the treatment prevents this risk. The long-term risks of rTMS treatment are unknown.

Precautions

Individuals with increased risk of seizure—including those with epilepsy or a seizure disorder, a history of seizures, or a family history of epilepsy or a seizure disorder—should not receive TMS. Other people at increased risk for seizures, such as those with increased intracranial pressure due to **trauma** or other causes, those taking medications that increase the risk or seizures, or anyone with serious heart disease, should not receive TMS.

The magnetic force generated by TMS will attract metallic objects and repel magnetic objects. Therefore, individuals with intracranial metallic or magnetic objects such as shrapnel or plates, screws, or clips from surgical procedures should not receive TMS unless the effects of the magnetic force on the object are known. Similarly, individuals with cardiac pacemakers, electrodes inside the heart, or implanted medication pumps should not receive TMS. Pregnant women or those who might be pregnant should not receive TMS.

Resources

BOOKS

Albers, Lawrence J., MD, Rhoda K. Hahn, MD, and Christopher Reist, MD. *Handbook of Psychiatric Drugs.* Laguna Hills, CA: Current Clinical Strategies Publishing, 2010.

American Psychological Association. *Publication Manual of the American Psychological Association,* 6th ed. Washington, DC: American Psychological Association, 2009.

Eisenberg, Ronald, JD MD FACR., and Alexander Margulis, MD. *A Patient's Guide to Medical Imaging.* New York, NY: Oxford University Press, 2011.

Graham, George. *The Disordered Mind: An Introduction to Philosophy of Mind and Mental Illness.* New York, NY: Routledge, 2010.

Marcolin, M. A., and F. Padberg, eds. *Transcranial Brain Stimulation for Treatment of Psychiatric Disorders.* Basel, Switzerland: Karger Publishers, 2007.

Virani, Adil S., et al., eds. *Clinical Handbook of Psychotropic Drugs,* 19th ed. Cambridge, MA: Hogrefe Publishing, 2011.

PERIODICALS

Barrett, Anna M., Elizabeth E. Galletta, and Paul R. Rao. "Transcranial magnetic stimulation (TMS): potential progress for language improvement in aphasia." *Topics in Stroke Rehabilitation* 18, no. 2 (2011): 87.

Bishnoi, Ram, et al. "Utility of repetitive transcranial magnetic stimulation as an augmenting treatment method in treatment-resistant depression." *Indian Journal of Psychiatry* 53, no. 2 (2011): 145.

Dannon, Pinhas, et al. "Deep transcranial magnetic stimulation for the treatment of auditory hallucinations: a preliminary open-label study." *Annals of General Psychiatry* 10 (2011): 3.

ORGANIZATIONS

American College of Physicians, 190 N. Independence Mall West, Philadelphia, PA, 19106-1572, (215) 351-2600, (800) 523-1546, http://www.acponline.org.

American Medical Association, 515 N. State Street, Chicago, IL, 60610, (312) 464-5000, http://www.ama-assn.org.

American Psychiatric Association, 1000 Wilson Boulevard, Suite 1825, Arlington, VA, 22209, (703) 907-7300, apa@psych.org, http://www.psych.org.

Mental Health America (NMHA), 2000 N. Beauregard Street, 6th Floor, Alexandria, VA, 22311, (703) 684-7722, (800) 969-6642, Fax: (703) 684-5968, http://www1.nmha.org.

National Alliance on Mental Illness (NAMI), Colonial Place Three, 2107 Wilson Blvd., Suite 300, Arlington, VA, 22201, (703) 524-7600, (800) 950-NAMI (6264) Fax: (703) 524-9094, http://www.nami.org/Hometemplate.cfm.

National Institutes of Health (NIH), 9000 Rockville Pike, Bethesda, MD, 20892, (301) 496-4000, http://www.nih.gov/index.html.

National Institute of Mental Health (NIMH), 6001 Executive Boulevard, Room 8184, MSC 9663, Bethesda, MD, 20892, (301) 443-4513, (866) 615-6464, Fax: (301) 443-4279, nimhinfo@nih.gov, http://www.nimh.nih.gov/index.shtml.

U.S. Food and Drug Administration (FDA), 10903 New Hampshire Ave., Silver Spring, MD, 20993, (888) 463-6332, http://www.fda.gov.

U.S. National Library of Medicine, 8600 Rockville Pike, Bethesda, MD, 20894, http://www.nlm.nih.gov/medlineplus/medlineplus.html.

Ruth A. Wienclaw, PhD
Laura Jean Cataldo, RN, EdD

Transient tic disorder *see* **Tic disorders**

Transsexualism *see* **Gender identity disorder**

Transvestic fetishism

Definition

Transvestic **fetishism**, or transvestic disorder, is characterized by the desire to dress in clothing traditionally attributed to the opposite sex. It is classified by the mental health professional's handbook, the ***Diagnostic and Statistical Manual of Mental Disorders*** (*DSM*), as a paraphilia. The **paraphilias** are a group of mental disorders characterized by **obsession** with unusual sexual practices or with sexual activity involving nonconsenting or inappropriate partners (such as children or animals). Paraphilias are not inherently causes for psychiatric diagnoses, but when the paraphilia causes distress, harm, or otherwise impairs everyday functioning for the person or others, it is considered a disorder. The essential feature of transvestic fetishism is recurrent intense sexual urges and sexually arousing fantasies involving dressing in clothing

A transvestite male applies makeup. (© *Custom Medical Stock Photo, Inc. Reproduced by permission.*)

associated with members of the opposite sex. A **diagnosis** of transvestic fetishism is made only if an individual has acted on these urges and is markedly distressed by them. In other systems of psychiatric classification, transvestic fetishism is considered a sexual deviation.

Demographics

Except for **sexual masochism**, in which the gender ratio is estimated to be 20 males for each female, paraphilias such as transvestic fetishism are practically never diagnosed in females, although a few cases have been reported. This lopsided gender ratio may be partly due to the fact that contemporary Western societies allow women to dress in a wide range of clothing styles influenced by menswear, whereas the reverse is not the case. While it is not at all unusual to see women wearing jeans, tailored trousers, Western-style boots, or even tuxedos in some circumstances, men wearing dresses or high-heeled shoes look distinctly out of place. Virtually no information is available on family patterns of the disorder.

Description

A person with a transvestic fetish derives sexual gratification from dressing in clothing appropriate for a member of the opposite sex. The participation in transvestism usually is gradual. Over time, a person with a transvestic fetish assumes the role and appearance of a member of the opposite gender and may be difficult to distinguish from members of the opposite sex. A so-called mature transvestic fetish involves adopting all of the mannerisms, clothing, materials and other items associated with persons of the opposite sex. It is important to note that this activity is closely associated with achieving sexual gratification rather than a desire to actually be of the opposite gender (gender dysphoria).

Though transvestic fetishism primarily occurs in males, proposed changes for the fifth edition of the *DSM* (*DSM-5*) account for different types of transvestic disorder, including if the person is sexually aroused only by the clothing (fetishism), by the thought of being a female if a male (autogynephilia), or by the thought of being a male if a female (autoandrophilia).

Causes and symptoms

Causes

The basis for a transvestic fetish is obtaining sexual gratification by dressing in clothing appropriate for the opposite sex. The cause may begin as adolescent curiosity. A person with a transvestic fetish may not be aware of its roots. Transvestic fetishism sometimes begins when a young boy dresses up in the clothes of an older sister or his

KEY TERMS

Cognitive-behavioral therapy—A type of psychotherapy in which people learn to recognize and change negative and self-defeating patterns of thinking and behavior.

Gender dysphoria—A disorder in which an individual experiences prolonged, significant distress or dissatisfaction with his or her biologic gender.

Orgasmic reorientation—A form of behavioral therapy that attempts to help people learn to respond sexually to culturally appropriate stimuli.

Paraphilias—A group of mental disorders characterized by obsession with unusual sexual practices or with sexual activity involving nonconsenting or inappropriate partners.

mother. The activity is continued because it is enjoyable, but the reasons for the enjoyment remain unconscious. In some cases, a boy's mother may initiate the cross-dressing by dressing him as if he were a girl.

A transvestic fetish is not an indication of a person's sexual orientation. According to the revised fourth edition of the *DSM* (*DSM-IV-TR*), most men who practice cross-dressing are basically heterosexual in their orientation, though some do have occasional sexual encounters with other men.

Symptoms

Early symptoms of transvestic fetishism involve touching or wearing items of clothing that are considered typically feminine. This initial interest may progress to wearing undergarments or other items that can be hidden from the view of others while providing arousal to the wearer. Over time, the extent of dressing in women's clothing expands, sometimes to the point of dressing as a woman on a regular basis. A developed transvestic fetish often involves feminine hair styling and the use of women's cosmetics and accessories.

In some individuals diagnosed with transvestic fetishism, the motivation for cross-dressing may change over time from a search for sexual excitement to simple relief from **stress**, **depression**, or anxiety.

In some cases, individuals with a transvestic fetish discover that they are unhappy with their biological sex, a condition known as gender dysphoria. They may elect to have hormonal and surgical procedures to change their bodies. Some may choose to have gender reassignment surgery. The incidence of gender dysphoria and

subsequent gender reassignment among persons diagnosed with transvestic fetishism is not known.

Diagnosis

Individuals with transvestic fetishism may or may not seek **psychotherapy** on their own account. In some instances, the person has agreed to consult a **psychiatrist** because his wife or girlfriend is distressed by the cross-dressing. The actual diagnosis of transvestic fetishism is most commonly made by taking a history or by direct observation. The diagnosis is made only if the individual has been markedly distressed by an inability to dress in such a manner or if the disorder is interfering with his education, occupation, or social life. The DSM diagnostic criteria also requires the behavior to occur for at least six months; dressing in women's clothing for such occasions as Halloween or a costume party is not sufficient for a diagnosis of transvestic fetishism.

Treatment

In the earliest period of behavior therapy, transvestic fetishes were narrowly viewed as inappropriate behavior that was confined to a limited range of situations. Sometimes they were treated with **aversion therapy**, usually with electric shocks. This approach was largely unsuccessful. Individuals with fetishes also have been treated by using a form of behavioral therapy known as orgasmic reorientation, which attempts to help people learn to respond sexually to culturally appropriate stimuli. This treatment also has had limited success.

Most people who have a transvestic fetish never seek treatment from professionals. Most are capable of achieving sexual gratification in culturally appropriate situations. Their preoccupation with cross-dressing is viewed as essentially harmless to others, since transvestism is not associated with criminal activities. American society has developed more tolerance for persons with a transvestic fetish, thus further reducing the demand for professional treatment.

Prognosis

The prognosis for treatment of transvestic fetishism is poor, as most persons with this disorder do not desire to change. Most cases in which treatment was demanded by a spouse as a condition of continuing in a marriage have not been successful. The prognosis for personal adjustment is good, however, as a person with a transvestic fetish and his related activities do not usually disturb others.

Prevention

The classification of transvestic fetishism as a mental disorder is highly controversial, as is the need for treatment and prevention. To address these concerns, revisions for the *DSM-5* acknowledge that transvestic behavior should only be considered a disorder if it causes a person significant distress; the behavior in itself is not considered a disorder.

In cases where transvestic fetishism may arise out of parental pressures, such as may be the case when parents wish they had a child of the opposite gender and treat their child as such, experts agree that providing gender-appropriate guidance in culturally appropriate situations will prevent the formation of a transvestic fetish. The origin of some cases of transvestism may be a random association between clothing inappropriate for a person's gender and sexual gratification. There is no reliable way to predict the formation of such associations. Supervision during childhood and adolescence, combined with acceptance of a child's biological sex, may be the best deterrent that parents can provide.

Resources

BOOKS

Clinton, Tim, and Laaser, Mark. *The Quick-Reference Guide to Sexuality and Relationship Counseling*. Grand Rapids, MI: Baker Books, 2010.

Laws, D. Richard, and O'Donohue, William T., eds. *Sexual Deviance: Theory, Assessment, and Treatment*. 2nd ed. New York, Guilford Press, 2008.

Rowland, David, and Luca Incrocci. *Handbook of Sexual and Gender Identity Disorders*. Hoboken, NJ: John Wiley & Sons, 2008.

PERIODICALS

Blanchard, Ray. "The DSM Diagnostic Criteria for Transvestic Fetishism." *Archives of Sexual Behavior*, 39, no. 2 (April 2010): 363–372.

Wright, Susan. "Depathologizing Consensual Sexual Sadism, Sexual Masochism, Transvestic Fetishism, and Fetishism." *Archives of Sexual Behavior*, 36, no. 6 (December 2010): 1229–1230.

ORGANIZATIONS

American Psychiatric Association, 1000 Wilson Blvd., Suite 1825, Arlington, VA, 22209-3901, (703) 907-7300, apa@psych.org, http://www.psych.org.

American Psychological Association, 750 1st Street NE, Washington, DC, 20002-4242, (202) 336-5500; TDD/TTY: (202) 336-6123, (800) 374-2721, http://www.apa.org.

Gay, Lesbian, Bisexual, and Transgender National Help Center, 2261 Market Street, PMB #296, San Francisco, CA, 94114, (415) 355-0003, Fax: (415) 552-5498, info@GLBTNationalHelpCenter.org, http://www.glbtnationalhelpcenter.org.

L. Fleming Fallon, Jr., MD
Tish Davidson, AM

Tranxene *see* **Clorazepate**

Tranylcypromine

Definition

Tranylcypromine is classified as a monoamine oxidase inhibitor (MAOI). It is used to treat serious **depression**. In the United States, tranylcypromine is sold under the brand name Parnate and under its generic name.

Purpose

Tranylcypromine is used primarily to treat depression that does not respond to other types of drug therapy. It is also used occasionally to treat **panic disorder**, **agoraphobia**, and **bulimia nervosa**, though these uses are not approved by the U.S. Food and Drug Administration (FDA).

Description

Tranylcypromine is a member of a class of drugs called **monoamine oxidase inhibitors**. Monoamine oxidase, or MAO, is an enzyme found throughout the body. In the **brain**, MAO breaks down norepinephrine and **serotonin**, two naturally occurring chemicals that are important for maintaining mental well-being and preventing depression. Monoamine oxidase inhibitors such as tranylcypromine reduce the activity of MAO, resulting in more norepinephrine and serotonin left in the brain, which helps alleviate depression.

Tranylcypromine is especially effective for treating complicated types of depression that have not responded to more traditional **antidepressants**. However, tranylcypromine affects the MAO enzyme in many other areas of the body, not just the brain, which results in a large number of serious side effects and drug interactions.

Recommended dosage

The typical starting dosage of tranylcypromine in adults is 10 mg taken twice per day. This dosage is sometimes increased to 30 mg per day after a two-week period. The maximum recommended amount is 60 mg per day. Those over age 60 are usually started on a dose of 2.5 mg per day. After this, their doctors will make an individualized decision about increasing the dosage. Older adults typically take smaller doses and do not take more than 45 mg per day. A doctor must make an individual determination of whether to give tranylcypromine to youths under the age of 18 years, because guidelines for this age group have not been developed.

The benefits of this drug may not become apparent for several weeks. Patients should be aware of this and

KEY TERMS

Depression—A mental state characterized by feelings of sadness, despair, and discouragement.

Norepinephrine—A chemical messenger in the brain thought to play a role in mood regulation.

Schizophrenia—A major mental illness marked by psychotic symptoms, including hallucinations, delusions, and severe disruptions in thinking.

Seizure—A convulsion, or uncontrolled discharge of nerve cells that may spread to other cells throughout the brain.

Serotonin—A chemical messenger in the brain thought to play a role in mood regulation.

continue taking the drug as directed, even if they do not see an immediate improvement.

Precautions

People taking tranylcypromine should not eat foods rich in tyramine. These foods include yeast or meat extracts, fermented sausage, overripe fruit, sauerkraut, cheese, and fava beans. Alcohol should not be consumed, and the same holds true for alcohol-free beer and wine. Large amounts of caffeine-containing food and beverages, such as chocolate, tea, coffee, and cola should be avoided. The treating doctor needs to approve the use of any drug, including prescription, over-the-counter drugs, and herbal treatments, that patients take while taking tranylcypromine.

Tranylcypromine should be used with great caution in pregnant and nursing women only after the risks and benefits of treatment have been assessed. The drug may not be appropriate for people with a history of **seizures**, children under age 18 years, people at risk for **suicide**, those with severe depression, or persons with a history of **schizophrenia**. The drug should also be used with caution in patients with glaucoma or diabetes mellitus. People with these conditions should discuss the risks and benefits of this drug with their physicians, and a decision to treat should be made on an individual basis. People with a history of high blood pressure, congestive heart failure, severe liver disease, severe kidney disease, severe heart disease, and blood vessel problems in the brain should not take tranylcypromine.

Children and adults up to age 24 are at an increased risk for developing suicidal thoughts and actions when taking antidepressant drugs, including tranylcypromine. Patients of any age taking an antidepressant medication should be monitored for signs of worsening depression or changes in behavior.

Tranylcypromine should not be stopped suddenly. Instead, the dose should be gradually reduced, then discontinued.

Side effects

Tranylcypromine should be stopped if symptoms of unusually high blood pressure develop. These symptoms include severe chest pain, severe headache, nausea, vomiting, stiff or sore neck, enlarged pupils, and significant changes in heart rate. If these symptoms develop, it should be considered an emergency. Patients should get medical help immediately. Generally, these serious side effects are rare.

More common but less serious side effects include light-headedness or dizziness when arising from a sitting position. These symptoms need to be reported to a doctor but are not considered an emergency. Less common symptoms that should be reported include pounding heartbeat, swelling of the lower extremities, nervousness, and diarrhea. Rare but reportable symptoms include fever, skin rash, dark urine, slurred speech, yellowing of the eyes or skin, and staggering when walking. Common but not serious side effects include decreased sexual performance, increased appetite, muscle twitching, trembling, blurred vision, and reduced urine output.

Overdose symptoms include confusion, seizures, severe dizziness, hallucinations, severe headache, severe drowsiness, significant changes in blood pressure, difficulty in sleeping, breathing difficulties, and increased irritability.

Interactions

Tranylcypromine interacts with a long list of drugs. Some of these interactions can cause death. Patients must make sure every healthcare professional who takes care of them (for example, doctors, dentists, podiatrists, optometrists, pharmacists, nurses) knows that they take tranylcypromine, as well as all of the other prescription or nonprescription drugs and herbal remedies that they take.

The combination of tranylcypromine with any type of stimulant can increase the risk of developing serious increases in blood pressure. Tranylcypromine when taken with antidiabetic drugs can reduce blood sugar levels to far below normal. The combination of tranylcypromine with **barbiturates** can prolong the effects of the barbiturate drug.

Tranylcypromine should never be combined with other antidepressant drugs, especially the **selective serotonin reuptake inhibitors (SSRIs)**, because of potentially severe or fatal reactions, including increased risk of dangerously high blood pressure. Patients taking tranylcypromine should stop the drug, then wait at least 14 days before starting any other antidepressant. The

QUESTIONS TO ASK YOUR DOCTOR

- What kind of changes can I expect to see or feel with this medication?
- Does it matter what time of day I take this medication?
- Should I take this medication with or without food?
- What are the side effects associated with this medication?
- Will this medication interact or interfere with other medications I am currently taking?
- What symptoms or adverse effects are important enough that I should seek immediate treatment?

same holds true when discontinuing another antidepressant and starting tranylcypromine.

Dangerously high blood pressure has resulted from the combination of **MAOIs** and antianxiety (anxiolytic) drugs such as **buspirone** (BuSpar). Patients taking tranylcypromine should stop the medication and wait at least ten days before starting buspirone.

Alcohol combined with tranylcypromine can lead to significantly increased blood pressure. Tranylcypromine combined with the blood pressure drug guanethidine (Ismelin) can reduce the beneficial effects of the guanethidine. When tranylcypromine is combined with levodopa (Dopar, Larodopa), a drug used to treat Parkinson's disease, severely increased blood pressure can develop. Tranylcypromine combined with lithium can cause fever. Meperidine (Demerol), when combined with tranylcypromine, can cause fever, seizures, increased blood pressure, and agitation. Tranylcypromine combined with norepinephrine can cause increased response to norepinephrine. Tranylcypromine combined with reserpine (Serpalan, Serpasil) can produce greatly increased blood pressure. When tranylcypromine is combined with the migraine drug sumatriptan (Imitrex), significantly increased concentrations of the latter drug develop that can produce potentially toxic effects.

Resources

BOOKS

Albers, Lawrence J., Rhoda K. Hahn, and Christopher Reist. *Handbook of Psychiatric Drugs.* Laguna Hills, CA: Current Clinical Strategies Publishing, 2010.

American Society of Health-System Pharmacists. *AHFS Drug Information 2011.* Bethesda, MD: American Society of Health-System Pharmacists, 2011.

Graham, George. *The Disordered Mind: An Introduction to Philosophy of Mind and Mental Illness.* New York: Routledge, 2010.

Holland, Leland Norman, and Michael Patrick Adams. *Core Concepts in Pharmacology.* 3rd ed. New York: Prentice Hall, 2011.

North, Carol, and Sean Yutzy. *Goodwin and Guze's Psychiatric Diagnosis.* New York: Oxford University Press, 2010.

Preston, John D., John H. O'Neal, and Mary C. Talaga. *Handbook of Clinical Psychopharmacology for Therapists.* 6th ed. Oakland, CA: New Harbinger Publications, 2011.

PERIODICALS

Frieling, Helge, and Stefan Bleich. "Tranylcypromine: New Perspectives on an 'Old' Drug." *European Archives of Psychiatry and Clinical Neuroscience* 256, no. 5 (Aug. 2006): 268–73.

McGrath, Patrick J., et al. "Tranylcypromine Versus Venlafaxine Plus Mirtazapine Following Three Failed Antidepressant Medication Trials for Depression: A STAR*D Report." *American Journal of Psychiatry* 163, no. 9 (Sept. 2006): 1531–41.

Thase, Michael E. "Bipolar Depression: Issues in Diagnosis and Treatment." *Harvard Review of Psychiatry* 13, no. 5 (Sept.–Oct. 2005): 257–71.

Tulen, Joke H. M., et al. "Sustained Effects of Phenelzine and Tranylcypromine on Orthostatic Challenge in Antidepressant-Refractory Depression." *Journal of Clinical Psychopharmacology* 26, no. 5 (Oct. 2006): 542–44.

Valenstein, Marcia. "Keeping Our Eyes on STAR*D." *American Journal of Psychiatry* 163, no. 9 (Sept. 2006): 1484–86.

ORGANIZATIONS

American Psychiatric Association, 1000 Wilson Boulevard, Suite 1825, Arlington, VA, 22209, (703) 907-7300, apa@psych.org, http://www.psych.org.

Mental Health America, 2000 N. Beauregard Street, 6th Floor, Alexandria, VA, 22311, (703) 684-7722, (800) 969-6642, Fax: (703) 684-5968, http://www1.nmha.org.

National Alliance on Mental Illness (NAMI), Colonial Place Three, 2107 Wilson Blvd., Suite 300, Arlington, VA, 22201, (703) 524-7600, (800) 950-NAMI (6264), Fax: (703) 524-9094, http://www.nami.org/Hometemplate.cfm.

National Institute of Mental Health (NIMH), 6001 Executive Boulevard, Room 8184, MSC 9663, Bethesda, MD, 20892, (301) 443-4513, (866) 615-6464, Fax: (301) 443-4279, nimhinfo@nih.gov, http://www.nimh.nih.gov/index.shtml.

U.S. Food and Drug Administration, 10903 New Hampshire Ave., Silver Spring, MD, 20993-0002, (888) INFO-FDA (463-6332), http://www.fda.gov.

Mark Mitchell, MD
Ruth A. Wienclaw, Ph.D.
Laura Jean Cataldo, RN, Ed.D.

Trauma

Definition

The English word *trauma* (plural, *traumata*) is simply the Greek word for "wound" written in the letters of the Roman rather than the Greek alphabet. It is used to refer to both physical and psychological injuries. In medicine, trauma is a physical wound or injury, often sudden, resulting from a violent blow or accident. In psychiatry, the term refers to damage to the mind and emotions resulting from a single event or series of experiences that overwhelm a person's ability to cope or to integrate the memories and feelings associated with the traumatic event(s).

Demographics

Physical trauma is the sixth-leading cause of death worldwide and accounts for 10% of all human deaths. In the United States, traumatic injury is the leading cause of death for persons between the ages of 1 and 44, with about 180,000 trauma deaths each year. About two-thirds of these deaths are accidental.

Psychological traumata vary widely in frequency and severity in the general population. It is estimated that between 50% and 90% of people in North America will undergo a traumatic experience at some point in life, but only 7%–8% will develop **post-traumatic stress disorder** (PTSD) or a complex post-traumatic syndrome. The lifetime prevalence of rape and sexual assault is estimated at 15%–20% for women and 3%–5% for men, although many researchers maintain that rapes for both sexes are under-reported. With regard to child **sexual abuse**, between 15% and 25% of women in North America and 5% to 15% of men report being sexually abused in childhood. In terms of combat-related trauma, about a quarter of the men and women deployed to Iraq and Afghanistan and during the Gulf War met or still meet the criteria for **acute stress disorder** (ASD) or PTSD.

Mass traumata, such as major industrial explosions, severe natural disasters, the loss of a large airplane or ship, or large-scale terrorist attacks, are rare but may have a disproportionate impact on survivors and first responders. Mass traumata are also more likely to lead to survivor guilt, a condition in which a person feels that they did something wrong or should feel guilty about surviving a disaster when others did not.

Description

Psychological or psychiatric trauma has two dimensions, objective and subjective. It may or may not be associated with physical trauma; in general, physical traumata that cause permanent damage to the senses or other body functions, or that result in disfigurement (particularly to the face), are more likely to have psychological sequelae than those that heal completely. The objective aspect of psychological trauma is its external description or definition, such as "rape," "airplane crash," or "earthquake." The subjective

---

Common symptoms following exposure to trauma

Behavioral	Cognitive/mental	Emotional	Physical
Antisocial acts	Change in alertness	Agitation	Chills
Change in activity	Confusion	Anxiety	Difficulty breathing
Change in appetite	Hypervigilance	Apprehension	Dizziness
Change in communication	Increased or decreased awareness of surroundings	Denial	Elevated blood pressure
Change in sexual functioning	Intrusive images	Depression	Fainting
Change in speech pattern	Memory problems	Emotional shock	Fatigue
Emotional outbursts	Nightmares	Fear	Grinding teeth
Inability to rest	Placing blame on others	Feeling overwhelmed	Headaches
Increased alcohol consumption	Poor abstract thinking	Grief	Muscle tremors
Intensified startle reflex	Poor attention	Guilt	Nausea
Pacing	Poor concentration	Inappropriate emotional response	Pain
Suspiciousness	Poor decision making	Irritability	Profuse sweating
Social withdrawal	Poor problem solving	Loss of emotional control	Rapid heart rate
			Twitches
			Weakness

SOURCE: Department of Veterans Affairs and Department of Defense, Management of Post-Traumatic Stress Working Group, *VA/DoD Clinical Practice Guideline for Management of Post-Traumatic Stress*, 2010.

Guidelines provided by the Department of Veterans Affairs and available online at http://www.healthquality.va.gov/PTSD-FULL-2010c.pdf. *(Table by PreMediaGlobal. © 2012 Cengage Learning.)*

dimension is the survivor's experience of being overwhelmed and rendered helpless by the event or incident. It is the individual's subjective experience that defines the event as traumatic for that person.

Causes and symptoms

Different people tend to respond differently to the same traumatic event; for example, some survivors may develop PTSD, some may have a time-limited **stress** reaction, and others may appear to be unaffected. The type of traumatic event or incident, however, may have some effect on the victims' response:

- Intentional human-caused traumata (e.g., war, criminal assault, rape, or torture) can be more distressing than technological accidents (e.g., transportation disasters, oil spills, plant explosions) or natural disasters (e.g., floods, hurricanes, tornadoes, blizzards, earthquakes, or volcanic eruptions).

- Repeated stressors, such as physical or sexual abuse, domestic violence, and military combat, are more likely to lead to PTSD than single episodes of trauma, as are stressors of long duration (e.g., kidnapping, some natural disasters, or warfare). The National Cancer Institute (NCI) maintains that the duration of the illness and its treatment helps to explain the emergence of PTSD in cancer patients.

- Multifaceted traumata may be a greater risk factor for experiencing a trauma-related disorder than simple traumata. For example, a person caught in a tornado may witness the death of, or injury to, loved ones in addition to suffering the loss of their home and personal possessions, and possibly their job, as well as physical injury to their own body.

- Traumata experienced in childhood are more likely to have long-term effects than those experienced in adult life.

- Unpredictable traumata (e.g., most industrial accidents, airplane and railroad crashes, or terrorist attacks) are more shocking than those that could be at least partly predicted or foreseen (e.g., hurricanes, tornadoes, or some epidemics) and thus may produce a more severe traumatic response.

- Traumata inflicted by a parent, caregiver, or other trusted adult may have a more serious effect on the victim than would similar actions inflicted by a stranger.

Post-traumatic stress disorder and acute stress disorder

PTSD and ASD are two of the more common disorders associated with trauma. Although the conditions are distinct, they do share some similar symptoms, including:

- flashbacks or recurring nightmares of the traumatic event

- avoidance of persons, places, or things that might spark a memory of the event

- a constant state of hyperarousal, a condition characterized by irritability, anxiety, insomnia, lack of concentration, and extreme startle response

- detachment from people or surroundings

Complex trauma

Complex trauma is a term with two different meanings, depending on whether it is applied to children or adults. According to the National Child Traumatic Stress Network, the term refers to a child's "exposure to multiple or prolonged traumatic events and the impact of this exposure on their development." Complex trauma in children may be either sequential or simultaneous and may include psychological maltreatment, **neglect**, physical and sexual abuse, and domestic violence. This type of trauma is chronic, begins in early childhood, and occurs within the primary caregiving system. It is estimated that about 30% of children nationwide in North America are exposed to complex trauma, and as many as 50% of children in some distressed communities; however, only about 12% of these children receive treatment. Rates of **self-mutilation** and nonsuicidal self-injury are as high as 62% among these children. Developmental trauma disorder (DTD) appears to be increasingly used as a synonym for complex trauma in children.

Complex trauma is also sometimes used to describe a condition in adults more accurately referred to as complex PTSD or C-PTSD. C-PTSD is a concept that Judith Herman developed in the 1997 edition of her book *Trauma and Recovery*. Herman maintained that the *DSM-IV* criteria for PTSD did not adequately account for the symptoms of survivors of chronic repetitive trauma, such as domestic violence, hostage situations, other forms of captivity, torture, or other abusive situations from which escape is difficult. Herman identified psychological fragmentation; the loss of a sense of safety, trust, and self-worth; a tendency to be revictimized; and insecure or disorganized forms of attachment to others as the symptoms that most clearly differentiate C-PTSD from PTSD. She also described three phases in the recovery of adults with C-PTSD: re-establishing a sense of safety, remembering and mourning what was lost in the traumatic experience, and reconnecting with the survivor's community and the larger society. Although some medical journals have published papers on C-PTSD, the disorder was not recognized by *DSM-IV*, although it is possible that *DSM-5* could include it under the category of "Other specified trauma- or stressor-related disorder."

Rape trauma syndrome

Rape trauma syndrome (RTS) is a term first coined by Ann Burgess and Lynda Holmstrom in 1974 to describe a complex form of psychological trauma to a rape victim (male or female) reflected in disruptions of the survivor's emotional, cognitive, physical, and interpersonal behaviors. RTS is a syndrome with two phases, an acute phase that lasts from several days to several weeks after the assault, and a longer "reorganization phase." Survivors react in different ways during the acute phase. Some survivors are expressive, meaning that they show their emotions by crying, yelling, or being openly angry. Others are controlled; they may be completely silent about the rape and go about their daily routines as if nothing has happened. Neither type of response is considered superior to the other.

The second phase of RTS is the reorganization phase, in which the survivor tries to recover the sense of safety and ability to trust others that he or she had before the rape. The survivor must cope with intense feelings of guilt and shame as well as fear and anxiety. In some cases, the survivor may feel disconnected or dissociated from her or his body. Male survivors are more likely than females to have questions about their sexual identity and orientation; they are also more likely to postpone or avoid treatment. One study of 100 male rape survivors found that the average time interval between the assault and seeking therapy was 16 years.

In addition to the emotional symptoms of RTS, many survivors also experience a variety of physical symptoms ranging from tension headaches and generalized muscle pain to specific symptoms in the parts of the body that were penetrated during the assault. Survivors of oral rape may have a variety of mouth and throat complaints, nausea and vomiting, and bulimia or anorexia, while survivors of vaginal or anal rape may suffer from abdominal cramping, dysmenorrhea, constipation, or diarrhea.

Indirect trauma

Indirect trauma, also called vicarious trauma or empathic strain, is a condition that may develop in therapists and others who work with trauma survivors over long periods of time. The symptoms of indirect trauma are similar to those of survivors; the care provider may experience nightmares, intrusive thoughts, intense anxiety, avoidance behaviors, **sleep disorders**, difficulty regulating emotions, and disruptions in personal or professional relationships. Indirect trauma may also involve a form of survivor guilt, such as when first responders feel that they are to blame for not having rescued everyone from a disaster, or when a therapist feels guilty about not being able to relieve a patient's suffering quickly.

Diagnosis

The subjective aspect of psychological trauma complicates assessment and evaluation of trauma survivors. A person who thinks that he or she may have PTSD or another trauma-related disorder should consult a **psychiatrist** or other health care provider with special training in the assessment of trauma survivors. In addition, the person should ask whether the doctor specializes in the type of trauma that the survivor underwent, and whether the doctor is also experienced in assessing members of the survivor's age group. There are different tests or question sets that can be used to evaluate adult and child survivors for symptoms of a disorder, and it requires specialized training to decide which test to administer in a given case and then interpret the results.

DSM-IV and DSM-5

The fourth edition of the ***Diagnostic and Statistical Manual of Mental Disorders***, first published in 1994 and revised in 2000, defined two trauma-related disorders—PTSD and ASD—under the larger category of anxiety disorders. A third disorder associated with trauma, adjustment disorder, was placed in a separate category of its own. The *DSM-5*, slated for publication in 2013, has revised this classification, introducing a new category, titled Trauma- and Stressor-Related Disorders, which includes the three trauma-related disorders defined by *DSM-IV* plus five new diagnostic categories, three of which are restricted to children.

The eight disorders listed under the proposed *DSM-5* category are as follows:

• Reactive attachment disorder of infancy or early childhood. This disorder was moved from the *DSM-IV* category of "Disorders Usually First Diagnosed in Infancy, Childhood, or Adolescence" to the new diagnostic category.

• Disinhibited social engagement disorder. Previously defined as a subtype of reactive attachment disorder in *DSM-IV*, the diagnosis describes children who lack the normal ability to select appropriate attachment figures and demonstrate excessive familiarity with, or closeness to, relative strangers.

- Post-traumatic stress disorder in preschool children. This disorder is essentially a form of PTSD as found in children below the age of six years. Some of the criteria are similar to those for developmental trauma disorder, another proposed new diagnostic category.

- Acute stress disorder (ASD). The major revisions proposed for *DSM-5* are the division of symptoms into four categories (intrusive, dissociative, avoidance, and arousal); the addition of "learning that the [traumatic] event(s) occurred to a close relative or close friend" as well as witnessing or experiencing the event oneself; and the specifier that "[the criterion of exposure] does not apply to exposure through electronic media, television, movies or pictures, unless this exposure is work-related."

- Post-traumatic stress disorder (PTSD). As with ASD, proposed changes include the addition of "learning that the [traumatic] event(s) occurred to a close relative or close friend" as well as witnessing or experiencing the event oneself; and the specifier that "[the criterion of exposure] does not apply to exposure through electronic media, television, movies or pictures, unless this exposure is work-related."

- Adjustment disorders. The major difference between the *DSM-IV* definition of adjustment disorder and the proposed changes for *DSM-5* is the addition of a distinct subtype called *bereavement-related disorder*.

- Other specified trauma- or stressor-related disorder.

- Unspecified trauma- or stressor-related disorder.

Developmental trauma disorder

The *DSM-5* working group lists developmental trauma disorder (DTD) among the "Conditions Proposed by Outside Sources." The new diagnostic category has been discussed among experts in **child abuse** since the 1980s, on the grounds that the criteria for PTSD in adults fail to detect the symptoms of recurrent traumata in childhood, and that as a result, affected children do not receive proper treatment. Only 5%–10% of children exposed to interpersonal abuse, domestic violence, and other recurrent dangers meet criteria for PTSD; however, over 50% of such children have problems with affect regulation, attention and concentration, negative self-image, impulse control, aggression, and risk-taking. As a result, the children are usually diagnosed as having one or more of a set of unrelated conditions, including **bipolar disorder**, **attention deficit hyperactivity disorder (ADHD)**, **conduct disorder**, phobic anxiety, reactive attachment disorder, and separation anxiety, and they are usually treated with medications only, rather

than **psychotherapy**. The diagnostic category of "developmental trauma disorder" would allow clinicians to effectively recognize and treat the core symptoms in these children—impaired capacity for emotional and behavioral regulation, and attachment-related difficulties.

A tentative set of criteria for the disorder was drawn up by Bessel van der Kolk in 2005 and revised by the National Child Traumatic Stress Network (NCTSN) in 2009. There are seven criteria in the present proposal:

- A. Exposure. The child or adolescent has experienced or witnessed multiple or prolonged adverse events over a period of at least one year beginning in childhood or early adolescence, including direct experience or witnessing of repeated and severe episodes of interpersonal violence and disruption of protective caregiving as the result of repeated changes in primary caregiver, repeated separation from the primary caregiver, or exposure to severe and persistent emotional abuse.

- B. Affective and emotional dysregulation. The child or adolescent exhibits at least two of the following: inability to recover from states of fear, shame, or anger, including prolonged tantrums or immobility; problems with such bodily functions as eating, sleeping, and elimination; diminished awareness of emotions, sensations, or bodily states; and inability to vocalize emotions or sensations.

- C. Attentional and behavioral dysregulation. The child experiences at least three of the following: inability to focus attention appropriately; preoccupation with threats or, conversely, a failure to perceive them; active thrill-seeking or risk-taking; lack of goal-directed behavior; and repeated or habitual acts of self-harm.

- D. Self- and relational dysregulation. The child demonstrates at least three of the following: impaired sense of identity; preoccupation with caregiver's safety; extreme distrust of, or aggressive action toward, others; inappropriate attempts to seek intimacy with adults or peers, including, but not limited to, sexual or physical contact; excessive reliance on others for safety or reassurance; inability to show empathy for others in pain or, conversely, showing excessive distress.

- E. Post-traumatic symptoms. The child shows at least one symptom in two of the three symptom clusters of adult PTSD (criteria B, C, and D).

- F. Duration. The symptoms in criteria B, C, D, and E must be present for at least six months.

- G. Functional impairment. The child suffers clinically significant distress or impaired function in at least two of six areas: academic, family, peer group, legal system, physical health, and vocational preparation or planning.

Treatment

Treatment for trauma-related disorders usually involves a combination of approaches rather than a single form of treatment. In addition, a person in an ongoing traumatic situation, such as a violent family situation or abusive relationship, needs to be removed from the traumatic environment prior to therapy in order for treatment to be effective.

Traditional

There are several different forms of psychotherapy that are used in the treatment of trauma survivors. According to the **National Institute of Mental Health** (NIMH), psychotherapy for adults with PTSD and acute stress disorder usually lasts about 6–12 weeks but may take longer. Therapies include:

- Cognitive-behavioral therapy (CBT). CBT may include exposure therapy, in which the survivor is exposed in a safe place to situations or images that they are avoiding, as reminders of the trauma; cognitive restructuring (sometimes called "cognitive processing" therapy when used to treat survivors of PTSD), in which the survivor learns to reframe memories of the traumatic event, particularly those that lead to feelings of guilt or shame; and stress inoculation training, in which the survivor learns to identify the cues that trigger traumatic memories and to cope with them by using relaxation and deep-breathing techniques.

- Psychodynamic psychotherapy. This approach is helpful to survivors with unresolved issues from childhood or adolescence that resurfaced as a result of the traumatic experience. It may be combined with CBT.

- Group therapy and family therapy. These approaches are often recommended for survivors of specific traumata (e.g., rape, combat, workplace violence, or accidents) or mass disasters.

- Supportive therapy. *Supportive therapy* refers to any form of treatment intended to relieve the patient's symptoms rather than to bring about changes in the patient's behaviors or basic character structure.

There were 120 **clinical trials** underway as of mid-2011 for various medications and psychotherapy in the treatment of psychological trauma, and an additional eight studies of medications (topiramate and **risperidone**) or cognitive processing therapy for women with rape trauma syndrome.

Therapists and other healthcare providers affected by indirect trauma are advised to consult a supervising therapist or another specialist in trauma treatment if self-care—activities such as getting adequate rest; eating a healthful diet; balancing their trauma work with other work; getting support from friends, family, and colleagues; and acknowledging the difficulties of the work—do not help.

Drugs

Medications for trauma- and stressor-related disorders include the **selective serotonin reuptake inhibitors (SSRIs)**; mood stabilizers like valproate (Depakote), **carbamazepine** (Tegretol), and topiramate (Topamax) to treat flashbacks, nightmares, and other symptoms of hyperarousal; and benzodiazepine tranquilizers to treat sleep disorders. The only two **SSRIs** specifically approved by the U.S. Food and Drug Administration (FDA) for the treatment of PTSD are **sertraline** (Zoloft) and **paroxetine** (Paxil). Other SSRIs that may be prescribed include **fluoxetine** (Prozac) and **citalopram** (Celexa). However, it is important for trauma survivors with a coexisting **substance abuse** disorder to be treated for that before being given any psychoactive drugs.

Alternative

One form of complementary therapy that is often recommended to trauma survivors is relaxation training. Sometimes called "anxiety management training," relaxation training includes breathing exercises and similar techniques intended to help the patient prevent hyperventilation and relieve the muscle tension associated with the fight-or-flight reaction of anxiety. **Yoga**, aikido, tai chi, and other forms of movement therapy are also reported to help patients work with the physical as well as the emotional tensions that are associated with trauma-related anxiety.

Other complementary therapies that are reported to relieve the symptoms of PTSD and other trauma-related disorders include massage therapy, **art therapy**, journaling, and **music therapy**. However, there is little research support for these therapies.

Some trauma survivors benefit from spiritual or religious counseling. Because traumatic experiences often affect people's spiritual views and beliefs, counseling with a trusted religious or spiritual advisor may be part of a treatment plan. A growing number of pastoral counselors in the major Christian and Jewish bodies in North America have advanced credentials in trauma therapy. Native Americans are often helped to recover from PTSD by participating in traditional tribal rituals for

KEY TERMS

Affect—In psychology, an observed emotional expression or response.

Cognitive processing therapy—A term that is sometimes used for the cognitive restructuring aspect of cognitive-behavioral therapy as it is applied to treatment for PTSD.

Cue—In psychology, a sensory stimulus or signal that can be extracted or distinguished from surrounding stimuli by a perceiver.

Dissociation—Partial or complete disruption of a person's normal memory and psychological functioning. Dissociative symptoms are commonly experienced by persons with PTSD.

Exposure therapy—An approach to treating trauma survivors that helps them to cope with trauma-related thoughts, feelings, and situations by exposing them to these reminders of the trauma in a safe situation.

Indirect trauma—A term used to refer to symptoms of trauma in therapists, first responders, and others who treat trauma survivors. It is sometimes called *vicarious trauma*.

Polytrauma—The medical term for injury to more than one part of the body or more than one type of injury (such as burn injuries in addition to broken bones).

Post-traumatic stress disorder (PTSD)—A psychological reaction that continues long after a highly stressful event and is characterized by depression, anxiety, flashbacks, and nightmares.

Psychoactive—Referring to any substance that crosses the blood-brain barrier and acts primarily upon the central nervous system, leading to changes in mood, perception, thinking, feeling, or behavior.

Sequela (plural, sequelae)—In medicine, a pathological condition resulting from a disease, injury, or other trauma. For example, PTSD may be a sequela of rape or abuse.

Supportive therapy—An approach to psychotherapy that seeks to encourage the patient or offer emotional support to him or her rather than attempt behavioral changes.

Survivor guilt—A mental condition in which a person feels that he or she did something wrong by surviving a disaster in which others died. It can also affect therapists and first responders who feel that they did not do enough to rescue or help people caught in a disaster.

Syndrome—A group of signs or symptoms that occur together and characterize or define a particular disease or disorder.

cleansing memories of war and other traumatic events. These rituals may include sweat lodges, prayers and chants, or consultation with a shaman or tribal healer.

Treatment of mass trauma

Treatment of survivors of a mass accident or disaster is different from treating survivors of an individual or small-scale attack or event. While most people in mass critical events can be helped by getting to safety, obtaining food and water, getting medical help if injured, contacting loved ones, and getting accurate information about what is being done to help, some survivors do not get better on their own after a mass disaster and may even find their **depression** or PTSD becoming worse with time. One reason for this phenomenon is widespread destruction of the community's infrastructure (e.g., buildings, roads, bridges, railroads, water supply, or airports), often involving loss of jobs, schools, and basic housing as well as difficulty finding health care, purchasing food, or paying bills. In many cases, families may have to move to a different location hundreds of miles away. Hospitals and trauma centers in the affected area may be overwhelmed by the scale of the disaster, meaning that some survivors do not receive the psychological or physical care they need in a timely fashion, especially when doctors and other healthcare providers may be struggling with their own injuries, lack of supplies and transportation, and emotional reactions to the situation.

One approach to psychotherapy following mass trauma that is still considered experimental is the use of Internet- and phone-based therapy to treat survivors who could not be assessed immediately following the disaster.

Prognosis

There is considerable discussion among psychiatrists and other therapists regarding the classification of different types of psychological traumata, particularly in regard to complex forms of traumatization and the specification of the age group affected. There is a growing recognition that trauma affects the development

QUESTIONS TO ASK YOUR DOCTOR

- Will therapy help me cope with my experience?
- Can you recommend a support group for trauma survivors?
- Do you think that medication will help my symptoms?
- Are there any side effects to medications?
- Will I experience any long-term effects as a result of my trauma?
- How can I help my child cope with the aftereffects of trauma?
- How can I tell the difference between a healthy reaction to trauma and an abnormal reaction to trauma?

and maturation of children and adolescents in a variety of ways; that symptoms in children and adolescents differ from those in adults; and that proper **diagnosis** of young survivors is essential to effective treatment. At present, however, researchers have not reached agreement on the most appropriate names for trauma-related disorders, their diagnostic criteria, or their relationship to other mental disorders.

Resources

BOOKS

American Psychiatric Association. *Diagnostic and Statistical Manual of Mental Disorders*. 4th ed., text rev. Washington, DC: American Psychiatric Association, 2000.

Arnold, Cheryl, and Ralph Fisch. *The Impact of Complex Trauma on Development*. Lanham, MD: Jason Aronson, 2011.

Courtois, Christine A., and Julian D. Ford, eds. *Treating Complex Traumatic Stress Disorders: An Evidence-Based Guide*. New York: Guilford Press, 2009.

Ledray, Linda, Ann Wolbert Burgess, and Angelo P. Giardino, eds. *Medical Response to Adult Sexual Assault: A Resource for Clinicians and Related Professionals*. St. Louis, MO: STM Learning, 2011.

Mendelsohn, Michaela, et al. *The Trauma Recovery Group: A Guide for Practitioners*. New York: Guilford Press, 2011.

PERIODICALS

Argentero, P., and I. Setti. "Engagement and Vicarious Traumatization in Rescue Workers." *International Archives of Occupational and Environmental Health* 84 (January 2011): 67–75.

Beaudoin, C.E. "Hurricane Katrina: Addictive Behavior Trends and Predictors." *Public Health Reports* 126 (May-June 2011): 400–409.

Beck, C.T. "Secondary Traumatic Stress in Nurses: A Systematic Review." *Archives of Psychiatric Nursing* 25 (February 2011): 1–10.

Carlson, E.B., et al. "Development and Validation of a Brief Self-Report Measure of Trauma Exposure: the Trauma History Screen." *Psychological Assessment* 23 (June 2011): 463–77.

Chard, K.M., et al. "A Comparison of OEF and OIF Veterans and Vietnam Veterans Receiving Cognitive Processing Therapy." *Journal of Traumatic Stress* 23 (February 2010): 25–32.

Cukor, J., et al. "Prevalence and Predictors of Posttraumatic Stress Symptoms in Utility Workers Deployed to the World Trade Center Following the Attacks of September 11, 2001." *Depression and Anxiety* 28 (March 2011): 210–17.

Hall, B., and M. Place. "Cutting to Cope—A Modern Adolescent Phenomenon." *Child Care, Health and Development* 36 (September 2010): 623–29.

Keogh, A. "Rape Trauma Syndrome: Time to Open the Floodgates?" *Journal of Forensic and Legal Medicine* 14 (May 2007): 221–24.

Lewis, S.P., et al. "The Scope of Nonsuicidal Self-Injury on YouTube." *Pediatrics* 127 (March 2011): e552–e557.

Liberman, Moishe, et al. "The History of Trauma Care Systems from Homer to Telemedicine." *McGill Journal of Medicine*, Spring 2004. http://www.med.mcgill.ca/mjm/issues/v07n02/feature_rev/feature_rev.htm (accessed August 2, 2011).

Raphael, B., and H. Ma. "Mass Catastrophe and Disaster Psychiatry." *Molecular Psychiatry* 16 (March 2011): 247–51.

Shalev, A.Y., et al. "Barriers to Receiving Early Care for PTSD: Results From the Jerusalem Trauma Outreach and Prevention Study." *Psychiatric Services* 62 (July 2011): 765–73.

Wolmer, L., et al. "Preventing Children's Posttraumatic Stress after Disaster with Teacher-Based Intervention: A Controlled Study." *Journal of the American Academy of Child and Adolescent Psychiatry* 50 (April 2011): 340–48.

OTHER

van der Kolk, Bessel, et al. "Proposal to Include a Developmental Trauma Disorder Diagnosis for Children and Adolescents in DSM-V." http://www.cathymalchiodi.com/dtd_nctsn.pdf (accessed August 11, 2011).

WEBSITES

American Academy of Experts in Traumatic Stress (AAETS). "Rape Trauma Syndrome." http://www.aaets.org/article210.htm (accessed August 12, 2011).

American Psychiatric Association. "Conditions Proposed by Outside Sources." DSM-5 Development. http://www.dsm5.org/ProposedRevisions/Pages/ConditionsProposedbyOutsideSources.aspx (accessed August 7, 2011).

———. "Trauma- and Stressor-Related Disorders." DSM-5 Development. http://www.dsm5.org/proposedrevision/pages/traumaandstressorrelateddisorders.aspx (accessed August 7, 2011).

Center for the Study of Traumatic Stress (CSTS). "Dealing with the Effects of Trauma—A Self-Help Guide." http://www.centerforthestudyoftraumaticstress.org/csts_items/SHG_Effects_of_trauma.pdf (accessed August 8, 2011).

International Society for Traumatic Stress Studies (ISTSS). "Self-Care for Providers: Indirect Trauma." http://www.istss.org/SelfCareForProviders/3050.htm (accessed August 7, 2011).

National Center for PTSD. "Cognitive Processing Therapy: Effective Treatment for Veterans with PTSD." This is a 15-minute video about CPT. http://www.ptsd.va.gov/public/videos/CPT/cpt_dvd.asx (accessed August 11, 2011).

———. "Coping with Traumatic Stress Reactions." U.S. Department of Veterans Affairs. http://www.ptsd.va.gov/public/pages/coping-traumatic-stress.asp (accessed August 29, 2011).

———. "FAQs about PTSD Assessment." http://www.ptsd.va.gov/public/pages/faqs-ptsd-assessment.asp (accessed August 11, 2011).

———. "Prolonged Exposure Therapy for PTSD." http://www.ptsd.va.gov/public/pages/prolonged-exposure-therapy.asp (accessed August 11, 2011).

———. "PTSD Overview." http://www.ptsd.va.gov/public/pages/fslist-ptsd-overview.asp (accessed August 3, 2011).

National Institute of Mental Health (NIMH). "Coping with Traumatic Events." This is a gateway page that includes two video presentations and links to NIMH publications about trauma-related disorders. http://www.nimh.nih.gov/health/topics/coping-with-traumatic-events/index.shtml (accessed August 8, 2011).

Sidran Institute. "What Is Psychological Trauma?" http://www.sidran.org/sub.cfm?contentID=88&sectionid=4 (accessed August 9, 2011).

ORGANIZATIONS

American Academy of Experts in Traumatic Stress (AAETS), 203 Deer Road, Ronkonkoma, New York, United States 11779, (631) 543-2217, Fax: (631) 543-6977, info@aaets.org, http://www.aaets.org/index.htm

Center for the Study of Traumatic Stress (CSTS), Uniformed Services University of the Health Sciences (USU), 4301 Jones Bridge Road, Bethesda, MD, United States 20814, (301) 295-2470, Fax: (301) 319-6965, cstsinfo@usuhs.mil, http://www.centerforthestudyoftraumaticstress.org/index.php

International Society for Traumatic Stress Studies (ISTSS), 111 Deer Lake Road, Suite 100, Deerfield, IL, United States 60015, (847) 480-9028, Fax: (847) 480-9282, http://www.istss.org/Home.htm

National Center for PTSD, 810 Vermont Avenue, NW, Washington, DC, United States 20420, (802) 296-6300, ncptsd@va.gov, http://www.ptsd.va.gov/index.asp

National Child Traumatic Stress Network (NCTSN), National Center for Child Traumatic Stress (NCCTS), University of California, Los Angeles, 11150 W. Olympic Blvd., Suite 650, Los Angeles, CA, United State 90064, (310)

235-2633, Fax: (310) 235-2612, http://www.nctsn.org/about-us/contact-us, http://www.nctsn.org/

National Institute of Mental Health (NIMH), 6001 Executive Boulevard, Room 8184, MSC 9663, Bethesda, MD, United States 20892-9663, (301) 443-4513, Fax: (301) 443-4279, (866) 615-6464, nimhinfo@nih.gov, http://www.nimh.nih.gov/index.shtml

Sidran Institute, PO Box 436, Brooklandville, MD, United States 21022-0436, (410) 825-8888, Fax: (410) 560-0134, info@sidran.org, http://www.sidran.org/index.cfm

Rebecca J. Frey, Ph.D.

Traumatic brain injury

Definition

Traumatic **brain** injury (TBI) is a physical injury to brain tissue that temporarily or permanently impairs brain function. TBI is sometimes known as acquired brain injury. TBIs can be evaluated as mild, moderate, or severe, depending on whether the person was knocked out and how long they were unconscious. In a mild TBI, also known as a concussion, the person either does not lose consciousness at all or is unconscious for 30 minutes or less. In a moderate TBI, the person is unconscious longer than 30 minutes but less than 6 hours. Unconsciousness lasting longer than 6 hours indicates a severe TBI.

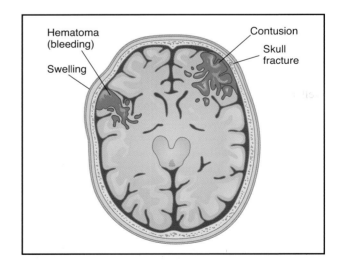

Possible signs of a traumatic brain injury include brain swelling, hematoma (bleeding), a contusion (bruise), or a skull fracture. (*Illustration by Electronic Illustrators Group.* © *2012 Cengage Learning.*)

Demographics

Estimates for the number of Americans affected by TBI vary. One source estimates that the number of persons in the United States who have had a TBI ranges between 2.5 and 6.5 million, making it a major public health problem that costs the country more than $48 billion annually. Yearly estimates range from 180 to 220 cases per 100,000 population, or 600,000 TBIs annually. As many as 10% of these injuries are fatal, resulting in almost 550,000 persons hospitalized annually in the United States with head injuries. According to the U.S. Centers for Disease Control and Prevention (CDC), 52,000 individuals die from traumatic brain injuries each year in the United States, with almost twice that number suffering permanent disability. TBI is a contributing factor in 30% of all injury-related deaths in North America. Since 75% of head injuries are classified as mild, it is likely that many mild injuries go unreported.

With regard to sex and race, in North America, males are twice as likely to be hospitalized for a TBI as females. This sex ratio in found worldwide. African Americans and Native Americans have higher rates of TBIs than other ethnic groups in the United States. With regard to age, half of all hospital admissions for TBIs involve people 24 years of age or younger.

Infants, children under five years of age, and adults 75 years and older are also at higher risk for TBI than the general population because they are most susceptible to falls around the home. Other factors predisposing the very young and the very old to TBI include physical **abuse**, such as violent shaking of an infant or toddler known as shaken baby syndrome.

Description

No two brain injuries are exactly the same; TBIs vary greatly in regard to changes in brain structure as well as severity. Mild TBIs may produce only microscopic changes in the structure of the brain, while severe TBIs may produce gross (major) damage. The nature and extent of injury depend on the mechanism of the injury and the amount of force involved. There are three main types of brain injuries: contusions (bruising of the brain tissue), axonal injuries (injuries to the axons, the long slender projects of nerve cells that carry nerve impulses away from the body of the cell), and hematomas (bleeding in the brain).

Immediate complications of TBI may include **seizures**, enlargement of the fluid-filled chambers within the brain (hydrocephalus or post-traumatic ventricular enlargement), leaks of cerebrospinal fluid, infection, injury to blood vessels or to the nerves supplying the head and neck, pain, bed sores, failure of multiple organ systems, and trauma to other areas of the body.

Long-term survivors of a TBI may suffer from persistent problems with behavior, thinking, and communication disabilities, as well as epilepsy; loss of sensation, hearing, vision, taste, or smell; ringing in the ears (tinnitus); coordination problems; and/or paralysis. Recovery from cognitive deficits is most dramatic within the first six months after TBI, and less apparent subsequently.

Risk factors

Risk factors for TBIs include:

- age—children younger than 4 years, adolescents between 16 and 19, and adults over 65 are at increased risk.
- male sex
- African American, Native American, or Hispanic ethnicity
- participation in contact sports, diving, or mountain climbing
- employment in construction, mining, and other occupations requiring blasting or wearing a hard hat
- frontline military combat
- drug or alcohol abuse
- driving under the influence of drugs or alcohol

Causes and symptoms

Causes

The causes of TBIs are commonly classified as either closed- or open-head injuries. Either type of injury may cause direct damage to brain tissue (crushing or tearing of brain tissue itself), or the damage may result from the cascade of events resulting from the original injury. In some cases, there is increased intracranial pressure (ICP), resulting from the fact that the skull is a closed space filled with cerebrospinal fluid that cannot be compressed and brain tissue that allows only minimal compression. Any swelling from edema or a hematoma inside the skull leads to a rise in the ICP. This process reduces the amount of blood flow to the brain, which in turn can lead to ischemia (inadequate blood supply) of the brain tissue.

CLOSED-HEAD INJURIES. A closed head injury is a type of TBI in which the head is hit by or strikes an object without breaking the skull. In a penetrating head injury, an object such as a bullet fractures the skull and enters brain tissue.

Diffuse brain damage associated with closed head injury may result from back-and-forth movement of the brain against the inside of the bony skull. This is sometimes called coup-contrecoup injury. "Coup," French for "blow," refers to the brain injury directly under the point of maximum impact to the skull. "Contrecoup," French for "opposite the blow," refers to the brain injury opposite the point of maximum impact. Coup-contrecoup injury may occur in a rear-end collision, with high-speed stops, or with violent shaking of a baby, because the brain and skull are of different densities and therefore travel at different speeds. The impact of the collision causes the soft, gelatinous brain tissue to jar against bony ridges on the inside of the skull.

Because of the movement of these injuries and the position of the brain within the skull, the frontal lobes (behind the forehead) and temporal lobes (underlying the temples) are most susceptible to this type of diffuse damage. These lobes house major brain centers involved in speech and language, so problems with communication skills often follow closed head injuries of this type.

Depending on which areas of the brain are injured, other symptoms of closed head injury may include difficulty with concentration, memory, thinking, swallowing, walking, balance, and coordination; weakness or paralysis; changes in sensation; and alteration of the sense of smell.

The consequences of a TBI can be relatively subtle or completely devastating, depending on the severity and mechanism of injury. Diffuse axonal injury (DAI), or shear injury, may follow contrecoup injury even when there is no damage to the skull or obvious bleeding into the brain tissue. A DAI involves damage to the axon, which is the part of the nerve that communicates with other nerves. The injured axon degenerates and releases harmful substances that can damage neighboring nerves. DAI is typically the underlying injury in shaken baby syndrome.

SKULL FRACTURES. Skull fractures caused by severe blunt trauma are considered a type of open-head injury. When the skull cracks or breaks, the resulting skull fracture can cause a contusion—an area of bruising of brain tissue associated with swelling and blood leaking from broken blood vessels. A depressed skull fracture occurs when fragments of the broken skull sink or are pushed downward from the skull surface and press against the surface of the brain. In a penetrating skull fracture, bone fragments enter brain tissue. Either type of skull fracture can cause bruising of the brain tissue, called a contusion. Contrecoup injury can also lead to brain contusion.

Some skull fractures are likelier than others to lead to a severe TBI. They include:

• Skull fractures in persons who already have a neurological disorder or impairment.

• Depressed skull fractures.

• Fractures of the occipital bone and the basilar bones of the skull. The basilar bones are strong, thick bones that require a very strong impact to break them, which implies a force strong enough to cause significant damage to the brain tissue itself.

• Fractures in infants. There is a risk of the fracture widening as the baby's skull is still growing.

• Fractures involving the carotid canal. The carotid canal is a passageway through the temporal bone of the skull that allows the internal carotid artery to enter the skull. A fracture in the area of the carotid canal can result in dissection of the carotid artery.

HEMATOMAS. If the physical trauma to the head ruptures a major blood vessel, the resulting bleeding into or around the brain is called a hematoma. Bleeding between the skull and the dura, the thick, outermost layer covering the brain, is termed an epidural hematoma. When blood collects in the space between the dura and the arachnoid membrane, a more fragile covering underlying the dura, it is known as a subdural hematoma. An intracerebral hematoma involves bleeding directly into the brain tissue.

All three types of hematomas can damage the brain by putting pressure on vital brain structures. Intracerebral hematomas can cause additional damage as toxic breakdown products of the blood harm brain cells, cause swelling, or interrupt the flow of cerebrospinal fluid around the brain.

EXTERNAL CAUSES. Transportation accidents involving automobiles, motorcycles, bicycles, and pedestrians account for half of all TBIs and for the majority of TBIs in individuals under the age of 75. At least half of all TBIs are associated with **alcohol use**. Sports injuries cause about 3% of TBIs; other accidents leading to TBI may occur at home, at work, or outdoors.

In those aged 75 and older, falls are responsible for most TBIs. Other situations leading to TBI at all ages include violence, implicated in about 20% of TBIs. Firearm assaults are involved in most violent causes of TBI in young adults, whereas **child abuse** is the most common violent cause in infants and toddlers. In shaken baby syndrome, a baby is shaken with enough force to cause severe countrecoup injury.

Symptoms

Symptoms, complaints, and neurological or behavioral changes following TBI depend on the location(s) of the brain injury and on the total volume of injured brain. Usually, TBI causes focal brain injury involving a single area of the brain where the head is struck or where an object such as a bullet enters the brain. Although damage is typically worst at the point of direct impact or entry, TBI may also cause diffuse brain injury involving several other brain regions.

The symptoms of TBI may occur immediately or they may develop slowly over several hours, especially if there is slow bleeding into the brain or gradual swelling. Depending on the cause, mechanism, and extent of the injury, the severity of immediate symptoms of TBI can be mild, moderate, or severe, ranging from mild concussion to deep coma or even death.

With concussion, the injured person may experience a brief or transient loss of consciousness, much like fainting or passing out, or merely an alteration in consciousness described as "seeing stars" or feeling dazed or "out of it." At the other extreme, coma refers to a profound or deep state of unconsciousness in which the individual does not respond to the environment in any meaningful way.

Approximately 40% of patients with TBI develop postconcussion syndrome within days to weeks, with symptoms including headache, dizziness or a sensation of spinning (vertigo), memory problems, trouble concentrating, sleep disturbances, restlessness, irritability, **depression**, and anxiety. This syndrome may persist for a few weeks, especially in patients with depression, anxiety, or other psychiatric symptoms before the TBI.

With more severe injuries, there may also be immediate numbness or weakness of one or more limbs, blindness, deafness, inability to speak or understand speech, slurred speech, lethargy with difficulty staying awake, persistent vomiting, loss of coordination, disorientation, or agitation. In addition to some of these symptoms, young children with moderate to severe TBI may also experience prolonged crying and refusal to nurse or eat.

When a person with a TBI regains consciousness, some symptoms are immediately apparent, while others are not noticed until several days or weeks later. Symptoms that may be obvious right away after mild TBI include headache, changes in vision such as blurred vision or tired eyes, nausea, dizziness, lightheadedness, ringing in the ears, bad taste in the mouth, or altered sense of smell, which is usually experienced as loss of the sense of taste.

While the injured person is preoccupied with headache or pain related to other physical trauma, symptoms such as difficulty in thinking or concentrating may not be evident. Often these more subtle symptoms may appear only when the individual attempts to return to work or to other mentally challenging situations. Similarly, personality changes, depression, irritability,

and other emotional and behavioral problems may initially be attributed to coping with the **stress** of the injury, and their severity may not be fully recognized until the individual is recuperating at home. Other symptoms that may appear immediately or that may be noticed only while the individual is returning to usual activities are confusion, **fatigue** or lethargy, altered sleep patterns, and trouble with memory, concentration, attention, and finding the right words or understanding speech. Seizures may occur soon after a TBI or may first appear up to a year later, especially when the damage involves the temporal lobes.

Diagnosis

Diagnosis of a TBI is suspected on the basis of the clinical signs and symptoms and confirmed by diagnostic imaging.

Examination

Recognizing a serious head injury, starting basic first aid, and seeking emergency medical care can help the injured person avoid disability or even death. When encountering a potential TBI, helpers on the scene should try to find out what happened from the injured person, from clues at the scene, and from any eyewitnesses. Because spinal cord injury often accompanies serious head trauma, it is prudent to assume that there is also injury to the spinal cord and to avoid moving the person until the paramedics arrive. Spinal cord injury is a challenging diagnosis; nearly one-tenth of spinal cord injuries accompanying TBI are initially missed.

Signs apparent to the observer that suggest serious head injury and mandate emergency treatment include shallow or erratic breathing or pulse; a drop in blood pressure; broken bones or other obvious trauma to the skull or face such as bruising, swelling, or bleeding; one pupil being larger than the other; or clear or bloody fluid drainage from the nose, mouth, or ears.

Symptoms reported by the injured person that should also raise red flags include severe headache, stiff neck, vomiting, paralysis or inability to move one or more limbs, blindness, deafness, or inability to taste or smell. Other ominous developments may include initial improvement followed by worsening symptoms, deepening lethargy or unresponsiveness, personality changes including irritability or unusual behavior, or loss of coordination.

When emergency personnel arrive, they will stabilize the patient, evaluate the patient's signs and symptoms, and assess the nature and extent of other injuries, such as broken bones, spinal cord injury, or

KEY TERMS

Closed-head injury—A head injury in which the skull is not cracked or fractured.

Coma—A decreased level of consciousness with deep unresponsiveness.

Computed tomography (CT) scan—A neuroimaging test that generates a series of cross-sectional x rays of the head and brain.

Concussion—Injury to the brain causing a sudden but temporary impairment of brain function.

Contrecoup—An injury to the brain opposite the point of direct impact.

Contusion—A focal area of swollen and bleeding brain tissue.

Dementia pugilistica—A term for "punch-drunk" syndrome of brain damage caused by repeated head trauma.

Depressed skull fracture—A fracture in which pieces of broken skull press into brain tissue.

Diffuse axonal injury (DAI; also called shear injury)—Traumatic damage to individual nerve cells resulting in breakdown of overall communication between nerve cells in the brain.

Epidural hematoma—Bleeding into the area between the skull and the dura, the tough, outermost brain covering.

Executive functions—An umbrella term for the group of mental processes responsible for planning, abstract thinking, logical deduction, choosing appropriate behaviors and inhibiting inappropriate behaviors, and distinguishing between relevant and irrelevant sensory information.

Glasgow coma scale—A measure of the level of consciousness and neurological functioning after TBI.

Hematoma—Bleeding into or around the brain caused by trauma to a blood vessel in the head.

Intracerebral hematoma—Bleeding within the brain caused by trauma to a blood vessel.

Ischemia—An inadequate flow of blood to a part of the body, caused by narrowing or blockage of the blood vessels supplying it.

Penetrating head injury—TBI in which an object pierces the skull and enters brain tissue.

Post-concussion syndrome—A complex of symptoms including headache following mild TBI.

Post-traumatic amnesia (PTA)—Difficulty forming new memories after TBI.

Post-traumatic dementia—Persistent mental deterioration following TBI.

Sequela (plural, sequelae)—In medicine, a pathological condition resulting from a disease, injury, or other trauma. For example, PTSD may be a sequela of a traumatic brain injury.

Shaken baby syndrome (SBS)—A severe form of TBI resulting from shaking an infant or small child forcefully enough to cause the brain to jar against the skull.

Stabilization—A set of procedures for preventing shock in an injured person by protecting the airway, controlling bleeding (if any), keeping the person warm, and preventing injury to the spinal cord.

Subdural hematoma—Bleeding between the dura and the underlying brain covering.

Syndrome—A group of signs or symptoms that occur together and characterize or define a particular disease or disorder.

Ventriculostomy—Surgery that drains cerebrospinal fluid from the brain to treat hydrocephalus or increased intracranial pressure.

damage to other organ systems. Medical advances in early detection and treatment of associated injuries have improved the overall outcome in TBI. Severely injured victims transported rapidly by helicopter or ambulance have better outcomes compared to those who cannot be transported quickly.

When possible, persons with severe head injuries are taken to a hospital with a dedicated trauma center. Such centers have specialized staff and equipment, and their patients have better outcomes compared to those

taken to general hospitals. The initial evaluation measures vital signs such as temperature, blood pressure, pulse, and breathing rate, while the neurological examination assesses reflexes, level of consciousness, ability to move the limbs, and pupil size, symmetry, and response to light.

Neurological features are standardized using the Glasgow Coma Scale (GCS), a test scored from 1 to 15 points. Each of three measures (eye opening, best verbal response, and best motor response) is scored separately, and the combined score helps determine the severity of TBI. A total score of 3 to 8 reflects a severe TBI, 9 to 12 a moderate TBI, and 13 to 15 a mild TBI. The lowest possible score, 3, usually indicates a fatal injury. There is a modified version of the GCS for use with infants and children.

Tests

Definitive diagnosis of a TBI is provided by **imaging studies**. Sophisticated imaging tests can help differentiate the variety of unconscious states associated with TBI and can help determine their anatomical basis. Until neck fractures or spinal instability have been ruled out with skull and neck x rays, or with head and neck **computed tomography** (CT) scans for more severe injuries, the patient should remain immobilized in a neck and back restraint.

By constructing a series of cross-sectional slices, or x-ray images through the head and brain, CT scans can diagnose bone fractures, bleeding, hematomas, contusions, swelling of brain tissue, and blockage of the ventricular system that circulates cerebrospinal fluid around the brain. In later stages after the initial injury, scans may also show shrinkage of brain volume in areas where neurons have died.

Using magnetic fields to detect subtle changes in brain tissue related to differences in water content, **magnetic resonance imaging** (MRI) scans show more detail than x rays or CT. However, MRI takes more time than CT and is not as readily available, making it less suited for routine emergency imaging.

For patients with seizures or for those with more subtle episodic symptoms thought to be seizures, an electroencephalogram (EEG) may reveal abnormalities in the electrical activity of the brain, or brain waves. Other diagnostic techniques that may be helpful include cerebral angiography, transcranial Doppler ultrasound, and **single photon emission computed tomography** (SPECT).

Treatment

Although no specific treatment may be needed for a mild head injury, it is crucial to watch the person closely for any developing symptoms over the next 24 hours. Over-the-counter pain relievers like acetaminophen or ibuprofen may be used for mild headache. Aspirin should not be given, however, because it can increase the risk of bleeding.

If the person is sleeping, he or she should be awakened every two to three hours to determine alertness and orientation to name, time, and place. Immediate medical help is needed if the person becomes unusually drowsy or disoriented, develops a severe headache or stiff neck, vomits, loses consciousness, or behaves abnormally.

Emergency care and surgery

Treatment for moderate or severe TBI should begin as soon as possible by calling 911 and beginning emergency care until the EMT team arrives. This care includes stabilizing the head and neck by placing the hands on both sides of the person's head to keep the head in line with the spine and prevent movement, which could worsen spinal cord injury. Bleeding should be controlled by firmly pressing a clean cloth over the wound. If a skull fracture is suspected, it should be covered with sterile gauze dressing without applying pressure. If the person is vomiting, the head, neck, and body should be rolled to the side as one unit to prevent choking without further injuring the spine.

Although the initial brain damage caused by trauma is often irreversible, the goal is to stabilize the patient and prevent further injury. To achieve these goals, the treatment team must insure adequate oxygen supply to the brain and the rest of the body, maintain blood flow to the brain, control blood pressure, stabilize the airway, assist in breathing or perform CPR if necessary, and treat associated injuries. Recent research has found that increasing the patient's caloric intake by 50% during the first two weeks after the TBI helps reduce inflammation and gives the brain the energy it needs to heal.

About half of severe head injuries require neurosurgery for hematomas or contusions. Swelling of the injured brain may cause increased intracranial pressure (ICP) within the closed skull cavity. ICP can be measured with an intraventricular probe or catheter inserted through the skull into the fluid-filled chambers (ventricles) within the brain. Placement of the ICP catheter is usually guided by CT scan. If ICP is elevated, ventriculostomy may be needed. This procedure drains cerebrospinal fluid from the brain and reduces ICP. Drugs that may decrease ICP include mannitol and **barbiturates**.

Drugs

Although some patients need medication for psychiatric and physical problems resulting from the TBI, prescribing drugs may be problematic, because TBI patients are more sensitive to side effects.

Rehabilitation

Both in the immediate and later stages of TBI, rehabilitation is vital to optimal recovery of the patient's ability to function at home and in society. Rehabilitation is a highly individualized process and is based on each patient's specific strengths and abilities.

Problems with orientation and thinking and communication problems should be addressed early, often during the hospital stay. The focus is typically on improving alertness, attention, orientation, speech understanding, and swallowing problems.

As the patient improves, rehabilitation should be modified accordingly. Physical therapy, occupational therapy, speech or language therapy, physiatry (physical medicine), psychology or psychiatry, and social support should all play a role in TBI rehabilitation. Appropriate settings for rehabilitation may include the patient's home, the hospital outpatient department, inpatient rehabilitation centers, comprehensive day programs, supportive-living programs, independent-living centers, and school-based programs. Families should become involved in rehabilitation, in modifying the home environment if needed, and in **psychotherapy** or counseling as indicated.

Prognosis

The prognosis of TBIs is highly individualized and varies with their severity and cause: 91% of TBIs caused by firearms (two-thirds of which may represent suicide attempts) are fatal, compared with only 11% of TBIs from falls.

Following TBI, patients may be at increased risk of such other long-term problems as Parkinson's disease, **Alzheimer's disease**, "punch-drunk" syndrome (**dementia** pugilistica), and post-traumatic dementia. Some patients may have difficulty returning to work following TBI, as well as problems with school, driving, sports, housework, and social relationships.

Mental health issues

Mental disorders and behavioral problems are common sequelae of TBIs. The most common are depression and behavioral problems. A report published in the August 2011 edition of the journal *Schizophrenia Bulletin* found that persons with TBIs may also be at risk for developing schizophrenia, being 1.6 times more likely to develop the disorder than persons in the general population. A major reason for the development of mental disorders after TBI is that the parts of the brain most susceptible to traumatic injury—the frontal and temporal lobes—are the portions of the brain that are responsible for executive functions (judgment, reasoning, decision making, evaluating a situation, processing information, etc.). These portions of the brain contain such structures as the hippocampus, which

helps to form long-term memory; Broca's and Wernicke's areas, which govern speech; and the amygdala, which processes emotions and is also responsible for memory consolidation. Thus, damage to the frontal and temporal lobes can have long-term behavioral and psychiatric consequences.

DEPRESSION. Depression is a common mood disorder that affects TBI patients; about half of all persons with a TBI will be diagnosed with major depression within a year after injury. Many TBI patients with depression also have concurrent **anxiety disorders**. Depression following a TBI usually results from a combination of factors that include physical changes in the brain after injury; emotional reactions to such changes as job or role loss, short- or long-term disability, loss of self-sufficiency and other losses; a personal or family history of depression; and genetic susceptibility to mood disorders.

Depression following a TBI is treated in the same way as depression in the general population, most often with a combination of antidepressant medications and cognitive behavioral or **group therapy**. Some patients with depression following a TBI report being helped by **yoga**, other gentle forms of **exercise**, **acupuncture**, and **biofeedback**.

Behavioral problems

Behavioral problems are another common sequela of a TBI. The problematic behaviors most frequently encountered in TBI patients are agitation, impulsive behaviors, loss of inhibition, and loss of motivation. Aggressive outbursts toward others, cursing, yelling, inappropriate sexual behaviors, self-injury, property destruction, and noncompliance with treatment can all hinder relationships with family members, return to work, and reintegration within the larger community. Assessment of the frequency and severity of behavioral problems is an important part of evaluation. For example, occasional temper tantrums in the home are one matter, but aggression may evolve to violence, placing friends and family in dangerous situations. Although some problem behaviors may not be physically dangerous to others, having them repeated literally hundreds of times a day can damage family relationships as well as the possibility of employment.

One way to understand behavioral problems in patients with TBIs is that they result from a combination of changes in the functioning of the patient's brain and negative feedback from the surrounding environment. The affected person may not be able to detect and respond to the social cues and feedback that remind most people of the limits of acceptable behavior. In return, healthcare workers as well as family members may respond to the problem behaviors by reprimanding or punishing the individual, which often makes the behavioral problems worse.

An additional complication in addressing problem behaviors in patients with TBIs is that there is no consensus regarding the best therapeutic approach. There are many different schools of psychiatry and psychotherapy, and treatment recommendations based on one theory of human behavior may vary considerably from recommendations based on a different theory. No two TBIs are identical, nor are the patients affected by them. Some general recommendations for treating behavioral problems are as follows:

- The individual should have a complete neurological examination and imaging studies to determine as precisely as possible which parts of the brain have been injured, along with the severity of the damage.
- Mild behavioral problems can often be managed in community settings or outpatient clinics with a combination of behavioral therapy and medications. The patient should be involved in the design of the treatment plan as much as possible.
- Some behavioral problems can also be managed by changing the patient's environment to minimize confusion and frustration.
- Severe behavioral problems often require inpatient treatment. The patient's family or friends, however, should make sure that the facility is staffed by physicians, psychologists, speech pathologists, and other therapists with extensive training and specific expertise in treating behavior problems resulting from TBIs. Other concerns include the safety of the facility (to prevent self-injury) and its security (to prevent the patient's wandering away).

Cognitive dysfunction

Cognition refers to a set of mental functions that include attention, memory, language, problem solving, logic, and decision making. Memory itself is a complex set of active storage processing that encodes information rather than just passively storing it. Cognitive skills assist memory by identifying what is important to remember in a given situation and by rearranging what is stored in memory when a person learns new information. In many cases, what appears to be memory loss in patients with TBIs is really a consequence of other cognitive deficits, such as difficulty concentrating or damage to vision and other forms of sensory perception.

In general, cognitive deficits are most noticeable immediately after the person emerges from coma (if they have lost consciousness). Although there are exceptions,

a common rule of thumb is that recovery of cognition is most rapid in the first 6 to 12 months after injury, and proceeds at a slower pace for the next one to three years. With regard to assessment of the person's cognitive abilities, most doctors recommend waiting until the person's condition has stabilized sufficiently to allow them to participate in a meaningful assessment.

Cognitive assessments serve several purposes, including identification of specific cognitive abilities and deficits, evaluating treatment outcomes, monitoring the patient's recovery, designing a treatment program, assessing the person's educational and occupational future, and documenting symptoms for legal purposes, particularly for decisions about the person's competency or applying for Medicaid or Social Security benefits. The cognitive assessment is usually repeated, as it is not unusual for new symptoms to appear as previous symptoms resolve. An example would be the appearance of difficulties with impulse control after the patient's initial loss of interest in activity has disappeared.

There are different treatment strategies for different cognitive deficits, although most involve long-term therapy; recovery of cognitive skills is a slow process that usually takes years, not months. Assistive technologies, such as wristwatches that beep to remind the person of a task or computer software that helps with organizing and managing complex information, are useful to many patients. Those with low mental stamina or difficulties with concentration may be helped by fatigue management strategies or by medications that have been shown to improve alertness and the ability to focus attention. With regard to impairment-specific treatments, speech-language therapy and treatment for loss of visual/spatial coordination have yielded better results than memory training strategies. Deficits in executive skills have been effectively treated by a combination of individualized psychotherapy and coaching in real-life situations, including the workplace.

Veterans' issues

TBI has been described as the "signature" injury of the conflicts in Iraq and Afghanistan; the rate of such injuries is higher in veterans of Iraq and Afghanistan compared to Vietnam veterans (12%). Veterans' advocates believe that between 10% and 20% of Iraq veterans (150,000 to 300,000 men and women) have some level of TBI. Among wounded troops, the rate of TBI is as high as 33%. The major causes of TBIs in recent veterans are blasts, motor vehicle accidents, and gunshot wounds. Unfortunately, TBI is underdiagnosed and therefore undertreated in military personnel. In 2008, the U.S. Department of Defense awarded a four-year grant to the Brain Trauma Foundation (BTF) to develop an eye-tracking device that can be used in the field to instantly

QUESTIONS TO ASK YOUR DOCTOR

- Do you know of any nearby rehabilitation facilities that specialize in treating TBIs?
- What are my best treatment options?
- Will my TBI have long-term effects?

determine if a soldier or airman has suffered any brain damage as a result of blast injury or another type of head injury.

Because many veterans with TBIs have coexisting PTSD or **substance abuse** disorders, they typically take longer than civilians to recover from these head injuries. Women veterans with TBIs are more likely than male veterans to be diagnosed with concurrent depression. Veterans with TBIs are also almost twice as likely to attempt **suicide** as veterans who did not suffer such injuries. Treatment for TBIs in veterans is similar to that for civilians, with rehabilitation programs that address **cognitive retraining**, psychosocial adjustment, communication and leisure skills, and vocational issues. The U.S. Veterans Administration (VA) maintains 4 polytrauma rehabilitation centers and 21 polytrauma network sites for veterans with the most severe TBIs.

Prevention

Not all accidents or other causes of TBIs can be prevented. People can, however, lower their risk by taking the following safety measures:

- Athletes should wear protective headgear for such sports as mountain climbing, martial arts, football, baseball, bicycling, motorcycling, rollerblading, and skateboarding. They should make sure their helmets and other protective gear are properly fitted. Coaches should insist that players are taught the rules of safe play and that they follow them. Players should report all head injuries to the team doctor even if they seem minor at the time.

- Adults and children should be careful when diving in shallow water, particularly in bodies of water with rocky shores and bottoms.

- Drivers and passengers should always wear seat belts when traveling in a motor vehicle, and people should never drive when under the influence of alcohol or other drugs.

- People in occupations requiring hardhats should wear them at all times, particularly in mining and construction work. Even a small object dropped from the upper floors of a building can cause a serious head injury.

- Elderly persons or parents of small children should check their house or apartment for loose rugs, poor lighting, slippery floors, and other problems that increase the risk of falls, which are a common cause of TBIs in the very old and very young.

Resources

BOOKS

Erdman, John, Maria Oria, and Laura Pillsbury. *Nutrition and Traumatic Brain Injury: Improving Acute and Subacute Health Outcomes in Military Personnel.* Washington, DC: National Academies Press, 2011.

Kerpelman, Larry C. *Pieces Missing: A Family's Journey of Recovery from Traumatic Brain Injury.* Minneapolis, MN: Two Harbors Press, 2011.

Phillips, Joseph R. *Hidden Wounds: Traumatic Brain Injury and Post Traumatic Stress Disorder in Service Members.* New York: Nova Science Publishers, 2011.

Roberts, Richard J., and Mary Ann Roberts. *Mild Traumatic Brain Injury: Episodic Symptoms and Treatment.* San Diego, CA: Plural Publishing, 2011.

Silver, Jonathan M., Thomas W. McAllister, and Stuart C. Yudofsky, eds. *Textbook of Traumatic Brain Injury.* 2nd ed. Arlington, VA: American Psychiatric Publishing, 2011.

Stone, C. Keith, and Roger L. Humphries, eds. *Current Diagnosis and Treatment: Emergency Medicine.* 6th ed. New York: McGraw-Hill, 2008.

PERIODICALS

Farrer, T. J., and D. W. Hedges. "Prevalence of Traumatic Brain Injury in Incarcerated Groups Compared to the General Population: A Meta-Analysis." *Progress in Neuro-Psychopharmacology and Biological Psychiatry* 35 (March 30, 2011): 390–94.

Gould, K. R., et al. "The Nature, Frequency and Course of Psychiatric Disorders in the First Year after Traumatic Brain Injury: A Prospective Study." *Psychological Medicine* 41 (October 2011): 2099–109.

Hart, T., et al. "Major and Minor Depression after Traumatic Brain Injury." *Archives of Physical Medicine and Rehabilitation* 92 (August 2011): 1211–19.

Hettich, T., et al. "Case Report: Use of the Immediate Post Concussion Assessment and Cognitive Testing (ImPACT) to Assist with Return to Duty Determination of Special Operations Soldiers Who Sustained Mild Traumatic Brain Injury." *Journal of Special Operations Medicine* 10 (Fall 2010): 48–55.

Iverson, K. M., et al. "Psychiatric Diagnoses and Neurobehavioral Symptom Severity among OEF/OIF VA Patients with Deployment-related Traumatic Brain Injury: A Gender Comparison." *Women's Health Issues* 21 (July–August 2011), Suppl. 4: S210–S217.

Max, J. E., et al. "Anxiety Disorders in Children and Adolescents in the First Six Months after Traumatic Brain

Injury." *Journal of Neuropsychiatry and Clinical Neurosciences* 23 (Fall 2011): 29–39.

Meares, S., et al. "The Prospective Course of Postconcussion Syndrome: The Role of Mild Traumatic Brain Injury." *Neuropsychology* 25 (July 2011): 454–65.

Reeves, R. R., and R. L. Panguluri. "Neuropsychiatric Complications of Traumatic Brain Injury." *Journal of Psychosocial Nursing and Mental Health Services* 49 (March 2011): 42–50.

Simpson, G. K., et al. "Suicide Prevention after Traumatic Brain Injury: A Randomized Controlled Trial of a Program for the Psychological Treatment of Hopelessness." *Journal of Head Trauma Rehabilitation* 26 (July–August 2011): 290–300.

Weeks, D. L., et al. "Association of Antidepressant Medication Therapy with Inpatient Rehabilitation Outcomes for Stroke, Traumatic Brain Injury, or Traumatic Spinal Cord Injury." *Archives of Physical Medicine and Rehabilitation* 92 (May 2011): 683–695.

Williams, W. H., et al. "Self-reported Traumatic Brain Injury in Male Young Offenders: A Risk Factor for Re-offending, Poor Mental Health and Violence?" *Neuropsychological Rehabilitation* 20 (December 2010): 801–12.

Zafonte, R. "Diagnosis and Management of Sports-Related Concussion: A 15-year-old Athlete with a Concussion." *Journal of the American Medical Association* 306 (July 6, 2011): 79–86.

Zatzick, D.F., and D.C. Grossman. "Association between Traumatic Injury and Psychiatric Disorders and Medication Prescription to Youths Aged 10–19." *Psychiatric Services* 62 (March 2011): 264–271.

OTHER

Centers for Disease Control and Prevention (CDC). "Traumatic Brain Injury in Prisons and Jails: An Unrecognized Problem." http://www.cdc.gov/traumaticbraininjury/pdf/Prisoner_TBI_Prof-a.pdf (accessed August 29, 2011).

Veterans Administration (VA). "Traumatic Brain Injury: A Guide for Patients." http://www.mentalhealth.va.gov/docs/tbi.pdf (accessed August 29, 2011).

WEBSITES

Brain Injury Association of America (BIAA). "Brain Injury in the Community." http://biausa.fyrian.com/brain-injury-community.htm (accessed August 29, 2011).

Brain Trauma Foundation (BTF). "More about Concussion." https://www.braintrauma.org/more-about-concussion (accessed August 26, 2011).

Centers for Disease Control and Prevention (CDC). "Traumatic Brain Injury." http://www.cdc.gov/TraumaticBrainInjury/index.html (accessed August 27, 2011).

Crippen, David W. "Head Trauma." http://emedicine.medscape.com/article/433855-overview (accessed August 27, 2011).

Mayo Clinic staff. "Traumatic Brain Injury." MayoClinic.com. http://www.mayoclinic.com/health/traumatic-brain-injury/DS00552 (accessed August 26, 2011).

Merck Manual Online. "Traumatic Brain Injury." http://www.merckmanuals.com/professional/sec22/ch330/ch330a.html (accessed August 27, 2011).

Olson, David A. "Head Injury." Medscape Reference. http://emedicine.medscape.com/article/1163653-overview (accessed July 5, 2011).

National Center for PTSD. "Traumatic Brain Injury and PTSD." http://www.ptsd.va.gov/public/pages/traumatic_brain_injury_and_ptsd.asp(accessed August 4, 2011).

National Institute of Neurological Disorders and Stroke (NINDS). "Traumatic Brain Injury Information Page." http://www.ninds.nih.gov/disorders/tbi/tbi.htm *accessed August 26m 2011).

Rettner, Rachael. "Head Trauma may Boost Schizophrenia Risk." MSNBC.com. (August 19, 2011). http://www.msnbc.msn.com/id/44202899/ns/health-mental_health (accessed November 13, 2011).

Research Channel. "Living with Traumatic Brain Injury" [half-hour video from the University of Washington Medical Center]. http://www.youtube.com/watch?v=FgtHvBF4t-E&feature=related (accessed August 28, 2011).

ORGANIZATIONS

American Academy of Neurology (AAN), 1080 Montreal Ave., Saint Paul, MN, United States 55116, (651) 695-2717, (800) 879-1960, Fax: (651) 695-2791, http://www.aan.com.

American College of Emergency Physicians (ACEP), PO Box 619911, Dallas, TX, United States 75261-9911, (972) 550-0911, (800) 798-1822, Fax: (972) 580-2816, http://www.acep.org.

Brain Injury Association of America (BIAA), 1608 Spring Hill Rd., Ste. 110, Vienna, VA, United States 22182, (703) 761-0750, (800) 444-6443, Fax: (703) 761-0755, http://www.biausa.org.

Brain Trauma Foundation (BTF), 7 World Trade Center, 34th Fl., 250 Greenwich St., New York, NY, United States 10007, (212) 772-0608, http://www.braintrauma.org/contact/, http://www.braintrauma.org.

National Center for PTSD, 810 Vermont Ave. NW, Washington, DC, United States 20420, (802) 296-6300, ncptsd@va.gov, http://www.ptsd.va.gov/index.asp.

National Institute of Mental Health, 6001 Executive Boulevard, Room 8184, MSC 9663, Bethesda, MD, United States 20892-9663, (301) 443-4513, (866) 615-6464, Fax: (301) 443-4279, nimhinfo@nih.gov, http://www.nimh.nih.gov/index.shtml.

National Institute of Neurological Disorders and Stroke (NINDS), PO Box 5801, Bethesda, MD, United States 20824, (301) 496-5751, (800) 352-9424, http://www.ninds.nih.gov.

Rebecca J. Frey, Ph.D.

Trazodone

Definition

Trazodone is an oral antidepressant. It is sold in the United States under the brand name Desyrel and is also available under its generic name.

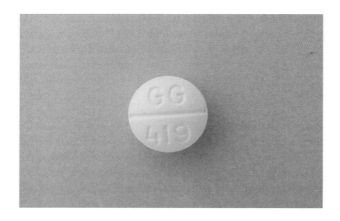

Trazodone, 50 mg. (© *Custom Medical Stock Photo, Inc. Reproduced by permission.*)

Purpose

Trazodone is used to treat **depression** and to treat the combination of symptoms of anxiety and depression. Like most **antidepressants**, trazodone has also been used in limited numbers of patients to treat **panic disorder**, **obsessive-compulsive disorder**, **attention deficit hyperactivity disorder**, **enuresis** (bed-wetting), eating disorders such as **bulimia nervosa**, **cocaine** dependency, and the depressive phase of **bipolar disorder**, but it should be noted that trazodone is not approved by the U.S. Food and Drug Administration (FDA) for these uses.

Description

Trazodone acts to change the balance of naturally occurring chemicals in the **brain** that regulate the transmission of nerve impulses between cells. Its action primarily increases the concentration of norepinephrine and **serotonin** (both chemicals that stimulate nerve cells) and, to a lesser extent, blocks the action of another brain chemical, acetylcholine. Trazodone is classified as an atypical antidepressant, but it shares many of the properties of tricyclic antidepressants (**amitriptyline**, **clomipramine**, **desipramine**, **doxepin**, **imipramine**, **nortriptyline**, **protriptyline**, and **trimipramine**). It also shares some of the properties of **selective serotonin reuptake inhibitor** (SSRI) antidepressants (such as **fluoxetine**, **paroxetine**, and **sertraline**).

The therapeutic effects of trazodone, like other antidepressants, appear slowly. Maximum benefit is often not evident for at least two weeks after starting the drug. People taking trazodone should be aware of this and continue taking the drug as directed even if they do not see immediate improvement.

Recommended dosage

As with any antidepressant, the dosage of trazodone must be carefully adjusted to produce the desired therapeutic effect. Trazodone is available as 50 mg, 100 mg, and 150 mg film-coated tablets that cannot be divided, as well as in 150 mg and 300 mg oral tablets that can be split. Therapy is usually started at a total of 150 mg per day divided into two or three doses. This dose is increased by 50 mg every three or four days until the desired effects are seen. Daily doses may be increased to a maximum of 400 mg per day in outpatients and up to 600 mg per day in hospitalized patients. In cases of extreme depression, daily doses of up to 800 mg have been used in hospitalized patients. To minimize daytime drowsiness, a major portion of the daily dose can be given at bedtime.

Precautions

Children and adults up to age 24 are at increased risk of developing suicidal thoughts and actions when taking antidepressant drugs, including trazodone. Patients of any age taking an antidepressant medication should be monitored for signs of worsening depression or changes in behavior. Trazodone is not approved for use in children younger than 18.

Although lower in anticholinergic side effects than the tricyclic antidepressants, trazodone should be used cautiously and with close physician supervision in people, especially the elderly, who have benign prostatic hypertrophy, urinary retention, and glaucoma, especially angle-closure glaucoma (the most severe form). Before starting treatment, people with these conditions should discuss the relative risks and benefits of treatment with their doctors to help determine if trazodone is the right medication for them.

Trazodone may increase heart rate and **stress** on the heart. Trazodone is associated with an increased risk of death in patients with heart disease. In rare cases where patients with cardiovascular disease must take trazodone, they should be monitored closely for cardiac rhythm disturbances and signs of cardiac stress or damage. Trazodone is also associated with an increased risk of bleeding, especially internal bleeding within the gastrointestinal tract.

The most common problem with trazodone is sedation (drowsiness and lack of mental and physical alertness). This side effect is especially noticeable early in therapy. In most patients, sedation decreases or disappears entirely with time, but until then patients taking trazodone should not perform hazardous activities requiring mental alertness or coordination, including driving or operating machinery. The sedative effect is increased when trazodone is taken with other central nervous system depressants, such as alcoholic beverages, sleeping medications, other **sedatives**, or antihistamines. It may be dangerous to take trazodone in combination with these substances.

Side effects

Trazodone shares side effects common to many antidepressants. The most frequent of these are dry mouth, constipation, and urinary retention, though these are less common than with tricyclic antidepressants. Increased heart rate, sedation, irritability, dizziness, and decreased coordination can also occur. As with most side effects associated with antidepressants, the intensity is highest at the beginning of therapy and tends to decrease with continued use.

Dry mouth, if severe to the point of causing difficulty in speaking or swallowing, may be managed by dosage reduction or temporary discontinuation of the drug. Patients may also chew sugarless gum or suck on sugarless candy in order to increase the flow of saliva. Some artificial saliva products may give temporary relief.

Men with prostate enlargement who take trazodone may be especially likely to have problems with urinary retention. Symptoms include having difficulty starting a urine flow and more difficulty than usual passing urine. In most cases, urinary retention is managed with dose reduction or by switching to another type of antidepressant. In extreme cases, patients may require treatment with bethanechol, a drug that reverses this particular side effect. In rare cases, trazodone has also been known to cause priapism, a prolonged and painful penile erection. People who think they may be experiencing any side effects from this or any other medication should tell their physicians.

Interactions

Because both trazodone and members of the class of antidepressants known as **monoamine oxidase inhibitors (MAOIs)** may increase serotonin levels in the brain, the combination of these drugs can lead to a serious condition known as **serotonin syndrome**. Symptoms of serotonin syndrome include a prolonged rapid heart rate, hypertension (high blood pressure), flushing of the skin, hallucinations, tremors, and hyperthermia (increased body temperature). It is dangerous to take trazodone in combination with MAOIs, such as **phenelzine** (Nardil) or **tranylcypromine** (Parnate). The same holds true when combining trazodone with an SSRI antidepressant, such as fluoxetine (Prozac), paroxetine, or sertraline.

Trazodone may increase the blood pressure–lowering effects in patients who are taking antihypertensive

> ## KEY TERMS
>
> **Acetylcholine**—A naturally occurring chemical in the body that generally produces effects that are the opposite of those produced by dopamine and norepinephrine. Central nervous system well-being is dependent on a balance between acetylcholine, serotonin, dopamine and norepinephrine.
>
> **Anticholinergic**—Related to the ability of a drug to block the nervous system chemical, acetylcholine. When acetylcholine is blocked, patients often experience dry mouth and skin, increased heart rate, blurred vision, and difficulty urinating. In severe cases, blocking acetylcholine may cloud thinking and cause delirium.
>
> **Benign prostatic hypertrophy**—Enlargement of the prostate gland.
>
> **Norepinephrine**—A neurotransmitter in the brain that acts to constrict blood vessels and raise blood pressure. It works in combination with serotonin.
>
> **Serotonin**—A widely distributed neurotransmitter that is found in blood platelets, the lining of the digestive tract, and the brain, and that works in combination with norepinephrine. It causes very powerful contractions of smooth muscle, and is associated with mood, attention, emotions, and sleep. Low levels of serotonin are associated with depression.

medications. Patients who take these drugs together should have their blood pressure monitored regularly so that their antihypertensive medications can be adjusted if their blood pressure becomes too low.

The sedative effects of trazodone are increased by medications used for other mental disorders such as **schizophrenia**. The anticholinergic effects of trazodone may be additive with other anticholinergic drugs such as **benztropine**, **biperiden**, **trihexyphenidyl**, and antihistamines.

Resources

BOOKS

American Society of Health-System Pharmacists. *AHFS Drug Information 2008*. Bethesda, MD: American Society of Health-System Pharmacists, 2008.

PERIODICALS

Jayaram, Geetha, and Pravin Rao. "Safety of Trazodone as a Sleep Agent for Inpatients." *Psychosomatics* 46, no. 4 (July–August 2005): 367–69.

Luparini, Maria Rita, et al. "A Cortical GABA-5HT Interaction in the Mechanism of Action of the Antidepressant Trazodone." *Progress in Neuro-Psychopharmacology & Biological Psychiatry* 28, no. 7 (November 2004): 1117–27.

Mayers, Andrew G., and David S. Baldwin. "Antidepressants and Their Effect on Sleep." *Human Psychopharmacology: Clinical and Experimental* 20, no. 8 (December 2005): 533–59.

McNeill, Alisdair. "Chorea Induced by Low-Dose Trazodone." *European Neurology* 55, no. 2 (2006): 101–102.

Mendelson, Wallace B. "A Review of the Evidence for the Efficacy and Safety of Trazodone in Insomnia." *Journal of Clinical Psychiatry* 66, no. 4 (April 2005): 469–76.

Mizoguchi, Yoshito, and Akira Monji. "Low-Dose-Trazodone-Induced Disorganized Type Psychosis." *Journal of Neuropsychiatry & Clinical Neurosciences* 17, no. 2 (May 2005): 253–4.

WEBSITES

Drugs.com "Trazodone (Trazodone hydrochloride)." http://www.drugs.com/pro/trazodone.html (accessed October 27, 2011).

PubMed Health. "Trazodone." http://www.ncbi.nlm.nih.gov/pubmedhealth/PMH0000530 (accessed November 13, 2011).

ORGANIZATIONS

National Institute of Mental Health, 6001 Executive Blvd., Rm. 8184, MSC 9663, Bethesda, MD, 20892-9663, (301) 433-4513; TTY: (301) 443-8431, Fax: (301) 443-4279, (866) 615-6464; TTY: (866) 415-8051, nimhinfo@nih.gov, http://www.nimh.nih.gov.

U.S. Food and Drug Administration, 10903 New Hampshire Ave., Silver Spring, MD, 20993-0002, (888) INFO-FDA (463-6332), http://www.fda.gov.

Jack Raber, Pharm.D.
Ruth A. Wienclaw, PhD

The Treatment for Adolescents with Depression Study (TADS)

Definition

The Treatment for Adolescents with Depression Study (TADS) was a clinical trial sponsored by the National Institutes of Health that examined the effectiveness of short- and long-term medication and **psychotherapy** treatments for teenagers (aged 12–17) with **major depressive disorder** (MDD).

MDD is a mood disorder also known as major depression, clinical depression, or unipolar depression. A person with MDD has experienced at least five of the nine symptoms below for two weeks or more, for most of the time almost every day, and this is a change from their prior level of functioning. One of the symptoms must be either (a) depressed mood, or (b) loss of interest. Recurrent MDD is diagnosed when two or more of these depressive periods occur with at least two months between episodes.

• Depressed mood (may be manifested as irritable mood).
• A significantly reduced level of interest or pleasure in most or all activities.
• A considerable loss or gain of weight (may also be an increase or decrease in appetite).
• Difficulty falling or staying asleep (insomnia), or sleeping more than usual (hypersomnia).
• Behavior that is agitated or slowed down (observable by others).
• Feeling fatigued, or having diminished energy.
• Thoughts of worthlessness or extreme guilt (not about being ill).
• Ability to think, concentrate, or make decisions is reduced.
• Frequent thoughts of death or suicide (with or without a specific plan), or suicide attempt.

It is estimated that 3 to 5% of adolescents in the United States have MDD. Depression occurs both in boys and in girls, although it is more prevalent in girls, and it is one of the most common disorders of adolescence. MDD frequently interferes with home, school, and family life, and often causes a high degree of family **stress**. **Suicide** is the third leading cause of death among teenagers, with approximately 50% of the deaths associated with depression.

Description

TADS was conducted at 13 academic and community clinics across the United States and enrolled 439 participants. The first participant entered TADS in the spring of 2000 and the last one in the summer of 2003. The initial findings were gathered from data from the first 12-week treatment period. The study showed that the antidepressant **fluoxetine** and **cognitive-behavioral therapy** combined produced the best success rate in treating depression in adolescents; 71% of participants receiving both medication and cognitive-behavioral therapy improved at the end of 12 weeks of treatment. Medication alone was also an effective treatment; 61% of participants improved; cognitive-behavioral therapy alone improved 44% of the cases; and 35% percent of the subjects improved with clinical management and placebo combined. Cognitive behavioral therapy taught the adolescent participant and their family skills to help relieve the depression.

TADS participants were randomly assigned to four treatment arms: 1) fluoxetine medication alone, 2) clinical management with placebo, 3) cognitive behavior therapy (CBT, talking with a therapist), and 4) combination of medication and CBT. The treatment phase was conducted in stages. Stage I lasted 12 weeks and included 6–14 visits to the clinic.

At the end of the first 12-week stage participants were advised of the treatment group to which they were assigned. Participants in the placebo group who did not improve during the first 12 weeks, or whose depression returned within 3 months, were offered any one of the other three treatments in the study—active medication, CBT, or both. The placebo condition was used only in stage I. During stage II (6 weeks, 2–6 clinic visits) and stage III (18 weeks, 3 clinic visits) participants received one of three treatments: 1) fluoxetine alone, 2) CBT alone, or 3) fluoxetine with CBT. Only participants who responded to one of the active treatments in stage I continued with treatment in stages II and III. Participants who responded well in stage I continued with their original treatment in stage II and later in stage III.

Fluoxetine is the generic name for Prozac, a selective **serotonin** reuptake inhibitor (SSRI). **SSRIs** primarily affect serotonin, a neurotransmitter in the **brain** that plays a pivotal role in depression. **Neurotransmitters** modulate mood, emotion, sleep, and appetite. Fluoxetine is the only medication approved by the FDA to treat depression in adolescents. However, since the TADS study, more recent studies suggest that antidepressant use in adolescents may be associated with a higher incidence of suicidal behavior and suggest close observation and caution.

CBT is a form of psychotherapy that emphasizes modifying everyday thoughts and behaviors, with the aim of positively influencing emotions. The precise therapeutic techniques vary according to particular client and issue, but commonly include keeping a diary of significant events and associated feelings, thoughts, and behaviors; questioning and testing assumptions or habits of thoughts that might be unhelpful and unrealistic; gradually facing activities that may have been avoided; and trying out new ways of behaving and reacting. Relaxation and distraction techniques are also commonly used.

Results

The study determined that the combination of fluoxetine with CBT was significantly better than fluoxetine alone or CBT alone in treating the symptoms of depression in adolescents. Fluoxetine alone was found to be a superior treatment to CBT alone. Clinically

significant suicidal thinking, which was present in 29% of the sample at the beginning of the study, while improved significantly in all four treatment arms, was most improved in the fluoxetine with CBT group. The data suggest that the combination of fluoxetine with CBT offered the most favorable tradeoff between benefit and risk for adolescents with MDD.

Resources

BOOK

American Psychiatric Association. *Diagnostic and Statistical Manual of Mental Disorders.* 4th ed., text rev. Washington, DC: American Psychiatric Association, 2000.

PERIODICALS

Bhatia, S. K., and S. C. Bhatia. "Childhood and Adolescent Depression." *American Family Physician* 75, no. 1 (2007): 73–80.
Emslie, G., et al Columbia Suicidality Classification Group; TADS Team. "Treatment for Adolescents with Depression Study (TADS): Safety Results." *Journal of the American Academy of Child and Adolescent Psychiatry* 45, no. 12 (2006):1440–55.
March, J., S. Silva, and B. Vitiello. TADS Team. "The Treatment for Adolescents with Depression Study (TADS): Methods and Message at 12 Weeks." *Journal of the American Academy of Child and Adolescent Psychiatry* 45, no. 12 (2006): 1393–1403.
Simon, G. E. "The Antidepressant Quandary: Considering Suicide Risk when Treating Adolescent Depression." *New England Journal of Medicine* 355, no. 26 (2006): 2722–23.
Vitiello, B., et al. TADS Team. "Functioning and Quality of Life in the Treatment for Adolescents with Depression Study (TADS)." *Journal of the American Academy of Child and Adolescent Psychiatry* 45, no. 2 (2006): 1419–26.

ORGANIZATIONS

National Institute of Mental Health, 6001 Executive Blvd., Rm. 8184, MSC 9663, Bethesda, MD, 20892-9663, (301) 433-4513; TTY: (301) 443-8431, Fax: (301) 443-4279, (866) 615-6464; TTY: (866) 415-8051, nimhinfo@nih.gov http://www.nimh.nih.gov.
National Institutes of Health, 9000 Rockville Pike, Bethesda, MD, 20892, (301) 496-4000; TTY: (301) 402-9612, http://www.nih.gov.

Andrew J. Bean, PhD

Triazolam

Definition

Triazolam is a hypnotic drug. It is a member of the benzodiazepine family of drugs. In the United States, it is

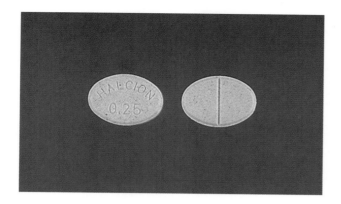

Halcion (triazolam), 25 mg. *(U.S. Drug Enforcement Administration)*

KEY TERMS

Amnesia—A general medical term for loss of memory that is not due to ordinary forgetfulness. Amnesia can be caused by head injuries, brain disease, or epilepsy as well as by dissociation.

Euphoria—A feeling or state of well-being or elation.

Hypnotic—A type of medication that induces sleep.

Insomnia—A chronic inability to sleep or to remain asleep throughout the night.

Tachycardia—A pulse rate above 100 beats per minute.

sold under the brand name Halcion as well as under its generic name.

Purpose

Triazolam is used for the short-term (generally seven to ten days) treatment of **insomnia**. Continued usage for more than two to three weeks requires a complete re-evaluation of the person receiving the drug.

Description

Triazolam increases the speed with which people achieve sleep, increases the duration of sleep, and decreases the likelihood of being awakened during sleep. The effect of triazolam decreases after 14 days of continuous use. In such cases, sleep patterns frequently return to those experienced prior to beginning use of triazolam; sometimes they are worse. This is called rebound insomnia.

Recommended dosage

The recommended dose of triazolam is 0.25 mg before going to bed. People with smaller body masses and older individuals can receive a comparable effect with 0.125 mg of triazolam. The lowest effective dosage of the drug should be used to minimize adverse reactions.

Precautions

Because of problems with rebound insomnia, patients should not receive triazolam for more than seven consecutive days. Daytime anxiety may occur after as few as 10 days of continuous usage. If this occurs, triazolam use should be discontinued.

Triazolam can cause serious birth defects. Women should not take this medicine if they are pregnant, think they may be pregnant, or are trying to get pregnant.

People using triazolam should exercise caution when driving or using power tools or machinery, due to the drug's sedative effects. People who use triazolam to reduce jet lag on long flights should be aware of a condition sometimes called "traveler's amnesia." This is a condition in which the traveler completes the flight and carries on with normal activities, including driving, but never fully awakens and has no memory of these activities. The period of **amnesia** may last for a few minutes or a few hours. Traveler's amnesia is most common when the traveler has had too little sleep or has been drinking alcohol.

Side effects

Triazolam has relatively few side effects. Those that have been reported include drowsiness, headache, dizziness, nervousness, a feeling of being light-headed, problems with coordination, nausea, and vomiting.

Less frequent side effects include euphoria, tachycardia, **fatigue**, confusion, impaired memory, muscle cramping, pain, and **depression**.

Interactions

Triazolam increases the effect of drugs and substances that depress the central nervous system. This class of drugs includes anesthetics, narcotics, **sedatives** and other sleeping pills, atropine, and alcohol.

Some drugs and foods increase the effects of triazolam and may also increase the chances of having side effects. These include cimetidine, isoniazid, oral contraceptives, and grapefruit juice.

Resources

BOOKS

Adams, Michael, and Norman Holland. *Core Concepts in Pharmacology.* 3rd ed. Upper Saddle River, NJ: 2010.

Foreman, John C., and Torben Johansen. *Textbook of Receptor Pharmacology.* 2nd ed. Boca Raton, FL: CRC Press, 2002.

Page, Clive P., et al. *Integrated Pharmacology*. 3rd ed. St. Louis, MO: Elsevier, 2006.

PERIODICALS

Mintzer, Miriam Z., et al. "Dose Effects of Triazolam on Brain Activity During Episodic Memory Encoding: A PET Study." *Psychopharmacology* 188, no. 4 (November 2006): 445–61.

Vansickel, Andrea R., Lon R. Hays, and Craig R. Rush. "Discriminative-Stimulus Effects of Triazolam in Women and Men." *American Journal of Drug and Alcohol Abuse* 32, no. 3 (2006): 329–49.

OTHER

Pfizer, Inc. *Halcion (Triazolam Tablets U.S.P.)*. http://www.pfizer.com/pfizer/download/uspi_halcion.pdf (accessed October 28, 2011).

WEBSITES

PubMed Health. "Triazolam." http://www.ncbi.nlm.nih.gov/pubmedhealth/PMH0000809 (accessed November 13, 2011).

ORGANIZATIONS

American Academy of Clinical Toxicology, 6728 Old McLean Village Drive, McLean, VA, 22101, (703) 556-9222, Fax: (703) 556-8729, admin@clintox.org, http://www.clintox.org.

American Academy of Family Physicians, 11400 Tomahawk Creek Parkway, Leawood, KS, 66211-2672, (913) 906-6000, (800) 274-2237, Fax: (913) 906-6075, contactcenter@aafp.org, http://www.aafp.org.

American Medical Association, 515 N State Street, Chicago, IL, 60610, (312) 464-5000, (800) 621-8335, http://www.ama-assn.org.

American Psychiatric Association, 1000 Wilson Blvd., Ste. 1825, Arlington, VA, 22209-3901, (703) 907-7300, apa@psych.org, http://www.psych.org.

American Society for Clinical Pharmacology and Therapeutics, 528 North Washington Street, Alexandria, VA, 22314, (703) 836-6981, http://www.ascpt.org.

American Society for Pharmacology and Experimental Therapeutics, 9650 Rockville Pike, Bethesda, MD, 20814-3995, (301) 634-7060, Fax: (301) 634-7061, http://www.aspet.org.

L. Fleming Fallon, Jr., MD, Dr.P.H.
Ruth A. Wienclaw, PhD

Trichotillomania

Definition

Individuals with trichotillomania repetitively pull out their own hair. Trichotillomania is an impulse-control disorder, although some researchers view it as a type of affective or **obsessive-compulsive disorder**. Nail-biting, skin-picking, and thumb-sucking are considered to be related conditions.

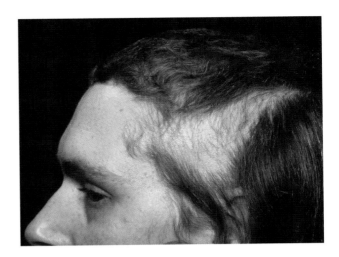

The bald patch on this man's scalp shows the effects of trichotillomania. (© *Custom Medical Stock Photo, Inc. Reproduced by permission.*)

Demographics

Once regarded as rare, trichotillomania is now considered more common, affecting 1–4% of people in the general population. When the tension-release requirement is excluded, trichotillomania occurs in adult females (3.4%) more often than adult males (1.5%). Among children, both genders are affected equally. Nonclinical levels of hair-pulling behavior may be as high as 15.3% among university students.

Description

Trichotillomania involves hair-pulling episodes that result in noticeable hair loss. Although any area of the body can be a target, the most common areas are the scalp, followed by the eyelashes, eyebrows, and pubic region. Hair-pulling can occur without the individual's awareness but is frequently preceded by a sense of increasing tension and followed by a sense of relief or gratification, common features of behavioral **addiction** disorders. The resulting hair loss can be a source of embarrassment or shame. Because of a tendency to hide symptoms and because professionals are relatively unfamiliar with the disorder, individuals either may not seek or are not offered treatment. Untreated trichotillomania can result in impaired social functioning, reduced quality of life, and medical complications.

Causes and symptoms

Causes

Psychoanalytic theories explain compulsive hair-pulling behavior as a way of dealing with unconscious conflicts or childhood **trauma** (such as **sexual abuse**). Behavioral theories assume that symptoms are learned, that a child may imitate a parent who engages in hair-pulling. The behavior may also be learned independently if it serves a purpose. For example, hair-pulling may begin as a response to **stress** and then develop into a habit. Biological theories address a genetic basis. For instance, people with trichotillomania often have a first-degree relative with an obsessive-compulsive spectrum disorder.

Researchers have also evaluated similarities between trichotillomania and **Tourette syndrome**. One group at Duke noted that the parent of a patient with Tourette syndrome in one of their studies displayed symptoms of trichotillomania. The researchers identified a link between mutations in a specific gene and the incidence of Tourette syndrome among the families in this study. Intrigued because the parent carried the mutation but did not exhibit symptoms of Tourette, the researchers completed a study analyzing the potential link between carrying the gene and having trichotillomania. They confirmed a link between the hair-pulling behavior and the mutant form of the gene, called SLITRK1, which is involved in the formation of connections among **brain** cells (called neurons). Two mutations in this gene appear to be linked to trichotillomania, and the researchers suggested that the mutant protein that results may cause missed connections among neurons, leading to the hair-pulling urges.

Symptoms

According to the **diagnosis** of trichotillomania:

- noticeable hair loss (alopecia) due to recurrent hair-pulling

- tension immediately before hair-pulling, or when attempting to resist hair-pulling

- reduction of tension, or a feeling of pleasure or gratification, immediately following hair-pulling

- significant distress or impairment in social, occupational, or other important areas of functioning

In addition, the *DSM-IV-TR* requires that the patient's hair-pulling not be due to another medical or mental disorder. The tension-release requirement is controversial because 17% of people who otherwise qualify for this diagnosis do not experience this.

Symptoms usually emerge in early adolescence. Episodes may last a few minutes or a few hours during periods of stress or relaxation. Those with trichotillomania may prefer hairs with unique textures or qualities. The pulling may include rituals, such as twirling hair off or examining the root. Half of those individuals with trichotillomania engage in oral behaviors—running hair across the lips or through the teeth, biting off the root (trichophagy), or eating hair (trichophagia). They usually try to control their behavior in the presence of others and may hide the affected areas. Symptoms may come and go for weeks, months, or years at a time.

Diagnosis

Other possible causes of symptoms must first be ruled out. Hair loss may have a medical cause, such as a dermatological condition. Hair-pulling may have another psychological cause, such as a delusion or **hallucination in schizophrenia**.

If individuals deny symptoms, hair-pulling behavior can be assessed by objective measures such as the presence of short, broken hairs or damaged follicles. Some **psychological assessment** instruments are also available. These include the Massachusetts General Hospital Hair Pulling Scale (MGH-HPS), a seven-item, self-report measure of the symptoms of hair-pulling. Also the Alopecia Rating assesses the level of hair loss, and the Trichotillomania Interference Checklist interviews patients to assess the effects of pathological hair-pulling on various quality-of-life and health parameters.

Severity of symptoms is also important. Twisting or playing with hair when nervous does not qualify as trichotillomania. If symptoms are minor or undetectable, a diagnosis should be given only if the individual expresses significant distress. Children should be given the diagnosis only if symptoms persist because hair-pulling may be a temporary phase, much like thumb-sucking.

Treatment

Treatment usually starts by determining the current frequency and severity of symptoms. This information, which serves as a measure of progress, is gathered by (a) self-report, (b) reports from significant others, (c) objective measures, such as saving pulled hairs, videotapes, or measuring areas of hair loss, or (d) a combination of these methods.

Primarily, three categories of therapy have been used in the treatment of trichotillomania:

- Psychoanalysis focuses on childhood experiences and unresolved conflicts during early development.

- Medications. Those typically used are antidepressants with serotonergic properties (also used with obsessive-compulsive disorders). Clomipramine (Anafranil) has proven most effective. The **selective serotonin reuptake inhibitors** (SSRIs) have had mixed results. Some researchers recommend low doses of antipsychotic drugs (neuroleptics) in conjunction with SSRIs. Medications are usually combined with behavior therapy.

KEY TERMS

Alopecia—Hair loss.

Selective serotonin reuptake inhibitors (SSRIs)—Commonly prescribed drugs for treating depression. SSRIs affect the chemicals that nerve cells in the brain use to send messages to one another. These chemical messengers (neurotransmitters) are released by one nerve cell and taken up by others. Neurotransmitters not taken up by other nerve cells are taken up by the same cells that released them. This process is termed "reuptake." SSRIs work by inhibiting the reuptake of serotonin, an action that allows more serotonin to be taken up by other nerve cells.

Serotonergic—Containing, activating, or otherwise involving serotonin, which is a chemical that aids in the transmission of nerve impulses.

Trichobezoar—A hairball that results from a buildup of swallowed hairs becoming lodged in the digestive system.

Trichophagia—Eating hair.

Trichophagy—Biting hair.

• Behavior therapy. Habit-reversal training is the most accepted approach. It teaches individuals to monitor their hair-pulling and substitute it for healthier behaviors. Alternative forms of behavior therapy include biofeedback and hypnosis.

Prognosis

The effects of trichotillomania can be very serious. Associated feelings of shame may result in avoidance of social situations; chewing hair can result in dental erosion; and eating hair may result in hairballs (trichobezoars) becoming lodged in the stomach or large intestine, which can lead to anemia, abdominal pain, nausea and vomiting, hematemesis (vomiting blood), or bowel obstruction or perforation.

Studies show low success rates with medications and traditional **psychoanalysis**. Behavioral therapy has reported long-term success rates of 90% or more. Follow-up sessions are encouraged to prevent **relapse**. A major issue in prognosis is whether an individual receives treatment. Professionals may not recognize or know how to treat trichotillomania effectively. Conversely, individuals with the disorder may be too embarrassed to address their symptoms.

Prevention

No specific information is available regarding prevention.

Resources

BOOKS

American Psychiatric Association. *Diagnostic and Statistical Manual of Mental Disorders*. 4th ed., text rev. Washington, DC: American Psychiatric Publishing, 2000.

Franklin, Martin E., and David F. Tolin. *Treating Trichotillomania: Cognitive-Behavioral Therapy for Hairpulling and Related Problems*. New York: Springer: 2010.

Grant, Jon E., and Dan J. Stein, Douglas Woods, and Nancy J. Keuthen. *Trichotillomania, Skin Picking, and Other Body-Focused Repetitive Behaviors*. Washington, DC: American Psychiatric Publishing: 2011.

PERIODICALS

Dia, David A. "'I Can't Stop Pulling my Hair!' Using Numbing Cream as an Adjunct Treatment for Trichotillomania." *Health and Social Work* 33, no. 2 (2008): 155.

Edson, Aubrey L., Martin E. Franklin, and Jennifer B. Freeman. "Behavior Therapy for Pediatric Trichotillomania: Exploring the Effects of Age on Treatment Outcome." *Child and Adolescent Psychiatry and Mental Health* 4 (2010): 18.

Parakh, Preeti, and Mona Srivastava. "The Many Faces of Trichotillomania." *International Journal of Trichology* 2, no. 1 (2010): 50.

WEBSITES

Duke Center for Human Genetics. "Trichotillomania." 2005. http://www.chg.duke.edu/diseases/ttm.html (accessed October 28, 2011).

Duke Medicine News and Communications. "Hair-pulling Disorder Caused by Faulty Gene in Some Families." September 27, 2006. Available online at DukeHealth.org: http://www.dukehealth.org/news/9887 (accessed November 10, 2011).

ORGANIZATIONS

Trichotillomania Learning Center, Inc, 207 McPherson Street, Ste. H, Santa Cruz, CA, 95060, (831) 457-1004, Fax: (831) 426-4383, info@trich.org, http://www.trich.org.

Sandra L. Friedrich, MA
Emily Jane Willingham, PhD

Trifluoperazine

Definition

Trifluoperazine is a phenothiazine antipsychotic agent. In the United States, this drug is sold under the brand name Stelazine.

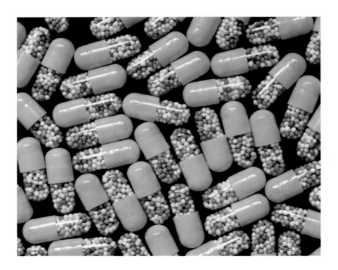

Stelazine (trifluoperazine), 2 mg. (© Adam Hart-Davis/Photo Researchers, Inc.)

Purpose

Trifluoperazine is a drug used to treat **schizophrenia**. It may also be used to treat anxiety in persons who have not had success with other medications.

Description

Trifluoperazine is an effective agent in treating symptoms of psychotic behavior. When used for the treatment of **schizophrenia**, trifluoperazine reduces the symptoms of emotional withdrawal, anxiety, tension, hallucinations, and paranoia.

Recommended dosage

The dosage of trifluoperazine should be adjusted to the lowest level needed to control symptoms. The drug may be given orally or by intramuscular injection (a shot).

A useful initial dosage of trifluoperazine for psychotic adults is 2–5 mg two times each day. A common total dosage is 15–20 mg per day. Some people may require up to 40 mg or more per day. When using deep intramuscular injection, 1–2 mg every four to six hours is usually sufficient to control symptoms within 24 hours. Total intramuscular trifluoperazine should not exceed 10 mg per day.

Control of psychotic symptoms in children between the ages of 6 and 12 can usually be achieved with 1–2 mg per day, given in 1 mg increments. Trifluoperazine is not recommended for use in children younger than 6.

Precautions

Trifluoperazine may cause bone marrow and blood disorders. It has also been associated with sudden

KEY TERMS

Anxiety—An abnormal and overwhelming sense of apprehension and fear often marked by physiological signs (as sweating, tension, and increased pulse), by doubt concerning the reality and nature of a threat, and by self-doubt about the capacity to cope with an issue.

Hallucination—An occurrence when a person sees or hears things that are not really there. Hallucinations can result from nervous system abnormalities, mental disorders, or the use of certain drugs.

Schizophrenia—A major mental illness marked by psychotic symptoms, including hallucinations, delusions, and severe disruptions in thinking.

cardiac death (heart attack). Some newborns born to mothers who took trifluoperazine during pregnancy displayed symptoms of withdrawal, including increased agitation and trouble breathing; women who are pregnant or planning to become pregnant should not take trifluoperazine.

Trifluoperazine is not approved by the U.S. Food and Drug Administration (FDA) for use in treating the behavioral symptoms of dementia in elderly patients. Patients taking trifluoperazine for this purpose are at increased risk of death during treatment.

Trifluoperazine increases the level of prolactin in the blood, a hormone that stimulates the mammary glands in the breast. This is a potential problem for people with a personal or family history of breast cancer and may increase the risk of breast cancer. For this reason and the other serious side effects associated with trifluoperazine, health professionals must carefully evaluate the benefits and risks of the drug before administering it.

Side effects

Relatively common side effects that accompany trifluoperazine include drowsiness, dizziness, rash, dry mouth, **insomnia**, **fatigue**, muscular weakness, anorexia, blurred vision, some loss of muscular control, and amenorrhea (lack of menstruation) in women.

Dystonia (difficulty walking or moving) may occur with trifluoperazine use. This condition may subside in 24 to 48 hours even when the person continues taking the drug, and it usually disappears when trifluoperazine is discontinued.

Trifluoperazine use may lead to the development of symptoms that resemble Parkinson's disease. These symptoms may include a tight or mask-like expression

QUESTIONS TO ASK YOUR DOCTOR

- What kind of changes can I expect to see or feel with this medication?
- Does it matter what time of day I take this medication?
- Should I take this medication with or without food?
- What are the side effects associated with this medication?
- Will this medication interact or interfere with other medications I am currently taking?
- What symptoms or adverse effects are important enough that I should seek immediate treatment?

on the face, drooling, tremors, pill-rolling motions in the hands, cogwheel rigidity (abnormal rigidity in muscles characterized by jerky movements when the muscle is passively stretched), and a shuffling gait. Taking the anti-Parkinson drugs **benztropine** mesylate or **trihexyphenidyl** hydrochloride along with the trifluoperazine usually controls these symptoms.

Trifluoperazine has the potential to produce a serious side effect called **tardive dyskinesia**. This syndrome consists of involuntary, uncoordinated movements that may appear late in therapy and may not disappear even after the drug is discontinued. Tardive dyskinesia involves involuntary movements of the tongue, jaw, mouth, face, or other groups of skeletal muscles. The incidence of tardive dyskinesia increases with age and with increasing dosage of trifluoperazine. Women are at greater risk than men for developing tardive dyskinesia. There is no known effective treatment for tardive dyskinesia, although gradual (but rarely complete) improvement may occur over a long period.

An occasionally reported side effect of trifluoperazine is **neuroleptic malignant syndrome**. This is a complicated and potentially fatal condition characterized by muscle rigidity, high fever, alterations in mental status, and cardiac symptoms such as irregular pulse or blood pressure, sweating, tachycardia (fast heartbeat), and arrhythmias (irregular heartbeat). People who think they may be experiencing any such side effects from this or any other medication should tell their physicians immediately.

Interactions

Trifluoperazine may reduce the effectiveness of oral anticoagulant (blood-thinning) drugs. It should not be taken with the drug metoclopramide (Reglan). The blood concentration of the drug phenytoin is increased by trifluoperazine, which may lead to phenytoin toxicity. **Propranolol** increases theconcentration of trifluoperazine. The blood pressure–lowering effects of guanethidine may be diminished by trifluoperazine. The use of diuretics with trifluoperazine may cause a sudden decrease in blood pressure often accompanied by dizziness due to a change in body position (known as orthostatic hypotension).

Trifluoperazine increases the effect of drugs and substances that depress the central nervous system. These drugs include anesthetics, opiates, **barbiturates**, atropine, and alcohol. These substances should be avoided or used sparingly by people taking trifluoperazine.

Several herbal supplements may interact with trifluoperazine; patients should inform their doctors of all drugs and supplements they are currently taking.

Resources

BOOKS

Albers, Lawrence J., MD, Rhoda K. Hahn, MD, and Christopher Reist, MD. *Handbook of Psychiatric Drugs.* Laguna Hills, CA: Current Clinical Strategies Publishing, 2010.

American Society of Health-System Pharmacists. *AHFS Drug Information 2011.* Bethesda: American Society of Health-System Pharmacists, 2011.

Graham, George. *The Disordered Mind: An Introduction to Philosophy of Mind and Mental Illness.* New York, NY: Routledge, 2010.

Holland, Leland Norman, and Michael Patrick Adams. *Core Concepts in Pharmacology,* 3rd ed. New York, NY: Prentice Hall, 2011.

North, Carol, and Sean Yutzy. *Goodwin and Guze's Psychiatric Diagnosis.* New York, NY: Oxford University Press, 2010.

Preston, John D., John H. O'Neal, and Mary C. Talaga. *Handbook of Clinical Psychopharmacology for Therapists,* 6th ed. Oakland, CA: New Harbinger Publications, 2011.

WEBSITES

PubMed Health. "Trifluoperazine." http://www.ncbi.nlm.nih.gov/pubmedhealth/PMH0000585 (accessed November 13, 2011).

ORGANIZATIONS

American Psychiatric Association, 1000 Wilson Boulevard, Suite 1825, Arlington, VA, 22209, (703) 907-7300, apa@psych.org, http://www.psych.org.

Mental Health America, 2000 N. Beauregard Street, 6th Floor, Alexandria, VA, 22311, (703) 684-7722, (800) 969-6642, Fax: (703) 684-5968, http://www1.nmha.org.

National Alliance on Mental Illness (NAMI), Colonial Place Three, 2107 Wilson Blvd., Suite 300, Arlington, VA, 22201, (703) 524-7600, (800) 950-NAMI (6264), Fax: (703) 524-9094, http://www.nami.org/Hometemplate.cfm.

National Institute of Mental Health (NIMH), 6001 Executive Boulevard, Room 8184, MSC 9663, Bethesda, MD, 20892, (301) 443-4513, (866) 615-6464, Fax: (301) 443-4279, nimhinfo@nih.gov, http://www.nimh.nih.gov/index.shtml.

U.S. Food and Drug Administration, 10903 New Hampshire Ave., Silver Spring, MD, 20993-0002, (888) INFO-FDA (463-6332), http://www.fda.gov.

L. Fleming Fallon, Jr., MD, Dr.P.H.
Ruth A. Wienclaw, Ph.D.
Laura Jean Cataldo, RN, Ed.D.

Trihexyphenidyl

Definition

Trihexyphenidyl is classified as an anti-parkinsonian agent. It is sold in the United States under the brand name Artane and is also available under its generic name.

Purpose

Trihexyphenidyl is used to treat a group of side effects (called parkinsonian side effects) that includes tremors, difficulty walking, and slack muscle tone. These side effects may occur in patients who are taking antipsychotic medications used to treat mental disorders such as **schizophrenia**.

Description

Some medicines, called antipsychotic drugs, that are used to treat schizophrenia and other mental disorders

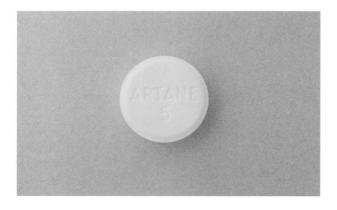

Artane (trihexyphenidyl), 5 mg. (© *Custom Medical Stock Photo, Inc. Reproduced by permission.*)

can cause side effects that are similar to the symptoms of Parkinson's disease. Such patients do not have Parkinson's disease, but they may experience shaking in muscles while at rest, difficulty with voluntary movements, and poor muscle tone. These symptoms are similar to the symptoms of Parkinson's disease.

One way to eliminate these undesirable side effects is to stop taking the antipsychotic medicine. Unfortunately, the symptoms of the original mental disorder usually come back, so in most cases simply stopping the antipsychotic medication is not a reasonable option. Some drugs such as trihexyphenidyl that control the symptoms of Parkinson's disease also control the parkinsonian side effects of antipsychotic medicines.

Trihexyphenidyl works by restoring the chemical balance between **dopamine** and acetylcholine, two neurotransmitter chemicals in the **brain**. Taking trihexyphenidyl along with the antipsychotic medicine helps to control symptoms of the mental disorder, while reducing parkinsonian side effects. Trihexyphenidyl is in the same family of drugs (commonly known as anticholinergic drugs) as **biperiden** and **benztropine**.

Recommended dosage

Trihexyphenidyl is available in 2 mg and 5 mg tablets and an elixir containing 2 mg per teaspoonful. For the treatment of tremors, poor muscle tone, and similar side effects, trihexyphenidyl should be started at a dose of 1 to 2 mg orally two to three times daily or as needed, to a maximum daily dose of 15 mg per day. Parkinson's-like side effects caused by antipsychotic drugs may come and go, so trihexyphenidyl may not be needed on a regular basis. Trihexyphenidyl may also be prescribed to prevent these side effects before they actually occur. This is called prophylactic (preventative) therapy.

Precautions

Trihexyphenidyl should never be used in children under age three. It should be used cautiously and with close physician supervision in older children and in people over age 60. Trihexyphenidyl, like all anticholinergic drugs, decreases sweating and the body's ability to cool itself. People who are unaccustomed to being outside in hot weather should take care to stay as cool as possible and drink extra fluids. People who are chronically ill, have a central nervous system disease, or who work outside during hot weather may need to avoid taking trihexyphenidyl.

People who have the following medical problems may experience increased negative side effects when taking trihexyphenidyl. People with these problems should discuss their conditions with their physicians before starting the drug:

- glaucoma, especially closed-angle glaucoma
- intestinal obstruction
- prostate enlargement
- urinary bladder obstruction

Although rare, some patients experience euphoria while taking trihexyphenidyl and may abuse it for this reason. Euphoria can occur at doses only two to four times the normal daily dose. Patients with a history of drug abuse should be observed carefully for trihexyphenidyl abuse.

Side effects

Although trihexyphenidyl helps to control the side effects of antipsychotic drugs, it can produce side effects of its own. A person taking trihexyphenidyl may have some of the following reactions, which may vary in intensity:

- dry mouth
- dry skin
- blurred vision
- nausea or vomiting
- constipation
- disorientation
- drowsiness
- irritability
- increased heart rate
- urinary retention

Dry mouth, if severe to the point of causing difficulty speaking or swallowing, may be managed by reducing or temporarily discontinuing trihexyphenidyl. Chewing sugarless gum or sucking on sugarless candy may also help to increase the flow of saliva. Some artificial saliva products may give temporary relief.

Men with prostate enlargement may be especially prone to urinary retention. Symptoms of this problem include having difficulty starting a urine flow and more difficulty passing urine than usual. This side effect may be severe and require discontinuation of the drug. Urinary retention may require catheterization. People who think they may be experiencing any side effects from this or any other medication should tell their physicians.

Patients who take an overdose of trihexyphenidyl are treated with forced vomiting, removal of stomach contents and stomach washing, activated charcoal, and respiratory support if needed. They are also given physostigmine, an antidote for anticholinergic drug poisoning.

Interactions

When drugs such as trihexyphenidyl are taken with **antidepressants** such as **amitriptyline, imipramine, trimipramine, desipramine, nortriptyline, protriptyline, amoxapine,** and **doxepin** or with many antihistamines that also have anticholinergic properties, the effects and side effects of trihexyphenidyl are usually intensified.

Drugs such as trihexyphenidyl decrease the speed with which food moves through the stomach and intestines. Because of this, the absorption of other drugs taken may be enhanced by trihexyphenidyl. Patients receiving trihexyphenidyl should be alert to unusual responses to other drugs they might be taking and report any changes to their physician.

Resources

BOOKS

American Society of Health-System Pharmacists. *AHFS Drug Information 2008.* Bethesda, MD: American Society of Health-System Pharmacists, 2008.

PERIODICALS

Nappo, Solange Aparecida, et al. "Trihexyphenidyl (Artane): A Brazilian Study of Its Abuse." *Substance Use and Misuse* 40, no. 4 (2005): 473–82.

Jack Raber, Pharm.D.
Ruth A. Wienclaw, PhD

Trilafon *see* **Perphenazine**
Trileptal *see* **Oxcarbazepine**

Trimipramine

Definition

Trimipramine is an oral tricyclic antidepressant. It is sold in the United States under the brand name Surmontil.

Purpose

Trimipramine is used primarily to treat **depression** and to treat the combination of symptoms of anxiety and depression. Like other **antidepressants** of this chemical and pharmacological class, trimipramine has also been used in limited numbers of patients to treat **panic disorder, obsessive-compulsive disorder, attention deficit** hyperactivity disorder, enuresis (bed-wetting), eating disorders such as **bulimia nervosa**, **cocaine** dependency, and the depressive phase of bipolar (manic-depressive) disorder, although not all of these uses are approved by the U.S. Food and Drug Administration (FDA).

Description

Tricyclic antidepressants act to change the balance of naturally occurring chemicals in the **brain** that regulate the transmission of nerve impulses between cells. Trimipramine acts primarily to increase the concentration of norepinephrine and **serotonin** (both chemical messengers in nerve cells) and, to a lesser extent, to block the action of another brain chemical, acetylcholine. Trimipramine shares most of the properties of other tricyclic antidepressants, such as **amitriptyline**, **amoxapine**, **clomipramine**, **desipramine**, **imipramine**, **nortriptyline**, and **protriptyline**. Studies comparing trimipramine with these other drugs have shown that trimipramine is no more or less effective than other antidepressants of its type. Its choice for treatment is as much a function of physician preference as any other factor.

The therapeutic effects of trimipramine, like other antidepressants, appear slowly. Maximum benefit is often not evident for at least two weeks after starting the drug. People taking trimipramine should be aware of this and continue taking the drug as directed even if they do not see immediate improvement.

Recommended dosage

The recommended dosage can vary based on the patient's age and situation. The initial dose of trimipramine for depression in an adult begins at 75 mg per day. This dosage can be increased as necessary, usually plateauing at a maximum of 200 mg a day. For patients who are hospitalized, the dose may exceed the 200 mg per day cutoff. This drug is not recommended for children and teenagers, but if it is prescribed, the recommended dosage for teenagers is an initial 50 mg per day that may be gradually increased by the doctor to a typical maximum of 100 mg per day. For children age 12 years and younger, the dose will be determined by the doctor. For the elderly, the initial dose is 50 mg per day, which can be increased as the doctor deems necessary, but typically no higher than 100 mg per day.

Precautions

Like all tricyclic antidepressants, trimipramine should be used cautiously and with close physician supervision in people, especially the elderly, who have benign prostatic hypertrophy, urinary retention, and glaucoma, especially angle-closure glaucoma (the most severe form). Before starting treatment, people with these conditions should discuss the relative risks and benefits of treatment with their doctors to help determine if trimipramine is the right antidepressant for them.

Some studies have shown that children and teenagers up to age 24 who take antidepressants such as trimipramine may have an increased risk of committing self-harm or **suicide**. Children under the age of 18 should not normally take this drug; if a child is prescribed the drug, parents or caregivers should closely monitor the child, as serious symptoms can develop suddenly. Any signs that a patient is considering self-harm or suicide warrants an immediate call to the doctor. These signs might include worsening depression, panic attacks, difficulty falling asleep, irritability, planning to engage in self-harm or to attempt suicide, or abnormal excitement.

Trimipramine may increase the possibility of having **seizures**. Patients should tell their physician if they have a history of seizures, including seizures brought on by the abuse of drugs or alcohol. These people should use trimipramine only with caution and be closely monitored by their physician. Trimipramine may also increase heart rate and **stress** on the heart. It may be dangerous for people with cardiovascular disease, especially those who have recently had a heart attack, to take this drug or other antidepressants in the same pharmacological class. In rare cases where patients with cardiovascular disease must receive trimipramine, they should be monitored closely for cardiac rhythm disturbances and signs of cardiac stress or damage.

A common problem with tricyclic antidepressants is sedation (drowsiness, lack of physical and mental alertness). This side effect is especially noticeable early in therapy. In most patients, sedation decreases or disappears entirely with time, but until then patients taking trimipramine should not perform hazardous activities requiring mental alertness or coordination. The sedative effect is increased when trimipramine is taken with other central nervous system depressants, such as alcoholic beverages, sleeping medications, other **sedatives**, or antihistamines. It may be dangerous to take trimipramine in combination with these substances.

Side effects

Trimipramine shares side effects common to all tricyclic antidepressants, including dry mouth, constipation, urinary retention, increased heart rate, sedation, irritability, dizziness, and decreased coordination. As with most side effects associated with tricyclic antidepressants, the intensity is highest at the beginning of therapy and tends to decrease with continued use.

Dry mouth, if severe to the point of causing difficulty speaking or swallowing, may be managed by dosage reduction or temporary discontinuation of the drug. Patients may also chew sugarless gum or suck sugarless candy to increase the flow of saliva. Some artificial saliva products may give temporary relief.

Men with prostate enlargement who take trimipramine may be especially likely to have problems with urinary retention. Symptoms include having difficulty starting a urine flow and more difficulty than usual passing urine. In most cases, urinary retention is managed with dose reduction or by switching to another type of antidepressant. In extreme cases, patients may require treatment with bethanechol, a drug that reverses this particular side effect. People who think they may be experiencing any side effects from this or any other medication should tell their physicians.

Interactions

Dangerously high blood pressure has resulted from the combination of tricyclic antidepressants, such as trimipramine, and members of another class of antidepressants known as **monoamine oxidase inhibitors (MAOIs)**. Because of this, trimipramine should never be taken in combination with **MAOIs**. Patients taking any MAOIs, for example **phenelzine** (Nardil) or **tranylcypromine** (Parnate), should stop taking the MAOI and wait at least 14 days before starting trimipramine or any other tricyclic antidepressant. The same holds true when discontinuing trimipramine and starting an MAOI.

Trimipramine may decrease the blood pressure–lowering effects of **clonidine**. Patients who take both drugs should be monitored for loss of blood pressure control and the dose of clonidine increased as needed.

The sedative effects of trimipramine are increased by other central nervous system depressants such as alcohol, sedatives, sleeping medications, or medications used for other mental disorders such as **schizophrenia**. The anticholinergic effects of trimipramine are additive with other anticholinergic drugs such as **benztropine**, **biperiden**, **trihexyphenidyl**, and antihistamines.

Resources

BOOKS

Stahl, Stephen. *The Prescriber's Guide: Antidepressants; Stahl's Essential Psychopharmacology.* 4th edition. New York: Cambridge University Press: 2011.

WEBSITES

PubMed Health. "Trimipramine." U.S. National Library of Medicine. http://www.ncbi.nlm.nih.gov/pubmedhealth/PMH0000191 (accessed November 12, 2011).

ORGANIZATIONS

American Society of Health-System Pharmacists, 7272 Wisconsin Ave., Bethesda, MD, 20814, (866) 279-0681, custserv@ashp.org, http://www.ashp.org.

U.S. National Library of Medicine, 8600 Rockville Pike, Bethesda, MD, 20894, http://www.nlm.nih.gov.

United States Food and Drug Administration, 10903 New Hampshire Ave., Silver Spring, MD, 20993, (888) 463-6332, http://www.fda.gov.

Jack Raber, Pharm.D.
Emily Jane Willingham, PhD

Trisomy 21 *see* **Down syndrome**
Tryptophan *see* **Serotonin**

Undifferentiated somatoform disorder

Definition

Undifferentiated somatoform disorder occurs when a person has physical complaints for more than six months that cannot be attributed to a medical condition. If there is a medical condition present, the complaints must be far more severe than can be accounted for by the presence of the medical problem.

Demographics

Undifferentiated somatoform disorder is relatively common. It is estimated that between 4% and 11% of the population experience the disorder at some time in their lives. Women are more likely than men to have undifferentiated somatoform disorder, as are the elderly and people of lower socioeconomic backgrounds. Young women who have low socioeconomic status are the most likely group to have undifferentiated somatoform disorder. Fifty percent of the people with this disorder have other psychological or psychiatric disorders as well, such as anxiety or depression.

Description

The physical complaints that are expressed by people with undifferentiated somatoform disorder are many and varied. The similarity between all physical complaints associated with undifferentiated somatoform disorder is an absence of medical evidence for the symptoms or for their severity.

The physical complaints usually begin or worsen when the patient is under **stress**. People with undifferentiated somatoform disorder experience problems functioning in their daily lives due to the physical symptoms that they experience. Seeing multiple doctors in an effort to find a physical cause for the reported symptoms is typical of people with this disorder. Undifferentiated

somatoform disorder is also sometimes referred to as somatization syndrome.

Causes and symptoms

The symptoms of undifferentiated somatoform disorder vary widely from person to person. Some of the most common physical complaints are pain, **fatigue**, appetite loss, and various gastrointestinal problems. The physical complaints generally last for long periods. Patients with undifferentiated somatoform disorder tend to complain of many different physical problems over time.

No matter what symptoms a person complains about, the overarching characteristic of the complaints is that no physical reason can be found for them. Laboratory tests and thorough examinations by doctors will reveal no medical reason for the pains or problems the person is having. The physical problems, however, persist after the person has been told no explanation can be found.

The causes of undifferentiated somatoform disorder are not clear. Some experts believe that problems in the family when the affected person was a child may be related to the development of this disorder. **Depression** and stress are thought to be other possible causes. In people who worry about even minor medical conditions, paying obsessive attention to any minor changes or sensations that their bodies experience may be a factor in developing the disorder. They give the feelings undue weight and worry unnecessarily about them.

Diagnosis

A person with undifferentiated somatoform disorder usually begins by visiting physicians looking for treatments for physical complaints. Later, he or she may be referred to a mental health professional. Referring physicians may continue to see the patient, however, so that a trusting relationship can be established and so the patient does not continue to bounce from doctor to doctor.

Mental health professionals use the handbook called the ***Diagnostic and Statistical Manual of Mental Disorders*** to diagnose mental disorders. The book lists diagnostic criteria for undifferentiated somatoform disorder and requires that the following conditions be met in order for the clinician to diagnose this disorder:

• There must be no underlying medical cause evident that could explain the patient's physical complaints. If there is a medical condition that could be related to the complaints, the symptoms reported must be far worse than any that could be explained by the existing medical problems.

• The unexplained physical symptoms must persist for at least six months.

• The symptoms must cause problems in the patient's daily life or relationships or interfere with the patient achieving his or her goals.

• There cannot be another mental disorder that accounts for the complaints.

• The patient cannot knowingly make false complaints of physical distress.

Somatization disorder

Somatization disorder is very similar to undifferentiated somatoform disorder, and the two can be easily confused. The symptoms are the same, but the diagnostic criteria are much more specific for somatization disorder. To be diagnosed with somatization disorder, the patient must have four different pain symptoms, two gastrointestinal symptoms, one sexual symptom, and one pseudoneurological symptom. These symptoms can occur at different times. The symptoms must be present for several years and must have begun before the patient was 30 years old. Just as with undifferentiated somatoform disorder, the complaints must not be traceable to any medical cause.

Hypochondriasis

Patients with hypochondriasis usually have a specific **diagnosis** in mind when they visit a doctor, unlike most patients with undifferentiated somatoform disorder who have complaints but do not have a cause in mind.

Treatment

Most treatments of undifferentiated somatoform disorder focus on treating any underlying psychological problems or stresses that may be causing the disorder.

When the disorder occurs in conjunction with another mental health problem such as depression, treating that problem often helps to resolve or lessen the symptoms of undifferentiated somatoform disorder. Some studies indicate that **antidepressants** are effective in treating this disorder. Patients also may benefit from programs intended to teach them how to manage stress and to understand the correlation between psychological stressors and physiological symptoms. These programs also teach people how to cope with criticism and how to stop negative behavior patterns.

Prognosis

For many people, undifferentiated somatoform disorder is a lifelong disorder. Often, the physical complaints increase or decrease in relation to stressors in the affected person's life. Many people with this disorder are eventually diagnosed with another mental disorder or with a legitimate medical problem. For some people, treatment can be successful at lessening or completely resolving symptoms.

Prevention

There are no known ways to prevent undifferentiated somatoform disorder; it is possible, however, for people who appear to be developing the disorder to enroll in programs designed to teach them coping strategies and about the relationship between psychological factors and physical symptoms.

Resources

BOOKS

American Psychiatric Association. *Diagnostic and Statistical Manual of Mental Disorders.* 4th ed., text rev. Washington, DC: American Psychiatric Publishing, 2000.

PERIODICALS

Koh, K. B., E. H. Choi, Y. J. Lee, and M. Han. "Serotonin-Related Gene Pathways Associated with Undifferentiated Somatoform Disorder." *Psychiatry Research* 189, no. 2 (2011): 246–50.

Koh, K. B., J. I. Kang, J. D. Lee, and Y. J. Lee. "Shared Neural Activity in Panic Disorder and Undifferentiated Somatoform Disorder Compared with Healthy Controls." *Journal of Clinical Psychiatry* 71, no. 12 (2010): 1576–81.

Tish Davidson, A.M.

Vaginismus

Definition

Vaginismus occurs when the muscles around the outer third of the vagina contract involuntarily when vaginal penetration is attempted during sexual intercourse.

Demographics

Although many women experience sexual disorders, it is hard to gather accurate data regarding the frequency of specific problems. Many cases go unreported. Vaginismus is thought to occur most often in women who are highly educated and of high socioeconomic status.

Description

Vaginismus is a reflex response to pressing on the vagina. Women with vaginismus do not intentionally contract their vaginal muscles; rather, the muscles of the outer vagina tighten automatically, often causing pain. Vaginismus can occur with any type of attempted vaginal penetration such as by a penis, speculum, tampon, or other object. Sometimes it occurs with mere touching. Pushing harder increases the pain and most women with vaginismus cannot tolerate sexual intercourse. Vaginismus does not affect a woman's desire for sexual intercourse. Most women with vaginismus enjoy sexual activity that does not involve penetration and many have orgasms through clitoral stimulation.

There are different types of vaginismus:

- Lifelong vaginismus is the most common type and begins the first time vaginal penetration is attempted.
- Acquired vaginismus begins after a period of normal sexual functioning, often after a physical condition causes an episode of painful intercourse or after a woman has intercourse while emotionally distressed.

- General vaginismus occurs whenever vaginal penetration is attempted.
- Situational vaginismus occurs only in specific situations, such as with a certain sexual partner or during a gynecological examination.

Causes and symptoms

According to the health professional's handbook, the ***Diagnostic and Statistical Manual of Mental Disorders*** (fourth edition, or *DSM-IV-TR*), in order for a condition to be diagnosed as vaginismus, the response must be due to psychological factors or a combination of psychological and medical factors, but not to medical factors alone. This entry focuses on the psychological causes and treatments of vaginismus.

Causes

There are many possible causes of vaginismus. One example is an upbringing in which sex was considered wrong or sinful—as in the case of some strict religious backgrounds. This is common among women with this disorder. Concern that penetration is going to be painful, such as during a first sexual experience, is another possible cause. It is also thought that women who feel threatened or powerless in their relationship may subconsciously use this tightening of the vaginal muscles as a defense or silent objection to the relationship. A traumatic childhood experience, such as sexual molestation, may cause lifelong vaginismus. Acquired-type vaginismus is often the result of sexual assault or rape.

Symptoms

The major symptom of vaginismus is the severe contraction of the outer vaginal muscles as the vagina is about to be penetrated. This may completely prevent penetration or make it difficult and painful. Women with vaginismus may be unable to consciously relax their vaginal muscles even when they truly desire to have sexual intercourse or allow penetration. Pelvic examinations may also be painful, and some women cannot tolerate inserting a tampon.

Diagnosis

Diagnosing sexual disorders such as vaginismus can often be very difficult. This is mainly due to the discomfort many people feel when discussing sexual relations, even with their physicians. Cultural norms and taboos often deter women from seeking help when they are experiencing problems. When a physician or gynecologist is consulted, involuntary spasm during pelvic examination can confirm the **diagnosis** of vaginismus, and a complete physical exam and medical and sexual history will rule out any physiological causes for the condition. When psychological causes are suspected, the patient should be referred to a **psychiatrist**, **psychologist**, or sex therapist.

DSM-IV-TR

The *DSM-IV-TR* criteria require that for a diagnosis of vaginismus, the spasm of the muscles in the outer third of the vagina must be involuntary and recurring or persistent and must interfere with sexual intercourse; the symptoms must cause physical or emotional distress or problems with relationships; and the symptoms must exist independently of another disorder, mental or physical, that could account for them.

DSM-5

Proposed changes for the *DSM-5* (fifth edition, 2013) subsume the diagnoses of vaginismus and **dyspareunia** (pain associated with sexual intercourse) into one condition, known as genito-pelvic pain/penetration disorder. A diagnosis will require that the patient experience one or more of the following symptoms over a six-month period:

- inability to have sexual intercourse
- vulvovaginal or pelvic pain during intercourse attempts
- anxiety or fear resulting from the pain or the act of intercourse
- significant tension of the pelvic floor muscles during attempted penetration

The subtypes of lifelong vs. acquired and generalized vs. situational will still apply.

Treatment

There are many different treatments of vaginismus. Therapists may use behavioral, hypnotic, psychological,

educational, or **group therapy** techniques. Multiple techniques are often used simultaneously for the same patient. Unless physical causes are present, treatment is aimed at reducing the anxiety and fear associated with penetration.

Traditional

PSYCHOTHERAPY. There are three settings in which psychological treatment can occur. These are in individual, couple, or group settings. Individual therapy often focuses on identifying and resolving underlying causes for vaginismus, such as childhood **trauma** or rape. When a woman has a trusting relationship with her therapist, insecurities or fears around sex resulting from factors such as parental attitudes or religious upbringing can often be revealed and successfully resolved.

Couples therapy, or dual-sex therapy, is based on the concept that any sexual problems should be addressed by the couple, rather than by the affected individual alone. The therapist interacts with the partners individually and as a couple, addressing the couple's sexual history and any other relationship problems. Confronting these issues may help to reveal and resolve the causes of vaginismus, especially when the disorder represents a nonverbal form of protest against some aspect of the relationship. The couple is educated about the condition and taught various activities that may be helpful in overcoming the disorder.

Group therapy also can be effective for treating vaginismus. Couples or individuals who have the same or similar sexual disorders are brought together in a group. This setting can provide comfort and support for women or couples who feel embarrassed or ashamed of the disorder. Witnessing others discussing sex and sexual problems in an open and honest forum can encourage patients to become more open and honest themselves. Group therapy also exerts a certain amount of positive pressure and encouragement to open up and express oneself and to follow through with "homework," which may include masturbation or certain kinds of foreplay.

HYPNOTHERAPY. Hypnotherapy is effective for some patients with vaginismus. Hypnotherapy tends to focus on overcoming the condition itself, rather than resolving any underlying causes or conflicts. It often entails a number of sessions during which the patient and therapist define the goals of hypnotherapy. When the actual hypnosis occurs, suggestions are aimed at resolving underlying fears or concerns and at alleviating symptoms. For example, the patient may be told that she can have intercourse without pain and that she will be able to overcome her muscle spasms. During hypnosis, the problems causing the vaginismus may be explored, or an attempt may even be made to reverse the feelings or fears causing the disorder. Exploring causal relationships, as well as suggesting to the woman she can overcome her vaginal muscle spasms, can be very effective for certain patients.

OTHER TREATMENTS. Behavioral therapy, including **cognitive-behavioral therapy** (CBT), is also used to treat vaginismus. When behavioral therapy is chosen, it is assumed that the vaginismus is a learned behavior that can be unlearned. Behavioral therapy generally involves desensitization. Patients are exposed to situations that they find create a mild sense of psychological discomfort or anxiety. Once these situations are conquered, the patient is exposed to sexual situations that they find more threatening, until eventually coitus is achieved without difficulty.

Another type of treatment for vaginismus involves desensitization over a period of time using systematic vaginal dilation. In the beginning of the treatment, the woman touches near or inserts a small object into her vagina. Over time, she inserts larger and larger vaginal dilators. Eventually, a dilator the size of a penis can be inserted comfortably and sexual intercourse can be achieved. There is some debate about this procedure, as it treats the symptoms and not the underlying causes of the vaginismus disorder.

Desensitization procedures are somewhat controversial because they address the symptoms but not the cause of vaginismus. The exercises should be pursued under the direction of an experienced therapist or other healthcare provider. They should involve the sexual partner and gradually include intimate contact before culminating in sexual intercourse.

Prognosis

Vaginismus is one of the most treatable sexual disorders, with a success rate of at least 63%. Because the causes of vaginismus vary, different treatments are successful with different women. In general, a treatment plan that combines two or more therapeutic techniques supervised by a specialist in sex therapy has the greatest likelihood of success. Untreated vaginismus can lead to unsatisfying sexual relationships, tension, and emotional distress between partners.

Prevention

There are no known preventions for vaginismus; however, maintaining open and honest communication within a sexual relationship may help prevent the disorder. Seeking prompt treatment if vaginismus does occur can minimize problems.

KEY TERM

Coitus—Sexual intercourse.

Resources

BOOKS

American Psychiatric Association. *Diagnostic and Statistical Manual of Mental Disorders.* 4th ed., text rev. Washington, DC: American Psychiatric Publishing, 2000.

Goldstein, Andrew, Caroline F. Pukall, and Irwin Goldstein, eds. *Female Sexual Pain Disorders.* Hoboken, NJ: Wiley-Blackwell, 2009.

Meana, Mart. "Painful Intercourse: Dyspareunia and Vaginismus." In *Systemic Sex Therapy,* edited by Katherine M. Hertlein, Gerald R. Weeks, and Nancy Gambescia. New York: Routledge, 2009.

Sadock, Benjamin J., and Virginia A. Sadock, eds. *Comprehensive Textbook of Psychiatry.* Vol. 2. 7th ed. Philadelphia: Lippincott Williams and Wilkins, 2000.

PERIODICALS

Binik, Yitzchak M. "The DSM Diagnostic Criteria for Vaginismus." *Archives of Sexual Behavior* 39, no. 2 (April 2010): 278–91.

Kleinplatz, Peggy J. "Sex Therapy for Vaginismus: a Review, Critique, and Humanistic Alternative." *The Journal of Humanistic Psychology* 38, no. 2 (Spring 1998): 51–82.

Sadovsky, Richard. "Management of Dyspareunia and Vaginismus." *American Family Physician* 61, no. 8 (April 15, 2000): 2511.

Ter Kuile, Moniek M., et al. "Therapist-Aided Exposure for Women With Lifelong Vaginismus: A Replicated Single-Case Design." *Journal of Consulting and Clinical Psychology* 77, no. 1 (February 2009): 149–59.

ORGANIZATIONS

American College of Obstetricians and Gynecologists, PO Box 96920, Washington, DC, 20090-6920, (202) 638-5577, http://www.acog.org.

American Psychological Association, 750 1st Street NE, Washington, DC, 20002-4242, (202) 336-5500; TDD/TTY: (202) 336-6123, (800) 374-2721, http://www.apa.org.

Tish Davidson, A.M.

Vagus nerve stimulation

Definition

Vagus nerve stimulation (VNS) is a type of adjunctive therapy that involves electrical stimulation of the vagus nerve, which is the tenth of the twelve

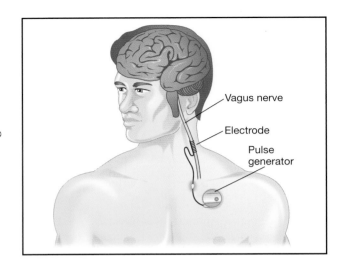

In vagus nerve stimulation, a device called a pulse generator is implanted in the chest. The device sends electrical pulses via a lead wire to the vagus nerve.
(Illustration by Electronic Illustrators Group. © 2012 Cengage Learning.)

cranial nerves. It arises from the medulla (the lower part of the **brain** stem) and controls such varied functions as heart rate, sweating, the rhythmic contractions of the intestines (peristalsis), speech, and keeping the airway open for breathing. The name *vagus* comes from the Latin word for "wandering" because the nerve takes a roundabout course through the body from the brain stem to the digestive tract. The vagus nerve is also known as "cranial nerve X" and the "pneumogastric nerve" because it has branches that innervate both the lungs and the stomach.

The most common form of VNS in current use involves the surgical implantation of a battery-powered stimulator. The procedure was approved by the Food and Drug Administration (FDA) to treat partial-onset epilepsy in 1997 and treatment-resistant **depression** in 2005. The VNS device is sometimes referred to as a "pacemaker for the brain." It is placed under the skin on the chest wall, and a wire runs from it to the vagus nerve in the neck.

A newer, noninvasive form of VNS known as transcutaneous vagus nerve stimulation (t-VNS) was developed by a German company, Cerbomed, founded in 2005. In 2009, the company conducted a pilot test of a new device called NEMOS, which consists of a stimulator and an electrode that the patient attaches to the ear and wears like an earphone for four to five hours per day. Intended for patients with treatment-resistant epilepsy, t-VNS is based on the fact that a branch of the vagus nerve runs directly under the skin of portions of the outer ear.

This branch of the nerve can be stimulated transcutaneously (through the skin) with electrical impulses. No surgery is necessary to use the device. NEMOS was presented at the Fourth International Epilepsy Colloquium in Marburg, Germany, at the end of June 2011. The device had not been approved by the FDA for use in the United States as of late 2011; however, the company has applied for several U.S. patents. Investigational applications of t-VNS include treatment of chronic tinnitus (ringing in the ears), migraine headaches, and **schizophrenia**.

Purpose

The goal of VNS is to change the functioning of various brain and somatic systems by reducing the frequency of **seizures** in the case of epilepsy or by inducing a more positive mood in the case of treatment refractory depression (TRD). In epilepsy, treatment has been concurrent with pharmaceuticals used to reduce seizures. Although approved by the FDA in 2005 for use in treating major depression that has not responded to at least four depression treatments, solid evidence for the efficacy of VNS in depression had not been established as of 2011.

Clinical applications of VNS that were still considered investigational as of 2011 are the treatment of such inflammatory conditions as arthritis, colitis, myocardial infarction, and congestive heart failure. In 2000, a researcher in New York discovered that stimulation of the vagus nerve reduces the release of cytokines, small cell-signaling protein molecules that help to regulate the immune system. Slowing the release of cytokines produced in the spleen helps to protect against organ damage resulting from excessive cytokine production. Thus, it may be possible to use VNS instead of drugs like infliximab (Remicade) or etanercept (Enbrel) to treat rheumatoid arthritis and other autoimmune diseases associated with inflammation.

Description

Research has not been able to establish exactly how VNS works, except to note a multiplicity of effects on the brain and body by stimulating the vagus nerve. That nerve, the tenth cranial nerve, originates in the brain and travels through the mid-brain. Branching into left and right vagus nerves, it runs down the neck and to the thorax and abdomen. The functions of the vagus nerve are many and various, ranging from the stimulation and release of **neurotransmitters** in the brain to issues related to breathing, swallowing, and the vocal chords, to the functioning of the digestive tract. The vagus nerve has been shown to create changes in the functioning of the hypothalamus, the amygdala, and the cingulate gyrusstructures that affect neurotransmitter release and reuptake; mood; and seizure activity, among other things. Because the vagus nerve runs through the middle of the brain, it influences many areas of the brain indirectly, so that while some brain cells increase their activity with VNS, others decrease in synaptic activity. The manufacturers of the only FDA-approved VNS treatment in the United States for epilepsy and depression have used the omnipresent effects of vagus nerve stimulation to bolster their claims as to its efficacy as a treatment for those two disorders.

Implantation and maintenance

VNS involves the surgical implantation of an electrical stimulation device alongside the vagus nerve in the area of the carotid artery, located in the neck. The pulse generator device, which is about the size of a pocket watch, is implanted on the left side of the body, just below the collarbone. Electrodes from the pulse generator are then implanted on the left side of the neck and wrapped around the left vagus nerve. The electrodes are connected to the pulse generator by a wire. The surgical procedure takes about an hour and is usually done as an outpatient procedure.

After implantation, the surgeon tests the device and closes the incisions. Further changes are made with the use of a special wand, a software package, and a portable computer, so patients need not undergo any more invasive procedures related to adjusting the intensity of the electrical impulse. The device is usually set to stimulate the vagus nerve for 20 seconds every five minutes. As an additional control, patients are provided with a strong handheld magnet. When the magnet is held over the skin covering the pulse generator, it prevents it from operating. If patients experience problems with the pulse, they can use the magnet to control it until they get to the physician. The patented collection of pulse generator, leads, software, and programming devices was at one time called the NeuroCybernetic Prosthesis System, or NCP, but the name appears to have been dropped after the FDA sent the manufacturer, Cyberonics, a warning letter in 2001. The FDA had received reports of 83 deaths and several dozen infections linked to the NeuroCybernetic Prosthesis System. The FDA accused the company of improperly reporting and recording the adverse events and of failing to investigate the causes of the deaths.

The pulse generator, which contains a battery with a lifespan of one to 16 years, sends out an electrical impulse whose strength, frequency, and duration are determined by the physician. The impulse travels through the wire to the electrodes, which transmit the pulse to the vagus nerve. VNS was originally used for patients with refractory episodic epilepsy who were deemed unsuitable for epilepsy surgery, but it has been increasingly prescribed for patients whose illnesses are less severe.

Origins and history

VNS was first described in the medical literature as a treatment for epilepsy in 1990. The first VNS implant for treatment-resistant depression was performed in the United States in 1998. Physicians using VNS for patients with epilepsy had reported that patients seemed more alert, and combining anecdotal observations with the fact that some anticonvulsant drugs have also been used in depression treatment, the manufacturer of the VNS system decided to test its efficacy as a treatment for treatment-resistant depression.

As of 2011, about 60,000 patients worldwide had received implanted VNS devices for the treatment of epilepsy. The reported VNS depression research to date has had low numbers of participants, and much research has been directly or indirectly funded by Cyberonics, leaving reported findings open to debate. In fact, in May 2006, the Public Citizen's Health Research Group sent a letter to the FDA requesting that the organization require Cyberonics to withdraw its advertisement from WebMd.com and issue a corrective statement. The group said that the Cyberonics ad "greatly exaggerated" the findings from the clinical studies, and called the advertisement "false and misleading." The nonprofit then pointed out 10 items in a two-paragraph advertisement, explaining why they were false, exaggerated, or both. In September 2006, the group followed up with a second letter to the FDA, requesting denial of Medicare reimbursement for the VNS device when implanted to treat depression.

In another case, one journal editor resigned over having failed to disclose that he and eight other researchers had been funded by Cyberonics in regards to a published study on VNS. Other researchers have included statements in their published papers on VNS, acknowledging that they received funding from the company. In view of the company's legal problems, it is significant that the Mayo Clinic's description of VNS as a treatment for depression urges caution: "For most people, vagus nerve stimulation doesn't significantly ease depression symptoms [although] it does seem to make a significant difference for some people. Some mental health experts don't recommend its use for depression at all, and most health insurance companies don't cover the procedure for depression treatment."

Transcutaneous VNS

Transcutaneous VNS, or t-VNS, is a noninvasive form of VNS. NEMOS, the device currently undergoing **clinical trials** in Europe, will be marketed in Germany for the treatment of epilepsy in September 2012. It consists of an electrode worn over the ear that is attached to a stimulator unit. The ear electrode stimulates a branch of the vagus nerve that runs below the skin of the concha of the ear. The patient uses the device for three one- or two-hour sessions each day, in the morning, at noon, and in the evening. The small size of the device allows it to be used unobtrusively in the workplace as well as at home.

The stimulator unit records data as well as sending electrical impulses to the ear electrode; this data collection allows the patient's physician to fine-tune the strength of the impulses and otherwise supervise the therapy. In addition to its portability and ease of use, NEMOS eliminates the risk of infection from a surgically implanted VNS.

Benefits

The benefits of VNS are partial or (in some cases) complete relief of the symptoms of the condition for which it was implanted. It is not a cure for either epilepsy or depression.

Precautions

The physician's manual published by the VNS manufacturer contains in the introduction a document subtitled *Indications, Contraindications, Warnings and Precautions*. This 20-page document must be considered the primary resource for precautionary information, as there is not yet much research available beyond that which the manufacturer, Cyberonics, has funded. Precautionary information for this section has been taken from this document, which can be found online at http://www.vnstherapy.com/depression/hcp/Manuals/default.aspx.

The difference among contraindications, warnings, and precautions as published by the manufacturer seem unclear, as they combine VNS requirements, pre-existing health conditions, procedures that cannot be performed on people using VNS, age limitations, and therapeutic devices that cannot be used in conjunction with VNS. The VNS system is only to be used on the left vagus nerve and is approved for children over the age of 12 in cases of epilepsy and for patients over the age of 18 for depression.

Procedures and devices that can damage the implant, the patient's tissue, or both, and consequently that should not be used with VNS:

- diathermy, or cauterization; causes a concentration of heat in the implant, which can damage the implant, destroy tissue, and even lead to death
- radiation therapy
- external and internal defibrillation devices
- electrosurgery
- therapeutic ultrasound
- full-body MRI

Pre-existing conditions under which VNS should not be prescribed:

- having only one vagus nerve
- having metal plates or other implants such as pacemakers
- pregnancy
- dysphagea (problems with swallowing)
- obstructive sleep apnea (OSA) (a condition that causes patients to stop breathing while asleep)
- previous heart attacks and other cardiac abnormalities
- respiratory illness such as asthma or dyspnea
- brain injury
- injury to the central nervous system (CNS)
- dysautonomis (disease of the autonomic nervous system)
- vasovagal syncope (a condition in which the blood vessels dilate and the heart rate slows, causing fainting)
- ulcers
- hoarseness
- having other concurrent forms of brain stimulation treatments
- suicidal thoughts or ideas
- bipolar disorder
- schizophrenia or schizoaffective disorders
- delusional disorders

With regard to t-VNS, the German manufacturer lists only four contraindications:

- age below 18
- pregnancy
- skin infection or open wound on the part of the ear where the electrode is worn
- use of a pacemaker or other active implanted device

Preparation

Patients must be informed of the risks of the procedure, and those with contraindicated health conditions must be ruled out before surgery. Patients who elect to have VNS should have the procedure and equipment

KEY TERMS

Adjunctive therapy—Any treatment that is secondary or subordinate to a primary therapy.

Concha—The hollow shell-shaped portion of the external ear nearest the ear canal.

Cytokine—Any of a group of small protein molecules (including interferon, interleukin, and tumor necrosis factor) secreted by certain cells in the immune system that modulate certain functions associated with the immune response.

Obstructive sleep apnea—A disorder caused by obstruction of the upper airway during sleep and characterized by repeated pauses in breathing during sleep despite efforts to breathe. It is sometimes a side effect of VNS.

Tinnitus—A ringing or buzzing sensation in the ear in the absence of an external cause or stimulus. It is not a disease by itself but a symptom that may have a number of different causes.

Transcutaneous—Through the skin.

thoroughly explained, and will be taught the use of the handheld magnet in case it is needed.

Aftercare

The surgical procedure takes about an hour, but there are two incisions and, as with any implant, risk of infection. Wound care must be addressed, and patients require follow-up appointments with their physicians to monitor the effects of the treatment and adjust the strength or frequency of the electrical impulse. Changes in patients' health also need to be monitored, as so many conditions are contraindicated in the use of VNS. For example, in the case of treatment-resistant depression, if a depressed patient becomes suicidal or experiences a **manic episode**, use of VNS is contraindicated.

Obese patients and others with a history of **sleep disorders** should be monitored for signs of obstructive sleep apnea during postsurgical follow-up.

Risks

With regard to surgically implanted VNS devices, along with the risk of infection there is the potential for breakage, migration, or corrosion. The first 1990 report on the device noted that the electrodes had to be redesigned after the first group of devices showed an unacceptably high rate of breakage. Other issues may

have to do with irritation to the vagus nerve, which can result in hoarseness or permanent nerve damage. Because VNS affects the rate of respiration during sleep, patients with an implanted device are at increased risk of developing obstructive sleep apnea. Some psychiatrists have also reported manic episodes in depressed patients treated with VNS. According to the Mayo Clinic, other side effects of VNS implantation include difficulty swallowing, nausea, tingling, neck pain, chest pain or spasms, breathing problems during **exercise**, and paralysis of the vocal cords. Because of these risks, it is imperative that the surgeon receive specialized training for implanting the VNS.

People who have cardiac arrhythmia are at risk, and occurrences of bradycardia (slowed heartbeat) or asystole (heart stoppage) during or after implantation have been reported. The manufacturer states that safety has not been established for patients who suffer bradycardia or asystole during implantation. Although there is implant information for cardiac patients, it is listed under the heading of contraindications.

Patients should be warned to avoid anything that may generate a strong electrical or magnetic field, as the field could affect the functioning of the VNS system. This includes strong magnets, hair clippers, and anti-shoplifting tag deactivators. The magnet used with the VNS can affect televisions, credit card strips, and computer disks. The pulse generator in the VNS is said to affect pocket transistor radios and hearing aids.

Another consideration is the high cost of an implanted VNS device. According to an article published in the *New York Times* in 2006, the device itself costs about $15,000, with implantation surgery costing an additional $10,000.

With regard to t-VNS, the German manufacturer reports a 10% risk of itchy skin and an 8% risk of numbness or localized discomfort at the point where the electrode is placed on the ear. No serious adverse affects had been reported as of late 2011.

Research and general acceptance

According to published studies, VNS has a fairly low rate of success in epilepsy patients as well as in patients with major depression. According to the manufacturer, 40% to 50% of patients report a reduction of seizures of 50% or more, 18 months after implantation. The rate of complete freedom from seizures in patients with partial-onset epilepsy that cannot be managed by medications is less than 10%.

Even though the benefits of VNS as a treatment for depression have not been established, as of 2011 there were

QUESTIONS TO ASK YOUR DOCTOR

- What is your opinion of VNS as a treatment for epilepsy?
- What is your opinion of VNS as a treatment for depression?
- Have you ever treated a patient with an implanted VNS device? Did they find it helpful?
- Do you think that transcutaneous VNS is a promising new development?

nine clinical trials under way of VNS as a treatment for the disorder, along with 10 studies of VNS as a treatment for epilepsy. VNS was also being studied as a treatment for vegetative states following **traumatic brain injury**, heart failure, ischemic heart disease, rheumatoid arthritis, fibromyalgia, and obesity. Four additional clinical trials were under way of transcutaneous vagus nerve stimulation (t-VNS) as a treatment for schizophrenia, chronic pain, tinnitus, and treatment-refractory epilepsy.

Resources

BOOKS

Donovan, Charles E., III. *Out of the Black Hole: A Patient's Guide to Vagus Nerve Stimulation and Depression*. St Louis, NC: Wellness Publishers, 2006.

Higgins, Edmund S., and Mark S. George. *Brain Stimulation Therapies for Clinicians*. Washington, DC: American Psychiatric Pub., 2009.

Rey, Joseph M., and Boris Birmaher, eds. *Treating Child and Adolescent Depression*. Philadelphia: Wolters Kluwer Health/Lippincott Williams and Wilkins, 2009.

PERIODICALS

Burakgazi, A.Z., et al. "The Correlation between Vagus Nerve Stimulation Efficacy and Partial Onset Epilepsies." *Journal of Clinical Neurophysiology* 28 (August 2011): 380–382.

Elliott, R.E., et al. "Vagus Nerve Stimulation for Children with Treatment-resistant Epilepsy: A Consecutive Series of 141 Cases." *Journal of Neurosurgery. Pediatrics* 7 (May 2011): 491–500.

Gerson, R., et al. "Mania Following Vagus Nerve Stimulation: A Case Report and Review of the Literature." *Epilepsy and Behavior* 20 (January 2011): 138–140.

Gigante, P.R., and R.R. Goodman. "Alternative Surgical Approaches in Epilepsy." *Current Neurology and Neuroscience Reports* 11 (August 2011): 404–408.

Grimm, S., and M. Bajbouj. "Efficacy of Vagus Nerve Stimulation in the Treatment of Depression." *Expert Review of Neurotherapeutics* 10 (January 2010): 87–92.

Howland, R.H., et al. "The Emerging Use of Technology for the Treatment of Depression and Other Neuropsychiatric Disorders." *Annals of Clinical Psychiatry* 23 (February 2011): 48–62.

Noe, K.H., et al. "Treatment of Depression in Patients with Epilepsy." *Current Treatment Options in Neurology* 13 (August 2011): 371–379.

Parhizgar, F., et al. "Obstructive Sleep Apnea and Respiratory Complications Associated with Vagus Nerve Stimulators." *Journal of Clinical Sleep Medicine* 7 (August 15, 2011): 401–407.

Terry, R., et al. "An Implantable Neurocybernetic Prosthesis System." *Epilepsia* 31 (1990), Suppl. 2: S33–S37.

Wozniak, S.E., et al. "Vagal Nerve Stimulator Infection: A Lead-Salvage Protocol." *Journal of Neurosurgery. Pediatrics* 7 (June 2011): 671–675.

OTHER

Feder, Barnaby. "Battle Lines in Treating Depression." *New York Times*, September 10, 2006. http://www.nytimes.com/2006/09/10/business/yourmoney/10cyber.html?adxnnl=1&pagewanted=all&adxnnlx=1316484059-Xd/Wuk7s5DZ8YrhgFUqE7w (accessed September 18, 2011).

Food and Drug Administration (FDA). *Summary of Safety and Effectiveness Data*. http://www.fda.gov/ohrms/dockets/ac/04/briefing/4047b1_02_Summary%20of%20Safety%20and%20Effectiveness.pdf (accessed September 17, 2011).

WEBSITES

Cerbomed Gmbh. "NEMOS: Frequently Asked Questions." http://www.cerbomed.com/index.php?lang=en#faq (accessed September 17, 2011).

Cyberonics, Inc. "VNS Therapy." http://us.cyberonics.com/en/vns-therapy (accessed September 17, 2011).

Mayo Clinic. "Vagus Nerve Stimulation for Depression." http://www.mayoclinic.com/health/vagus-nerve-stimulation/MY00183 (accessed September 17, 2011).

Medscape. "Epilepsy and Seizures." http://emedicine.medscape.com/article/1184846-overview (accessed September 17, 2011).

Public Citizen's Health Research Group. "Letter Requesting the Halt of Ads for Vagus Nerve Stimulator Device," May 18, 2006. http://www.citizen.org/Page.aspx?pid=636 (accessed September 18, 2011).

Public Citizen's Health Research Group. "Letter Requesting that Medicare Deny Reimbursement for Vagus Nerve Stimulation Device for Treatment-Resistant Depression," September 6, 2006. http://www.citizen.org/Page.aspx?pid=632 (accessed September 18, 2011).

WebMD. "Epilepsy: Vagus Nerve Stimulation (VNS)." http://www.webmd.com/epilepsy/guide/vagus-nerve-stimulation-vns (accessed September 17, 2011).

ORGANIZATIONS

Cerbomed Gmbh, Henkestrasse 91, Erlangen, Germany 91052, +49 9131 9202 76 0, Fax: +49 9131 9202 76 92, info@cerbomed.com, http://www.cerbomed.com/index.php?lang=en.

Cyberonics, Inc, 100 Cyberonics Boulevard, Houston, TX, 77058, Fax: (281) 218-9332, (800) 332-1375, http://us.cyberonics.com/en.

National Institute of Neurological Disorders and Stroke (NINDS), PO Box 5801, Bethesda, MD, 20824 (301) 496-5751, (800) 352-9424, http://www.ninds.nih.gov.

Public Citizen, Inc, 1600 20th Street NW, Washington, DC, 20009, (202) 588-1000, hrg1@citizen.org, http://www.citizen.org/Page.aspx?pid=183.

U.S. Food and Drug Administration (FDA), 10903 New Hampshire Ave., Silver Spring, MD, 20993, (888) 463-6332, http://www.fda.gov/default.htm.

Lorena S. Covington, M.A.
Rebecca J. Frey, Ph.D.

Valerian

Description

Valerian (*Valeriana officinalis*) is one of at least 300 species of the Valerianaceae family. This plant is native to Europe and west Asia; it is naturalized throughout North America. A common name for this hardy perennial is garden heliotrope. Valerian has been valued for its soothing qualities for at least a millennium. The name valerian may have come from the Latin *valere* meaning "to be strong" or "to be in good health." Chaucer (c. 1343–1400) called the herb setewale. Other common names are all-heal, vandal root, and Capon's tail.

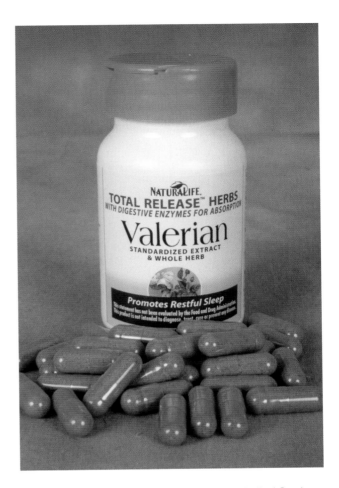

Bottle of valerian supplements. (© *Custom Medical Stock Photo, Inc. Reproduced by permission.*)

Purpose

Valerian has been used as a medicinal herb for more than a thousand years, especially for mild cases of **insomnia**. Research shows that proper use of valerian promotes sleep, reduces night awakenings, and increases dream recall in most people. A team of pharmacologists in Argentina reported that they had isolated two flavonoids, 6-methylapigenin and hesperidin, as the compounds in valerian with sedative and sleep-enhancing properties. A German study of more than 900 children suffering from pathological restlessness and/or difficulty falling asleep reported in 2006 that a twice-daily dose of 160 mg of valerian and 80 mg of lemon balm significantly decreased restlessness and difficulty falling asleep. The researchers suggested this combination may be a safer and more practical alternative to prescription medications.

Historically, valerian has been highly regarded as a tranquilizer that acts without narcotic effects. It has been thought to act as a pain reliever, antispasmodic, sedative, and carminative, but only its use in treating insomnia has been shown the most effective in **clinical trials**, and even those results have been conflicting.

Description

Valerian grows in lime-rich soil near streams or in damp, low meadows where it may reach a height of 5 ft. (1.5 m). It is also found in drier environments at higher elevations, where it grows to just 2 ft. (0.6 m). Roots harvested from the drier environment may be more medicinally potent. This variety is sometimes known as sylvestus.

Valerian's short vertical rhizome is dark yellow-brown in color and has round rootlets. These rootlets produce hollow, fluted stems with opposite leaves and a single leaflet at the tip, with as many as ten pairs of toothed leaflets. The upper leaves are attached at their base and emerge from a white sheath along the stem. The stems remain erect and unbranched until the very top, where the small, white flowers, tinged with pink, bloom in clusters in the middle of summer.

Preparations

Valerian's rhizome and root make up the medicinal part of this herb. Fresh root will produce the highest quality of medicinal extract and should be harvested in the autumn of its second year. Valerian works well in combination with other tranquilizing herbs such as **passionflower** (*Passiflora incarnata*) to safely induce sleep or skullcap (*Scutellaria laterifolia*) to relieve nervous tension. The somewhat bitter, unpleasant taste of the tea may be masked by adding peppermint oil, or the user can take the herb in capsule form. Combinations contain equal parts of each herb. The herb may be drunk as an herbal tea, used as a tincture, or swallowed in capsule form one hour before bedtime.

It is important to note that there is no standard dosage for valerian and that the potency of valerian products can vary drastically from brand to brand. In 2006, ConsumerLab.com tested 16 brands of valerian products and found that most had a lower potency than what was printed on the label and/or contained contaminants. One of the products was contaminated with lead, which can damage almost every system in the human body, and two others were contaminated with cadmium, a heavy metal that can cause kidney damage.

Precautions

Valerian should not be used in large doses or for an extended period. People should not take it continuously for more than two to three weeks. Users of valerian may become tolerant to its effects with prolonged use. Increasing the dose of the herb to achieve desired effects may result in negative side effects. Prolonged use, according to some research, could result in liver damage and central nervous system impairment. Women who are pregnant or breast-feeding should not use valerian, as the herb's effects on the fetus or infant have not yet been tested. Patients undergoing surgery should stop taking valerian at least two weeks before their procedure.

Side effects

Large doses of valerian may occasionally cause headache, muscle spasm, heart palpitations, dizziness, gastric distress, sleeplessness, and confusion. Uninterrupted use may cause **depression**.

KEY TERMS

Carminative—A medication or preparation that prevents the formation of intestinal gas or allows it to be expelled.

Flavonoid—Any of a group of plant compounds with an aromatic nucleus, often found as a pigment.

Rhizome—A fleshy plant stem that grows horizontally under or along the ground; roots are sent out below this stem and leaves or shoots are sent out above it.

Interactions

Although valerian has been regarded as a relatively safe herb, it should not be used with other **sedatives**, including alcoholic beverages, **benzodiazepines**, **barbiturates**, or antihistamines. Long-term safety studies (longer than one month) of valerian had not been conducted as of early 2011.

Resources

BOOKS

Barnes, Joanne, Linda A. Anderson, and J. David Phillipson. *Herbal Medicines (Includes CD-ROM)*. 3rd. ed. London: Pharmaceutical Press, 2007.

PDR for Nonprescription Drugs, Dietary Supplements, and Herbs 2009. Montvale, NJ: PDR Network, 2009.

Woolven, Linda, and Ted Snider. *Healthy Herbs: Everyday Guide to Medicinal Herbs and Their Use*. Markham, ON, Canada: Fitzhenry & Whiteside, 2006.

PERIODICALS

Bone, Kerry. "Valerian: A Safe and Effective Herb for Sleep Problems." *Townsend Letter for Doctors and Patients* (April 2005): 44.

Brown, Donald. "Valerian and Lemon Balm Safely and Effectively Treat Restlessness and Dyssomnia in Children" *Original Internist* (December 2006).

Castleman, Michael. "Rest Assured: Valerian, a Safe and Effective Herbal Sleep Aid, Will Help You Close the Door on Insomnia." *Natural Health* (March 2007): 98.

WEBSITES

National Center for Complementary and Alternative Medicine. "Valerian." National Institutes of Health. http://nccam.nih.gov/about/ataglance (accessed December 18, 2011).

ORGANIZATIONS

American Institute of Homeopathy, 101 South Whiting Street, Suite 16, Alexandria, VA, 22304, (888) 445-9988, admin@homeopathyusa.org, http://homeopathyusa.org.

Homeopathic Medical Council of Canada, 31 Adelaide Street East, Box 605, Toronto, ON, M5C 2J8, (416) 788-4622, Ontario@HMCC.ca, http://www.hmcc.ca.

National Center for Complementary and Alternative Medicine, 9000 Rockville Pike, Bethesda, MD, 20892, info@nccam.nih.gov, http://nccam.nih.gov.

U.S. Food and Drug Administration, 10903 New Hampshire Ave., Silver Spring, MD, 20993, (888) 463-6332, http://www.fda.gov.

Clare Hanrahan
Ken R. Wells

Valium *see* **Diazepam**

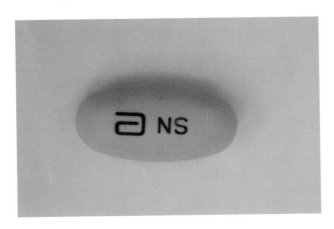

Valproic acid

Definition

Valproic acid is an anticonvulsant (antiseizure) drug. In the United States, valproic acid is also known as valproate and is sold under brand name Depakene.

Purpose

The U.S. Food and Drug Administration (FDA) recognizes valproic acid for the treatment of epilepsy and for mania that occurs with **bipolar disorder**. Valproic acid is also approved for the prevention of migraine headaches.

Description

Valproic acid's properties in preventing **seizures** were first discovered in Europe in 1963. The medication was first used clinically in the United Stated in 1978.

Valproic acid is effective in treating a variety of seizure types, which include simple and complex absence seizures, partial seizures, and tonic-clonic seizures (grand mal seizures). Valproic acid is also effective in treating the manic episodes of patients with bipolar disorder. Patients who have bipolar disorder resulting from a head injury and patients who do not respond to or who cannot tolerate conventional lithium therapy (normally the therapy of choice for bipolar disorder) can be treated with valproic acid. In addition, valproic acid provides a 50% or greater reduction in the frequency of migraine headaches. Valproic acid is also safe and effective in preventing headaches that arise as a side effect of taking a class of drugs known as **selective serotonin reuptake inhibitors** (SSRIs). These drugs include **sertraline** (Zoloft), **paroxetine** (Paxil), **fluoxetine** (Prozac), **fluvoxamine** (Luvox), and **citalopram** (Celexa).

Valproic acid comes in 250 mg gelatin capsules and in a 250 mg/5mL syrup.

Recommended dosage

The dosage of valproic acid used to treat epilepsy depends on the type of seizures the patient has. The doses are determined based on the patient's weight.

The initial dose of valproic acid used to treat mania is 750 mg daily. This dose is then reduced to the lowest dose that will achieve the desired effects. Another dosage strategy is based on patient weight. The starting dose is 30 mg per 2 lb (1 kg) of body weight on days one and two followed by 20 mg per kg of body weight taken daily on days three through ten.

For prevention of migraine headaches, a dose of 250 mg twice daily is beneficial. It may take up to 1,000 mg of valproic acid to control migraine attacks.

Precautions

Valproic acid may cause life-threatening damage to the liver and pancreas. Before starting valproic acid therapy, every patient should have a blood test to assess his or her liver function. The risk of valproic acid causing liver damage is greatest during the first six months of treatment. Liver function tests should be done once a month during the first three months, then every three to six months for as long as the patient continues to take the drug. Vomiting, lethargy, anorexia, and jaundice (yellowing of the skin) may precede signs of liver damage. If a patient develops severe or unusual abdominal pain, this may be a sign of pancreatitis (inflammation of the pancreas). Pancreatitis can occur in both children and adults. It can develop shortly after valproic acid is started or after several years of use.

Patients who are younger than two years old should not take valproic acid. When it is necessary for children

Depakote (valproic acid), 500 mg. (© *Custom Medical Stock Photo, Inc. Reproduced by permission.*)

KEY TERMS

Absence seizure—Absence (petit mal) seizures usually begin with a brief loss of consciousness and last between one and 10 seconds. People having a petit mal seizure become very quiet and may blink, stare blankly, roll their eyes, or move their lips. A petit mal seizure lasts 15–20 seconds. When it ends, the individual resumes whatever he or she was doing before the seizure began, and may not realize that anything unusual happened.

Anorexia—Loss of appetite.

Tonic-clonic seizure—This is the most common type of seizure among all age groups and is categorized into several phases beginning with vague symptoms hours or days before an attack. These seizures are sometimes called grand mal seizures.

under age two to take valproic acid, the drug should be used cautiously and with close physician monitoring.

Pregnant women or women who are planning to become pregnant should not take valproic acid, as the drug is harmful to the fetus and may cause birth defects, including **intellectual disability**.

Side effects

Side effects of valproic acid may include nausea, vomiting, indigestion, and either diarrhea or constipation. Headaches, dizziness, lack of coordination, confusion, **fatigue**, tremor, drowsiness, and seizures have also been associated with the use of valproic acid. Behavioral changes associated with the drug including irritability, longer and deeper sleep, hyperactivity, increased sociability, increased sadness, happiness or aggression, are seen more often in children than in adults taking valproic acid.

Less than 1% of patients experience appetite changes. These changes may include either diminished or increased appetite. Skin rash, photosensitivity, (acute sensitivity to the sun) hair loss, and other hair changes have also been reported in people using valproic acid.

Interactions

Using valproic acid with other anticonvulsant drugs, such as phenobarbital, **clonazepam**, and **lamotrigine** may cause excessive sedation (drowsiness and lack of physical and mental alertness).

Valproic acid may diminish the benefits of phenytoin, another commonly used anticonvulsant. Severe central nervous **depression** has been reported with the use of valproic acid and another anticonvulsant called primidone.

Taking aspirin during valproic acid therapy may cause valproic acid levels to increase to toxic (poisonous) levels. Other medications that may cause valproic acid toxicity are the antibiotic erythromycin and the antidepressant **amitriptyline**. Drugs that can decrease the effectiveness of valproic acid include **carbamazepine** and cholestyramine. **Ginkgo biloba**, an herbal supplement commonly available in the United States, may be prepared with a chemical called 4′-O-methylpyridoxine. If this chemical remains in the herbal preparation, it can cause seizures and reduce the effectiveness of valproic acid.

Resources

BOOKS

Lacy, Charles F. *Drug Information Handbook with International Trade Names Index.* Hudson, OH: Lexi-Comp, Inc. 2011.

Sadock, Benjamin J., and Virginia A. Sadock, eds. *Comprehensive Textbook of Psychiatry.* Vol. 2. 7th ed. Philadelphia: Lippincott Williams and Wilkins, 2000.

WEBSITES

PubMed Health. "Valproic Acid." http://www.ncbi.nlm.nih.gov/pubmedhealth/PMH0000677 (accessed November 13, 2011).

ORGANIZATIONS

U.S. Food and Drug Administration, 10903 New Hampshire Ave., Silver Spring, MD, 20993-0002, (888) INFO-FDA (463-6332), http://www.fda.gov.

Ajna Hamidovic, Pharm.D.

Vascular dementia

Definition

Vascular **dementia** is a group of disorders characterized by the severe loss of mental functioning resulting from cerebrovascular disease. Vascular dementia is often caused by repeated strokes.

Demographics

In most countries, vascular dementia is a much less common form of dementia than **Alzheimer's disease**

(AD), though the reverse is true in Japan, where it is more common than AD. Overall, vascular dementia is the second most common form of dementia, after AD. About 10%–20% of patients who experience dementia have the vascular form of the disorder. The difference in prevalence in different countries may result from different lifestyle factors rooted in the culture.

About 1.5% of individuals are affected by vascular dementia in the United States. Vascular dementia is more common in men than in women, which may be because men are more likely than women to suffer from strokes. Vascular dementia becomes increasingly prevalent as people grow older. The number of people affected by vascular dementia rises dramatically during and after age 70. Vascular dementia usually occurs at a younger age than AD.

Description

Vascular dementia is caused by cerebrovascular disease and occurs almost always in the elderly. People with vascular dementia generally experience a decline in thought processes (cognitive function) that follows specific steps. This decline is often punctuated by small strokes—ruptures of tiny blood vessels in the **brain**. People experiencing vascular dementia often have problems with memory, abstract thinking, object identification or recognition, speech creation, speech comprehension, and motor activities.

Causes and symptoms

Vascular dementia is thought to be caused by small strokes that interfere with blood flow to the brain. Usually, vascular dementia is caused by many small strokes over time, rather than one large **stroke**. Sometimes this is referred to as multi-infarct dementia (MID). If the vascular dementia is caused by one large stroke, or develops in less than three months, then it is called acute onset vascular dementia. Acute onset vascular dementia is rare.

The signs of dementia often begin with impaired memory function. Sometimes a person has difficulty learning new things or remembering new events, and sometimes the person has difficulty recalling events or things that he or she used to know. Other signs of dementia include impairment in other areas of thought processing. Sometimes a person with vascular dementia may have difficulty producing coherent speech or may have other language impairments, such as problems understanding spoken or written language. The signs of vascular dementia are similar to those of Alzheimer's disease.

KEY TERMS

Acute onset vascular dementia—Vascular dementia caused by a single stroke or with an onset of fewer than three months.

Alzheimer's disease—An incurable disease of older individuals that results in the destruction of nerve cells in the brain and causes gradual loss of mental and physical functions.

Delirium—A disturbance of consciousness marked by confusion, difficulty paying attention, delusions, hallucinations, or restlessness. It can be distinguished from dementia by its relatively sudden onset and variation in the severity of the symptoms.

Dementia—A chronic condition in which thinking and memory are progressively impaired. Other symptoms may also occur, including personality changes and depression.

Hypertension—Persistently high blood pressure.

Multi-infarct dementia (MID)—Dementia caused by a series of many small strokes over a period longer than three months.

Difficulty with motor activities is a problem for some people with vascular dementia. Things that require hand-eye coordination, such as tying shoes or undoing buttons, are examples of motor activities that may be impaired. People with vascular dementia may also have difficulty recognizing familiar objects or may be unable to name them. Problems organizing things, putting events in sequence, or performing other types of abstract thinking may be present.

Some people with vascular dementia exhibit neurological signs that indicate the presence of cerebrovascular disease. They may have weakness of the arms or legs, abnormal reflexes, or abnormalities in the way they walk (gait abnormalities). Some people also exhibit behavioral disturbances related to the dementia, such as violence or aggression, often toward his or her caretaker. The patient may act impulsively and irritably or sometimes scream.

Diagnosis

The first step in the **diagnosis** of vascular dementia is to verify that dementia is present. The *Diagnostic and Statistical Manual of Mental Disorders*, fourth edition, text revision (*DSM-IV-TR*), the handbook used by medical professionals in diagnosing mental disorders, indicates that impairments to memory must be present for a diagnosis of vascular dementia. Memory problems can include difficulties in learning and retaining new information or problems remembering past events or things that were learned before dementia took root.

In addition to memory impairment, the *DSM-IV-TR* specifies that one or more other impairments must be present. These impairments can include language problems, such as not being able to form speech and/or not being able to understand language, either spoken or written; problems performing activities that require hand-eye coordination, such as tying shoes, even though motor function is normal; problems recognizing or identifying objects, although the person is able to use his or her sense organs fully; problems doing tasks such as organizing, planning events, or putting things into sequence; or problems thinking abstractly. To meet the criteria for diagnosis, the memory problems and other impairments must cause the patient either significant distress or must impair his or her functioning in activities of daily life, such as by affecting the person's job or relationships with family or friends. The *DSM-IV-TR* specifies that the symptoms must show a decline in cognitive functioning and that the problems cannot occur during the course of an event that is categorized as **delirium**. There must be evidence that the problem is a result of cerebrovascular disease.

If dementia occurs without any other significant signs or symptoms, then it is classified as uncomplicated. There are three other possible *DSM-IV-TR* classifications based on the predominant feature of the dementia: vascular dementia with delirium, vascular dementia with **delusions**, and vascular dementia with depressed mood. If there are significant behavioral disturbances occurring as a result of the dementia, then the disturbances are specified.

Vascular dementia and AD are similar in many ways and can be confused. The most significant difference between the two is that vascular dementia can be diagnosed using physiological evidence of cerebrovascular disease. Also, AD generally occurs first as a slow loss of memory function, and then as a gradual decline into eventual dementia. Vascular dementia, however, generally occurs suddenly. The patient often declines in a stepwise fashion, with each step occurring after a small stroke.

Treatment

The treatments for vascular dementia focus on attempts to slow or halt the progression of the disorder and alleviate some of the symptoms. The disorder cannot be cured or reversed. The most common way to treat vascular dementia is to try to prevent further strokes.

QUESTIONS TO ASK YOUR DOCTOR

- Are my symptoms such as memory loss signs of dementia?
- Is the dementia vascular dementia or Alzheimer's disease?
- What steps can I take to help slow or halt the progression of the disease?
- Are there dietary changes that could help reduce the risk of additional strokes?
- Is there any light-to-moderate exercise you could recommend to help reduce the risk of additional strokes?

Treatments include diet and drug treatment for hypertension (high blood pressure), aspirin therapy, **smoking cessation**, avoidance of heavy **alcohol use**, and **stress reduction**. Some drugs that are used to treat mild AD are being studied for their effectiveness in treating vascular dementia.

Prognosis

Vascular dementia is a disorder that cannot be reversed. The progression of the disorder can, however, be slowed. Using drugs along with lifestyle changes to prevent more strokes from occurring may help slow the progression of vascular dementia.

Prevention

Vascular dementia is generally associated with a series of strokes causing increasing mental impairment. Measures generally recommended by physicians to prevent strokes may be effective in helping to prevent vascular dementia. These include such things as quitting smoking, decreasing cholesterol levels, treating hypertension by reducing sodium (salt) intake, decreasing alcohol consumption, and making other lifestyle changes. Some studies have shown that drinking moderate daily amounts of alcohol, particularly red wine, may help to prevent dementia, but further research is needed.

Resources
BOOKS

Banejee, Sube, and Lawrence, Vanessa. *Managing Dementia in a Multicultural Society*. Hoboken, NJ: John Wiley and Sons, 2010.

Jacobsen, Sarah R., ed. *Vascular Dementia: Risk Factors, Diagnosis, and Treatment.* Hauppauge, NY: Nova Science, 2011.

Wahlund, Lars-Olof, Timo Erkinjuntti, and Serge Gauthier. *Vascular Cognitive Impairment in Clinical Practice.* New York: Cambridge University Press, 2009.

PERIODICALS

Aarsland, Dag, et al. "Is Physical Activity a Potential Preventive Factor for Vascular Dementia? A Systematic Review." *Aging and Mental Health* 14, no. 4 (May 2010): 386–395.

Heyanka, Daniel J., et al. "Distinguishing Alzheimer's Disease from Vascular Dementia: An Exploration of Five Cognitive Domains." *International Journal of Neuroscience* 120, no. 6 (June 2010): 409–414.

Yeager, Catherine A., et al. "Alzheimer's Disease and Vascular Dementia: The Complex Relationship Between Diagnosis and Caregiver Burden." *Issues in Mental Health Nursing* 31, no. 6 (June 2010): 376–384.

ORGANIZATIONS

American Aging Association, 2103 Cornell Rd., Room 5125, Cleveland, OH, 44106, (216) 368-3671, Fax: (216) 368-8964, americanaging@case.edu, http://www.americanaging.org.

American Association of Cardiovascular and Pulmonary Rehabilitation, 401 North Michigan Ave., Suite 2200, Chicago, IL, 60611, (312) 321-5146, Fax: (312) 673-6924, aacvpr@aacvpr.org, http://www.aacvpr.org.

National Institute on Aging, Bldg. 31, Rm. 5C27, 31 Center Drive, MSC 2292, Bethesda, MD, 20892, (301) 496-1752, (888) TTY: (800) 222-4225, Fax: (301) 496-1072, http://www.nia.nih.gov.

Tish Davidson, AM

Venlafaxine

Definition

Venlafaxine is an antidepressant available in the United States under the trade name of Effexor or Effexor XR.

Purpose

Venlafaxine is used to treat **depression** and **generalized anxiety disorder**. It has also been used to treat **obsessive-compulsive disorder** and irritable bowel syndrome.

Description

Venlafaxine is an antidepressant. It has actions common to both the cyclic **antidepressants**, such as

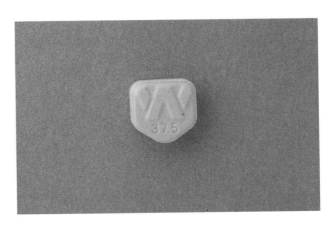

Effexor (venlafaxine), 37.5 mg. (© *Custom Medical Stock Photo, Inc. Reproduced by permission.*)

imipramine (Tofranil) and **amitriptyline** (Elavil), and the **selective serotonin reuptake inhibitors (SSRIs)**, such as **fluoxetine** (Prozac), **sertraline** (Zoloft), and **paroxetine** (Paxil). It is believed that venlafaxine works by increasing levels of the neurotransmitters norepinephrine and **serotonin** in the **brain**.

The therapeutic effects of venlafaxine, like other antidepressants, appear slowly. Maximum benefit is often not evident for at least two weeks after starting the drug. People taking venlafaxine should be aware of this and continue taking the drug as directed even if they do not see immediate improvement.

Venlafaxine is available in 25 mg, 37.5 mg, 50 mg, 75 mg, and 100 mg rapid-release tablets and 75 mg and 150 mg extended-action capsules.

Recommended dosage

The recommended initial dose of venlafaxine is 75 mg daily taken as two or three equal doses. The dose may be increased in 75 mg increments every four days as needed until symptoms of depression or anxiety resolve. Most commonly, dosages range between 150 mg to 225 mg daily, although in severe situations 375 mg per day may be needed. Once patients are stabilized using the rapid-acting tablets, they may be converted over to the appropriate dose of extended-release capsules.

Venlafaxine is broken down by the liver and eliminated from the body by the kidneys. As a result, the dose of venlafaxine must be lowered in people with liver or kidney disease. In people with liver disease, the daily dosage of venlafaxine should be cut in half. In patients with kidney disease, the daily dosage of venlafaxine should be reduced 25%–50%, depending upon the extent of kidney damage. When stopping venlafaxine, the dosage should be reduced gradually over a period of at least two weeks before the drug is totally stopped.

Precautions

Patients taking venlafaxine should be monitored closely for **insomnia**, anxiety, mania, significant weight loss, **seizures**, and thoughts of **suicide**. Children and adults up to age 24 are at increased risk for developing suicidal thoughts and behaviors when taking an antidepressant drug, including venlafaxine. Patients of any age who are taking antidepressants should be monitored for signs of worsening depression or changes in behavior.

Caution should also be exercised when prescribing venlafaxine to patients with impaired liver or kidney function, the elderly (over age 60), children, individuals with **bipolar disorder** or a history of seizures, people with diabetes, persons with narrow-angle glaucoma, and individuals expressing ideas of committing suicide. People with diabetes should monitor their blood or urine sugar more carefully, since venlafaxine may affect blood sugar.

Care should be taken to weigh the risks and benefits of this drug in women who are or wish to become pregnant, as well as in breast-feeding mothers.

Until individuals understand the effects that venlafaxine may have, they should avoid driving, operating dangerous machinery, or participating in hazardous activities. Alcohol should not be used while taking venlafaxine.

Side effects

More common side effects include decreased sexual drive, restlessness, difficulty sitting still, skin rash, hives, and itching. Less common side effects include fever and/or chills and pain in joints or muscles.

Rare side effects include pain or enlargement of breasts and/or abnormal milk production in women, seizures, fast heart rate, irregular heartbeats, red or purple spots on the skin, low blood sugar and its symptoms (anxiety, chills, cold sweats, confusion, difficulty concentrating, drowsiness, excess hunger, rapid heart rate, headache, shakiness or unsteadiness, severe **fatigue**), low blood sodium and its symptoms (including confusion, seizures, drowsiness, dry mouth, severe thirst, decreased energy), **serotonin syndrome** (characterized by at least three of the following symptoms: diarrhea, fever, sweatiness, mood or behavior changes, overactive

---

QUESTIONS TO ASK YOUR DOCTOR

- What kind of changes can I expect to see or feel with this medication?
- Does it matter what time of day I take this medication?
- Should I take this medication with or without food?
- What are the side effects associated with this medication?
- Will this medication interact or interfere with other medications I am currently taking?
- What symptoms or adverse effects are important enough that I should seek immediate treatment?

---

reflexes, fast heart rate, restlessness, shivering or shaking), excitability, agitation, irritability, pressured talking, difficulty breathing, and odd body or facial movements.

Interactions

Venlafaxine interacts with a long list of other medications. Anyone starting this drug should review the other medications they are taking with their physician and pharmacist for possible interactions. Patients should always inform all of their healthcare providers, including dentists, that they are taking venlafaxine.

Dangerously high blood pressure has resulted from the combination of antidepressants, such as venlafaxine, and members of another class of antidepressants known as **monoamine oxidase inhibitors** (MAOIs). Because of this, venlafaxine should never be taken in combination with MAOIs. Patients taking any MAOIs, for example **phenelzine** (Nardil) or **tranylcypromine** (Parnate), should stop taking the MAOI and wait at least 14 days before starting venlafaxine or any other antidepressant. When stopping treatment with venlafaxine, patients should wait five weeks before taking an MAOI.

Some other drugs such as **trazodone** (Desyrel), sibutramine (Meridia), and sumatriptan (Imitrex) also interact with venlafaxine and cause a syndrome known as **neuroleptic malignant syndrome**, characterized by irritability, muscle stiffness, shivering, muscle spasms, and altered consciousness.

KEY TERMS

Depression—A mental state characterized by excessive sadness. Other symptoms include altered sleep patterns, thoughts of suicide, difficulty concentrating, agitation, lack of energy, and loss of enjoyment in activities that are usually pleasurable.

Generalized anxiety disorder—A general form of fear that can dominate a person's life.

Insomnia—A sleep disorder characterized by waking in the middle of the night and having difficulty returning to sleep, or waking too early in the morning.

Mania—An elevated or euphoric mood or irritable state that is characteristic of bipolar disorder.

Narrow-angle glaucoma—An eye disorder caused by a buildup of fluid pressure inside the eyeball due to an abnormally small angle between the iris (the colored portion of the eye) and the cornea (the transparent front part of the eye).

Norepinephrine—A chemical messenger in the brain thought to play a role in mood regulation.

Obsessive-compulsive disorder—A disorder in which affected individuals have an obsession (such as a fear of contamination, or thoughts they do not like to have and cannot control) and feel compelled to perform certain acts to neutralize the obsession (such as repeated hand washing).

Seizure—A convulsion, or uncontrolled discharge of nerve cells that may spread to other cells throughout the brain.

Serotonin—A chemical messenger in the brain thought to play a role in mood regulation.

Serotonin syndrome—A condition characterized by at least three of the following symptoms: diarrhea, fever, extreme perspiration, mood or behavior changes, overactive reflexes, fast heart rate, restlessness, shivering, or shaking. The condition occurs when there is too much serotonin in the body.

The sedative effects (drowsiness or lack of mental clarity) of venlafaxine are increased by other central nervous system depressants such as alcohol, **sedatives**, sleeping medications, or other medications used for mental disorders such as **schizophrenia**. Patients taking blood thinners, including aspirin, are at risk for increased bleeding when taking venlafaxine.

Resources

BOOKS

Albers, Lawrence J., Rhoda K. Hahn, and Christopher Reist. *Handbook of Psychiatric Drugs*. Laguna Hills, CA: Current Clinical Strategies Publishing, 2010.

American Society of Health-System Pharmacists. *AHFS Drug Information 2011*. Bethesda: American Society of Health-System Pharmacists, 2011.

Graham, George. *The Disordered Mind: An Introduction to Philosophy of Mind and Mental Illness*. New York: Routledge, 2010.

Holland, Leland Norman, and Michael Patrick Adams. *Core Concepts in Pharmacology*. 3rd ed. New York: Prentice Hall, 2011.

North, Carol, and Sean Yutzy. *Goodwin and Guze's Psychiatric Diagnosis*. New York: Oxford University Press, 2010.

Preston, John D., John H. O'Neal, and Mary C. Talaga. *Handbook of Clinical Psychopharmacology for Therapists*. 6th ed. Oakland, CA: New Harbinger Publications, 2011.

PERIODICALS

Baca, Enrique, et al. "Venlafaxine Extended-Release in Patients Older than 80 Years with Depressive Syndrome." *International Journal of Geriatric Psychiatry* 21, no. 4 (April 2006): 337–43.

Davidson, Jonathan, et al. "Treatment of Posttraumatic Stress Disorder with Venlafaxine Extended Release." *Archives of General Psychiatry* 63, no. 10 (Oct. 2006): 1158–65.

Johnson, Ellyn M., et al. "Cardiovascular Changes Associated With Venlafaxine in the Treatment of Late-Life Depression." *American Journal of Geriatric Psychiatry* 14, no. 9 (Sept. 2006): 796–802.

Kim, Tae-Suk, et al. "Comparison of Venlafaxine Extended Release Versus Paroxetine for Treatment of Patients with Generalized Anxiety Disorder." *Psychiatry and Clinical Neurosciences* 60, no. 3 (June 2006): 347–51.

McGrath, Patrick J, et al. "Tranylcypromine Versus Venlafaxine Plus Mirtazapine Following Three Failed Antidepressant Medication Trials for Depression: A STAR*D Report." *American Journal of Psychiatry* 163, no. 9 (Sept. 2006): 1531–41.

Montgomery, Stuart A. "Escitalopram Versus Venlafaxine XR in the Treatment of Depression." *International Clinical Psychopharmacology* 21, no. 5 (Sept. 2006): 297–309.

Nemeroff, Charles B., and Michael E. Thase. "A Double-Blind, Placebo-Controlled Comparison of Venlafaxine and Fluoxetine Treatment in Depressed Outpatients." *Journal of Psychiatric Research* 41, nos. 3–4 (April–June 2007): 351–59.

Post, R. M., et al. "Mood Switch in Bipolar Depression: Comparison of Adjunctive Venlafaxine, Bupropion and Sertraline." *British Journal of Psychiatry* 189, no. 2 (Aug. 2006): 124–31.

Tiihonen, Jari, et al. "Antidepressants and the Risk of Suicide, Attempted Suicide, and Overall Mortality in a Nationwide Cohort." *Archives of General Psychiatry* 63, no. 12 (Dec. 2006): 1358–67.

Yazicioglu, Bengi, et al. "A Comparison of the Efficacy and Tolerability of Reboxetine and Sertraline Versus Venlafaxine in Major Depressive Disorder: A Randomized, Open-Labeled

Clinical Trial." *Progress in Neuro-Psychopharmacology & Biological Psychiatry* 30, no. 7 (Sept. 2006): 1271–76.

WEBSITES

PubMed Health. "Venlafaxine." U.S. National Library of Medicine. http://www.ncbi.nlm.nih.gov/pubmedhealth/PMH0000947 (accessed November 13, 2011).

ORGANIZATIONS

American Psychiatric Association, 1000 Wilson Boulevard, Suite 1825, Arlington, VA, 22209, (703) 907-7300, apa@psych.org, http://www.psych.org.

National Alliance on Mental Illness (NAMI), Colonial Place Three, 2107 Wilson Blvd., Suite 300, Arlington, VA, 22201, (703) 524-7600, (800) 950-NAMI (6264), Fax: (703) 524-9094, http://www.nami.org/Hometemplate.cfm.

National Institute of Mental Health (NIMH), 6001 Executive Boulevard, Room 8184, MSC 9663, Bethesda, MD, 20892, (301) 443-4513, (866) 615-6464, Fax: (301) 443-4279, nimhinfo@nih.gov, http://www.nimh.nih.gov/index.shtml.

U.S. Food and Drug Administration, 10903 New Hampshire Ave., Silver Spring, MD, 20993-0002, (888) INFO-FDA (463-6332), http://www.fda.gov.

Kelly Karpa, R.Ph.,Ph.D.
Ruth A. Wienclaw, Ph.D.
Laura Jean Cataldo, RN, Ed.D.

Veterans' mental health *see* **Military mental health**

Violence *see* **Mental health and violence**

Vivactil *see* **Protriptyline**

Vivitrol

Purpose

Vivitrol (**naltrexone** for extended-release injectable suspension) is a once-monthly injection used in the treatment of alcohol dependence in patients who are able to abstain from alcohol at least seven to ten days prior to treatment.

Description

Naltrexone, the active ingredient in Vivitrol, is an opioid antagonist that blocks the effects of alcohol; it is not an aversive therapy that pairs a strong feeling of dislike or disgust with alcohol. Naltrexone has few, if any, intrinsic actions other than as an opioid antagonist. It produces withdrawal symptoms in patients physically dependent on **opioids**. Vivitrol should be used as only one component of a comprehensive alcoholism

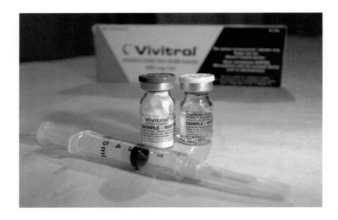

Vivitrol injection. (© *Mark Dye/Star Ledger/Corbis*)

management program that includes counseling, self-help **support groups**, or other psychosocial support.

Recommended dosage

The recommended dosage of Vivitrol is 380 mg once a month. Vivitrol is delivered by intramuscular gluteal injection and should not be administered intravenously. Patients missing a dose should be given the next dose as soon as possible. Vivitrol must be administered by a healthcare professional.

Before starting treatment with Vivitrol, the patient should abstain from alcohol in an outpatient setting, not be actively drinking, not be in acute opiate withdrawal, and be opioid free for at least seven to ten days.

Precautions

In excessive doses, naltrexone has been found to cause liver damage. Therefore, Vivitrol is not recommended for use in cases of acute hepatitis or liver failure. Careful consideration should be given before administering Vivitrol to patients with liver disease. Vivitrol should be discontinued in the event of signs of acute hepatitis.

Vivitrol should not be given to patients with a physiological dependence on opioids or who are in opioid withdrawal. To prevent withdrawal, Vivitrol should not be administered to patients receiving opioid analgesics. In cases where Vivitrol blockade needs to be reversed for pain management, patients should be monitored in a setting enabled for cardiopulmonary resuscitation.

Side effects

Vivitrol counteracts the effects of opioid-containing medications, including analgesics, cough and cold medications, and antidiarrheal preparations.

Vivitrol is generally well tolerated. In **clinical trials**, serious adverse reactions occurred in patients receiving Vivitrol at a similar rate to patients receiving a placebo. Mild to moderate adverse events were seen in most patients. The most common of these were nausea, vomiting, headache, dizziness, **insomnia**, **fatigue**, and injection site reaction.

In clinical trials, suicidal tendencies (including thoughts of **suicide**, suicide attempts, and completed suicides), although infrequent, occurred more often in patients treated with Vivitrol (1%) than in patients receiving a placebo (0). Similarly, depression-related events were higher for patients taking Vivitrol (1%) than for those taking a placebo (0). Patients taking Vivitrol should be monitored for **depression** or suicidal thinking.

Side effects and other reactions reported include:

- blood and lymphatic system disorders (e.g., swollen, firm, or possibly tender lymph nodes; increased white blood cell count)
- cardiac disorders (e.g., palpitations, atrial fibrillation, myocardial infarction, angina pectoris, angina unstable, congestive heart failure, atherosclerosis)
- eye disorders (e.g., conjunctivitis)
- gastrointestinal disorders (e.g., constipation, toothache, flatulence, gastroesophageal reflux disease, hemorrhoids, colitis, gastrointestinal hemorrhage, paralysis/obstruction of the intestine, perirectal abscess)
- general disorders (e.g., fever, lethargy, rigors, chest pain or tightness, weight loss)
- liver disorders (e.g., gallstones)
- infections and infestations (e.g., influenza, bronchitis, urinary tract infection, gastroenteritis, tooth abscess, pneumonia)
- immune system disorders (e.g., seasonal allergy, hypersensitivity reaction)
- injection site reactions (e.g., pain, tenderness, skin reactions)
- metabolism and nutrition disorders (e.g., anorexia, appetite disorders, increased appetite, heat exhaustion, dehydration, elevated blood cholesterol)
- musculoskeletal and connective tissue disorders (e.g., pain in limbs, muscle spasms, joint stiffness)
- nausea, particularly after initial injection
- nervous system disorders (e.g., headache and migraine, dizziness, fainting, sleepiness, abnormality of the sense of taste, disturbance in attention, mental impairment, convulsions, ischemic stroke, cerebral arterial aneurysm)

> ## KEY TERMS
>
> **Alcohol dependence**—A chronic disease with both neurological and genetic factors. Diagnostic criteria include increased tolerance for alcohol, withdrawal symptoms, loss of control over the use of alcohol, and/or impaired function. Alcohol dependence is distinguished from alcohol abuse, alcohol withdrawal syndrome, and other alcohol-induced syndromes.
>
> **Analgesic**—A medication to reduce or eliminate pain.
>
> **Opioid**—A synthetic narcotic that resembles natural opiates.
>
> **Placebo**—A preparation without pharmacological effect that is given in place of a drug in clinical trials to determine the effectiveness of the drug under study; a "sugar pill."

- psychiatric disorders (e.g., irritability, decreased libido, abnormal dreams, alcohol withdrawal syndrome, agitation, euphoric mood, delirium)
- respiratory, thoracic, and mediastinal disorders (e.g., shortness of breath, sinus congestion, chronic obstructive airways disease)
- skin and subcutaneous tissue disorders (e.g., increased sweating, night sweats)
- vascular disorders (e.g., elevated blood pressure, hot flushes, deep venous thrombosis, pulmonary embolism)

Interactions

Although Vivitrol is a powerful drug with prolonged effects for blocking the action of opioids, the blockade can be overcome. However, such action is extremely dangerous. Any attempt by the patient to overcome the blockage by taking higher amounts of opioids or large dose of heroin while on Vivitrol could lead to serious injury, coma, or death.

A number of drugs may interact with Vivitrol. Patients should inform their doctor of all drugs they are currently taking before starting treatment. It has been shown, however, that patients treated simultaneously with Vivitrol and antidepressant medications (e.g., **sertraline**, **citalopram**, **paroxetine**, **fluoxetine**, trazodone, **bupropion** hydrochloride) had similar safety profiles to patients taking Vivitrol without **antidepressants**.

Resources

BOOKS

American Psychiatric Association. *Diagnostic and Statistical Manual of Mental Disorders*. 4th ed., text rev. Washington, DC: American Psychiatric Publishing, 2000.

WEBSITES

Cephalon, Inc. "U.S. Government Organizations Release Positive Information About VIVITROL for the Treatment of Alcoholism." http://investors.cephalon.com/phoenix. zhtml?c=81709&p=irol-newsArticle&ID=1000756&highlight= (accessed October 29, 2011).

Cephalon, Inc. "Vivitrol (naltrexone for extended-release injectable suspension): Prescribing Information." 2010. http://www.vivitrol.com/pdf_docs/prescribing_info.pdf (accessed October 29, 2011).

Hilt, Emma. "Naltrexone Extended-Release Prescribing Information Strengthened." Medscape Medical News. May 5, 2010. http://www.medscape.com/viewarticle/721288 (accessed October 29, 2011).

Ruth A. Wienclaw, Ph.D.

Vocational rehabilitation

Definition

Vocational rehabilitation (VR) is a set of services offered to individuals with mental or physical disabilities. These services are designed to enable participants to attain skills, resources, attitudes, and expectations needed to compete in the interview process, get a job, and keep a job. Services offered may also help an individual retrain for employment after an injury or mental disorder has disrupted previous employment.

Purpose

Vocational rehabilitation services prepare qualified applicants to achieve a lifestyle of independence and integration within their workplace, family, and local community. This transition is achieved through work evaluation and job readiness services, job counseling services, and medical and therapeutic services. For individuals with psychiatric disabilities, situational assessments are generally used to evaluate vocational skills and potential.

Precautions

Vocational rehabilitation as operated by state agencies is not an entitlement program. Only individuals considered eligible can receive VR services. Eligibility criteria require that an individual be at least 16 years old, unemployed or under-employed, and have a physical or mental disability that results in a substantial barrier to employment, such as psychotic disorders, alcohol and other drug abuse dependence, mental and emotional disorders, attention deficit disorders, specific learning disabilities, or physical or sensory disabilities. In addition, the individual must be able to benefit from VR services. An individual must also need help to prepare for, find, and succeed in paid employment. When resources are limited, individuals with the most significant disabilities must be served first.

Description

Vocational rehabilitation services are based on individual needs and defined as any goods or services an individual might need to be employable, such as assistive technology devices and services. For instance, a person who is blind would need screen reading software to access a computer and people with a cognitive or mental disability might need a talking electronic reminder device programmed to prompt them when it is time to perform certain tasks.

Vocational rehabilitation can be provided by private organizations, but is not typically funded under **managed care** arrangements. Thus, most people apply to state vocational rehabilitation agencies that are funded through federal and state monies. Typically, state agencies have offices in their state's major cities and towns. State VR agencies do not necessarily offer the same services or deliver services in the same way in every state, so individuals seeking services must learn how to access the VR program in their own state. The federal VR component is administered by the U.S. Department of Education Rehabilitation Services Administration and authorized by the Rehabilitation Act of 1973 as amended in the 1988 reauthorization.

Most vocational rehabilitation services are free for eligible applicants; however, applicants may be asked to use other benefits, such as insurance, Pell grants or other financial aid for training or higher education, to pay part of program costs.

Best practices in vocational rehabilitation include individual choice, person-centered planning, integrated setting, natural supports, rapid placement, and career development. The term *integrated setting* refers to placing individuals in usual employment situations rather than making placements into sheltered workshops or other segregated settings. Natural supports are the person's already existing support network, including family members, service providers, and friends, who can help the person reach a goal, such as the employment of their choice. Person-centered planning is a technique in which a plan for a person's future is developed by a team consisting of the person and his or her natural supports, and the team develops a practical plan based on the person's wishes and dreams. Each teammember agrees to perform certain tasks identified in the plan to help the person reach goals. Unfortunately, not all VR programs incorporate all of these best practices.

Preparation

Vocational rehabilitation transition planning services are required for all public and private education students aged 16 and over, who have Individualized Education Plans (IEPs) or Rehabilitation Act Section 504 Plans. Transition services help students make the transition from school to employment, training or higher education. Older individuals who have acquired disabilities and are applying for VR services must undergo medical and psychological assessments at their local VR office to determine the extent of their disabilities, except for individuals receiving SSDI or SSI who are presumed eligible without assessments. Applicants may receive treatment and counseling, if needed, before training and employment. All VR services are described in an applicant's Individualized Plan for Employment (IPE). Applicants may design the IPE either on their own or with the assistance of their assigned VR counselor, usually a person with a master's degree in rehabilitation counseling.

Aftercare

A vocational rehabilitation counselor will help applicants access an employment agency to help locate a job. Counselors may provide support (supported employment programs) if applicants need support to keep a job. This support may include job coaching, which includes working with the person in the workplace until the person is comfortable with the work. The counselors also act as resources if a job does not work out by assessing what happened and counseling the person on how to improve performance or change habits that were not looked on with favor in the workplace.

Risks

Applicants may not be satisfied with the pace of progress toward their employment goal through VR, or they may not believe their wishes or talents and skills are being taken seriously. Applicants wanting to start their own businesses or engage in telecommuting may not be successful in receiving vocational rehabilitation assistance. Applicants may find that VR counselors tend to

KEY TERMS

IEP (Individualized Education Plan)—Under federal law governing special education, every child in public schools who is determined through assessment to have special mental disability needs has an IEP. An IEP is typically developed by a team of professionals that may include special education teachers; physical, occupational and speech therapists; psychologists; parents or guardians; and others who may be called on to provide expertise. The team meets at least once a year to set goals for the next school year and to assess progress on already established goals. Parents who are not satisfied with school-based assessments have the right to ask for independent assessments that must be paid for by the school system.

Integrated setting—Placing individuals in usual employment situations rather than making placements into sheltered workshops or other segregated settings.

Natural supports—Using a person's already existing support network to help the person reach a goal, such as the employment of their choice.

Person-centered planning—A technique in which a plan for a person's future is developed by a team consisting of the person, family members, service providers and friends (natural supports). The team develops a practical plan based on the person's wishes and dreams. Each team member agrees to perform certain tasks identified in the plan to help the person reach goals.

Section 504—This section of the Rehabilitation Act of 1973 provides that no person may be discriminated against because of a physical disability—for instance, a child who uses a wheelchair. If a science class is on the second floor and the building has no elevator, the school must find a way to ensure that children in wheelchairs have access to that science class. An educational plan for a child who has both cognitive and physical disabilities is developed under an IEP.

recommend low-level and low-paying jobs traditionally recommended for VR applicants, such as food service and janitorial work. Applicants may also be turned away by VR counselors because the counselors decide the applicant's disability is too severe for the person to benefit from VR services. An additional risk for individuals with mental disorders is a usual lack of coordination between VR and mental health systems.

To address these problems in the VR system, the U.S. Congress passed the Ticket To Work Act in 1999. Under this Act, persons with mental or physical disabilities receive a ticket worth a certain amount of money. They may take this ticket to any private or public entity that provides job training and placement, including state VR programs. The entities providing the employment-related services are able to redeem the tickets for payment only after the person has been gainfully employed for a certain period of time.

Results

Individuals with mental or physical disabilities will receive the assessments, counseling, training, placement, accommodations and long-term supports needed to allow them to engage in the gainful employment of their choice.

Resources

PERIODICALS

Cook, Judith A. "Research-Based Principles of Vocational Rehabilitation for Psychiatric Disability." University of Chicago National Reserach and Training Center on Psychiatric Disability. Issue 4 (September 1999).

Harding, Courtney. "Some Things We've Learned about Vocational Rehabilitation of the Seriously and Persistently Mentally Ill." Presented at the Boston University Colloquium, Brookline, MA: April 17, 1996.

Lehman, Anthony F. "Vocational Rehabilitation in Schizophrenia." *Schizophrenia Bulletin* 21, no. 4 (1995): 645–56.

MacDonald-Wilson, K., et al. "Unique Issues in Assessing Work Function Among Individuals with Psychiatric Disabilities." *Journal of Occupational Rehabilitation* 11, no. 3 (2001): 217–32.

Maronne, J., et al. "If You Think Work Is Bad for People with Mental Illness, Then Try Poverty, Unemployment, and Social Isolation." *Psychiatric Rehabilitation Journal* 23, no. 2 (2000): 187–193.

WEBSITES

Office of Special Education and Rehabilitation Services. "Rehabilitation Services Administration (RSA) Programs and Projects." http://www2.ed.gov/about/offices/list/osers/rsa/programs.html (accessed December 18, 2011).

U.S. Social Security Administration. "About Ticket to Work." http://ssa.gov/work/aboutticket.html (accessed December 18, 2011).

ORGANIZATIONS

Association for Persons in Supported Employment, PO Box 1280, Rockville, MD, 20849, (301) 279-0060, Fax: (301) 251-3762, http://www.apse.org.

Office of Special Education and Rehabilitative Services, Rehabilitation Services Administration, 400 Maryland Ave., SW, Washington, DC, 20202-2800, (202) 245-7488, http://rsa.ed.gov.

State Rehabilitation Councils, 1902 Market Street, Camp Hill, PA, 17011, (888) 250-5175, http://www.parac.org.

Geoffrey Grimm, Ph.D., LPC

Voyeurism

Definition

Voyeurism is a psychosexual disorder in which a person derives sexual pleasure and gratification from looking at naked bodies and genital organs or observing the sexual acts of others. The voyeur is usually hidden from view of others. Voyeurism is a form of paraphilia. Other **paraphilias** include **exhibitionism**, **fetishism**, and **pedophilia**.

A variant form of voyeurism involves listening to erotic conversations. This is commonly referred to as telephone sex, although it is usually considered voyeurism primarily in the instance of listening to unsuspecting people.

Demographics

Voyeurism is more common in men but does occasionally occur in women. However, the prevalence of voyeurism is not known. Contemporary society in the United States is increasingly voyeuristic (as illustrated by the popularity of reality television); however, **diagnosis** is made only when voyeurism is a preferred or exclusive means of sexual gratification. Paraphilias in total are generally believed to occur much more frequently in men than women, with about 20 men diagnosed for each woman diagnosed.

Description

The object of voyeurism is to observe unsuspecting individuals who are naked, in the process of undressing, or engaging in sexual acts. The person being observed usually is a stranger to the observer. The act of looking or peeping is undertaken for the purpose of achieving sexual excitement. The observer generally does not seek to have sexual contact or activity with the person being observed.

If orgasm is sought, it is usually achieved through masturbation. This may occur during the act of observation or later, relying on the memory of the act that was observed.

Frequently, a voyeur may have a fantasy of engaging in sexual activity with the person being observed. In reality, this fantasy is rarely acted out.

A number of states have statutes that render voyeurism a crime. Such statutes vary widely regarding definitions of voyeurism. Most states specifically prohibit anyone from photographing or videotaping another person without consent while observing that person in the privacy of his home or some other private place.

Causes and symptoms

Professionals do not agree about the causes of voyeurism, but its symptoms are generally accepted as having to do with violating the privacy of others for personal sexual gratification.

Causes

There is no scientific consensus concerning the basis for voyeurism. Some experts attribute the behavior to an initially random or accidental observation of an unsuspecting person who is naked, in the process of disrobing, or engaging in sexual activity. Successive repetitions of the act tend to reinforce and perpetuate the voyeuristic behavior.

Other experts view this and other paraphilias as having an obsessive-compulsive element, and some findings describe these behaviors in a category of compulsive-impulsive sexual behaviors or behaviors that fit in the inclusive term of **process addiction**. For example, those with symptoms of compulsive-impulsive sex behavior related to process addiction may have frequent, intrusive thoughts about sex and engage repeatedly in sex behaviors that can spiral out of control.

Single case studies have suggested some effectiveness in treating paraphilic behaviors with drugs used to treat **bipolar disorder**, implying a potential link to bipolar disorders. People with pedophilia, which is also characterized as a paraphilia, have abnormalities in **brain imaging studies** that are similar to those observed in imaging studies of people with **obsessive-compulsive disorder**. Disruption of the pathways of **dopamine** and **serotonin** (both nerve-signaling molecules) is implicated in these disorders. People who engage in paraphilic behavior may also have a higher rate of substance use, novelty seeking, and sexual risk-taking behaviors.

Symptoms

The act of voyeurism is the repeated observation of an unsuspecting person who is naked or who is in the process of disrobing or engaging in sexual activity that provides sexual arousal to the viewer, who usually remains hidden from the individual being observed. The onset of voyeuristic activity is usually before the age of 15.

Diagnosis

According to the handbook used by mental health professionals to diagnose mental disorders, the

KEY TERMS

Bipolar disorder—A psychiatric disorder characterized by periods of mania alternating with periods of depression.

Dopamine—A neurochemical made in the brain that is involved in many brain activities, including movement and emotion.

Paraphilia—A group of sexual disorders involving fantasies, desires, or behaviors with uncommon objects or in uncommon situations generally not found sexually arousing by others and that are not generally accepted by society.

Serotonin—5-Hydroxytryptamine; a substance that occurs throughout the body with numerous effects, including neurotransmission. Low serotonin levels are associated with mood disorders, particularly depression and obsessive-compulsive disorder.

Diagnostic and Statistical Manual of Mental Disorders (*DSM*), two criteria are required to make a diagnosis of voyeurism:

• An individual must experience recurrent, intense, and sexually arousing fantasies, urges, or behaviors that involve the act of observing a person who is naked, disrobing, or engaging in sexual activity, and who is unaware of being observed.

• The actions must cause significant distress or impairment in areas of everyday functioning, or the person must have sought sexual stimulation from observing three or more persons on at least three separate occasions.

Revisions for the fifth edition of the *DSM* (*DSM-5*) proposed changing voyeurism to voyeuristic disorder, in order to help differentiate between paraphilias and paraphilic disorders. Paraphilias are not inherently causes for psychiatric diagnoses, but when the paraphilia causes distress, harm, or otherwise impairs everyday functioning for the person or others, it is considered a disorder.

Treatment

For treatment to be successful, a person with voyeuristic disorder must want to modify existing patterns of behavior. This initial step is difficult for most patients to admit and then take, and usually individuals must be compelled to accept treatment, often as the result of a court order.

QUESTIONS TO ASK YOUR DOCTOR

- Could my behavior or sexual preferences indicate voyeurism?
- Can you recommend a mental health professional who is experienced in treating this disorder?
- Will my insurance cover treatment for this disorder?
- Are there any support groups in this area?
- What are the laws concerning voyeuristic behavior in this state?

Behavioral therapy is commonly used to try to treat voyeurism. The voyeur must learn to control the impulse to watch nonconsenting victims and acquire more acceptable means of sexual gratification. Outcomes of behavioral therapy are not known. There are no direct drug treatments for voyeurism.

Voyeurism is a criminal act in many jurisdictions. It is usually classified as a misdemeanor. As a result, legal penalties are often minor. The possibility of exposure and embarrassment may deter some persons from engaging in voyeurism. It is not easy to prosecute cases of voyeurism, as intent to watch is difficult to prove. In defense statements, perpetrators of voyeurism usually claim that the observation was accidental.

Prognosis

Once voyeuristic activity is undertaken, it commonly does not stop. Over time, it may become the main form of sexual gratification for the voyeur. Its course tends to be chronic.

The prognosis for completely eliminating voyeuristic actions is poor, largely because most persons with voyeuristic disorder have no desire to change their pattern of behavior. Because voyeurism involves nonconsenting partners and is against the law in many jurisdictions, the possibility of embarrassment may deter some individuals.

Prevention

Most experts agree that providing guidance regarding culturally acceptable behavior will help to prevent the development of a paraphilia such as voyeurism. The origin of some instances of voyeurism may be accidental observation with subsequent sexual gratification. There is no way to predict when such an event and association may occur.

Members of society can reduce the incidence of voyeurism by drawing curtains, dropping blinds, or closing window curtains. Reducing opportunities for voyeurism may reduce the practice.

Resources

BOOKS

Clinton, Tim, and Mark Laaser. *The Quick-Reference Guide to Sexuality and Relationship Counseling.* Grand Rapids, MI: Baker Books, 2010.

Hock, Roger R. *Human Sexuality,* 2nd ed. Upper Saddle River, NJ: Prentice Hall, 2010.

Laws, D. Richard, and William T. O'Donohue, eds. *Sexual Deviance: Theory, Assessment, and Treatment,* 2nd ed. New York, Guilford Press, 2008.

Rowland, David L., and Luca Incrocci, eds. *Handbook of Sexual and Gender Identity Disorders.* Hoboken, NJ: John Wiley and Sons, 2008.

PERIODICALS

Hinderliter, Andrew C. "Disregarding Science, Clinical Utility and the DSM's Definition of Mental Disorder: The Case of Exhibitionism, Voyeurism, and Frotteurism." *Archives of Sexual Behavior* 39, no. 6 (December 2010): 1235–37.

Langstrom, Niklas. "The DSM Diagnostic Criteria for Exhibitionism, Voyeurism, and Frotteurism." *Archives of Sexual Behavior* 39, no. 2 (April 2010): 317–24.

ORGANIZATIONS

American Academy of Child and Adolescent Psychiatry, 3615 Wisconsin Ave. NW, Washington, DC, 20016-3007, (202) 966-7300, Fax: (202) 966-2891, http://www.aacap.org.

American Psychological Association, 750 1st St. NE, Washington, DC, 20002-4242, (202) 336-5500; TDD/TTY: (202) 336-6123, (800) 374-2721, apa@psych.org, http://www.apa.org.

L. Fleming Fallon, Jr, MD
Tish Davidson, AM

Vyvanse *see* **Lisdexamfetamine**

Wechsler Intelligence Scales

Definition

The Wechsler Intelligence Scales are a series of **intelligence tests** used to assess general cognition in children and/or adults. The series of tests consists of the Wechsler Preschool and Primary Scale of Intelligence (WPPSI) for children from three to seven years of age, the Wechsler Intelligence Scale for Children (WISC) for children from six to 16 years of age, and the Wechsler Adult Intelligence Scale (WAIS) for adults 16 years and older.

Purpose

The purpose of the Wechsler Scales is to test cognitive abilities (intelligence) in children and adults by providing various index scores that indicate different verbal and non-verbal (performance) abilities.

A five-year-old child is assessed using the Wechsler Intelligence Scale for Children. (© *Custom Medical Stock Photo, Inc. Reproduced by permission.*)

Description

Origins

The Wechsler Intelligence Scales were developed by Romanian-born American **psychologist** David Wechsler (1896–1981). In 1939, Dr. Wechsler developed the first of his tests, the Wechsler Adult Intelligence Scale, while working at the Bellevue Hospital Center in Manhattan, New York City. In 1949, he developed the Wechsler Intelligence Scale for Children, and in 1967, the Wechsler Preschool and Primary Scale of Intelligence. These tests were originally developed by Wechsler as a way to learn more about his patients at Bellevue after he realized that existing intelligence tests were not adequate for his purposes and, especially, that those tests did not provide very much validity for older children and adults.

Wechsler believed that intelligence was based on performance and not on capacity. As such, he viewed intelligence as an individual's ability to solve problems. He stated in 1944, "Intelligence is the aggregate or global capacity of the individual to act purposefully, to think rationally and to deal effectively with his environment." Wechsler developed his Scales by introducing two parts for the testing in intelligence: Verbal and Performance (non-verbal). Each part was then subdivided into subtests. He assigned an arbitrary value of 100 to the mean intelligence, to stand for the average or expected value of intelligence. Wechsler then added or subtracted 15 points from 100 for each standard deviation above or below the mean, respectively.

Components

As a widely used series of intelligence tests developed by clinical psychologist David Wechsler, their most distinctive feature is a division into a verbal section and a nonverbal (or "performance") section, with separate scores available for each one. Verbal intelligence—the component most often associated with academic accomplishment—implies the ability to reason abstractly in terms using either words or mathematical symbols.

Performance intelligence suggests the ability to perceive relationships and piece individual parts together logically into a whole. The inclusion of the performance section in the Wechsler scales is especially helpful in assessing the cognitive ability of non-native speakers and children with speech or language disorders. The test can be of particular value to school psychologists screening for specific learning disabilities because of the number of specific subtests that make up each section.

For all of the Wechsler scales, separate verbal and performance scores, as well as a total score, are computed. These are then converted using a scale divided into categories (such as average and superior), and the final score is generally given as one of these categories rather than as a number or percentile ranking.

WPPSI

The Wechsler Preschool and Primary Scales of Intelligence (WPPSI) has traditionally been geared toward children ages four to six years of age, although the newest version of the test (WPPSI-III, publication year: 2002) broadens the age range downward to two years, six months, and upward to seven years, three months. The younger age limit allows earlier testing for such children. Originally developed in 1967, it has been revised in 1989 (WPPSI-II) and 2002 (WPPSI-III).

WPPSI-III provides subtests and related scoring in verbal and performance (non-verbal), along with a composite scoring that assesses general intellectual ability. Two age divisions are included in the test. The test takes 30 to 45 minutes to administer for children from two years, six months, to three years, eleven months, and 45 to 60 minutes for children from four years to seven years, three months. Compared to older children, younger children take fewer subtests that measure verbal comprehension and perceptual organization skills, and processing speed skills. In both groups, less acquired knowledge is required of the child test takers when compared to earlier versions of the test. In addition, the third edition of the WPPSI contains more simplified instructions and scoring procedures that enhance the ability of the administrator to examine children.

In all, 14 subtests are provided. These are:

- Block Design (recreate one- or two-color blocks)

- Information (Performance: respond to question by selecting one picture from four options; Verbal: respond to question from general-knowledge topics)

- Matrix Reasoning (fill in incomplete matrix from four or five response options)

- Vocabulary (Performance: name pictures displayed; Verbal: give definitions for words verbally stated by administrator)

- Picture Concepts (choose one picture from rows of pictures with common characteristic)

- Symbol Search (decide whether target symbol matches any symbol in group)

- Word Reasoning (identify common concept in series of clues)

- Coding (copy symbols paired with geometric shapes)

- Comprehension (answer questions based on general principles and social situations)

- Picture Completion (look at pictures, and indicate what important parts are missing)

- Similarities (find missing part of an incomplete sentence containing two concepts)

- Receptive Vocabulary (select one of four pictures based on what the administrator says)

- Object Assembly (arrange pieces of puzzle within a time limit)

- Picture Naming (name pictures as displayed in book)

The Verbal section includes the five subtests of Information, Vocabulary, Comprehension, Object Assembly, and Picture Naming. The Performance section includes all 14 subtests as with the Verbal section.

The scoring of the WPPSI-III includes a Verbal IQ score and a Performance IQ score, along with a Full Scale IQ score. In addition, a score for Processing Speed Quotient is produced for children from four years to seven years, three months. A General Language Composite score is available for children from both age divisions.

WISC

The Wechsler Intelligence Scale for Children (WISC), now in its third revision (WISC-IV, publication year 2003), is designed for children and adolescents from the ages of six years to 16 years, 11 months. Each version is re-standardized to compensate for the Flynn Effect, to ensure that the biases against women and minorities are eliminated, and to ensure that the administration of the test is as easy as possible. Originally developed in 1949, it has been revised in 1974 (WISC-R) and 1991 (WISC-III). The current version is WISC-IV, which was first produced in 2003. It takes approximately 60 to 90 minutes to administer the core subtests, and about 10 to 15 minutes for each supplemental test.

In all, 15 subtests are provided. They are divided into: Verbal Comprehension (VCI), Perceptual Reasoning

(PRI), Processing Speed (PSI), and Working Memory (WMI). For VCI, the five subtests are:

- Vocabulary (define words)
- Similarities (state why two words are alike or different)
- Comprehension (answer questions pertaining to social situations or well-known concepts)
- Information (supplemental subtest; answer questions pertaining to general knowledge)
- Word Reasoning (supplemental subtest; solve clues that help to identify word)

For PRI, the four subtests are:

- Block Design (arrange red-and-white blocks based on pre-provided pattern)
- Picture Concepts (select which pictures (one from each row) go together from two or three rows of pictures)
- Matrix Reasoning (select one picture (from a choice of five) that fits an array of pictures with one missing spot)
- Picture Completion (supplemental subtest; identify missing part from common art objects)

For WMI, the three subtests are:

- Digit Span (repeat sequence of numbers stated by administrator, either as stated or in reverse order)
- Letter-Number Sequencing (repeat sequence of numbers and letters stated by administrator, in pre-determined order)
- Arithmetic (supplemental subtest; complete problems orally stated by administrator)

For PSI, the three subtests are:

- Coding (children under eight years: mark rows of shapes with different lines according to particular code; children over eight: transcribe digit-symbol code)
- Symbol Search (mark whether target symbols appear in rows of symbols or not)
- Cancellation (supplemental, answer based on visual-perceptual speed)

A Full Scale score (FSIQ) is generated from the subtests. Scores are also generated from the four indices (VCI, PRI, WMI, and PSI).

WAIS

The Wechsler Adult Intelligence Scale (WAIS), now in its third revision (WAIS-IV, publication year 2008), is designed for adolescent and adult intelligence. Each version is re-standardized to compensate for the Flynn Effect, to ensure that the biases against women and minorities are eliminated, and to ensure that the administration of the test is as easy as possible. Originally developed in 1955, it has been revised in 1974 (WISC-R) and 1991 (WISC-III). The current version is WISC-IV, which was first released in 2008. It takes approximately 60 to 90 minutes to administer the core subtests, and about 10 to 15 minutes for each supplemental test.

The WAIS-IV consists of 10 core subtests and five supplemental subtests. Four index scores are included: Verbal Comprehension Index (VCI), Perceptual Reasoning Index (PRI), Working Memory Index (WMI), and Processing Speed Index (PSI).

For VCI, the five subtests (which are similar in meaning but not exactly the same as in the WISC) are:

- Similarities (asks such questions as "In what ways are a cat and dog similar?")
- Vocabulary (asks questions such as "What is an airplane?")
- Information ("What is the capital of the United States?")
- Comprehension (supplemental subtest; "What does *The sky is as thick as pea soup* mean?")

For PRI, the five subtests are:

- Block Design (abstract problem solving and spatial perception)
- Matrix Reasoning (inductive reasoning and nonverbal problem solving)
- Visual Puzzles (nonverbal reasoning)
- Picture Completion (supplemental subtest; ability to see details quickly)
- Figure Weights (supplemental subtest; analogical and quantitative reasoning)

For WMI, the three subtests are:

- Digit Span (repeat sequence of numbers in different ways, such as *Repeat 7-9-3-5 in reverse order*)
- Arithmetic (mathematics problems using memory, such as administrator may ask "How much money do you have if you are given two quarters, three dimes, and four five-dollar bills?")
- Letter-Number Sequencing (supplemental subset; repeat sequence of numbers and letters stated by administrator, but in a different order, such as "State 7-A-Z-9-3-5-T but, first, the numbers in numerical order and, second, the letters in alphabetical order.")

For PSI, the three subtests are:

- Symbol Search (ability to perceive a situation visually and to do it quickly)

KEY TERMS

IQ—The acronym for intelligence quotient.

Percentile—A statistical measure that shows, on a scale of 100, whether a distribution is below or above it.

Standard deviation—A statistical measure of the difference to an arithmetical mean.

• Coding (mental speed and visual-motor coordination)

• Cancellation (supplemental, visual-perceptual speed).

A Full Scale score (FSIQ) is generated from the subtests. Scores are also generated from the four indices (VCI, PRI, WMI, and PSI).

Preparation

Preparation for the Wechsler Intelligence Scales is neither needed nor recommended.

Risks

The Wechsler Intelligence Scales are some of the most frequently used tests by psychologists and other professionals to assess general intellectual ability. Analysis and research into the way they are administered, however, indicates that errors are sometimes made in scoring and administering the tests. Such errors lessen the accuracy of the Wechsler tests. For instance, sometimes professionals place more emphasis on differences between the Verbal IQ and Performance IQ scores than they should. In other cases, they make conclusions regarding **brain** damage based only on the test, when other screening instruments should be included. Research has also shown that the ethnicity of the administrator may have an effect on the scoring of individual of minority groups.

Despite criticisms, the Wechsler Intelligence Scales remain a good way to access general intelligence when performed by a trained, unbiased professional.

Results

Administering and scoring of the three Wechsler Scales are very similar. Each of the three tests has a series of subtests grouped into two general areas: Verbal Scales and Performance Scales. The Verbal Scales measure general knowledge, reasoning, language, and memory skills, and the Performance Scales assess problem solving, spatial, and sequencing abilities.

The tests are administered by trained professionals. Raw scores are first generated and then converted to standard scores with a mean and standard deviations from that average. In addition, scores in the Verbal battery are summed and converted to a Verbal IQ score; the same is done for the Performance scores, providing the Performance IQ score. The Verbal and Performance IQ scores are added together and are then converted to an overall Full Scale IQ score. The Verbal, Performance, and Full Scale IQ scores are considered "normative" IQ scores, which means, in this specific case, that they have a mean of 100 and a standard deviation of 15.

A Full Scale IQ score higher than 130 indicates that the test taker is in the highest intelligence category. Scores in the 120s are considered very high in intelligence, and in the 110s they are above normal, while scores from 90 to 109 are considered normal-average, and in the high 80s low-average. Scores below 85 are considered low in mental functioning, with the lower the score the less ability to function mentally.

Resources

BOOKS

Drummond, Robert J. *Assessment Procedures for Counselors and Helping Professionals*. Boston: Pearson, 2010.

Green, Susan K. and Robert L. Johnson. *Assessment is Essential*. Boston: McGraw-Hill Higher Education, 2010.

Hart, Diane. *Authentic Assessment: A Handbook for Educators*. Menlo Park, CA: Addison-Wesley, 1994.

McAfee, Oralie, and Deborah J. Leong. *Assessing and Guiding Young Children's Development and Learning*. Upper Saddle River, NJ: Pearson, 2011.

McCullough, Virginia E. *Testing and Your Child: What You Should Know about 150 of the Most Common Medical, Educational, and Psychological Tests*. New York City: Plume, 1992.

Mindes, Gayle. *Assessing Young Children*. Boston: Pearson, 2011.

Walsh, W. Bruce, and Nancy E. Betz. *Tests and Assessment*, 4th ed. Upper Saddle River, NJ: Prentice Hall, 2001.

Wechsler, David. *Manual for the Wechsler Adult Intelligence Scale*. New York: The Psychological Corporation, 1955.

Wechsler, David. *Manual for the Wechsler Intelligence Scale for Children*. New York: The Psychological Corporation, 1949.

Wechsler, David. *Manual for the Wechsler Preschool and Primary Scale of Intelligence*. New York: The Psychological Corporation, 1967.

WEBSITES

David Wechsler (1896–1981) Psychologist. Human Intelligence, Indiana University. (July 25, 2007), http://www.indiana.edu/~intell/wechsler.shtml (accessed October 28, 2010).

Wechsler Adult Intelligence Scale—Fourth Edition (WAIS—IV). Pearson. http://www.pearsonassessments.com/HAIWEB/Cultures/en-us/Productdetail.htm?Pid=015-8980-808(accessed October 28, 2010).

Wechsler Intelligence Scale for Children™—Fourth Edition (WISC™—IV). Pearson. http://www.pearsonassessments.com/HAIWEB/Cultures/en-us/Productdetail.htm?Pid=015-8979-044 (accessed October 27, 2010).

Wechsler Preschool and Primary Scale of Intelligence™—Third Edition (WPPSI™—III. Pearson. http://www.pearsonassessments.com/haiweb/cultures/en-us/productdetail.htm?pid=015-8989-317 (accessed October 27, 2010).

William Arthur Atkins

Wellbutrin *see* **Bupropion**

Wernicke-Korsakoff syndrome

Definition

Wernicke-Korsakoff syndrome is a severe memory disorder usually associated with chronic excessive alcohol consumption, although the direct cause is a deficiency in the B vitamin thiamin.

The *Diagnostic and Statistical Manual of Mental Disorders,* fourth edition, text revision (DSM-IV-TR), the professional handbook that aids clinicians in diagnosing patients' mental disorders, refers to Korsakoff syndrome as alcohol-induced persisting amnestic disorder and includes it under the category of substance-induced persisting amnestic disorders.

Demographics

When **diagnosis** is based on postmortem findings, the estimated prevalence of Wernicke-Korsakoff syndrome is between 1% and 2% of the population. The classic presentation with acute onset of Wernicke's encephalopathy is fairly rare, about 0.05% of all hospital admissions, although this does not account for patients who do not seek medical attention. Wernicke-Korsakoff syndrome usually follows many years of chronic alcoholism or malnutrition and is seldom seen among people under 20. Most patients are 40 years of age or older. The disorder is apparently more common in alcoholic individuals who are particularly vulnerable to malnutrition such as indigent or homeless people.

Description

The disorder was first identified in the late nineteenth century. The first phase of the condition, called Wernicke's encephalopathy, was described by German neurologist and **psychiatrist** Karl Wernicke in 1881. He noted three key symptoms in three patients—two with alcoholism and one who had swallowed sulfuric acid. These patients suffered from mental confusion, eye **movement disorders**, and ataxia (poor motor coordination). A few years later, S. S. Korsakoff, a Russian psychiatrist, began publishing reports describing a syndrome of anterograde amnesia—an inability to form new memories—and confabulation in individuals with severe alcoholism or certain medical illnesses. (Confabulation refers to the practice of filling in gaps in memory by fabrication.) By 1900, researchers and clinicians studying alcoholism recognized a connection between the two conditions. The typical syndrome begins with acute Wernicke's encephalopathy, with Korsakoff syndrome emerging when the acute phase resolves. The symptoms of Wernicke's encephalopathy appear suddenly. The most prominent symptom initially is mental confusion including memory problems. On examination, patients have difficulty moving their eyes to follow a visual stimulus due to paralysis of the muscles controlling eye movements. For instance, patients may have trouble looking upward or to the side with one or both eyes. Problems maintaining balance while standing or walking, a condition known as ataxia, are frequently observed as well. If left untreated, most of these symptoms may resolve spontaneously, but the severe memory disorder characteristic of Korsakoff syndrome remains.

The typical person with Korsakoff syndrome appears fairly normal on first impression. Intelligence is intact and individuals with the syndrome can carry on a conversation quite naturally. They are usually able to recall and talk about incidents that took place before the onset of the disorder and recognize family members and old friends without much difficulty. The ability to form new memories is nearly absent, however. In the course of conversation, people with Korsakoff syndrome may repeat comments or questions several times. They will fail to recognize people they met minutes before or greet a friend with excitement and surprise after a brief trip to another room. These are the characteristics of anterograde **amnesia**. Research shows that anterograde amnesia results from a failure of memory formation and storage. New information is processed normally but almost immediately forgotten, never making it into the regions of the **brain** where memories of the past are stored. People with Korsakoff syndrome thus have no memories of events that happened after the onset of the illness. Many previously stored memories are still available, however, explaining why individuals with Korsakoff syndrome can usually remember the distant past quite well.

Causes and symptoms

Causes

Wernicke-Korsakoff syndrome is caused by thiamin deficiency. It is most commonly observed in people with alcoholism because heavy drinkers often eat poorly, and alcoholism interferes with absorption of nutrients from the digestive system. It can also occur in people who are malnourished for other reasons, including hyperemesis gravidarum (excessive vomiting during pregnancy) or an eating disorder. Thiamin helps produce the energy-containing molecules needed to make neurons function properly. Insufficient thiamin can lead to damage to or death of neurons.

Thiamin deficiency damages regions of the brain, particularly the thalamus and the mammillary bodies. The thalamus is a structure deep within the brain that serves many important functions. It is often called the major relay station of the brain, and many neurons make connections in the thalamus. The mammillary bodies are part of the hypothalamus, located just below the thalamus. The mammillary bodies receive many neural connections from another part of the brain called the hippocampus, which appears to be the primary part of the brain involved in the formation of memories. Neurons in the mammillary bodies make connections with the thalamus, which in turn makes connections with the cortex of the brain, where long-term memories are stored. This may explain why damage to the mammillary bodies and thalamus can lead to anterograde amnesia. Memories formed in the hippocampus are never stored since connections between hippocampus and cortex are disrupted.

Eye movement disorders observed in the acute phase of the condition are probably due to damage to other nearby brain regions that make connections to the nerves controlling eye muscles. These nerves emerge from the brainstem located right below the thalamus and mammillary bodies. Nerves involved in balance also make connections with other nerves in the brain stem, but a separate part of the brain called the cerebellum may also contribute to ataxia.

Symptoms

Mental confusion, eye movement disturbances, and ataxia are the primary symptoms of Wernicke's encephalopathy—the first, acute stage of Wernicke-Korsakoff syndrome. At first glance, confusion and ataxia may resemble the effects of severe alcohol intoxication, but they persist after intoxication wears off. Some patients with Wernicke's encephalopathy will recover completely without residual memory deficits, particularly if they are treated quickly with thiamin. Patients with this acute phase may not be recognized because they may not necessarily exhibit all three "classic" symptoms; therefore, their cases may be overlooked.

About 80%–90% of alcoholics with Wernecke's go on to develop Korsakoff's **psychosis**, the chronic stage of Wernicke-Korsakoff syndrome. This stage is distinguished by anterograde amnesia, and most untreated patients with Wernicke's encephalopathy will develop this severe memory disorder, which prevents them from forming lasting memories of events or information encountered after the onset of the initial symptoms. Symptoms of Korsakoff syndrome may also develop spontaneously in many patients who never show signs of Wernicke's encephalopathy. Once patients develop Korsakoff's amnesia, recovery is unlikely.

Loss of memory for past events is called retrograde amnesia. Many people with Korsakoff syndrome have some retrograde amnesia in addition to anterograde amnesia, particularly for events that occurred shortly before the onset of illness, but most can recall the distant past without difficulty.

Immediate memory is not affected. For instance, an individual with Korsakoff syndrome could repeat a sentence or string of numbers immediately after hearing them, although this information would likely be forgotten within half a minute. Preservation of immediate memory allows individuals with Korsakoff syndrome to interact with others and respond to questions. Implicit memory is also preserved, so people with Korsakoff syndrome can learn new motor skills or develop conditioned reactions to stimuli. For example, individuals who play computer games can show improved performance each time they play, even if they cannot explicitly remember having played the game before.

Confabulation is another striking feature of Korsakoff syndrome, although it is not always observed. Confabulation refers to falsification of memory. The individual appears to be making up stories to cover up for inability to remember. Confabulation often seems to involve a confusion of the past and present. For example, if patients with Korsakoff syndrome are asked why they are in the hospital, they may say they just had a baby, are recovering from pneumonia, undergoing medical tests, or even applying for a job.

Patients with Wernicke-Korsakoff syndrome may also show signs of **apathy** and a lack of spontaneous behavior. Emotional expression may be lacking as well.

Autopsies often reveal brain lesions characteristic of Wernicke-Korsakoff syndrome in alcoholic patients who showed general cognitive problems like those seen in **dementia**, but who never developed anterograde amnesia. These findings suggest that onset may be gradual in some patients, or, as some experts suspect, that there is a genetic component to susceptibility and manifestation of the disorder.

Diagnosis

Wernicke's encephalopathy is diagnosed when patients seek medical attention and have the classic trio of signs: mental confusion, eye movement disorders, and ataxia, although not every patient will exhibit all three signs. The diagnosis of Korsakoff syndrome is given when anterograde amnesia is present in an individual with a history of chronic, heavy drinking or malnutrition. When Korsakoff syndrome follows Wernicke's encephalopathy, the entire Wernicke-Korsakoff syndrome diagnosis is appropriate. The diagnosis is supported by neuroimaging or autopsy findings showing degeneration of the thalamus and mammillary bodies and loss of brain volume in the area surrounding the fourth ventricle—a fluid-filled cavity near the brain stem.

Although the *DSM-IV-TR* criteria for alcohol-induced persisting amnestic disorder apply to most people with Wernicke-Korsakoff syndrome, there are some differences between the two diagnoses. Despite research findings suggesting that severe amnesia is not a necessary symptom of Wernicke-Korsakoff syndrome, the *DSM-IV-TR* requires the presence of either antero-grade or retrograde amnesia for a diagnosis of alcohol-induced persisting amnestic disorder. One additional cognitive symptom is also required. Symptoms listed in the *DSM-IV-TR* include language disturbance (aphasia), inability to carry out motor activities (apraxia), inability to recognize objects (agnosia), or deficits in planning, initiation, organization, and abstraction (executive functions). Individuals with Wernicke-Korsakoff syndrome frequently demonstrate problems with executive functions that contribute to the symptoms of confabulation and apathy. Aphasia, apraxia, and agnosia are not common signs of Wernicke-Korsakoff syndrome.

The *DSM-IV-TR* also requires that memory impairment must significantly impair a person's ability to perform normal activities and functions, and it must represent a decline from a previous level of functioning. Amnesia cannot occur exclusively during states of **delirium**, alcohol intoxication, or withdrawal, or be exclusively associated with dementia. Both of these requirements are consistent with the usual presentation of Wernicke-Korsakoff syndrome.

Finally, the *DSM-IV-TR* requires evidence that amnesia is caused by use of alcohol. Such evidence can include an extensive history of heavy drinking; or physical examination or laboratory findings revealing other signs of heavy **alcohol use**, such as abnormal liver function tests. Despite this *DSM-IV-TR* requirement,

Wernicke-Korsakoff syndrome can occur in the absence of heavy alcohol use. Emergence of the disorder in people without alcoholism is much less common today than it was in the past, however, since vitamins are now added to many foods. In practice, most people who show the hallmark symptoms of Wernicke-Korsakoff syndrome also qualify for the *DSM-IV-TR* diagnosis.

Treatment

Nutritional

Individuals with signs of Wernicke's encephalopathy should be treated with thiamin immediately. In many cases, prompt administration of thiamin reverses the symptoms and prevents amnesia from developing. Thiamin can be administered intravenously or directly into the digestive system. Unfortunately, thiamin is less effective in the chronic phase of the condition. Based on autopsy findings suggesting the presence of Wernicke-Korsakoff syndrome in people with milder cognitive problems who do not show the classic signs of the disorder, researchers have examined the usefulness of thiamin treatment in people with alcohol dependence who are at risk of developing the syndrome. Results suggest that thiamin treatment improves performance on memory tests in this group, and that higher thiamin doses are associated with better performance. These findings suggest that thiamin treatment can help prevent Wernicke-Korsakoff syndrome in heavy drinkers. Other nutritional treatments may include use of magnesium sulfate to address magnesium deficits common in people with alcoholism, and potassium acid phosphate to address potassium deficiencies.

Medication

Recent reports suggest that **donepezil** and **rivastigmine**, drugs used to treat **Alzheimer's disease**, may improve memory in patients with Wernicke-Korsakoff syndrome. Both drugs affect the action of the neurotransmitter acetylcholine, which is important for the formation of memories. Patients treated with these drugs showed improvements on memory tests and were more able to recognize hospital staff and family members. Although improvements appear to be rather modest, these drugs may be useful for patients who do not respond to thiamin. **Antidepressants** that increase levels of **serotonin** may also be helpful, although the reasons why are not clear since these drugs are not effective with other memory disorders.

Conditioning

The fact that implicit memory is not affected by Wernicke-Korsakoff syndrome has led some researchers

KEY TERMS

Anterograde amnesia—Amnesia for events that occurred after a physical injury or emotional trauma but before the present moment.

Apathy—Lack of feelings or emotions.

Cognitive—Pertaining to the mental processes of memory, perception, judgment, and reasoning.

Encephalopathy—Brain disease that causes damage or degeneration.

Explicit memory—Consciously recalled memory for facts or events.

Implicit memory—Unconsciously recalled memory for skills, procedures, or associations.

Neurons—Nerve cells in the brain that produce nerve impulses.

Neurotransmitter—A chemical in the brain that transmits messages between neurons, or nerve cells.

Retrograde amnesia—Amnesia for events that occurred before a traumatic injury.

Serotonin—A widely distributed neurotransmitter that is found in blood platelets, the lining of the digestive tract, and the brain, and that works in combination with norepinephrine. It causes very powerful contractions of smooth muscle, and is associated with mood, attention, emotions, and sleep. Low levels of serotonin are associated with depression.

Syndrome—A group of symptoms that together characterize a disease or disorder.

to explore the use of classical conditioning procedures in helping patients to remember specific people. In classical conditioning, animals and people learn to associate a stimulus with an outcome. The most famous example is the pairing of a ringing bell with food. Dogs naturally salivate when given food. In a famous experiment, Ivan Pavlov rang a bell immediately before serving food to dogs. After doing this repeatedly, Pavlov found that the dogs salivated upon hearing the bell ring even when the food was not presented. This form of learning does not rely on the hippocampus and cortex but appears to involve neurons in other parts of the brain. Patients with Wernicke-Korsakoff syndrome who are given specific rewards for correctly choosing a picture of a face that matches a face they have seen previously are more able to choose the correct face than those who do not receive the rewards. Although these individuals do not explicitly remember the face they saw previously, they are still able to make the correct choice. Working with patients in this way could enable them to recognize familiar people and differentiate them from strangers.

Prognosis

The prognosis for full recovery from Wernicke-Korsakoff syndrome is poor. Once chronic Korsakoff's amnesia ensues, approximately 80% of patients will never fully recover the ability to learn and remember new information. Because they cannot learn from experience, individuals with Wernicke-Korsakoff syndrome almost always require some form of custodial care. They are usually unable to work, although some can perform simple tasks they learned prior to onset of the condition if closely supervised. The mortality rate is between 10% and 20%, usually from liver failure or infection, but sometimes as a result of the irreversible effects of prolonged thiamin deficiency.

Prevention

Wernicke-Korsakoff syndrome can be prevented with a nutritious diet containing sufficient thiamin. Because severe chronic alcoholism is the most common cause of thiamin deficiency, treatment of alcohol dependence is extremely important. To prevent Wernicke-Korsakoff syndrome among people who are unable to stop drinking or among particularly vulnerable individuals like homeless drinkers, some researchers and clinicians have advocated supplementing alcoholic beverages with thiamin.

Resources

BOOKS

American Psychiatric Association. *Diagnostic and Statistical Manual of Mental Disorders.* 4th ed., text rev. Washington, DC: American Psychiatric Publishing, 2000.

Hochhalter, Angela K., et al. "Using Animal Models to Address the Memory Deficits of Wernicke-Korsakoff Syndrome." In *Animal Research and Human Health: Advancing Human Welfare Through Behavioral Science,* edited by Marilyn E. Carroll and J. Bruce Overmier. Washington, DC: American Psychological Association, 2001.

Mesulam, M.-Marsel. *Principles of Behavioral and Cognitive Neurology.* 2nd ed. Oxford: Oxford University Press, 2000.

Nolte, John. *The Human Brain: An Introduction to Its Functional Anatomy.* 6th ed. St. Louis: Mosby, 2008.

Walsh, Kevin, and David Darby. *Neuropsychology: A Clinical Approach.* 5th ed. Edinburgh: Churchill Livingstone, 2005.

PERIODICALS

Ambrose, Margaret L., Stephen C. Bowden, and Greg Whelen. "Thiamin Treatment and Working Memory Function of Alcohol-dependent People: Preliminary Findings." *Alcoholism: Clinical and Experimental Research* 25, no. 1 (January 2001): 112–16.

Angunawela, Indira I., and Andrew Barker. "Anticholinesterase Drugs for Alcoholic Korsakoff Syndrome." *International Journal of Geriatric Psychiatry* 16, no. 3 (2001): 338–39.

Cochrane, M., et al. "Acetylcholinesterase Inhibitors for the Treatment of Wernicke-Korsakoff Syndrome: Three Further Cases Show Response to Donepezil." *Alcohol and Alcoholism* 40, no. 2 (March/April 2005): 151–54.

Harding, Antony, et al. "Degeneration of Anterior Thalamic Nuclei Differentiates Alcoholics with Amnesia." *Brain* 123, no. 1 (2000): 141–54.

Iga, Jun-Ichi, et al. "A Case of Korsakoff's Syndrome Improved by High Doses of Donepezil." *Alcohol and Alcoholism* 36, no. 6 (2001): 553–55.

WEBSITES

Martin, Peter R., Charles K. Singleton, and Susanne Hiller-Sturmhoefel. "The Role of Thiamine Deficiency in Alcoholic Brain Disease." U.S. National Institute of Alcohol Abuse and Alcoholism, 2004. http://pubs.niaaa.nih.gov/publications/arh27-2/134-142.htm (accessed October 29, 2011).

Memory Disorders Project. "Memory Loss and the Brain" Rutgers University. http://www.memorylossonline.com (accessed October 29, 2011).

U.S. National Institute of Neurological Disorders and Stroke. "Wernicke-Korsakoff Syndrome Information Page." http://www.ninds.nih.gov/disorders/wernicke_korsakoff/wernicke-korsakoff.htm (accessed October 29, 2011).

U.S. National Institute on Alcohol Abuse and Alcoholism. "Alcohol's Damaging Effects on the Brain." http://pubs.niaaa.nih.gov/publications/aa63/aa63.htm (accessed October 29, 2011).

Xiong, Glen L. "Wernicke-Korsakoff Syndrome." Medscape Reference. http://emedicine.medscape.com/article/288379-overview (accessed October 29, 2011).

ORGANIZATIONS

Family Caregiver Alliance, 180 Montgomery Street, Ste. 900, San Francisco, CA, 94104, info@caregiver.org, http://www.caregiver.org.

Medical Council on Alcohol, 5 St. Andrew's Place, London, UK NW1 4LB, (020) 7487-4445, Fax: (020) 7935-4479, mca@medicalcouncilalcol.demon.co.uk, http://www.m-c-a.org.uk.

National Institute on Alcohol Abuse and Alcoholism, 5635 Fishers Lane, MSC 9304, Bethesda, MD, 20892-9304, http://www.niaaa.nih.gov.

Danielle Barry, MS
Emily Jane Willingham, PhD

Wide range achievement test

Definition

The Wide Range Achievement Test (WRAT) is an achievement test that measures basic abilities to read, spell, and comprehend writing and to solve mathematics calculations and problems. Achievement tests refer to skills that individuals learn through direct instruction or intervention. In addition, the WRAT is a screening test that can be administered to determine if a more comprehensive achievement test is needed. The WRAT is currently in its fourth edition: WRAT-4.

Purpose

The WRAT-4, the latest edition of the test, measures basic skills in reading, arithmetic, spelling, and comprehension. The test covers ages from five to 94 years and takes approximately 15 to 45 minutes to administer, dependent primarily on the age of the test taker (15 to 25 minutes for those from five to seven years of age, and 35 to 45 minutes for those eight years or older).

The fourth edition has four subtests: Sentence Comprehension, Word Reading, Spelling, and Math Computation. The Sentence Comprehension subtest is new to this latest edition of the WRAT, providing for a way to assess reading comprehension in test takers. Overall, the WRAT-4 provides reliable measurement for fundamental academic skills, along with **diagnosis** of learning disabilities, progression of academic ability over time, evaluation of achievement discrepancies, progression of remedial learning, and evaluation of instructional needs.

Description

American psychologists Sidney William Bijou (1908–2009) and Joseph Jastak first developed the WRAT in 1941. Its various editions have been used

---

KEY TERMS

Achievement test—Any of a number of tests that assess developed knowledge or skill.

Arithmetic—The branch of mathematics involving problems of addition, subtraction, multiplication, and division.

Psychometric—The branch of psychology that deals with the measurement of mental capacities, traits, and processes.

---

widely as a measure of basic academic skills used for learning, thinking, reading, spelling, and calculating of arithmetic.

The WRAT-4 has two alternative, but equivalent, testing forms (Green and Blue). One form is administered with the second form available if needed. Both Green and Blue testing forms can be administered together, if necessary, as a pre-test and a post-test arrangement, using either one at the start. When both tests forms are used, a combined scored is obtained and a more comprehensive evaluation is provided. Each testing form consists of one Word Reading subtest, one Math Computation (arithmetic) subtest, one Spelling subtest, and one Sentence Comprehension subtest. The Word Reading and Sentence Comprehension subtests can be administered individually, but the other two tests, the Spelling and Math Computation subtests, may be given in groups.

The Word Reading subtest consists of various letters and individual words that the examinee is asked to name or pronounce. The Spelling subtest consists of writing one's name, various letters, and numerous words dictated to the examinee and used in a sentence. The spelling items increase with difficulty. The Math Computation subtest consists of counting, reading number symbols, and solving simple arithmetic problems that are verbally presented to the examinee. It also consists of using paper and a pencil to calculate up various arithmetic problems. The Sentence Comprehension subtest assesses reading comprehension through the use of various sentences.

Preparation

Preparation by the test taker is not necessary nor advised.

Risks

Although screening instruments may save time, these instruments can sometimes have misleading results. For instance, the scores may overestimate or underestimate a person's skills or the test does not measure other important achievement abilities.

Precautions

To obtain a more in-depth result of an examinee's abilities, a more comprehensive achievement test must be administered. For example, the WRAT-4 does not provide assessment of fundamental skills such as reading comprehension, writing abilities, and applying mathematical concepts to real-life situations. Finally, psychometric testing requires a clinically trained examiner. Therefore, the test should only be administered and interpreted by a trained examiner.

QUESTIONS TO ASK YOUR DOCTOR

- Do you know of a properly trained administrator for the WRAT?
- If I should need additional assessment, what are other appropriate tests to use after the WRAT is completed?
- Will health insurance cover the test in whole or part?

Results

The WRAT-4 is an easy and sound measure of fundamental academic skills. It was standardized on a representative sample of the U.S. population using approximately 3,000 people from the ages of five to 94 years. It was improved over the previous edition, WRAT-3, by adding grade-based norms, which helps to assess students in grades kindergarten through twelfth grade. In addition, the new edition has been improved with respect to age-based norms, allowing test takers up to the age of 94 years, as opposed to a maximum of 75 years in edition three.

Scoring consists of a "1" for a correct answer and a "0" for an incorrect answer. The raw scores are converted to standard scores. These are scores that allow the examiner to compare the individual's score to other people who have taken the test. Additionally, by converting raw scores to standard scores the examiner has uniform scores and can more easily compare an individual's performance on one test with the individual's performance on another test. The average score for each test of the WRAT-4 is 100. An examiner can also obtain grade-equivalent scores, percentile ranks, and normal curve equivalents. A poor performance in any of the three areas assessed by this instrument can indicate the need for further testing.

Specifically, the WRAT-4 uses the following: a score summary table, which provides raw scores and standard scores, along with confidence intervals, percentile ranks, grade equivalents, and other such measures; a standard score profile, which provides a graphic representation of standard scores and confidence intervals; and a standard score comparison table, which provides relative performance data on subtests.

Resources

BOOKS

Boyer, Bret A., and M. Indira Paharia, editors. *Comprehensive Handbook of Clinical Health Psychology.* Hoboken, NJ: John Wiley and Sons, 2008.

Groth-Marnat, Gary. *Handbook of Psychological Assessment.* 4th edition. Hoboken, NJ: John Wiley and Sons, 2003.

Hersen, Michel, editor. *Comprehensive Handbook of Psychological Assessment.* Hoboken, NJ: John Wiley and Sons, 2004.

Kellerman, Henry, and Anthony Burry. *Handbook of Psychodiagnostic Testing: Analysis of Personality in the Psychological Report.* New York: Springer, 2007.

Leeming, David A., Kathryn Madden and Stanton Marlan, eds. *Encyclopedia of Psychology and Religion.* New York: Springer, 2010.

Sattler, Jerome M. *Assessment of Children: Cognitive Foundations.* San Diego, CA: J.M. Sattler, 2008.

PERIODICALS

"Sidney W. Bijou, Child Psychologist, Is Dead at 100." *New York Times,* (July 21, 2009). http://www.nytimes.com/2009/07/22/science/22bijou.html?_r=1 (accessed January 7, 2011).

WEBSITES

"Reynolds Intellectual Assessment Scales/Wide Range Achievement Test 4 Discrepancy Interpretive Report (RIAS/WRAT4-DIR)." Par. (2010), http://www4.parinc.com/Products/Product.aspx?ProductID=RIAS/WRAT4/DIR (accessed January 7, 2011).

"Wide Range Achievement Test 4 (WRAT4)." Western Psychological Services. http://portal.wpspublish.com/portal/page?_pageid=53,118660&_dad=portal&_schema=PORTAL (accessed January 7, 2011).

ORGANIZATIONS

American Psychiatric Association, 1000 Wilson Blvd., Ste. 1825, Arlington, VA, 22209-3901, (703) 907-7300, apa@psych.org, http://www.psych.org.

American Psychological Association, 750 1st St. NE, Washington, DC, 20002-4242, (202) 336-5500; TDD/TTY: (202) 336-6123, (800) 374-2721, http://www.apa.org.

National Association of School Psychologists, 4340 East West Highway, Ste. 402, Bethesda, MD, 20002, (301) 657-0270, (866) 331-5277, Fax: (301) 657-0275, http://www.nasponline.org.

Keith Beard, Psy.D.

Wilson disease

Definition

Wilson disease, or WD, is a rare inherited disorder that causes excess copper to accumulate in the body. It is also known as hepatolenticular degeneration. Steadily increasing amounts of copper circulating in the blood are deposited primarily in the **brain**, liver, kidneys, and the cornea of the eyes. WD is fatal if it is not recognized and treated. It is named for a U.S. neurologist, Samuel A. K. Wilson, who first described it in 1912.

Demographics

Wilson disease affects approximately 1 in 30,000 to 1 in 100,000 individuals and can affect people from many different populations. Approximately one in 90 individuals are carriers of the gene for Wilson disease.

Description

Under normal conditions, copper that finds its way into the body through the diet is processed within the liver. This processed form of copper is then passed into the gallbladder, along with the other components of bile (a fluid produced by the liver, which enters the small intestine in order to help in digestive processes). When the gallbladder empties its contents into the first part of the small intestine (duodenum), the copper in the bile enters and passes through the intestine with the waste products of digestion. In healthy individuals, copper is then passed out of the body in stool.

In Wilson disease, copper does not pass from the liver into the bile, but rather begins to accumulate within the liver. As copper levels rise in the liver, the damaged organ begins to allow copper to flow into the bloodstream, where it circulates. Copper is then deposited throughout the body, building up primarily in the kidneys, the brain and nervous system, and the eyes. Wilson disease, then, is a disorder of copper poisoning occurring from birth.

Causes and symptoms

Causes

Wilson disease is inherited in an autosomal recessive manner. Autosomal recessive refers to the pattern of inheritance where each parent carries a gene for the disease on one of his or her chromosome pairs. When each parent passes on the chromosome with the gene for Wilson disease, the child will be affected with the disease. Both males and females can be affected with Wilson disease. If an individual is a carrier of the Wilson disease gene, they do not have any symptoms of this disease. In order to be affected, an individual must inherit two copies of the gene, one from each parent. Many cases of Wilson disease may not be inherited but occur as a spontaneous mutation in the gene.

The gene for Wilson disease is located on chromosome number 13. The name of the gene is called ATP7B and is thought to be involved in transporting copper. More than 200 different mutations of this gene have been identified, making **diagnosis** by genetic testing difficult.

Symptoms

Symptoms typically present between the ages of 3 and 60, with age 17 considered to be the average age at diagnosis. About half of all patients experience their first symptoms in the liver. The illness causes swelling and tenderness of the liver, sometimes with fever, mimicking more common disorders, such as viral hepatitis and infectious mononucleosis. Abnormal levels of circulating liver enzymes reveal that the liver is being seriously damaged. This form of damage is referred to as fatty degeneration. Without medical **intervention**, the liver damage will progress to actual cirrhosis. An often-fatal manifestation of liver disease is called fulminant hepatitis. This extremely severe inflammation of the liver (hepatitis) results in jaundice, fluid leaking into the abdomen, low protein circulating in the blood, abnormalities of the blood clotting system, swelling of the brain, and anemia due to the abnormal destruction of red blood cells.

Neurological symptoms are the first to occur in half of all patients due to copper accumulation in the brain and nervous system. The average age of onset for neurological symptoms is 21. These symptoms include tremors of the hands, uncontrollable movements of the limbs, stiffness, drooling, difficulty swallowing, difficulty talking, and headache. There is no change in patient's intelligence.

About one-third of all patients with Wilson disease have a variety of psychiatric symptoms as the first signs of the disease. These symptoms include inability to cope, **depression**, irritability, increased anger, and inappropriate behavior. Often times patients have trouble completing tasks at work or in school.

Other symptoms that can affect patients with Wilson disease, and that may occur before or after a diagnosis has been made, include joint disorders, symptoms of arthritis, and skeletal problems such as osteoporosis. Patients have occasionally been affected with kidney stones and abnormal handling of glucose in their body, and women may have menstrual cycle irregularities including stopping their regular cycle temporarily.

Diagnosis

The diagnosis of Wilson disease can be performed relatively easily through several different tests; however, because Wilson disease is so rare, diagnosis is often unfortunately delayed. The tests used to diagnose Wilson disease can be performed on patients who have and who have not already shown symptoms of the disease. It is extremely important to make a diagnosis as soon as possible, since liver damage can occur before there are any signs of the disease.

An easy way to diagnose Wilson disease is to measure the amount of a glycoprotein found in the blood called ceruloplasmin. Low levels of ceruloplasmin can diagnose the disease in about 80% of affected patients. This procedure is not as effective for women taking birth control pills, pregnant women, or infants younger than six months of age.

A second test involving an eye examination to detect a characteristic ring of copper deposited in a membrane of the cornea (referred to as Kayser-Fleischer rings) is very easy to perform and is very useful in diagnosing patients who have already exhibited symptoms. This test is not as effective in persons without symptoms. This diagnostic test cannot be used by itself to make a diagnosis because some patients with liver disease but not Wilson disease will test positive.

A third test for diagnosing Wilson disease involves measuring the amount of copper in the liver. This can be accomplished by sampling a portion of the liver, called a biopsy. This is one of the most effective ways to diagnose Wilson disease, but the procedure itself is more difficult to perform than the others.

Other tests are also useful, such as measuring the amount of copper passed into the urine daily (high in Wilson disease). Another lab test measures the ability of a patient's ceruloplasmin to bind with a form of copper (decreased in Wilson disease). Some patients can be diagnosed through a DNA test to determine whether or not they carry two genes for Wilson disease. This test does not always prove to be useful in certain patients and is of most use when used to test the brothers and sisters of affected patients.

Molecular genetic testing is not particularly valuable in diagnosing Wilson disease because of the large number of possible gene mutations.

Treatment

Treatment involves life-long administration of either D-penicillamine (Cuprimine, Depen) or trientine hydrochloride (Syprine). Both of these drugs remove copper deposits throughout the body by binding to the copper which then leaves the body in the urine. This type of treatment is called chelation therapy. **Zinc** acetate (Galzin) and a low-copper diet are other ways in which to treat Wilson disease.

Penicillamine has a number of serious side effects:

• joint pain
• neurological problems
• systemic lupus erythematosus
• decreased production of all blood elements
• interference with clotting
• allergic reactions

Careful monitoring is necessary. When patients have side effects from penicillamine, the dose can sometimes be lowered to an effective level that causes fewer difficulties. Alternatively, steroid medications may be required to reduce certain sensitivity reactions. Trientine has fewer potential side effects, but must still be carefully monitored.

KEY TERMS

Anemia—A blood condition in which the level of hemoglobin or the number of red blood cells falls below normal values. Common symptoms include paleness, fatigue, and shortness of breath.

Bile—A substance produced by the liver, and concentrated and stored in the gallbladder. Bile contains a number of different substances, including bile salts, cholesterol, and bilirubin.

Biopsy—The surgical removal and microscopic examination of living tissue for diagnostic purposes.

Cell—The smallest living units of the body which group together to form tissues and help the body perform specific functions.

Ceruloplasmin—A protein circulating in the bloodstream that binds with copper and transports it.

Chelation therapy—A method of removing copper or other heavy metals from the body by giving medications that bind to the metal and allow it to be excreted.

Chromosome—A microscopic thread-like structure found within each cell of the body and consists of a complex of proteins and DNA. Humans have 46 chromosomes arranged into 23 pairs. Changes in either the total number of chromosomes or their shape and size (structure) may lead to physical or mental abnormalities.

Cirrhosis—A chronic degenerative disease of the liver, in which normal cells are replaced by fibrous tissue. Cirrhosis is a major risk factor for the later development of liver cancer.

Deoxyribonucleic acid (DNA)—The genetic material in cells that holds the inherited instructions for growth, development, and cellular functioning.

Gallbladder—A small, pear-shaped organ in the upper right hand corner of the abdomen. It is connected by a series of ducts (tube-like channels) to the liver, pancreas, and duodenum (first part of the small intestine). The gallbladder receives bile from the liver and concentrates and stores it. After a meal, bile is squeezed out of the gallbladder into the intestine, where it aids in digestion of food.

Gene—A building block of inheritance, which contains the instructions for the production of a particular protein, and is made up of a molecular sequence found on a section of DNA. Each gene is found on a precise location on a chromosome.

Glucose—One of the two simple sugars, together with galactose, that makes up the protein, lactose, found in milk. Glucose is the form of sugar that is usable by the body to generate energy.

Hepatitis—A viral disease characterized by inflammation of the liver cells (hepatocytes). People infected with hepatitis B or hepatitis C virus are at an increased risk for developing liver cancer.

Jaundice—Yellowing of the skin or eyes due to excess of bilirubin in the blood.

Toxic—Poisonous.

Treatment with zinc acetate is also an effective way to remove excess copper from the body. Zinc is a metal that works to block copper absorption and bind copper in the intestinal cells until it is all released into the stool approximately one week later. The benefit of treatment with zinc is there are no toxic side effects; however, the zinc is a slower acting agent than the other drugs. It takes four to eight months for the zinc to be effective in reducing the overall amount of copper in the body.

Patients with Wilson disease are encouraged to follow a diet low in copper, with an average copper intake of 1 mg per day. Foods to be avoided for the high levels of copper include liver and shellfish. Patients are also instructed to monitor their drinking water for excess levels of copper and drink distilled water instead.

Patients may be given a liver transplant in the event of liver failure as a complication of Wilson disease. Liver transplantation has been reported to have a relatively favorable outcome, in some cases decreasing the patient's neurologic symptoms.

Prognosis

Without treatment, Wilson disease is always fatal. With treatment, symptoms may continue to worsen for the first six to eight weeks. After this time, definite improvement should begin to be seen. However, it may take several years (two to five) of treatment to reach maximal benefit to the brain and liver. Even then, many patients are not returned to their original level of functioning. Patients with Wilson disease need to maintain some sort of anticopper treatment for the rest of their lives in order to prevent copper levels from rising in the body. Interruptions in treatment can result in a **relapse** of the disease which is not reversible and can ultimately lead to death.

Resources

BOOKS

Porter, Robert S., and Justin L. Kaplan, eds. *The Merck Manual of Diagnosis and Therapy*. 19th ed. Whitehouse Station, NJ: Merck Research Laboratories, 2011.

PERIODICALS

Daniel, K.G., et al. "Copper Storage Diseases: Menkes, Wilsons, and Cancer." *Frontiers in Bioscience* 9 (September 1, 2004): 2652–2662.

Georghe, L., et al. "Wilson's Disease: A Challenge of Diagnosis. The 5-Year Experience of a Tertiary Centre." *Romanian Journal of Gastroenterology* 13, no. 3 (September 2004): 179–185.

Velez-Pardo, C., et al. "New Mutation (T1232P) of the ATP-7B Gene Associated with Neurologic and Neuropsychiatric Dominance Onset of Wilson's Disease in Three Unrelated Colombian Kindred." *Neuroscience Letters* 367, no. 3 (September 9, 2004): 360–364.

ORGANIZATIONS

American Liver Foundation, 39 BRd.way, Suite 2700, New York, NY, 10006, (212) 669-1000, Fax: (212) 483-8179, http://www.liverfoundation.org.

National Organization for Rare Disorders, PO Box 1968, Danbury, CT, 06813-1968, (203) 744-0100, (800) 999-6673, Fax: (203) 798-2291, http://www.rarediseases.org.

Wilson Disease Association, 5572 North Diversey Blvd., Milwaukee, WI, 53217, (414) 961-0533, (866) 961-0533, info@wilsonsdisease.org, http://www.wilsonsdisease.org.

Katherine S. Hunt, MS
Rebecca J. Frey, PhD

WISC *see* **Wechsler intelligence scales**

Women's mental health *see* **Gender issues in mental health**

XY

Xanax *see* **Alprazolam**

Yoga

Definition

Yoga is an ancient system of breathing practices, physical exercises and postures, and **meditation** intended to integrate the practitioner's body, mind, and spirit. It originated in India several thousand years ago, and its principles were first written down by the scholar Patanjali in the second century B.C. The word *yoga* comes from a Sanskrit word *yukti* and means "union" or "yoke." In modern times, yoga is practiced both as directed by its ancient foundations and as a way to maintain fitness and health. In fact, some people use yoga to help relieve certain mental and physical conditions, such as **stress**, anxiety, and injuries. Yoga has not been medically verified to be beneficial for some of these problems. It is recommended to consult with a medical professional before trying yoga for such medical problems.

Adults in a yoga class. (© *Ira Block/National Geographic Image Collection/Alamy*)

Purpose

Traditionally, yoga is a method joining the individual self with the Divine, Universal Spirit, or Cosmic Consciousness. Physical and mental exercises are designed to help achieve this goal, also called self-transcendence or enlightenment. On the physical level, yoga postures, called *asanas*, are designed to tone, strengthen, and align the body. Flexibility to the back, shoulders, hips, and hamstring muscles are improved with yoga, providing greater range of motion to these muscles and joints and others. These postures are performed to make the spine supple and healthy and to promote blood flow to all the organs, glands, and tissues. Many yoga postures require that individuals support their own weight, which also helps to improve balance and strength in the legs (such as with the tree pose) or the arms (such as with the downward facing dog pose).

Yoga uses breathing techniques (*pranayama*) and meditation (*dyana*) to quiet, clarify, and discipline the mind. Mental calm can be achieved with yoga and its practice of controlling the breathing process. Overall, such physical activity and mental focus in yoga help to relieve stress. In essence, yoga can be a **stress management** technique as participants become more aware of their body and mind.

Yoga can also be used as an aerobic type of **exercise** for staying fit and healthy. Rather than as a series of slow movements, a form of yoga taught in Western countries is called power yoga. Also called by the Sanskrit term *Vinyasa Yoga*, power yoga consists of a series of slower moves at the beginning to warm up the body. Later, more active poses are performed, which are not as long as the other types of yoga but are quicker in movement for the participants and more challenging to their muscles.

Demographics

In 2008, the Harris Interactive Service Bureau conducted a poll for the magazine *Yoga Journal*. The survey, called "Yoga in America," found that 6.9% of adults, or 16.5 million people, practice yoga in the United

States. Of these, 77.1% are female and 22.9% are male. According to age, 29.1% are 18–34 years, 41.6% are 35–54 years, and 18.4% are 55 years or older.

Description

There are six major branches of yoga: hatha, raja, karma, bhakti, jnana, tantra and raja. Hatha yoga is the type most familiar to Westerners. Karma yoga emphasizes selfless work as a service to others. Bhakti yoga, also called devotional yoga, is the path of cultivating an open heart and single-minded love of God. It is one of the most popular types of yoga in India. Jnana yoga is the sage or philosopher's approach; it cultivates wisdom, intellect, and discernment, and is considered the most difficult type of yoga. Tantra yoga emphasizes transcending the self through religious rituals, including sacred sexuality. Raja yoga, or royal yoga, is a spiritual path of self-renunciation and simplicity. It is a combination of bhakti, karma, and jnana yogas.

Hatha yoga

Hatha yoga, sometimes called physical yoga, is the best-known form of yoga in the West because it is often taught as a form of physical therapy. A typical hatha yoga practice consists of a sequence of asanas, or physical poses, designed to exercise all parts of the body in the course of the practice. The asanas incorporate three basic types of movement: forward bends, backward bends, and twists. Practitioners of hatha yoga have over 200 asanas to choose from in creating a sequence for practice. The postures have traditional Indian names, such as eagle pose, half moon pose, or mountain pose. There are steps for entering and leaving the pose, and the student is taught to concentrate on proper form and alignment. The pose is held for a period of time (usually 10–20 seconds), during which the practitioner concentrates on breathing correctly. Mental focus and discipline are necessary in order to maintain one's poise and balance in the asana. At the close of the practice, most students of yoga rest in a position that allows for a period of meditation. Most yoga practices take about an hour, although some are as short as 20 minutes.

Different styles of hatha yoga are taught in the United States, the best known being iyengar, bikram, kripalu, and ashtanga yoga. Iyengar yoga, which was developed by Indian yoga teacher B.K.S. Iyengar (1918–), also called bellur krishnamachar sundararaja iyengar, emphasizes attention to the details of a pose and the use of such props as blocks and belts to help students gain flexibility. It puts strict emphasis on form and alignment, and the props make it easier for beginners to get into the yoga postures. Bikram yoga, taught on the West Coast by

Indian yoga guru Bikram Choudhury (1946–), is practiced in heated rooms intended to make participants sweat freely as they warm and stretch their joints and muscles. Kripalu yoga, sometimes called the yoga of consciousness, emphasizes breathing exercises and the proper coordination of breath and movement. It also teaches awareness of one's psychological and emotional reactions to the various poses and movements of the body. Ashtanga yoga, developed by Indian yoga teacher Sri Krishna Pattabhi Jois (1915–2009), is the basis of so-called power yoga. Ashtanga yoga is a physically demanding workout that is not suitable for beginners.

A typical hatha yoga routine consists of a sequence of asanas designed to work all parts of the body, with particular emphasis on making the spine supple and healthy and increasing circulation. Hatha yoga asanas utilize three basic movements: forward bends, backward bends, and twisting motions. Each asana is named for a common object or creature it resembles, like the cobra, locust, bow, eagle, and tree poses. A pose is held for some time, depending on its level of difficulty and one's strength and stamina, and the practitioner is also usually aware of when to inhale and exhale at certain points in each posture, as breathing properly is another fundamental aspect of yoga. Breathing should be deep and through the nose. Mental concentration in each position is also important, which improves awareness, poise, and posture. During a yoga routine there is often a position in which to perform meditation, if deep relaxation is one of the goals of the sequence.

Yoga routines can take anywhere from 20 minutes to two or more hours, with one hour being a good time investment to perform a sequence of postures and a meditation. Some yoga routines, depending on the teacher and school, can be as strenuous as the most difficult workout, while others merely stretch and align the body, keeping the breath and heart rate slow and steady. Yoga achieves its best results when it is practiced as a daily discipline and can be a lifelong exercise routine, offering deeper and more challenging positions as a practitioner becomes more adept. The basic positions can increase a person's strength, flexibility, and sense of well-being almost immediately, but it can take years to perfect and deepen them, which is an appealing and stimulating aspect of yoga.

Yoga as complementary therapy

One of the advantages of yoga as a complementary therapy is its adaptability to patients with a wide variety of physical and psychiatric conditions. There are a number of different schools of yoga—over 40, according to one expert in the field—and even within a particular school or tradition, the asanas and breathing exercises can be tailored to the patient's needs. One can find special yoga courses for children; for people over 50 years of age; for people with fibromyalgia, arthritis, or back problems; for cancer patients; and for people who are overweight or obese (extremely overweight). Although most people who participate in yoga attend classes, it is possible to learn the basic postures and breathing techniques at home from beginners' manuals or videos. Patients who feel self-conscious about exercising in the presence of others may find yoga appealing for this reason. In addition, yoga does not require expensive equipment or special courts, tracks, or playing fields. An area of floor space about 6 feet by 8 feet (1.8 m by 2.4 m), a so-called sticky mat to keep the feet from slipping, and loose clothing that allows the wearer to move freely are all that is needed.

Origins

Yoga originated in ancient India and is one of the longest surviving philosophical systems in the world. Some scholars have estimated that yoga is as old as 5,000 years; artifacts detailing yoga postures have been found in India dating from 3000 B.C. Yoga masters (*yogis*) claim that it is a highly developed science of healthy living that has been tested and perfected through the centuries. Yoga was first brought to the United States in the late 1800s when Swami Vivekananda (1862–1902), an Indian teacher and yogi, presented a lecture on meditation in Chicago, Illinois.

Yoga slowly began gaining followers and flourished during the 1960s when there was a surge of interest in Eastern philosophy. After that, yoga knowledge in the United States became more extensive, with many students going to India to study and many Indian experts coming to the United States to teach, resulting in the establishment of a wide variety schools. Yoga practice remains popular in the United States, and teachers and practitioners are easily located across the country.

Millions of Americans do yoga regularly or occasionally. Physical therapists and professional sports teams use yoga stretches, and movie stars and *Fortune* 500 executives tout the benefits of yoga. Many prestigious schools of medicine have studied and introduced yoga techniques as proven therapies for illness and stress. Some medical schools, such as the one at the University of California at Los Angeles (UCLA), even offer yoga classes as part of their physician training program.

Benefits

Yoga is often recommended as an adjunct to **psychotherapy** or standard medical treatments. Its integration of the mental, physical, and spiritual dimensions of being is helpful to patients struggling with distorted cognitions or pain syndromes. The stretching, bending, and balancing involved in the asanas help to align the head and spinal column; stimulate the circulatory system, endocrine glands, and other organs; and keep muscles and joints strong and flexible. Yoga programs have been shown to reduce the risk of heart disease by lowering blood pressure and anxiety levels. The breath control exercises emphasize slow and deep abdominal breathing. They benefit the respiratory system, help to induce a sense of relaxation, and are useful in pain management. The meditation that is an integral part of classical yoga practice has been shown to strengthen the human immune system. In addition, pain relief can be achieved with the use of yoga. When the body is more flexible and strong, many types of pain are relieved, such as pain in the back.

Yoga also guides the individual toward self-control (*yama*), involving abstinence, truthfulness, honesty, and not doing harm to other living things. In addition, the individual is instructed in contentment and austerity and in devotion to the Supreme Being, what is called *niyama*. Yoga also helps individuals to look inward into the soul (what is called restraint of the senses, or *pratyahara*); to concentrate on one object, such as a body part, in order to avoid being sensitive to external disturbances (*dharana*); and to achieve complete contemplation (*samadhi*). It should be remembered that yoga is not a religion, but a way of living, with health and peace of mind as its aims.

Yoga provides the same benefits as any well-designed exercise program, increasing general health and stamina, reducing stress, and improving those conditions brought about by sedentary lifestyles. Yoga has the added advantage of being a low-impact activity that uses only gravity as resistance, which makes it an excellent physical therapy routine.

Meditation has been much studied and approved for its benefits in reducing stress-related conditions. The landmark book, *The Relaxation Response* (1975), by Harvard University cardiologist Herbert Benson (1935–), showed that meditation and breathing techniques for relaxation could have the opposite effect of stress, reducing blood pressure and other indicators. Since that publication, much research has reiterated the benefits of meditation for **stress reduction** and general health. The American Medical Association recommends meditation techniques as a first step before medication for treating borderline hypertension.

Modern psychological studies have shown that even slight facial expressions can cause changes in the involuntary nervous system; yoga utilizes the mind/body connection. That is, yoga practice contains the central ideas that physical posture and alignment can influence a person's mood and self-esteem and also that the mind can be used to shape and heal the body. Yoga practitioners claim that the strengthening of mind/body awareness can bring eventual improvements in all facets of a person's life.

Yoga exercises are also recommended as a way to tone muscles and nerves, as a way to reduce weight, and as an overall way to improve health and prolong life.

Preparation

Yoga can be performed by those of any age and condition, although not all poses should be attempted by everyone. Yoga is also an accessible form of exercise; all that is needed is a flat floor surface large enough to stretch out on, a mat or towel, and enough overhead space to extend the arms. It is a good activity for those who cannot go to gyms, who do not like other forms of exercise, or have busy schedules. Yoga should be done on an empty stomach, and teachers recommend waiting at least two to three hours after meals to engage in yoga. Loose and comfortable clothing should be worn, and the feet are usually left bare.

Risks

Most reported injuries in yoga result from lack of concentration or attempts to perform difficult poses without working up to them. People who have consulted a physician before starting yoga and practice under the supervision of an experienced teacher are unlikely to suffer injury. Beginners sometimes report muscle soreness and **fatigue** after performing yoga, but these side effects diminish with practice.

Patients with a history of heart disease, severe back injuries, inner ear problems or other difficulties with balance, glaucoma, or recent surgery should consult a physician before beginning yoga. Certain yoga positions should not be performed with a fever or during menstruation. Pregnant women are usually advised to modify their yoga practice during the first trimester.

People diagnosed with a dissociative disorder should not attempt advanced forms of pranayama (yogic breathing) without the supervision of an experienced teacher. Some yogic breathing exercises may trigger symptoms of derealization or **depersonalization** in these patients.

Beginners should exercise care and concentration when performing yoga postures and not try to stretch too much too quickly, as injury could result. A stretch or posture should be stopped if there is pain, dizziness, or

---

QUESTIONS TO ASK YOUR DOCTOR

- How do you think yoga will benefit me?
- Do I have any physical limitations that would prohibit my undertaking yoga?
- What tests or evaluation techniques will you perform to see if yoga has been beneficial for me?
- What other treatment options do you recommend for me?
- Will yoga interfere with my current medications?
- What symptoms or behaviors are important enough that I should seek immediate treatment?

---

fatigue. Some advanced yoga postures, such as headstand and full lotus position, can be difficult and require strength, flexibility, and gradual preparation, so beginners should get the help of a teacher before attempting them.

One additional precaution is often necessary for Westerners. Yoga is not a competitive sport, and a "good" practice is defined as whatever one's body and mind are capable of giving on a specific day. Westerners are, however, accustomed to pushing themselves hard, comparing their performances to those of others, and assuming that exercise is not beneficial unless it hurts—an attitude summed up in the phrase "no pain, no gain." Yoga teaches a gentle and accepting attitude toward one's body rather than a punishing or perfectionistic approach. A person should go into the stretches and poses gradually, not forcibly or violently. Stretching should not be done past the point of mild discomfort, which is normal for beginners; frank pain is a warning that the body is not properly aligned in the pose or that the joints are being overstressed. Most people beginning yoga will experience measurable progress in their strength and flexibility after a week or two of daily practice.

The mental component of yoga is just as important as the physical postures. Concentration and awareness of breath should not be neglected. While performing the yoga of breathing (pranayama) and meditation (dyana), it is best to have an experienced teacher, as these powerful techniques can cause dizziness and discomfort when done improperly.

KEY TERMS

Asana—A position or stance in yoga.

Dyana—The yoga term for meditation.

Hatha yoga—A form of yoga using postures, breathing methods, and meditation.

Meditation—Technique of concentration for relaxing the mind and body.

Pranayama—Yogic breathing techniques.

Yogi (feminine, yogini)—A trained yoga expert.

Research and general acceptance

Although Western medical researchers have been studying yoga only since the 1970s, **clinical trials** in the United States have demonstrated its effectiveness in treating stress-related illnesses, anxiety, **premenstrual syndrome**, and mood disorders. Other reports indicate that yoga merits further research in the treatment of **obsessive-compulsive disorder** (OCD) and **substance abuse**. Studies done in Germany have focused on the psychological benefits of yoga. Many have been randomized, controlled studies, which are the most strenuous ones available to prove or disprove the validity of a hypothesis.

In 2008, researchers from the University of Utah studied yoga and its association with reducing pain. Forty-two participants were studied: 12 were experienced in yoga, 14 had fibromyalgia (hypersensitivity to pain), and 16 were overall healthy individuals. All of the participants were subjected to the pain caused by pressing down with a thumbnail. Functional magnetic resonance image (fMRI) scans were performed on each person to measure activity within the **brain** caused by the pain. The people with fibromyalgia showed the most pain response with the least amount of pressure. By contrast, the yoga practitioners reported the least amount of pain when compared to the other two groups. The researchers concluded that yoga can help individuals control their stress levels when pain is present.

The Harvard University Medical School also reports that yoga is being studied for people with **post-traumatic stress disorder** (PTSD), such as sometimes found among military combatants. One such study looked at military veterans from Australia who had fought in Vietnam. All of the participants were taking at least one type of antidepressant on a daily basis and were also considered daily heavy drinkers of alcohol. Some of the veterans were enrolled in a five-day course that included yoga, along with education on stress reduction. A control group did not receive this training.

Using the Clinician Administered PTSD Scale (CAPS), the researchers found that scores dropped from 57 (moderate to severe symptoms) to 42 (mild to moderate symptoms), on average, after six weeks. The veterans were re-evaluated six months later and it was found that their scores remained at these lower levels. The control group did not show improvement during this period. Based on this study and others, the Walter Reed Army Medical Center in Washington, DC, started offering yoga classes to U.S. service men and women returning from combat in Iraq and Afghanistan in the hope that it would help to counter PTSD. Studies are ongoing to determine the results of this treatment.

Other studies performed in the 2000s and early 2010s showed that yoga is helpful with **depression**, stress, fatigue, headaches, back pain, sleep problems, and symptoms of **schizophrenia** and **bipolar disorder**. Further studies showed improvements in mood and quality of life for breast cancer survivors, patients with epilepsy, the elderly, and people caring for patients with **dementia**.

Training and certification

Yoga is usually best learned from a yoga teacher or physical therapist, but yoga is simple enough that one can learn the basics from good books on the subject, which are plentiful. Yoga classes are generally inexpensive, averaging around ten dollars per class, and students can learn basic postures in just a few classes. Many Young Men Christian Associations (YMCAs), colleges, and community health organizations offer beginning yoga classes as well, often for nominal fees. If yoga is part of a physical therapy program, its cost can be reimbursed by insurance.

Resources

BOOKS

Butera, Robert J. *The Pure Heart of Yoga: Ten Essential Steps for Personal Transformation*. Woodbury, MN: Llewellyn, 2009.

Christensen, Alice. *The American Yoga Association's Easy Does It Yoga*. New York: Fireside/Simon & Schuster, 1999.

Coulter, David H. *Anatomy of Hatha Yoga: A Manual for Students, Teachers, and Practitioners*. Honesdale, PA: Body and Breath, 2010.

Iyenger, B. K.S. *Yoga Wisdom & Practice*. New York: DK, 2009.

Rountree, Sage. *The Athlete's Pocket Guide to Yoga: 50 Routines for Flexibility, Balance, and Focus.* Boulder, CO: VeloPress, 2009.

Williams, Nancy. *Yoga Therapy for Every Special Child: Meeting Needs in a Natural Setting.* Philadelphia: Jessica Kingsley, 2010.

WEBSITES

"Yoga for Anxiety and Depression." Harvard Health Publications Harvard Medical School. http://www.health.harvard.edu/newsletters/Harvard_Mental_Health_Letter/2009/April/Yoga-for-anxiety-and-depression (accessed August 16, 2011).

Yoga Journal Releases 2008 "Yoga in America" Market Study. Yoga Journal. (February 26, 2008). http://www.yogajournal.com/advertise/press_releases/10 (accessed July 21, 2011).

Mayo Clinic staff. "Yoga: Tap into the Many Health Benefits." MayoClinic.com, January 16, 2010. http://www.mayoclinic.com/health/yoga/CM00004 (accessed August 16, 2011).

ORGANIZATIONS

American Yoga Association, PO Box 19986, Sarasota, FL, 34276, info@americanyogaassociation.org, http://www.americanyogaassociation.org.

International Association of Yoga Therapists, PO Box 12890, Prescott, AZ, 86304, (928) 541-0004, mail@iayt.org, http://www.iayt.org.

Yoga Science Foundation, 759 South State St., No. 24, Ukiah, CA, 95482, http://www.yrec.org.

Rebecca J. Frey, PhD
William A. Atkins, BB, BS, MBA

Z

Zaleplon

Definition

Zaleplon is classified as a hypnotic drug. Such drugs help people sleep. Zaleplon is available in the United States under the brand name Sonata.

Purpose

Zaleplon is a drug that is used to treat short-term **insomnia**.

Description

The U.S. Food and Drug Administration approved Zaleplon in 1999 to treat short-term sleep problems. Zaleplon is thought to act by mimicking a chemical in the **brain** that helps to facilitate sleep. It is different from other sleeping pills in that it begins to work almost immediately and its effects are rather short-lived (a few hours). These properties make it beneficial both for people who have troubling falling asleep at bedtime and for people who awaken in the middle of the night and

Zaleplon, 10 mg. (© *Custom Medical Stock Photo, Inc. Reproduced by permission.*)

have trouble falling back to sleep. Zaleplon may be taken in the middle of the night so long as the person can sleep at least four more hours before having to awaken.

Zaleplon is available as capsules. The drug is broken down by the liver. It is a controlled substance and can be habit-forming.

Recommended dosage

The usual dose of zaleplon for adults is 5–20 mg. For healthy adults, 10 mg is a common dosage. However, people over age 65, small adults with low body weight, and people with serious health problems (especially liver disease) should take a dose at the low end of this range (usually 5 mg). Zaleplon is taken immediately before bedtime. It usually takes only about 30 minutes for the sleep-inducing actions of zaleplon to be felt, and sleep-facilitating effects appear to last only a few hours. If zaleplon is taken with a meal, it will take longer to work. For the fastest sleep onset, it should be taken on an empty stomach. The maximum dose for one day is 20 mg. Under no circumstances should a person take more than 20 mg in one day.

Precautions

Zaleplon should be taken exactly as directed by a physician. A person who forgets a dose of zaleplon should skip the dose and take the next dose at the regularly scheduled time.

Because zaleplon is used to help people fall asleep, it should only be taken when the patient is preparing for a full night's sleep (seven to eight hours). Some patients taking sleep medications have engaged in sleep-related behaviors, including eating, talking, and even driving while asleep, with no recollection of the events. Zaleplon should not be used with other drugs (over-the-counter or prescription) that also cause drowsiness. It should be used only with close physician supervision in people with liver disease and in the elderly because these individuals are especially sensitive to the sedative properties of zaleplon. Zaleplon should not be used before driving, operating machinery, or performing other activities that require mental alertness. People with a history of drug abuse, psychiatric disorders, or **depression** should be carefully monitored when using zaleplon, since the drug may worsen symptoms of some psychiatric disorders and can become a drug of abuse.

If zaleplon is needed for more than seven to ten days, patients should be re-evaluated by a physician to determine whether another disorder is causing their difficulty sleeping. When zaleplon or other sleeping pills are used every night for more than a few weeks, they begin to lose their effectiveness, and/or people may become dependent upon them to fall asleep. Zaleplon can be addictive. People using zaleplon should not suddenly stop taking the drug because withdrawal symptoms, including sleep disturbances, may occur even if zaleplon has been used for only a short time.

Side effects

There is a risk of severe allergic reaction upon taking a sleep medication for the first time. Some sleeping pills such as zaleplon can cause aggressiveness, agitation, hallucinations, and **amnesia** (memory problems). A patient experiencing these side effects should call a physician immediately. A physician should also be called immediately if a person taking zaleplon develops a fast or irregular heartbeat, chest pains, skin rash, or itching.

The most common side effects of zaleplon are less serious and include dizziness, drowsiness, impaired coordination, upset stomach, nausea, headache, dry mouth, and muscle aches. Other side effects that may occur include fever, tremor, or eye pain. Many side effects appear worse at higher doses so it is important to use the lowest dose that will induce sleep.

Interactions

Any drug that causes drowsiness may lead to substantially decreased mental alertness and impaired motor skills when taken with zaleplon. Examples include alcohol, **antidepressants** such as **imipramine** or **paroxetine**, antipsychotics like **thioridazine**, and some antihistamines.

Because zaleplon is broken down by the liver, it may interact with other drugs also broken down by the liver. For example, the drug rifampin, which is used to treat tuberculosis, may cause zaleplon to be less effective. Alternatively, cimetidine (Tagamet), a drug commonly used to treat heartburn, may cause people to be more sensitive to zaleplon.

Resources

BOOKS

Preston, John D., John H. O'Neal, and Mary C. Talaga. *Handbook of Clinical Psychopharmacology for Therapists.* 5th ed. Oakland, CA: New Harbinger Publications, 2008.

Wolters Kluwer Health. *Drug Facts and Comparisons 2012.* 66th ed. St. Louis: Lippincott, Williams & Wilkins, 2011.

PERIODICALS

Bain, Kevin T. "Management of Chronic Insomnia in Elderly Persons." *American Journal of Geriatric Pharmacotherapy* 4, no. 2 (June 2006): 168–92.

Conn, David K., and Robert Madan. "Use of Sleep-Promoting Medications in Nursing Home Residents: Risks versus Benefits." *Drugs and Aging* 23, no. 4 (2006): 271–87.

Glass, Jennifer, et al. "Sedative Hypnotics in Older People with Insomnia: Meta-Analysis of Risks and Benefits." *British Medical Journal* 331, no. 7526 (November 2005): 1–7.

McCall, W. "Diagnosis and Management of Insomnia in Older People." *Journal of the American Geriatrics Society* 53, no. 7 Suppl. (July 2005): S272–S277.

Rosenberg, Russell P. "Sleep Maintenance Insomnia: Strengths and Weaknesses of Current Pharmacologic Therapies." *Annals of Clinical Psychiatry* 18, no. 1 (January–March 2006): 49–56.

Kelly Karpa, R.Ph., PhD
Ruth A. Wienclaw, PhD

Zinc

Definition

Zinc (chemical symbol Zn) is a mineral and a metal that is essential for a healthy immune system, production of certain hormones, wound healing, bone formation, and clear skin. It is required in very small amounts and is thus known as an essential trace element. Despite this low requirement, zinc is found in nearly every cell of the body and is key to the proper function of more than 300 enzymes.

Purpose

Zinc is vital for the body to function normally, both physically and mentally, and has been shown to help sustain intellectual (cognitive) function, mood control, healthy skin, strong vision, blood-clotting ability, cell division, wound repair, and proper taste and smell. Normal growth and development cannot occur without zinc. Zinc is also important in promoting mental health and has increasingly been found to reduce symptoms of certain mental disorders. Research has found that

Recommended Dietary Allowance (RDA) of zinc

Age group	RDA
Children, 0–6 months	2 mg
Children, 7–12 months	3 mg
Children, 1–3 years	3 mg
Children, 4–8 years	5 mg
Children, 9–13 years	8 mg
Teenage females, 14–18 years	9 mg
Teenage males, 14–18 years	11 mg
Adult females (19+)	8 mg
Adult males (19+)	11 mg
Pregnant teenage females	12 mg
Pregnant adult females	11 mg
Breast-feeding teenage females	13 mg
Breast-feeding adult females	12 mg

SOURCE: Office of Dietary Supplements, National Institutes of Health.

(Table by PreMediaGlobal. Reproduced by permission of Gale, a part of Cengage Learning.)

symptoms of **schizophrenia, autism, attention deficit hyperactivity disorder (ADHD), Down syndrome**, Wilson's disease, and other mental health problems may be reduced with zinc supplementation. However, too much zinc can be harmful to persons with other mental illnesses, such as **Alzheimer's disease**.

Description

Zinc deficiency is a serious health problem in the world, although it is relatively uncommon in the United States. The World Health Organization (WHO) estimates that zinc deficiency affects about one-third of the world's population. Although this deficiency is considered to be mild to moderate in most cases, it can result in mental health problems, such as **depression**.

General symptoms of zinc deficiency include:

- depression
- impotence in men, low fertility in men and women
- poor growth in infants and children, along with delayed sexual maturation in adolescents
- night blindness
- pale skin, along with skin problems, such as acne
- eye sores
- lowered alertness levels
- poor hair growth, along with hair loss
- diarrhea
- lack of menstrual period
- frequent infections, such as pneumonia
- loss of appetite, weight loss

- reduced ability to taste or smell
- poor wound healing

Symptoms of too much zinc in the body include:

- nausea
- vomiting
- loss of appetite
- stomach cramping
- diarrhea
- headaches
- lower immunity levels
- low levels of high-density lipoprotein (HDL) cholesterol—the so-called "good cholesterol"

Many of these symptoms could be signs of other medical problems. It is wise to see a medical professional if such symptoms are present.

Zinc and mental health

Over the past 40 years, research has found a correlation between mental health and zinc. American physician and biochemist Carl Curt Pfeiffer (1908–1988) discovered in the 1970s that low amounts of zinc and manganese (Mn) in children can adversely affect their learning ability, as well as lead to an increased risk of **intellectual disability**. Pfeiffer also reported that zinc and vitamin B_6 supplements helped to control pyroluria-type schizophrenia (a type of schizophrenia characterized by an abnormal number of pyrroles in the body) in the vast number of cases he studied. Since the Pfeiffer-led study, many people with pyroluria-type schizophrenia are successfully treated with a combination of zinc and vitamin B_6.

Zinc has also been found to help symptoms of **ADHD**. Studies performed in the last quarter of the twentieth century showed that children with low levels of zinc, manganese, and vitamin B_6 (along with excessive amounts of copper [Cu] and lead [Pb]) were hyperactive. Canadian **psychiatrist** and biochemist Abram Hoffer (1917–2009) showed that zinc, along with other vitamins and minerals, helped children minimize symptoms associated with autism and ADHD. A separate study performed at Capella University, in Minneapolis, Minnesota, concluded that zinc supplements given along with **methylphenidate** (Ritalin), an ADHD medication, showed positive results in treating the symptoms of attention deficit and hyperactivity in ADHD children. In 2005, a study published in the *Journal of Child and Adolescent Psychopharmacology* further correlated that a relationship exists between zinc and inattentiveness in children. Other studies have supported the evidence that zinc can improve symptoms of ADHD, such as impulsiveness and hyperactivity, in children who regularly take zinc along with their traditional ADHD treatment.

Additionally, zinc may play a role in helping people with Down syndrome (DS). Studies showed that a deficiency of zinc adversely affects the nervous, neuroendocrine, and immune systems of people with DS. A 2004 study reported in the journal *Down Syndrome Research and Practice* that zinc levels in the hair of children with DS were significantly less than in other children. The researchers concluded that some of the problems found in DS children could be due to low levels of zinc. Since this study, others have suggested that oral zinc supplements be used to correct immune and endocrinological disorders associated with DS.

In 2008, American clinical **psychologist** Ann M. DiGirolamo, an assistant professor at Rollins School of Public Health (Emory University), and Guatemalan physiologist Manuel Ramirez-Zea, a principle investigator at the Institute of **Nutrition** of Central America and Panama (Guatemala City), reported that low levels of zinc increase the risk of depression and ADHD, especially in people already at high risk for these two mental illnesses. Their study, based on 30 years of research, was published in the *American Journal of Clinical Nutrition*.

Wilson's disease, or hepatolenticular degeneration, is a neurodegenerative disease that is caused by the inability of the body to metabolize copper. In this disease, copper builds up to abnormally large levels in the **brain**, liver, and other organs. Symptoms often include depression, clumsiness, difficulty speaking, problems walking, and involuntary shaking. For its treatment, medications are prescribed that reduce the amount of copper in the body. Chelating agents are used for this reduction method. This process allows copper to be taken into the bloodstream so that it can be released through urine. Two chelating agents are penicillamine (Cuprimine, Depen) and trientine (Syprine). To prevent a buildup of copper into the body from the foods that are eaten, zinc is used.

In the 2010s, zinc has often been promoted as an aid for memory. This may be true to the extent that vitamin B_6 and **neurotransmitters** are not properly utilized without it. However, in the case of people with Alzheimer's disease (AD), zinc can cause more harm than good. Some experiments indicate that zinc actually decreases intellectual function of patients with AD. Under these circumstances, it is best to adhere to the recommended dietary allowance (RDA) for zinc of 11 mg for adult males and 8 mg for adult females.

Overall, zinc has been found to generally help in reducing symptoms associated with some mental health

problems when used in conjunction with conventional treatments. When used alone, zinc has not been found to be as beneficial. Further studies are warranted to better learn about zinc's role in helping with mental health conditions.

Recommended dosage

For treating symptoms of ADHD, the U.S. National Institutes of Health (NIH) recommends using from 55 mg of zinc sulfate (15 mg elemental zinc) to 150 mg (40 mg elemental) each day. It has also been suggested that zinc may promote weight gain and improve symptoms of depression in patients with **anorexia nervosa**; the NIH recommended dosage for this purpose is 100 mg of zinc gluconate per day. Exact dosage amounts should be confirmed with a physician. Without medical supervision, the daily tolerable upper intake levels (UL) of zinc are:

- children under the age of 6 months, 4 mg
- children aged 7 to 12 months, 5 mg
- children aged 1 to 3 years, 7 mg
- children aged 4 to 8 years, 12 mg
- children aged 9 to 13 years, 23 mg
- adolescents aged 14 to 18 years (including pregnancy and lactation), 34 mg
- adults aged 19 years and older (including pregnancy and lactation), 40 mg

Natural sources

Oysters are tremendously high in zinc. Some sources, such as whole grains, beans, and nuts, have good zinc content, but the fiber in these foods prevents it from being absorbed well. Foods with high amounts of zinc include red meat; poultry, such as chicken and turkey; crabs and lobsters; fortified breakfast cereals; and dairy products such as milk, cheese, and yogurt. Pure maple syrup also is a good source of zinc.

Supplemental sources

Zinc supplements are available as oral tablets in various forms as well as lozenges. Zinc gluconate is the type most commonly used in lozenge form to kill upper respiratory viruses. Consumers should look for brands that do not use citric acid or tartaric acid for flavoring, as these appear to impair the effectiveness. The best-absorbed oral types of zinc may include zinc citrate, zinc acetate, or zinc picolinate. Zinc sulfate is the most likely to cause stomach irritation. Topical formulations are used for acne and skin injuries. Oral zinc should not be taken with foods or substances that will reduce its absorption, such as coffee, bran, protein, phytates, calcium, or phosphorus. Supplements should be stored in a cool, dry location, away from direct light, and out of the reach of children.

Precautions

It is not uncommon to have mild to moderately low levels of zinc, although serious deficiency is rare. Symptoms can include an increased susceptibility to infection, rashes, hair loss, poor growth in children, delayed healing of wounds, rashes, acne, male infertility, poor appetite, decreased sense of taste and smell, and possible swelling of the mouth, tongue, and eyelids.

A more serious, chronic deficiency can cause severe growth problems, including dwarfism and poor bone maturation. The spleen and liver may become enlarged. Testicular size and function both tend to decrease. Cataracts may form in the eyes, the optic nerve can become swollen, and color vision is sometimes affected by a profound lack of zinc. Hearing is sometimes affected as well.

Since meats are the best sources of zinc, people on a restricted diet, such as strict vegetarians and vegans, are among the groups more likely to be deficient. The absorption of zinc is inhibited by high-fiber foods, so people who have **diets** that are very high in whole grain and fiber need to take supplements separately from the fiber. Zinc is needed in larger amounts for women who are pregnant, lactating, or breastfeeding. Deficiency during pregnancy may lower fetal birth-weight, as well as increase maternal risk of toxemia. A good prenatal vitamin is likely to contain an adequate amount of zinc. People over the age of 50 years do not absorb zinc as well as younger people, nor do they generally have adequate intake, and they may require a supplement. Alcoholics generally have poor nutritional status to begin with, and alcohol also depletes stored zinc.

There is an increased need for most vitamins and minerals for people who are chronically under high **stress**. Those who have had surgery, severe burns, wasting illnesses, or poor nutrition may require larger amounts of zinc than average.

Interactions

The absorption of vitamin A is improved by zinc supplements, but they may interfere with the absorption of other minerals taken at the same time, including calcium (Ca), magnesium (Mg), iron (Fe), and copper (Cu). Supplements of calcium, magnesium, and copper should not be taken at the same time as the zinc. Iron should only be taken if a known deficiency exists.

KEY TERMS

Acrodermatitis enteropathica—Hereditary metabolic problem characterized by dermatitis, diarrhea, and poor immune status. Oral treatment with zinc is curative.

Enzyme—A biological catalyst that increases the rate of a chemical reaction without being used up in the reaction.

Hemochromatosis—A hereditary condition that results in excessive storage of iron in various tissues of the body.

Pyrrole—A heterocyclic aromatic organic compound with chemical formula C_4H_4NH.

RDA—The abbreviation for "recommended dietary allowance," which is the amount of vitamins and minerals needed to provide adequate nutrition in most healthy people; the amount varies depending on age, gender, and physical conditions, such as pregnancy; sometimes RDA is called "daily value" (DV) in the United States.

Schizophrenia—A severe mental illness in which a person has difficulty distinguishing what is real from what is not real. It is often characterized by hallucinations, delusions, and withdrawal from people and social activities.

Sickle cell anemia—An inherited disorder in which red blood cells contain an abnormal form of hemoglobin, a protein that carries oxygen. The abnormal form of hemoglobin causes the red cells to become sickle-shaped. The misshapen cells may clog blood vessels, preventing oxygen from reaching tissues and leading to pain, blood clots, and other problems.

Thiazide and loop diuretic medications, sometimes used for people with high blood pressure, congestive heart failure, or liver disease, increase the loss of zinc. Levels are also lowered by oral contraceptives. Zinc can decrease the absorption of tetracycline and quinolone class antibiotics, antacids, soy, or manganese, and should not be taken at the same time of day.

Drinking coffee at the same time as taking zinc can reduce the absorption by as much as half. Even moderate amounts of alcohol impair zinc metabolism and increase its excretion. Chelation with ethylenediaminetetraacetic acid (EDTA) can deplete zinc, so patients undergoing chelation need to supplement with zinc, according to the instructions of the health care provider.

QUESTIONS TO ASK YOUR DOCTOR

• In what way do you think zinc will benefit me?

• Will zinc interfere with my current medications?

• What symptoms or adverse effects are important enough that I should seek immediate treatment?

Make sure to inform the medical professional who regularly makes regular physical examinations as to any dietary supplements and medicines that are being taken. Zinc can interact with many over-the-counter or prescription medications.

Complications

Some diseases increase the risk of zinc deficiency. Sickle cell anemia, diabetes, and kidney disease can all affect zinc metabolism. People with Crohn's disease, sprue (celiac disease), chronic diarrhea, or babies with acrodermatitis enteropathica (a metabolic disorder affecting the absorption of zinc) also have an increased need for zinc. People who are anorexic also are at increased risk of having insufficient amounts of zinc within the body, as are people with hookworm, cirrhosis, chronic renal disease, and severe **trauma**. Consult a health care provider for appropriate supplementation instructions.

Toxicity can occur with excessively large doses of zinc supplements and can produce symptoms including fever, cough, abdominal pain, nausea, vomiting, diarrhea, drowsiness, restlessness, and gait abnormalities. If doses greater than 100 mg per day are taken chronically, anemia, immune insufficiency, heart problems, and copper deficiency can result. High doses of zinc can also cause a decrease in high-density lipoprotein (HDL), or "good" cholesterol.

People who have hemochromatosis, are allergic to zinc, or are infected with human immunodeficiency virus (HIV) should not take supplemental zinc. Ulcers in the stomach or duodenum may be aggravated by supplements as well. Those with glaucoma should use caution if using eye drops containing zinc. Overuse of supplemental zinc during pregnancy can increase the risk of premature birth and stillbirth, particularly if the supplement is taken in the third trimester. This increase in adverse outcomes has been documented with zinc dosages of 100 mg taken three times daily.

Zinc may cause irritation of the stomach and is best taken with food in order to avoid nausea. The lozenge form used to treat colds has a strong taste and can alter the sense of taste and smell for up to a few days.

Resources

BOOKS

Marian, Mary J., Pamela Williams-Mullen, and Jennifer Muir Bowers. *Integrating Therapeutic and Complementary Nutrition.* Boca Raton, FL: CRC, 2006.

Micozzi, Marc S. *Fundamentals of Complementary and Alternative Medicine.* New York: Saunders, 2010.

Pelletier, Kenneth R. "Western Herbal Medicine: Nature's Green Pharmacy." Chapter 6 in *The Best Alternative Medicine.* New York: Simon and Schuster, 2007.

Physician's Desk Reference. *PDR for Nonprescription Drugs, Dietary Supplements, and Herbs 2009,* 30th ed. New York: Physician's Desk Reference, 2008.

Purchon, Nerys. *The Essential Natural Health Bible: The Complete Home Guide to Herbs and Oils, Natural Remedies and Nutrition.* NSW, Australia: Millennium House, 2011.

Therapeutic Research Faculty. *Natural Medicines Comprehensive Database 2007.* Stockton, CA: Natural Medicines Database, 2006.

Ulbricht, Catherine E. *Davis's Pocket Guide to Herbs and Supplements.* Philadelphia: F.A. Davis, 2011.

PERIODICALS

Yenigun, Ayse, et al. "Hair Zinc Level in Down Syndrome." *Down Syndrome Research and Practice* 9, no. 2 (2004): 53–57. http://dx.doi.org/10.3104/reports.292 (accessed September 2, 2011).

WEBSITES

Mayo Clinic staff. "Wilson's Disease." MayoClinic.com (September 24, 2009). http://www.mayoclinic.com/health/wilsons-disease/DS00411 (accessed August 30, 2011).

Mayo Clinic staff. "Zinc Supplement." MayoClinic.com (November 1, 2010). http://www.mayoclinic.com/health/drug-information/DR602313 (accessed August 30, 2011).

"Zinc." Office of Dietary Supplements, National Institutes of Health. http://ods.od.nih.gov/factsheets/Zinc-Health Professional (accessed August 30, 2011).

ORGANIZATIONS

American Botanical Council, 6200 Manor Road, Austin, TX, 78723, (512) 926-4900, Fax: (512) 926-2345, abc@herbalram.org, http://abc.herbalgram.org.

American Psychiatric Association, 1000 Wilson Boulevard, Suite 1825, Arlington, VA, 22209, (703) 907-7300, apa@psych.org, http://www.psych.org.

National Center for Complementary and Alternative Medicine Clearinghouse, 9000 Rockville Pike, Bethesda, MD, 20892, info@nccam.nih.gov, http://nccam.nih.gov.

Natural Standard, One Davis Square, Somerville, MA, 02144, (617) 591-3300, Fax: (617) 591-3399, http://naturalstandard.com.

Office of Dietary Supplements, National Institutes of Health, 6100 Executive Boulevard, Room 3B01, MSC 7517, Rockville, MD, 20892-7517, (301) 435-2920, Fax: (301) 480-1845, ods@nih.gov, http://ods.od.nih.gov.

United States Pharmacopoeia, 12601 Twinbrook Parkway, Rockville, MD, 20852-1790, (800) 227-8772, http://www.usp.org.

Judith Turner
Teresa G. Odle
William A. Atkins

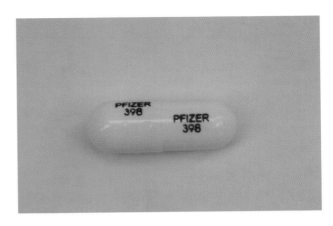

Geodon (ziprasidone), 60 mg. (© *Custom Medical Stock Photo, Inc. Reproduced by permission.*)

Ziprasidone

Definition

Ziprasidone is an atypical antipsychotic drug used to treat **schizophrenia**. It is also used to treat acute manic or mixed episodes associated with **bipolar disorder**. It is available with a prescription under the brand name Geodon.

Purpose

Ziprasidone is in a class of drugs called antipsychotics. It is used to control symptoms of schizophrenia, or for acute symptoms associated with bipolar disorder. It may also be used in conjunction with lithium or valproate (Depakote) as maintenance treatment for bipolar disorder. Ziprasidone is one of the newer antipsychotic drugs—often called atypical antipsychotics—that is less likely to cause significant adverse side effects than conventional antipsychotic medications.

Description

The U.S. Food and Drug Administration (FDA) approved ziprasidone for treatment of schizophrenia in 2001, for treatment of acute manic or mixed episodes associated with bipolar disorder in 2004, and as maintenance treatment of bipolar disorder in 2009. In people with schizophrenia or bipolar disorder, chemical systems in the **brain** are out of balance. Mental well-being is partially related to maintaining a balance between naturally occurring chemicals called **neurotransmitters**. Ziprasidone is thought to modify the actions of several neurotransmitters and restore appropriate function to the chemical systems.

Recommended dosage

The dosage of ziprasidone varies widely from one individual to another. A common initially dosage is 20 mg of ziprasidone taken twice daily. The dosage is gradually increased until symptoms of schizophrenia subside. Dosages of up to 100 mg may be taken twice daily. Dosing for treatment of bipolar disorder generally ranges from 40–80 mg twice daily. Ziprasidone should be taken with food.

For acute treatment of agitation in schizophrenia, ziprasidone may be administered intramuscularly (as an injection) at a dose of 10–40 mg (maximum) per day.

Precautions

Ziprasidone may interact with other medications to caused altered heart rhythms (arrhythmia). It should not

---

QUESTIONS TO ASK YOUR DOCTOR

- What kind of changes can I expect to see or feel with this medication?
- Does it matter what time of day I take this medication? If so, what is the recommendation?
- What are the side effects associated with this medication?
- Will this medication interact or interfere with other medications I am currently taking?
- What symptoms or adverse effects are important enough that I should seek immediate treatment?

KEY TERMS

Delusions—Irrational beliefs that defy normal reasoning and remain firm even when overwhelming proof is presented to dispute them. Delusions are distinct from culturally or religiously based beliefs that may be seen as untrue by outsiders.

Neurotransmitter—One of a group of chemicals secreted by a nerve cell (neuron) to carry a chemical message to another nerve cell, often as a way of transmitting a nerve impulse. Examples of neurotransmitters include acetylcholine, dopamine, serotonin, and norepinephrine.

Schizophrenia—A major mental illness marked by psychotic symptoms, including hallucinations, delusions, and severe disruptions in thinking.

Seizure—A convulsion, or uncontrolled discharge of nerve cells that may spread to other cells throughout the brain.

Serotonin—A chemical messenger in the brain thought to play a role in mood regulation.

be taken by people with a history of irregular or prolonged heart rhythms (long QT syndrome), those with heart failure, or individuals who have recently had a heart attack. People with a history of heart disease should discuss the risks and benefits of treatment with their doctor before starting ziprasidone. Ziprasidone may also lower blood pressure to dangerously low levels, possibly causing a person to faint. It should not be taken by people who have slow heartbeats or low levels of potassium or magnesium in their blood; people taking medication to regulate their blood pressure should have their blood pressure monitored and their treatment modified as needed.

Individuals with a history of **seizures**, even seizures brought on by drug or alcohol abuse, should use ziprasidone cautiously and with close physician supervision, as it may increase the risk of seizures. Ziprasidone may also increase body temperatures to dangerously high levels. People who **exercise** strenuously, those exposed to extreme heat, individuals taking drugs with anticholinergic effects (this includes many common **antidepressants**), and persons prone to dehydration should use the drug cautiously and be alert to dehydration-related side effects.

Elderly persons with increased risk of developing pneumonia should be carefully monitored while taking ziprasidone. Because there is a high incidence of suicide in all patients with psychotic illnesses, people using ziprasidone should be observed carefully for signs of suicidal behavior. Women who are pregnant or breast-feeding should not take ziprasidone, as it may harm the fetus. Some newborns born to mothers who had taken ziprasidone during pregnancy exhibited withdrawal symptoms, including respiratory problems and tremor.

In June 2008, the FDA announced a requirement for manufacturers of ziprasidone (and other antipsychotic drugs) to issue a warning label regarding the adverse effects of using ziprasidone to treat behavioral problems in older individuals with dementia-related **psychosis**, including death. Studies showed that older adults with **dementia** taking antipsychotics such as ziprasidone were at increased risk of having a **stroke** or mini-stroke during treatment and, in some cases, an increased chance of death during treatment, though the reason for the finding was unclear. The use of ziprasidone in treating older adults with dementia-related psychosis is not approved by the FDA.

Side effects

The most common reason that ziprasidone is stopped is the development of a rash. Another common side effect is drowsiness. This side effect is usually worse when starting the drug and becomes less severe with continued use. People performing tasks that require mental alertness such as driving or operating machinery should refrain from doing so until they see how the drug affects them. Other side effects that may occur are abnormal, involuntary twitching (5%) and respiratory disorders (8%). Nausea, constipation, indigestion, and dizziness due to low blood pressure occur in more than 5% of people taking ziprasidone.

Other less common side effects include rapid heartbeat, low blood pressure, agitation, tremor, confusion, **amnesia**, dry mouth, increased salivation, joint pains, and abnormal vision.

The incidence of some adverse effects such as low blood pressure, loss of appetite, abnormal involuntary movements, sleepiness, tremor, cold symptoms, rash, abnormal vision, dry mouth, or increased salivation appears to increase at higher dosages.

People taking ziprasidone should alert their healthcare provider immediately if they develop a rash or hives, since this could indicate a potentially serious adverse reaction. Patients should also notify their health care provider right away if they experience any abnormal involuntary muscle movements. People who think they may be experiencing side effects from this or any other medication should tell their physicians.

Interactions

Ziprasidone interacts with many other drugs, and patients should let their physician know of all the other medications they are taking before starting treatment with ziprasidone. Ziprasidone may produce irregular heart rhythms and other cardiac problems when used with other drugs, including quinidine, dofetilide, **pimozide**, sotalol, erythromycin, **thioridazine**, moxifloxacin, and sparfloxacin; these drugs should not be taken in combination with ziprasidone.

Drugs that cause drowsiness, such as antidepressants, antihistamines, some pain relievers, and alcohol, may increase the sedative effects of ziprasidone. Individuals taking **zolpidem** (Ambien, Ambien CR) concomitantly with ziprasidone should be monitored for central nervous system effects such as respiratory **depression** and should avoid activities requiring mental alertness and motor coordination.

Other drugs taken in combination with ziprasidone may alter the effects of ziprasidone. Drugs such as **carbamazepine**, used to treat seizures, increases liver metabolism and may cause ziprasidone to be less effective. Alternatively, drugs such as ketoconazole, used to treat fungal infections, slow liver metabolism and may increase negative side effects associated with ziprasidone. Ziprasidone may also decrease the effects of drugs used to treat Parkinson's disease such as levodopa.

Resources

BOOKS

Albers, Lawrence J., Rhoda K. Hahn, and Christopher Reist. *Handbook of Psychiatric Drugs.* Laguna Hills, CA: Current Clinical Strategies Publishing, 2010.

American Society of Health-System Pharmacists. *AHFS Drug Information 2011.* Bethesda: American Society of Health-System Pharmacists, 2011.

Graham, George. *The Disordered Mind: An Introduction to Philosophy of Mind and Mental Illness.* New York: Routledge, 2010.

Holland, Leland Norman, and Michael Patrick Adams. *Core Concepts in Pharmacology.* 3rd ed. New York: Prentice Hall, 2011.

North, Carol, and Sean Yutzy. *Goodwin and Guze's Psychiatric Diagnosis.* New York: Oxford University Press, 2010.

Preston, John D., John H. O'Neal, and Mary C. Talaga. *Handbook of Clinical Psychopharmacology for Therapists.* 6th ed. Oakland, CA: New Harbinger Publications, 2011.

PERIODICALS

Barak, Yoram, Doron Mazeh, Igor Plopski, and Yehuda Baruch. "Intramuscular Ziprasidone Treatment of Acute Psychotic Agitation in Elderly Patients with Schizophrenia." *American Journal of Geriatric Psychiatry* 14, no. 7 (July 2006): 629–33.

Frederickson, Anne M., John M. Kane, and Peter Manu. "Does Antipsychotic Polypharmacy Increase the Risk For Metabolic Syndrome?" *Schizophrenia Research* 89, no. 1–3 (2007): 91–100.

Gentile, Salvatore. "Extrapyramidal Adverse Events Associated With Atypical Antipsychotic Treatment of Bipolar Disorder." *Journal of Clinical Psychopharmacology* 27, no. 1 (2007): 35–45.

Ginsberg, David L. "Ziprasidone-Induced Torsade de Pointes." *Primary Psychiatry* 13, no. 8 (2006): 27–29.

Glick, Ira D. "Understanding the Results of CATIE in the Context of the Field." *CNS Spectrums* 11, no. 7 (July 2006): 40–47.

Harvey, Philip D., Christopher R. Bowie, and Antony Loebel. "Neuropsychological Normalization with Long-Term Atypical Antipsychotic Treatment: Results of a Six-Month Randomized, Double-Blind Comparison of Ziprasidone vs. Olanzapine." *Journal of Neuropsychiatry and Clinical Neurosciences* 18, no. 1 (2006): 54–63.

Joyce, Amie T., et al. "Effect of Initial Ziprasidone Dose on Length of Therapy in Schizophrenia." *Schizophrenia Research* 83, no. 2–3 (2006): 285–92.

Kane, John M., Sumant Khanna, Sunita Rajadhyaksha, and Earl Giller. "Efficacy and Tolerability of Ziprasidone in Patients with Treatment-Resistant Schizophrenia." *International Clinical Psychopharmacology* 21, no. 1 (Jan. 2006): 21–28.

Kinon, Bruce J., et al. "A 24-Week Randomized Study of Olanzapine Versus Ziprasidone in the Treatment of Schizophrenia or Schizoaffective Disorder in Patients with Prominent Depressive Symptoms." *Journal of Clinical Psychopharmacology* 26, no. 2 (2006): 157–62.

Malhotra, Anil K., et al. "Ziprasidone-Induced Cognitive Enhancement in Schizophrenia: Specificity or Pseudospecificity?" *Schizophrenia Research* 87, no. 1–3 (2006): 181–84.

Stroup, T. Scott, et al. "Effectiveness of Olanzapine, Quetiapine, Risperidone, and Ziprasidone in Patients with Chronic Schizophrenia Following Discontinuation of a Previous Atypical Antipsychotic." *American Journal of Psychiatry* 163, no. 4 (2006): 611–22.

Ziegenbein, Marc, and Iris T. Calliess. "Clozapine and Ziprasidone: A Useful Combination in Patients With Treatment-Resistant Schizophrenia." *Journal of Neuropsychiatry and Clinical Neurosciences* 18, no. 2 (Spring 2006): 246–47.

ORGANIZATIONS

American Psychiatric Association, 1000 Wilson Boulevard, Suite 1825, Arlington, VA, 22209, (703) 907-7300, apa@psych.org, http://www.psych.org.

National Alliance on Mental Illness (NAMI), Colonial Place Three, 2107 Wilson Blvd., Suite 300, Arlington, VA, 22201, (703) 524-7600, (800) 950-NAMI (6264), Fax: (703) 524-9094, http://www.nami.org/Hometemplate.cfm.

National Institute of Mental Health (NIMH), 6001 Executive Boulevard, Room 8184, MSC 9663, Bethesda, MD, 20892, (301) 443-4513, (866) 615-6464, Fax: (301)

443-4279, nimhinfo@nih.gov, http://www.nimh.nih.gov/index.shtml.

U.S. Food and Drug Administration, 10903 New Hampshire Ave., Silver Spring, MD, 20993-0002, (888) INFO-FDA (463-6332), http://www.fda.gov.

Kelly Karpa, RPh, PhD
Ruth A. Wienclaw, PhD
Laura Jean Cataldo, RN, EdD

Zoloft *see* **Sertraline**

Zolpidem

Definition

Zolpidem is classified as a hypnotic drug. These drugs help people sleep. In the United States, zolpidem is sold as tablets under the brand name Ambien.

Purpose

Zolpidem is a drug that is used to treat **insomnia**. Zolpidem is especially helpful for people who have trouble falling asleep. However, once individuals have fallen asleep, zolpidem also helps them continue to sleep restfully. Zolpidem should be used only for short periods, approximately seven to ten days. If sleeping pills are needed for a long period, an evaluation by a physician is recommended to determine if another medical condition is responsible for the insomnia.

Description

Although the way zolpidem helps people sleep is not entirely understood, it is believed to mimic a chemical in

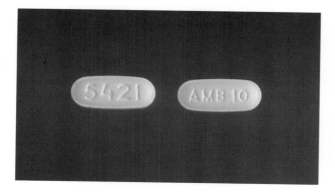

Zolpidem (Ambien), 10 mg. *(U.S. Drug Enforcement Administration)*

the **brain** called gamma-aminobutyric acid (GABA) that naturally helps to facilitate sleep. Zolpidem is a central nervous system depressant, which means that it slows down the nervous system. Unlike some sleeping pills, zolpidem does not interfere with the quality of sleep or usually leave the user feeling sedated in the morning. As a result, most people using zolpidem usually awake feeling refreshed.

Recommended dosage

The usual dose of zolpidem in adults is 5–10 mg. For healthy adults, 10 mg is commonly recommended. However, people taking other drugs that cause drowsiness; people who have severe health problems, especially liver disease; and older people (over age 65) should take a lower dose usually 5 mg. Zolpidem should be taken immediately before bedtime and only if the person can count on getting seven or eight hours of uninterrupted sleep. It usually takes only about 30 minutes for the sleep-inducing actions of zolpidem to be felt. Unlike some sleeping pills, the sleep-facilitating effects appear to last six to eight hours.

If zolpidem is taken with a meal, it will take longer to work. For the fastest sleep onset, it should be taken on an empty stomach. The maximum dose for one day is 10 mg. People who miss a dose of zolpidem should skip the missed dose and take the next dose at the regularly scheduled time. Under no circumstances should a person take more than 10 mg in one day. Zolpidem should be taken exactly as directed by the prescribing physician.

Precautions

Because zolpidem is used to help people fall asleep, it should not be used with other drugs (either over-the-counter, herbal, or prescription) that also cause drowsiness (for example, antihistamines or alcohol). Zolpidem should be used only with close physician supervision in people with liver disease and in the elderly, because these individuals are especially sensitive to the sedative properties of zolpidem. Zolpidem should not be used before driving, operating machinery, or performing activities that require mental alertness. People with a history of drug abuse, psychiatric disorders, or **depression** should be carefully monitored when using zolpidem since zolpidem may worsen symptoms of some psychiatric disorders.

If zolpidem is needed for more than seven to ten days, patients should be reevaluated by a physician to determine if another disorder is causing their difficulty in sleeping. When zolpidem or other sleeping pills are used every night for more than a few weeks, they begin to lose their effectiveness, and people may become dependent upon them to fall asleep. Zolpidem can be habit-forming when taken over a long period. People using zolpidem should

KEY TERMS

Antidepressant—A medication used to treat the symptoms of depression.

Antihistamine—A medication used to alleviate allergy or cold symptoms such as runny nose, itching, hives, watering eyes, or sneezing.

Antipsychotic—A medication used to treat psychotic symptoms of schizophrenia such as hallucinations, delusions, and delirium. May be used to treat symptoms in other disorders as well.

not stop taking the drug suddenly but should gradually reduce the dose over a few days before quitting, even if zolpidem has been used only for a short time.

Side effects

Some sleeping pills such as zolpidem can cause aggressiveness, agitation, hallucinations, **amnesia** (partial or complete loss of memory), rapid heartbeat, and chest pains. These side effects are rare but patients should call their physician immediately if such side effects occur. Other serious side effects include anaphylaxis (severe allergic reaction) and angioedema (facial swelling).

Some patients taking sleep medications have engaged in sleep-related behaviors, including eating, talking, and even driving while asleep, with no recollection of the events. More common side effects include headache, nausea, muscle aches, and drowsiness. Although drowsiness is desired when trying to fall asleep, a few people continue to feel drowsy the next day. Daytime drowsiness may cause people, especially the elderly, to be less coordinated and more susceptible to falls. Other less common side effects include anxiety, confusion, dizziness, and stomach upset.

Interactions

Any drug that causes drowsiness may lead to substantially decreased mental alertness and impaired motor skills when taken with zolpidem. Some examples include alcohol, **antidepressants** such as **imipramine** or **paroxetine**, antipsychotics such as **thioridazine**, and antihistamines (commonly found in allergy and cold medications).

The effectiveness of zolpidem may be reduced if taken with rifampin, an antibiotic that is commonly used to treat tuberculosis infections.

Resources

BOOKS

Physicians' Desk Reference 2011. 66th ed. Montvale, NJ: PDR Network, 2011.

Preston, John D., John H. O'Neal, and Mary C. Talaga. *Handbook of Clinical Psychopharmacology for Therapists.* 5th ed. Oakland, CA: New Harbinger Publications, 2008.

Wolters Kluwer Health. *Drug Facts and Comparisons 2012.* 66th ed. St. Louis: Lippincott, Williams & Wilkins, 2011.

PERIODICALS

Conn, David K., and Robert Madan. "Use of Sleep-Promoting Medications in Nursing Home Residents: Risks versus Benefits." *Drugs and Aging* 23, no. 4 (2006): 271–87.

Glass, Jennifer, et al. "Sedative Hypnotics in Older People with Insomnia: Meta-Analysis of Risks and Benefits." *British Medical Journal* 331, no. 7526 (November 2005): 1–7.

Hajak, G., et al. "Continuous versus Non-Nightly Use of Zolpidem in Chronic Insomnnia: Results of a Large-scale, Double-blind, Randomized, Outpatient Study." *International Clinical Psychopharmacology* 17, no. 1 (January 2002) 9–17.

Hart, Carl L., et al. "Combined Effects of Methamphetamine and Zolpidem on Performance and Mood During Simulated Night Shift Work." *Pharmacology, Biochemistry and Behavior* 81, no. 3 (July 2005): 559–68.

Lucchesi, Lígia M., et al. "Acute Neurophysiological Effects of the Hypnotic Zolpidem in Healthy Volunteers." *Progress in Neuro-Psychopharmacology and Biological Psychiatry* 29, no. 4 (May 2005): 557–64.

Meléndez, Jaime, et al. "Zolpidem and Triazolam Do Not Affect the Nocturnal Sleep-Induced Memory Improvement." *Psychopharmacology* 181, no. 1 (August 2005): 21–26.

Moen, Marit D., and Greg L. Plosker. "Zolpidem Extended Release in Insomnia: Profile Report." *Drugs and Aging* 23, no. 10 (2006): 843–46.

Rosenberg, Russell P. "Sleep Maintenance Insomnia: Strengths and Weaknesses of Current Pharmacologic Therapies." *Annals of Clinical Psychiatry* 18, no. 1 (January–March 2006): 49–56.

Staner, Luc, et al. "Next-Day Residual Effects of hypnotics in DSM-IV Primary Insomnia: A Driving Simulator Study with Simultaneous Electroencephalogram Monitoring." *Psychopharmacology* 181, no. 4 (October 2005): 790–98.

Wesensten, Nancy Jo, et al. "Daytime Sleep and Performance Following a Zolpidem and Melatonin Cocktail." *Sleep: Journal of Sleep and Sleep Disorders Research* 28, no. 1 (January 2005): 93–103.

Kelly Karpa, R.Ph., PhD
Ruth A. Wienclaw, PhD

Zyban *see* **Bupropion**

Zyprexa *see* **Olanzapine**

ORGANIZATIONS

The following is an alphabetical compilation of relevant organizations listed in the *Resources* sections of the main body entries. Although the list is comprehensive, it is by no means exhaustive. It is a starting point for gathering further information. U.S. government organizations and agencies are alphabetized under the first letter of the primary name (e.g., U.S. Food and Drug Administration is listed under "F"). Many of the organizations listed provide information for multiple disorders and have links to additional related websites. E-mail addresses and web addresses listed were provided by the associations; Gale, Cengage Learning is not responsible for the accuracy of the addresses or the content of the websites.

 A

Academy for Eating Disorders
111 Deer Lake Rd., Ste. 100
Deerfield, IL 60015
Phone: (847) 498-4274
Fax: (847) 480-9282
E-mail: info@aedweb.org
Web site: http://www.aedweb.org

U.S. Administration on Aging
1 Massachusetts Ave. NW
Washington, DC 20001
Phone: (202) 401-4634
Web site: http://www.aoa.gov

AGS Foundation for Health in Aging
40 Fulton St., 18th Fl.
New York, NY 10038
Phone: (212) 755-6810
Fax: (212) 832-8646
Toll free: (800) 563-4916
Web site: http://www.healthinaging.org

Albert Ellis Institute
45 E 65th St.
New York, NY 10021
Phone: (212) 535-0822
Fax: (212) 249-3582
Toll free: (800) 323-4738
E-mail: info@albertellis.org
Web site: http://www.rebt.org

Alzheimer Europe
145, route de Thionville
Luxembourg, L-2611
Phone: +352 29 79 70
Fax: +352 29 79 72
E-mail: info@alzheimer-europe.org
Web site: http://www.alzheimer-europe.org

Alzheimer's Foundation of America
322 8th Ave., 7th Fl.
New York, NY 10001
Fax: (646) 638-1546
Toll free: (866) 232-8484
E-mail: info@alzfdn.org
Web site: http://www.alzfdn.org

American Academy of Addiction Psychiatry (AAAP)
400 Massasoit Ave., Ste. 307, 2nd Fl.
East Providence, RI 02914
Phone: (401) 524-3076
Fax: (401) 272-0922
Web site: http://www.aaap.org

American Academy of Child and Adolescent Psychiatry
3615 Wisconsin Ave. NW
Washington, DC 20016-3007
Phone: (202) 966-7300
Fax: (202) 966-2891
Web site: http://aacap.org

American Academy of Clinical Toxicology
6728 Old McLean Village Dr.
McLean, VA 22101
Phone: (703) 556-9222
Fax: (703) 556-8729
E-mail: admin@clintox.org
Web site: http://www.clintox.org

American Academy of Experts in Traumatic Stress (AAETS)
203 Deer Rd.
Ronkonkoma, NY 11779
Phone: (631) 543-2217
Fax: (631) 543-6977
E-mail: info@aaets.org
Web site: http://www.aaets.org

American Academy of Family Physicians
11400 Tomahawk Creek Pkwy.
Leawood, KS 66211-2672

Phone: (913) 906-6000
Fax: (913) 906-6075
Toll free: (800) 274-2237
E-mail: contactcenter@aafp.org
Web site: http://www.aafp.org

American Academy of Medical Acupuncture
1970 E Grand Ave.
El Segundo, CA 90245
Phone: (310) 364-0193
E-mail: administrator@medicalacupuncture.org
Web site: http://www.medicalacupuncture.org

American Academy of Neurology (AAN)
1080 Montreal Ave.
Saint Paul, MN 55116
Phone: (651) 695-2717
Fax: (651) 695-2791
Toll free: (800) 879-1960
E-mail: memberservices@aan.com
Web site: http://www.aan.com

American Academy of Pain Medicine
4700 W. Lake
Glenview, IL 60025
Phone: (847) 375-4731
Fax: (847) 375-6477
E-mail: info@painmed.org
Web site: http://www.painmed.org

American Academy of Pediatrics (AAP)
141 Northwest Point Blvd.
Elk Grove Village, IL 60007-1098
Phone: (847) 434-4000
Fax: (847) 434-8000
Web site: http://www.aap.org

American Academy of Private Practice in Speech-Language Pathology and Audiology
7349 Topanga Canyon Blvd.
Canoga Park, CA 91303
Web site: http://www.aappspa.org

American Academy of Psychiatry and the Law (AAPL)
PO Box 30, One Regency Dr.
Bloomfield, CT 06002
Phone: (860) 242-5450
Fax: (860) 286-0787
Toll free: (800) 331-1389
E-mail: http://www.aapl.org/contact.htm
Web site: http://www.aapl.org

American Academy of Sleep Medicine
2510 N Frontage Rd.
Darien, IL 60561
Phone: (630) 737-9700
Fax: (630) 737-9790
E-mail: inquiries@aasmnet.org
Web site: http://www.aasmnet.org

American Aging Association
2103 Cornell Rd., Rm. 5125
Cleveland, OH 44106
Phone: (216) 368-3671
Fax: (216) 368-8964
E-mail: americanaging@case.edu
Web site: http://www.americanaging.org

American Art Therapy Association
225 N Fairfax St.
Alexandria, VA 22314
E-mail: info@arttherapy.org
Web site: http://www.americanarttherapyassociation.org

American Association of Acupuncture and Oriental Medicine
PO Box 162340
Sacramento, CA 95816
Fax: (916) 443-4766
Toll free: (866) 455-7999
Web site: http://www.aaaomonline.org

American Association of Cardiovascular and Pulmonary Rehabilitation
401 N Michigan Ave., Ste. 2200
Chicago, IL 60611
Phone: (312) 321-5146
Fax: (312) 673-6924
E-mail: aacvpr@aacvpr.org
Web site: http://www.aacvpr.org

American Association for Clinical Chemistry
1850 K St. NW, Ste. 625
Washington, DC 20006
Fax: (202) 887-5093
Toll free: (800) 892-1400
Web site: http://www.aacc.org

American Association for Geriatric Psychiatry (AAGP)
7910 Woodmont Ave., Ste. 1050
Bethesda, MD 20814-3004
Phone: (301) 654-7850
Fax: (301) 654-4137
E-mail: main@aagponline.org
Web site: http://www.aagponline.org

American Association on Intellectual and Developmental Disabilities (AAIDD)
501 3rd St. NW, Ste. 200
Washington, DC 20001
Phone: (202) 387-1968
Fax: (202) 387-2193
Toll free: (800) 424-3688
Web site: http://www.aaidd.org

American Association for Marriage and Family Therapy (AAMFT)
112 S Alfred St.
Alexandria, VA 22314-3061
Phone: (703) 838-9808
Fax: (703) 838-9805
Web site: http://www.aamft.org

American Association of Naturopathic Physicians
4435 Wisconsin Ave. NW, Ste. 403
Washington, DC 20016
Phone: (202) 237-8150
Fax: (202) 237-8152
Toll free: (866) 538-2267
Web site: http://www.naturopathic.org

American Association of Neuromuscular and Electrodiagnostic Medicine
2621 Superior Dr. NW
Rochester, MN 55901
Phone: (507) 288-0100

E-mail: aanem@aanem.org
Web site: http://www.aanem.org

American Association of Sexuality Educators, Counselors, and Therapists (AASECT)
1444 I St. NW, Ste. 700
Washington, DC 20005
Phone: (202) 449-1099
Fax: (202) 216-9646
E-mail: info@aasect.org
Web site: http://www.aasect.org

American Association of Sleep Technologists
2510 N Frontage Rd.
Darien, IL 60561
Phone: (630) 737-9704
Fax: (630) 737-9788
E-mail: AAST@aastweb.org
Web site: http://www.aastweb.org

American Association of Suicidology
5221 Wisconsin Ave. NW
Washington, DC 20015
Phone: (202) 237-2280
Fax: (202) 237-2282
Web site: http://www.suicidology.org

American Board of Psychiatry and Neurology
2150 E Lake Cook Rd., Ste. 900
Buffalo Grove, IL 60089
Phone: (847) 229-6500
Fax: (847) 229-6600
E-mail: questions@abpn.com
Web site: http://www.abpn.com

American Board of Registration for Electroencephalographic Technologists
2509 W Iles Ave., Ste. 102
Springfield, IL 62704
Phone: (217) 726-7980
Fax: (217) 726-7989
E-mail: abreteo@att.net
Web site: http://www.abret.org

American Botanical Council
6200 Manor Rd.
Austin, TX 78723
Phone: (512) 926-4900
Fax: (512) 926-2345
Toll free: (800) 373-7105
E-mail: abc@herbalram.org
Web site: http://abc.herbalgram.org

American Chronic Pain Association
PO Box 850
Rocklin, CA 95677
Fax: (916) 632-3208
Toll free: (800) 533-3231
E-mail: ACPA@pacbell.net
Web site: http://www.theacpa.org

American College of Neuropsychopharmacology
5034-A Thoroughbred Ln.
Brentwood, TN 37027
Phone: (615) 324-2360
Fax: (615) 523-1715
E-mail: acnp@acnp.org
Web site: http://www.acnp.org/default.aspx

American College of Physicians
190 N Independence Mall W
Philadelphia, PA 19106-1572
Phone: (215) 351-2400
Toll free: (800) 523-1546
Web site: http://www.acponline.org

American Council for Drug Education
50 Jay St.
Brooklyn, NY 11201
Phone: (646) 505-2061
E-mail: acde@phoenixhouse.org
Web site: http://www.acde.org

American Dance Therapy Association
10632 Little Patuxent Pkwy., Ste. 108
Columbia, MD 21044
Phone: (410) 997-4040
Fax: (410) 997-4048
Web site: http://www.adta.org

American Epilepsy Society
342 N Main St.
West Hartford, CT 06117-2507
Phone: (860) 586-7505
Fax: (860) 586-7550
Web site: http://www.aesnet.org

American Foundation for Suicide Prevention
120 Wall St., 29th Fl.
New York, NY 20016-3007
Phone: (212) 363-3500
Fax: (212) 363-6237
Toll free: (888) 333-2377
E-mail: inquiry@afsp.org
Web site: http://www.afsp.org

American Geriatrics Society (AGS)
40 Fulton St., 18th Fl.
New York, NY 10038
Phone: (212) 308-1414
Fax: (212) 832-8646
E-mail: info.amger@americangeriatrics.org
Web site: http://www.americangeriatrics.org

American Health Assistance Foundation
22512 Gateway Center Dr.
Clarksburg, MD 20871
Fax: (301) 948-4403
Toll free: (800) 437-2423
E-mail: info@ahaf.org
Web site: http://www.ahaf.org

American Hospice Foundation
2120 L St. NW, Ste. 200
Washington, DC 20037
Phone: (202) 223-0204
Fax: (202) 223-0208
Toll free: (800) 347-1413
Web site: http://www.americanhospice.org

American Hospital Association
325 7th St. NW
Washington, DC 20004-2802
Phone: (202) 638-1100
Web site: http://www.aha.org

American Institute of Homeopathy
101 S Whiting St., Ste. 16
Alexandria, VA 22304
Toll free: (888) 445-9988
E-mail: admin@homeopathyusa.org
Web site: http://homeopathyusa.org

American Institute of Stress
124 Park Ave.
Yonkers, NY 10703
Phone: (914) 963-1200
Fax: (914) 965-6267
E-mail: Stress125@optonline.net
Web site: http://www.stress.org

American Lung Association
1301 Pennsylvannia Ave. NW, Ste. 800
Washington, DC 20004
Phone: (202) 785-3355
Fax: (202) 452-1805
E-mail: info@lungusa.org
Web site: http://www.lung.org

American Massage Therapy Association
500 Davis St., Ste. 900
Evanston, IL 60201-4695
Phone: (847) 864-0123
Fax: (847) 864-5196
Toll free: (877) 905-0577
E-mail: info@amtamassage.org
Web site: http://www.amtamassage.org

American Medical Association (AMA)
515 N State St.
Chicago, IL 60610
Phone: (312) 464-5000
Toll free: (800) 621-8335
Web site: http://www.ama-assn.org

American Music Therapy Association
8455 Colesville Rd., Ste. 1000
Silver Spring, MD 20910
Phone: (301) 589-3300
Fax: (301) 589-5175
Web site: http://www.musictherapy.org

American Neurological Association
5841 Cedar Lake Rd., Ste. 204
Minneapolis, MN 55416
Phone: (952) 545-6284
E-mail: ana@llmsi.com
Web site: http://www.aneuroa.org

American Neuropsychiatric Association
700 Ackerman Rd., Ste. 625
Columbus, OH 43202
Phone: (614) 447-2077
E-mail: anpa@osu.edu
Web site: http://www.anpaonline.org/home.php

American Organization for Bodywork Therapies of Asia
1010 Haddonfield-Berlin Rd., Ste. 408
Voorhees, NJ 08043-3514
Phone: (856) 782-1616
Fax: (856) 782-1653
E-mail: office@aobta.org
Web site: http://www.aobta.org

American Physical Therapy Association
1111 N Fairfax St.
Alexandria, VA 22314-1488
Phone: (703) 684-APTA (2782); TDD: (703) 683-6748
Toll free: (800) 999-APTA (2782)
Web site: http://www.apta.org

American Polarity Therapy Association
122 N. Elm St., Ste. 512
Greensboro, NC 27401
Phone: (336) 574-1121
Fax: (336) 574-1151
E-mail: aptaoffices@polaritytherapy.org
Web site: http://www.polaritytherapy.org

American Psychiatric Association (APA)
1000 Wilson Blvd., Ste. 1825
Arlington, VA 22209-3901
Phone: (703) 907-7300
Toll free: (888) 357-7924
E-mail: apa@psych.org
Web site: http://www.psych.org

American Psychoanalytic Association
309 E 49th St.
New York, NY 10017
Phone: (212) 752-0450
Fax: (212) 593-0571
E-mail: info@aspa.org
Web site: http://www.apsa.org

American Psychological Association (APA)
750 1st St. NE
Washington, DC 20002-4242
Phone: (202) 336-5500; TDD/TTY: (202) 336-6123
Toll free: (800) 374-2721
E-mail: apa@psych.org
Web site: http://www.apa.org

American Psychotherapy Association
2750 E Sunshine St.
Springfield, MO 65804
Phone: (417) 823-0173
Toll free: (800) 205-9165
Web site: http://www.americanpsychotherapy.com

American Sleep Apnea Association
6856 Eastern Ave. NW, Ste. 203
Washington, DC 20012
Phone: (202) 293-3650
Fax: (202) 293-3656
Web site: http://www.sleepapnea.org

American Sleep Association
614 S 8th St., Ste. 282
Philadelphia, PA 19147
Phone: (443) 593-2285
E-mail: sleep@1sleep.com
Web site: http://www.sleepassociation.org

American Society of Addiction Medicine
4601 N Park Ave., Upper Arcade #101
Chevy Chase, MD 20815
Phone: (301) 656-3920
Fax: (301) 656-3815
E-mail: email@asam.org
Web site: http://www.asam.org

American Society of Clinical Hypnosis
140 N Bloomingdale Rd.
Bloomingdale, IL 60108
Phone: (630) 980-4740
Fax: (630) 351-8490
E-mail: info@asch.net
Web site: http://www.asch.net

American Society for Clinical Pharmacology and Therapeutics
528 N Washington St.
Alexandria, VA 22314
Phone: (703) 836-6981
E-mail: info@ascpt.org
Web site: http://www.ascpt.org

American Society of Electroneurodiagnostic Technologists
402 E Bannister Rd., Ste. A
Kansas City, MO 64131-3019
Phone: (816) 931-1120
Fax: (816) 931-1145
E-mail: info@aset.org
Web site: http://www.aset.org

American Society of Health-System Pharmacists
7272 Wisconsin Ave.
Bethesda, MD 20814
Toll free: (866) 279-0681
E-mail: custserv@ashp.org
Web site: http://www.ashp.org

American Society for Pharmacology and Experimental Therapeutics
9650 Rockville Pike
Bethesda, MD 20814-3995
Phone: (301) 634-7060
Fax: (301) 634-7061
Web site: http://www.aspet.org

American Sociological Association
1430 K St. NW, Ste. 600
Washington, DC 20005
Phone: (202) 383-9005
Fax: (202) 638-0882
Web site: http://www.asanet.org

American Speech-Language-Hearing Association (ASHA)
2200 Research Blvd.
Rockville, MD 20850-3289
Phone: (301) 296-5700; TTY: (301) 296-5650
Fax: (301) 296-8580
Toll free: (800) 638-8255
Web site: http://www.asha.org

American Stroke Association
7272 Greenville Ave.
Dallas, TX 75231
Toll free: (800) 242-8721
Web site: http://www.heart.org

American Thyroid Association
6066 Leesburg Pike, Ste. 550
Falls Church, VA 22041
Phone: (703) 998-8890
Fax: (703) 998-8893
E-mail: thyroid@thyroid.org
Web site: http://www.thyroid.org

American Yoga Association
PO Box 19986
Sarasota, FL 34276
E-mail: info@americanyogaassociation.org
Web site: http://www.americanyogaassociation.org

Angelman, Rett & Prader-Willi Syndromes Consortium (ARPWSC), Rare Diseases Clinical Research Network
University of Alabama at Birmingham
Birmingham, AL 35294-1150
Phone: (205) 934-1130
Fax: (205) 975-6330
E-mail: jlane@uab.edu
Web site: http://rarediseasesnetwork.epi.usf.edu/arpwsc

Anxiety Disorders Association of America
8730 Georgia Ave.
Silver Spring, MD 20910
Phone: (240) 485-1001
Fax: (240) 485-1035
E-mail: information@adaa.org
Web site: http://www.adaa.org

The Arc
1660 L St. NW, Ste. 301
Washington, DC 20036
Phone: (202) 534-3700
Fax: (202) 534-3731
Toll free: (800) 433-5255
E-mail: info@thearc.org
Web site: http://www.thearc.org

ARCH National Respite Network and Resource Center, Chapel Hill Training-Outreach Project
800 Eastowne Dr., Ste. 105
Chapel Hill, NC 27514
Phone: (919) 490-5577
Fax: (919) 490-4905
Web site: http://www.chtop.com

Art Therapy Credentials Board
3 Terrace Way
Greensboro, NC 27403-3660
Phone: (336) 482-2856
Fax: (336) 482-2852
Toll free: (877) 213-2822
E-mail: atcb@nbcc.org
Web site: http://www.atcb.org

Assertive Community Treatment Association
PO Box 2428
Brighton, MI 48116
Phone: (810) 227-1859
Fax: (810) 227-5785
E-mail: acta@actassociation.org
Web site: http://www.actassociation.org

Associated Bodywork & Massage Professionals
25188 Genesee Trail Rd.
Golden, CO 80401
Fax: (800) 667-8260
Toll free: (800) 458-2267
Web site: http://www.abmp.com

Association for the Advancement of Behavior Therapy
305 7th Ave., 16th Fl.
New York, NY 10001
Phone: (212) 647-1890

Fax: (212) 647-1865
Web site: http://www.abct.org

The Association for the Advancement of Gestalt Therapy
Web site: http://www.aagt.org

Association for Applied Psychotherapy and Biofeedback
10200 W 44th Ave., Ste. 304
Wheat Ridge, CO 80033
Phone: (303) 422-8436
Toll free: (800) 477-8892
E-mail: aapb@resourcecenter.com
Web site: http://www.aapb.org

Association for Behavioral Analysis International
550 W Centre Ave., Ste. 1
Portage, MI 49024
Phone: (269) 492-9310
Fax: (269) 492-9316
Web site: http://www.abainternational.org

Association for Behavioral and Cognitive Therapies
305 7th Ave., 16th Fl.
New York, NY 10001
Phone: (212) 647-1890
Fax: (212) 647-1865
Toll free: (866) 615-6464
Web site: http://www.abct.org

Association for Comprehensive Neurotherapy
PO Box 2198
Broken Arrow, OK 34688-1967
Phone: (561) 798-0472
Fax: (561) 798-9820
E-mail: acn@latitudes.org
Web site: http://www.latitudes.org

Association for the Development of the Person-Centered Approach
Web site: http://www.adpca.org

Association for Frontotemporal Degeneration
290 King of Prussia Rd., Radnor Station Bldg. 2, Ste. 320
Radnor, PA 19103
Phone: (267) 514-7221
Toll free: (866) 507-7222
Web site: http://www.theaftd.org

Association for Persons in Supported Employment
PO Box 1280
Rockville, MD 20849
Phone: (301) 279-0060
Fax: (301) 251-3762
Web site: http://www.apse.org

Association for Play Therapy, Inc
3198 Willow Ave., Ste. 110
Clovis, CA 93703
Phone: (599) 294-2128
Fax: (559) 294-2129
E-mail: info@a4pt.org
Web site: http://www.a4pt.org

Association for the Treatment of Sexual Abusers
4900 SW Griffith Dr., Ste. 274
Beaverton, Oregon 97005
Phone: (503) 643-1023

Fax: (503) 643-5084
E-mail: atsa@atsa.com
Web site: http://www.atsa.com

Association for Treatment and Training in the Attachment of Children
PO Box 533
Lake Villao, IL 60046
Phone: (847) 453-8224
Fax: (847) 356-7856
E-mail: questions@attach.org
Web site: http://www.attach.org

Attention Deficit Disorder Association (ADDA)
PO Box 7557
Wilmington, DE 19803-9997
Toll free: (800) 939-1019
E-mail: info@add.org
Web site: http://www.add.org

Augustine Fellowship, Sex and Love Addicts Anonymous
PO Box 119, New Town Branch
Boston, MA 02258
Phone: (617) 332-1845

Autism Network International (ANI)
PO Box 35448
Syracuse, NY 13235-5448
Web site: http://autreat.com

Autism Society
4340 East-West Hwy., Ste. 350
Bethesda, MD 20814
Phone: (301) 657-0881
Toll free: (800) 3-AUTISM (328-8476)
Web site: http://www.autism-society.org

Autism Speaks
1 E 33rd St., 4th Fl.
New York, NY 10016
Phone: (212) 252-8584
Fax: (212) 252-8676
Toll free: (888) AUTISM2 (288-4762)
E-mail: contactus@autismspeaks.org
Web site: http://www.autismspeaks.org

B

The Balanced Mind Foundation (formerly the Child & Adolescent Bipolar Foundation)
820 Davis St., Ste. 520
Evanston, IL 60201
Phone: (847) 492-8510
E-mail: info@thebalancedmind.org
Web site: http://www.thebalancedmind.org

The Bazelon Center for Mental Health Law
1101 15th St. NW, Ste. 1212
Washington, DC 20005
Phone: (202) 467-5730
E-mail: info@bazelon.org
Web site: http://www.bazelon.org

Beck Institute for Cognitive Therapy and Research
One Belmont Ave., Ste. 700
Bala Cynwyd, PA 19004-1610

Phone: (610) 664-3020
Fax: (610) 664-4437
E-mail: beckinst@gim.net
Web site: http://www.beckinstitute.org

Benson-Henry Institute for Mind Body Medicine
151 Merrimac St., 4th Fl.
Boston, MA 02114
Phone: (617) 643-6090
Fax: (617) 643-6077
E-mail: mindbody@partners.org
Web site: http://www.massgeneral.org/bhi

Better Sleep Council
501 Wythe St.
Alexandria, VA 22314-1917
Web site: http://www.bettersleep.org

Biofeedback Certification International Alliance
10200 W 44th Ave., Ste. 310
Wheat Ridge, CO 80033
Phone: (303) 420-2902
Fax: (303) 422-8894
Toll free: (866) 908-8713
E-mail: info@bcia.org
Web site: http://www.bcia.org

Borden Institute
1546 Porter St., Ste. 207
Fort Detrick, MD 21702
Phone: (301) 619-3470
Fax: (301) 619-3471
E-mail: bordeninfo@amedd.army.mil
Web site: http://www.bordeninstitute.army.mil/index.html

Brain Aneurysm Foundation
269 Hanover St., Bldg. 3
Hanover, MA 02339
Phone: (781) 826-5556
Fax: (781) 826-5566
E-mail: office@bafound.org
Web site: http://www.bafound.org

Brain and Behavior Research Foundation
60 Cutter Mill Rd., Ste. 404
Great Neck, NY 11021
Phone: (516) 829-0091
Fax: (516) 487-6930
E-mail: info@bbrfoundation.org
Web site: http://www.bbrfoundation.org

Brain Injury Association of America (BIAA)
1608 Spring Hill Rd., Ste. 110
Vienna, VA 22182
Phone: (703) 761-0750
Fax: (703) 761-0755
Toll free: (800) 444-6443
Web site: http://www.biausa.org

Brain Trauma Foundation (BTF)
7 World Trade Center, 34th Fl., 250 Greenwich St.
New York, NY 10007
Phone: (212) 772-0608
Web site: http://www.braintrauma.org

British Columbia Institute Against Family Violence
74640 Kitsilano RPO
Vancouver, British Columbia V6K 4P4
Canada

Phone: (604) 669-7055
Toll free (within Canada): (877) 755-7055
E-mail: ngrunberg@bcifv.org

Bureau of Justice Assistance
810 7th St. NW, 4th Fl.
Washington, DC 20531
Phone: (202) 616-6500
Fax: (202) 305-1367
Toll free: (866) 859-2687
Web site: http://www.ojp.usdoj.gov/BJA/index.html

 C

Callier Center for Communication Disorders
University of Texas at Dallas
1966 Inwood Rd.
Dallas, TX 75235
Phone: (214) 905-3000
Fax: (214) 905-3022
Web site: http://www.utdallas.edu/calliercenter

Cambridge Center for Behavioral Studies
PO Box 7067
Cummings Center, Ste. 340F
Beverly, MA 01915
Phone: (978) 369-2227
Fax: (978) 369-8584
Web site: http://www.behavior.org

Canadian Movement Disorder Group
Web site: http://www.cmdg.org

Canadian Symposium for Parental Alienation Syndrome (CS-PAS)
150 Hollidge Blvd., Ste. 252
Aurora, Ontario L4G 8A3
Canada
Phone: (647) 476-3170
E-mail: info@cspas.ca
Web site: http://cspas.ca

Center for Brain and Cognition, University of California, San Diego
0109 Mandler Hall, 9500 Gilman Dr.
La Jolla, CA 92093-0109
Phone: (858) 534-6240
Fax: (858) 534-7190
E-mail: ramalab@ucsd.edu
Web site: http://cbc.ucsd.edu/index.html

Center for Internet Addiction Recovery
PO Box 72
Bradford, PA 16701
Phone: (814) 451-2405
Fax: (814) 368-9560
Web site: http://www.netaddiction.com

Center for Mind-Body Medicine
5225 Connecticut Ave. NW, Ste. 415
Washington, DC 20015
Phone: (202) 966-7338
Fax: (202) 966-2589
Web site: http://www.cmbm.org

Center for Mindfulness in Medicine, Health Care, and Society
University of Massachusetts Medical School
55 Lake Ave. N
Worcester, MA 01655
Phone: (508) 856-2656
Fax: (508) 856-1977
E-mail: mindfulness@umassmed.edu
Web site: http://www.umassmed.edu/cfm/home/index.aspx

Center for Psychological Studies, Nova Southeastern University
3301 College Ave.
Fort Lauderdale-Davie, FL 33314-7796
Toll free: (800) 541-6682, ext. 25700
Web site: http://www.cps.nova.edu

Center for Science in the Public Interest
1220 L St. NW, Ste. 300
Washington, DC 20005
Phone: (202) 332-9110
Fax: (202) 265-4954
Web site: http://www.cspinet.org

Center for Studies of the Person
1150 Silverado, Ste. 112
La Jolla, CA 92037
Phone: (858) 459-3861
Web site: http://www.centerfortheperson.org

Center for the Study of Anorexia and Bulimia
1841 Broadway, 4th Fl.
New York, NY 10023
Phone: (212) 333-3444
Fax: (212) 333-5444
E-mail: casb@icpnyc.org
Web site: http://www.csabnyc.org

Center for the Study of Traumatic Encephalopathy
Boston University
Phone: (617) 638-6143
E-mail: cbaugh@bu.edu
Web site: http://www.bu.edu/cste

Center for the Study of Traumatic Stress (CSTS)
Uniformed Services University of the Health Sciences (USU)
Department of Psychiatry
4301 Jones Bridge Rd.
Bethesda, MD 20814
Phone: (301) 295-2470
Fax: (301) 319-6965
E-mail: cstsinfo@usuhs.mil
Web site: http://www.centerforthestudyoftraumaticstress.org/index.php

U.S. Centers for Disease Control and Prevention
1600 Clifton Rd.
Atlanta, GA 30333
Phone: (404) 639-3534
Toll free: 800-232-4636
E-mail: inquiry@cdc.gov
Web site: http://www.cdc.gov

U.S. Centers for Medicare & Medicaid Services
7500 Security Blvd.
Baltimore, MD 21244-1850
Toll free: (800) 633-4223
Web site: http://www.medicare.gov

Centre for Addiction and Mental Health
33 Russell St.
Toronto, Ontario M5S 2S1
Canada
Phone: (416) 535-8501
Toll free: (800) 463-6273
Web site: http://www.camh.net

Children and Adults with Attention Deficit/Hyperactivity Disorder (CHADD)
8181 Professional Pl., Ste. 150
Landover, MD 20785
Phone: (301) 306-7070
Fax: (301) 306-7090
Toll free: (800) 233-4050
Web site: http://www.chadd.org

Cocaine Anonymous World Services
21720 S Wilmington Ave., Ste. 304
Long Beach, CA 90810-1641
Phone: (310) 559-5833
Fax: (310) 559-2554
E-mail: cawso@ca.org
Web site: http://www.ca.org

Colorado Learning Disabilities Research Center (CLDRC)
Institute for Behavioral Genetics, University of Colorado Boulder
1480 30th St.
Boulder, CO 80303
Phone: (303) 492-7362
Fax: (303) 492-8063
E-mail: info@ibg.colorado.edu
Web site: http://ibgwww.colorado.edu/cldrc

Compassionate Friends
PO Box 3696
Oak Brook, IL 60522
Phone: (630) 990-0010
Fax: (630) 990-0246
Toll free: (877) 969-0010
Web site: http://www.compassionatefriends.org

U.S. Consumer Product Safety Commission
4330 East-West Hwy.
Bethesda, MD 20814
Phone: (301) 504-7923
Web site: http://www.cpsc.gov

Council of State Governments Justice Center
100 Wall St., 20th Fl.
New York, NY 10005
Phone: (212) 482-2320
Web site: http://www.justicecenter.csg.org

D

U.S. Department of Health & Human Services
200 Independence Ave. SW
Washington, DC 20201
Phone: (202) 619-7800
Toll free: (877) 696-6775
Web site: http://www.hhs.gov

U.S. Department of Housing and Urban Development
451 7th St. SW
Washington, DC 20410
Phone: (202) 708-1112
Web site: http://www.hud.gov

U.S. Department of Veterans Affairs (VA)
810 Vermont Ave. NW
Washington, DC 20420
Toll free: (800) 827-1000; Mental health crisis line: (800)
    273-8255 (press 1)
Web site: http://www.va.gov

Depression and Bipolar Support Alliance (DBSA)
730 N Franklin St., Ste. 501
Chicago, IL 60654-7225
Fax: (312) 642-7243
Toll free: (800) 826-3632
E-mail: info@dbsalliance.org
Web site: http://www.dbsalliance.org

Disaster Psychiatry Outreach
One Gustave L. Levy Pl., PO Box 1228
New York, NY 10029-6574
Phone: (646) 233-1215
E-mail: info@disasterpsych.org
Web site: http://www.disasterpsych.org.

Dougy Center
PO Box 86852
Portland, OR 97286
Phone: (503) 775-5683
Toll free: (866) 775-5683
E-mail: help@dougy.org
Web site: http://www.grievingchild.org

U.S. Drug Enforcement Administration
Mailstop AES
8701 Morrissette Drive
Springfield, VA 22152
Toll free: (800) 882-9539
Web site: http://www.justice.gov/dea

Dual Recovery Anonymous
PO Box 8107
Prairie Village, KS 66208
Phone: (913) 991-2703
Web site: http://www.draonline.org/index.html

E

Emotions Anonymous
PO Box 4245
St. Paul, MN 55104-0245
Phone: (651) 647-9712
Fax: (651) 647-1593
Web site: http://www.emotionsanonymous.org

Epilepsy Foundation
8301 Professional Pl.
Landover, MD 20785-7223
Fax: (301) 577-2684
Toll free: (800) 332-1000
E-mail: contactus@efa.org
Web site: http://www.epilepsyfoundation.org

**Eunice Kennedy Shriver National Institute of Child Health
    and Human Development (NICHD)**
Bldg 31, Rm. 2A32, MSC 2425, 31 Center Dr.
Bethesda, MD 20892
Fax: (866) 760-5947
Toll free: (800) 370-2943; TTY: (888) 320-6942
E-mail: NICHDInformationResourceCenter@mail.nih.gov
Web site: http://www.nichd.nih.gov

European College of Neuropsychopharmacology (ECNP)
PO Box 85410
Utrecht 3508 AK
The Netherlands
Phone: +31 30 2538567
Fax: +31 30 2538568
E-mail: secretariat@ecnp.eu
Web site: http://www.ecnp.eu

F

Families for Depression Awareness
395 Totten Pond Rd., Ste. 404
Waltham, MA 02451
Phone: (781) 890-0220
Fax: (781) 890-2411
Web site: http://www.familyaware.org

Family Caregiver Alliance
180 Montgomery St., Ste. 900
San Francisco, CA 94104
Phone: (415) 434-3388
Toll free: (800) 445-8106
E-mail: info@caregiver.org
Web site: http://www.caregiver.org

Federation of Families for Children's Mental Health
9605 Medical Center Dr.
Rockville, MD 20850
Phone: (240) 403-1901
Fax: (240) 403-1909
E-mail: ffcmh@ffcmh.org
Web site: http://ffcmh.org.

Fetal Alcohol Spectrum Disorders Center for Excellence
2101 Gaither Rd., Ste. 600
Rockville, MD 20850
Toll free: (866) 786-7327
E-mail: fasdcenter@samhsa.hhs.gov
Web site: http://www.fascenter.samhsa.gov

Fetal Alcohol Syndrome (FAS) World Canada
2448 Hamilton Rd.
Bright's Grove, Ontario N0N 1C0
Canada
Phone: (519) 869-8026
Web site: http://www.faslink.org

Fisher Center for Alzheimer's Research Foundation
One Intrepid Square, W 46th St. & 12th Ave.
New York, NY 10036
Toll free: (800) 259-4636
Web site: http://www.alzinfo.org

U.S. Food and Drug Administration (FDA)
10903 New Hampshire Ave.
Silver Spring, MD 20993

Toll free: (888) 463-6332
Web site: http://www.fda.gov

Freedom from Fear
308 Seaview Ave.
Staten Island, NY 10305
Phone: (718) 351-1717
E-mail: help@freedomfromfear.org
Web site: http://www.freedomfromfear.org

Friends: The National Association of Young People Who Stutter
c/o Lee Caggiano, 38 S Oyster Bay Rd.
Syosset, NY 11791
Toll free: (866) 866-8335
E-mail: LCAGGIANO@aol.com
Web site: http://www.friendswhostutter.org

Fuqua Center for Late-Life Depression
Wesley Woods Health Center, 4th Fl., 1841 Clifton Rd. NE
Atlanta, GA 30329
Phone: (404) 728-6948
Web site: http://www.fuquacenter.org

 G

Gamblers Anonymous, International Service Office
PO Box 17173
Los Angeles, CA 90017
Phone: (626) 960-3500
Fax: (626) 960-3501
Toll free: (888) GA-HELPS (424-3577)
E-mail: isomain@gamblersanonymous.org
Web site: http://www.gamblersanonymous.org

Gay, Lesbian, Bisexual, and Transgender National Help Center
2261 Market St., PMB #296
San Francisco, CA 94114
Phone: (415) 355-0003
Fax: (415) 552-5498
E-mail: info@GLBTNationalHelpCenter.org
Web site: http://www.glbtnationalhelpcenter.org

Genetic Alliance
4301 Connecticut Ave. NW, Ste. 404
Washington, DC 20008-2369
Phone: (202) 966-5557
Fax: (202) 966-8553
E-mail: info@geneticalliance.org
Web site: http://www.geneticalliance.org

Geriatric Mental Health Foundation
7910 Woodmont Ave., Ste. 1050
Bethesda, MD 20814
Phone: (301) 654-7850
Fax: (301) 654-4137
E-mail: web@GMHFonline.org
Web site: http://www.gmhfonline.org

Global and Regional Asperger's Syndrome Partnership
135 E 15th St.
New York, NY 10003
Phone: (646) 242-4003
E-mail: info@grasp.org
Web site: http://www.grasp.org.

GROWW (Grief Recovery Online)
11877 Douglas Rd., #102-PMB101
Alpharetta, GA 30005
Web site: http://www.groww.org

 H

Hazelden Foundation
PO Box 11
Center City, MN 55012-0011
Phone: (651) 213-4200
Toll free: (800) 257-7810
E-mail: info@hazelden.org
Web site: http://www.hazelden.org

Hoarding of Animals Research Consortium (HARC)
c/o Gary Patronek, Animal Rescue League of Boston, 10 Chandler St.
Boston, MA 02116
Phone: (617) 426-9170
Fax: (617) 426-3028
E-mail: cfapp@tufts.edu
Web site: http://www.tufts.edu/vet/hoarding

Homeopathic Medical Council of Canada
31 Adelaide St. E, Box 605
Toronto, Ontario M5C 2J8
Canada
Phone: (416) 788-4622
E-mail: Ontario@HMCC.ca
Web site: http://www.hmcc.ca

The Hormone Foundation
8401 Connecticut Ave., Ste. 900
Chevy Chase, MD 20815-5817
Fax: (301) 941-0259
Toll free: (800) 467-6663
E-mail: hormone@endo-society.org
Web site: http://www.hormone.org

 I

I CAN [children's communication charity]
8 Wakley St.
London, United Kingdom, EC1V 7QE
Phone: 0845 225 4071 or 020 7843 2510
Fax: 0845 225 4072 or 020 7843 2569
E-mail: info@ican.org.uk
Web site: http://www.ican.org.uk

Imagery International
1574 Coburg Rd. #555
Eugene, OR 97401
Toll free: (800) 494-9985
E-mail: information@imageryinternational.com
Web site: http://imageryinternational.org

Insight Meditation Society
1230 Pleasant St.
Barre, MA 01005
Phone: (978) 355-4378
Web site: http://www.dharma.org

Institute for Traditional Medicine
2017 SE Hawthorne Blvd.
Portland, OR 97214
Phone: (503) 233-4907
Web site: http://www.itmonline.org

International Association of Yoga Therapists
PO Box 12890
Prescott, AZ 86304
Phone: (928) 541-0004
E-mail: mail@iayt.org
Web site: http://www.iayt.org

International Center for Alcohol Policies
1519 New Hampshire Ave. NW
Washington, DC 20036
Phone: (202) 986-1159
Fax: (202) 986-2080
E-mail: info@icap.org
Web site: http://www.icap.org

International Dyslexia Association (IDA)
40 York Rd., 4th Fl.
Baltimore, MD 21204
Phone: (410) 296-0232
Fax: (410) 321-5069
E-mail: http://www.interdys.org/ContactUs.htm
Web site: http://www.interdys.org

International League Against Epilepsy
342 N Main St.
West Hartford, CT 06117-2507
Phone: (860) 586-7547
Fax: (860) 586-7550
Web site: http://www.ilae-epilepsy.org

International Neuropsychiatric Association
INA Secretariat Office Neuropsychiatric Institute Euroa
    Centre
The Prince of Wales Hospital, NSW Australia 2031
Phone: 612 93823816
Fax: 612 93823774
E-mail: angie.russell@unsw.edu.au
Web site: http://www.inawebsite.org

International Neuropsychological Society
700 Ackerman Rd., Ste. 625
Columbus, OH 43202
Phone: (614) 263-4200
Fax: (614) 263-4366
Web site: http://www.the-ins.org

International OCD Foundation Hoarding Center
PO Box 961029
Boston, MA 02196
Phone: (617) 973-5801
Fax: (617) 973-5803
E-mail: info@ocfoundation.org
Web site: http://www.ocfoundation.org/hoarding

International Paruresis Association
PO Box 65111
Baltimore, MD 21209
Toll free: (800) 247-3864
Web site: http://www.paruresis.org

International Psychoanalytical Association
Broomhills, Woodside Ln.

London, United Kingdom N12 8UD
Phone: +44 20 8446 8324
Phone: +44 20 8445 4729
E-mail: ipa@ipa.org.uk
Web site: http://www.ipa.org.uk

International Psychogeriatric Association (IPA)
550 Frontage Rd., Ste. 3759
Northfield, IL 60093
Phone: (847) 501-3310
Fax: (847) 501-3317
Web site: http://www.ipa-online.org

International Rett Syndrome Association
4600 Devitt Dr.
Cincinnati, OH 45246
Fax: (513) 874-2520
Toll free: (800) 818-7388
Web site: http://www.rettsyndrome.org

International Society for ECT and Neurostimulation (ISEN)
5454 Wisconsin Ave., Ste. 1220
Chevy Chase, MD 20815
Phone: (301) 951-7220
Fax: (301) 299-4918
E-mail: contact@isen-ect.org
Web site: http://www.isen-ect.org

International Society for Interpersonal Psychotherapy
University of Iowa, Department of Psychiatry, 1-293 Medical
    Education Bldg.
Iowa City, IA 52242
Phone: (391) 353-4230
Fax: (391) 353-3003
E-mail: scott-stuart@uiowa.edu
Web site: http://interpersonalpsychotherapy.org

International Society for Mental Health Online (ISMHO)
E-mail: https://www.ismho.org/contact.asp
Web site: https://www.ismho.org/home.asp

International Society of Psychiatric Genetics (ISPG)
5034-A Thoroughbred Ln.
Brentwood, TN 37027
Phone: (202) 336-5500
Web site: http://www.ispg.net

International Society for the Study of Personality Disorders
University of Michigan Health System, Psychiatry MCHC-6,
    Box 5295, 1500 E Medical Center Dr.
Ann Arbor, MI 48109-5295
Phone: (734) 936-8316
Fax: (734) 936-9761
Web site: http://www.isspd.com

**International Society for the Study of Subtle Energies and
    Energy Medicine**
2770 Arapahoe Rd., Ste. 132
Lafayette, CO 80026
Phone: (303) 425-4625
Fax: (866) 269-0972
Web site: http://www.isssseem.org

**International Society for the Study of Trauma and
    Dissociation**
8400 Westpark Dr., 2nd Fl.
McLean, VA 22102
Phone: (703) 610-9037

Fax: (703) 610-0234
Web site: http://www.isst-d.org

International Society for Traumatic Stress Studies (ISTSS)
111 Deer Lake Rd., Ste. 100
Deerfield, IL 60015
Phone: (847) 480-9028
Fax: (847) 480-9282
Web site: http://www.istss.org

International Stuttering Association (ISA)
c/o Joseph Lukong Tardzenyuy, Secretary, 1018 S Payne St.
New Ulm, MN 56073
E-mail: admin@stutterisa.org
Web site: http://www.stutterisa.org

J

Jin Shin Do Foundation for Bodymind Acupressure
PO Box 416
Idyllwild, CA 92549
Phone: (951) 659-5707
Web site: http://www.jinshindo.org

The Johns Hopkins Hospital, Sexual Behaviors Consultation Unit
600 N Wolfe St., Meyer 144
Baltimore, MD 21287
Phone: (410) 583-1661
Fax: (410) 583-2693
Web site: http://www.hopkinsmedicine.org/psychiatry/specialty_areas/sexual_behaviors

Johns Hopkins University Center for Epigenetics in Common Human Disease
855 N Wolfe St.
Baltimore, MD 21205
Phone: (410) 614-3489
Web site: http://www.hopkinsmedicine.org/epigenetics

K

The Kempe Foundation for the Prevention and Treatment of Child Abuse and Neglect
The Gary Pavilion at Children's Hospital Colorado
Anschutz Medical Campus
13123 E 16th Ave., B390
Denver, CO 80045
Phone: (303) 864-5300
Web site: http://www.kempe.org

Kleine-Levin Syndrome Foundation
PO Box 5382
San Jose, CA 95150-5382
Phone: (408) 265-1099
Fax: (408) 269-2131
E-mail: facts@klsfoundation.org
Web site: http://www.klsfoundation.org

Kristin Brooks Hope Center
615 7th St., NE
Washington, DC 20002
Phone: (202) 536-3200

Toll free: (800) 442-4673
Web site: http://www.hopeline.com

L

Leadership Council on Child Abuse and Interpersonal Violence
c/o Joyanna Silberg, PhD, 6501 N Charles St., PO Box 6815
Baltimore, MD 21285-6815
E-mail: desk1@leadershipcouncil.org
Web site: http://www.leadershipcouncil.org/index.html

Learning Disabilities Association of America (LDA)
4156 Library Rd.
Pittsburgh, PA 15234-1349
Phone: (412) 341-1515
Fax: (412) 344-0224
E-mail: http://www.ldanatl.org/contact/contact.cfm
Web site: http://www.ldanatl.org

M

MAAP Services for Autism, Asperger Syndrome, and PDD
PO Box 524
Crown Point, IN 46308
Phone: (219) 662-1311
Fax: (219) 662-0638
E-mail: info@maapservices.org
Web site: http://www.maapservices.org

March of Dimes Foundation
1275 Mamaroneck Ave.
White Plains, NY 10605
Phone: (914) 997-4488
Web site: http://www.marchofdimes.com

Matrix Institute on Addictions
Web site: http://www.matrixinstitute.org

Medical Council on Alcohol
5 St. Andrew's Place
London, United Kingdom NW1 4LB
Phone: 011 4420 7 7487 4445
Fax: 011 4420 7 7935 4479
E-mail: mca@medicalcouncilalcol.demon.co.uk
Web site: http://www.m-c-a.org.uk

Mental Health America
2000 N Beauregard St., 6th Fl.
Alexandria, VA 22311
Phone: (703) 684-7722
Fax: (703) 684-5968
Toll free: (800) 969-6642
E-mail: infoctr@mentalhealthamerica.net
Web site: http://www.mentalhealthamerica.net

Mental Health Foundation
PO Box 322
Albany, NY 12201
E-mail: info@mentalhealthfoundation.net
Web site: http://www.mentalhealthfoundation.net

Movement Disorder Society
555 E Wells St., Ste. 1100

Milwaukee, WI 53202
Phone: (414) 276-2145
Fax: (414) 276-3349
E-mail: info@movementdisorders.org
Web site: http://www.movementdisorders.org

Munchausen by Proxy Survivors Network
PO Box 806177
St. Clair Shores, MI 48080

N

Narcolepsy Network
110 Ripple Ln.
North Kingstown, RI 02852
Phone: (401) 667-2523
Fax: (401) 633-6567
Toll free: (888) 292-6522
E-mail: narnet@narcolepsynetwork.org
Web site: http://www.narcolepsynetwork.org

Narcotics Anonymous
PO Box 9999
Van Nuys, CA 91409
Phone: (818) 773-9999
Fax: (818) 700-0700
E-mail: fsmail@na.org
Web site: http://www.na.org

National Academy of Neuropsychology
7555 E Hampden Ave., Ste. 525
Denver, CO 80231
Phone: (303) 691-3694
Fax: (303) 691-5983
E-mail: office@nanonline.org
Web site: http://nanonline.org

National Alliance on Mental Illness (NAMI)
3803 N Fairfax Dr., Ste. 100
Arlington, VA 22203
Phone: (703) 524-7600
Fax: (703) 524-9094
Toll free: (800) 950-NAMI (6264)
Web site: http://www.nami.org

National Aphasia Association
350 7th Ave., Ste. 902
New York, NY 10001
Toll free: (800) 922-4622
E-mail: naa@aphasia.org
Web site: http://aphasia.org

National Association of Anorexia Nervosa and Related Eating Disorders, Inc.
PO Box 640
Naperville, IL 60566
Phone: (630) 577-1330
E-mail: anadhelp@anad.org
Web site: http://www.anad.org

National Association of Cognitive-Behavioral Therapists
PO Box 2195
Weirton, WV 26062
Phone: (304) 723-3982
Toll free: (800) 853-1135

E-mail: nacbt@nacbt.org
Web site: http://www.nacbt.org

National Association for Continence
PO Box 1019
Charleston, SC 29402-1019
Toll free: (800) 252-3337
Web site: http://www.nafc.org

National Association for Holistic Aromatherapy
PO Box 1868
Banner Elk, NC 28604
Phone: (828) 898-6161
Fax: (828) 898-1965
E-mail: info@naha.org
Web site: http://www.naha.org

National Association of School Psychologists
4340 East-West Hwy., Ste. 402
Bethesda, MD 20002
Phone: (301) 657-0270
Fax: (301) 657-0275
Toll free: (800) 331-5277
Web site: http://www.nasponline.org

National Association on Sexual Addiction Problems
22937 Arlington Ave., Ste. 201
Torrance, CA 90501
Phone: (213) 546-3103

National Association of Social Workers
750 First St. NE, Ste. 700
Washington, DC 20002-4241
Phone: (202) 408-8600
Web site: http://www.naswdc.org

National Black Association for Speech-Language and Hearing
700 McKnight Park Dr., Ste. 708
Pittsburgh, PA 15237
Phone: (412) 366-1177
Fax: (412) 366-8804
E-mail: NBASLH@nbaslh.org
Web site: http://www.nbaslh.org

National Cannabis Prevention and Information Centre (NCPIC)
PO Box 684
Randwick, NSW Australia 2031
Phone: +612 9385 0208
E-mail: info@ncpic.org.au
Web site: http://ncpic.org.au

National Center for Complementary and Alternative Medicine (NCCAM)
9000 Rockville Pike
Bethesda, MD 20892
E-mail: info@nccam.nih.gov
Web site: http://nccam.nih.gov

National Center on Elder Abuse (NCEA)
University of California—Irvine, Program in Geriatric Medicine
101 The City Dr. S
200 Building
Orange, CA 92868
Fax: (714) 456-7933
Toll free: (855) 500-ELDR (3537)
E-mail: ncea-info@aoa.hhs.gov
Web site: http://www.ncea.aoa.gov

National Center for Learning Disabilities (NCLD)
381 Park Ave. S, Ste. 1401
New York, NY 10016
Phone: (212) 545-7510
Fax: (212) 545-9665
Toll free: (888) 575-7373
E-mail: ncld@ncld.org
Web site: http://www.ncld.org

National Center for Posttraumatic Stress Disorder, U.S. Department of Veterans Affairs
810 Vermont Ave. NW
Washington, DC 20420
Phone: (802) 296-6300
E-mail: ncptsd@va.gov
Web site: http://www.ncptsd.va.gov

National Center for Responsible Gambling
1299 Pennsylvania Ave. NW, Ste. 1175
Washington, DC 20004
Phone: (202) 552-2689
Fax: (202) 552-2676
E-mail: info@ncrg.org
Web site: http://www.ncrg.org

National Center on Sleep Disorders Research
6701 Rockledge Dr.
Bethesda, MD
Phone: (301) 435-0199
Fax: (301) 480-3451
Web site: http://www.nhlbi.nih.gov/sleep

National Certification Commission for Acupuncture and Oriental Medicine
76 S Laura St., Ste. 1290
Jacksonville, FL 32202
Phone: (904) 598-1005
Fax: (904) 598-5001
Web site: http://www.nccaom.org

National Child Traumatic Stress Network (NCTSN)
University of California, Los Angeles
11150 W. Olympic Blvd., Ste. 650
Los Angeles, CA 90064
Phone: (310) 235-2633
Fax: (310) 235-2612
E-mail: http://www.nctsn.org/about-us/contact-us
Web site: http://www.nctsn.org

National Chronic Fatigue Syndrome and Fibromyalgia Association
PO Box 18426
Kansas City, MO 64133
Phone: (816) 737-1343
Web site: http://www.ncfsfa.org

National Clearinghouse on Alcohol and Drug Information
PO Box 2345
Rockville, MD 20847
Fax: (240) 221-4292
Toll free: (877) SAMHSA-7; Spanish: (877) 767-8432; TDD: (800) 487-4889
Web site: http://ncadi.samhsa.gov

National Coalition Against Domestic Violence
1120 Lincoln St., Ste. 1603
Denver, CO 80203

Phone: (303) 839-1852; TTY: (303) 839-1681
Fax: (303) 831-9251
Web site: http://www.ncadv.org

National Coalition for the Homeless
2201 P St. NW
Washington, DC 20037
Phone: (202) 462-4822
Fax: (202) 462-4823
E-mail: info@nationalhomeless.org
Web site: http://www.nationalhomeless.org

National Coalition for Homeless Veterans
333 1/2 Pennsylvania Ave. SE
Washington, DC 20003-1148
Phone: (202) 546-1969
Fax: (202) 546-2063
Toll free: (800) 838-4357
E-mail: info@nchv.org
Web site: http://www.nchv.org

National Committee for the Prevention of Elder Abuse
151 1st Ave., No. 93
New York, NY 10003
Fax: (212) 420-6026
Toll free: (800) 677-1116
Web site: http://www.preventelderabuse.org

National Consortium on Stigma and Empowerment (NCSE)
Illinois Institute of Technology, Institute of Psychology
3424 S. State St.
Chicago, IL 60616
Web site: http://www.stigmaandempowerment.org

National Council on Alcoholism and Drug Dependence, Inc. (NCADD)
244 E 58th St., 4th Fl.
New York, NY 10022
Phone: (212) 269-7797
Fax: (212) 269-7510
Toll free: (800) 622-2255
E-mail: national@ncadd.org
Web site: http://www.ncadd.org

National Council for Community Behavioral Healthcare
1701 K St. NW, Ste. 400
Washington, DC 20006
Phone: (202) 684-7457
Fax: (202) 386-9391
E-mail: communications@thenationalcouncil.org
Web site: http://www.thenationalcouncil.org

National Council of Juvenile and Family Court Judges (NCJFCJ)
PO Box 8970
Reno, NV 89507
Phone: (775) 784-6012
Fax: (775) 784-6628
E-mail: staff@ncjfcj.org
Web site: http://www.ncjfcj.org

National Dissemination Center for Children with Disabilities
1825 Connecticut Ave. NW, Ste. 700
Washington, DC 20009
Phone: (202) 884-8200
Fax: (202) 884-8441

Toll free: (800) 695-0285
E-mail: nichcy@aed.org
Web site: http://www.nichcy.org

National Down Syndrome Society (NDSS)
666 Broadway, 8th Fl.
New York, NY 10012
Fax: (212) 979-2873
Toll free: (800) 221-4602
E-mail: info@ndss.org
Web site: http://www.ndss.org/index.php

National Eating Disorders Association
165 W 46th St.
New York, NY 10036
Phone: (212) 575-6200
Fax: (212) 575-1650
Toll free: (800) 931-2237
E-mail: info@NationalEatingDisorders.org
Web site: http://www.nationaleatingdisorders.org

National Education Alliance for Borderline Personality Disorder
PO Box 974
Rye, NY 10580
E-mail: info@neabpd.com
Web site: http://www.borderlinepersonalitydisorder.com

National Family Caregivers Association
10400 Connecticut Ave., Ste. 500
Kensington, MD 20895-3944
Phone: (301) 942-6430
Fax: (301) 942-2302
Toll free: (800) 896-3650
E-mail: info@thefamilycaregiver.org
Web site: http://www.nfcacares.org

National Health Care for the Homeless Council
PO Box 60427
Nashville, TN 37206-0427
Phone: (615) 226-2292
Fax: (615) 226-1656
Web site: http://www.nhchc.org

National Human Genome Research Institute (NHGRI)
Bldg. 31, Rm. 4B09, 31 Center Dr., MSC 2152, 9000
    Rockville Pike
Bethesda, MD 20892-2152
Phone: (301) 402-0911
Fax: (301) 402-2218
Web site: http://www.genome.gov

National Institute on Aging (NIA)
Bldg. 31, Rm. 5C27, 31 Center Dr., MSC 2292
Bethesda, MD 20892
Phone: (301) 496-1752
Fax: (301) 496-1072
Toll free: (800) 222-2225; TTY: (800) 222-4225
Web site: http://www.nia.nih.gov

National Institute on Alcohol Abuse and Alcoholism (NIAAA)
5635 Fishers Ln., MSC 9304
Bethesda, MD 20892-9304
Phone: (301) 443-3860
Web site: http://www.niaaa.nih.gov

National Institute of Biomedical Imaging and Bio-engineering
31 Center Dr., 1C14
Bethesda, MD 20892-8859
Phone: (301) 469-8859
Web site: http://www.nibib.nih.gov

National Institute on Deafness and Other Communication Disorders (NIDCD)
31 Center Dr., MSC 2320
Bethesda, MD 20892-2320
Phone: (301) 496-7243
Fax: (301) 770-8977
Toll free: (800) 241-1044
E-mail: nidcdinfo@nidcd.nih.gov
Web site: http://www.nidcd.nih.gov

National Institute on Drug Abuse (NIDA)
6001 Executive Blvd., Rm. 5213
Bethesda, MD 20892
Phone: (301) 442-1124; Spanish: (240) 221-4007
E-mail: information@nida.nih.gov
Web site: http://www.nida.nih.gov

National Institute of Justice (NIJ)
810 7th St. NW
Washington, DC 20531
Web site: http://www.nij.gov

National Institute of Mental Health (NIMH)
6001 Executive Blvd., Rm. 8184, MSC 9663
Bethesda, MD 20892
Phone: (301) 443-4513
Fax: (301) 443-4279
Toll free: (866) 615-6464
E-mail: nimhinfo@nih.gov
Web site: http://www.nimh.nih.gov

National Institute of Neurological Disorders and Stroke (NINDS)
NIH Neurological Institute, PO Box 5801
Bethesda, MD 20824
Phone: (301) 496-5751; TTY: (301) 468-5981
Toll free: (800) 352-9424
Web site: http://www.ninds.nih.gov

National Lead Information Center
422 S Clinton Ave.
Rochester, NY 14620
Fax: (585) 232-3111
Toll free: (800) 424-5323
Web site: http://www.epa.gov/lead/nlic.htm

U.S. National Library of Medicine
8600 Rockville Pike
Bethesda, MD 20894
Web site: http://www.nlm.nih.gov

National Mental Health Consumers' Self-Help Clearinghouse
1211 Chestnut St., Ste. 1207
Philadelphia, PA 19107
Phone: (215) 751-1810
Fax: (215) 636-6312
Toll free: (800) 553-4539
E-mail: info@mhselfhelp.org
Web site: http://mhselfhelp.org

National Organization on Fetal Alcohol Syndrome
1200 Eton Ct. NW, 3rd Fl.
Washington, DC 20007
Phone: (202) 785-4585
Fax: (202) 466-6456
E-mail: information@nofas.org
Web site: http://www.nofas.org

National Organization for Rare Disorders
55 Kenosia Ave., PO Box 1968
Danbury, CT 06813-1968
Phone: (203) 744-0100
Fax: (203) 798-2291
Toll free: (800) 999-6673
Web site: http://www.rarediseases.org

National Organization for the Reform of Marijuana Laws (NORML)
1600 K St. NW
Washington, DC 20006
Phone: (202) 483-5500
Fax: (202) 483-0057
E-mail: norml@norml.org
Web site: http://norml.org

National Psychological Association for Psychoanalysis
40 W 13th St.
New York, NY 10011
Phone: (212) 924-7440
Fax: (212) 989-7543
E-mail: info@npap.org
Web site: http://www.npap.org

National Resource Center on ADHD
8181 Professional Pl., Ste. 150
Landover, MD 20785
Toll free: (800) 233-4050
Web site: http://www.help4adhd.org

National Safety Council
1121 Spring Lake Dr.
Itasca, IL 60143-3201
Phone: (630) 285-1121
Fax: (630) 285-1315
Toll free: (800) 621-7615
E-mail: customerservice@nsc.org
Web site: http://www.nsc.org

National Schizophrenia Foundation
403 Seymour Ave., Ste. 202
Lansing, MI 48933
Phone: (517) 485-7168
Fax: (517) 485-7180
Toll free: (800) 482-9534
E-mail: inquiries@nsfoundation.org

National Sexual Violence Resource Center (NSVRC)
123 N Enola Dr.
Enola, PA 17025
Phone: (717) 909-0710
Fax: (717) 909-0714
Toll free: (877) 739-3895
E-mail: resources@nsvrc.org
Web site: http://www.nsvrc.org

National Sleep Foundation
1010 N Glebe Rd., Ste. 310
Arlington, VA 22201

Phone: (703) 243-1697
E-mail: nsf@sleepfoundation.org
Web site: http://www.sleepfoundation.org

National Stroke Association
9707 E Easter Ln., Ste. B
Centennial, CO 80112
Fax: (303) 649-1328
Toll free: (800) 787-6537
E-mail: info@stroke.org
Web site: http://www.stroke.org

National Suicide Prevention Lifeline
Toll free: (800) 274-TALK (8255)
Web site: http://www.suicidepreventionlifeline.org

Natural Standard
One Davis Sq.
Somerville, MA 02144
Phone: (617) 591-3300
Fax: (617) 591-3399
E-mail: questions@naturalstandard.com
Web site: http://naturalstandard.com

Neuroleptic Malignant Syndrome Information Service
Box 1069
Sherburne, NY 13460-1069
Phone: (607) 674-7920
Fax: (607) 674-7910
E-mail: info@nmsis.org
Web site: http://www.nmsis.org

New York Online Access to Health
Web site: http://www.noah-health.org/en/mental

New York State Psychiatric Institute, Columbia University Medical Center
1051 Riverside Dr.
New York, NY 10032
Phone: (212) 543-6000
Web site: http://www.nyspi.org

North American Family Institute
26 Howley St.
Peabody, MA 01960
Phone: (978) 538-0286
Fax: (978) 531-9313
Web site: http://www.nafi.com

O

Obsessive Compulsive Foundation
PO Box 961029
Boston, MA 02196
Phone: (617) 973-5801
Web site: http://www.ocfoundation.org

OCD Center of Los Angeles
11620 Wilshire Blvd., Ste. 890
Los Angeles, CA 90025
Phone: (310) 824-5200
E-mail: http://www.ocdla.com/contactus.html
Web site: http://www.ocdla.com/index.html

U.S. Office of Dietary Supplements, National Institutes of Health
6100 Executive Blvd., Rm. 3B01, MSC 7517
Rockville, MD 20892-7517
Phone: (301) 435-2920
Fax: (301) 480-1845
E-mail: ods@nih.gov
Web site: http://ods.od.nih.gov

Office of Fair Housing and Equal Opportunity, U.S. Department of Housing and Urban Development
451 7th St. SW
Washington, DC 20410
Web site: http://portal.hud.gov/hudportal/HUD?src=/program_offices/fair_housing_equal_opp

Office of Juvenile Justice and Delinquency Prevention, U.S. Department of Justice
810 7th St. NW
Washington, DC 20531
Phone: (202) 307-5911
Web site: http://www.ojjdp.gov

Office of Special Education and Rehabilitative Services, U.S. Department of Education
400 Maryland Ave., SW
Washington, DC 20202-2800
Phone: (202) 245-7488
Web site: http://rsa.ed.gov

Office on Women's Health, U.S. Department of Health and Human Services
200 Independence Ave., SW
Washington, DC 20201
Toll free: (800) 994-9662; TDD: (888) 220-5446
Web site: http://www.womenshealth.gov

Olweus Bullying Prevention Program
Toll free: (800) 328-9000
E-mail: olweusinfo@hazelden.org
Web site: http://www.olweus.org/public/index.page

Overeaters Anonymous
PO Box 44020
Rio Rancho, NM 87174-4020
Phone: (505) 891-2664
Fax: (505) 891-4320
Web site: http://www.oa.org

P

PAIRS Foundation
1675 Market St., Ste. 207
Weston, FL 33326
Toll free: (877) PAIRS-4U (724-7748)
E-mail: info@pairs.com
Web site: http://www.pairs.com

Parents Anonymous, Inc
675 W Foothill Blvd., Ste. 220
Claremont, CA 91711-3475
Phone: (909) 621-6184
Fax: (909) 625-6304
E-mail: Parentsanonymous@parentsanonymous.org
Web site: http://www.parentsanonymous.org

The Partnership at Drugfree.org
352 Park Ave. S, 9th Fl.
New York, NY 10010
Phone: (212) 922-1560
Fax: (212) 922-1570
Web site: http://www.drugfree.org

Personality Disorders Awareness Network
490 Sun Valley Dr., Ste. 205
Roswell, GA 30076
Phone: (770) 642-4236 x61
Fax: (770) 642-4239
E-mail: info@bpdan.org
Web site: http://www.bpdan.org

Pick's Disease Support Group
E-mail: info@pdsg.org.uk
Web site: http://www.pdsg.org.uk

Postpartum Support International
PO Box 60931
Santa Barbara, CA 93160
Phone: (805) 967-7636
Toll free: (800) 944-4773
Web site: http://www.postpartum.net

President's Committee for People with Intellectual Disabilities, Administration for Children and Families, U.S. Department of Health and Human Services
Aerospace Center, Ste. 210, 370 L'Enfant Promenade SW
Washington, DC 20447
Phone: (202) 619-0634
Fax: (202) 205-9519
Toll free: (800) 424-3688
Web site: http://www.acf.hhs.gov/programs/pcpid

Prevent Child Abuse America
228 S Wabash Ave., 10th Fl.
Chicago, IL 60604
Phone: (312) 663-3520
Fax: (312) 939-8962
E-mail: mailbox@preventchildabuse.org
Web site: http://www.preventchildabuse.org

Public Citizen, Inc
1600 20th St. NW
Washington, DC 20009
Phone: (202) 588-1000
E-mail: hrg1@citizen.org
Web site: http://www.citizen.org/Page.aspx?pid=183

Q

Qigong Human Life Research Foundation
PO Box 5327
Cleveland, OH 44101

R

Rape, Abuse & Incest National Network (RAINN)
2000 L St. NW, Ste. 406
Washington, DC 20036

Phone: (202) 544-1034
Toll free: (800) 656-HOPE
E-mail: info@rainn.org
Web site: http://www.rainn.org

Rational Recovery
Box 800
Lotus, CA 95651
Phone: (530) 621-2667
Fax: (530) 621-4374
Web site: https://rational.org/index.php?id=1

ReSTART
1001 290th Ave. SE
Fall City, WA 98024-7403
Phone: (425) 417-1715
Toll free: (800) 682-6934
E-mail: restart@netaddictionrecovery.com
Web site: http://www.netaddictionrecovery.com

Restless Legs Syndrome Foundation
1904 Banbury Rd.
Raleigh, NC 27608-4428
Phone: (919) 781-4428
Web site: http://www.rls.org

S

Schizophrenia.com
Web site: http://www.schizophrenia.com

Selective Mutism Group—A Division of Childhood Anxiety Network, Inc.
Web site: http://www.selectivemutism.org

Sensory Processing Disorder Foundation
5420 S. Quebec St., Ste. 135
Greenwood Village, CO 80111
Phone: (303) 794-1182
Fax: (303) 322-5550
Web site: http://www.sinetwork.org

Sex Addicts Anonymous
PO Box 70949
Houston, TX 77270
Toll free: (800) 477-8191
E-mail: info@saa-recovery.org
Web site: http://www.sexaa.org

Sexuality Information and Education Council of the United States
1706 R St., NW
Washington, DC 20009
Phone: (202) 265-2405
Fax: (202) 462-2340
Web site: http://www.aasect.org

SHARE Pregnancy and Infant Loss Support
402 Jackson St.
St. Charles, MO 63301
Fax: (636) 947-7486
Toll free: (800) 821-6819
Web site: http://www.nationalshare.org

Shyness Research Institute
4201 Grant Line Rd.

New Albany, IN 47150
Phone: (812) 941-2295
Fax: (812) 941-2591
E-mail: bcarducc@ius.edu
Web site: http://www.ius.edu/shyness

Sidran Institute
PO Box 436
Brooklandville, MD 21022-0436
Phone: (410) 825-8888
Fax: (410) 560-0134
E-mail: info@sidran.org
Web site: http://www.sidran.org/index.cfm

SIDS Alliance
1314 Bedford Ave., Ste. 230
Baltimore, MD 21208
Toll free: (800) 221-SIDS
Web site: http://www.sidsalliance.org

Society for Clinical and Experimental Hypnosis
PO Box 252
Southborough, MA 01772
Phone: (508) 598-5553
Fax: (866) 397-1839
E-mail: info@sceh.us
Web site: http://www.sceh.us

Society for the Exploration of Psychotherapy Integration
E-mail: geostricker@gmail.com
Web site: http://sepiweb.org

Society for Light Treatment and Biological Rhythms
824 Howard Ave.
New Haven, CT 60610
E-mail: sltbrinfo@gmail.com
Web site: http://www.sltbr.org

Society for the Psychological Study of Men and Masculinity (Division 51), American Psychological Association
750 1st St. NE
Washington, DC 20002-4242
Phone: (202) 216-7602
Fax: (202) 218-3599
E-mail: kcooke@apa.org
Web site: http://www.apa.org/about/division/div51.aspx

Stanford University School of Medicine Center for Narcolepsy
450 Broadway St., Pavilion B, 2nd Fl.
Redwood City, CA 94063
Phone: (650) 725-6517
Fax: (650) 725-4913
Web site: http://med.stanford.edu/school/Psychiatry/narcolepsy

The Stanley Medical Research Institute, Research on Schizophrenia and Bipolar Disorder
E-mail: info@stanleyresearch.org
Web site: http://www.stanleyresearch.org/dnn

State Rehabilitation Councils
1902 Market St.
Camp Hill, PA 17011
Toll free: (888) 250-5175
Web site: http://www.parac.org

STOP Cyberbullying
Phone: (201) 463-8663

E-mail: parry@aftab.com
Web site: http://www.stopcyberbullying.org/index2.html

Structured Clinical Interview for DSM Disorders (SCID)
c/o Biometrics Research Department, Columbia University at
    NYSPI
1051 Riverside Dr., Unit 60
New York, NY 10032
Phone: (212) 543-5524
Fax: (212) 543-5525
E-mail: scid4@columbia.edu
Web site: http://www.scid4.org

Stuttering Foundation of America (SFA)
3100 Walnut Grove Rd., Ste. 603
Memphis, TN 38111-0749
Phone: (901) 452-7343
Fax: (901) 452-3931
Toll free: (800) 992-9392
E-mail: info@stutteringhelp.org
Web site: http://www.stutteringhelp.org/Default.aspx?tabid=4

Substance Abuse and Mental Health Services Administration
    (SAMHSA)
1 Choke Cherry Rd.
Rockville, MD 20857
Fax: (240) 221-4292
Toll free: (877) SAMHSA-7 (726-4727); TTY: (800) 487-4889
E-mail: SAMHSAInfo@samhsa.hhs.gov
Web site: http://www.samhsa.gov

T

Therapeutic Touch International Association
PO Box 419
Craryville, NY 12521
Phone: (518) 325-1185
Fax: (509) 693-3537
E-mail: nhpai@therapeutic-touch.org
Web site: http://www.therapeutictouch.org

Tourette Syndrome Association, Inc.
42-40 Bell Blvd.
Bayside, NY 11361-2861
Phone: (718) 224-2999
Web site: http://www.tsa-usa.org

Tourette Syndrome Foundation of Canada
5945 Airport Rd., Ste. 195
Mississauga, Ontario L4V 1R9
Canada
Phone: (905) 673-2255
Fax: (905) 673-2638
Toll free: (800) 361-3120
Web site: http://www.tourette.ca

Tragedy Assistance Program for Survivors
1777 F St. NW, Ste. 600
Washington, DC 20006
Phone: (202) 588-TAPS (8277)
Fax: (202) 509-8282
Toll free: (800) 959-TAPS (8277)
E-mail: info@taps.org
Web site: http://www.taps.org

Treatment Advocacy Center
200 N Glebe Rd., Ste. 730
Arlington, VA 22203
Phone: (703) 294-6001
Fax: (703) 294-6010
E-mail: info@treatmentadvocacycenter.org
Web site: http://www.treatmentadvocacycenter.org

Treatment and Research Advancements Association for
    Personality Disorder
23 Greene St.
New York, NY 10013
Phone: (212) 966-6514
Toll free: (888) 4-TARA-APD
E-mail: tara4bpd@gmail.com
Web site: http://www.tara4bpd.org

Trichotillomania Learning Center, Inc.
207 McPherson St., Ste. H
Santa Cruz, CA 95060-5863
Phone: (831) 457-1004
Fax: (831) 426-4383
E-mail: info@trich.org
Web site: http://www.trich.org

U

Uniformed Services University of the Health Sciences
    (USU)
4301 Jones Bridge Rd.
Bethesda, MD 20814
Phone: (301) 295-1219
Fax: (301) 295-3757
Toll free: (800) 515-5257
Web site: http://www.usuhs.mil

United States ... **For U.S. agencies, see specific agency**
    name (e.g., Food and Drug Administration).

United States Pharmacopoeia
12601 Twinbrook Pkwy.
Rockville, MD 20852-1790
Toll free: (800) 227-8772
Web site: http://www.usp.org

University of Minnesota Clinic, Center for Sexual Health
1300 S 2nd St.
Minneapolis, MN 55454
Phone: (612) 624-7821
Web site: http://www.fm.umn.edu/phs/clinic/home.html

University of North Carolina School of Medicine,
    Department of Psychiatry
110 Conner Dr., Ste. 4
Chapel Hill, NC 27514
Phone: (919) 929-7449
Web site: http://www.psychiatry.unc.edu

V

Vipassana Meditation Center
PO Box 24
Shelbourne Falls, MA 01370

Phone: (413) 625-2160
Web site: http://www.dhamma.org/en/schedules/schdhara.shtml

W

Weight-control Information Network
1 WIN Way
Bethesda, MD 20892-3665
Phone: (202) 828-1025
Fax: (202) 828-1028
Toll free: (877) 946-4627
E-mail: win@info.niddk.nih.gov
Web site: http://win.niddk.nih.gov/index.htm

Wellesley Centers for Women (WCW)
Wellesley College, 106 Central St.
Wellesley, MA 02481-8203
Phone: (781) 283-2500
E-mail: wcw@wellesley.edu
Web site: http://www.wcwonline.org

Wilson Disease Association
5572 N Diversey Blvd.
Milwaukee, WI 53217
Phone: (414) 961-0533
Toll free: (866) 961-0533
E-mail: info@wilsonsdisease.org
Web site: http://www.wilsonsdisease.org

Workplace Bullying Institute (WBI)
PO Box 29915

Bellingham, WA 98228
E-mail: http://www.workplacebullying.org/aboutwbi/contact/
Web site: http://www.workplacebullying.org

World Association for Person-Centered and Experiential Psychotherapy and Counseling
PO Box 142
Ross-on-Wye, United Kingdom HR9 9AG
Phone: 011 44 1989 763 901
Web site: http://www.pce-world.org

World Professional Association for Transgender Health (WPATH)
1300 S 2nd St., Ste. 180
Minneapolis, MN 55454
E-mail: wpath@wpath.org
Web site: http://www.wpath.org

Worldwide Education and Awareness for Movement Disorders (WE MOVE)
5731 Mosholu Avenue
Bronx, NY 10471
E-mail: wemove@wemove.org
Web site: http://www.wemove.org

Y

Yoga Science Foundation
759 S State St., No. 24
Ukiah, CA 95482
Web site: http://www.yrec.org

GLOSSARY

The glossary is an alphabetical compilation of terms and definitions listed in the *Key Terms* sections of the main body entries. Although the list is comprehensive, it is by no means exhaustive.

A

A1 ALLELE. An allele related to reward deficiency syndrome (RDS).

A1 D2. A chromosome sequence related to reward deficiency syndrome (RDS).

ABSENCE SEIZURE. A seizure characterized by a short-term (15–20 seconds) but abrupt lack of conscious activity. Individuals become very quiet and may blink, stare blankly, roll their eyes, or move their lips, but once the seizure ends, they may not even realize that anything unusual happened. Also called a petit mal seizure.

ABSTINENCE. Refraining from sexual intercourse for a period of time.

ABSTRACT REASONING. The ability to analyze information and solve problems.

ABUSE. Physical, emotional, or sexual harm.

ACAMPROSATE. Also called Campral, a medication used since 1989 in Europe and since 2004 in the United States to reduce the craving for alcohol.

ACETYLCHOLINE. A naturally occurring chemical in the body that transmits nerve impulses from cell to cell. Acetylcholine causes blood vessels to dilate, lowers blood pressure, and slows the heartbeat. Central nervous system well-being is dependent on a balance among the neurotransmitters acetylcholine, dopamine, serotonin, and norepinephrine.

ACETYLCHOLINESTERASE. The chemical responsible for the breakdown of acetylcholine.

ACHIEVEMENT TEST. Any of a number of tests that assess developed knowledge or skill.

ACRODERMATITIS ENTEROPATHICA. Hereditary metabolic problem characterized by dermatitis, diarrhea, and poor immunity. Oral treatment with zinc is curative.

ACTIVITIES OF DAILY LIVING (ADLs). A general term for routine activities of self-care (e.g., brushing teeth, dressing, bathing) and independent functioning (e.g., managing money, preparing meals, cleaning house).

ACUPOINT. A pressure point stimulated in acupressure.

ACUPRESSURE. A form of massage in which certain points of the body are pressed with the fingers and hands to produce a desired effect.

ACUTE. Having a sudden onset and lasting a short time.

ACUTE ONSET VASCULAR DEMENTIA. Vascular dementia caused by a single stroke or with an onset of fewer than three months.

ADAPTIVE BEHAVIOR. A person's ability to accomplish tasks and adapt to and function in an environment.

ADAPTIVE FUNCTIONING. A term used to describe a person's having the intellectual, social, and practical skills needed to live independently.

ADDICTION. A strong physical or psychological dependence on a physical substance.

ADDICTIVE DISORDER. A disorder involving repeated participation in a certain activity, despite negative consequences and/or attempts to stop the behavior. Alcohol abuse is an example.

ADDICTIVE PERSONALITY. The concept that addiction is the result of a pre-existing character disposition.

ADENOSINE. A nucleoside that plays multiple physiological roles in energy transfer and molecular signaling, as a component of ribonucleic acid (RNA), and as an inhibitory neurotransmitter that promotes sleep.

ADHD. Attention deficit hyperactivity disorder.

ADJUNCT THERAPY. A form of treatment that is not strictly necessary but is helpful to a therapy regimen (e.g., music or art therapy).

ADJUSTMENT DISORDER. A disorder defined by the development of significant emotional or behavioral symptoms in response to a stressful event or series of events. Symptoms may include depressed mood, anxiety, and impairment of social and occupational functioning.

ADRENAL GLAND. A small gland located above each kidney that produces many different hormones, including estrogen, progesterone, and stress hormones.

ADRENALINE ADDICTION. A drug-like dependency on the physiological effects of participating in activities that trigger adrenaline release (such as skydiving or gambling).

AEROBIC EXERCISE. Activity that increases the body's requirement for oxygen, thereby increasing respiration and heart rate.

AFFECT. In psychology, an observed emotional expression or response, such as through facial expressions, hand gestures, or tone of voice. Types of affect include flat (inanimate, no expression), blunted (minimally responsive), inappropriate relative to the context, and labile (abrupt changes in type and intensity of emotion).

AFFECTIVE DISORDER. A disorder involving an inappropriate or unexpected emotional experience or reaction relative to the circumstance (for example, feeling sad when there is no easily identifiable reason, as in depression).

AGE OF CONSENT. The minimum age at which a person is considered legally competent to consent to sexual acts. It should not be confused with the voting age, driving age, legal drinking age, or marriageable age. In most jurisdictions in the United States, the age of consent is 16 or 18, but it may be set as low as 12 or as high as 21.

AGE-ASSOCIATED MEMORY IMPAIRMENT (AAMI). A condition in which an older person suffers some memory loss and takes longer to learn new information. AAMI is different than dementia because it is not progressive and does not represent a serious decline from the person's previous level of functioning. Benign senescent forgetfulness is another term for AAMI.

AGITATION. Excessive restlessness or emotional disturbance that is often associated with anxiety, psychosis, or other mental disorder (such as Alzheimer's disease).

AGNOSIA. Inability to recognize familiar people, places, and objects.

AGONIST. Any chemical that binds to a receptor on a cell surface and stimulates that cell to respond.

AGORAPHOBIA. An anxiety disorder characterized by fear of crowds, open or public spaces, or situations that might trigger panic attacks, and from where exits (or help) may be inaccessible or impeded.

AIDS. Acquired immunodeficiency syndrome.

AKATHISIA. Agitated or restless movement, usually affecting the legs. Movement is accompanied by a sense of discomfort and an inability to sit, stand still, or remain inactive for periods of time. Akathisia is a common side effect of some neuroleptic (antipsychotic) medications.

ALCOHOL. An organic chemical and the active agent in beer, wine, and liquor; chemically known as ethanol.

ALCOHOL POISONING. A potentially life-threatening condition caused by consuming large amounts of alcohol within a short time period, negatively affecting heart rate, breathing, and the gag reflex.

ALCOHOL USE DISORDERS INVENTORY TEST (AUDIT). A test for alcohol use developed by the World Health Organization (WHO). Its ten questions address three specific areas of drinking over a 12-month period: the amount and frequency of drinking, dependence upon alcohol, and problems that have been encountered due to drinking alcohol.

ALCOHOLIC ENERGY DRINK. Caffeinated alcoholic beverages; malt liquors that, in addition to high alcohol content, have added caffeine and sometimes other stimulants.

ALCOHOLISM. Chronic and compulsive use of alcohol that interferes with everyday life.

ALIENATOR. In parental alienation disorder, the alienator is the parent attempting to negatively affect the child's opinion of the other (targeted or alienated) parent.

ALLELE. One member of a pair or a series of genes that occupies a specific position on a specific chromosome.

ALLERGIC REACTION. A physiological reaction to certain substances, such as ragweed or grass, that occurs when susceptible persons come into close proximity with the substance.

ALOPECIA. Hair loss (also, loss of feathers or wool in animals).

ALS. Amyotrophic lateral sclerosis.

ALTER. An alternate or secondary personality in a person with dissociative identity disorder. Each alter has a unique way of looking at and interacting with the world.

ALTRUISM. An unselfish willingness to help others.

ALVEOLAR. Pertaining to alveoli, which are tiny air sacs at the ends of the small air passages in the lungs.

ALZHEIMER'S DISEASE. A progressive, neurodegenerative disease characterized by loss of function and death of nerve cells in several areas of the brain, leading to loss of mental functions, including memory and learning. Alzheimer's disease is the most common cause of dementia.

AMBIVALENCE. A state of having conflicting feelings about a person or situation.

AMBULATION. Ability to walk.

AMENORRHEA. Abnormal absence of menstrual periods in a woman.

AMNESIA. Partial or complete loss of memory, or gaps in memory, that is not due to ordinary forgetfulness. Amnesia can be caused by diseases, seizures, medications, tumors, physical injuries, and emotional traumas (dissociation).

AMNESTIC. Having to do with, or related to, amnesia.

AMPHETAMINES. A group of powerful and highly addictive substances that stimulate the central nervous system. Amphetamines may be prescribed for various medical conditions but are often purchased illicitly and abused.

AMYGDALA. An almond-shaped brain structure in the limbic system that is activated in acute stress situations to trigger the emotion of fear.

AMYLOID. A waxy translucent substance, composed mostly of protein, that forms plaques (abnormal deposits) in the brain.

AMYOTROPHIC LATERAL SCLEROSIS (ALS). A degenerative disease that affects nerves of the brain and spinal cord, resulting in eventual paralysis; also known as Lou Gehrig's disease.

ANABOLIC. Causing muscle and bone growth and a shift from fat to muscle in the body.

ANALGESIC. A medication used to reduce or eliminate pain.

ANANKASTIC PERSONALITY DISORDER. The European term for obsessive-compulsive personality disorder.

ANCILLARY. Subordinate or secondary.

ANDROGENIC. Causing testosterone-like, masculinizing effects.

ANDROGYNY. The condition of having the characteristics of both a man and a woman, or not being clearly identified as male or female. Androgyny may refer to a person's physical characteristics, to psychological characteristics, or to behavior.

ANECDOTAL. Based on personal experience or reported individual observations, as opposed to controlled experiments or proven facts.

ANEMIA. A blood condition in which the level of hemoglobin or the number of red blood cells falls below normal values. Common symptoms include paleness, fatigue, and shortness of breath.

ANESTHESIA. A drug-induced loss of sensation or feeling. General anesthesia produces total unconsciousness, whereas local anesthesia produces numbness only around the site where the drug was introduced.

ANEURYSM. A symptomless bulging of a blood vessel, due to a weak arterial wall. Ruptured aneurysms can result in stroke or even death.

ANGINA. Severe pain and a feeling of constriction around the heart.

ANGIOEDEMA. Patches of swelling of the skin, subcutaneous layers, mucus membranes, and sometimes internal organs.

ANGIOGRAPHY. A procedure used to investigate the condition of blood vessels, usually via a combination of radiological imaging (x ray) and injection of a contrast medium, which highlights its path through the body. Angiography is used to check for blockage, bleeding, or any other abnormality.

ANOREXIA. Loss of appetite or unwillingness to eat. Can be caused by medications, depression, or many other factors.

ANOREXIA NERVOSA. A serious eating disorder characterized by a pathological fear of gaining weight. Anorexia nervosa causes disturbed eating behaviors and can lead to severe weight loss and malnutrition.

ANOXIA. Lack of oxygen.

ANTABUSE. Trade name for disulfiram (DSF), a chemical used to treat alcoholism by causing a severe physiological reaction to any amount of alcohol.

Glossary

ANTAGONIST. A substance whose actions counteract the effects of, or work in the opposite way from, another chemical or drug.

ANTERIOR. Situated toward the head or front.

ANTEROGRADE AMNESIA. A type of amnesia characterized by the inability to form new memories, with existing memories left unaffected.

ANTICHOLINERGIC. Related to the ability of a drug to block the neurotransmitter acetylcholine. When acetylcholine is blocked, patients often experience dry mouth and skin, increased heart rate, blurred vision, and difficulty urinating. In severe cases, blocking acetylcholine may cloud thinking and cause delirium.

ANTICHOLINERGIC TOXICITY. A poisonous effect brought about by ingestion of medications or other toxins that block acetylcholine receptors. When these receptors are blocked, the person taking the medication may find that he or she gets overheated, has dry mouth, has blurry vision, and retains urine.

ANTICHOLINERGICS. Drugs that block the action of acetylcholine, a naturally occurring chemical that is involved in communication between nerve cells.

ANTICOAGULANT. A medication (such as warfarin [Coumadin] or Heparin) that decreases the blood's clotting ability, preventing the formation of new clots. Although anticoagulants do not dissolve existing clots, they can stop them from getting larger. These drugs are commonly called blood thinners.

ANTICONVULSANT. A drug used to relieve or prevent seizures.

ANTIDEPRESSANT. Any of a group of medications given to relieve mood disorders, including anxiety disorders as well as major depression. Antidepressants include monoamine oxidase inhibitors (MAOIs), tricyclic (TCAs) and tetracyclic (TeCAs) antidepressants, selective serotonin reuptake inhibitors (SSRIs), and serotonin-norepinephrine reuptake inhibitors (SNRIs).

ANTIEMETIC. A preparation or medication given to stop vomiting.

ANTIHISTAMINE. A medication used to alleviate allergy or cold symptoms such as runny nose, itching, hives, watering eyes, or sneezing.

ANTIHYPERTENSIVE. A drug used to treat hypertension (high blood pressure).

ANTIOXIDANT. A substance that protects the body from damaging reactive oxygen molecules (free radicals). These reactive oxygen molecules can come from inside the body or from environmental pollution and are thought to play a role in the aging process and the development of degenerative disease.

ANTIOXIDANT ENZYME. An enzyme that can counteract the damaging effects of oxygen in tissues.

ANTIPSYCHOTIC. A drug used to treat serious mental disorders that cause hallucinations or delusions, such as schizophrenia or psychosis.

ANTISEPTIC. A substance that inhibits the growth of microorganisms.

ANTISOCIAL BEHAVIOR. Behavior that differs significantly from the norms of society and is considered harmful to society.

ANTISOCIAL PERSONALITY. A personality characterized by attitudes and behaviors at odds with society's customs and moral standards, including illegal acts.

ANTISOCIAL PERSONALITY DISORDER. A psychological condition in which a person appears to be unaware of, or indifferent to, the feelings of others and to normal social rules and standards.

ANTISPASMODIC. A medication or preparation given to relieve muscle or digestive cramps.

ANXIETY. A psychological state characterized by strong feelings of worry, nervousness, apprehension, or agitation; may also be accompanied by physical symptoms, including sweating, tension, and increased pulse.

ANXIETY DISORDERS. A group of disorders characterized by anxiety, including generalized anxiety disorder, panic disorder, and post-traumatic stress disorder (PTSD).

ANXIOLYTIC. Any of a group of medications prescribed to relieve anxiety. Also called tranquilizers, anxiolytics include benzodiazepines, some of the selective serotonin reuptake inhibitors (SSRIs), barbiturates, and buspirone.

APATHY. Lack of feelings or emotions.

APHASIA. Loss of previously acquired ability to speak or understand written or spoken language.

APHONIA. Inability to speak caused by a functional disturbance of the voice box or vocal cords.

APNEA. A brief suspension or interruption of breathing.

APOLIPOPROTEIN E (APOE). A protein that transports cholesterol throughout the body. One form of this protein, APOE e4, is associated with a 60% risk of late-onset Alzheimer's disease.

APOTEMNOPHILIA. A word coined by John Money in 1977 to describe the condition now known as body integrity identity disorder (BIID).

APPERCEPTION. The process of understanding something in terms of previous experience.

APRAXIA. An inability to perform purposeful movements that is not caused by paralysis or loss of feeling.

ARITHMETIC. The branch of mathematics involving problems of addition, subtraction, multiplication, and division.

ARRHYTHMIA. Any disturbance in the normal rhythm of the heartbeat.

ARSON. The deliberate setting of fires for criminal purposes, usually to collect insurance money or to cover up evidence of another crime. It is distinguished from pyromania by its connection with planning and forethought rather than failure of impulse control.

ART THERAPY. The use of art to assess or treat an individual's development, abilities, personality, interests, concerns, or conflicts.

ARTERIOSCLEROSIS. A chronic condition characterized by a thickening and hardening of the arteries and the build-up of plaque on the arterial walls. Arteriosclerosis can slow or impair blood circulation.

ASANA. A position or stance in yoga.

ASPERGER SYNDROME. A developmental disorder that is similar to mild autism. It is characterized by impaired social interaction, repetitive patterns of behavior, and restricted interests, but with normal language and cognitive development and often above-average abilities in a narrow field.

ASSERTIVE. Confidently self-assured; able to express oneself constructively and directly.

ASSERTIVE COMMUNITY TREATMENT (ACT). A service-delivery model for providing comprehensive, highly individualized, and locally based treatment directly to patients with serious and persistent mental illness.

ASSISTED SUICIDE. A form of suicide in which individuals voluntarily bring about their own death with the help of another person, usually a physician, relative, or friend. Assisted suicide is sometimes called physician-assisted death (PAD).

ASTRINGENT. A substance or compound that causes contraction or constriction of soft tissue.

ASYLUM. An older term for psychiatric hospitals; it is rarely used except in historical studies of psychiatric treatment.

ATAQUE DE NERVIOS. A culture-specific anxiety syndrome found among some Latin American groups in the United States and in Latin America. It resembles panic disorder in some respects but also includes dissociative symptoms and frequently occurs in response to stressful events.

ATRIAL FIBRILLATION. A condition in which the upper chambers (atria) of the heart contract rapidly instead of pumping in an organized way. The irregular contractions do not allow the chambers to empty of blood, which can allow blood clots to form and is associated with a higher risk of stroke.

ATROPHY. Shrinkage or deterioration.

ATTACHMENT. The bond developed between an infant and his or her primary caregiver within the first 12 to 18 months of life.

ATTACHMENT DISORDER. A general term used to describe emotional and behavioral problems in children or adults that result from a failure to form healthy attachments in early childhood to parents or other primary caregivers.

ATTENTION DEFICIT HYPERACTIVITY DISORDER (ADHD). A condition characterized by lack of concentration, impulsive or inappropriate behavior (relative to age level), and hyperactivity.

ATYPICAL ANTIPSYCHOTICS. A group of medications for the treatment of psychotic symptoms that were introduced in the 1990s. The atypical antipsychotics include clozapine, risperidone, quetiapine, ziprasidone, and olanzapine. They are sometimes called serotonin dopamine antagonists, or SDAs.

AUDIOLOGIST. A healthcare professional with special training in testing people for hearing loss or other hearing disorders.

AUDITORY. Pertaining to the sense of hearing.

AURA. An energy field that is thought to emanate from the human body and to be visible to people with special psychic or spiritual powers.

AURICULAR ACUPUNCTURE. Acupuncture using only points found on the ears.

AUTISM. A severe developmental disorder that usually begins before three years of age and affects a child's social as well as intellectual development; often includes impairment of verbal and nonverbal communication skills.

AUTISM SPECTRUM DISORDER (ASD). One of a group of disorders with similar symptoms, including an impaired ability to communicate and form normal social relationships, with symptoms ranging in severity depending on the condition. ASDs include (in order of severity) Asperger syndrome, autism, pervasive developmental disorder not otherwise specified, and childhood disintegrative disorder.

AUTISTIC PSYCHOPATHY. The original name for Asperger syndrome; it is still used occasionally as a synonym for the disorder.

AUTOGENIC TRAINING. A relaxation technique with parallels to hypnosis and meditation. It consists of six exercises that use visualization and verbal cues to relax the body.

AUTOIMMUNE DISEASE. A condition in which the immune system's antibodies or T cells attack the body's own molecules, cells, or tissues as if they were foreign invaders.

AUTOMATIC BEHAVIOR. Activities that are carried out while a person is partially awake but is not conscious of his or her behavior and cannot recall the event afterward; occurs with some sleep disorders.

AUTOMATIC THOUGHTS. Thoughts that automatically come to mind when a particular situation occurs. Cognitive-behavioral therapy seeks to challenge automatic thoughts.

AUTONOMIC NERVOUS SYSTEM. The part of the nervous system that governs the heart, involuntary muscles, and glands.

AUTOSOMAL DOMINANT. A pattern of genetic inheritance where only one abnormal gene is needed to display the trait or disease.

AVERSANT. A chemical or medication with unpleasant effects that is used to deter a person from engaging in a specific activity; used in aversion therapy.

AVERSION. A strong feeling of unpleasantness, dislike, or disgust toward a certain object or activity.

AVERSION THERAPY. An approach to treatment in which an unpleasant or painful stimulus is linked to a behavior in order to condition the patient to dislike or avoid the behavior.

AXON. The long extension of a nerve fiber that generally conducts impulses away from the body of the nerve cell.

AYURVEDIC MEDICINE. The traditional medical system of India. Ayurvedic treatments include specialized diets, exercises, herbal treatments, meditation, massage, and breathing techniques.

B

BACK-UP REINFORCER. In a token economy system, a desirable item, privilege, or activity that is purchased with tokens and that serves as a delayed reward and as motivation to display a target (desired) behavior (which is how tokens are earned).

BACTERICIDAL. An agent that destroys bacteria (e.g., *Staphylococci aureus, Streptococci pneumoniae, Escherichia coli, Salmonella enteritidis*).

BARBITURATES. A class of medications that cause sedation and drowsiness. They may be prescribed legally but are also used as drugs of abuse.

BASAL GANGLIA. Masses of gray matter located in the cerebral hemispheres of the brain that control movement as well as some aspects of emotion and cognition.

BASELINE DATA. Information regarding the frequency and severity of behavior, gathered before treatment begins.

BATTERY. A number of separate items (such as tests) used together. In psychology, refers to a group or series of tests given with a common purpose, such as personality assessment or measurement of intelligence.

BEHAVIOR DISORDERS. Disorders characterized by disruptive behaviors, such as conduct disorder, oppositional defiant disorder, and attention deficit hyperactivity disorder.

BEHAVIOR MODIFICATION. An approach to therapy based on the principles of operant conditioning. Behavior modification seeks to replace undesirable behaviors with preferable behaviors through the use of positive or negative reinforcement.

BEHAVIORAL. Related to the way a person acts.

BEHAVIORAL CONTRACT. A behavioral contract is a written agreement that defines the behaviors to be performed and the consequences of the specified behaviors.

BEHAVIORAL COUPLES THERAPY (BCT). Traditional behavioral couples therapy (TBCT); relationship therapy based on behavioral psychology models.

BEHAVIORAL HEALTH. A broad term for any condition related in any way to mental health.

BEHAVIORAL INHIBITION. A set of behaviors that appear in early infancy and that are displayed when the child is confronted with a new situation or unfamiliar people. These behaviors include agitated movement, crying, and general irritability, followed by withdrawing from the situation and seeking comfort from a familiar person. Such behaviors are associated with an increased risk of social phobia and panic disorder in later life. Behavioral inhibition in children appears to be linked to anxiety and mood disorders in their parents.

BEHAVIORAL MEDICINE. The branch of medicine that studies mind-body relationships.

BEHAVIORAL THERAPY. An approach to treatment that focuses on learning how to replace an undesirable behavior with a desired behavior.

(LA) BELLE INDIFFÉRENCE. A psychiatric symptom sometimes found in patients with conversion disorder, in which the patient shows a surprising lack of concern about the nature or implications of his or her physical symptom(s).

BEM SEX ROLE INVENTORY (BSRI). A 60-item self-administered test that researchers often use to measure psychological androgyny in test subjects. It was devised in 1971 by Sandra Bem.

BENIGN PROSTATE HYPERTROPHY. Enlargement of the prostate gland.

BENZENE. A colorless toxic liquid with a chemical formula of C_6H_6, where C stands for carbon and H for hydrogen.

BENZODIAZEPINES. A group of central nervous system depressants used to relieve anxiety or to induce sleep.

BEREAVEMENT. The emotional experience of loss after the death of a friend or relative.

BETA BLOCKERS. Drugs that block beta-adrenergic receptors in the central nervous system, reducing the action of adrenaline, the body's natural fight-or-flight chemical. When these sites are blocked, heart rate, blood pressure, and anxiety levels decrease.

BETA-AMYLOID PLAQUES. Senile plaques; structures in the brain, composed of dead or dying nerve cells and cell debris surrounding deposits of beta-amyloid protein, that are diagnostic of Alzheimer's disease. Beta-amyloid forms when amyloid precursor protein (APP) is not broken down properly.

BEZOAR. A hard ball of hair or vegetable fiber that may develop in the stomach of humans as the result of ingesting nonfood items.

BIAS. A point of view, preference, or judgment.

BIBLIOTHERAPY. The use of books (usually self-help or problem-solving) to improve understanding of personal problems and/or to heal painful feelings.

BILE. A substance produced by the liver and concentrated and stored in the gallbladder. Bile contains a number of different substances, including bile salts, cholesterol, and bilirubin.

BINGE DRINKING. Consumption of multiple alcoholic beverages in a short time frame, with the goal of intoxication.

BINGEING. An excessive amount of food consumed in a short period of time. Usually, while a person binge eats, he or she feels disconnected from reality and feels unable to stop. The bingeing may temporarily relieve depression or anxiety, but after the binge, the person usually feels guilty and depressed.

BIOFEEDBACK. A technique in which patients learn to control certain body functions, such as temperature or pulse rate, in response to external stimuli, such as stress.

BIOFIELD THERAPIES. A subgroup of energy therapies that make use of energy fields (biofields) thought to exist within or emanate from the human body. Biofield therapies include such approaches as Reiki, therapeutic touch, qigong, and polarity balancing.

BIOLOGICAL MARKER. An indicator or characteristic trait of a disease that facilitates differential diagnosis (the process of distinguishing one disorder from other similar disorders).

BIOLOGICAL PSYCHIATRY. An approach to psychiatry that attributes mental disorders to biochemical or other biological malfunctions of the central nervous system, rather than factors such as environment or experience; it tends to favor drug treatments for mental disorders rather than psychotherapies.

BIOPSY. The surgical removal and microscopic examination of living tissue for diagnostic purposes.

BIOPSYCHOSOCIAL HISTORY. A history of experiences and other factors that influence behavior, including medical, educational, occupational, and interpersonal histories, as well as any alcohol or drug use or criminal activity.

BIOPSYCHOSOCIAL MODEL. An approach to human health that holds that a combination of biological, psychological, and social factors should be taken into account when evaluating a patient, rather than physical factors alone.

BIOSOCIAL. A psychological model that asserts that both social and biological factors contribute toward the development of personality.

BIPOLAR DEPRESSION. Depression with the presence of at least one manic episode.

BIPOLAR DISORDER. A mood disorder marked by alternating episodes of extremely low mood (depression) and exuberant highs (mania); formerly known as manic-depressive disorder.

BLADDER. A muscular sac in the lower abdomen that holds urine until it is discharged from the body.

BLENDED FAMILY. A family formed by the remarriage of a divorced or widowed parent. It includes a new husband and wife, plus some or all of their children from previous marriages.

BLOGGING. Creating and maintaining an online personal blog, in most cases allowing readers to add comments. The term comes from the word weblog, or online diary.

BLOOD ALCOHOL CONCENTRATION OR CONTENT (BAC). A measure of the amount of alcohol in the body; in most states, legal alcohol intoxication is defined as a BAC of at least 0.08 grams per deciliter of blood.

BLOOD-BRAIN BARRIER. A specialized, semi-permeable layer of cells around the blood vessels in the brain that controls which substances can leave the circulatory system and enter the brain.

BLUNTED AFFECT. A lack of display of emotion or feelings, including monotone voice and expressionless face.

BODY DYSMORPHIC DISORDER. A psychiatric disorder marked by preoccupation with an imagined physical defect.

BODY IMAGE. A person's perceptions of, beliefs about, and emotional attitudes toward his or her body.

BODY MASS INDEX, OR BMI. A measure of body fat, calculated as weight in kilograms over the square of height in meters.

BODYWORK. Any technique involving hands-on massage or manipulation of the body.

BORDERLINE PERSONALITY DISORDER. A severe and usually lifelong mental disorder characterized by violent mood swings and severe difficulties in sustaining interpersonal relationships.

BOTULINUM TOXIN. Any of a group of potent bacterial toxins or poisons produced by different strains of the bacterium *Clostridium botulinum*. The toxins cause muscle paralysis and force the relaxation of a muscle in spasm.

BRADYCARDIA. Slow heartbeat, defined as a rate of less than 60 beats per minute.

BRAIN STEM. The part of the brain consisting of the midbrain, pons, and medulla oblongata. The brain stem connects the forebrain and cerebrum to the spinal cord and regulates heart and respiratory function, the sleep cycle, and the nerves that convey sensory information to the face and neck.

BRAIN-DERIVED NEUROTROPHIC FACTOR (BDNF). A brain protein that helps maintain nerves and promotes the growth of new nerve cells (neurons).

BRIEF PSYCHOTIC DISORDER. An acute, short-term episode of psychosis lasting no longer than one month. This disorder may occur in response to a stressful event.

BRONCHIOLES. Tiny tubes in the lungs.

BRUXISM. Habitual, often unconscious, grinding of the teeth.

BULIMIA NERVOSA. A serious eating disorder characterized by compulsive overeating followed by purging, usually by way of self-induced vomiting or the use of laxatives or diuretics.

BULLYCIDE. Suicide attributed to the victim's having been bullied.

BUPRENORPHINE. A medication that blocks some of the withdrawal effects during heroin detoxification.

BURNOUT. An emotional condition marked by fatigue, loss of interest in a job or activity, or frustration. Burnout is usually regarded as the result of prolonged stress.

C

CACHEXIA. Physical wasting and malnutrition, usually from chronic disease.

CAGE. A four-question assessment used to detect alcoholism.

CAPD. Central auditory processing disorder; the inability to differentiate, recognize, or understand sounds, though hearing and intelligence are normal.

CARCINOID SYNDROME. The pattern of symptoms (often including asthma and diarrhea) associated with carcinoid tumors of the digestive tract or lungs.

CARMINATIVE. A medication or preparation that prevents the formation of intestinal gas or allows it to be expelled.

CARRIER OIL. An oil used to dilute essential oils for use in massage and other skin care applications.

CASE MANAGER. A professional who designs and monitors implementation of comprehensive care plans for individuals seeking mental health or social services.

CASTRATION. Desexing a person or animal by surgical removal of the testes (in males) or ovaries (in females).

CATAPLEXY. Sudden episode of muscle weakness (often causing a person to fall), usually triggered by intense emotion. It is regarded as a diagnostic sign of narcolepsy.

CATATONIA. Psychomotor disturbances that can include stupor, rigidity, muteness, or purposeless and bizarre movements.

CATATONIC SCHIZOPHRENIA. Schizophrenia accompanied by catatonic symptoms.

CATECHOLAMINES. A set of neurotransmitters released by the hypothalamic-pituitary-adrenal system in the brain in response to acute stress. The catecholamines include dopamine, norepinephrine, and epinephrine.

CATHA EDULIS. Leaves of an East African bush that can be chewed for their stimulant effect.

CATHARSIS. A powerful emotional release, usually preceded by emotional tension and followed by a feeling of great relief.

CATHETERIZATION. Placing a tube in the bladder so that it can be emptied of urine.

CELL. The smallest living unit of the body, which groups together with other cells to form tissues and help the body perform specific functions.

CENTRAL NERVOUS SYSTEM. The part of the nervous system that includes the brain and spinal cord.

CENTRAL NERVOUS SYSTEM DEPRESSANT. Any drug that lowers the level of stimulation or excitement in the central nervous system.

CENTRAL NERVOUS SYSTEM STIMULANT. Any drug that raises the level of activity in the central nervous system.

CEREBELLUM. The part of the brain between the brain stem and back of the cerebrum, consisting of two lateral lobes and a median lobe and involved especially in muscle coordination and maintenance of bodily equilibrium.

CEREBRAL CORTEX. The convoluted gray matter on the surface of the cerebrum that coordinates motor and sensory information and cognitive function.

CEREBRAL PALSY. A movement disorder caused by a permanent brain defect or injury present at birth or shortly after. It is frequently associated with premature birth. Cerebral palsy is not progressive, meaning that it does not worsen with age.

CEREBROSPINAL FLUID (CSF). The fluid that circulates through the central nervous system to maintain uniform pressure on the brain and spinal cord.

CEREBRUM. The largest area of the brain, consisting of the two cerebral hemispheres and connecting structures. The cerebrum is responsible for conscious mental processes, including movement and language.

CERULOPLASMIN. A protein circulating in the bloodstream that binds with and transports copper.

CERVIX. The neck or narrow lower end of a woman's uterus.

CHAKRA. One of the seven major energy centers in the body, according to traditional Indian yoga.

CHARACTER. An individual's set of emotional, cognitive, and behavioral patterns learned and accumulated over time.

CHARLES BONNET SYNDROME (CBS). A disorder characterized by visual hallucinations following a sudden age-related deterioration in a person's vision, most commonly glaucoma or macular degeneration. CBS is named for a Swiss doctor who first described it in his visually impaired grandfather in 1780.

CHELATION THERAPY. A method of treating heavy metal poisoning by giving medications that remove heavy metals from the bloodstream. The medications that are used are called chelating agents.

CHI. The traditional Chinese term for vital energy or the life force. The word is also spelled "ki" or "qi" in English translations of Japanese and Chinese medical books.

CHOLESTEROL. A steroid alcohol in cells and body fluids that serves as a precursor for hormones and other steroids.

CHOLINESTERASE INHIBITORS. Drugs that may slow the progression of Alzheimer's disease by inhibiting the enzymes that break down the neurotransmitter acetylcholine.

CHOREATHETOID MOVEMENTS. Repetitive dance-like movements that do not have any type of rhythm.

CHORIONIC VILLUS SAMPLING (CVS). A prenatal test that involves taking a small sample of the placenta, the organ that forms inside the uterus during pregnancy and supplies the baby with oxygen and nutrients carried by the blood. The placental tissue is then tested for chromosome abnormalities or other genetic diseases.

CHROMOSOME. A microscopic thread-like structure found within each cell of the body that consists of proteins and DNA. Humans have 46 chromosomes arranged into 23 pairs. Changes in either the total number of chromosomes or their shape and size (structure) may lead to physical or mental abnormalities.

CHRONIC. A disease or condition that progresses slowly but persists or reoccurs over time.

CHRONOTHERAPY. A sleep disorder treatment that involves adjusting sleep and wake times to help reset the patient's biological clock.

CIMETIDINE. A drug that decreases the amount of acid in the stomach, used to treat conditions such as ulcers, gastroesophageal reflux disease, and heartburn.

CIRCADIAN RHYTHM. Any physiological, mental, or behavioral activity that recurs in 24-hour cycles. The sleep-wake cycle is an example of a circadian rhythm.

CIRRHOSIS. A chronic degenerative disease of the liver, in which normal cells are replaced by fibrous tissue. Cirrhosis is a major risk factor for the later development of liver cancer.

CIVIL COMMITMENT. The involuntary confinement of persons who cannot care for themselves, as determined by a court of law.

CLASSICAL CONDITIONING. In psychology, a process in which a previously neutral stimulus eventually produces a specific response by being paired repeatedly with another stimulus that produces that response. The best-known example of classical conditioning is Pavlov's dogs, who were conditioned to salivate when they heard a bell ring (the previously neutral stimulus) because the sound had been paired repeatedly with their feeding time.

CLEFT PALATE. A failure of the two sides of the palate within the mouth to meet during fetal development.

CLINICAL. Pertaining to or founded on observation and treatment of participants, as distinguished from theoretical or basic science.

CLINICAL TRIAL. A controlled scientific experiment designed to investigate the effectiveness of a drug or treatment in curing or lessening the symptoms of a disease or disorder.

CLITORIS. The most sensitive area of the external genitals. Stimulation of the clitoris causes most women to reach orgasm.

CLONUS. Muscular spasm involving repeated, rhythmic contractions. Clonus may be spontaneous or inducible and may involve major body muscles or eye muscles.

CLOSED-HEAD INJURY. A head injury in which the skull is not cracked or fractured.

CLOZAPINE. An atypical antipsychotic medication used to treat schizophrenia. Clozapine is often given to patients who are not seeing improvement with other medications or who are developing adverse side effects (such as tardive dyskinesia).

CLUSTER SUICIDE. Refers to the phenomenon of additional suicides being attempted or completed after one suicide has occurred within a small community, such as a high school.

COGNITION. Conscious intellectual activity, including thinking, imagining, reasoning, remembering, and learning.

COGNITIVE. Associated with conscious intellectual activity.

COGNITIVE DISSONANCE. A conflict of anxiety resulting from the difference in personal beliefs and actions.

COGNITIVE PROCESSING THERAPY. A term that is sometimes used for the cognitive restructuring aspect of cognitive-behavioral therapy, especially in treatment for post-traumatic stress disorder (PTSD).

COGNITIVE RESTRUCTURING. An approach to psychotherapy that focuses on helping clients examine distorted patterns of perceiving and thinking in order to change their emotional responses to people and situations.

COGNITIVE STYLE. The way in which individuals process and use information to perform cognitive tasks, such as reasoning, learning, thinking, understanding, making decisions, and using memory.

COGNITIVE THERAPY. A form of psychotherapy that focuses on changing clients' emotional reactions by correcting distorted patterns of thinking and perception.

COGNITIVE-BEHAVIORAL THERAPY (CBT). A type of psychotherapy in which people learn to recognize and change negative and self-defeating patterns of thinking and behavior.

COITUS. Sexual intercourse.

COLD TURKEY. A slang term for suddenly and completely stopping the use of a substance or engagement in an activity.

COLIC. Excessive crying and irritability in babies, which may be caused by numerous problems such as stomach discomfort.

COMA. A state of prolonged unconsciousness.

COMBAT STRESS REACTION. A general term for mental health symptoms experienced after combat, such as depression, fatigue, dissociative symptoms, lack of concentration, or irritability. It is not identical to post-traumatic stress disorder (PTSD) but may be a precursor of it.

COMMAND HALLUCINATION. A type of auditory hallucination in which a person hears voices ordering him or her to perform a specific act.

COMMUNITY MENTAL HEALTH CENTERS. Organizations that manage and deliver a comprehensive range of mental health services, education, and outreach to residents of a given community.

COMMUNITY MENTAL HEALTH CENTERS ACT OF 1963. Federal legislation that provides grants for the operation of community mental health centers and related services.

COMMUNITY MENTAL HEALTH CLINIC (CMHC). A community-based provider of mental health services.

COMMUNITY-BASED. Used to describe any organization or initiative stemming from non-government, local, and independent sources.

COMORBID PSYCHOPATHOLOGY. The presence of other mental disorders in a patient together with a primary disorder that is the immediate focus of therapy.

COMORBIDITY. The presence of one or more diseases or disorders in a patient in addition to a primary disease or disorder.

COMPLIANCE. Adherence to a treatment plan or medication regimen.

COMPLICATED GRIEF. An abnormal response to bereavement that includes unrelieved yearning for the deceased, the total loss of positive beliefs or worldview, and general dysfunction.

COMPULSION. A strong impulse to perform an act, particularly one that is irrational or contrary to a person's disposition.

COMPULSIVE GAMBLING DISORDER. An impulse control disorder in which an individual cannot resist gambling despite repeated losses.

COMPUTED TOMOGRAPHY. An imaging technique in which cross-sectional x rays of the body are compiled to create a three-dimensional image of the body's internal structures; also referred to as a CT or CAT scan.

CONCHA. The hollow shell-shaped portion of the external ear nearest the ear canal.

CONCUSSION. Injury to the brain causing a sudden but temporary impairment of brain function.

CONDUCT DISORDER. A behavioral and emotional disorder of childhood and adolescence in which children display physical aggression and infringe on or violate the rights of others. Youths diagnosed with conduct disorder may set fires, exhibit cruelty toward animals or other children, sexually assault others, or lie and steal for personal gain.

CONFABULATION. Using false or imagined details to explain physical phenomena or to fill in memory gaps.

CONFLICT RESOLUTION. Various methods used by psychologists and other such professionals to eliminate sources of conflict in clients.

CONGENITAL. Present at birth.

CONSERVATOR. Legal guardian.

CONTACT DERMATITIS. Skin irritation as a result of contact with a foreign substance.

CONTRACEPTIVE. Birth control; an object or medication intended to prevent conception and pregnancy.

CONTRECOUP. An injury to the brain opposite the point of direct impact.

CONTROL GROUP. A group in a research study that does not receive the treatment being tested. For example, in an experiment testing the effectiveness of a new drug, the control group might receive the current drug of choice while the experimental group receives the new drug under investigation.

CONTUSION. A focal area of swollen and bleeding brain tissue.

CONVERSION. In psychiatry, a process in which a repressed feeling, impulse, thought, or memory emerges in the form of a bodily symptom.

CONVERSION DISORDER. A type of somatoform disorder in which unconscious psychological conflicts or other factors manifest as physical symptoms.

CONVULSION. An uncontrollable motion of a limb of the body or the body itself.

CO-OCCURRING DISORDERS. Sets of mental illnesses—usually substance abuse and at least one other disorder—that appear together in a single individual.

Also referred to as dual diagnosis or co-morbidity disorders.

COPING. In psychology, a term that refers to how a person responds to stress.

COPROLALIA. A vocal tic characterized by the uttering of obscene, hostile, or inappropriate words.

COPROPRAXIA. A motor tic characterized by the display of unacceptable or obscene gestures.

COROLLARY DISCHARGE. A mechanism in the brain that allows persons to distinguish between self-generated and external stimuli or perceptions.

CORONARY OCCLUSION. Blockage of the arteries supplying the blood to the heart.

CORPORA CAVERNOSA. The pair of columns of erectile tissue on either side of the penis that, together with the corpus spongiosum, produce an erection when filled with blood.

CORPUS CALLOSUM (PLURAL, CORPORA CALLOSA). A thick bundle of nerve fibers lying deep in the brain that connects the two cerebral hemispheres and coordinates their functions.

CORPUS SPONGIOSUM. The column of erectile tissue in the penis that contains the urethra.

CORTEX. The outer layer of the cerebrum in the brain, where sensation and perception are processed and integrated into thoughts, memories, and abilities and where actions are planned and initiated.

CORTICAL. Regarding the cortex, or the outer layer of the brain.

CORTICOSTEROID. A steroid hormone produced by the adrenal gland and involved in metabolism and immune response.

CORTICOSTEROID DRUG. A medication that acts like a type of hormone (cortisol) produced by the adrenal gland of the body. Corticosteroid drugs (also just called steroids) help treat inflammation, infection, or trauma to the body.

CORTISOL. A steroid hormone produced by the adrenal gland that is released in response to stress. Cortisol suppresses the immune system and slows down bone formation.

COVERT. Concealed, hidden, or disguised.

COVERT SENSITIZATION OR CONDITIONING. A form of aversion therapy in which a patient imagines or views images of an undesirable behavior, followed by imagining or viewing images of an aversive (negative) consequence.

C-REACTIVE PROTEIN (CRP). A protein whose levels in blood rise rapidly in response to inflammation. It can be measured to test for the presence of inflammation and response to treatment; it is also used as a rough indication of a patient's risk of heart disease.

CREATINE. A nitrogen-containing substance found in muscle.

CREUTZFELDT-JAKOB DISEASE. A degenerative disease of the central nervous system caused by a prion, or "slow virus."

CRIMINAL JUSTICE SYSTEM. The system instituted by federal, state, and local governments to control and deter crime and to punish persons who violate laws.

CRIMINALIZATION. The de facto societal trend over several decades of sending people with mental disabilities to jails and prisons instead of to treatment institutions.

CRITICAL INCIDENT. An event that is stressful enough to overwhelm the coping skills of a person or group; also known as a "crisis event."

CROSS-DRESSING. Wearing clothes and other accessories associated with the opposite sex.

CUE. Any behavior or event in a person's environment that stimulates a particular response. For example, the smell of liquor may be a cue for some people to pour themselves a drink.

CYBERBULLYING. The use of electronic devices, including computers, cell phones, and other mobile devices, to bully by means of hurtful messages, spreading rumors, or misusing social media.

CYCLIC AMP. A small molecule of adenosine monophosphate (AMP) that activates enzymes and increases the effects of hormones and other neurotransmitters.

CYCLOTHYMIA. A milder form of bipolar disorder characterized by alternating hypomania and less severe depressive episodes.

CYCLOTHYMIC DISORDER. A mood disorder in which hypomanic episodes and depressive episodes both occur over the course of at least two years, with symptom-free periods lasting no more than two months.

CYTOCHROME P450 (CYP450). Enzymes present in the liver that metabolize drugs.

CYTOGENETICS. The branch of genetics concerned with the structure and function of the individual cell, particularly its chromosome content.

CYTOKINE. Any of a group of small protein molecules (including interferon, interleukin, and tumor necrosis factor) secreted by certain cells in the immune system that modulate specific functions associated with the immune response.

D

D1, D2, ETC. Dopamine receptor proteins.

DAWN SIMULATION. A form of light therapy in which the patient is exposed while asleep to gradually brightening white light over a period of an hour and a half.

DE FACTO. Acting as; fulfilling a role, even though the occupation of the role is not legally recognized.

DECISION TREE. A decision support model used in medical and psychiatric diagnosis that consists of a tree-like chart or diagram listing various symptoms, tentative diagnoses, and diagnostic decisions and their possible consequences.

DECOCTION. An herbal extract produced by mixing an herb with cold water, bringing the mixture to a boil, and letting it simmer to evaporate the excess water. Decoction is usually chosen over infusion when the botanical or herb in question is a root, seed, or berry.

DECONDITIONING. Loss of physical strength or stamina resulting from bed rest or lack of exercise.

DECREASED PENETRANCE. Individuals who inherit a changed disease gene but do not develop symptoms.

DEFENSE. An unconscious mental process that protects the conscious mind from unacceptable or painful thoughts, impulses, or desires. Examples of defenses include denial, rationalization, projection, and repression.

DEFENSE MECHANISMS. Indirect strategies used to reduce anxiety rather than directly facing the issues causing the anxiety.

DEINSTITUTIONALIZATION. A movement to close public mental institutions and transfer patients to community treatment programs, with the goal of better serving people with mental disabilities. The movement shifted the responsibility for care from large (often governmental) agencies to families and community organizations.

DELIRIUM. A disturbance of consciousness marked by confusion, difficulty paying attention, delusions, hallucinations, or restlessness. It can be distinguished from other conditions by its relatively sudden onset and variation in the severity of the symptoms.

DELUSION. A false belief that persists despite evidence to the contrary.

DELUSIONAL DISORDER. A mental illness characterized by the presence of nonbizarre delusions (situations that could occur in real life) in the absence of other mood or psychotic symptoms.

DELUSIONAL DISORDER OF THE PERSECUTORY TYPE. A psychotic disorder characterized by a patient's belief that others are conspiring against him or her.

DEMENTIA. A disease characterized by the progressive deterioration of intellectual functions, such as memory, reasoning, and language. Other symptoms include changes in personality, deterioration in personal grooming, and disorientation. Alzheimer's disease is a type of dementia.

DEMENTIA PUGILISTICA. A delayed-onset form of dementia caused by repeated head injury; often occurs in boxers.

DENDRITES. Fibers of a brain cell that receive signals from other brain cells.

DENIAL. A psychological defense mechanism that reduces anxiety by excluding recognition of a problem or stressor from the conscious mind.

DEOXYRIBONUCLEIC ACID (DNA). The genetic material in cells that holds the inherited instructions for growth, development, and cellular functioning.

DEPENDENCE. A state in which a person requires a steady concentration of a particular substance in order to avoid withdrawal symptoms.

DEPENDENT PERSONALITY DISORDER. Personality disorder characterized by a constant, unhealthy need to be liked and appreciated by others at all costs.

DEPERSONALIZATION. A dissociative symptom in which a patient feels that his or her body is unreal, is changing, or is dissolving.

DEPERSONALIZATION NEUROSIS. Another name for depersonalization disorder.

DEPRESSANT. Any psychoactive substance that lowers the function or activity level of a specific part of the body or brain. Depressants are sometimes referred to as "downers." These include anxiolytics, sedatives, antipsychotics, opioids, and anesthetics as well as such nonprescription substances as alcohol.

DEPRESSED SKULL FRACTURE. A fracture in which fragment pieces of broken skull press into brain tissue.

DEPRESSION. A mental state characterized by excessive sadness and loss of interest in life; other symptoms may include altered sleep or eating patterns, loss of concentration, agitation, lack of energy, and, in severe cases, attempts at self-harm or suicide.

DEREALIZATION. A dissociative symptom in which a person's external environment is perceived as unreal or dreamlike.

DERMATITIS ARTEFACTA. A disorder characterized by the deliberate and conscious self-infliction of skin lesions.

DERMATOLOGIST. A physician who specializes in the diagnosis and treatment of disorders of the skin, scalp, hair, and nails.

DESENSITIZATION. The reduction or elimination of an overly intense reaction to a cue, achieved by controlled repeated exposures to the cue.

DESIGNER AMPHETAMINES. Substances close in chemical structure to classic amphetamines that provide both stimulant and hallucinogenic effects.

DETOXIFICATION. A process in which toxins (including drugs and alcohol) are eliminated from the body. In cases of substance abuse, the symptoms of withdrawal may be treated concurrently.

DEVELOPMENTAL. Referring to human development.

DEVELOPMENTAL DAMAGE. A term that some therapists prefer to personality disorder, on the grounds that it is more respectful of the patient's capacity for growth and change.

DEVELOPMENTAL DISABILITIES. Disabilities that are present from birth and that delay or prevent normal development, such as intellectual disability or autism.

DEVOTEE. With regard to body integrity identity disorder, someone who is sexually attracted to amputees or disabled persons.

DIABETES. Also called diabetes mellitus, a disease characterized by an inability to process sugars in the diet, due to a decrease in or total absence of insulin production. Type 1 diabetes (juvenile diabetes) involves failure of the body to produce insulin, while type 2 diabetes (adult-onset diabetes) involves failure of the body's cells to use insulin properly.

DIABETIC NEUROPATHY. Condition existing in people with diabetes in which their nerve endings, particularly in the legs and feet, become less sensitive. Minor injuries, such as blisters or callouses, are not felt and can thus become infected and develop into more serious problems.

DIAGNOSTIC AND STATISTICAL MANUAL OF MENTAL DISORDERS (DSM). The handbook published by the American Psychiatric Association that mental health professionals use to diagnose mental disorders.

DIALECTICAL BEHAVIOR THERAPY (DBT). A type of cognitive-behavioral therapy designed specifically to treat borderline personality disorder.

DIATHESIS. The medical term for predisposition.

DIENCEPHALON. The "between brain" or "interbrain," located beneath the cerebral hemispheres and consisting of the thalamus and hypothalamus.

DIFFERENTIAL DIAGNOSIS. Comparing and contrasting the signs, symptoms, and laboratory findings of two or more diseases to determine which is causing a patient's condition.

DIFFERENTIATION. The ability to retain one's identity within a family system while maintaining emotional connections with the other members.

DIFFUSE AXONAL INJURY (DAI). Traumatic damage to individual nerve cells resulting in breakdown of overall communication between nerve cells in the brain; also called a shear injury.

DIFFUSION TENSOR IMAGING (DTI). A refinement of magnetic resonance imaging (MRI) that allows doctors to measure the flow of water and track the pathways of white matter in the brain. DTI can detect abnormalities in the brain that do not show up on standard MRI scans.

DIGRAPH. A pair of letters that represents a single speech sound. In English, the *th* in "thumb" and the *ei* in "vein" are examples of digraphs.

DIMINISHED CAPACITY. The inability of a person to understand the nature of his or her behavior when committing a criminal act.

DIPLOPIA. A disorder of vision in which a single object appears double (double vision).

DISENFRANCHISED GRIEF. Grief that is not openly expressed because the bereavement cannot be publicly acknowledged.

DISFLUENCY. Any difficulty in fluent speech, including stuttering.

DISINGENUOUS. Insincere, deceitful, dishonest.

DISORDER OF SEX DEVELOPMENT (DSD). The term that is increasingly preferred for an atypical pattern of chromosomal, genital, or gonadal development; also known as disorder of sex differentiation.

DISRUPTIVE BEHAVIOR DISORDER. A broader term that includes two similar disorders: oppositional defiant disorder and conduct disorder.

DISSOCIATION. A psychological mechanism in which the mind splits off certain aspects of an event (usually traumatic) from conscious awareness. Dissociation can affect the person's memory, sense of reality, and sense of identity.

DISSOCIATIVE AMNESIA. A dissociative disorder characterized by loss of memory for a period or periods of time in a person's life; may occur as a result of a traumatic event.

DISSOCIATIVE DISORDERS. Medical disorders characterized by disruptions or breakdowns of awareness, identity, memory, and/or perception.

DISSOCIATIVE IDENTITY DISORDER (DID). Also called multiple personality disorder, a mental condition in which a person displays multiple distinct personalities (alter egos).

DISULFIRAM. A medication that helps reinforce abstinence in people who are recovering from alcohol abuse. If a person taking disulfiram (Antabuse) drinks even a small amount of alcohol, he or she experiences facial flushing, headache, nausea, and vomiting.

DIURETIC. A substance that removes water from the body by increasing urine production.

DNA (DEOXYRIBONUCLEIC ACID). The hereditary material that makes up genes and influences the development and functioning of the body.

DNA METHYLATION. The imprinting process of introducing methyl into a gene, suppressing its usual function.

DO NOT RESUSCITATE ORDER (DNR). A directive specifying that if a patient's heart stops, he or she should not receive cardiopulmonary resuscitation (CPR).

DONEPEZIL HYDROCHLORIDE. A drug that increases the levels of acetylcholine in the brain; sold under the trade name Aricept.

DOPAMINE. A chemical in brain tissue that serves to transmit nerve impulses (a neurotransmitter) and helps to regulate movement, emotions, concentration, impulse control, judgment, attention span, and psychostimulation; may be involved in disease states such as addiction, ADHD, and depression.

DOPAMINE AGONIST. A drug that binds to dopamine receptors and produces effects that are similar to dopamine.

DOPAMINE ANTAGONIST. A substance that binds to dopamine receptors, preventing dopamine from binding and triggering its response.

DOUBLE ANXIETY. Acute anxiety from a recent stressful event combined with underlying persistent anxiety associated with generalized anxiety disorder.

DOUBLE-BLIND PLACEBO-CONTROLLED STUDY. A study in which patients are divided into two groups—those who will receive a medication, and those who will receive a placebo (a pill that looks like the medication but has no active ingredients). Neither the patients nor their physicians know which pill any specific patient is receiving.

DOUBLE-BLIND STUDY. A research study in which neither the participants nor the researchers know whether the subjects are receiving the experimental treatment or a placebo or control treatment.

DOWN SYNDROME. A genetic disorder characterized by an extra chromosome 21 (trisomy 21), intellectual disability, and susceptibility to early-onset Alzheimer's disease.

DREAM ANXIETY DISORDER. Another name for nightmare disorder.

DRUG ABUSE. Repeated use of controlled substances, prescription or over-the-counter drugs, or alcohol despite damage to personal health, thought processes, relationships, or functioning at work or school; also, using a substance for purposes other than which it is intended.

DSM. Diagnostic and Statistical Manual of Mental Disorders.

DYANA. The yoga term for meditation.

DYSARTHRIA. Difficulty talking and speaking caused by impairment of the muscles used in speech, often as a result of damage to the brain or nerves.

DYSCALCULIA. Difficulty in performing mathematical computations; also called mathematical learning disorder.

DYSFUNCTIONAL. Degraded ability or inability to function emotionally.

DYSGRAPHIA. A writing disorder characterized by illegible handwriting.

DYSKINESIA. Difficulty in performing voluntary muscular movements.

DYSLEXIA. A variable learning disability that is usually characterized by difficulty reading, writing, and spelling; also called developmental reading disorder (DRD) or specific reading disability.

DYSMENORRHEA. Painful menstruation.

DYSPAREUNIA. Painful sexual intercourse.

DYSPHORIA. A persistent mood of sadness, discomfort, or general unease. The English word comes from two Greek words meaning "difficult" or "hard" and "to bear."

DYSPRAXIA. Developmental dyspraxia is an impairment or immaturity of the organization of movement. It is a defect in the way the brain processes information, resulting in messages not being correctly or fully transmitted. The term dyspraxia comes from the word "praxis," meaning "doing" or "acting." Dyspraxia is associated with problems of perception, language, and thought.

DYSSOMNIA. A type of sleep disorder characterized by problems with the amount, quality, or timing of sleep.

DYSTHYMIA. A less severe but chronic (ongoing) form of depression.

DYSTHYMIC DISORDER. A mood disorder that is less severe than depression but usually more chronic.

DYSTONIA. A neurological disorder characterized by involuntary muscle spasms. The spasms can cause a painful twisting of the body and difficulty walking or moving.

E

EATING DISORDERS. Psychological disorders characterized by disturbances in eating patterns, abnormal attitudes toward food, and unhealthy efforts to control weight. Types of eating disorders include anorexia nervosa, binge eating disorder, and bulimia nervosa.

ECHOLALIA. Involuntary repeating the last word, phrase, or sentence spoken by someone else (or heard in the surrounding environment).

ECHOPRAXIA. The imitation of the movement of another individual.

ECSTASY. A drug that produces both stimulant and hallucinogenic effects; also known as MDMA.

EGO. In Freudian psychology, the conscious, rational part of the mind that experiences and reacts to the outside world.

EGO-SYNTONIC. Consistent with one's sense of self, as opposed to ego-alien or dystonic (foreign to one's sense of self).

EJACULATION. The discharge of semen by the male reproductive organs.

ELECTROCARDIOGRAM (EKG). A test that measures the electrical activity of the heart as it beats. An abnormal EKG can indicate possible cardiac disease.

ELECTROCONVULSIVE THERAPY (ECT). A psychological treatment in which a series of controlled electrical impulses are delivered to the brain in order to induce a seizure. ECT is used to treat major depression and severe mental illnesses that do not respond to other forms of treatment.

ELECTROENCEPHALOGRAPHY (EEG). A diagnostic test that measures electrical activity in the brain.

ELECTROLYTES. Ions—such as sodium, potassium, calcium, magnesium, chloride, phosphate, bicarbonate, and sulfate—that are dissolved in bodily fluids such as blood and that regulate or affect most metabolic processes.

ELECTROMAGNETIC RADIATION. Radiation including gamma rays, x rays, ultraviolet light, visible light, infrared radiation, microwaves, and radio waves.

ELIMINATION. The medical term for expelling waste from the body.

EMETIC. A medication that causes vomiting.

EMMENAGOGUE. A medication or substance given to bring on a menstrual period.

EMOTIONALLY FOCUSED THERAPY FOR COUPLES (EFT-C). A widely used, evidence-based system of therapy that emphasizes the individual emotions of each partner.

EMPIRICAL. Based on information gathered by scientific observation or experiments, as distinct from pure theory.

ENCEPHALITIS. Inflammation of the brain.

ENCEPHALOPATHY. An abnormality in the structure or function of tissues of the brain.

ENDOCRINE DYSFUNCTION. A problem relating to inadequate or excessive production of hormones.

ENDOGENOUS DEPRESSION. Depression arising from causes within a person, such as chemical or hormonal imbalances.

ENDOMETRIOSIS. A condition in which the tissue that is normally present in the lining of the uterus grows elsewhere in the body.

ENDORPHINS. A group of peptide compounds released by the body in response to stress or traumatic injury; may also be produced during exercise. Endorphins react with opiate receptors in the brain to reduce or relieve pain and improve mood.

ENDOTRACHEAL INTUBATION. The insertion of a flexible tube into the trachea for purposes of anesthesia, airway protection, and mechanical lung ventilation.

ENFLEURAGE. A technique for extracting essential oils from flower petals by placing them on a layer of purified fat.

ENTEROCHROMAFFIN CELLS. Specialized cells in the thin layer of tissue lining the cavity (lumen) of the digestive tract. Also known as Kulchitsky cells, enterochromaffin cells provide about 90% of the human body's supply of serotonin.

ENTRAINMENT. The patterning of body processes and movements to the rhythm of music.

ENURESIS. Involuntary urination.

ENVIRONMENTAL INFLUENCE. Any component of the cause of a behavior or condition that is perceived to be developed from experience.

ENZYMES. Proteins that trigger chemical reactions in the body.

EOSINOPHILIA MYALGIA SYNDROME (EMS). A chronic, painful disease of the immune system that causes joint pain, fatigue, shortness of breath, and swelling of the arms and legs. EMS can be fatal.

EPHEBOPHILIA. Sexual desire on the part of an adult for youths in the early stages of puberty, as distinct from prepubertal children.

EPHEDRINE. An amphetamine-like substance used as a nasal decongestant.

EPICANTHIC FOLD. A fold in the inner corner of the skin of the upper eyelid, found in about half of children with Down syndrome.

EPIDEMIOLOGY. A field of medical science dealing with the incidence, distribution, and control of disease in a population.

EPIDURAL HEMATOMA. Bleeding into the area between the skull and the dura, the tough, outermost brain covering.

EPIGENETICS. The study of heritable changes in an organism's appearance or gene expression, caused by chemical reactions and factors other than changes in the organism's DNA sequences.

EPIGENOME. A collection of chemical compounds (from food, medications, and other sources) that marks the human genome (a person's complete set of DNA) in certain ways, determining whether certain genes will be turned "on" (active) or "off" (inactive).

EPILEPSY. A neurological disorder characterized by recurrent seizures. Seizures are caused by a disturbance in the electrical activity in the brain and can cause loss of consciousness, muscle spasms, rhythmic movements, abnormal sensory experiences, or altered mental states.

EPINEPHRINE. Also known as adrenaline, the hormone secreted by the adrenal glands in response to stress.

EROTOMANIA. The false belief that a person is the object of another person's love or sexual desire.

EROTOMANIC DELUSIONS. Erotomanic delusions involve the mistaken belief that someone is in love with the delusional person. Often, the other person is a public figure of some prominence, such as an actress, rock star, or political figure.

ESSENTIAL OIL. A volatile oil extracted from the leaves, fruit, flowers, roots, or other components of a plant and used in aromatherapy, perfumes, and foods and beverages.

ESSENTIAL TREMOR. An uncontrollable (involuntary) shaking of the hands, head, and face; also called familial tremor if it is inherited.

ESTROGEN. The primary female sex hormone.

ETHANOL. The chemical name for beverage alcohol. It is also sometimes called ethyl alcohol or grain alcohol to distinguish it from isopropyl or rubbing alcohol.

ETHICS. The branch of philosophy that deals with questions of morality (good and evil, right and wrong).

ETIOLOGY. The cause or origin of a disease or disorder. The word is also used to refer to the study of the causes of disease.

EUGEROIC. A type of medication that promotes wakefulness.

EUNUCH. A castrated male, often one castrated at an early age with noticeable hormonal consequences.

EUPHORIA. A feeling or state of well-being or elation.

EUTHANASIA. The act of putting humans or animals to death painlessly or allowing them to die by withholding medical services, usually because of an incurable disease.

EUTHYMIA. A feeling of well-being often associated with individuals with bipolar disorder when they are not having a manic or a depressive episode.

EXCESSIVE DAYTIME SLEEPINESS (EDS). A condition characterized by a persistent sense of mental cloudiness, lack of energy, depressed mood, or extreme state of exhaustion.

EXCORIATION. The medical term for abrasion of the upper layer of skin caused by mechanical means, most often scratching or picking.

EXECUTIVE FUNCTIONS. An umbrella term for the group of mental processes responsible for planning, abstract thinking, logical deduction, self-control, and prioritization.

EXISTENTIAL FACTORS. Realities of life including death, isolation, freedom, and meaninglessness that must be faced by all individuals.

EXPLICIT MEMORY. Consciously recalled memory for facts or events.

EXPOSURE THERAPY. A form of cognitive-behavioral therapy in which individuals with phobias are exposed to their fears while accompanied by the therapist. The length of exposure is gradually increased until the association between the feared situation and the individual's experienced panic symptoms is no longer present.

EXTENDED FAMILY FIELD. A person's family of origin plus grandparents, in-laws, and other relatives.

EXTERNALIZING DISORDERS. Disorders in which a person acts out inner turmoil or conflict on the external environment. The three major characteristics of externalizing disorders are disruptive, hyperactive, and aggressive behaviors.

EXTINCTION. The elimination or removal of a person's reaction to a cue as a result of exposure treatment.

EXTRAPYRAMIDAL. Related to the motor system in the brain.

EXTRAPYRAMIDAL SYMPTOMS (EPS). A group of side effects associated with antipsychotic medications and characterized by involuntary muscle movements, including contraction and tremor.

F

"FACEBOOK DEPRESSION." A term used to describe a mood disorder associated with low self-esteem and depressed mood triggered by excessive concern with online social media.

FACTITIOUS DISEASES. Conditions in which symptoms are deliberately manufactured by patients in order to gain attention and sympathy. Patients with factitious diseases do not fake symptoms for obvious financial gain or to evade the legal system.

FACTITIOUS DISORDER. A false or exaggerated disorder in which the physical or psychological symptoms are controlled or produced by the patient.

FADING. In a token economy system, refers to gradually decreasing the amount or frequency of a reinforcer so that the target behavior will begin to occur independent of any rewards.

FAIR HOUSING ACT OF 1968. Federal legislation regarding access to housing that prohibits discrimination based on race, color, national origin, sex, religion, disability, or familial status.

FAMILY SYSTEMS THEORY. An approach to treatment that emphasizes the interdependency of family members rather than focusing on individuals in isolation from the family. This theory underlies the most influential forms of contemporary family therapy.

FARADIC. A type of discontinuous alternating electric current sometimes used in aversion therapy; named for the nineteenth-century British physicist Michael Faraday.

FASCIA (PLURAL, FASCIAE). A band or sheath of connective tissue that covers, supports, or connects the muscles and the internal organs.

FAST FOURIER TRANSFORM (FFT). A mathematical process used in the analysis of electroencephalograms (EEGs) to investigate the composition of an EEG signal.

FATHERS' RIGHTS MOVEMENT. A social movement that emerged in the 1980s in response to what members consider gender bias in favor of women in family law.

FAT-SOLUBLE VITAMIN. A vitamin that dissolves and can be stored in body fat or the liver.

FECES. Waste products eliminated from the large intestine; excrement.

FELONY. A major crime, such as sexual assault, aggravated assault and battery, grand theft, rape, burglary, arson, and similar acts.

FEMALE ATHLETE TRIAD. A group of three disorders often found together in female athletes, consisting of disordered eating, amenorrhea (absence of menstrual periods), and osteoporosis.

FETAL ALCOHOL SPECTRUM DISORDERS. A range of birth defects, including intellectual disability, poor growth, nervous system dysfunctions, and malformations, that result from heavy maternal alcohol consumption during pregnancy.

FETAL TISSUE TRANSPLANTATION. A method of treating Parkinson's and other neurological diseases by grafting brain cells from human fetuses onto the basal ganglia. Human adults cannot grow new brain cells but developing fetuses can; grafting fetal tissue stimulates the growth of new brain cells in affected adult brains.

FETUS. The stage of development between embryo and newborn.

FIBROMYALGIA. A chronic condition in which patients experience widespread musculoskeletal pain and fatigue.

"FIGHT-OR-FLIGHT" RESPONSE. A function of the autonomic nervous system that prepares the brain to make an immediate decision to deal with a sudden threat.

FINE MOTOR SKILLS. Control of the smaller muscles of the body, especially in the hands, feet, and head, for activities such as writing and crafts.

FLASHBACK. The reemergence of a memory as a vivid recollection of sounds, images, and sensations associated with the (often traumatic) event. The person having such a memory typically feels as if he or she is reliving the event.

FLAVONOIDS. Plant pigments that have a variety of effects on human physiology (such as anti-inflammatory, anticarcinogenic, or antioxidant effects).

FLOODING. A type of exposure treatment in which patients are exposed to anxiety-provoking or feared situations all at once and until the anxiety and fear subside.

FLUNITRAZEPAM (ROHYPNOL). A central nervous system depressant that is not legal in the United States but that is used illegally as a date-rape drug.

FOOD ALLERGY. An abnormal reaction to a food.

FOOD FREQUENCY QUESTIONNAIRE. A listing of how often a person consumes foods from certain food groups in a given period of time.

FORENSIC. Pertaining to courtroom procedures or evidence used in courts of law.

FORMICATION. The medical term for the sensation of insects crawling on or under the skin.

FRAGILE X SYNDROME. A genetic condition related to the X chromosome that affects mental, physical, and sensory development.

FREE RADICALS. Reactive molecules created during cell metabolism that can cause tissue and cell damage like that which occurs in aging and diseases such as cancer.

FREE-FLOATING. A term used in psychiatry to describe anxiety that is unfocused or lacking an apparent cause or object.

FREUDIAN ANALYSIS. A psychological treatment based on the theories developed by Sigmund Freud, in which the therapist seeks to help the patient resolve conflicts and traumas buried in the subconscious.

FRONTAL CORTEX. The part of the human brain associated with aggressiveness and impulse control.

FRONTAL LOBE. A part of the brain that is involved in processes such as muscle movement, speech production, working memory, planning, reasoning, and judgment.

FROTTAGE. The act of touching or rubbing against the body or genitals of a nonconsenting individual.

FROTTEURISM. The practice of rubbing one's pelvis or (for males) erect penis against a nonconsenting person for sexual gratification. Frotteurism is a type of paraphilia and is considered a form of sexual assault.

FUGUE. A dissociative experience during which those affected develop amnesia regarding their past and identity, and as a result travel far from home.

FUNCTIONAL MAGNETIC RESONANCE IMAGING (FMRI). A special type of magnetic resonance imaging (MRI) scan that measures changes in blood flow and blood oxygenation within the body.

G

GADOLINIUM. A very rare metallic element useful for its sensitivity to electromagnetic resonance, among other things. Traces of it can be injected into the body to enhance magnetic resonance imaging (MRI) scans.

GALACTORRHEA. Lactation occurring in the absence of pregnancy.

GALANIN. A neurotransmitter with roles in various physiological processes, including regulation of the stress response.

GALLBLADDER. A small, pear-shaped organ in the upper right-hand corner of the abdomen. It is connected by a series of ducts (tube-like channels) to the liver, pancreas, and duodenum (first part of the small intestine). The gallbladder receives bile from the liver and concentrates and stores it. After a meal, bile is squeezed out of the gallbladder into the intestine, where it aids in digestion of food.

GAMMA CAMERA. A device inside the machine used in single-photon emission computed tomography

(SPECT) that forms images of the gamma rays emitted by the radionuclides used in tracers in nuclear medicine.

GAMMA HYDROXYBUTYRATE (GHB). A central nervous system depressant that has been abused in the United States for euphoric, sedative, bodybuilding, and date-rape purposes.

GAMMA RAYS. Extremely short-wavelength electromagnetic radiation released during the process of radioactive decay.

GAMMA-AMINOBUTYRIC ACID (GABA). A neurotransmitter that helps to lower or reduce the level of excitement in the nerves, leading to muscle relaxation, calmness, sleep, and the prevention of seizures.

GANSER SYNDROME. A rare subtype of factitious disorder accompanied by dissociative symptoms. It is most often seen in male patients under severe stress in prison or courtroom settings.

GASTRITIS. Inflammation of the lining of the stomach.

GASTROSTOMY. A surgical opening into the stomach.

GENDER DYSPHORIA. A disorder in which an individual experiences prolonged, significant distress or dissatisfaction with his or her biological gender.

GENE. The basic unit of genetic material carried in a particular place on a chromosome. Genes are passed on from parents to child during conception and determine how traits such as blood type are inherited and expressed.

GENERALIZATION. A person's ongoing use of new behaviors that were previously modeled for him or her. Generalization is also called transfer of training or maintenance.

GENERALIZED ANXIETY DISORDER. An anxiety disorder characterized by daily irrational worry that is often excessive and uncontrolled.

GENERIC. A term that refers to a medication that is not protected by a registered trademark.

GENETIC DISEASE. A disease caused by genes inherited from one or both parents.

GENETIC INFLUENCE. Any component of the cause of a behavior or condition that is inherited biologically from a person's parents.

GENITALS. The reproductive organs in either sex, especially the external reproductive organs.

GENOGRAM. A family tree diagram that represents the names, birth order, sex, and relationships of the members of a family. Therapists use genograms to detect recurrent patterns in the family history and to help the members understand their problems.

GENOME. The complete set of DNA in a cell.

GERM CELL. A cell involved in reproduction. In humans, the germ cells are the sperm (male) and egg (female). Unlike other cells in the body, germ cells contain only half the standard number of chromosomes.

GESTALT THERAPY. A therapeutic approach that focuses on increasing awareness of feelings and impulses in the present.

GILLBERG'S CRITERIA. A six-item checklist for Asperger syndrome developed by Christopher Gillberg, a Swedish researcher. It is widely used as a diagnostic tool.

GINKGO. An herb from *Ginkgo biloba*, a shade tree native to China with fan-shaped leaves and fleshy seeds with edible kernels.

GLANS. The tip of the penis.

GLASGOW COMA SCALE. A measure of level of consciousness and neurological functioning after a traumatic brain injury (TBI).

GLAUCOMA. A group of eye diseases characterized by increased pressure within the eye, significant enough to damage eye tissue and structures. If untreated, glaucoma results in blindness.

GLIAL CELLS. The support cells of nervous tissue, especially in the brain, spinal cord, and ganglia, interspersed between signal-transmitting neurons. There are three main types of neuroglia: astrocytes, oligodendrocytes, and microglia.

GLUCOSE. One of the two simple sugars (the other being galactose) that makes up the protein lactose, found in milk. Glucose is the form of sugar that is used by the body to generate energy.

GLUTAMATE. An excitatory amino acid neurotransmitter that carries messages to and from nerve cells in the brain.

GLUTAMATERGIC SYSTEM. The neurotransmitter system in the central nervous system that plays a role in memory formation and information processing; it is also believed to play a role in depression and other mood disorders.

GLYCOGEN. The form of glucose (sugar) that is stored in the liver and muscles.

GONAD. The organ that makes gametes (germ cells). The gonads in males are called testicles and produce sperm; those in females are called ovaries and produce eggs.

GONADOTROPIN-RELEASING HORMONE. A hormone produced by the brain that stimulates the pituitary gland to release hormones that trigger ovulation.

GRANDIOSE DELUSIONS. Grandiose delusions are delusions that magnify a person's importance; the person experiencing the delusion may believe him- or herself to be a famous person, to have magical superpowers, or to be someone in a position of enormous power (such as a king or president).

GRANDIOSITY. Exaggerated and unrealistic self-importance; inflated self-assessment.

GRIEF REACTION. The normal depression felt after a traumatic major life occurrence, such as the loss of a loved one.

GROOMING. Deliberately establishing an emotional connection with someone in order to manipulate them psychologically.

GROSS MOTOR SKILLS. Control of the large muscles of the body, including the arms, legs, back, abdomen, and torso, for activities such as sitting, crawling, walking, and running.

GROUP PSYCHOTHERAPY. A form of therapy in which a small, carefully selected group of individuals meets regularly with a therapist to assist each individual in emotional growth and personal problem solving.

GROUP THERAPY. Therapy based on group interaction and designed to provide support, constructive criticism, and a forum for consultation and reference.

GUANETHIDINE. An antihypertensive drug used to treat high blood pressure.

GUIDED IMAGERY. A relaxation technique where individuals actively imagine themselves in a scene (usually a different location, such as a relaxing beach, or a trigger situation, such as handling a problem situation successfully), typically guided by another person describing the scene.

GUSTATORY. Pertaining to the sense of taste.

GYRI. Convoluted ridges between the sulci, or grooves on the surface of the brain.

H

HABITUATION. The reduction of a person's emotional or behavioral reaction to a cue by repeated or prolonged exposure.

HALLUCINATIONS. False sensory perceptions, such as hearing sounds or seeing people or objects that are not there. Hallucinations can also affect the senses of smell, touch, and taste.

HALLUCINOGEN. A drug or other substance that induces hallucinations.

HAPTIC. Pertaining to the sense of touch; sometimes called tactile hallucinations.

HATHA YOGA. A form of yoga that focuses on postures, breathing methods, and meditation.

HEALTH MAINTENANCE ORGANIZATION (HMO). A healthcare organization that provides managed care group health insurance, in which members pay a stated amount on a regular basis and in turn receive medical care from participating physicians, hospitals, and other providers.

HEBEPHILIA. Sexual attraction on the part of an adult to children in the early stages of puberty.

HEMATOMA. An accumulation of blood, often clotted, in a body tissue or organ, usually caused by a break or tear in a blood vessel.

HEMIPLEGIA. Paralysis of one side of the body.

HEMOCHROMATOSIS. A hereditary condition that results in excessive storage of iron in various tissues of the body.

HEPATITIS. A viral disease characterized by inflammation of the liver cells (hepatocytes).

HEREDITARY ATAXIA. One of a group of hereditary degenerative diseases of the spinal cord or cerebellum. These diseases cause tremor, spasm, and wasting of muscle.

HERITABILITY. The effects of differences in genetics (among the population) in producing differences in behavior.

HERTZ. A unit of frequency equal to one cycle per second.

HIERARCHY. In exposure therapy, a list of feared items or situations, ranked from least fearsome to most fearsome.

HIGH-DENSITY SEX OFFENSES. Several offenses within a short period of time.

HIGH-FUNCTIONING AUTISM (HFA). A subcategory of autistic disorder consisting of children diagnosed with IQs of 70 or higher.

HIPPOCAMPUS. A part of the brain's limbic system that is involved in forming, storing, and processing memories and in regulating mood.

HISTAMINE. Substance released during allergic reactions.

HISTONE. A type of protein that serves as a "spool" for wrapping DNA within a chromosome.

HISTRIONIC. Very dramatic or excessive in behavior; theatrical.

HIV. Human immunodeficiency virus.

HOLISTIC. In medicine, a practice that focuses on treating the patient as a whole (rather than just treating the disease); addresses the physical, social, emotional, and spiritual needs of a patient.

HOMEOSTASIS. The tendency of a system to maintain its internal stability and resist change.

HOMOCYSTEINE. An amino acid with the chemical formula $HSCH_2CH_2CH(NH_2)CO_2H$.

HORMONE. A chemical messenger produced by the body that is involved in regulating specific bodily functions such as growth, development, reproduction, metabolism, and mood.

HOST. The dominant or main alternate personality in a person with dissociative identity disorder (DID).

HUMAN TRAFFICKING. Illegal trade in human beings, whether adults or children, for the purposes of reproductive slavery, prostitution, other forms of sexual exploitation, or forced labor.

HUMANISTIC THERAPY. Sometimes also called "humanistic psychology," a perspective that stresses that people are basically good but deviate from that tendency through mental and social problems. It uses a holistic approach that focuses on individual potential and growth, along with self-actualization.

HUMORAL. A term describing a hormonal substance secreted by an endocrine gland (such as the thyroid).

HUNTINGTON'S DISEASE. A midlife-onset inherited disorder characterized by progressive loss of brain function and control over voluntary movements. It is sometimes called Huntington's chorea.

HYDROCEPHALUS. The excess accumulation of cerebrospinal fluid around the brain, often causing enlargement of the head.

HYDROGEN. The simplest, most common element known in the universe. It is composed of a single electron (negatively charged particle) circling a nucleus consisting of a single proton (positively charged particle).

HYDROTHERAPY. This term literally means "water treatment" and involves the use of water in physical therapy as well as treatment of physical and emotional illness.

HYMEN. A membrane that partially or completely covers the vaginal opening in females prior to first intercourse.

HYPERACTIVITY. Describes activity that is unusually active and restless, accompanied by an inability to concentrate for any extended period.

HYPERALIMENTATION. A method of refeeding persons with anorexia by infusing liquid nutrients and electrolytes directly into central veins through a catheter.

HYPERAROUSAL. A state of increased emotional tension and anxiety, often including jitteriness and a heightened startle response.

HYPEREMESIS. Severe vomiting during pregnancy. Hyperemesis appears to increase a woman's risk of postpartum depression.

HYPERSEXUALITY. A clinically significant level of desire to engage in sexual behaviors; usually associated with lowered sexual inhibitions.

HYPERSOMNIA. An abnormal increase of 25% or more in time spent sleeping. Patients usually have excessive daytime sleepiness.

HYPERSOMNOLENCE. Excessive daytime sleepiness in spite of sufficient nighttime sleep.

HYPERTENSION. High blood pressure.

HYPERTENSIVE CRISIS. A steep rise in blood pressure that can lead to brain hemorrhage or heart failure.

HYPERTHERMIA. Elevated body temperature.

HYPERTHYROIDISM. Condition resulting from the production of excess thyroid hormone, causing an increased basal metabolic rate and an increased need for food to meet the demand of the metabolic activity; generally, however, weight loss results.

HYPERVIGILANCE. A state of abnormally intense wariness or watchfulness that is often found in survivors of trauma or long-term abuse.

HYPERVIGILANT. Extreme attention and focus to both internal and external stimuli.

HYPNAGOGIC. Pertaining to drowsiness.

HYPNAGOGIC HALLUCINATIONS. Auditory or visual hallucinations that occur while falling asleep.

HYPNOPOMPIC. Persisting after sleep.

HYPNOSIS. The means by which a state of extreme relaxation and suggestibility is achieved.

HYPNOTIC. A medication that causes sleep.

HYPOCHONDRIASIS. An anxiety disorder in which the individual believes that real or imagined symptoms are indicative of a serious or life-threatening illness or condition.

HYPOCRETINS. A pair of closely related neuropeptide hormones that promote wakefulness, secreted by a small group of cells in the hypothalamus. The hypocretins are also called orexins and are identified as hypocretin-1 (orexin-A) and hypocretin-2 (orexin-B).

HYPOGONADISM. Functional incompetence of the male gonads, with impaired production of hormones and sperm cells.

HYPOKALEMIA. Abnormally low levels of potassium in the blood. Hypokalemia is a potential medical emergency, as it can lead to disturbances in heart rhythm.

HYPOKINESIA. A condition of abnormally diminished motor activity.

HYPOMANIA. A milder form of mania that is characteristic of bipolar II disorder.

HYPOPNEA. Shallow or excessively slow breathing, usually caused by partial closure of the upper airway during sleep, leading to disruption of sleep.

HYPOTENSION. Low blood pressure.

HYPOTHALAMIC-PITUITARY-ADRENAL (HPA) SYSTEM. A part of the brain involved in the human stress response. The HPA system releases cortisol, the primary human stress hormone, and neurotransmitters that activate other brain structures associated with the body's fight-or-flight reaction.

HYPOTHALAMUS. A part of the forebrain that controls heartbeat, thirst, hunger, body temperature and pressure, blood sugar levels, and other functions.

HYPOTHESIS. An assumption, proposition, or educated guess that can be tested empirically (verified by scientific fact or observation).

HYPOTHYROIDISM. A disorder in which the thyroid gland produces too little thyroid hormone, causing a decreased rate of metabolism.

HYPOTONIA. The medical term for poor muscle tone.

HYPOVENTILATION. An abnormally low level of blood oxygenation in the lungs.

HYPOXIA. Oxygen deficiency.

HYSTERIA. In nineteenth-century psychiatric use, a neurotic disorder characterized by violent emotional outbursts and disturbances of the sensory and motor (movement-related) functions. The term "hysterical neurosis" is still used by some psychiatrists as a synonym for conversion disorder.

I

ICTAL EEG. A type of electroencephalogram (EEG) done to determine the type of seizure characteristic of a person's disorder. During this EEG, seizure medicine may be discontinued in an attempt to induce a seizure during the testing period.

ID. A construct in Freudian psychodynamic theory that represents the irrational, self-centered aspects of human thought.

IDENTIFICATION WITH AN AGGRESSOR. In psychology, an unconscious process in which a person adopts the perspective or behavior patterns of a captor or abuser.

IDENTIFIED PATIENT (IP). In a family unit, the member whose symptom has emerged or is most obvious.

IDENTITY DIFFUSION. A character formation that is scattered or spread around rather than an identity that becomes solidified or consolidated.

IDIOGRAPHIC. An approach to interpreting the results of a projective test within the context of the individual subject's record.

IDIOPATHIC. Arising spontaneously or from an unknown or obscure cause.

IEP (INDIVIDUALIZED EDUCATION PLAN). Under federal law governing special education, every child in public schools who is determined through assessment to have special mental disability needs has an IEP. An IEP is typically developed by a team of professionals that may include special education teachers; physical, occupational, and speech therapists; psychologists; parents or guardians; and others who may be called on to provide expertise.

ILLUSION. A false interpretation of a real sensory image or impression.

IMITATIVE BEHAVIOR. Behaviors of a therapist or group member that are imitated, consciously or unconsciously, by other group members.

IMMUNOSUPPRESSANT. Medications that suppress or lower the body's immune system, primarily used to help the body accept a transplanted organ.

IMPAIRMENT. A physical or mental defect at the level of a major body system or organ.

IMPLICIT MEMORY. Unconsciously recalled memory for skills, procedures, or associations.

IMPULSE CONTROL DISORDERS. A group of emotional disorders characterized by the repeated inability to refrain from performing a particular action that is harmful either to oneself or others.

IN VIVO. A Latin phrase that means "in life."

INCEST. Unlawful sexual contact between people who are biologically related. Many therapists also use the term to refer to inappropriate sexual contact between members of a family unit, including stepparents and stepsiblings.

INCIDENCE. A measurement of the risk of developing a specific disease or disorder within a given time period in a specific population.

INCONTINENCE. The inability to control the release of urine or feces.

INDIRECT TRAUMA. A term used to refer to symptoms of trauma in therapists, first responders, and other persons who treat trauma survivors. It is sometimes called vicarious trauma.

INDIVIDUAL PSYCHOTHERAPY. A relationship between therapist and patient designed to foster the patient's emotional growth and personal problem-solving skills.

INFORMATION GIVING. Imparting of information about a disease or condition as part of the therapeutic process.

INFUSION. The most potent form of extraction of a herb into water. Infusions are steeped for a longer period of time than teas.

INHALANT. A substance a person can sniff, or inhale, to get high.

INSANITY DEFENSE. The common term for the defense that an accused person makes to argue against his or her actions having criminal intent because of an underlying mental illness.

INSIDIOUS. Progressing gradually and inconspicuously but with serious effects.

INSOMNIA. A chronic inability to sleep or to remain asleep throughout the night.

INSULIN. A hormone made by the pancreas that controls blood glucose (sugar) levels by moving excess glucose into muscle, liver, and other cells for storage.

INSULIN RESISTANCE. A condition in which a person's natural insulin becomes less effective in lowering the blood sugar level.

INTEGRATED SETTING. Placing individuals with disabilities in usual employment situations rather than making placements into sheltered workshops or other segregated settings.

INTEGRATIVE BEHAVIORAL COUPLES THERAPY (IBCT). A widely used and highly individualized form of behavioral couples therapy, developed by Andrew Christensen and Neil Jacobson in the 1990s.

INTELLECTUAL DISABILITY. Significant impairment in intellectual function, usually associated with an intelligence quotient (IQ) below 70.

INTERICTAL. Occurring between seizures.

INTERMEDIATE CARE FACILITY. An inpatient facility that provides periodic nursing care.

INTERMITTENT EXPLOSIVE DISORDER. A personality disorder in which an individual is prone to intermittent episodes of aggression and rage, particularly when the response is deemed inappropriate or extreme for the situation.

INTERNALIZING DISORDERS. Disorders related to issues within the self; depression and the anxiety disorders are two common types of internalizing disorders.

INTEROCEPTIVE. Referring to stimuli or sensations that arise inside the body.

INTERPERSONAL LEARNING. Learning that takes place via feedback from others.

INTERPERSONAL THERAPY. Also called "talking therapy," this type of psychological counseling is focused on determining how dysfunctional interpersonal relationships of the affected individual may be causing or influencing symptoms of depression.

INTER-RATER RELIABILITY. The degree to which judgments about a person are consistent among raters or diagnosticians.

INTERSEX. A term that is sometimes used to refer to having a sexual anatomy that is not standard for either a male or a female. It covers a number of different conditions but is considered a convenient umbrella term for discussing disorders of sex development.

INTERVENTION. A confrontation of a substance abuser by a group of interested people who propose immediate medical treatment. An intervention is also a method of treatment used in therapy.

INTOXICATION. The presence of significant behavioral or psychological changes following ingestion of a substance.

INTRACEREBRAL HEMATOMA. Bleeding within the brain caused by trauma to a blood vessel.

INTROJECTION. The unconscious incorporation of another person's ideas or attitudes into one's personality.

ION. Charged molecule, such as sodium or chloride, used in neuronal signaling in the brain.

ION CHANNEL. Physical opening on the surface of neurons that allows the passage of charged ions.

IONIZING RADIATION. Electromagnetic radiation that can damage living tissue by disrupting and destroying individual cells. All types of nuclear decay radiation (including x rays) are potentially ionizing. Radio waves do not damage the organic tissues they pass through.

IQ. Intelligence quotient, or a measure of the intelligence of an individual based on the results of a standardized test.

IRRITABLE BOWEL SYNDROME. Disorder involving dysfunction of the gastrointestinal tract that may include symptoms of constipation, diarrhea, or both.

IRRITATIVE HALLUCINATIONS. Hallucinations caused by abnormal electrical activity in the brain.

ISCHEMIA. An inadequate flow of blood to a part of the body, caused by a narrowing or blockage of the blood vessels supplying it.

 J

JAUNDICE. Yellowing of the skin or eyes due to excess bilirubin in the blood.

JET LAG. A temporary disruption of the body's sleep-wake rhythm following high-speed air travel across several time zones. Jet lag is most severe in people who have crossed eight or more time zones in 24 hours.

JOHREI. A form of energy therapy that originated in Japan in the 1920s. It emphasizes the channeling of spiritual energy to heal people of toxins by raising their spiritual vibrations.

JOINT CONTRACTURES. Stiffness of the joints that prevents full extension.

JUNGIAN ANALYSIS. A psychological treatment based on the theories of Carl Jung, in which the patient strives to understand the internal, often mythical images in thoughts and dreams.

 K

KARYOTYPE. The number and appearance of a complete set of chromosomes in a species or an individual organism. The arrangement of microphotographs of the chromosomes in a standard photographic format is called a karyogram.

KAVALACTONES. Medically active compounds in kava root that act as local anesthetics in the mouth and as minor tranquilizers.

KAVAPYRONES. Compounds in kava root that act as muscle relaxants and anticonvulsants.

KEGEL EXERCISES. Repetitive contractions to tone the pubococcygeus muscle of the pelvic floor for enhancing sexual response during intercourse or controlling incontinence.

KETAMINE. An anesthetic, used predominately by veterinarians to treat animals, that can be abused or used as a date-rape drug.

KI. The Japanese spelling of *qi*, the traditional Chinese term for vital energy or the life force.

KILOGRAM. A metric unit of weight equaling 2.2 lb.

KLEINE-LEVIN SYNDROME. A disorder that occurs primarily in young males and is marked by episodes of hypersomnia, hypersexual behavior, and excessive eating, occurring three or four times a year.

KLEPTOMANIA. A disorder of impulse control characterized by repeated stealing or shoplifting of items that the person does not need or that are of little or no value.

KORO. A culture-specific syndrome involving the belief that a person's external genitalia are shrinking or retracting and may disappear; it occurs primarily in Southeast Asia.

KUNDALINI. In Indian yoga, a vital force or energy at the base of the spine that is activated or released by certain yoga postures or breathing techniques. This release is called the "awakening" of the kundalini. Some Westerners have had kundalini experiences that were diagnosed as psychotic episodes or symptoms of schizophrenia.

L

LABIA. The outside folds of tissue that surround the clitoris and the opening of the urethra in women.

LABILE AFFECT. A display of frequently changing emotion or mood.

LANUGO. A soft, downy body hair that develops on the chest and arms of women with anorexia.

LAPSE. A single, isolated occurrence of a symptom or negative behavior.

LARYNGOSPASM. Spasms that close the vocal apparatus of the larynx (the organ of voice production).

LAXATIVE. Substance or medication that encourages a bowel movement.

LEARNED HELPLESSNESS. The tendency to give up on solving a problem when efforts appear to bring no results.

LEARNING DISORDER. A condition characterized by difficulty in learning that has an unknown cause.

LEAST RESTRICTIVE ENVIRONMENT. Refers to care options that involve the least amount of restraint and the greatest degree of independence possible, while still meeting the individual's needs and maintaining safety.

LESION. Any abnormality in or injury to body tissue.

LEVODOPA (L-DOPA). A substance used in the treatment of Parkinson's disease. Levodopa can cross the blood-brain barrier that protects the brain. Once in the brain, it is converted to dopamine and thus can replace the dopamine lost in Parkinson's disease.

LEWY BODIES. Areas of injury found on damaged nerve cells in certain parts of the brain associated with dementia.

LEWY BODY DEMENTIA. A type of dementia characterized by the presence of abnormal, sphere-shaped clumps of protein in nerve cells in the brain. Lewy body resembles Alzheimer's disease but progresses more rapidly. Common symptoms include confusion and recurring visual hallucinations.

LEXICAL. Relating to the individual words that make up a language.

LIBIDO. Sex drive; level of sexual desire.

LIDOCAINE. A local anesthetic.

LIMBIC SYSTEM. A group of structures in the brain that includes the amygdala, hippocampus, olfactory bulbs, and hypothalamus. The limbic system is associated with homeostasis and the regulation of emotions.

LOFEXIDINE. A medication approved for use in Great Britain to aid in the opioid detoxification process.

LOW AFFECT. Severe lack of interest and emotions; emotional numbness.

LUTEAL PHASE. The period of time between ovulation and menstruation.

LUX. The International System (IS) unit for measuring illumination, equal to one lumen per square meter.

LYSERGIC ACID DIETHYLAMIDE (LSD). The first synthetic hallucinogen, discovered in 1938.

M

MACERATION. A technique for extracting essential oils from plant leaves and stems by crushing the plant parts and soaking them in warm vegetable oil.

MACROSOCIAL. Pertaining to the wider society, as distinct from such smaller social groupings as families, neighborhoods, etc.

MAGNETIC FIELD. A region around a magnetized body or a current-carrying circuit, in which a magnetic force can be detected.

MAGNETIC RESONANCE IMAGING (MRI). An imaging technique that uses electromagnetic radiation and a strong magnetic field to obtain detailed images of soft tissues such as the brain.

MAGNETOENCEPHALOGRAPHY (MEG). A newer form of brain imaging that captures and records the brain's magnetic fields, produced by electrical currents occurring naturally in brain tissue. MEG can identify split-second changes in brain activity.

MAJOR DEPRESSION. A psychological condition in which a person experiences one or more disabling attacks of depression lasting two or more weeks.

MAJOR DEPRESSIVE DISORDER. A clinical psychiatric diagnosis of chronic depressed mood that interferes with normal life activities.

MALADAPTIVE. Unsuitable or counterproductive; for example, maladaptive behavior is inappropriate to a given situation.

MALADROITNESS. Another word for awkwardness or clumsiness.

MALINGERING. Pretending to be physically or mentally ill in order to be relieved of an unwanted duty or obtain some other obvious benefit.

MANIA. An elevated or euphoric mood or irritable state that is characteristic of bipolar disorder. Mania is characterized by mental and physical hyperactivity, disorganization of behavior, and inappropriate elevation of mood.

MANIC. Referring to mania, a state characterized by excessive activity, excitement, or emotion.

MANTRA. A sacred word or formula repeated over and over to concentrate the mind.

MAO-B INHIBITORS. Inhibitors of dopamine or noradrenaline reuptake by monoamine oxidase.

MAOIs. Monoamine oxidase inhibitors.

MASOCHISM. A condition in which people obtain sexual satisfaction through pain or humiliation inflicted by themselves or by another person. The term is sometimes used more generally to refer to a tendency to find pleasure in submissiveness or self-denial.

MASTER STATUS ATTRIBUTE. A term used in sociology for a characteristic that is the most important definer of an individual's social status or identity, one that overshadows other traits and affects the person's behavior in most situations. Common master status attributes are race, sex, sexual orientation, level of education, age, and mental illness or disability.

MATRIX. In statistics, variables that may influence a particular outcome are placed into a grid (matrix), either in columns or in rows. Statistical calculations can be performed that assign different weights to each variable, and the differential weighting of variables can be seen to affect the outcome (positive or negative).

MEDICAID. A program jointly funded by state and federal governments that reimburses hospitals and physicians for the care of individuals who cannot pay for their own medical expenses. These individuals may be in low-income households or may have chronic disabilities.

MEDICAID HOME AND COMMUNITY BASED-WAIVER. Legislation regarding the use of Medicaid funds for care services; allows certain federal requirements to be bypassed so that states can use the funds more flexibly for accessing home- and community-based services, rather than using hospitals or intermediate-care facilities.

MEDICAL MODEL OF MENTAL ILLNESS. An approach to psychiatric diagnosis and treatment patterned on the process of diagnosis and treatment of physical disease.

MEDICARE. A federal health insurance program in the United States that provides medical care and hospital treatment for people over a certain age (usually 65 years).

MEDITATION. Technique of concentration for relaxing the mind and body.

MEDROXYPROGESTERONE ACETATE (MPA). A female hormone that may be prescribed for male patients with sexual sadism or other paraphilias. MPA helps to control sexual urges in men by speeding up the clearance of testosterone from the bloodstream.

MELATONIN. A hormone involved in regulation of the sleep-wake cycle and other circadian rhythms.

MENARCHE. The first menstrual period.

MENINGES. The three membranes that enclose the brain and spinal cord, consisting of the dura mater, arachnoid mater, and pia mater.

MENOPAUSE. A period of decreasing hormonal activity in women, when ovulation stops and conception is no longer possible.

MENTAL DISORDER. A psychiatric disorder of mental faculties.

MENTAL HEALTH. Appropriate adaptation to everyday psychosocial challenges.

MENTAL ILLNESS. Any psychiatric disorder that causes unusual (atypical) behavior.

MENTAL STATUS EXAMINATION (MSE). A clinical evaluation in which the doctor assesses a patient's external appearance, attitude, behavior, mood and affect, speech, thought processes, thought content, perception, cognition, insight (or lack thereof), and judgment.

MERIDIANS. In traditional Chinese medicine, a network of pathways or channels that convey *qi* (also sometimes spelled *chi*), or vital energy, through the body.

MERYCISM. Another name for rumination disorder.

MESOLIMBIC PATHWAY. The "reward pathways" of the brain.

METABOLISM. All of the physical and chemical changes that occur in cells to allow growth and maintain body functions. These include processes that break down substances (such as food) to yield energy and processes that build up other substances necessary for life.

METABOLITE. Chemical compound that occurs as a result of a parent drug being broken down and metabolized in the body. A metabolite may be a medically active or inactive compound, depending on the drug in question.

METFORMIN. A drug developed to treat type 2 diabetes that has been used experimentally to treat weight gain in patients with schizophrenia.

METHADONE. A drug often prescribed legally as a replacement for heroin. It induces a slight high but blocks heroin from producing a more powerful euphoric effect. It may be used in heroin detoxification to ease the process, or it may be used daily after detoxification as maintenance therapy. Methadone maintenance therapy is controversial.

METHAMPHETAMINE. A drug that is approved by the U.S. Food and Drug Administration to treat attention deficit hyperactivity disorder but that is also the most common illegally produced amphetamine.

METHYLATION. A process in which chemical tags called "methyl groups" (made of one carbon and three hydrogen atoms) attach themselves to a DNA molecule in specific locations, affecting the level of a gene's activity.

METHYLPHENIDATE. A mild central nervous system stimulant that is used to treat hyperactivity.

MICROSLEEP. A brief episode of sleep lasting from a fraction of a second to 30 seconds. It may result from sleep deprivation, sleep apnea, or oxygen deprivation as well as from narcolepsy.

MILD COGNITIVE IMPAIRMENT (MCI). A transitional phase of memory loss in older people that precedes dementia or Alzheimer's disease.

MILLIGRAM (MG). One-thousandth of a gram. A gram is the metric measure that equals about 0.035 ounces.

MILLON CLINICAL MULTIAXIAL INVENTORY (MCMI-II). A self-report instrument designed to help clinicians assess *DSM-IV*-related personality disorders and clinical syndromes. It provides insight into 14 personality disorders and 10 clinical syndromes.

MINERAL. An inorganic substance found in the earth that is necessary in small quantities for the body to maintain health. Examples: zinc, copper, iron.

MINNESOTA MULTIPHASIC PERSONALITY INVEN-TORY (MMPI-2). A comprehensive assessment tool widely used to diagnose personality disorders.

MISDEMEANOR. A minor crime, such as petit larceny (petty theft), that is punishable by not more than one year in prison.

MIXED MANIA. A mental state in which symptoms of both depression and mania occur simultaneously.

MODALITY. The medical term for a method of treatment.

MODELING. A behavioral therapy technique in which a patient first observes and then imitates a desired behavior.

MONOAMINE OXIDASE INHIBITORS (MAOIs). A group of antidepressant drugs that decrease the activity of monoamine oxidase, a neurotransmitter found in the brain that affects mood.

MOOD DISORDER. Any of a group of mental disorders involving a disturbance of mood, along with either a full or partial excessively happy (manic) or extremely sad (depressive) syndrome not caused by any other physical or mental disorder. Mood refers to a prolonged emotion.

MORPHEME. The smallest meaningful speech sound.

MORTALITY RATE. A measure of the number of deaths in a specific population, usually expressed per 1,000 per year.

MOSAIC. A term referring to a genetic situation in which a person's cells do not have the exact same composition of chromosomes.

MOTIVATIONAL ENHANCEMENT THERAPY. Therapy that focuses on increasing motivation for change by empathically comparing and contrasting the consequences and benefits of changing or not changing.

MOTIVATIONAL THERAPY. An approach to treatment for learning disorders that emphasizes problem-solving skills, the ability to set and attain goals, and ways to counteract negative thinking and poor self-image.

MOTOR SKILLS. Skills pertaining to or involving muscular movement.

MOURNING. The public expression of bereavement, including funerals and other rituals, special clothing, and symbolic gestures.

MOVEMENT EDUCATION. The active phase of body-work, in which clients learn to move with greater freedom and to maintain the proper alignment of their bodies.

MOXIBUSTION. An acupuncture technique that involves burning of the herb moxa or mugwort.

MULTIAXIAL. Refers to a type of classification system that involves numeric measurement along more than one dimension and that is not based on assignment to mutually exclusive categories.

MULTI-INFARCT DEMENTIA (MID). Dementia caused by a series of many small strokes over time; also called vascular dementia.

MULTIMODAL. Involving several types of therapeutic interventions, such as heat or ice packs, electrical stimulation, or ultrasound; sometimes refers to a mix of physical and psychological therapies.

MULTIPLE PERSONALITY DISORDER (MPD). An older term for dissociative identity disorder (DID).

MULTIPLE SCLEROSIS. A disease characterized by patches of hardened tissue in the brain or spinal cord, paralysis, and/or muscle tremors.

MUTATION. A change in a gene. A gene mutation may alter a trait or characteristic of an individual or may manifest as a disease; the mutation can also be transmitted to offspring.

MUTISM. The inability or refusal to speak.

MYASTHENIA GRAVIS. A chronic disease with symptoms that include muscle weakness and sometimes paralysis.

MYELIN. A white, fatty substance that covers and protects nerves.

MYOCARDIAL DISEASE. Disease of the muscular layer of the heart wall.

MYOCARDIUM. The specialized involuntary muscle tissue found in the walls of the heart.

MYOCLONUS. An abrupt spasm or twitching in a muscle or group of muscles.

N

NALTREXONE. A medication originally developed to treat addiction to heroin or morphine that is also used to treat alcoholism. It works by reducing the craving for alcohol rather than by producing vomiting or other unpleasant reactions.

NARCISSISTIC PERSONALITY DISORDER. Personality characterized by continually exaggerating one's own positive qualities and refusing to recognize personal defects or flaws.

NARCISSISTIC PERSONALITY INVENTORY (NPI). The most widely used English-language diagnostic instrument for narcissistic personality disorder. Based on the *DSM-III* criteria for NPD, the NPI is frequently used in research studies as well as patient assessment.

NARCOLEPSY. A disorder characterized by frequent and uncontrollable attacks of deep sleep.

NARCOTHERAPY. A form of psychotherapy that involves the administration of a drug that makes the patient drowsy.

NARCOTIC. A drug derived from opium or compounds similar to opium. Such drugs are potent pain relievers and can affect mood and behavior. Long-term use of narcotics can lead to dependence and tolerance.

NARROW-ANGLE GLAUCOMA. An eye disorder caused by a buildup of fluid pressure inside the eyeball due to an abnormally small angle between the iris (the colored portion of the eye) and the cornea (the transparent front part of the eye).

NASOGASTRIC INTUBATION. A process in which a tube is inserted down the throat and into the stomach.

NATURAL SUPPORTS. Existing relationships that can serve as part of a person's support network to help that person reach a goal.

NEGATIVE SYMPTOMS. Symptoms of schizophrenia characterized by the absence or elimination of certain behaviors, such as initiative, speech, or affect.

NEGATIVISM. Behavior characterized by resistance, opposition, and refusal to cooperate with requests, even reasonable ones.

NEPHRITIS. Inflammation of the kidney.

NERVOUS TIC. A repetitive, involuntary action, such as the twitching of a muscle or repeated blinking.

NEURALGIA. Pain that extends along the course of a nerve.

NEUROENDOCRINE SYSTEM. The part of the autonomic nervous system responsible for growth and hormonal regulation.

NEUROFIBRILLARY TANGLES. Accumulations of twisted protein fragments inside nerve cells in the brain that are diagnostic of Alzheimer's disease.

NEUROGENESIS. The development of new nerve cells in the brain, whether before birth or during adulthood.

NEUROGENIC. Referring to a disorder associated with damage to the central nervous system.

NEUROLEPTIC DRUGS. Antipsychotic drugs, including major tranquilizers, used in the treatment of psychoses such as schizophrenia.

NEUROLEPTIC MALIGNANT SYNDROME. An unusual but potentially serious complication that develops in some patients who have been treated with antipsychotic medications. NMS is characterized by changes in blood pressure, altered states of consciousness, rigid muscles, and fever. Untreated NMS can result in coma and death.

NEUROLEPTIC-INDUCED ACUTE DYSTONIA. A severe form of neurological movement disorder, caused by the use of neuroleptic drugs.

NEUROLEPTIC-INDUCED AKATHISIA. A disorder characterized by physical restlessness (the inability to sit still, for example) and excessive movement, caused by the use of neuroleptic drugs; research indicates it is likely the most common of neuroleptic-induced movement disorders.

NEUROLEPTIC-INDUCED PARKINSONISM. Symptoms similar to Parkinson's disease that may appear in people taking neuroleptic (antipsychotic) medications. These symptoms include tremors in muscles and a shuffling gait.

NEUROLEPTIC-INDUCED TARDIVE DYSKINESIA. A potentially irreversible neurological disorder caused by the use of antipsychotic/neuroleptic medications, with symptoms involving uncontrollable movement of various body parts.

NEUROLEPTICS. Drugs that treat psychosis, such as hallucinations.

NEUROLOGICAL. Relating to neurology, or the branch of medicine dealing with the function and structure of the nervous system, along with its associated diseases and disorders.

NEUROLOGICAL CONDITIONS. A condition that has its origin in some part of the patient's nervous system.

NEURONAL SIGNALING. The pathway by which neurons communicate, which can be electrical or chemical.

NEURONS. Nerve cells in the brain that produce nerve impulses.

NEUROPATHIC. Relating to neural damage.

NEUROPATHIC PAIN. State of pain related to the nervous system; also known as neurogenic pain.

NEUROPROTECTIVE. Conveying some form of protection to the nervous system from injury.

NEUROPSYCHOLOGICAL. Relating to neuropsychology, or the branch of neurology that studies behavior disorders such as memory loss, speech impairment, epilepsy, and others.

NEUROTRANSMITTER. A naturally occurring chemical in the body that carries chemical messages to nerve cells, often by transmitting nerve impulses. Central nervous system well-being is dependent on a balance among the neurotransmitters acetylcholine, dopamine, serotonin, and norepinephrine.

NEUROTRANSMITTER RECEPTOR. A physical recipient for chemicals called neurotransmitters. Receptors sit on the surface of cells that make up body tissues, and once bound to the neurotransmitter, they initiate the chemical signaling pathway associated with neurotransmitters.

NICOTINE. A colorless, oily chemical found in tobacco that makes people physically dependent on smoking. It is poisonous in large doses.

NIGHT TERROR. Commonly called sleep terror disorder; a disorder in which a person wakes up fearful and anxious but with no recollection of the source of the fear.

NIGHTMARE. A frightening dream that occurs during REM (rapid eye movement) sleep.

NIMBY PHENOMENON. Acronym for "Not In My Backyard," describing the common opposition displayed by citizens toward the placement of group homes or other social service facilities in their neighborhoods.

NOCTURNAL MYOCLONUS. A disorder in which a person is awakened repeatedly during the night by cramps or twitches in the calf muscles; sometimes called periodic limb movement disorder (PLMD).

NOMOTHETIC. An approach to interpreting the results of a projective test in which the subject's answers are measured against a normative comparison sample.

NON-AMBULATORY. Unable to walk.

NONDISJUNCTION. Nonseparation of a chromosome pair during either meiosis or mitosis.

NON-RAPID EYE MOVEMENT (NREM) SLEEP. The first phase of a sleep cycle, in which there is little or no eye movement.

NONSTEROIDAL ANTI-INFLAMMATORY DRUGS (NSAIDs). A class of pain relief medications that also decreases inflammation, such as ibuprofen (Advil), naproxen (Aleve) and acetylsalicylic acid (Aspirin).

NONVERBAL LEARNING DISABILITY (NLD). A learning disability syndrome identified in 1989 that may overlap with some of the symptoms of Asperger syndrome.

NORADRENERGIC. Acts similarly to norepinephrine.

NOREPINEPHRINE. Also called noradrenaline, a chemical messenger in the brain that regulates attention and that powers the "fight-or-flight" stress response; precursor of epinephrine.

NUCLEAR FAMILY. The basic family unit, consisting of father, mother, and their biological children.

NUCLEAR MEDICINE. A branch of medicine that makes use of radioisotopes (also called radionuclides) to evaluate the rate of radioactive decay in diagnosing and treating various diseases.

NUCLEOTIDES. Building blocks of genes, which are arranged in specific order and quantity.

NUCLEUS ACCUMBENS. A structure deep inside and near the center of the brain that makes up a major part of the pathway of pleasure and reward and that is implicated in addictive behavior.

O

OBJECT RELATIONS. In psychology, a phrase that refers to the way in which a subject describes relationships with other people in their environment, and the ways in which he or she has internalized interpersonal relationships.

OBSESSION. A persistent image, idea, or desire that dominates a person's thoughts or feelings.

OBSESSIVE THINKING. Thoughts that overcome a person's thought processes; a compulsive way of thinking in which the same thought repeats, preventing other thoughts.

OBSESSIVE-COMPULSIVE DISORDER. A disorder in which affected individuals have an obsession (such as a fear of contamination, or thoughts they do not like to have and cannot control) and feel compelled to perform certain acts to neutralize the obsession (such as repeated hand washing).

OBSTRUCTIVE SLEEP APNEA. A disorder caused by obstruction of the upper airway during sleep and characterized by repeated pauses in breathing during sleep despite efforts to breathe.

OCCIPITAL BONE. The bone that forms the back part of the skull.

OFF-LABEL. The use of a prescription medication to treat conditions outside the indications approved by the U.S. Food and Drug Administration (FDA). It is legal for physicians to prescribe these drugs, but it is not legal for pharmaceutical companies to advertise drugs for off-label uses.

OLFACTORY. Pertaining to the sense of smell.

OLFACTORY NERVE. The cranial nerve that regulates the sense of smell.

ONSET. The point in time at which the symptoms of a disorder first became apparent.

OPERANT. Conditioning in which the desired response is reinforced by an introduced stimulus.

OPERANT CONDITIONING. A psychological process in which a desired behavior is followed with positive or rewarding stimuli.

OPIATE BLOCKER. A type of drug that blocks the effects of natural opiates in the system. This type of drug makes some people appear more responsive to their environment.

OPIATES. A class of drugs that is either derived from opium (e.g., morphine, hydromorphone, oxymorphone, heroin, codeine, hydrocodone, oxycodone) or resembles these opium derivatives (such as meperidine); commonly referred to as narcotics.

OPIOID. Any of a group of potent pain-relieving drugs derived from the opium poppy or synthesized in the laboratory.

OPIOID ANTAGONIST. A type of receptor antagonist (drug) that acts on opioid receptors.

OPPOSITIONAL DEFIANT DISORDER. A psychiatric disorder characterized by an ongoing pattern of excessively hostile, angry, and disobedient behavior that is directed toward authority figures.

ORAL PHASE. The first of Freud's psychosexual stages of development in which satisfaction is focused on the mouth and lips. During this stage, sucking and eating are the primary means of gratification.

OREXINS. Another name for the hypocretins.

ORGANIC BRAIN DISORDER. An organic brain disorder refers to impaired brain function due to damage or deterioration of brain tissue.

ORGANIC BRAIN SYNDROME. A class of disorders characterized by progressive deterioration of mental processes caused by temporary brain dysfunction or permanent brain damage. Symptoms include delusions, dementia, amnesia, and delirium that are not caused by drugs, alcohol, or as a side effect of medication.

ORGANIC ILLNESS. A physical, biologically based illness.

ORGASM. Another word for sexual climax.

ORGASMIC REORIENTATION. A form of behavioral therapy that attempts to help people learn to respond sexually to culturally appropriate stimuli.

OROFACIAL DYSKINESIA. Involuntary movements of the face.

ORTHOSTATIC HYPOTENSION. A sudden decrease in blood pressure due to a change in body position, as when moving from a sitting to standing position.

OSTEOPATHY. A system of medical practice that believes that the human body can make its own remedies to heal infection. It originally used manipulative techniques but also includes surgical, hygienic, and medicinal methods when needed. Doctors of osteopathy are referred to as osteopaths or DOs.

OSTEOPOROSIS. The thinning of bone and loss of bone density.

OVERCOMPENSATION. An attempt to overcome or correct a behavior by going too far in the opposite direction.

OXIMETRY. The measurement of blood oxygen levels.

P

PAIN STATES. Refers to the four-way classification of pain disorder as being (1) acute with psychological factors, (2) acute with psychological factors and a general medical condition, (3) chronic with psychological factors, or (4) chronic with psychological factors and a general medical condition.

PALILALIA. Involuntary echoing of the last word, phrase, sentence, or sound vocalized by oneself.

PANIC ATTACK. A period of intense fear or discomfort combined with a feeling of doom and a desire to escape. Panic attacks may be unexpected or triggered by specific internal or external cues.

PANIC DISORDER. An anxiety disorder in which an individual experiences sudden, debilitating attacks of intense fear.

PARADIGM. The commonly accepted foundations among a group of similar theories, usually derived from a philosophy, including assumptions, terminology, measurements, and expectations.

PARAMETER. A characteristic or factor that is measured during a test of a complex process or activity like sleep.

PARANOIA. An unwarranted sense of suspicion or of being persecuted, sometimes reaching delusional proportions.

PARANOID PERSONALITY DISORDER. A personality disorder characterized by unwarranted suspicion, jealousy, hypersensitivity, social isolation, and a tendency to detect malicious intent in the words and actions of others.

PARAPHILIA. The medical term for a condition in which a person is sexually aroused by nonhuman objects, animals, corpses, children and other nonconsenting partners, or other individuals or situations that are not part of normative stimulation.

PARASOMNIA. A type of sleep disorder characterized by abnormal changes in behavior or body functions during sleep, specific stages of sleep, or the transition between sleeping and waking.

PARCOPRESIS. Fear of having a bowel movement in a public place.

PARENS PATRIAE. The legal concept by which the state has the responsibility to protect those with mental disabilities from self-harm.

PARESTHESIA. An abnormal sensation of tingling or "pins and needles."

PARIETAL LOBE. The middle portion of each cerebral hemisphere of the brain; associated with bodily sensations.

PARIETAL-OCCIPITAL. Relating to the parietal and occipital bones or lobes.

PARKINSONIAN. Related to symptoms associated with Parkinson's disease.

PARKINSON'S DISEASE. A disease of the nervous system most common in people over age 60, characterized by a shuffling gait, muscle stiffness, and tremors.

PARTIAL AGONIST. A substance that partially activates a receptor in the brain, while blocking the neurotransmitter for that receptor from binding to it.

PARURESIS. Fear of urinating in a public place.

PATHOLOGICAL. Uncontrollable in nature; relating to disease.

PAVOR NOCTURNUS. Another term for sleep terror disorder.

PEDOPHILIA. A sexual perversion in which children are the preferred sexual object.

PELVIS. The basin-like cavity in the human body below the abdomen, enclosed by a framework of four bones.

PENETRATING HEAD INJURY. A type of traumatic brain injury in which an object pierces the skull and enters brain tissue.

PENIS. The external male sex organ.

PERCENTILE. A statistical measure that shows, on a scale of 100, whether a distribution is below or above it.

PERINEAL. An anatomical area located between the external genitals and the anus.

PERIODIC LIMB MOVEMENTS IN SLEEP (PLMS). Random movements of the arms or legs that occur at regular intervals of time during sleep.

PERIPHERAL NERVE. A nerve in a distant location from the brain that receives information in the form of an impulse from the brain and spinal cord.

PERIPHERAL NERVOUS SYSTEM. The part of the nervous system that lies outside the brain and spinal cord. It connects the central nervous system with sensory organs, muscles, blood vessels, and glands.

PERISTALSIS. Waves of muscular contraction in the intestines that push food along during the process of digestion.

PERSEVERATION. Continuous involuntary repetition of speech or behavior.

PERSISTENT PULMONARY HYPERTENSION (PPHN). A life-threatening disorder seen in newborn babies in which blood does not properly enter the lungs.

PERSONALITY. The organized pattern of behaviors and attitudes that makes a human being distinctive. Personality is formed by the ongoing interaction of temperament, character, and environment.

PERSONALITY DISORDER. A maladaptive pattern of behavior, affect, and/or cognitive style displayed in a broad range of settings. The pattern deviates from the accepted norms of the individual's culture and can occur over a lifetime.

PERSONALITY INVENTORY. A type of psychological test that is designed to assess a client's major personality traits, behavioral patterns, coping styles, and similar characteristics. The MMPI-2 is an example of a personality inventory.

PERSONALITY TEST. Various standardized tasks that are used to determine aspects of personality or emotional status.

PERSONALIZATION. The tendency to relate large-scale events or general patterns of events to the self in inappropriate ways. For example, a person who regards the loss of a loved one in an accident as punishment for having quarreled with that person before the accident is said to be personalizing the event. This tendency increases a person's risk of developing acute stress disorder or post-traumatic stress disorder after a traumatic event.

PERSON-CENTERED PLANNING. A technique in which a plan for a person's future is developed by a team consisting of the person, family members, service providers, and friends (natural supports). The team develops a practical plan based on the person's wishes and dreams. Each team member agrees to perform certain tasks identified in the plan to help the person reach his or her goals.

PERSON-CENTERED THERAPY. A therapeutic approach that believes the client's own drive toward growth and development is the most important factor in healing.

PERVASIVE DEVELOPMENTAL DISORDERS (PDDs). A group of five disorders—including Asperger syndrome, autism, Rett disorder, childhood disintegrative disorder (CDD), and pervasive developmental disorder not otherwise specified (PDD-NOS)—that are characterized by developmental delays or impairments.

PHARMACODYNAMICS. The study of the effects of drugs on the human body.

PHARMACOKINETICS. The study of the absorption, distribution, and elimination of drugs from the body.

PHENOMENOLOGICAL THERAPY. A therapeutic approach that focuses on the interpretations individuals place on their experiences.

PHENOTHIAZINES. A class of drugs widely used in the treatment of psychosis.

PHENOTYPES. Observable traits or characteristics.

PHENYLKETONURIA (PKU). An enzyme deficiency present at birth that disrupts metabolism and causes brain damage. If left untreated, the disease progresses into intellectual disability.

PHOBIA. An intense, abnormal, or illogical fear of something specific, such as heights or open spaces.

PHONEME. The smallest detectable sound within a spoken word.

PHONICS. A method of teaching reading and spelling based on the phonetic interpretation of single letters, letter combinations, and syllables.

PHONOLOGICAL DISORDER. A developmental disorder of childhood in which the child fails to use speech sounds that are appropriate for his or her age level and native language or dialect.

PHOSPHODIESTERASE-5 (PDE5). An enzyme that is involved in the loss of penile erection.

PHOTOMULTIPLIER. A device that is designed to be extremely sensitive to electromagnetic radiation, especially within the ultraviolet, visible, and near-infrared ranges of the electromagnetic spectrum.

PHOTON. The smallest amount of electromagnetic radiation that possesses both particle and wave properties.

PHOTOTHERAPY. Also called light therapy, a therapy in which the patient is exposed to a bright light to compensate for reduced exposure to sunlight.

PHOTOTOXIC. Causes a harmful skin reaction when exposed to sunlight.

PHYSIOLOGIC. Describes physiology, particularly normal, healthy, physical functioning.

PHYSOSTIGMINE. A short-acting drug that enhances levels of acetylcholine (a neurotransmitter) between neurons in the brain.

PICA. An abnormal appetite or craving for non-food items, often such substances as chalk, clay, dirt, laundry starch, or charcoal.

PICK'S DISEASE. A rare type of primary dementia that affects the frontal lobes of the brain. It is characterized by a progressive loss of social skills, language, and memory, leading to personality changes and sometimes loss of moral judgment.

PILATES. An exercise regimen specifically designed to improve overall physiological and mental functioning.

PINEAL GLAND. A small endocrine gland in the brain that produces melatonin.

PITUITARY GLAND. A small endocrine organ in the brain that is associated with various hormones that control and regulate other endocrine organs. The pituitary affects most basic bodily functions, including growth and development.

PLACEBO. An inactive substance or preparation given to a control group in a clinical trial to test the effectiveness of the real medication or treatment; usually study participants do not know if they are receiving the drug or the placebo.

PLAQUE. A sticky cholesterol-containing substance that builds up on the walls of blood vessels, reducing or blocking blood flow.

PLATELET. A small, irregularly shaped cell fragment that plays an important role in blood clotting. Platelets are also called thrombocytes.

POINT-OF-SERVICE. A healthcare organization that provides managed-care group health insurance and has characteristics of both health maintenance organizations (HMOs) and preferred provider organizations (PPOs).

POLYGENIC. A trait or disorder that is determined by several different genes. Most human characteristics, including height, weight, and general body build, are polygenic, as is the development of certain diseases.

POLYPHARMACY. The use of a number of different medications by the same patient. Polypharmacy is most common among the elderly and those taking psychiatric medications.

POLYSOMNOGRAPHY. Laboratory measurement of a patient's basic physiological processes during sleep, used to diagnose sleep disorders. Polysomnography usually measures heart rate, eye movements, brain waves, muscle activity, breathing, changes in blood oxygen concentration, and body position.

POLYTRAUMA. The medical term for injury to more than one part of the body or more than one type of injury (such as burn injuries in addition to broken bones).

PORNOGRAPHY. Sexually explicit pictures, writings, or other material produced for the purpose of sexual arousal.

PORPHYRIA. A disease of the metabolism characterized by skin lesions, urine problems, neurologic disorders, and/or abdominal pain.

POSITIVE AFFIRMATION STATEMENTS. Statements repeated to oneself, either aloud or mentally, that reflect positive attitudes of self-worth.

POSITIVE REINFORCEMENT. A procedure or response that rewards a desired behavior.

POSITIVE SYMPTOMS. Symptoms that are characterized by the production or presence of abnormal or excessive behaviors, including hallucinations and thought-process disorder.

POSITRON. A positively charged particle; also called an "antielectron," the antimatter counterpart of the electron.

POSITRON EMISSION TOMOGRAPHY (PET). A medical imaging technique that allows for the scanning of the metabolic activity of the body's organs, which is useful to diagnosis cancer, locate brain tumors, and investigate other disorders.

POST-CONCUSSION SYNDROME. A complex of symptoms, including headache, following a mild traumatic brain injury.

POST-DEPLOYMENT SYNDROME (PDS). A term developed to describe a constellation of mental disorders found in veterans of the conflicts in Iraq and Afghanistan. PDS includes post-traumatic stress disorder, generalized anxiety disorder, major depression, chronic pain, and traumatic brain injury.

POSTPARTUM. Following childbirth.

POST-TRAUMATIC AMNESIA (PTA). Difficulty forming new memories after a traumatic brain injury.

POST-TRAUMATIC DEMENTIA. Persistent mental deterioration following a traumatic brain injury.

POST-TRAUMATIC STRESS DISORDER (PTSD). A condition that develops in response to a highly stressful or traumatic event, typically characterized by depression, anxiety, flashbacks, nightmares, and avoidance of reminders of the traumatic experience.

POSTURAL TREMOR. A continuous quiver that affects body posture and movement.

PRADER-WILLI SYNDROME. A rare genetic disorder that causes a constant feeling of hunger.

PRAGMATIC LANGUAGE IMPAIRMENT (PLI). A term that is used by some researchers as an equivalent to social communication disorder. PLI was previously known as semantic pragmatic disorder (SPD).

PRAGMATICS. A subfield of linguistics that explores the ways in which context contributes to the meaning of language. In ordinary usage, pragmatics refers to a person's ability to know what is appropriate to say, where and when to say it, and the give-and-take nature of conversation.

PRANAYAMA. Yogic breathing techniques.

PREFERRED PROVIDER ORGANIZATION (PPO). A healthcare organization that provides managed-care group health insurance and that has contracted with a group of doctors, hospitals, and other providers to provide health care at reduced rates for its clients.

PREFRONTAL CORTEX. Area of the brain involved in attention span, judgment, response to external stimuli, memory, motor function, and impulse control.

PREMENSTRUAL MOLIMINA. The normal signs that indicate that menses will soon occur.

PRENATAL EXPOSURE. Coming in contact with a fetus during pregnancy.

PRESENILE DEMENTIA. The original name for Alzheimer's disease.

PRESENILIN (PSEN). Proteins that are involved in processing amyloid precursor protein (APP). Mutations in the genes encoding these proteins can cause early-onset Alzheimer's disease.

PRESSURE ULCERS. Also known as pressure sores or bed sores, these can develop in patients who are unable to move. If not treated properly, they can become infected.

PRETENDER. With regard to body integrity identity disorder (BIID), a person who uses assistive devices or other props in public in order to appear disabled.

PREVALENCE. The number of cases of a disease or disorder existing in a specific population at a given point in time.

PRIAPISM. Painful involuntary penile erection that persists over long periods of time.

PRIMARY ENURESIS. Bed-wetting in a child who has not yet developed bladder control.

PRIMARY GAIN. In psychiatry, the principal psychological reason for the development of a patient's symptoms.

PRIMARY NARCISSISM. Sigmund Freud's term for a normal phase in early childhood development in which the infant has not yet learned to distinguish between itself and its world, seeing other people and things in its environment as extensions of itself.

PRIMARY PERSONALITY. The core personality of a patient with dissociative identity disorder.

PRIMARY PROGRESSIVE APHASIA. A disorder in which there is progressive loss of language skills.

PRIMARY SLEEP DISORDER. A sleep disorder that cannot be attributed to a medical condition, another mental disorder, prescription medications, or other substances.

PRION. An infectious agent consisting of protein in a misfolded form. Its name is a combination of "protein" and "infection."

PROCESS ADDICTION. A term used to describe addiction to an activity or behavior rather than a substance; also known as behavioral addiction or non-substance-related addiction.

PRODROMAL. The early stage or the start of a disease, before specific or characteristic symptoms occur.

PRODRUG. The inactive form of a drug that is metabolized into an active compound inside the body.

PROGRESSIVE MUSCLE RELAXATION. Relaxation exercises that involve slowly tensing and then relaxing each muscle group in the body separately in a systematic order.

PROGRESSIVE SUPRANUCLEAR PALSY. A rare disease that gradually destroys nerve cells in the parts of the brain that control eye movements, breathing, and muscle coordination. The loss of nerve cells causes palsy, or paralysis, that slowly gets worse as the disease progresses. The palsy affects ability to move the eyes, relax the muscles, and control balance.

PROJECTION. A psychological process in which a person unconsciously attributes unacceptable feelings to someone else.

PROJECTIVE TEST. A psychological test for assessing thinking patterns, observational abilities, attitudes, and feelings based on open-ended responses to ambiguous (having more than one meaning) stimuli; often used to evaluate personality disorders.

PROLACTIN. A hormone that stimulates milk production and breast development.

PROPRIOCEPTION. A person's normal sense of posture, balance, direction of movement, and location in space.

PROPRIOCEPTIVE. Pertaining to proprioception.

PROSTAGLANDINS. A group of unsaturated fatty acids involved in the contraction of smooth muscle, control of inflammation, and many other body processes.

PROSTATE. A walnut-shaped gland surrounding the urethra in males at the base of the urinary bladder. The prostate gland secretes the fluid that combines with the male sperm cells to form semen.

PROXY. An individual who makes decisions on behalf of another.

PSEUDODEMENTIA. A term for a type of depression with symptoms resembling those of dementia. The term "dementia of depression" is now preferred.

PSEUDOSEIZURE. A fit that resembles an epileptic seizure but is not associated with abnormal electrical discharges in the patient's brain.

PSYCHIATRIC. Relating to psychiatry.

PSYCHIATRIC BOARDING. The practice of holding patients with mental illness in emergency department corridors and waiting areas because of the lack of hospital beds or other facilities.

PSYCHIATRIC DISORDERS. Any behavioral or psychological condition that impairs basic bodily functions and increases the risk of death and disability.

PSYCHIATRIST. A medical doctor who has completed specialized training in the diagnosis and treatment of mental illness. Psychiatrists can diagnose mental illnesses, provide mental health counseling, and prescribe medications.

PSYCHIC. Relating to the mind rather than the body.

PSYCHIC NUMBING. An inability to respond emotionally to people or situations; this numbing affects positive as well as negative emotions.

PSYCHOACTIVE. Referring to any substance that crosses the blood-brain barrier and acts primarily upon the central nervous system, leading to changes in mood, perception, thinking, feeling, or behavior.

PSYCHOANALYSIS. The study of human psychological functioning and behavior.

PSYCHOANALYTIC. Understanding human motivations, emotions, and mental processes according to theories and concepts originally developed by Sigmund Freud.

PSYCHOANALYTIC THERAPY. Therapy based on the psychodynamic theory of Sigmund Freud.

PSYCHODIAGNOSTIC. Various methods used to examine and analyze the factors that form human behavior, especially abnormal behavior.

PSYCHODRAMA. A form of group therapy that has group members act out parts of important people in the lives of individual group members.

PSYCHODYNAMIC. Referring to the mental, emotional, or motivational forces or processes that form human attitudes and behaviors, especially unconscious processes that develop in early childhood.

PSYCHODYNAMIC GROUPS. Psychotherapy groups that utilize the principles of unconscious needs and motivations developed by Sigmund Freud.

PSYCHODYNAMIC PSYCHOTHERAPY. A therapeutic approach to helping persons find relief from emotional pain.

PSYCHODYNAMIC THEORISTS. Therapists who believe that the origins of mental problems lie in a person's internal conflicts and complexes.

PSYCHODYNAMIC THERAPY. A therapeutic approach that assumes that dysfunctional or unwanted behavior is caused by unconscious, internal conflicts and focuses on gaining insight into and resolving these conflicts.

PSYCHOGENIC. Originating in the mind, or in a mental process or condition. The term "psychogenic" is sometimes used as a synonym for "conversion."

PSYCHOLOGICAL. Refers to mental processes, including thoughts, feelings, and emotions.

PSYCHOLOGICAL ASSESSMENT. A process of gathering and synthesizing information about a person's psychological makeup and history for a specific purpose, which may be educational, diagnostic, or forensic.

PSYCHOLOGIST. A mental health professional who treats mental and behavioral disorders by providing support and insight to encourage healthy behavior patterns and personality growth. Psychologists also study the brain, behavior, emotions, and learning.

PSYCHOMETRIC PSYCHOLOGY. A branch of psychology that deals with measurement of mental capacities, processes, and traits.

PSYCHONEUROIMMUNOLOGY. The study of the relationships among the mind, nervous system, and immune response.

PSYCHOPATHOLOGY. The study of the causes and development of psychiatric disorders in humans.

PSYCHOPATHY. A serious personality disorder characterized by antisocial, aggressive, and violent behavior and thoughts, along with a lack of empathy for personal actions.

PSYCHOSEXUAL CONFLICTS. In Freudian categories, internal conflicts related to problems at a particular stage of childhood development. Freud associated each developmental stage with a particular part of the human body, such as the mouth or the phallus.

PSYCHOSIS. A general psychiatric term for a condition in which the patient loses touch with reality. It is marked by such symptoms as hallucinations, delusions, personality changes, and disordered thinking. Psychosis is usually one feature of an overarching disorder, not a disorder in itself.

PSYCHOSOCIAL. A term that refers to the emotional and social aspects of psychological disorders.

PSYCHOSOMATIC. A type of physical illness caused by mental factors.

PSYCHOSTIMULANT. A type of drug that increases the activity of the parts of the brain that produce dopamine.

PSYCHOTHERAPEUTIC DRUGS. Drugs used to treat psychiatric disorders, such as tranquilizers, sedatives, analgesics, and stimulants.

PSYCHOTHERAPY. The treatment of mental and behavioral disorders by providing support and insight to encourage healthy behavior patterns and personality growth.

PSYCHOTIC. Relating to psychosis, or a psychiatric disorder characterized by hallucinations, a distorted view of reality, and other such mental problems.

PSYCHOTIC DISORDER. Any psychiatric disorder involving a loss of touch with reality, made evident by such symptoms as hallucinations, delusions, and incoherence; examples of psychotic disorders include schizophrenia and mania.

PSYCHOTROPIC DRUG. A drug that acts on or influences the activity of the mind.

PSYCHOTROPIC MEDICATION. Medication that has an effect on the mind, brain, behavior, perceptions, or emotions. Psychotropic medications are used to treat mental illnesses because they affect a patient's moods and perceptions.

PTOSIS. Drooping of the upper eyelid.

PUNITIVE. Concerned with, or directed toward, punishment.

PURGING. Inappropriate actions taken to prevent weight gain, often after bingeing, including self-induced vomiting or the misuse of laxatives, diuretics, enemas, or other medications.

PYROMANIA. An impulse control disorder characterized by repeatedly setting fires.

PYRROLE. A heterocyclic aromatic organic compound with chemical formula C_4H_4NH.

Q

QI. The traditional Chinese term for vital energy or the life force. The word is also spelled *ki* or *chi* in English translations of Japanese and Chinese medical books.

QIGONG. An exercise practice derived from traditional Chinese medicine and designed to facilitate energy flow throughout the body.

QUALITATIVE. Relating to quality.

QUANTITATIVE. Relating to quantity.

QUANTITATIVE REASONING. The ability to complete mathematical problems and to apply mathematics on a practical level.

QUICKENING. A term that refers to the movements or other signs of life of a fetus in the womb.

R

RADIO WAVES. Electromagnetic energy of the frequency range corresponding to that used in radio communications, usually 10,000 cycles per second to 300 billion cycles per second. Radio waves are the same as visible light, x rays, and all other types of electromagnetic radiation but are of a higher frequency.

RADIOACTIVE. Relating to radiation emitted by certain substances.

RADIONUCLIDE. An atom with an unstable nucleus that emits gamma rays during the process of its radioactive decay. Radionuclides, also known as radio-isotopes, are used to make the tracers used in some imaging studies.

RADIOPHARMACEUTICAL. A radioactive drug.

RANDOMIZATION. The process of randomly assigning participants in an experiment to the various treatment groups, so that each individual has an equal chance of being assigned to any of the groups.

RAPHE NUCLEI. A group of nine pairs of compact clusters of nerve cells found in the brainstem that secrete serotonin for use in the brain.

RAPID CYCLING. Four or more manic, hypomanic, mixed, or depressive episodes within a 12-month period.

RAPID EYE MOVEMENT (REM) SLEEP. A stage of sleep during which the sleeper's eyes move back and forth rapidly. Most dreams occur during REM sleep.

RAPPORT. A relation of empathy and trust between a therapist and patient.

RATIONAL EMOTIVE THERAPY. A form of psychotherapy developed by Albert Ellis and other psychotherapists based on the theory that emotional response is based on the subjective interpretation of events, not on the events themselves.

RAYNAUD'S SYNDROME. A disorder of the circulatory or vascular system characterized by abnormally cold hands and feet because of constricted blood vessels in these areas.

RDA. The abbreviation for recommended dietary allowance, which is the amount of vitamins and minerals needed to provide adequate nutrition in most healthy people. The amount varies depending on age, gender, and physical conditions, such as pregnancy; sometimes RDA is called "daily value" (DV) in the United States.

REALITY TESTING. A phrase that refers to a person's ability to distinguish between subjective feelings and objective reality.

REBOUND EFFECT. A physical reaction to stopping a medication characterized by the reappearance of the symptom(s) that the medication was given to suppress.

REBUS. A puzzle in which syllables of words and names are represented by pictures of objects that sound similar or by letters.

RECEPTOR. In biochemistry, a substance (usually a protein) found on the surface of a cell that interacts with specific other molecules, drugs, hormones, or antibodies.

RECIDIVISM. A tendency to return to a previous activity or behavior, especially criminal or deviant behavior.

RECREATIONAL DRUGS. The use of a drug with the intention of creating a psychoactive (heightened) mental experience; for the most part, such use is illegal.

REFOCUSING TECHNIQUES. Techniques that direct a person's attention away from overwhelming, negative thoughts and emotions by focusing on inner peace and managing one issue at a time.

REGIMEN. A regulated course of treatment for a medical or mental disorder.

REGISTERED DIETITIAN. A person who has met certain education and experience standards and is well-qualified to provide nutrition counseling.

REGRESSION. In psychology, a return to earlier, usually childish or infantile, patterns of thought or behavior.

REGURGITATION. The return of partly digested food from the stomach to the mouth. Regurgitation may be either an intentional act or an involuntary physical reaction.

REHABILITATE. To restore; to put back into good condition.

REINFORCEMENT. In behavioral therapy, the ability of a behavior to produce effects that will make the user want to perform the behavior again. In modeling, reinforcement refers to rewarding the model's demonstration of a skill or the client's performance of the newly acquired skill in practice or in real-life situations.

REINFORCEMENT SCHEDULE. The frequency and amount of reinforcers administered.

REINFORCER. Anything that causes an increase of a particular behavior.

RELAPSE. A recurrence of symptoms after a period of improvement or recovery.

RELATIVE DEPRIVATION. A feeling of deprivation based on comparison with neighbors and relatives.

RELAXATION RESPONSE. The body's inactivation of stress responses and return of stress hormone levels to normal after a threat has passed.

RELAXATION TECHNIQUES. Techniques used to relieve stress. Exercise, biofeedback, hypnosis, and meditation are all effective relaxation tools. Relaxation techniques are used in cognitive-behavioral therapy to teach patients new ways of coping with stressful situations.

RELEASE HALLUCINATIONS. Hallucinations that develop after partial loss of sight or hearing and that represent images or sounds formed from memory traces rather than present sensory input. They are called "release" hallucinations because they would ordinarily be blocked by incoming sensory data.

RELIABILITY. The ability of a test to yield consistent, repeatable results.

REM. Rapid eye movement; a stage of the normal sleep cycle characterized by rapid eye movements, increased forebrain and midbrain activity, and dreaming.

REM LATENCY. After a person falls asleep, the amount of time it takes for the first onset of REM sleep.

REMEDY ANTIDOTE. Certain foods, beverages, prescription medications, aromatic compounds, and other environmental elements that counteract the efficacy of homeopathic remedies.

REMISSION. In the course of an illness or disorder, a period of time when symptoms are absent.

REMOTE THERAPY. A general term for therapy delivered by electronic communication technologies; includes Internet-based therapy along with telephone therapy and videoconferencing.

REPETITIVE STRESS INJURY (RSI). A type of injury to the musculoskeletal and nervous systems associated with occupational strain or overuse of a specific part of the body. Bodywork therapies are often recommended to people suffering from RSIs.

RESILIENCE. In psychiatry, the ability of a person to respond positively to, or bounce back from, trauma or hardship. Resilience is considered a process of interaction between the person and his or her environment rather than a one-time action.

RESPITE CARE. Temporary care of a patient to provide the usual caregivers with a period of physical, mental, and emotional rest.

RESPONSE COST. A behavioral technique that involves removing a stimulus from an individual's environment so that the response directly preceding the removal is weakened. In a token economy system, response cost is a form of punishment involving loss of tokens due to inappropriate behavior, which consequently results in decreased ability to purchase back-up reinforcers.

RESPONSE TO INTERVENTION (RTI). An approach to diagnosis of learning disorders based on a child's response (or lack of response) to early interventions with learning problems.

RESPONSE-CONTINGENT. An approach to treatment in which rewards or punishments are given in response to a particular behavior, in order to encourage or correct the behavior.

RESTLESS LEGS SYNDROME (RLS). A neurological disorder characterized by aching, burning, or creeping sensations in the legs that can only be relieved by moving the legs, often resulting in insomnia.

RETROGRADE AMNESIA. Amnesia for events that occurred before the onset of an amnestic disorder.

RETROPERITONEAL. The anatomical area between the peritoneum (lining of the abdominal cavity) and the muscular and connective tissues of the abdominal wall.

RETT SYNDROME. An inherited progressive neurodevelopmental disorder that affects females, usually beginning in infancy. Rett syndrome is characterized by cognitive and motor deterioration, slow brain growth, and intellectual disability.

REVIEW OF SYSTEMS (ROS). A systematic checklist of the various organ systems in the human body—ear, nose, and throat; respiratory; cardiovascular; gastrointestinal; genitourinary; musculoskeletal; skin and hair; and neurological—used to ensure that all relevant physical signs and symptoms have been taken into account during a medical or psychiatric evaluation.

RHIZOME. A fleshy plant stem that grows horizontally under or along the ground; roots are sent out below this stem and leaves or shoots are sent out above it.

RISK ASSESSMENT. The process of gathering and interpreting data useful in estimating the probability that an individual will display a certain behavior.

RISK MANAGEMENT. Using the results of a risk assessment to tailor intervention strategies intended to reduce the likelihood that an individual will demonstrate a certain behavior.

ROLE. The set of customary or expected behavior patterns associated with a particular position or function in society.

ROLE PLAYING. A technique used in therapy in which participants act out roles relevant to real-life situations in order to change their attitudes and behaviors.

ROLE TRANSITION. Life changes that require an adjustment in social or occupational status or self-image.

RORSCHACH TEST. A popular projective psychological test, in which a subject's interpretations of a series of ten standard inkblots are used to assess personality and emotional traits and diagnose disorders; also known as the Rorschach psychodiagnostic test.

RUMINATE. To chew or rechew regurgitated food.

RUNNER'S HIGH. A feeling of exhilaration that occurs when a period of strenuous exercise activates the release of endorphins. While typically associated with long-distance runners, the experience of such a high has been reported by dancers and athletes in other sports.

RUSSELL'S SIGN. Scraped or raw areas on a patient's knuckles caused by self-induced vomiting.

S

SADISM. A mental disorder in which sexual arousal and gratification are obtained by inflicting pain or humiliation on another person.

"SATISFACTION WITH LIFE." Term coined by psychologist Ed Diener as a level of satisfaction determined by acceptance of the past, contentment with the present, and optimism for the future.

SCABIES. A contagious skin infection in humans and other animals caused by a tiny parasite that burrows under the skin and causes intense itching.

SCALE. A subset of test items from a multi-item test.

SCAPEGOATING. The emergence of behavioral problems in one family member, usually the identified patient, who is often punished for problems within the entire family.

SCHEMAS. Fundamental core beliefs or assumptions that are part of the perceptual filter people use to view the world. Cognitive-behavioral therapy seeks to change maladaptive schemas.

SCHIZOAFFECTIVE DISORDER. Having symptoms of both schizophrenia and bipolar disorder.

SCHIZOPHRENIA. A severe mental illness in which a person has difficulty distinguishing what is real from what is not real. It is often characterized by hallucinations, delusions, language and communication disturbances, and withdrawal from people and social activities.

SCHIZOPHRENIFORM DISORDER. A short-term variation of schizophrenia that has a total duration of one to six months.

SCINTILLATOR. A material that exhibits the property of luminescence (also called "scintillation") when it is excited by ionizing radiation.

SCREENING TEST. A test given as a preliminary tool that helps to later target a more thorough analysis.

SEASONAL AFFECTIVE DISORDER (SAD). A mood disorder characterized by depression, weight gain, and sleepiness during the winter months.

SECONDARY ENURESIS. Bed-wetting in a child who had previously established bladder control but has begun to wet the bed again, usually as the result of emotional stress.

SECONDARY GAIN. In conversion disorder, a term that refers to other benefits that a patient obtains from a conversion symptom. For example, a patient's loss of function in an arm might require other family members to do the patient's share of household chores, or they might give the patient more attention and sympathy than he or she usually receives.

SECTION 504. The section of the Rehabilitation Act of 1973 that provides that no person may be discriminated against because of a physical disability For example, if a child uses a wheelchair, his or her school must find a way to ensure that children in wheelchairs have access to all classes.

SEDATION. A state of emotional or physical relaxation. The term is usually used to refer to this condition when it is produced by a medication.

SEDATIVE. A medication that induces relaxation and sleep.

SEIZURE. A sudden attack, spasm, or convulsion.

SELECTIVE SEROTONIN NOREPINEPHRINE REUPTAKE INHIBITORS (SSNRIs). Drug class that acts to specifically inhibit the reuptake of serotonin and norepinephrine with little effect on other types of neurotransmitters, thereby decreasing side effects associated with broader-acting drugs.

SELECTIVE SEROTONIN REUPTAKE INHIBITORS (SSRIs). A class of antidepressants that works by blocking the reabsorption of serotonin in brain cells, raising the level of the chemical in the brain.

SELF-DELIVERANCE. A term for assisted suicide, more commonly used in Great Britain than in the United States.

SELF-HELP GROUPS. Groups that fall outside the realm of psychotherapy groups but that offer help to individuals with a particular problem or concern. These groups are typically not led by professionals.

SELF-STIGMA. Loss of self-esteem and personal effectiveness that develops when a person being treated for a mental health issue internalizes public prejudice against people diagnosed with mental disorders.

SEMANTIC DEMENTIA. A disorder in which there is progressive loss of knowledge about words and word meanings.

SEMANTICS. A subfield of linguistics that focuses on the meaning of words; in ordinary usage, the ability to use words correctly and understand their meanings.

SEMEN. A thick whitish fluid containing sperm, produced by the male reproductive organs.

SEMINAL FLUID. Fluid composed of semen from the testes and prostatic secretions.

SEMINAL VESICLES. Sac-like structures that border the male urethra and serve as storage depots for the seminal fluid.

SEMI-STRUCTURED INTERVIEW. A type of psychiatric interview in which the interviewer can ask new questions in the course of the interview, depending on the interviewee's answers to previous questions (does not follow a set format).

SENSITIZATION. To make sensitive or susceptible.

SENSORIMOTOR. Relating to sensory and motor coordination of the nervous system.

SEQUELA (PLURAL, SEQUELAE). In medicine, a pathological condition resulting from a disease, injury, or other trauma.

SEROTONERGIC. Containing, activating, or otherwise involving serotonin.

SEROTONIN. 5-Hydroxytryptamine; a substance that occurs throughout the body with numerous effects, including neurotransmission. Low serotonin levels are associated with mood disorders, particularly depression and obsessive-compulsive disorder.

SEROTONIN SYNDROME. A potentially life-threatening drug reaction involving an excess of the neurotransmitter serotonin, usually occurring when too many medications that increase serotonin are taken together.

SEROTONIN TRANSPORTER (SERT). A protein that removes serotonin from the spaces between neurons (synaptic clefts) and thus terminates its action. In effect, SERT recycles serotonin by returning it to the neuron that originally released it (the presynaptic neuron).

SEX HORMONES. Hormones that are responsible for sexual characteristics and reproductive functioning.

SEXUAL ASSAULT NURSE EXAMINER (SANE). A nurse with specialized training in the care and forensic examination of victims of sexual assault.

SEXUAL VIOLENCE. Actual, attempted, or threatened sexual contact with a person who is nonconsenting or unable to give consent.

SHAKEN BABY SYNDROME (SBS). A severe form of traumatic brain injury resulting from shaking an infant or small child forcefully enough to cause the brain to jar against the skull.

SHAMAN. In certain indigenous tribes or groups, a person who acts as an intermediary between the natural and supernatural worlds. Shamans are regarded as having the power or ability to cure illnesses.

SHARED PSYCHOTIC DISORDER. Also known as *folie à deux,* shared psychotic disorder is an uncommon disorder in which the same delusion is shared by two or more individuals, one of whom has no established mental illness.

SHIATSU. Japanese form of acupressure massage.

SHIFT. The transition of control from one personality to another in a person with dissociative identity disorder. Usually shifts occur rapidly, within seconds, but in some cases a more gradual changeover is observed. Also referred to as a switch.

SIBLING RIVALRY. Competition among brothers and sisters in a nuclear family.

SICKLE CELL ANEMIA. An inherited disorder in which red blood cells contain an abnormal form of hemoglobin, a protein that carries oxygen. The abnormal form of hemoglobin causes the red cells to become sickle shaped. The misshapen cells may clog blood vessels, preventing oxygen from reaching tissues and leading to pain, blood clots, and other problems.

SKILLED NURSING FACILITY. An inpatient facility that provides 24-hour nursing services to individuals in need of extended care.

SLEEP APNEA. A condition in which a person temporarily stops breathing during sleep.

SLEEP CYCLE. A period of NREM (non-rapid eye movement) sleep followed by a shorter phase of REM (rapid eye movement) sleep. Most adults have four to six sleep cycles per night.

SLEEP DISORDER. Any condition that interferes with sleep.

SLEEP DRUNKENNESS. A condition associated with primary hypersomnia in which the person has an abnormally prolonged period of transition from sleep to wakefulness; is disoriented, drowsy, and uncoordinated; and may behave in an excited or violent fashion.

SLEEP HYGIENE. Beneficial behavior and environmental choices that precede sleep and tend to help produce a good night's sleep.

SLEEP LATENCY. The amount of time that it takes to fall asleep. Sleep latency is measured in minutes and is important in diagnosing depression.

SLEEP PARALYSIS. An abnormal episode of sleep in which the patient cannot move for a few minutes, usually occurring on falling asleep or waking up. It is often found in patients with narcolepsy.

SLEEP TERROR DISORDER. A sleep disorder in which a person wakes up fearful and anxious but with no recollection of the source of the fear.

SOCIAL COMMUNICATION DISORDER. A communication disorder in which persons have trouble understanding the pragmatics of conversation, or the appropriate use of language depending on the context or social situation.

SOCIAL LEARNING THEORY. A subset of learning theories based on the concept that human behavior originates in and is affected by the interplay among the person's learned experiences, previous behaviors, and environmental influences.

SOCIAL MEDIA. A general term for both Web-based and mobile technologies that facilitate social (as distinct from commercial or academic) interaction online.

SOCIAL MODELING. A process of learning behavioral and emotional-response patterns from observing one's parents or other adults.

SOCIAL PHOBIA. An anxiety disorder characterized by a strong and persistent fear of social or performance situations.

SOCIALIZATION. The process through which a person learns his or her roles in society. It includes the society's customs, traditions, and professional roles as well as gender roles.

SOCIOECONOMIC STATUS. Perceived status of an individual, family, or community based on average income, education level, and social status.

SODOMY. Anal sex; the term is sometimes used to describe anal rape.

SOLUTION-FOCUSED THERAPY. A type of therapy that involves concrete goals and an emphasis on future direction rather than past experiences.

SOMATIC. Relating to the body, rather than the mind.

SOMATIC CONCERN. Excessive concern about the body, particularly in relation to illness.

SOMATIC EDUCATION. The integration of bodywork with self-awareness, intelligence, and imagination.

SOMATIZATION. When mental or emotional distress manifests as physical symptoms.

SOMATIZATION DISORDER. A disorder in which patients seek medical treatment for physical ailments with no discernible organic cause.

SOMATOFORM DISORDERS. A category of psychiatric disorders characterized by physical complaints that appear to be medical in origin but that cannot be explained in terms of a physical disease, the results of substance abuse, or by another mental disorder.

SOMNAMBULISM. Another term for sleepwalking.

SPECIFIC PHOBIA. A type of phobia in which the object or situation that arouses fear is clearly identifiable and limited. An older term for specific phobia is simple phobia.

SPEECH-LANGUAGE PATHOLOGIST. A professional with special training in the evaluation and treatment of persons with voice, speech, and language disorders.

"SPEED RUN." The episodic bingeing on amphetamines.

SPHENOIDAL ELECTRODES. Fine wire electrodes that are implanted under the cheek bones, used to measure temporal seizures.

SPLITTING. In regards to narcissistic personality disorder, a psychological process that occurs during childhood, in which the child separates aspects of him- or herself that the parents value from those that they disregard.

SPONTANEOUS REMISSION. Recovery from a disease or disorder that cannot be attributed to medical or psychiatric treatments.

SPORADIC. Occurring at random in persons with no known risk factors or genetic mutations.

SNRI. Selective serotonin norepinephrine reuptake inhibitor.

SSRI. Selective serotonin reuptake inhibitor.

STABILIZATION. Preventing shock in an injured person by protecting the airway, controlling bleeding (if any), keeping the person warm, and preventing injury to the spinal cord.

STALKING. The willful and repeated following, watching, and/or harassing of another person, usually with the intent of forcing the victim into a dating or sexual relationship.

STANDARD DEVIATION. A statistical measure of dispersion; that is, how much a set of values differs from an arithmetic mean.

STANDARDIZATION. The administration of a test to a sample group of people for the purpose of establishing scoring norms.

STANDARDIZED TEST. A test that follows a regimented structure, with each individual's scores compared to others within a group.

STATE CHILDREN'S HEALTH INSURANCE PROGRAM (SCHIP; CHIP). A state-administered health insurance program for lower- and middle-income children who are without private health insurance and whose family incomes are above the Medicaid eligibility limits.

STATUTORY RAPE. Sexual activity, often coercive, in which one party is below the age of consent.

STEAM DISTILLATION. A process of extracting essential oils from plant products through a heating and evaporation process.

STEROIDS. A class of hormones and drugs that includes sex and stress hormones and anti-inflammatory medications, contraceptives, and growth-promoting substances.

STEROLS. Steroid alcohols, such as cholesterol, that are widely distributed in the body.

STIGMA. Any attribute that is generally perceived as negative by society (regardless of fact).

STIMULANT. A type of psychoactive substance that increases alertness or wakefulness. Stimulants may be prescribed to treat disorders such as autism or attention deficit hyperactivity disorder but are also illegally abused.

STIMULANT ABUSE DISORDERS. Also called stimulant use disorders, any disorder that involves the abuse of stimulant drugs.

STIMULUS. An agent that directly elicits a response, such as a thought, emotion, or action, including images, smells, sounds, words, or ideas.

STIMULUS FADING. A form of behavior modification in which goals of gradually increasing difficulty are set for the client.

STOOLS. Feces; bowel movements.

STREET DRUG. A substance purchased from a drug dealer. It may be a legal substance sold illicitly (without a prescription and not for medical use), or it may be a substance that is illegal to possess.

STRESS. A physical and psychological response that results from being exposed to a demand or pressure.

STRESS HARDINESS. A personality characteristic that enables persons to stay healthy in stressful circumstances. It includes belief in one's ability to influence the situation, commitment to or full engagement with one's activities, and a positive view of change.

STRESS MANAGEMENT. A category of popularized programs and techniques intended to help reduce or eliminate stress.

STRESSOR. A stimulus or event that provokes a stress response in an organism. Stressors can be categorized as acute or chronic and as external or internal to the organism.

STRIATUM. Area of the brain involved in psychostimulation and addiction.

STROKE. A temporary loss of normal blood flow to an area of the brain, caused by blockage or rupture of a blood vessel.

STRUCTURAL INTEGRATION. Term used to describe the method and philosophy of life associated with Rolfing, a type of bodywork therapy.

STRUCTURED INTERVIEW. A type of interview often used by researchers to gather data, in which subjects are asked a series of standardized questions in the same order with the same wording. The questions are usually closed-ended (the choice of answers is fixed in advance), although some structured interviews may include a few open-ended questions.

STUPOR. A state of sluggishness or impaired consciousness.

SUBDURAL ELECTRODES. Strip electrodes that are placed under the dura mater (the outermost, toughest, and most fibrous of the three membranes [meninges] covering the brain and spinal cord) to locate the foci of epileptic seizures prior to epilepsy surgery.

SUBDURAL HEMATOMA. Active bleeding or a blood clot inside the dura (leathery covering of the brain). This causes swelling of the brain and if left untreated can cause death.

SUBJECTIVE. Referring to a person's unique internal thoughts and feelings, as distinct from the objects of those thoughts and feelings in the external world.

SUBJECTIVE UNITS OF DISTRESS (SUDS) SCALE. A scale used by patients during exposure treatment to rate their levels of fear and anxiety with numbers from 0–100.

SUBSTANCE ABUSE. Illicit or excessive use of a drug or other substance that has a pronounced effect on the mind or body without any therapeutic application.

SUBTHRESHOLD. A term used in psychiatry to describe a condition that has significant clinical features but does not meet the full criteria of any major disorder.

SUICIDE GESTURE. Attempted suicide by way of a low-lethality method, low level of intent or planning, and little physical damage; sometimes called pseudocide.

SUICIDE MAGNET. A bridge, tall building, or geographic location that acquires a reputation as a location for suicide attempts.

SULCI. The furrows or grooves on the surface of the brain between convolutions.

SUNSETTING. Confusion or agitation in the evening; also called sundowning.

SUPEREGO. According to Freud, the part of the mind that represents traditional parental and societal values. The superego is the source of guilt feelings.

SUPERIOR MESENTERIC ARTERY SYNDROME. A condition in which a person vomits after meals due to blockage of the blood supply to the intestine.

SUPPORT GROUP. A group whose primary purpose is to provide empathy and emotional support to its members. Support groups are less formal and less goal-directed than group therapy sessions.

SUPPORTIVE THERAPY. An approach to psychotherapy that seeks to encourage the patient or offer emotional support rather than attempt behavioral changes.

SUPRACHIASMATIC NUCLEUS (SCN). A pair of nerve clusters in the hypothalamus in the brain that receives light input from the retina via the optic nerve and regulates circadian rhythms.

SURVIVOR'S GUILT. A psychological reaction in trauma survivors that takes the form of guilt feelings for having survived or escaped a trauma without serious injury when others did not.

SYDENHAM'S CHOREA. A serious manifestation of acute rheumatic fever that commonly occurs in children ages 7 through 14, peaking at age 8. This disease of the central nervous system is characterized by emotional instability, purposeless movements, and muscular weakness.

SYMPATHETIC NERVOUS SYSTEM. The part of the nervous system that prepares the body to react to situations of stress or emergency; physical effects include increased heart rate and blood pressure, sweating, and pupil dilation.

SYNAPSE. A connection between a neuron (nerve cell) and another cell (which may be a neuron or another type of cell) that allows the neuron to transmit a chemical or electrical signal to the receiving cell.

SYNCOPE. A brief lapse of consciousness caused by a temporarily insufficient flow of blood to the brain.

SYNDROME. A group of signs or symptoms that occur together and characterize or define a particular disease or disorder.

SYSTEMIC LUPUS ERYTHEMATOSUS (SLE). A chronic inflammatory autoimmune disorder.

SYSTOLIC. Referring to the rhythmic contraction of the heart (systole) as the blood in the chambers is forced out. Systolic blood pressure is blood pressure measured during the systolic phase.

T

TACHYCARDIA. A pulse rate above 100 beats per minute.

TACTILE. The perception of touch.

TAI CHI. A martial art involving controlled movements specifically designed to improve physical and mental well-being.

TARDIVE AKATHISIA. A disorder in which an individual continuously feels restless.

TARDIVE DYSKINESIA (TD). A disorder characterized by involuntary and repetitive body movements that sometimes develops after long-term use of antipsychotic medications.

TARDIVE DYSTONIA. Involuntary, abnormal movements of the neck and shoulder muscles.

TARGET BEHAVIOR. The specific behavior to be increased or decreased during the course of a treatment.

TAU PROTEIN. A protein involved in maintaining the internal structure of nerve cells. Tau protein is damaged in Alzheimer's disease and forms neurofibrillary tangles.

TEMPERAMENT. A person's natural or genetically determined disposition.

TEMPORAL. Relating to the temples.

TEMPORAL LOBE. A part of the brain that is involved in processing auditory and visual information, emotion and motivation, and understanding language.

TEMPOROMANDIBULAR JOINT DYSFUNCTION. A condition resulting in pain in the head, face, and jaw. Muscle tension or abnormalities of the bones in the area of the hinged joint (the temporomandibular joint) between the lower jaw and the temporal bone are usually the cause.

TERATOGEN. An agent or chemical that causes a birth defect.

TERMINATION. The process of ending a therapy group; an important part of a group therapy.

TERRITORIAL AGGRESSION. The response of aggressively defending a defined space perceived as being threatened by a member of the same species.

TEST ANXIETY. A name for the stress and intensity of emotional upset that students experience before they take exams.

TESTOSTERONE. The primary male sex hormone.

THALAMUS. The middle part of the diencephalon (a part of the human forebrain), responsible for transmitting and integrating information from the senses.

THANATOLOGIST. A specialist in the study of death and the psychological mechanisms for coping with death.

THEMATIC APPERCEPTION TEST (TAT). A clinical psychology projective test where patients make up stories or descriptions for a set of pictures; used for diagnostic, psychodynamic, and personality assessments.

THERAPEUTIC ALLIANCE. The technical term for the cooperative relationship between a therapist and a client, considered essential for successful psychotherapy.

THERAPEUTIC VALUE. The potential benefit of an object or situation in terms of its ability to enhance functioning (social, emotional, intellectual, occupational, etc.) in an individual.

THERAPEUTIC WRITING. A treatment technique in which patients are asked to write an account of a traumatic event and their emotional responses to it.

THERMISTOR. An electrical device whose resistance decreases with rises in temperature.

THOUGHT DISORDER. A condition characterized by incomprehensible language, either written or spoken.

THROMBOCYTOPENIA. A condition involving abnormally low numbers of platelets (blood-clotting agents) in the blood; usually associated with hemorrhaging (bleeding).

THUJONE. A natural chemical compound found in sage as well as in wormwood and certain other spices. In large quantities, it can cause hallucinations and convulsions.

THYROID. A gland in the neck that produces the hormone thyroxine, which is responsible for regulating metabolic activity in the body.

TIC. A sudden involuntary behavior that is difficult or impossible for the person to suppress. Tics may be either motor (related to movement) or vocal and may become more pronounced under stress.

TINCTURE. An alcohol-based herbal extract prepared by soaking parts of the plant in a mixture of alcohol and water.

TINNITUS. Perceived ringing, buzzing, whistling, or other noise heard in one or both ears that has no external source. It is not a disease by itself but a symptom that may have a number of different causes.

TISSUE PLASMINOGEN ACTIVATOR (tPA). A drug that is sometimes given to patients within three hours of a stroke to dissolve blood clots within the brain; also used to treat heart attack victims.

TOKEN. In a token economy system, any item that can be seen and collected (such as stickers or points in a point tally) that has no value on its own but that is used as an immediate reward for desirable behavior to later be redeemed for a larger reward.

TOLERANCE. A progressive decrease in the effectiveness of a drug with long-term use, requiring higher doses to achieve the desired effect.

TOMOGRAPHY. A scanning technique that uses electromagnetic radiation (such as gamma rays or x rays) or ultrasound to produce a three-dimensional image of a structure.

TONIC. A preparation or medicine that invigorates, strengthens, or restores tone to body tissues.

TONIC-CLONIC SEIZURE. A seizure involving the entire body, characterized by unconsciousness, muscle contraction, and rigidity; also called grand mal or generalized seizures.

TONIFICATION. Acupuncture technique for strengthening the body.

TORPOR. Sluggishness or inactivity.

TOURETTE SYNDROME. A neurological disorder characterized by involuntary motor or vocal tics.

TOXIC. Poisonous.

TOXOCARIASIS. Infection with roundworm larvae, commonly transmitted by the feces of dogs and cats.

TOXOPLASMOSIS. A parasitic infection caused by the intracellular protozoan *Toxoplasmosis gondii*. Humans are most commonly infected by swallowing the oocyte form of the parasite in soil (or kitty litter) contaminated by feces from an infected cat or by swallowing the cyst form of the parasite in raw or undercooked meat.

TRACER. A substance containing a radioisotope, injected into the body and followed in order to obtain information about various metabolic processes in the body.

TRACHEOSTOMY. A surgical procedure in which an artificial opening is made in the patient's windpipe to relieve airway obstruction.

TRAIT ANXIETY. A type of persistent anxiety found in some patients with generalized anxiety disorder. Trait anxiety is regarded as a feature (trait) of a person's temperament.

TRANQUILIZER. A medication that induces a feeling of calm and relaxation; also known as an anxiolytic.

TRANSABLED. A word coined by people with body integrity identity disorder (BIID) to express their need to be disabled.

TRANSCENDENTAL MEDITATION. A meditation technique based on Hindu practices that involves the repetition of a mantra (positive affirmation).

TRANSCUTANEOUS. Through the skin.

TRANSIENT ISCHEMIC ATTACK (TIA). Temporary blockage of blood flow to the brain often resulting in slurred speech, vision disturbances, and loss of balance. The episode is brief and the damage is often short-term (not permanent); also called mini-stroke or warning stroke.

TRANSLOCATION. The transfer of one part of a chromosome to another chromosome during cell division. A balanced translocation occurs when pieces from two different chromosomes exchange places without loss or gain of any chromosome material. An unbalanced translocation involves the unequal loss or gain of genetic information between two chromosomes.

TRANSVESTIC FETISHISM. A paraphilia in which a person is sexually aroused by wearing the clothing of the other sex (as distinct from cross-dressing for a theater role or costume party).

TRAUMA. A severe injury or shock to a person's body or mind.

TRAUMATIC GRIEF. Grief resulting from bereavement under traumatic circumstances, such as natural or transportation disasters, acts of terrorism, and murder.

TREATMENT. In reference to mental disorders, the process of helping persons adapt to and overcome the challenges of their disorder.

TREMOR. Involuntary shaking.

TREPANATION. An operation in which a hole is cut through the skull in order to access the brain.

TRIAGE. A process for determining the order and priority of emergency treatment for injured people (civilians or military personnel), the order and priority of emergency transport, and the injured person's transport destination.

TRIANGLING. A process in which two family members diminish the tension between them by drawing in a third member.

TRICHOBEZOAR. A hairball that results from a buildup of swallowed hairs becoming lodged in the digestive system.

TRICHOPHAGIA. Eating hair.

TRICHOTILLOMANIA. A disorder marked by repeated pulling and tugging of one's hair, usually resulting in noticeable hair loss on the scalp or elsewhere on the body.

TRICHURIASIS. Infection with the larvae of roundworms. These parasites may live for 10–20 years in humans.

TRICYCLIC ANTIDEPRESSANTS (TCAs). An older group of antidepressant drugs.

TRIGEMINAL NEURALGIA. A disorder of the trigeminal nerve that causes severe facial pain.

TRIGGER. Any situation (people, places, times, events, etc.) that causes a person to experience a negative emotional reaction, which is often accompanied by a display of symptoms or problematic behavior.

TRIGLYCERIDES. A type of fat in the blood. High levels of triglycerides can increase the risk of coronary artery disease.

TRISOMY. The condition of having three identical chromosomes, instead of the normal two, in a cell.

TRYPTOPHAN. An essential amino acid produced in the body by the action of trypsin (a digestive enzyme) on protein molecules.

TSUBO. In shiatsu, a center of high energy located along one of the body's meridians. Stimulation of the *tsubos* during a shiatsu treatment is thought to rebalance the flow of vital energy in the body.

TUBAL LIGATION. A surgical procedure in which a woman's fallopian tubes are cut or blocked to prevent an egg from reaching the uterus for fertilization.

TUBEROUS SCLEROSIS. A genetic disease that causes skin problems, seizures, and intellectual disability.

TUMOR. An abnormal growth of body cells, which may be malignant (harmful) or benign (harmless).

24-HOUR RECALL. A listing of the type and amount of all foods and beverages consumed by a person in a 24-hour period.

TWIN STUDY. Research studies that use pairs of twins to study the effects of heredity and environment on behavior or another characteristic.

TYRAMINE. Intermediate product between the chemicals tyrosine and epinephrine in the body and a substance normally found in many foods, especially in protein-rich foods that have been aged or fermented, pickled, or bacterially contaminated, such as cheese, beer, yeast, wine, and chicken liver.

TYROSINE. The amino acid from which epinephrine is synthesized.

U

ULTRASOUND. A noninvasive test in which high-frequency sound waves are reflected off a patient's internal organs, allowing them to be viewed.

UNIVERSALITY. The feeling of being isolated, unique, and separate from others, often experienced by therapy group members.

UNNA SLEEVE. A dressing made of gauze impregnated with glycerin, zinc oxide, and calamine that can be used to protect skin injured by compulsive picking from further injury. It is named for the German dermatologist who invented it.

URETHRA. The tube that discharges urine (and in males, semen) from the bladder to the outside of the body.

URETHRITIS. Inflammation of the urethra.

URINARY INCONTINENCE. Inability to control urination.

URINARY RETENTION. Excessive storage of urine in the body.

URINARY SYSTEM. The kidney, urethra, bladder, and associated organs that process urine and eliminate it from the body.

U.S. FOOD AND DRUG ADMINISTRATION (FDA). The U.S. Department of Health and Human Services agency responsible for ensuring the safety and effectiveness of all drugs, biologics, vaccines, and medical devices. The FDA also works with the blood banking industry to safeguard the nation's blood supply.

UTERUS. The hollow muscular sac in which a fetus develops; sometimes called the womb.

V

VAGINA. The part of the female reproductive system that opens to the exterior of the body and into which the penis is inserted during sexual intercourse.

VAGINISMUS. An involuntary tightening of the vaginal muscles that makes sexual intercourse painful, difficult, or impossible.

VAGUS NERVE STIMULATION (VNS). An experimental treatment for depression that involves implanting a stimulator device that sends electrical impulses at timed intervals to the left vagus nerve.

VALIDITY. The ability of a test to measure accurately what it claims to measure.

VASCULAR. Pertaining to the bloodstream (arteries, veins, and blood vessels).

VASOCONGESTION. A pooling of blood in dilated blood vessels.

VASOCONSTRICTOR. Any substance that causes blood vessels to narrow or tighten.

VENTRAL TEGMENTAL AREA. Produces dopamine and signals to the nucleus accumbens and the rest of the striatum.

VENTRICULAR SYSTEM. The system of small cavities in the brain that forms, circulates, and drains the cerebrospinal fluid.

VENTRICULOSTOMY. Surgery that drains cerebrospinal fluid from the brain to treat hydrocephalus or increased intracranial pressure.

VERBAL REASONING. The ability to understand and reason using concepts involving words (within a particular language).

VESTIBULAR. Pertaining to the vestibule; regarding the vestibular nerve of the ear, which is linked to the ability to hear sounds.

VESTIBULAR SYSTEM. The system that helps to maintain balance and orient the body.

VETERAN'S ADMINISTRATION (VA) HOSPITALS. Medical facilities operated by the federal government explicitly for veterans of the U.S. military.

VICARIOUS. Acquired through imagined participation in the experience of others. Modeling is a form of vicarious learning.

VIPASSANA. A Buddhist meditative practice that emphasizes deep attentiveness to the present moment.

VIRTUAL REALITY. A realistic simulation of an environment, produced by a computer system using interactive hardware and software.

VISUALIZATION. A technique that employs the imagination to visualize specific events or behaviors.

VISUAL-MOTOR. The ability to coordinate vision and bodily movements.

VISUAL-SPATIAL. The ability to see how objects relate within the "big picture."

VISUOMOTOR. Pertaining to visual and motor processes.

VOLATILE. Something that vaporizes or evaporates quickly when exposed to air.

VOYEURISM. A paraphilia that involves watching unsuspecting people, usually strangers, undress or engage in sexual activity.

VULVAR VESTIBULITIS SYNDROME (VVS). Vulvar vestibulitis syndrome is thought to be the most frequent cause of dyspareunia in premenopausal women. A chronic, persistent clinical syndrome, VVS is characterized by severe pain on vestibular touch or attempted vaginal entry.

W

WANNABE. In reference to body integrity identity disorder, a person who feels a need for an amputation or impairment.

WEIGHT CYCLING. Repeatedly gaining and losing weight.

WELFARE-TO-WORK. Several American public reforms of the late 1990s and early 2000s designed to move individuals from public assistance programs to paying jobs.

WERNICKE-KORSAKOFF SYNDROME. A condition of the brain caused by alcohol abuse coupled with malnutrition; also called alcohol encephalopathy.

WILSON'S DISEASE. An inborn defect of copper metabolism in which free copper may be deposited in a variety of areas of the body. Deposits in the brain can cause tremor and other symptoms of Parkinson's disease.

WITHDRAWAL SYMPTOMS. A group of physical or mental symptoms that may occur when a drug is discontinued after prolonged regular use.

WRAPAROUND PROGRAMS. A form of mental health service delivery that strives to accommodate all family members based on self-defined needs, flexibly incorporating both formal and informal community services.

X

X RAY. A type of electromagnetic radiation, between gamma rays and ultraviolet, with a wavelength of between 0.01 and 10 nanometers.

Y

YIN/YANG. Universal characteristics used to describe aspects of the natural world.

YOGA. A physical, mental, and meditative discipline and practice that began in India.

YOGI (FEMININE, YOGINI). A trained yoga expert.

Z

ZEN MEDITATION. A discipline that teaches the mind to relax. Zen meditation involves sitting in prescribed positions in order to calm the body and mind, with the goal of slowing heart rate and breathing to reach a reflective meditative state.

ZOONOSIS (PLURAL, ZOONOSES). Any contagious disease that can be transmitted from nonhuman animals to humans or from humans to nonhuman animals. Zoonoses include viral, bacterial, parasitic, fungal, and prion diseases.

ZYGOMATIC ARCH. Cheekbone. A quadrilateral bone forming the prominence of the cheek. It articulates (touches or moves) with the frontal, sphenoid, maxillary, and temporal bones.

INDEX

In the index, references to individual volumes are listed before colons; numbers following a colon refer to specific page numbers within that particular volume. **Boldface** references indicate main topical essays. Photographs and illustration references are highlighted with an *italicized* page number. Tables are also indicated with the page number followed by a lowercase, italicized *t*.

A

A1D2 sequence, 2:1287, 1288

AACAP. *See* American Academy of Child and Adolescent Psychiatry

AAMA. *See* American Academy of Medical Acupuncture

AAMFT. *See* American Association for Marriage and Family Therapy

Abandonment
  borderline personality disorder, 1:233, 235
  dependent personality disorder, 1:441

Abilify. *See* Aripiprazole

Abnormal Involuntary Movement Scale (AIMS), 1:**1–3**, *2t*

Abreu, Jose, 1:681

Absence seizures, 2:1347, 1348

Abstinence
  addiction, 1:26
  alcohol, 1:56
  cannabis, 1:276
  cocaine, 1:351
  detoxification, 1:468
  Matrix model, 2:939
  opioids, 2:1077–1081
  self-help groups, 2:1360
  smoking, 2:1439, 1440
  See also Withdrawal

Abstract reasoning, 1:71–72, 434

Abuse, 1:**3–8**
  acute stress disorder, 1:18
  body dysmorphic disorder, 1:219
  bodywork therapies, 1:231
  borderline personality disorder, 1:233–234
  bulimia nervosa, 1:251
  bullying as, 1:257
  conversion disorders, 1:389
  dependent personality disorder, 1:441

depersonalization and depersonalization disorder, 1:444, 447

dissociation and dissociative disorders, 1:506, 515

legal issues concerning recovered memories, 1:510

neglect, 2:1032–1033

post-traumatic stress disorder, 2:1187

reactive attachment disorder, 2:1259, 1260

See also Child abuse; Domestic violence; Elder abuse; Sexual abuse; Substance abuse and related disorders

Academy for Guided Imagery, 1:722, 724

Academy of Neurology, 1:68

Acamprosate, 1:26, 55, 199

Acceptance, 1:710, 2:947

Acetaldehyde, 2:1045

Acetaminophen, 1:68

Acetylcholine
  Alzheimer's disease, 1:60
  borderline personality disorder, 1:234
  donepezil, 1:523
  doxepin, 1:534
  neurotransmitters, 2:1041
  nortriptyline, 2:1052
  rivastigmine, 2:1294
  tacrine, 2:1549
  trihexyphenidyl, 2:1614
  Wernicke-Korsakoff syndrome, 2:1651

Acetylcholinesterase inhibitors
  galantamine, 1:662–664
  ginkgo biloba, compared to, 1:702

Achenbach's Child Behavior Checklist, 2:1378

Achievement tests, 1:862–863, 2:1653–1654

Acne excoriée. *See* Dermatillomania

Acquired brain injury. *See* Traumatic brain injury

Activities of daily living (ADL)
  Alzheimer's disease, 1:61
  dementia, 1:430, 433
  economic and financial stress, 1:549
  grief, 1:713
  intellectual disabilities, 1:820
  reading disorders, 2:1263
  schizophrenia, 2:1323
  vascular dementia, 2:1634

Acupressure, 1:**8–11**, 2:1191

Acupuncture, 1:**11–16**, *12*
  alcohol use and related disorders, 1:56
  bipolar disorder, 1:216
  cocaine abuse, 1:351
  generalized anxiety disorder, 1:688
  major depressive disorder, 2:918
  mental illness, 2:1095
  mini-mental state examination, 2:985
  opioid disorders, 2:1081
  pain disorder, 2:1104
  postpartum depression, 2:1185
  restless leg syndrome, 2:1281
  sexual abuse, 2:1395
  sleep disorders, 2:1431
  smoking cessation, 2:1441
  specific phobias, 2:1465
  stress management/reduction, 2:1498
  traumatic brain injuries, 2:1600

Acute akathisia, 2:941

Acute Depression Medication Trial, 2:1476–1477

Acute dystonia, 2:940, 943

Acute lead poisoning, 1:881

Acute stress disorder, 1:**16–21**
  adjustment disorders, compared to, 1:30
  anxiety disorders, 1:113, 114

Alzheimer's disease, 1:*59*, **59–73**
  amnesia, 1:83
  anosognosia, 1:98–101
  art therapy, 1:*131*
  autism, compared to, 1:160
  caregivers, 2:1372
  CATIE study, 1:289
  cognitive retraining, 1:363
  delusions, 1:423, 425
  dementia, 1:430, 431–432, 435, 437
  donepezil, 1:523–524
  Down syndrome, 1:531–532, 824
  electroencephalography, 1:565
  following traumatic brain injuries,
    2:1600
  galantamine, 1:663
  genetics, 1:689–690, 2:1089
  ginkgo biloba, 1:700, 702
  ginseng, 1:706
  hallucinations, 1:729
  imaging studies, 1:801
  Kraepelin, Emil, 1:487
  memantine, 2:950–951
  mini-mental state examination, 2:985
  music therapy, 2:1013
  neurotransmitters, 2:1042
  paranoia, 2:1115, 1116
  Pick's disease, as distinct from,
    2:1167
  positron emission tomography,
    1:241, 2:1179
  rivastigmine, 2:1294–1295
  saffron, 2:1304
  sage, 2:1306, 1307
  SAMe, 2:1311
  seizures, 2:1346
  senior mental health, 2:1370
  sexual abuse, 2:1391
  sleep deprivation, 2:1422
  stigma, 2:1489
  tacrine, 2:1549–1550
  urinary incontinence, 1:574
  vascular dementia, compared to,
    2:1634
  zinc, 2:1667, 1668
  See also Dementia
AMA. *See* American Medical
  Association (AMA)
Amantadine, 1:*73*, **73–74**
  dopamine, 1:527
  late-life depression, cause of, 1:875
  for medication-induced movement
    disorders, 2:943
Ambien. *See* Zolpidem
Amenorrhea

  anorexia nervosa, 1:95
  bulimia nervosa, 1:252
  compulsive exercise, 1:374
American Academy of Child and
  Adolescent Psychiatry, 1:**75–76, 853**
American Academy of Medical
  Acupuncture (AAMA), 1:16
American Academy of Sleep Medicine,
  1:780
American Association for Marriage and
  Family Therapy (AAMFT), 1:624,
  2:934–935
American Board of Medical Specialties,
  2:1369
American Board of Psychiatry and
  Neurology, 2:1214
American Dance Therapy Association,
  1:411, 413, 414
American Law Institute, 2:956
American Medical Association (AMA)
  acupuncture, 1:12, 15
  addiction, 1:24
  alcoholism definition, 1:48
  elder abuse, 1:557
American Music Therapy Association,
  2:1014
American Psychiatric Association,
  1:**76–77**
  adjustment disorders, 1:30
  antisocial personality disorder, 1:110
  aversion therapy, 1:164, 356
  *Diagnostic and Statistical Manual of
    Mental Disorders*, 1:484
  electroconvulsive therapy,
    1:559–560, 2:918
  *Practice Guideline for the
    Psychiatric Evaluation of Adults*,
    1:482–483
  psychiatrists, 2:1215
  reading disorder, 2:1263
American Psychological Association,
  1:**77–78**
  aversion therapy, 1:164
  biofeedback training, 1:208
  Hare Psychopathy Checklist paper,
    1:753
  informed consent, 1:808
  Internet addiction disorder, 1:829
  psychologists, 2:1226
  Thematic Apperception Test, 2:1557
American Recovery and Reinvestment
  Act, 1:769
American Speech-Language-Hearing
  Association, 2:1466–1467
American Stroke Association, 2:1507
Americans with Disabilities Act (ADA),
  1:601, 2:1488

Amitriptyline, 1:*78*, **78–80**
  apathy, 1:123
  chlordiazepoxide with, 1:316
  depersonalization and
    depersonalization disorder, 1:445
  depression, 1:452
  diets, 1:496
  vs. 5-HTP, 1:646
  late-life depression, 1:877
  postpartum depression, 2:1185
  sleepwalking disorder, 2:1437
Amnesia, 1:**80–83**
  Alzheimer's disease, 1:61, 63
  chlordiazepoxide, 1:317
  co-occurring disorders, 1:393–394
  diazepam, 1:490
  dissociation and dissociative
    disorders, 1:506, 507
  dissociative amnesia, 1:17, 18, 505,
    508–511
  dissociative fugue, 1:512–513
  dissociative identity disorder,
    1:514–518
  electroconvulsive therapy, 1:562
  late-life depression, 1:876
  Rohypnol, 1:102
  Wernicke-Korsakoff syndrome,
    2:1649–1652
  See also Dissociative amnesia
Amniocentesis
  Down syndrome, 1:530
  intellectual disability, 1:823
Amobarbital, 1:465
Amotivational syndrome, 1:276
Amoxapine, 1:**83–85**
  late-life depression, 1:877
  medication-induced movement
    disorders, 2:940
  schizotypal personality disorder,
    2:1337
Amphetamines and related disorders,
  1:**85–88**, *86*, *88*, **88–92**
  antianxiety drugs with, 1:103
  delusions, 1:427
  dermatillomania, 1:455
  hypersomnia, 1:780
  Kleine-Levin syndrome, 1:870
  medication-induced movement
    disorders, 2:941
  methamphetamine, compared to,
    2:969
  narcolepsy, 2:1026
  panic attacks, 2:1112
  paranoia, 2:1119
  psychopharmacology, 2:1230

D

Index

N

Q

Social skills *(continued)*
  executive function, 1:592–593
  pyromania, 2:1248
  reactive attachment disorder,
    2:1258–1262
Social skills training, 2:**1452–1455**
  Asperger syndrome, 1:139
  attention deficit hyperactivity
    disorder, 1:154
  borderline personality disorder,
    1:234
  delusional disorder, 1:424
  dependent personality disorder,
    1:442
  exhibitionism, 1:601
  Internet addiction disorder, 1:832
  major depressive disorder, 2:917,
    919
  modeling, 2:997
  pervasive developmental disorders,
    2:1153
  sexual masochism, 2:1407
  sexual sadism, 2:1409
  social phobia, 2:1451
  token economy system, 2:1573
Social stigma. *See* Stigma
Social support. *See* Support systems
Social workers, 2:**1456**
Socialization
  agoraphobia, 1:45
  gender identity disorder, 1:672–673
  gender roles, 1:678
Sociocultural factors. *See* Culture
Socioeconomic status, 1:310, 685
Sociopathy. *See* Antisocial personality
  disorder
Sodium lactate, 2:1111
Sodium oxybate
  hypersomnia, 1:780
  narcolepsy, 2:1027
Sodium valproate, 1:409
Software. *See* Computers
Soiling. *See* Encopresis
Somatic experiences
  delusions, 1:422, 426
  post-traumatic stress disorder, 2:1191
  schizophrenia, 2:1325
Somatization disorder, 2:**1456–1459**
  Clinical Assessment Scales for the
    Elderly, 1:329
  dissociation and dissociative
    disorders, 1:506
  electroconvulsive therapy, 1:562
  histrionic personality disorder
    comorbidity, 1:756

somatoform disorders, 2:1459–1461,
    1460
  undifferentiated somatoform
    disorder, as distinct from, 2:1620
Somatoform disorders, 2:**1459–1461**
  conversion disorder, 1:387–392
  hypochondriasis, 1:788–792
  St. John's wort, 2:1309
  undifferentiated somatoform
    disorder, 2:1619–1620
Somatostatin, 2:1042
Somnambulism. *See* Sleepwalking
  disorder
Sonata. *See* Zaleplon
Soteria House, 1:402
Southern Illinois University, 1:668
Soviet Union, 2:957
Soy, 2:1201
Spanking, 1:300
Spatial neglect, 1:99
Specific Fear Inventory, 2:1112
Specific phobias, 1:113, 2:**1461–1466**
SPECT. *See* Single photon emission
  computed tomography (SPECT)
Speech and language
  Alzheimer's disease, 1:62, 63
  Asperger syndrome, 1:136, 137
  autism, 1:158–159
  childhood disintegrative disorder,
    1:305
  Cognistat, 1:353
  cognitive remediation, 1:361
  dementia, 1:433
  developmental coordination disorder
    link, 1:470
  expressive language disorder,
    1:608–609
  Gestalt therapy, 1:698
  Halstead-Reitan Battery, 1:743
  incoherence, 1:247
  Kaufman Assessment Battery for
    Children, 1:862
  learning disorders, 1:885, 888
  mental status examination, 2:962
  mini-mental state examination, 2:986
  mixed receptive-expressive language
    disorder, 2:993–995
  phonological disorder, 2:1161–1163
  Pick's disease, 2:1166–1168
  psychosis, 2:1234
  reading disorder, 2:1263, 1264
  Rett syndrome, 2:1284–1285
  schizophreniform disorder, 2:1332
  selective mutism, 2:1351, 1352
  social communication disorder,
    2:1443–1445

speech-language pathology, 2:1467,
    1467
  stuttering, 2:1514–1518
  Wernicke-Korsakoff syndrome,
    2:1651
  See also Communication
Speech sound production disorder. *See*
  Phonological disorder
Speech Sounds Perception Test, 1:743
Speech-language pathology,
  2:**1466–1467**, *1467*
  learning disorders, 1:888
  phonological disorder, 2:1163
  Pick's disease, 2:1168
  social communication disorder,
    2:1444–1445
  stuttering, 2:1517–1518
  traumatic brain injuries, 2:1601
Spinal tap, 2:1026
Spiral CT scans, 1:378, 379
Spiritual abuse, 1:5
Spiritual counseling
  adjustment disorders, 1:31
  post-traumatic stress disorder, 2:1191
  trauma, 2:1591
Spirituality
  self-help groups, 2:1361
  stress management/reduction, 2:1502
  12-step programs, 2:1363
Spironolactone, 2:1200
"Splitting," 1:233, 235
Sports
  dementia pugilistica, 1:431
  exercise, benefits of, 1:594
  steroids, 2:1481
  traumatic brain injuries, 2:1596, 1602
SSNRIs. *See* Serotonin-norepinephrine
  reuptake inhibitors (SNRIs)
SSRI discontinuation syndrome, 1:586
SSRIs. *See* Selective serotonin reuptake
  inhibitors (SSRIs)
Stalking, 1:4, 4*t*, 5, 2:1391
Standards of Care (World Professional
  Association for Transgender Health),
  1:674
Stanford Sleepiness Scale, 1:780
Stanford-Binet intelligence scales,
  2:**1467–1470**
STAR*D study, 2:1232, **1470–1474**,
  1471*t*
State Children's Health Insurance
  Program, 1:368
States
  acupuncture training, 1:16
  assertive community treatment, 1:143
  binge drinking prevention, 1:199

T

U

X

Y

Z